The Tropical Look

The Tropical Look

An Encyclopedia of Dramatic Landscape Plants

ROBERT LEE RIFFLE

TIMBER PRESS
Portland, Oregon

This book is for
Diane Laird,
who wanted it so much she made it happen,

and

Alton Marshall,
friend and plantsman extraordinaire

All photos by the author unless otherwise indicated.

ISBN 0-88192-422-9

Printed in Hong Kong

Timber Press, Inc.
The Haseltine Building
133 S.W. Second Avenue, Suite 450
Portland, Oregon 97204, U.S.A.

Library of Congress Cataloging in Publication Data

Riffle, Robert Lee.
The tropical look : an encyclopedia of dramatic landscape plants / Robert Lee Riffle.
    p.   cm.
Includes bibliographical references (p.   ) and index.
ISBN 0-88192-422-9
1. Landscape plants—Encyclopedias. 2. Tropical plants—Encyclopedias.
3. Landscape plants—United States—Encyclopedias.
4. Tropical plants—United States—Encyclopedias. I. Title.
SB407.R545   1998
635.9′5237′03—dc21   97-41819
CIP

Contents

Color plates follow pages 160 and 256

5

Acknowledgments

I would like to thank first Sally Roth, garden writer and editorial staff member of *Fine Gardening* magazine, who started this project and without whom it would never have happened.

Larry Schokman, director of horticulture at The Kampong, the home of the late David Fairchild and now a part of the National Tropical Botanical Garden, is one of the most knowledgeable and enthusiastic plantsmen it has been my pleasure to meet. I owe him a great debt of gratitude for sharing that wisdom and excitement, for guiding me through the paradise that "Fairy" started, and for contributing many valuable and excellent photographs to this endeavor.

Special thanks are due Roger L. Hammer of Homestead, Florida, who opened his garden and his wonderful knowledge of tropical plants to me one winter day and contributed a number of photographs for this book.

To Kitty Morgan, publications chairperson of the Tropical Flowering Tree Society, I am most appreciative for making my last photographic sojourn in Florida so easy, so pleasant, and so productive.

Dr. Henry Donselman was kind enough to read a large portion of the manuscript and offer his expert advice and comments.

I would also like to thank Cathy Ryan, horticulturist at Fairchild Tropical Garden, for her enthusiastic and valuable assistance while I was photographing the glories of that tropical garden.

Lance Walheim of California Citrus Specialties and author of *Citrus: A Complete Guide to Selecting and Growing More than 100 Varieties for California, Arizona, Texas, the Gulf Coast and Florida* read the citrus section and generously offered his expert advice and comments.

Lynn McKamey, owner of Rhapis Gardens in Gregory, Texas, reviewed the sections on the genera *Cissus, Cycas, Polyscias,* and *Rhapis* in great detail and gave me expert accounts of her experiences with these plant groups. Muchas gracias, LM.

Lib Tobey, director of Heathcote Botanical Garden in Fort Pierce, Florida, was kind enough to take time from her busy schedule and show me the garden and share her plant experiences with me.

Grant Stephenson, owner of Horticultural Consultants in Houston, Texas, and one of the country's experts on the cultivation of palms, hardy and otherwise, contributed much of his store of knowledge to me about this noble group of plants.

The ingratiating Shirley Hackney was most generous in contributing valuable and excellent drawings for the glossary and text.

Patrick Mulcahey of San Francisco read the beginnings of the manuscript and was kind enough to communicate to me his professional writer's reaction and advice.

To those correspondents who contributed additional valuable photographs a heartfelt "Thank You!" They are Perry D. Slocum, founder of Slocum Water Gardens and Perry's Water Gardens and co-author of the invaluable and complete *Water Gardening, Water Lilies and Lotuses;* Steven Timbrook, executive director, Ganna Walska Lotus Land in Santa Barbara, California; Sean Hogan of Portland, Oregon, garden writer, plant explorer, horticulturist and contributor to several excellent books on tropical and desert plants; and Dr. Jim Racca of Iowa, Louisiana, member of the Bromeliad Society of America.

I want again to thank Diane Laird of Seattle, Washington, who kept me writing when times were not so good and constantly provided not only the needed cheerleading, unerring eye, and educated mind, but also one of the writer's best friends: Starbucks coffee beans.

And last but not least I want to acknowledge my very longtime companion, Jesse R. McIntyre, who endured day after day and night after night of my selfish and usually irascible writing stint at the infernal computer machine, asking only occasionally if it would make me happy in the long run. The answer was finally, "Yes; I think so."

Introduction

The lure of the beauty of tropical landscapes like those found in Hawaii, Key West, Puerto Rico, Costa Rica, Bali, and other exotic locales is undeniable. Such beauty has an almost irresistible appeal for people who do not live in such places, and for most of those who do. Indeed, this fascination with the tropical look has been used by Madison Avenue to sell all kinds of products, useful and otherwise. It is the stuff dreams are made of. It is also the subject of this book.

The Tropical Look Defined

The tropical look is a bit difficult to define with words alone, but its components include all palms, all plants with relatively large or boldly shaped foliage and flowers, and all plants with colored or variegated leaves and large and spectacular flowers or flower clusters. It is very hard to imagine a tropical looking landscape without the conspicuous and dramatic accent of palms. It is this one plant family that is most synonymous with the tropics and the look thereof; no other group of plants can quite match the effect of these noble plants in the landscape. The tropical look is also based generally upon evergreen plants, especially large-leaved evergreen herbaceous plants like bananas, bold-leaved trees, and ferns. In short, the tropical look is one of flamboyant form and contrast. This look is mainly derived by means of subjects with exceptional foliage, punctuated by the luminosity of tropical blossoms.

Author's Apologia

The biggest impetus for writing this volume has been the conviction that the tropical look is not taken advantage of to the extent it could and should be, even in regions that have a tropical or subtropical climate, especially in the United States. Roses, pansies, phlox, lilies, daylilies and the many other common flowering perennials that fill most gardens, tropical or otherwise, are beautiful enough, but these lovelies pale compared to such things as banyan trees, bananas, palms, almost all ferns, and such spectacular flowering plants as aloes, royal poinciana trees, yellow flame trees, African tulip trees, the blue trumpet vine, or the overwhelmingly beautiful Easter-lily vine.

The Tropical Look in Cooler Climates, Homes, Greenhouses, and Conservatories

Many of these glories of the tropical regions are completely adaptable as houseplants and even more (almost all of them in fact) are perfect candidates for conservatories and atriums. Many people do not realize how many tropical looking plants can be grown well outdoors outside of the truly tropical and subtropical regions.

Gardeners who live in U.S.D.A. hardiness zones 8 and higher (minimum temperature higher than 10°F), an area encompassing most of southern and southwestern United States, the west coasts of the United States and Canada, and almost all of Great Britain, for example, will find a wealth of landscape plants in this book from which to choose. Obviously, those who live in zones as warm or warmer than zone 10 (minimum temperature 30°F) will have the widest range of choices available.

There are three basic ways of attaining the tropical look in a landscape away from the tropics. First, one can use plants that have tropical looking characteristics but which also have some degree of hardiness. Second, some protection—-burlap wrapping, poly sheeting, and so forth—-can be given to tender plants. Finally, the gardener may choose to use plants that "die back" to the roots in freezing temperatures, but which will grow again quite vigorously when warmer temperatures return in the spring. This book discusses all three methods; the most convincing-looking plantings usually have combinations of all of them. Each plant entry provides complete data as to how much cold a plant can stand, the best methods of protecting a plant from winter cold, and whether it can "spring back" from the roots.

Tropical Plants versus the Tropical Look

There are two ways of defining the tropics. Geographically speaking, the tropics are the area of the earth between latitudes 23° 27' north and south of the equator. This definition, however, is not very useful to us, as the tropics have many areas of high elevation and cold temperatures. Horticulturally speaking, any climate in which the minimum temperature never goes below freezing is tropical. For our purposes, a truly "tropical" plant is any plant that cannot sustain freezing temperatures. I should state clearly that a "tropical looking" plant need not be strictly tropical, either in the geographical or horticultural sense.

It is not always the case that a plant whose origin is tropical actually looks tropical. A salient example is the genus *Araucaria*, including the monkey-puzzle tree and the Norfolk Island pine. The latter tree is completely tropical in its origins and temperature requirements and yet does not have the look we are after. Therefore this genus, along with several other completely tropical groups, is not here included. In addition, tropical looking plants whose statures are of less than "landscape proportions" and whose natures are not amenable to mass plantings are not included. We have to draw limits somewhere or we would end up with many volumes dealing with many plants that are better subjects for specialized editions aimed at collectors.

In general those plants that are only attractive when in bloom and whose flowering periods do not last a significantly long time are not included here. Such a group is, of course, the orchid family. For the most part these plants with their amazingly beautiful and intricate blossoms are of quite modest proportions and, when in bloom, can light up and bejewel the landscape of which they are a part. Vegetatively, however, they are usually of quite modest size and their stems and leaves are usually anything but beautiful or impressive in and of themselves. Other groups of tropical or subtropical plants not here included are *Crinum*, *Hippeastrum*, and *Hymenocallis:* their beauty is mostly limited to their production of flowers whose lives are not that long. This is all another way of saying that the present volume deals with tropical looking landscape subjects whose appeal is of at least a reasonably permanent status. There is but one true annual plant genus listed in this book, although many genera can be and are used as annuals.

The Tropical Deserts and Their Tropical Looking Plants

Many people do not think of deserts as tropical in either appearance or climatic characteristics, yet most desert regions are tropical or subtropical climatically. The climax community aspect of these areas is uniquely exotic, tropical, and colorful. Furthermore, the dominant species are often quite large and of exceptional beauty and appeal. Their forms have the flamboyance and the exotic appeal required for the tropical look. Again, this is a roundabout way of saying that the "wet" tropical look is not the only one. Many cactus and succulent species are included in this book because they partake of the look in an exceptional and unique way.

Landscaping with Tropical Looking Plants

The reader new and uninitiated to the beauties and delights of the tropical landscape may at first be overwhelmed by the different and spectacular plants and concepts delineated in the descriptions that follow, just as the person unfamiliar with lilacs, roses, lupines, and daylilies might wonder, upon first encountering their descriptions and photos, exactly how to treat them in the landscape. Of course there is no "exact" way to treat any landscape subject, but to help the uninitiated in the quest, the descriptions are followed by useful lists of the main groups of tropical looking landscape subjects. Each group's salient characteristics and general landscaping uses are identified.

Winter Temperatures and the U.S.D.A. Growing Zones

The hardiness zones given in this book are those of the United States Department of Agriculture. These are meant to convey no other information than the average low temperatures one can expect in a given area the zone encompasses. It should be pointed out that if one lives in U.S.D.A. zone 9 it is not the case that one will never see temperatures below 20°F. Such temperatures will be exceptional but by no means unheard of.

Some garden writers and many garden catalog authors are wont to be (too) generous and liberal in assigning a specific plant to a zone or range of zones. Conversely other writers, frequently of a professorial bent, tend to be extremely conservative in assigning plants to the zones, preferring to be very safe and never sorry. I tend rather towards the latter philosophy with the exception that many of the plants discussed in this book are fast-growing perennial subjects that can rapidly "spring back" from their roots or stems if damaged by cold. For these plants I give the range of zones in which they will survive to come back another day, which information is indicated in the text.

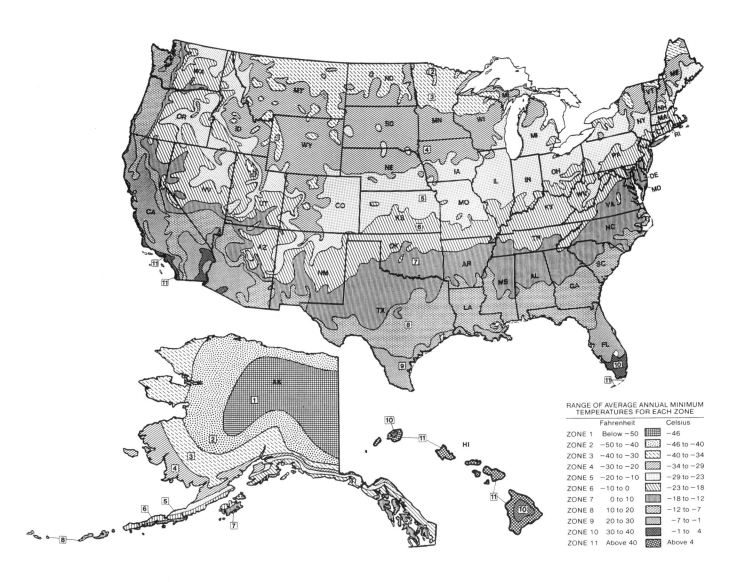

RANGE OF AVERAGE ANNUAL MINIMUM
TEMPERATURES FOR EACH ZONE

	Fahrenheit	Celsius
ZONE 1	Below −50	−46
ZONE 2	−50 to −40	−46 to −40
ZONE 3	−40 to −30	−40 to −34
ZONE 4	−30 to −20	−34 to −29
ZONE 5	−20 to −10	−29 to −23
ZONE 6	−10 to 0	−23 to −18
ZONE 7	0 to 10	−18 to −12
ZONE 8	10 to 20	−12 to −7
ZONE 9	20 to 30	−7 to −1
ZONE 10	30 to 40	−1 to 4
ZONE 11	Above 40	Above 4

HARDINESS ZONE
TEMPERATURE RANGES

°F	ZONE	°C
below −50	1	below −45
−50 to −40	2	−45 to −40
−40 to −30	3	−40 to −34
−30 to −20	4	−34 to −29
−20 to −10	5	−29 to −23
−10 to 0	6	−23 to −17
0 to 10	7	−17 to −12
10 to 20	8	−12 to −7
20 to 30	9	−7 to −1
30 to 40	10	−1 to 5

Botanical Names

The use of and especially the pronunciation of Latinized botanical names are often difficult for the uninitiated—and sometimes not so easy for the "expert." So why use these scientific names if they are difficult? The answer is threefold: many of the plants described in the following text have no English common name; many of them have many different common names that vary from one region to another; and there is only one botanical name for each species or hybrid or cultivar.

A botanical name consists of usually two but often three words; the name is a binomial or trinomial. The genus name, whose initial letter is always capitalized, is followed by the species name, whose initial letter is usually lowercased. The third name is that of a naturally occurring variety or a cultivar (a cultivated variety), the latter a form or variety of the species that is found only in horticulture and not in nature. These two or three words uniquely define a group of plants; no other group of plants has the same binomial or trinomial.

This classification is in some ways analogous to the naming of people. For example, "Brown, Joe" defines a person in terms of his name, but it is obvious that it does not uniquely define the person's name. You can bet money that there is more than one Joe Brown in the world. "Joe Lee Brown" goes quite a bit further in uniquely naming the person, but that trinomial is most likely not unique either. Botanical names are more precise.

The trinomial with genus, species, and variety, *Aechmea caudata* var. *variegata*, defines a unique subset of plants within the larger set of those known as "*Aechmea caudata*." In this case the plants in the smaller set have variegated leaves as opposed to the larger group that does not. The trinomial *Dracaena deremensis* 'Warneckii' works in the same way except that the third name refers to a horticultural form, not one found in nature. Note that the genus and species names as well as names of naturally occurring varieties are always printed in italics, whereas the horticultural form or variety names—the cultivar names—are not. Instead, they are always printed inside single quotation marks.

The experienced gardener may be wondering at this point about the nomenclature and inscription of hybrids. They are written as "*Bauhinia ×blakeana*" if the cross was made within the genus, in this case *Bauhinia*, and as "*×Fatshedera lizei*" for crosses made between two genera, in this case *Fatsia* and *Hedera*. Most hybrids are artificially created, but some are found naturally between different but related species and even separate genera that inhabit adjacent regions in the natural world.

That botanical names apply to groups of plants is one reason these names can be unique—unique for the population or group of plants under consideration. There is not just one *Aechmea caudata* plant in the world; there is a population of these plants with

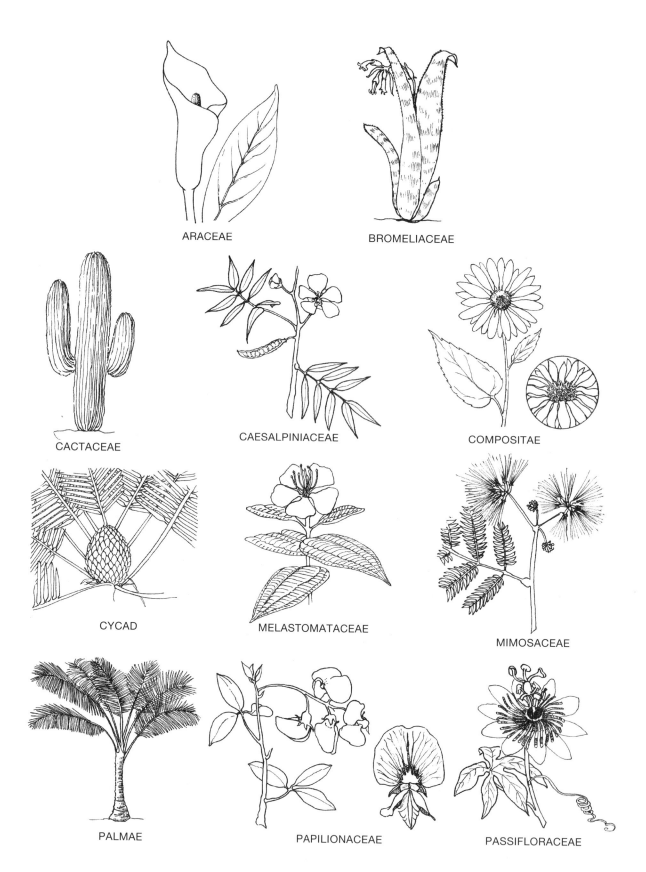

ARACEAE

BROMELIACEAE

CACTACEAE

CAESALPINIACEAE

COMPOSITAE

CYCAD

MELASTOMATACEAE

MIMOSACEAE

PALMAE

PAPILIONACEAE

PASSIFLORACEAE

Figure 1. Some tropical looking families and groups of plants.

enough constant similarities between the individual members to be referred to with a binomial or trinomial description.

It is useful and quite interesting also to know the even broader relationships of plants; all *Aechmea* species are related to a much larger group of plants with common characteristics, the bromeliads. This much larger assemblage of plants is the family of plants known as "bromeliads," members of the bromeliad family, Bromeliaceae. A family is simply a larger group of plants with common characteristics.

Humankind's passion for classification does not stop at this level, of course; above the family level are classifications of ever broader scope up to the level of distinguishing plants from animals, a very basic distinction. The concept of a family of plants is often very useful as it can tell the plant lover much information about the type of plant and its needs. For example the bromeliad family consists of plants found only in the Western Hemisphere, the Americas, and most of them are tropical in origin and epiphytic in nature, with flowers all of a similar and basic form.

How to Use this Book

The Pronouncers

Just as with almost all words in the English language, there is no one and only correct way to pronounce botanical names. Some people say "toe-MAH-toe" and some say "ta-MAY-doe"; some people say "SAL-ix" and some say "SAY-lix" for the botanical genus name of the willow tree, *Salix*. Both are correct. The "pronouncers" in the header of the plant descriptions to be found in the encyclopedic portion of the book are to be used as a guide; they are not set in stone.

The primary stress syllable of a word in the pronouncers is indicated by upper case letters. In long botanical names it is sometimes desirable not only to indicate the syllable that receives the primary stress but also a syllable that takes a secondary stress. For example, in the binomial "*Carpentaria acuminata*" (a-kyoo´-mi-NAIT-a), the pronunciation of "*acuminata*" is somewhat difficult to understand and execute if the syllable receiving a secondary stress is not indicated. One needs it to find a "rhythm" for the pronunciation to get a handle on its utterance. In this case it is the second syllable of the word that should receive the secondary stress and this fact is indicated by the ´ mark following the syllable. A few general rules about the use of the pronouncers:

In all cases, only one syllable is to be pronounced between each hyphen in the pronouncers.

- a is short as in the word *cat* or even shorter when at the end of a word
- e is short as in the word *elf*
- i is short as in the word *in*
- o is long as in the word *open*
- u is short as in the word *up*
- g is hard as in the word *get*
- ow is to be pronounced as the "ou" in *ouch* and not as the "ow" in *show*
- th is to be pronounced as the "th" in *thing* and not as the "th" in *the*

Alternative pronunciations as for the genus name *Costus* (KOAST-us / KAHST-us) illustrate the dictum that there is no one and only correct way to pronounce most words. This fact is also very commonly exhibited in specific epithets that end in "ata" or "ana." For example, "baileyana" is pronounced "bay-lee-YAHN-a" or "bay-lee-AN-a"; it is completely a matter of preference.

The Encyclopedia Headers and Text

The headers that precede the descriptive text of each species are to be interpreted as follows:

ARUNDINARIA (a-run´-di-NAHR-ee-a)	Genus name and pronunciation
Gramineae: The Grass, Bamboo Family	Family name & examples of members
BAMBOO CANE	Common name(s)
Dwarf to medium-sized running-type bamboos	General description of plant
Zones vary according to species	USDA hardiness zones for the plants
Sun to partial shade	Light requirements of the plants
Average but regular amounts of moisture	Moisture requirements of the plants
Rich, friable well-drained soil	Soil type preferences of the plants
Can be invasive	Special considerations of the plants
Propagation by rhizome division	Propagation techniques for the plants

Synonyms for the botanical names are indicated in the text immediately after the binomial (or trinomial) and its pronouncer and appear as: "*Freycinetia cumingiana* (kum-in´-jee-AHN-a) (synonym *Freycinetia multiflora*)." The synonyms come about usually because of the publication of two names. This phenomenon was much more common in the earlier part of the twentieth century and in the previous centuries because of the relative difficulty and slowness of communication. The rules of nomenclature require that the first published name take precedence over the later name else confusion would reign supreme; thus the occurrence of synonyms in the literature.

Tropical Looking Plants
A through Z

ACACIA (a-KAY-shya / a-KAY-see-a)
Mimosaceae (Fabaceae, Leguminosae), subfamily
 Mimosoideae: The Mimosa Family
ACACIA; MIMOSA; WATTLE
Large shrubs or large trees; narrow or pinnate leaves;
 evergreen or deciduous; yellow flowers
Zones vary according to species
Sun to part sun
Drought tolerant
Average well-drained soil
Propagation by seed

Acacia is one of the great genera of flowering trees and shrubs in the drier areas of the tropics and subtropics, with most of the 1000 or so species indigenous to Australia and Africa. About 75 percent of the species are Australian, although it is some of the African species that form the largest and most magnificent trees. The Australian species are by far the more spectacular in flower but seldom noble of size or form. Almost all the species have yellow flowers, though some are nearly white, and all the flowers are borne in clusters. The flower clusters are of two shapes, balls and spikes. As is typical of the family (or subfamily), the stamens of the individual blossoms create the show. The leaves are also of two types. The first type consists of flattened and broadened leaf stems that function as leaves and are called "phyllodes." In some species these phyllodes are so reduced in size as to be mere prickles or short spines. The second type of leaf consists of true leaves, which are bipinnate or rarely tripinnate. All species with phyllodes are Australasian or Hawaiian. Some species exhibit both leaf types during their life span: phyllodes when young and pinnately compound true leaves when older. The pinnate and true leaf is thought to be primitive in an evolutionary sense, preceding the evolution of the phyllode in this genus.

Many *Acacia* species (especially the Australian phyllodal species) find the climatic conditions of the southeastern United States and similar climates less than ideal. They like the Mediterranean conditions of California, southern Europe, and Australia, where the air is normally drier and the nights cooler. And yet there are several Australian species that do well enough in humid climes and a few that are indigenous to these areas. These species should be planted more than they are at present. Common names for the trees vary from continent to continent, being called wattles in Australia, thorn trees in Africa, and mostly mimosa in the United States and Great Britain.

All species are drought tolerant to some extent, relatively fast growing (some grow very fast), and relatively short-lived. Exceptions are mainly the giant African species like *Acacia galpinii* and *A. albida* that grow relatively slowly and live to a great age. Most tree species attain less than 50 feet of height but Edwin A. Menninger quotes in his book, *Fantastic Trees,* a report from South Africa which estimates that some *A. galpinii* specimens along the Magalakwini River in Transvaal (a province of northeastern South Africa) reached a height of about 400 feet in the nineteenth century. If this estimate is accurate it would make these long-gone trees the tallest ever known to grow on earth. The acacia trees of the southern African savannahs so familiar to Westerners in the movies and documentaries on lions and Africa in general are *A. giraffe,* so named because giraffes eat these trees. They are sometimes called camel thorn, as the word *cameleopard* (head like a camel and spots like a leopard) was once applied to giraffes.

Acacia abyssinica (ab-i-SIN-i-ka) is, as the specific epithet implies, native to Ethiopia and is hardy in zones 9 through 11. This lovely tree has large bipinnate leaves almost a foot long. Except for the color of the bark and flowers, the tree looks much like a *Jacaranda* species. It has no thorns. The tree grows to as much as 30 feet but needs to be trained to a single trunk when young to attain this stature. Unlike many other bipinnate species, it has a rather open, graceful and airy, flattish-topped crown. The foliage is medium green in color. While naturally evergreen, the leaves may drop in a sudden cold spell or under conditions of prolonged drought. The white to yellow flower heads are ball-shaped, as much as an inch wide, and come in clusters of three to six. They appear in midspring and are only slightly fragrant. While naturally drought tolerant to some extent, the tree looks very much better when watered during such conditions. This beautiful thing is worth growing for its lovely leaves alone. The flowers are an irresistible lagniappe. The species has the undistinguished common name of Abyssinian acacia.

Acacia albida (al-BY-da) occurs naturally in tropical East Africa, southern Ethiopia, Uganda, Kenya, Tanzania, northern Mozambique, and into northeastern South Africa and is not adaptable outside zones 10 and 11. It grows to as much as 90 or 100 feet in its native habitats, but is usually no more than 60 feet tall in cultivation. It is one of the noblest and most beautiful trees. The form is that of an inverted triangle. The massive trunk and large limbs are a light to dark gray in color, supporting a broad and somewhat flattened canopy of blue-green foliage. The trees dominate the landscape like a major geological feature and are an irresistible force of beauty. The bipinnate leaves are somewhat less than a foot long, and the leaflets are a beautiful bluish to grayish green in color. The leaves are accompanied by pairs of inch-long straight white thorns with red tips found at the base of the leaf stalk. The tree is somewhat deciduous with drought or cold. The yellowish white flowers appear throughout most of the year and are in 4-inch-long cylindrical spikes. The dark orange-brown pods are twisted often into hoops or circles, thus leading to one of the vernacular names, apple ring acacia. Another common name is winter thorn. The tree is drought tolerant when established, but grows much faster and is more beautiful with adequate and regular supplies of moisture.

Acacia auriculiformis (aw-rik´-yoo-ly-FOR-mis) is native to areas of New Guinea and northern Australia. It is a lovely, foolproof tree in the nearly frost-free areas of zones 10 and 11, where it grows very fast to as much as 40 feet and almost as wide. It has a dense crown of bright green 8-inch-long, sickle-shaped phyllodes. The shape of the leaves supposedly leads to the common name of ear-leaf acacia, but there is not much of an earlike appearance. The flowers appear heavily in spring and intermittently throughout the summer and fall. They are tiny buttonlike affairs in 3-inch-long spikes, but are very bright yellow in color and make quite a show. The pods are about 4 inches long and are curled or coiled, appearing more like ears than do the leaves, and they remain on the tree for too long a period to be desirable. The tree grows fast and can tolerate drought and poor as well as saline soil and conditions. Its disadvantages are that it is short-lived, the pods are not attractive, and the wood is brittle.

Acacia baileyana (bay-lee-YAHN-a) is indigenous to New South Wales in Australia. It is probably the most widely planted *Acacia* species, because it is one of the most spectacular in the genus when in flower. It naturally makes a large and spreading shrub, but it can be trained to a single trunk when young and often grows to 20 feet or more in height. The small bipinnate leaves are only about 2 inches long and consist of many tiny bluish to silvery green leaflets. The little trees bloom in late winter and early spring, at which time they are covered in 3-inch-long racemes of little golden yellow balls of fragrance. ***Acacia baileyana* 'Purpurea'** (poor-POOR-ee-a) is an attractive cultivar with purplish bronzy new leaves. The tree is one of the hardier of the Australian species and is adaptable to zones 9b through 11. It has a vernacular name of golden wattle in its native Australia and the moniker of mimosa elsewhere.

Acacia berlandieri (bur-lan´-dee-ER-ee / bur-LAN-dyur-eye) is native to southern Texas and adjacent Mexico, and hardy in zones 9 through 11 and marginal in zone 8. It is naturally a large and spreading shrub to 10 feet or so in height but, as so many other shrubby *Acacia* species, can be trained into a small tree form. The dark green bipinnate leaves are usually about 6 inches long, but may reach 8 inches or more. They are finely pubescent, especially when young, and are evergreen on the plant unless extreme cold hits them. The flowers appear intermittently from fall through spring in loose-flowered racemes of half-inch-wide white balls, which are not as sweetly scented as those of *A. baileyana* or *A. farnesiana*. They are favorites of bees and result in an excellent white honey. The species is sometimes called thornless cat's claw in Texas. Soil with impeded drainage is anathema to this shrub.

Acacia choriophylla (kor´-ee-o-FYL-la) (synonym *A. choriophyllodes*) is indigenous to the Florida Keys, the Bahamas, and Cuba, and is hardy in zones 10 and 11. The tree grows to as much as 30 feet with a dense and rounded crown but is usually smaller in stature. The bipinnate leaves are exceptionally handsome and are as much as 9 inches long with 6- to 10-inch-long leathery dark green oblong leaflets, somewhat reminiscent of those of the *Ceratonia siliqua* (carob tree) or *Sophora secundiflora* (Texas mountain laurel). The flowers appear in loose-flowered panicles from the leaf axils in half-inch-wide deep yellow or golden heads. Common names include thornless acacia and tamarindillo (tah-mah-rin-DEE-yo).

Acacia choriophyllodes. See *A. choriophylla*.

Acacia erioloba. See *A. giraffe*.

Acacia farnesiana (far-nee´-zee-AN-a) is probably originally native only to parts of Mexico and tropical America, but is now found in the southernmost parts of Texas and Florida. It is hardy to about 25°F, therefore dependable only in zones 9b through 11. It is also found in most other warm regions (most likely having been spread around the globe before records were kept) and is considered by some botanists to have originated in Africa. Common names are sweet acacia, huisache, popinac, and cassie. It may be grown as a large multitrunked shrub or trained as a picturesque small spreading tree to as much as 30 feet in height and at least as wide. The deciduous bipinnate leaves are 4 to 5 inches long, dark green, and feathery, and the bases of the leaf stalks have a pair of small sharp thorns. The tree usually makes a rounded crown of dense dark green foliage and zigzagging branches with a quaintly crooked dark trunk. Near the seacoast, however, they become beautifully flat-topped with a quaintly attractive leaning stem. Most leaves usually remain on the tree if the winter is mild. In any case their growth is renewed just after the flowers cover the tree in January or February with small, deep golden yellow balls whose fragrance is legendary and reminiscent of daffodils or oleander. Some trees start blooming in late autumn. The plant is not particular as to soil as long as it is well drained and, while it is drought tolerant, always looks better and holds its leaves longer with an adequate supply of water. It needs at least part sun and grows and blooms better with full sun. Growth under optimum conditions is moderately fast. Plate 1.

Acacia galpinii (gal-PIN-ee-eye) occurs naturally in northeastern South Africa and Mozambique and is hardy in zones 10 and 11. It is one of the largest trees in the genus and, other than the great *A. albida,* is the most magnificent. It grows slowly to as much as 80 or even 90 feet with a widespreading canopy above a massive gray to tan trunk with flaking bark. The bipinnate leaves are large, usually more than a foot long, with many small grayish green leaflets. They are accompanied by short brown and shiny curved thorns. The flowers are borne in clusters of 3-inch-long spikes from the leaf axils. The pods are dark brown or black and quite large, up to 10 inches long.

Acacia giraffe (ji-RAF-fee) (synonym *A. erioloba*) occurs naturally in northeastern South Africa, Mozambique, Tanzania, Kenya, and Uganda and is hardy in zones 10 and 11. It is one of the world's most recognizable trees due mainly to the number of excellent documentary and narrative films photographed in its native habitat. The tree is wonderfully picturesque and grows slowly to 40 or sometimes 50 feet with an inverted triangle-shaped form and a great spreading flat canopy of relatively sparse foliage. The bluish to grayish green bipinnate leaves are about 6 inches long and consist of 5 to 11 small leaflets. They are accompanied in the leaf axils by large curved thorns that usually have expanded bases. The tree loses its leaves in cold or drought. The flowers are in small yellow balls and appear after rains in the tree's native habitats and mainly in spring in wetter climates. The fat black pods are about 6 inches long and are curved into semicircles. They are relished by livestock as well as giraffes. The tree is very drought tolerant and can survive for years without much moisture because of its deep roots. It adapts well to almost any soil as long as it is fast draining. As already alluded to, the tree is called camel thorn.

Acacia karroo (ka-ROO) is indigenous to a large area of Africa from southeastern South Africa through Botswana and Zimbabwe into Mozambique. It is not adaptable outside zones 10 and 11. It is a large shrub or small tree slowly growing to as much as 40 feet in height. The tree has many similarities, especially its overall form and shape, to *A. giraffe* (camel thorn), but is smaller and shorter with an even flatter top. The leaves are small and the deep green leaflets tiny. They are accompanied at the juncture of leaf and stem by pairs of large white thorns with inflated bases. The flowers appear throughout the year but principally in the summer and are clustered in fragrant golden balls, which almost cover the tree in the summer. This tree is one of the world's most drought tolerant and grows in any well-drained soil.

Acacia koa (KO-a) is indigenous to the Hawaiian Islands where it is found on all sloping ground except for the driest sites. It is hardy in zones 10 and 11 and marginal in zone 10a. The species is probably the most magnificent of the phyllodal species. The tree grows to 70 feet with a widespreading and open crown above a truly massive short trunk, which may be as much as 10 feet in diameter. The great limbs grow almost horizontally and are picturesquely somewhat contorted. The phyllodes are sickle-shaped, dark green in color, and about 6 inches long. The pale yellow flowers are borne in ball-shaped clusters in the spring. Few trees are as nobly beautiful as this species, which is one of the glories of the endemic Hawaiian flora. It is not drought tolerant and needs regular and adequate supplies of moisture. It is known locally as the koa tree.

Acacia macracantha (mak-ra-KANTH-a) (synonym *A. macracanthoides*) is native to a large area of tropical America from the West Indies through Central America and into Venezuela, and is hardy in zones 10 and 11. It is by nature a large shrub, but may be trained to tree form although it is rather difficult to keep the form to one trunk. As a tree the plant reportedly grows to 40 feet. It usually attains no more than 25 feet in cultivation. It is a striking landscape subject with a spreading and fairly open crown of rather large bright green bipinnate leaves to 6 inches long, reminiscent of small *Jacaranda* leaves. The leaf axils and sometimes parts of the trunk bear tough and sharp 2-inch-long spines in pairs. The flower heads also usually come in pairs from the leaf axils and are in ball-shaped bright yellow clusters. The tree blooms mainly in winter, but is reported to flower sporadically all year long. Vernacular names include long-spine acacia and steel acacia.

Acacia macracanthoides. See *A. macracantha.*

Acacia minuta. See *A. smallii.*

Acacia nilotica (ny-LO-ti-ka / ny-LAHT-i-ka) is originally native to a vast area from tropical Africa through India and Sri Lanka and is hardy in zones 10 and 11. It is another of the species with similarities to *A. farnesiana* (sweet acacia), although its leaves are slightly larger and the flowers are not as fragrant. It is often shrubby in nature, but is easily trained into tree form and grows to as much as 40 feet in height. The globose flower heads are a bright yellow. The plant carries the common names of stuntwood and gum arabic, the latter name because at one time the congealed sap was valued for making candies. *Acacia senegal* has now just about replaced it for that purpose.

Acacia pinetorum (pyn-e-TOR-um) is indigenous to southern Florida and the West Indies and is adaptable only to zones 10 and 11. It is a small tree or large shrub with many similarities to *A. farnesiana* (sweet acacia), including growth habit and paired spines. It is usually completely evergreen, does not usually grow as large as sweet acacia, and its leaves are about half the size and usually a duller green. The flower heads are also slightly smaller than those of sweet acacia but have basically the same color and a fragrance almost as sweet. One advantage it has over sweet acacia is that it seems to be more tolerant of drought and saline soil. A denizen of the southern Florida pinelands, this species has the common name of pine acacia.

Acacia schaffneri. See *A. tortuosa.*

Acacia smallii (SMAHL-lee-eye) (synonym *A. minuta*) occurs naturally from southern California through Texas and Mexico and over into northwestern Florida. It is another small *Acacia* species that is very similar to *A. farnesiana* (sweet acacia) and *A. pinetorum* (pine acacia). Some taxonomists consider it only a variety of *A. farnesiana*. It is much hardier than the pine acacia and is a good candidate for zones 8 through 11. In addition, it is more attractive than the pine acacia, growing larger to 20 or even 30 feet sometimes. In general, it is more free-flowering than sweet acacia, often flowering in summer and fall. This species (if it is, indeed, a distinct species from *A. farnesiana*) has common names of huisache, sweet acacia, and Small's acacia, the preferred name being the latter.

Acacia tortuosa (tor-tyoo-O-sa) (synonym *A. schaffneri*) is native from southwestern Texas down through Mexico into northern South America and the Galapagos Islands but is hardy in zones 8b through 11. It grows naturally as a large spreading shrub with rather coiling and tentacle-like branches but, with care, may be trained (if started early) into a picturesque small single-trunked tree with contorted trunk and branches to as much as 20 feet in height. The bipinnate leaves are deciduous and small, only 2 inches or less in length, with tiny light green leaflets. The flower heads are ball-shaped, and the blossoms are fragrant and much reminiscent of those of *A. farnesiana*. They appear just before or with the leaves in early spring. This strange and exotic-looking small tree or large shrub is adapted in a landscaping sense to the cactus and succulent garden setting. The vernacular name is, appropriately enough, twisted acacia.

Acacia wrightii (RYT-ee-eye) is native to central southwestern Texas and adjacent Mexico as well as the Mexican state of Sonora. It is hardy in zones 8b through 11 and marginal in zone 8a. The tree grows slowly to 30 feet and is often found as a very large shrub. As a tree it forms a widespreading and somewhat irregularly shaped canopy above a short gray or light brown ridged trunk. The bipinnate leaves are small and only about 3 inches long with usually 10 oblong or obovate medium green leaflets. The tree is usually free of thorns, but some individuals have a few short, sharp brown spines at the base of each leaf. The tree is almost completely evergreen but loses its leaves in extreme drought or cold. The flowers appear in spring and summer, especially after rain, and are in cylindrical yellowish white clusters. The fat, curved pods are about 4 inches long. This species thrives in dry and somewhat alkaline soil.

ACALYPHA (ak-a-LY-fa)
Euphorbiaceae: The Euphorbia, Spurge Family
COPPER LEAF PLANT; CHENILLE PLANT
Shrubs with large colorful leaves and flowers
Zones 10b and 11 as dependable perennials; almost
    anywhere as annuals
Sun
Average but regular amounts of moisture
Average well-drained soil
Propagation by seed and cuttings

A very large genus of more than 400 species of herbaceous to woody shrubs in tropical and subtropical regions. They have mostly large and highly colored leaves and sometimes spectacular flower spikes. All the cultivated species, hybrids, and varieties with colored leaves are indiscriminately referred to as copper leaf plants. They must have good drainage and are not completely dependable as perennial subjects outside regions like southern Florida as they do not take well to wet winters, even frost-free wet winters. They are planted for year-round effect and often look quite good after cold with the return of warm weather along the northern Gulf Coast. Both the species described below grow to a maximum height of 12 to 15 feet in frost-free climates.

Acalypha hispida (HIS-pi-da) is native to extrasylvan sites in Malaysia. The leaves are dark green, ovate to elliptic, as much as 8 inches long and 4 inches wide. The leaves are not the reason to grow the chenille plant; the flowers are. The female flower clusters are a brilliant red in color, and the individual blossoms, though tiny, are in long pendent narrow tail-like spikes, which have a decidedly velvety look and which are as much as 18 inches long. There are white-flowered and purplish-flowered cultivars, but the red-flowered plants are the most spectacular. The plants need some sun to bloom well, but grow satisfactorily in partial shade. They may be pruned to just about any desired size and are often used as hedges. Plate 2.

Acalypha wilkesiana (wilks-ee-AHN-a) is indigenous to sunny sites on the islands of the South Pacific. With this species and its cultivars the leaves are the main attraction. They are profuse, large, often 10 inches long and almost as wide, and are a bronzy green in color daubed with copper, purple, and red. The leaves are seldom flat in the type but are usually puckered into a boat shape (i.e., they are somewhat concave in cross section). The individual plants, unlike the above species, are not bisexual. The female spikes are shorter than those of *A. hispida* and are red but not spectacular. As seen from a distance, they give the plants an almost spidery look. There are many cultivars of this species (often the cultivars are from hybrid stock), some with green leaves and shallowly scalloped and wavy white margins like *Acalypha wilkesiana* **'Godseffiana'** (gahd-sef´-fee-AHN-a). There are few more spectacularly colored plants that are as easy to grow well, and they rival *Codiaeum* (croton) varieties in this respect. Like *A. hispida*, this species is often pruned into informal hedges. It needs sun to look its best and to prevent legginess. Plate 3.

ACCA. See *Feijoa*.

ACHIMENES (a-KIM-i-neez)
Gesneriaceae: The Gloxinia (Sinningia) Family
JAPANESE PANSY; ORCHID PANSY; NUT
  ORCHID
Low herbaceous flowering perennials
Zones 9 through 11
Partial Shade
Water lovers; perfect drainage
Rich, friable sandy soil
Propagation by seed and cuttings

A genus of about 25 species of small perennial herbs in tropical America. They have fibrous roots growing from fleshy rhizomes, lovely oppositely arranged mostly velvety leaves, and beautiful funnel-shaped flowers that are solitary or in small clusters. This genus boasts some of the world's most beautiful flowering plants. Every species, hybrid, and cultivar has velvety leaves reminiscent of *Coleus* species and other members of the mint family, and all have beautiful flowers, which are shaped like small flaring trumpets and come in every color. Most species are no more than 2 feet tall, and many are significantly smaller. The smaller ones may be used as a groundcover, and the others are an excellent substitute for the ubiquitous *Impatiens* species as bedding plants.

The average gardener probably never thinks of the genus as being amenable to outdoor cultivation, but it is not only possible in the climate zones cited above, but also rather easy to accomplish. These tropical plants have a dormant period and can be grown as any other landscape subject with a dormant period, such as *Kaempferia* (peacock ginger) and *Caladium* species. The requirements during the dormant period of *Achimenes* are a well-drained site where water never stands and a climate in which the soil does not freeze and stays at least as warm as 50°F. All *Achimenes* species grow from scaly rhizomes, which look like wormy versions of pine cones. These underground roots should never be allowed to dry out during the growing season, yet they will not tolerate standing water. The less water the rhizomes receive during the winter the better. The plants love a brightly lit site but not much sun. The substrate is important in their successful culture as they (like all gesneriads) have delicate and fine roots that do not like heavy soils. A loose, composted medium is adequate, especially one amended with regular applications of mild, organic fertilizer during the growing season. Fish emulsion is excellent, as is manure tea, and kelp.

ACHRAS. See *Manilkara*.

ACOELORRAPHE
(a-seel-o-RAY-fee)
Palmae (Arecaceae): The Palm Family
EVERGLADES PALM; SILVER SAW PALM;
  PAUROTIS
Medium-sized clumping fan-leaved palm with many
  trunks
Zones 9b through 11
Sun to part shade
Water lover
Average soil
Propagation by seed and root division

A monotypic genus formerly known as *Paurotis*. *Acoelorraphe wrightii* (RYT-ee-eye) is a clumping palm indigenous to southern Florida, the Bahamas, Cuba, Central America, and parts of Mexico. Nothing is more beautiful than a mature clump of this palm with its slender trunks of varying heights—the essence of the tropical look with a wild yet elegant aspect. The trunks usually grow slowly to around 20 feet, but some specimens attain 30 or 40 feet. Each trunk is covered in a beautiful pattern of old leaf bases and fibers. The palmate leaves are 3 feet or more in diameter on long graceful leaf stalks that are armed with teeth, and the leaf color is bright green above with a silvery sheen beneath. The plants have been known to resprout from the roots after freezing to the ground at 15°F. Damage to the leaves starts below 25°F, and the trunks are usually killed to the ground by a temperature of 20°F or lower. These plants tolerate poor soil and even dry situations, but only look good with adequate water and a fairly rich soil. This palm species is one of the few that tolerates occasionally boggy conditions. Like many other clumping palm species, the Everglades palm looks better with some judicious thinning of its trunks in older clumps. Plate 4.

ACROCOMIA (ak-ro-KO-mee-a)
Palmae (Arecaceae): The Palm Family
GRU-GRU PALMS
Single-trunked, spiny feather-leaved palms
Zones vary according to species
Full sun
Average but regular amounts of moisture
Average soil
Propagation by seed

A genus of only three species of pinnate-leaved palms in tropical America, all of which are armed with vicious spines on the trunks, leaf petioles, and often the leaves. One species is acaulescent; that is, its trunks are underground and non-apparent. The other two species have columnar, straight trunks, which, when old, are reminiscent of the trunks of royal palms (*Roystonea*). Some trunks have bulges making the whole stem spindle-shaped. In some species, the old and dying leaves fall cleanly from the trunk, leavings rings of beautiful but vicious spines around the light-colored trunk. The leaves of other types adhere to the trunk for years until the leaf bases rot and fall off, leaving a smooth trunk with no spines. Some taxonomists think that the two species described below are varieties of each other, the type being named *Acrocomia aculeata.*

Acrocomia mexicana (mex-i-KAHN-a) is native to southern Mexico, Belize, and Honduras. This palm is smaller than *A. totai* and has persistent leaf bases, giving the tree from a distance a very hairy and almost spidery aspect. The leaves are plumose like those of *A. totai* but are a darker green. The tree also grows slowly to about 30 feet. It is more tender than *A. totai,* and temperatures below 30°F can be fatal. Thus it is a landscape subject only for zones 10b and 11. Besides grugru, the palm has monikers of corojo and coyoli. It is as hard to find for sale as *A. totai,* but certainly worth the effort.

Acrocomia totai (to-TAH-ee) is native to Paraguay, eastern Bolivia, and northern Argentina. It is a very striking landscape subject in zones 9b through 11 when planted where the spines on the trunks and leaves of young plants are not a problem. The trunks reach a maximum height of 40 feet, and the leaves are deciduous. When the dead leaves fall from the trunk, they leave a light-colored, fairly massive column free of spines except near the summit. Alas, the plants grow rather slowly. The grassy green leaves are especially noteworthy as the leaflets spring from the spiny rachises at several angles, not all in one plane, thus giving a boa or cylindrical effect in the landscape. The palms need regular watering until they are established, after which they are relatively drought tolerant. Damage to the leaves starts at about 26°F, severe damage is sustained at 22°F, and death of the palm usually occurs with temperatures below 20°F. This species is not readily available as the seed is slow and often difficult to germinate and young plants pose a mechanical problem for growers. Plate 5.

ACROSTICHUM

(ak-ro-STYK-um / a-KRAHST-i-kum)
Polypodiaceae: The Largest Fern Family
SWAMP FERN; GIANT LEATHER FERN
Immense, coarse, pinnate-leaved ferns
Zones 9 through 11
Sun
Water lover
Wet, humusy soil
Propagation by spores and root divisions

A genus of only three species of fern. They are aquatic or nearly so and are commonly found along riverbanks, along and in estuaries, and in mangrove swamps in tropical and subtropical regions. One species, *Acrostichum danaeifolium* (day´-nee-eye-FO-lee-um), is native to central and southern Florida, the West Indies, and northern South America. It is sometimes planted for erosion control to fill in wet and swampy sites and to create bold landscape effects. It is more useful than beautiful, although "spectacular" might also be applicable. The stiff leaves arise from a tough creeping and clumping rhizome and are as much as 10 or 12 feet long and a foot or more wide, with a stout midrib and yellow-green rough-surfaced segments. They are covered in a beautiful cinnamon-colored tomentum when they first unfurl. The plant is not completely hardy in zone 9, but reliably resprouts from the roots there if frozen back. Plate 6.

ACTINOPHLOEUS. See *Ptychosperma.*

ADANSONIA (ad-an-SO-nee-a)

Bombacaceae: The Bombax, Baobab Family
BAOBAB; MONKEY-BREAD TREE; DEAD RAT TREE
Immense spreading deciduous tree with massive trunk
Zones 10 and 11; marginal in zone 10a
Sun
Very drought tolerant
Almost any well-drained soil
Propagation by seed

The genus has nine species of unusual and spectacular trees in the drier parts of Africa, Madagascar, and Australia. Some consider these trees more grotesque than beautiful. In their harsh native environments they often are, but planted in areas with regular amounts of rainfall distributed more or less evenly throughout the year they can be strikingly beautiful and impressive ornamental additions to the landscape. In their native habitats the trees develop incredibly massive trunks with age. These trunks, which are as much as 33 feet in diameter and larger than any single-trunked tree, contain great pockets of water to see the plant through the dry seasons of their arid birthplaces. *Adansonia digitata* (dij-i-TAHT-a) is native to the drier parts of tropical Africa and is sometimes planted as a specimen tree on estates and in parks. It makes a dramatic and spectacular landscape subject with its relatively short, immensely thick trunk and contorted limbs. The tree is usually deciduous in the winter months if the season is dry or cold, but in warm, moist winters it may be completely evergreen except for the briefest leaf fall just before the flowers appear. The blossoms are as unusual as the tree that produces them: they are pendulous on long stalks, arising from the ends of the branches, usually before or with the new leaves. The white, fleshy petals do not last long. The pistil and stamens are on a short, thick stalk protruding from the corolla, and the female part is hidden by the very numerous purple extended stamens. From these flowers within a few months are produced large, elongated, brown fruits, which are suspended on long stalks from the ends of the sometimes leafless branches. The appearance of the fruit has led to the graphic vernacular name of dead-rat tree. The large, very tropical looking leaves consist of five to nine dark green, glossy, palmately compound 6-inch-long leaflets. Each leaflet has a strong and lighter colored midrib. This completely tropical species endures but a few degrees of frost. In addition, the plants succumb in soils whose drainage is impeded in any way. The trees are reputed to live as long as 5000 years. Plates 7 and 8.

ADENANTHERA (ad-e-NANTH-e-ra)
Mimosaceae (Fabaceae, Leguminosae), subfamily
    Mimosoideae: The Mimosa Family
RED SANDALWOOD; BEAD TREE
Medium-sized evergreen tree; large pinnate leaves,
    yellow-white flowers, coiled pods with red seeds
Zones 10 and 11
Sun
Water lover
Sandy, humusy, moist, well-drained soil
Propagation by seed and cuttings

There are four species in this Australasian genus. All have large bipinnate leaves and small white or yellow flowers in long racemes. Only one species is commonly cultivated. **Adenanthera pavonia** (pa-VO-nee-a) is native to Southeast Asia, India, and Sri Lanka, and grows in cultivation to about 30 feet but is sometimes much larger in its native haunts. The tree has a broad open crown of medium green bipinnate foliage atop a smooth light gray trunk. The leaves, which are 10 to 12 inches long and composed of 10 to 12 oblong 2-inch-long leaflets, fall in cold weather or under drought stress. The white and yellow flowers appear in dense and narrow racemes that are as much as 10 inches long. They are followed by 8-inch-long brown pods that coil upon opening to reveal bright red lens-shaped seeds. Called Circassian seeds, they are reputedly edible if roasted. This handsome tree has fallen out of favor in southern Florida because it has spread into native flora as birds disperse its seeds.

ADENIUM (a-DEN-ee-um)
Apocynaceae: The Oleander, Frangipani, Vinca
    Family
DESERT ROSE
Succulent shrub or small tree; thick rubbery
    branches; large rose-colored flowers
Zones 10b and 11
Full sun
Drought tolerant
Light, porous sandy soil
Propagation by seed and cuttings

A small genus in southeastern Africa and into Arabia, thought by some taxonomists to have only one species. The succulent deciduous shrubs and small trees have thick, milky, poisonous sap. **Adenium obesum** (o-BEE-sum) hails from arid southeastern Africa, the island of Socotra, and the southern Arabian Peninsula. The shrub slowly grows to as much as 10 feet in height with a usually smooth dark gray to brown trunk, which is swollen at its base. The plant can be easily trained into a small tree form. The attractive leaves are thick, leathery, dark green with a lighter midvein, obovate in shape, 3 to 6 inches long, and sometimes lobed. They are reminiscent of *Pittosporum* or small *Plumeria* leaves. Bunched mainly at the ends of the few branches, they create a picturesque "bonsai" look to the little tree or shrub. The foliage is normally deciduous in cold or drought conditions during the winter, but may also remain on the tree, sometimes accompanied by flowers if there is rain. This oddity is extremely beautiful when in bloom but somewhat difficult to maintain in non-desert regions, even in the warmest areas. It needs perfect drainage, full sun, and mostly dry warm winters, but wants regular watering when in growth during the summer. The reward is the flaring trumpet-shaped, rose-colored flowers, which usually cover the tree in cycles during the summer growing season. **Adenium obesum var. multiflorum** (mul-ti-FLOR-um) has superior flowers, magnificently colored white with scarlet edges. It is also rather more floriferous. Plate 9.

ADHATODA. See *Justicia adhatoda*, *Megaskepasma erythrochlamys*.

ADIANTUM (ad-ee-ANT-um)
Adiantaceae: The Maidenhair Fern Family
MAIDENHAIR FERNS
Small to medium-sized delicate, lacy ferns
Zones vary according to species
Part shade
Water lovers
Humusy, moist, well-drained soil of varying pH
Propagation by rhizome division and spores

Adiantum is the maidenhair fern genus, most of whose 300 or so species are in the American tropics, with some in temperate North America and a few in Australasia and Africa. They have creeping rootstocks which, usually slowly but sometimes quickly, form beautiful colonies. All species have much-divided, lacy, and usually quite delicate-appearing fronds. The fronds are of two general shapes: (1) oblong to linear in outline and bipinnate or tripinnate and (2) much divided, rather wide, and triangular-shaped. Many species have distinctive fan-shaped leaflets, and most have bronzy to pinkish new foliage. All are water lovers but also demand perfect drainage. None of the species likes hot dry conditions. Some species prefer soils with a relatively high pH and are fond of limestone and limestone-based soils, often sprouting up on brick walls or the cracks in cement floors. Others like neutral or even acidic soils. All need a humusy and relatively light medium. Few thrive in heavy clay. Most species grow in partial to full shade, but some adapt to full sun. Many species, even if hardy, die back to the roots in freezing weather. Most species have wiry stipes that are usually black or dark in color, but a few have red, brown, or orange stipes. All have a length of stipe below the rachis. The members of this very variable genus of ferns tend to freely mutate, adding to the great diversity of the populations of most individual species.

Adiantum capillus-veneris (cap-PIL-lus-VEN-e-ris) is called the southern maidenhair fern or the Venus maidenhair fern and is distributed almost worldwide in the warmer parts of the earth, including most warmer parts of the United States. It is hardy in zones 7 through 11. The beautiful billowy, light green, generally triangular-shaped leaves, composed of very many small fan-shaped leaflets, make this small fine-leaved fern an outstanding choice for contrast in the close-up landscape. There is always a look of movement, like a rippling stream, to these lovely leaves, even when they are not touched by a breeze. The fronds are deciduous in cold winter areas but generally evergreen in zones 9 through 11. The species is found mainly in association with limestone soils and is therefore intolerant of soils that are very acidic, although it flourishes on neutral to slightly acidic soils. It needs part to full shade, a light humusy soil, and a regular supply of moisture. Southern maidenhair is a variable species. Of the several cultivars available, some have relatively large and quite deeply cleft leaflets, others have distantly spaced leaflets, and still others have dense and compact leaves. Some plants are quite compact; others are open and airy. All require the same culture: a loose, fast-draining humusy soil that is not too acidic, nearly constant moisture, and partial shade.

Adiantum caudatum (kaw-DAY-tum) is a beautiful small fern with linear-shaped once-pinnate leaves that is native to a wide area of the tropical world from South Africa through southern India, Indonesia, and Malaysia, northward through New Guinea and the Philippines. It is hardy in zones 9b through 11. Common names are walking fern and trailing maidenhair. The leaves are gracefully arched and a grayish green in color with unusual oblong leaflets each of which is straight on one side and cleft into five or more lobes on the other side. This species is an excellent groundcover in partial shade and humusy soil as each frond can root at the tip. It also looks superb hanging from soil pockets in walls or other structures. This species is one of a group that demands slightly alkaline soil (a pH above 7.5) and moist conditions with perfect drainage.

Adiantum diaphanum (dy-AF-a-num) is called the filmy maidenhair. It is native to a large area from Australia and New Zealand northward through New Guinea to Japan, and is hardy in zones 9 through 11. This nice dark green, linear-leaved small clumping fern readily proliferates in partially shaded sites by its underground rhizomes, making an excellent groundcover for shady moist sites. In form this maidenhair is somewhat similar to *A. caudatum* (walking fern), but the leaves are thicker and more leathery. The new fronds are a beautiful silvery mint green in color. This fern should have a rich, composted soil and is not a lime (high pH) lover.

Adiantum formosum (for-MO-sum) is a large spreading evergreen fern native to Australia and New Zealand. It is hardy in zones 9 through 11. This outstandingly beautiful and lush fern has great triangular deep green fronds that may reach a height of 4 feet or more. The underground rhizomes spread rather quickly, but their control is easy. This species makes lovely colonies of tropical beauty in partially shaded moist sites with light, rich humusy soil but demands regular water and a soil which, unlike that needed by many other maidenhairs, is slightly acidic. The plant will freeze to the ground if temperatures fall below 28°F, but will spring back from the roots with the return of warm weather if the top inch of soil does not freeze.

Adiantum hispidulum (his-PID-yoo-lum) is a small, leathery-leaved, semi-evergreen fern native to Australasia and is hardy in zones 8 through 11. It is variously termed rosy maidenhair fern, Australian maidenhair fern, and rough maidenhair fern. The stipes are forked into two branches, and the fronds are dark green, very narrow, leathery, and shiny, creating a wonderfully lush appearing small fern that grows to 2 feet in height. The new growth is a beautiful rose color. The fern is quite easy to grow in almost any exposure including full sun and in a wide variety of soil types as long as there is sufficient moisture, humus, and good drainage.

Adiantum polyphyllum (pah-lee-FYL-lum), the giant maidenhair fern, is native to the Caribbean Islands and northern South America. This noble large, leathery triangular-leaved fern looks more like a tree fern than the usual maidenhair. The new leaves are an attractive light pink, a wonderful combination with the leathery light green of the more mature fronds and the dark stipes. The plant is not particularly hardy, being adapted only to zones 9b through 11. It readily takes to sites in part shade to nearly full sun if there is an abundant supply of moisture. It is not that particular as to soil if the medium is loose and humusy.

Adiantum pulverulentum (pul-ver´-oo-LENT-um) is a large leathery-leaved tropical fern from the Caribbean and northern South America. It is hardy in zones 10 and 11. It does not look like most other maidenhairs: the leaves are neither triangular nor linear, but rather more typical of most other genera of fern. Each bipinnate leaf is about 2 feet long, including the stipe, and carries many shiny dark green leaflets. While this species needs a rich, moist, and well-drained soil, it does not like one that is very acidic. It is a water lover that cannot adapt to full sun.

Adiantum raddianum (rad-dee-AHN-um) is native to most of tropical America and is the paradigm maidenhair fern, the essence of robust delicacy. Hardy in zones 9b through 11, it grows to 3 feet or more and is an exceptionally variable species that has produced numerous cultivars with variously shaped leaflets and varying plant statures. The type is a small to medium-sized, triangular-leaved, very delicate appearing fern. There are innumerable cultivars of this loveliest of maidenhairs, and some are breathtakingly and airily beautiful—great fountains or miniature trees of lacy animation. Some of the most outstanding cultivars are **'Excelsum'**, **'Fritz-Leuth'**, **'Ideal'**, **'Kensington Gem'**, **'Matador'**, and **'Maximum'**, all of which are bigger growing and more luxuriant than the type. The plants require an adequate and steady moisture supply, part shade, and a light well-drained humusy soil. The optimum pH range for these ferns is wide, and they luxuriate in soils with acidic to basic pH.

Adiantum seemannii (say-MAHN-nee-eye) is a large (to 3 feet) triangular-leaved pinnate fern with very large, ovate to diamond-shaped, dark green leaflets, which are beautifully glaucous beneath. It occurs naturally from Mexico through Central America to northern South America and is hardy in zones 10 and 11. This beautiful fern needs a humusy, non-acidic soil in a partially shaded site with abundant moisture.

ADONIDIA. See *Veitchia merrillii.*

AECHMEA (EEK-mee-a / eek-MEE-a)
Bromeliaceae: The Bromeliad, Pineapple Family
LIVING VASE
Small to large, tubular to spreading rosettes; thick
   spiny-margined leaves; showy flower spikes
Zones vary according to species
Shade to sun
Average but regular amounts of moisture
Light, porous, humusy soil; leaf mold or epiphytic
   mix
Propagation by removing offsets or suckers

A large and very variable genus of about 175 species, with the most diversity of plant form in the bromeliad family. Most species are epiphytic, but many are terrestrial. All produce offsets. This genus is one of the commonest bromeliad genera available because most species are easy to cultivate. All have spines on the leaves, but some of the teeth are quite small and can be found only on the lowermost leaves. Plant shape varies from almost narrow and tubular vases to broad and spreading rosettes of leaves. Some are tiny indeed, having statures measured in a few inches, while others are 10 feet across and 5 feet or more in height. Very many have brilliantly colored leaves and equally spectacular and long-lasting inflorescences. Most species have tall, branched flower spikes but some, like *Aechmea fasciata,* have compact spikes nestled just above the center of the leaf rosette and others have globular or cylindrical inflorescences. All species produce berries, and some of the fruits are spectacularly colored and long-lasting. Some species are fairly hardy to cold and flourish year-round even in the warmer parts of zone 9. There are so many hybrids and cultivars that it is often difficult to find the unadulterated species. Some of the hybrids, cultivars, and naturally occurring varieties are dramatically different in their respective characteristics and often are unusually beautiful. The epiphytic species need a light, well-drained medium to do their best, while the terrestrial species may be planted in humusy soil, if it is well drained, or in pure leaf mold. The epiphytes may be grown on large trees or walls if there is a depression or pocket for some amount of medium. The soil pocket and the plant often need to be contained in a basket or netting of some sort until the plant's roots are established. All species need regular watering, which is most easily accomplished by simply filling the center of the rosettes when they are dry. All species readily sucker, but the offshoots should not be removed (for propagation purposes) until the "mother plant" starts to wither after flowering, usually several months later.

Aechmea amazonica. See *A. chantinii.*

Aechmea angustifolia (an-gust´-i-FO-lee-a) (synonym *A. cylindrica*) is found naturally in Costa Rica through Panama to Peru and Bolivia and is hardy in zones 10 and 11. The medium-sized tubular-shaped grayish-green-leaved plant grows as often on the forest floor in leaf mold as it does epiphytically on the trees. The leaves are narrow and remotely toothed. The flower spike is about 18 inches tall and is narrow with yellow flowers and red bracts. The berries are compact on the spike and are a shiny white, turning a beautiful blue with age. The plant requires a shady or partly shaded site and is a water lover. It is closely related to *A. cylindrata* and likes the same treatment.

Aechmea bernoulliana. See *A. mexicana.*

Aechmea bracteata (brak-tee-AIT-a) occurs naturally from Mexico to Colombia and Venezuela in the trees and on the ground and is sometimes called the Amazon zebra plant. It is hardy in zones 10 and 11. This large species has a tubular-shaped and green-leaved rosette. The plant is imposing in stature, since it is much as 4 feet tall and 6 feet wide. The leaves are narrow and armed with widely spaced large teeth. The inflorescence is 4 feet or more in height, unbranched, with brilliant red bracts and light yellow flowers followed by tightly packed black berries. This species, which grows in partial shade or full sun, is a water and humidity lover. A red-leaved form is often sold as *A. schiedeana* or *A. macracantha.*

Aechmea bromeliifolia (bro-mel´-ee-eye-FO-lee-a) (synonym *A. tinctoria*) is often referred to as the wax torch plant. It also has a wide-ranging natural habitat from Belize to Argentina and is hardy in zones 9b through 11. This very variable species has a spectrum of sizes (from 18 inches to 3 feet in height) and shapes (from a narrow cylinder to an open vase). It is a mostly medium-sized plant, which grows as a terrestrial and as an epiphyte in partial shade to full sun, often covering large areas of bare soil as a terrestrial in its native habitats. The leaves are 1 to 2 feet long, olive green in color, and strongly recurved at the tips with curved spines along the margins. The beautiful inflorescence consists of rosy red bracts from which emerges a dense spike shaped like a pine cone. On the spike are borne white or light yellow flowers that soon turn black, resulting in an almost unique color combination of black and white. The species is a water lover.

Aechmea bromeliifolia **'Rubra'** has red leaves.

Aechmea calyculata (ka-lik-yoo-LAIT-a) is native to the wet forests of southern Brazil and northern Argentina where it grows as an epiphytic medium-sized broad rosette of soft yellow-green leaves about 2 feet long with tiny inconsequential teeth on the margins and gorgeous darker green mottling. It is happy in partial shade to full sun in zones 9b through 11 and wants a regular and consistent supply of moisture. The beautiful bright yellow globular to pyramidal inflorescence is held well above the foliage.

Aechmea caudata (kaw-DAIT-a) is a large epiphytic, narrow vaselike plant with stiff arching narrow light green leaves as much as 3 feet long. It is native to the southern coast of Brazil and is hardy in zones 10 and 11. It likes part shade to full sun and regular water. This quite variable species has several noteworthy cultivars. *Aechmea caudata* **var.** *variegata* (vair-ee-a-GAIT-a) has cream-colored stripes on the leaves, a branched and compact inflorescence, yellow flowers, and orange bracts.

Aechmea chantinii (shan-TIN-ee-eye) (synonym *A. amazonica*) is often called the Amazon zebra plant. One of the world's most beautiful bromeliads, this very choice large, vase-shaped plant is native to the Amazon rain forests, where it grows on large trees, often near their tops, in partial shade to full sun. It is hardy in zones 10b and 11. The green leaves are banded with silver or yellow markings and are thick and tough, 2 to 3 feet long with small teeth on the margins. They are widespreading with pointed tips that are usually recurved. The plant is similar in form to the ubiquitous *A. fasciata* but is more beautiful because of the leaf markings. The flower stalk is often 3 feet or more in height and is branched. The flowers are bright yellow with large, scarlet bracts beneath. This truly spectacular bromeliad wants humidity, warmth, and a regular supply of water. *Aechmea chantinii* **'Amazonica'** has deep purple and light pink transverse bands on the undersurfaces of the leaves. *Aechmea chantinii* **'Samurai'** and *Aechmea chantinii* **'Shogun'** are two outstanding cultivars from Japan. They have, along with the banded markings, wonderful yellow or silver stripes on the leaves. See Plate 10.

Aechmea coelestis (see-LES-tis) hails from the southern Brazilian highlands where it grows as an epiphyte in partial shade to full sun. It is a medium-sized, tubular-shaped plant whose gray leaves are stiff and fairly broad, with ends that do not usually curl as in many other species, but whose color is quite attractive. The 18-inch-tall inflorescence is pyramidal and has pink bracts and purple flowers. The species is reasonably hardy with adequate moisture in zones 9b through 11. *Aechmea coelestis* **var.** *albo-marginata* has leaves with a band of white along their edges.

Aechmea cylindrata (sil-in-DRAIT-a) is a little gem from southern Brazil, growing both as an epiphyte and a terrestrial and is one of the hardiest in the genus. It flourishes in zones 9 through 11 and is a medium-sized spreading, vaselike plant. The leaves are solid light green, concave in cross section and often almost tube-like, remotely toothed on their margins, and rounded at the tips. The inflorescence is held well above the foliage and is long cylindrical in shape with violet-magenta bracts and blue flowers, which produce long-lasting pink fruit. The species thrives in part shade to full sun and is a fast grower, making impressive clumps from the many suckers.

Aechmea cylindrica. See *A. angustifolia.*

Aechmea dichlamydea **var.** *trinitensis* (dy-kla-MID-ee-a trin-i-TEN-sis) is a very beautiful epiphytic plant occurring naturally only on the islands of Trinidad and Tobago and adjacent coastal Venezuela. It is hardy in zones 10b and 11. A large, wide, vaselike plant, it has grayish green leaves as much as 3 feet long and 3 inches wide. The inflorescence is a thing of wonder: a much-branched salmon-colored to rose-colored stalk more than 3 feet tall with blue and purple bracts and white and blue flowers. The plant needs water and partial shade.

Aechmea fasciata (fas-see-AIT-a), usually called the silver vase plant or the urn plant, is epiphytic and native to southern Brazil. Hardy in zones 10 and 11, it is the most popular and widely sold bromeliad. The plant makes a spreading, vase-shaped rosette with thick leaves, which are as much as 2 feet long and 3 inches wide, mint-green in color, with wide silver cross bars and small teeth along the margins. The squat and conical inflorescence consists of bright pink bracts and violet flowers. One reason for its great popularity is its ease of culture in partial shade to full sun with a regular supply of water. *Aechmea fasciata* **var.** *marginata* (mar-ji-NAIT-a) has green leaves with creamy white margins. *Aechmea fasciata* **var.** *purpurea* (poor-POOR-ee-a) has leaves with a rose to purple cast, especially near the tips. *Aechmea fasciata* **var.** *variegata* (vair-ee-a-GAIT-a) has light yellow-green leaves with an outer dark green margin.

Aechmea fosteriana (fahs-ter-ee-AHN-a) is a dramatically colored, tubular vase of light green leaves whose undersides are banded with purplish brown. It is native to the coastal forests of Brazil and is therefore hardy only in zones 10b and 11. The plant grows as an epiphyte and as a terrestrial to about 2 feet in height with stiff, erect leaves margined with heavy spines. The pendent inflorescence consists of red bracts and yellow flowers. The species tolerates partial shade but looks its finest with sun.

Aechmea fulgens (FUL-genz) is native to southern Brazil as both an epiphyte and a terrestrial. It is dependably hardy in zones 10 and 11, where it appreciates shade or partial shade and an adequate supply of water. It spreads by creeping rootstocks. There are two distinct naturally occurring varieties. Both forms are quite beautiful with long-lasting flower spikes, and both are sometimes called the coral-berry bromeliad. *Aechmea fulgens* **var.** *fulgens* is a medium-sized plant with gray-green leaves and beautiful solid red, pyramidal inflorescences bearing tiny blue flowers. As an epiphyte, it climbs tree trunks by its creeping stolons. *Aechmea fulgens* var. *discolor* (DIS-kul-or) has slightly larger leaves that are the same gray-green color on top but with an attractive purple hue and a powdery dusting beneath. The inflorescence is like that of *A. fulgens* var. *fulgens*. *Aechmea fulgens* var. *discolor* 'Magnificent' is bigger, bolder, and more cold tolerant, and has a larger inflorescence.

Aechmea gigantea. See *A. sphaerocephala*.

Aechmea kuntzeana (koont-zee-AHN-a) is native to southwestern Brazil and eastern Bolivia and is hardy in zones 10b and 11. This gigantic and wonderfully beautiful terrestrial species looks almost as much like a vase-shaped *Agave* species as it does a bromeliad. The light green leaves are as much as 3 feet long, very broad and thick, and are margined with large and vicious but spectacular black spines. The inflorescence reaches as much above the rosette as the rosette is tall and consists of a very erect much-branched spike with small yellow-white bracts and flowers above exceptionally large rosy red pendent bracts.

Aechmea macracantha. See *A. bracteata*.

Aechmea mariae-reginae (MAHR-ee-eye-REJ-i-ny), a large epiphytic spreading vase-shaped plant from the Costa Rican lowlands, is hardy in zones 10b and 11. The 4-foot-long remotely spiny and relatively broad leaves are a deep and shiny green and are generally lance-shaped. If grown in full sun, the leaves take on a rosy cast. The inflorescence is possibly the most beautiful in the genus. It has a group of deep pink or purplish red, foot-long limp and hanging bracts above which is the 2-foot-tall narrowly cylindrical unbranched white to yellow flower cluster. Unlike other bromeliads, this one bears male and female flowers on separate plants. This species wants partial shade to sun with frequent water. It is of outstanding beauty. See Plate 10.

Aechmea mexicana (mex-i-KAHN-a) (synonym *A. bernoulliana*) occurs naturally from southern Mexico through Central America and is hardy in zones 10 and 11. It grows as an epiphyte and forms a large, spreading open rosette. The broad, thick light green leaves, which are as much as 30 inches long and mottled with darker green, turn rose to orange in the sun. The inflorescence is a 2-foot-tall panicle that bears tiny pink flowers, which produce white berries. The plant likes partial shade to full sun and frequent watering. This species is very bold and attractive.

Aechmea nidularioides (nid'-yoo-lair-ee-OY-deez) is indigenous to the tropical rain forests of northeastern Peru and southeastern Colombia. It is hardy in zones 10 and 11 and marginal in zone 10a. The large rosette may reach a diameter of 4 feet and a height of 3 feet. The lance-shaped leaves are long, somewhat recurved, and a wonderful satiny reddish green, often with darker red or lighter green striations above. The leaf margins are spiny. The spectacular inflorescence rises about a foot above the rosette and consists of a cluster shaped like a pine cone with boat-shaped and keeled bright orange to red bracts usually tipped with white. The flowers are white. This species is very choice. Plate 11.

Aechmea orlandiana (or-land'-ee-AHN-a) hails from the coastal forests of Brazil where it grows as an epiphyte and as a terrestrial in partial shade to full sun. It is a compact, tubular-shaped colorful plant with 2-foot-long stiff, pale green leaves with stout spines on the margins and wavy bands and splotches of red to black across the leaf blade. Like the leaves of many other *Aechmea* species, the leaves of this one have a rosy cast in full sun. The inflorescence is scarlet with light yellow flowers. The plant is not hardy to cold and needs to be grown in zones 10b and 11. Several cultivars are even more beautiful than the species and have bands of white or orange usually flecked with red spots.

Aechmea paniculigera (pan-ik'-yoo-LIJ-e-ra) is native to the West Indies where it grows in partial shade and full sun as an epiphyte. It is hardy in zones 10 and 11. This large, vase-shaped plant has tough, broad light green leaves, which are 3 feet long by 3 inches or more wide, and which have margins with distantly spaced spines. The inflorescence is about 2 feet tall with bannerlike ovate red to rosy bracts beneath a spectacular cylindrical spike of densely packed purple or deep pink flowers. The berries are cream colored.

Aechmea penduliflora (pen-dyoo'-li-FLOR-a) (synonym *A. schultesiana*) grows in partial shade to full sun on trees and terrestrially from Costa Rica to Brazil. It is hardy in zones 10b and 11. It is a real beauty if grown in good light, which causes the strap-shaped, dark green, remotely toothed leaves to turn a cinnamon-rose hue. The plant is a medium-sized open, vaselike rosette. A veritable rainbow of color when in bloom and fruit, it has inflorescences branched with a few crimson bracts beneath and small yellow flowers that are followed by white berries, which change to pink and finally blue. This very choice plant requires frequent waterings.

Aechmea phanerophlebia (fan'-er-o-FLEE-bee-a) grows in partial shade to full sun as an epiphyte and as a terrestrial in southern Brazil. It is hardy in zones 9b through 11. This rather large plant is a beautiful and exotic-looking species because of its form (a tight tubular rosette) and the lovely olive green leaves that are horizontally banded with white. The margins of the leaves are quite spiny. The inflorescence is held well above the foliage and appears from any distance rather like a bottle brush, being evenly cylindrical and consisting of bright rose bracts and tiny purple flower petals.

Aechmea racinae (RAS-i-nee) from the shady rain forest of Brazil is sometimes referred to as Christmas jewels because of the brightly colored pendent flower spikes and fruit that form and color up around the turn of the year. It is a small, water-loving epiphytic vase-shaped plant with beautiful remotely toothed glossy green leaves about a foot long. The wonderful inflorescence with its long drooping stem bearing scarlet bracts with small yellow and black-spotted flowers gives the visual effect of a small pendulous-flowered heliconia.

The flowers are followed by luminous orange berries, which last for months—a real beauty! This species is not hardy to cold and should not be grown outside zones 10b and 11.

Aechmea retusa (re-TOOS-a) is indigenous to Ecuador and northern Peru and is hardy in zones 10 and 11 and marginal in zone 10a. An epiphytic species, it forms a large, rather tall, and usually narrow rosette of fairly stiff leaves that are deep green above and a beautiful purplish red beneath. The large and spirally branched inflorescence consists of large lance-shaped orange-red bracts among the yellow-bracted and orange-bracted yellow flowers. Plate 12.

Aechmea schiedeana. See *A. bracteata.*

Aechmea schultesiana. See *A. penduliflora.*

Aechmea sphaerocephala (sfee-ro-SEF-a-la) (synonym *A. gigantea*) hails from the Rio de Janeiro area of Brazil and is hardy only in zones 10b and 11. It grows terrestrially in wet areas in partial shade to full sun and is an immense, tubular vase-shaped plant. The leaves are as long as 9 feet, concave in cross section and uniformly green with large vicious spines on the margins. The large inflorescence is 6 inches or more in diameter, green, and completely spherical with blue to purple flowers. The rounded flower cluster is held above erect rosy red bracts. This plant is a startling sight when in bloom, but alas, it rarely does so in cultivation.

Aechmea tillandsioides (til-land´-zee-OY-deez) is yet another species with more than one distinct form in nature. All the forms are epiphytic, water-loving, medium-sized tubular-shaped plants with narrow leaves needing part shade to full sun. All are tender to cold, and their cultivation is limited to zones 10b and 11. *Aechmea tillandsioides* **var.** *kienastii* (kee-NAST-ee-eye) hails from southern Mexico to the Amazon Basin. It has graceful, spiny, dark green leaves and a distinct upright tubular shape. The leaves are widely spaced up the "vase." The dark rose inflorescence is branched with dark pink bracts and yellow flowers, followed by white berries that slowly change to light blue. The bracts remain on the scape with the berries and keep their color, resulting in all three colors being present simultaneously. *Aechmea tillandsioides* **var.** *tillandsioides* is found all over the Amazon Basin, Venezuela, and Guiana. It is larger in all respects than the type, and the leaves are broader and gray-green with stout brown spines. The inflorescence is a brilliant red throughout.

Aechmea tinctoria. See *A. bromeliifolia.*

Aechmea zebrina (ze-BREEN-a / ze-BRYN-a) occurs naturally in Colombia, Ecuador, and eastern Peru where it grows as an epiphyte in partial shade to full sun in the wet tropical forest. It is hardy in zones 10b and 11. This beautiful medium-sized tubular-shaped plant has rather stiff and thick dark green leaves heavily banded with white. The tall erect yellow flower spike bears large ovate and brilliant red bracts beneath the much-branched clusters of orange- and yellow-bracted yellow flowers.

AEONIUM (ee-O-nee-um)

Crassulaceae: The Sedum, Sempervivum Family
Common names vary according to species
Succulent rosettes of green or green and red leaves, often atop small branching shrubs
Zones vary according to species
Sun to part shade
Average but regular amounts of moisture; most are somewhat drought tolerant
Loose, porous, fast-draining soil
Propagation by seed and removal of suckers

A genus of about 30 species of beautiful succulent plants allied most closely to *Sempervivum* (hens-and-chickens) but also to *Crassula* and *Sedum*. They are all native to islands in the Mediterranean, the Canary Islands, and northern Africa, with most species originating in the Canary Islands. All have the rosette form common to the just-mentioned genera but, in addition, *Aeonium* species have stems that are often branching, which can make them shrubs of considerable size. All have fleshy and rather soft usually spatulate-shaped leaves very often tinged with or completely suffused with red, orange, or purple. All have yellow, red, white, or pink flowers in panicles that arise from the centers of the rosettes of leaves, usually in spring, but often in winter or early summer. The plants flower only when mature and then the flowering parts gradually die off much like species of *Agave* (century plants). Most species produce more stems from beneath the withered parts. Some of the larger species are sometimes mistaken for members of the genus *Agave*, although they are not related and *Aeonium* leaves are neither spiny nor tough like *Agave* leaves. Aeoniums are unexcelled for beauty in a raised bed or the cactus and succulent garden. None of them can take very much cold or poor drainage, but most acclimate nicely to partial shade. Unlike most cactus species, none of them is truly drought tolerant, and they like to be watered when dry during the fall through spring growing season. Most species are dormant or semidormant in the summer.

Aeonium arboreum (ahr-BOR-ee-um), as the specific name implies, is almost arboreal in form and attains at least 3 feet in height. It is native to Morocco in northern Africa and the southern Mediterranean islands and is hardy in zones 10 and 11. The leaves, borne at the ends of the few branches in rather flat rosettes, are 6 inches wide, glossy, light green to yellow-green, long-spatulate, and margined with fine white hairs. The large pyramidal panicles consist of many bright yellow 10-petaled flowers with long extruded stamens of the same color. *Aeonium arboreum* **'Atropurpureum'** (at´-ro-poor-POOR-ee-um) is a beautiful cultivar with vegetative parts colored deep copper to dark purple in the summer. It needs full sun to attain the most color. The darker forms of this cultivar are often referred to as zwartkop (black tree). The plants take only a few degrees of frost.

Aeonium canariense (ka-nair´-ee-ENS-ee) is, of

course, from the Canary Islands. It is often called velvet rose or green velvet rose because of the beautifully symmetrical and large (to 2 feet across) deep, cup-shaped rosette it forms. The stem is very short, almost nonexistent. The dark green leaves are as much as 10 inches long and covered in thick, white, somewhat sticky hairs. In full sun the tips of the leaves have a distinct rosy hue. The inflorescence can be almost 3 feet tall with bright yellow flowers. The plant readily suckers, resulting in large mounds of rosettes. It is dependably hardy in zones 10 and 11. Damage starts at 28°F, but plants will spring back from temperatures in the low 20s.

Aeonium decorum (de-KOR-um) is another species from the Canary Islands. This beauty has small highly colored ovate to obovate, puckered green and copper to red leaves with scarlet margins. The spring-blooming inflorescence is relatively large as are the deep pink flowers thereupon. A small branched shrub, usually less than a foot high, it is tender to temperatures below 30°F, making it dependable in zones 10 and 11. It is sometimes called the copper pinwheel.

Aeonium holochrysum (ho-lo-KRY-sum) is native to the Canary Islands and is a tall (to 3 feet) branched plant with large (10 inches across) rosettes of narrowly spatulate, smooth green leaves, which often turn chocolate brown in drought. The flowers are a deep golden color, and the inflorescence is a fat cylinder. This species is hardy to 28°F, making it adaptable to zones 10 and 11 and marginal in zone 9b.

Aeonium nobile (NO-bi-lee) is native to the Canary Islands and is hardy in zones 9b through 11. It is a spectacular plant in or out of flower. The rosettes are as much as 2 feet wide and consist of very fleshy pale green sticky leaves, which are concave in cross section. The inflorescence is of a stature commensurate with the rosette of leaves: 2 feet wide with fleshy, purple involucral leaves. The flowers are deep orange to scarlet and, alas, have an unpleasant odor. The plant produces no suckers or offshoots and dies entirely after flowering. It must be propagated by seed.

Aeonium tabulaeforme (tab´-yoo-ly-FORM-ee) is indigenous to the Canary Islands. It forms an unusual flat, platelike rosette of closely packed grassy green narrowly spatulate leaves with fine hairs on the margins. The plant dies after flowering without producing offshoots. The inflorescence is much branched, 2 feet in height, with bright light yellow flowers. The plant is hardy to about 30°F and thus adaptable only to zones 10 and 11.

Aeonium undulatum (un-dyoo-LAIT-um) is indigenous to the Canary Islands. It is a large, stout-stemmed and much-branched shrub growing to as much as 10 feet in height with large rosettes (12 inches wide) of spatulate, very broad, wavy-margined dark green leaves. The inflorescence is a broad pyramid of bright yellow flowers. This species is hardy to 30°F, making it adaptable only in zones 10 and 11.

AGAVE (a-GAH-vay)
Agavaceae: The Agave Family
CENTURY PLANT
Small to immense rosettes of thick, tough swordlike
    leaves; tall candelabra-like flower spikes
Zones vary according to species
Sun to part sun
Drought tolerant
Light, porous, sandy, well-drained soil
Propagation by transplanting of suckers and by seed

A genus of more than 300 species of small to giant, stout and succulent herbs, all native to tropical and subtropical America but mostly Mexico. None are found naturally in the Southern Hemisphere, only a few are found in northern South America, and there are more in the southwestern United States than in the West Indies, Florida, Central America, and northern South America. All the species have thick and stout, fleshy straplike leaves in rosettes, usually with spines on the margins. Sometimes the spines, especially the terminal spine, are vicious. Almost all the species are trunkless, but a few produce stems to as much as 6 feet high. Most species flower only after attaining some age and then die, but usually sucker and produce offshoots that renew the landscape subject. The inflorescences are usually of considerable size and arise from the center of the rosette of leaves, often to a great height. The flower clusters occupy only the top half or so of the inflorescence. All the species need well-drained soil and at least half a day's sun. They appreciate watering in drought conditions, but succumb to rot if the soil drainage is impeded. All the species are generally referred to as century plants. The leaf fibers of many of them are used for making rope and twine, and the rosette hearts of other species are used in Latin America to make an alcoholic drink known as "mescal."

Agave americana (a-mer´-i-KAHN-a) is native to the northern half of Mexico and is hardy in zones 9 through 11 and marginal in zone 8a. It makes a very imposing statement in the landscape and is probably the most famous of the agaves, with common names of century plant and maguey (mah-GAY). The plant is gigantic at maturity: the leaves are as much 8 feet long and often a foot wide, resulting in a rosette of amazing proportions, as much as 12 feet in diameter and almost as tall. The leaves, which are bluish green or grayish green, are very thick and fleshy but curve downward the last third of their length. The margins are spiny with hooked thorns, and the terminal spine is large and deadly. The flower spike, which appears anywhere from age 12 to 20, can reach to 40 feet but is usually about 25 feet in height with flattish flower clusters in candelabra-like spacing on the top third of the stem. Each 3-inch-long yellow flower is narrow and tube-shaped. *Agave americana* 'Variegata', along with other cultivars, is more commonly planted than the species. It has bluish green leaves with yellow or white stripes that are seldom as wide as those of the type and, in addition, are often picturesquely twisted and turning. The cultivars are not quite as hardy to cold as is the type. Plates 13, 14, and 16.

Agave angustifolia (an-gust-i-FO-lee-a) is native to the West Indies. It makes a suckering rosette that is 5 or 6 feet wide with many stiff, narrowly lanceolate 3-foot-long bluish green leaves. Each leaf has small whitish or bluish teeth on the margins and a stout terminal spine that is usually tipped in red. The inflorescence is as much as 12 feet tall with panicles of greenish yellow flowers adorning the top half. The plants are hardy in zones 9b through 11. *Agave angustifolia* **'Marginata'** (mar-ji-NAIT-a) has leaves margined in white.

Agave atrovirens (at-ro-VY-renz) is a very picturesque species from the Oaxaca area of Mexico. It is hardy in zones 9b through 11. The green to bluish gray leaves are fat and thick, almost ovate, as much as 6 feet long and 2 feet wide, concave above and keeled below, with a long spine at the apex and small teeth along the margins. The inflorescence is a magnificent 30-foot-tall spike with many red-blossomed flat-topped flower clusters. This plant is the chief source of the alcoholic beverage known as *pulque* (POOL-kay) and, therefore, the plant is usually called pulque or pulque agave.

Agave attenuata (at-ten´-yoo-AIT-a), a central western Mexican species, is sometimes called the dragon-tree agave as it makes a trunk as much as 5 feet tall with age. The plant also freely suckers, resulting in a beautiful mass of green to gray, 5-foot-long leaves, which are spineless on the margins, rather narrow at the base, wide in the center, and tapering to a soft point. The inflorescence is a thing of wonder: as much as 12 feet long, beautifully arching, with greenish yellow flowers the whole length of the flower spike. This very beautiful species appreciates a richer and more moist soil than most agaves and flourishes in partial shade as well as full sun. Not very hardy, the plant is adapted to zones 9b and 11 and is marginal in zone 9a. There is a variegated cultivar with creamy white stripes on the leaves. Plates 15, 27, and 252.

Agave echinoides (ek-i-NOY-deez) is indigenous to the southern half of Mexico and is hardy in zones 9 through 11. It forms a many-leaved rosette with quite narrow cylindrical, almost pencil-shaped, gray to green 6-inch-long leaves. The leaf margins are spineless, but the tip of the leaf carries a vicious spine. The younger leaves are mostly erect, but the older ones grow more and more horizontally, according to their age, giving the whole plant a very full pincushion or hedgehoglike visual effect. The plant is very drought tolerant and demands full sun. The inflorescence reaches 5 feet in height with yellow or red flowers along the top third of the flower spike.

Agave fernandi-regis (fer-NAN-dee-RAY-gis) is very similar to *A. victoriae-reginae*. It is native to the same area and has the same hardiness and cultural requirements.

Agave ferox (FER-ahx) is indigenous to a large region of central and western Mexico and is hardy in zones 9 through 11 and marginal in zone 8b. It forms rosettes that are about 6 feet wide. The rosettes consist of very fat, brilliantly deep green, glossy, stiff, and keeled 3-foot-long leaves that are margined with black teeth and taper to a long vicious spine. The incredible inflorescence is 30 feet tall and layered with clusters of brilliant yellow flowers. The species is one of the most magnificent in the genus and is amazingly hardy to cold for such a tropical looking succulent. Plate 16.

Agave filifera (fi-LIF-e-ra) is a small species from Mexico with flowerlike rosettes of many curved, sword-shaped, concave stiff leaves that are each 10 to 12 inches long. The leaves are bright green in color with a fine white line along the spineless margins (and sometimes in the centers of the leaves) ending in a sharp point. The leaf margins, especially on the younger leaves, split into loose, curling white filaments, which has led to the common name of thread agave. The leaves often have a purple or bronzy hue in full sun. The inflorescence is 4 to 6 feet high with whitish green flowers gradually changing to dark red. The plant is hardy in zones 8 through 11 and marginal in zone 7b. It grows in partial shade as well as full sun. *Agave filifera* **'Compacta'** is a very small, compact cultivar that is less than a foot in diameter.

Agave franzosinii (frahn-zo-SIN-ee-eye) is native to southern Mexico and is hardy in zones 10 and 11. It grows to as much as 12 feet wide and 10 feet tall with great 8-foot-long bluish green to bluish gray fleshy linear-lanceolate spiny-margined leaves that usually are pendulous on their tips and often twisted to some extent like those of *A. americana* forms. The leaf tips have short, vicious spines. The inflorescence is as much as 40 feet high with pale yellow flowers. One of the most beautiful and spectacular species, it is, alas, tender to cold.

Agave guadalajarana (gwahd´-a-la-HAHR-a-na) occurs naturally in southwestern Mexico and is hardy in zones 10 and 11 and marginal in zone 9b. It forms a 3-foot-wide spreading rosette of fleshy flat and somewhat outwardly curving gray or bluish gray leaves that are obovate in outline. The margins and leaf tip are armed with beautiful red spines. The plant looks like a giant blue spiny-petaled rose. The inflorescence is as tall as 18 feet and has tufts of purplish red flowers. This plant is striking and beautiful.

Agave havardiana. See *A. scabra*.

Agave lechuguilla (lay-choo-GEE-ya) is indigenous to southern New Mexico, southwestern Texas, and adjacent northern Mexico, and is hardy in zones 8 through 11 and marginal in zone 7b. It is almost universally termed lechuguilla where it is native. The plant forms a medium-sized, very spiny yellow-green to reddish purple erect rosette. The 2-foot-long leaves are stiff and concave in cross section with widely spaced spines on the margins and a vicious dagger point at the tips.

Leaf color is variable, being generally yellowish green but often deep rose or even purple in cold weather or under conditions of drought. The plants sucker very freely, making, with time, somewhat extensive colonies by the creeping rhizomes. The individual rosettes, which flower at three or four years of age, are not very long lived, but the constant suckering ensures the perpetuation of the landscape subject. The inflorescence is from 4 to 12 feet tall and consists of tightly packed green and yellow tubular flowers on the top half or two-thirds of the spike.

Agave macroacantha (mak´-ro-a-KANTH-a) occurs naturally in southern Mexico and is hardy in zones 10 and 11, although it often survives to maturity in zone 9b. It forms foot-wide fairly erect, urn-shaped rosettes of stiff linear keeled bluish gray to bluish white leaves margined with small curved spines and an abrupt and very sharp black terminal spine. The inflorescence is about 9 feet tall with brownish red flowers.

Agave neglecta (ne-GLEK-ta) is a native of southern Florida, where it is called wild century plant or blue century plant. The plants are hardy in zones 9 through 11. The linear leaves, which are about 6 feet long, are stiff and erect as they arise from the center of the rosette, but then they spread outward and narrow to a brown spine. The inflorescence is as much as 30 feet high with yellow-green flowers.

Agave parrasana (pair-a-SAHN-a) from southwestern Texas and adjacent northern Mexico is hardy in zones 8 through 11. It makes a medium-sized spiny light blue rosette. The very wide ovate leaves are a beautiful blue gray and are concave in cross section with stout black spines on the margins and a long black terminal spine. The slightly open rosette resembles a big blue rose. The flower spike grows to 12 or 15 feet in height with clusters of yellow blossoms.

Agave parryi (PAIR-ee-eye) hails from southern New Mexico and adjacent northern Mexico and is widely known as mescal. It is a beautiful compact and dense gray to grayish blue rosette of stiff, very fleshy, thick ovate to obovate leaves that are margined with small spines and a stout black terminal spine. The leaves, which are usually no more than 12 inches long, are completely erect and do not recurve at the ends but rather are somewhat inwardly curving at this point. The rosette has a flowerlike appearance, much like an artichoke. The inflorescence is relatively large, as much as 12 feet or more in height, with the flower clusters along the top half. Each flower opens red and changes to sulfur-yellow. This very beautiful agave is amazingly hardy, being adaptable to zones 7 through 11. Plate 17.

Agave salmiana (sahl-mee-AHN-a) is native to central Mexico and is hardy in zones 9b through 11. This magnificent and imposingly beautiful species grows to a height of 10 feet. It has very stiff, broad, sword-shaped 8-foot-long powdery blue to bluish gray keeled leaves. The margins are covered with short white spines and the spiny dark tips are steel-like. The inflo-rescence is as much as 30 feet tall and consists of tiers of greenish yellow blossoms. The plant is often called pulque.

Agave scabra (ha-vahr´-dee-AHN-a) (synonyms *A. havardiana, A. wislizenii*) is indigenous to the elevated portions of the Chihuahuan Desert of southwestern Texas and adjacent northern Mexico and is hardy in zones 8 through 11. This small but beautiful species grows to about 2 feet or so in height (not including the inflorescence), with bluish gray thick fat leaves, margined with backward pointing spines, and provided with straight black spines at the tips. The inflorescence is about 15 feet in height with bright golden yellow flower clusters only near the tip.

Agave sisalana (sis-a-LAHN-a) is native to the Yucatán area of Mexico. This striking plant is a large dark green fan of long, narrow swordlike leaves, almost spineless, except for the tips. It is known as hemp agave, sisal, and sisal hemp. Each leaf is as much as 5 feet long, stiff and straight, but concave in cross section. With age the plant may form a trunk up to 3 feet in height. It produces many suckers from the base of the rosette and sometimes plantlets from the bracts of the inflorescence beneath the flower clusters. The flower spike may reach 30 feet in height, and the flowers are greenish white and fragrant. The fairly tender plant is hardy in zones 9b through 11. It is widely grown in the tropics for the leaf fibers, which are used in making rope. Some individuals are allergic to the sap.

Agave stricta (STRIK-ta) is quite similar to *A. echinoides*, but is a larger plant with leaves to 3 feet long and purple flowers. It wants the same culture and has the same hardiness as *A. echinoides*.

Agave utahensis (yoo´-tah-EN-sis) is native to southern Utah, northwestern Arizona, and southern Nevada, and is hardy in zones 6 through 11. It is a small but attractive species with olive green 8- to 10-inch-long stiff upwardly arching leaves armed with large stout white spines on the margins and provided with white spines on the leaf tips. *Agave utahensis* **var.** *eborispina* (ee-bor´-i-SPYN-a) has incredibly long, upwardly curving white apical spines. The summer inflorescence is about 8 feet tall with small clusters of yellow flowers.

Agave victoriae-reginae (vik-TOR-ee-eye-REJ-in-eye) is native to northern Mexico and, because of the beauty of the compact variegated rosette, has the well-deserved common name of queen agave. The leaves are spineless except for the small spine at the tip. Never more than a foot long, they are very stiff, erect, and usually somewhat curved inward, and they are dark green and margined above and below with a white stripe. This slow-growing but choice plant is hardy in zones 9 through 11, although it has survived zone 8b. The plant dies after flowering without making suckers and, therefore, is propagated only by seed. The inflorescence is relatively small (to 4 feet) and pale green. Plate 18.

Agave wislizenii. See *A. scabra*.

AGLAONEMA

(ag-lay-O-nee-ma / a-GLAW-nee-ma)
Araceae: The Calla Lily, Jack-in-the-Pulpit Family
CHINESE EVERGREEN
Small herbaceous foliage plants with mostly
    variegated leaves
Zones 10 and 11; marginal in zone 10a
Shade to part-shade
Average but regular amounts of moisture
Rich, humusy, well-drained soil
Propagation by rhizome division and cuttings

A genus of about 50 species of showy small herbs in tropical East Asia from the Philippines to southeastern China, to Thailand and New Guinea. There are very many hybrids and cultivars, with new ones constantly being introduced to the market. In form the plants very much resemble those of the genus *Dieffenbachia* (dumbcanes). In the unadulterated species, the leaves are often solid green or different shades of green, while almost all the cultivars and hybrids have highly variegated leaves, *Aglaonema* 'Silver Queen' being an outstanding example.

Because of their size (never more than 2 feet in height), their tolerance of shady conditions, and their variegation and beauty of form, these plants make superb groundcover or understory subjects. They are wonderfully shade tolerant if the shade is not too dense, as they need some light to maintain their best color. Almost all the species, cultivars, and hybrids clump, making in time a nice groundcover colony. They often form roots on the lower parts of their stems, allowing them to creep and spread.

The flowers are typical of the family Araceae, being tiny, white or cream, and tightly packed onto a short spadix inside the boatlike green to yellow spathe. The fruits are red or orange berries, often quite colorful and attractive.

Aglaonemas can stand very little frost, but they do not languish and look ragged with sustained cool to cold temperatures (as do many other tropicals) as long as the temperature remains above freezing. They can endure dry air, but flourish when the relative humidity is high, which is not much of a problem for areas like southern Florida. They like to be moist, but can also endure for short periods almost drought conditions. They are durable, tough and easy.

The hybrids and cultivars of *Aglaonema* are too numerous and their genetic heritage too complex to attempt a definitive listing with descriptions. A few of my favorite forms and species are described here.

***Aglaonema commutatum* 'Treubii'** (TROY-bee-eye) has long, linear bluish green leaves marked with grayish green to silvery spreading splotches from the midrib outward. It is sometimes called the ribbon aglaonema.

***Aglaonema costatum* 'Foxii'** (FOX-ee-eye) has 12-inch-long dark green cordate-acuminate leaves with a broad white stripe along the midrib and white spots scattered throughout the blade. It is sometimes referred to as the spotted evergreen.

Aglaonema crispum (krisp-um) (synonyms *A. roebelinii*, *Schismatoglottis roebelinii*) is native to the Philippines and is sometimes called the painted drop-tongue. It has foot-long broad-elliptic green leaves with a band of silvery gray between the midrib and the margin.

***Aglaonema nitidum* 'Curtisii'** (ni-TY-dum kur-TIS-ee-eye) has foot-long leaves that are bluish green with silver to gray bands radiating from the midrib.

***Aglaonema roebelinii*.** See *A. crispum*.

Aglaonema rotundum (ro-TUN-dum) is indigenous to the island of Sumatra. The 6-inch-long leaves are ovate to orbicular, glossy dark green above with a pink to white midrib and lateral curved veins, and purplish red beneath.

***Aglaonema* 'Silver King'** has long (18 inches) and long-tipped narrow leaves that are silvery gray with blotches of bluish green. The plant is large and lush. It grows quickly and suckers freely.

***Aglaonema* 'Silver Queen'** has narrow, foot-long lance-shaped olive green leaves with a pinnate pattern of silvery gray markings from the midrib outward. The plant is large and lush. It grows quickly and suckers freely.

AIPHANES (EYE-fa-neez / ah-EE-fa-neez)

Palmae (Arecaceae): The Palm Family
COYURE PALMS
Medium-sized, slender-trunked, very spiny feather-
    leaved palms with exotically shaped leaves
Zones 10b and 11
Shade to sun
Water lovers
Rich, moist, well-drained soil
Propagation by seed

A genus of 22 species of small to medium-sized pinnate-leaved palms, all in tropical America and all very tropical, graceful, and beautifully exotic looking. They are very prickly, spiny, and thorny to some degree in all their parts, even the inflorescences. Furthermore, they are also quite tender and can be successfully cultivated in mainland United States only in southern Florida. They flourish wonderfully in moist and truly tropical regions. Most species are single trunked, but a few sucker, and some have hidden underground trunks. Most species have leaflets that are distinctly jagged on their ends, but others have almost completely entire leaflets. Most hail from high rainfall areas and cannot stand drought conditions. They relish rich, humusy soil, although many species from the Caribbean islands can flourish on limestone-based soil. None of them like full sun when young as they start out their lives as understory subjects. They grow relatively fast for palms if their cultural requirements are met.

Aiphanes acanthophylla (a-kanth´-o-FYL-la) (synonym *A. minima*), a native of Puerto Rico, is one of the two most commonly planted species in southern

Florida. It is often referred to as coyure palm. The trunk is composed of alternating rings of stout black spines and clean, light-colored areas and attains a maximum height of 30 feet. The flat leaves are 6 feet or more in length, and the leaflets are 1 to 2 inches wide and a foot or more in length, with squared and slightly jagged ends. The palm is fast growing and very beautiful.

Aiphanes caryotifolia (kair´-ee-ot-i-FO-lee-a) (synonym *A. aculeata*) is native to Colombia, Venezuela, and Ecuador. It is one of the two most commonly planted species in southern Florida. Like *A. acanthophylla,* it is often referred to as coyure palm. It is of the same stature as the above palm, but the trunk is slightly thinner and even lighter in color and has the same alternating bands of spines and clear trunk. The leaves are about 6 feet long, and the leaflets are wide and roughly deltoid with very jagged ends, giving the leaf as a whole a distinctly "ruffled" appearance. This ruffled aspect of the gracefully arching leaves and the thin trunk combine to make this one of the world's most beautifully graceful and exotic looking palms.

Aiphanes erosa (e-RO-sa) is native to the West Indian island of Barbados and is sometimes called the macaw palm. The trunk is covered with black spines, but is darker than the trunk of *A. caryotifolia* and is also of lesser stature, attaining a maximum of about 15 feet. The leaves are about 6 feet long with leaflets similar to those of *A. acanthophylla,* but the leaves stand out somewhat more erect from the trunk than do those of the coyure palm. The mature fruit is a beautiful deep red in color and is preceded by clusters of fragrant white flowers. Some botanists think this species is but a variety of *A. acanthophylla.* Plate 19.

ALBIZIA (al-BIZ-ee-a)

Mimosaceae (Fabaceae, Leguminosae), subfamily
    Mimosoideae: The Mimosa Family
Common names vary according to species
Medium-sized to giant, pinnate-leaved, evergreen or
    deciduous trees
Zones vary according to species
Sun
Average but regular amounts of moisture
Average soil
Propagation by seed

A large genus of about 150 species of mostly trees in tropical and warm climate areas around the earth. Some are deciduous, but most are evergreen or almost evergreen. All have ferny bipinnate leaves and globular flower clusters like plumes or powder puffs. Many are drought tolerant to some degree. The genus name is sometimes erroneously spelled "Albizzia."

Albizia julibrissin (jool-i-BRIS-sin) is the mimosa of the South, sometimes also called the silk tree. It occurs naturally from Iran eastward to Japan and is one of the most commonly planted trees throughout the South and Deep South—and with good reason. Both the leaves and the wonderfully fragrant pink flowers are beautiful. It is, alas, falling out of favor with landscapers and the public in general because it is planted as if it were a drought-tolerant cactus or succulent. Then, when it is generally neglected, it shows premature leaf drop, general decline, and disease and insect infestation. If the tree is planted in decent soil and receives adequate watering in times of drought, it is one of the most beautiful deciduous trees for zones 7 through 9. If the leaves remain green with good culture, the 8-inch brown seed pods are not nearly so noticeable or objectionable during the late summer. It can grow to 40 feet or more, but is usually about 20 feet tall and as wide. It is not well adapted to the soil and climate of tropical Florida, although it will grow there. In limestone soil the tree needs soil amendment to prevent chlorosis. *Albizia julibrissin* var. *rosea* (RO-zee-a / ro-ZAY-a) is a readily available variety with deeper pink flowers. Plate 20.

Albizia lebbeck (LEB-bek) is much more tender to cold than *A. julibrissin.* It is indigenous to a large part of tropical Asia, including northern Australia, and is hardy only in zones 10 and 11. It is a massive and very fast growing shade tree attaining 50 feet or more in cultivation and supposedly 100 feet in its native habitats. It ultimately makes a broad spreading crown atop a relatively short thick trunk. The bipinnate leaves are dark green, and the leaflets are oblong to obovate and large, as much as 2 inches long. The leaves are shed for a brief period in the spring. The fragrant flowers are greenish yellow globes that are 2 inches in diameter. They are followed by large, long-lasting, light-brown leguminous seed pods, which rattle in the breeze after the leaves have fallen in winter, leading to the sexist common name of woman's-tongue tree. It is also sometimes called siris tree or monkey-pod tree. The tree is drought tolerant when established but, like *A. julibrissin,* looks better with an adequate supply of moisture. It has three faults: it readily suckers from far-traveling roots, it readily reseeds, and it is messy with the litter of its pods.

Albizia saman. See *Samanea saman.*

ALBIZZIA. See *Albizia.*

ALEURITES

    (a-LOOR-i-teez / al-yoo-RYE-teez)
Euphorbiaceae: The Euphorbia, Poinsettia Family
TUNG OIL TREES
Medium to large trees with large heart-shaped leaves;
    showy white flowers; interesting large nuts
Zones vary according to species
Sun
Average but regular amounts of moisture
Sandy, well-drained soil
Propagation by seed and mature cuttings

A genus of six species of deciduous and evergreen trees in tropical and subtropical Asia and the islands of the South Pacific. They all have large, very decorative mostly heart-shaped leaves with oil glands, and some have beautiful flowers. All the species have the milky sap typical of the family, and the seeds of several yield valuable oils.

Aleurites cordata (kor-DAIT-a) is native to southeastern China, the southern Japanese islands, and Taiwan. The tree is not particularly hardy to cold and should be confined to zones 9b through 11. It grows to about 25 feet with an equal width. The almost evergreen leaves are large, more than a foot wide, ovate to cordate, and with three to five lobes or teeth on the margins. The flowers are small and not particularly ornamental, but the large flattened warty fruits are quite interesting. An oil used in lamps is derived from the seeds, resulting in the common name of Japanese wood-oil tree.

Aleurites fordii (FORD-ee-eye) is native to central Asia and is hardy in zones 8 through 11. It grows to 35 feet and about as wide. Known as the tung oil tree or Chinese wood-oil tree, it was, at one time, widely planted in the Deep South with the intention of creating a commercial nut oil industry. The deciduous leaves are as much as a foot wide, long ovate-cordate, sometimes slightly lobed or toothed, and softly hairy with distinct depressions on top corresponding with the main veins of the leaf. The flowers are beautiful 2-inch-wide flaring trumpets of pure white with red, yellow, or orange throats and appear in spring with or before the leaves. The 3-inch-diameter fruits are poisonous, but are important for the oil expressed from the seeds, which is used in the making of paints and lacquers. The tree grows on poor dry soil and is drought tolerant but, of course, looks better with decent soil and an adequate supply of moisture.

Aleurites moluccana (mo-LUK-ka-na) is native to the islands of the South Pacific. The candlenut tree or varnish tree grows quickly to 60 or 70 feet in height and about 30 feet wide. It is hardy in zones 10 and 11 and marginal in zone 10a. The mature evergreen leaves are 8 to 15 inches wide with three to five lobes, strongly veined light to dark green, and reminiscent of large glossy maple leaves. The juvenile foliage may or may not be lobed and is covered in white soft hairs, which later turn to a rusty-colored pubescence. The flowers are small pure white stars in terminal branched panicles. The fruits are as glorious as the leaves and contrast beautifully with the varicolored leaves. Light-colored, rough-textured globular drupes, the fruits are reminiscent of large grapes or figs. Since fruits and flowers appear simultaneously on the tree, they create a true symphony of texture and color. The seeds have been used for millennia by islanders for fuel, illumination, and dyes and the wood for making canoes and houses. Plates 21 and 22.

Aleurites montana (mahn-TAN-a) is the mu tree or mu-oil tree and occurs naturally from southeastern China to northern Myanmar (Burma). It is slightly hardier than *A. moluccana* and is appropriate for zones 9b through 11. The tree grows to 25 or 30 feet in height and about as wide. The semi-evergreen leaves are long-ovate, a foot or more wide and often longer, strongly palmate-veined, and have three to five lobes. The tree is almost completely covered in April and May with masses of inch-wide pure white star-shaped flowers. The fruit in late summer is light-colored, elliptic, and about 2 inches in diameter.

ALLAGOPTERA (al-la-GAHP-te-ra)
Palmae (Arecaceae): The Palm Family
SEASHORE PALM
Small trunkless clumping pinnate-leaved palm; large
    plumose leaves
Zones 9 through 11
Sun
Drought and salt tolerant
Sandy, well-drained soil
Propagation by seed and root division

A small genus of only four species of pinnate-leaved palms that are indigenous to South America. Only one species is common in cultivation. *Allagoptera arenaria* (air-e-NAHR-ee-a) is native to the seacoast of the Bahía region of Brazil where it thrives on the dunes and in the saline scrublands farther inland. The 5- to 6-foot-long arching leaves are plumosely pinnate and the leaflets are arranged in distinct whorls. The leaflets are dark green on top and rather silvery beneath with a distinct and lighter-colored midrib, each one slightly less than a foot long, linear-lanceolate, and usually twisted to some extent. The woody inflorescence is strange and interesting, but usually hidden among the leaves. This strikingly attractive small palm is quite valuable for seaside plantings. The plant survives in clay or other soils, but does not grow well. It wants to be in almost pure sand. As one of the palm species subject to acquiring the always-fatal virus disease, lethal yellowing, it should not be planted in areas where this disease is present.

ALLAMANDA (al-la-MAN-da)
Apocynaceae: The Oleander, Frangipani, Vinca
    Family
ALLAMANDA
Sprawling evergreen shrubs and vines; trumpet-
    shaped yellow or violet flowers
Zones 10 and 11
Sun
Average but regular amounts of moisture
Rich, humusy, well-drained soil
Propagation by cuttings and seed

A genus of a dozen or so vines and shrubs all native to tropical America. All have milky sap that is irritating to the skin of some people and poisonous fruit. The leaves are oppositely arranged or in whorls, and the yellow or purplish flowers are large, showy, and funnel-shaped, with five expanded corolla lobes. Only three species are in general cultivation, but there are several varieties and cultivars. Included here are some of the world's most beautiful flowering vines. None, alas, is hardy to freezing temperatures.

Allamanda cathartica (ka-THART-i-ka) is the most commonly planted species, especially the cultivar *A. cathartica* 'Hendersonii'. Both plants are often called golden trumpet vine. The species has leathery light green linear-elliptic leaves, which are in whorls of three to four or in opposite pairs. They are 5 to 6 inches long, almost stalkless, and rather densely packed on far-ranging stems. The stems have only a slight tendency to twine and, therefore, must be trained and tied to a support if a vine is wanted. Otherwise the plants can be used as sprawling shrubs or clipped to more traditional shrub form, even a hedge. They are excellent as fast-growing espalier subjects. If trained as a vine the stems reach a maximum of about 50 feet in length. The flowers arise from the leaf axils and are short flaring, deep yellow trumpets as much as 4 inches wide with an orange to brown throat. *Allamanda cathartica* **'Hendersonii'** (hen-dur-SO-nee-eye) has larger flowers, to 6 inches or more in width, of a deep yellow or deep golden color. The flower buds are gorgeously milk-chocolate-colored, and the throats of the open flowers are brown. The variety is even looser growing than the species and takes the same pruning techniques. Both bloom almost constantly, especially in warm weather, but tolerate no frost. Not even the roots are hardy, although there are instances of the plants resprouting from temperatures in the upper 20s. *Allamanda cathartica* **'Williamsii'** (WILL-yum-zee-eye) is less often seen but eminently worthy of being planted. It is smaller in all parts, but the flowers are delicately fragrant and semi-double, and the plant is even more floriferous than *A. cathartica* or *A. cathartica* 'Hendersonii'. It is also rather more root hardy, often springing back from the roots if frozen down. Plate 23.

Allamanda **'Golden Sprite'** is a wonderful compact hybrid between *A. cathartica* and *A. neriifolia*. It is not a vine and does not sprawl as do the other *Allamanda* species dealt with here, but rather is a small and fairly compact shrub to 3 feet in height. The small, glossy evergreen foliage is like that of a dwarf golden trumpet vine, and the small brilliant yellow flowers are chocolate brown in bud. The plant is as floriferous as its parent, *A. neriifolia*. It needs the same culture as all the others.

Allamanda neriifolia (ner´-ee-eye-FO-lee-a), the bush allamanda, is a smaller, more compact and shrub-like plant than *A. cathartica* and attains a maximum height of 6 or 7 feet with about the same width. The leaves are similar to and arranged the same as the above hybrid but are smaller, darker green, and not as glossy or as leathery. The flowers are also smaller: 2-inch-long trumpets with a flare of the same width. The color is golden yellow with a deeper yellow throat with brown stripes. The plant is at least as floriferous as *A. cathartica*. The unusual fruits are soft, spiny balls.

Allamanda violacea (vee-o-LAY-see-a) has, as the specific epithet implies, more or less violet-colored flowers. The habit of the plant is like that of *A. cathartica*, sprawling or vinelike. The leaves are similar in outline to those of *A. cathartica*, but not as long and are not flat but rather troughed and ridged, felty above and definitely hairy beneath. The plant is not as floriferous as any of the above, and the flowers generally appear only in late summer and autumn, but are well worth the wait. This species is usually grafted onto *A. cathartica* rootstock as it is a weak grower on its own roots.

ALOCASIA
(al-o-KAY-sha / al-o-KAY-see-a)
Araceae: The Calla Lily, Jack-in-the-Pulpit Family
ELEPHANT-EAR; ELEPHANT'S EAR; TARO
Mostly stemless plants with large heart-shaped, often variegated or colored leaves
Zones vary according to species but most are entirely tropical
Light requirements vary according to species
Water lovers
Rich, moist humusy soil
Propagation by rhizome division and seed

A genus of about 70 large perennial rhizomatous herbs in tropical Asia. All have heart-shaped or arrow-shaped, usually deeply sagittate and long-petioled, leathery, glossy and waxy leaves, which sometimes are of great size, lobed or cut, and variegated or beautifully marked with various colors, and always of great beauty. All have the leaves emerging from usually short above-ground stems, although a few species make significant stems or trunks. Almost all species slowly sucker and form clumps with time. All require rich soil, abundant moisture, humidity, and warmth, although some can go into a dormant period, dying down in cold weather and returning from the rhizomatous roots with the advent of warm weather. The inflorescences of all species consist of a spathe and spadix typical of the family. In this case the flower spike is green to white and not very exciting. All species tolerate and even flourish in shade, but have more color in adequate light. Indeed some thrive in full sun.

Alocasia ×*amazonica* (am-a-ZAHN-i-ka) is a hybrid between *A. lowii* and *A. sanderiana*. Compared to *A. sanderiana*, it has slightly broader leaves with much less indentation on the margins, but it is an equally thrilling sight. It is sometimes called African mask.

Alocasia cucullata (kuk-yoo-LAIT-a) is found naturally from India and Sri Lanka and northeastward to Myanmar (Burma). This species has relatively small leaves for an alocasia (mostly less than a foot long) that are remotely sagittate on long petioles. The heart-shaped leaves are uncolored and unmarked, but are dark green and leathery and long-pointed. The rhizomatous roots are relatively hardy for an alocasia, and the roots are known to have survived 15°F and may be successfully grown in zones 9 through 11 in shade or sun. The plant is more than a water lover. It is almost aquatic and is very useful for growing in shallow water. Although it does not insist on having its roots in standing water, it can be said to be a true bog plant. These plants are sometimes called Chinese taro or Chinese ape (AH-pay). Plate 24.

Alocasia cuprea (KYOO-pree-a) is from Borneo and is as exotic as its place of origin. It is hardy in zones 10 and 11. The large, thick leathery leaves are peltate with the basal lobes almost completely united. They are long-cordate, usually 20 inches long and 12 inches wide, glossy dark green with a metallic sheen and puckered along the prominent veins. The raised area of the leaf is a lighter green than the background, and the back of the leaf is purple. This species is more tender than *A. cucullata* or *A. plumbea,* but the plants have been observed to sprout from the rootstock following temperatures in the upper 20s. The plant is not a sun lover and needs full to partial shade. *Alocasia cuprea × A. korthalsii* (kor-TAL-zee-eye) is called the mauro alocasia and is a stunningly beautiful cross with pink petioles. Compared to *A. cuprea × A. longiloba,* it has broader, less sagittate leaves, which are lighter green in color but similarly marked with white. *Alocasia cuprea × A. longiloba* (lahn-ji-LOB-a) is equally beautiful with deeply sagittate grayish green narrower leaves, slightly wavy margins, and white main veins. It is sometimes referred to as the mauro alocasia.

Alocasia 'Hilo Beauty', a cultivar of unknown parentage, is root hardy in zones 9b (possibly in 9a) through 11. It is a fairly small leaved plant, but is quite graceful and colorful. The 8- to 12-inch-long leaves are held on long purplish brown succulent petioles. The leaf blade is broadly ovate-sagittate in shape, a deep fir green in color, with many irregular silvery green to gray blotches. This exciting beautifully leaved plant is a true water lover and is often used at the margins of ponds or pools as a semi-aquatic in shade or sun. Plate 369.

Alocasia lowii (LO-wee-eye) is a very beautiful species from Malaya. It is hardy in zones 10 and 11 and marginal in zone 10a. It has long-ovate deeply sagittate, arrowhead-shaped leaves about 12 inches long and 8 inches wide. The color of the leaf is a deep metallic bluish green, and the main veins are white or gray. The plant does not want sun and is happy in shade or partial shade. *Alocasia lowii* var. *grandis* (GRAN-dis) has some of the most beautiful leaves in the plant world. They are larger and broader than the type and less deeply sagittate, and the white veining is not limited to the main veins but also creates a fine network of variegation between these veins.

Alocasia macrorrhiza (mak-ro-RY-za) is a very massive plant that is native to a large part of tropical Asia from Sri Lanka through India to Malaya and Indonesia. It is surprisingly hardy considering its native habitats, being appropriate for zones 9b through 11. Unlike most *Alocasia* species, it makes a significant stem or trunk, which can reach a height of 6 feet. The leaves, which are bright medium green and as much as 4 feet wide and 6 feet long, are held on long petioles as much as 4 feet long. Leaf and petiole are in the same plane, giving the leaf the unusually stiff aspect of facing heavenward. The plants are not as tender to cold as their exotic appearance would seem to indicate. The leaves are damaged by temperatures below freezing, but the trunks will resprout if the temperature does not go below 25°F. If protected, the plants can withstand even lower temperatures. They grow in almost total shade to full sun and are true bog plants, thriving in several inches (but no deeper) of water along the edges of ponds and pools. Several common names are applied to this great aroid, the commonest being giant alocasia and giant elephant's ear, but giant taro and giant ape (AH-pay) are also used. There is a variegated-leaved cultivar that does not grow as large as the species but is quite effective against a dark green background. Plate 25.

Alocasia odora (o-DOR-a) is native to northeastern India, northern Myanmar (Burma), and southern China. It is similar to *A. macrorrhiza,* but has an even larger stature. It requires the same climatic and cultural conditions as *A. macrorrhiza.*

Alocasia plumbea (plum-BAY-a) from Java is similar to *A. macrorrhiza* except for size and color: it makes a short trunk, and the leaves are in the same plane as the long dark purple petiole. The leaf surface is a deep olive green, and the underside is dark purple. The leaf blade is as much as 3 feet long, cordate-sagittate in shape, with slightly wavy margins. The plant is at least as hardy as *A. macrorrhiza* and may successfully be grown in zones 9 through 11 in shady or sunny sites. It is sometimes called the purple taro.

Alocasia sanderiana (san´-dur-ee-AHN-a) is a stunning beauty native to the Philippines. Not hardy to cold, it thrives only in shady or partially shady sites in zones 10 and 11 and is marginal in zone 10a. The leaves are deeply sagittate and light green with deeply indented margins, and the veins are white. This species is one of the most common decorative alocasias. Plate 26.

Alocasia watsoniana (wat-so´-nee-AHN-a) is native to Indonesia and one of the world's most beautiful plants. The large leaf, as much as 3 feet long and almost as wide, is peltate on the petiole, medium-sagittate, leathery, and somewhat puckered. It is the variegation, however, which is the main attraction: a network of gray to light green (rather similar to the markings on *A. lowii* var. *grandis*) on a background of bluish to dark olive green. The undersides of the leaves are rose to purple. The plant is not sun tolerant and must be grown in partial shade. It is hardy in zones 10b and 11.

ALOE (AL-o-ee)
Liliaceae: The Lily Family
ALOE (AL-o / AY-lo)
Succulent rosettes of leaves or trees with rosettes at
　branch ends; tall spikes of red and yellow flowers
Zones vary according to species
Part to full sun
Drought tolerant

Average, light, sandy, well-drained soil
Propagation by seed and transplanting of suckers;
    stem cuttings usually root

A large genus of more than 300 species of succulent herbs, shrubs, and trees native mostly to Africa, especially South Africa. The succulent leaves of all species are in rosettes. Arborescent species have rosettes only at the ends of the usually branching trunks and stems. Almost all species have teeth on the margins of the thick, tough ovate to long-lanceolate leaves and a spine at the end of the leaf. All have racemes of tubular, usually pendent yellow, orange, or red flowers on relatively tall spikes. The plants are frequently mistaken for those in the genus *Agave* and vice versa. All are easy to grow and maintain if given some sun and excellent drainage. All species described here are native to South Africa unless otherwise indicated. They grow and bloom mostly in the winter, but some are ever-growing and ever-blooming. The plants should receive the minimum amount of moisture possible in their dormant period which, unfortunately for regions like southern Florida, usually coincides with summer. These are some of the most striking and beautiful succulent plants. They are wonderfully powerful in the landscape, both as to form and, for very many species, the spectacular flower spikes. The smaller clump-forming species are almost overwhelmingly impressive when planted en masse, especially when they are in bloom.

Aloe africana (af-ri-KAHN-a) is sometimes called the spiny aloe and is very beautiful when in bloom. Its deep red flowers change to bright yellow as they age, resulting in a multicolored 3-foot-tall flower spike. The plants bloom several times a year. The leaves, which are 2 feet long with a bluish cast to the dark green, are concave in cross section and recurved, with large dark colored teeth on the margins. The plant makes a trunk as much as 12 feet high which, in time, is branched. The species is easy to cultivate in full sun in zones 9b through 11.

Aloe arborescens (ahr-bor-ES-senz) is found in northern South Africa. Older specimens make very impressive and beautiful masses of leaves, but these plants are dependably hardy only in zones 10 and 11 and marginal in zone 9b. Some specimens reach as much as 12 feet in height with candelabra-like branching, but most form large mounds of rosettes. The deep grayish to bluish green thick leaves are linear-lanceolate and often more than 2 feet long. The ends of the leaves are usually recurved with teeth along the margins. The late winter inflorescences bear scarlet, tubular-shaped flowers on 3-foot-tall unbranched spikes. Cold damage to the leaves starts at 30°F, but the trunks are hardier and have sometimes survived temperatures in the low 20s. Common names are tree aloe, torch plant, candelabra aloe, and octopus plant. Plate 27.

Aloe aristata (air-i-STAIT-a) makes no trunk, but is a charming tiny thing that is very useful for edging or filling soil pockets in the cactus and succulent garden.

The thick numerous leaves are long-lanceolate and usually less than 6 inches long. They have small white dots on the blades, white teeth on the margins, and a thread-like soft point at the end. The orange flowers appear in winter on 2-foot-long unbranched spikes. These fairly tender plants are dependably hardy in zones 9b through 11. Common names are torch plant and lace aloe.

Aloe bainesii (BAIN-zee-eye) is one of the largest tree types in the genus. Older specimens are an impressive sight in the landscape. The slow-growing trees can reach heights of more than 50 feet with massive whitish, smooth, very thick many-branched woody trunks. The recurved leaves are troughed, as much as 3 feet long, and toothed on the margins. The pinkish flowers are borne intermittently all year on 2-foot-long spikes. The plants are not very hardy to cold and are best limited to culture in zones 10 and 11. Although they might survive temperatures in the 20s, they will be cut back with each freeze, obviating the main reason for growing them, the beautiful tree form.

Aloe barbadensis (bar-ba-DENS-is) (synonym *A. vera*) is native to the islands off northwestern Africa, Madeira, the Canary Islands, and the Cape Verde Islands. This very succulent looking aloe has 2-foot-long lanceolate, erect light green leaves, which are toothed on the margins and which form vase-shaped rosettes. The deep yellow flowers appear in the winter and spring and hang from the top third of the 3-foot-tall spikes. The sap of this aloe is used medicinally for the treatment of burns and skin abrasions. The plants are of exceptionally easy culture in zones 9 through 11. Common names are aloe vera, medicinal aloe, and Barbados aloe. Plate 28.

Aloe camperi (KAMP-e-ry) occurs naturally in tropical East Africa. It is hardy in zones 10 and 11 and marginal in zone 9b. It is a stemmed and branching plant that grows to about 3 feet tall. The leaves usually hide the stems. The rosettes are about 2 feet wide and consist of 2-foot-long stiff grayish green lance-shaped leaves with prominent light-colored downward-pointing spines along the leaf margins. The inflorescence is especially beautiful in autumn and winter with inch-long orange to red flowers that are a deep scarlet color in bud.

Aloe dichotoma (dy-KAHT-o-ma) is native to southern South Africa northwestward into Namibia. It is hardy in zones 10 and 11, and marginal in zone 9b. This magnificent tree has thick trunks and many thick branches, each ending in a wonderful rosette of leaves. The leaves are 14 to 18 inches long, linear-lanceolate, and thick grayish green to bluish green, with tiny spines along their margins. The winter flowers are yellow and are borne in small foot-high panicles.

Aloe excelsa (ek-SEL-sa) occurs naturally in tropical East Africa and is hardy in zones 10 and 11. It forms a 20-foot-tall trunk with age but is seldom branched. The rosette is composed of several thick light green recurved leaves. The leaves are concave above and keeled beneath, and bear regularly spaced short spines along their margins. The glorious winter inflorescence is 3 to 5 feet in height and much branched, and bears very many yellow or orange to scarlet blossoms. Plate 29.

Aloe ferox (FER-ahx) is native to South Africa and is hardy in zones 9b through 11. This trunk-forming species sometimes grows to as much as 10 feet. The trunk is usually unbranched and clothed, for most of its length, with dead leaves. The terminal flattish leaf rosette is 4 or 5 feet wide with 3-foot-long grayish green fat stiff lance-shaped somewhat concave leaves armed with black marginal teeth and tipped with half-inch-long sharp spines. The widely branched late winter inflorescence is as much as 5 feet tall with very many closely set fiery reddish orange flower buds whose efflorescence reveals yellow-orange corollas. The plant is breathtakingly beautiful when in bloom. It is more handsome as a young plant than a mature specimen, although older plants underplanted with smaller species blend magnificently into the succulent landscapes. Plate 30.

Aloe marlothii (mar-LO-tee-eye) is a massive plant to 20 feet tall with, usually, a trunk 3 feet or more in diameter. It has thick, stiff, linear-lanceolate leaves as much as 5 feet long that are bluish gray to bluish green, concave in cross section, with large purple teeth along the margins. The plants bloom off and on most of the year with flower spikes about 3 feet high and branched in candelabra fashion. The branches are mostly covered with non-drooping yellow to orange flowers. This very beautiful but tender species is dependably hardy in zones 10 and 11. Plate 31.

Aloe mitriformis (mit-ri-FOR-mis) is native to southern South Africa and is hardy in zones 9b through 11. It is a clumping species that forms usually unbranched stems as tall as 6 feet. The stems are usually reclining to some extent. The ovate-lanceolate leaves are about 10 inches long, fat, keeled beneath, and a bluish green usually suffused with red. The leaf margins are armed with stout orange to red spines and the leaf tip is sharp and pointed. The summer inflorescence is about 2 feet tall and sparsely branched, with many gorgeous tubular scarlet to deep orange blossoms at its apex.

Aloe petricola (pet-ri-KO-la) grows to about 2 feet tall with clumping rosettes of curved lanceolate gray-green spiny-margined ascending fleshy leaves. The wonderful winter inflorescence is as much as 4 feet tall with pale yellow flowers near its base and brick red blossoms on the upper two-thirds of the spike. This species is dependably hardy in zones 9b through 11.

Aloe plicatilis (ply-KAYT-i-lis) is sometimes called the fan aloe. It is quite exotic and unusual because of the smooth foot-long, strap-shaped, completely spineless and smooth grayish green leaves, which are arranged not in rosettes but all in one plane, like a fan. With time the plant makes a branched trunk to 12 feet or more in height with the lovely fans of leaves at the ends of the branches. The red to orange flowers are rather large on a loose-flowered 2-foot-high spike. The

plant, which blooms in summer, is hardy in zones 10 and 11. Plate 32.

Aloe saponaria (sap-o-NAHR-ee-a) is indigenous to Zimbabwe and Botswana in south-central Africa. It is usually stemless but sometimes has a short trunk. It grows into a mound of 18-inch-wide rosettes of dark green broadly lanceolate leaves marked with yellowish white blotches. The orange to red flowers are borne in spring and summer atop a branched panicle about 3 feet in height. The plant freely suckers and grows rather fast. It is hardy in zones 9 through 11 and is sometimes called soap aloe.

Aloe speciosa (spee-see-O-sa) is a sparsely branched tree type growing to as much as 20 feet. It has immense terminal rosettes of 30-inch-long ovate-lanceolate, thick, olive green to bluish green leaves whose margins bear stout, short red thorns. The great leaves are keeled underneath and often exhibit a lovely brownish red suffusion in winter when the 4-foot-tall inflorescences form. The flower stalks are sparsely branched, but the spectacular flowers are borne on more than half their length. The individual blossoms are about 2 inches long and generally tubular, and are a fiery reddish orange in bud, opening to a greenish yellow color. The plant is not adaptable outside zones 10 and 11. Plate 33.

Aloe striata (stry-AIT-a) grows to about 3 feet with an often reclining unbranched stem in older plants. The gray to bluish gray leaves are almost 2 feet long, lance-olate in shape, keeled beneath, with a red margin and a short sharp point at the end. The winter inflorescence is broad, branched, and about 3 feet tall. The individual blossoms are a brick red or coral red in color. The plants are adaptable to zones 9b through 11. They are sometimes called the coral aloe.

Aloe variegata (vair-ee-a-GAIT-a) occurs naturally in southern South Africa and northwestward into Namibia. It is hardy in zones 9b through 11. This small clumping plant is usually no more than a foot in height. The leaves are very thick, tough, and stiff, lanceolate-triangular, and about 6 inches long, with a white margin and beautiful whitish spots on the blades. The plants bloom in winter with 2-foot-tall racemes of narrow brick-red tubular flowers, each about 2 inches long. The species is sometimes called the partridge breast aloe as well as the tiger aloe.

Aloe vera. See *A. barbadensis.*

ALPINIA (al-PIN-ee-a)
Zingiberaceae: The Ginger Family
Common names vary according to species
Clumping, reedlike stems; cannalike leaves in one
    plane; terminal, orchidlike flowers
Zones 9a (sometimes 8a) and 9b as foliage plants;
    zones 10 and 11 as dependable flowering plants
Sun to part-shade
Water lovers
Rich, moist, well-drained soil
Propagation by rhizome division

A large genus of more than 200 perennial clumping Asian herbs, mostly tropical. The large, rhizomatous roots are fairly hardy and usually resprout after temperatures in the teens. The stems, however, will not flower until the second season of growth, making these plants usually non-flowering subjects in all but zones 10 and 11. The long-lanceolate leaves are alternate on the stems and are usually arranged in one plane or almost in one plane. The inflorescences usually appear atop the individual stems. The foliage is fragrant if bruised or crushed, sometimes powerfully so. The flowers are in spikes or panicles, and each is somewhat orchidlike with one of the lobes of the corolla (usually called the "lip") larger and more showy than the others. After flowering the individual stems start to slowly die and are best cut to the ground to encourage the growth of new canes.

Alpinia auroecarpa. See *A. luteocarpa.*

Alpinia calcarata (kal-ka-RAIT-a) is native to the Indian subcontinent and is sometimes referred to as the Indian ginger. It is reportedly root hardy in zone 8b. The stems attain a maximum height of 5 or 6 feet. The narrow leaves are about a foot long and 2 inches wide, dull dark green above and lighter beneath. The flowers, which are white with yellow and red variegation on the lip, are among the most beautiful in the genus. Plate 34.

Alpinia formosana (for-mo-SAHN-a) is indigenous to the southern Japanese islands and Taiwan (formerly Formosa) and is root hardy in zone 8b. It is similar to *A. zerumbet,* but grows to only about 6 feet in height and has leaves that are only about 2 feet long. *Alpinia formosana* **'Variegata'** has leaves that are beautifully striped with white and flowers that are white with a red blotch on the crinkled lip.

Alpinia japonica (ja-PAHN-i-ka) is native to the southern Japanese islands, Taiwan, and the adjacent Chinese mainland. It is root hardy in zone 8, where it sometimes reputedly even flowers. It grows to only 2 (sometimes 3) feet in height and has foot-long bright green leaves, which are silky above and pubescent beneath. The inflorescence carries stalkless small red and white flowers of typical *Alpinia* form.

Alpinia luteocarpa (loo´-tee-o-KARP-a) (synonym *A. aureocarpa*) is native to Thailand and is not root hardy outside zones 10 and 11 and is somewhat marginal in zone 10a. It is an extraordinary clumping species that grows to 4 or 5 feet in height. It has many thin stems and very closely set stiff but fleshy 4- to 6-inch-long lance-shaped leaves that are a deep olive green above and reddish purple beneath. The small flowers are a yellowish white in color, but the plant seldom blooms in cultivation. This species is called the bamboo ginger in the nursery trade.

Alpinia mutica (MYOOT-i-ka) hails from Malaysia and is similar except in stature and hardiness to *A. zerumbet;* it is not root hardy outside zones 9 through 11. The plant usually grows to less than 6 feet in height and is less floriferous than *A. zerumbet,* and the blossoms are not quite as waxy or showy. It also carries the common names of shell ginger and orchid ginger.

Alpinia nutans. See *A. zerumbet.*

Alpinia purpurata (pur-pyoo-RAIT-a), the red ginger, is native to the islands of the South Pacific and is root hardy only in zones 10 and 11. The plant is large, reaching a height of 12 feet or more. The leaves are often 3 feet long and 6 inches wide, glossy and dark green, with slight ridges along the veins, and a strong and distinctly lighter-colored midrib. The flower spikes are a foot or more long, but the small whitish flowers are not the real attraction; rather the brilliant scarlet bracts that subtend them are. There are at least two cultivars. *Alpinia purpurata* **'Jungle Queen'** has pink inflorescences. *Alpinia purpurata* **'Tahitian Ginger'** has shortened, very fat inflorescences that are a darker red than those of the species. All are noble and spectacular plants and the essence of the tropical look. Plate 35.

Alpinia sanderae (SAND-ur-eye) is native to New Guinea and seldom blooms in cultivation. It is the variegated leaves that are the attraction, leading to the common name of variegated ginger. The stem grows only to about 3 feet in height. The leaves, which are about a foot long and 1 or 2 inches wide, appear to be white with dark green central bands near the center, but the reverse is, of course, the case. The plant is tender and is root hardy only in zones 9b through 11. Plate 36.

Alpinia speciosa. See *A. zerumbet.*

Alpinia zerumbet (ZER-um-bet) (synonyms *A. nutans, A. speciosa*) is commonly called shell ginger (for its white or pinkish glossy, waxy looking and feeling unopened buds), pearls-of-the-Orient, or shellflower. It hails from subtropical parts of China and the southern Japanese islands. This majestic beauty is probably the most widely planted *Alpinia* species in warmer regions. The stems often reach a height of 12 feet before flowering, and the flower clusters and individual flowers are magnificent. The many-flowered inflorescence is a foot long and heavy to the point that it is pendent. Indeed, the drooping cluster in bud is reminiscent of a bunch of shell-pink or white grapes. Each bud opens into a 3-inch-wide pink and white flower whose lip is fringed and mottled with red and yellow. *Alpinia zerumbet* **'Variegata'** (vair-ee-a-GAIT-a) is a beautiful cultivar with leaves about as large as those of the species and stems a bit shorter. The variegation on the leaves is more spectacular and even more beautiful than that of *A. sanderae,* being more zebralike and with yellow instead of white. The flowers are similar to the species, but not quite as large or as brilliantly marked. Plates 37 and 38.

ALSOPHILA. See *Cyathea.*

ALSTONIA (al-STO-nee-a)
Apocynaceae: The Oleander, Frangipani, Vinca Family
SCHOLAR'S TREE; DEVIL TREE; PALI-MARA; MILKWOOD

Tall, light-colored, straight-trunked tree with tiered
    branches, large leaves in whorls
Zones 10b and 11
Sun
Water lover
Rich, moist, well-drained soil
Propagation by seed

A genus of about 45 trees and shrubs distributed throughout the tropics, all with milky sap, large leaves in whorls, small white, usually fragrant flowers in terminal clusters, and long podlike fruits. Only one species is planted outside botanical gardens in the United States. It is a very noble and very beautiful large tree, which has the essence of the tropical look. *Alstonia scholaris* (sko-LAIR-is / SKAHL-a-ris) is indigenous to a wide area of the Old World tropics from Africa through India, Southeast Asia, Malaysia, and northern Australia. It grows to as much as 100 feet in its native habitat, but usually attains no more than 60 to 70 feet in cultivation. The great smooth and light-colored trunk is almost straight with just enough variation to be exquisitely picturesque and with the limbs generally in tiers from the top two-thirds of the bole. The lustrous 9-inch-long leaves, which are elliptic to oblanceolate in shape and a deep green above and paler green beneath, are arranged in whorls near the ends of the branches and are deeply veined above and below. The summer flowers appear in rounded terminal clusters and are small and greenish white with an outstanding fragrance. The flowers give way to 2-foot-long very thin beanlike pods, which split open when mature to release the fluffy milkweedlike seeds. The tree is arrestingly attractive, grows fairly fast, and is basically free of pests and diseases. It should be much more widely planted in tropical and nearly tropical areas than it is at present.

AMHERSTIA (am-HURST-ee-a)
Caesalpiniaceae (Leguminosae), subfamily
    Caesalpinioideae: The Cassia, Royal Poinciana
    Family
PRIDE OF BURMA
Spreading medium-sized tree; immense pinnate
    foliage; large clusters of pink flowers
Zone 11
Sun
Water lover
Rich, moist, well-drained soil
Propagation by seed and cuttings

A monotypic genus native to Myanmar (Burma). *Amherstia nobilis* (NO-bi-lis) is often referred to as the world's most beautiful flowering tree or as the queen of flowering trees. It is a small tree in cultivation usually not exceeding about 25 feet in height. The leaves, which are 3 feet long with oblong, even-numbered leaflets 6 to 12 inches long, are light green above with a bluish white bloom below. The new growth is limp and beautifully colored bronze, purple, and pink. It soon changes to pure bronze and finally green, stiffening in the process to become flat and horizontal. The inflorescence is a long, pendulous and loose-flowered raceme, rather like an inverted candelabrum. The individual flowers are pink to red, orchidlike or birdlike in shape, with the uppermost petal 2 or 3 inches wide, spreading, diamond-shaped, and tipped with bright yellow and streaked with deeper red. The blossoms are accompanied by large scarlet bracts beneath or above, since the inflorescence is pendent. The very long pinkish red stamens hang downwards from the rest of the flower and curl upwards, creating an exquisite tableau of "birds in flight." The 6-inch-long seed pods are oblong and a beautiful crimson in color, but the seeds are often inviable. The tree must have regular water, high humidity, and rich well-drained soil. Plate 39.

AMPHIBLEMMA (am-fee-BLEM-ma)
Melastomataceae: The Tibouchina Family
No known English common name
Small velvety-leaved, large-leaved shrub; pink to
    purple flowers
Zones 10 and 11; recovers from frost in zone 9b
Part shade
Water lover
Humusy, rich, moist, well-drained soil
Propagation by seed and cuttings

A small genus of about 15 species of very beautiful herbs and subshrubs from tropical West Africa. As is typical for the family, they have large leaves and lovely flowers. All the species require moist, tropical conditions and rich soil. One is fairly commonly planted. *Amphiblemma cymosum* (sy-MO-sum) is native to Sierra Leone and has leaves that are typical of the members of this family: lengthwise depressed veins on a usually velvety leaf. The small shrub grows to no more than 5 or 6 feet. The leaves are even more of a reason to grow the plant than are the lovely pink to purple flowers—the combination is very beautiful indeed. The large, velvety blades are held on long leaf stalks and are 7 inches long, long-cordate, satiny on the upper surfaces and reddish beneath with five to seven lengthwise depressed veins. The flowers are 1 to 2 inches wide, pink or red, five-petaled and in (as the specific name implies) broad flat cymes. The plant revels in moisture, humidity, rich soil, and partial shade. Damage starts at 32° to 30°F, but the plant springs back from freezing temperatures of 24° to 26°F.

AMPHITECNA (am-fi-TEK-na)
Bignoniaceae: The Catalpa, Jacaranda, Trumpet-
    Vine Family
BLACK CALABASH; WILD CALABASH;
    CALABASH TREE
Small evergreen tree; dense compact crown of large
    dark green leaves
Zones 10 and 11

Sun
Drought tolerant
Sandy, well-drained soil
Propagation by seed

A genus of 18 species of small trees in tropical America, all with relatively large bell-shaped flowers and, unlike most other members of the family, hard-shelled, gourdlike fruit. The genus was formerly called *Enallagma*. Only one species is commonly planted. ***Amphitecna latifolia*** (lat-i-FO-lee-a) is a wonderful small tree from the West Indies, Mexico, and Central America. It has dark green, leathery, elliptic to obovate leaves, each 6 to 8 inches long, with a pointed or notched apex. The limbs ascend almost vertically, creating an oblong and dense canopy. The tree is often maintained as a large and dense shrub or a densely sheared hedge. The flowers appear in winter and spring and are 2- to 3-inch-long, fringed, and purple or purplish white upright bells with a yellow stripe and a somewhat disagreeable odor. The hard-shelled fruits mature in autumn and are 3 to 4 inches long, egg-shaped, and green, but not edible. The tree can grow in slightly saline environments and revels in the limy soils of southern Florida which, along with its ability to withstand drought conditions, adds to its landscape utility.

AMYRIS (a-MY-ris / AM-i-ris)

Rutaceae: The Citrus Family
TORCHWOOD TREES
Evergreen shrubs and small trees; aromatic bark; pinnate leaves; panicles of fragrant flowers
Zones vary according to species
Sun
Average but regular amounts of moisture
Sandy, well-drained soil
Propagation by seed

A genus of about 20 species of trees and shrubs in the warmer parts of the Americas. They all have evergreen compound leaves that are aromatic with a distinct citruslike odor and clusters of white fragrant flowers.

***Amyris balsamifera*,** if it is a distinct species, is so similar to *A. elemifera* as to warrant description under that more widespread species.

Amyris elemifera (el-e-MIF-e-ra) (synonym *A. maritima*) is native to the southeastern half of Florida, the Florida Keys, and the West Indies, and is hardy in zones 10 and 11. It is a small tree, no more than about 15 feet in height, and more often a large shrub. The leaves are compound, usually with three drooping leaflets but sometimes five. Each dark green and leathery leaflet is 1 to 3 inches long and ovate to ovate-lanceolate with tapering points and remotely serrate margins that are reminiscent of *Pyrus kawakami* (evergreen pear). The trees bloom in spring and autumn, at which time they are covered in panicles of tiny four-petaled yellowish white and very fragrant flowers. The fruits, which are bluish black half-inch berries with glandular dots on the surface, are reportedly edible. These little trees are somewhat drought tolerant and flourish on the limy and calcareous soils of southern Florida's hammocks. They can also tolerate some saline conditions, but are not for the beach. They look and grow their best with an ample supply of water. All parts of the trees are aromatic and resinous, and even the green wood burns, leading to the vernacular name.

Amyris madrensis (ma-DREN-sis) is native to extreme southern Texas and adjacent Mexico and is adaptable in zones 9b through 11. It is a beautiful small tree that attains a maximum height of about 30 feet with a slender and open crown of pinnate and aromatic leaves and a smooth trunk of mottled shades of gray. The pinnate leaves are about 4 inches long with five to nine leaflets that are each usually less than an inch long. The leaflets are leathery and lustrous above and pale green and pubescent below. The flowers are in 3-inch-wide clusters, which spring from the leaf axils in spring and summer. They are white and very fragrant and result in ovoid purplish aromatic berries. This choice little tree is sometimes called the mountain torchwood because it grows abundantly in the Sierra Madre Oriental of Mexico.

ANANAS (an-AN-us)

Bromeliaceae: The Pineapple, Bromeliad Family
PINEAPPLE
Large terrestrial, spiny-leaved rosettes; pineapple fruit
Zones 10 and 11
Part to full sun
Water lovers
Light, porous, rich, very well drained soil
Propagation by transplanting of suckers and by seed

The pineapple genus has only eight species native mostly to Brazil and adjacent countries. One of its species was the first bromeliad to be discovered by Europeans because it was carried to the West Indies centuries earlier and cultivated by the native peoples whom Columbus and his crew found there. All the species are sun lovers and have long narrow leaves that are usually armed with marginal teeth. All have compound, usually yellow, more or less elongated fruit atop which new plants form. All are also suckering plants. The suckers make bigger and more fruitful plants than those derived from the fruit crowns. The inflorescences are on short to medium-length stems and are thick and squat with purple flowers. The plants are tender and are killed back by any temperature below 30°F, but are easily and successfully protected against temperatures as low as 25°F with a simple covering of leaves or cloth. These plants need regular and adequate supplies of water but, at the same time, demand perfect drainage and will quickly die from rot in waterlogged soils. They usually fruit in the second year of growth after transplanting of offshoots.

Ananas bracteatus (brak-tee-AIT-us) is sometimes called the red pineapple. It is native to most of Brazil. The dark green very spiny leaves are large, to as much as 6 feet long, and very narrow, less than 2 inches wide. The flower stem is about 2 feet tall with red leaves, red bracts, and brownish red to almost scarlet-colored fruit. Although edible, the fruit is slightly smaller, seedier, and not as meaty as that of *A. comosus*, the commercial pineapple. *Ananas bracteatus* var. *albomarginata* is a beautifully variegated, naturally occurring variety. *Ananas bracteatus* var. *striatus* (stry-AIT-us) is even more beautiful and exotic, especially when in fruit. It has dark green leaves striped lengthwise with creamy white. *Ananas bracteatus* **'Tricolor'** is one of the world's most beautiful plants with its smooth-margined long narrow leaves with longitudinal bands of olive green, yellow and red, and the amazingly scarlet fruit atop which even more of those gorgeous leaves spring. I cannot recommend this cultivar highly enough. Plate 40.

Ananas comosus (ko-MO-sus) is the pineapple of commerce. It is so widely cultivated that it seems endemic to most of the tropical world. It has numerous commercial cultivars. *Ananas comosus* **'Porteanus'** (por-tee-AHN-us) is quite handsome with its nearly spineless olive green leaves striped with yellow, which often exhibit a reddish hue. *Ananas comosus* var. *variegata* (vair-ee-a-GAIT-a), the most beautiful form of the species, has longitudinal striping of the green leaves with pink and white near their bases. Plate 41.

ANDIRA (an-DEER-a / an-DY-ra)

Papilionaceae (Fabaceae, Leguminosae), subfamily
    Papilionoideae: The Bean, Pea Family
CABBAGE-BARK; CABBAGE TREE; ANGELIN;
    ALMENDRO; PARTRIDGE WOOD
Medium-sized tree with ragged bark, large pinnate
    leaves, pink to purple fragrant flowers
Zones 10b and 11
Sun
Average but regular amounts of moisture
Rich, humusy, well-drained soil
Propagation by seed and cuttings

A genus of about 20 species of leguminous trees in tropical America and Africa, only one of which is regularly planted. *Andira inermis* (in-ER-mis) is indigenous to tropical West Africa and a large area of tropical America. In its native habitat it can grow to 100 feet with a buttressed trunk and a dense rounded crown, but in cultivation it seems to attain a maximum height of 50 feet. The common name of cabbage-bark tree refers to the exfoliating bark of mature trees, which has the odor of the cole. The 18-inch-long pinnate leaves are composed of 9 to 15 leathery ovate to elliptic leaflets. The tree blooms mostly in late spring, but flowering has been reported in summer as well. The terminal inflorescences are as much as a foot tall and consist of

panicles of very many dark pink to purple or violet pealike fragrant flowers. From a distance the tree is reminiscent of a giant crepe-myrtle or lilac in bloom. The plant is quite tender when young and is anything but hardy when mature. Any temperatures below freezing damage it.

ANDROLEPIS

(an-DRAHL-e-pis / an-dro-LEEP-is)
Bromeliaceae: The Pineapple, Bromeliad Family
No known English common name
Large vase-shaped and spreading bromeliad; thick
    erect reddish leaves; tall spikes of white flowers
Zones 10 and 11; marginal in zone 10a
Sun to partial sun
Water lover
Humusy, well-drained soil, leaf mold, or epiphytic
    mix
Propagation by transplanting of suckers and by seed

A monotypic genus native to Belize, Guatemala, Costa Rica, and Honduras. *Androlepis skinneri* (SKIN-nur-eye) (synonym *A. donnell-smithii*) grows to 3 feet and may be grown either as an epiphyte or as a terrestrial. The rosette consists of 3-foot-long stiff and mostly unarching lanceolate to obovate thick leaves with spiny margins. Leaf color is apple green in shady situations, but a deep rose to a dark wine color on the upper surface in sun. The inflorescence, which is as much as 6 feet tall, is a whitish thick stalk with white basal bracts and short compact racemes of yellow or yellowish white small flowers. It resembles a tall, erect, cylindrical whitish yellow candle that blends beautifully with the rose-colored or wine-colored leaf. This plant is wonderfully dramatic in the landscape, especially when in flower. It needs warmth, sun for color, and high humidity levels. Plate 42.

ANEMOPAEGMA

(an´-e-mo-PEEG-ma)
Bignoniaceae: The Catalpa, Jacaranda, Trumpet-
    Vine Family
YELLOW TRUMPET VINE
Vigorous high-climbing, tendril-bearing evergreen
    vines; yellow trumpet flowers
Zones 9 through 11
Part shade to full sun
Average but regular amounts of moisture
Humusy, well-drained soil
Propagation by seed

A genus of about 40 species in South America, mostly Brazil. All have compound opposite leaves with two or three leaflets. If there are only two leaflets, the end of the leaf is a tendril. The genus is closely allied to *Macfadyena* (synonym *Doxantha*), with which it is often confused. The vines, however, do not cling to surfaces as do those of *Macfadyena unguis-cati* (cat-claw) and need some sort of projecting structure on which to wrap their tendrils. Only one species is commonly planted. ***Anemopaegma chamberlaynii*** (sham-bur-LAY-nee-eye) (synonym *Bignonia chamberlaynii*) is native to Brazil. The shiny dark green leaves are large, with two oblong-ovate leaflets 7 or 8 inches long, and end with a hooked tendril. The flowers are bright yellow, funnel-shaped flaring trumpets 3 inches or more across and are reminiscent of those of the cat-claw, but are somewhat larger. The flower clusters are on longer pedicels, and the throats of the flowers are marked with purple and white. Unlike *Macfadyena* species, *A. chamberlaynii* blooms in summer and for a longer time. Considering its origin, it is a relatively hardy plant that is damaged by temperatures in the mid-20s but is root hardy to about 20°F without mulch, and even lower with mulch. This most desirable flowering vine should be planted much more extensively than it is.

ANGIOPTERIS (an-jee-AHP-te-ris)
Marattiaceae: The Marattia Fern Family
KING FERN; GIANT FERN; MULE'S-FOOT
   FERN
Tree fern; thick trunk; immense bipinnate leaves
Zones 10 and 11; marginal in zone 10a
Partial shade
Water lover
Rich, humusy, moist acidic soil
Propagation by spores

A monotypic genus native to Polynesia, New Guinea, northeastern Australia, and Malaysia. ***Angiopteris evecta*** (ee-VEK-ta) is a tree fern with leaves supposedly larger than those of any other fern species. The trunk is very stout and thick, as much as 2 feet in diameter, but only 6 to 10 feet in height when mature. The immense leaves can grow to 12 or even 15 feet long with unusually fleshy and leathery dark green leaflets. The plant is found naturally in very wet tropical rain forests. Drought kills it, so it should not be attempted in regions that do not have regular and copious amounts of rainfall or where the gardener cannot provide these conditions. It also needs protection from all but the lightest frosts and a site out of the full sun in hot climates. Few sights are more impressive than these wonderful and gigantic leaves ascending over masses of other lower vegetation. The tree form, however, is not that apparent since the trunk is relatively short compared to the size of the leaves and, therefore, the typical and graceful silhouette of other tree ferns is lacking. As a centerpiece or planted so that it towers over other shade-loving plants, it is supreme. Plate 43.

ANNONA (an-NO-na)
Annonaceae: The Cherimoya Family
Common names vary according to species
Small to medium-sized trees with large leaves and
   large, edible fruit
Zones vary according to species

Part shade to full sun
Average but regular amounts of moisture
Rich, humusy, well-drained soil
Propagation by seed and air-layering

A fairly large genus of about 100 species of small semideciduous trees in tropical America with relatively large, simple, and entire leaves; fleshy, usually fragrant flowers; and large compound fruit. Most fruits are edible (a few are delicious), with generally large, black, hard, and poisonous (if chewed) seeds.

Annona cherimola (cher-i-MO-la), the cherimoya (cher-i-MOY-ya) or custard apple, is native to mountain valleys of Peru and Ecuador where the summers are mild, the relative humidity is not excessive, and the winters are cool but frost-free. It is probably the tastiest species, but is not entirely happy along the Gulf Coast region and in Florida, where the summers are hot and the relative humidity high. In the Upper Gulf Coast, where the winters are usually rather wet, the cherimoya is subject to root rot if the soil remains soggy when it is in its state of relative dormancy. To minimize this problem, it is best to plant the cherimoya in a well-drained site. Nonetheless, the tree must have an adequate supply of moisture during the growing season in late spring and summer. Although this species is not recommended for southeastern United States if good fruit is wanted, it makes a fine tropical looking tree and, in cooler climates like those of coastal southern California or the Mediterranean, an excellent fruiting specimen. It grows into an erect but low-branched and spreading specimen to no more than 25 feet in height but usually less. It is not completely evergreen but rather loses most of its leaves for a brief period in the spring. It is an attractive tree with a spreading, picturesque habit and can be pruned to a large multi-trunked shrub or small tree form. The leaves are 10 inches long, somewhat variable in shape but generally ovate to elliptic, and a dull deep green with velvety undersides. The inch-long flowers appear in midsummer and are drooping, three-petaled, fleshy, yellow to brownish, and fragrant. The deep green to yellow-green fruit, shaped like an ox's heart, grows slowly over the fall and winter to a large 6 by 4 inches, with large overlapping scales covering the outside of the fruit. Each scale has a small, darker-colored tubercle in its center. The fruit is usually ripe in mid to late spring, and the ripeness is indicated by the color becoming definitely yellowish. Because the trees suffer damage starting at about 26°F and severe damage or death at temperatures in the low 20s, they are therefore appropriate subjects in zones 9b through 11. Another problem with the fruiting in the colder parts of its area is that the developing fruit is more tender than the leaves and branches and will be damaged by sub-freezing temperatures. Regional names in Latin America are chirimoya and cherimalla.

Annona diversifolia (di-vurs´-i-FO-lee-a) is native to lowland parts of western Mexico and Central America. The tree has smaller leaves than those of *A. cheri-*

mola and slightly larger, lighter-colored fruit on a small spreading tree no more than 20 feet in height. The evergreen leaves are about 6 inches long, elliptic to oblanceolate in shape, thin but glossy above, duller beneath, and fragrant when crushed or bruised. The new foliage is bronze in color. The flowers are long-stalked and maroon in color with fleshy and furry petals. The fruit is variable in shape and texture, only hinting at the scaliness of *A. cherimola*, and is usually egg-shaped but often heart-shaped. The surface can be studded with triangular-shaped tubercles or relatively smooth. The color varies from light green to deep pink or even purple. The tree is not hardy to cold, and its successful culture is limited to zones 10b and 11. Temperatures below 30°F are often fatal. Common names are ilama and anona blanca.

Annona glabra (GLAB-ra) is native to southern Florida, most of northern South America, and the Galapagos Islands. It is hardy in zones 9b through 11. The tree can grow to 40 feet or more in height and almost as wide. It is naturally found in swampy areas, including saline mangrove environments. The evergreen leaves, which are somewhat variable in size and shape, are usually ovate-acuminate but sometimes almost oblong and obtuse. They are usually about 8 inches long and are smooth and glossy above, and paler and slightly pubescent below. The fragrant flowers are large, succulent, and yellowish with red spots near the base of the outer petals. The backs of the inner petals are a deep red. The smooth fruit is usually round but sometimes ovoid. The species is known as pond apple or alligator apple.

Annona muricata (myoor-i-KAIT-a) is native to most of the West Indies and northern South America. The various regional names include soursop, prickly custard apple, and guanabana. The tree is small, usually multitrunked, and never more than 25 feet in height. The evergreen leaves are not as large as those of most other species in the genus (being about 6 inches long at the most), but they are a beautiful dark green, very smooth and glossy above, elliptic to obovate, not completely flat but rather concave, and very reminiscent of many leaves in the genus *Ficus*. The leaves are, alas, malodorous if crushed or bruised. The tree may flower anywhere on the trunk or branches. The three-petaled flowers are thick and plump, about 2 inches long, ovoid in shape, greenish yellow outside and pale yellow within. The mature yellow fruit, which is 12 inches or more in length and often weighs 15 pounds or more, is oval or heart-shaped and covered with large but soft spines on all but the lowest parts. The tree is quite tender and not hardy outside zones 10b and 11.

Annona reticulata (re-tik-yoo-LAIT-a) is native to the West Indies and northern South America, where it is known to reach a height of 40 feet or more. In cultivation, it usually is significantly smaller. Commonly called custard apple and bullock's heart, it is hardy in zones 10 and 11. The dark green evergreen leaves are about 8 inches long, smooth, generally lanceolate to oblong in outline, and ill-smelling when crushed or bruised. The flowers are yellow, thick-petaled, and about an inch long. The fruit is less than 6 inches long, globular to heart-shaped, and smooth with only hints at the scaliness of most other species. Fruit color is yellow or brown with a rosy blush. The fruit is said to be of inferior quality for eating. The plant needs a regular supply of water and deep rich soil to look and fruit its best.

Annona squamosa (skwah-MO-sa) is native to the West Indies and northern South America. English vernacular names are sugar apple, sweetsop, and custard apple. It makes a 20-foot-tall tree with an open spreading crown of zigzagging branches. The smooth, dull green leaves are variable in shape and size, but usually about 6 inches long and lanceolate to oblong in outline. Unlike the leaves of the two preceding species, the leaves of sweetsop are fragrant when crushed. The three-petaled flowers are about 2 inches long, fleshy, and green and yellow. The bluish green 5-inch-long fruit, which is round to heart-shaped with a rough-scaly outside, is tubercular due to the overlapping carpels. The tree is somewhat drought tolerant, but drops its leaves and fruit if so stressed. It is hardy in zones 10 and 11. Plate 44.

Annona squamosa × *A. cherimola* is called the atemoya (ah-tay-MO-ya) and is not found in nature, but is a cross made in the early twentieth century between the cherimoya and the sugar apple. It is a medium-sized, spreading semievergreen tree similar in appearance to the cherimoya, except the leaves are smaller and the fruit is very "scaly," a result of the mature carpels being so enlarged as to give the fruit an almost porcupine-like appearance. The plant is slightly more tender to cold than the cherimoya, but slightly hardier than the sweetsop. It is adaptable to zones 10 and 11. Its biggest advantage over the cherimoya is that it fruits well in warm and humid climates.

ANTHURIUM (an-THOOR-ee-um)
Araceae: The Calla Lily, Jack-in-the-Pulpit Family
TAIL-FLOWER; PATENT-LEATHER FLOWER;
    FLAMINGO-LILY
Stemless large-leaved foliage plants often with highly
    colored inflorescences
Zones 10b and 11 (a few come back in zones 10a and
    9b)
Part to full shade
Water lovers
Moist, rich, humusy, well-drained soil
Propagation by seed, transplanting of suckers, and
    stem cuttings

An immense genus of almost 1000 species of aroids in tropical America with wonderful variation in form, leaf, and flower type. Most are terrestrial plants, but some are epiphytic. Some are grown for their foliage, some for the fantastic flowers, and some for both flowers and foliage. Most have large heart-shaped leaves, but many have much-divided leaves. All have thick and leathery leaves. Some have callalike inflorescences typical of the family, but many have large, beautifully expanded long-lasting and highly colored spathes, the "patent-leather-flowers." All require near-tropical conditions, but some can take a modicum of frost and spring back from the roots. All species grow well with low light, but need humidity, ample moisture, rich soil, and warmth.

Anthurium andraeanum (an-dree-AHN-um) is native to the rain forests of southwestern Colombia. It is the plant most people have in mind when the name "patent-leather flower" or "anthurium" is used. It is one of the most popular of florists' plants. The long-petioled leathery leaves, which are dark green with prominent lighter veins, are long-ovate and sagittate. The flowers are long-stalked and held well above the leaves. The cordate to orbicular and flattish leathery spathe does, indeed, have the appearance of puckered patent leather and is cordate to orbicular in shape and salmon to red in color. The yellowish spadix is stalkless, long, and downwardly curved. The plants are completely tropical and dependable only in zones 10 and 11, and marginal in zone 10a. This species is one of the parents of innumerable hybrids, all of which resemble approximately the type but have spathes in many shapes, sizes, and colors, from white to purple. Additional common names are flamingo lily and oilcloth flower. Plates 45 and 46.

Anthurium clarinervum (klair-i-NURV-um) is native to the rain forests of southern Mexico and is not adaptable outside zones 10b and 11. It is quite similar to *A. crystallinum,* but has smaller and more rounded leaves that are never more than a foot wide. It is, nevertheless, of exceptional beauty. Plate 47.

Anthurium crystallinum (kris-ta-LYN-um) is native to the tropical rain forests of Colombia and Peru and is one of the species that is grown for its leaves rather than its flower. One of the glories of the tropical plant world, the leaves are immense, cordate to elliptic in shape, as much as 2 feet long, and more than a foot wide. Their texture is smooth and leathery. Their color is dark emerald green with cream-colored to silver main veins. The inflorescence is held above the foliage, and the whitish spathe is long-linear. The spadix is a long, narrow drooping yellowish "tail" and leads to the common name strap flower. The plant is tropical in its requirements and adaptable only to zones 10b and 11.

Anthurium hookeri (HOOK-e-ry) is native to parts of the West Indies and northern South America and has the common name of bird's-nest anthurium because the leaves are somewhat reminiscent of *Asplenium australasicum* (bird's-nest fern). The leaves also look like leathery versions of *Nicotiana tabacum* (tobacco) leaves. In any case, they are very beautiful. Growing on very short leaf stalks, they give the plant the effect of a rosette. The leaves are to 3 feet or more in length, elliptic to oblanceolate in shape, and a light green in color with the midrib and lateral veins slightly depressed and yellowish in color. The flower is attractive, but not very showy. The spathe is linear, straplike, and whitish or gray, changing to a dull, washed-out purple. The spadix is long-conical and a deep, bright violet. The plant tolerates temperatures to about 30°F and recovers from the roots if frozen back in zones 9b through 11.

Anthurium warocqueanum (war-ahk´-ee-AN-um) is native to the rain forests of Colombia. The leaves are very attractive and somewhat similar to those of *A. crystallinum* but longer and narrower. The lobes are almost obscured because they are so large that they overlap. This species is a climber, with aerial rootlets much like those of a *Philodendron* or *Monstera* species. It is very tropical and can only be successfully grown in zones 10b and 11.

ANTIDESMA (ant-i-DES-ma)
Euphorbiaceae: The Euphorbia, Spurge Family
BIGNAY; CHINESE LAUREL
Large tree with dense crown of drooping branches,
    glossy leaves, multicolored fruit
Zones 10 and 11
Sun
Water lover
Average well-drained soil
Propagation by cuttings and seed

A genus of perhaps 70 species of trees and shrubs in tropical Africa, Asia, Australia, and the islands of the South Pacific. All have small insignificant flowers, but mostly large and attractive leaves and fairly spectacular clusters of berrylike fruit. Only one species is commonly planted in the United States. *Antidesma bunius* (BOO-nee-us) is indigenous to a vast area from India and Sri Lanka to Australia and northwards to the Philippines. It is hardy in zones 10 and 11, although sometimes surviving for several years in zone 9b. In its native habitats the tree sometimes attains a height of as much as 100 feet, but in cultivation it is hardly ever more than 50 feet tall and is usually less. It is a truly beautiful ornamental with elliptic to oblong, almost stalkless, shiny and leathery, luminously green leaves, which are as much as 10 inches long. The insignificant rusty-colored flowers are single-sexed with male and female flowers on separate trees. Female trees are to be preferred because of the beautiful fruit they produce; male trees are usually superfluous unless viable seed is desired. The quarter-inch-wide berries are in long clusters reminiscent of grapes. Each fruit matures at a different rate, resulting in colors of green, white, red-purple, and black all in one cluster. When mature, the fruit is edible and reportedly tastes much like a cranberry. The tree is a superbly ornamental shade tree for warm climates. Plate 48.

ANTIGONON (an-TIG-o-nun)
Polygonaceae: The Buckwheat, Sea-Grape Family
QUEEN'S WREATH VINE; CORAL VINE;
    CONFEDERATE VINE

Large evergreen coarse-leaved vine; long tresses of
    pink flowers
Zones 8 through 11
Part to full sun
Average but regular amounts of moisture
Any well-drained soil
Propagation by seed and by cuttings or division of
    tuberlike roots

A small genus of only three species of tendril-climbing vines from Mexico and Central America with alternate entire usually cordate leaves. Only one species is
planted. It is grown for the large and usually pendent racemes of small, pink, red, or white flowers. ***Antigonon
leptopus*** (LEP-to-pus) is one of the most familiar and
dependable vines for zones 8 through 11. It is a fast and
rampant grower, but needs support as it is not a clinger,
climbing rather by forked tendrils on stems and flower
clusters. It climbs to 40 feet or more in one season in
zones 9 through 11. The long-ranging stems are often
seen "jumping" from fences or pergolas to ramble over
nearby trees and telephone and electrical lines. Since it
is not a particularly dense vine, its "jumping" habit is
not usually a problem. The deeply veined leaves are a
light, dull green and rough to the touch, ovate to lanceolate, and 4 or 6 inches long with a distinctly pointed
tip. The flowers, which are wonderful long racemes of
deep pink and white, appear intermittently all year if
the weather is warm, but most heavily in late spring
through autumn. The plants are drought tolerant sun
lovers, but with prolonged dry conditions tend to lose
their leaves, stop blooming, and may even die back. The
vine also starts dying back if the temperature falls much
below 30°F. Temperatures below 20°F kill the roots,
unless they are mulched. Whether frosted back or not is
often a moot point as the vine tends to bloom mostly on
newer growth and is often purposefully cut back to the
ground in late fall to make new growth, even in tropical
sites. If left to itself in frost-free areas, it can be a wonderful screening subject. The sight of the flowers at the
tops of large trees is an enchanting phenomenon in the
landscape. ***Antigonon leptopus*** **'Album'** (AL-bum),
a white-flowered cultivar, is not quite as floriferous as
the species and does not show up in the landscape as
well as the type. Plate 49.

APHELANDRA (af-e-LAN-dra)
Acanthaceae: The Acanthus Family
Common names vary according to species
Small shrubs with large variegated leaves and striking
    flower spikes
Zones 10b and 11
Sun to part shade
Water lover
Rich, humusy, well-drained soil
Propagation by cuttings and seed

A fairly large genus of about 170 herbs, shrubs, and
small trees in tropical America, almost all of which have
large and colorfully variegated leaves and brilliant reddish yellow or orange flowers in terminal spikes. The
flowers are small and yellow or white, but the surrounding brilliantly colored bracts make the show.
These species closely resemble those in the genus *Sanchezia,* and the two genera are often confused. They are
very tender perennials but will spring back from the
roots if cut down by frost and, if the roots are mulched,
will sometimes survive even in zone 9b. The plants usually need pinching after growing a while to keep them
compact and to prevent legginess.

Aphelandra aurantiaca (aw-ran-TY-ak-a) (synonyms *A. fascinator, A. nitens*) hails from Mexico, Central America, and northern South America. This handsome plant grows to about 5 feet in height with elliptic
to lanceolate, long-acuminate dark green leaves to 8
inches or more in length. The veins are marked with a
lighter shade of green. The flowers are scarlet and orange-yellow in short terminal spikes. The slightly more
compact cultivar ***Aphelandra aurantiaca*** **'Roezlii'**
(ROZ-lee-eye) is a much more striking and desirable
plant. The flowers are larger, the dark green leaves are
veined in bright white or silver, and the undersides of
the leaves are purplish with a silvery hue. Both the species and its cultivar are sometimes referred to as fiery
spike.

Aphelandra chamissoniana (sham´-i-so´-nee-
AH-na) from Brazil is sometimes called yellow pagoda.
It has 5-inch-long, narrowly elliptical leaves whose veins
are distinctly marked with white. The inflorescence is
erect to 6 inches or more, and the flowers are deep
golden-yellow.

Aphelandra fascinator. See *A. aurantiaca.*
Aphelandra nitens. See *A. aurantiaca.*

Aphelandra squarrosa (skwahr-RO-sa) from Brazil is perhaps the choicest of the species. Often called
the zebra plant, it can reach a height of 6 feet or more,
and the large, foot-long elliptic to ovate, deep olive
green leaves have veins prominently marked with white.
The inflorescence is 6 inches or more in height and is
composed of many bright yellow to orange flower bracts.
Several cultivars are available. ***Aphelandra squarrosa***
'Fritz Prinsler' is similar to the species but has longer
leaves with a darker green background. ***Aphelandra
squarrosa*** **'Louisae'** is also similar to the species, but
is more compact with leaves and flower spikes that are
larger than those of the species but not as large as those
of 'Fritz Prinsler'.

APOROCACTUS (a-POR-o-kak-tus)
Cactaceae: The Cactus Family
Common names vary according to species
Small slender, creeping, golden fine-spined cactus
    with brilliant flowers
Zones 10 and 11
Sun
Drought tolerant
Light, sandy, well-drained soil
Propagation by cuttings and seed

A genus of only two species of lovely little cactus plants with ridged, creeping, rooting, pendent, and spiny stems and brilliantly colored flowers. All are native to Mexico and Central America. They are especially nice planted in soil pockets of stone walls or boulders, where their trailing habit can be appreciated, but they are equally at home along the edges of the succulent and cactus garden.

Aporocactus conzattii (kahn-ZAT-tee-eye), from around Oaxaca, Mexico, has large many-petaled bright scarlet flowers 3 or more inches wide. They are borne on 3-foot stems during the summer.

Aporocactus flagelliformis (fla-jel´-i-FOR-mis) is native to a large area from Mexico through the drier parts of Central America. The stems are as long as 6 feet and grayish green with many thin ridges from which the tiny spines arise. The 3-inch-long reddish purple flowers are tubular and seem to be made of a flower within a flower, much like those of the Christmas cactus (*Schlumbergera* species), with recurved petals and light-yellow stamens and style. This species is sometimes called the rattail cactus.

ARALIA. See *Dizygotheca, Polyscias, Tetrapanax.*

ARCHONTOPHOENIX

(ahr-kon´-to-FEE-nix)
Palmae (Arecaceae): The Palm Family
KING PALM
Tall feather-leaved palms with large crownshafts and
   straight smooth trunks
Zones 10 and 11
Part-shade to full sun
Water lovers
Rich, deep, humusy, moist, well-drained soil
Propagation by seed

A small genus of six species of large pinnate-leaved palms from northeastern Australia. They are some of the world's most beautiful trees, palm or otherwise. Indeed, the genus name is translated as "king palm tree." In their native habitat these palms grow to 80 feet or more, while in cultivation 50 feet is about the maximum height. The always straight trunks are light in color, relatively slender, with usually faint rings, and are topped by the striking green to reddish brown crownshafts beneath the crown of large arching leaves. The dark green to grassy green leaves are short-petioled and flat. The leaflets are all in one plane, but their ends droop to some extent. The leaf rachises arch most gracefully along their lengths, but do not usually hang much below the horizontal plane. The inflorescences arise from the base of the crownshafts and encircle the trunk with branched and drooping racemes of tiny white or purplish flowers, which give way to masses of small, half-inch pink to red fruit. The palms luxuriate in partial shade when they are young in areas with hot summers, but can take full sun at any age unless suddenly exposed to it. The trees can survive with average but regular amounts of moisture and can tolerate dry spells when established. They are basically rain forest species, however, and look their best with a dependable and regular supply of moisture. All species grow fairly fast for palms and all look especially beautiful, as do most single-trunked palms, when trees of varying heights are planted in groups of three or more. The trees are difficult to transplant successfully if they are of size.

Archontophoenix alexandrae (al-ex-AN-dree) is the most tender of the species, being dependable only in zones 10b and 11, especially when young. Besides king palm, it is sometimes called the Alexander palm, King Alexander palm, or Alexandra palm. The grayish trunks are somewhat bulged near the base, and the rings are ridged and lighter in color than those of *A. cunninghamiana*. The leaf stalks are short and no more than a foot long. The leaf blades are usually 6 to 10 feet long, and the long, linear-lanceolate leaflets are as much as 3 feet long by about 2 or 3 inches wide, and are yellowish to grassy green above and gray to white beneath. There are at least two naturally occurring varieties. *Archontophoenix alexandrae* var. *beatricae* (bee-AT-ri-see) has a more bulging trunk at the base than does the type. The rings near the base are enlarged to the point that they resemble steps, and the leaves are also slightly more erect from the apex of the trunk. *Archontophoenix alexandrae* var. *kuranda* (koo-RAN-da) has a thicker trunk and a longer, taller crownshaft than does the type.

Archontophoenix cunninghamiana (kun´-ning-ham-ee-AHN-a) is similar to *A. alexandrae* but is slightly smaller in stature and slightly more cold-hardy. It is successfully grown in zones 10 and 11. In addition, it does not have the bulging base of *A. alexandrae* nor the whitish undersides to the leaflets, and the leaflets are somewhat wider and are not "ribbed" like those *A. alexandrae*. The palm has survived for several years at a time in zone 9b, but it is tender enough that it can not be relied upon as a landscape subject there. Plate 50.

Archontophoenix purpurea (poor-POOR-ee-a) (synonym *A. alexandrae* 'Mt. Lewis') is quite similar to *A. alexandrae* except for its wonderful crownshaft, which is distinctly bulbous at its base and is a definite reddish brown to reddish purple in color. It is somewhat slower growing than other *Archontophoenix* species, but is reported to be hardier to cold and is probably a quite safe candidate for zones 10 and 11, possibly even marginal in zone 9b.

ARECA (a-REEK-a / AIR-ee-ka)
Palmae (Arecaceae): The Palm Family
ARECA PALMS
Slender-trunked feather palms; prominently ringed
   trunks, green crownshafts
Zones 10b and 11

Sun to partial shade
Water lovers
Rich, humusy, well-drained soil
Propagation by seed and (for clumping species)
    transplanting of rooted suckers

A genus of about 50 palms in India, Sri Lanka, Southeast Asia, Malaysia, the Philippines, and the Solomon Islands. They are all truly tropical in their requirements and cannot be grown where frost occurs. Some are clustering, but most are solitary-trunked, and a few form stilt roots. They have slender and beautifully graceful, mostly green trunks with prominent rings of leaf scars atop which are smooth green or red crownshafts. The leaves are relatively few, lending an open and graceful appearance to the crown of leaves. All the species hail from rain forests and need ample and regular amounts of moisture. Some do not tolerate full sun well as they are understory subjects in the forest.

Areca catechu (KAT-e-choo / KAT-e-kyoo) is well known, having the vernacular name of betel-nut palm, which was made famous by the Bloody Mary character in the Rodgers and Hart musical and movie, *South Pacific*. It is native to a large area of Southeast Asia, Malaysia, and the Solomon Islands (but not the Hawaiian Islands where the movie was filmed). It grows rather quickly to a maximum height of about 30 feet and is a solitary-trunked or nonsuckering palm with a beautiful and straight green trunk (except for the lower portion in old specimens) and 8-foot-long deep green leaves atop a bright green crownshaft. The leaflets, which are relatively wide (6 inches) and about 2 feet long, are fairly widely spaced along the rachis and are squared but incised at their ends. The inflorescence is a much-branched drooping panicle of yellowish white fragrant flowers about 3 feet long and directly beneath the crownshaft. The fruits are orange to red, and the seeds (the betel nuts) contain a mild narcotic that native peoples have chewed for millennia with the leaves of *Piper methysticum* (pepper plant), usually with lime juice and tobacco, to obtain some sort of "high"—and stain and rot their teeth. This beautiful, very lush, and tropical looking palm, unfortunately, is not hardy outside frost-free areas.

Areca langloisiana. See *A. vestiaria.*

Areca lutescens. See *Chrysalidocarpus lutescens.*

Areca triandra (try-AN-dra) is indigenous to eastern India, Southeast Asia, Sumatra, Borneo, and the Philippines. A clustering species, it has very thin and graceful green trunks that reach a height of about 15 feet. In all other respects, including cultural requirements, it is similar to *A. catechu*. Few other clustering palms have the delicate grace of this one.

Areca vestiaria (ves-tee-AHR-ee-a) (synonym *A. langloisiana*) is native to eastern Indonesia. It is usually a suckering species, but is sometimes single-trunked. The 30-foot trunks are usually brownish rather than green, are beautifully marked with dark rings, and when older usually develop stilt roots at their bases. The leaves are similar to those of *A. catechu*, but the leaflets are even broader and the leaf stalks are very short. The crownshaft is glorious: it is plump at the base and a beautiful orange or orange-red in color. This species is possibly the most beautiful in the genus.

ARECASTRUM. See *Syagrus romanzoffiana.*

ARENGA (a-RENG-a)
Palmae (Arecaceae): The Palm Family
Common names vary according to species
Medium-sized to large pinnate-leaved, clustering or
    single-trunked palms
Zones vary according to species
Part to full sun
Water lovers
Rich, humusy, moist, well-drained soil
Propagation by seed and (for clumping species)
    transplanting of rooted suckers

A genus of about 17 species of pinnate-leaved palms in tropical Asia and Australia. Some species are single trunked, while others are clustering, but almost all are monocarpic. The stems, however, do not flower until they are mature (often many years) and the flowering may last for several years because the inflorescences emerge from the rings of leaf scars around the trunk and progress from top to bottom, usually one per year. With the clustering species, there are always new trunks forming to take their places. The fruits of all species are poisonous and corrosive to the skin.

Arenga engleri (ENG-lur-eye) is native to the southern Japanese islands and Taiwan and is the hardiest species in the genus, adaptable to zones 9b through 11 and marginal in zone 9a. It is one of the finest landscape subjects for the southern Texas coast, deep central Florida, southern Florida, the southern half of the coastal areas of Florida, and the rest of the subtropical world. It is a clustering species with trunks as much as 10 feet tall and covered with a network of black fibers and old leaf stalks. The clumps can measure as much as 20 feet across and, like the clumps of many clustering palm species, usually look better if some of the young trunks are cut out and the clumps thinned to prevent the landscape effect from being nothing but a mass of leaves. The leaves, which are on long petioles, are as much as 9 feet long, flat, erect, and ascending but gracefully arching. The leaflets are dark green above and silvery beneath, about 18 inches long, and linear except for the terminal leaflet, which is usually oblong to deltoid. All the leaflets are slightly jagged near their apices. The inflorescences are short and mostly hidden by the mass of leaves, but they are an attractive orange in color and delightfully fragrant. The immature fruits are green, changing to orange and finally purple when they ripen. Plate 51.

Arenga microcarpa (myk-ro-KARP-a) hails from New Guinea and is the most beautiful *Arenga* species of those planted in the continental United States. It is similar to *A. engleri*, but larger in all respects. The individual ringed trunks may attain a maximum height of 25 feet and are free of fiber and leaf bases near the bottom. The leaves are longer (to 12 feet or more) and wider (to 5 feet) than those of *A. engleri*, but the leaflets are narrower. The plants are tender and are adaptable only to zones 10 and 11.

Arenga pinnata (pin-NAIT-a) (synonym *A. saccharifera*) is a single-trunked palm indigenous to Malaysia and hardy in zones 10 and 11. It is an imposing palm of giant stature. The massive trunks reach a maximum height of about 20 feet and are covered with tough black fibers and large triangular-shaped old leaf bases. The leaves are 20 feet or more in length, and the long, linear, straplike leaflets are dark green above and almost white beneath. They originate from several angles off the leaf rachis and give the leaf a distinctly plumose appearance. The palm is commonly referred to as the sugar palm because indigenous peoples have for millennia made sugar (and, of course, liquor) from the sweet sap that flows from the severed male flower spathes. The nearly indestructible fibers are also used as cordage and matting.

Arenga saccharifera. See *A. pinnata*.

Arenga tremula (TREM-yoo-la) is native to the Philippines and is slightly less hardy than *A. engleri*, being dependable only in zones 10 and 11 and marginal in zone 9b. The plant is in other respects similar to *A. engleri:* it is of relatively low stature (trunks to 12 feet in height) and clustering. The most salient difference in the landscape is that the leaflets of *A. tremula* are not as stiff as those of *A. engleri* and are, therefore, more pendulous, giving a more fernlike aspect to this palm.

ARGUSIA. See *Mallotonia*.

ARGYREIA (ahr-ji-REE-a)
Convolvulaceae: The Morning Glory Family
WOOLLY MORNING GLORY; WOOD ROSE
Large twining vine with large felty heart-shaped
    leaves and purplish pink trumpet flowers
Zones 9 through 11
Part to full sun
Average but regular amounts of moisture
Not particular as to soil
Propagation by seed and cuttings

A large genus of almost 100 species of twining, pubescent vines from tropical Asia and Australia. All have trumpet-shaped flowers, like morning glory, with large felty leaves. Only one species is commonly planted. *Argyreia nervosa* (ner-VO-sa) (synonym *A. speciosa*) from India is a fast grower to 25 feet or more. The foot-wide dark green cordate leaves are white and densely pubescent beneath. The flowers, which appear in summer, are almost identical to those of most *Ipomoea* species (except that these have large lemon yellow calyces)

and are rose to purple with much darker-hued throats. This rampant strong-growing heavy vine only blooms with size (although the vine is worth growing for the great, tropical looking leaves alone) and therefore needs room to develop and something sturdy on which to twine. The fruits mature into lovely flowerlike affairs with the texture of hard leather or soft wood, leading to one of the common names. The plant freezes with temperatures below 30°F, but is capable of resprouting from the root in zone 9. Plate 52.

Argyreia speciosa. See *A. nervosa*.

ARISTOLOCHIA (air-is´-to-LOK-ee-a)
Aristolochiaceae: The Aristolochia (Birthwort)
    Family
BIRTHWORT
Twining vines with large heat-shaped leaves and
    fantastic birdlike flowers
Zones vary according to species
Sun to partial shade
Water lovers
Average soil
Propagation by seed and cuttings

A large genus of about 300 species of perennial vines from warm or tropical areas. All have relatively large, usually cordate, pubescent leaves and flowers whose shapes generally resemble that of meerschaum pipes or swanlike birds, often with long "tails" at the bottom of the flowers. The vines climb by twining their stems around something; they do not cling. The often gigantic and fantastically shaped flowers are also usually malodorous, their colors are seldom bright and cheery, and it is not everyone who can appreciate their particular brand of exotic beauty. Edwin A. Menninger once referred to them as "astonishingly ugly flowers that often stink." They are also exotic and fantastic. The contortions of the flower's perianth and the odor produced seem to be evolutionary adaptations to pollination by flies. The flowers are bisexual with the female part (the ovary, style and stigma) becoming sexually active a day or so before the male parts (the stamens). The fly-attracting odor is emitted only while the female parts are active. The crooks and crannies in the interior of the flower and the inward facing hairs therein keep the poor insects trapped until the anthers have released pollen and the stigmas received pollen, at which time both stigmas and anthers wither and the hairs close, releasing the fly to visit another flower.

Aristolochia brasiliensis (bra-zil´-ee-EN-sis) (synonym *A. ornithocephala*) is indigenous to southeastern Brazil and is hardy in zones 10 and 11. The leaves are as interesting and as attractive as the flowers, being 8 inches or more in width and kidney-shaped to orbicular. The large birdlike flower is dull yellow with purple veins and splotches and has an almost indescribable shape: an inflated pouchlike tube on the bottom and a flaring, hood-shaped affair on a long stalk above the pouch with a long erect "fin" at the back of the hood. The stalk of the "hood" usually lengthens after the first day, and the hood hangs beneath the rest of the flower.

Aristolochia durior (DOO-ree-or) (synonyms *A. macrophylla, A. sipho*) is native to a large part of the eastern half of the United States and is hardy in zones 5 through 11. In the United States it is called the Dutchman's-pipe. A fast and large (to 30 feet or more) grower when established, it is grown more for its foot-wide kidney-shaped to orbicular deep green glossy deciduous leaves than its purplish brown flowers, which are not very large and are mostly hidden by the dense foliage. As the common name implies, the small flowers are shaped like a curved pipe.

Aristolochia elegans (EL-e-ganz) (synonym *A. littoralis*) hails from Brazil and is commonly called calico flower. The leaves and flowers are small but rather attractive. Edwin Menninger refers to it as "the least offensive of the genus." The vine is not the rampant grower that *A. durior* is. The leaves are cordate and about 4 inches wide. The velvety flowers, which are on long peduncles, are about 3 inches in diameter and white with purple veining on the outside and inside. They are shaped in general like the bowl of a Dutchman's pipe. The plant is root hardy in zones 9 through 11. Unlike most others in the genus, the flower produces no odor. Plate 53.

Aristolochia gigantea (jy-GANT-ee-a) is also native to Brazil and is hardy in zones 10 and 11. The flower is truly immense and spectacular. It is a pouch almost 2 feet long, more than a foot across, and white with purple veining on the outside and inside. The leaves are cordate and as much as 6 inches long. There is definitely an odor to the flowers.

Aristolochia gigas. See *A. grandiflora.*

Aristolochia grandiflora (grand-i-FLOR-a) (synonym *A. gigas*), variously called pelican-flower, swan-flower, goose-flower, and duck-flower, is native to the West Indies and Central America. It is hardy in zones 10 and 11 and produces a gargantuan flower. It is, however, except for the odor of its newly opened blossoms, much more beautiful than the flower of *A. gigantea*. The vine is a lush, fast grower with large cordate leaves to 10 inches or more in length. The flowers resemble those of *A. elegans* except they are much larger (usually about 20 inches across) and have a long "tail" (usually about 3 feet long). The common name of pelican flower seems most apt for this species. Plate 54.

Aristolochia littoralis. See *A. elegans.*

Aristolochia macrophylla. See *A. durior.*

Aristolochia ornithocephala. See *A. brasiliensis.*

Aristolochia sipho. See *A. durior.*

ARMATOCEREUS
(arm´-a-toe-SEER-ee-us / ahr-mat´-o-SEER-ee-us)
Cactaceae: The Cactus Family
No known English common name

Large treelike columnar and ribbed cactuses; white nocturnal flowers
Zones 10 and 11
Sun
Drought tolerant
Sandy, well-drained soil
Propagation by seed and cuttings

A genus of about 10 large, columnar and usually treelike cactus species with ribbed stems and nocturnal white-petaled tubular flowers with brownish outer sepals. The flowers are formed along the stems on the crests of the ribs. The egg-shaped fruits are colored yellow, orange, or red, and are covered with spines.

Armatocereus cartwrightianus (kart-ryt´-ee-AHN-us) (synonym *Lemaireocereus cartwrightianus*) is native to western Ecuador and northwestern Peru. It grows to as much as 30 feet with a stout foot-wide trunk and many olive green "arms" or branches. Each branch has seven or eight ribs along whose crests grow the regularly spaced areoles with many vicious brown and white spines. The branches are segmented into oblong divisions. Each division is about 2 feet long and 6 to 8 inches wide. The nocturnal flowers come in summer and are 3-inch-long white tubes with flaring lobes and brownish sepals. The fruits are a bright red in color. The mature plants are quite a sight. This is one of the most spectacular cactus species.

Armartocereus laetus (LY-tus / LEE-tus) (synonym *Lemaireocereus laetus*) is indigenous to western Ecuador and Peru. It grows to 15 or 20 feet and forms a short squat trunk with many ascending branches. The branches or stems are grayish green in color and segmented into 2- to 3-foot-long portions. Each branch has about eight ribs along whose crests the regularly spaced areoles bear white or gray spines. The nocturnal summer flowers are white and are followed by greenish yellow fruits.

Armatocereus oligogonus (o-lig´-o-GOAN-us / ah-li-GAHG-o-nus) occurs naturally in western Peru. It grows to 10 or 15 feet with basal branching to form several stems, which are segmented into 2-foot-long linear-ovate tapering joints that are about 6 inches wide at the base and 2 or 3 inches wide at the end. Each segment has four or five winglike ribs along whose crests the brown or gray spines grow. The nocturnal 3-inch-long flowers are white and are followed by brownish red fruits. This species is one of the most picturesque cactus species.

Armatocereus rauhii (RAW-ee-eye) is indigenous to northwestern Peru. It is a tree form growing to 20 or 25 feet with a short stout trunk and several tall grayish green to bluish green branches or stems. Each branch is divided into 2-foot-long segments with a dozen or so linear ribs along whose crests the gray to black spines grow. The nocturnal flowers, which are red and about 3 inches long, are followed by spiny red fruit. The form of this spectacular and noble plant is strongly reminiscent of *Carnegiea gigantea* (sahuaro).

ARRABIDAEA. See *Saritaea*.

ARTABOTRYS (ahr-TAB-o-tris)
Annonaceae: The Cherimoya Family
YLANG-YLANG VINE
Dense evergreen tendril-climbing shrub; large,
    leathery leaves; fragrant flowers
Zones 10 and 11
Sun to partial shade
Water lovers
Rich, humusy, moist, well-drained soil
Propagation by seed

A large genus of about 100 species of vines and clambering shrubs in tropical Africa through Indonesia with white or yellow flowers and large evergreen leaves. Only one species is commonly planted. ***Artabotrys hexapetalus*** (hex-a-PET-a-lus) (synonym *A. odoratissimus, A. uncinatus*) is native to southern India and Sri Lanka. It is a woody clambering shrub that is often trained as a vine. The plant climbs by hooked tendrils, which develop from the flower clusters. The alternately spaced 6-inch-long deep green leaves are glossy, leathery, linear-lanceolate, and entire. The six-petaled flowers develop opposite a leaf in clusters of two, each flower being about 2 inches wide and half as long, greenish yellow, and intensely and penetratingly fragrant. The yellow inch-long plum-shaped fruits are also highly fragrant. The plant must be tied to a trellis, lattice, or other structure when first planted, while the flowers and tendrils form.

ARTOCARPUS (art-o-KARP-us)
Moraceae: The Fig, Mulberry Family
BREADFRUIT; JACKFRUIT
Massive trees with immense leaves; spectacular fruits
Zones vary according to species
Sun
Water lovers
Rich, humusy, moist, well-drained soil
Propagation methods vary according to species

A genus of about 50 species of large-leaved trees in tropical Asia and the islands of the South Pacific. A few species are semi-evergreen but most are entirely evergreen. All have relatively large compound fruit (known as "syncarps") like the pineapple or, in this case, more accurately like the fig. Some species such as *Artocarpus altilis* (breadfruit) and *A. heterophylla* (jackfruit) produce edible fruit. Many are large forest trees whose timber is valuable.

Artocarpus altilis (AL-ti-lis) (synonym *A. incisa*) is native to Indonesia and Polynesia and is known as the breadfruit. The tree is variable in habit, but usually makes a columnar to round-headed tree to 60 feet in height, often with the branches low. The dark green leathery and glossy leaves are immense, as much as 3 feet long, and ovate in outline, but with such deep pinnate clefts as to almost obscure the shape. The young leaves are soft and pubescent, the upper surface soon turning leathery and glossy, the lower surface becoming rough to the touch. The tree bears male and female flowers on the same plant. The male inflorescence is greenish yellow and oblong, while the female spike is spherical. The immature fruit is green to yellow and covered in small blunt spines, but the mature fruit is only rather pebbly and yellow in color. Each fruit is round to ovoid, as much as 8 inches in diameter, and can weigh up to 10 pounds. The tree is one of the world's most beautiful and is the very essence of the tropics and the tropical look. It also is very sensitive to cold and can tolerate no frost. It refuses to flourish outside zone 11, although sometimes it is successfully grown (but never fruiting) in zone 10b. Indeed, sustained temperatures below 40°F can cause damage. There are at least two varieties of breadfruit, one of which is seedless. The other has seeds and is sometimes called the breadnut, which is unfortunate since another tree (*Brosimum alicastrum*) is also and more correctly known by this name. When cooked, the fruits of the type and its seedless cultivar are staples of the diet of many Polynesian peoples, but the fruit of *Artocarpus* is not nearly as widely eaten as it was when Captain Bligh of the HMS *Bounty* tried to import it to the islands of the Caribbean to feed plantation slaves. This wonder of the vegetable kingdom is propagated by cuttings or by transplanting its suckers for the seedless variety. The variety with large seeds may also be propagated by these methods as well as by planting the seeds.

Artocarpus heterophylla (het´-ur-o-FYL-la) (synonym *A. integrifolia*) is native to India through Malaysia. It attains about the same height as the breadfruit, but usually has a straighter trunk and a more columnar shape. The stiff and glossy leaves, while large and beautiful, are nothing like those of the breadfruit. They are elliptic to obovate, to 8 inches long, and completely without sinuses or lobes. The tree is cauliflorous. The fruits are oblong, spectacular, and truly colossal, to 2 feet long. When mature they are spiny and brown, and weigh as much as 40 pounds. The tree, which is almost as tender as the breadfruit tree, is hardy in zones 10b and 11. It is propagated by seed or cuttings.

Artocarpus incisa. See *A. altilis*.
Artocarpus integrifolia. See *A. heterophylla*.

ARUNDINARIA (a-run´-di-NAIR-ee-a)
Gramineae (Poaceae): The Grass, Bamboo Family
BAMBOO CANE
Dwarf to medium-sized running-type bamboos
Zones vary according to species
Sun to partial shade
Average but regular amounts of moisture
Rich, friable well-drained soil
Can be invasive
Propagation by rhizome division

A small genus of about 30 running bamboo species, mostly in China and North America but also in Africa.

All species have long-lasting culm sheaths and culms that are round in cross section but are relatively small in diameter. They make rather dense groves and the rhizomes spread quickly and far. Some botanists think that there is only one species, *Arundinaria gigantea,* in the genus and that the others belong to several related bamboo genera. The descriptions here follow the taxa as described in *Hortus III.*

Arundinaria amabilis (a-MAHB-i-lis) is native to the southern parts of China and northern Indochina, although it is no longer found in the wild. It is called Tonkin cane bamboo and Tonkin bamboo. In spite of its place of origin, it is hardy in zones 9 through 11 and is root hardy in zone 8. It is one of the larger species in the genus. Mature plants can produce culms as tall as 30 feet with a diameter of 2 inches. The canes are straight and sparsely branched near their bottoms, which, coupled with the strength and resiliency of the stems, makes the species the premier bamboo for fishing poles, plant stakes, and handicrafts. The oblong-lanceolate leaves are as much as a foot long and are a dark green above with a bluish white bloom beneath.

Arundinaria argenteostriata (ahr-jen´-tee-o-stry-AIT-a) (synonym *Bambusa argenteostriata*) is native to Japan and is hardy in zones 8 through 11 and root hardy in zone 7. It is a wonderful plant for shade and groundcover where a large subject is needed. It grows to 3 feet or sometimes more. The lanceolate leaves are large, to a foot or more in length, with white longitudinal stripes. This plant grows in full sun, but looks best in partial shade. It is a choice, peaceful-looking variegated plant for contrast in shady areas.

Arundinaria auricoma. See *A. viridistriata.*

Arundinaria disticha (DIS-ti-ka) (synonyms *Bambusa nana, B. pygmaea, Pleioblastus distichus, Sasa disticha*) is native to Japan and is hardy in zones 8 through 11 but useful in zone 7, where it is root hardy. It is valuable as a tall groundcover because it only grows to 1 or 2 feet in height. It is often called dwarf fernleaf bamboo because the thin leaves are long-lanceolate, about 6 inches long, with a decidedly fernlike appearance.

Arundinaria gigantea (jy-GANT-ee-a) (synonym *A. tecta*) is native to most of the southeastern United States and is hardy in zones 6 through 11 and probably root hardy in colder areas. It is the canebrake of legend and literature and is also called southern canebrake. It grows to 30 feet in height under optimum conditions, with foot-long, long-cordate to lanceolate, dark green leaves. It is a useful plant for screening purposes and erosion control on banks.

Arundinaria pygmaea (pig-MEE-a) (synonyms *Bambusa pygmaea, Sasa pygmaea*) is native to Japan and is hardy in zones 7 through 11. One of the tiniest bamboo plants, it grows to a maximum height of a foot and is an extremely useful and attractive groundcover. It is appropriately called pygmy bamboo. The canes are purplish, and the leaves are usually less than 6 inches long. This species is an aggressive spreader but, because of its small size, is fairly easy to contain. There is hardly a

better choice for erosion control and for holding together the soil on slopes in full sun.

Arundinaria tecta. See *A. gigantea.*

Arundinaria viridistriata (vir-id´-ee-stry-AIT-a) (synonyms *A. auricoma, Bambusa argentea, Phyllostachys argenteostriata*) is yet another great bamboo from Japan. It is perhaps the choicest of the variegated dwarf bamboos. Growing to about 2 feet in height, it has large 8-inch-long leaves, which are long-cordate to long-lanceolate and wonderfully striped lengthwise with bands of gold. The species is hardy in zones 7 through 11.

ARUNDO (a-RUN-do)
Gramineae (Poaceae): The Grass, Bamboo Family
GIANT REED; GIANT CANE; GIANT
    FEATHER-REED GRASS
Heavy bamboolike giant grasses usually growing in
    moist places
Zones 7 through 11
Sun
Water lover
Rich, humusy, moist, well-drained soil
Invasive
Propagation by rhizome division and seed

A genus of five species of tall reedlike grasses in warm regions of the Old World. Only one species is planted in the United States. ***Arundo donax*** (DO-nax) would appear to be a native plant so well does it grow in the South and Southwest, but it is an import from southern Europe and was first brought to the American tropics by the Spaniards in the sixteenth century. The canes grow to 20 feet and have big, bold, lanceolate leaves that are 3 inches wide and 2 or more feet long. Unlike the canes of true bamboos, mature canes flower every year with terminal much-branched linear panicles, which are 2 or more feet tall and which are the color of ripe wheat panicles. The plant is definitely invasive and is best suited for large areas and erosion control. ***Arundo donax* var. *variegata*** (vair-ee-a-GATE-a) is a superior landscape subject because of the attractively variegated leaves, striped lengthwise with bright yellow. It is somewhat less hardy to cold than the type.

ASPIDISTRA (ass-pi-DIS-tra)
Liliaceae: The Lily Family
CAST-IRON PLANT
Clumping rosettes of dark green ovate, straplike
    leaves to 3 feet long
Zones 8 through 11
Full to partial shade
Average but regular amounts of moisture
Light, humusy, well-drained soil
Propagation by root division

A genus of eight species of herbaceous perennials from the Himalayas, China, and Japan. The plants form stemless rosettes of long-petioled leaves from fairly thick and tough rhizomatous roots. The leaves of all eight species are thick, tough, and leathery, and make excellent tall groundcover plants. Only one species is commonly planted. *Aspidistra elatior* (ee-LAY-tee-or) is one of the most useful landscape subjects in all parts of the country that do not have severe winters. The plants never grow more than 3 feet in height, and the shape and color of the leaves are amenable to very many landscape situations from tall groundcover to specimen plants in containers. There is a soft, soothing aspect to the venerable, dark green glossy, wide strap-like blades. The plant is called cast-iron plant for good reason: it is almost indestructible and tolerates mild drought conditions, poor soil, and neglect. Like most plants, though, it appreciates an adequate and dependable supply of moisture and soil that is at least average in fertility. The one thing it does not tolerate is full sun. One of the most egregious mistakes made in southern plantings is the placing of cast-iron plant in full sun where the leaves turn yellow, the tips burn, and the plant languishes and is subject to dying out. The plant flourishes in sites with full shade to half-sun morning and late afternoon. *Aspidistra elatior* '**Variegata**' (vair-ee-a-GAIT-us) is not that attractive.

ASPIDIUM. See *Rumohra*.

ASPLENIUM (ass-PLEN-ee-um)
Polypodiaceae: The Largest Fern Family
BIRD'S-NEST FERNS
Epiphytic ferns with large leaves in rosettes
Zones 10 and 11
Shade to partial shade
Water lovers
Leaf mold or epiphytic potting mix with peat or
    sphagnum
Propagation by rhizome division and spores

A very large genus of about 700 species of very variable ferns, both epiphytic and terrestrial, with pinnate to entire leaves. The species discussed here are epiphytic, though they are often grown as terrestrials. They demand warmth, humidity, and a constant supply of moisture.

Asplenium bulbiferum (bul-BIF-e-rum) is indigenous to the north island of New Zealand, tropical Australia, and parts of India and is one of the world's most satisfactory landscape subjects. The beautiful, very lacy fronds are about 3 feet long, linearly triangular, and usually a lovely light green in color. The stipe of the leaf is thick and dark in color, almost black, but the leaf blade is so large that it is usually bent and picturesquely curving towards the earth. The tripinnate leaves bear plantlets, making the leaves all the heavier. (The specific epithet *bulbiferum* is not completely accurate as the leaf does not bear bulbs.) The exceptionally airy and graceful plants are unqualified successes placed almost anywhere, but look especially wonderful with *Impatiens*

species, as do all ferns, or with bromeliads. They luxuriate in partial shade to almost full shade, and their only other requirements are moist soil and warmth. Because of its viviparous habit, this plant is usually called the mother fern.

Asplenium nidus (NY-dus) occurs naturally in a very large area of tropical Asia from the southernmost islands of Japan southward to northern Australia. The universally accepted common name in English-speaking countries is the bird's-nest fern (the specific epithet *nidus* is Latin for "nest"). This startlingly beautiful plant has stiff erect, linear-lanceolate to oblanceolate bright green leaves that are as much as 5 feet long with a strong and prominent dark midrib. The variable species has leaf types ranging from completely flat on the margins to strongly wavy. The leaf colors also vary, some being very dark green, others only light green. *Asplenium nidus* var. *plicatum* (ply-KAIT-um) has deeply ridged narrow dark green leaves. The plants take no frost and are sometimes damaged even in zone 10a. The fern may be grown in the ground if the soil or medium is loose, relatively low in pH, and well drained. It also may be kept in pots attached to tree trunks or may be planted into soil pockets of stone walls or in the crotches of large trees. The plants do not take full sun without damage or discoloration. Plate 55.

Asplenium serratum (ser-RAIT-um), a terrestrial fern native to southern Florida, the West Indies, and northern South America, is sometimes planted in zones 10 and 11. It is similar to most forms of *A. nidus*, though slightly hardier to cold, and grows about as large with leaves that are finely serrate on the margins. It wants the same conditions as *A. nidus*. Common names are American bird's-nest fern and wild bird's-nest fern.

ASTROCARYUM
(ass-tro-KAHR-ee-um)
Arecaceae: The Palm Family
STAR-NUT PALM
Beautiful, medium-sized to very tall, very spiny
    feather-leaved palms
Zones 10b and 11
Sun to partial shade
Water lovers
Rich, humusy, well-drained soil
Propagation by seed

A genus of 47 species of very spiny pinnate-leaved palms in the West Indies, Mexico, Central America, and parts of South America. A few are clumping palms, but most are solitary-trunked. Some have plumelike leaves because the leaflets spring from the rachis at different angles; many others have the leaflets all in one plane. All are of exceptional beauty at every stage of growth, and all have stout and vicious spines on most of their anatomy, which make the plants difficult to handle. These palms are not recommended for planting in high traffic areas. Their spininess is one reason these beauties are still rare and difficult to find, but they are worth the effort. Many (mostly the smaller species) are understory rain forest plants and do very well in shade or partial shade; others are more adapted to the sun.

Astrocaryum aculeatum (a-kyoo´-lee-AIT-um) occurs naturally on the island of Trinidad and the adjacent northern South American mainland down into Brazil. It is one of the most magnificent palm species. The trunk grows to as much as 70 feet and 12 to 15 inches in diameter. Except for the lowest portions, the trunk is covered in long black spines. The 18-foot-long leaves have their leaflets arranged at different angles along the rachis. Nothing on earth is more beautiful than a grove of these palms with individuals of varying heights.

Astrocaryum alatum (a-LAIT-um) is quite similar to and as beautiful as *A. mexicanum,* but hails only from Central America. Plate 56.

Astrocaryum mexicanum (mex-i-KAHN-um) is a solitary-trunked species indigenous to Mexico and Central America where it is a denizen of lowland rain forests. It will, however, adapt to full sun if it is not in seedling stage. It is one of the world's loveliest palm species, especially when grown in an area protected from high winds, as the untattered leaves are gloriously beautiful. The palm only grows to a maximum height of 15 feet or so. The trunk is covered in strong and sharp spines attendant on the old leaf bases. The leaves are as much as 10 feet long with leaflets that are as much as 2 feet long. Arising in one plane from the rachis, which also bears black spines, the leaflets are arranged into two or more groups along the rachis. The leaflets are united within the groups, thus sometimes giving the impression of an undivided leaf. They are a bright green color above and silvery beneath. The flowers and fruit are encased in a spiny boat-shaped spathe. There is no more exotic and lush palm for the nearly tropical areas.

ASYSTASIA

(as´-iss-TAY-zee-a / as´-iss-TAY-zhya)
Acanthaceae: The Acanthus Family
COROMANDEL; GANGES PRIMROSE;
    SUTTER'S GOLD
Trailing vinelike plant with light green heart-shaped
    leaves and white to purple flowers
Zones 9b through 11
Sun to part shade
Average but regular amounts of moisture
Humusy, well-drained soil
Propagation by cuttings

A genus of about 70 species of usually trailing or clambering herbaceous plants native to tropical areas of Africa, India, and Australasia. Only one species is commonly planted in the United States. *Asystasia gangetica* (gan-JET-i-ka) (synonym *A. coromandeliana*) hails from tropical Africa and Malaysia. It is one of the prettiest groundcovers available to gardeners in nearly frost-free regions. It is not a soil-binder or candidate for erosion control, but does creep and, where a

filler is needed in sun or partial shade, it is a little gem. The plants may also be pruned to make shrublets and can be trained as true vines. They grow to a maximum height of 2 feet and have 4-inch-long cordate, membranous leaves with prominent veins. The little inch-wide trumpet-shaped flowers are white or yellow when they first open, but soon change to pink and then deep violet. These transformations give an attractive aspect to an area planted in coromandel, as there are several colors at any one time. The flowers appear off and on throughout the year, but most abundantly in the summer months. Temperatures below about 24°F kill the leaves, stems, and roots.

AUCUBA (AWK-yoo-ba / aw-KOO-ba)

Cornaceae: The Dogwood Family
AUCUBA
Evergreen shrub with large, ovate leathery, often
    variegated leaves
Zones 7 through 9
Shade to partial shade
Average but regular amounts of moisture
Rich, humusy, well-drained soil
Propagation by cuttings

A genus of only three species of evergreen shrubs found from the lower Himalayas through southern China to Japan, with purple flowers and variously colored berries. Only one species is planted outside botanical gardens. *Aucuba japonica* (ja-PAHN-i-ka) is sometimes referred to as the Japanese laurel. It grows slowly to perhaps 12 feet in height and width and has dark green ovate to oblong toothed leaves to 8 inches long, usually bunched up near the ends of the branches. The tiny flowers come in mid-spring in terminal panicles and are purplish red. The male and female flowers are on separate plants, so that both types of shrubs are needed for the females to produce the long-lasting berries during the summer, which become bright red by fall. The plant is useful for creating a semi-tropical look in shady situations where a shrub is wanted. It is mostly pest-free and somewhat drought tolerant, but, like most plants, looks better and grows faster with adequate moisture. It is extremely easy of culture in shade or partial shade. It is not such a good performer in tropical areas as it likes a drop in temperature in the winter to look its best. There are several cultivars that are more planted than the type. *Aucuba japonica* 'Crotonifolia' (kro-tahn´-i-FO-lee-a) has leaves so heavily splotched with golden-yellow as to look like a yellow leaf with some dark green splotches. It is quite choice. *Aucuba japonica* 'Fructo-alba' (frook´-to-AL-ba) has white-variegated leaves and pinkish white berries. *Aucuba japonica* 'Goldieana' (gol-dee-AN-a) has very dark green leaves with white to yellow maculation usually near the center of the leaf. *Aucuba japonica* 'Picturata' (pik-tyoo-RAIT-a) has more linear leaves with the central part light yellow to white. *Aucuba japonica* 'Serratifolia' (ser-rait´-i-FO-lee-a) has very pretty leaves with deeply serrated leaf margins that give the shrub the aspect of a holly bush. *Aucuba japonica* **'Variegata'** (vair-ee-a-GAIT-a) is commonly called the gold-dust plant and is probably the most widely planted cultivar, having deep green leaves speckled with light yellow.

AVERRHOA (av-er-RO-a)

Oxalidaceae: The Oxalis Family
Common names vary according to species
Small evergreen trees with large pinnate leaves and
    large yellow fruit
Zones vary according to species
Sun
Water lovers
Rich, deep, moist, well-drained, relatively acidic soil
Propagation by seed and air-layering

The genus consists of two species from southeastern tropical Asia. Both species produce edible fruit. Both have relatively large, odd-pinnate evergreen leaves whose leaflets, like many members of the Caesalpiniaceae, Mimosaceae, and Papilionaceae (Fabaceae), are somewhat sensitive to touch and illumination, and tend to fold up against the leaf rachis when touched or with the descent of darkness. The flowers are somewhat cauliflorous and are borne in the leaf axils and on the main branches.

Averrhoa bilimbi (bil-IM-bee) is indigenous to Malaysia, where it is known as the bilimbi, but is usually referred to as the cucumber tree in English-speaking countries. It is a medium-sized tree with a short trunk and a rounded crown, attaining a maximum height of perhaps 50 feet. The odd-pinnate leaves are usually clustered near the tips of the branches and are about 2 feet long with many felty, narrowly ovate to narrowly oblong, pointy-tipped, grassy green leaflets that hang somewhat limply from the rachis and give the tree a lovely tropical appearance. The flowers are purple-red with greenish yellow stamens and are borne in small hairy clusters on the branches and trunks. The waxy fruits are shaped like cucumbers but are not curved and are 2 to 4 inches long with five shallow ribs. Green when immature and light yellow or white when mature, the fruits look somewhat like small bananas. The plant bears flowers and fruits on the trunk as well as the branches and twigs. The fruit, which is not usually eaten fresh because it is sharply acidic in taste, is made into pickles and relish and is used as a condiment in many vegetable dishes. The tree tolerates no frost and is dependable only in zones 10b and 11.

Averrhoa carambola (kar-AM-bo-la / kar-am-BO-la) is native to the same general region as *A. bilimbi* (cucumber tree), but is called star fruit (from the cross sections of the fruit, which are shaped like a star or starfish) or carambola. It is a slow-growing, medium-sized tree generally resembling the cucumber tree but reaching a maximum height of only 30 feet or so with a very dense crown when grown in good soil. The odd-pinnate leaves are also smaller than those of the cucumber tree and have fewer leaflets, usually only 9, sometimes 11. The leaflets, which are distinctly cordate and 1 to 3 inches long, are smaller near the trunk and progressively larger towards the end of the rachis. They are grassy green and shiny above, whitish and pubescent below. The tiny hairy fragrant flowers appear in spring and summer in small clusters in the leaf axils and are white to pink with purple markings. The very attractive fruit ripens in the summer through autumn and is a large (to 6 inches long), oblong 5-ribbed waxy-yellow to orange berry. This species is only slightly hardier than *A. bilimbi* and is suitable for zones 10 and 11, but mature trees are occasionally found in 9b. Although not that particular as to soil, the tree certainly looks better and flowers and fruits better with good soil and an adequate and regular supply of water. It does not tolerate a cold and soggy soil and demands perfect drainage. The fruit, which ranges in taste from quite sour to somewhat sweet, is eaten raw or mixed into salads, cooked into stews, curries, and puddings, and made into preserves. Of the several named forms, many people consider *Averrhoa carambola* **'Maha'** the best.

AVICENNIA (av-i-SEN-nee-a)

Avicenniaceae: The Black Mangrove Family
BLACK MANGROVE; HONEY MANGROVE
Large evergreen leathery-leaved mangrove tree with
    aerial roots emerging from the water
Zones 9b through 11
Sun
Water lover; marine aquatic
Sandy, humusy wet soil
Propagation by seed

A genus of about 12 species of mangrove trees, only one of which is found in the United States. It occurs naturally throughout tropical America and is the hardiest species of mangrove, at one time growing on the northern Gulf Coast of Texas. It is also found on the coasts of West Africa. *Avicennia nitida* (ni-TY-da / ni-TEE-da) is a small shrub in the most northerly parts of its range, but a large tree to as much as 80 or more feet tall in truly tropical areas. It grows rather slowly into a sprawling, shallow-rooted, dense-headed tree with succulent and leathery, linear-lanceolate leaves to 4 or 5 inches long. The leaves are yellow-green to olive green and smooth above, but softly pubescent and whitish beneath. In saline environments the leaves are usually covered with encrustations of salt, which the tree has separated from the water its roots take up. The small white fragrant flowers appear intermittently throughout the year and are favorites of bees. They are followed by capsules that germinate (as do all other mangrove species) on the tree, sending out a root from the bottom of the fruit. Because of its bottom heaviness, the fruit drops into the water or soil, where its root quickly becomes established or it floats off to another part of the coast to carry on the species. Like all other mangroves, the tree's roots send up many pneumato-phores that are usually about 6 inches high with the diameter of a pencil. The tree is not the most beautiful tree in the world, but is nevertheless quite attractive and extremely useful for planting where water and salinity prevent other trees from growing. It can also be planted farther inland away from the tide if the ground is constantly moist. Plate 57.

AZADIRACHTA (a-zad′-i-RAK-ta)

Meliaceae: The Mahogany, Chinaberry Family
NEEM TREE; MARGOSA TREE
Large evergreen tree; large pinnate leaves; large
    clusters of fragrant white flowers; yellow berries
Zones 10 and 11; marginal in zone 9b
Sun
Average but regular amounts of moisture; drought
    tolerant when established
Average well-drained soil
Propagation by seed and cuttings

A genus of only two tree species in India eastward to Malaysia. One species has been planted in its native haunts for years as an ornamental and for its wood and the medicinal extracts of its bark. This species is now sought after in the Western world as its bark was discovered to yield a hormone that interrupts the life cycle of many harmful insects. *Azadirachta indica* (IN-di-ka) (synonym *A. nim*) is native to monsoonal India and Sri Lanka where it grows to 50 feet or more. It has a fairly open canopy of large odd-pinnate glossy leaves that are as much as 2 feet long with pendent lanceolate and somewhat sickle-shaped leaflets with finely serrate margins. The leaves and the form of the tree are quite reminiscent of *Juglans* (walnut) species or an especially healthy *Carya* (pecan) species. The flowers are borne in the spring in loose-flowered axillary panicles. Each blossom is star-shaped, greenish white in color, and somewhat fragrant. The inflorescences are not spectacular in the landscape because they are half hidden by the leaves. The fruits are clusters of small orange berries that are relished by birds. In India the species is used for planting along streets and avenues, and it is a very good shade tree anywhere the climate is amenable. The tree is damaged by temperatures below 30°F, but recovers quickly from those of 28°F or above. It is drought tolerant when established.

BACTRIS (BAK-tris)

Palmae (Arecaceae): The Palm Family
PEACH PALM
Large clumping, very spiny plumosely pinnate-leaved
    palm
Zones 10b and 11
Sun
Water lover
Rich, humusy, moist, well-drained soil
Propagation by seed

A large genus of more than 200 species of small to large, usually very spiny pinnate-leaved palms in tropical America. Most are suckering species. In the palm family only the genus *Calamus* has a greater number of species. The old name for the genus was *Guilelma*. *Bactris gasipaes* (GAS-i-peez) is a noble and beautiful tall-growing, usually suckering tree to 60 feet in height. It is no longer found outside cultivation, but its origin is most probably Central or South America. The trunks are light brown in color and strongly ringed. Each ring sports stout black spines. The leaves are about 12 feet long on 3-foot-long spiny petioles. The gracefully arching 2-foot-long grassy-green leaflets arise from several angles along the spiny rachis, giving the blade a somewhat plumose appearance. The spineless inflorescences appear among the leaves and produce pendent masses of 2- to 4-inch-long plum-shaped, orange to reddish orange edible fruits, which are much relished by the native peoples. The palm is a superb and tropical looking landscape subject but, because of the spines, must be judiciously placed in the landscape.

BAMBUSA (bam-BOOS-a)

Gramineae (Poaceae): The Grass Family
BAMBOO
Giant woody, clumping bamboos
Zones vary according to species
Sun to partial sun
Average but regular amounts of moisture
Average well-drained soil
Propagation by rhizome division

A large genus of about 120 species of tall clumping-type bamboos in tropical and subtropical Asia and tropical America. Some of the most useful landscape bamboo species are found in this genus.

Bambusa argentea. See *Arundinaria viridistriata*, *B. multiplex*.

Bambusa argenteostriata. See *Arundinaria argenteostriata*, *B. multiplex* 'Silverstripe'.

Bambusa arundinacea (a-run′-di-NAY-see-a) (synonym *B. bambos*) is from tropical India and is one of the best bamboos for making a large screen. Commonly called giant thorny bamboo, it can grow to 80 feet or more in cultivation (and even larger in its native habitat) and makes a very dense clump of great golden yellow culms. Each culm is as much as 8 inches in diameter. The lower branches have strong and sharp spines, probably to protect the succulent and edible young shoots from predation by deer and other animals. The leaves are linear-lanceolate, to 8 inches or more long. Because the plant is tender and its aboveground growth succumbs to temperatures in the upper 20s, the plant's successful cultivation is limited to zones 10 and 11. Mature specimens, however, can be expected in the warmer parts of zone 9b. It takes the roots of newly planted clumps a year to become established, and the growth until that time is liable to be scrubby and the culms small and tangled. When the new culms emerge, their growth rate is quite fast and many new shoots are produced each year. In areas with hot summers this species is best planted, like most bamboo, in the autumn, so that the roots and shoots do not have to contend with the high temperatures of late spring and summer.

Bambusa bambos. See *B. arundinacea.*

Bambusa beecheyana (beech-ee-YAHN-a) (synonym *Sinocalamus beecheyanus*) is native to southeastern China and is commonly called beechey bamboo. It is a lovely, open clumper with gracefully arching culms to as much as 40 feet in height. The culms have relatively short internodes, are a maximum of 4 or 5 inches in diameter, and are not completely round in cross section. The light green leaves are as much as a foot long and 3 inches wide and are oblong to lanceolate in shape. The aboveground growth is hardy to about 20°F and can be grown in zones 9 through 11. The stems sprout from the roots in zone 8b. This bamboo makes an unusually beautiful grove. The young shoots are considered among the choicest for eating in southern China.

Bambusa glaucescens. See *B. multiplex.*

Bambusa multiplex (MULT-i-plex) (synonyms *B. argentea, B. glaucescens, B. nana*) is native to southeastern China. It is the most commonly planted bamboo in Florida, the Gulf States, and California, where it is called hedge bamboo. Along with *B. vulgaris,* it is the most widely planted bamboo in the tropics. The plant makes a good hedge as (unlike many species of *Phyllostachys* and some tropical species) there are leaves all the way from the top of the culms to the ground, and the clumps are dense with stems. It is also one of the hardiest of the clumping bamboos and is successful in zones 9 through 11 as are its varieties and cultivars. The deep green culms are relatively thin, attaining a maximum width of only an inch, and are gracefully arching. They emerge from the soil almost any time of the year if the weather is warm, but most abundantly in summer and fall, and they reach a usual height of 30 feet although some of the cultivars attain only 12 feet or so. The leaves are typically as long as 8 inches, linear-lanceolate, and dark green above and silvery beneath. The cultivars of *B. multiplex* show a great diversity of leaf form and color, and some of them are much more common in cultivation than is the species. ***Bambusa multiplex* 'Alphonse Karr'** (synonym *B. nana*) grows magnificently to 30 feet or so. The culms are as large as 2 inches in diameter and are a beautiful dark green striped with yellow or orange. ***Bambusa multiplex* 'Fernleaf'** grows to about 15 feet in height with small leaves, which give the branches somewhat the look of a large fern and lead to the common name fernleaf bamboo. This plant tends to grow larger and the leaves become much larger with ample water and good soil. Thus it is more useful in containers than in the ground if the ferny look is wanted. It is also very good as a dense hedge. ***Bambusa multiplex* var. *riviereorum*** (riv´-ee-er-ee-OR-um) is sometimes called the Chinese goddess bamboo. It is quite beautiful and has small leaves rather like the fernleaf bamboo, but generally even smaller than the latter, and it usually only reaches about 12 feet in height. ***Bambusa multiplex* var. *riviereorum* 'Tiny Fern'** is a dwarf form. ***Bambusa multiplex* 'Silverstripe'** (synonyms *B. argenteostriata, B. nana*) is perhaps the most attractive cultivar of a very attractive species. It grows large, to 30 or 40 feet in height, and has large leaves striped with white. White stripes also usually appear on the culms between the internodes. Plate 58.

Bambusa nana. See *Arundinaria disticha, B. multiplex, B. multiplex* 'Alphonse Karr', *B. multiplex* 'Silverstripe'.

Bambusa oldhamii (old-HAM-ee-eye) (synonyms *Dendrocalamus latiflorus, Sinocalamus oldhamii*) is also from southeastern China and Taiwan. It is one of the most beautiful tropical clumping bamboos that can be grown in zones 9b through 11; it is marginal in zone 9a. The clumps are fairly open and the culms, which reach a height of as much as 50 feet (usually 30 to 40 feet), are as much as 4 inches in diameter. Besides Oldham bamboo, it is sometimes called Oldham timber bamboo. The stems grow tall and straight but are light in weight, and the wind through a grove can chime them against each other. They are a vivid green for the first year or so but gradually change in color to a deep yellow if planted in the sun. The leaves are large (to a foot or more long), and linear-lanceolate with a decidedly pointed tip, and the branches clothe the culms almost to the ground, making this an excellent choice for giant hedges or for screening. This giant grass is equally useful as a specimen plant when sited where its form and size can be appreciated.

Bambusa pygmaea. See *Arundinaria pygmaea.*

Bambusa textilis (TEX-ti-lis / tex-TY-lis) is also from southern China but is hardy to 15°F or even lower, making it probably the largest and most attractive clumping bamboo that can be successfully grown in zones 8b through 11. It should be tried in zone 8a. The slender (often only 2 inches in diameter) blue-green stems sometimes reach a height of 50 feet but more commonly are 40 feet in cultivation. They are bare of branches and leaves for more than half their height, giving an almost startling aspect to clumps planted as specimens where their form can be appreciated. The leaves are a maximum of 8 inches long and are linear-ovate and a dark green in color. This species does not make a very good screen subject since most of the stem length is free of branches and leaves, but as a grove or specimen plant it is quite spectacular.

Bambusa tuldoides (tool-DOY-deez), from southern China, is called punting-pole bamboo from one of its many uses in its native habitat. It is mostly hardy in zones 9 through 11, but in severe winters may be killed to the ground in zone 9a, with root survival. The stems are slender, attaining no more than about 2 inches in diameter, but often grow to 50 feet in height, making a very graceful specimen plant. The clumps are dense, and many culms are produced each year with established plants. The leaves are relatively small (to 5 inches long) for so tall a species. They are dark green and generally oblong in shape. This bamboo is equally beautiful as a specimen plant or as a giant hedge or screen.

Bambusa ventricosa (ven-tri-KOS-a) is yet another species from southern China and, like *B. tuldoides*, is completely hardy in zones 9 through 11. Its most distinctive feature, the shortened and swollen nodes, is apparent only when the plant is grown as a bonsai or when consistently grown in poor, dry soil. Under these conditions the stems grow only to 6 or 8 feet in height and evince the quite picturesque greatly swollen nodes, which phenomenon leads to the common names of Buddha bamboo or Buddha's belly bamboo. Otherwise, the plant is quite similar in morphology and cultural requirements to *B. tuldoides*.

Bambusa vulgaris (vul-GAIR-is) is the most commonly planted bamboo in the world. So long has it been in cultivation and so widespread is its popularity that its original habitat is not precisely known but is probably southern India, including Sri Lanka. It is not, therefore, terribly surprising that its most common name is common bamboo. Of course, beauty alone would not have made it the world's premier bamboo, but its many utilitarian and economic uses in the past would. Because it is not very hardy to cold and is damaged by temperatures below 30°F, it is dependable only in zones 10 and 11, although it has often reached maturity in zone 9b. It makes a very open clump and can almost be called "invasive," since the new culms, unlike those of most other clumping types of bamboo, emerge from the soil after traveling a relatively great distance. In fact, they travel as much as 3 feet, rather like the running types of bamboo. The species makes a beautiful and tropical looking subject with its prominent nodes and long internodes. The mature culms, which grow to 50 or 60 feet in height, are clothed within 3 or 4 feet of the bottom with branches and leaves. The leafless region often has adventitious roots around the nodes. The relatively few branches are many-branched, and the leaves are large (to a foot long), lanceolate, and dark green. The typical color of the mature culms is dark green, but some stems grown in the more tropical parts of the globe develop a beautiful golden color. *Bambusa vulgaris* **var.** *striata* (synonym *B. vulgaris* var. *vittata*) is rare but well worth the search as it has golden stems heavily striped with dark green. It is truly magnificent and one of the tropical world's most beautiful plants.

BARLERIA (bar-LER-ee-a)
Acanthaceae: The Acanthus Family
Common names vary according to species
Herbaceous, often spiny shrubs with white, blue, or
    yellow flowers
Zones 9b through 11; marginal in zone 9a
Sun
Average but regular amounts of moisture
Humusy, well-drained soil
Propagation by seed and cuttings

A large genus of about 250 species of tropical evergreen herbs and small shrubs, often with spines, having simple leaves that are usually hairy to some extent. The flower colors range from white to yellow and orange, to magenta, purple, and blue. The form of the flower is a tube whose end flares into five corolla lobes. One lobe is distinct and usually larger than the other four. The plants make perfect and nearly everblooming hedges in tropical or nearly frost-free areas but need to be pruned when young to maintain a compact shape.

Barleria cristata (kris-TAIT-a) is native to India and Myanmar (Burma) but is called the Philippine violet. It grows to a maximum of 6 feet in height but is usually less. The leaves are hairy, oblong to lanceolate and 3 or 4 inches long. The quite attractive flower is reminiscent of that of many *Ruellia* species, being a 2-inch-wide trumpet-shaped blossom with five corolla lobes of blue, purple, or white. The lobes are in two groups, the lower petal usually larger than the upper four. The plant blooms most of the summer and autumn and can be used as a low hedge or tall groundcover in shady to partially sunny sites where many other flowering subjects would not bloom well. It is even more floriferous with sun. There are bi-colored cultivars with white and lilac colors. This plant has naturalized itself in parts of southern Florida as it readily self sows. Plate 59.

Barleria lupulina (loop-yoo-LYN-a) is native to the island of Mauritius. It grows only to about 2 feet in height. The leathery 4-inch-long leaves are linear-lanceolate and dark green, with a distinct red midvein, and are extremely attractive. There are usually small spines in the leaf axils. The inch-wide yellow to orange flowers appear in terminal spikes of overlapping bracts, reminiscent of the flower spikes of many bromeliads and hop vines. The plants bloom in cycles in spring, summer, and fall.

Barleria obtusa (ahb-TOOS-a) is a 3-foot-shrub native to South Africa. It has 3-inch-long dark green elliptic to lanceolate leaves and clusters of blue 2-inch-wide flowers, which appear in late winter and spring and sometimes also in summer. The flowers appear to have four petals, but actually the two bottom lobes of the five-lobed flowers are fused.

Barleria repens (REEP-enz) is native to South Africa. This wonderful creeping vinelike plant roots at the stem nodes, which makes it a singularly attractive groundcover. It grows to about 2 feet and creates a dense cover in sunny or partially sunny locations. The leaves are small, elliptic in shape, and dense on the vines. The flowers, which are exceptionally large for such small plants, are a bright coral red in color and about 2 inches wide.

BARRINGTONIA (bair-ring-TO-nee-a)
Lecythidaceae: The Brazil-Nut Family
FISH POISON TREE
Large evergreen, large-leaved tree; shaving-brush-like
    fragrant flowers

Zones 10b and 11
Sun
Water lovers
Sandy, moist, well-drained, humusy soil
Propagation by seed

A genus of about 30 species of medium-sized, large-leaved, evergreen broad-crowned trees in Madagascar, India, and Sri Lanka, through Malaysia, the Philippines, northern Australia, and the islands of the South Pacific. The leathery leaves are similar to those of many *Ficus* species or *Magnolia grandiflora* (southern magnolia) and often turn a beautiful red or bronzy hue before they fall. The spectacular, fragrant flowers are nocturnal with great masses of long protruding stamens. Most species are indigenous to tropical seashores as well as farther inland, and all are quite tolerant of salty air, salt spray, and saline soil. The trees are the very essence of the tropical look and should be planted much more widely in the warmer parts of southern Florida and in similar climates. ***Barringtonia asiatica*** (ay-zee-AT-i-ka) (synonym *B. speciosa*) is found in the shoreline forests of Madagascar, India, Sri Lanka, the Philippines, and the islands of the South Pacific. It grows to 70 feet or more and is a widespreading tree, often with buttresses at the base of the trunk. The great leathery, strongly veined obovate leaves are as much as 2 feet long and are graced with a strong central midrib and transverse veins, which are lighter in color than the bright glossy green surrounding them. The leaves are found mostly at the ends of the tree's great thick, contorted branches and turn a beautiful reddish to purplish bronze before they fall from the tree. The fragrant nocturnal flowers are in terminal racemes. Each flower is as much as 8 inches in diameter and consists of four ovate fleshy white petals from which spring very many long pure white stamens tipped with pink and purple anthers. The fruit is a four-angled, heart-shaped brown capsule with one poisonous seed, which is surrounded by a spongy, fibrous husk that is light and full of air pockets. These pockets create the buoyancy of the fruits, which allows for their consequent wide dissemination around the tropical seas. The Pacific Island peoples use the fruits as floats for their fishing nets. They also use the poisonous seeds to stun the fish, which practice has led to one of the common names, the fish-poison tree. The trees are tropical but successful in zones 10b and 11 and, although, ideally adapted to the saline environment of tropical beaches, nevertheless grow superbly inland.

BAUHINIA (baw-HIN-ee-a)
Caesalpiniaceae (Leguminosae), subfamily
    Caesalpinioideae: The Cassia, Royal Poinciana
    Family
BAUHINIA
Trees, shrubs, and vines with two-lobed leaves;
    orchidlike flowers
Zones vary according to species

Sun
Average but regular amounts of moisture
Sandy, humusy, well-drained soil
Propagation by seed, cuttings, air-layering, and
    (sometimes) transplanting of suckers

A large genus of as many as 300 species of trees, shrubs, and large vines in warm or tropical regions around the world. All the species have distinctive two-lobed leaves that are generally shaped like a cloven-hoof print. Many of the plants have thorns. Most have unusual and quite distinctive and recognizable flowers reminiscent of orchids in shape, with five spreading petals. The uppermost petal, called "the standard," is usually larger than and differently colored from the other four. The trees are, as a group, called orchid trees, and they may be entirely evergreen or briefly deciduous. The flowers are mostly quite beautiful, although the trees are often less so, being sometimes weak and brittle of trunk and stem and easily damaged by strong wind. Furthermore, the trees are somewhat messy because of the seed pods. These plants resent limy soil and have ratty and browning foliage when grown in such a medium. Soil amendments with compost or peat moss and regular irrigation are required. In spite of these shortcomings, the trees are universally admired and planted because of their flowers.

Bauhinia ×blakeana (blaik-ee-AHN-a) is called the Hong Kong orchid tree because it originated in that region as a sterile hybrid, most likely a cross between *B. purpurea* and *B. variegata*. It is commonly considered to be the most beautiful orchid tree. Evergreen and fast growing, it makes a fairly large tree to 40 feet or more with rather long trailing branches. The leaves are especially beautiful, to 8 or more inches wide, dark olive green, thick, and almost succulent. The flowers are large (to 6 inches wide) and have the typical form of the genus. The standard petal is not so differently colored from the other petals as it is in most other *Bauhinia* species. The blossoms appear on the tree from early October through the following spring and are a deep rose, almost red in color. The four smaller petals have lighter veining, while the standard petal has darker veining. The flowers have an outstanding fragrance that is powerful yet delicate and impossible to describe. One great advantage this tree has over most others is that, being sterile, it sets no messy fruit pods. Alas, the tree is not very hardy to cold. Temperatures of 30°F and lower defoliate it and kill the flower buds. Damage to the twigs and branches starts at about 28°F, with death of the tree occurring below 25°F. Thus this hybrid is successful only in zones 10 and 11, although occasional mature specimens are found in zone 9b. The trees are not very particular as to soil and, once established, are moderately drought tolerant although they seem to do best with dependable water and a fairly deep soil of average fertility. Many trees are sold bearing the name "Hong Kong Orchid Tree," although they are not the sterile hybrid just described. According to Derek Burch of

Horticultural Masterworks in Miami, gardeners should "ask searching questions about the propagation technique used" as "the presence of seed pods is an almost certain disqualification." Plate 60.

Bauhinia corymbosa (kor-im-BO-sa) (synonym *Phanera corymbosa*) is a large-growing dense evergreen tendril-climbing vine from southeastern China. It is hardy in zones 9b through 11 and makes a beautiful thick cover of typically shaped, deeply cleft 1- to 2-inch-wide dark green leaves with distinct parallel veins. The pinkish white flowers appear in summer in many-flowered, loose clusters. The five petals of each blossom are equal in size and shape (almost rectangular) with long, narrow fluted bases and shallowly scalloped margins. Among the most beautiful features of the flowers are the long scarlet stamens. The vine climbs by its tendrils, which need a support onto which they can hold. This species is not drought tolerant and will do best in sun, with a fairly rich and humusy, moist well-drained soil. It is a breathtaking sight when in bloom.

Bauhinia forficata (for-fi-KAIT-a) is native to Peru, Brazil, and Argentina, and is probably the hardiest of the large and large-flowered orchid trees. It is a safe and quite dependable candidate for zones 9b through 11, often making mature specimens in zone 9a. It forms a tree to 20 or 30 feet in height with long, drooping spiny branches. The leaves, which cover the branches densely, are large, 4 to 5 inches long, evergreen, and wonderfully dark green with the typical shape of those in the genus. The flowers are exceptional in size and color: as much as 8 inches in width and a brilliant white in color. All five petals are the same size and linear-lanceolate to long-obovate. The flowers appear in dense terminal clusters through the late spring, summer, and fall, opening at night but closing up in the heat of a midsummer's day unless the day is overcast or cool. Some sources cite the common name Brazilian orchid tree. A much more appropriate moniker would seem to be white orchid tree. No other bauhinia is more floriferous or more dependable. It should be planted much more than it is in zone 9. The tree makes a wonderfully imposing statement in the landscape when in bloom, with only two faults: it is thorny, and it freely suckers. Plate 61.

Bauhinia galpinii. See *B. punctata.*

Bauhinia kappleri. See *B. monandra.*

Bauhinia monandra (mo-NAN-dra) (synonym *B. kappleri*) is native to Myanmar (Burma) and is called the butterfly flower or pink orchid tree. It is a small deciduous tree to only 20 feet or so in height (rarely to 40 feet) with large leaves to 8 inches wide. The large flowers are quite beautiful. They open white with the standard petal heavily splotched with red or pink and margined with yellow, and the other four petals bedecked with red dots. Soon all the white changes to rose-pink, creating a wonderful, multicolored panorama over the tree, which blooms profusely from late spring to fall. The tree is, unfortunately, not hardy and is dependable only in zones 10 and 11.

Bauhinia punctata (punk-TAIT-a) (synonym *B. galpinii*) is a small, rather sprawling tree or shrub from tropical Africa and South Africa. Growing to 10 feet or more in height, it climbs (by the twining branch tips) if trained to a support and is very fine as an espalier. It has rather small leaves and flowers, but the flowers are a delectable brick red or scarlet and they appear on the tree for most of the year. The plant has been referred to as the nasturtium bauhinia, and there is a slight resemblance in the flowers of the one to the other but no one would confuse them. The more appropriate common name is red bauhinia, but pride of the Cape is also used. The flowers are about 3 inches across, and all the petals are the same size and shape. Each petal is fluted at the base and expands into an ovate to oblong to almost squared limb. The little tree cannot take much cold and is not adaptable outside zones 10 and 11 although sometimes reaching maturity in the warmer parts of zone 9b. Plate 62.

Bauhinia purpurea (poor-POOR-ee-a) is indigenous to a wide area of the Asian tropics from India through Malaysia, but is dependably hardy in zones 9b through 11. It is a large shrub or medium-sized, usually multitrunked tree, to as much as 30 feet in height. It can be trained into a standard single-trunked tree with a somewhat contorted trunk. The leaves are only slightly cleft and are almost orbicular in outline. The flowers are the classic orchid-tree shape and size, to 6 inches across, and are pink to purple to lavender (sometimes almost white) with a larger standard petal with darker veins. The tree is deciduous from about December until March, but the flowers appear in autumn, usually before the leaves fall in late September to mid-December. This species is sometimes referred to as the butterfly tree but always as an "orchid tree."

Bauhinia tomentosa (toe-men-TOE-sa) is native to a very large area from tropical southeastern Africa through India to southeastern China. It is a small tree (or more often a large shrub) to maybe 20 feet in height with 3-inch-wide leaves. It is not hardy to cold and, even though it is known to sprout from the roots after being frozen to the ground, is dependable only in zones 10 and 11. The leaves are typical of the genus and almost round in outline. The flowers, which are so much unlike those of most other *Bauhinia* species that it is hard for the casual observer to accept including this species in the genus, are shaped like a cup. The petals overlap to the point that, seen from any distance, there is no apparent separation of them. The flowers look more like many hibiscus flowers than they do those of other *Bauhinia* species. The flower color is a bright yellow, and the standard petal has a single red to brown spot. The more common of the two common names is St. Thomas tree because the little tree is naturalized on that island. Bell bauhinia is also used and is quite accurately descriptive of the flower shape.

Bauhinia variegata (vair-ee-a-GAIT-a) is native to northern India, northern Indochina, and southeastern China. It is quite similar to *B. purpurea* (and is often confused with it), but has differences of flower color and time of bloom. It also is hardy in zones 9b through 11. The tree is usually briefly deciduous, but this seems to depend on the amount of cold or moisture as much as anything. Freezing temperatures will defoliate the tree, as will drought in winter. Lacking either of these phenomena, the tree may lose its leaves in early spring in any case. It blooms in late winter to late spring and is often bare of leaves (or nearly so) when the flowers make their appearance. The flowers are as much as 6 inches across and have the classic shape with the petals pink to magenta and the standard petal heavily marked with deep purple. Most sources report that the petals of *B. variegata* overlap whereas those of *B. purpurea* do not. This trait is usually the case but is not completely diagnostic. Both species seem rather variable in flower color and size of flower petals, as well as time of flowering. ***Bauhinia variegata* 'Candida'** (kan-DEED-a) is a beautiful cultivar with pure white flowers of the same size and shape as the type, usually with faint greenish veins on the standard petal. It is very choice and looks more like a white *Cattleya* orchid than anything that produces beanlike pods.

BEAUCARNEA (bo-KAR-nee-a)
Agavaceae: The Agave Family
PONYTAIL PALM; BOTTLE PALM
Treelike perennials; trunks basally swollen; long, narrow grasslike leaves in rosettes
Zones 9b through 11
Sun
Average but regular amounts of moisture; somewhat drought tolerant
Sandy, humusy, well-drained soil
Propagation by seed

A small Mexican genus of about six species of large succulent perennials, sometimes of treelike proportions and often forming a basally swollen trunk. The leaves are in large and dense terminal rosettes, with each long blade narrow and grasslike. The genus is considered by some taxonomists to be a subset of the genus *Nolina*. These are, of course, not true palms nor are they closely related to palms.

Beaucarnea gracilis (GRAS-i-liss) is sometimes planted. It has much shorter leaves (a maximum of 3 feet long) than *B. recurvata* that are only slightly recurved, but it grows to almost the same height as *B. recurvata*. The flowers are reddish.

Beaucarnea recurvata (rek-yoor-VAIT-a) (synonym *Nolina tuberculata*) is native to the drier parts of the state of Veracruz in Mexico. Besides ponytail palm, it is sometimes called the elephant's foot tree because of the greatly swollen trunk base, which is bulblike in young plants but spreading and somewhat amorphous (the nearest comparison is to that of old *Phytloacca dioica* trees) in mature plants. The tree can reach as much as 20 or even 30 feet in height but is always rather sparsely branched in comparison to more traditional trees. The trunks of young plants are tan-colored; they become gray with age and form thick, fissured bark and a basal portion that may be several feet wide. The leaf rosettes are at the ends of the few branches, and each leaf is as long as 6 feet or even more, narrow (usually less than an inch wide), grasslike, and recurved with almost smooth margins. The plant, after attaining some size, produces large terminal panicles of tiny, yellowish white six-petaled flowers. Seed should not be expected from any species unless trees of differing sexes are planted, as the male and female flowers are on separate trees. The trees are tender to cold when young and are often killed by temperatures below 26°F, but older plants have been known to survive 20°F. Veracruz is not a desert region of Mexico, and the plants should not be treated like most cactus. That is, they are somewhat drought tolerant but are not true succulents and appreciate water during times of drought. The important consideration is that the soil never be soggy and the drainage never impeded. The plants grow in partial shade but look their best in full sun. They are slow growing, taking years to form a treelike structure. There are several other species, but none are very common. Plate 63.

Beaucarnea stricta (STRIK-ta) is similar to *B. gracilis* but has its leaves margined with light yellow. Plate 64.

BEAUMONTIA (bo-MAHNT-ee-a)
Apocynaceae: The Oleander, Frangipani, Vinca Family
EASTER-LILY VINE; HERALD'S TRUMPET
Large heavy evergreen twining vine; large leathery leaves; large white, lilylike fragrant flowers
Zones 10 and 11; marginal in zone 10a
Sun
Water lover
Rich, humusy, moist, well-drained soil
Propagation seed and cuttings; root division of old plants

A small genus of about nine woody flowering vines indigenous to India and Malaysia. They have large entire leaves and large trumpet-shaped flowers in terminal clusters. They are all tropical, can stand but a few degrees of frost, and need deep, moist rich soil. Only one species is commonly planted outside botanical gardens. ***Beaumontia grandiflora*** (grand-i-FLOR-a) is native to the foothills of the Himalayas in northern India and Nepal and is one of the world's most beautiful vines. It is naturally a sprawling, clambering, semi-twining large shrub that can even be grown as a small tree. With guidance it can be maintained as a large and spectacular vine, often growing to as much as 50 feet in height if it has a strong support. In time the woody trunks stand alone without help but must be guided when young. Under optimal conditions the vine makes an almost impenetrable screen of large overlapping leaves. The leaves are outstanding enough that the vine could be grown for them alone. As much as 10 inches long by 4 inches wide, with prominent and lighter-colored veins, they are slightly wavy-margined, elliptic to obovate, glossy dark green above and pubescent below. The wonderfully fragrant flowers are in large terminal clusters. Each flower is a pendent trumpet, 4 inches long and 4 inches wide, pure white, sometimes tinged with pink on the margins, with faint green veins throughout. Large plants can have as many as 100 or more flowers at a time. The decorative fruit is typical of the family: a long, cylindrical woody pod, which splits lengthwise to reveal silky floss. Alas, the plant bears fruit only under completely tropical conditions. The Easter-lily vine blooms in late winter and spring and should be pruned only after the flowering season as the blossoms come on year-old wood, not new growth. Plants are damaged when the temperature reaches 28°F, and they are killed to the ground with temperatures below 25°F but usually sprout from the roots. If the resprouting precedes a subsequently milder winter, flowers will be produced the following year, making this vine marginal but possible in zone 9b. It can grow to 15 feet or more in one good year. Plate 65.

BEGONIA (beh-GO-nee-a / bee-GOAN-ya)
Begoniaceae: The Begonia Family
BEGONIA
Small to large herbs, usually with showy leaves and/or
  flowers
Zones vary according to species
Sun to shade
Water and humidity lovers
Rich, humusy, moist, well-drained soil
Propagation by seed, cuttings, and root division;
  bulbils in some species

A very large genus of almost 1000 species of mostly herbaceous perennials from tropical and subtropical regions. Most species have usually asymmetrical, showy leaves and large clusters of often long-lasting flowers. Some species are large and shrublike and become woody, but most are smaller and succulent, while some are vinelike or creeping. The genus is usually divided into two large sections according to the way the plants grow and the type of root system: fibrous-rooted and tuberous-rooted. Most horticulturists further divide these sections. Since we are dealing in this book with landscape subjects rather than collections for house or greenhouse, only those species, hybrids, and cultivars that fit our landscape parameters are covered, whatever the type of root system or the plant's habit. The tuberous begonias do not do well in the hot summer regions as they are derived from mountainous species and resent very hot and humid summers. Such classes as the *Hiemalis* hybrids are subject to mildew and rot in such climates.

Begonia flowers are unisexual, with both male and female flowers on the same plant. They are usually in axillary clusters, and the forms of the flowers are distinctive. The male flowers consist of sepals and petals in multiples of two with many stamens and bright yellow pollen masses in the center of the flower. The female flowers have two to five sepals and petals, indistinguishable in color or size, topped by three styles and stigmas, all atop a three-sided ovary. Both sexes occur in the same flower clusters. Some species form bulbils in the leaf axils, which may be used for propagation. Other than this, the most common method of propagation is the rooting of cuttings. The seeds are very fine and difficult to handle.

The following species, hybrids, and cultivars include some of the most beautiful leaves and flowers in the genus. Some are groundcovers; some are shrubs. All blend with and look superb with many kinds of ferns.

Begonia acetosa (ai-si-TOE-sa) (synonym *B. cantareira*) is native to Brazil and is not hardy outside zones 10b and 11. It is a compact growing, stemless herb with gigantic velvety leaves that are asymmetrically heart-shaped, bronzy olive green above and purplish red beneath, and are held on foot-long leaf stalks. The flowers are white in many-flowered clusters a foot or so above the foliage. This stunning plant is suitable for accent in a low border and demands water with very good drainage, warmth, and partial shade.

Begonia ×argenteo-guttata (ahr-jen´-tee-o-gut-TAIT-a) is a naturally occurring hybrid in Brazil between *B. albo-picta* and *B. olbia*. It is hardy in zones 10 and 11. This erect, almost shrublike plant grows to 5 feet in height, with 5-inch-long, ovate-acuminate leaves, which are shallowly toothed along the margins. The leaves are a dark, glossy green with strongly marked darker veins and heavily spotted with silver. This color combination leads to the common name of trout-leaf begonia. The flowers appear in few-flowered clusters in the leaf axils and are white tinged with pink. This very bold and dramatic species wants a very bright location out of full sun and moist, humusy, well-drained soil.

Begonia cantareira. See *B. acetosa*.

Begonia cathayana (kath-ay-YAHN-a) is indigenous to the Yunnan province of China, but is relatively hardy considering its tropical origin and is adaptable to zones 10 and 11. It makes a small, succulent, velvety shrub to 3 feet or more in height. The 6-inch-long leaves are among the most beautiful in the genus. They are asymmetrically cordate and long-acuminate, with deep basal lobes, and are shallowly toothed along the margins. The coloration is dark olive green with red veins and an inner outline of silver on top, while the undersides of the leaves are crimson. The flowers are in axillary clusters and are reddish orange to white. This species is exquisite and easy to grow if given moisture, sandy-humusy soil, and good drainage.

Begonia coccinea (kahk-SIN-ee-a) is native to the low mountainous area northeast of Rio de Janeiro, Brazil, and is hardy in zones 10 and 11. It is the original angel-wing begonia, so-called because of the shape of the leaves. The leaves are succulent, cupped, thick, obliquely long-ovate, and a dark green in color, with wavy and reddish margins. The plant grows to 4 or 5 feet in height and has red, long-lasting flowers. It needs moisture, partial shade, and regular feeding with an organic fertilizer such as fish emulsion.

Begonia ×credneri (KRED-nur-eye) is a naturally occurring hybrid in Brazil between *B. metallica* and *B. scharffiana*. It is beautiful with obliquely ovate leaves almost a foot long, and prominent and depressed veins. The plant grows to about 3 feet in height with dense, rounded axillary inflorescences of large pink flowers on long thick peduncles. Hardy in zones 10 and 11, it thrives on much light (it can be acclimated to almost full sun) and water, and should be fed regularly in spring and summer.

Begonia deliciosa (dee-lis´-ee-O-sa), a tender beauty from Borneo, is hardy in zones 10 and 11. The plant grows to about 2 feet and has reddish brown, succulent stems with large (as much as a foot wide) deep olive green palmate leaves, which are much spotted with silver above and are red underneath. The fragrant flowers are light pink. The plant wants rich soil and much light and moisture in spring and summer. It is not dependable in zone 9b, but has been known to resprout from the rhizomatous roots if the temperature does not fall below the mid 20s.

Begonia dichotoma (dy-KHAHT-o-ma) is a large plant from Venezuela. It is sometimes called the kidney begonia because of the shape of the leaves, which are orbicular to broadly ovate and as much as 12 inches long and almost as wide. The plant grows very large, sometimes to as much as 12 feet in height. The small white flowers are in long-petioled clusters, usually reaching above the foliage. This begonia is not adaptable outside zones 10 and 11 and needs partial shade to partial sun, rich soil, feeding in spring and summer, and a regular supply of moisture.

Begonia discolor. See *B. grandis*.

Begonia evansiana. See *B. grandis*.

Begonia fusca (FYOOS-ka) is a very choice species from southern Mexico and Central America. It is adaptable only to zones 10 and 11, although it has been known to resprout from its rhizomatous roots in zone 9. It is a large plant that grows to as much as 6 feet in height. The wonderfully felty leaves, which are held on long leaf stalks and are almost orbicular, sometimes as much as a foot wide, are dark green with prominent and lighter veins. The white or pink flowers are held well above the foliage in large panicles. The plant needs some sun to bloom and look good and the usual rich soil and regular supply of water.

Begonia goegoensis (go´-ee-go-EN-sis) is an exquisite creeping groundcover from Sumatra. It only grows a foot tall and, being quite tender, is successful only in zones 10b and 11. The 9- to 10-inch-wide succulent leaves, which are broad-ovate to orbicular, peltate, and puckered, are dark olive green in color with bronzy patches. They have prominent lighter veins above and are red beneath. The flowers are light to dark pink. The plant does not stand full sun and must have rich soil and regular water.

Begonia grandis (GRAN-dis) (synonyms *B. discolor*, *B. evansiana*) is native to the southern islands of Japan, Taiwan, and adjacent mainland China. Despite its semitropical heritage, it is quite hardy, being adaptable to zones 7 through 11 because it is capable of going dormant, dying back to the ground in winter. It is, therefore, not surprisingly called the hardy begonia. The plant grows to 3 feet or more in height, and the beautiful leaves are about 6 inches long, dark green, obliquely (but not dramatically so) ovate-acuminate, with prominent reddish veins. The fragrant flowers are light beige-pink and are carried in drooping clusters. The plants can take almost full sun but look better in partial shade. They need a rich, fibrous soil and regular water. This species is one of those that forms bulbils in the leaf axils.

Begonia haageana. See *B. scharffii*.

Begonia heracleifolia (her-ak´-lee-eye-FO-lee-a) is native to southern Mexico and adjacent Central America. It is called the star begonia or the star-leaf begonia because the long-petioled, foot-wide, hairy, bronzy green leaves are deeply and palmately cleft into five to nine toothed lobes. The fragrant flowers are white to pink. The plant is successfully grown in zones 10 and 11 but will resprout from its rhizomatous roots in zone 9b.

Begonia imperialis (im-peer´-ee-AL-iss) hails from tropical Mexico and is a superb border subject. Hardy in zones 10 and 11, it usually sprouts from the rhizomatous roots in zone 9b. The plant grows no more than 18 inches tall and has 6-inch-wide cordate brownish leaves whose veins are marked with a light, mint green. The flowers are white.

Begonia luxurians (luk-ZHOOR-ee-anz) is native to the rain forests of Brazil. It grows to as much as 4 or 5 feet tall with incredible palmately divided leaves with 7 to as many as 17 segments radiating from the end of the leaf stalk and forming a complete circle of narrowly lanceolate leaflets. Each leaf segment usually has its edges upturned and its margins finely serrate. Leaf color is a bronzy to reddish bronzy green above and a pale green beneath. The pinkish white to deep pink flowers are formed in broad many-stemmed clusters, and the flower stalks are coral to red in color. This beauty can tolerate very little cold and is appropriate only in zones 10 and 11, although it is happy in frost-free but cooler Mediterranean climates.

Begonia masoniana (ma-so´-nee-AHN-a) is indigenous to Indochina and can stand no frost. It thus is a candidate only for zones 10b and 11, although it resprouts from the rhizomatous root if the temperature does not fall much below 30°F. This very choice begonia grows to a couple of feet in height, with some of the most beautiful leaves in the plant kingdom. They are obliquely cordate, 6 inches long by 4 inches wide, bullate, light green, marked with reddish brown in the center. The markings on the leaves are somewhat in the shape of the iron cross medal of honor, leading to the common name of iron-cross begonia. The flowers are greenish white and rather insignificant. The plant wants very bright shade or partial sun, rich humusy, well-drained soil, and regular feeding and watering.

Begonia nelumbiifolia (ne-lumb´-ee-eye-FOE-lee-a) is native to a wide area from southern Mexico through Central America to northern South America. In spite of its quite tropical origins it has been successfully grown in zones 10 and 11 and will probably resprout from its rhizomatous roots in zone 9b. The leaves are immense, to almost 2 feet in width, round, peltate, and felty and, because of their shape and size, the plant is called the lily-pad begonia. The white flowers are in tall, branched cymes, held well above the foliage. This species is almost overwhelmingly spectacular. It needs morning or afternoon sun only; rich, moist soil; and regular watering.

Begonia paulensis (paw-LEN-sis) is native to Brazil. This glorious-leaved gem tolerates no frost and is successful only in zones 10b and 11. The plant grows to about 18 inches in height. The leaves have raised ridges of a quilted manner on top and are red beneath. Leaf shape is irregularly orbicular to irregularly ovate, sometimes irregularly reniform. The leaves are as much as 10 inches wide, peltate, glossy, waxy and dark green. There is a distinct lighter spot on top of the leaf above the junction of the leaf stalk. From that spot radiates a network of lighter veins. The plants want very bright shade or partial and filtered sun with rich, moist soil and a constant and regular supply of moisture.

Begonia peponifolia (pep-o´-ni-FO-lee-a) is found in tropical Mexico and some Caribbean islands. It is successfully grown in zones 10 and 11 and is another beautiful giant round-leaved species. The specific epithet means "squash-leaved" and this is an apt description, except that these leaves are dark green and glossy, and as much as 2 feet wide. The flowers are white but not very impressive. The plant can take some sun but does not like full sun.

Begonia popenoei (poap-e-NO-ee) is native to Central America and is similar to *B. peponifolia* in appearance and culture. The flowers, however, are much more attractive: large, white, and in big panicles held well above the foliage.

Begonia pustulata (pus-tyoo-LAIT-a) hails from Mexico and Guatemala. It is one of the most beautiful species in the genus but is hardy only in zones 10 and 11. The plants are rather low growing, spreading, and trailing, and are excellent as a groundcover. The leaves are obliquely cordate, about 6 inches long, and warty or pebbly blistered. Mint green in color, they have wonderful silvery markings along the veins and a fine network of tiny white veins between the main channels. They are rose-colored beneath. The white to light pink flowers are quite attractive but are half-hidden by the foliage. The species is sometimes called blister begonia because of the texture of the leaves. This beauty demands warmth, moisture, and rich, very well drained soil and needs bright light or high, filtered shade.

Begonia rex is native to northeastern India (Assam). The common names are rex begonia and beefsteak begonia. The unadulterated species, which is probably no longer found in cultivation, grows to about 2 feet in height. The leaves are large, wrinkled, obliquely cordate, wavy-margined, and toothed. They are deep metallic-green in color with a reddish hue beneath and a band of silver above. This tender plant is adapted to zones 10 and 11 but commonly sprouts from the root in zone 9b. It is the main parent of a legion of dazzlingly beautiful and incredibly diverse hybrids and cultivars of these hybrids. ***Begonia* 'Edna Korts'** has cordate, long-acuminate lobed leaves that are dark green with an inner band of silver. ***Begonia* 'Fireflush'** has rounded, obliquely cordate, glistening emerald green leaves with scarlet veins and a dark center and margins. The flowers are large and white. ***Begonia* 'Frau Hoffman'** has large, obliquely cordate and long-acuminate leaves that are silvery in color with the toothed margins, central veins, and undersurfaces a deep violet. ***Begonia* 'Helen Taupel'** has long-cordate, shallowly lobed and toothed leaves to a foot long with chocolate-colored centers and rose, white, or red margins. ***Begonia* 'Her Majesty'** carries large broad tapering, obliquely ovate leaves that are deep purple with an inner light-green zone. ***Begonia* 'Merry Christmas'** has large, smooth leaves with chocolate-red centers, an adjoining zone of pink and white, and yellow-green margins with pink spots. ***Begonia* 'Mikado'** has obliquely cordate, silvery white leaves with deep purple centers and margins. ***Begonia* 'Salamander'** has obliquely long-cordate leaves almost a foot long that are dark olive green blotched with silver. ***Begonia* 'Silver Queen'** boasts leaves that are rounded, obliquely cordate, puckered above, deep emerald green, and heavily splotched with creamy white. All hybrids and cultivars are resentful of direct sun but need bright shade or high, filtered shade, moisture, and well-drained, rich soil. Plate 66.

Begonia rotundifolia (ro-tund´-i-FO-lee-a) is native to Haiti and yet is relatively hardy for a begonia, being adaptable to zones 9b through 11. It is a wonderful groundcover, slowly covering area by its creeping rhizomes. The plant grows to no more than a foot in height. The leaves are about 3 inches across, light glossy green, and almost orbicular. They are held on bright red leaf stalks. The pinkish white flowers are carried well above the foliage in small clusters. The plant blooms for a long period in summer and fall. This species is one of the few that takes almost full sun. It also needs moisture and a loose rich soil.

Begonia scharffii (SHARF-fee-eye) (synonym *B. haageana*) is native to Brazil and, in zones 10 and 11, is one of the most dependable, beautiful, and sturdy plants in the genus. It grows to 4 feet or more in height and has lovely velvety foot-long, obliquely ovate and long-acuminate, bronzy-green leaves with red veins and reddish brown undersides. It is a very free-flowering species with large white and red blossoms that come and go in cycles year-round. The plant can be acclimated to full sun but needs adequate moisture and rich humusy soil.

***Begonia* Semperflorens-Cultorum** (sem-pur-FLOR-enz-kul-TOR-um) is a large group of hybrids and cultivars with distinct and recognizable traits. Common names are wax-leaf begonia, bedding begonia, and wax plant. This group includes some of the most useful and brilliant flowering plants for sites with partial to full sun. The plants are not hardy outside zones 10 and 11, but will grow back from the roots in zones 9b and often zone 9a. They are much used for summer annual bedding plants as they are ever-blooming if the temperature stays above freezing, and the flowers come in every color except blue. They are even somewhat drought tolerant and do not need a rich soil or much fertilizer. Most grow to no more than a foot in height, but a few can become 2 or more feet tall. Most are compact in habit but some are trailing, making them useful for decorating walls or for use in hanging baskets. The leaves, which are mostly small, obliquely ovate to round, and no more than 2 inches wide (although some cultivars have larger leaves), are usually glossy green (sometimes with reddish margins), but many are bronzy hued.

Begonia valdensium (val-DENS-ee-um) hails from Brazil. It is one of the most attractive species in the genus with giant foot-wide, obliquely ovate to almost orbicular, long-acuminate leaves that are a deep, rich green in color with prominent cream-colored veins. The plant grows to 3 feet in height and is adaptable only to zones 10 and 11. The flowers are pinkish white in small clusters held well above the foliage. The plant is sometimes called philodendron-leaf begonia. Very bright shade or partial sun (mornings and afternoons) and rich, moist, well-drained soil are to its liking.

BELOPERONE. See *Justicia*.

BERRYA (BER-ree-a)
Tiliaceae: The Linden Tree Family
No known English common name
Large evergreen tree; large heart-shaped leaves; large clusters of pink flowers; winged pods
Zones 10b and 11
Sun to partial shade
Average but regular amounts of moisture; drought tolerant when established
Humusy, sandy, well-drained soil
Propagation by seed

A genus of four species of large trees native to tropical Asia and Malaysia. The trees have large entire leaves and hard wood that is valuable as timber, especially in Asia. The white, pink, or purple flowers are in large terminal cymes. The unusual inch-long seed pods are attractive with six to eight "wings." One species is sparingly planted in tropical regions of the United States. ***Berrya cordifolia*** (kor-di-FO-lee-a) (synonym *B. am-*

monilla) grows to as much as 80 or 90 feet in its native habitat and usually to about 50 or 60 feet in cultivation. It forms a beautiful straight trunk bare of branches for half its height and a spreading and dense crown. The foot-long leaves are ovate and cordate in shape, somewhat thin in texture, and a dark green in color with prominent and lighter colored midribs and lateral veins. The flowers are borne in foot-tall erect terminal panicles. Each five-petaled blossom is an inch or more wide and light pink to light violet in color. This magnificent tree should be much more widely cultivated in tropical regions than it is at present. Plates 67 and 68.

BERTOLONIA (bert-o-LO-nee-a)
Melastomataceae: The Tibouchina Family
JEWEL PLANTS
Small often creeping Brazilian herbs with showy multicolored leaves
Zones 10b and 11
Very bright shade
Water lovers
Rich, humusy, moist, well-drained soil
Propagation by seed and cuttings

A genus of 14 perennial herbs from tropical American rain forests. All have exquisitely beautiful velvety-hairy foliage in shades of green, purple, bronze, white, and pink, with the beautiful parallel venation so characteristic of the family. In addition, the small flowers, borne in erect inflorescences above the leaves, can be very attractive. All species are quite tender and need constant humidity and warmth with rich, moist soil. They make perfect partial shade groundcovers in frost-free climates.

Bertolonia hirsuta (heer-SOOT-a) grows to less than a foot in height. It has deep green, velvety ovate 4- to 6-inch-long leaves with cinnamon-colored central veins. The flowers are white.

Bertolonia houtteana (hoot-tee-AHN-a) grows to only a foot or so in height and has 7-inch-long, ovate to elliptic, olive green ridged leaves. The five prominent longitudinal leaf veins and many cross veins are colored pink, and pink dots are interspersed between the veins. The undersides of the leaves are greenish purple. The flowers are pink.

Bertolonia lowiana (lo-wee-AHN-a) usually grows to less than a foot in height with ovate, corrugated, velvety, 4- to 7-inch-long bronzy green leaves. The flowers are large and pink.

Bertolonia maculata (mak-yoo-LAIT-a) grows to only 6 inches or so in height. It has 4-inch-long hairy leaves that are a deep green with light green on the central veins and a reddish bronze hue along the margins; the undersides of the leaves are blood red. The flowers are a light pink. ***Bertolonia maculata* 'Wentii'** (WENT-ee-eye) has slightly larger deep green leaves with yellow to silver longitudinal veins.

Bertolonia marmorata (mar-mo-RAIT-a) is a trailing plant with quilted cordate 7-inch-long emerald green somewhat convex leaves. The main veins are painted in white or silver, and the undersides of the leaves are purple. The flowers are large and pink. The plant can be trained as a small vine. ***Bertolonia marmorata* var. *aenea*** (EEN-ee-a) has green leaves that are beautifully tinged with bronze. ***Bertolonia marmorata* 'Sanderiana'** has olive green to bronzy green leaves that are heavily blotched with silver.

Bertolonia sanguinea (san-GWIN-ee-a) is a trailing, vinelike plant with 4-inch-long, ovate-elliptical bronze-green leaves. The veins are silver, and the undersides of the leaves are blood red.

BIGNONIA (big-NO-nee-a)
Bignoniaceae: The Catalpa, Jacaranda, Trumpet-
  Vine Family
CROSS VINE
Large evergreen vine; reddish orange trumpet-shaped
  flowers
Zones 6 through 11
Sun
Water lover
Rich, humusy, moist, well-drained soil
Propagation by seed and cuttings

A monotypic genus, although many "trumpet vines" were originally classified in this genus.

Bignonia australis. See *Pandorea pandorana*.

Bignonia capensis. See *Tecomaria capensis*.

Bignonia capreolata (kap'-ree-o-LAIT-a) is native from Virginia to southern Illinois, down to Texas and across to northern Florida. Known as the cross vine, it climbs by adhesive disks, which cling to almost any rough surface, making the plant very useful for covering walls but also making it unsuitable for painted wooden surfaces. Growth is rampant, and the plant, which can climb to 50 feet or more, makes a dense screen of leaves that is not bothered by pests or wind. The 6-inch-long leaves are pinnate but have only two leaflets. Each leaflet is a glossy, dark green in color and ovate or oblong in shape. The leaves have a bronzy, purplish reddish hue in the winter. The narrow trumpet-shaped flowers are quite beautiful, but the vine only blooms once, in late spring into early summer. Flowers, which are usually about 2 inches long and orange-red to almost yellow, are carried in axillary clusters in groups of two to five. Each blossom has a lighter color on the inside of the petals and a darker shade inside the throat, creating an almost two-toned effect. Although the vine does not bloom all that long, it makes quite a spectacle when it does. The plant is a water lover but, once established, exhibits a modicum of tolerance to drought. It is quite useful for screening purposes and as a cover. In a confined space it must be regularly pruned, but this is not a great problem as the flowers are produced on new wood. ***Bignonia capreolata* 'Atrosanguinea'** (at'-ro-san-GWIN-ee-a) has longer, narrower leaves with darker, almost purplish colored flowers.

Bignonia chamberlaynii. See *Anemopaegma chamberlaynii*.

Bignonia cherere. See *Distictis buccinatorius*.

Bignonia chinensis. See *Campsis grandiflora*.

Bignonia grandiflora. See *Campsis grandiflora*.

Bignonia ignea. See *Pyrostegia venusta*.

Bignonia jasminoides. See *Pandorea jasminoides*.

Bignonia magnifica. See *Saritaea magnifica*.

Bignonia radicans. See *Campsis radicans*.

Bignonia stans. See *Tecoma stans*.

Bignonia venusta. See *Pyrostegia venusta*.

BILLBERGIA (bil-BURG-ee-a)
Bromeliaceae: The Pineapple, Bromeliad Family
VASE PLANTS
Small to large vase-shaped rosettes of often highly
  colored leaves; spectacular flowers
Zones vary according to species
Partial shade to partial sun
Water lovers
Leaf mold or epiphytic potting mix
Propagation by transplanting of suckers and by seed

A genus of about 50 different species, mostly in Brazil, but also in Mexico, Central America, and other parts of South America. The plants are often mistaken for those in the genus *Aechmea*, but *Billbergia* species usually have many fewer leaves to a plant, the leaves are only remotely and very finely toothed on the margins, the rosettes are usually much more slender, narrower, and taller, and the inflorescences are mostly pendent. *Billbergia* species are, if possible, even easier to grow than are *Aechmea* species, and they grow fast and readily produce offsets. Some of the most attractive inflorescences of bromeliads are found in this genus, and some of the color combinations are nothing short of spectacular. Alas, the flowers do not last as long as those of most *Aechmea* species, but the plants grow and propagate even faster than do those of the latter genus. All species are epiphytic, but, like many other bromeliads, they seem to grow as well on the ground in soil as they do on trees or other natural structures. In nature they often fall from the trees and grow quite happily in the soil. Some species are found at relatively high elevations in their native habitats and are not completely adaptable to hot summers, but the ones that are adaptable are unexcelled as garden subjects in warm regions.

Billbergia amoena (a-MEEN-a / a-MOYN-a) is native to eastern Brazil on trees, rocks, and other exposed sites and in deep forests. Because of its adaptability, it is also one of the most variable species of bromeliad as to both color and size, and has several naturally occurring forms. The inflorescence consists of large bright pink to red bracts from which emerge the green flowers tipped in dark blue; this is the case for all the forms of this species. The plants are hardy in zones 10 and 11 and grow in mostly shade to almost full sun, though the leaf colors are brighter with some sun. ***Billbergia amoena* var. *amoena*** grows to about 2 feet in height and has fairly wide (2 inches) glossy, apple-green leaves about 2 feet long, which form a slender rosette. *Billbergia amoena* var. *rubra* (ROOB-ra) is the largest of the forms and grows to a height of 3 feet or more. It forms a tall tubular rosette with leaves as much as 3 inches wide and colored pink to red with white and yellow spots. *Billbergia amoena* var. *viridis* (VEER-i-dis) also has the same basic rose-to-red leaf colors as *B. amoena* var. *rubra,* but is even more spectacular, with irregular horizontal bars of green. It is a very striking plant and very useful in the landscape.

Billbergia brasiliensis (bra-zil-ee-EN-sis) (synonym *B. leopoldii*) from southern Brazil grows into a beautiful 3-foot-high tubular rosette of erect, 2-inch-wide olive green leaves with broad silver bands of irregular spacing and width. The whole leaf is often suffused with a rosy cast. The inflorescence consists of large pink bracts subtending the satiny blue flowers, which have long extruded stamens of the same color. The plant is hardy in zones 10 and 11 and likes partial shade.

Billbergia leopoldii. See *B. brasiliensis.*

Billbergia nutans (NYOO-tanz) is native to the forests of southern Brazil, northern Argentina, and Uruguay, and is adaptable to zones 9b through 11. It only grows to a foot or so in height with very narrow, somewhat channeled, grasslike, gracefully recurved olive green leaves that turn a reddish hue in full sun. The flower sepals are pink, the petals green and edged with blue, and the bracts bright pink on long, nodding spikes. The plants grow fast, sucker freely, and form rather large clumps in or out of soil. There are two common names: queen's tears (because of the long and pendulous inflorescence) and friendship plant (because of the ease of dividing the clumps and giving one or more slips to a friend).

Billbergia pyramidalis (peer-a-MID-a-lis) is indigenous to southern Brazil and grows to about 3 feet in height. For a *Billbergia* species, it makes an unusually wide and open rosette. The leaves, which grow to almost 3 feet long and are 2 or more inches wide with squared, blunt tips, are a grassy green in color with faint, darker striations. The inflorescence is short, erect, and pyramidal in shape with brilliant orange-pink bracts and blue-tipped petals. *Billbergia pyramidalis* var. *striata* (stry-AIT-a) is one of the most beautiful forms in the genus with wide olive green leaves margined in bright yellow above and a silvery undersurface. The plants are not hardy outside zones 10 and 11.

BISCHOFIA (bis-SHO-fee-a)
Euphorbiaceae: The Euphorbia, Spurge Family
TOOG TREE; BISHOPWOOD
Fast growing tall, almost evergreen, large-leaved tree
Zones 10 and 11
Sun
Water lover
Average well-drained soil
Propagation by seed

A monotypic genus from a very wide area of Southeast Asia and Polynesia. *Bischofia javanica* (ja-VAHN-i-ka) grows to 70 feet or more and, because of the dense crown of foliage, makes an excellent shade tree in warm climates. The smooth trunks grow fairly straight and are grayish brown in color. The leaves are quite beautiful and are divided into three large 5- to 8-inch-long ovate, somewhat troughed, dark green often bronzy hued, long-acuminate, shiny succulent leaflets with prominent midveins. The fragrant flowers are a greenish white and appear in winter in large terminal clusters followed by large clusters of yellow to brown or black berries. Male and female flowers are found on separate trees, and only female trees bear fruit. The trees are usually evergreen but in spells of drought or cold will temporarily lose most leaves, which turn a bright red before falling. The tree is subject to scale and whitefly infestation, and its brittle limbs break easily in high winds. It is, nevertheless, of great beauty and is recommended for planting away from structures.

BISMARCKIA (biz-MARK-ee-a)
Palmae (Arecaceae): The Palm Family
BISMARCK PALM
Tall solitary-trunked bluish-leaved fan palm
Zones 9b through 11
Sun
Average but regular amounts of moisture
Humusy, well-drained soil
Propagation by seed

A monotypic genus native to Madagascar and one of the most majestic palm species. *Bismarckia nobilis* (NO-bi-lis) is a spectacular palm because of its size and color. The relatively thin trunk is usually no more than a foot in diameter and may reach 80 feet in height, although reportedly it grows to more than 100 feet in its native habitat. The bluish green costapalmate leaves are immense, to 10 feet or more in width, and are very heavy, thick, and massive. Usually there is a waxy bloom on the leaf stalks and new leaves, which are often also margined with a reddish hue. Plants grow slowly, especially when young, and are difficult to transplant because of the developing underground trunk. They are impossible as bare root subjects, but once the trunk is evident the palms are not that difficult to move. Once established, the Bismarck palm is rather drought tolerant but, like most other plants, it grows and looks better with an adequate supply of moisture. These palms are somewhat similar, especially when mature, to those of the genus *Latania* (Latan palms), but unlike the latter, are taller, have a more slender trunk, and have larger leaves that are not as folded. Plate 258.

BIXA (BIX-a)
Bixaceae: The Bixa Family
LIPSTICK TREE; ANNATTO
Large evergreen shrub; large leaves; pink and white
    flowers; red spiny fruit

Zones 10 and 11; marginal in zone 10a
Sun
Average but regular amounts of moisture
Average well-drained soil
Propagation by seed and cuttings

A monotypic genus native to Amazonia. ***Bixa orellana*** (o-ray-YAHN-a / o-REL-la-na / o-rel-LAHN-a) is a small tree, hardly ever growing to more than 20 feet in height and usually growing into a large bush rather than a tree form unless trained to do so. The leaves are a light glossy green and are long-cordate, to 7 inches long, with prominent veins, especially the midvein; they also often have a reddish bronzy hue, especially when young. The lovely 2-inch-wide pink to white flowers appear all spring and summer and often into the fall in many-flowered terminal panicles and are succeeded by 2-inch-long, almond-shaped, brilliant scarlet to scarlet-brown fruit capsules covered in soft spines. The plants are often pruned into tall hedges for which purpose they are excellent if they are pruned regularly. For millennia native peoples made a dye from the seed arils of the tree. This practice was later industrialized and plantations were created to export food colorings and dyes for cosmetics (especially lipsticks) to Europe and America. Plate 69.

BLECHNUM (BLEK-num)

Blechnaceae: The Dwarf Tree Fern Family
Common names vary according to species
Medium-sized pinnate evergreen ferns, some with
    short trunks
Zones 9b through 11
Shade to partial shade
Water lovers
Rich, humusy, moist, well-drained soil
Propagation by spores

A large genus of about 200 species of medium-sized to rather large ferns from warm regions in all parts of the world. All are somewhat coarse in appearance, but are quite valuable landscape subjects. None of them does very well in full sun.

Blechnum brasiliense (bra-zil´-ee-EN-see) is native to Brazil and Peru and is a good subject for zones 9b through 11. It is a trunk-forming species, although small in stature (to 3 feet in height) relative to most tree ferns. The leathery, glossy dark green, stiff, and erect leaves are 3 feet or slightly more long and are pinnately segmented. Each segment is connected at its base to the adjacent segments. The plants are reminiscent in appearance to cycads. ***Blechnum brasiliense*** 'Crispum' (KRIS-pum) has smaller leaves whose margins are reddish when young and wavy, giving a rather ruffled look.

Blechnum gibbum (GIB-bum) is native to the islands of the South Pacific north of Australia and yet is mostly hardy in zones 9b through 11, although the fronds are sometimes damaged in zone 9b. It makes a relatively short trunk to 4 or 5 feet in height with time. The dull green gracefully arching leathery leaves are deeply and pinnately segmented, with the segment bases usually completely separated from the adjacent ones. The species is elegant and a valuable addition to the landscape repertoire, being especially effective as an emergent from a mass of lower growing ferns or other tropical looking plants. ***Blechnum gibbum*** 'Moorei' and ***Blechnum gibbum*** 'Platyptera' (pla-TIP-tur-a) are not as attractive as the type, because they have fewer but larger and more erect leaves. The type and the cultivars are often called the dwarf tree fern.

Blechnum serrulatum (ser-oo-LAIT-um) is indigenous to a large area from the southern half of Florida all the way down through eastern South America and is hardy in zones 9 through 11. In Florida it is usually called the swamp fern or saw fern. It is an attractive pinnate-leaved fern, which never has more than two or three fronds up at any one time. Each leaf is 2 to 3 feet long with the pinnae joined at their bases and is a light to medium green in color.

BLIGHIA (BLIG-hee-a / BLY-ee-a)

Sapindaceae: The Soapberry, Golden-Rain Tree
    Family
AKEE; AKEE APPLE
Small evergreen tree; large pinnate foliage; orange
    fruit
Zones 10 and 11
Sun
Average but regular amounts of moisture
Average well-drained soil
Propagation by seed and air-layering

A genus of four species of evergreen trees in tropical West Africa. These have pinnate leaves, greenish white flowers, and three-sectioned fleshy fruits. Only one is commonly planted in the United States. ***Blighia sapida*** (SAP-i-da) is a beautiful, fast-growing tree that grows to as much as 40 feet in height with a short, thick, smooth gray trunk and a dense crown of foliage. The leaves are even-pinnate with three to five pairs of elliptic to obovate-oblong leaflets 6 to 12 inches long. The inner leaflets are shortest, the outer ones progressively longer. The leaves are glossy dark green above with prominent veins and are paler and pubescent below. The fragrant, five-petaled white flowers are hairy on pendulous stems. The pear-shaped fruits are orange to pinkish red, leathery, three-lobed, and about 3 inches long. They split into three cream-colored parts with one or more large shiny black seeds evident. The flesh of the fruit is said to be edible at certain stages of maturity but, unless at the right stage, is very poisonous, as are the seeds. This beautiful tree is therefore unsuitable for planting where small children might have access to the fruit. The genus was named after Captain Bligh of the infamous H.M.S. *Bounty* fame.

BOCCONIA (bo-KOAN-ee-a)

Papaveraceae: The Poppy Family
PLUME POPPY
Evergreen shrubs or small trees; large, pinnately
  lobed leaves; large panicles of flowers
Zones 9b and 10a as a shrub; zones 10b and 11 as a
  tree
Sun
Average but regular amounts of moisture; somewhat
  drought tolerant
Average well-drained soil
Propagation by seed and cuttings

A small genus of nine species of very large-leaved and very tropical looking shrubs or small trees from Mexico and Central America with thick orange latex, which is used by native peoples as a dye. These trees are unlike other plants in the poppy family. For one thing the flowers look nothing like garden poppies; in fact they have no petals and are in large terminal clusters on the plants. The only two species planted in the United States are rather similar. Both are unexcelled for creating a tropical effect in sunny, well-drained sites. The leaves are not entirely dissimilar to those of *Artocarpus* (breadfruit tree). The plants are marginally hardy in zone 9a, but usually sprout from the roots after a freeze, and in zone 9b they are often frozen back but recover quickly.

Bocconia arborea (ahr-BOR-ee-a) is indigenous to the western states of Mexico from Durango southwards and into Guatemala. It makes a large shrub or small tree to 25 feet in height with a corky bark. The leaves, which are as much as 18 inches long and as much as a foot wide, are very deeply and pinnately cleft to two-thirds or three-quarters of the way to the strong and prominent midrib. They are elliptic in outline, smooth and dark green on the upper surface, and gray and pubescent on the lower surface. The greenish white flowers are in large, terminal panicles and are followed by small, tear-shaped black fruit. Plate 70.

Bocconia frutescens (froo-TES-senz) is found in the eastern states of Mexico all the way down into Honduras in sunny and well-drained sites. The plant is usually a large shrub but sometimes a small tree with smooth, gray bark and giant leaves to 2 feet long. The oblong leaves have deep pinnate divisions and a very prominent, reddish hued midvein. They are reddish pubescent below and smooth and dark green above. The flowers are in large terminal racemes, like those of *B. arborea*, but are greenish purple in color. The fruit pods are similar to the pods of *B. arborea*.

BOMBACOPSIS (bahm-ba-KAHP-sis)

Bombacaceae: The Bombax, Baobab Family
POCHOTE; CEDRO ESPINOSO; CEDRO
  MACHO
Large buttressed, deciduous spiny tree with large
  palmate leaves
Zones 10b and 11
Sun
Water lover that survives with average but regular
  amounts of moisture
Humusy, moist, well-drained soil
Propagation by seed

A genus of 21 large tree species in tropical America that are quite similar to *Bombax* species, with large usually buttressed trunks, which are often covered with spiny tubercles. Only one species is planted outside specialty and botanic gardens. Some botanists put this genus into *Pachira*.

Bombacopsis fendleri (FEND-lur-eye) (synonyms *B. quinata*, *Pachira fendleri*) is native to the drier hillsides of the wet, lowland forests of Nicaragua down to northern South America (Colombia). The tree is fantastic (some would say "grotesque") and not to everyone's liking, but spectacular to many. Although it grows usually with a single massive and buttressed trunk with corky-fissured bark, it is sometimes found as a multi-trunked entity with a widespreading crown of massive branches. All but the lowest portions of the tree are covered with large, conical tubercles ending in a spine. In its native habitats the tree can grow to 100 feet or more in height, but in cultivation it is usually no more than 70 to 80 feet tall. The leaves are palmately divided into five obovate leaflets. Each leaflet is 7 or 8 inches long, glabrous, and a shiny dark green in color. The tree is usually deciduous from January through February, although periods of drought at any time may bring on leaf drop. The flowers usually appear while the tree is leafless in February or early March and are typical of the family with 5 recurved petals that are reddish brown on the outside and white inside. There are very many long white to pink stamens (as many as 100 or more) protruding from the flower. The fruit is a 3-inch-long, five-sided brown capsule that opens after a few weeks to expose a mass of soft brownish gray "wool" and small brown seeds. The trees are sometimes slightly damaged in the colder parts of zone 10a but recover quickly.

Bombacopsis quinata. See *B. fendleri.*

BOMBAX (BAHM-bax)

Bombacaceae: The Bombax, Baobab Family
RED SILK-COTTON TREE; RED KAPOK TREE
Large widespreading, deciduous tree; large palmate
  leaves; showy red flowers
Zones 10 and 11
Sun
Water lover
Deep, humusy, moist, well-drained soil
Propagation by seed and cuttings

A genus of eight species of tall and spreading, deciduous, and often spiny large-leaved trees native to tropical areas of the Southern Hemisphere. They usually produce their large and characteristically shaped flowers when they are leafless. All have palmately divided leaves. Only one species is regularly planted in mainland United States. It is one of the world's most beautiful flowering trees.

Bombax ceiba (SEE-ba / SAY-ba) (synonym *B. malabaricum*) is native to a wide area of tropical Asia from India to Vietnam. It is a large soft-wooded, spreading tree to 70 or 80 feet or more in height with the branches in great, tiered whorls. The trunk is usually buttressed and quite spiny when young. The leaves are palmately divided into as few as three and as many as seven giant 10-inch-long glossy dark green leaflets, which are lighter colored beneath. Like many other trees in this family, this one is briefly deciduous usually in late winter just before the flowers appear. The spectacular blossoms are immense, to 7 or more inches across, with many red stamens, and five succulent and thick, shining scarlet or orange-red recurved petals. The flowers secrete a nectar, which is loved by birds and other wildlife and by native peoples in India who use the petals in curries. The fruit is typical of the family, a 6-inch-long brown pod that eventually splits open to reveal a mass of white, cottony fibers in which small seeds are embedded. The floss is used by native peoples for stuffing, much like the fiber of another member of the bombax family, *Ceiba pentandra* (kapok). Plate 71.

Bombax ellipticum. See *Pseudobombax ellipticum.*
Bombax malabaricum. See *B. ceiba.*

BORASSUS (bo-RAS-sus)
Palmae (Arecaceae): The Palm Family
PALMYRA PALM; LONTAR PALM; TODDY PALM
Tall and massive fan-leaved palms
Zones 10 and 11; marginal in zone 10a
Sun
Average but regular amounts of moisture
Average well-drained soil
Propagation by seed

A genus of six species of large to immense fan-leaved palms in tropical Africa, India, southern China, and Malaysia. One species has been carried around the tropics and used for so long by humankind that its place of origin is unclear.

Borassus aethiopium (ee-thee-O-pee-um) (synonym *B. aethiops*) is native to tropical Africa and is a veritably stunning palm species. It is similar to *B. flabellifer* but is larger in all its parts except for the diameter of the trunk. It grows to 90 feet or more in height in its native habitat. Plate 72.

Borassus aethiops. See *B. aethiopium.*
Borassus flabellifer (fla-BEL-i-fur) is a giant among the fan-leaved palms, growing rather slowly under cultivation to 70 feet or more in height. It has a massive trunk that is 3 feet in diameter, gray, ringed, and usually covered with split leaf bases on its younger parts. The leaves are 10 feet wide with many deeply cleft segments and a 6-foot-long petiole armed with massive black spines. The leaves have a decidedly bluish cast when young and often retain the color to some extent even when the palms are mature. The male and female flowers are on separate trees and come in 6-foot-long drooping panicles. The fruits (on the female trees) are quite large, to 8 inches in diameter and a light-brown in color when mature; they are edible and sweet. Not only the fruit, but every other part of this palm has been used for millennia by native peoples in tropical Asia to whom the plant is secondary in importance only to the coconut. It is of primary importance for some inland peoples where the coconut does not usually grow. For people who fancy tropical beauty in southern Florida, Puerto Rico, Hawaii, and similar climates, it is important for being able to add striking nobility to a large landscape. This palm is not that commonly planted in the United States, however, as the seedlings have very long taproots and are best planted as seed where the landscape subject is wanted. Plate 73.

BORZICACTUS (BOR-zee-kak-tus)
Cactaceae: The Cactus Family
No known English common name
Ribbed cactus plants; large red flowers
Zones 10 and 11
Sun to partial sun
Drought tolerant
Sandy, humusy, well-drained soil
Propagation by seed and cuttings

A small genus of about 10 species of beautiful ribbed, columnar or prostrate-stemmed cactus species in South America, all with spectacular red or pink tubular or bell-shaped flowers forming along the golden spiny stems. All these species have been transferred into other related genera, leaving *Borzicactus* empty and now an invalid name. These changes, however, are not yet reflected in most of the literature nor in the names used by growers and retailers.

Borzicactus fieldianus (feel-dee-AHN-us) (synonym *Cleistocactus fieldianus*) hails from Peru. It is a spectacular sprawling, half-erect cactus with stems as long as 20 feet, each one with six or seven tubercled ribs, and each "knob" having a small areole with a few short spines. It is summer-blooming, and the flowers are 3-inch-long red tubes with a small inch-wide disk of red petals. The plant appreciates being in a site somewhat protected from the hottest midday sun.

Borzicactus leucotrichus (lyoo-ko-TRY-kus) (synonym *Oreocereus leucotrichus*) is native to southern Peru and northern Chile. It is a many-ribbed and quite spiny column about 4 inches thick and 2 feet or more in height. The flowers, which appear in summer in small clusters mainly atop the spiny columns, are 3-inch-long pubescent red tubes. The ends of the tubes flare into a 1- to 2-inch many-petaled scarlet disk with numerous purplish stamens.

Borzicactus samaipatanus (sa-my´-pa-TAIN-us) (synonym *Cleistocactus samaipatanus*) is indigenous to Bolivia. It makes a cluster of 2-inch-thick many ribbed, brown-spined 4- to 6-foot-long columns. The columns are mostly erect, but the older ones become somewhat prostrate. The summer flowers appear along the top third or so of the stem and are curved tubes about 3 inches long. The tubes expand into 3- or 4-inch-wide disks of many petals. Each petal is a deep red in color with orange-red margins. This wonderful landscape subject is beautiful year-round.

BOUGAINVILLEA (boo-gan-VIL-lee-a)

Nyctaginaceae: The Four-O'Clock, Bougainvillea
    Family
BOUGAINVILLEA
Large evergreen thorny vines and scrambling shrubs;
    spectacular masses of flowers
Zones 10 and 11 as permanent perennials; zone 9b as
    returning perennials
Sun
Average but regular amounts of moisture; somewhat
    drought-tolerant
Sandy, humusy, well-drained soil
Propagation by cuttings

A small genus of 14 species of spiny shrubs, trees, and vines in South America, all with small tubular short-lived flowers in clusters near the ends of the stems. The flowers are surrounded by large, brilliantly colored and long-lasting bracts. Only the shrubby or vining species and their hybrids and cultivars are commonly planted in the United States. These are descendants of three Brazilian species: predominantly *Bougainvillea spectabilis,* but also *B. glabra* and *B. peruviana.* The botanical distinctions between these species are subtle, and the "pure" species are almost never found in the nursery trade.

All the vining types in cultivation have long and rangy, thorny canes with mostly dark green heart-shaped leaves that are often pubescent with reddish or bronzy young growth. A few cultivars have foliage beautifully variegated with cream or white; these do not grow as large as the non-variegated types. They all need to be tied to sturdy supports to fulfill their potential as vines until they can obtain enough footholds via their spines. While they make excellent seaside subjects, strong winds tear the leaves, pull the canes off their supports, and shatter the flowers before their time. All the plants can be maintained as shrubs by frequent pruning of the spreading canes. Since the plants bloom on new wood, the practice is not detrimental to flower production. Each pruning should be done immediately after the current crop of flowers has faded away. Nothing, however, is more appealing and even spectacular than the tall vines on a wall or cascading over the top of a wall. As a vine or climbing shrub the plants reach at least 20 feet, often quite a bit more. They also make excellent giant groundcovers if allowed to just sprawl, with possibly a little judicious pruning for guidance. Some of the newer hybrids and cultivars never really make vines, but stay low and relatively compact, and make excellent color subjects planted in a flower border.

Flower (bract) colors include white, yellow, orange, pink, many shades of red, magenta, purple—every color except true blue. Several double-flowered types are sold, but the extra bracts add nothing to the beauty of the plants, and the cultivars in question have a tendency to hold the faded bracts, resulting in a rather ugly, messy appearance.

The plants are quite tender to cold and are damaged by temperatures of 30°F or lower and are frozen to the ground by temperatures below 25°F. Almost all the varieties, however, will come back from the roots after the return of warm weather. They are, of course, completely evergreen in zones 10b and 11, almost completely so in zone 10a, marginal in zone 9b, and almost never hardy in zone 9a. Most cultivars grow so rapidly that, even in zone 9a, the winter "dormancy" is not that great a problem in the landscape.

Bougainvillea have brittle roots, which do not hold soil very well. This characteristic presents a problem when planting, since the roots do not recover from being broken. Metal containers should first have holes punched in their sides and then be placed in the ground without removing the plants, so that the soil level in the container matches the soil level outside the container; the metal will soon rust and disintegrate. With plastic pots, the bottom of the pot should be cut out before placing the pot in the ground; then the sides of the pot should be cut in at least two places opposite each other, and soil gradually filled in around the root ball as the cut sides are removed. If the plastic-bound plants are to be planted into a bed of other plants where their bases will not be seen, the sides of the pots may be cut and the whole pot planted at the proper level, allowing the roots to grow out the bottom and out the slits in the sides of the pot into the surrounding soil. In nearly frost-free climes, it is not necessary to dig a hole. The pots can simply be put on bare ground where the roots will penetrate the soil beneath and, in time, the trunks (of the large vine types) will split the pots.

There is controversy whether to feed bougainvillea and, indeed, just what, if anything, makes them bloom. Part of the confusion comes about because of the differing genetic heritages of the plants involved. Some are seasonal bloomers and do most flower production in the cooler and shorter days of late autumn, winter, and early spring; others (the majority) are year-round bloomers in cycles of about three months or so, sometimes more often. Also, some cultivars simply do not produce as many flowers or flower as often as do others. Fertilizing the plants is usually not necessary, but since the flowers are produced on new growth, if the plants are not producing new growth, a 3–1–2 fertilizer may be in order. The best fertilizer is, of course, the best soil, and this means compost, humus, or manure. Feeding (and pruning) should be done at the end of each bloom cycle. Probably the two most important considerations in the successful growing of bougainvillea are sun and good drainage. Soggy or frequently flooded sites are anathema to these plants, and they refuse to bloom without some sun. Plate 74.

Bougainvillea ×*buttiana* is a cross between *B. peruviana* and *B. glabra*. Its cultivars are definitely worth growing.

'**Apple Blossom**' is a medium-sized vine with white bracts flushed with rose.

'**Golden Glow**' is an outstanding large vine with brilliant yellow-gold bracts.

'**Hawaiian Yellow**' is a sport of 'Golden Yellow' with pure yellow bracts.

'**Mrs. Butt**' makes a large vine with intensely red bracts.

'**Phoenix**', a sport of 'Mrs. Butt', is a rather large vine with variegated leaves and red bracts.

'**Texas Dawn**' is an open-growing large vine with light purple bracts.

Bougainvillea glabra (GLAB-ra) is a sprawling shrub that can be easily trained into either a vine or a small tree. Unpruned it can grow to as much as 20 feet in height with masses of magenta flowers (a color that is somewhat difficult to combine with other colors) in cycles throughout the year. It is slightly hardier to cold than the other two species or the big, free-flowering hybrids. It also has fewer thorns than the others. Some of the oldest (and best) named cultivars are derivatives of this species.

'**Cypheri**' is a large, rampant, and fast-growing vine with deep, almost glowing, purple bracts.

'**Easter Parade**' is a medium-sized vine with light pink bracts.

'**Elizabeth Angus**' makes a large vine with vibrantly purple bracts.

'**Key West White**' (synonym 'Alba') is a somewhat diffuse grower with pure white bracts.

'**Magnifica**' is large, bushy grower with bright purple bracts.

'**Sanderiana**' is a dense, medium-sized vine with deep purple bracts.

'**Singapore Beauty**' is a large, dense vine with magenta bracts.

'**Singapore White**' is a white-flowered sport of 'Singapore Beauty'.

Bougainvillea peruviana (pe-roo´-vee-AHN-a) is a loose and open-growing, relatively small sprawling shrub with thorns and relatively small rose-colored bracts. It blooms in cycles throughout the year in response to periods of rain following dry periods in Brazil. Neither the species nor its cultivars are now in cultivation in the United States, but cultivars of *Bougainvillea* ×*buttiana,* a cross between *B. peruviana* and *B. glabra*, are definitely worth growing.

Bougainvillea spectabilis (spek-TAB-i-lis) (synonym *B. brasiliensis*) is the main parent of the many differently colored and free-flowering hybrids and cultivars now for sale. It is a vigorous and big dense vine with rose to reddish flowers, mostly in late fall, winter, and spring in response (in its native haunts) to rain following dry periods. It is quite thorny, and the thorns are usually curved. The leaves are large, ovate to almost orbicular, wavy margined, and pubescent beneath. There are several noteworthy cultivars of this species.

'**African Sunset**' is a modest grower with orange bracts that turn red.

'**Alex Buchart**' makes a large vine with bright red bracts.

'**Carnarvon**' is a large vine with bright red bracts.

'**Dauphine**' makes a fairly small compact vine with large red bracts.

'**Grimleyi**' is a medium-sized vine with large, drooping clusters of reddish orange-red bracts.

'**Laidlaw**' is a large vine with rusty red bracts.

'**Lateritia**' is a fairly small shrubby vine with brick red bracts.

'**Picta-Aurea**' is a large, dense vine with variegated (white) leaves and bright purple bracts.

'**Pink Gem**' is a very large vine with bright pink bracts.

'**Rosa Catalina**' is another large vine with pink bracts.

'**Speciosa**' is a dense and vigorous vine with deep purple bracts.

'**Splendens**' is a very large and vigorous vine with outstanding large magenta bracts.

'**Thomasi**' is a large vine with pink bracts.

SHRUBBY OR COMPACT HYBRIDS: The free-flowering hybrids (and cultivars thereof) are, in general, more dependable bloomers than the above species and their cultivars. '**Brilliant Variegated**' has leaves splotched with silver and deep brick red flowers. '**Crimson Jewel**' is a profuse and frequent bloomer with metallic bronzy orange to bronzy red flowers. '**Hawaii**' (synonym 'Raspberry Ice') has bright red flowers and makes a fountain-shaped spreading mound with leaves beautifully margined in gold or deep yellow. '**La Jolla**' has brilliant deep red flowers.

VINING HYBRIDS: Like the shrubby hybrids, these free-flowering hybrids (and cultivars thereof) are, in general, more dependable bloomers than the above species and their cultivars. '**Afterglow**' is a rangy plant, which often has more stem than leaves, but is covered when in bloom with deliciously deep yellow to orange flowers. The flowers age to a dusty pink and make a stunning display cascading over a wall. '**Barbara Karst**' is one of the most dependable, hardiest, most popular, and most widely planted bougainvillea with brilliant vivid purplish red flowers on a vigorous and tall vine. '**Blondie**' is a medium-sized vine with beautiful orange bracts, which change to pink. '**Jamaica White**' has pretty white flowers on a vine of modest proportions. '**James Walker**' is one of the best, with abundant purplish red flowers on a large and vigorous vine. '**Lavender Queen**' is a choice large vine with great masses of pale lavender to purple flowers, mostly in winter and spring. '**Mary Palmer's Enchantment**' is probably the best of the white-flowered large and vigorous vining types. **'Miss Manilla'** is a very large and dense vine with lovely orange bracts, which turn bright pink. **'Pink Tiara'** is one of the best of the pink-flowered vining types. **'San Diego Red'** (synonym 'Scarlett O'Hara') is, next to 'Barbara Karst', the most widely planted, most dependable, and most popular vining bougainvillea. Great masses of vivid pure red flowers are produced over a long season on a wonderfully strong-growing vine.

BOWENIA (bo-WEN-ee-a)
Zamiaceae: The Zamia (a Cycad) Family
FERN CYCADS
Small fernlike cycads
Zones 10 and 11
Shade to partial shade
Water lover
Rich, humusy, moist, well-drained soil
Propagation by seed; division of tuberous roots is
    precarious and uncertain

A genus of two species of small fernlike cycads from the rain forests of eastern Queensland in Australia. Unlike all other cycads these have bipinnate leaves. Both species are similar in appearance, with a long leaf stalk, a twice-branched rachis, oblong to elliptic leaflets, and a very large underground tuber but no aboveground trunks. They cannot stand much cold but are eminently worth cultivating in zones 10 and 11 for their lovely graceful fronds of lustrous green. The plants do not hold many leaves at a time—only one leaf at a time is produced—allowing the rosette of leaves an open and airy form, which is never more than 5 feet in height. They are lovely plants for a shady, close-up border or path. The leaves and seeds are poisonous.

Bowenia serrulata (ser-oo-LAIT-a) is native to most of eastern Queensland. The plant has rather wide (to 2 feet) open leaves as much as 5 feet long, whose distinctly elliptic to ovate, light green shiny leaflets have finely toothed margins. The fronds never number more than 10 to a plant at any one time. The plant can take a little sun but not the intense midday sun of hot summer areas.

Bowenia spectabilis (spek-TAB-i-lis) is indigenous to northern Queensland in shady rain forests and grows in rich, heavy moist soil. It usually has fewer fronds to a plant than does *B. serrulata*. Furthermore, each leaf is narrower, with more closely spaced and darker green leaflets whose margins are entire and whose shape is more oblong or ovate than elliptic.

BRACHYCHITON
(braik-ee-KY-ton / bra-KY-kee-tun)
Sterculiaceae: The Cacao, Cola-Nut Family
Common names vary according to species
Large, sometimes deciduous trees; large leaves; large
    mostly red flowers

Zones 10 and 11; marginal in zone 9b
Sun
Drought tolerant
Average well-drained soil
Propagation by seed and cuttings

A genus of about 30 species of tall trees, often with swollen trunks, in Australia. All the species are quite variable not only in size of tree, shape of trunk, and form of leaf, but also in flower color and profusion and time of bloom. Most of them are briefly deciduous in late spring, when the flowers usually appear. The blossoms are generally bell-shaped and red with strongly recurved petals.

Brachychiton acerifolia (ay´-sur-i-FO-lee-a) is indigenous to Queensland and New South Wales. It is called the flame tree or the Australian flame tree in the United States. In its native habitat it reaches 100 feet or more in height, but usually grows relatively fast to about half that height in cultivation. The tree's crown, which is variable in shape, is usually narrowly pyramidal or oblong but may also be widespreading. The trunk is usually straight and is greenish in its upper parts; it may be enlarged or swollen at the base. The leaves are large, 10 to 12 inches wide, deep glossy green above and paler beneath, and are usually palmately lobed with three to seven divisions, but are sometimes entire. Most leaves drop for a relatively brief period in late spring or early summer, when the flowers appear. The flowers are borne in loose racemes, which appear near the ends of the branches. The entire inflorescence is a flaming red in color. The flowers are usually less than an inch long and are bell-shaped. A large tree in full bloom is an unforgettably spectacular sight. Sometimes only a part of the tree blooms, but it is still a spectacle because the leaves will have fallen from the part that blooms. The tree is mostly hardy in zones 9b through 11, but if a severe freeze occurs and the temperature falls below 26°F for very long, the flower-bearing wood will be lost for the following season. A temperature of 20°F or lower usually kills the tree to the ground.

Brachychiton discolor (DIS-kul-or) is, like *B. acerifolia*, native to parts of Queensland and New South Wales. It grows faster than the flame tree into a taller (to 80 feet or more in cultivation), more spreading tree, with leaves similar to those of the flame tree. The leaves have three, five, or seven lobes, and are glossy above but rusty pubescent beneath. The tree tends to be evergreen in tropical climates, but usually becomes deciduous with cold. It is at least as hardy as *B. acerifolia* and probably slightly more so. The inflorescences are larger than those of the flame tree, as are the lavender-pink bell-shaped flowers, but they are never as numerous as those of the former tree. They manage, however, to make this tree exceptionally beautiful when in bloom in the spring. The fruit of this tree is also ornamental: 6-inch long elliptical cinnamon-colored fuzzy pods.

BRAHEA (BRAH-ya / bra-HAY-a)

Palmae (Arecaceae): The Palm Family
Common names vary according to species
Stiff-leaved fan palms with fairly thick trunks
Zones vary according to species
Sun
Drought tolerant
Average well-drained soil
Propagation by seed

A genus of 16 species of palmate-leaved palms in western Mexico and dry areas of Guatemala and El Salvador. They are all slow growing but often quite ornamental, many with a decidedly bluish cast to the leaf color, which is spectacular in a green landscape. They have an overall appearance to the more familiar *Washingtonia* species, but are generally smaller and much slower growing, have stiffer leaves, and are more drought tolerant. They are wonderful alternatives to any landscape dominated by *W. robusta* (Mexican fan palm). The genus was formerly named *Erythea,* and this name is still widely applied, especially in the trade. The species are noteworthy for their giant inflorescences, often several times longer than the leaf crown. The genus is one of the very few that tolerates true drought —with often poor and rocky soil. The palms demand perfect drainage, and several species resent high humidity or acidic soils.

Brahea armata (ahr-MAHT-a) (synonyms *Erythea armata, E. roezlii*) is native to northwestern Mexico and Baja California and is hardy in zones 9 through 11. It is called the blue hesper palm and the Mexican blue palm. The tree grows very slowly to as much as 40 feet in height. The trunk of a mature tree is straight, about 18 inches in diameter, and usually free of leaf bases for most of its height, showing only the crowded rings. The dead leaves may be removed from younger trees to improve their appearance. The waxy-coated leaves, which are on 3- to 5-foot-long petioles that are armed with stout teeth, are 3 to 5 feet wide and divided halfway to the petiole into thin stiff segments. Leaf color varies from a definite green to almost pure grayish blue. The icy blue color is, of course, the more desirable one to most people. The inflorescences are spectacular. They are 15 or more feet long and extend and hang down well beyond the crown of leaves. The individual flowers are not showy, but the size of the cluster is almost startling. This beauty is fairly temperamental and is difficult to transplant successfully. It is shorter-lived and does not look its best (not usually as blue) in constantly humid regions, but it is so attractive that it is grown anywhere it is hardy. It is beautiful at any age and, because it is so slow growing, makes a wonderful close-up landscape subject for a long time. Plate 75.

Brahea brandegeei (bran-DEJ-ee-eye) (synonym *Erythea brandegeei*) is also indigenous to Baja California and is hardy in zones 9 through 11. It is called the San Jose palm, San Jose fan palm, or San Jose hesper palm. It grows somewhat faster than *B. armata* and has a more slender trunk to as much as 50 feet or more in height with persistent leaf bases on all but the oldest trunk parts. The leaf bases form a very attractive pattern, lending an almost artificially sculptured look to the trunk, but in humid climes where these leaf bases are more easily removed, the resulting marred pattern is egregious. The leaves are similar in form and size to those of *B. armata,* but their color is light green above and gray or whitish beneath. Plate 76.

Brahea calcarea. See *B. dulcis.*

Brahea decumbens (dee-KUM-benz) occurs naturally in northeastern interior Mexico and is hardy in zones 9b through 11. This unusual palm has solitary trunks that are prostrate and creep along the ground. Because the plants sucker, they create veritable palm thickets as much as 8 feet tall. The waxy and shiny blue-green leaves are rather small, and their outline is almost a full circle with several stiff segments. This species makes a beautiful and very striking large groundcover and is quite drought tolerant.

Brahea dulcis (DOOL-sis / DUL-sis) (synonym *B. calcarea*) is indigenous to southwestern and northeastern Mexico down to Guatemala. It is more tender to cold than most other *Brahea* species and is not hardy outside zones 10 and 11, although there are mature specimens in the warmer parts of zone 9b. This beautiful palm is more at home in humid regions than are most other species. The leaves are large, to 7 feet wide, and are usually bluish green above and grayish beneath. The tree grows slowly to about 20 feet and has a nice smooth and ringed trunk, usually completely free of leaf bases. The fruits are a golden yellow and reportedly edible and sweet. This one is sometimes called the rock palm.

Brahea edulis (ED-yoo-liss) (synonym *Erythea edulis*) is native to western Mexico and is at least as hardy *B. dulcis* and *B. decumbens*. It is a good candidate for zones 9b through 11. It grows slowly to 40 feet or so in height, but is not as slow growing as *B. armata,* and its trunk is similar to but even stouter than that of *B. armata.* The leaves are borne on 3-foot-long petioles that have teeth along their margins and are 3 to 5 feet wide, a grassy green in color, and somewhat similar to those of *Livistona chinensis* (Chinese fan palm). The black round fruit is said to be edible. Like *B. armata* the palm is not completely happy in humid climates and needs a generally richer soil than most other *Brahea* species. It is usually called the Guadelupe palm.

BRASSAIA. See *Schefflera.*

BREYNIA (BRAY-nee-a)

Euphorbiaceae: The Euphorbia, Spurge Family
SNOW-BUSH
Large shrub with leaves splotched red, pink, and
   white
Zones 10 and 11; marginal in zone 9b
Sun to partial sun

Average but regular amounts of moisture
Average well-drained soil
Propagation by cuttings

A genus of about 24 species of shrubs and trees in Southeast Asia, Australia, and the islands of the South Pacific, only one of which is planted in the United States.

Breynia disticha (DIS-ti-ka) (synonym *B. nivosa*) is native to the islands of the South Pacific. It reaches a maximum height of 10 feet with the same width, although it is usually no more than half that size in cultivation. The leaves, which are small, 2 inches long, and mostly elliptic to ovate in shape, are alternately arranged along the pendent red, zigzagging branches, giving each branch almost the appearance of a large pinnate leaf. The species has leaves blotched with cream or white. *Breynia disticha* 'Roseo-picta' (ro´-zee-o-PIK-ta), the form usually planted, has leaves that are mottled with pink, red to violet and white, sometimes to the point of obscuring any green in the leaf. The effect is quite nice, almost as if the shrub were in bloom. The flowers are quite insignificant in any landscaping sense. The plant does not have much color in shade, where it becomes loose and straggly. It is damaged by a temperature of 30°F or below, is killed to the ground by anything below 25°F, but sometimes sprouts from the roots if the temperature does not fall below 20°F.

Breynia nivosa. See *B. disticha.*

BROMELIA
(bro-MEL-ee-a / bro-MEEL-ee-a)
Bromeliaceae: The Pineapple, Bromeliad Family
HEART-OF-FLAME; PINGUIN
Large rosettes of very spiny arching, tough narrow
    leaves marked with red
Zones 9b through 11
Sun
Average but regular amounts of moisture; drought
    tolerant when established
Sandy, humusy, well-drained soil
Propagation by seed and transplanting of offsets

The genus *Bromelia* is the type genus of the family (the genus that is the basis for the name of a family). There are about 50 species, all found in tropical America but mostly in Brazil. They are terrestrial and form large, very spiny-leaved rosettes. All are large plants, spreading by underground stolons called "ratoons" by which they form thickets of beautiful spiny leaves. While not exactly invasive these plants can present a dilemma as they spread and their spininess can lead to problems if the plants are grown where people and pets are liable to wander. These species are quite similar to those in the genus *Ananas* (pineapple) when not in bloom. All the species are very tolerant of saline soil and salt-laden air and are perfect seaside landscape subjects. The following two species are among the largest and most spectacular bromeliads.

Bromelia balansae (ba-LAHN-see) is native to Paraguay and northern Argentina where its rosettes grow to 4 or 5 feet in height and 6 feet wide. The leaves, which are narrow (an inch or so wide) but 4 to 6 feet long, have viciously sharp spines on the margin, a bright, glossy green to olive green upper surface, and a white bloom on the under surface. The heart of the rosette turns a vivid deep almost glowing red in spring and early summer when the plant reaches flowering size. The inflorescence is a thick, relatively short (to 4 feet in height) spike with dense white hairs, bright red spiny bracts beneath, and maroon and white flowers above. The plants are untouched by temperatures above 30°F and recover from temperatures in the mid-20s. They are often used for "living fences" because of their size, quick growth, suckering habit, and vicious spines. These are wonderfully carefree and spectacular plants, especially when in bloom. Plate 77.

Bromelia pinguin (PIN-gwin / peen-GEEN) is native to a wide area including the West Indies, parts of Mexico, Central America, and northern South America. It is very similar to *B. balansae* and indeed, the former is often mislabeled in nurseries and botanical gardens as the latter. The important differences for the gardener and landscaper are that *B. pinguin* is a slightly larger and (if possible) even spinier plant that is not as colorful as *B. balansae* when the latter flowers. Nonetheless, *B. pinguin* makes a striking and spectacular plant in its own right with its larger but less colorful inflorescence and great 7-foot-long spiny leaves.

BROWNEA (BROWN-ee-a)
Caesalpiniaceae (Leguminosae), subfamily
    Caesalpinioideae: The Cassia, Royal Poinciana
    Family
ROSE OF VENEZUELA
Small tree; large spectacular pinnate leaves; large
    round clusters of red or orange flowers
Zones 10b and 11
Sun to part shade
Water lovers
Rich, humusy moist soil on the acidic side
Propagation by seed

A genus of about 24 species of shrubs and small to large trees in tropical America. They have large even-pinnate leaves with large leathery leaflets that are limp and a beautiful translucent pinkish brown to rosy bronze when new but soon mature to green while simultaneously stiffening. The flowers are in large usually pendulous clusters that are mostly round and are either formed in the leaf axils or on the branches as well as the trunk. The individual flowers are tubular or bell-shaped with emergent anthers and stamens. All the species are intolerant of frost, need a fairly fertile soil, and must not be subjected to drought conditions. These requirements and the slow-growing nature of the species may partially explain the relative scarcity of these plants in tropical regions of the United States, but the plants are no more demanding than many other beauties that are avidly sought out and readily planted in the tropics and subtropics. All the species are more than worthy of cultivation, but only two species are common.

Brownea coccinea. See *B. latifolia*.

Brownea grandiceps (GRAND-i-seps) is indigenous to northern Venezuela and the island of Trinidad. It grows to as much as 30 feet in cultivation and twice that in its native haunts. The leaves, which are at least as beautiful as the flowers, are as much as 3 feet long with 5 to 11 pairs of 7-inch-long oblong to lanceolate leathery leaflets. Each leaflet has a pointed usually curved "tail," and the leaves may drop under cold or drought conditions. The trees bloom in spring and early summer, and the flowers are borne in round, hanging, almost stalkless clusters near the ends of the branches. Each flower head is as much as 10 inches across and looks as much like an *Ixora* flower head as those of any other tree. Each blossom is a 3- or 4-inch-long tube of deep pink or crimson and is densely packed into the flower head with its 50 or so neighboring blossoms. The plant is most effective when pruned to tree form with a certain amount of trunk so that the flowers may be more easily seen. Plate 78.

Brownea latifolia (lat-i-FO-lee-a) (synonym *B. coccinea*) is also indigenous to Venezuela but is a much smaller tree. It grows to about 20 feet with a spreading habit and rather pendent branches. The leaves are 12 to 18 inches long with five or six pairs of 6-inch-long leaflets. The little tree blooms mainly in summer. The flower heads are about 6 inches wide, and the individual blossoms have long protruding yellow stamens.

BRUGMANSIA (brug-MAN-zee-a)
Solanaceae: The Petunia, Potato, Tomato Family
ANGEL'S TRUMPET
Large spreading, large-leaved shrubs and small trees;
    giant pendent trumpetlike flowers
Zone 9b as returning perennials, zones 10 and 11 as
    year-round subjects
Sun to part shade
Water lovers
Humusy, moist, well-drained soil
Propagation by seed and cuttings

A genus of only five species of soft-wooded shrubs and trees native to the South American Andean region. They usually have large leaves and always more or less pendulous flowers that are fragrant to a lesser or greater degree. These plants were once included in the genus *Datura*, whose flowers are similar in general shape and are closely allied to those of *Brugmansia*. The two genera may be most easily distinguished by their flowers and fruits. The flowers of *Brugmansia* species are pendent and drooping (at least to some extent), while those of *Datura* are held erect or at right angles to the stems, and the fruits of the *Brugmansia* are elongated smooth pods, while those of *Datura* are globose and covered in spinelike protrusions. Furthermore, although the flow-

ers of both genera have a five-pointed corolla, the points of most *Brugmansia* species are recurved to at least some extent. In addition, *Brugmansia* species, which make larger plants than do *Datura* species (some *Brugmansia* species grow to 30 feet or more in height), provide soft wood when grown to maturity, whereas *Datura* species are annuals and seldom make wood. All parts of *Brugmansia* plants are poisonous, including the flowers and seeds.

All *Brugmansia* species are indigenous to elevated areas in South America that are of moderate to great altitude. Several of the largest growing species (*B. arborea*, *B. aurea*, and *B. sanguinea*) are indigenous to these high mountain regions and do not fare well in warm and humid areas, and are not therefore usually in cultivation in the southeastern United States and similar climates. These cold country species do figure, however, in the parentage of many forms now available everywhere. These mountainous habitats are quite moist year-round and yet are, of course, mostly of sloping ground. These facts are two of the clues to successful cultivation of *Brugmansia*: moisture and good soil drainage.

None of the species, hybrids, or cultivars are hardy to cold, but most will come back from the roots in zone 9b and sometimes in zone 9a. Temperatures of 30°F damage the foliage; temperatures of 25°F or lower usually freeze the plants to the ground; and temperatures below 20°F are usually fatal but the plants sometimes spring back with the return of warm weather. Whether the plants return from a freeze depends on several factors, not the least important of which is the heritage of the plant (the hybrids are, in general, more tender) and the age of the plant. For example, plants that are repeatedly cut to the ground by cold in successive winters seem to lose strength and within relatively few years will probably die, even if their roots never freeze.

There are several hybrids and cultivars now whose parentage is uncertain, but most probably involve the species *Brugmansia versicolor*. The taxonomy of these plants is still in flux, and what follows is doubtless subject to revision, as far as names go.

Brugmansia arborea (ahr-BOR-ee-a) (synonyms *Datura arborea*, *D. cornigera*) is indigenous to the high Andes region and is not in cultivation in the southeastern United States (indeed, it seems to be rarely cultivated in the United States). Plants so labeled here are usually *B.* ×*candida*, which see. This small tree to only 12 feet or so in height has velvety pubescent and strongly ribbed ovate usually toothed leaves about 6 inches long. The fragrant white pendent flowers have recurved pointed lobes and are small for the genus, usually no more than 6 inches long, with green veins and a large green calyx.

Brugmansia aurea (OW-ree-a / AW-ree-a) (synonyms *Datura affinis*, *D. aurea*, *D. pittieri*) is another species from the high elevations in the eastern Andes regions. It is not in cultivation in the hot and humid southeastern United States and similar climes and seems rarely cultivated outside its native haunts except under glass. This strikingly handsome tree can attain 20 or 30 feet in height. The large strong, ribbed foot-long, linear-cordate and tapering dark green leaves are usually toothed on the margins of young plants but entire on older ones. The beautiful pendulous flowers are usually a deep golden yellow, but may also be almost white. They are 10 or more inches long and trumpet-shaped with spreading corolla lobes that terminate in long recurved "tails." The blossoms are quite fragrant.

Brugmansia ×*candida* (kan-DEED-a) (synonyms *Datura candida, D.* ×*candida*) is a hybrid of *B. aurea,* a white-flowered or yellow-flowered species from high elevations in Ecuador, and *B. versicolor,* a white-flowered or peach-colored species from the lower Andean regions of Ecuador. It grows fast to 12 or 15 feet in height with foot-long, dull green ovate to elliptic leaves that are usually toothed on the margins. The flowers are a foot or more long, pure white, often tinged with pink or yellow, and are intensely, almost overpoweringly fragrant. The plant blooms all year in cycles of about 6 weeks but most heavily in summer and autumn. There is a pure white double-flowered cultivar, a "trumpet within a trumpet," and a gorgeous golden-yellow-flowered form.

Brugmansia ×*insignis* (in-SIG-nis) is a second generation hybrid between *B. suaveolens,* a white-flowered species from southeastern Brazil, and *B. versicolor.* It has foot-long narrowly ovate leaves with toothed margins. The immense flowers are pink, sometimes almost red, or white, or combinations thereof and are a foot or more long with a delicate and delicious fragrance. They are more bell-shaped than trumpet-shaped and have usually six recurved and pointed lobes. The plant grows to at least 12 feet in height. It is a year-round bloomer, but blooms most heavily in fall, winter, and spring.

Brugmansia sanguinea (san-GWIN-ee-a) (synonyms *Datura rosei, D. sanguinea*) is a tree type with red and yellow flowers. Native to high elevations in the Andes, it is unable to cope with the heat of the Gulf Coast, the southeastern United States, and similar climates, and is not usually grown nor available in those areas. It is, however, grown in cooler tropical and subtropical areas like coastal California, the Riviera, northern New Zealand, and southeastern Australia. The red angel's trumpet is a magnificent flowering tree that attains a height of 30 feet or more, although it is often more shrublike. The velvety bright green foot-long leaves are long-ovate, deep-ribbed, acuminate, and as much as a foot long. The narrowly trumpet shaped and pendent flowers are also a foot long, and their colors are remarkable. As the flowers emerge from the large and fleshy calyx, they are light yellow; the yellow changes to pink by the middle of the tube, and the pink changes to scarlet at the corolla lobes, which are abruptly long pointed with the points recurving toward the calyx. There are varieties and cultivars that are pure red and pure yellow.

Brugmansia suaveolens (swahv-ee-O-lenz) (synonyms *Datura gardneri, D. suaveolens*) is native to the low mountains of southeastern Brazil. It grows to at least 12 feet in height, often more, and has ovate to elliptic dark green leaves to a foot long and usually 6 to 8 inches wide. The fragrant flowers are about a foot long, with the points of the corolla only slightly recurved. The flowers often are only half-pendulous, giving the impression of large tubular white stars. There are yellow and pink forms. Plate 79.

Brugmansia versicolor (VUR-si-kul-or) (synonyms *Datura mollis, D. versicolor*) grows to 15 feet or more in height with foot-long, dark bluish green, heavily veined elliptic to lanceolate leaves. The flowers are perhaps the most beautiful of all the species: 18 to almost 24 inches long, with long, recurved points to the corolla. They open almost pure white with a delicate blush of pink or apricot and soon change to almost pure pink or orange-pink. There is also a beautiful pure white cultivar. Plate 80.

BRUNFELSIA

(brun-FEL-zee-a / brun-FEL-zha)
Solanaceae: The Petunia, Potato, Tomato Family
Common names vary according to species
Medium to large evergreen shrubs; white to purple
  fragrant flowers
Zones vary according to species
Sun to partial shade
Average but regular amounts of moisture
Humusy, well-drained soil
Propagation by seed and cuttings

A genus of about 36 shrubs and small trees in tropical America with tubular or bell-shaped flowers with flaring corolla lobes. When in bloom most of these plants lend an almost unique form and color to the tropical planting. All have fragrant flowers to some extent and some are very fragrant, but the lavender and white forms exude a scent that is not completely pleasant to everyone. The species are never found on calcareous soil, and such conditions should be amended with shredded peat moss or humus, including leaf mold if it can be obtained.

Brunfelsia americana (a-mer´-i-KAHN-a) is native to islands in the West Indies. It is usually a large shrub to 8 feet or so in height but, with good soil, sun, and adequate water, it can attain the proportions of a small tree to 20 feet or so in height with a dense crown of foliage. It does not reach tree size outside zones 10 and 11, but is widely grown and adaptable to zone 9b as a shrub. The leaves are elliptic to obovate in shape, 4 to 6 inches long, and a deep glossy green in color with the prominent veins a lighter color. The flowers appear in spring and early summer at the ends of the branches and are 3-inch-wide "wheels" at the end of 4-inch-long very narrow tubes. Opening pure white, the flowers soon change to a creamy yellow. They are mildly fragrant during the day, but almost overpoweringly so at night, and thus have been given the vernacular name lady-of-the-night. The shrub or tree is somewhat drought tolerant, but grows ever so much better with adequate moisture.

Brunfelsia australis (aw-STRAL-is) is indigenous to southern Brazil, Paraguay, and northern Argentina ("australis" does not necessarily mean "Australia" but rather simply "southern"). An occasional common name is Paraguay jasmine. This species can make a large shrub to 10 feet or more in height with glossy green ovate to obovate leaves to 6 inches long. The about 2-inch-wide flowers come in cycles from late spring through midsummer and into the fall. They open a deep rich purple with a white eye but fade to white within a day or so, resulting in several colors of flower on the same plant. This parti-colored phenomenon has led to the much more common name of yesterday-today-and-tomorrow. The shrub is hardy in zones 10 and 11 and will come back from the roots in zone 9b. It grows wonderfully in partial shade but is intolerant of drought.

Brunfelsia calycina. See *B. pauciflora.*

Brunfelsia grandiflora (grand-i-FLOR-a) is indigenous to western Venezuela through Colombia and Peru to Bolivia. It makes a large shrub to 12 feet or more in height and can be trained to a small tree form. The dark green leaves are lanceolate in shape and as much as 10 inches long. The plants, which bloom all year but are most floriferous in fall, winter, and spring, have 2-inch-wide flowers that are purple with a white center. This species needs sun to flower well and, like *B. australis,* is adaptable only to zones 9b through 11. Some botanists consider this species to be a form of *B. pauciflora,* which also carries the vernacular name of yesterday-today-and-tomorrow.

Brunfelsia pauciflora (paw-si-FLOR-a) (synonym *B. calycina*) is native to southern Brazil and is hardy in zones 9b through 11, although it usually survives even in zone 9a. It makes a shrub to 8 feet or more in height with dark green, oblong-lanceolate leathery leaves to 6 inches long. The flowers are about 3 inches across and open blue to purple with a white eye, then gradually change to white. This color change occasions the common name yesterday-today-and-tomorrow, which is also applied to *B. australis* and to *B. grandiflora.* The plant needs protection from the heat of the midday sun in hot summer regions.

BRYOPHYLLUM. See *Kalanchoe.*

BUCIDA (BYOOS-i-da / byoo-SYD-a)
Combretaceae: The Combretum Family
BLACK OLIVE
Medium-sized evergreen trees; dense, rounded crown of foliage
Zones 10 and 11; marginal in zone 10a
Sun
Average but regular amounts of moisture; drought tolerant when established

Average soil
Propagation by seed

A small genus of about six species of slow-growing trees in extreme southern Florida, the Caribbean region, and Central America. All have small insignificant flowers and small leathery leaves.

Bucida buceras (BYOO-ser-us / boo-SER-us) makes a beautiful specimen tree of 40 to 50 feet with its dense crown of dark green leathery elliptic-obovate leaves 3 or 4 inches long in whorls near the ends of the terminally pendent branches. The whorls of leaves are accompanied by thorns an inch or so long, but there are no spines on the inner branches or trunk. The only real fault the tree has is that it is quite slow growing, taking many years to reach maturity. It is one of the best landscape subjects for seaside planting as it takes wind without damage and tolerates saline soil and salty sea breezes. It also needs no soil amendment in the calcareous soils of southern Florida and, in addition, tolerates drought once established. While it could never be mistaken for the true olive tree, the young plants do have a certain resemblance to olive trees with their small evergreen leaves and tiered branches.

Bucida spinosa (spi-NO-sa) is native to the Florida Keys, the Bahamas, and Cuba. It is quite similar to *B. buceras* and grows just as slowly, but is a much smaller plant, only to 12 or so feet in height. It makes a quite attractive large shrub and may also be trained into a dwarf tree.

BULNESIA (bul-NEE-zee-a / bul-NEE-zhya)
Zygophyllaceae: The Lignum-Vitae Family
VERA; VERAWOOD; BULNESIA
Medium-sized evergreen tree; small pinnate leaves; extremely showy yellow flowers
Zones 10b and 11
Sun
Average but regular amounts of moisture; drought tolerant when established
Average well-drained soil
Propagation by seed and cuttings

A small genus of about nine species of trees and shrubs in South America, all with jointed branches that are swollen at the nodes, pinnate leaves, and five-petaled showy flowers. ***Bulnesia arborea*** (ahr-BOR-ee-a) is native to the coastal areas of northern Colombia and northern Venezuela. In its native habitats it sometimes reaches 80 feet or more in height, but in cultivation it cannot be expected to attain more than 40 or 50 feet and that only in the warmer regions. The trunk is fairly tall and straight, and the canopy is rounded and dense but graceful and spacious. It is a truly beautiful and magnificent tree when mature with choice leaves and flowers. The leaves, which are small, only 4 or 5 inches long, with 1- to 2-inch-long oblong leaflets, give an airy and delicate appearance to the tree. The 3-inch-wide flowers consist of five yellow to orange petals.

Each petal is narrow and fluted at the base, expanding into an ovate to almost squared end. The fruits are winged, yellowish green capsules. This wonderful tree grows moderately fast and is virtually carefree in a tropical or nearly tropical climate. Besides its beauty, it is fairly drought tolerant when established. It is difficult to be too enthusiastic about its qualities as a landscape subject for color, shade, and form. The wood is dense and heavy and was formerly much in demand, being similar to but not as fine as that of *Guaiacum* (lignum-vitae) species. Plates 81 and 82.

BURBIDGEA (bur-BIJ-ee-a)
Zingiberaceae: The Ginger Family
BURBIDGEA
Small, green-leaved, red-stemmed perennial; orange, birdlike flowers
Zones 10 and 11
Partial shade
Water lover
Humusy, moist, well-drained soil
Propagation by root division and seed

A genus of six species of perennial rhizomatous-rooted small herbs in Borneo. They are similar to *Alpinia* species in form but are smaller and more compact than most of those species. All have terminal inflorescences with three-petaled flowers. One petal (the "lip" or labellum) is larger and more erect than the other two. One species has become popular in nearly tropical climates as a large groundcover or as an accent in partially shady borders. *Burbidgea schizocheila* (skitz-o-KYL-a / skitz-o-KEEL-a) is a very lovely little thing that is quite tender to frost but will resprout from the root if the temperature does not fall below the upper 20s. The plants are generally 2 feet tall or less, but with good soil, water, and warmth will occasionally grow to 3 feet. The succulent and scandent stems are brownish red, and the 6-inch-long leaves are waxy and succulent ellipses of medium green above and brownish or purplish red beneath. The flower clusters, which are terminal on the stems and which rise well above the foliage mass, consist of six to eight or so orange-yellow flowers with three petals, one of which is larger than the other two. The plants bloom off and on all year if not frosted and slowly make wonderful little clumps by the creeping rhizomes. The plants cannot take full sun in hot summer areas but are quite beautiful in high dappled shade.

BURSERA (BURS-e-ra / bur-SER-a)
Burseraceae: The Gumbo-Limbo Family
GUMBO-LIMBO; WEST INDIAN BIRCH; TOURIST TREE; TURPENTINE TREE
Widespreading, deciduous, pinnate-leaved tree; beautiful shiny scaly red bark
Zones 10 and 11; marginal in zone 10a
Sun
Average but regular amounts of moisture; drought tolerant when established
Average well-drained soil
Propagation by branch (not twig) cuttings and seed

A genus of about 40 species of shrubs and trees in tropical America, most of which are deciduous. All species have aromatic or resinous sap, scaly and flaking bark, pinnate leaves, and small flowers in axillary panicles or racemes. Only the native Florida species is planted in the United States outside botanical gardens. *Bursera simaruba* (sim-a-ROO-ba) is indigenous to a large area including extreme southern Florida, the West Indies, and parts of Mexico and Central America. It is one of the most picturesque and beautiful trees available for tropical and subtropical regions. The gumbo-limbo can quickly reach a height of 60 feet and is a widespreading, massive-looking tree with very characteristic light reddish brown freely exfoliating bark, which, from a distance, looks almost oily—definitely smooth and shiny. The limbs, which are usually few but heavy and massive, are rather weak and will break in strong winds. The leaves are odd-pinnate on short petioles with 3 to 11 ovate to elliptic 3-inch-long leaflets that have prominent yellowish green midveins. The upper surfaces are shiny dark green and the lower surfaces are a paler green. The trees are usually deciduous from late December until early March, but this is often also not the case and in wet winter years they may be virtually evergreen. The insignificant greenish white flowers appear in small clusters in early spring followed by small brownish red to purple-red berries, which mature in midsummer. Once established the trees are drought tolerant, fast growing, tolerant to salty air, and, to some extent, saline soil. The trunks and limbs are startlingly beautiful in winter, especially if backed by green. The trees do not tolerate frost but recover fast if temperatures do not fall below 28°F. The species is very easily propagated as almost any sizable branch (not twigs) roots if simply stuck into the ground. The common name tourist tree comes from the always red and peeling bark.

BUTEA (BOO-tay-a)
Papilionaceae (Fabaceae, Leguminosae), subfamily Papilionoideae: The Bean, Pea Family
FLAME OF THE FOREST; PARROT TREE
Crooked trunked deciduous tree; spectacular red and orange flowers
Zones 10b and 11
Sun
Average but regular amounts of moisture; drought tolerant when established
Humusy, well-drained soil
Propagation by seed and transplanting of suckers

A genus of about six deciduous trees and lianas in India and Myanmar (Burma) with large pinnate leaves of only three leaflets and spectacular pealike flowers when leafless. Only one species is planted. **Butea monosperma** (mo-no-SPUR-ma / mo-no-SPER-ma) (synonym *B. frondosa*) is indigenous to most of India into Myanmar (Burma). It is a picturesque tree to 50 feet in its native haunts and to about 40 feet in cultivation, with a crooked sinuous trunk and gray bark and branches. Some think it grotesque and ugly and, instead of "picturesque," would use the terms "distorted" and "deformed" except when it is in flower. The leaves are pinnate but with only three very large and leathery leaflets that are finely pubescent beneath. The terminal leaflet is larger (8 inches wide and orbicular in shape) than the other two, which are rhomboidal and about 6 inches long. The tree loses most of its leaves December through February, when it blooms (most often in February). The flowers are in 6-inch-long densely flowered panicles, which almost cover the tree. Each blossom is shaped like a claw or a parrot's beak because of the large "keel" petal and is subtended by a velvety black calyx. All the petals are a vivid reddish orange to pure red in color. The flowers are covered in fine silky hairs, which impart a silvery sheen to the inflorescence. The pods are about 5 inches long, light bluish green in color, and glisteningly silky. This outstanding bloomer is tolerant of drought when established and is immune to salty winds and somewhat saline soil. It is even more picturesque when contorted by coastal winds. Planted inland, it looks its best not as a specimen tree but incorporated into other vegetation over which it can tower and show off its spectacular blooming season. Plate 83.

BUTIA (BYOOT-ee-a / BYOO-sha)
Palmae (Arecaceae): The Palm Family
PINDO PALM; JELLY PALM
Medium-sized palm; bluish green gracefully arching
     pinnate leaves
Zones 8b through 11
Sun
Average but regular amounts of moisture; drought
     tolerant when established
Sandy, humusy, well-drained soil
Propagation by seed

A genus of eight single-trunked palm species found in the drier parts of southern Brazil, Paraguay, Uruguay, and northern Argentina. The different species are all similar, varying mainly in the color of the leaves and in the thickness and the height of the trunk. The species freely hybridize, so that it is nearly impossible to attach a specific name to many of the palms. In addition, this genus has the fortunate ability of "mating" with at least two other genera, *Jubaea* and *Syagrus* (synonym *Arecastrum*), producing marvelous intergeneric hybrids. These hybrid palms are probably the hardiest pinnate-leaved palms (see (*Butiagrus*); they have survived temperatures in the low teens, but are usually damaged, sometimes severely so, by temperatures of 15°F or less.
Butia capitata (cap-i-TAIT-a) is the most common species planted in the United States and is an out-

standing landscape subject for creating a tropical effect. The stiff yet gracefully arching and much recurved bluish or silvery green feathery fronds are very pleasing as are the light to dark gray trunk with the adhering leaf bases. Nothing stands out quite like this palm against the darker greens of other palms or trees. It makes a trunk in some cases as tall as 25 feet but usually is shorter, and can be from a foot in diameter to almost 3 feet thick. The leaves are about 6 feet long, strongly arched and recurving at their tips with stiffly arching leaflets that are concave in cross section. The leaf petioles sometimes are as long as the leaf and are armed with inch-long spines. The flowers are in large drooping clusters accompanied by a large obovate, woody spathe. They are not that decorative, unlike the gigantic clusters of ripe fruits, which are round or egg-shaped when mature in late summer and fall and bright orange. The edible fruits are sweet and very good for making jelly. There is much variation in this species as to color and amount of curvature of the leaves, thickness of the trunk, and color and size of the fruit. Some of the world's most beautiful palms are mature specimens of the thinner-trunked forms with the thick crowns of nearly blue, strongly arched and recurving leaves.
Butia eriospatha (er-ee-o-SPAYTH-a) is native to southern Brazil and differs from *B. capitata* in having a thicker and usually shorter trunk and mostly green leaves rather than the bluish cast that the leaves of *B. capitata* exhibit. The leaf bases are covered in a beautiful brown and delicate tomentum. It is a very graceful palm and has the same basic cultural requirements as *B. capitata*.
Butia yatay (ya-TAH-ee) is indigenous to northern Argentina, Uruguay, and Paraguay. It has the same cultural requirements as *B. eriospatha*. It is similar in leaf color to *B. capitata,* but usually grows taller and has a somewhat more open crown of leaves. The trunk is exceptional in that it usually retains all the old leaf bases, which phenomenon creates a quite exotic and appealing appearance. The palm is most highly recommended.

×BUTIAGRUS (byoo-tee-AG-rus)
Palmae (Arecaceae): The Palm Family
MULE PALM
Tall dark green feather-leaved palm
Zones 8b through 11
Sun
Average but regular amounts of moisture
Rich, humusy, well-drained soil
Propagation usually impossible

An intergeneric hybrid between *Butia capitata* (pindo palm) with *Syagrus romanzoffiana* (queen palm). This genus does not occur in nature, but came about as a result of the happy chance of the two genera being grown near each other in Florida. The progeny of this cross exhibits the best features of each parent: the hardiness of the pindo palm, the graceful form and color of the queen palm's leaves, and the relatively quick growth of the queen palm. The fly in the ointment is that almost all the fruits produced by this hybrid have sterile seeds, making this wonderful palm still fairly rare and expensive to obtain. And yet, it is not only one of the world's most beautiful palms, it is also the most beautiful palm that can be grown in the colder areas of the palm-growing regions. According to Grant Stephenson of Horticultural Consultants in Houston, Texas, this wonderful hybrid has survived temperatures in the mid teens in northern Florida.

It is not known just how tall the tree grows, but there are specimens already with 20 feet of trunk. The trunks, like those of the queen palm, are mostly clear of leaf bases, wonderfully straight, and beautifully ringed for most of their length on the older palms. As young palms they have a large amount (like the queen palm) of brown fiber near the leaf crown. The leaves are not quite as long as those of the queen palm, but they are beautifully arched and a darker green than either of the parents. In addition, the leaflets are not stiff and arched like those of the pindo palm but rather have more of the limpness and gracefulness of those of the queen palm. Large specimens look much like *Howea* species (kentia palms) and sometimes even coconut palms.

This palm has some of the pindo palm's drought tolerance but looks and grows much better with an adequate and regular supply of water, and really appreciates a rich soil that is not too alkaline. It is one of the world's finest landscape subjects whether the garden be tropical or not. Its only faults are its relative rarity and the cost of obtaining it. Plate 84.

BUTIARECASTRUM.

See ×Butiagrus.

CAESALPINIA (see-sal-PIN-ee-a)

Caesalpiniaceae (Leguminosae), subfamily
    Caesalpinioideae: The Cassia, Royal Poinciana
    Family
Common names vary according to species
Evergreen trees and shrubs; pinnate foliage; showy
    red or yellow flowers
Zones vary according to species
Sun
Average but regular amounts of moisture
Sandy, humusy, well-drained soil
Propagation by seed

A wonderful genus of about 70 species of trees, shrubs, and vines from tropical areas around the world. Some species have spines. All the species have bipinnate, fernlike leaves and showy white, yellow, orange, or red flowers. Many of these plants were formerly placed in the genus *Poinciana*, but this is no longer a valid genus or name. Some current vernacular names include the word "poinciana."

Caesalpinia bonduc (BAHN-dook) (synonym *C. crista*) is so widespread on tropical seashores that its true origin is obscure but is most likely tropical America. It has common names of nicker nut, gray nickers, and molucca bean. It is completely hardy only in zones 10 and 11, but will come back from the root in zone 9b and sometimes in zone 9a. It is viciously thorny in all its parts, but is exceptionally attractive of leaf; the flowers are less than spectacular. The plant is quite useful in the landscape because of its imperviousness to salinity, its drought tolerance, and its ability to control erosion. It is a sprawling evergreen shrub only a few feet in height but clambering along the soil or sand dunes to as much as 30 feet with stems covered in hooked spines. The leaves are 18 inches long and bipinnate, with elliptic to oblong shiny green leaflets about 3 inches long; there are spines even on the undersides of the leaflets. The flowers are insignificantly greenish yellow and come in fall and winter. The plant is extremely drought tolerant and can be trained into a virtually impenetrable barrier. It is of paramount importance on tropical beaches, where it binds sand dunes. It should not be planted near other ornamental plants as it tends to smother them.

Caesalpinia coriaria (kor-ee-AHR-ee-a) (synonym *Libidibia coriaria*) is a large shrub or a beautiful small, dense-crowned, spreading tree to 30 feet in height. Native to the West Indies, parts of Mexico, and Central America, it is hardy in zones 10 and 11 and marginal in zone 10a. The leaves are about 6 inches long and bipinnate with many small, dark green leaflets about an inch long. The flowers appear mostly in summer, but may be evident at any time of the year; they are white or yellowish, not spectacular, but sweetly fragrant. The tree is sometimes called divi-divi, dibi-dibi, or libi dibi, names usually applied to the flat seed pods, which are curled like the letter *S* and from which tannin is derived.

Caesalpinia crista. See *C. bonduc.*

Caesalpinia gilliesii (gil-LEEZ-ee-eye) (synonym *Poinciana gilliesii*) is called the yellow bird-of-paradise, Mexican bird-of-paradise, and paradise poinciana. Native to relatively dry areas of Argentina and Uruguay, it is quite hardy to cold and is a good subject for zones 8 through 11. It has naturalized in western and southern Texas, including the Davis and Chisos Mountains, southern New Mexico, Arizona, and areas along the Gulf Coast. It makes a medium to large-sized shrub to as much as 10 feet in height with 6-inch-long leaves of 6 to 12 pairs of small medium-green, inch-long leaflets. The flowers are spectacular, in terminal pyramid-shaped loose racemes. Each is a bright clear yellow cup shape (i.e., the petals do not spread as they do in many other species of the genus), with 10 very long, protruding, scarlet curved stamens. The flowers are formed all spring, summer, and fall. The pods form quickly and are to be found at the bases of the flower clusters still with flowers; they are about 3 inches long, pubescent, and reddish brown when mature. The plant is very drought tolerant when established and often grows on poor soil. It is a good candidate for the cactus garden or rock garden and needs full sun to bloom well.

Caesalpinia granadillo (grann-a-DIL-o / grahn-a DEE-yo) (synonym *Libidibia granadillo*) is native to northern South America where it is known as granadillo or ebano, although the Florida nursery trade calls it the bridal-veil tree. It is not hardy to cold and will not make a tree outside zones 10b and 11. This very beautiful high-branched and open-crowned vase-shaped tree grows to 30 or 40 feet in height (twice this in its native habitat). It has dark gray bark that naturally exfoliates to reveal the lovely pure white inner bark, very much like *Platanus* (plane tree, sycamore) species. The leaves are about a foot long with relatively large oblong medium green leaflets. The bright clear yellow flowers come in summer, are about 2 inches wide, and are carried in loose clusters at the ends of the branches.

Caesalpinia mexicana (mex-i-KAHN-a) is native to Mexico. It makes a beautiful and picturesque open-headed small tree to as much as 30 feet in height but usually less. The bipinnate leaves are 6 to 8 inches long with as many as 100 dark green oblong leaflets. The very beautiful five-petaled flowers are fragrant, each about 2 inches wide, deep yellow with a red splotch on the standard petal, and are borne in large, loose-flowered terminal racemes. The tree blooms all summer and often into late autumn. It will come back from its roots after a freeze, but cannot usually make a tree outside zones 10 and 11, although as a shrub it usually can be dependable even in zone 9a. It blooms in partial shade, but flowers more in full sun. The tree is not drought tolerant in spite of its native habitat and should receive adequate and regular irrigation.

Caesalpinia pulcherrima (pull-KERR-i-mah) (synonym *Poinciana pulcherrima*) is native to the West Indies and is the most spectacular-flowering species in the genus. It grows quickly to about 15 feet in height if not frozen back, but must be trained to make a small tree form even in frost-free areas. It is a large shrub otherwise and, because it grows fast, is dependably so in zones 9 through 11, and sometimes sprouts from its roots in zone 8b. It is often grown as an annual in colder climates. While it is very beautiful as a small tree in bloom, it tends to lose leaves in cool winters and can become rather unattractive unless pruned back then, even in zones 10 and 11. The leaves are as much as 2 feet long with many small, glaucous, light green to bluish green oblong leaflets. All plants have reddish stiff hairs along the younger branches and stems, which in some plants become relatively soft spines. The flowers appear in spring (if the plants were not frozen back the previous winter), summer, and autumn, and are borne in terminal, pyramid-shaped racemes that are as much as 2 feet tall. Each flower has four large open, spatulate-shaped petals with crinkled edges and fluted bases, a smaller inner petal, and 10 long red stamens. The petals open either yellow or red with yellow margins and age to pure red; each flower is as much as 3 inches wide. *Caesalpinia pulcherrima* var. *flava* is a pure yellow form. There is also a form with purplish pink and yellow blossoms. Common names are dwarf poinciana, red bird-of-paradise, Barbados flower-fence, pride of Barbados, and peacock flower. Plates 85 and 365.

CALADIUM (ka-LAY-dee-um)
Araceae: The Calla Lily, Jack-in-the-Pulpit Family
CALADIUM
Tuberous-rooted, stemless plants; large, colorful, heart-shaped to lance-shaped leaves
Zones 9 through 11 as permanent landscape subjects; anywhere as annuals
Shade to partial shade (some new cultivars for sun)
Water lovers
Rich, humusy, moist, well-drained soil
Propagation by root division and rhizome division

These plants are so familiar they hardly need description, and there are too many cultivated varieties to list here. Almost all the showy varieties now in cultivation are derived from **Caladium bicolor,** which is native to areas of Venezuela and Colombia. Leaf shapes vary from almost orbicular to narrowly sagittate and leaf size varies from less than a foot long to over 2 feet. Among the many hybrids and cultivars is found every color except blue, although pink, red, and white with varying or no amounts of green predominate. The flowers are typical of the family but are not showy. Their formation takes from the tuberous root energy that is better used to make leaf growth. Therefore the flowers should be cut off, which tends to delay the onset of the dormant period.

The plants may be started from the tubers once the weather is warm and the soil temperatures remain above 60°F. This usually means daytime temperatures of at least 80°F and night temperatures no less than 60°F for several weeks. The roots should be planted about twice as deep as the greatest thickness of the tuber. The plants may also be purchased already leafed out and, as long as the soil is warm enough, may be planted out directly.

The plants have a dormant period and at some time in October or November the leaves usually start dying back and the plants stop producing them. This dormancy is not dependent on day length, but rather on the time since the tubers start producing leaves. In the tropics the gorgeous leaves can be had year-round with the proper planting dates. Gardeners in areas with hard freezes should lift the tubers, cut the fading leaves away, let the soil around the tubers dry and then shake it off, dust the tubers with sulfur or a fungicide, and store them in dry sawdust, excelsior, or completely dry sphagnum at no less than 55°F for the winter. In areas where the winters are relatively warm, the tubers are subject to rot if there is much rain and the soil drainage is poor, and even if the roots do not rot, the leaves are usually less vigorous the following season and do not last as long as those from stored or new tubers.

All the varieties grow in partial shade and many prefer near total shade, but there are new varieties with narrow leaves that can take full or nearly full sun. If the gardener is willing to water plants daily, the tubers of all varieties may be planted in soil as shallow as 3 or 4 inches. This fact makes caladiums one of the few groups of colorful plants that can go among the roots of large trees like oaks. The best fertilizer is fish emulsion once a month. Plate 86.

Caladium lindenii. See *Xanthosoma lindenii.*

CALATHEA

(kal-a-THEE-a / ka-LAY-thee-a)
Marantaceae: The Maranta Family
Common names vary according to species
Small clumping plants with short-stemmed rosettes
    of large, variegated, colorful leaves
Zones vary according to species
Shade to partial shade
Water lovers
Sandy, humusy, moist, well-drained soil
Propagation by root division, rhizome division, and
    transplanting of suckers

A large genus of about 300 species of clumping herbs in tropical America, mostly Brazil. Most species are similar to those of *Maranta* and, except for the trained botanist or gardener already familiar with them, some species are almost impossible to distinguish from species in that genus. *Calathea* species have large glossy, variegated leaves, often with a metallic sheen. All have three-lipped flowers (usually white to rose or yellow) in dense spikes, but most are insignificant in beauty compared to the leaves. Some of the world's most beautiful and most tropical looking leaves are to be found among these species. No plants give more dazzling yet subtle tropical color than these. All are tender to cold, but some are more tolerant of it than others. The soil should never dry out but, at the same time, the drainage must not be impeded in any way lest root rot occur.

Calathea bachemiana (bah-kem´-ee-AHN-ah) is native to tropical Brazil and is hardy in zones 10 and 11. It is a relatively small plant growing only to about 18 inches. The leaves are narrow and lance-shaped, about 10 inches long and 2 inches wide, and are a lovely silver with a dark green midrib, leaf margin, and main lateral veins; the undersides are purplish.

Calathea bella (BEL-la) (synonyms *C. kegeliana, Maranta kegeljanii*) is native to the rain forests of central Brazil and is hardy in zones 10 and 11. It grows to about 2 feet tall and has glossy foot-long, ovate to elliptic leaves that are 6 or 7 inches wide and borne on thin petioles about the same length. The leaves are silvery gray-green marked with darker green along the midvein and subsidiary parallel veins.

Calathea concinna (kahn-SIN-na) is indigenous to western Brazil and is not adaptable outside zones 10 and 11. It is a bushy clumping plant, growing to as much as 18 inches. The foot-long glossy leaves are a deep olive green with dark bluish green sickle-shaped irregular lateral stripings between the midrib and the leaf margin and with deep reddish purple undersides.

Calathea crotalifera (kro-ta-LIF-e-ra) is indigenous to southern Mexico, Central America, and south to Ecuador. It is a large-growing plant with large bright green leaves. The cordate leaves are held on 3-foot-long petioles and are as much as 2 feet long with a prominent midrib and gray-green undersides. The strange inflorescences arise directly from the ground and reach a height of 2 or 3 feet. The upper third or so bears disk-like, two-ranked bright yellow to orange-red bracts enclosing the tiny yellow flowers, the whole affair strongly reminding one of the rattles at the ends of a snake's tail. The scientific generic name of the rattlesnake is *Crotalaria*, which has been used for the specific epithet of this *Calathea* species to mean "like a rattlesnake." This species grows in zones 9b through 11.

Calathea insignis. See *C. lancifolia.*
Calathea kageliana. See *C. bella.*
Calathea lancifolia (lants-i-FO-lee-a) (synonyms *C. insignis, Maranta insignis*) is also native to Brazil, but is slightly more tolerant of cold than *C. bella* and may be hardy in zones 9b through 11. It is a striking species that grows to about 2 feet with stiff and erect 18- to 24-inch-long linear-lanceolate, wavy-margined leaves. The top of the leaves is olive green with a darker midrib and many dark green spots, while the undersides are a beautiful purplish red. This species is called rattlesnake plant because of the spotted leaves. It spreads slowly and makes a very fine tall groundcover.

Calathea makoyana (mak-o-YAHN-a) from Brazil is one of the loveliest foliage plants. It is called peacock plant because of the brilliant variegation and coloring of the leaf. The plant grows to about 2 feet. The broad-ovate leaves are about 8 inches long on 6-inch-long red petioles; their upper surfaces are olive green or yellowish green with a coppery green leaf margin, red midrib, and dark bronzy green areas along the lateral veins. The undersides of the leaves have the same pattern of markings as the upper surface, but the colors are a rich purplish red on the veins. The plants are tender to cold and are adaptable only to zones 10 and 11.

Calathea ornata (or-NAYT-a) is a wonderful large plant indigenous to tropical northern South America. Hardy in zones 10 and 11, it grows to 3 or even 5 feet in height and has long-petioled, 2-foot-long, ovate to elliptic leaves. The upper surface is dark green, marked with bright pink to orange-pink lines, while the undersurface is purplish red.

Calathea roseopicta (ro´-zee-o-PIK-ta) is a small but exquisite plant indigenous to tropical Brazil. It grows only to a foot or so in height with foot-long asymmetrical, wide-ovate leaves on short stalks. The blades are a deep dark green with a strong red or silvery midrib and a thin outline of red, silvery pink, or white near the margins above and a reddish purple color beneath. The plants are adaptable only to zones 10 and 11. Plate 87.

Calathea stromata (stro-MAHT-a) is native to Brazil and hardy in zones 10 and 11. It is a low growing, creeping plant, never more than a foot tall, with elegantly beautiful 6-inch-long oblong leaves. The upper surfaces are an icy silvery bluish green with alternating dark bluish green sickle-shaped markings along each side of the midrib. The undersides of the leaves are a deep wine red.

Calathea veitchiana (vee-chee-AHN-a) is indigenous to the rain forests of eastern Ecuador and northeastern Peru and is hardy in zones 10 and 11. It is a large plant, growing to 4 or more feet tall. The leaves are about a foot long, ovate to elliptic in shape, dark green with yellowish green feathery markings along and adjacent to the midrib, and a scalloped and feathery zone of pale green between the midrib and the margin; the undersurfaces of the leaves repeat the pattern with the substitution of purple-red for the areas of light green. This plant is called the peacock plant because of the intricate and very colorful variegation of the leaves.

Calathea warscewiczii (war-see-WIK-zee-eye) is a symphony of different shades of green. Native to Costa Rica, it is adaptable to zones 10 and 11. It is a large plant and a strong grower. The long-petioled leaves are a foot or more long, oblong-lanceolate in shape, dark green with a yellow-green midrib and light green feathering along the lateral veins out to a yellow-green thin leaf margin. The undersides of the leaves are a deep and vibrant purple-red. Plate 88.

Calathea zebrina (ze-BREEN-a) is indigenous to the Rio de Janeiro area of Brazil and is hardy in zones 10 and 11. It is the most beautiful species of the genus. The plant grows to more than 3 feet in height, and the immense elliptic 2- or 3-foot-long leaves make exceptionally bold statements with their deep, dark, almost black, green background color, yellowish green midrib and bands of olive green along the lateral veins. They are held on foot-long reddish purple petioles, and the undersides of the leaves are a brilliant purplish red. Alas, the plant is tender and adaptable only to zones 10 and 11. Plate 89.

CALLIANDRA (kal-lee-ANN-dra)
Mimosaceae (Fabaceae, Leguminosae), subfamily
  Mimosoideae: The Mimosa Family
POWDER PUFF; FLAME PLANT
Shrubs and small trees; lush, pinnate foliage; red and
  pink powder-puff-like flower clusters
Zones vary according to species
Sun
Average but regular amounts of moisture
Sandy, humusy, well-drained soil
Propagation by seed and cuttings

A large genus of about 200 species of evergreen shrubs and small trees in tropical America with bipinnate foliage and powder-puff-like red or pink flowers with tiny petals but very many long, brilliantly colored stamens. Most species are relatively drought tolerant.

Calliandra emarginata (ee-mar-ji-NAIT-a) (synonym *C. minima*) is native from southern Mexico into Honduras. It is a medium-sized, rather dense shrub that does not grow to more than 8 feet and is usually smaller in stature. The leaves are small for the genus and consist of only a pair of pinnae, each with three oblong and sickle-shaped leaflets that open pinkish bronze and soon turn dark green. The plant blooms year-round with raspberry-shaped red flower buds that open into 3-inch-wide pompons of scarlet all along the branches. It is ever-blooming with sun and the plant is covered in flowers. It blooms decently enough in partial shade under which condition it has a more open and graceful form. It is not as drought tolerant as some of the other *Calliandra* species and appreciates an adequate and regular water supply. It is dependably hardy in zones 9b through 11 and comes back in zone 9a. It carries the common name of dwarf powder puff. It is unexcelled for year-round show in warm winter areas. Plate 90.

Calliandra guildingii. See *Calliandra tweedii*.

Calliandra haematocephala (hee´-ma-toe-SEF-a-la) (synonym *C. inaequilatera*) is native to Bolivia. It is a large shrub or small tree growing to a maximum height of 20 feet and must be trained when young if a tree form is desired. The bipinnate leaves are quite lush and are about 8 inches long with many dark green 3-inch-long oblong, sickle-shaped leaflets that open coppery pink. The plant flowers in late autumn, winter, and spring with 6-inch-wide globular flower clusters of hundreds of great purplish red, raspberry-shaped buds, each one opening to reveal hundreds of scarlet 3-inch-long stamens. I do not know why the plants are called pink powderpuff as I have never seen a pink one, only vivid red; the name should be red powder puff. The plants are hardy only in zones 10 and 11, but usually come back in zone 9b. Plates 91 and 92.

Calliandra inaequilatera. See *C. haematocephala*.
Calliandra minima. See *C. emarginata*.

Calliandra surinamensis (soor´-i-na-MEN-sis) is native to Guyana, Surinam, and northern Brazil. It is a large, spreading shrub or a small widespreading tree in frost-free climes to 10 feet in height and as wide. The fine leaves are about 3 inches long with 8 to 12 pairs of half-inch-long leaflets. The fragrant flowers appear in late winter and spring and are a true pink in color. The species is hardy in zones 10 and 11, but usually comes back in zone 9b. It is sometimes called pink powder puff. Plate 93.

Calliandra tweedii (TWEED-ee-eye) (synonyms *C. guildingii, Inga pulcherrima*) is native to northern Brazil and is called Trinidad flame-bush or Brazilian flame-bush. This widespreading, open shrub to 10 feet or less has very fine, small leaflets that are quite airy and graceful in appearance. The stems are pliable, and the shrub's habit is sufficiently sprawling that it is sometimes trained as a vine or espalier to which function it is admirably suited. The 3- or 4-inch-wide flower clusters are scarlet and spherical, like the other *Calliandra* species, but are not as dense with stamens. The shrub blooms in spring, summer, and fall. It is dependably hardy in zones 10 and 11, but resprouts from the roots in zone 9b.

CALLISIA (kal-LIS-ee-a)
Commelinaceae: The Spiderwort Family
INCH PLANT
Succulent leaves in rosettes or along creeping stems;
    white fragrant flowers
Zones 10 and 11
Shade to partial shade
Average but regular amounts of moisture
Sandy, humusy, well-drained soil
Propagation by rhizome division, seed, and cuttings

A genus of 20 species of small succulent-leaved mostly creeping perennials in tropical America closely allied to *Tradescantia* (spiderwort). The species are often mistaken for *Tradescantia* species, and both genera have three-petaled flowers. Although *Callisia* species look like water-loving plants, most are rather drought tolerant when established.

Callisia elegans (EL-e-ganz) (synonyms *Setcreasea striata*, *Spironema elegans*) is indigenous to tropical Mexico and is, as its specific epithet indicates, elegant. It grows to about 2 feet tall with succulent and watery stems much reminiscent of the old-fashioned *Tradescantia* (spiderwort) species. The beautiful dark green leaves are arranged opposite each other in one plane, are ovate to broadly lanceolate, and are striped longitudinally above with silvery white lines and reddish purple beneath. The flowers are three-petaled and pure white.

Callisia fragrans (FRAY-granz) (synonyms *Spironema fragrans*, *Tradescantia dracaenoides*) is native to southwestern Mexico. The succulent-looking leaves are borne in rosettes resembling some of the small bromeliad species or of a *Rhoeo* (Moses-in-a-boat) species or a fanciful combination thereof. The leaves are a glossy medium green but take on a reddish purple hue in the sun, are a foot long and narrowly lanceolate to long-elliptic. The upper leaf surface exhibits a prominent and lighter-colored midrib. The plants have creeping rhizomes that send up suckers, which makes the species a very good tall groundcover in nearly frost-free regions. The plants thrive in full sun to partial shade. The rosettes occasionally produce curled spikes of white fragrant three-petaled flowers in the spring. *Callisia fragrans* **'Melnickoff'** has leaves beautifully striped with white or yellow.

CALOCARPUM. See *Pouteria*.

CALODENDRUM (kal-o-DEN-drum)
Rutaceae: The Citrus Family
CAPE CHESTNUT
Evergreen tree; glossy leaves; spectacular clusters of
    rose-colored flowers in summer
Zones 10 and 11
Sun
Water lover
Humusy, slightly acidic, moist, well-drained soil
Propagation by cuttings

A monotypic genus native to South Africa, Zambia, and Zimbabwe. *Calodendrum capense* (ka-PEN-say) slowly grows to 40 or sometimes 50 feet in height with a smooth gray bark and a spreading crown usually as wide as the tree is tall. The 6-inch-long bright glossy green leaves are long-elliptic in shape and usually somewhat upturned at their margins. The tree is deciduous in dry or cold winters. It is worth growing for the beautiful foliage alone, but the flower clusters are simply spectacular, making this tree one of the world's most spectacular when in flower. Each terminal cluster is dome-shaped to almost pyramidal, about a foot high and as wide, and consists of about a dozen 5-inch-wide fragrant flowers with narrow, recurved white to rose-colored petals, five long pink stamens, and five modified petal-like pink stamens with crimson dots. The seed capsules are interesting: a warty round dark brown nut that splits into five "petals," revealing 10 shiny black triangular-shaped seeds. While not a denizen of swampy areas, the tree must have an adequate and regular supply of water lest it die back. It sometimes survives in zone 9b for many years, but a severe freeze in this zone is bound to decimate it occasionally.

CALONYCTION. See *Ipomoea alba*.

CALOPHYLLUM (kal-o-FYL-lum)
Guttiferae (Clusiaceae): The Autograph Tree,
    Garcinia Family
Common names vary according to species
Large evergreen trees; large leathery, strongly veined
    leaves
Zones vary according to species
Sun
Average but regular amounts of moisture
Humusy, well-drained soil
Propagation by seed

A genus of about 180 species of mostly large trees in tropical areas of Asia and America. The leaves are invariably large and leathery with strong midribs and lateral veins. The flowers are small and most often visually insignificant in the landscape but often quite fragrant. The two species described below are tolerant of both salty air and saline soil.

Calophyllum antillanum. See *C. brasiliense*.

Calophyllum brasiliense (bra-zil´-ee-ENS-ee) (synonym *C. antillanum*) is indigenous to the West Indies, parts of Mexico, and northern South America. The tree grows to a height of 40 or maybe 50 feet in cultivation (taller in nature) with a dense, rounded, dark green crown. The beautiful glossy dark green leaves, which are reminiscent of those of *Magnolia grandiflora*, are elliptic, somewhat notched on the ends, and to 8 inches long with light green midribs and lateral veins. The white flowers usually appear in the spring in small loose-flowered racemes and have a spicy orange-blossom aroma. The attractive fruits are perfectly spherical and yellowish green. The tree is very adaptable and easy to grow in locations where hard frosts do not occur and is mostly dependable in zones 10 and 11, although it is sometimes damaged in zone 10a. It is sometimes referred to as Brazilian beautyleaf or Santa Maria.

Calophyllum inophyllum (in-o-FYL-lum) is indigenous to southern India through Malaysia. It is similar in form and dimensions to *C. brasiliense*, but is even bolder and more attractive with slightly larger leaves and flowers. It is also slightly less hardy to cold and is adaptable only to zones 10b and 11. It is often called Indian laurel or mastwood. The glossy and leathery dark green leaves are as much as 8 inches long with a yellow midrib and light green lateral veins. The tree blooms in the summer with 8-inch-long racemes of intensely fragrant white flowers. The fruit is similar to that of *C. brasiliense*. Plate 94.

CALOTROPIS (kal-o-TRO-pis)
Asclepiadaceae: The Milkweed, Madagascar Jasmine
    Family
GIANT MILKWEED
Shrubs and soft-wooded small trees; large, felty
    leaves; unusual flowers; milky sap
Zones 10 and 11 as small trees; zone 9b as shrubs
Sun
Drought tolerant
Sandy, humusy, well-drained soil
Propagation by seed and cuttings

About six species of shrubs and small trees in tropical Africa, the Middle East, India, and Malaysia, all with soft, fibrous wood and milky latexlike sap. All species have large, usually pubescent, succulent, strongly veined leaves, which mostly lack petioles and clasp the stems at the leaf bases. The flowers are typical of the family: wheel-shaped, with a five-parted corolla, and a corona of stamens and stigmas. Because of the coronal flowers, the plants are sometimes called crown flower. The species bloom off and on most of the year. Many people are allergic to the milky sap of the two species described below.

Calotropis gigantea (jy-GAN-tee-a) is found from Iran eastward through India and into southern China. A large shrub or small tree (it will probably have to be trained as such), it is a strikingly beautiful curiosity suitable for a specimen plant in a rock garden, cactus garden, or dry, sunny border. It also makes a fine hedge plant. It grows to about 15 feet, but is usually somewhat smaller. The younger branches have a bluish white glaucous and waxy bloom, while the older branches and trunk become woody with thick corky bark. The leaves are about 8 inches long and are obovate to almost deltoid in shape. They are succulent looking and grayish green in color with prominent yellowish veins, and are covered, especially underneath, with a white fuzz. The lavender or waxy-white flowers are also succulent looking with five reflexed and slightly twisted divisions to

the corolla and a plump, five-angled corona consisting of fused anthers and stigma. The fruit is a swollen dry pod that opens to reveal many seeds covered in white silky fibers. The species has very many human uses in its native habitats including medicinal preparations and cordage. It is associated with the god Shiva by the Hindus of India, and the flowers are made into leis by the Hawaiian peoples and are a favorite of the monarch butterfly.

Calotropis procera (PRO-se-ra / pro-SER-a) has an even wider natural range than does *C. gigantea*, and includes tropical East Africa. It is just as beautiful as the former species, but is slightly smaller in stature. It is best used as a shrub and even then usually needs to be pruned to keep it from becoming leggy. The light green, strongly veined leaves are oblong to elliptic and about 8 inches long. The flowers are even more attractive than are those of the preceding species. The corolla segments are not reflexed nor twisted, but rather form a cup and are thick, succulent, and white with purple tips. The flowers are much beloved of butterflies.

CALYCOPHYLLUM.
See *Warszewiczia*.

CALYPTRANTHES
    (kal-ip-TRANTH-eez)
Myrtaceae: The Myrtle, Eucalyptus Family
SPICEWOOD; PALE LID-FLOWER; MYRTLE-
    OF-THE-RIVER
Evergreen shrubs and small trees; tough, glossy, dark
    green leaves; small berries
Zones 10 and 11; marginal in zone 10a
Sun
Average but regular amounts of moisture
Sandy, humusy, well-drained soil
Propagation by seed

A large genus of about 100 species of small trees and shrubs in tropical America with oppositely arranged entire leaves, small clusters of petal-less flowers with many long stamens and flower buds with lids. Only two species are presently in cultivation outside botanical gardens. The genus name is sometimes erroneously spelled "Calythranthes."

Calyptranthes pallens (PAL-lenz) is indigenous to extreme southern Florida, the Florida Keys, the West Indies, Mexico, and Guatemala. It is naturally a shrub, but sometimes can attain tree form (if so trained) and a height of 20 feet. The entire tree is aromatic, especially the leaves, resulting in one of the vernacular names of spicewood. Another common name is pale lid-flower from the shape of the flower buds. The leathery and dark green leaves are about 3 inches long, elliptical in shape, and tapering at the ends; they somewhat resemble those of *Camellia sinensis* and are a beautiful rosy pink when new. The greenish white flowers do not resemble camellias, but are very typical of the family Myrtaceae: they are tiny, in clusters from the leaf axils and without petals, have many relatively long stamens, and appear mainly in summer. The flower buds are topped by a circular caplike feature whose lid flips back upon efflorescence to release the stamens. The fruits are berries and are red aging to black or dark purple. This most attractive shrub or small tree has been successfully used for some years as hedge material.

Calyptranthes zuzygium (zoo-ZIJ-ee-um) occurs naturally in extreme southern Florida, the Bahamas, eastern Mexico, and most of Central America. It is similar to *C. pallens*, but usually makes a larger shrub or tree to as much as 30 feet in height. In addition, the leaves are slightly smaller, almost stalkless, and not as shiny, and their midveins are stronger. The flower clusters are usually not as large as those of *C. pallens*, but the flowers are similar, as is the fruit.

CALYTHRANTHES.
See *Calyptranthes*.

CAMPHORA. See *Cinnamomum camphora*.

CAMPSIS (CAMP-sis)
Bignoniaceae: The Catalpa, Jacaranda, Trumpet-
    Vine Family
TRUMPET VINE; TRUMPET CREEPER
Large deciduous woody vines; aerial roots; pinnate
    leaves; large trumpet-shaped flowers
Zones vary according to species
Sun
Average but regular amounts of moisture
Humusy, well-drained soil
Propagation by seed and cuttings; root divisions of
    mature plants

A genus of two species. Both are large-growing, deciduous, woody vines that climb by aerial rootlets. They have spectacular red, yellow, or orange trumpet-shaped flowers in summer, followed by long, thin pods full of seeds. Both species need sun to produce all the bloom of which they are capable, and they very much appreciate a rich, humusy soil. Although somewhat drought tolerant when established, they nevertheless are more satisfactory with an adequate supply of water. Like most vines that grow to the tops of forest trees, both species like to have their heads in the full sun with their bases and their roots cool and protected by shade.

Campsis chinensis. See *C. grandiflora*.

Campsis grandiflora (gran-di-FLOR-a) (synonyms *Bignonia chinensis*, *B. grandiflora*, *Campsis chinensis*, *Tecoma chinensis*, *T. grandiflora*) is native to east-central China and is hardy in zones 8 through 11. It is a strong-growing vine that can reach a maximum height of 30 feet. It does not support itself well when young and needs a structure like a lattice upon which to climb. It also usually needs some guidance, such as tying the pliable branches to the structure, until it is old enough

to form strong aerial rootlets. The leaves are about a foot long and are composed of seven to nine dark green ovate to lanceolate toothed leaflets that are 2 to 3 inches long. The large and spectacular flowers are long, flaring scarlet trumpets 3 or 4 inches wide at their mouths, and are produced from midsummer into the fall.

Campsis radicans (RAY-di-kanz) (synonyms *Bignonia radicans*, *Tecoma radicans*) is native to a large area of the eastern United States. Very hardy to cold, it grows in zones 6 through 11. This very large and rampant-growing vine freely suckers. As a result it should not be planted where its invasive habit will cause problems; it is best used as a large landscape subject in outlying areas. It differs from *C. grandiflora* in the following five ways: it is a much larger vine, to 50 feet or more in height, and climbs all but the tallest trees; the leaves are slightly larger with 7 to 11 leaflets; the flowers are smaller, usually only about 2 inches wide; the vine flowers for a longer period, from late spring through summer and into the fall; and the flower color is more orange-red than pure red. *Campsis radicans* 'Flava', the most outstanding of the several cultivars, has pure deep yellow flowers. *Campsis radicans* 'Praecox' has deeper-colored and redder flowers than does the species.

Campsis ×tagliabuana (tahl-ya-boo-AHN-a) is a hybrid cross between the above two species. *Campsis ×tagliabuana* 'Madame Galen' is usually the only available form of this hybrid. It combines the traits of both its parents into a less aggressively growing vine that makes many fewer suckers and is more controlled and amenable to close-up planting. In addition, it is more freely flowering than is *C. grandiflora*, the flowers are larger than those of *C. radicans*, and the color is a deep salmon. It grows to a height of 30 feet or more and is hardy in zones 7 through 11.

CANANGA (ka-NAYN-ga)
Annonaceae: The Cherimoya Family
YLANG-YLANG; ILANG-ILANG (EE-lahng);
    PERFUME TREE
Large evergreen tree of straight trunk, pendent
    branches; very fragrant yellow flowers
Zones 10b and 11
Sun
Average but regular amounts of moisture
Sandy, humusy, well-drained soil
Propagation by seed; cuttings are sometimes
    successful

There are only two species in this genus of trees, and only one is commonly planted outside botanical gardens. *Cananga odorata* (o-doe-RAYT-a) (synonym *Canangium odoratum*) is indigenous to Myanmar (Burma), Malaysia, the Philippines, and northern Australia. In its native habitat it grows quickly into a rather narrow-headed tree to 75 feet or more with an unusually straight trunk, but in cultivation it is rarely over 50 feet or so in height and is sometimes grown as a large shrub with constant pruning, since the tree blooms when young and on new growth. The bright green glossy leaves are oblong, long-acuminate, 10 or more inches long, and about 3 inches wide with ridges along the lateral veins; they are usually somewhat drooping, especially in the heat of midday. The branches, being long and slender, also tend to droop, which gives a quite picturesque "weeping" habit to the entire tree. The flowers are exceptional not because they are showy and certainly not because they make a spectacular display from any distance, but because of their sweet, penetrating fragrance that lets one know without seeing the tree that it is not too far away. They are to this day used in the fine perfume industry. The flowers have six narrow and somewhat twisted, drooping, 3- or 4-inch-long succulent petals (actually three sepals and three petals) that open green but soon change to pure yellow or greenish yellow or orange. The tree blooms sporadically throughout the year but heaviest in late autumn in southern Florida which, alas, is the only venue in the continental United States where it is hardy. The tree blooms when quite young. Each blossom produces a syncarp of inch-long plumlike green fruits in the form of a pin cushion, which mature to a decidedly black hue. The only disadvantage to the tree is that the slender and pendulous branches are brittle and easily break in strong winds. Plates 95 and 96.

CANANGIUM. See *Cananga*.

CANAVALIA (kan-a-VAL-ee-a)
Papilionaceae (Fabaceae, Leguminosae), subfamily
    Papilionoideae: The Bean, Pea Family
BEACH BEAN; BAY BEAN; SWORDBEAN
Creeping, spreading vine; three-part compound
    leaves; red stems; purple and pink pealike flowers
Zones 10 and 11
Sun
Drought tolerant
Average or poor soil
Propagation by seed

A genus of 50 or so species of vines throughout the tropics. Several species are cultivated mostly for cattle feed and are not particularly attractive. One is quite useful for seaside plantings and erosion control and is rather attractive and definitely tropical looking. *Canavalia maritima* (ma-RIT-i-ma) (synonym *C. obtusifolia*) is so widespread on tropical seacoasts that its original habitat is uncertain; it is probably in Polynesia. The leaves are pinnate with only three rather large 4- or 5-inch-long leaflets that are light green, elliptic to oblong, tough, and leathery, with deep and prominent midrib and lateral veins. The flowers appear in few-flowered erect clusters held well above the leaves and are dark pink to purple. The plant blooms in cycles year-round. It is unexcelled for helping to bind seaside dunes or any other site that has full sun, poor soil, and drought con-

ditions. It is capable of being content with average or more-than-average but regular amounts of moisture as long as the soil has perfect drainage and the plant is in full sun. It climbs to some extent.

CANELLA (ka-NEL-la)
Canellaceae: The Canella Family
WILD CINNAMON; PEPPER CINNAMON;
    WHITE CINNAMON; CANEEL
Evergreen aromatic tree; lustrous leaves; clusters of
    white, red, and purple flowers; attractive fruit
Zones 10 and 11; marginal in zone 10a
Sun
Drought tolerant
Sandy, well-drained soil
Propagation by seed

A monotypic genus native to southern Florida and the West Indies. *Canella winterana* (win-tur-AHN-a) (synonyms *C. alba*, *Winterana canella*) is a very beautiful large shrub or small tree, depending on how much water it receives. It grows slowly to as much as 40 feet and, in spite of its mainly windswept native habitat, usually has a rather straight trunk whose inner bark has a cinnamon or clove fragrance. This bark has been used commercially as a substitute for cinnamon and as an additive in adulterated spice mixtures and pipe tobacco; the outer bark is poisonous and has been used as an insecticide. The light green leaves are also poisonous; they are leathery but lustrous, elliptic to ovate or obovate or even spatulate, and 4 or 5 inches long, and are found clustered near the ends of the branches, giving a picturesque appearance to the tree. The flowers appear in terminal clusters year-round but most abundantly in the winter. They are less than an inch wide but nevertheless beautiful; the five white to red to purple petals are cup-shaped with bright yellow anthers in the middle of the cup. The aromatic berries resulting from the flowers are also quite attractive, being a quarter-inch wide and a bright red in color. It is suggested that, in spite of the many uses of the berries and inner bark, the gardener eschew ingestion of any part of the plant as there is a fine line between inner and outer bark as well as between fruit and stem. There is hardly a more attractive tree or shrub native to the state of Florida, and its ornamental value is outstanding and most highly recommended. Plate 97.

CANISTRUM (ka-NIS-trum)
Bromeliaceae: The Pineapple, Bromeliad Family
No known English common name
Large rosettes of thick spiny-margined leaves; starlike
    flower clusters
Zones 10 and 11
Shade to partial shade
Water lovers
Leaf mold or epiphytic soil mix
Propagation by transplanting of suckers and by seed

A genus of six bromeliad species in northern Brazil and the island of Trinidad. Technically epiphytic plants, they are never found at great heights but rather near the ground on tree trunks and rocks in shady and moist conditions. All species are relatively large plants, usually 2 or 3 feet in height and often of even greater girth. The inflorescences are somewhat unusual in that they are short, compact, and subtended and surrounded by large, colorful bracts that are longer than the flower spikes, giving the impression of a flower spike in a basket or of a single large flower with large petals and a dense center. "Canistrum" is Latin for "basket." None of the species can tolerate much cold.

Canistrum aurantiacum (aw-ran-TY-a-kum) is native to Brazil. It can be grown either as an epiphyte or as a terrestrial. The spiny-margined leaves are about 2 feet long, erect but gracefully recurved at the tips, and apple green in color with darker green blotches. The inflorescence is a foot high with orange-red bracts and a dense, compact head of orange-yellow flowers.

Canistrum fosterianum (fahs-ter´-ee-AHN-um) is native to Brazil. It forms a tubular vase-shaped rosette with 3-inch-wide by 2-foot-long spiny-margined, gray green or olive green leaves with brown splotches and stripes. The inflorescence has pink bracts and white flowers and looks something like a big old-fashioned pink rose.

Canistrum lindenii (lin-DEN-ee-eye) is a beautiful plant native to northern Brazil. The size of the plant and the form and color of the inflorescence are very variable. *Canistrum lindenii* **var.** *lindenii* is a large-spreading rosette that is 3 or more feet wide with broad waxy light green leaves flecked with dark green. The inflorescence has white bracts and greenish white flowers. *Canistrum lindenii* **var.** *roseum* (ROE-zee-um) is a larger variety with darker leaves whose undersides are pink. The inflorescence has pinkish red bracts and green and white flowers, a superbly beautiful combination of colors.

CARICA (KAIR-i-ka / ka-REEK-a)
Caricaceae: The Papaya Family
PAPAYA; PAWPAW
Tall herbaceous plants; large divided leaves atop
    palmlike trunk; large showy fruit
Zones 10b and 11; often grown as a foliage annual in
    long-season climates
Sun
Water lovers
Sandy, humusy, moist, well-drained soil
Propagation by seed

A genus of perhaps 25 species in tropical America. They are soft-wooded small trees with large deeply lobed leaves growing atop the trunks. Only one species is commonly planted in areas with hot summers. They are among the most tropical looking plants on earth, and they are often grown in zone 9b and even zone 9a as tender perennials or annuals for this effect.

Carica papaya (pa-PAH-ya) is now found throughout the tropics and has been so long in cultivation that its exact point of origin is obscure but is probably Central America. It is usually a single-trunked herbaceous "tree" growing very quickly to as much as 20 or more feet in height. The large, much-divided dark green leaves (somewhat similar to those of *Philodendron selloum* or *Artocarpus* species) arise in a spiral from the top of the trunk. Damage to the trunk often results in multiple stems. With age and size the light-colored trunks become softly woody near the base and usually have faint to prominent rings of leaf scars. The leaves are variable, but usually almost orbicular or ovate in outline. They are usually about 2 feet wide, but may be almost 3 feet wide and as long if ovate. There are usually five to seven deep lobes (sometimes cut almost to the petiole) to each leaf with strong and prominent lighter colored midribs to each lobe and lighter colored lateral veins. The flowers appear year-round and are small and greenish yellow in color and not especially showy. The plants naturally produce male and female flowers on separate trees, but there are now cultivars with bisexual or only female blossoms. The fruits are small to large, round to pear-shaped, green when young but maturing to yellow-green or yellow to orange; they can be from 3 or 4 inches in width or length to as much as a foot or more long and weigh from 8 ounces to 20 pounds, always with many small black seeds in the center of the fruit. Female plants produce round fruit if a male plant is nearby, while the bisexual plants make pyriform fruit. Papaya plants are almost completely frost intolerant and are damaged by any temperature below freezing, but they are such fast growers that they are often planted for their habit and foliage in zone 9 (and sometimes in even colder zones) in early spring as annuals. New varieties are now appearing that flower and fruit much sooner than the species. The plants love moisture, but at the same time must have excellent drainage; prolonged flooding kills them. Plate 98.

CARISSA (ka-RIS-sa)
Apocynaceae: The Oleander, Frangipani, Vinca
    Family
Common names vary according to species
Large evergreen spiny shrubs; glossy dark green
    leaves; white fragrant flowers; red fruit
Zones vary according to species
Sun
Drought tolerant
Sandy, well-drained soil
Propagation by seed and cuttings

A genus of about 36 species of large shrubs and small trees in tropical Africa, Asia, and India, almost all of which have leathery leaves, spines, milky sap, fragrant flowers, and edible leathery fruit.

Carissa carandas (ka-RAN-das) is native to India, Sri Lanka, Myanmar (Burma), and western Indonesia, and is sometimes called karanda. It is a straggly, spreading, half-climbing large shrub to 15 feet in height that may be trained to a small weeping tree form. The variable leaves are narrowly lanceolate to oblong or even ovate, dark green, leathery and glossy on the upper surface, and lighter green and dull beneath. The shrub has pairs of 2-inch-long sharp spines in most leaf axils. The fragrant white five-petaled flowers appear all spring and summer in terminal clusters of 2 to 12. Each blossom is tubular with flaring ends that form a star. The small half-inch-wide edible fruits are red or black when mature and contain a sweetly acid pulp. The plants are beautiful when in bloom and very useful for planting in dry, sunny, sandy sites with poor soil, although they grow lush in average good soil with regular amounts of moisture. Like its cousin *C. macrocarpa*, this species makes an outstanding hedge if kept pruned. It is hardy in zones 10 and 11 and somewhat marginal in zone 10a.

Carissa edulis (ED-yoo-lis) is native to tropical East Africa. It is similar to *C. carandas* but with the following four differences: the plant grows larger, to 30 feet; the leaves are never more than 2 inches long; the plant is not as thorny; and the flower buds are pink or wine colored. It has the same cultural requirements as *C. carandas.*

Carissa grandiflora. See *C. macrocarpa.*

Carissa macrocarpa (mak-ro-KARP-a) (synonym *C. grandiflora*) is indigenous to northern South Africa and is called the Natal plum. It can grow to 20 feet in frost-free regions and can be trained into a very beautiful small tree. It is hardy in zones 10 and 11 and returns from frosts in zone 9b. The branches and the ends of the twigs have forked spines an inch or more long. The shiny, dark green leaves are ovate and acuminate to 3 or 4 inches long. The five-petaled, starlike flowers are white, succulent, and 2 or more inches wide; they are also deliciously fragrant with the aroma of orange blossoms, especially at night. The fruit is a plum-shaped scarlet berry about 2 inches long; it is edible, with the taste of sweet cranberries. The plants bloom nearly year-round, and therefore flowers and fruit are to be found simultaneously on the plant in most seasons. There is no better plant for screening purposes: the shrub is not only beautiful, but also dense (when grown in full sun) and, because of the thorns, an effective barrier. It is also very tolerant of salty air and saline soil and is a perfect beach plant. There are dwarf cultivars that grow no more than a foot or so in height, low and creeping forms that are perfect for groundcover, and thornless varieties. Some cultivars combine both lowly stature and lack of thorns. As with most good things there are drawbacks; all the cultivars are prone to making growth that reverts to the species characteristics, and they usually require a certain amount of pruning to keep the cultivar from totally reverting. They are generally worth the trouble though, as they are so good looking and useful. In fact, the unadulterated species is now harder to find than one or more of the many cultivars. It, too, is worth searching for; nothing is better or more attractive for a hedge in hot, dry or saline sites. Plate 99.

CARLUDOVICA (kar-loo-DOE-vi-ka)
Cyclanthaceae: The Panama-Hat Plant Family
PANAMA-HAT PLANT; PANAMA-HAT PALM
Large, stemless, long-petioled palmate-leaved
  perennials
Zone 11; marginal in zone 10b
Shade to partial shade
Water lover
Humusy, moist, well-drained soil
Propagation by root division and seed

Of the three species in this tropical American genus, only one is commonly planted in far southern Florida and other tropical or nearly tropical regions. *Carludovica palmata* (pahl-MAIT-a / pahl-MAHT-a), called the Panama-hat palm, is native to low, warm, wet sites from Central America down through South America to Bolivia. The leaves are 3 or more feet wide and arise from the ground on 6-foot-long petioles; they are divided into three to five large segments, each of which is further (but more shallowly) cleft into several pendent segments. The inflorescences are somewhat like those of most palms: small and many-flowered with large spathes. These are very beautiful plants, similar to the trunkless palmetto palms of the southern United States but much more delicate and more lush appearing. Few plants are more tropical looking. Alas, they are very tender to cold and impossible to grow year-round outside tropical regions. Plate 100.

CARMONA. See *Ehretia microphylla.*

CARNEGIEA
  (kar-NAY-gee-a / kar-nay-GEE-a)
Cactaceae: The Cactus Family
SAGUARO CACTUS; SAHUARO
Immense ribbed cactus trees with multiple "arms"
  and nocturnal white flowers
Zones 9b through 11
Sun
Drought tolerant
Sandy, humusy, well-drained soil
Propagation by seed

A monotypic genus in the Sonoran desert of southern Arizona and northwestern Mexico. *Carnegiea gigantea* is familiar enough to almost everyone as to hardly need description. It is one of the most precious and picturesque things in nature. Old plants can attain a height of 60 feet or sometimes more, and their wonderful pleated and ribbed spiny columns take on the universal appeal when the plants are old enough to form those characteristic great ascending arms. These colossal forms bloom in spring with circular rows of fleshy white flower disks around the tops of the columns. Each disk surrounds a central mass of golden stamens and stigma. The flowers open at night and close during the heat of the day. The scarlet egg-shaped fruits mature in late summer and are relished for their sweet but seedy pulp by all sorts of animals including humans.

The cactus is very slow-growing, and up until the age of 50 years or later the plants are usually unbranched. This makes armed specimens extremely expensive and in great demand. Many plants are "rustled" out of the wild. This would not be so catastrophic if the plants were fast growing and reproduced in their native habitat. They do not reproduce in the wild because the wolves, mountain lions, and other primary predator populations have been decimated due to urban expansion, hunting, development, and agricultural interests, which in turn has allowed the rodent population to explode in these areas. Since the sahuaro fruit and seeds are relished by rodents, they are usually eaten before they can germinate. The gardener should never purchase a branched *Carnegiea* species! None can have come from a "cactus farm"; and those that do usually have a tag indicating that they were grown commercially from seed; if in doubt demand to see proof. Some old and branched specimens are collected "legally," but these are rare and extremely costly, and purchasing them only encourages more of them to be taken. Get a seedling a foot or so in height and enjoy its magnificence even at that size with the knowledge that at least some of the older plants are still there for future generations to see. Plant the Sahuaro in full sun in a raised cactus garden. It will not usually survive temperatures below 20°F. Plates 101 and 296.

CARPENTARIA (karp-en-TAHR-ee-a)
Palmae (Arecaceae): The Palm Family
CARPENTARIA PALM
Tall thin-trunked elegant, fast-growing feather palm
Zones 10b and 11
Sun
Water lover
Sandy, humusy, moist, well-drained soil
Propagation by seed

A monotypic palm genus found only in the tropical rain forests of northeastern Australia. *Carpentaria acuminata* (a-kyoo´-mi-NAIT-a) (synonym *Kentia acuminata*) is of exceptional beauty with its single thin, very graceful trunk and emerald green arching leaves arising from the long, smooth and shiny green crownshaft. The trunks can attain 40 feet or more of height and are almost white in some trees, a dark beige in others, with faintly ringed or almost completely smooth trunks. The leaves are on short petioles and are deep green on top but have a distinctly bluish cast beneath. They are 6 feet long or sometimes longer, strongly arched, and concave in cross section due to the leaflets springing from the rachis at an angle. The flower clusters appear all year in cycles from the base of the crownshaft. The flowers are greenish white, and the subsequent fruits mature to a bright red. The palms are true water lovers; they will not perform well and will even die from lack of adequate irrigation. They are impossi-

ble to grow outside the frost-free or nearly frost-free areas and are often damaged (even killed) in zone 10a. The tree is extremely fast growing for a palm species.

CARYOTA (kair-ee-OAT-a)
Palmae (Arecaceae): The Palm Family
FISHTAIL PALMS
Single or clustering trunked palms; dense, large, bipinnate foliage
Zones 10b and 11
Sun
Average but regular amounts of moisture
Humusy, well-drained soil
Propagation by seed and (for multitrunked species) transplanting of suckers

A small genus of about 12 species of bipinnate-leaved palms from the tropical parts of Asia. It is the only palm genus with bipinnate leaves. All species produce stems (trunks) that die after flowering. The dead stems are not a landscape problem with the clustering types, since new trunks are constantly being produced to replace the flowered stems, but they may be a problem with the single-trunked species. It should also be noted that, when flowering, the trunks produce many inflorescences starting from the top of the stem and progressing downwards to the bottom leaf axil, and this process may take several years to come to fruition. All species have large leaves with many leaflets, which are usually deltoid in shape with jagged ends. All species have fruit with oxalic acid crystals, which are irritating to the skin and mucous membranes; thus, wear gloves when handling these fruits. Nothing else quite matches the superlative effect of these palms in the landscape if they are placed well. All are tender and impossible to grow outside zones 10 and 11, although small protected specimens of *C. mitis* are to be found in zone 9b, where they are temporary landscape subjects.

Caryota mitis (MY-tis) is a clustering species from Myanmar (Burma), Indonesia, and the Philippines. It is the most commonly planted species and grows to a maximum height of 25 feet in cultivation. The palm makes a giant shrub unless the trunks are thinned, as the constant suckering habit insures that there will be foliage from top to bottom of a clump. Either form, thinned or natural, is spectacularly beautiful. The clumps are usually no more than 6 feet wide. The leaves are 10-foot-long giant triangles in outline, but the leaf outline is seldom apparent unless the trunks are thinned.

Caryota rumphiana (rump-fee-AHN-a) occurs naturally in Southeast Asia, Malaysia, Indonesia, and northern Australia. It is one of the world's most sumptuously beautiful and exotic trees, palm or otherwise. The solitary trunk grows to as much as 60 feet, often more, and is usually bulging in its middle with the great 20-foot-long bipinnate leaves forming an elongated, massive, and fantastically beautiful crown. The tree is very fast growing for a palm species, and its only fault is that it dies after flowering and fruiting. It is sometimes called the giant fishtail palm.

Caryota urens (YOO-renz) is native to India, Sri Lanka, and Malaya. It is a single-trunked species growing to a height of 30 feet or more in cultivation, with a ringed, robust, and thick trunk to 2 feet in diameter. The crown is elongated so that there are many large (to 12 or more feet long) leaves sort of in layers for an extended length of the trunk and not just a ring of leaves at the top of the trunk as in most other palms. This palm is an almost startlingly beautiful sight in the landscape. It is sometimes called toddy palm or jaggery palm as native peoples use the sugary sap to make an alcoholic beverage.

CASASIA (ka-SAY-zee-a / ka-SAY-zhya)
Rubiaceae: The Coffee, Gardenia, Ixora Family
SEVEN-YEAR APPLE
Evergreen shrub resembling *Pittosporum;* white
    flowers; small yellow fruit
Zones 10 and 11; somewhat marginal in zone 10a
Sun
Drought tolerant
Sandy, well-drained soil
Propagation by seed

A genus of about 10 species of shrubs and small trees in southern Florida, Mexico, and the Caribbean region. They have large oppositely arranged leathery leaves and clusters of tubular flowers with five flaring corolla lobes. Some taxonomists combine this genus with *Genipa.* Only one species is at present commonly planted if the genus is considered separate from *Genipa.* ***Casasia clusiifolia*** (kloo´-see-eye-FO-lee-a) (synonym *Genipa clusiifolia*) is found in Bermuda, southern Florida, the Bahamas, and the West Indies. It grows into a spreading shrub to about 12 feet in height. The bright green 6-inch-long coriaceous oblong to obovate leaves are clustered near the ends of the branches and have prominent and lighter colored midribs. The flowers are truly beautiful: 2-inch-wide very fragrant stars that appear in spring and early summer. The fruits are ovoid, plum-shaped, and about 3 inches long, and change in color from green to gold to almost black at maturity. They are relished by wildlife and are sometimes eaten by humans, and reportedly have an insipid licorice-like flavor. The shrub is one of the finest and most beautiful for seaside plantings as it is drought tolerant and flourishes in salty air and saline soil.

CASIMIROA (ka-sim´-i-RO-a)
Rutaceae: The Citrus Family
WHITE SAPOTE
Evergreen tree; large, shiny, palmate leaves; round
    yellow fruit
Zones 9b through 11
Sun
Average but regular amounts of moisture

Sandy, humusy, well-drained soil
Propagation by seed and air-layering

A genus of about six species of shrubs and trees native to elevated sites in Mexico and Central America. They all have palmately compound leaves, small flowers in terminal or axillary clusters, and large berrylike fruit. One species is planted in subtropical regions for its beautiful leaves and its fruit. ***Casimiroa edulis*** (ED-yoo-lis) is a very ornamental tree, growing from 20 to 50 feet in height with a picturesque slightly contorted trunk that has light gray, thick and warty bark with many conspicuous lenticels and long, drooping branches. The leaves are palmately compound to 6 inches long and 8 inches wide. The leaflets vary in number from three to seven; each one is elliptic to ovate in shape, dark green above, lighter and pubescent beneath, and as much as 6 inches long. The tree blooms in midwinter on new wood. The small, unspectacular yellow-green flowers are borne in loose terminal or axillary panicles. The large, ornamental fruit matures from early summer to autumn, is round to ovoid, and is green until mature at which point it turns yellow to golden; it is edible and sweet and should be picked while still green and allowed to mature in a cool dry environment off the tree. Because it is native to highland areas in the tropics, the species is not the best for fruit production in hot summer areas. In fact, it dislikes heat and humidity, preferring winters that are dry and cool but not cold. It is eminently worth growing for its ornamental qualities alone. The tree is hardy to the upper or even mid 20s when established and is sometimes grown in zone 9a as a large shrub. The plants should be tip pruned when young to induce branching lest the tree develop a narrow and unnaturally linear crown.

CASSIA (KAS-ee-a / KASH-ya)
Caesalpiniaceae (Leguminosae), subfamily
    Caesalpinioideae: The Cassia, Royal Poinciana
    Family
CASSIA; SENNA; SHOWER TREES
Large shrubs or small trees; large compound leaves;
    large yellow or pink flowers
Zones vary according to species
Sun
Average but regular amounts of moisture
Sandy, humusy, well-drained soil
Propagation by seed and cuttings

A large genus of more than 500 species of herbs, shrubs, and trees in tropical areas around the world. All have even-pinnate foliage and five-petaled, large-stamened flowers either spreading or cup-shaped, usually in clusters. All need some sun to bloom well and well-drained soil. Most are fast-growing shrubs or trees; some grow very fast. Within the genus are found some of the world's most spectacular flowering landscape subjects. Some of the species (usually the more herbaceous ones) have a rather rank odor to the leaves, which some people find objectionable; others find the odor not that displeasing but rather very "plantlike." There is much discrepancy in reference materials regarding this genus; some authors put most species into the genus *Senna* which, by most authorities, is now considered an invalid name. Adding to the confusion is the nature of the individual species to freely hybridize and thus provide a spectrum of characteristics adherent to many of them.

Cassia alata (a-LAIT-a) (synonym *Senna alata*) is indigenous to tropical America. It grows very fast to 15 feet or more if not frozen back, and it is not deciduous (at least in warm winters) as some sources suggest. In wet and completely tropical regions it is a 30-foot tree. It should be tip-pinched when young to encourage a spreading habit lest it become a very tall and slender thing that high winds topple because of its great leaves. The leaves are glorious enough to warrant cultivation of the plant for their sake alone. The 2- to 3-inch-long dark green oblong to obovate leaflets are arranged in 6 to 20 opposite pairs on rachises as much as 3 feet long. At dusk or when bruised the leaflets close up tight against their oppositely arranged partners. The flower spikes are spectacular, 2 or more feet tall, and composed of large bright yellow cup-shaped flowers that open from the bottom up and occasion the common name of candlestick plant. It is also sometimes called ringworm cassia because concoctions of the leaves have been used to treat that condition. In spite of what some sources indicate, the plant blooms at any time of year if it is large enough and the weather is warm enough. If it is frozen back or if the plants are not started until spring, the blooming period is then in late summer and fall. The spent flower stems should be cut to the ground in frost-free areas to force new growth and to create a spreading shrub. The plant is grown in zones 8 and 9a as a self-sowing annual and in zones 9b through 11 as a perennial shrub or even a tree. The fruits are 6-inch-long, four-angled pods that are not especially attractive when they turn brown—another reason to cut back the spent flowering stems. Plate 102.

Cassia bicapsularis (by-kaps´-yoo-LAIR-is) (synonym *C. candolleana*, *Senna bicapsularis*) is widespread in the American tropics, though its exact native habitat is uncertain. It is similar to *C. corymbosa,* but has larger leaves and more leaflets per leaf, as many as 10. It is also somewhat more tender to cold than is *C. corymbosa* and is only evergreen in zones 10 and 11 but comes back from the roots in zone 9. The leaves and especially the seeds are poisonous but not deadly if eaten.

Cassia candolleana. See *C. bicapsularis.*

Cassia carnaval. See *C. excelsa.*

Cassia corymbosa (kor-im-BO-sa) (synonym *Senna corymbosa*) is native to southern Brazil, northern Argentina, and Uruguay, and is a perennial dormant in the winter in zone 8a, a usually dependable evergreen perennial in zone 9a, and a dependable evergreen in zones 9b through 11. The plant grows to 12 feet or more in height and makes an unusually wide shrub or

can be trained into a broad-crowned small tree in zones 9 through 11. It can also be grown as an espalier or vine if trained early as the branches are spreading, pliable, and rather clambering. The leaves are usually no more than 8 inches long and are composed of six (rarely four) narrow, linear, deep green leaflets widely spaced along the rachis. The plant blooms off and on year-round in frost-free areas but most heavily in late summer, autumn, and winter. The deep golden yellow flowers are in terminal corymbs and are open with the petals spreading and have long extruded anthers.

Cassia didymobotrya (dy´-dee-mo-BOAT-ree-a) (synonyms *C. nairobensis*, *Senna didymobotrya*) is indigenous to tropical East Africa and is completely hardy in zones 9b through 11 but is also grown in zone 9a where it usually resprouts from the root if frozen back. The plant has become naturalized in southern Florida and southern California, and is drought tolerant when established. It is a very fast but rangy-growing large shrub to 10 or 12 feet in height; like *C. corymbosa* it is often trained as a sprawling vinelike subject. The leaves are a foot or more long with as many as 30 elliptic leaflets. The inflorescences are quite showy, a foot or more in height, and composed of many densely packed 2-inch-wide bright yellow flowers with spreading petals. The flower cluster is reminiscent of that of *C. alata*. The plant blooms from spring to fall, but most heavily in late summer and fall. It is sometimes called the popcorn cassia because to some people the blossoms smell like popcorn.

Cassia excelsa (ek-SEL-sa) (synonym *C. carnaval*) is indigenous to southern Brazil and northern Argentina. It is one of the fastest-growing, showiest, and hardiest tree type cassias, but inexplicably neglected in most of the southeastern United States. Sometimes called the crown-of-gold tree, it is dependably hardy as a tree in zones 9b through 11, a very large shrub or small tree in zone 9a, and a shrub in zone 8b. The plant grows to 25 or 30 feet in height in frost-free regions. The leaves are large (to 2 feet long), heavy, and very attractive with 20 to 40 leaflets each 2 inches long. The fragrant flowers come in late summer and fall in large, loose clusters of 2-inch-wide open yellow blossoms.

Cassia fistula (FIST-yoo-la) is native to India and is sometimes called Indian laburnum but most often golden shower tree in this country. A truly spectacular tree when in flower, it is quite tender and not hardy outside zones 10 and 11; indeed, it is sometimes damaged in the colder parts of zone 10a. It grows to 25 or 30 feet in height if not frozen back. The leaves are as much as 2 feet long with 8 to 16 large (to 8 inches long), ovate and (unlike most other *Cassia* species) glossy leaflets that look more like leaves of *Ficus benjamina* than leaflets of *Cassia.* The tree is briefly deciduous in spring, usually with the emergence of the flowers. The golden to almost white flowers appear from spring to midsummer but most heavily in June in 18-inch-long pendent racemes. The 3-foot-long by half-inch-wide cylindrical pods turn from dark green to black when mature. The leaves and especially the seeds are poisonous but not deadly if eaten. Plate 103.

Cassia florida. See *C. siamea*.

Cassia gigantea. See *C. siamea*.

Cassia glauca. See *C. surattensis*.

Cassia grandis (GRAN-dis) is indigenous to Central America and is a large, spreading, beautiful tree species, sometimes growing to as much as 60 feet in height. It is dependably hardy only in zones 10 and 11 and marginal in zone 10a. The leaves are usually about a foot long and are composed of 3-inch-long oblong leaflets with silvery pubescence underneath. The flowers usually appear in April just before the renewal of the leaves, which fall in midwinter. They are borne in 8-inch-long racemes, and each flower is about an inch wide and pink with a yellow throat. This species is called the pink shower tree or horse cassia.

Cassia javanica (ja-VAHN-i-ka) is indigenous to Indonesia, but is not as tender to cold as the above species, being completely adaptable to zones 10 and 11. It makes a broad-spreading, briefly deciduous tree to as much as 40 feet in height. The leaves are usually about 18 inches long with 16 to more than 30 three-inch-long oblong leaflets. The branches grow such that each leaflet is often mistaken for a single leaf. The flowers are pink or white and appear in great masses along the branches in summer. Because of the flower color, the tree is sometimes called the apple blossom cassia. No plant is more spectacular than this one in full bloom. **Cassia javanica × C. fistula,** the rainbow cassia or rainbow shower tree, is a large deciduous tree with great masses of pink (or red), yellow, and white flowers all summer. It has the same cultural requirements and climatic limitations as its parents. Plate 104.

Cassia multijuga (mul-TIJ-yoo-ga) (synonym *Senna multijuga*) is native to northern South America. It is hardy in zones 10 and 11, although it can be grown as a tender shrub in zone 9b. It is a large shrub or small tree to 25 feet in height with foot-long, lacy leaves composed of 40 to 80 leaflets, each less than an inch long. The plant blooms in late summer and fall with 12-inch-tall terminal panicles of golden 2-inch-wide open flowers. It needs to be trained when young if a tree form is wanted.

Cassia nairobensis. See *C. didymobotrya*.

Cassia nodosa (no-DOE-sa), called pink shower tree, is treated by some botanists as a separate species, although to gardeners it is very similar to *C. javanica*.

Cassia siamea (sy-AM-ee-a) (synonyms *C. florida, C. gigantea, Senna siamea*) is native to Southeast Asia and is one of the loveliest cassias. It is hardy in zones 10 and 11 and marginal in zone 10a. It is a widespreading tree to 40 feet tall in cultivation and has foot-long leaves composed of 16 to 20 leathery oblong 3-inch-long leaflets. The flowers come in spring and early summer in broad terminal, pyramidal panicles of golden yellow blossoms, each less than an inch wide. The species is sometimes called the kassod tree. The leaves and especially the seeds are poisonous but not deadly if eaten.

Cassia spectabilis (spek-TAB-i-lis) is native to parts of South America and is one of the more tender species, dependable only in zones 10b and 11. The tree grows to 30 or 40 feet with a large spread. The large leaves are almost as beautiful as the flowers; they are 2 or more feet long, and the lance-shaped leaflets are 3 inches long and softly hairy. The terminal and erect flower spikes are as much as 2 feet tall and are composed of 2-inch-wide golden yellow flowers. This tree is incredibly spectacular in and out of bloom.

Cassia splendida (splen-DEE-da) (synonym *Senna splendida*) is native to Brazil. It is used as a tender shrub in zone 9a and a hardy shrub in zones 9b through 11. It is a large shrub to 10 feet in height with leaves similar to those of *C. corymbosa*, with 4 elliptic to oblong 3-inch-long leaflets. The deep gold flowers are also similar to those of *C. corymbosa* but are larger, each as much as 2 inches wide. The plants tend to bloom in cycles year-round, but are most floriferous in the fall and winter when they are much welcomed. The species is sometimes called golden wonder or the golden wonder senna. Plate 105.

Cassia surattensis (soor-a-TENS-is) (synonym *C. glauca*) is native to Southeast Asia, northern Australia, and Polynesia. It is possibly the least cold hardy of the shrubby cassias, being dependable only in zones 10 and 11 although sometimes grown as a tender shrub or annual in zone 9b. In the truly tropical parts of southern Florida it can be trained into a lovely little tree form, but it naturally wants to be a large shrub. The leaves are usually less than a foot long with 12 to 20 elliptic, 2-inch-long light green leaflets. The inch-wide golden flowers are in rather flat racemes near the ends of the branches but are sometimes half hidden by the leaves. They are, nevertheless, of great beauty and make quite a show off and on all year. The species is sometimes called scrambled egg tree.

CASTANOSPERMUM
(ka-stan´-o-SPUR-mum)
Papilionaceae (Fabaceae, Leguminosae), subfamily Papilionoideae: The Bean, Pea Family
MORETON BAY CHESTNUT; AUSTRALIAN CHESTNUT
Large tree; large pinnate leaves; entire tree covered with yellow, orange, red flowers in summer
Zones 10 and 11 (sometimes planted and long surviving in zone 9b)
Sun
Average but regular amounts of moisture
Sandy, humusy, well-drained soil
Propagation by seed

A monotypic genus in Australia, from New South Wales up through Queensland, and on the island of New Caledonia. **Castanospermum australe** (aw-STRAL-ee) makes a large tree to 90 feet in Australia. It is somewhat variable in shape, but usually has a rather wide, spreading and dense crown of lustrous 18-inch-long pinnate leaves composed of 7 to 15 elliptic to oblong leathery 5-inch-long leaflets. The flowers appear in summer on the twigs, branches, and (sometimes) the trunk. They are shaped like those of *Lathyrus* (sweet pea) species and open yellow but soon change to orange and then red. The fruit is a striking 10-inch-long pod that contains large seeds similar to a shelled chestnut. The Australian aborigines are said to have eaten them roasted, but Europeans evidently find them unpalatable. The seeds are also reportedly poisonous unless cooked. This is an incredibly beautiful tree for sufficiently warm climates. It is somewhat drought tolerant and, although it is naturally not a fast grower, it grows faster and looks better with an ample and regular supply of moisture.

CECROPIA (se-KROAP-ee-a)
Moraceae: The Fig, Mulberry Family
CECROPIA; SNAKEWOOD
Medium sized soft-wooded trees; hollow stems;
    beautiful large, deeply divided leaves
Zones 10b and 11
Sun
Water lovers
Sandy, humusy, moist, well-drained soil
Propagation by seed

A large genus of about 100 species in the wet lowlands of tropical America. These are fast-growing, soft-wooded, large-leaved trees with milky sap, which are grown for their incredibly beautiful great palmately lobed leaves. The trees never make a dense crown of foliage, but have branches more or less in whorls or tiers around the smooth, light-colored trunks wherever there is enough sun on the trunk. This phenomenon gives an open and quite graceful aspect to the crown of foliage. The trunks and branches of all the species are hollow and, in their native habitats, are inhabited by insects, usually biting ants. The male and female flowers are produced on separate trees, and the flowers of both sexes are greenish white and not very attractive or significant in the landscape. The fruits are 6-inch-long slender pods that are also rather insignificant ornamentally; they are edible but reportedly insipid. Both species described below have peltate leaves, although only one has this characteristic alluded to in its botanical name. Native peoples make musical instruments from the hollow trunks of these trees, thus the vernacular names trumpet tree or trumpet-wood. These are among the world's most tropical looking plants. Few phenomena are as beautiful as the view from below up into the open crown of giant *Cecropia* leaves backlit by the sky. None of the species is hardy to cold. Some taxonomists place this genus in a separate family, Cecropiaceae.

Cecropia palmata (pahl-MAIT-a) is native to the West Indies and northern South America and is a very fast growing tree to 50 feet in height with a rather slender, soft-wooded trunk supporting a broad and open crown of large felty leaves at the ends of the branches.

The leaves are magnificent: as much as 18 inches wide with 7 to 11 deeply cleft lobes cut almost to the center of the leaf. Each lobe has a strong yellowish orange midrib and depressed lateral veins. The undersides of the leaves are whitish or silvery pubescent and a spectacular sight when the wind turns them up. Plate 106.

Cecropia peltata (pel-TAIT-a / pel-TAHT-a) is native to the West Indies, Mexico, Central America, and northern South America. It is similar to *C. palmata*, but the leaves are not as large (only to a foot in width) nor as deeply divided. The leaves are the principal diet of the tree sloths in Central and South America, whose unhurried and measured gait is apparently ignored by the ants living in the stems.

CEIBA (SEE-ba / SAY-ba)
Bombacaceae: The Bombax, Baobab Family
KAPOK; SILK-COTTON TREE; SHAVING-
    BRUSH TREE
Immense buttress-trunked deciduous trees; large
    palmately divided leaves
Zones 10b and 11
Sun
Average but regular amounts of moisture; drought
    tolerant when established
Rich, humusy, well-drained soil
Propagation by seed

The genus has fewer than a dozen species of large to very large deciduous trees in the tropical areas of the Americas. Some of the trees attain a height of 150 feet with an equal crown diameter in their native habitats. The branches, like those of the genus *Cecropia,* tend to be arranged in tiers or whorls around the tall trunks. All are famous for the immense buttresses found at the bases of the mature specimens of most species. These sinuous flanges of trunk are sometimes 25 feet high at their point of origin and often spread to more than 30 feet from the base of the trunk, diminishing in height the farther from the tree they reach but never diminishing in thickness. According to Edwin A. Menninger, this thickness factor never varies for any given tree and is usually from 6 to 12 inches in width. In nature the trees do not usually manifest much buttressing until they reach full sunlight and, what is more important, the wind above the canopy of the forest. The trunk may be as much as 10 feet in diameter just above the buttresses and is amazingly straight all the way up to the crown of the tree. The trees usually have stout fat spines on the trunks when young and persistently so on the upper parts of the trunks and branches. Inexplicably, some trees do not have spines regardless of the age of the trunks and branches.

All the species are deciduous for varying lengths of time where they are native, a period that corresponds to the dry season. In southern Florida, however, they are sometimes only briefly deciduous. All species have palmately divided leaves and relatively small, bell-shaped blossoms in loose-flowered axillary clusters. Although not related to mallows, *Ceiba* flowers are somewhat similar with five fleshy petals that are densely pubescent on the outside and five stamens united into an extruding column that is five-parted on top. The fruits are woody or leathery pods with many seeds embedded in a mass of cottonlike fiber. The cotton of *C. pentandra* was formerly of great value commercially and is termed "kapok." All species are fast growers, but quite tender to cold.

The trees are somewhat drought tolerant when established but grow and look ever so much better with an adequate water supply. Also, these are forest trees and they are not well adapted to the poor and calcareous soil found in most of southern Florida. These spectacularly beautiful trees are very massive. They are not for the average homeowner's lot, but rather for parks and estates. There are no other trees to match them in beauty and size other than some of the giant banyan trees.

Ceiba aesculifolia (ees´-kyoo-li-FO-lee-a) is native to southwestern Mexico and Guatemala where it grows to 80 feet or more in height. In cultivation it usually grows no more than 40 to 50 feet tall. The glossy leaves are about 10 inches wide and are divided into five to eight elliptic to oblanceolate 5-inch-long leaflets. The 3-inch-wide flowers are purple on the outside and white or yellowish within; they appear mostly in early spring before the leaves come out but also sporadically in the summer.

Ceiba pentandra (pen-TAN-dra) is most likely native to tropical America but has been in cultivation worldwide for so long that its exact origins are not known. The tree can grow to 150 feet in height in its native haunts, but is usually no more than 100 feet tall in cultivation, with a spread of crown as wide as the tree is high. The leaves are up to a foot wide with five to seven 6-inch-long leaflets. Like the flowers of *C. aesculifolia*, those of *C. pentandra* appear in early spring usually before the leaves. They are not particularly attractive and are a dull white to yellow or pink in color. The woody pods are about 6 inches long and are elliptic to spindle-shaped. From them is obtained the valuable fiber kapok, formerly much used for stuffing furniture, pillows, life preservers, and so forth, but mostly now superseded by synthetic materials. Because most of the natural fiber came from the Far East where the kapok plantations were, much literature on this tree indicates a worldwide natural distribution for the tree rather than the American tropics. Plate 107.

CEPHALOCEREUS

(sef´-a-lo-SEER-ee-us)
Cactaceae: The Cactus Family
OLD MAN CACTUS
Tall columnar ribbed cactus covered in white hair
Zones 10 and 11; marginal in zone 9b
Sun
Drought tolerant

Sandy, well-drained soil
Propagation by seed and cuttings

A genus of only three cactus species in central Mexico. They are mostly unbranched columnar, ribbed plants that bear long white hairlike growths especially when young. Some are tall growing. One species is common as a landscape subject in tropical and subtropical succulent gardens and arid regions. *Cephalocereus senilis* (se-NIL-is / SEN-i-lis) grows to as much as 40 feet with age and is usually unbranched but may form several columns from the base of the short trunk. The stems are deep green with whitish yellow spines and are as much as a foot wide with age. The young plants and young growth on older plants are covered with long white hairs that impart a unique and spectacular texture to succulent plantings. Old stems have the look of Sahuaro columns beneath the white-haired tops. This cactus only blooms when mature, at 15 to 20 years of age, with nocturnal 2-inch-long deep pink blossoms in a circle atop the columns. The cactus is particularly beautiful when individuals of varying heights are planted in groups and, if one is fortunate enough to have an old and multitrunked specimen, few things can compare to its loveliness. The plants must have perfect drainage, especially in winter. Although mature plants are undamaged by temperatures of 26°F or above, young plants are often killed by temperatures below freezing. Plates 108 and 178.

CERATOZAMIA (se-rait´-o-ZAY-mee-a)

Zamiaceae: The Zamia (a Cycad) Family
No known English common name
Palmlike or fernlike, tough, stiff leaves atop a short
    pineapple-like trunk
Zones 9b through 11
Partial shade to partial sun
Water lover
Sandy, humusy, well-drained soil
Propagation by seed

A genus of 11 species of slow-growing, graceful cycads from elevated forest regions in Mexico, Belize, and Guatemala. Because of their forest habitats, these species do not like sites in full sun, especially in hot climates. Only one species is commonly planted. *Ceratozamia mexicana* (mex-i-KAHN-a) is native to the Ciudad Victoria region of northeastern Mexico and can withstand but a few degrees of frost. The plants are similar in general form to the ubiquitous *Cycas revoluta* (sago palm), but the trunks are much shorter, the 5-foot-long leaves are more delicate and lighter in color, the leaf crown is never as full, and the leaflets are much broader and are usually spaced farther apart on the rachis. There is some similarity between this species and several palm species in the genus *Chamaedorea*. In time the plants form short trunks but this takes many years. The plant usually reaches about 6 feet in height and about 4 feet in width. These little palmlike cycads are very graceful in appearance and are perfect in a moist and shady border.

CERBERA (SUR-be-ra)
Apocynaceae: The Oleander, Frangipani, Vinca Family
SEA MANGO
Large shrub or small tree; large shiny leaves; white flowers; plumlike fruit
Zones 10b and 11
Sun
Water lover
Humusy, moist, well-drained soil
Propagation by seed and cuttings

A genus of about six species in the islands of the Indian Ocean including Madagascar, through India and Malaysia to Australia. They are evergreen shrubs and trees with large alternately arranged leaves bunched at the ends of the branches and terminal clusters of frangipani-like flowers. Only one species is common in cultivation. *Cerbera manghas* (MAHN-gahs) (synonym *C. odollan*) is native to India and Malaysia. It is closely related to *Plumeria* (frangipani) species. It grows to 20 or 30 feet in cultivation in frost-free areas, but attains a height of 50 feet or more in its native habitats. The dark green shiny, leathery leaves are long-elliptic to linear-obovate in shape and as much as 10 inches long with a strong and lighter colored midrib. Like those of the frangipani, the leaves tend to cluster at the ends of the branches. The 3-inch-wide flowers are almost as attractive as those of the plumeria. Appearing mainly in spring and summer but sporadically throughout the year, they are arranged in large, terminal clusters and are white, usually with a red or yellow "eye." The fruits are 4 inches long, plumlike, and bright green when immature and shades of red when mature; they much resemble those of a small mango (*Mangifera* species), but they are poisonous. The tree grows naturally on and near the seacoast and is completely tolerant of saline soil and salty spray and air, making it a perfect candidate for those conditions in nearly tropical areas. It also grows inland as long as there is a constant supply of moisture. The fruits and milky sap in these plants are poisonous.

CEREUS (SEER-ee-us)
Cactaceae: The Cactus Family
CEREUS
Large columnar ribbed cactuses; large, white nocturnal flowers
Zones vary according to species
Sun to part sun
Drought tolerant
Sandy, humusy, well-drained soil
Propagation by seed and cuttings

This genus formerly included all columnar species of cactus; subsequent studies have led to the segregation of many of these into differing genera. As it now stands there are about 50 species of *Cereus*, all columnar (although some are not erect columns) with ribs and areoles on the ribs from which the spines arise in a radiating fashion. All the species are large, fast-growing plants and, while drought tolerant like most of their relatives, nevertheless need more water and more fertile soil than the "typical" cactus plant. They should never suffer drought conditions in their summer growing season, but need less water in the winter. The fruits are edible and usually red to purple when mature. The plants are superbly beautiful and very dramatic in a large rock garden or succulent garden.

Cereus aethiops (EE-thee-ahps) is native to Argentina and is one of the hardier species in the genus, dependably hardy in zones 9b through 11. The plants grow to no more than 8 feet in height. They seldom branch and do not cluster. The stems have eight plump ribs and are bluish green, often with a purplish cast in full sun. The plants bloom in summer with 8-inch-long, many-petaled silky white and pale pink nocturnal flowers with brown sepals.

Cereus argentinensis (ahr-jen´-ti-NENS-is) is native to Argentina and is hardy in zones 10 and 11. In its native habitat the plant makes a true tree to 30 feet or more in height. The stems are bluish or grayish green and have four or five strong, deep ribs. The flowers appear in summer and are as much as 10 inches long, and funnel-shaped, with silky white inner petals and green outer petals and sepals.

Cereus azureus (a-ZOOR-ee-us / az-yoo-REE-us) is found in southern Brazil and northern Argentina and is hardy in zones 10 and 11. It grows to about 10 feet with definitely bluish stems that have six or seven deep ribs. The summer flowers are as much as a foot long, and funnel-shaped, with white inner petals and reddish brown sepals.

Cereus chalybaeus (kal-i-BEE-us) is indigenous to northern Argentina and Uruguay and is one of the hardier species, being dependable in zones 9b through 11. It grows to about 8 feet with few branches and has blue to dark green stems with five or six deep narrow ribs. The 8-inch-wide flowers are widespreading with white inner petals and red to wine-colored outer petals and sepals.

Cereus forbesii (FORB-zee-eye) (synonym *C. validus*) is native to northern Argentina and is hardy in zones 9b through 11. It grows into a branched tree 20 feet high in its native land and has six deep, narrow, notched ribs with long, tough reddish brown spines. The new growth is definitely bluish in color but later turns a deep green. The flowers are relatively small, only to 3 or so inches long, with white silky petals often tipped with pink.

Cereus jamacaru (zhah-ma-KAR-oo) is a very variable species indigenous to northeastern Brazil. Hardy in zones 10b and 11, it makes a massive branched and treelike plant to 30 or 40 feet tall. The stems have from 4 to 10 ribs and are usually dark green in color without a hint of blue. The white flowers are as much as a foot long. Some forms are almost spineless, while others have very many long spines.

Cereus marginatus. See *Pachycereus marginatus*.

Cereus peruvianus (pe-roo´-vee-AHN-us) (synonym *C. uruguayanus*) is probably native to southeastern Brazil and northern Argentina, but is no longer found in the wild. It is intolerant of all but the lightest frost and is adaptable only in zones 10 and 11, although sometimes surviving in zone 9b. It is sometimes called hedge cactus or Peruvian apple cactus. This large plant clusters from the base and grows to 10 or 12 feet in height. The stems have five to eight deep but plump ribs and are light green when young but turn bluish green or grayish green when mature. The fragrant flowers are about 6 inches long and mostly white. **Cereus peruvianus 'Monstrosus'** (mahn-STRO-sus), a commonly found cultivar, is sometimes called curiosity plant. It has ribs that are divided and broken up into sinuous and wavy crests. It is smaller and slower growing than the type. Plate 109.

Cereus thurberi. See *Stenocereus thurberi*.
Cereus uruguayanus. See *C. peruvianus*.
Cereus validus. See *C. forbesii*.

CHALCAS. See *Murraya*.

CHAMAEDOREA (kay-mee-DOR-ee-a)
Palmae (Arecaceae): The Palm Family
Common names vary according to species
Small, delicate-looking pinnate-leaved clustering or
    solitary-trunked palms
Zones vary according to species
Shade to partial shade
Water lovers
Humusy, moist, well-drained soil
Propagation by seed and (for clumping species)
    transplanting of suckers

A large genus of about 100 species of medium-sized to tiny, mostly moderately fast-growing even-pinnate-leaved palms in Mexico, Central America, and South America, with the majority of the species in Central America. Most species are solitary-trunked palms, but some are clustering and almost all species are understory plants, meaning that they live and grow beneath the overhead canopy of the tropical forest. Nearly all grow in rain forest conditions at varying altitudes, from lowland forest to cloud forest. All have slender trunks resembling bamboo culms. Most species flower and fruit when relatively young, and all produce male and female flowers on separate plants. Many plants sold in nurseries are hybrids and do not fit the description of any one individual species; this is especially true of forms like *C. erumpens* and *C. seifrizii*. The sap of all species is said to be irritating to the skin to some extent. Some of the loveliest and most graceful small palm species are found in this genus.

Chamaedorea atrovirens. See *C. cataractarum*.

Chamaedorea cataractarum (kat-a-RAK-ta-rum / kat-a-rak-TAR-um) (synonym *C. atrovirens*) is native to southern Mexico and makes a very lovely clump of dark green fernlike foliage. The trunks are so short as to be nonexistent for all practical purposes, which gives the clumps of leaves as much the appearance of a graceful cycad as a palm. Young plants are very tender to cold, but mature plants can withstand a modicum of frost and are dependable in zones 10 and 11. The gracefully arching leaves are 3 to 5 feet long. The inflorescences are mostly hidden by the leaf crowns, but are greenish yellow and are followed by bright red berry-like fruits. A clue to the environmental conditions wanted by this species is in the specific epithet "cataractarum," meaning "of cataracts or waterfalls"; the plants are often flooded in their native habitats. In Florida nurseries this species is known as the cat palm.

Chamaedorea costaricana (koast-a-REEK-a-na / koast´-a-ree-KAHN-a) is a fast-growing, clustering species native to Central America from elevations of about 2000 feet to more than 6000 feet. It rather resembles a dense clump of fine-textured bamboo and is usually called bamboo palm, but so are several other species in this genus. The trunks grow to about 12 feet in height, but because there are many stems to a clump, individual trunks are usually obscured by the wall of foliage created by the trunks of varying heights. The clumps, which are much more beautiful if thinned somewhat to allow the lovely green and ringed trunks to show, spread to about 6 feet wide, sometimes more. The individual leaves are 2 to 4 feet long with 40 or more linear-lanceolate light green foot-long leaflets, the terminal pair usually wider than the others. The flower spikes are orange and hang in clusters from the leaves. The little berrylike fruits are black when mature. This beautiful palm is hardy in zones 10 and 11.

Chamaedorea elegans (EL-e-ganz) (synonyms *Collinia elegans*, *Neanthe bella*) is a single-trunked species from southern Mexico and Guatemala. It is hardy in zones 10 and 11, although the plant has frequently sprouted from its root after being frozen back in zone 9. No species more deserves its descriptive specific epithet than this lovely little palm: it is delicate and elegant from youthfulness unto old age. The slender green trunks are ringed with leaf scars and grow slowly to a maximum height of 4 or 5 feet with relatively compact crowns of diaphanously pinnate leaves. The leaves are variable in form with from 20 to 40 leaflets that may be narrow or broad. The light green to olive green leaf is generally 2 to 3 feet long on mature plants, and the leaflets 6 to 10 inches long. The branched inflorescence is erect and carries many sulfur-yellow flowers. The tiny fruits are black when mature. This palm is probably the world's most widely grown and sold palm (most being sold as houseplants) due to its ease of culture especially regarding light levels and water requirements. It loves bright shade and does well with less water than most *Chamaedorea* species, although it should never be drought stricken. Commonly called parlor palm, it is unexcelled as an accent in shady borders and, if expense is not a problem, makes one of the most beautiful of tall groundcovers. Few landscapes are more striking than an area devoted to this palm with small plants on the perimeter and larger plants towards the center of the mass. It is worth plunging pots of this palm into shady borders during the frost-free seasons in almost any zone for the great beauty it lends to such areas.

Chamaedorea ernesti-augusti (er-nest´-ee-aw-GUST-ee) is indigenous to southeastern Mexico, Belize, and Honduras, and is hardy in zones 10 and 11. The palm is similar to *C. metallica* with the two notable exceptions that it grows to about three times the height of *C. metallica* and has leaves that are a pure light green with no metallic sheen.

Chamaedorea erumpens (ee-RUMP-enz) is native to southern Mexico, Belize, and Honduras, and is hardy in zones 10 and 11. It is another *Chamaedorea* species called bamboo palm. A densely clustering species, it is similar in form and stature to *C. seifrizii*, but the leaflets are wider, especially the terminal leaflets. The leaves reach about 2 feet in length, but have only about 20 leaflets per blade. The trunks grow to as much as 12 feet in height. Flowers and fruit resemble those of *C. seifrizii;* indeed, some botanists consider *C. erumpens* to be a form of *C. seifrizii*. The palm is beautifully graceful, especially up close. It is intolerant of full sun.

Chamaedorea metallica (me-TAL-li-ka) is a single-trunked species originating in eastern tropical Mexico and is not dependably hardy outside zones 10 and 11 although many mature specimens are to be found in zone 9b. It is an oddity in the genus and among palms in general: the leaves are pinnate but usually undivided (i.e., the leaf looks as though the individual leaflets had fused). In addition, the leaves are stiff and tough, are held approximately erect, and have depressions radiating out from the rachis that correspond to the outlines of the "fused" leaflets. The leaf color is also unusual, a deep, dark bluish green with a metallic sheen. Some older plants exhibit leaflets that are separate, but this is rather rare. The plant thrives in shade. The little palms never grow more than 4 or 5 feet in height. The flowers are cream colored and not especially attractive, nor are the subsequent fruits.

Chamaedorea microspadix (myk-ro-SPAY-dix) is native to eastern Mexico and is probably the hardiest species in the genus, being dependable in zones 9 through 11 and having been known to resprout after freezing back in zone 8. It is a fast-growing clustering species whose trunks attain 6 or 8 feet of stature with leaves covering most of the trunk. The leaves are usually about 2 feet long with 16 to 20 fairly widely spaced dark green leaflets. As in many other *Chamaedorea* species, the terminal pair of leaflets is larger than the others. The pendent inflorescence is as much as 2 feet long and carries many small whitish flowers; it is quite attractive but the bright red fruits that result from it are almost spectacular. This palm is very nice for shade and is perfect for adding form and color to difficult places. Plate 110.

Chamaedorea radicalis (rad-i-KAL-is) is a clustering species indigenous to northeastern Mexico. It is about as hardy as *C. microspadix,* being dependable in zones 9 through 11 and often surviving winters in zone 8. It is possibly the most beautiful of the "hardy" *Chamaedorea* species. Often apparently trunkless, it sometimes has several slender trunks reaching as much as 3 feet in height. The large gracefully arching leaves are 3 to 4 feet long with foot-long thick, dark green leaflets. The inflorescence is held well above the foliage and consists of many small yellowish orange flowers, which give way to the very colorful half-inch-wide bright orange berries.

Chamaedorea seifrizii (sy-FRITZ-ee-eye / see-FRITZ-ee-eye) is a clumping species native to southeastern Mexico, Belize, Honduras, and Guatemala. It is hardy in zones 10 and 11. The trunks grow rather quickly to 10 feet or more in height with leaves widely spaced on the upper half of the stems. The leaves are about 2 feet long and are dark green with narrow, linear leaflets all the same size. The palm flourishes in shade, but also tolerates some sun if it is neither full sun nor the midday sun of hot climates. It is a graceful species that looks especially good against a wall or other light background where its form can be fully appreciated. Besides bamboo palm, it is sometimes called reed palm.

Chamaedorea tepejilote (tay-pay´-hee-LO-tay) is a single-trunked species from southern Mexico southwards to Colombia. A tender palm, it is hardy only in zones 10 and 11 and is sometimes damaged in zone 10a. It grows rather quickly to a height of 12 feet or so with a beautiful dark green, ringed trunk and large (to 5 or more feet long) bright green leaves whose leaflets are long-lanceolate and about 8 inches long. The flowers are a bright yellow, and the large fruits (half inch or more in diameter) are black.

CHAMAERANTHEMUM
(kay-mee-RANTH-i-mum)
Acanthaceae: The Acanthus Family
No known English common name
Creeping tropical herbs; variegated leaves; white
    flowers
Zones 10b and 11
Shade to partial shade
Water lovers
Sandy, humusy, moist, well-drained soil
Propagation by seed

A genus of only four species of herbs and small shrubs in Central and South America with variegated leaves and terminal clusters of white flowers. Only one species is common.

Chamaeranthemum alatum. See *Pseuderanthemum alatum.*

Chamaeranthemum venosum (ve-NO-sum) is native to tropical Brazil. It is a prostate and creeping, stem-rooting herb no more than 6 inches in height with exquisitely beautiful velvety, 4-inch-long elliptic to obovate, succulent grayish to olive green leaves whose veins are streaked with white. The half-inch-wide flowers are in small clusters and are white and starlike, often suffused with pink. This is a beautiful groundcover species for frost-free or nearly frost-free regions.

CHAMAEROPS (ka-MEE-rahps)
Palmae (Arecaceae): The Palm Family
MEDITERRANEAN FAN PALM; EUROPEAN
    FAN PALM
Clustering fan-leaved palm with gracefully curved
    trunks and stiff leaves on spiny stalks
Zones 8b through 11
Sun
Drought tolerant
Sandy, humusy, well-drained soil
Propagation by seed and transplanting of suckers

A monotypic genus from southern Mediterranean Europe and northern Africa.

Chamaerops excelsa. See *Trachycarpus*.

Chamaerops humilis (HYOO-mi-lis) is sometimes a single-trunked species in its native lands, especially in the drier parts of these areas, but in cultivation usually forms clusters of trunks. The trunks may grow slowly to a height of 20 feet and hardly ever have a girth of more than a foot, each one leaning outward from the center of the cluster. This characteristic is possibly the most attractive aspect to the species, lending a formal yet very graceful appearance to a large clumped specimen. The trunks are always covered in the picturesque leaf stubs unless very old. The stiff leaves are variable, but are usually almost round in outline, gray-green to bluish green in color, about 3 feet in diameter, and very deeply divided (almost to the petiole) into many linear segments. The petiole is usually longer than the leaf and is armed with vicious spines. The inflorescence is erect and much-branched and carries many yellow or greenish yellow flowers followed by yellow to brown fruits on female plants. The palm has been in cultivation long enough for there to be varieties or forms of the species, some of which vary from the type in hardiness and color, leaf size, size of the palm, and so forth. All forms demand a well-drained soil and do not tolerate flooding for any length of time. Although drought tolerant when established, the plants look and perform better with adequate and regular irrigation. No clustering palm makes a more dramatic specimen on lawns or against the background of a wall or differently colored foliage, or otherwise isolated from its surroundings where the form and texture of its leaning trunks and starburstlike leaves can be fully appreciated. Plate 111.

CHLOROPHYTUM (klor-o-FYT-um)
Liliaceae: The Lily Family
SPIDER PLANT
Small evergreen creeping perennials; narrow straplike
    usually variegated leaves; white flowers
Zones 10 and 11 as permanent perennials; zone 9 as
    returning perennials
Partial shade
Water lovers
Sandy, humusy, moist, well-drained soil
Propagation by root division, rhizome division,
    plantlets on stems, and seed

A large genus of more than 200 species of perennial herbs found on all continents except Europe and North America. Only one species is commonly planted. *Chlorophytum comosum* (ko-MO-sum) (synonym *C. capense*) is native to southern and tropical Africa. It grows to a foot in height with 18-inch-long soft linear straplike leaves ascending stemless from the ground in rosette fashion. The plants send out long stems on which are borne plantlets identical to the "mother" plant and which root when they touch the ground, making this an excellent (if unspectacular) groundcover. The flowering stems are more or less erect and held well above the foliage, with white six-petaled flowers that often produce fruit with seeds. The flower scapes usually have tufts of leaves which, after the fruit is produced, form aerial roots and can be snipped off and planted. Much more attractive than the species are the variegated forms; in fact it is now difficult to find the non-variegated type for sale. *Chlorophytum comosum* 'Mandaianum' (man-day-AHN-um) has leaves with a broad yellow center stripe. *Chlorophytum comosum* 'Picturatum' has a wide central yellow stripe down each leaf often with faint green lines within, and usually faint bands of yellow in the green margin. *Chlorophytum comosum* 'Variegatum' has its leaves margined with white. *Chlorophytum comosum* 'Vittatum' has leaves with a central band of white.

CHORISIA (ko-RIS-ee-a)
Bombacaceae: The Bombax, Baobab Family
FLOSS-SILK TREE; SILK-FLOSS TREE
Stout spiny-trunked trees; large deciduous palmate
    leaves; large lilylike white and pink flowers
Zones vary according to species
Sun
Drought tolerant
Sandy, humusy, well-drained soil
Propagation by seed and air-layering

There are perhaps only two species in this genus of briefly deciduous trees in southern Brazil and northern Argentina. They are fast-growing, as much as 6 or more feet per year, soft-wooded trees attaining maximum heights of 30 to as much as 50 feet with thick trunks covered in fat, tough spines. The shape of mature trees varies from pyramidal or conical to widespreading but is usually the latter form. The trunks are green when young, turning gray with age. The spines on the trunks sometimes disappear with age. Other trees are always covered with spines. The leaves are circular in outline and palmately compound with five to seven 6-inch-long leaflets. The flowers appear from summer through early winter, depending on the species, at which time the leaves often fall. Cold causes the leaves to drop as does drought, but the trees are native to fairly dry areas and must have perfect drainage. The fruits are not often seen in cultivation, but are similar to those of *Bombax,* and the floss within the pods was also formerly used as kapok. The trees are beautiful in and out of bloom, with a distinctly tropical appearance. There are several cultivars with various colors, but they are difficult to find labeled. Plate 112.

Chorisia insignis (in-SIG-nis) is slightly hardier and smaller than *C. speciosa* and is at home in zones 10 and 11 and worth trying (with occasional damage) in zone 9b. The leaves are glossy and smooth-margined, and the leaflets are often pendent to some extent. The waxy, five-petaled flowers are variable in color and even shape from one tree to another, but generally are 6 inches wide and about as long, and have the shape of regal lilies. They usually open with a yellow or gold color to the petals and a deeper yellow to orange or even purple color in the flower's throat, all soon changing to white.

Chorisia speciosa (spee-see-O-sa) is slightly more tender than *C. insignis* and is hardy in zones 10 and 11. The leaves are stiffer than those of *C. insignis,* and the leaflets are usually slightly serrulate and do not droop. The flowers are wider spreading than those of *C. insignis* (more like tiger lilies in shape than regal lilies); they are pink to almost red with white to yellow throats and brown or purple dots or striations. The white or yellowish color in the center of the flower may extend almost to the ends of the petals in some specimens. Plates 113 and 114.

CHRYSALIDOCARPUS

(kry´-sa-lid´-o-KAR-pus)
Palmae (Arecaceae): The Palm Family
Common names vary according to species
Single or multitrunked pinnate palms with beautifully
    ringed trunks
Zones 10b and 11
Sun
Water lovers
Sandy, humusy, well-drained soil
Propagation by seed

A genus of about 20 slender-trunked, feather-leaved palm species in Madagascar and adjacent islands with lovely, gracefully arching leaves. All are native either to riparian sites or areas of high rainfall and, while they survive periods of inadequate moisture, should not be subjected to these conditions if possible.

Chrysalidocarpus cabadae (KAB-a-dee) (synonym *Dypsis cabadae*) is unknown in the wild, but is probably indigenous to Madagascar. It is a clustering type, but never makes a dense clump and often takes several years to start suckering. The individual trunks grow relatively fast to 30 feet or more in height. The deep green 10- to 12-foot-long leaves have 50 to more than 100 leaflets, which are 2 feet long by 2 inches wide and arched near the ends of the leaves, so that the leaf is trough-shaped for part of its length. The long sheathing leaf bases create a beautiful grayish green crownshaft. The palm is outstandingly beautiful for the leaves, but it is the trunks that are so exceptionally attractive; they are tall, slender, very smooth bright to olive or even grayish green with widely spaced, very distinct light gray or white rings of leaf scars that create one of the most exotic and beautiful palm trunks. The flowers are yellow, and the subsequent half-inch-long egg-shaped fruits are bright red. Plate 115.

Chrysalidocarpus lucubensis (loo-kyoo-BEN-sis) (synonym *C. madagascariensis* var. *lucubensis*) is a single-trunked palm growing fairly rapidly to a height of 30 feet or slightly more. It is considered by some authorities to be a variety of the very similar *C. madagascariensis.* The trunks are tapering towards the apex and slightly more massive than those of *C. cabadae,* and the rings of leaf scars are not as widely spaced nor as distinct. The leaves are about the same size and color of the above species, but the arching and somewhat drooping leaflets arise from different angles from the rachis, giving the leaf a rather plumelike appearance. The crownshaft is not as large or as spectacular as that of *C. cabadae.* The flowers are yellow, and the fruit is black. While the trunks are not as beautiful as those of *C. cabadae,* the leaves are perhaps more beautiful because of their plumose aspect and the gracefully drooping leaflets, each leaf making a stunning silhouette.

Chrysalidocarpus lutescens (loo-TES-senz) (synonyms *Areca lutescens, Dypsis lutescens*), another clustering species, is almost universally called areca palm in the United States, often called the butterfly palm, and sometimes called the bamboo palm (as are several other palms). The latest taxonomic research segregates this palm into the genus *Dypsis,* but it is here retained under *Chrysalidocarpus* as the change is not yet found in the trade. The species is hardy in zones 10 and 11, although it is sometimes damaged in zone 10a. It is one of the glories of the plant world; few plants are as breathtakingly graceful as a well-grown clump of this palm, although it is often planted badly in a landscaping sense, leading to a ho-hum attitude among gardeners. The individual trunks usually grow to about 10 feet in height, but sometimes, especially in the more tropical areas, reach 25 feet. The palm forms many stems (trunks) to each clump, and often only the outermost and lower parts of the trunks are visible. These trunks do resemble bamboo stems, but then so do those of *C. cabadae.* In any case, they are a very lovely dark green to yellow green in color with closely spaced brown to yellow rings of leaf scars. The crownshafts are long, smooth, and grayish green to almost white. Each trunk has but a few gracefully arching leaves, which individually are about 8 feet long with 2-foot-long yellow petioles and rachises. The 80 to 100 leaflets have a prominent yellow midrib and arch from the rachis, so that the leaf is trough-shaped. The palm grows rather fast with adequate water and good soil, but is slow and starved-looking on dry and poor soil. In its native habitat it mostly grows in full sun near riverbanks where it always has water. It grows well in shady situations, but grows slowly and does not have as much color as it does in sunny sites. Like the clumps of many other clustering palm species, the clumps of *C. lutescens* are usually more beautiful if judiciously and occasionally thinned. Plate 116.

Chrysalidocarpus madagascariensis (mad´-a-gas-kair´-ee-EN-sis) is so similar to *C. lucubensis* that some taxonomists consider the latter to be only a variety of this species. The main difference between the two is that *C. madagascariensis* is a clustering species. As such it seems even more desirable.

CHRYSOBALANUS
(kry-so-BAL-a-nus)
Chrysobalanaceae: The Coco-Plum Family
COCO-PLUM; ICACO
Large shrubs and small evergreen trees; glossy leaves; white and purple fruit
Zones 10 and 11
Sun
Average but regular amounts of moisture
Sandy, humusy, well-drained soil
Propagation by seed and cuttings

A genus of four species of large shrubs to small trees in tropical and subtropical America and tropical Africa. They have large leathery entire leaves arranged alternately on the stem, clusters of small greenish white flowers, and berrylike fruits. Only one species is planted in the United States. *Chrysobalanus icaco* (EE-ka-ko / ee-KAHK-o) is indigenous to southern Florida from the Fort Pierce area in the east and the Fort Myers area in the west southwards through the West Indies, Central America, and northern South America. In its northernmost range it is a small shrub, and in its southernmost range it grows to as much as 30 feet in height, but must usually be pruned and trained if a tree form is wanted. It is difficult to train into a tree in windswept locations. As a tree the trunk is seldom straight but usually picturesquely crooked with dark brown fissured bark and a dense crown of foliage; as a shrub the plant is clothed to the ground in leaves, which are from 1 to 4 inches long, obovate to almost orbicular with rounded or notched apices, leathery, lustrous and dark green above but paler and yellowish beneath. The leaves are seldom flat, but are usually somewhat folded along the prominent and yellowish midrib. The white flowers are tiny and borne in terminal or axillary panicles. The fruits are plumlike, about 2 inches long, and may be white or purple. *Chrysobalanus icaco* **var.** *pellocarpus* (pel-lo-KARP-us), with white fruits, is said to be more tolerant of saline conditions than the purple-fruited variety. Both varieties bloom and fruit nearly year-round. They grow near the seacoast and farther inland, making them excellent choices for seaside plantings.

CHRYSOPHYLLUM
(kry-so-FYL-lum)
Sapotaceae: The Sapodilla Family
SATIN-LEAF
Medium-sized, dense-crowned trees; green and bronzy leaves; purple fruit
Zones 10 and 11; marginal in zone 10a
Sun
Average but regular amounts of moisture
Sandy, humusy, well-drained soil
Propagation by seed and cuttings

A genus of about 80 species of trees in tropical America, West Africa, and Australasia. All have alternately arranged leaves, tiny flowers, and often large, mostly edible fruit. They are tender, especially when young and, although one species is native to the southern Florida mainland, it is often nipped by frost even there. It has been many times successfully grown to maturity in southern Texas, but is always eventually killed back.

Chrysophyllum cainito (ky-NEET-o) is native to the West Indies and possibly Central America and northern South America. In its native habitat it sometimes reaches almost 100 feet in height, but in cultivation it is quite smaller, usually only to 60 feet. The crown is usually as wide as the height of the tree, and it has a straight but rather short trunk (i.e., the branches commence low on the trunk). The young branches are covered in short velvety light brown hairs. The elliptic leaves are about 6 inches long, dark green and lustrous above with a prominent and lighter colored midrib, but glisteningly silky and copper-colored beneath with an almost metallic sheen. This invariable color phenomenon of the leaves has led to the common name of satin-leaf, but the species is more often called star apple (because a cross section of the berry reveals seed cells that radiate in a starlike or asterisk-like fashion from the central core of the fruit) or caimito (ky-MEET-o). The purplish white to yellowish flowers are tiny and are borne in small axillary clusters in summer. The fruits are shaped more or less like pomegranates and vary in color from dark red to dark purple when mature. They are usually about 4 inches wide and are said to be delicious when they are fully ripe; otherwise they are gummy and astringent. The fruit does not naturally fall from the tree when ripe and must be removed manually. Signs of ripeness are the commencement of wrinkling in the outer skin and a softening of the whole fruit. The fruit is usually ripe from early to late spring. While somewhat drought tolerant when established, the trees never do very well in prolonged drought and need a fairly rich soil and protection from frost when young.

Chrysophyllum oliviforme (o-liv´-i-FORM-ee) is indigenous to extreme southern Florida and the West Indies and always bears the vernacular name of satin-leaf. It is similar to *C. cainito*, but has usually smaller leaves, does not grow as tall (a maximum height of about 30 feet), and produces invariably purple fruits that are an inch or less in diameter. The tree is at least as tender as *C. cainito* and slightly more tolerant of drought.

CINNAMOMUM (sin-na-MO-mum)

Lauraceae: The Laurel, Avocado, Sassafras Family
Common names vary according to species
Massive trees with glossy evergreen, aromatic foliage
Zones vary according to species
Sun
Average but regular amounts of moisture
Average well-drained soil; calcareous soils need
    organic amendment to lower pH
Propagation by seed

A large genus of about 250 species of trees and shrubs indigenous from Japan to Australia. All are aromatic to some extent and all have glossy and leathery, usually large leaves, clusters of tiny flowers, and berrylike fruit.

Cinnamomum aromaticum (air-o-MAT-i-kum) (synonym *C. cassia*) is native to southern China and Myanmar (Burma). It is a generally inferior source of cinnamon bark and is variously called cassia-bark tree, Chinese cinnamon, bastard cinnamon, and cassia. It grows to a maximum height of about 40 feet in cultivation and is fairly tender, being at home as a tree only in zones 10 and 11 and as a shrub in zones 9b through 11. The leaves are distinctly parallel-veined with three prominent nerves; they are also oblong to lanceolate and very long acuminate, the "tail" often being almost half the length of the 6- to 7-inch-long leaf. Like that in most species in the genus, the new growth is spectacularly colored, in this case cream-colored blushed with red. The inflorescences are axillary erect panicles of tiny yellowish flowers. The fruit is a black berry. The bark of this tree was the source of the first cinnamon known to Europeans. It was not used as a culinary spice, but rather as incense, as an analgesic drug, and to flavor wine.

Cinnamomum camphorum (kam-FOR-um) (synonym *Camphora officinalis*) is native from southern Japan to eastern China and Taiwan. Its only common name in the United States is the camphor tree. The tree grows to almost 100 feet with an almost equal spread in its native habitat, but usually attains no more than 50 feet in cultivation. It generally has a few low and heavy, almost ponderous branches. The bark is a dark cinnamon color when young, turning gray to brown with age; it is fissured on trunks that are as much as 5 feet in diameter. The 5-inch-long apple green leaves are ovate-elliptic, long-acuminate, leathery, and glossy and are reminiscent of those of *Ficus benjamina* (weeping or Chinese banyan). The foliage rustles in the slightest breeze, giving a shimmering quality to the tree's broad, dense crown. The leaves and wood are strongly aromatic of camphor when bruised or crushed and are the natural source of that essential oil. One of the most appealing aspects of the tree is the pink and bronze-colored new growth in late winter, spring, and often

during the summer. The tiny greenish yellow flowers are in small axillary panicles and are not significant ornamentally. The fruits are small berries, black when mature; they can be a nuisance above sidewalks, patios, or parking areas. This is one of the most beautiful shade trees for the Gulf Coast and warmer regions of the southeastern United States. It is at home in zones 9 through 11 as a tree and zone 8 as a shrub. The tree is sometimes allowed or trained to grow as a multitrunked small tree or large shrub, which effect is often quite beautiful, especially if the individual trunks are stripped of lower branches. Older trees are difficult to transplant and are slow growing until they become established or attain a few years of age, although they grow somewhat rapidly thereafter. Plate 117.

Cinnamomum cassia. See *C. aromaticum.*
Cinnamomum officinalis. See *C. camphorum.*
Cinnamomum zeylanicum (zay-LAHN-i-kum) is indigenous to Sri Lanka (formerly Ceylon) and southern India, as the specific epithet indicates. It is hardy in zones 10b and 11. The tree grows to about 30 feet in height. The leaves are quite beautiful: parallel-veined with three prominent nerves, ovate-lanceolate, and 7 or more inches long. The new foliage is a spectacular rose to bronzy crimson in color. The yellowish flowers are numerous and tiny, and the fruits are small black berries. The bark is the source of cinnamon, which is now mostly produced synthetically. The common name is cinnamon tree.

CISSUS (SIS-sus)

Vitaceae: The Grape Family
GRAPE IVY; TREEBINE
Fleshy, large-leaved, mostly evergreen vines
Zones vary according to species
Light requirements vary according to species
Water requirements vary according to species
Sandy, humusy, well-drained soil
Propagation by seed and cuttings

This is a large and very varied genus of about 350 species of vines and some shrubs mostly in tropical areas around the world. Most are tendril-bearing vines and have rather large and fleshy evergreen leaves that are divided or compound; a few are deciduous. Some are desert-dwelling succulent plants. All have small and mostly insignificant flowers that form small berries. Many of the vines are extremely attractive and very lush and tropical looking, often with long-hanging thick and fleshy aerial roots of a tan to red color.

Cissus adenopoda (ad-e-NAHP-o-da / a-dee'-no-PO-da) is native to tropical West Africa and is not reliably hardy outside zones 10 and 11, although the tuberous root usually survives in zone 9. It is a fast-growing, tendril-bearing vine that reaches 12 feet or more in one season and ultimately as much as 20 feet or more in frost-free regions. The large and very beautiful leaves are trifoliate. Each leaflet is about 6 inches long and ovate to elliptic in shape with shallow-toothed margins and depressed main veins. The upper surfaces of the leaflets are dark green with a definite coppery and metallic sheen and are covered in soft purple hairs; the undersides of the leaves are a lovely purplish red. The vine wants partial shade (never full sun) and humusy soil. It is not drought tolerant.

Cissus amazonica (am-a-ZAHN-i-ka) is known only in cultivation, but may be native to the Amazon region of Brazil. It is tender and appropriate only for zones 10b and 11. The tendril-bearing vine is not a terribly rampant grower and even in frost-free regions does not grow very big or high; it is a vine for tracery and up-close beauty on a patio or other intimate site. The fleshy leaves are fairly closely and densely set along the stems and are about 6 inches long, linear-lanceolate, long-acuminate with cordate bases. The top surfaces of the leaves are a metallic grayish green with the main veins marked in bright silver with brown margins; the undersides of the leaves are wine red. This beauty needs partial shade, rich, humusy soil, and adequate moisture.

Cissus antarctica (ant-ARK-ti-ka) is native to Queensland and northern New South Wales in Australia and is hardy in zones 10 and 11. It is not a rampant grower and never gets more than about 12 feet in height, but is densely clothed with leaves. It is quite valuable as a tropical looking subject for shady sites, although it does quite well in partial sun. The succulent leaves are ovate-cordate in shape, usually deeply toothed on the margins but sometimes almost entire, and a deep shiny green with the main veins golden brown. The tendril-bearing vine grows in almost full shade and does not require an abundance of moisture, but should not be allowed to suffer prolonged drought conditions. A sandy, humusy, well-drained soil is perfect. Common names are kangaroo vine and kangaroo treebine.

Cissus discolor (DIS-kul-or) is native to Southeast Asia and Indonesia and is a tender plant not adaptable outside zones 10b and 11. The leaves are among the most beautiful of any vine. They are long-cordate to lanceolate with a distinct and elongated tip and 7 to 8 inches long. Leaf color is deep velvety green with red veins and silver (sometimes pink) markings on the upper surface; the lower surface is felty and maroon in color as are the petioles. The tendril-bearing vine is not rampant, but grows to almost 20 feet with good care. It thrives in part shade to part sun and needs adequate moisture and rich, well-drained soil. Because of the variegated leaves the vine is sometimes called the rex-begonia vine.

Cissus gongylodes (gahn-JIL-o-deez / gahn-ji-LO-deez) is indigenous to southern Brazil, southeastern Peru, and Paraguay, and is completely hardy only in zones 10 and 11, although the roots often survive in zone 9. This wonderful tendril-bearing vine is the essence of tropical beauty. It grows fast and high to 20 feet or more with squared succulent stems and clings by tendrils with suction-cup-like disks. The leaves are divided into three leaflets, the middle one larger (to 7 or 8 inches long) than the other two and rhombic in shape like an unequal-sided diamond. All three leaflets have depressed and hairy veins and are toothed or lobed, sometimes deeply so, especially the middle one. The tendril-bearing vine produces many long aerial roots that are pink to deep red in color and create a truly tropical atmosphere. The vine goes semidormant in late autumn and may become deciduous. Before it goes dormant it produces large, fleshy tuberlike growths at the ends of the stems. These grow and become pendent and generally fall from the stems in early winter to make new plants. The vine grows in shade to partial sun and needs a rich, moist but well-drained soil.

Cissus hypoglauca (hy-po-GLAWK-a) is a fast and vigorous grower from southeastern Australia, which is hardy in zones 9b through 11. It is a vine but bears no tendrils, climbing rather by aerial rootlets. Because of this characteristic, it makes an excellent groundcover and grows in sun or partial shade. The glossy bronzy green and leathery leaves are divided into four or five elliptic to ovate leaflets that are only remotely toothed along their margins; the leaf undersides are covered in a bluish gray bloom. The plant climbs to 40 or 50 feet on any rough surface and covers much ground in one season as a groundcover. It needs only average amounts of water and, once established, is somewhat drought tolerant.

Cissus incisa (in-SY-sa) (synonym *C. trifoliata*) occurs naturally from Missouri south to northern Mexico, west to Arizona and east to Florida and is hardy in zones 6 through 11. It is a deciduous, but very fast growing tendril-bearing vine that can attain a height of 30 feet in one growing season. The tendrils have holdfasts that allow the plant to cling to almost any surface that is not completely smooth. The beautiful leaves are 2 or 3 inches wide and 3 inches long, thick and succulent, medium green in color and variable in shape; most are divided into three lobes, but some are often deltoid and unlobed or remotely lobed, always toothed. The vine grows in partial shade or full sun and is drought tolerant. It is not particular as to soil and, because it is tolerant of saline conditions, makes a fine seaside groundcover or wall covering. Common names are marine ivy, possum grape, and cow-itch vine. The crushed stems and leaves emit what to most people is a disagreeable odor, akin to burning rubber.

Cissus porphyrophyllum. See *Piper porphyrophyllum.*

Cissus rhombifolia (rahm-bi-FO-lee-a) is native to the West Indies and northern South America and is hardy in zones 9b through 11. The vine climbs by forked tendrils to a height of 20 feet or more. The glossy, deep green leaves are divided into three rhomboidal, toothed leaflets that have a reddish bronzy-colored pubescence on their undersides. The vine grows in sun or shade. It is often called grape-ivy. ***Cissus rhombifolia* 'Mandiana'** (man-dee-AHN-a), a very attractive cultivar, has wider and thicker leaflets.

Cissus sicyoides (sis-ee-OY-deez) is native to a

wide area from tropical West Africa to South America and up to southeastern Mexico. Adaptable only in zones 10 and 11, it is a rather fast and strong grower to 20 feet or more in height, with fleshy, perfectly cordate deep green leaves whose tips are long-acuminate and whose margins are remotely toothed. This tendril-bearing vine has many long aerial roots similar to those of *C. gongylodes* but greenish and not red in color. The vine is sometimes called princess vine. It grows in shade or partial sun and needs adequate moisture and a fairly rich soil. **Cissus sicyoides 'Albonitens',** an unusually beautiful cultivar, has a silvery and metallic sheen to the upper surface of the leaves.

Cissus trifoliata. See *C. incisa.*

Cissus voinieranum. See *Tetrastigma voinieranum.*

CITHAREXYLUM (sith-a-REX-i-lum)
Verbenaceae: The Verbena, Lantana Family
FIDDLEWOOD
Small to medium evergreen trees; linear leathery
    leaves; long spikes of fragrant white flowers
Zones 10 and 11; marginal (as a shrub) in zone 9b
Sun
Average but regular amounts of moisture
Sandy, humusy, well-drained soil
Propagation by seed

A genus of about 70 species of evergreen shrubs and trees in tropical America with leathery leaves, fragrant white or yellow flowers, and beadlike berries.

Citharexylum fruticosum (froot-i-KO-sum) is native to southern Florida and the West Indies. It is a very attractive little tree or large shrub that grows slowly to as much as 30 feet in height with a usually leaning trunk and a rather oblong or pyramidal crown. The leaves are mostly elliptic but sometimes almost oblong in shape with cuneate bases and acuminate tips. The leaves are seldom more than 6 inches long and are bright green and glossy above, paler beneath. The tree blooms most of the year with 6-inch-long, loose axillary spikes of tiny tubular white fragrant flowers with five corolla lobes. The fruits are small brown or black berries.

Citharexylum spinosum (spi-NO-sum) is indigenous to the West Indies. It is similar to *C. fruticosum* but is larger in all respects and sometimes grows slowly to as much as 50 feet in height. The leaves are 8 or more inches long and similar to those of *C. fruticosum;* they usually turn an attractive bronze color with cool weather. The flower spikes are as much as a foot long with small tubular white flowers with five corolla lobes. The fruits are dark purple berries.

×CITROFORTUNELLA
(sit´-ro-for-tyoo-NEL-la)
Rutaceae: The Citrus Family
Common names vary according to species
Evergreen aromatic, mostly thorny trees and shrubs;
    fragrant white flowers; showy edible fruit

Zones vary according to species and variety
Sun
Average but regular amounts of moisture
Deep, sandy, humusy, well-drained soil
Propagation by grafting

A small genus of three naturally occurring intergeneric hybrids between a *Citrus* species and a *Fortunella* species. One species is known commonly as the calamondin orange, the other two are limequats.

×**Citrofortunella floridana** (flor-i-DAHN-a), the eustis limequat, is a hybrid between *Citrus aurantiifolia* (Mexican lime) and a *Fortunella* (kumquat) species. The little tree has the overall appearance of the Mexican lime, but the leaves are more like those of a kumquat, and are usually troughed or somewhat folded lengthwise. Flowers appear mainly in the spring, sometimes later. The little fruits are very attractive, a bright yellow when mature, perfectly round, and about 2 inches in diameter. The tree only grows to about 6 feet in height and is hardy in zones 9 through 11 to the low 20s.

×**Citrofortunella microcarpa** (myk-ro-KARP-a) (synonym ×*C. mitis*), the calamondin orange, is a hybrid between *Citrus reticulata* and a *Fortunella* species. The aromatic tree is very attractive and can grow to 25 feet in height with a cylindrical and slender, dense crown of dark foliage. The leaves are glossy, broad-ovate to elliptic, 2 to 4 inches long, dark green above and paler beneath. The inch-wide, pure white, intensely fragrant flowers are truly wonderful. The little fruits are usually less than 2 inches in diameter, but are a brilliant reddish orange in color, with an easily peeled loose and somewhat puffy skin, a delightful aroma, and a deliciously acidic taste; they are mostly round but may also be oblate. The tree is hardy in zones 9b through 11 and is often grown even in zone 9a although with occasional damage. It also does wonderfully in the truly tropical regions. It is not very particular as to soil and grows well in the "gumbo" of the Gulf Coast and in the limy soils of southern Florida. It is truly one of the most beautiful of the "citrus" varieties.

×**Citrofortunella swinglei** (SWING-lee-eye), the tavares limequat, is a hybrid between *Citrus aurantiifolia* and a *Fortunella* species. It is very similar to ×*Citrofortunella floridana*.

×CITRONCIRUS (sit-rahn-SY-rus)
Rutaceae: The Citrus Family
CITRANGE
Semideciduous trees; trifoliate leaves; fragrant
    flowers; edible fruit
Zones 8 through 11
Sun
Average but regular amounts of moisture
Deep, sandy, humusy, well-drained soil
Propagation by grafting

An intergeneric hybrid between the genera *Poncirus* and *Citrus*. ×**Citroncirus webberi** (WEB-ur-eye), a cross between *Poncirus trifoliata* (trifoliate orange) and a hybrid of *Citrus sinensis* (the orange), has the vernacular name of citrange. It is, because of its trifoliate orange parent, semideciduous in cold weather and is very hardy and flourishes in zones 8 through 11. It grows to 10 feet or more in height. The leaves are trifoliate, dark green, and about 4 inches wide. The flowers are small white fragrant stars, and the fruits are small, roundish and orange colored. It is not the prettiest of the citrus tribe, but is nonetheless quite attractive, especially in flower and fruit. ×***Citroncirus webberi*** has been crossed with a *Fortunella* (kumquat) species to produce citrangequat, one of the hardiest citrus varieties. Citrangequat is successfully grown in zones 8b through 11 and often in zone 8a. It is a beautiful little tree usually with trifoliate leaves, growing to 10 or 12 feet in height. The tree flowers almost year-round (except in the coldest weather) and the blossoms are lusciously fragrant and reminiscent of gardenias. The fruit is oval to almost round, 2 or 3 inches in diameter, and a pure orange in color. There are at least two cultivars of this hybrid, the most attractive of which is *Citrus* 'Macciaroli'.

CITRUS (SIT-rus)
Rutaceae: The Citrus Family
CITRUS
Evergreen aromatic, mostly thorny trees and shrubs;
    fragrant white flowers; showy edible fruit
Zones vary according to species and variety
Sun
Average but regular amounts of moisture
Deep, sandy, humusy, well-drained soil
Propagation by seed and air-layering; most varieties
    are grafted

A small genus of 16 species and near countless hybrids and cultivars, some of whose parentage is uncertain. All the species are native to India, southern China, Southeast Asia, or Malaysia. They are mostly denizens of coastal flood plains interspersed with the tropical rain forests of these regions, although a few citrus relatives are found in upland areas. The leaves and fruits are very aromatic, and the flowers exhibit some of the most wonderful fragrances to be found among the flowering plants. The starlike blossoms are white, although many are purplish in bud; the petals and sepals are five and are generally thick and succulent. The fruits are edible and range from intensely sour (such as lemon, lime, and sour orange) to lusciously sweet.

Most *Citrus* species and relatives have compound leaves that are usually reduced to one leaflet, a condition termed "unifoliolate." They also have unusual petioles that are winged with a leaflike appendage, obovate in shape, and sometimes almost as large as the blade itself. Most species bloom most heavily in spring, with the fruit maturing from late summer to the next spring. The more tropical the climate, the more frequently citrus varieties tend to bloom. In completely tropical climates there is usually year-round production of flowers and fruit, which can lead to a marketing problem since

the color of mature fruit is almost the same as that of the unripened fruit. Fruit color ranges from green to yellow, orange, and almost red.

The fruit in the warmer regions does not always show the intensity of color that is associated with citrus fruit in markets because a certain differential in temperature between night and day is responsible for much of this dazzling color (i.e., the skins of southern Florida oranges are not generally as colorful as those grown in California or the Gulf Coast). Compensating for the duller colors is the significantly higher sugar content of citrus grown in warm areas. In addition, the higher humidity of most of the southeastern United States results in generally larger size and higher juice content of the fruit; most juice oranges are grown in Florida, and most commercial lemons are grown in California. Few plants are more beautiful than a round-crowned, glossy-leaved citrus tree covered in deliciously fragrant blossoms and succulent fruit of various shades of yellow, gold, red, or orange.

Almost all named citrus varieties are grafted onto a rootstock, which is different in species and often genus from the named hybrid or cultivar. This is done because the rootstock, usually a *Citrus* species or relative, is hardier to adverse conditions and is more disease resistant than the cultivar or hybrid plant's roots. In addition, the rootstock may make the named variety grow as a dwarf, which is desirable in many circumstances where space is restricted. Even though citrus need regular irrigation and must not be subjected to drought conditions, no *Citrus* species or cultivar is capable of surviving in soil that does not have good drainage; prolonged flooding or standing water kills the trees.

Citrus aurantiifolia (aw-rant´-ee-eye-FO-lee-a), called the lime, key lime, bartender's lime, or Mexican lime, is the most tender *Citrus* species, being adaptable only in southern Florida, far southern Texas, coastal southern California, and elsewhere in zones 10 and 11. Any temperature below 30°F will severely damage the plants. The species is native to Southeast Asia and southern India, areas of monsoonal rainfall that are completely tropical. These trees grow year-round and tend to flower mostly after or concurrently with rainy periods. The main fruit production is in spring, summer, and fall. There are but few varieties, and the Mexican lime is one of the few species of *Citrus* usually grown on its own roots. It is naturally a large shrub to 15 feet in height, densely clothed in leaves with small spines in the leaf axils; it must be trained and pruned if a tree form is desired. The dark green and very aromatic leaves are mostly elliptic in shape and only 3 or 4 inches long. The large flowers are 2 or more inches wide and not as fragrant as those of most other *Citrus* species. The round to elliptical and very acidic fruit is also about 2 inches in diameter and yellow when ripe. The tree seems immune to the calcareous soils of southern Florida and, in general, is not that particular as to soil type if it is well drained. There are spineless cultivars, but they do not fruit as well as the type. The Bearss' or Persian lime or Tahitian lime (synonym *C. latifolia*) is probably a hybrid, most likely between the citron (*C. medica*) and the Mexican lime (*C. aurantiifolia*). It is similar in all respects to the species except for thorniness, acidity, and hardiness: it is much less sour than the Mexican lime, sometimes almost sweet, less thorny, and hardy in zones 9b through 11 although sometimes suffering damage in zone 9b. It is a very beautiful little tree, more attractive than the species.

Citrus aurantium (aw-RANT-ee-um) is indigenous to Vietnam and is called the sour orange or bitter orange. It is one of the hardier species in the genus and flourishes in zones 9b through 11. These beautiful little trees grow to as much as 20 feet or more in height (although there are varieties that are shrubby) with compact crowns of dark green foliage above smooth brown trunks. The long-petioled 6-inch-long leaves are ovate to elliptic or even obovate, depending on the variety. The wonderfully fragrant large 2-inch-wide flowers produce fruits that are 3 to 4 inches in diameter, rather pulpy-skinned, and imperfectly round with thick rinds and very acidic flesh; the centers of the fruit are hollow. Most people find the fruit much too sour to eat fresh, but it is greatly esteemed for making marmalades, candies, and preserves, and is used, as are Mexican limes, for flavoring drinks and for seasoning fish and other viands. Of the several varieties and cultivars of sour orange, the three most common are described here. ***Citrus aurantium* var. *bergamia*** (ber-GAHM-ee-a), called the bouquet or bouquet de fleurs, is a compact and thornless little tree with intensely fragrant flowers and beautiful elliptic to obovate bright green leaves. ***Citrus aurantium* var. *myrtifolia*** (mur-ti-FO-lee-a), called chinotto or myrtle-leaved orange, is another compact, shrubby, and thornless little tree with small leaves and pulpy-skinned, yellowish orange fruit that is favored for candies. ***Citrus aurantium* 'Seville'** is a wonderful landscape subject. It makes a near perfect small tree to 20 feet or more in height. All three forms bear fruit that ripens from early winter to early spring, but can remain on the tree for almost a year in good condition. With their brilliant reddish orange fruits and glossy leaves one could hardly ask for more attractive objects in the subtropical landscape.

Citrus grandis. See *C. maxima*.

Citrus ichangensis (ee-chang-EN-sis) is indigenous to southwestern China, the area north of Myanmar (Burma) and Vietnam. It is known as the papeda, ichang lemon, or ichang-papeda. It is the hardiest species in the genus and is adaptable in zones 8b through 11, although it is sometimes damaged in zone 8. Unlike most other species of *Citrus* it is found in upland areas and therefore demands perfect drainage. This large shrub or small tree grows to as much as 15 feet with a usually upright and linear form. The leaves are generally lanceolate-acuminate in shape and 4 to 5 inches long with very large, winged, almost leaflike obovate petioles. The flowers are small, as is the fruit, which is a very attractive orange in color and is shaped like a small lemon. The hybrid known as Yuzu seems to be a cross between *C. ichangensis* and *C. reticulata* (mandarin orange) with small bright yellow fruit and leaves similar in shape to those of *C. ichangensis* but smaller. It has reportedly survived 10°F without damage, making it suitable for zones 8 through 11 and is possibly hardy even in zone 7. It loses its leaves and goes dormant with freezing weather.

Citrus latifolia. See *C. aurantiifolia*.

Citrus limon (LIM-ahn) is the lemon. It is possibly a hybrid between *C. medica* (citron) and *C. aurantiifolia* (Mexican lime), although its nativity and original habitat are unknown. The tree grows to 20 feet or so in height, but must usually be trained to tree form as its natural bent is to be a large shrub with rangy stems. Most commercial supermarket varieties of lemon do not flower and fruit well in hot and humid climates, although they can make lovely landscape subjects and nevertheless produce some fruit in these areas. The leaves are mostly elliptic to oblong and 3 to 5 inches long. The flowers are large, tinged with purple, and very fragrant. Two forms are widely grown in Florida and the Gulf Coast: *C. limon* 'Meyer' and *C. limon* 'Ponderosa.'

'Eureka' does best in climates that are not drenched with high humidity year-round and that have cooler nights than areas like Florida and the Gulf Coast. It is the prime variety grown in southern California for marketing, where it makes a beautiful small tree to 20 feet or more in height and is hardy in zones 9b through 11.

'Lisbon' should be considered in a landscape if the fruits are not the main attraction. It is a very large (to 30 feet), fast-growing, and beautiful tree, and is probably the hardiest of the lemons. It is a good candidate for zones 9a through 11, although it does not fruit well along the Gulf Coast or in Florida because of the humidity.

'Meyer' (synonym *Citrus meyerii*) is probably a hybrid between a lemon and a sweet orange. It is dependably hardy in zones 9b through 11 and often successfully grown in zone 9a as damage only starts at about 25°F and the trees sprout back even from temperatures below 20°F. The trees are almost thornless and grow normally to about 12 feet; they produce typically sized bright yellow and rather sweet fruit intermittently most of the year.

'Ponderosa' (synonym *Citrus ponderosa*) is not quite as hardy as the Meyer lemon and is a smaller, more spreading and much thornier tree with truly immense and quite acidic fruit, often larger than a typical grapefruit.

Citrus ×limonia (li-MOAN-ee-a), known as the Rangpur lime or sometimes as the mandarin lime, is a hybrid between *C. limon* (lemon) and *C. reticulata* (Mandarin orange). It is hardy in zones 9 through 11 and sometimes successfully grown in zone 8b. This small, spreading tree has few thorns and usually pendent branches sometimes reaching a height of 20 feet. The attractive leaves are elliptic to obovate in shape and as much as 5 inches long; new growth is purplish to reddish in color. The plant blooms and fruits intermittently most of the year. The fruit is usually perfectly round but may be oblate and has a flavor like a very sour orange; it is usually used as a substitute for the true limes. The fruit is a bright almost reddish orange color and as much as 3 inches in diameter. This is a very attractive little tree or shrub when in flower and fruit.

Citrus maxima (MAX-i-ma) (synonym *C. grandis*), the pummelo, pommelo, or shaddock, is native to a vast area from Thailand to Polynesia. It is the largest growing *Citrus* species; the type can grow to as much as 50 feet in height but usually attains no more than 20 to 30 feet. The leaves are as much as 8 inches long and vary from ovate to elliptic in shape. The large (to 3 inches wide), fragrant, yellowish white flowers result in very large, round to pear-shaped yellow to greenish yellow fruits that are as much as 12 inches in diameter and that sometimes weigh as much as 20 pounds; they are of unparalleled beauty hanging on the tree. These great yellow orbs have a pinkish flesh that is sweet but not juicy compared to more commercial citrus varieties. The tree is not widely grown in the United States, although it is a simply superb landscape subject (the most beautiful *Citrus* species in my opinion) and is hardy in zones 9b through 11. *Citrus maxima* **'Chandler'** is the most commonly sold and planted form. *Citrus maxima* **'Reinking'** is a much larger and more beautiful tree.

Citrus medica (MED-i-ka) is the citron. It is an ancient fruit and the first known to the Western world. The thorny and straggly shrub only grows to about 12 feet in height and must be studiously trained if a tree form is desired. The leaves are ovate-lanceolate to as much as 8 inches long. The 2-inch-wide fragrant, purple-tinged flowers form very large (as much as a foot long) yellow, pulpy-skinned, very fragrant fruit that is generally oblong in shape but extremely variable in some of its varieties. It is a tender species and is not dependable outside zones 10 and 11. There are several naturally occurring varieties, the two most common of which are described here. *Citrus medica* **var.** *ethrog,* the etrog or ethrog citron, has a spindle-shaped fruit that is not juicy but has a very aromatic rind. This rind is used not only candied, but is also the ceremonial fruit of the Jewish Feast of the Tabernacles. *Citrus medica* **var.** *sarcodactylus,* the Buddha's hand citron or fingered citron, is the world's most unusual *Citrus* variety. It is a large, pulpy-skinned oblong fruit that is apically divided into several recurved segments, which are more than half the total length of the fruit. It is exotic, and some would say grotesque, but nevertheless fascinating to contemplate—a startling sight on the trees.

Citrus otaitense, the otaheite orange, is a dwarf and nonacidic form of *C.* ×*limonia.*

Citrus ×*paradisi,* (pair-a-DEE-see), the grapefruit, is most likely a hybrid between *C. maxima* (pummelo) and *C. sinensis* (orange) and is hardy in zones 9b through 11 although it is planted in zone 9a. It much resembles one of its parents, *C. maxima.* The trees usually do not grow more than 20 feet tall and have few thorns and lovely spreading and rounded crowns of dark green foliage above stout gray trunks. The leaves are ovate to linear-ovate, about 6 inches long, and only minutely serrate on the margins. The 2-inch-wide white flowers yield globose to pear-shaped yellow fruit in clusters, each of which is usually about 6 inches in diameter and has white to pink to red flesh. The fruit takes a year or sometimes longer to mature. Several forms do well along the warmer parts of the Gulf Coast and in Florida, including those listed here. *Citrus* ×*paradisi* **'Duncan'** is the hardiest and has juicy white flesh. *Citrus* ×*paradisi* **'Flame'** has red flesh. *Citrus* ×*paradisi* **'Marsh'** has white or pink flesh. *Citrus* ×*paradisi* **'Mexican Red'** also has red flesh. *Citrus* ×*paradisi* **'Redblush',** known in Texas as "Ruby Red," has dark pink to red flesh and a reddish tint on the outside of the fruit. *Citrus* ×*paradisi* **'Rio Red'** has red flesh, as does *Citrus* ×*paradisi* **'Star Ruby'.** Grapefruit varieties are among the few *Citrus* hybrids that usually come true from seed and can be grown successfully on their own roots. They do not, however, grow nearly as fast this way and can take many years to flower and fruit. They also lack the hardiness and disease resistance they have when grown on other rootstocks All grapefruits need much heat if the fruit is not to be bitter. They grow best on deep alluvial soil (as is found in the Rio Grande Valley of Texas) with regular irrigation. Grapefruit trees make magnificent landscape subjects, second in beauty only to the pummelo.

Citrus reticulata (re-tik´-yoo-LAIT-a) is native to Laos, Vietnam, and the Philippines. Common names for the species, hybrids, and cultivars include tangerine, satsuma orange, mandarin, and mandarin orange. The name "tangerine" is most often applied (and should be confined) to those types with a distinctly reddish color to the fruit. Some of the cultivars and hybrids are among the most cold hardy citrus species. The type makes a thorny spreading, broad-crowned tree to as much as 25 feet. The leaves are lanceolate in shape and usually about 5 inches long. The fruit is oblate in shape, about 3 inches wide, and a bright reddish orange in color, with a sweet and only slightly acidic taste. The most salient characteristic of the fruit is the ease of separation of the skin and segments. Plate 118.

Among the available cultivars of *Citrus reticulata* are the following. *Citrus reticulata* **'Clementine'** (synonym 'Algerian Tangerine') is believed to be a hybrid but the other parent is unknown. It is not as hardy as the calamondin and should not be grown outside zones 9 through 11. The tree usually grows no more than about 15 feet in height and has a nice weeping habit with branches densely clothed in leaves. The 2- to 4-inch-long leaves are lanceolate to elliptic in shape and a medium green in color. The fruit is round to pear-shaped, reddish orange, very sweet, and juicy. For best fruit production, a second tree of the same type or another tangerine variety should be planted nearby. *Citrus reticulata* **'Dancy'** is the most widely grown and sold tangerine variety. It seems to be a sport of a mandarin orange that originated in Morocco. The word *tangerine* is an archaic word meaning "from or of Tangiers." This cultivar grows rather quickly into an almost thornless tree to 20 feet in height or even more with a usually oblong and fairly narrow crown of foliage. The leaves are ovate-elliptic and about 4 inches long. The fruit is oblate to pear-shaped with a slightly puffy skin that is loose, very easy to peel, and a deep orange-red to almost scarlet in color. The flesh is acidic, but sweet and very juicy. The tree is hardy in zones 9 through 11 and does best where heat is abundant. ***Citrus reticulata*** **'Mediterranean Mandarin'** (synonym 'Willowleaf Mandarin') is dependably hardy in zones 9 through 11 but is also grown in 8b. It makes a small, spreading, dense-crowned tree with narrow bright green willow-like leaves and has very few or no thorns. The fruit is oblate, yellow-orange in color, and has a juicy and sweet flesh. ***Citrus reticulata*** **'Satsuma'** is a very hardy mandarin orange that is dependable in zones 8b through 11. It is one of the least attractive varieties of citrus, but the fruit is sweet and delicious. The tree grows slowly to 12 feet or more in height and has an open and spreading habit. The shape of the fruit is variable and ranges from almost round and smooth to pyriform and pulpy; the color is always orange without much red. There are several varieties of satsuma but by far the most common is ***Citrus reticulata*** **'Owari Satsuma'.** Another variety that is reputed to be even hardier to cold than the owari is ***Citrus reticulata*** **'Kimbrough'.**

Among the available hybrids of *Citrus reticulata* are ×*Citrofortunella microcarpa* (which see) and the following. ***Citrus*** **'Changsha'** (synonym 'Changsa') is usually classed as a tangerine because of the distinctly reddish hue of the fruits. It is most likely a hybrid between a mandarin orange and one of the cultivars of *C. ichangensis.* It is small spreading and slow-growing tree with 3- to 4-inch-long elliptic-acuminate leaves. It is extremely hardy to cold and is suitable for zones 8a through 11, although it performs best outside the truly tropical areas. The fruit is not particularly good, being insipidly sweet with an aftertaste that is objectionable to most palates, but the little tree is attractive. ***Citrus*** **'Fairchild Tangerine'** is a hybrid between the clementine tangerine and a tangelo (which is a cross between the grapefruit and a mandarin orange). It is a small, thornless, spreading tree with lanceolate leaves that are as much as 6 inches long. It is hardy in zones 9 through 11. The 3-inch fruits are generally oblate in shape, very sweet in flavor, deep reddish orange in color, with a smooth skin that is peeled with some difficulty. The tree needs other tangerine varieties nearby for pollination and best fruit production. ***Citrus*** **'Page'** is a hybrid between the clementine tangerine and the minneola tangerine. It is hardy in zones 9 through 11. This vigorous grower sometimes reaches a height of 25 feet, has a dense round crown of foliage, and is almost thornless. The fruit is unlike that of other tangerines in that it is

usually not reddish in color but looks like a round sour orange. It makes one of the most beautiful citrus trees. ***Citrus*** **'Wilking'** is a hybrid between two other Mandarin cultivars and is hardy in zones 9 through 11. It is an attractive tree that usually grows to a maximum height of 15 feet and has a dense and rounded crown. The leaves are linear-lanceolate, long-acuminate, and rather willowlike. The fruit is a deep orange in color, oblate in shape, and about 3 inches in diameter.

Citrus sinensis (sin-EN-sis), the sweet orange or simply the orange, is thought by some taxonomists to be only a variety of the sour orange. It is probably native to northwestern India, Myanmar (Burma), and southern China, but is no longer found in the wild. The beautiful trees usually grow to 25 or 30 feet in height with round crowns and somewhat pendent branches when mature, although very old trees are known to attain as much as 50 feet of height. The plants usually have stout spines on the younger branches. The leaves are ovate to elliptic in shape and usually finely serrate on the margins, dark glossy green in color, and 4 to 6 inches long. The pure white 2-inch-wide starlike flowers have a heavy and very sweet fragrance. The fruit is globular, yellow to orange in color when ripe, and unlike *C. aurantium* (sour orange), has a solid center. *Citrus sinensis* and its cultivars are hardy in zones 9b through 11 and marginal in zone 9a; damage usually starts at about 25°F, is severe at 20°F, and fatal at 15°F or below. Because sweet orange varieties mostly ripen late, even if the tree is not damaged by cold, the fruit may be. Not one of the cultivars is good on its own roots; all are sold grafted onto various rootstocks.

The best and most available varieties of sweet orange for the Gulf Coast and Florida include the following. ***Citrus sinensis*** **'Hamlin'** is a medium-sized (usually about 15 feet in height) dense-crowned tree that is one of the hardiest of the sweet oranges. ***Citrus sinensis*** **'Marrs'** is a small tree (usually no more than 8 feet in height) that is best grown as a large shrub. It is a heavy fruit bearer. ***Citrus sinensis*** **'Parson Brown'** (synonym 'Parson') is a relatively hardy, large, and beautiful tree whose fruit ripens early. It is a prime candidate for the Gulf Coast. ***Citrus sinensis*** **'Pineapple'** is a rather tender large tree to 20 feet that is best grown only in zones 9b through 11. ***Citrus sinensis*** **'Valencia'**, the world's most widely grown orange, is a large and beautiful tree that is reasonably hardy to cold but whose fruit ripens late and is usually damaged in areas colder than zone 9b.

The navel oranges are not completely adapted to the humid subtropical regions like Florida and the Gulf Coast, but are some of the most widely grown orange varieties in California and the subtropical desert southwest. The original navel orange is now called the "Washington navel"; it is a medium-sized dense tree with outstandingly good large fruit. Hybrids of *Citrus sinensis* include ×*Citroncirus webberi* (which see).

Citrus ×***tangelo,*** commonly called tangelo, is the result of crosses between varieties of *C. reticulata* (tangerine) and *C. ×paradisi* (grapefruit) or *C. maxima* (pummelo). The trees are rather large and quite attractive, combining the traits of both parents. They are candidates for zones 9 through 11. The fruits range from the size of a mandarin orange to that of the grapefruit and often have a collar or neck at the stem end; like the mandarins, they are usually easy to peel and have a sweet and acidic flesh. *Citrus ×tangelo* '**Minneola**' grows large with a dense crown of very attractive large leaves; its fruits are a vibrant orange, about the size of a small grapefruit and have a distinct collar. *Citrus ×tangelo* '**Orlando**' is the hardiest of the tangelos and is similar to 'Minneola' except that the fruits are not collared and the tree does not grow quite as large. *Citrus ×tangelo* '**Sampson**' makes the most beautiful tree and grows to the size of a grapefruit tree with bright yellow fruit of the same size. *Citrus ×tangelo* '**Seminole**' makes a large and attractive tree with reddish orange 4-inch fruit.

CLEISTOCACTUS
(KLEES-toe-kak-tus)
Cactaceae: The Cactus Family
Common names vary according to species
Tall slender, many-ribbed cactuses; dense spines;
    tubular flowers
Zones vary according to species
Sun
Drought tolerant
Sandy, humusy, well-drained soil
Propagation by seed and cuttings

A genus of about 70 erect slender cylindrical-columned, many-ribbed cactus species branching from near the base. All have long hairlike white to yellow spines densely covering the stems and clusters of narrow tubular flowers that never open very widely. The Greek word *kleisto* means "closed." The flowers are usually red, but some species have yellow or green along with the red color. These cactuses are not completely typical of desert dwellers (indeed, many are not denizens of true deserts) and should not be allowed to suffer prolonged conditions of drought.

Cleistocactus baumannii (baw-MAN-nee-eye) is indigenous to eastern Bolivia, northern Argentina, Paraguay, and Uruguay. It is not dependably hardy outside zones 10 and 11. The stems reach a height of 3 or 4 feet with dense yellowish spines. The flowers come in summer and are a brilliant orange-red.

Cleistocactus brookei (BROOK-ee-eye) is native to eastern Bolivia and is a good landscape subject for zones 9b through 11. The stems are not completely erect and are somewhat sprawling, rising only to about 6 feet in height. They are very densely covered with white to yellowish spines and look fuzzy from any distance. The plants bloom in summer with narrow usually curved bright red flowers. This species is one of the most beautiful in the genus, and it is difficult to resist hugging these teddy-bear-like stems.

Cleistocactus buchtienii (book-TEE-nee-eye) is indigenous to eastern Bolivia and is hardy in zones 9b through 11. The stems reach 7 or 8 feet in height, are many-ribbed, and are fairly stout. The spines are not as dense on this species as they are on many others, and they are distinctly reddish in color. The flowers are purplish red and are as long as 3 inches.

Cleistocactus candelilla (kahn-de-LEE-ya) is native to southeastern Bolivia and is hardy in zones 9b through 11. The stems grow to about 3 feet and are not completely erect but usually reclining or leaning. They are very densely covered with long spines that are red when young but age to a dull white or gray. The flowers are a fiery red with yellow tips and are about 2 inches long. This species is exceptionally beautiful.

Cleistocactus fieldianus. See *Borzicactus fieldianus*.

Cleistocactus jujuyensis (joo-joo-YEN-sis) is native to northern Argentina and southern Bolivia and is hardy in zones 9b through 11. It is one of the most attractive species in the genus; the plant freely branches from the base, resulting in lovely and picturesque groups of yellow-white columns of varying heights. The stems are about 3 feet tall and are densely clothed in white to yellowish spines. The flowers are 2 inches long and orange-red in color.

Cleistocactus samaipatanus. See *Borzicactus samaipatanus*.

Cleistocactus smaragdiflorus (sma-rag´-di-FLOR-us) is native to northern Argentina, Uruguay, and Paraguay, and is hardy in zones 10 and 11. The stems grow to 6 or 7 feet in height and are more decumbent than erect. They are completely covered in light to dark brown spines. The flowers are red at the base and yellow and green near the tips.

Cleistocactus strausii (STROWSS-ee-eye) is native to southern Bolivia and northern Argentina and is a wonderful landscape subject for zones 9b through 11. The plant freely branches from the base and has erect stems about 6 feet tall, which are completely covered in pure white spines. The flowers are a deep raspberry red and are clothed in short white spines. This species is possibly the most beautiful species in cultivation and is sometimes called silver torch.

Cleistocactus vulpis-cauda (vool´-pis-KAW-da) is indigenous to Bolivia and is hardy in zones 9b through 11. The trailing stems are covered in russet-colored spines and give a foxtail resemblance to the plants. The Latin words *vulpis* and *cauda* mean "fox" and "stem," respectively. The flowers are orange with red tips. This cactus is superb in a rock garden and on or above rock walls in full sun.

CLEMATIS (KLEM-a-tis / kle-MAT-is)
Ranunculaceae: The Ranunculus, Anemone,
    Clematis Family
EVERGREEN CLEMATIS
Evergreen vine; drooping, linear leaves; white,
    fragrant spring flowers

Zones 7 through 9a
Sun
Average but regular amounts of moisture
Sandy, humusy, well-drained soil
Propagation by seed and cuttings

A large genus of more than 200 species of mostly vines that are typically deciduous, small, and herbaceous. The one tropical looking species is evergreen and large, and becomes woody. ***Clematis armandii*** (ahr-MAN-dee-eye) is native to central and western China and the Himalayan region. The vine grows to at least 20 feet in height by twisting petioles and is quite dense except at the base. It is usually good to plant some sort of cover at the base of the stems to hide the bare trunks and help shade the roots, which is usually necessary in the hotter climes. This hardy vine has some of the most beautiful and tropical looking leaves of any plant. They are leathery, a deep dark green, and trifoliate, with the middle leaflet usually longer than the other two, 5 or 6 inches long, and linear-cordate or oblong in shape with three prominent parallel veins. The flowers come in February or March in masses of airy panicles from the leaf axils. Each blossom is pure white and as much as 3 inches wide, with five or six widely separated lanceolate petals and a round center of stamens and pistils. The fruit is typical of the genus, a long, silky plume. The plants need guidance and patience from the gardener when first planted as they usually just sit until their roots become adjusted to the transplanting trauma; adequate irrigation and shade is important for them at this time. Once established the vine is quite vigorous and grows fast. It may take an entire season to become established, but it is worth the effort for such a beautiful plant. It is not a lover of acidic soils; manure and agricultural lime are recommended for such situations.

CLERODENDRUM
(kler-o-DEN-drum)
Verbenaceae: The Verbena, Lantana Family
Common names vary according to species
Evergreen shrubs and small trees; usually large bold
  leaves; large panicles of mostly red flowers
Zones vary according to species
Sun to partial shade
Average but regular amounts of moisture
Humusy, well-drained, slightly acidic soil
Propagation by seed, cuttings, and (sometimes)
  transplanting of suckers

A large genus of about 200 species of shrubs, trees, and a few vines from tropical areas around the world, mostly the Eastern Hemisphere. The generic name is sometimes spelled "*Clerodendron*," which is a prettier sounding word though incorrect. All the species have showy flowers either because of the beauty of the individual flowers or the number of flowers in the panicles. All have flowers with relatively long, protruding, and often arched stamens, and every flower color is repre-

sented. None of the species is really hardy to cold, but some come back from the roots and grow strongly after a freeze. Almost all have showy, colored fruits. Some of the world's most beautiful flowers (as well as beautiful leaves) are found in this genus.

Clerodendrum buchananii (byook-a-NAN-ee-eye) is indigenous to Java and is hardy in zones 10 and 11, although it is grown in zone 9 as a marginal or annual shrub. It grows to 7 or 8 feet if not knocked back by cold. The wonderful soft, velvety dark green leaves are a foot long and are ovate in outline. The flowers are in great panicles similar to those of *C. paniculatum* but not quite as large, and the flowers are more orange-red in color than the fiery red of *C. paniculatum*. The flowers are followed by blue fruits.

Clerodendrum bungei (BUN-jee-eye) is native to southern China, Myanmar (Burma), and eastern India, and is adaptable in zones 8 through 11 and possibly in the warmer parts of zone 7. It is a very beautiful plant with a problem for most gardeners: it is invasive. The plant has mostly unbranched stems that grow to as much as 10 feet in height. The dark green leaves often have a purplish cast and are about a foot wide and strongly toothed on the margins; they are usually hairy to some extent, especially beneath. The flowers appear most heavily in late spring, but may be found in summer and fall also. They are in large densely packed (to 8 inches wide) convex, rounded corymbs. Each flower is a dark violet color in bud and, when fully open, is a short tube that expands into five starlike petals of pure pink. Because the central flowers open first, a flower head usually has two colors. The fragrance of the flowers is, to most proboscises, heavenly sweet, a mixture of honeysuckle and carnation, but some people find the odor unpleasant. The leaves, when crushed or bruised, are somewhat malodorous. The plant suckers with spreading roots that can travel as much as 20 feet before sending up a stem. These suckers are easily pulled up, but they are prolific. The shrub is naturalized in many parts of the U.S. Deep South. It grows in full sun or part shade and seems to flourish in most soil types, but is not drought tolerant. It is sometimes called gloryflower, but in the Deep South it is universally known as cashmere bouquet. Plate 119.

Clerodendrum fragrans. See *C. philippinum*.

Clerodendrum indicum (IN-di-kum) occurs naturally in northeastern India and Myanmar (Burma) and is hardy in zones 10 and 11. It grows 6 to 8 feet in height with 8-inch-long narrowly elliptic leaves. The inflorescence is as much as 2 feet long with many long tubular pure white flowers, each of which has expanded corolla lobes similar in form to most other species. The lovely fruits are dark blue in color. Plate 120.

Clerodendrum minahassae (min-a-HAH-see) is native to Indonesia, the Philippines, and Malaysia. A large shrub in zone 9b and a small tree in zones 10 and 11, it freezes back to the ground in zone 9 but usually resprouts from the roots. If not killed back, it reaches a height of 12 feet or more. It is easily trained into a very handsome little tree as it is vigorous and grows fast. The leaves are 8 to 10 inches long and are elliptic to oblong to obovate in shape with depressed veins. The flowers are borne in loose-flowered cymes. Each blossom is as much as 5 inches long with narrow reflexed, pure white petals, and very long thin deep red stamens, the whole subtended by (above) a fleshy bright red calyx. The little trees bloom in cycles all year long if not killed back by frost. These gorgeous plants need ample water and rich soil, but flourish in sun or partial shade. This very elegant plant has gossamer, airy flowers and colorful fruit. Plates 121 and 122.

Clerodendrum nutans. See *C. wallichii.*

Clerodendrum paniculatum (pan-ik´-yoo-LATT-um) is native to Southeast Asia and is a startlingly beautiful shrub in and out of flower. Although it grows in zones 9 through 11, it is marginal and freezes back in the former zone. It is commonly called the pagoda flower. The shrub grows to 6 or 8 feet in height with leaves that are lovely enough to warrant growing the plant for their sake alone; they are more than a foot wide, orbicular to ovate in shape, with deeply depressed veins, usually three to five lobes, and slight pubescence. The vivid carmine to scarlet flowers appear all year long (but mostly in summer) in giant 18-inch-tall, densely flowered tiered terminal panicles that resemble a Chinese pagoda. Each flower is a 3-inch-long tube ending in a 2-inch-wide fan of flaring petals with long protruding stamens. Some plants have yellow and even white on the petals. This wonderful plant needs fairly rich soil and ample water. It grows best in full sun, although it does well in partial shade. It suckers but is not truly invasive. Plate 123.

Clerodendrum philippinum (fi-LIP-pi-num) (synonym *C. fragrans*) is native to eastern China, the Philippines, and the southern Japanese islands, and is adaptable to zones 9 through 11 although marginal in zone 9a. It is commonly called the glory tree or glorybower, and glorious it is. It is not really a tree, but a medium-sized shrub growing to 10 feet or so in height. The habit is like that of *C. bungei* in that the stems are seldom branched; it suckers like *C. bungei* but is not as invasive. The dark green leaves are about a foot across, ovate to triangular in shape, pubescent, and deeply veined. The fragrant flowers are in densely flowered terminal clusters. Each little blossom is shaped as a little round rose, ivory-colored with a peach blush, sometimes also with a bluish hue. Like *C. bungei* the shrub looks best when underplanted to mask its bare stem bases.

Clerodendrum quadriloculare (kwad´-ri-lahk-yoo-LAIR-ee) is indigenous to the Philippines and is hardy in zones 10b and 11. It is arguably the most beautiful species in the genus. The shrub grows to 20 feet and may be trained to a small tree form, but is usually grown as a large shrub. The plant has reddish purple stems and leaves that are among the most beautiful in the plant world: foot long, lanceolate to ovate-lanceolate in shape, deep green with heavy and lighter colored veins on the upper surface, and a beautiful reddish purple to dark purple beneath. The great terminal flower clusters appear in late winter, spring, and summer and are more than a foot high, with many inch-wide white five-petaled flowers with very long pink tubes and protruding white stamens; often the clusters are heavy enough to droop. The petals are recurved and often also blushed with pink. They are an incredible sight and a veritable symphony of color and form, which has led to the vernacular name of shooting stars. This gorgeous little tree wants rich, moist soil that is well drained, and it needs sun to bloom. Plate 124.

Clerodendrum speciosissimum (spee´-see-o-SIS-si-mum) is indigenous to Sri Lanka, Sumatra, and Java. It is root hardy in zone 9a, relatively dependable in 9b, and hardy in zones 10 and 11. It is similar in stature, leaf shape, and flower color to *C. paniculatum* and *C. buchananii*, but the leaves are not quite as large and the terminal flower panicles are not as gigantic. It is not quite as spectacular as *C. paniculatum*, but is a very beautiful thing in and out of bloom. It flourishes in full sun or partial shade, but must have an ample supply of water and rich soil. It can be trained to a trellis as a vine.

Clerodendrum ×*speciosum* (spee-see-O-sum) is a hybrid between *C. splendens* and *C. thomsoniae*. It is quite similar in all respects to *C. thomsoniae* except for color of flowers which, in this case, have no white parts except for the stamens; the ballooned calyces are purplish red, and the petals rosy hued to deep red. Plate 125.

Clerodendrum splendens (SPLEN-denz) is native to tropical West Africa from Senegal to the Republic of Congo and down to Angola. It is hardy in zones 10 and 11, although it is grown in zone 9 where it is often root hardy. It is a twining and sprawling shrublike vine that grows to only 12 feet or so, but freely suckers so that it makes a widespreading and dense cover. The ovate to oblong 6-inch-long leaves are deep green and glossy, with deepset veins that give an almost corrugated appearance to the upper surface. The flowers are in dense, many-flowered, terminal panicles with scarlet to orange-red petals and purple calyces. This exquisite little vine does well in sun or partial shade, but needs rich soil and ample water. It works equally well as a large groundcover.

Clerodendrum thomsoniae (tomp-SO-nee-eye) is a scrambling, twining, vinelike shrub native to tropical West Africa. It is not truly hardy outside zones 10 and 11, although it is grown in zone 9 where it is often root hardy. The plant is sometimes partly deciduous in the winter. It is commonly called the bleeding-heart vine or bag-flower. It grows to 20 feet or so with the proper support and makes a dense cover with adequate moisture and partial shade. It likes to be mulched or to have its base shaded by other plants. The dark green leaves are ovate, elliptic or oblong-ovate, 6 or 7 inches long, and glossy above with deeply depressed veins. The plant blooms all year in frost-free areas with panicles of flowers that are cream-colored, heart-shaped greatly expanded four-angled calyces from which protrude the ray of crimson petals and long white stamens. The flowers are followed by round dark blue fruits embedded in the center of the papery calyx, which turns pink or purple after the flowers fade. Since the calyces last a long time and the vine is nearly ever-blooming, there are usually three colors visible simultaneously on the plants. Several cultivars of this vine are available with white, pink, or red flowers. Plate 126.

Clerodendrum trichotomum (try-KAHT-o-mum) is indigenous to Japan, eastern China, and Taiwan, and is hardy in zones 8 through 11 and marginal in zone 7. This deciduous large shrub or small tree can attain a height of 20 feet, sometimes more. It must be trained when young to tree form, as its natural inclination is to be a large, many-stemmed shrub. The soft, usually hairy leaves are ovate to linear-ovate and about 5 inches long. The plants bloom in summer and fall, and the flowers appear in large, loose-flowered clusters near the ends of the branches. The individual blossoms are long-stalked, five-petaled, fragrant, white, and protrude from the ends of pink to scarlet heart-shaped, balloonlike calyces. The fragrance is much relished by some people who compare it to a sachet; others think it vile. The fruits are round turquoise-colored marblelike berries encased in the persistent calyces that turn almost white. *Clerodendrum trichotomum* var. *fargesii* (far-GAY-zee-eye) is glabrous, smaller, and reputedly hardier to cold than the type. The tree flourishes in sun or partial shade and is not particular as to soil type, but does not look good and grows slowly without adequate water. The little tree suffers under the unwieldy vernacular name of harlequin glorybower.

Clerodendrum ugandense (oo-gahn-DENS-ee) is native to tropical Africa and is hardy in zones 10 and 11 and marginal in zone 9b. It is a sprawling shrub that may be trained as a vine. It attains a maximum height of 9 feet, but is usually smaller. The leaves are, for a *Clerodendrum* species, rather nondescript. They are elliptic in shape, faintly toothed on the margins, dark to medium green in color, about 5 inches long, smooth, and rather glossy. The flowers are exceptional, especially up close. They are almost orchidlike with small red calyces from which project four blue obovate petals and one purple-"lipped" petal; the very long purple stamens are recurved and projected upwards from the rest of the flower, the appearance of the whole affair giving rise to the common and unfortunate name of butterfly bush (unfortunate because several other garden shrubs are also burdened with this common name, *Buddleia* species chief among them). The plant does best in partial shade with adequate water and a rich soil. Plate 127.

Clerodendrum wallichii (wahl-LIK-ee-eye) (synonym *C. nutans*) is native to Southeast Asia and is not very hardy, being adaptable successfully only to zones 10 and 11 and marginal in zone 9b. This very alluring large shrub grows vigorously in frost-free areas to 12 feet or so in height, often with a single stem and long, almost weeping branches. The glossy and leathery, dark green, strongly veined leaves are almost a foot long and are linear-lanceolate in shape with curved "tails." The splendid flower panicles are as much as 18 inches long and are pendent. The flower stalks are a lovely coral red as are the small calyces. The five pure white petals are as much as 3 inches wide, are obovate in shape, and form a semicircle. The very long, curved stamens sweep down like a sixth petal and consist of white silky filaments and brilliant orange-red anthers—truly a glorious bower. The plant grows well in sun or partial shade.

CLEYERA (klay-YER-a)
Theaceae: The Camellia, Tea Family
CLEYERA
Large shrubs and small trees; lustrous evergreen
    leaves
Zones 8 through 10
Sun or partial shade
Average but regular amounts of moisture
Sandy, humusy, well-drained acidic soil
Propagation by cuttings

A genus of 17 species of evergreen tropical and subtropical shrubs and trees in eastern Asia and tropical America with alternately arranged simple glossy leaves, small flowers, and berrylike fruits. Only one species is commonly planted. *Cleyera japonica* (ja-PAHN-i-ka) is indigenous to Japan, the southern Korean peninsula, and northeastern China. It is a lovely dense evergreen shrub that grows to 15 or even 20 feet in height and can easily be trained into a very picturesque little tree or clipped as a hedge. Older plants tend to have the leaves clustered near the ends of the branches. The dark green leaves are 3 to 6 inches long, elliptic in shape, and shiny and glossy with a distinct and reddish midrib; new leaves have a deep cinnamon hue, sometimes with purple overtones. The plant blooms in autumn with axillary clusters of small, fragrant white flowers, which produce red berries that last all winter. The species grows in full sun with adequate irrigation, but looks better in part shade and demands a good, slightly acidic soil with humus. It languishes and usually dies in dry, limy soils and is not a drought-tolerant plant.

CLITORIA (kli-TOR-ee-a)
Papilionaceae (Fabaceae, Leguminosae), subfamily
    Papilionoideae: The Bean, Pea Family
BUTTERFLY PEA
Slender twining vine; pinnate leaves; blue and white
    sweet pealike flowers
Zones 9 through 11
Sun
Average but regular amounts of moisture
Sandy, humusy, well-drained soil
Propagation by seed and cuttings

A genus of about 70 species of herbs, shrubs, and vines with pinnate leaves and papilionaceous flowers distributed in warm regions around the world. Only one is commonly planted. ***Clitoria ternatea*** (tur-NAIT-ee-a) is probably native to Malaysia, but has become naturalized in so many warm-climate areas that no one is sure just where its origin was. It grows to only about 15 feet in height, but does so rather quickly in warm weather. It usually needs guidance when young to climb and a trellis, lattice, or chain link fence is perfect for it, although it is really a plant for viewing up close. The leaves are very attractive and 6 to 8 inches long, and consist of five to seven ovate to oblong leaflets. The 2-inch-long flowers consist of a large royal blue standard marked with white or orange at the center; some plants have purple or even white flowers, and some have double blossoms. The vine is not very particular as to soil, but must have adequate water and some sun to bloom well.

CLIVIA (KLIV-ee-a / KLYV-ee-a)
Amaryllidaceae: The Amaryllis Family
KAFFIR LILY
Stemless herb with thick, dark green straplike leaves; orange-red flowers
Zones 9b through 11
Partial shade
Average but regular amounts of moisture
Sandy, humusy, well-drained soil
Propagation by root division and seed

A genus of four species of evergreen tuberous-rooted perennials with thick straplike leaves arranged oppositely in a single plane and with umbels of flowers atop solid scapes that arise directly from the ground. All are indigenous to South Africa. Only one species is commonly planted. ***Clivia miniata*** (min-ee-AIT-a) grows to about 2 feet in height. The thick dark green leaves are almost reason enough to grow the plant, and the flowers are spectacular. They appear in winter and early spring in many-flowered round umbels. Each flower is a 3-inch-long red funnel with a yellow throat, similar to those of the large-flowered hybrid *Hippeastrum* (amaryllis) species, but smaller and more delicate looking. The overall visual effect is that of quiet molten lava. The plant is clumping but slow to do so. ***Clivia miniata* var. *citrina*,** a beautiful completely yellow-flowered variety, is still fairly rare and therefore very expensive. The clumps should be divided only when it is obvious that the vigor of the plants is compromised, which condition takes many years to occur. They want bright shade but not direct sun, especially in hotter regions. They are not drought tolerant but, at the same time, must have excellent drainage. They can be grown in zone 9a with protection. Plate 128.

CLUSIA (KLOO-see-a)
Guttiferae (Clusiaceae): The Autograph Tree, Garcinia Family
AUTOGRAPH TREE; PITCH-APPLE; MONKEY APPLE

Large shrubs and small trees; beautiful large thick leathery leaves; roselike flowers; whitish fruit
Zones 10b and 11 as a large shrub or small tree; zone 10a as a shrub
Sun
Average but regular amounts of moisture; drought tolerant when established
Sandy, humusy, well-drained soil
Propagation by seed and cuttings

A genus of about 145 species of evergreen trees and shrubs in tropical America, most of which are epiphytic or partially epiphytic for part of their lives. All have horizontally growing branches and large thick and leathery leaves without conspicuous lateral veins. Their flowers are usually large and fleshy, and the fruits are leathery. Only one species is commonly grown outside botanical gardens. ***Clusia rosea*** (RO-zee-a / ro-ZAY-a) (synonym *C. major*) is native to the Bahamas, the Florida Keys, the West Indies, and southeastern Mexico down to northern South America. In the wetter parts of its native habitats it may attain a height of 50 feet, but in cultivation on the Florida mainland is usually no more than about 30 feet tall. The trees often start out as epiphytes much like *Ficus aurea* (strangler fig), the seeds sprouting in the crotches of large trees to send down roots to the ground and eventually developing a trunk that often kills the host tree. The olive green to dark green leaves are 8 inches long, mostly obovate and cuneate in shape but sometimes elliptic, and usually exhibiting a notched end; they have a strong, usually brownish midvein but no apparent lateral veins. The leaves are tough, stiff, and leathery and occasion the common name of autograph tree because they are persistent and can be written (carved) on. This practice, of course, disfigures them, which is a travesty as they are among the most beautiful leaves of any tree. The tree blooms during the summer with three-flowered terminal inflorescences of lovely pink or white 3-inch-wide flowers that have a beautiful and distinct central ring of either stamens or stigmas (the male and female flowers are produced on separate trees). The whitish green to beige tomatillo-shaped fruits are 3 inches in diameter. When mature, they unfold to reveal linear-ovate, yellow and reddish banana-shaped segments surrounding a central "crown" that contains the seeds embedded in black, poisonous resin. The tree grows fairly rapidly and has wandering roots much like those of many *Ficus* species. It is perfectly at home in sandy or saline soil and makes an especially wonderful seaside landscape subject. Plates 129 and 130.

CLYTOSTOMA
(kly-TAHS-toe-ma / kly-toe-STO-ma)
Bignoniaceae: The Catalpa, Jacaranda, Trumpet-Vine Family
VIOLET-TRUMPET VINE; ARGENTINE TRUMPET-VINE

Evergreen tendril-climbing leafy vines; lavender
    trumpet-shaped flowers in spring
Zones vary according to species
Sun
Average but regular amounts of moisture
Average well-drained soil
Propagation by cuttings

The genus contains eight species of vines native to
South America with pinnate leaves that have two or
three leaflets and a terminal tendril. The five-lobed
flowers are funnel-shaped or bell-shaped and occur in
pairs in the leaf axils or terminally.

Clytostoma binatum (by-NAIT-um) is native to
the same general area as *C. callistegioides,* but is slightly
less hardy to cold and is dependable only in zones 9b
through 11. It is similar in most respects to *C. callistegioides,* but has brighter green leaves and smaller flowers
(an inch long) that are reddish purple with white
throats. The flowers are even prettier than those of the
more common *C. callistegioides.*

Clytostoma callistegioides (kal´-lis-tee-jee-OY-
deez) is native to southern Brazil and northern Argentina and grows to 20 feet or more. It is hardy in zones 10
and 11 as a perennial but sprouts from the root in zone
9b and sometimes in zone 9a. The vine tends, like many
others, to become bare of leaves at the base, but above
is dense and ever so attractive, growing to the tops of
fences or walls and cascading down therefrom. The
leaves are composed of two 4-inch-long elliptic-oblong
glossy dark green leaflets, the third leaflet as a terminal
tendril. The flowers appear in spring in great abundance in terminal clusters of two blossoms; they are 5-
inch-long light lavender trumpets with 3-inch-wide flaring ends that are shallowly five-lobed and are streaked
with purple. The plants occasionally put out flowers in
summer and fall, but this is not a dependable characteristic. The vine needs little attention once established;
it is beautiful and virtually carefree, but is not completely drought tolerant and needs water in prolonged
dry periods.

COBAEA (ko-BEE-a)
Polemoniaceae: The Phlox Family
CUP-AND-SAUCER VINE; MEXICAN IVY;
    CATHEDRAL BELLS
Large dark green vine; cup-and-saucer-like greenish
    white and purple flowers
Zones 9b through 11 as year-round perennials; zones
    9a and 8b as resprouting perennials; anywhere as
    annuals
Sun
Average but regular amounts of moisture
Sandy, humusy, well-drained soil
Propagation by seed

A genus of 10 vines native to tropical America. All
have pinnate foliage with a terminal and branching tendril, and all have bell-shaped corollas with prominent

and persistent calyces beneath. Only one species is
commonly planted. *Cobaea scandens* (SKAN-denz)
is native to tropical Mexico. It is a rampant, dense, and
fast-growing vine to as much as 40 or 50 feet in the near
tropical areas. It climbs by tenacious tendrils that cling
to any rough surface and should not be planted on
painted wood where it defaces the surface. The leaves
are 8 to 10 inches long and are composed of four to six
elliptic dark green leaflets with a terminal tendril; some
of the other leaflets infrequently produce tendrils at
their ends. The plant blooms profusely all spring (if in a
warm zone), summer, and fall. The flowers are unusual,
2-inch-long bell-shaped "cups" (the corolla) sitting on
a saucerlike disk formed by the calyx lobes. The color of
the flowers usually changes from a greenish white to a
dull purple, but the calyx often remains green or white.
Because of their muted colors, the flowers are not spectacular in the landscape, but they are nevertheless fascinating and beautiful up close. The vine is perfect as a
fast-growing cover or screen.

COCCOLOBA (ko-ko-LOAB-a)
Polygonaceae: The Buckwheat, Sea-Grape Family
SEA GRAPE; PIGEON PLUM
Large-leaved evergreen trees; showy large clusters of
    berries
Zones vary according to species
Sun
Drought tolerant
Sandy, humusy, well-drained soil
Propagation by seed, cuttings, air-layering

A large genus of about 150 species of trees, shrubs,
and vines in tropical America. Most have large (some
are truly immense) evergreen leaves, but some are
briefly deciduous. All have rather large clusters of small
flowers, which result in often showy clusters of berries.
Many species have variable leaves, with the juvenile
ones much larger than the mature ones.

Coccoloba diversifolia (dy-vurs´-i-FO-lee-a) (synonyms *C. floridana, C. laurifolia*) is native to southern
Florida, the West Indies, and northern South America,
and is hardy only in zones 10b and 11 but often survives as a small tree in zone 10a. The tree grows to as
much as 70 feet in height, but is usually smaller in cultivation. It has a rather narrow and upright crown of
dark green foliage. The leathery dark green leaves are
oblong in shape and about 4 inches long, although some
plants exhibit the tendency of the genus to produce
much larger juvenile leaves. The white flowers appear in
great abundance on slender spikes in the spring and
result in 3-inch-long clusters of dark purple quarter-
inch-wide berries in late summer, which are supposedly
edible. It is often called pigeon plum or dove plum. This
tree is exceptionally beautiful and is also drought tolerant and immune to saline soil and air, making a splendid seaside subject in the warmest parts of Florida and
similar climates.

Coccoloba floridana. See *C. diversifolia.*
Coccoloba grandifolia. See *C. pubescens.*
Coccoloba laurifolia. See *C. diversifolia.*
Coccoloba pubescens (pyoo-BES-senz) (synonym *C. grandifolia*) is indigenous to islands of the West Indies and is tender and not adaptable outside zones 10b and 11. It is a spectacular tree that can attain a height of 80 feet in its native habitat; no one seems to know just how large it grows in cultivation. The tree grows naturally into a somewhat narrow and sparsely branched crown of foliage with light brown wood. The light green leaves are generally less than a foot wide but, incredibly, sometimes as much as 3 feet wide, almost stalkless, orbicular, puckered, and heavily veined with a rusty pubescence on the upper veins and heavily so on the undersides of the leaf. The leaves are so large that the margins droop in spite of their thick texture. The flowers are borne in 2-foot-high terminal spikes, and the small fruits are green to reddish. The tree is rather difficult to combine appropriately into the landscape but, when it is, like against a high wall or in the center of a protected area, it is outstandingly beautiful and very tropical appearing. It is often cut back to cause the leaves to grow as large as possible and to keep the tree at a manageable height as the limbs are brittle and break easily in strong winds. The plant is almost impossible to propagate by cuttings and seldom flowers and fruits in cultivation, which means that it is difficult to find and expensive when found. It is worth the search as it is a startlingly beautiful and dramatic landscape subject. It is sometimes referred to as the moralin tree in Puerto Rico. Plate 131.

Coccoloba uvifera (oo-VIF-e-ra) is native to the Caribbean Basin, including southern Florida, the Bahamas, the West Indies, and the coasts of southern Mexico, Central America, and northern South America. It is hardy as a very large shrub or small tree in zones 10 and 11, but often survives as a shrub in zone 9b. It is called the sea-grape because of its seaside habitat and its drooping clusters of grapelike fruit. Near the sea the tree is usually only a large, multistemmed, suckering shrub with leaves from bottom to top, but farther inland it can slowly grow to 25 feet or so in height with an irregular and fissured gray trunk. It is always rather sprawling in habit and is not a suitable as a street tree. The leaves are very beautiful, 6 to 10 inches, wide, reniform to orbicular in shape, deep green, shiny, rubbery, and leathery, with usually red prominent midveins and lighter and distinct lateral veins. The new leaves are a beautiful coppery color, and the old and dying leaves turn an orange-red before falling. The tiny white flowers are in foot-long spikes, and the fruit is in a similar drooping cluster, each pear-shaped berry less than an inch wide. The fruits are purple when mature, but the individual fruits ripen at different rates and there are several colors in a cluster, from green to white and purple. There is a very attractive cultivar with variegated leaves. The tree can be pruned into a very impressive hedge and is the supreme seaside subject, tolerating almost any degree of salinity. It is drought tolerant when established, but looks better and grows much faster with regular watering. Like the leaves of *Clusia rosea* (autograph tree), the leaves of this species were used for writing notes by the early Spaniards. The fruit is reputedly edible.

COCCOTHRINAX (ko´-ko-TRY-nax)
Palmae (Arecaceae): The Palm Family
SILVER FAN PALM
Lovely graceful slender-trunked, circular-leaved fan palms
Zones 10 and 11; marginal in zone 10a
Sun
Drought tolerant
Sandy, humusy, well-drained soil
Propagation by seed

A genus of 14 palm species in southern Florida and the West Indies, mostly in Cuba. They are slender, single-trunked, sometimes hairy-trunked palms with orbicular, many-segmented palmate leaves. Most are relatively small, the largest attaining perhaps 25 feet in height. These palms are tough and fairly immune to hostile conditions, growing in poor, limy soil and withstanding drought and heat. All are relatively immune to saline soil and air. Alas, they are tender to cold; none withstand temperatures below 28°F. The genus is closely allied to and often confused with *Thrinax.*

Coccothrinax acuminata. See *C. miraguama.*
Coccothrinax alta (AHLT-a) (synonyms *C. barbadensis*, *C. radiata*, *Thrinax altissima*) is indigenous to Puerto Rico and the Virgin Islands. It is called the silver palm because of the color of the undersides of the leaves. The palm grows larger than most other species in the genus and slowly to as much as 25 feet in height. The very slender (never more than 6 inches in diameter) trunk is smooth and gray in color when old, but covered in brown leaf base fibers in its upper portion. The nearly perfectly round leaves are rather small for a palm of this height and give an alluringly graceful aspect to the whole tree; they are 3 feet wide on 3-foot-long petioles and olive green above and silvery beneath.

Coccothrinax argentata (ahr-jin-TAIT-a) is native to southern Florida and the Bahamas. It, too, is called the silver palm or Florida silver palm. It grows slowly to a maximum height of about 15 feet on dry and calcareous soil mostly in the scrub pinelands of southern Florida and the Florida Keys. The leaves are not as circular in outline as many other species in the genus, and the petioles are only about 2 feet long. Very deeply segmented, the leaves gracefully droop at the ends and are a beautiful and bright silvery hue underneath.

Coccothrinax argentea (ahr-JEN-tee-a) is native to Hispaniola and grows to as much as 30 feet in height. It is probably the largest species in the genus. It is wonderfully graceful with a very slender trunk that is mostly free of fiber and leaf bases. The 4- or 5-foot-wide leaves are held on 3- to 4-foot-long petioles and are stiffer than those of the above species but are nonetheless extremely graceful. Like the leaves of *C. argentata,* the leaves of *C. argentea* are not quite circular and are olive green above and silvery beneath. There are few plants more beautiful than mature specimens of this palm. They look especially wonderful in groups with individuals of different heights.

Coccothrinax barbadensi. See *C. alta.*

Coccothrinax crinita (kri-NEET-a) is native to the savannahs of Cuba and is one of the most unusual species in the genus. It is called the old man palm because of its very hairy trunks. It grows very slowly to 15 or 20 feet in height with a slender trunk hidden in a thick mass of brown to gray, matted hairs. The beautiful, nearly circular leaves are bright green above and grayish green beneath, contrasting very nicely with the gray or brown trunks.

Coccothrinax fragrans (FRAY-granz) is native to Cuba and Hispaniola. It sometimes attains a height of 20 feet with a smooth gray trunk. The beautiful leaves are circular in outline, about 4 feet wide, bright green above, and grayish green to silver beneath; they are carried on 5-foot-long petioles that give an especially airy and graceful aspect to the crown. The flowers are fragrant.

Coccothrinax miraguama (mir-a-GWAHM-a) (synonym *C. acuminata*) is indigenous to Cuba and is one of the larger and faster growing species of the genus. It usually grows to 20 or 25 feet in height. The trunks are somewhat variable in thickness and in the amount of fiber adhering to them: they are usually covered in fibers and leaf bases for most of their height but may be almost completely free of these, in which case they are quite smooth and grayish in color. The perfectly circular dark green leaves are among the most attractive in the genus: as much as 6 feet wide, silvery beneath, and very deeply segmented, they are held on 3-foot petioles. This palm is almost incredibly beautiful.

Coccothrinax radiata. See *C. alta.*

COCCULUS
(KOAK-yoo-lus / KAHK-yoo-lus)
Menispermaceae: The Moonseed Family
SNAIL-SEED; MOONSEED; LAUREL-LEAVED
   SNAILSEED
Small evergreen tree or large shrub; lustrous deeply
   veined leaves
Zones 9b through 11
Sun or shade
Water lover
Average soil
Propagation by seed and cuttings

A small genus of 11 species of evergreen and deciduous sprawling shrubs and small trees in North America and tropical and temperate eastern Asia. At least two species are planted in the United States, but only one has a tropical look. **Cocculus laurifolia** (law-ri-FO-lee-a) is native to a very large area of Asia from the southern Japanese islands through southern China to the Himalayas. It is a sprawling, widespreading shrub that makes a dense crown of foliage and can be trained as an espalier if tied to a support or even made into a small 15- to 20-foot tree if staked and trained to one strong leader. It is grown in parts of zone 9a, but is not reliably hardy there. The 6-inch-long dark green leaves are very beautiful, elliptic to oblong, shiny, and glossy with three yellowish prominent and parallel veins. The plant seldom flowers in cultivation in the United States; when it does the tiny yellowish green flowers are in small spikes and the berries are black. This plant is superb as an espalier or as a small tree. Leaves and stems are poisonous if eaten.

COCHLIOSTEMA
(kahk´-lee-AHS-te-ma / koak´-lee-o-STEM-a)
Commelinaceae: The Spiderwort Family
No known English common name
Large epiphytic rosette of long straplike leaves; large
   clusters of fragrant purple and white flowers
Zones 10b and 11
Partial shade to partial sun
Water lover
Rich, humusy moist soil or epiphytic mix
Propagation by root division and seed

A genus of only two species of large epiphytic plants in Central America and South America. One species is occasionally grown. **Cochliostema odoratissimum** (o´-do-ra-TISS-i-mum) makes large stemless rosettes of oblong-lanceolate leaves that are as much as 4 feet long, deep olive green above and purplish red with darker longitudinal lines beneath. The plants bloom year-round with inflorescences that are short-stalked conical foot-long heads of blossoms arising from the leaf axils of the rosette; the individual flowers are fleshy, light purple to violet in color, with three large greenish yellow sepals, three purplish petals (one of which is larger and longer than the others), three fleshy stamens, and three staminodes with purple hairs. The plant is spectacular in or out of bloom. It can be grown as an epiphyte or as a terrestrial if the soil is loose, humusy, and well draining. It also makes a beautiful potted plant, but it is as an epiphyte perched on a large tree that it is most charming. It tolerates no frost and needs good air circulation as well as protection from the noonday sun.

COCHLOSPERMUM
(koak-lo-SPUR-mum)
Bixaceae: The Bixa Family
BUTTERCUP TREE; WILD COTTON; SHELL
   SEED
Medium-sized deciduous tree; large single roselike
   yellow flowers; palmately lobed leaves
Zones 10b and 11
Sun
Average but regular amounts of moisture; drought
   tolerant when established

Sandy, humusy, well-drained soil
Propagation by seed and cuttings

A genus of about 15 species of soft-wooded deciduous trees and shrubs in tropical America with large palmately lobed leaves, large yellow flowers in clusters before the leaves appear in spring, and fruit with abundant floss around the seeds. One species is commonly planted in tropical areas for its outstandingly spectacular display of flowers. ***Cochlospermum vitifolium*** (vit-i-FO-lee-um) is native to tropical Mexico (from Sonora to Oaxaca on the west coast and across to Veracruz and Yucatán on the east coast), Central America, and northern South America. The tree grows quickly to a height of 30 to 40 feet, sometimes more, with a spreading open-branched crown of medium green foliage. The leaves are very attractive, as much as a foot wide, and palmately divided into usually five and sometimes seven deep lobes with serrate margins. The flowers start appearing in late winter or early spring before the leaves come out; they are 4 to 5 inches wide, golden yellow in color, with five apically notched corolla lobes and centers of great masses of stamens. They look very much like large single yellow roses, and they usually cover the tree. The tree blooms when young at about 3 feet in height and often is in bloom for as long as 3 months. The dark brown 3-inch-long obcordate velvety fruits are five-sectioned capsules that enclose shell-like seeds covered in a white cottony floss. The tree is outstandingly spectacular when in flower against a dark green background. It should receive a protected site as the branches are soft but brittle and break rather easily in strong winds. It is used as a hedge in parts of Mexico, constantly pruned back to 6 feet or less. ***Cochlospermum vitifolium*** 'Plenum' is a fully double form with flowers that are attractive up close, but otherwise do not add much to the landscape. Plates 132 and 133.

COCOS (KO-koas)
Palmae (Arecaceae): The Palm Family
COCONUT PALM
Tall slender leaning trunked palm; large pinnate
     leaves; clusters of large, hard-shelled fruit
Zones 10b and 11; marginal in zone 10a
Sun
Average but regular amounts of moisture; drought
     tolerant when established
Sandy, humusy, well-drained soil
Propagation by seed

A monotypic genus that is ubiquitous on tropical seacoasts. ***Cocos nucifera*** (noo-SIF-e-ra) is the paradigm of the tropics and tropical beauty. While quite commonplace in tropical areas, it is one of the most beautiful trees on earth, as most tropical dwelling people who venture away from its grace can attest to after returning home. Its area of origin is not known. It has been carried around and planted by ancient seafaring peoples of the tropics since well before written history;

much research, however, has put a high probability on its having originated on the islands in the Indian Ocean or those of Polynesia.

The tree can grow to more than 100 feet in height but is usually no more than 70 feet or so tall in cultivation. As young plants with only a few feet of trunk, the palms are extraordinarily beautiful with their great arching feather leaves as much as 20 feet long, strong yellowish rachises, and gracefully drooping leaflets. The 3- to 4-foot-long petioles are light green to yellow in color with the bases covered in a dense wrapping of brown fibers. The color of the leaves varies from yellow green to dark green according to genetic heritage, locality, and soil or cultural conditions. The trunks, even on very old palms, are hardly ever more than a foot in diameter and, with the height of mature palms, creates one of the world's most picturesquely graceful sights. The base of the trunk is always swollen, sometimes bulbous, and the upper part is always covered in crescent-shaped leaf scars and often shows vertical cracks.

The palms start blooming and fruiting at a relatively early age, often with no more than 3 feet of trunk growth. The inflorescences appear in 5-foot-long panicles just below the crown of leaves and are accompanied by a large tubular woody spathe, which is usually deciduous before the fruits form. The latter are about a foot long, three-sided and, when fully mature, bright yellow to green or brown depending on the cultivar and the age of the fruit. They are exceedingly handsome on the tree, hanging as they do in great clusters just below the crown of leaves. And, yes, they can be fatal if they fall from any height onto a person's head. The edible nut has a brittle and brown-hairy shell; encased in the middle of the tough-husked fruit, it must be liberated from the shell for consumption.

Although synonymous with tropical seacoasts, the coconut palm flourishes inland as well, even in elevated sites. While drought tolerant and blessed with the ability to grow in poor and limy soil, the palms (like so many other drought-tolerant plants) look and grow ever so much better with good soil and adequate water. In the tropics on coconut plantations the trees are fed and irrigated regularly. As with most other palms, the coconut looks best in a landscaping sense planted in groups. One of the most picturesque palm tableaux is to plant an odd number of trees of varying heights in a group with each tree no more than 10 feet from the other; their trunks naturally bend towards the optimum lighting conditions for each tree and the gardener will have a very natural appearing island of the ultimate in tropical beauty.

The coconut has been grown to maturity as far north as Cape Canaveral on the east coast of Florida and Clearwater on the west coast as well as in the Brownsville area of Texas. It is inevitable, however, that trees grown in these areas eventually succumb to a bad freeze. Many people think it worth the trouble of having to occasionally remove the dead trunks if they can have several years with these beauties. A temperature of 32°F often defoliates the world's most graceful palm and anything below 30°F is usually fatal, although some have survived brief periods of 28°F.

"Lethal yellowing" is an always fatal disease to which coconuts and too many other palms in Florida are subject. Formerly almost all the coconut palms in southern Florida were of 'Tall Jamaican' variety, which has proved to be very susceptible to the disease. *Cocos nucifera* **'Tall Jamaican'**, the tallest and most graceful form of the species, is also reputedly hardier to cold than the more disease-tolerant varieties. At present there are only four coconut cultivars that show any real resistance to the disease. *Cocos nucifera* **'Golden Malayan Dwarf'** has very bright yellow small fruit. *Cocos nucifera* **'Green Malayan Dwarf'** has vivid green fruit. *Cocos nucifera* **'Maypan'**, which is especially useful because of its size and fast growth, is larger in all parts than the type. Its trunk is exceptionally thick, and the leaves are very long and strong. *Cocos nucifera* **'Panama Tall'** is an especially beautiful large tree. It should go without saying that healthy, well cared for and unstressed palms (as for all other garden subjects) are usually more resistant to all pests and diseases. Plates 134 and 135.

   Cocos plumosa. See *Syagrus romanzoffiana.*
   Cocos schizophylla. See *Syagrus schizophylla.*

CODIAEUM (ko-DY-ee-um / ko-DEE-um)
Euphorbiaceae: The Euphorbia, Spurge Family
CROTON
Large-leaved shrubs with variegated leaves in
   dazzling array of colors
Zones 10 and 11; marginal in zone 10a
Sun to partial shade
Average but regular amounts of moisture; drought
   tolerant when established
Sandy, humusy, well-drained soil
Propagation by cuttings

A genus of six species of evergreen trees and shrubs native to Malaysia and Polynesia. Only one is planted outside botanical gardens. *Codiaeum variegatum* **var.** *pictum* (vair-ee-a-GAIT-um PIK-tum) is almost as ubiquitous in tropical plantings as is the coconut palm. The species is very variable and has resulted in almost innumerable cultivars with many leaf shapes and every hue except blue represented in the leaf color. The leaves are often a foot long, naturally thick and leathery and, although it is hardly noticeable in the highly colored varieties, prominently veined. Depending on the cultivar, the leaves may be narrow or sickle-shaped, broad obovate or ovate, deeply lobed, spirally twisted, almost entirely green or so highly colored that there is no green apparent in the leaf. Most plants require full sun to achieve the brightest leaf color, while others (mostly the more deeply green leaved cultivars) need partial shade. Most grow to 8 or even 10 feet in height (and about as wide) if not killed back by cold. The larger growing kinds need special pruning to create

from them a standard or small tree form. All are able, when established, to withstand drought conditions, if those conditions are not too prolonged. They are not completely hardy in zone 10a; some damage can usually be expected in that zone, but if the freeze does not last too long, the plants come back quickly with the return of warm weather. Prolonged freezing temperatures kill the shrubs outright. There is nothing more colorful and exciting than a group of crotons accenting an area of green tropical leaves. Great masses of the highly colored varieties seem excessive and ill-advised because of their gaudiness. Plates 136 and 137.

COFFEA (KAHF-fee-a / KOAF-fee-a)
Rubiaceae: The Coffee, Gardenia, Ixora Family
COFFEE
Large evergreen shrub; large glossy leaves; white,
   fragrant flowers; red and black berries
Zones 10b and 11
Partial shade
Water lover
Humusy, moist, well-drained soil on the acidic side
Propagation by seed, cuttings, and air-layering

A genus of almost 40 species of evergreen shrubs and trees in tropical Asia and Africa. They have large oppositely arranged leaves, axillary clusters of small funnel-shaped white flowers and berrylike fruit. *Coffea arabica* (a-RAB-i-ka), the coffee tree, is indigenous to elevated sites in tropical East Africa and is not perfectly at home in hot climates although it does well enough as an ornamental and curiosity. The tree grows to about 30 feet in height in its native habitats; on plantations the trees are kept at no more than 12 feet to facilitate harvest of the berries. If pruned when young to train it to form, it makes a lovely little tree with a straight trunk, horizontal branches, and a dense and dark green crown of foliage. The leaves are 6 to 8 inches long and elliptic in shape, with pointed leaf tips, wavy margins, and deeply veined blades. The resemblance of the leaves to those of *Gardenia jasminoides* (to which the coffee tree is related) is striking. The flowers appear in spring (sometimes also in summer) in small clusters in the leaf axils; they are white, five-petaled, and very fragrant (quite reminiscent of gardenias) but last only a day. The fruits take only a few weeks to ripen into half-inch oval berries that are first green, then red, and finally blackish purple. There are normally two seeds in each fruit, each with a flat and grooved side; these are the "beans" of commercial coffee. The plants revel in a rich, moist but well-drained soil that is on the acidic side; limy soils should be well amended with compost and leaf mold if possible. The plants need protection from the full sun in hot climates.

COLEUS (KO-lee-us)
Labiatae (Lamiaceae): The Mint Family
COLEUS

Herbaceous subshrubs with highly colored leaves;
    spikes of blue and white flowers
Zones 10 and 11 as permanent perennials; marginal
    in zone 9, resprouting from roots; annual
    elsewhere
Sun to partial shade
Water lover
Rich, humusy, moist, well-drained soil
Propagation by seed or cuttings

The genus name is correctly *Solenostemon*, but only botanists use it. Instead, the genus is universally known to gardeners and horticulturists as *Coleus*. It has about 60 species of succulent-stemmed herbs in Southeast Asia and Malaysia, but only a few species and their hybrids and cultivars are grown. The number and varieties of these hybrids and cultivars are legion. They rival crotons in form and color if not in size; their leaves may be colored red, purple, brown, orange, yellow, green, pink, or combinations thereof. Unlike most croton varieties, these lovelies do best in partial shade and are perfect for semishady borders, especially mixed with ferns, caladiums, impatiens, and so forth. There are dwarf varieties with small leaves, but most varieties grow to 3 feet or more in height. The leaves are generally ovate to lanceolate in shape with toothed margins, but there are many variations on this theme and some leaves are curled with ruffled margins. The flower spikes are sometimes almost as tall as the plants, and, while the individual flowers are quite attractive up close, they should be cut off as they form to keep the plants vigorous and to prevent legginess. The plants tend to die out if the flowers are allowed to set seed. It is also a good idea to pinch back the tips of the plants when they are young to encourage bushiness and a compact growth habit. The plants are not drought resistant and need regular and adequate watering and a rich and well-drained soil. While they will grow in full sun, the leaf colors tend to be washed out in such sites and deep shade will also reduce the vibrancy of leaf color, although there are cultivars, usually termed "Sun Coleus," that keep their colors in sun in all but the hottest climates. These wonderful plants are nearly foolproof for color in part shade and they are indispensable in the tropical garden.

COLLINIA. See *Chamaedorea elegans*.

COLOCASIA
(kahl-o-KAY-see-a / kahl-o-KAY-shya)
Araceae: The Calla Lily, Jack-in-the-Pulpit Family
ELEPHANT-EAR; ELEPHANT'S-EAR; TARO
Almost stemless herbs with very large peltate heart-
    shaped leaves
Zones 10b and 11 as year-round perennials; zones 8b
    through 10a as returning perennials
Sun to shade
Water lovers

Rich, humusy, moist soil
Propagation by root division

A genus of six species of tuberous-rooted, perennial, large-leaved herbs in tropical Asia. All have large, sagittate or cordate, peltate leaves and grow from underground tuberous rhizomes that spread to form colonies. The inflorescences are typical of the family. None have top growth that withstands freezing temperatures, but the tuberous rootstocks survive if the ground does not freeze and the freezing temperatures do not last too long. The leaves are the very essence of the tropical look and indispensable in the tropical garden. The plants are of extremely easy culture given rich soil and abundant moisture.

Colocasia affinis (AF-i-nis) is native to northern Myanmar (Burma), southern China, northern Laos, and northern Vietnam but is sometimes called the Egyptian taro. Its choice leaves are smaller than those of most other species, usually no more than a foot long, and are cordate to almost orbicular in shape and emerald green in color with purple to black blotches between the lateral veins. ***Colocasia affinis* 'Jenningsii'** (jen-NING-zee-eye) (synonym *C. antiquorum* var. *illustris*) is a gorgeous, larger-leaved cultivar with vivid green leaves interlarded with a deep brownish purple color between the lateral veins. It is sometimes called the black caladium. The plants are true water lovers and are often grown aquatically, their roots under a few inches of water, where they add great beauty to the margins of ponds and pools.

Colocasia antiquorum (ant-i-KWOR-um) is considered by many botanists and some horticulturists to be a form of *C. esculenta*. This may be so but the differences in appearance between the two are great enough to warrant segregation here, especially since they are usually offered in the trade as separate species. The leaves are rather small, like those of *C. affinis* and are held on long petioles. They are a deep green with bronzy purple to black markings between the veins. These are true water-loving plants and can be grown aquatically around the fringes of ponds or streams as long as the leaves are able to reach air and sun. They grow in partial sun to full sun, but they tend to die out in deep shade. Plate 138.

Colocasia esculenta (ess-kyoo-LENT-a) is native to most of tropical eastern Asia and has been naturalized throughout the wet tropical world. It is planted in the United States all over the Southeast and the Gulf Coast as well as southern California and all of Florida. This is the edible taro, though the tubers are poisonous unless cooked. It is also called the yam in the Pacific areas because of the edible tubers it produces, and in India is known as the dasheen. The great cordate to sagittate 3-foot-long leaves are a uniform deep to almost yellow-green with indistinct veins. Few plants give a greater impression of the tropics. It is strongly suggested that the home grower eschew ingestion of these or any other rootstocks in this genus (and, indeed, in the family) as many of these plants have oxalic acid crystals in their sap. The plants thrive around the margins of ponds and pools with their roots in a few inches of water where they provide superb form and texture.

Colocasia fallax (FAL-lax) is quite similar in all respects to *C. affinis* and *C. antiquorum* except that the dark markings on the leaves are confined to a smaller area near the center of the leaf.

COLVILLEA (kol-VIL-lee-a)
Caesalpiniaceae (Leguminosae), subfamily
    Caesalpinioideae: The Cassia, Royal Poinciana
    Family
COLVILLEA
Evergreen tree; great bipinnate leaves; spectacular
    orange and red flower clusters
Zones 10b and 11
Sun
Average but regular amounts of moisture
Sandy, humusy, well-drained soil
Propagation by seed

A monotypic genus from Madagascar and tropical East Africa. *Colvillea racemosa* (ray-se-MO-sa) is one of the world's most spectacular flowering trees. It grows to 50 feet with an open, fairly spreading to rather narrow yet sparsely branched crown of dark green, ferny, bipinnate leaves similar to those of *Delonix regia* (royal poinciana) but twice as large. In fact, the whole tree when not in bloom looks very much like the poinciana. The usually smooth, grayish brown trunk is fairly thick for a tree its size, and the tree's form is beautifully picturesque. The great leaves are as much as 3 feet long with very many half-inch-long elliptic dark green leaflets. They are deciduous in winter except in the most tropical areas. The tree blooms in the fall. The inflorescences are long pendent racemes that appear atop the branches in late summer and fall and are as much as 2 feet long; they are composed of fiery orange-red velvety buds that open from the top down to reveal the small red petals and long yellow stamens, creating the effect of giant red or orange wisteria flower clusters. The fruit is a roundish, brownish pod. There is no more spectacular tree when in bloom. Plates 139 and 140.

COMBRETUM (kahm-BREE-tum)
Combretaceae: The Combretum Family
COMBRETUM; BOTTLEBRUSH VINES
Large woody vines with slender stems; brilliant red
    comblike flower clusters
Zones 10 and 11; marginal in zone 10a
Sun
Average but regular amounts of moisture
Sandy, humusy, well-drained soil
Propagation by seed and cuttings

A large genus of about 250 species of trees, shrubs, and climbing shrubs distributed throughout all the tropical regions of the globe except Australia. The shrub species climb by modified leaf petioles that become spinelike and serve as "footholds." They sometimes need to be tied to a strong support on which to climb. The flowers are often in one-sided racemes and have the appearance of highly colored combs. The fruits are papery and winged and are often also highly colored.

Combretum coccineum (kahk-SIN-ee-um) is native to Madagascar. It is similar to *C. grandiflorum* but has larger leaves, to 10 inches long. The vine blooms mainly in spring, but flowers can appear at almost any time of the year. The flowers and fruit are similar to those of *C. grandiflorum*, but the fruits are an intense red.

Combretum fruticosum (froot-i-KO-sum) is indigenous to tropical Mexico and Central America. It is not much of a climber and is best grown as a very lovely sprawling shrub to 12 feet or more in height. The leaves are very attractive, rather like those of ornamental *Ficus* trees; they are 6 to 7 inches long, long-elliptic to obovate, and a glossy deep green with prominent and lighter colored veins. The plant blooms mostly in spring with 8-inch-long, one-sided spikes of brilliant orange to reddish orange fragrant, nectar-filled flowers.

Combretum grandiflorum (grand-i-FLOR-um) is a rampantly growing, large woody vining shrub from tropical West Africa. It can reach a height of 30 feet in frost-free areas and is the most commonly planted of the vining *Combretum* species. The glossy, bright green, ovate-elliptic leaves are 6 inches long, the new ones a bright reddish orange in color. The brilliant red flowers issue forth mostly in winter, but can appear at any time of the year. They are in one-sided spikes resembling thick red combs. Each flower is an inch-long narrow scarlet tube. The parchmentlike five-winged fruits are yellowish green, changing to red and finally brown; they are in spikes shaped rather like pine cones and are quite attractive. The leaves of this vine often but not always turn red at their tips when the plant blooms. Plate 141.

Combretum microphyllum (myk-ro-FYL-lum) is indigenous to Mozambique in tropical East Africa. It is a sprawling shrub that can be trained to a vine form. The leaves are no more than 3 inches long and are variable in shape, usually ovate, but can be oblong; they are usually deciduous in cold weather. The plant blooms mostly in late summer and fall when it is covered in bright red flowers; in truly tropical climes it may bloom at any time of the year. The intensity and profusion of the flowers occasion the common names of burning bush and flame creeper. The fruits are similar to those of the other species and are chartreuse to red in color.

CONGEA (KAHN-jee-a / KAHN-gee-a)
Verbenaceae: The Verbena, Lantana Family
WOOLLY CONGEA; SHOWER ORCHID
Sprawling vinelike shrub; fuzzy leaves; cascades of
    white and pink flowers
Zones 10 and 11
Sun

Average but regular amounts of moisture
Average well-drained soil
Propagation by seed and cuttings

A genus of seven species of climbing shrubs in Asia. All have small flowers subtended by persistent and colorful bracts. Only one is commonly planted. **Congea tomentosum** (toe-men-TOE-sum) is indigenous to Myanmar (Burma) and Thailand and has leaves as pretty as its flowers. They are about 7 inches long, strongly veined, ovate to long-ovate, short-tipped, and covered with hairs especially on their lower surfaces. The plant blooms in winter and usually into early spring with small clusters of tiny white flowers surrounded by three velvety, inch-long bracts shaped like a propeller; these bracts start out white in color, change to pink, lilac, or purple, and last for many weeks.

CONOCARPUS (kahn-o-KARP-us)
Combretaceae: The Combretum Family
SILVER BUTTON-BUSH; BUTTONWOOD;
  BUTTON MANGROVE
Silvery-leaved tree with crooked trunk; cinnamon-
  colored round fruit
Zones 10 and 11; marginal in zone 9b
Sun
Drought tolerant
Sandy, well-drained soil
Propagation by seed and cuttings

A genus of only two tree species in tropical America and Africa. Both species grow near tidal estuaries and seashores and, therefore, are very tolerant of saline and calcareous soil conditions. Neither, however, is a true mangrove and neither can grow in salt water as do the mangroves. They have leathery leaves with salt-excreting glands at their bases. The flowers are in conelike terminal panicles. Only the American species is commonly planted in the United States. **Conocarpus erectus** (ee-REK-tus) is usually a low spreading tree with a rounded crown but, under the most favorable conditions, may reach 50 feet in height; specimens near windy shores are always shorter and more reclining. The thick, fleshy, grayish green leaves are generally about 4 inches long and are elliptic to obovate in shape with a prominent midvein. The tiny whitish green flowers are borne densely in round heads as are the small scalelike purplish brown fruits. The plant is often used as a hedge or screen near the seashore. **Conocarpus erectus var. sericea** (se-RIS-ee-a) has very beautiful leaves that are covered in silvery gray hairs. It is now planted more widely than the type, but is slightly less hardy to cold and probably should be limited to zones 10 and 11. Few plants are as well adapted to seashore life and none make a better seaside landscape subject than this species and its variety.

COPERNICIA (ko-pur-NEE-see-a)
Palmae (Arecaceae): The Palm Family

Common names vary according to species
Fan-leaved palms often with massive trunks that are
  often covered in shag
Zones vary according to species
Sun to high shade
Drought tolerant
Sandy, humusy, well-drained soil
Propagation by seed

A genus of about 13 species of fan-leaved palms in tropical America, mainly Cuba. Most have large to very large, stiff, almost artificially formal-looking leaves; some have leaves that are almost stalkless, while others have long petioles armed with curved teeth. Some species have leaf crowns in which the leaves are very densely packed, making them appear as much like yuccas as palms, especially in those species where the leaf bases are persistent on the trunk. Many species have their leaves coated with wax, and one species has a very tough wax (carnauba) that is valuable commercially. Most have relatively short trunks, but some are tall and majestic. Most species are single-trunked palms, but a few are suckering. All are rather slow growing, some very slow growing. All are unusual and dramatic landscape subjects.

Copernicia alba (AL-ba) (synonym *C. australis*) is indigenous to southern Brazil and northern Argentina and is one of the hardier species in the genus, dependable in zones 9b through 11 and marginal in zone 9a. With great age the palm can grow to 80 feet and is one of the tallest in the genus, but in cultivation it is seldom more than half that stature. The trunk is unusually straight and relatively narrow for such a tall palm (less than a foot in diameter) and has the most unusual characteristic of shiny dark brown and persistent leaf bases arranged in a spiral pattern. The leaves are tough, stiff, and almost orbicular in shape, but with deeply cleft wax-coated segments. This noble, very attractive palm needs more water than most species. It occurs naturally on savannahs that are sometimes flooded in the rainy season. Plate 142.

Copernicia australis. See *C. alba*.

Copernicia baileyana (bay-lee-AHN-a) is native to Cuba and is hardy in zones 10b and 11. It is a spectacular palm because of its large dark green very stiff leaves that are tightly packed into the crown and its massive trunk which, when old, looks like a giant white concrete pillar. The palm grows slowly to a height of 35 to 40 feet in cultivation. The perfectly straight trunk can be 2 or 3 feet in diameter in mature palms and is smooth and gray to almost white in color. The wax-covered leaves are as much as 6 feet in diameter and are divided into many very stiff and erect segments to one-third of their depth; they are held on 5-foot-long petioles and are almost circular in outline. Seen against the sky, the leaves seem to have a halo created by the regularly spaced comblike outer segments. There are few sights to compare to a group of these mature palms. Plate 143.

Copernicia cerifera. See *C. pruinifera.*

Copernicia hospita (HAHS-pi-ta) is native to Cuba and is hardy in zones 10b and 11. It grows to 40 or even 50 feet in height with a dense crown of bluish green to bright green, stiff wedge-shaped leaves that are almost stalkless. The leaves have a "hastula," a projecting growth of cone-shaped tissue at the juncture of petiole and leaf blade. The trunk is usually covered for much of its length with old leaves that form a "skirt"; some palms look like haystack yucca plants. This species is spectacular and unusual, but very slow growing.

Copernicia macroglossa (mak-ro-GLAHS-sa) is native to Cuba and is fairly tender to cold but usually successful in zones 10 and 11. It is a small palm, only growing to about 12 or 15 feet in height. The trunk is slender, but is usually covered in a skirt of old leaves. The crown of dark green stiff leaves is very dense, and the leaves are almost stalkless, giving the palm the aspect of a *Yucca* species. Because of the skirt of old leaves, this palm can also have the look of a haystack. It is sometimes called the Cuban petticoat palm. Plate 144.

Copernicia pruinifera (proo-i-NIF-e-ra) (synonym *C. cerifera*) is indigenous to northeastern Brazil in the flood plain of the Amazon and is hardy in zones 10 and 11. The most distinct aspect of this palm is its trunk which, like that of *C. alba*, is covered in its lower portions with old leaf bases in a more or less circular arrangement (i.e., the leaf bases cease adhering to the trunk after a certain age). The trunk grows to as much as 40 feet and is more slender and graceful than that of *C. alba*. The grass green waxy leaves are about 4 feet in diameter, are circular in outline, and are deeply divided into many segments; they are held on 3-foot-long petioles, giving a graceful, open aspect to the crown. This very picturesque palm often has a trunk that leans to some extent. It is commonly called the carnauba waxpalm because of the commercially valuable wax obtained from the leaves.

CORDIA (KOR-dee-a)
Boraginaceae: The Heliotrope Family
Common names vary according to species
Evergreen small trees; large leaves; clusters of large
    white, yellow, or red trumpet flowers
Zones vary according to species
Sun
Average but regular amounts of moisture; drought
    tolerant when established
Average well-drained soil
Propagation by seed and air-layering

A large genus of about 300 species of trees and shrubs in tropical areas around the world. They have funnel-shaped red, white, or yellow flowers in clusters. Most species are evergreen, but a few are deciduous.

Cordia boissieri (boy-see-ER-ee) is native to southern Texas and adjacent Mexico. It is hardy as a shrub in zones 8b and 9a and as a small tree in zones 9b through 11. It grows to a maximum height of 25 or 30 feet, but usually less, and forms a rounded crown with dark gray, fairly stout trunk and branches. The evergreen leaves are 5 or 6 inches long, ovate to oblong in shape, and are dark green and rough-hairy above and velvety grayish green beneath. The flowers are borne in large clusters all spring, summer, and fall and often into the winter months in frost-free areas. Each blossom is pure white and trumpet-shaped with five lobes at the flaring apex; the corolla is 2 inches long by 3 inches wide, crinkled, and usually wavy-margined with a yellowish throat. Common names are anacahuita (a-nahk-a-WEE-ta), wild olive, and Texas wild olive. The leaves and flowers are quite attractive, and the whiteness of the flowers against the dark green leaves is startlingly beautiful in the landscape. Plate 145.

Cordia lutea (LOOT-ee-a) is native to western Peru and Ecuador and is hardy in zones 10 and 11 and marginal in zone 10a. It is a large shrub, growing 12 to 15 feet tall, and can be trained to a small tree form when young. The leaves are elliptic to obovate to almost round, thick, rough in texture, and deeply veined. The plant blooms most of the year in tropical climes with terminal rounded clusters of 2-inch-long funnel-shaped pure yellow flowers. Plate 146.

Cordia sebestena (seb-es-TEEN-a) is native to extreme southern Florida, the West Indies, and northern South America, and is hardy in zones 10b and 11. It grows 25 to 30 feet in height and usually has a slender crown but is variable in form and may be low and spreading; the trunk is seldom straight. The beautiful dark green leaves are as much as 8 inches long, ovate to oblong in shape, rough and hairy above and smooth and light green beneath. The midrib and the lateral veins are lighter than the leaves in color, and the lateral veins are depressed, sometimes to the point of making the leaf look corrugated. The tree blooms all year but most heavily in summer. The flowers are borne in terminal clusters and are funnel-shaped, 2 inches long by 3 inches wide with bright yellow stamens. The scarlet to orange corolla expands into six crinkled lobes. The common name is geiger tree. This beauty is tolerant of saline soil and air and is perfect for seaside color. Plate 147.

CORDYLINE (kor-di-LYN-ee)
Agavaceae: The Agave Family
Common names vary according to species
Yuccalike sparsely branched trees; long straplike,
    usually colored leaves
Zones vary according to species
Sun to partial shade
Water requirements vary according to species
Sandy, humusy, well-drained soil
Propagation by cuttings

A genus of 15 species of woody sparsely branched shrubs and trees with long, usually narrow leaves at the ends of the trunks and branches forming a palmlike or giant yucca form. They are found in India, Australasia, and Polynesia. The inflorescence is a terminal, many-flowered panicle with green to yellow flowers that are often fragrant.

Cordyline australis (aw-STRAL-is) (synonym *Dracaena australis*) is indigenous to New Zealand and is hardy in zones 9b through 11 and marginal in zone 9a. In its native habitat it grows to true tree proportions; in cultivation in the United States it seldom grows to more than 25 feet in height. It should be cut back when young to force branching, which makes a much more picturesque form, especially if the separate trunks are of differing heights. The grayish green to dark green leaves are about 3 feet long, narrow (2 inches wide), stiff but soft, the newer (upper) ones erect and the older ones pendent, giving the "head" of leaves on each trunk a full starburstlike effect. The tree looks like a tropical yucca and is excellent for the succulent garden, although it is not a true desert plant. It also can blend very well with other tropical looking plants and is a perfect contrast and accent to more typical foliage. It looks especially nice as a specimen plant near pools and is a good candidate for seaside plantings, although it cannot tolerate truly saline soil conditions. The inflorescences are terminal on each trunk and consist of 3-foot-long panicles of fragrant white flowers. The plant is not particular as to soil type, but needs a soil deep enough to accommodate its taproot. One thing it must have is perfect drainage. It is drought tolerant when established, but looks better and grows faster with adequate and regular supplies of water. It is intolerant of shade and dies out under such conditions. *Cordyline australis* **'Atropurpurea'** (at´-ro-poor-POOR-ee-a) is a very handsome cultivar with purplish bronze leaves. It grows slower than the type and not as tall. Usually it is no more than 15 feet tall. *Cordyline australis* **'Variegata'** has leaves with a yellow stripe in the center and yellow margins. From a distance the leaves appear almost totally yellow. It also is slower growing than the species, to about 15 feet in height.

Cordyline congesta. See *C. stricta*.

Cordyline fruticosa. See *C. terminalis*.

Cordyline stricta (STRIK-ta) (synonyms *C. congesta, Dracaena stricta*) is native to eastern Australia (Queensland and New South Wales) and is hardy in zones 10 and 11 and marginal in zone 9b. It grows to 12 or 15 feet in height and is slender-trunked and sparsely branched. The soft leathery leaves are dark green with a purplish hue and are about 2 feet long and only an inch or so wide; new growth is usually purplish red. The lavender flowers come in spring in large terminal panicles followed by purplish berries. The plant grows in shade to part shade, but does not like full sun in hot climates. This elegant plant can add the drama of its yuccalike form to shady sites where most other plants of the type do not grow well. It looks best when pruned to trunks of varying heights and thinned so that it is not a mass of foliage. It needs more water than *C. australis*.

Cordyline terminalis (tur-mi-NAL-is) (synonyms *C. fruticosa, Dracaena amabilis, D. terminalis*) is indigenous to Southeast Asia and Polynesia and is hardy in zones 10b and 11 although usually surviving in zone 10a. It is called the ti plant or Hawaiian good-luck plant. It is so popular in Hawaii that it has almost become a symbol of that state. It is commonly sold as ti logs, which are simply sections of the plant's canes that may be rooted by placing them horizontally in moist soil with good drainage. The plant grows to 12 feet or so in tropical climates with slender, ringed, usually unbranched stems atop which the 3-foot-long, elliptic to lanceolate, 6-inch-wide leaves grow, rather like a feather duster. The variably formed leaves are carried on grooved petioles (unlike *C. australis* and *C. stricta*), and they may be solid light to dark green, purplish black, red, yellow, pink, or a combination of these colors in a bewildering array of horticultural varieties most of which are named. The type has solid green leaves. There are also dwarf forms that are useful for edging. Normally the plant grows with a single stem and does not branch even if cut back, but there are forms that branch to some extent. This growth habit creates a rather weedy aspect if the ti plant is grown as a specimen in a site where its entire stems are evident. It is, however, quite beautiful when intermingled with other foliage to hide the bases of its stems. It adapts to full sun, but luxuriates in partial shade. It is not drought tolerant. Plate 148.

CORNUTIA (kor-NOO-tee-a)

Verbenaceae: The Verbena, Lantana Family
No known English common name
Evergreen small tree and large shrub; large leaves; tall spikes of blue flowers
Zone 9b as a shrub; zones 10 and 11 as a small tree
Sun
Average but regular amounts of moisture
Humusy, well-drained soil
Propagation by seed and cuttings

A genus of about 15 species of evergreen shrubs and trees in southern Mexico and Central America. All have aromatic and hairy leaves, four-sided stems (new growth), and spikes of flowers similar to those of *Vitex*. Only one species is common in cultivation. *Cornutia grandifolia* (gran-di-FO-lee-a) is indigenous to hillsides in southern Mexico and Central America where it grows quickly to 20 or 30 feet in height and about as broad. The velvety leaves are usually a foot or more long, are broad-ovate and long-acuminate in shape, and are usually slightly toothed on the margins; they are a medium green in color and are strongly fragrant if bruised or crushed. The tree is sometimes deciduous in very dry winters. The inch-wide flowers have four to five petals, are fragrant, and are borne in immense spikes as much as 18 inches high and sometimes a foot wide. The flower color is blue to purplish blue. Because of its beauteous leaves and giant blue flower clusters in spring and summer, this fast-growing and lush small tree is a very valuable addition to gardens in nearly frost-free regions.

CORYPHA (ko-RYF-a / ko-REEF-a)
Palmae (Arecaceae): The Palm Family
TALIPOT PALM; GEBANG PALM
Tall and massive fan-leaved palms with leaves of
    immense proportions
Zones 10b and 11
Sun
Average but regular amounts of moisture
Average well-drained soil
Propagation by seed

A genus of eight palmate-leaved palm species in India and Australasia. All the species have gigantic leaves, but *Corypha umbraculifera* has larger leaves than any other palmate-leaved palm. The plants are monocarpic, which can create a major mechanical problem in the landscape. Were it not for the incredibly spectacular beauty of the leaves, especially when young, and the many years it takes for the palms to flower, these species would be outcasts; even so they are best relegated to estate-sized gardens, botanical gardens, and other gardens in which the death of the great trunks does not pose a threat to adjacent gardens or structures. The palms grow quite slowly when young but faster with the advent of trunk formation. Only two species are commonly planted. Both dominate the landscape in a manner in which hardly any other plant can.

Corypha elata. See *C. utan*.

Corypha umbraculifera (um-brak´-yoo-LIF-e-ra) is the talipot palm. Its origins are obscured because of its long history of cultivation; in fact, it is no longer found in the wild except in association with human habitation. The tree grows to 80 feet or more with a 3-foot diameter trunk that is covered in old leaf bases until it attains some height; thereafter it is usually smooth, ringed, and a deep gray in color. The leaves are larger than those of any other fan palm: they are generally from 18 to more than 20 feet wide on 10-foot-long, spiny petioles and are almost circular in outline but deeply divided into about 100 segments. The final glory of the palm is its inflorescence that forms at the apex of the trunk, causing the leaves (and trunk) to eventually die off. This phenomenon occurs when the tree is between 30 and 80 years old, usually nearer the latter number than the former. The giant terminal panicle of white flowers rises 30 feet or more above the last leaf formation; it may be as wide as it is tall and, indeed, is shaped like a giant Christmas tree atop an immense and dying palm. There are millions of the tiny flowers in the inflorescence. There is nothing quite like the talipot palm if the plant lover has space and lives long enough to see it to maturity and fruition.

Corypha utan (OO-tahn) (synonym *C. elata*) is called the gebang palm and has the same problems associated with determining its original habitat as *C. umbraculifera*, although there is some evidence for its being indigenous to Myanmar (Burma) and Thailand. It is similar to *C. umbraculifera* except that it is not quite as large in any of its parts. Plate 149.

COSTUS (KOAST-us / KAHST-us)
Costaceae: The Costus Family
SPIRAL GINGER; SPIRAL FLAG
Herbaceous small shrubs; fleshy leaf spirals around
    stem; terminal clusters of flowers
Zones vary according to species
Partial shade to sun
Water lovers
Rich, moist, well-drained soil
Propagation by root division, rhizome division, and
    sometimes cuttings

A genus of about 100 species of rhizomatous perennial herbs with fleshy leaves more or less spirally arranged on fleshy stems that are reedlike in appearance. The inflorescences are mostly terminal (infrequently a scape), but always conelike with overlapping bracts from which the tubular and usually crinkly petaled flowers emerge. The blossoms usually expand into an almost circular shape at their apices. All species bloom in the summer or fall in warm weather. The latest taxonomic thinking places the genus (along with three other genera) into a separate family, Costaceae, but for many years it was included with the gingers, the Zingiberaceae. These beautiful perennials have been unaccountably neglected for the most part. There are probably fewer than a dozen species commonly cultivated. They deserve much wider recognition and cultivation. Many of them are root hardy in zone 9 and even the warmer parts of zone 8; they all need a fairly long growing season to produce their flowers and they generally need some sun to bloom well. The leaves of many are attractive enough to warrant cultivation for their sake alone.

Costus afer (AF-er) is a giant species from tropical West Africa that grows to as much as 10 or 12 feet in height with spiraling stems. The leaves are no more than 6 inches long and are generally lanceolate and acuminate. The terminal inflorescence is squat and densely packed with many pinkish bracts and flowers with white, watery, almost transparent petals, each with a yellow stripe. The plants are hardy in zones 10 and 11 and root hardy in zone 9.

Costus arabicus (a-RAB-i-kus) is native to Brazil and is hardy in zones 10 and 11, although it is probably root hardy in zone 9b. It grows to 5 or 6 feet and has 9-inch-long elliptic leaves that are emerald green above and purplish beneath. The white and yellow flowers emerge from red and green bracts.

Costus cuspidatus (kusp-i-DAYT-us) (synonym *C. igneus*) is indigenous to Brazil. It only grows to about 2 feet, but has wonderful large leaves that are as much as 8 inches long and oblong-lanceolate in shape, dark green above and tinged with reddish purple beneath. The large orange to reddish orange flowers are as much as 3 inches wide and are almost circular in outline; they emerge from a few-flowered short spike.

Costus igneus. See *C. cuspidatus*.

Costus malortieanus (ma-lor´-tee-AHN-us) is indigenous to northern South America and Central

America and is one of the most beautiful species in the genus. It is hardy in zones 10 and 11 and root hardy in zone 9b and sometimes in zone 9a. It grows to 3 feet under optimum conditions with succulent leaves that are usually about a foot long and are broadly elliptic to obovate. The leaves are a grayish to emerald green with darker lengthwise striations and are densely covered with short soft hairs that create a silky appearance and feel. The flowers are bright yellow marked with red stripes. Besides spiral flag and spiral ginger, the plant is sometimes called the stepladder plant.

Costus speciosus (spee-see-O-sus) is one of the largest and certainly one of the showiest and most beautiful species in the genus; it can grow to as much as 9 feet with thick, succulent stems and leaves. Native to a wide area from India through Southeast Asia into New Guinea, it is reliably hardy in zones 10 and 11 and root hardy in zone 9. The thick and succulent leaves are about 12 inches long, elliptic-acuminate in shape, and dark green and silky with very fine hairs above and pubescence beneath. The flowers are large, round, and white with orange and yellow centers; they emerge from dark green to purplish, brown-tipped large bracts. Because of the crinkly texture of the flowers the plant is often called crepe ginger. There are several forms of the plant including dwarf, variegated-leaved, and a pink-flowered variety. Plate 150.

Costus spicatus (spy-KAIT-us) is indigenous to Hispaniola and is dependably hardy in zones 10 and 11 and root hardy in zone 9 and the warmer parts of zone 8. The plant can grow to as much as 8 feet in height, but usually reaches no more than 4 or 5 feet. The leaves are as much as 10 inches long, medium green in color, and narrowly elliptic or obovate in shape. The inflorescence is a cylinder with densely packed yellow-green to brilliant red bracts from which emerge small pink or yellow flowers.

COTYLEDON (ko-TIL-e-dun)
Crassulaceae: The Sedum, Sempervivum Family
Common names vary according to species
Small fleshy shrubs; usually spatulate-shaped fat
    leaves; clusters of bell-shaped flowers
Zones vary according to species
Partial sun
Drought tolerant
Sandy, humusy, well-drained soil
Propagation by cuttings and seed

A small genus of only nine species of succulent-leaved shrubs from South Africa to Arabia. They are closely allied to *Crassula*, *Echeveria*, and *Sempervivum*. The leaves are oppositely arranged or in whorls and are stalkless and usually spatulate to obdeltoid in shape. The flowers are bell-shaped in many-flowered terminal clusters atop fairly tall stems, the individual blossoms usually pendent. The fat-leaved plants are the very essence of the word *succulent* and are quite attractive in a raised bed or the cactus and succulent garden. Although drought tolerant, the plants are not completely adaptable to the full sun of hot summer regions, and most species should not be subjected to it lest the juicy leaves be burned.

Cotyledon barbeyi (BAR-bee-eye) occurs naturally from South Africa through tropical East Africa to Arabia and is dependably hardy in zones 10 and 11. The plant grows into a much-branched shrub to about 6 feet in height if not cut back by frost. The leaves are jade green with a whitish bloom, spatulate in shape and usually curved inward, flat on top and keeled beneath, and are from 4 to 6 inches long. The half-inch-long flowers are greenish yellow to orange.

Cotyledon ladysmithiensis (lay´-dee-smith´-ee-EN-sis) is a small, dense-leaved shrublet native to Cape Province, South Africa, and is dependably hardy in zones 10 and 11 although sometimes grown to maturity in zone 9b. It reaches a foot or so in height and has irresistible 2- to 6-inch-long fat concave obovate leaves that are mint green in color, covered with white hairs, and apically notched like tiny claws; the notches are red to maroon in color. The flowers are yellow and orange. This species is commonly called cub's paws.

Cotyledon macrantha (mak-RANTH-a) is native to the Cape of Good Hope in South Africa and is hardy in zones 10 and 11 although sometimes successful in zone 9b. This beauty grows to about 3 feet and has its leaves densely packed on the stems, giving the aspect almost of a small *Aeonium* or *Aloe* species. The leaves are about 4 inches long, spatulate-shaped, concave, and emerald green in color with a whitish bloom and red margins; they are not as thick and fleshy as many others in the genus. The inflorescences are held well above the foliage and consist of small half-inch-long brilliant red, nodding bell-like flowers.

Cotyledon orbiculata (or-bik´-yoo-LAIT-a) occurs naturally from Namibia through South Africa and is similar to *C. macrantha* but has larger and thicker leaves and grows to half again as large. It has several leaf forms, the most beautiful of which has silvery or bluish leaves with red margins. The plant is dependably hardy in zones 10 and 11 and is often grown successfully in zone 9b. This is an outstandingly beautiful subject for the cactus and succulent garden.

Cotyledon tomentosa (toe-men-TOE-sah) is native to South Africa and is similar to *C. ladysmithiensis* except that the apical notches on the leaves are usually bright red rather than maroon and the entire plant is covered in dense white hair. It is dependably hardy in zones 10 and 11, although it is sometimes grown to maturity in zone 9b. The flowers are usually not pendent and are red on the outside and straw-colored on the inside.

Cotyledon undulata (un-dyoo-LAIT-a) is native to southern South Africa and is hardy in zones 10 and 11 and sometimes zone 9b. It grows to about 2 feet and has silvery gray obdeltoid 4- to 5-inch-long leaves that are scalloped and wavy-margined. The flowers are orange to yellow.

COUROUPITA

(koo-ROOP-i-ta / koo-roo-PEET-a)
Lecythidaceae: The Brazil-Nut Family
CANNONBALL TREE
Massive tree; large leathery leaves; spectacular
  flowers, large round woody fruit on trunk
Zones 10b and 11
Sun
Water lover
Rich, humusy, moist soil
Propagation by seed

A genus of only three species of tropical American trees distributed from Nicaragua to the Amazon Basin. Only one species is planted in the United States. *Couroupita guianensis* (gee-a-NEN-sis) is native to northern South America and the Amazon Basin. It is one of the most fascinating and beautiful botanical "curiosities." In its native haunts it can reach 100 feet in height, but is seldom more than 60 feet tall in cultivation. It usually forms a vase-shaped or elmlike crown with the 8- to 12-inch-long obovate and leathery leaves in whorls at the ends of the branches. The mature leaves tend to drop all at once and may do so more than once a year. The flowers and fruit are borne on long, vinelike peduncles that arise directly from the bark of the tree's trunk. The peduncles are not deciduous with maturation of the fruit, but rather remain on the tree, growing longer each year. From these stalks the inflorescences arise as racemes with 6-inch-wide flowers, which have been described as "orchidlike" but which look more like mutant peonies. In the center of the flower is a button-like yellow stigma surrounded by a round yellow pincushion-like mass of stamens borne atop a short stalk (androphore). This mass is surrounded by six pink to orange to scarlet and variably shaped (but generally oblong to obovate) petals. In addition, there is a strange appendage flaring out from the base of the androphore and arching over the center of the flowers; it also carries stamens, but these are plumelike and feathery and remind one of a cockscomb. The flowers are very fragrant with a strange and heady aroma that some find sweet and pleasing and others think unpleasant. The woody fruits take about 18 months to mature and, when they do, are cinnamon-colored, woody, 8 inches in diameter, and almost perfectly round. There are often flowers and mature to half-matured fruit on the trunk simultaneously. The origin of the vernacular name cannonball tree is obvious from the appearance of the individual fruits and the sound resulting from their rattling against each other in the wind on their long and twisted stalks. Plates 151 and 152.

CRASSULA (KRAS-yoo-la)

Crassulaceae: The Sedum, Sempervivum Family
Common names vary according to species
Succulent-leaved small shrubs; large, usually flat-
  topped flower clusters
Zones vary according to species
Partial sun
Drought tolerant
Sandy, humusy, well-drained soil
Propagation by cuttings, occasionally seed

A large genus of more than 300 species of fleshy-leaved herbs, shrubs, shrublets, and even vines. Some are tiny, others make small trees with more or less woody trunks; some are annuals, others are biennials, and very many are perennials. The flowers are in terminal usually rounded or flat clusters. Almost all the species are endemic to South Africa. These plants are somewhat similar to those in the genus *Cotyledon* and are not well adapted to full sun in hot summer regions. Only two of the perennial shrub species are of true landscape value.

Crassula arborescens (ahr-bo-RES-senz) is native to Cape Province, South Africa, and is successfully grown in zones 10 and 11 with occasional damage in zone 10a. It grows slowly to a maximum height of 6 feet with thick squat and rubbery trunks and branches; the oldest stems are semi-woody with parchmentlike, usually peeling bark. The plant makes a spreading, usually multitrunked, bonsai-treelike specimen. The leaves are variable in shape and size from 1 to almost 3 inches long and from almost round to obovate in shape. They are slightly curved inward, somewhat keeled below, and bluish green with a grayish bloom, usually reddish margins, and tiny red dots scattered on the leaf surface. The five-petaled starlike flowers are borne in small terminal clusters; they open pure white and age to pinkish white. The plants usually do not flower until they are several years old and need a considerable amount of sun to do so. The little tree is commonly called Chinese jade tree, silver dollar, and silver jade plant.

Crassula argentea. See *C. ovata*.

Crassula ovata (o-VAIT-a) (synonyms *C. argentea, C. portulacea*) is universally known as the jade tree in the United States and is the commoner of the two jade trees. It has suffered under several names in the nursery trade along with the botanical synonyms. It is native to South Africa from the Cape of Good Hope northeastward to the Durban area and is somewhat more tender than *C. arborescens*, being hardy only in zones 10b and 11. The plant grows to 10 feet with time, makes a multibranched bonsailike little tree, and is somewhat faster growing than *C. arborescens*. It is similar in all respects to the other *Crassula* species, but grows larger and faster and has light pink flowers. There are several cultivars. *Crassula ovata* 'Crosby's Dwarf' is a dwarf. *Crassula ovata* 'Sunset' has yellow leaves with red margins. *Crassula ovata* 'Tricolor' is a variegated form with green, pink, and white in the leaf. The species and its cultivars are outstanding beauties for creating a little world of their own in a cactus and succulent garden as they have the form of a miniature live oak when mature. Like *C. arborescens*, *C. ovata* needs some sun to bloom but, unlike *C. arborescens*, it blooms when younger and is definitely more floriferous.

Crassula portulacea. See *C. ovata*.

CRESCENTIA (kress-SENT-ee-a)
Bignoniaceae: The Catalpa, Jacaranda, Trumpet-
 Vine Family
CALABASH TREE; GOURD TREE
Small evergreen trees; flowers and large rounded fruit
 on trunk and older branches
Zones 10b and 11
Sun
Average but regular amounts of moisture
Sandy, humusy, well-drained soil
Propagation by seed and cuttings

A genus of six species of small trees, shrubs, and vines in tropical America. All the tree species produce flowers on the trunk and older branches. This cauliflorous habit is believed to be an adaptation to their being pollinated by bats who find it difficult to distinguish, via their echolocation, the flowers from the leaves. All the species produce relatively large, rounded, and hard-shelled fruit. Only two species are planted outside botanical gardens in the United States.

Crescentia alata (a-LAIT-a) is native to the southern and western Pacific slopes of Mexico down into Costa Rica. The tree grows to about 30 feet in height with a short trunk and a crown of long, mostly zigzagged whiplike branches. The leaves are quite distinctive: usually with three leaflets (although sometimes five) on large winged petioles (*alata* means "winged"), they create the visual effect of a cross, which phenomenon led the early explorers to attach religious significance to them. The whole dark green leaf is seldom more than 5 inches long. Because the tree does not produce many smaller subsidiary branches and because its branches are mostly clothed in leaves and the petioles are like leaves, the tree's crown appears almost like a mass of branches of a *Fouquieria* (ocotillo) species. The strange flowers are nearly stalkless and grow in pairs directly from the trunk and older branches. The five petals are fused into a more or less bell shape, which is also rather like a hood; they are 2 to 3 inches long and greenish yellow to purple brown with purple stripes. The fruits account for the common names of calabash tree and Mexican calabash tree. They are round or nearly round, about 5 inches in diameter, yellow-green, and are almost stalkless like the flowers. To some gardeners the tree is not especially beautiful, but is, indeed, interesting and certainly exotic appearing. It is drought tolerant to some degree but, at the same time, grows in monsoonal areas and withstands periodic flooding in the rainy season.

Crescentia cujete (koo-JET-ee) is native to the West Indies, the eastern and wetter parts of Mexico, and down into most of Central America. The tree is similar in growth habit to *C. alata*; it grows to about the same height and has an open crown with relatively thin and mostly pendulous branches that are clothed almost completely with leaves. The leaves appear in clusters on the branches and are larger and more attractive than are those of *C. alata*; they are as much as 6 inches long,

simple, oblanceolate to obovate in shape, dark green in color, and stalkless or almost so. The flowers are similar in all respects to those of *C. alata* but slightly more colorful. The fruits are spectacular large yellow-green berries that may be from 5 inches to more than a foot in diameter. They are usually almost completely round, but may also be elliptical in shape and are woody on the outside. They are used to this day by native peoples as water vessels and as musicians' rattles after the pulp (which is said to be poisonous) is removed.

CROSSANDRA
(krahs-SAN-dra / kro-SAHN-dra)
Acanthaceae: The Acanthus Family
CROSSANDRA; FIRECRACKER PLANT
Small evergreen, herbaceous shrubs; showy five-
 lobed orange, pink, or red flowers
Zones 10b and 11 as year-round perennials; zones
 10a and 9b as returning perennials
Partial shade
Water lovers
Sandy, humusy, well-drained soil
Propagation by cuttings and (sometimes) seeds

A genus of about 50 evergreen, small, mostly herbaceous shrubs or shrublets in India, Africa, and Madagascar. All have ovate leaves and bright, showy spikes of flowers, and bloom over a rather long period in the warm months. They are near perfect bedding plants for partially shady spots, blooming well with only bright shade, and they are unexcelled combined with impatiens, ferns, caladiums, and other shade-loving exotics. The plants are quite tender to frost, but will sprout from the roots in zone 10a and sometimes in zone 9b if freezing temperatures do not last too long. Only one species is common, although there are several color forms of it. *Crossandra infundibuliformis* (in-fun-dib´-yoo-ly-FOR-mis) is native to southern India and Sri Lanka. It grows to about 4 feet in height if not cut back by freezing temperatures. The leaves are narrowly ovate to lanceolate, from 2 to 5 inches long, and a wonderful dark green with distinct veining. The funnel-shaped flowers are borne in terminal spikes, have five spreading lobes, and are unique shades of apricot-orange to coral and red. No other plant gives more vibrant color to shady situations in the summer. The brown velvety spikes of seed pods, while rather ornamental, should be removed before they mature to help keep the plants in bloom.

CRYOSOPHILA (kry-o-SAHF-i-la)
Palmae (Arecaceae): The Palm Family
ROOTSPINE PALM; SILVER STAR PALM
Medium-sized, single slender-trunked, fan-leaved
 palm; short spinelike roots on trunk
Zones 10b and 11
Sun
Average but regular amounts of moisture

Sandy, humusy, well-drained soil
Propagation by seed

A genus of nine species of palmate-leaved palms in tropical America with elegantly thin trunks and circular leaves. The genus was formerly known as *Acanthorrhiza*. The trunks of all species have aerial roots, which are spinelike on the upper part of the trunks and function as true roots on the basal portion. There are two species available, but they are so outwardly similar as to warrant a single description. **Cryosophila argentea** (ahr-JEN-tee-a) (synonym *C. stauracantha*) and **Cryosophila warscewiczii** (war-see-WIK-zee-eye) are indigenous to Central America and southern Mexico and grow to about 25 feet in height with beautiful thin trunks slightly swollen at the base and covered, at least in the lower parts, with root spines (i.e., roots that do not normally reach the ground but become hard and spiny). The wonderful leaves are about 6 feet wide, are carried on petioles almost as long, and each forms a complete circle in outline but is divided into about 60 segments halfway to the center of the blade. *Cryosophila argentea* has leaves whose undersides are more or less silvery, while the leaves of *C. warszewiczii* are bright green on both sides. These elegant palms should be much more widely planted in far southern Florida and other tropical or nearly tropical moist regions. They are of unusual beauty and are tolerant of limy soil conditions.

CRYPTANTHUS (krip-TANTH-us)
Bromeliaceae: The Pineapple, Bromeliad Family
EARTH STAR
Small flattish rosettes of thick, tough, mostly
   variegated aloelike leaves
Zones 10 and 11; marginal in zone 10a
Partial shade to sun
Average but regular amounts of moisture
Light, porous, humusy soil or leaf mold
Propagation by root division, transplanting of
   suckers, and seed

A genus of 20 or so small but exquisite terrestrial bromeliad species from eastern Brazil. Most of these species form low, rather flat and spreading, more or less symmetrical rosettes of rigid and usually wavy-margined, spiny-margined leaves that are commonly colored and variegated and exhibit some of the most exotic and beautiful leaf patterns of all the bromeliads. The small white flowers are borne on inflorescences that hardly emerge from the center of the leaf rosettes and are perhaps the least exciting in the family, but are nevertheless quite attractive against the usually highly colored foliage. The gorgeous leaves more than make up for the less-than-spectacular blossoms. The plants slowly spread by creeping rootstocks called "stolons," and some produce offshoots between the leaves. No plants give a more exotic and picturesque effect as a groundcover or growing in soil pockets on trees or from rocks. Their only fault is that they are all relatively small plants.

Cryptanthus acaulis (a-KAW-lis) is indigenous to the Rio de Janeiro area of eastern Brazil and is a tiny but delectable little flat rosette of bright green 5-inch-long elliptic-shaped leaves with very wavy margins. The naturally occurring varieties are even choicer. **Cryptanthus acaulis** var. **argentea** has leaves whose upper surfaces are frosted with tiny white scales. **Cryptanthus acaulis** var. **ruber** has leaves tinged with a rosy or reddish suffusion.
Cryptanthus acaulis var. **bromelioides.** See *C. bromelioides*.
Cryptanthus acaulis var. **diversifolius.** See *C. diversifolius*.
Cryptanthus bahianus (bah-hee-AHN-us) is found in dry areas of eastern Brazil and is unlike other *Cryptanthus* species in two ways: the plants flourish in full sun and they form a stem rather like a small *Aloe* species. The 8-inch-long leaves are narrow with a wavy margin and a spiny tip and are an olive green in color that changes to almost a chocolate brown in full sun.
Cryptanthus beuckeri (BOIK-ur-eye) is indigenous to far southern Brazil and, unlike most other species, makes an open rosette with upward-turned leaves that have a distinct petiole and are broad-lanceolate in shape. The leaves are about 6 inches long and are pale green to brownish green, strongly mottled with darker green and cream-colored maculations; the undersides of the leaves are covered with tiny white scales. The species looks more like a small *Dracaena godseffiana* (gold-dust plant) than it does other *Cryptanthus* species.
Cryptanthus bivittatus (by-vit-TAIT-us) (synonym *C. rosea-picta*) is also from southern Brazil and is probably the most widely grown species of *Cryptanthus*. It is one of the most colorful of the species with 6-inch-long, wavy-margined straplike leaves, each with two longitudinal stripes of cream or pink on a dark brownish green background and reddish brown undersides. **Cryptanthus bivittatus** var. **atropurpureus** (at-ro-poor-POOR-ee-us) has dark pink leaves with dark stripes. **Cryptanthus bivittatus** var. **bivittatus** has pale green leaves with darker green stripes. A very large version of this variety is **Cryptanthus bivittatus** var. **bivittatus** 'Ludemannii' (loo-di-MAN-ee-eye), which grows to more than 2 feet in diameter with a height of about a foot.
Cryptanthus bromelioides (bro-mel-ee-OY-deez) (synonym *C. acaulis* var. *bromelioides*) is native to southern Brazil and is one of the larger species, reaching a height of 1 foot and a diameter of 2 feet. The olive green sword-shaped leaves are on petioles and are about a foot long; they have a distinctly bronzy sheen in half sun. **Cryptanthus bromelioides** 'Racinae' (RAS-i-ny) has leaves that are transversely marked with wavy bands of silver. **Cryptanthus bromelioides** var. **tricolor** (TRY-kul-or), a larger form, is also one of the most beautiful in the genus. The green leaves are longitudinally banded in cream and white, and the young growth suffused with pink.
Cryptanthus diversifolius (dy-vurs´-i-FO-lee-us)

(synonym *C. acaulis* var. *diversifolius*) has foot-long leaves that are dark reddish green to reddish brown in color, rounded on the apices, and fluted at the base. The blade is covered in tiny silvery scales.

Cryptanthus fosterianus (fahs-ter´-ee-AHN-us) is a plant of exceptional beauty with its wide 14-inch-long leaves that form a very flat and large rosette to 30 inches in diameter. The leaves range in color from dark pink to almost purple and have many transverse and wavy bands of silver.

Cryptanthus roseo-picta. See *C. bivittatus.*

Cryptanthus zonatus (zo-NAIT-us) is possibly the most beautiful species of *Cryptanthus.* The type has 9-inch-long wavy-margined leaves that are light green with transverse bands of silver. The bands are so wavy as to resemble the markings of a seismograph during an earthquake. ***Cryptanthus zonatus*** forma *fuscus* has leaves with a reddish brown background rather than light green.

CRYPTOCEREUS

(krip-toe-SEER-ee-us)
Cactaceae: The Cactus Family
ZIGZAG CACTUS
Spineless flat-stemmed, sprawling epiphytic cactus; large red or white nocturnal flowers
Zones 10 and 11
Partial shade to partial sun
Average but regular amounts of moisture
Light, porous, humusy soil or leaf mold
Propagation by seed and cuttings

A genus of two epiphytic cactus species in Mexico, Central America, and Ecuador (see also *Selenicereus* and *Weberocereus*). This is one of the cactus genera called "leaf cactus" because of the lobed, leaflike, and spineless stems. The genus is allied to the genus *Epiphyllum* (which see for cultural information) and often confused with it. The plants are not climbers, but may be tied to tree trunks or some other support; like the *Epiphyllum* species, they look best cascading from a "perch." They bloom mainly in spring and early summer.

Cryptocereus anthonyanus (an-toe´-nee-AHN-us) has 5-inch-long tubular-shaped flowers whose ends expand into many linear red and yellow sepals and petals in the center of which are the numerous yellow stamens and a large yellow many-parted stigma.

Cryptocereus imitans (IM-i-tanz) has flowers similar in shape and size to those of *C. anthonyanus,* but pure white in color.

CRYPTOSTEGIA

(krip-toe-STEE-jee-a / krip-toe-STEEJ-ya)
Asclepiadaceae: The Milkweed, Madagascar Jasmine Family
RUBBER VINE; MADAGASCAR RUBBER VINE
Glossy red-veined leaves on heavy vining shrub; pink to purple trumpet-shaped flowers
Zones 10 and 11
Sun
Average but regular amounts of moisture
Sandy, humusy, well-drained soil
Propagation by seed and cuttings

A genus of two, possibly three, species of twining vines in Madagascar and tropical East Africa. They have thick, leathery, glossy, opposite leaves and white to purple funnel-shaped flowers in terminal clusters. Two of the species are planted. Both species have milky poisonous latex that was once used in making rubber. The plants are often pruned to shrub size and make some of the most beautiful screening subjects available. They tolerate salty air, making them wonderful candidates for seaside gardens if not planted too close to the ocean.

Cryptostegia grandiflora (grand-i-FLOR-a) is indigenous to tropical East Africa and grows to about 20 feet in height with heavy ropelike stems. It makes a fine screen. The beautiful 5-inch-long leathery, glossy oblong leaves have a prominent and lighter colored midrib and are usually slightly folded into a concave cross section. The flowers are borne in summer in terminal few-flowered clusters of tube-shaped blossoms with flaring corollas; lilac to purple in color, they usually quickly fade to a washed-out white.

Cryptostegia madagascariensis (mad´-a-gas-ker´-ee-EN-sis) is native to the island of Madagascar. It is a twining shrub that reaches heights of 20 feet or more if it is not cut back by freezing temperatures. It also makes an excellent screening subject and has leaves very much like those of *C. grandiflora,* but with beautiful red midveins. The flowers are similar to those of *C. grandiflora* and appear in summer but have 3-inch-wide lobed corollas, are generally pink to lilac in color, and do not fade with age. The plant is in general more attractive than *C. grandiflora* and grows slightly faster and stronger.

CTENANTHE (ten-ANTH-ee)

Marantaceae: The Maranta Family
Common names vary according to species
Small fleshy herbaceous shrubs; large, mostly linear and variegated long-stalked leaves
Zones 10b and 11 as year-round perennials; zone 10a (sometimes zone 9b) as returning perennials
Bright shade
Water lovers
Humusy, well-drained soil
Propagation by root division, rhizome division, and cuttings

A genus of 15 species in tropical America (mostly Brazil). These rhizomatous herbs have variegated and often highly colored oblong to straplike leaves. They are closely allied to the genera *Calathea* and *Maranta,* and their uses in the landscape are the same—tall groundcovers and bold accent plants—but they grow more like large *Aglaonema* species than the other two aforementioned genera. The flowers come in terminal clusters and are usually not terribly showy. All forms are quite beautiful and exotic and add greatly to tropical shade plantings. None of them are frost tolerant, but they resprout from the rhizomes if the temperature does not fall much below 28°F for very long.

Ctenanthe compressa (kahm-PRESS-a) is native to east-central Brazil. The plant grows to 3 feet in height with lemony green long-petioled ovate to oblong leaves whose blades are 14 or more inches long with depressed veins.

Ctenanthe glabra (GLAB-ra) is native to eastern Brazil and is a large grower to 5 feet in height and almost as wide. The leaves are 12 to 14 inches long on 4- to 6-inch-long petioles and are oblong to almost rectangular in shape, a light green in color with pinnate dark green markings radiating from the midrib. This lovely plant slowly makes a rather large clump by its stoloniferous roots.

Ctenanthe kummerana (koo-mer-AHN-a) is indigenous to southeastern Brazil and is a very noble looking landscape subject that grows to about 3 feet. The 6- to 8-inch-long leaves are carried on 4-inch-long petioles, are ovate to linearly oblong in shape, and are a dark green in color on the upper surfaces with the veins marked in silver, and a beautiful maroon color beneath. The plants slowly clump.

Ctenanthe lubbersiana (loob-ber´-see-AHN-a) is indigenous to a wide area in Brazil and grows to about 2 feet in height with a much-branched and bushy aspect. The beautiful leaves have 4-inch-long petioles and are nearly perfect 8-inch oblongs with an apical "tail" that is slightly twisted. The leaf color is dark green with much yellowish white variegation. This species is a relatively fast grower and soon makes a nice clump of tropical and exotic looking foliage.

Ctenanthe oppenheimiana (ahp´-pen-hy-mee-AHN-a) is native to eastern Brazil. It grows to 3 or 4 feet in height and has gorgeous 18-inch-long linearly ovate to lanceolate leaves that are a deep, dark green with lateral swaths of yellowish white or silver above and a deep red beneath; leaf petioles are about 6 inches long. There is a cultivar with much more yellow on the upper surfaces of the leaves; it is not as choice as the type. This species is sometimes called the never-never plant.

Ctenanthe setosa (see-TOE-sa) is native to southeastern Brazil. It grows to 3 feet or sometimes more. The leaves are carried on long brownish petioles and are 18 or more inches long, a beautiful deep and metallic green with wide bands of silver or gray in a pinnate pattern from the midrib. The plant does not grow very thick, but makes a very attractive and delicate accent and silhouette in bright shade.

CUPANIA. See *Cupaniopsis.*

CUPANIOPSIS (kyoo-pay´-nee-AHP-sis)
Sapindaceae: The Soapberry, Golden-Rain Tree Family
CARROTWOOD TREE
Medium-sized spreading, evergreen tree; large, leathery pinnate leaves; yellow fruit
Zones 10 and 11; marginal in zone 10a
Sun
Average but regular amounts of moisture
Average well-drained soil
Propagation by seed

A genus of about 50 species of trees and shrubs in Australia, New Guinea, and the islands of the South Pacific. The species have alternately arranged pinnate leaves, small flowers in axillary clusters, and six-parted capsular fruits. Only one species is commonly planted. *Cupaniopsis anacardioides* (an´-a-kar-dee-OY-deez) (synonym *Cupania anacardioides*) is found in eastern Australia. The common name carrotwood tree refers to the tree's pinkish brown wood. The species grows into a round-crowned, densely foliaged tree 25 to 30 feet in height, sometimes to as much as 45 feet. The leaves are 10 to 12 inches long and consist of six to ten 5-inch-long oblong to obovate glossy dark green leaflets that are thick and leathery and have a prominent and lighter colored midvein. The flowers are borne in terminal racemes and are tiny, yellowish green and mostly inconspicuous. The tree blooms in midwinter, and the fruits, which mature by midsummer, are in clusters at the ends of the branches, each one no more than an inch in diameter, yellow to orange in color and divided into six sections. They look rather like tiny pumpkins. This lush little tree is perfect for small yards and patios and is much used in other parts of the world as a street tree as it is not messy and is always attractive. It is not tolerant of saline soil, but is quite happy in seaside gardens if not planted too close to the water.

CUPHEA (KYOO-fee-a)
Lythraceae: The Crepe-Myrtle Family
Common names vary according to species
Herbaceous or woody shrubs and shrublets; small leaves; showy flowers in all colors
Zones 10 and 11 as perennials; zone 9b as root hardy perennials; anywhere as tender annuals
Sun to partial shade
Average but regular amounts of moisture
Average well-drained soil
Propagation by seed and cuttings

A large and variable genus of about 250 species of shrubs or subshrubs found in tropical America and the warmer parts of the United States. Many of them are completely herbaceous; all have more or less hairy stems and leaves that are oppositely arranged or whorled on the stem. The flowers typically are swollen and extended, cylindrical and asymmetrical, composed of fused calyx and corolla (technically termed an *hy-*

panthium), which usually expands into six lobes. Every flower color known in the plant world is found in this genus.

Cuphea hyssopifolia (his-sahp´-i-FO-lee-a) is native to Mexico and Guatemala and grows to a maximum of about 2 feet with an equal spread. It is commonly called Mexican heather because of its stature, the tiny leaves, and the small flowers. The leaves are mostly less than an inch long and narrowly lanceolate to linear in shape and densely cover the little plants. The flowers are even more diminutive and are never more than a half inch long; they are tiny cylinders with six expanded lobes of blue to lavender or purple. This plant has become very popular and widely available in the 1990s. It is very useful for edging beds with color. There are dwarf forms and cultivars with white, pink, or red flowers. The species is everblooming except in frosty weather and, while it survives drought conditions, does much better with adequate and regular supplies of moisture.

Cuphea ignea (IG-nee-a) (synonym *C. platycentra*) is indigenous to Mexico and the West Indies and is commonly called cigar flower. It grows to 3 feet. The 3-inch-long leaves are lanceolate in shape and a medium green in color with a prominent and lighter colored midrib. The flowers are borne singly from the axils of the leaves and are inch-long cylinders of scarlet with a dark purple-red ring near the end tipped with white and yellow. The plants bloom year-round in frost-free areas and from midsummer to frost in colder climes.

Cuphea platycentra. See *C. ignea.*

CURCAS. See *Jatropha curcas.*

CURCULIGO (koor-KYOO-li-go)
Amaryllidaceae: The Amaryllis Family
PALM GRASS
Stemless rosettes of pleated and ribbed palm-like
    leaves
Zones 10 and 11; marginal in zone 9b
Partial shade
Water lovers
Rich, humusy, well-drained soil
Propagation by root division, rhizome division

A genus of about 36 species of rhizomatous or tuberous-rooted evergreen herbs in southern Japan, Southeast Asia, Indonesia, and Australia. The plants have no stems, but the leaves have rather long petioles and beautiful form (like juvenile palm leaves), and make very attractive clumps mixed with ferns, begonias, impatiens, and other low-growing tropicals. The leaves resemble bamboo leaves more than typical grasses, although they are not related to the grasses. The flowers of most species are attractive, but are at ground level and usually hidden by the leaves. *Cucurligo* species are not very tolerant of frost but usually resprout from the roots in zone 9. These plants demand a regular and adequate supply of water but, at the same time, must have perfect drainage. There is only one species that is commonly planted and is large enough for landscaping purposes. ***Curculigo capitulata*** (ka-pit´-yoo-LAIT-a) is native to a wide area from Southeast Asia, Indonesia, and northern Australia. The light green arching and recurved leaves are 3 feet long, linear in shape with longitudinal grooves, and are held on 2-foot-long petioles. The leaves are very graceful in their nodding arch and move with the slightest breeze, lending a subtle air of excitement to any planting that includes them.

CYATHEA (sy-AY-thee-ah)
Cyatheaceae: The Tree-Fern Family
TREE FERN
Very large ferns with significant fibrous trunks; large
    triangular lacy tripinnate leaves
Zones 9b through 11
Partial shade in hot climates; sun or partial shade in
    cool summer climates
Water lovers
Humusy, well-drained soil
Propagation by spores

A very large genus of about 600 species of tree ferns in tropical and subtropical areas around the world. Most are indigenous to lowland and wet tropical and subtropical areas, but a few are found in mountainous (and wet) areas where there is even occasional light frost. All the species need regular moisture with perfect drainage and humidity. None of them likes very hot weather such as is found in the desert and, if the heat is accompanied by low humidity, it can sometimes be fatal. Even in hot and humid areas such as the Gulf Coast and Florida, there are usually some days in summer and winter in which the relative humidity level is low and is accompanied by drying wind. Under such circumstances the plants need special attention, especially if the preceding conditions were humid, as the plants resent sudden changes in humidity and temperature. Most species are vigorous, fast growers and therefore heavy feeders. They need a rich but friable soil and most respond very favorably to supplemental feeding; fish emulsion and manures are best. Leaf mold is a near-perfect addition to the planting site and as a mulch. ***Cyathea cooperi*** (KOOP-ur-eye) (synonyms *Alsophila cooperi, Sphaeropteris cooperi*) is native to eastern Australia and is commonly called the Australian tree fern. It is probably the most commonly planted tree fern, at least in the Western world, and is one of the most beautiful and tropical subjects for the warm-climate garden. The plants in their native haunts often attain trunk heights of 40 feet, but this is rare in cultivation, especially in the continental United States. The older parts of the trunks are usually devoid of fibers but have very beautiful and picturesque rounded leaf scars. The great light green leaves are elliptic to triangular in outline, tripinnate, and may be as long as 15 or even 20 feet under ideal conditions but usually only about half that size elsewhere. The plants take full sun in areas with cooler summers, but in hot summer areas they need protection from the midday sun and grow luxuriantly in partial shade. Some of the literature indicates hardiness to about 20°F, but in my experience such temperatures, especially if prolonged, are usually fatal. Older plants will usually survive the low 20s, but will lose most of their already expanded fronds. Protection of the crozier goes a long way in assuring the plant's survival from cold, but this is not always mechanically possible for the home gardener. This species has suffered under several widely used botanical names and is often confused with and labeled as *Alsophila australis*, which is rarely seen in the continental United States. Plate 153.

CYBISTAX. See *Tabebuia*.

CYCAS (SY-kas)
Cycadaceae: The Cycad Family
Common names vary according to species
Palmlike slow-growing trunked plants; stiff green or
   bluish green pinnate leaves; large cones
Zones vary according to species
Sun to partial shade
Average but regular amounts of moisture
Sandy, humusy, well-drained soil
Propagation by seed, transplanting of suckers, and
   (sometimes) cuttings

A genus of about 40 species of fairly large cycads in tropical and subtropical areas of East Africa, Madagascar, India, Southeast Asia, Malaysia, the Philippines, the southern Japanese islands, New Guinea, and Australia. All have stiff palmlike pinnate leaves and make trunks of varying heights with adhering leaf bases; the trunks of a few species are subterranean. Many species sucker and produce offshoots from the bases of the parent trunks, and some form buds on almost any part of the trunk. (The buds may be removed and planted as cuttings.) The cones—all cycads are nonflowering plants and have cones analogous to those of the conifers—are unisexual and on separate plants. The male cones are cylindrical and consist of highly modified leaves that look like giant scales, while the female cones are spherical and consist of a globular cluster of highly modified leaves on which the spores and seeds are borne. New leaves are soft upon emergence, and the leaflets, but not the petioles, are coiled. The leaves mature after fully expanding into a flat or trough-shaped pinnate frond with dark green leaflets that have usually become quite stiff and even prickly; the leaflets turn into spines near the base of the leaf. While most species are drought tolerant to some extent, they grow faster and look better if not allowed to suffer from lack of water. All species are fairly to extremely slow growing. Species of this genus are very often mistaken by gardeners for palms, to which they are not related.

Cycas circinalis (seer-si-NAL-is) is found in India and Sri Lanka through Myanmar (Burma) and Southeast Asia, Indonesia, and into the islands of the South Pacific. It is hardy in zones 10 and 11 and marginal in zone 9b. This is arguably the most beautiful cycad species; it has a delicacy and grace that many other cycads lack. It is a clumping or suckering plant with individual trunks attaining, with great age, a maximum height of 12 feet and a diameter of about a foot. The leaf crown is especially full, and the gracefully arching leaves are as much as 10 feet long but usually no more than 8 feet in length. The leaflets grow almost at right angles from the rachis, and they are not nearly so stiff as those of most other species but are somewhat drooping. Each leaflet is a shiny medium to dark green and as much as a foot long. The most common of the vernacular names for the plant are queen sago or queen sago palm. Plate 154.

Cycas media (MEE-dee-a) is indigenous to northern and northeastern Australia and southeastern New Guinea. It is hardy in zones 10 and 11 and marginal in zone 9b. It is a very beautiful nonsuckering species that slowly makes a trunk to 10 or 12 feet in height with a fairly full crown of gracefully arching 6-foot-long bright glossy green leaves that are completely flat in cross section. It looks as much like a tree fern as it does a cycad or palm. This species is not as readily available as are *C. revoluta* or *C. circinalis*, but is well worth the search.

Cycas revoluta (rev-o-LOOT-a) is native to the southern Japanese islands of Ryuku and Satsuma and is hardy in zones 9 through 11 and marginal in zone 8. It is a freely suckering species that often makes large clumps with individual trunks as much as 10 feet in height and a foot in diameter. The trunks occasionally bud, producing offsets that can be removed and rooted. The leaves are from 4 to 6 feet long, very dark green, and gracefully arching. The leaflets are very stiff and grow at an angle from the rachis, so that the leaf is trough-shaped in cross section. At the same time, the margins of individual leaflets are mostly turned under. The leaf crown is never as full as that of *C. circinalis* and does not usually form a complete circle or globe of leaves. This is the most widely planted cycad in the world and has the common name of sago palm in the United States. Plates 155, 156, and 157.

Cycas taiwaniana (ty-wahn-ee-AHN-a) is native to the island of Taiwan and adjacent mainland China and is hardy in zones 9 through 11. It is similar to *C. revoluta* except that the leaves are flatter, slightly longer, and wider; the leaflet tips are not turned under and sometimes have a slightly bluish cast. The species is usually called the prince sago or prince sago palm in the nursery trade.

CYCLOSORUS. See *Thelypteris*.

CYDISTA. See *Pseudocalymma*.

CYPERUS (si-PER-us / sy-PER-us)
Cyperaceae: The Sedge Family
Common names vary according to species
Large aquatic perennials with tall, reedlike stems;
    palmlike flower heads with linear leaves
Zones vary according to species
Sun to part shade
Water lovers
Humusy, moist soil
Propagation by root division and seed

A very large genus of about 600 species of rhizomatous grasslike or rushlike plants, although they are not grasses, of varying statures but mostly large. They are distributed in the warmer parts of the world, chiefly in Asia and Africa. All have inflorescences surrounded by and intermingled with long linear leaflike bracts atop relatively tall stems that are leafless or have reduced and sheathing leaves only at their bases. Many are aquatic in nature and are valuable additions to the water and bog garden repertoire.

Cyperus alternifolius (ahl-turn´-i-FO-lee-us) is native to swampy areas of Madagascar and the islands of Réunion and Mauritius. The plants are evergreen perennials in zones 9b through 11 and root hardy in zone 9a. They have slender, usually triangular stems that reach a height of 5 to 8 feet and atop which 12 to 20 drooping 12-inch-long by half-inch-wide leaflike bracts radiate like the spokes of an umbrella, leading to the most common vernacular name of umbrella palm. The inflorescences also radiate from the tops of many stems; they are small clusters of grasslike brownish bracts and minute flowers on stalks somewhat shorter than the green bracts. The plants are fairly fast growing and make dramatic statements if placed as accents in the landscape; they grow in or out of shallow water. They do and look their best in moist soil and are not drought tolerant. Other common names for this species are umbrella plant and umbrella sedge. *Cyperus alternifolius* 'Gracilis', a dwarf cultivar, grows only a foot or so in height. *Cyperus alternifolius* 'Variegatus', a variegated form, is quite beautiful.

Cyperus papyrus (pa-PY-rus) is native to swampy areas and along riverbanks of tropical Africa. It is called giant papyrus, Egyptian paper reed, and Egyptian papyrus because it was used by the ancient Egyptians as a source of paper (papyrus). This plant is hardy in zones 9b through 11, though it sometimes dies back to its roots in zone 9b. It is a bold, exotic, and noble landscape subject. The stems are as much as 12 feet or even more tall. From the tops of these stems radiate 100 or more green or brownish green drooping foot-long threadlike inflorescences with dark brown bracts at their bases, the whole affair having the diaphanous appearance from a distance of a globular puff of green and tan-colored smoke. These fascinating plants require near full sun and, while they grow in moist soil, only reach their prime when grown as aquatics with a couple of inches of water above their rhizomatous roots. They are also not for small ponds as they dominate the aquatic landscape. In the right situation, however, nothing equals their presence. Plate 158.

CYRTOSPERMA (seer-toe-SPURM-a)
Araceae: The Calla Lily, Jack-in-the-Pulpit Family
No known English common name
Tuberous-rooted herbs; large colored arrow-shaped
    leaves; dramatic Jack-in-pulpit-like flowers
Zones 10b and 11
Partial shade to partial sun
Water lovers
Rich, humusy, moist soil
Propagation by root division and seed

A small genus of about 10 species in Southeast Asia, New Guinea, and some of the islands of the South Pacific. They are mostly aquatic or bog plants with sagittate leaves on long and usually knobby or spiny petioles with minute petal-less flowers clustered on a spadix and surrounded by a colored spathe. These are quite dramatic accent plants for moist and half-shaded soil in frost-free climates.

Cyrtosperma johnstonii (jahn-STON-ee-eye) is from the Solomon Islands. Its 2-foot-long leaves are a deep olive green with pink or red veins above and are dark green to almost black with a metallic sheen beneath. They have deep lobes at their bases that give a distinct arrow shape to the blade. They are carried on 3-foot-long knobby and prickly dark green petioles, which are mottled with pink and purple. The inflorescence is about 6 inches long and is brown or purple with tiny reddish flowers inside.

Cyrtosperma merkusii (mer-KYOO-zee-eye) is native to Malaysia, New Guinea, and the islands of the South Pacific. The giant arrow-shaped leaves are 4 or more feet long and are carried on 6- to 8-foot-long petioles, which are dark green mottled with brown and which bear stout prickles. The spathe is green or purple and holds brownish red flowers.

CYRTOSTACHYS (seer-toe-STAIK-iss)
Palmae (Arecaceae): The Palm Family
SEALING-WAX PALM; LIPSTICK PALM
Exquisitely thin-trunked clustering feather palms;
    bright red crownshafts and leaf stalks
Zone 11; marginal in zone 10b
Sun
Water lovers
Moist, humusy, well-drained soil
Propagation by seed

A genus of eight or nine slender-trunked clustering pinnate-leaved palms in Malaysia and the Solomon Islands, only one of which is planted outside botanical gardens. *Cyrtostachys lakka* (LAK-ka / LAHK-ka) (synonym *C. renda*) is native to Borneo, Sumatra, and Malaysia. It is a denizen of rain forests and is completely intolerant of drought. It also is one of the most tender of palms; temperatures below 40°F will cause it to sulk and sometimes even damage it. Nonetheless, it is so choice that it is grown in regions where these temperatures may be expected. In its native habitats it attains a trunk height of 30 feet, but in the United States (excluding Hawaii and Puerto Rico) it is usually no more than half this height. The gray to light brown trunks are heartbreakingly graceful and slender, no more than 6 inches in diameter, with evenly spaced and beautiful white rings of leaf scars. The glorious red to orange-red slender 3-foot-long crownshafts are the fillip that causes the heart to beat faster. Never has nature been more profligate in lavishing beauty on a single plant. The leaves in the crown are sparse (how else could such diaphanous trunks support them?) but elegantly spaced. Each leaf is about 4 feet long and stiffly but gracefully arched. The leaflets are 12 to 18 inches long and spring from the scarlet to orange-red rachis at an angle that creates a V shape to the leaf in cross section. The inflorescence and clusters of half-inch-wide fruits appear directly beneath the crownshaft and, in any other palm species, might be the highlight of the individual plant: the stems of the flower panicles are red and the round fruits produced are red and black. A mature clump of this species must be seen to be believed; it combines almost all the best aspects of the whole family into one species, and that is saying a lot!

DALBERGIA
(dal-BUR-jee-a / dal-BURG-ee-a)
Papilionaceae (Fabaceae, Leguminosae), subfamily
    Papilionoideae: The Bean, Pea Family
Common names vary according to species
Straight-trunked trees; briefly deciduous pinnate
    leaves; white or purplish pealike flowers
Zones vary according to species
Sun
Average but regular amounts of moisture
Sandy, humusy, well-drained soil
Propagation by seed

A genus of about 100 species of mostly vines, but also trees and shrubs in tropical and semitropical areas around the world. They have alternately arranged pinnate leaves, clusters of pealike flowers, and flat seed pods. The vining species are not terribly attractive, but many tree species are quite beautiful, although they are not much planted in the United States except for one.

Dalbergia lanceolaria (lants-ee-o-LAIR-ee-a) (synonym *D. frondosa*) is native to India and Sri Lanka and is hardy only in zones 10 and 11 and marginal in zone 10a. It is a tall and graceful tree to 60 feet or more in height with a straight trunk and an open crown of somewhat pendulous branches. The 6-inch-long leaves are composed of 7 to 11 leathery elliptic to ovate 2-inch-long leaflets, each with a shallow notch at its end. The leaves are usually briefly deciduous in late winter, depending on the amount of rain and cold. The very showy flowers, which appear before or with the growth

of the new leaves, are in 6-inch-wide terminal panicles. Each blossom is a light purple to lilac in color. The fruit is a 4-inch-long flat beanlike pod.

Dalbergia latifolia (lat-i-FO-lee-a) is native to the southern part of the Indian subcontinent and is hardy in zones 10b and 11. It grows very tall in India but is usually no more than 50 feet in height in cultivation. It makes an open-crowned tree with a straight trunk. The leaves are about 6 inches long and are composed of three to seven ovate to almost orbicular 3-inch-wide leaflets, which are arranged on the zigzagging rachis in such a manner that the leaf is hard to identify as being pinnate. Rather the leaflets appear at first glance to be single, whole leaves. The flowers appear in the spring in axillary racemes. Each small pealike flower is white or pale purple. The wood of this tree is much used for making furniture and is known as Indian rosewood or black rosewood.

Dalbergia sissoo (SIS-oo) is indigenous to India where it grows to 80 feet or more in height. It is slightly hardier to cold than *D. lanceolaria* or *D. latifolia* and is adaptable to zones 10 and 11 and marginal in zone 9b. It is the most commonly planted *Dalbergia* species in the continental United States and is similar to *D. latifolia* in height, form, and leaf size. The flowers are relatively drab compared to those of *D. lanceolaria* and even to *D. latifolia*. They are yellowish white in color but are wonderfully fragrant. The wood of this tree is very valuable for making fine furniture and is known as sissoo, Indian rosewood, and shisam. It is a fairly drought tolerant tree.

DASYLIRION
(day-zee-LEER-ee-ahn / das-ee-LEER-ee-ahn)
Agavaceae: The Agave Family
SOTOL; BEAR GRASS; DESERT SPOON;
    SPOON-LEAF
Large clumps of long narrow grasslike leaves with
    spiny margins; large erect panicles of flowers
Zones vary according to species
Sun
Drought tolerant
Sandy, well-drained soil
Propagation by transplanting of suckers and by seed

A genus of 15 or so large, agavelike perennial herbs from the arid areas of the southwestern United States and adjacent Mexico. Some of the species make trunks atop which the full and rounded rosettes of long, linear, tough, and usually thorny-margined leaves grow. All have leaves with greatly expanded bases (which leads to two of the vernacular names) and most have no or non-apparent trunks. All sucker and form clumps of rosettes with time. The plants resemble those of both *Agave* and *Yucca*, but the leaves are generally narrower and less succulent than those of either of these genera. The inflorescences are tall and narrow with the tiny greenish white or yellowish white flowers arranged in wormlike clusters and crowded along the upper half or third of the spike, which remains for a long time with the brown or orange-colored and papery or leathery small fruits maturing. The species make impressive accent plants for the cactus and succulent garden and need sites with excellent drainage, full sun, and water only in periods of prolonged drought.

Dasylirion bigelovii. See *Nolina bigelovii.*

Dasylirion glaucophyllum (glawk-o-FYL-lum) is indigenous to northeastern Mexico, and is hardy in zones 10 and 11 and marginal in zone 9b. It forms a short and stocky trunk with age but is mostly seen as a giant rosette of 4-foot-long very narrow ribbonlike and somewhat flexible leaves that are yellow-green to blue-green in color and whose margins are armed with hooked spines and small teeth between the spines. The gigantic inflorescence is as much as 18 or even 20 feet tall and is quite full and spectacular.

Dasylirion leiophyllum (lay-yo-FYL-lum) is native to southwestern Texas, southern New Mexico, and adjacent Mexico and is hardy in zones 8 through 11 and marginal in zone 7b. It forms a short trunk to as much as 3 feet with time. The dark green leaves are about 3 feet long, erect, and stiff, and are armed with rather vicious downward curving thorns along their margins. The inflorescence is as much as 12 feet tall and is fairly robust and thick. Plate 159.

Dasylirion longifolium. See *Nolina longifolia.*

Dasylirion longissimum (lahn-JIS-si-mum) is indigenous to central Mexico and is hardy in zones 9b through 11 and marginal in zone 9a. The plant forms a trunk to as much as 10 feet tall that is generally unbranched unless injured; it is usually covered with the adherent dead leaves. The leaves are quite unusual for the genus: they are very narrow, diamond-shaped in cross section, deep green in color, smooth-margined and rather pliable, arching gracefully to form a very large rounded rosette dense with the pliable but wiry leaves. The inflorescence is about 10 feet tall with orange flowers and brown fruit. Plates 160 and 161.

Dasylirion texanum (tex-AHN-um) occurs naturally in central and western Texas and northern Mexico. It is hardy in zones 7 through 11 and marginal in zone 6b. The species does not usually form a trunk and the leaf rosettes are quite similar to those of *D. wheeleri,* including the orientation of the curved thorns on the leaf margins. The inflorescence is as much as 15 feet tall.

Dasylirion wheeleri (WHEEL-ur-eye) is indigenous to extreme western Texas, southern New Mexico, southern Arizona, and adjacent Mexico and is hardy in zones 8 through 11. It makes 5-foot-high beautifully rounded and dense rosettes of stiff leaves, each of which is about 3 feet long. The plants form trunks, but these are not evident except in very old plants and sometimes remain underground. The leaves are usually less than an inch wide except at their bases and are armed on the margins with small thorns pointing towards the apex (outer end) of the leaf. The base of the leaf is wide and abruptly expanded from the rest of the blade, leading to

the common name of desert spoon, but the leaves must be pulled from the plant to observe this phenomenon. There are at least two forms of this plant, one with bright green leaves and one with decidedly bluish leaves. In nature these two forms intergrade into each other. In spring and summer the rosettes send up from their centers tall flowering stalks as much as 15 feet in height but always taller than the rosette of leaves. These stalks bear fat, worm-shaped racemes of tiny straw-colored flowers. Male and female flowers are on separate plants. Mexicans make an alcoholic drink, which is called *sotol,* from the cooked and then fermented trunks and leaf rosettes, which both contain much sugary sap.

DATURA (da-TOOR-a)
Solanaceae: The Petunia, Potato, Tomato Family
JIMSON WEED; DEVIL'S TRUMPET; THORN
    APPLE; ANGEL'S TRUMPETS
Medium-sized herbaceous shrubs; large leaves, white
    and purple trumpet-shaped flowers
Treat as annuals—most species are annuals and the
    perennial species are short-lived
Sun
Average but regular amounts of moisture
Sandy, well-drained soil
Propagation by seed

A small genus of eight species closely allied to the genus *Brugmansia,* which see for the differences between these two genera. Unlike that genus, *Datura* produces rounded fruits that are covered in spinelike protrusions. The taxonomic status of the genus has been and still is in a state of flux and confusion. Unlike *Brugmansia* species these plants are indigenous to more than one continent. Some have been cultivated for so long that their origins are obscured, and some taxonomists think the genus is entirely American. Most forms now in cultivation are from *D. inoxia, D. metel, D. stramonium,* or derivations therefrom. All parts of these plants are poisonous, and some are deadly. These bold and tropical looking subjects have large, attractive leaves and beautiful flowers similar to those in the genus *Brugmansia.* They grow fast, have few if any pests, thrive on average or even poor soil, are just short of drought tolerant, and are valuable additions to the repertory of the tropical garden.

Datura affinis. See *Brugmansia aurea.*
Datura arborea. See *Brugmansia arborea.*
Datura aurea. See *Brugmansia aurea.*
Datura candida. See *Brugmansia ×candida.*
Datura ×candida. See *Brugmansia ×candida.*
Datura chlorantha. See *D. metel.*
Datura cornigera. See *Brugmansia arborea.*
Datura cornucopia. See *D. metel.*
Datura fastuosa. See *D. metel.*
Datura gardneri. See *Brugmansia suaveolens.*
Datura guayaquilensis. See *D. inoxia.*
Datura humilis. See *D. metel.*
Datura inermis. See *D. stramonium.*

Datura inoxia (i-NOX-ee-a) (synonym *D. guayaquilensis*) is indigenous to the warmest parts of the southwestern United States down through Mexico and into Central America. The type is now exceedingly rare in cultivation. *Datura inoxia* subsp. *inoxia* (synonym *D. meteloides*) is more common than the type. It grows to 3 feet or more and is a spreading and mostly herbaceous plant. The leaves have a strong odor, are ovate in outline, 10 inches long, and dark green, are covered with tiny shaggy hairs, and usually have scalloped margins. The plant blooms almost throughout its life with flowers that are held erect or at right angles to the stem and grow from the leaf axils. They are 6-inch-long tubular white (rarely pinkish) beautifully fragrant trumpets that flare at the ends into a spreading disk with five large recurved "tails" alternating with five smaller "tails." *Datura inoxia* subsp. *quinquecuspida* (kwin-kwee-KUSP-i-da) (synonym *D. wrightii*) is the most widely grown form. It is a more spreading plant with leaves that are strongly veined and finely pubescent rather than shaggy. It also has slightly larger flowers, which have only five points to the corolla. It is a beautiful plant in flower.

Datura laevis. See *D. stramonium*.

Datura metel (meh-TEL) (synonyms *D. chlorantha, D. fastuosa, D. humilis*) has been naturalized in all the warm areas of the world but is thought by most researchers to have originated in China. It is similar to *D. inoxia* and its subspecies but is usually a larger plant with purple stems and larger flowers. The blossoms are white, but there are cultivars with yellow and purple flowers as well as a double-flowered form often listed as *Datura cornucopia*.

Datura meteloides. See *D. inoxia* subsp. *inoxia*.

Datura mollis. See *Brugmansia versicolor*.

Datura pittieri. See *Brugmansia aurea*.

Datura rosei. See *Brugmansia sanguinea*.

Datura sanguinea. See *Brugmansia sanguinea*.

Datura stramonium (stra-MO-nee-um) (synonym *D. laevis*) is native to the southern and southwestern United States and Mexico. Known as the jimson weed, it is similar to *D. inoxia* except that the leaves are not hairy. They do, however, smell bad when bruised. The white fragrant flowers are also somewhat smaller. There are double-flowered cultivars as well as a purple form.

Datura suaveolens. See *Brugmansia suaveolens*.

Datura versicolor. See *Brugmansia versicolor*.

DAUBENTONIA. See *Sesbania*.

DAVALLIA (da-VAL-lee-a)
Davalliaceae: The Hare's-Foot Fern Family
HARE'S-FOOT FERNS
Small to medium-sized very lacy ferns with creeping rhizomes
Zones vary according to species
Partial shade to sun

Average but regular amounts of moisture
Humusy, well-drained soil or leaf mold
Propagation by root division, rhizome division, and spores

A genus of about three dozen species of mostly epiphytic ferns in southern Europe, northern Africa, Madagascar, Australia, New Guinea, Borneo, Malaysia, Polynesia, and most of Asia including Japan and Korea. Most species have tripinnate leaves—some are even four-pinnate or five-pinnate—and most are evergreen, although some hail from monsoonal areas and are deciduous in the dry season, and others from cold regions are deciduous in winter. All species have leaves that are triangular in outline. All have creeping and wandering scaly rhizomes (the scales often appearing like hairs) which, in the terrestrial species, form clumps and, in the epiphytic species, allow the plants to climb and wander around trees, rocks, and other strata. The plants are especially beautiful when older, as they fill an area and cascade downwards, giving the lush effect of many fern plants. All the epiphytic species may be grown in the ground if the soil is loose and humusy enough; part leaf mold is perfect. Only the evergreen species are treated here, and all these, as opposed to some deciduous species, need regular and ample amounts of moisture but cannot tolerate a soggy or poorly draining medium.

Davallia divaricata (dy-vair-i-KAYT-a) is native to southern China, Southeast Asia, Malaysia, and Indonesia, and is hardy in zones 10 and 11. The tripinnate leaves of this large fern can attain 3 feet in length and 2 feet in width. They are dark green when mature, but the new leaves are reddish orange or even crimson when they unfold. This species grows both terrestrially and as an epiphyte, and thrives in a humusy compost-rich soil. The plant wants partial shade and should be protected from the midday sun. It does not like to dry out completely.

Davallia fejeensis (fee-jay-ENS-is) is indigenous to the Fiji Islands and is hardy only in zones 10 and 11 and is somewhat marginal in zone 10a. This epiphytic species is perfect for hanging in baskets, on trees, or planting in the crotches of trees. It is also beautiful in soil cavities in rocks. It grows to as much as 4 feet in height, and the leaves are as long as 3 feet. They arch and droop very gracefully and are a medium green in color. Like the leaves of several other species in this genus, these leaves may die back if cold or drought conditions ensue. The scaly, hairy rhizomes wander into the air and along whatever substrate they can find, looking to spread the beauty of the leaves. There are several cultivars, which vary in the degree of laciness of the fronds and in frond size. One is a dwarf form. The fern has common names of lacy hare's-foot fern and rabbit's-foot fern.

Davallia mariesii (ma-REEZ-ee-eye) is native to Japan and southern Korea and is hardy in zones 8 through 11 but is only evergreen in zones 9b and warmer. It is a small epiphytic species whose tripinnate or quadripinnate leaves are no longer than about 8 inches but are beautiful little triangles of glossy bright green. The rhizomes are famous for their peregrinating habit and in Japan are guided into forms of various animals and other shapes.

Davallia trichomanoides (try-ko´-ma-NOY-deez / trik´-o-ma-NOY-deez) is native to Malaysia, New Guinea, and Indonesia, and is hardy in zones 10 and 11. This small fern has tripinnate to quadripinnate leaves to 2 feet in length with a long tapering outline to the generally triangular shape. It is epiphytic but can be grown terrestrially and makes a beautiful and very lacy groundcover for nearly frost-free climates.

DELONIX (DEL-o-nix / de-LO-nix)
Caesalpiniaceae: The Cassia, Royal Poinciana, Tamarind Family
ROYAL POINCIANA; FLAMBOYANT TREE; FLAME TREE; PEACOCK FLOWER
Large spreading tree; large ferny foliage; spectacular red flowers cover tree in summer
Zones 10b and 11
Sun
Average but regular amounts of moisture
Average soil
Propagation by seed

A genus of 10 species of pinnate-leaved trees in Africa, Madagascar, and India. Outside botanical gardens, only one species is planted in the United States, although *Delonix elata* is almost as beautiful as *D. regia* (royal poinciana) and certainly should be more widely grown. ***Delonix regia*** (REE-jee-a) (synonym *Poinciana regia*) is endemic to the island of Madagascar. It is the world's most beautiful flowering tree. Other trees have even larger blossoms and are as floriferous, and still other trees have at least as beautiful a form, but no tree is quite as thrilling as this one when it is in bloom in late spring and early summer. There is something almost indescribable, protecting yet massive, dark and yet vibrant and, of course, flamboyant in the aspect of one of these regal elephants arrayed in red and yellow brilliance. Nothing in the tropical landscape is more beautiful.

The royal poinciana makes a very spreading and usually flat-topped or dome-topped tree to 40 feet or more in height with a relatively short and stout trunk. The width of the tree's canopy is often as great as or greater than its height. The main branches are also fairly thick and heavy, and they are never stiff and straight. In form the tree has the aspect of a great old *Quercus virginiana* (live oak) but, instead of the dark and fissured bark of the live oak, the royal poinciana has a smooth and light brown or gray-colored trunk. Unless the tree receives regular and deep watering it forms strong surface roots much like many species of *Ficus*. These roots only add to the overall beauty of the tree, but for many gardeners can be a problem near sidewalks and lawns.

This tree would be eminently worth growing for its form and leaves, even if it never flowered. The leaves are as much as 2 feet long and are bipinnate and fernlike. The tree is naturally deciduous in its native habitat, mainly because of the distinct dry season but, if the area in which it is grown has a wet winter and spring, this phenomenon is often lacking. When it does lose its leaves, it loses them anytime from late fall to early spring, for only a brief period, unless the weather remains dry, in which case the leafless period can last all winter. Cold weather usually also results in leaf drop.

The flowers come anywhere from early April to mid May in a breathtaking flush that covers the entire tree, leafless or not. Borne in broad clusters, each flower is reminiscent of those of most *Bauhinia* species: five-petaled, 4 inches wide, with vibrant orange to scarlet fluted petals that are linear at the base, expanding into a squared lobed or toothed limb. One of the five petals (the standard) is larger than the other four and is basically white, sometimes pinkish, speckled red, and bearing a streak of yellow in its center. Some trees have lightly scented blossoms, but this is not universal. The flowering period most often extends throughout the summer, peaking in June. although this also is variable. A pure yellow-flowered form that originated in the Caribbean is beautiful enough but not as spectacular as the glowing orange or scarlet of the type. The fruits are large and fascinating 2-foot-long brown pods.

The tree is not particular as to soil and thrives in any but those that are poorly drained, although it grows faster in a reasonably fertile medium. It is extremely fast growing and often puts on 5 feet of height each year until it is mature. It needs sun to flower. There is nothing more beautiful than a street or avenue planted with royal poinciana, and the flower show in spring and summer against a background of green is something that must be experienced to be believed. Plates 162, 163, and 164.

DENDROCALAMUS
(den-dro-KAL-a-mus)
Gramineae (Poaceae): The Grass, Bamboo Family
GIANT BAMBOO; MALE BAMBOO; CALCUTTA BAMBOO
Tall large-leaved clumping bamboos with immense canes
Zones vary according to species
Sun to partial shade
Average but regular amounts of moisture
Average well-drained soil
Propagation by root division and transplanting of suckers

A genus of about 30 species of giant clumping bamboos in tropical Asia. One species is among the world's most widely cultivated bamboos.

Dendrocalamus giganteus (jy-GANT-ee-us) (synonym *Sinocalamus giganteus*) is indigenous to India, Sri Lanka, Myanmar (Burma), Southeast Asia, and southern China. The biggest bamboo species, it grows to well over 100 feet in nature and as much as 70 or 80 feet in cultivation. It is quite tender to cold and is not practical outside zones 10b and 11. There is nothing to compare to the spectacle of a mature clump of this species with its giant ringed stems, which can be a foot or more in diameter. In tropical areas the new canes can grow more than a foot each day. The leaves are of a size commensurate with the canes: they are sometimes 2 feet long by 5 inches wide. Only the upper portions of the canes have branches and therefore leaves.

Dendrocalamus strictus (STRIK-tus) is native to southeastern China, India, and Java, and is dependably hardy in zones 10 and 11 but often planted and surviving in zone 9b. In its native habitats the canes can reach 90 feet in height; in cultivation they usually attain no more than 50 feet. It usually takes a year for the roots of newly planted clumps to establish themselves, but once established a clump produces new canes that can grow an inch or more a day. The new canes are a lovely deep green and very smooth, almost waxy. They mature to a straw or gold color with extremely hard wood. It is reported that these canes are solid if grown in dry regions but hollow, or almost so, if grown under wet conditions. The foliage consists of elongated thin branches, which arise in clusters from the nodes starting about halfway up the height of the canes and from which the foot-long lanceolate-shaped deep green leaves grow. This giant bamboo is beautiful and vigorous. Each clump makes a wonderful little grove of giant ringed trunks. This species is so widely grown because it is used for making paper in countries that have depleted their timber sources. Plate 165.

DEUTEROCOHNIA

(dyoo´-tur-o-KO-nee-a)
Bromeliaceae: The Pineapple, Bromeliad Family
No known English common name
Clumping rosettes of spiny-margined, aloelike leaves; tall stalks of red and yellow flowers
Zones 9b through 11; marginal in zone 9a
Sun to partial shade
Drought tolerant
Sandy, well-drained soil
Propagation by transplanting of suckers and by seed

A genus of seven unusual bromeliad species in Peru, Brazil, Paraguay, Chile, and Argentina. These unusual plants look more like members of the genus *Aloe* than almost all other bromeliads and are allied to the bromeliad genera *Dyckia, Hechtia,* and *Puya,* which are also denizens of desert or mountainous regions. They are tough and drought tolerant, thrive in full sun, and are also relatively hardy to cold for bromeliads since they are from elevated regions of tropical and subtropical areas. The genus is unaccountably rare in cultivation in spite of its very attractive and exotic-looking species, which should be much more widely planted. While the flowers are not as spectacular as those of many other bromeliads, the plants are wonderful additions to warm-climate rock gardens or succulent gardens and are perfect accents in the landscape. *Deuterocohnia schreiteri* (SHRY-tur-eye / SHRY-tur-ee) is sometimes found in collections of bromeliad lovers. It makes dense clumping rosettes of 2-foot-long aloelike, linear-lanceolate gray or silvery green leaves that often have a rosy or reddish cast and always have small and sharp teeth on their margins. The ends of the leaves are gracefully recurved downwards, and the leaf blade is narrow and leathery. With time these plants eventually form a short stem or trunk for each rosette. The inflorescence is also most unusual in that it is a permanent feature of the plant, lasting for years and becoming woody. The flowers are in loose-flowered racemes at the ends of the tall and thin woody flower stalks. They are narrow, tubular, and yellow with a few orange or red bracts at the bottom of the inflorescence. Plate 166.

DICHORISANDRA

(dy-kor´-i-SAN-dra)
Commelinaceae: The Spiderwort Family
BLUE GINGER; QUEEN'S SPIDERWORT
Reedlike stems 4 to 6 feet tall; large linear leaves in spiral arrangement; spikes of blue and violet flowers
Zone 9 through 11 as flowering perennials; zone 8 as foliage plants
Partial shade to sun
Water lovers
Rich, moist, humusy, well-drained soil
Propagation by root division, seed, and stem cuttings

A genus of about 24 herbaceous clumping perennials in tropical America with succulent reedlike stems and fleshy rhizomatous rootstocks. The only similarity to plants in the Zingiberaceae (ginger family) is the leaves; these plants are related to *Tradescantia* (spiderwort) or *Commelina* (dayflower) species. The leaves are large and often variegated, and the flowers three-petaled and purple, lavender, or blue. The plants are quite worth growing for the leaves alone. They need ample water always, good soil drainage, and a rich soil.

Dichorisandra musaica. See *Geogenanthus.*

Dichorisandra reginae (re-JY-nee) is native to moist tropical areas of Peru where it can grow to 4 feet, but it is usually no more than 2 feet tall in cultivation. The young growth of the stems is purple with green spots, later changing to dark green. The very dark green leaves, which are 7- to 8-inch-long ellipses with long, tapering "tails," are wonderfully variegated with silver stripes and a purplish red center stripe, while the undersides of the leaves are purple with silver stripes. This species has true blue flowers in compact clusters at the ends of the stems.

Dichorisandra thyrsiflora (thyr-si-FLOR-a) is indigenous to southeastern Brazil where it grows to 6 feet or even more in height; in cultivation it is seldom this tall. The glossy bright green leaves are a foot long and elliptic to lanceolate in shape with a tapering point; they are usually purplish red on their lower surfaces. The flowers are borne in foot-long vertical racemes at the ends of the stems. Each blossom is violet to almost pure blue and is quite beautiful.

DICKSONIA (dik-SO-nee-a)

Dicksoniaceae: The Tasmanian Tree Fern Family
TASMANIAN TREE FERN
Tall tree fern with fibrous thick trunk and large dark
    green tripinnate arching fronds
Zones 9 through 11; marginal in zone 8b
Partial shade to partial sun
Water lover
Rich, humusy, moist, well-drained soil
Propagation by spores

A genus of about 24 species of tree ferns in Southeast Asia, Australia, Tasmania, New Zealand, Polynesia, and South America. They are denizens of elevated sites where the climate is tropical or subtropical but also rather cool. As a consequence these beauties are not completely at home in the lowland tropics, are impossible in desert climates, and need some coddling in areas with hot summers even though the areas be moist. They do not tolerate full sun in these regions. Only one species is commonly planted in the continental United States. *Dicksonia antarctica* hails from southeastern Australia and the island of Tasmania. It is a slow-growing, great spreading tree fern with a thick trunk that may reach 20 feet or more with great age in cultivation, 40 feet or more in its native haunts. The trunk can be as thick as 2 feet in diameter and is covered in small fibrous "proto-roots"; it never forms a "clean" trunk even in old age. The wonderfully lacy leaves are oblong or rhomboidal in outline, not triangular as in many other tree ferns. The leaf petioles are covered in thick cinnamon-colored hairs, and the leaf blade is 6 to 8 feet long. There may be 50 or more fronds on a single tree, resulting in a veritable starburst of light to dark green fernlike growth atop the dark brown trunks. This lovely thing needs constant humidity, rich, moist but well-drained soil, and protection from hot drying winds. It also appreciates a mulch of leaf mold and monthly applications of fish emulsion fertilizer. It is quite hardy to cold for a tree fern and can withstand a temperature of 20°F or even lower if the cold is not accompanied by dry wind. It languishes and even dies in the full sun of hot summer areas such as the Gulf Coast and Florida, and the sudden onset of hot drying winds wreak havoc with the well-being of these ferns. The grower must be vigilant at these times and mist the entire plant as much as several times per day lest they succumb. In spite of this temperamental bent, the things are worth the trouble; no other fern has quite the cool yet tropical effect of this one.

DICTYOSPERMA

(dik´-tee-o-SPUR-ma)
Palmae (Arecaceae): The Palm Family
HURRICANE PALM; PRINCESS PALM
Ringed, slender-trunked feather-leaved palm with
    long, dark green arching leaves
Zones 10b and 11
Sun to partial shade
Water lover
Average well-drained soil
Propagation by seed

A monotypic genus from the Mascarene Islands, east of Madagascar; it is probably extinct in its native habitats. *Dictyosperma album* (AL-bum) (synonym *D. aureum*) is one of the world's most graceful and elegant palms. It forms a fairly slender (about 8 inches in diameter) and perfectly straight ringed and dark gray trunk, swollen at the base, with many thin vertical fissures. The stem attains a height of 40 feet or more atop which springs a fountain of 10- to 12-foot-long, gracefully arching, dark green, flat pinnate leaves whose midribs twist 90 degrees at their tips so that the ends of the leaves are usually parallel to the trunk. The leaflets are as much as 3 feet long and are pointed at their tips. The new leaves are slow to unfold their leaflets and remain in a thick, needlelike shoot for a while before the leaflets unfurl. In general appearance the palm is akin to *Archontophoenix* (king palm) and *Howea* (kentia) species, although, unlike the latter, it has a crownshaft that is swollen at its base and usually a light green in color but may be almost white or reddish hued. The leaf petioles are fairly short and they also may be light green, whitish, or reddish. The inflorescences are rather insignificant 18-inch-long strings of yellowish white flower stalks. Initially they are covered by strange paddle-shaped light brown leathery bracts, which give way to beautiful half-inch-wide dark purple to black shiny egg-shaped fruits. The common name hurricane palm comes from the unquestionable resistance of the leaves to shredding by strong winds. The leaves, however, are not resistant to hot dry winds, and the tree languishes in low humidity and high heat. It is fairly fast growing in rich and moist soil but is definitely slower growing and less attractive in poor and dry soils. It is completely hardy in zones 10b and 11 but is usually damaged in zone 10a. *Dictyosperma album* var. *rubrum* usually has red hued juvenile leaves and petioles, and definitely reddish crownshafts. Plate 167.

DIEFFENBACHIA

(deef-fin-BAHK-hee-a)
Araceae: The Calla Lily, Jack-in-the-Pulpit Family
DUMB CANE; MOTHER-IN-LAW'S TONGUE
Small to large herbaceous perennials with large
    variegated leaves
Zones 10b and 11; marginal in zone 10a
Partial shade to partial sun
Water lovers

Rich, humusy, moist, well-drained soil
Propagation by cuttings

A tropical American genus of about 25 species of large evergreen perennial herbs with wonderful large variegated strong-midribbed leaves near the ends of their stout, beautifully ringed and unbranched stems. Many forms are grown, but most of the pure, unadulterated species are now fairly hard to find, though well worth the trouble. Most plants now sold are hybrids or cultivars (of which there are very many), and most of these are based on *Dieffenbachia amoena* and *D. maculata*. Some of the forms have leaves so heavily variegated in white or yellow that the entire leaf seems almost of that color, while other species and cultivars are only subtly maculated. The flowers are typical of the family Araceae and somewhat resemble those of slender *Zantedeschia* (calla lily) species. They are quite attractive in and of themselves. None of these plants like full sun except in the mildest of summer regions. All relish moist, well-drained, not soggy, rich soil, and they are lovers of high relative humidity levels. They should also be protected from damaging winds. There are now many compact forms that seldom need to be cut back and that make superb accent plants, and some are low growing enough to be fine tall groundcovers. Most species tend to become leggy, to the point that they look almost like vines; under most landscaping circumstances, these should be pruned back to encourage a more shrublike form, usually with multiple "trunks." The plants are marginally hardy in zone 10a and are sometimes damaged there, but their growth is fast and strong and, if not severely damaged, they soon recover to resume their landscape role. Like the *Aglaonema* species they usually remain fresh and vigorous-looking with cool temperatures, but they do not tolerate prolonged periods below freezing. There are no better plants for providing color and form to shady sites in frost-free areas. The vernacular name dumb cane refers to the poisonous sap in all species, hybrids, and cultivars. This sap has calcium oxalate crystals, which are irritating to mucous membranes and can paralyze the vocal cords. Plate 168.

DILLENIA (dil-LEN-ee-a)
Dilleniaceae: The Dillenia Family
ELEPHANT APPLE
Tall large-leaved tree with rounded crown; large
    single roselike flowers; large green fruit
Zones 10 and 11; marginal in zone 10a
Sun
Average but regular amounts of moisture
Average well-drained soil
Propagation by seed

A fairly large genus of about 60 species of trees and shrubs in tropical Asia, Madagascar, and Australia. Almost all the species have large and beautiful leaves with strong pinnate venation and five-petaled single-roselike solitary flowers with many stamens. The fruits are big and fleshy and consist of large overlapping segments. Only one species is common in cultivation. *Dillenia indica* (IN-di-ka) is native to India and Malaysia and is a very beautiful, large-leaved tree that grows to as much as 60 feet with a relatively short and stout dark-colored trunk and a broad open crown. The giant leaves are mostly at the ends of the branches and are usually at least 14 inches long by 6 inches wide, slightly serrate on the margins, leathery and tough, and lanceolate to oblong-lanceolate in shape with very deep lateral veins, which create an almost corrugated appearance and texture. They are smooth above but quite rough to the touch beneath and are reminiscent of giant *Eriobotrya japonica* (loquat) leaves. The leaves drop in the winter if the weather turns cold or if a drought ensues. The spectacular white fragrant flowers appear in late spring and are as much as 8 inches wide; they consist of five oblong and evenly spaced 3-inch-long petals surrounding a central mass of golden yellow stamens above which rises the many-branched, octopus-like yellow-white pistil. Alas, the blossoms are mostly hidden by the giant leaves. The fruits are green, round, musk scented, and as much as 6 inches in diameter, and consist of the greatly swollen and fleshy overlapping sepals from the base of the flower. These segments enclose a sticky green mass with many seeds. As Edwin A. Menninger put it, the fruit "looks like a big green baseball with overlapping cover flaps." The outer segments are said to be edible with a strong and acidic taste, and Indian people use them in curries. Elephants evidently also relish the fruit. This tree is spectacularly attractive, has no problems or serious pests, needs no special treatment other than a nearly frost-free climate, and yet is fairly uncommon in cultivation in the United States, possibly because (like many other trees) it has the distinction of being a fruit tree whose fruits are supposedly not terribly tasty. Why isn't the beauty enough? Plate 169.

DIOON (dy-O-ahn / dy-OON)
Zamiaceae: The Zamia (a Cycad) Family
Common names vary according to species
Palmlike cycads with great heads of fernlike pinnate
    leaves atop thick dark trunks
Zones vary according to species
Sun to partial shade
Average but regular amounts of moisture
Humusy, well-drained soil

A cycad genus of 11 species in tropical and subtropical America; all but one species is endemic to Mexico. Most species occur in dry and exposed sites on hillsides, but a few are found in moist tropical areas. They are all slow growing but are very beautiful additions to the tropical garden.
   Dioon edule (ED-yoo-lee) is native to northeastern Mexico and is very hardy for a cycad species, being adaptable to zones 8 through 11 and marginal in zone 7a. The 5-foot-long leaves are mostly held erect and are flat in cross section, narrowly elliptic in outline, and a

beautiful shiny light green to bluish green in color. The juvenile leaves are soft and rubbery in texture and a bright yellow green, but the leaflets soon turn stiff. They are rather narrow and evenly spaced along the midrib, and each one ends in a point. The plant grows very slowly but in time forms a thick dark trunk to 3 feet or more. This species is fairly drought tolerant when established and is completely intolerant of soggy soils. It also does best in partly sunny positions with a humusy and very well drained soil. The seeds are edible and in Mexico are ground and made into tortillas.

Dioon spinulosum (spin-yoo-LO-sum) is indigenous to the state of Veracruz in Mexico and is hardy in zones 10 and 11, although large specimens are to be found in the warmer parts of zone 9b. It is one of the largest cycad species and in nature can attain a trunk height of 50 feet with great age, although in cultivation it is usually no more than 20 feet or so in height. The trees have truly gorgeous leaf crowns with many gracefully arching fronds that are long-elliptic in outline. The plants are especially attractive when young as the leaves can be appreciated up close, although they make spectacular specimens when old. They grow faster than *D. edule* but are still slow, and the trunks are more slender and graceful. The leaves are about 6 feet long with leathery light or bluish green lanceolate, somewhat drooping leaflets whose margins carry tiny spines. The female (seed-bearing) cones are immense and heavy heart-shaped affairs on fairly long stalks that get so heavy they often hang down beneath the leaf canopy. These beautiful plants start their lives as understory subjects in tropical forests, and they grow their best in partial shade. They also like warmth and humidity and prefer a soil that is slightly on the alkaline side (a relatively high pH), but are adaptable landscape subjects and can be successfully grown in a fairly wide spectrum of soil types. Plates 170 and 171.

DIOSCOREA (dee-o-SKOR-ee-a)
Dioscoreaceae: The Yam Family
Common names vary according to species
Large vines with large heart-shaped leaves; often with
　　rounded warty aerial tubers
Zones vary according to species
Sun to partial shade
Average but regular amounts of moisture
Humusy, deep, well-drained soil
Propagation by planting tubers, root division, aerial
　　tubers, cuttings, and seed

A large genus of about 600 species of tuberous-rooted twining vines in warm regions around the world. Most are found in areas of average or above average rainfall, but a few are strange and succulent desert dwellers with stony or tubercled roots mostly above ground. Among the nondesert species are to be found some of the world's most beautiful and tropical looking leaves. All species have tuberous roots, some of which are immense and edible and are food staples in

tropical countries; these are the tropical yams. The word *yam* is loosely applied in the United States, especially in the South, and usually to what is otherwise known as "sweet potato." The true sweet potato is actually the large tuberous root of an *Ipomoea* (morning glory) species and neither *Dioscorea* nor *Ipomoea* species are true potatoes nor are they related to the true potato, *Solanum tuberosum*. All *Dioscorea* species grow big roots and therefore need a fairly deep and friable soil, and they all revel in one amended with compost. While they are not bog plants, none of the nonsucculent species easily tolerate drought conditions.

Dioscorea batatas (ba-TAH-tas) is native to a large area of eastern Asia including China, the Philippines, Japan, and Korea, and is root-hardy in zones 7 through 11. This species with edible tubers is called Chinese yam and cinnamon vine, the latter name referring to the odor of the small whitish clustered flowers. The vine grows vigorously to 20 feet or more with twining stems that are usually striped with maroon. The leaves are from 6 to 12 inches long and are wide-cordate, almost diamond-shaped with basal lobes that almost overlap, and deeply depressed longitudinal (curved) and transverse veins that give a quilted effect to the blade. The flowers are insignificant except for their odor. The roots are gigantic, as much as 3 feet long, and are usually coiled or twisted. They are grown and eaten not only in the vine's native habitats, but also in parts of Europe.

Dioscorea bulbifera (bul-BIF-e-ra) is called the air potato and is indigenous to eastern China and the Philippines although, like the above species, it is root-hardy in zones 7 through 11. This species has very beautiful leaves, which are dark green, 6 or more inches wide, and cordate in shape, with deep lateral veins that render a quilted look and feel to the leaf blade. The vine twines to 20 feet or more and grows very quickly in warm weather. It will die back in the fall, with or without the advent of cold weather. Unlike the Chinese yam, air potato does not produce massive tubers; indeed, it sometimes has no underground tubers. It does, however, make globular aerial tubers, which can range in size from that of a pea to as much as 6 inches in diameter. The tubers are usually light to dark brown and always have little "warts" covering their surfaces. These aerial "potatoes" may be planted and usually grow if they are large enough. They are said by some to be edible; others say they are poisonous. It is probably best to avoid experimentation. Plate 172.

Dioscorea discolor (DIS-kul-or) is native to northern South America and is hardy in zones 10b and 11 as a permanent perennial and in zones 9 through 10a as a returning perennial. It climbs high and grows relatively quickly to 20 feet or more. The beautiful leaves are about 6 inches wide and as long and are broadly cordate in shape with an abrupt short point at the end. They are a medium green in color with the veins outlined in light mint green and with splotches of white or silver along the midrib and at random on the upper surface;

the under surface is a purplish red. This plant is sometimes called the ornamental yam, but so are most other species.

Dioscorea dodecaneura (do´-de-ka-NYOO-ra) is native to tropical Brazil and is similar to *D. discolor* with narrower leaf blades; it may be a variety of the latter. It has the same cultural requirements as the ornamental yam.

DIOSPYROS (dee-o-SPY-ros)
Ebenaceae: The Persimmon, Ebony Family
Common names vary according to species
Large trees; large evergreen leaves; large fruit
Zones vary according to species
Sun
Average but regular amounts of moisture
Rich, humusy, well-drained soil
Propagation by seed

A large genus of more than 450 species of trees and shrubs from all parts of the world, but mostly in warm regions. Some of the species are deciduous, such as *Diospyros virginiana* (persimmon) and *D. kaki*, but most are evergreen. The wood of most trees is exceedingly hard (and some of it exceedingly black in color) and is used for making piano keys and chess figures among other articles of commerce.

Diospyros digyna (DY-ji-na / di-JY-na) is indigenous to the lowlands of the West Indies, southern Mexico, and Central America, and is hardy only in zones 10 and 11 and marginal in zone 10a. For many years it has been erroneously called *D. ebenaster,* which is a synonym for another species, *D. ebenum* (ebony tree). *Diospyros digyna* grows to as much as 60 feet in nature but is usually no more than 40 feet in cultivation. It makes a rounded and dense-foliaged crown atop a fairly short, almost black trunk. The leaves are 8 inches long, elliptic to ovate in shape, and glossy with a prominent and lighter colored midrib. The flowers are insignificant small, whitish, and wonderfully fragrant. The fruits are like 5-inch-wide green and leathery tomatoes and include the persistent sepals as do tomatoes. The fruits are edible when ripe (soft) and give the tree its most common vernacular name of black sapote. Another common name is chocolate-pudding fruit from the color of the flesh of the ripe fruit. This is a gloriously attractive and very tropical looking shade tree.

Diospyros discolor (DIS-kul-or) (synonym *D. blancoi*) is native to the Philippines and is hardy in zones 10 and 11. It is a beautiful tree that grows slowly to 60 or 70 feet high in its native habitat but seldom attains more than 30 feet in cultivation in the continental United States. It usually has a somewhat narrow or oblong and fairly dense crown atop a stout dark trunk. The leaves are elliptic to oblong in shape with a pointed apex and are from 6 to 10 inches long, dark green, leathery and shiny above with a prominent midrib, and grayish green and pubescent beneath. The silky-pubescent new foliage has a beautiful pinkish hue. Male and female flowers appear on separate trees in summer and are not showy but are lightly fragrant. The fruits ripen in the fall to early winter and have a cheesy odor that some find pleasant and others not so pleasant. The fruits are 4 inches wide, globular in shape, with furry outer skin in any color from a deep yellow to orange, cinnamon, or reddish purple. The cheesy fragrance does not extend to the flesh of the fruit, which is a light yellow to white in color and is insipidly sweet and mealy. This outstanding ornamental is one of the most beautiful species of the entire genus. The tree is called velvet apple and, in the Philippines, mabolo.

Diospyros ebenaster. See *D. digyna, D. ebenum.*

Diospyros ebenum (EB-e-num) (synonym *D. ebenaster*) is native to India and Sri Lanka and is quite tender to cold, being adaptable only in zones 10b and 11. It grows to 60 feet or more in its native habitat with a massive, dark colored trunk and heavy limbs. It has lovely glossy and narrowly elliptic leaves that have a strong lighter colored midrib and are from 4 to 6 inches long. The white nocturnal flowers are not showy but are nicely fragrant and produce small dark-colored and leathery tomato-shaped fruits. The wood of this tree is the ebony of commerce, and contrary to the old simile, "black as ebony," the heartwood is pinkish with dark gray or black stripes. The tree has some overall similarity to *Persea americana* (avocado tree) and *Quercus virginiana* (live oak) and is a wonderfully tropical looking subject for frost-free regions.

Diospyros malabarica (mal-a-BAR-i-ka) is indigenous to a large area from India through Myanmar (Burma) and Thailand into Sumatra. It is rather similar to the two above species in general appearance, but the 6-inch-long narrowly oblong leaves are of exceptional beauty, especially the new leaves, which open a bright Chinese-lantern red. This pulchritudinous tree is tender and is not adaptable outside zones 10b and 11.

DIPLADENIA. See *Mandevilla.*

DISTICTIS (dis-TIK-tis)
Bignoniaceae: The Catalpa, Jacaranda, Trumpet-
    Vine Family
TRUMPET VINES
Large tendril-climbing vines; glossy leaves; large,
    spectacular red and purple trumpet flowers
Zones 10 and 11
Sun
Average but regular amounts of moisture
Rich, humusy, well-drained soil
Propagation by seed and cuttings

A small genus of only nine vine species in tropical America that climb by tendrils. The species have compound foliage of two or three leaflets, the third (and terminal) leaflet often modified into a tendril. None of the species are hardy to cold, but they will usually resprout from the root if the temperature does not fall below 25°F for very long. The three species described below are very spectacular in the landscape, especially *D. buccinatoria.*

Distictis buccinatoria (buk-sin´-a-TOR-ee-a) (synonyms *Bignonia cherere, Phaedranthus buccinatorius*) is indigenous to tropical nondesert areas of Mexico. It is called blood trumpet vine or blood-red trumpet vine. It grows fast to 20 feet or more in height and has leathery 3-inch-long dark green leaves that are divided into two leaflets with a terminal three-forked tendril sporting a tiny, clinging disklike organ. These little disks can damage wooden surfaces, especially painted wood. The stocky stems are usually clothed with leaves from the top of the vine to the ground. The plants bloom throughout the warm months with spectacular flowers in large terminal clusters that cover the entire vine if it receives full sun. The flowers are flaring orange-red to blood-red trumpets with yellow throats and tube, 4 inches long and about as wide. Each lobe of the corolla is usually cleft at its end.

Distictis cinerea. See *D. laxiflora.*

Distictis laxiflora (lax-i-FLOR-a) (synonym *D. cinerea*) is also from Mexico and, except for the color of the flowers, is outwardly quite similar to *D. buccinatoria.* This species does not grow as rampantly or as fast as the blood trumpet vine. The flowers are deep purple in bud and when first opened, but quickly turn a pale lavender and eventually white. Since all the flowers in a cluster do not open at the same time, there are usually several shades of purple and white in any given flower cluster. The flowers are deliciously fragrant with the scent of vanilla, and the vine is often called the vanilla trumpet vine.

Distictis 'Rivers' (synonym *D. riversii*) is a hybrid between *D. laxiflora* and *D. buccinatoria.* Called the royal trumpet vine, it is a vigorous and tall grower that is similar to its parents but has larger leaves and larger flowers. The flowers are purple to lavender with orange throats.

Distictis riversii. See *D. 'Rivers'.*

DIZYGOTHECA

(di-ZY-go-thee-ka / di-zy´-go-THEEK-a)
Araliaceae: The Aralia, Schefflera Family
FALSE ARALIA; THREAD-LEAF ARALIA
Slender open shrubs and small trees; large, palmate
    leaves of very slender segments
Zones 10b and 11
Partial shade
Water lover
Rich, humusy, well-drained soil
Propagation by seed

A small genus of about 15 species of shrubs and small trees in the islands of the South Pacific (New Caledonia and Polynesia). They are closely allied to the genus *Schefflera* and are placed in that genus by some taxonomists. All species have palmately lobed leaves, the divisions radiating from the petiole in all directions.

They are all understory plants in their native habitats and do not take well to full sun, especially in hot regions. The plants also should have protection from wind and need an ample and regular supply of moisture in a well-drained soil. Only one species is very commonly planted. ***Dizygotheca elegantissima*** (el´-e-gan-TIS-i-ma) (synonyms *Aralia elegantissima, A. laciniata, Schefflera elegantissima*) has leaves on juvenile plants that are composed of 6 to 10 very narrow, almost threadlike, 4- to 10-inch-long leaflets with wavy, notched margins. The leaflets are shiny and dark green above with a lighter colored midrib and are a deep brownish red beneath. The juvenile plants are seldom branched and have very straight stems or trunks. The adult plants branch in the upper part of their trunks, and this is when the character of the leaves changes from the very delicate-appearing and thin leaflet to a much broader one. Mature trees, which grow to as much as 12 or 15 feet, look like large compact fatsia plants with light colored trunks. The very delicate and lacy-looking juvenile form is best placed against a light background (like a wall) where its elegant leaves can be appreciated. The delicacy, even in mature plants, can be prolonged with constant bright shade rather than direct sun, and ample, regular watering.

DOMBEYA (dahm-BAY-ya)

Sterculiaceae: The Cacao, Cola-Nut Family
HYDRANGEA TREE; TROPICAL SNOWBALL;
    PINK BALL; MOUNTAIN ROSE; MEXICAN
    ROSE
Large shrubs and small trees; large palmately veined
    leaves; large clusters of white and pink flowers
Zones 10 and 11 as permanent landscape subjects;
    zone 9b as returning perennials
Sun
Average but regular amounts of moisture
Average well-drained soil
Propagation by seed and cuttings

A large genus of about 200 species of trees and shrubs in tropical eastern and southeastern Africa, Madagascar, and the Mascarene Islands east of Madagascar. Most species are evergreen; a few are deciduous. They all have large, palmately veined, usually palmately lobed hairy leaves in a dense crown of foliage and large, hydrangea-like clusters of pink or white five-petaled flowers, which usually have a honeylike fragrance. All are spectacular in and out of flower but, because the faded and discolored dried flowers remain on the plants, they should be cut off to keep the plants pristine looking. While almost all species are root hardy in zone 9b (and often zone 9a) the plants are mainly fall and winter bloomers. If the plants are constantly frozen back, the flowers are not usually forthcoming. Some of the species (like *Dombeya walichii*) are worth growing for the beautiful giant leaves.

Dombeya acutangula (ak-yoo-TANG-yoo-la) is indigenous to a wide area from tropical East Africa through Madagascar and the Mascarene Islands. It makes a large shrub or small tree to 25 feet in height but needs guidance to make a tree form. The leaves are usually less than a foot wide and variously lobed depending on the age of the plant. Juvenile plants have leaves with more lobes than do mature plants, but both mature and juvenile leaves have small teeth along the edges of the lobes. The flowers appear in late November through December and into January and are in 3-inch-wide loose clusters that are white, rarely pink.

Dombeya burgessiae (bur-JES-ee-eye) is native to tropical East Africa and is sometimes called the African wedding flower or African wedding tree. Its natural habit is to make a large multitrunked shrub, but it can be trained to a tree form that grows to as much as 20 feet. The leaves are a beautiful dark green, 10 inches wide, and broadly cordate in shape with prominent reddish yellow midribs and lateral veins. The flower clusters are not as massive or as densely flowered as many others in the genus, but the flowers are very attractive: large and pinkish white with a rose throat.

Dombeya ×cayeuxii (ky-YOO-zee-eye) is a hybrid between *D. burgessii* and *D. wallichii*. It closely resembles the latter species but has a usually more open and pendent head of flowers. Each blossom is rosy pink with a white center.

Dombeya dregeana. See *D. tiliacea.*

Dombeya elegans (EL-e-ganz) is native to the island of Réunion in the Mascarene Islands and is naturally a large shrub to about 15 feet that can be pruned and trained to a small tree form. The flowers clusters are somewhat similar to those of *D. wallichii* and are a similar color, but they are not pendent or as densely flowered. The smooth leaves are much smaller than those of *D. wallichii*, never more than 6 inches long, and are cordate in shape with toothed margins.

Dombeya natalensis. See *D. tiliacea.*

Dombeya rotundifolia. See *D. spectabilis.*

Dombeya 'Seminole' is a hybrid of unknown parentage. A large shrub to 12 or 15 feet, it is relatively compact and lush in form and sports 6- to 8-inch-long leaves that are cordate in outline but are usually three-lobed. This wonderful shrub is nearly everblooming in fall, winter, and early spring, and the erect flower clusters are about 6 inches wide with many small pure and deep pink roselike blossoms. Plate 173.

Dombeya spectabilis (spek-TAB-i-lis) (synonym *D. rotundifolia*) is native to tropical northeastern South Africa and adjacent Madagascar. It is one of the larger species, sometimes attaining a height of 40 feet, at least in its native lands. The softly pubescent leaves are broadly ovate to obovate to almost orbicular in shape and usually less than 8 inches wide. They are rusty-tomentose beneath. The tree is deciduous in the dry season of its native habitat and can be expected to lose its leaves in dry periods elsewhere, especially dry periods that coincide with winter. The flowers are in large clusters that are not pendent, and the individual flowers are a creamy white sometimes with a rosy blush. The

tree is called the wild pear in South Africa as it often blooms before the leaves appear and it has some similarity to a pear tree in bloom.

Dombeya tiliacea (til-ee-AY-see-a) (synonym *D. dregeana, D. natalensis*) is indigenous to South Africa and is usually a large shrub but may be pruned and trained to a small tree form with a maximum height of about 25 feet. The cordate and long-acuminate leaves are small for a *Dombeya* species and are, for the most part, no more than 5 inches long. They are a deep green in color, have pronounced veins, and do indeed resemble those of *Tilia ×vulgaris* (European linden). The exceptionally graceful flowers are in loose and few-flowered terminal clusters and are white to bluish white or greenish white, usually with a red center. The tree is called Natal cherry in South Africa.

Dombeya wallichii (wahl-LIK-ee-eye) is native to tropical East Africa and adjacent Madagascar. It grows to about 30 feet under optimum conditions with a very dense crown of foliage, but must be trained when young to a single-trunked tree form if that is what is desired. It is often grown as a truly giant, immense-leaved, and multitrunked shrub. The great softly pubescent leaves are frequently more than a foot long and at least a foot wide. They are broadly elliptic to diamond-shaped with three lobes, and the whole leaf bears dentation on all its margins. The flower clusters appear in winter, usually starting in early December, and are as much as 6 inches wide. Hanging from 6-inch-long hairy peduncles, the individual blossoms consist of numerous inch-wide bright pink flowers packed into a hemispherical ball of beauty. Unlike the flowers of many other species of *Dombeya*, they are only remotely fragrant, if at all. This species is the most widely planted *Dombeya* species around the world and is a spectacular landscape subject, adaptable as a tree or a giant umbrella-like shrub. Plate 174.

DORYANTHES (dor-ee-ANTH-eez)
Agavaceae: The Agave Family
SPEAR LILY
Gigantic rosettes of erect stiff sword-shaped fleshy leaves; tall imposing spikes of red flowers
Zones 10 and 11
Sun to partial shade
Average but regular amounts of moisture
Average well-drained soil
Propagation by transplanting suckers, (sometimes) by seed, and (sometimes) by aerial bulblets

A genus of only three species of giant succulent, agavelike perennial herbs in eastern Australia. The leaves have the appearance of the tough swords of *Agave* species, but they are fleshier and not spiny. In general appearance the plants look like melanges of *Agave* and *Yucca* species. Unlike almost all species of *Agave*, they do not die after flowering. Their culture is similar to that for *Agave* species, but they need more water (with perfect drainage) and flourish in partial shade. The plants are tender to cold but there are mature specimens in zone 9b. They are perfect for bold accents in succulent gardens or anywhere a dramatic landscape subject is appropriate. The plants sucker slowly and remain confined to their original space allotments for several years. The offshoots may be removed for propagation purposes. Occasionally the flower spikes produce bulblets along with flowers.

Doryanthes excelsa (ek-SEL-sa) is native to the state of New South Wales in Australia. It is a very impressive plant, which makes a rosette of 6-foot-long erect and stiff olive green to dark green sword-shaped leaves. There may be as many as 100 leaves in any rosette. The immense flower spikes are as much as 12 or even 14 feet tall with many large grayish green ovate bracts along its lower half. The flowers are packed into a great globular cluster on the top of the lofty spike. The individual flowers are six-petaled and scarlet to pinkish red, and look like narrow-petaled *Crinum* flowers. Furthermore, they exude nectar and are fought over by birds and insects. This species is sometimes called the globe spear-lily.

Doryanthes palmeri (PALM-ur-eye) is native to northeastern Australia. It makes a full rosette as much as 10 feet tall with as many as 100 leaves. Each leaf may be 8 feet long, is olive green to dark green, and is channeled longitudinally with several grooves along the length of the blade. The flower spikes are 15 or more feet tall and are covered for two-thirds of their length with large gray-green linear-ovate bracts. The top third of the spike is a one-sided gigantic inflorescence of large six-petaled flowers that look like narrow-petaled water lilies. Each flower is crimson to reddish brown on the outside and pinkish white inside. There is hardly a more impressive landscape subject, especially when in bloom. Plate 108.

DOXANTHA. See *Macfadyena*.

DRACAENA (dra-SEEN-a)
Agavaceae: The Agave Family
Common names vary according to species
Herbaceous to treelike and palmlike plants; swordlike
　　or ribbonlike leaves; large flower clusters
Zones vary according to species
Light requirements vary widely according to species
Average but regular amounts of moisture; some
　　species are drought tolerant
Humusy, well-drained soil
Propagation by cuttings and (for the species) seed

A genus of about 40 very variable species of small and mostly herbaceous perennials to large and woody treelike (or palmlike) plants distributed in the tropics and warm regions of the Old World and united into one natural group by the form of their flowers and terminal flower clusters. All have sword-shaped, often stalkless leaves of varying widths, which usually grow in a spiral fashion from the stem and are confined to the tops of the trunks or at the ends of the branches in older plants. The genus is closely allied to *Cordyline*, and some of the plants in one genus are still misnamed as being in the other genus. Few of these species are true water lovers, even those that hail from wet tropical areas, and a few are definitely drought tolerant. None are hardy to cold, although a few can withstand a few degrees of frost. Many smaller and more herbaceous species are utilized as some of the most popular and enduring houseplants and interior "decor" plants. None is grown for the tiny six-petaled flowers alone, but many have rather spectacular displays of them. Some of the most beautiful and useful of tropical looking plants are found within this genus.

Dracaena arborea (ahr-BOR-ee-a) is native to tropical West Africa and is hardy in zones 10 and 11 and marginal in zone 10a. It grows to a maximum height of 15 or sometimes even 20 feet with a slender grayish ringed trunk that is often unbranched and from atop which spring the dark green, soft but leathery strap-shaped leaves. Each leaf is 2 or 3 feet long by only 2 or 3 inches wide and droops gracefully in a full and luxuriant crown, which gives the appearance of a large tropical yucca or palm tree. The main landscape use of this small tree is as a thin and graceful accent where the form is needed. The tiny white flowers are in 4-foot-long drooping panicles and give way to bright red berries. This species thrives in sun or partial shade and needs a soil rather richer than that of most other species, with an adequate supply of water.

Dracaena australis. See *Cordyline australis.*

Dracaena deremensis (der-e-MEN-sis) is indigenous to tropical West Africa and is hardy in zones 10 and 11 and marginal in zone 10a. It grows to 15 feet or more in height and looks much like the ubiquitous houseplant called "corn plant" (*Dracaena fragrans*). The leaves are generally narrower than those of the corn plant, but, like them, are found only terminally or at the ends of the few branches. The leaves are usually 2 to almost 3 feet long by 2 to 3 inches wide and are linear-elliptic to linear-lanceolate in shape, a dark green in color, with longitudinal grooves running the length of the blade. The tiny flowers are in linear panicles. Each flower is red on the outside, white on the inside. This species needs protection from the full sun of hot regions and is not drought tolerant. There are many cultivars of this popular plant, most of which have variegated leaves. All are superb as large to small accent plants. *Dracaena deremensis* **'Bausei'** (BAU-zee-eye) has leaves slightly wider than the species, each one with a wide center stripe of white or cream and a pale green midrib. *Dracaena deremensis* **'Compacta'** (kahm-PAK-ta) is a very compact plant that grows more like a small agave or aloe, with foot-long lanceolate leaves bundled into a compact rosette that only grows to about 18 inches tall. *Dracaena deremensis* **'Janet Craig'** has leaves that are wider and longer than the species, to 3 or 4 feet long. They are solid dark green with deep longitudinal grooves. *Dracaena deremensis* **'Roehrs**

Gold' has leaves the size and shape of the type but with beautiful longitudinal striations of white and yellow. *Dracaena deremensis* **'Souvenir d'August Schryver'** has leaves somewhat shorter than those of the species. They are beautifully striped with dark and pale green in the center of the leaf, which has an outer marginal band of gold. *Dracaena deremensis* **'Warneckii'** (war-NEK-ee-eye) has leaves very much like the type but with narrow and linear white stripes. It is one of the most widely sold houseplants. *Dracaena deremensis* **'Warneckii Marginata'** (mar-ji-NAIT-a) is, as the cultivar name implies, a beautifully and more highly variegated form of *D. deremensis* 'Warneckii'.

Dracaena draco (DRAY-ko) is native to the Canary Islands and is hardy in zones 9b through 11. It is the famous dragon tree so widely grown in Mediterranean climates including southern California. It slowly grows to 20 or 30 feet in cultivation with an umbrella-shaped crown of branches and leaves but reaches 40 or 50 feet (or sometimes more) in its native habitat. It forms a very stout, swollen and often somewhat grotesque woody trunk that is much-branched above with the stiff 2- to 3-foot sword-shaped leaves at the ends of the massive branches. This fantastic tree should have a full sun exposure and is quite drought tolerant when established. It also endures saline soil and air and is a very good choice for seaside plantings where a very dramatic landscape statement is wanted. The sap of this tree is dark red in color and, according to European myth and legend, was supposed to be the blood of dragons. Plate 175.

Dracaena fragrans (FRAY-granz) is found naturally from Senegal to the Ivory Coast in West Africa and is hardy in zones 10 and 11 and marginal in zone 10a. It is the corn plant of interior decorators and retail nurseries, and one of the most widely sold and grown houseplant subjects. It grows to 15 feet or more, and the trunk becomes woody at the base but seldom branches until it is old, pruned, or injured. The soft, leathery dark green leaves are usually about 3 feet long by 3 or 4 inches wide and are linear-lanceolate to linear-elliptic in shape. In very old plants the upper trunk is sparsely branched and the plants have the appearance of giant green yucca trees. The plants flower in late autumn and winter, and the flowers are in clusters along a terminal spike that is usually long and heavy enough to be pendent. Each small whitish yellow flower is exceedingly fragrant. Most people find the odor quite appealing, but some cannot tolerate it. The plant grows wonderfully in partial shade but can withstand full sun. It should not be subjected to drought conditions as it loses most of its leaves although it will survive this stress. There are several cultivars, which are much more widely grown and available than is the type. *Dracaena fragrans* **'Lindenii'** (lin-DEN-ee-eye) has leaves the shape of the type, but they are beautifully variegated with a broad central stripe of dark green, thin longitudinal white striations, and a wide leaf margin of bright yellow. *Dracaena fragrans* **'Massangeana'** (mah-sahn-jee-AHN-a) has wider leaves than the type with a broad central stripe of yellow, thin green striations within that stripe, and a leaf margin of bright green. It is the most widely grown and sold *Dracaena* cultivar in the world. *Dracaena fragrans* **'Victoriae'** (vik-TOR-ee-eye) is a wonderfully beautiful form with broad and recurved leaves having the shape and length of 'Massangeana' leaves, and with a broad central stripe of dark green and a border of golden yellow often with longitudinal green striations. This cultivar does not grow as tall as the type. Plate 340.

Dracaena godseffiana. See *D. surculosa.*

Dracaena goldieana (gold-ee-AHN-ah) occurs naturally from Guinea to Nigeria in tropical West Africa and is hardy in zones 10 and 11. It is a tiny species compared to the others and usually only grows to 12 or 18 inches tall in cultivation but can reach 6 feet or more in its native habitat. Unlike the leaves of most other species, the leaves of this one have relatively long petioles. The soft and leathery leaf blade is 9 to 10 inches long by 5 inches wide, ovate to lanceolate in shape, and a dark green in color with many creamy white transverse bands. The botanical image is almost that of a zebra's hide and is truly exotic and tropical looking. The new leaves also have a pinkish tinge. It is not a plant for full sun, but is one of the most beautiful accent subjects in a partially shaded tropical border. The little plants look somewhat like some of the African succulents, such as *Haworthia* or even *Sansevieria* species.

Dracaena gracilis. See *D. marginata.*

Dracaena marginata (mar-ji-NAIT-a) (synonym *D. gracilis*) is indigenous to the large island of Madagascar and is hardy in zones 10 and 11 and marginal in zone 10a. The plant slowly grows to 15 feet or more with a slender, rubbery, picturesquely contorted and light-colored trunk that is much branched and ringed with leaf scars when old. This paradigm of elegance and grace is a garden designer's sculptural dream come true. It should be planted where its beautiful form can be silhouetted against a lighter (or darker) background, and is perfect as a single small multitrunked specimen. The linear straplike leaves are about 2 feet long and usually less than an inch wide at the ends of the sinuous branches. They are a dark green in color with darker longitudinal veins and have a red margin when the plant is grown in the sun. The plants do not flower in cultivation until they are old. The blossoms are in narrow terminal spikes rather similar to those of *D. fragrans.* There are several cultivated forms of this species. *Dracaena marginata* **'Magenta'** has attractive maroon-colored leaves. *Dracaena marginata* **'Tricolor',** the most beautiful cultivar, has leaves that are green with longitudinal creamy white stripes and pinkish margins.

Dracaena reflexa (ree-FLEX-a) (synonym *Pleomele reflexa*) is native to Madagascar, the island of Mauritius, and western India, and is hardy in zones 10 and 11. It makes a large shrub to 12 feet or more with many softly woody branches. In completely frost-free areas it may grow to more than twice this height. The narrow dark green leaves are tufted at the ends of the branches, usually less than a foot in length, and lanceolate to elliptic in shape. This plant looks as much like a broad-leaved bamboo as it does a *Dracaena* species, and its cultivars look like *Arundo donax* (giant variegated cane). **Dracaena reflexa 'Honoriae'** (o-NOR-ee-eye) has yellow-white stripes. **Dracaena reflexa 'Variegata'** is sometimes called the song of India. It has white-margined leaves that are quite attractive up close.

Dracaena sanderiana (sand´-ur-ee-AH-nah) is native to tropical West and Central Africa and is hardy only in zones 10 and 11 and marginal in zone 10a. It is a small plant, never growing to more than 5 feet in height, and is seldom branched. The leaves are usually no more than 8 inches long and are elliptic in shape with a beautiful strip of white along each margin. The plant makes a beautiful small accent in shady or partially sunny sites.

Dracaena surculosa (surk-yoo-LO-sa) (synonym *D. godseffiana*) is indigenous to tropical West Africa and is hardy in zones 10 and 11 and marginal in zone 10a. It is called the gold-dust plant or gold dust dracaena or spotted dracaena. The plant grows to only 3 or 4 feet and is unusual in the genus for having wiry narrow branching and spreading stems from which spring the leaves. The 5- to 8-inch-long leaves are elliptical in shape with a short and abrupt point at their ends, and are dark green with many white spots randomly but widely scattered along the length and breadth of the leaf blades. The flowers are in small spreading terminal panicles. Each whitish flower is very fragrant with a scent much akin to that of *D. fragrans* (corn plant). The flowers are followed by small bright red berries. Partial shade to almost full shade is the desideratum of these choice little plants in which environment they are perfect for brightening the gloom. They also make a groundcover of exceptional beauty. They like a fairly rich soil and are not drought tolerant. **Dracaena surculosa 'Florida Beauty'** has leaves so heavily spotted with white that the leaf blade seems to have a background of white or cream-spotted with dark green spots. **Dracaena surculosa 'Juanita'** bears leaves with a broad central stripe of creamy white. The margins are dark green with the typical white spots.

Dracaena thalioides (thail-ee-OY-deez) is indigenous to tropical Africa and Sri Lanka and is hardy in zones 10 and 11. Out of flower the plant looks much like a member of the genus *Aspidistra:* it has a maximum height of 3 feet and is a stemless (or almost stemless) rosette of dark green ribbed lanceolate leaves at the ends of long channeled petioles. It makes a good specimen plant for a low border and a nice silhouette in partly shaded sites with average amounts of moisture.

DRYNARIA (dry-NAHR-ee-a)
Polypodiaceae: The Largest Fern Family
OAK-LEAF FERN
Large epiphytic fern with large pinnate dark green
    leaves

Zones 10 and 11; marginal in zone 10a
Partial shade to partial sun
Average but regular amounts of moisture
Leaf mold or epiphytic mix

A genus of about 20 species of creeping rhizomatous-rooted large to gigantic epiphytic fern species in tropical Asia, tropical Australia, and some of the islands of the South Pacific. The fronds are of two kinds: the sterile fronds are relatively short and unstalked with shallow lobes, and the fertile fronds are large, long-stalked, and very deeply lobed or actually pinnate in form. One species is fairly commonly grown in the tropics on trees and terrestrially as well as in pots and hanging baskets. **Drynaria quercifolia** (kwers-i-FO-lee-a) (synonym *Polypodium quercifolium*) is native to an immense area of the tropical Eastern Hemisphere from southern China and Southeast Asia eastward to northern Australia and the island of Fiji. Its fertile fronds are as much as 3 feet long and are divided almost to the rachis into about 20 lance-shaped segments, each with a strong midvein. This fern is grace personified, arching from the limbs of a large tree or springing from the soil pockets of a stone wall.

DRYOPTERIS. See *Thelypteris.*

DYCKIA (DIK-ee-a)
Bromeliaceae: The Pineapple, Bromeliad Family
DYCKIA
Rosettes of tough straplike, curved, spiny-margined
    leaves; spikes of yellow and orange flowers
Zones vary according to species
Sun
Average but regular amounts of moisture; drought
    tolerant
Average well-drained soil
Propagation by transplanting suckers and by seed

A genus of about 100 terrestrial bromeliad species in South America where they grow in and among rocks, usually in full sun. None is naturally found north of the equator. All species have clumping stemless rosettes of tough succulent leaves armed with marginal teeth or spines and sharp terminal points. The leaves are scaly beneath, and the scales are sometimes arranged into longitudinal rows. The relatively tall inflorescences appear usually in the spring and arise from the side of the individual plants rather than from the centers of the rosettes. They are clumping plants and often spread so densely that it is difficult to distinguish individual plants in some massive clumps. All want at least partial sun and are not particular as to soil as long as it drains freely. They are perfect additions for the cactus and succulent garden, on a wall, or in a large pot where they cascade over the sides of the container.

Dyckia altissima. See *D. encholirioides.*

Dyckia brevifolia (brev-i-FO-lee-a) (synonym *D. sulphurea*) is native to southern Brazil in sunny sites that are subject to flooding in the rainy season. It is hardy in zones 10 and 11 and marginal in zone 9b. The plant has 8-inch-long dark green rather short, stiff, and only slightly recurved lanceolate-shaped leaves that are concave in cross section and have short and widely spaced teeth on the margins. The rosettes are usually less than a foot wide but sucker freely, making large clusters. The inflorescence may reach 3 feet in height, with widely scattered yellow bell-shaped flowers along its upper half.

Dyckia encholirioides (en´-ko-leer-ee-OY-deez) (synonym *D. altissima*) occurs naturally in central to southern Brazil and northeastern Argentina and is hardy in zones 9b through 11. It is a large and striking plant with many dark green 18-inch-long narrow very rigid leaves, giving the plant the appearance of a small *Agave* species. The undersides of the leaves have wonderful bright silver longitudinal lines. The 3-foot-tall inflorescence is spectacular because of the many bell-shaped orange flowers it carries.

Dyckia fosteriana (fahs-ter´-ee-AHN-a) is native to southern Brazil and is hardy in zones 10 and 11. It is one of the most attractive species in the genus, although it is a small plant. It forms perfect spiraled rosettes of 4- to 5-inch-long narrow curved silvery-colored arching and recurved leaves that are scalloped on the margins. Each projection of each scallop ends in a lighter colored spine. The orange flowers are carried on 2-foot-tall spikes. There are several forms of this plant varying in leaf color from almost green to silver to red or purple and bronze. This little bromeliad is very choice for viewing up close and is perfect planted in a sunny site on a stone wall or cascading over the tops of pots or ledges.

Dyckia marnier-lapostollei (mahrn´-yay-lap´-o-STOL-lee-eye) is indigenous to southern Brazil and is hardy in zones 10 and 11. It is the most beautiful *Dyckia* species. Although slightly less than a foot in length, each leaf is a glorious piece of architecture: fat and wide, grayish brown or silvery and bluish green, velvety broadly lance-shaped with a midrib variegation pattern like a fern frond and with backwards pointing teeth on the margin. The inflorescence is about 2 feet tall with a few orange-yellow flowers. This species is one of the most beautiful and exotic succulent plants whether bromeliaceous or not and is incredibly effective planted with rose-colored pebbles or against a dark background.

Dyckia sulphurea. See *D. brevifolia*.

DYPSIS. See *Chrysalidocarpus* and *Neodypsis*.

ECHEVERIA (ek-e-VER-ee-a)
Crassulaceae: The Sedum, Sempervivum Family
Common names vary according to species
Small or medium-sized rosettes of green, gray, or
　　colored fleshy leaves; tall spikes of flowers
Zones vary according to species
Sun to partial shade
Drought tolerant
Average well-drained soil
Propagation by root division, rhizome division, and
　　seed

A genus of about 150 species of succulent, mostly stemless herbs and subshrubs with fleshy, stalkless leaves arranged in rosettes. All species are American; most are from Mexico, but the area of distribution of the genus ranges from southern Texas to Argentina. The inflorescence is a relatively tall spike that arises from the leaf axils and is sometimes branched, often with small leaflike bracts on its lower parts. The flowers are yellow, orange, pink, or red, pendent, and bell-shaped, and are borne on the upper half of the spike. The plants are related to species of *Cotyledon, Crassula, Sedum,* and *Sempervivum,* but some look much like *Aeonium* species; they have the same landscape uses in the rock garden or succulent garden. Many species are wonderfully colored, and a few are relatively hardy to cold. They bloom primarily in summer. The smaller species should be planted where their beautiful form and color can be enjoyed up close. All are indispensable subjects for raised beds, cactus and succulent collections, and rock gardens.

Echeveria agavoides (ag-a-VOY-deez) is native to the plateau region of central Mexico and is hardy in zones 9 through 11. This lovely little plant has 8-inch-wide rosettes of deep green ovate, fat, and keeled leaves that end in a short but sharp point and often have distinctly reddish margins in full sun. The specific epithet means "agavelike," and the little rosettes do indeed resemble tiny agaves. The flowers are red, and the petals are tipped with yellow.

Echeveria albicans (AL-bi-kanz) is indigenous to the tropical plateau region of Mexico and is hardy in zones 9b through 11. It makes very beautiful and elegant clustering 8-inch-wide rosettes of spatulate-shaped bluish gray leaves with tiny points at their ends. The flowers are deep pink outside with yellow inside their little bells. This species is one of the most exquisitely beautiful succulent plants and should be planted where its color and form can be appreciated up close.

Echeveria chihuahuaensis (chee-wah´-wah-ENS-is) is indigenous to north-central Mexico and is hardy in zones 9 through 11. It makes a beautiful 4- to 5-inch-wide rosette of white to pink ovate to oblong, keeled and short-pointed leaves with reddish purple margins. The flowers are red and orange.

Echeveria crenulata (kren-yoo-LAIT-a) is native to south-central Mexico and is hardy in zones 10 and 11. It is a rather large plant with short, branching stems and great foot-long obovate to rhomboid-shaped wavy and crinkled yellow-green leaves with scalloped reddish margins that resemble those of a succulent lettuce plant. Some forms of the plant have leaves that are covered with a bluish white bloom. The flowers are pink outside and yellow inside. Like a lettuce plant, these unusual and striking little shrublets do not like full sun in areas with hot summers, and they need more water than most other species in the genus.

Echeveria derenbergii (der-en-BURG-ee-eye) is native to southern Mexico and is hardy in zones 10 and 11. It forms tight globular-shaped clustering rosettes of waxy 2-inch-long light green to bluish gray obovate leaves with short spiny tips and red margins. The plants have short-branched stems, but these are usually hidden by the leaves. The flowers are red and yellow and, unlike most other species, appear in winter and early spring. This species is sometimes called painted lady because of the red-tipped leaves.

Echeveria elegans (EL-e-ganz) is indigenous to the north-central plateau region of Mexico and is hardy in zones 9 through 11. It is one of the most widely grown *Echeveria* species and has been in cultivation for a very long time. It is indeed an elegant little plant that forms tight rounded clustering rosettes. The 3-inch-long spatulate-shaped leaves are keeled with a short pointed tip, and their color ranges from a bluish gray to bluish green, although some are almost white. The common names Mexican rose, Mexican snowball, pearl echeveria, and Mexican gem give a clue to the beauty of the plants and to their exquisite form, and the name hen-and-chickens refers to their clustering and spreading habit. The flowers are pink and yellow. ***Echeveria elegans*** '**Kesselringii**' has ice blue leaves. This little gem needs protection from the midday sun in regions with hot summers.

Echeveria gibbiflora (gib-i-FLOR-a) is indigenous to southern Mexico and is hardy in zones 10 and 11. It is one of the largest *Echeveria* species with stems that can grow to 3 feet in height. The leaves are obovate to spatulate in shape with notched ends in which are embedded a tiny short point; they are as much as 15 inches long, forming rosettes as wide as 3 feet. Leaf color varies from grayish green to purplish green. The plant resembles an *Aeonium* species more than other *Echeveria* species. The gracefully arching flower stalks can be as long as 5 feet with red flowers; unlike most other *Echeveria* species this one blooms in fall and winter. ***Echeveria gibbiflora*** '**Metallica**' (met-AL-lik-a) has leaves that are rosy purple with a decidedly bronzy cast. Other cultivars have crinkled or deformed leaves that are, in my opinion, not very attractive. This large succulent is strikingly effective as a background or focal point in the rock garden or cactus and succulent collection.

Echeveria ×imbricata (im-bri-KAIT-a) is a hybrid between *E. gibbiflora* 'Metallica' and *E. secunda* var. *glauca*. It is one of the most widely cultivated forms of the genus, especially in California. It is often called hen-and-chickens because of its strong resemblance to many *Sedum* species and its clustering growth habit. It is hardy in zones 9 through 11. The freely clustering and flattish rosettes are 6 inches wide and are composed of 3-inch-long grayish green to bluish gray fat obovate and concave leaves with short points. The flowers are orange to red. This veteran should not be eschewed in

consideration for the cactus and succulent garden as there is a reason for its widespread cultivation: it is beautiful.

Echeveria lauii (LOW-ee-eye) is indigenous to southern Mexico and is hardy in zones 10 and 11. This beautiful plant has perfectly round foot-wide rosettes of fat concave and keeled, ovate 4-inch-long leaves. The leaves are bluish white often edged in red and look as if they are carved from soapstone. The plants usually form short unbranched stems to 3 or 4 inches tall. The flowers are pink. This species is unusually choice.

Echeveria leucotricha (lyoo-ko-TRYK-a) is indigenous to the plateau region of south-central Mexico and is hardy in zones 10 and 11. It forms stems to 6 inches tall and has loose 6- to 8-inch-wide rosettes of 4-inch-long spatulate-shaped fat green leaves that appear almost white because of the velvety covering of short white hairs. In addition, the hairs are usually sparsely streaked in zones of rust to purplish red color, giving the leaves a distinct resemblance to those of *Kalanchoe tomentosa* (panda plant). The flowers are a rusty red in color.

Echeveria lindsayana (lind-za-YAHN-a) has uncertain origins, but is probably native to southern Mexico. It is hardy in zones 10 and 11. The 6-inch-wide rosettes are rather flat and consist of fat obovate and concave, greenish gray 3-inch-long leaves with a waxy whitish bloom and a short bristle at the end. The leaf margin and tip are suffused in red. The rosettes look as if they were chiseled from stone and invite one to touch them; indeed, some people are moved to want to eat them, so perfect do they appear. The 2-foot-high flower stalks bear scarlet flowers with yellow tips and throats. This exquisite little species should be planted where it can be appreciated up close.

Echeveria potosina (po-toe-SEE-na) is native to the north-central plateau region of Mexico and is hardy in zones 9b through 11. It makes a beautiful rosette similar to that of *E. elegans*, but is deeper colored. The leaves are definitely blue, often with a purplish hue, especially near the tips of the leaves, and the flowers are pink. ***Echeveria potosina*** '**Alba**' (AL-ba) is a white-flowered cultivar.

Echeveria pulvinata (pul-vi-NAIT-a) is indigenous to the southern plateau region of Mexico and is hardy in zones 10 and 11. Its lack of cold hardiness is unfortunate, because it is one of the choicest of the genus. The plants make short felty stems in time atop which reside the 5-inch-wide rosettes of very fat 2- to 3-inch long obovate to spatulate-shaped concave and keeled grayish green leaves. The leaves are densely covered in a fine silvery tomentum, which creates an almost glowing effect. In time the silvery felt turns a reddish brown, which adds to the beauty as there is then rusty red among the silver. The flowers are also red. This beauty is often called the plush plant because of the covering of white tomentum; it is also sometimes called the chenille plant, which is unfortunate because this name is widely used for *Acalypha hispida*.

Echeveria secunda (se-KUN-da) is native to the plateau regions of northern Mexico and is hardy in zones 9 through 11. It is a wonderful little clustering plant with 4-inch-wide rosettes of narrowly obovate leaves that are grayish blue to bluish green in color. Because of its clumping or clustering habit, this is another *Echeveria* species whose common name is hen-and-chickens; it is also sometimes called blue hen-and-chickens. The flowers are red outside and yellow within.

Echeveria setosa (se-TOE-sa) is indigenous to southern Mexico and is hardy in zones 10 and 11. It makes a somewhat flat rosette of many densely packed spatulate-shaped dark green leaves that are covered in short stiff white hairs. Because of the density of the hairs, the center of the rosette is white, which gives a wonderful contrast to the outer margins of the rosettes. The flowers are bright red with yellow-tipped petals.

ECHINOCACTUS (ee-KYN-o-kak-tus)
Cactaceae: The Cactus Family
Common names vary according to species
Stout ribbed, straight-spined barrel or columnar
 cactuses; yellow and red flowers atop plant body
Zones vary according to species
Sun
Drought tolerant
Sandy, average, well-drained soil
Propagation by seed

A small genus of about five large cactus species from the southwestern United States and Mexico. All have deeply ribbed plant bodies with very stout spines. The yellow or orange flowers grow out of a circular ring of woolly areoles in the top center of the plant. The plants are short thick columns or rounded and barrel-like. Among other characteristics distinguishing these barrel types from the barrel cactus genus *Ferocactus* are the spines, which in the latter genus are mostly hooked but in *Echinocactus* are straight. The larger species are quite spectacular in the cactus and succulent garden, but they need perfect drainage and are almost impossible to keep in wet and humid climates where they are subject to stem rot. The genus formerly consisted of hundreds of species, which included almost all globular-shaped cactus species. Unfortunately, many of these names are still used in the trade.

Echinocactus grandis. See *E. platyacanthus.*

Echinocactus grusonii (groo-SO-nee-eye) is native to the central plateau region of Mexico and is hardy in zones 9b through 11. It is a large barrel-type cactus with a body as much as 3 feet in height and more than 2 feet in diameter. Younger plants are completely round, while mature plants are very fat columns. The plants are green with two to three dozen deep ribs. The ribs are covered with so many clusters of golden yellow 2-inch-long spines that the overall appearance of the plant is yellow, resulting in the most common vernacular name of golden barrel cactus. This cactus blooms only when mature with a crown of yellow 2-inch-long flowers in summer. *Echinocactus grusonii* var. *inermis* is a naturally occurring variety that is completely spineless. Plate 176.

Echinocactus horizonthalonius (hahr´-i-zahnth-a-LO-nee-us) is indigenous to southwestern Texas, southeastern New Mexico, and adjacent northern Mexico, and is hardy in zones 8b through 11. It is one of the smaller species, never surpassing a foot in height, but is usually more than a foot in diameter. The body is squat and a deep green in color with 7 to 13 fat and bulging ribs. The ribs bear vicious, steely-hard light brown to reddish brown thick spines an inch long or more; some of the spines may be curved to some extent. The tough spines have led to common names of eagle's-claw cactus and mule-crippler cactus. The flowers appear in summer and are 3 inches long with many linear rosy petals.

Echinocactus platyacanthus (plait´-ee-a-KANTH-us) (synonym *E. grandis*) is native to central and northern Mexico and is hardy in zones 9b through 11. This barrel-type plant attains a maximum diameter of 2 feet with a total height of about a foot. The body is a bright yellowish green with as many as 60 very deep ribs on older plants. The short spines along the tips of the ribs are dark gray to black in color and do not cover the skin of the plants, so that the visual effect is that of a bright green deeply furrowed and flattish globe. The flowers are a bright yellow, and the plants bloom in the summer. This very beautiful species is visually quite satisfying planted among rocks and non-green succulents.

Echinocactus polycephalus (pah-lee-SEF-a-lus) is native to southeastern California, southern Nevada, western Arizona, southwestern Utah, and the state of Sonora in Mexico, and is hardy in zones 8 through 11. It is a clustering species that produces offsets. The plant body is a 1- to 2-foot-high dark green cylinder almost completely covered in reddish hued 3-inch-long spines. The yellow flowers are 2 to 3 inches long and appear in the summer. The species, one of the most spectacular of the relatively cold hardy cactus species, is also easy of culture in dry climates.

Echinocactus texensis (tex-ENS-is) (synonym *Homalocephala texensis*) is native to southern and southwestern Texas and adjacent northern Mexico and is hardy in zones 8 through 11. This species is similar in all respects, including cultural requirements, to *E. horizonthalonius*, except that the plant body is flatter and the flowers appear in spring rather than in summer.

ECHINOPSIS (eek-i-NAHP-sis)
Cactaceae: The Cactus Family
Common names vary according to species
Small to immense, globular to treelike ribbed
 columnar cactus plants; large showy flowers
Zones vary according to species
Sun to partial shade
Drought tolerant
Sandy, well-drained soil
Propagation by seed and cuttings

A genus of perhaps 80 species of cactus in South America. For many years these plants were in two separate genera, *Echinopsis* and *Trichocereus,* the former genus included all the low and globular forms (called sea urchin cactus and Easter-lily cactus) and the latter genus the large columnar and often treelike forms. The situation was nice for horticulturists, gardeners, and landscapers because of the great difference in size and form between the two genera. All these species have large flowers. Because all forms freely hybridize, there are many spectacularly flowered hybrids among the small globular plants formerly known only as *Echinopsis,* the flowers often significantly larger than the plants themselves. What they all now have in common are the ribbed plant bodies and the showy mostly nocturnal flowers; they all have the same cultural requirements, whether small or large. Only some of the landscape-size plants are dealt with here.

Echinopsis huascha (WAHS-ka) (synonym *Trichocereus huascha*) is indigenous to northwestern Argentina and is hardy in zones 9b through 11. One of the smaller columnar species, it grows only to about 5 feet tall. It is a clumping plant, branching from the base into several unbranched semierect many-ribbed long cylinders of dark green stems, each with at least a dozen distinct ribs with white areoles along the ribs' crests. The stems are never more than 3 inches thick. The spines are yellow to brownish yellow and are relatively small, and a clump of this cactus is most attractive and fuzzy-looking from a distance. The long-necked diurnal flowers are borne at the tops of the stems; they are about 4 inches long and as wide with many narrow petals and are, amazingly, either a pure bright lemon yellow or scarlet in color. This cactus species is exquisite because of its color—the small white areoles and yellowish small spines are quite striking against the finely ribbed and deep green cactus body—and because of its spectacular summer flowers.

Echinopsis pachanoi (PAK-a-noi) (synonym *Trichocereus pachanoi*) is native to western Ecuador and Peru and is hardy in zones 9b through 11. This wonderful cactus grows as tall as 20 feet with many clustering dusty green to bluish green stems arising from the base of the plant. Each trunk is deeply ribbed into six to eight broad crests along which the 1- to 3-inch-long white to golden brown spines grow; the spines do not grow in a dense manner, which adds to their beauty. The beautiful flowers grow from the tops of the columns, are long-necked and as much as 10 inches in length, have many white petals and brownish sepals, and are nocturnal and fragrant. Plate 177.

Echinopsis pasacana (pahs-a-KAHN-a) (synonym *Trichocereus pasacana*) is native to northwestern Argentina and southern Bolivia and is hardy in zones 10 and 11. This gigantic species grows to as much as 30 feet in its native habitat. It is treelike in its form with a stout trunk and massive branches (arms), which create a plant body with similarities to that of *Carnegiea gigantea* (sahuaro), but with so many gray to reddish brown spines that the grassy green of the stem and its very many ribs are all but obscured. The plant blooms in summer with 5-inch-long many-petaled diurnal white flowers at the tips of the arms. The red spine-covered globose fruits are supposed to be edible. This almost incredibly beautiful cactus species makes a good "replacement" for the slower-growing sahuaro. Plate 178.

Echinopsis santiaguensis (sahnt´-ee-a-GEN-sis) (synonym *Trichocereus santiaguensis*) is native to northwestern Argentina and is hardy in zones 10 and 11. The species is a tree form, growing to 20 feet or more with a stout short trunk and many sharply ascending fairly slender bluish green branches. Each branch bears a dozen or more deep ribs with small white areoles atop their crests. The spines are short and do not hide the ribs. The long-necked diurnal white summer flowers are as much as 10 inches long by 6 inches wide with many large wide white petals.

Echinopsis spachianus (spahk-ee-AHN-us) (synonym *Trichocereus spachianus*) is native to northwestern Argentina and is hardy in zones 10 and 11. It forms a clump of ascending unbranched columns to as much as 6 feet in height but usually about 3 feet tall. Each stem is dark green, slender, and deeply ridged with 10 to 15 ribs. The areoles are yellowish brown in color and bear many thin yellowish brown spines. The visual aspect of these short columns has led to the common name of torch cactus. The flowers are nocturnal and 8 inches long and almost as wide with many silky white petals and rosy brown sepals. This exceptionally beautiful species adds outstanding color and form to the cactus and succulent garden.

Echinopsis tarijensis (tahr-ee-HEN-sis) (synonym *Trichocereus poco*) occurs naturally in southern Bolivia and is quite similar to *E. pasacana* except that it does not grow as tall (only to about 10 feet), the stems are not quite as stout, and the flowers are red instead of white.

Echinopsis terscheckii (ter-SHEK-ee-eye) (synonym *Trichocereus terscheckii*) is indigenous to a large area of northwestern Argentina and is hardy in zones 9b through 11. The largest and grandest species in the genus, it grows to as much as 40 feet in its native habitat. It is a tree form with a relatively short stout trunk and a few thick ascending branches, forming a landscape subject quite similar in overall form and size to that of *Carnegiea gigantea* (sahuaro). The deep green branches are 6 to 8 inches in diameter with a dozen or so deep narrow ribs along whose crests are the small golden areoles bearing a dozen or so thin yellow spines. The species is a nocturnal summer bloomer with 8-inch-long funnel-shaped blossoms and many white petals and brown sepals. This giant cactus is magnificently beautiful and picturesque and is another good replacement for the much slower-growing sahuaro. Plate 179.

Echinopsis thelegonus (thee-le-GO-nus) (synonym *Trichocereus thelegona*) is indigenous to northwestern Argentina and is hardy in zones 9b through 11. It branches from the base to form semi-erect stems to as much as 6 feet long that are as often recumbent as erect but the ends are usually erect. Each deep green to bluish or grayish green branch is cylindrical and bears a dozen or so broad ribs that are segmented into hexagonal tubercles. The spines are stout and yellowish in color. The nocturnal summer flowers are immense, as much as 10 inches long and 8 inches wide, with many narrow silky white petals and a few rosy-brown sepals; they are as beautiful as the night-blooming cereus, *Selenicereus*. When planted en masse, this plant in bloom is one of the greatest spectacles in the cactus family.

ECHITES (EK-i-teez)
Apocynaceae: The Oleander, Frangipani, Vinca
  Family
RUBBER VINE; DEVIL'S POTATO
Large twining vine with leathery leaves; nocturnal
  fragrant white flowers
Zones 10 and 11; marginal in zone 10a
Sun
Average but regular amounts of moisture
Average well-drained soil
Propagation by seed, sometimes cuttings

A genus of about six vining species in southern Florida, the West Indies, tropical Mexico, and northern South America. All the species are beautiful of leaf and flower and easy of culture, but only one is much planted or readily available.

Echites andrewsii. See *Urechites*.

Echites umbellata (um-bel-LAIT-a) is native to southern Florida, the West Indies, Central America, and northern South America. The vine climbs fast to 20 feet or more by twining around its support. The dark green leathery leaves are about 3 inches long and oblong in shape with notched ends, and bear a strong midvein; they are usually puckered into a trough to some degree. The flowers arise from the leaf axils in small clusters. They are half-inch-long narrow tubes whose ends flare into five glistening twisted white corolla lobes; they open at night and are very fragrant. The root is an enlarged tuber vaguely reminiscent of a potato. As one of the common names implies, all parts of this plant are poisonous.

EHRETIA (e-RET-ee-a / e-REET-ee-a)
Boraginaceae: The Heliotrope Family
Common names vary according to species
Small to medium-sized evergreen trees; white, pink,
  or yellow flowers; colorful blue fruit
Zones vary according to species
Sun
Average but regular amounts of moisture
Average well-drained soil
Propagation by seed and cuttings

A genus of about 50 species of deciduous or evergreen trees and shrubs found in the tropics and subtropics around the world. The flowers are small and are borne in clusters from the leaf axils; they are mostly white or pink, sometimes yellow. The fruits are berrylike and are red or blue, maturing to black.

Ehretia anacua (a-NAHK-wa) is native to southern and southeastern Texas and eastern Mexico and is hardy in zones 8 through 11. Vernacular names are anaqua and nockaway. This beautiful tree grows to as much as 50 feet in height with a fissured and cinnamon-colored to gray trunk and a fairly dense and rounded crown. The stiff and leathery olive green leaves are 3 or more inches long, elliptic to ovate in shape, and very rough on their upper surfaces, and whitish green and hairy on their lower surfaces. The leaves are only half evergreen in harsh and or exceptionally dry winters. The rounded to pyramidal flower clusters, which form in spring and sometimes also in the fall, are composed of many small five-petaled white starlike fragrant flowers. The effect is rather like that of a gigantic *Spiraea* or *Viburnum* bush in bloom. The fruits are red to yellowish orange single-seeded berries about a third of an inch in diameter and are said to be edible and sweet. The plant is drought tolerant when established but, like so many other trees, looks better and grows faster with an adequate and regular supply of moisture. This lovely tree is at present planted mainly in southeastern and southern Texas; it deserves much wider acceptance and distribution as it is beautiful in form, leaf, flower, fragrance, and fruit, and is easy of culture.

Ehretia microphylla (myk-ro-FYL-la) (synonyms *Carmona retusa*, *Ehretia buxifolia*) is native to India, Southeast Asia, and the Philippines, and is hardy in zones 10 and 11. It has several common names: Fukien tea, Philippine tea, and false tea, as the leaves can be used as a tea substitute. It is a graceful and quite attractive smooth-trunked little tree to 30 feet, which usually needs guidance when young to attain tree form. The 2- to 3-inch long leaves are obovate in shape and almost stalkless; they are clustered near the ends of the slender branches and are a dark green but have a silvery sheen because of the many short white hairs on their upper surfaces. The tree blooms all year with small and few-flowered clusters of starlike white to pinkish flowers. The fruit is a quarter-inch-wide yellow or red seedless berry, which matures to a lustrous dark blue. Unlike *E. anacua*, *E. microphylla* is not drought tolerant.

EICHORNIA (yk-HORN-ee-a)
Pontederiaceae: The Water-Hyacinth, Pickerel-Weed
  Family
WATER HYACINTH; WATER ORCHID
Floating plants; rosettes of round puckered leaves;
  large violet, blue, yellow orchidlike flowers
Zones 8b through 11
Sun to partial shade
Aquatic or bog plant or both
Rich, wet soil
Invasive

Propagation by root division, rhizome division, and
transplanting of suckers

A genus of seven species of floating, clustering plants
in South America (mainly Brazil), all with long fine
roots that tap the soil in shallow waterways. Besides sexual reproduction, the plants propagate themselves either by sending out runners in the water or by offsets
from the parent plants becoming detached. *Eichornia
crassipes* (KRAS-i-peez), the one species commonly
grown in the United States, is indigenous to shallow
and slow-moving watercourses in tropical South America. It also can occasionally be found and grows well in
boggy conditions as long as the soil is constantly moist.
It is one of the most beautiful aquatic plants because of
the gorgeous flowers; it also is invasive in warm climates
and can be (and has been) a problem for navigation
along watercourses in the Gulf Coast and other warm
areas. The leaves are in perfectly round rosettes and are
broadly ovate to round with the margins usually turned
up or twisted to create a more or less concave and puckered blade. As much as 5 inches long, each leaf is carried on a long petiole whose base is swollen and bulbous
and filled with porous tissue, which keeps the petiole,
leaf, and rosette afloat. The plants bloom in cycles all
through the warm periods of the year, and the flowers
are borne in erect spikes and open from bottom to top.
Each 3-inch flower has six light blue to lilac or lavender-colored petals. The uppermost petal bears a triangular
yellow spot surrounded by deep blue or purple feathery
markings. While these plants will usually survive temperatures of 20°F, they will only thrive and bloom well
in areas with summer heat. Plate 180.

ELAEIS (e-LEE-is)
Palmae (Arecaceae): The Palm Family
AFRICAN OIL PALM
Large feather-leaved palm with knobby picturesque
    trunk
Zones 10b and 11
Sun
Average but regular amounts of moisture
Average soil
Propagation by seed

A genus of only two pinnate-leaved palm species, one
in tropical West and Central Africa, the other in Central
America and the Amazon region of South America. The
South American palm is rarely planted. *Elaeis giuneensis* (gin-ay-EN-sis) is a massive and exotic looking
palm that grows to about 40 feet or so in cultivation in
the continental United States, but reaches 60 feet in its
native habitat and in other wet tropical regions. The
trunk is robust and as much as 2 feet in diameter, but
seems fairly slender because of the height of the palm. In
older palms the trunk is covered with the very picturesque scars from the old leaf bases, which give it a
knobby, chiseled look. The 16- to 18-foot long leaves
are especially graceful with their limp 2-foot-long leaf-

lets that create an almost plumose appearance to the leaf
as a whole, since they arise from the rachis at different
angles and are arranged in clusters. The leaf petioles are
spiny. Young immature plants do not have the graceful
beauty of older palms as the leaves are much stiffer and
do not arch as they do in older specimens. The palms
produce male and female flowers on the same plant.
The male flower clusters, which are dramatically different from the female flower clusters are to be found in
relatively short branched wormlike clusters, while the
female flowers are in dense broad clusters. The fruits
are beautiful, but have little effect in the landscape as
they are almost completely hidden in the crown of
leaves. Because of the valuable oils extracted from the
fruit of this palm, it is second in economic importance
only to the coconut, and large areas of the tropical world
are now devoted to plantations of this tree. This palm is
for large areas and hardly any planting is more beautiful
than a group of widely spaced individuals of varying
heights. It does not demand special treatment and,
other than its total intolerance of temperatures below
30°F, is easy to grow. It is one of the few palm species
that tolerates temporary flooding of its roots.

ENCEPHALARTOS
(en-sef´-a-LAHR-tos)
Zamiaceae: The Zamia (a Cycad) Family
Common names vary according to species
Trunked clustering palmlike; stiff prickly often bluish
    pinnate leaves; large colorful cones
Zones vary according to species
Sun to partial shade
Average but regular amounts of moisture
Moderately fertile, well-drained soil
Propagation by seed, transplanting of suckers, and
    (sometimes) transplanting of trunk buds

A genus of 50 or so cycad species, all in the southern
half of Africa, half of them endemic to South Africa. A
few of the species keep their trunks hidden beneath the
soil but most of them have obvious aboveground stems.
Most species are clustering or clumping and a few
branch and produce offsets from the trunk. None of the
species have true spines or thorns, but the leaves of almost all are very stiff, and the leaflets often have sharp
points along their margins or tips. In addition, most
species have leaves that are trough-shaped in cross section because the leaflets arise from the rachis at an
angle. Some species are drought tolerant, but all look
and grow better with adequate and regular supplies of
moisture. The male and female flowers are on separate
plants, and the cones exhibit every color of the rainbow.
The seeds in the female cones often are even more colorful than the cones that bear them. Some of the most
exotic-looking plant species are found in this genus, and
many of them are so unusual that they cry out for architectural placement in the landscape, sites where they
can be appreciated as garden sculpture and where their
unusual forms and colors can be seen to advantage.

Encephalartos altensteinii (ahl-ten-STYN-ee-eye) is a somewhat variable suckering species native to wooded areas of extreme southeastern South Africa where it is found in both exposed and shaded sites. It is hardy in zones 9b through 11. The plant slowly forms a trunk to as much as 15 feet in height with a crown of mostly erect leaves. The medium to dark green leaves are 6 to 9 feet long on mature plants, and the stiff and uncrowded leaflets are about 6 inches long and an inch wide with a few prickles on their margins. The leaf is not flat because the leaflets arise from the rachis at an angle, giving a slight trough shape to the leaf as a whole; the leaves tend to be flatter in shady sites than when they are grown in the sun. Both male and female cones are about 18 inches long and are yellowish brown in color, but the female cone is fatter than the male. This species grows well in sun or partial shade. The cycad is sometimes referred to as bread tree because the trunks are full of starch similar to that of *Metroxylon sagu* (sago palm). It has long been used by the native peoples of South Africa.

Encephalartos cupidus (KYOOP-i-dus) is endemic to grassy areas in northeastern South Africa and is hardy in zones 9b through 11. It is a small clustering trunkless species with a sparse and open crown of stiff bluish green trough-shaped leaves each of whose widely spaced linear-lanceolate leaflets bears half a dozen or so sharp prickles. The plant freely suckers and may have as many 10 heads in one clump. The cones are a bright, light green and about 10 inches long. The female cones are much stouter than the male cones. This very colorful species needs full sun.

Encephalartos cycadifolius (sy-kad´-i-FO-lee-us) is endemic to mountainous regions of southern South Africa and is hardy in zones 9 through 11. It is a clustering species with a short, usually branched trunk and a crown of stiff 3-foot-long dark green leaves that strongly resemble those of *Cycas revoluta* (sago palm), except that they are stiffer. The leaflets have no prickles, and the male and female cones are about a foot long and yellow to orange in color.

Encephalartos eugene-maraisii (yoo-jeen´-mar-AY-zee-eye) is endemic to mountainous areas of South Africa and is hardy in zones 9 through 11. This suckering species has trunks to 9 feet in height and full crowns of stiff 8-foot-long silvery-blue to bluish green trough-shaped leaves whose 8-inch-long leaflets are linear-oblong in shape with smooth margins. The cones are grayish green, but are covered with reddish brown hairs resulting in an overall cinnamon color effect; male cones are narrow and about 14 inches long, while female cones are almost 2 feet in length and quite stout.

Encephalartos ferox (FER-ahx) is indigenous to coastal areas of Natal (northeastern South Africa) and Mozambique and is hardy in zones 10 and 11. This exotic and colorful species very rarely makes an above-ground trunk but suckers from the base with age. The stiff, erect, bright green glossy leaves are 3 to 6 feet long and almost flat with widely spaced 6-inch-long elliptic-lanceolate leaflets. The leaflets are usually scalloped and toothed at their apices and have prickles on their margins that cause these leaflets to look like those of *Ilex aquifolia* (European holly). The spectacular cones are 14 to 18 inches long and may be yellow, orange, or pink but are usually scarlet. The male cones are linear, and the female cones are fat and shaped like large pine cones. Unlike many other plants in this genus, these plants are not drought tolerant and languish under such conditions. They grow in full sun or partial shade and are tolerant of saline air and soil. Plate 181.

Encephalartos gratus (GRAT-us) is native to southern Central Africa (Malawi and Mozambique) and is hardy in zones 10 and 11. It sometimes suckers, but is usually single-trunked. The stout stems reach 8 feet or so in height with great age. The leaf crown is full and dense with many 6-foot-long dark green, often somewhat twisted leaves composed of lanceolate to oblong spiny-tipped leaflets. The male cones are linear-cylindrical in shape and about a foot long, while the female cones are as much as 2 feet long and are much fatter; both are pinkish brown to orange-red in color. These wild and woolly looking cycads flourish in full sun or partial shade.

Encephalartos hildebrandtii (hil-de-BRANT-ee-eye) is indigenous to Tanzania and Kenya and is hardy in zones 10 and 11. This large species can, in time, make a trunk to 15 feet or more in height; it is single-trunked for many years but eventually suckers. The leaf crown is full with many 8-foot-long almost flat bright green leaves composed of 6-inch-long lanceolate to oblong sparsely toothed leaflets; the plant looks more like a palm than do most other species, although the leaves are mostly erect and stiff.

Encephalartos horridus (HAHR-i-dus) is endemic to the scrub regions of southernmost South Africa and is hardy in zones 9b through 11. It is a suckering species, but does not usually form a trunk. The leaf crown is open and erect. The 3-foot-long leaves are a silvery blue to almost purple when they first unfold and slowly change to an icy blue or bluish green; they are recurved at the tips. The usually puckered leaflets are 4 inches long and lobed. Each lobe is tipped (as is the leaf margin) with sharp spines. The leaflets arise from the leaf rachis at several different angles, resulting in a leaf appearance that is unmistakable because of its color and form. The cones are about 14 inches long and yellowish green overlain with brownish red hairs. The male cones are more slender than the female cones. These plants need full sun to attain the best coloring; they are tolerant of average soil, but must have excellent drainage. The species is the most architectural cycad and needs a site appropriate to its exotic coloring and form. Plate 182.

Encephalartos latifrons (LAT-i-frahnz) is endemic to the scrub regions of southeastern South Africa and is hardy in zones 9b through 11. This beautiful and large species eventually forms a stout trunk to 8 or even 10 feet in height; it freely suckers when mature. The 7- to 8-foot-long leaves are glossy and dark green in color, V-shaped in cross section, and stiff and recurved at their ends. The 6-inch-long leaflets are deeply lobed, toothed, and puckered and are similar in appearance to those of *Ilex aquifolium* (European holly) and to those of *E. horridus* in shape. The cones are a deep olive green in color and are 18 inches to 2 feet long. The female cones are fatter than the male cones. This beautiful species is endangered in its native habitat and is rare in cultivation but is worth the search. There is something most alluring about the stiff curl of the leaves and the noble proportions of the trunk. It grows in sun or partial shade and is not particular as to soil as long as it is well draining.

Encephalartos lehmannii (lay-MAHN-nee-eye) is endemic to arid regions of South Africa and is hardy in zones 9 through 11. This small attractive clustering and suckering species has a short fat gray trunk and beautiful blue-green leaves. The 5-foot-long troughed stiff and erect leaves are recurved near their ends, and the 6-inch-long leaflets are mostly free of teeth. The cones are also bluish green and about 18 inches long with the usual phenomenon of the female cones being fatter than the male cones. This species is drought tolerant and happy on alkaline or neutral pH soils but demands perfect drainage. Plate 183.

Encephalartos longifolius (lahn-ji-FO-lee-us) is endemic to scrub and arid regions of southern South Africa and is hardy in zones 9b through 11. It is a large and beautiful species with a big crown of many leaves atop a fat and clustering trunk that can attain a height of 12 feet or more. The 6-foot-long leaves are deeply troughed and are a deep bluish green in color. The 8-inch-long leaflets are ovate-lanceolate in shape and have no teeth or prickles. The 2-foot-long cones are a deep olive green to tan in color, and the male cone is quite slender compared to the massive female cone. The trunks of this species have, like those of *E. altensteinii,* a starchy pith from which the aboriginal peoples made a type of bread. This species is drought tolerant when established.

Encephalartos natalensis (nah´-ta-LEN-sis) is endemic to Natal and Zululand in eastern South Africa and is hardy in zones 9b through 11. It is a large species with a very full and large crown of 9-foot-long dark green flat to slightly troughed leaves atop a usually solitary dark-colored trunk. The 10-inch-long leaflets are linear-elliptic to broadly lanceolate in shape and have a few short prickles along their margins. The cones are a deep yellow in color and are 18 inches to 2 feet long. The plant needs full sun to flourish. It is a very noble and majestic-looking cycad.

Encephalartos transvenosus (trans-ve-NO-sus) is endemic to east-central South Africa and is hardy in zones 10 and 11. It is the tallest growing and one of the fastest growing species in the genus and is known to attain a height of 40 feet in its native habitat. The crown is dense with many 8-foot-long bright green flat leaves consisting of 10-inch-long linearly ovate to lanceolate slightly toothed leaflets. The trunks sucker only with age and then sparsely. The cones are a deep golden brown and may be as long as 2 feet, the female cone stouter than the male cone.

Encephalartos trispinosus (try-spin-O-sus) is endemic to extreme southern South Africa and is adaptable to zones 9b through 11. It slowly forms a trunk as much as 3 feet in height and suckers freely after the trunk becomes apparent. It is a variable species with leaves that are always quite dramatic in appearance. Usually 4 to 6 feet long, the leaves are much recurved and a beautiful light blue-green or grayish green in color. The 6- to 8-inch-long leaflets are basically lance-shaped, and the lower parts of the leaflets usually have one or more large lobes. The cones are a bright yellow, with the female cones significantly larger than the males.

ENELLAGMA. See *Amphitecna.*

ENSETE (en-SET-ee)
Musaceae: The Banana Family
ABYSSINIAN BANANA; BLACK BANANA
Palmlike plants; very stout trunks and immense
    banana-like leaves often tinged with red
Zones 10 and 11 as permanent landscape subjects;
    zone 9b as returning perennials
Sun
Water lover
Rich, moist, well-drained soil
Propagation not practical for the home gardener

A genus of seven species of banana-like plants in tropical Africa and tropical Asia. Unlike true bananas (genus *Musa*), these plants are monocarpic and are never suckering. The trunks are relatively short and very stout compared to those of bananas, and the giant leaves are spirally arranged at the top of the stem. The flowers and fruit appear in great pendent grayish green to brown masses, and the fruit is not edible. Only one species is common in cultivation. *Ensete ventricosum* (ven-tri-KO-sum) (synonyms *Musa arnoldiana, M. ensete*) is native to tropical East Africa. The trunks attain a height of 40 feet in their native habitat, but are usually no more than 10 feet tall in cultivation. The leaves are as much as 20 feet long, usually no more than 12 feet, and are broader than most banana leaves. They are a deep green in color with a stout reddish midrib. *Ensete ventricosum* 'Maurellii' has leaves tinged with red, especially on their undersurfaces. These giants are among the most tropical looking subjects for the warm-climate gardener with enough space to accommodate them. They need protection from strong wind lest the leaves become tattered, they do not flourish without an abundant and regular supply of moisture and, while they grow in partial shade, they only look their best with full sun. The plants will lose their leaves when the temperature reaches 28°F, die to the ground from temperatures of 25°F or below, but come back if the temperature does not fall below about 22°F and the freeze is not prolonged. Plate 184.

Plate 1. *Acacia farnesiana.* Leu Gardens, Orlando, Florida

Plate 2. *Acalypha hispida.* Edison estate, Fort Myers, Florida

Plate 3. *Acalypha wilkesiana* 'Godseffiana'.
Houston, Texas

Plate 4. *Acoelorraphe wrightii.* Fairchild Tropical Garden, Miami,
Florida

Plate 5. *Acrocomia totai.* Ganna Walska Lotus Land, Santa Barbara, California. Photo by Steven Timbrook

Plate 6. *Acrostichum danaeifolium.* Edison estate, Fort Myers, Florida

Plate 7. *Adansonia digitata.* Homestead, Florida

Plate 8. *Adansonia digitata* inflorescence. Coconut Grove, Florida. Photo by Larry Schokman

Plate 9. *Adenium obesum* var. *multiflorum.* Earth Star Nursery, Houston, Texas

Plate 11. *Aechmea nidularioides* inflorescence. Photo by Jim Racca

Plate 10. *Aechmea chantinii* × *A. mariae-reginae.* Photo by Jim Racca

Plate 12. *Aechmea retusa.* Photo by Jim Racca

Plate 13. *Agave americana*. Ruth Bancroft Garden, Walnut Creek, California. Photo by Diane Laird

Plate 14. *Agave americana*, type and variegated. Leu Gardens, Orlando, Florida

Plate 15. *Agave attenuata*. Fairchild Tropical Garden, Miami, Florida

Plate 16. *Agave ferox* with *A. americana* inflorescence in background. Ruth Bancroft Garden, Walnut Creek, California. Photo by Diane Laird

Plate 17. *Agave parryi* in native habitat. Photo by Sean Hogan

Plate 18. *Agave victoriae-reginae.* Ruth Bancroft Garden, Walnut Creek, California. Photo by Diane Laird

Plate 19. *Aiphanes erosa.* Leu Gardens, Orlando, Florida

Plate 20. *Albizia julibrissin.* Houston, Texas

Plate 21. *Aleurites moluccana.* The Kampong, Coconut Grove, Florida

Plate 22. *Aleurites moluccana* leaves. The Kampong, Coconut Grove, Florida

Plate 23. *Allamanda cathartica* 'Hendersonii'. Author's garden, Houston, Texas

Plate 24. *Alocasia cucullata.* Fairchild Tropical Garden, Miami, Florida

Plate 25. *Alocasia macrorrhiza.* Fairchild Tropical Garden, Miami, Florida

Plate 26. *Alocasia sanderiana*. Author's garden, Houston, Texas

Plate 27. *Aloe arborescens* × *A. ferox* and *Agave attenuata*. Ganna Walska Lotus Land, Santa Barbara, California. Photo by Steven Timbrook

Plate 28. *Aloe barbadensis* with *Pereskia grandifolia* in bloom. Alton Marshal garden, Houston, Texas

Plate 29. *Aloe excelsa*. Parrot Jungle, Miami, Florida

Plate 30. *Aloe ferox*. Parrot Jungle, Miami, Florida

Plate 31. *Aloe marlothii*. Earth Star Succulents Nursery, Houston, Texas

Plate 32. *Aloe plicatilis*. Strybing Arboretum, San Francisco, California

Plate 33. *Aloe speciosa*. South Africa. Photo by Sean Hogan

Plate 35. *Alpinia purpurata*. Fairchild Tropical Garden, Miami, Florida

Plate 34. *Alpinia calcarata*. Houston, Texas

Plate 36. *Alpinia sanderae*. Mercer Arboretum, Houston, Texas

Plate 37. *Alpinia zerumbet*. Author's garden, Houston, Texas

Plate 38. *Alpinia zerumbet* 'Variegata'. Author's garden, Houston, Texas

Plate 39. *Amherstia nobilis* inflorescence. Sri Lanka. Photo by Larry Schokman

Plate 40. *Ananas bracteatus* var. *albomarginata.* Photo by Jim Racca

Plate 41. *Ananas comosus* var. *variegata.* Leu Gardens, Orlando, Florida

Plate 42. *Androlepis skinneri*. Fairchild Tropical Garden, Miami, Florida

Plate 43. *Angiopteris evecta*. Parrot Jungle, Miami, Florida

Plate 44. *Annona squamosa*. The Kampong, Coconut Grove, Florida. Photo by Larry Schokman

Plate 45. *Anthurium andraeanum* hybrid. Leu Gardens, Orlando, Florida

Plate 46. *Anthurium andraeanum* hybrid. Leu Gardens, Orlando, Florida

Plate 47. *Anthurium clarinervum.* Cornelius Nursery, Houston, Texas

Plate 48. *Antidesma bunius.* The Kampong, Coconut Grove, Florida

Plate 49. *Antigonon leptopus.* Mercer Arboretum, Houston, Texas

Plate 50. *Archontophoenix cunninghamiana.* Miami, Florida

Plate 51. *Arenga engleri.* Fairchild Tropical Garden, Miami, Florida

Plate 52. *Argyreia nervosa.* Homestead, Florida. Photo by Roger Hammer

Plate 53. *Aristolochia elegans.* Largo, Florida. Photo by Tom Kiehl

Plate 54. *Aristolochia grandiflora.* Photo by Larry Schokman.

Plate 55. *Asplenium nidus.* Ganna Walska Lotus Land, Santa Barbara, California. Photo by Steven Timbrook

Plate 56. *Astrocaryum alatum.* Fairchild Tropical Garden, Miami, Florida

Plate 57. *Avicennia nitida* trunks and pneumatophores. Selby Botanic Garden, Sarasota, Florida

Plate 58. *Bambusa multiplex*. Author's garden, Houston, Texas

Plate 59. *Barleria cristata*. Mounts Botanic Garden, West Palm Beach, Florida

Plate 60. *Bauhinia ×blakeana*. Brownsville, Texas

Plate 61. *Bauhinia forficata*. Alton Marshall garden, Houston, Texas

Plate 62. *Bauhinia punctata*. The Kampong, Coconut Grove, Florida. Photo by Larry Schokman

Plate 63. *Beaucarnea recurvata* in bloom. Parrot Jungle, Miami, Florida

Plate 64. *Beaucarnea stricta*. Ganna Walska Lotus Land, Santa Barbara, California. Photo by Steven Timbrook

Plate 65. *Beaumontia grandiflora*. Homestead, Florida. Photo by Roger Hammer

Plate 66. *Begonia rex* hybrid. Cornelius Nursery, Houston, Texas

Plate 67. *Berrya cordifolia*. Photo by Larry Schokman

Plate 68. *Berrya cordifolia* leaves and flowers. Photo by Larry Schokman

Plate 69. *Bixa orellana*. Fruit and Spice Park, Homestead, Florida

Plate 70. *Bocconia arborea*. Sinaloa State, Mexico

Plate 71. *Bombax ceiba*. The Kampong, Coconut Grove, Florida. Photo by Larry Schokman

Plate 72. *Borassus aethiopium.* Fairchild Tropical Garden, Miami, Florida

Plate 73. *Borassus flabellifer.* Brownsville, Texas

Plate 74. *Bougainvillea.* Gladys Porter Zoo, Brownsville, Texas

Plate 75. *Brahea armata.* Corpus Christi, Texas

Plate 76. *Brahea brandegeei.* Moody Gardens, Galveston, Texas

Plate 77. *Bromelia balansae.* Photo by Jim Racca

Plate 78. *Brownea grandiceps.* The Kampong, Coconut Grove, Florida. Photo by Larry Schokman

Plate 79. *Brugmansia suaveolens* hybrid. Alton Marshall garden, Houston, Texas

Plate 80. *Brugmansia versicolor.* The Kampong, Coconut Grove, Florida. Photo by Larry Schokman

Plate 82. *Bulnesia arborea* flowers and leaves. Homestead, Florida. Photo by Roger Hammer

Plate 81. *Bulnesia arborea.* The Kampong, Coconut Grove, Florida. Photo by Larry Schokman

Plate 83. *Butea monosperma.* The Kampong, Coconut Grove, Florida. Photo by Larry Schokman

Plate 84. ×*Butiagrus.* Growers' Mart, Houston, Texas

Plate 86. *Caladium* cultivar. Author's garden, Houston, Texas

Plate 87. *Calathea roseopicta.* Author's garden, Houston, Texas

Plate 85. *Caesalpinia pulcherrima.* Houston, Texas

Plate 88. *Calathea warscewiczii.* Leu Gardens, Orlando, Florida

Plate 89. *Calathea zebrina* cultivar. Leu Gardens, Orlando, Florida

Plate 91. *Calliandra haematocephala.* Edison estate, Fort Myers, Florida

Plate 90. *Calliandra emarginata.* Author's garden, Houston, Texas

Plate 92. *Calliandra haematocephala* flower. The Kampong, Coconut Grove, Florida. Photo by Larry Schokman

Plate 93. *Calliandra surinamensis.* The Kampong, Coconut Grove, Florida. Photo by Larry Schokman

Plate 94. *Calophyllum inophyllum.* Fairchild Tropical Garden, Miami, Florida

Plate 95. *Cananga odorata.* Roger Hammer garden, Homestead, Florida

Plate 96. *Cananga odorata* flowers. The Kampong, Coconut Grove, Florida

Plate 97. *Canella winterana.* The Kampong, Coconut Grove, Florida. Photo by Larry Schokman

Plate 98. *Carica papaya.* Brownsville, Texas

Plate 99. *Carissa macrocarpa.* Galveston, Texas

Plate 100. *Carludovica palmata.* Homestead, Florida. Photo by Roger Hammer

Plate 101. *Carnegiea gigantea.* Organ Pipe Cactus National Monument, Arizona

Plate 102. *Cassia alata.* Roger Hammer garden, Homestead, Florida

Plate 121. *Clerodendrum minahassae*. Author's garden, Houston, Texas

Plate 122. *Clerodendrum minahassae* in fruit. Homestead, Florida

Plate 123. *Clerodendrum paniculatum*. The Kampong, Coconut Grove, Florida. Photo by Larry Schokman

Plate 125. *Clerodendrum ×speciosum*. The Kampong, Coconut Grove, Florida. Photo by Larry Schokman

Plate 124. *Clerodendrum quadriloculare*. The Kampong, Coconut Grove, Florida. Photo by Larry Schokman

Plate 126. *Clerodendrum thomsoniae.* Heathcote Botanic Garden, Fort Pierce, Florida

Plate 127. *Clerodendrum ugandense.* Selby Botanic Garden, Sarasota, Florida

Plate 128. *Clivia miniata.* Alton Marshall garden, Houston, Texas

Plate 130. *Clusia rosea* leaves and fruit. The Kampong, Coconut Grove, Florida. Photo by Larry Schokman

Plate 129. *Clusia rosea.* Fairchild Tropical Garden, Miami, Florida

Plate 131. *Coccoloba pubescens.* Roger Hammer garden, Homestead, Florida

Plate 161. *Dasylirion longissimum* inflorescence. Photo by Sean Hogan

Plate 163. *Delonix regia* trunk and form. The Kampong, Coconut Grove, Florida

Plate 162. *Delonix regia* in full bloom. Photo by Larry Schokman

Plate 164. *Delonix regia* flowers and leaves. Homestead, Florida. Photo by Roger Hammer

Plate 165. *Dendrocalamus strictus.* Edison estate, Fort Myers, Florida

Plate 167. *Dictyosperma album* crownshaft. Selby Botanic Garden, Sarasota, Florida

Plate 166. *Deuterocohnia schreiteri.* Selby Botanic Garden, Sarasota, Florida

Plate 168. *Dieffenbachia* cultivars. Parrot Jungle, Miami, Florida

Plate 169. *Dillenia indica.* Edison estate, Fort Myers, Florida

Plate 170. *Dioon spinulosum.* San Antonio Botanic Gardens, San Antonio, Texas

Plate 171. *Dioon spinulosum* with female cone. Fairchild Tropical Garden, Miami, Florida

Plate 172. *Dioscorea bulbifera.* Maas Nursery, Seabrook, Texas

Plate 173. *Dombeya* 'Seminole' hybrid. Parrot Jungle, Miami, Florida

Plate 174. *Dombeya wallichii*. Edison estate, Fort Myers, Florida

Plate 175. *Dracaena draco* in mass planting. Ganna Walska Lotus Land, Santa Barbara, California. Photo by Steven Timbrook

Plate 204. *Ficus benghalensis* trunks. Edison estate, Fort Myers, Florida

Plate 205. *Ficus benjamina.* Parrot Jungle, Miami, Florida

Plate 206. *Ficus macrophylla.* Selby Botanic Garden, Sarasota, Florida

Plate 207. *Ficus mysorensis* trunk and root system. Edison estate, Fort Myers, Florida

Plate 208. *Ficus pseudopalma.* Fruit and Spice Park, Homestead, Florida

Plate 209. *Filicium decipiens* leaves. Selby Botanic Garden, Sarasota, Florida

Plate 211. *Gardenia taitensis.* Homestead, Florida. Photo by Roger Hammer

Plate 210. *Fouquieria splendens.* Photo by Sean Hogan

Plate 212. *Globba wintii.* Mercer Arboretum, Houston, Texas

Plate 213. *Gordonia lasianthus.* Newton Nursery, Houston, Texas

Plate 214. *Graptophyllum pictum.* Fairchild Tropical Garden, Miami, Florida

Plate 215. *Guaiacum officinale* leaves, flowers, and fruit. The Kampong, Coconut Grove, Florida. Photo by Larry Schokman

Plate 216. *Guaiacum sanctum.* Homestead, Florida. Photo by Roger Hammer

Plate 218. *Guzmania conifera.* Photo by Jim Racca

Plate 217. *Guihaia argyrata.* Fairchild Tropical Garden, Miami, Florida

Plate 219. *Guzmania lingulata* 'Superb'. Photo by Jim Racca

Plate 221. *Harpullia pendula* fruit. The Kampong, Coconut Grove, Florida. Photo by Larry Schokman

Plate 220. *Hamelia patens.* Author's garden, Houston, Texas

Plate 223. *Hedychium gardnerianum.* Alton Marshall garden, Houston, Texas

Plate 222. *Hechtia marnier-lapostollei.* Photo by Jim Racca

Plate 273. *Manihot esculenta* 'Variegata'. Mercer Arboretum, Houston, Texas

Plate 274. *Manilkara roxburghiana*. Fairchild Tropical Garden, Miami, Florida

Plate 275. *Manilkara zapota*. The Kampong, Coconut Grove, Florida. Photo by Larry Schokman

Plate 276. *Maranta leuconeura* var. *erythroneura*. Author's garden, Houston, Texas

Plate 277. *Markhamia obtusifolia*. Photo by Larry Schokman

Plate 278. *Medinilla magnifica*. The Kampong, Coconut Grove, Florida. Photo by Larry Schokman

Plate 279. *Megaskepasma erythrochlamys*. Roger Hammer garden, Homestead, Florida

Plate 280. *Miconia calvescens*. The Kampong, Coconut Grove, Florida

Plate 281. *Monstera deliciosa*. Author's garden, Houston, Texas

Plate 282. *Mucuna bennettii* inflorescence. Photo by Larry Schokman

ENTEROLOBIUM
(ent´-e-ro-LOAB-ee-um)
Mimosaceae (Fabaceae, Leguminosae), subfamily
    Mimosoideae: The Mimosa Family
ELEPHANT'S-EAR TREE; CONACASTE
Massive spreading, white-trunked tree; ferny green
    foliage; white flowers; coiled seed pods
Zones 10 and 11; marginal in zone 10a
Sun
Average but regular amounts of moisture
Average soil

A small genus of about six tree species in tropical
America from Mexico and the West Indies down to Argentina. They are all large and beautiful trees, but only
two of the species are in cultivation and only one of
those is common. The genus is closely allied to *Albizia*.
The great light-colored and smooth trunks form buttresses with time. The leaves are large, bright green, and
bipinnate, consisting of many small leaflets. The very
essence of airy gracefulness, they are deciduous in areas
where there are winter dry seasons, and cold also defoliates them. No species shows any real tolerance to
freezing temperatures. The tiny flowers are in dense
balls of greenish white blossoms which, like the other
members of the family, are mostly stamens (the petals
being minuscule) and appear in spring at or near the
time of releafing if the trees lose their leaves; they are
not particularly showy. The fruits are coiled and segmented pods that are dark brown or black and shiny
when mature and quite ornamental; they are said to be
edible and palatable to humans and are much used for
feeding livestock in the trees' native habitats. They are
very fast growing, easy of culture, and free of major
pests. These are trees that define the terms "tropical
looking" and "venerable." While they lose limbs to hurricanes and have aggressive root systems, they should
nevertheless not be shunned for planting in large areas
as they give canopy and beauty to a world whose trust
fund of these attributes is all too quickly dwindling.
There are much worse things in life than having to deal
with fallen limbs; lack of beauty is one of them.

Enterolobium contortisiliquum (kon-tort´-i-si-
LIK-wum) is native to southern Brazil, northern Argentina, and adjacent Paraguay. It is a massive tree,
growing to a height of 75 or 80 feet with an equal spread
and an immense trunk to more than 6 feet in diameter
although it usually branches low. The bark is mostly
smooth and a light gray to almost pure white in color; it
is also wrinkled and somewhat reminiscent of an elephant's hide, especially at the juncture of branch and
trunk. The pods of this species form incomplete circles.
Plate 185.

Enterolobium cyclocarpum (syk-lo-KARP-um)
is widespread from the West Indies, Mexico, Central
America, and northern South America. It is an even
larger growing species than *E. contortisiliquum* and can
attain a height of 100 feet or more with an equal spread.
It is much more commonly planted than is *E. contor-*

tisiliquum, but in most other respects is quite similar except that its pods are coiled into a complete or nearly
complete circle.

Enterolobium saman. See *Samanea saman.*

EPIPHYLLUM (ep-i-FYL-lum)
Cactaceae: The Cactus Family
ORCHID CACTUS
Spineless flat-stemmed sprawling epiphytic cactuses;
    large fragrant flowers, some nocturnal
Zones 10 and 11
Partial shade to partial sun
Average but regular amounts of moisture
Rich, porous, humusy soil or leaf mold
Propagation by cuttings

A small genus of about 15 species in Mexico, Central
America, and South America. They grow mainly on
fairly large trees on which have formed pockets of soil or
leaf mold in crotches or other depressions. All have
green, flat or sometimes rounded, leaflike stems usually scalloped to some extent on the margins; some
species having very deep marginal lobes. They, with
several other cactus genera, are sometimes called "leaf
cactus" because the plant bodies, the stems, look much
like leaves, although they do not form true leaves. The
stems usually grow no more than 3 feet or so in length,
but occasionally attain twice this length, or even more.
They do not climb but rather lean against their supports
and may be tied up on a support like a tree trunk.

These plants are grown not for the cactus bodies,
even though they are attractive, but for the large (4 to 6
inches in width) and spectacular flowers they produce.
The plants bloom in spring, summer, and fall. The flowers arise singly from the sides of the stems and consist of
a long tube at the end of which is the large spreading
cup of many flaring silky petals and sepals; in the center
of this cup are the many stamens and the single stigma.
The flower colors range from white to cream to yellow
and orange and even pale violet, most white-colored
species having blossoms that open only after dark and
close with the return of bright sunlight and heat.

As beautiful as the blossoms of these species are, they
somewhat pale compared to the flowers of the hybrids
between *Epiphyllum* and various other soft-bodied, similarly shaped, and closely allied cactus genera. These hybrids are placed in the genus *Phyllocactus* and sometimes
in *Epicactus*. The other parent genus is usually *Aporocactus, Disocactus, Heliocereus, Hylocereus, Nopalxochia*
(another leaf cactus genus), *Nyctocereus,* or *Selenicereus.*
All these hybrid plants have plant bodies more similar to
those of *Epiphyllum* than to the other parent, have the
same cultural requirements, and need similar growing
conditions and sites. Every color and hue of the rainbow is represented in the flowers of these hybrids except true blue, and the flowers are often of exceptional
size. All the hybrids produce diurnal flowers.

While considered succulents, these cactus species are
not drought tolerant and need a regular supply of water,

especially when they are actively growing and producing flowers in the warm months of the year. They also need a very friable, porous soil (the addition of leaf mold is perfect) and one that is on the acidic side and drains freely; without perfect drainage the plants are subject to root rot. Although the plants burn in full sun, especially in hot regions, they need adequate light levels to bloom. Very bright shade is perfect as is gentle early morning sun or late afternoon sun. Plates 186 and 187.

EPIPREMNUM (ep-i-PREM-num)
Araceae: The Calla Lily, Jack-in-the-Pulpit Family
POTHOS; GOLDEN POTHOS; DEVIL'S IVY
High-climbing vines with clinging roots; immense
    mature variegated and lobed leaves
Zones 10 and 11
Partial shade to sun
Water lovers
Rich, moist, well-drained soil
Propagation by cuttings

A genus of about eight species of very large climbers in Southeast Asia, the Philippines, Indonesia, Malaysia, and the islands of the South Pacific. The genus is allied to *Monstera*, *Pothos*, *Rhaphidophora*, and *Scindapsus*, and the members of one genus are often mistaken for those of one or more of the others. All have large to very large leaves whose juvenile forms are markedly different from the mature leaves; juvenile leaves are smaller and not lobed, whereas the mature leaves are lobed and gigantic. In reality it would seem that the leaf form, juvenile or mature, is not so much a function of age as it is of environment: the leaves never assume mature form, no matter how old the plant is, unless the plant climbs into nearly full sunlight. All species travel over large areas of ground until they reach a support upon which to ascend. These beauties climb by means of aerial rootlets growing directly from their often very thick stems. Fortunately, cuttings taken from the climbing stems tend to keep the large mature leaf form even when they can no longer climb. The inflorescence is typical of the family, with the spathe being early deciduous. As container and indoor subjects, these plants are abused and allowed to dry out almost completely between waterings. They usually survive such neglect but do not thrive; they are denizens of tropical rain forests. They grow well in partial shade to almost deep shade, but only attain their maximum size and form with sunlight for at least part of the day. Only two species are common in cultivation; one of them is very common as a house and indoor plant. All create the very essence of the tropical look: lushness, boldness, drama, yet with grace and delicacy.

Epipremnum aureum (AW-ree-um / OW-ree-um) (synonyms *Pothos aureus*, *Rhaphidophora aurea*, *Scindapsus aureus*) is native to the Solomon Islands in the South Pacific, northeast of Australia. The juvenile leaves are 4 to 8 inches long and heart-shaped with a tapered tip, and are usually variegated with yellow streaks and blotches. In this form it is perhaps the most common and widespread houseplant, especially in hanging baskets; it is also one of the most common lianas in the tropics. Mature leaves are 3 feet or more in length, oblong in outline, heart-shaped at their bases and deeply lobed into mostly oblong and apically truncated segments. The shapes of these mature leaves are reminiscent of those of *Monstera deliciosa* and are often mistaken for the variegated form of the latter species. There are several cultivars that vary in the amount and pattern of leaf variegation. The plant is gorgeous when climbing and makes a wonderful groundcover in tropical areas; it climbs anything it reaches except for very smooth and hard surfaces like the links in a chainlink fence or any other substrate into which the aerial rootlets cannot penetrate. Plate 188.

Epipremnum pinnatum (pin-NAIT-um) (synonym *Rhaphidophora pinnatum*) is indigenous to the Philippines, Malaysia, and down into the wet tropical area of northern Australia (Queensland). Mature leaves are solid dark green, 3 feet or more in length, and elliptic to oblong in outline, with regularly spaced curved lobes cut almost to the midrib. This species looks even more like *Monstera deliciosa* than does *E. aureum*. Plate 189.

EPISCIA
(e-PISH-ya / e-PIS-see-a / e-PIS-kee-a)
Gesneriaceae: The Gloxinia (Sinningia) Family
CARPET PLANT; LOVEJOY
Herbaceous creeping perennials; velvety, often
    variegated paired leaves; tubular flowers
Zones 10b and 11
Partial shade to partial sun
Water lovers
Rich, porous, humusy, well-drained soil or leaf mold
Propagation by root division, rhizome division, and
    cuttings

A genus of six species of herbs in tropical America. They have oppositely arranged hairy leaves and small clusters of beautiful trumpet-shaped flowers. They are small plants, seldom growing to more than a foot in height. All species send out creeping stolons that root at the tips and start another tuft of plant, thus making the genus superb for groundcovers.

The exquisite leaves are covered in a short silky tomentum, which makes them velvety to the touch and appearance. They are heart-shaped to elliptic (sometimes almost round) and puckered, with depressed veins above (which are often colored differently from the rest of the leaf), and are from 2 to 6 inches long. The leaves are arranged like those of most Labiatae (mint family) species: they grow in pairs of oppositely arranged leaves, each pair forming at a 90° angle to the pair beneath it. Leaf colors range from mint green to deep green and bronzy brown, and the main veins are often colored yellow or white; some leaves have a combination of these colors, some are variegated with white, yellow, or pinkish splotches, and some leaves are also colored purple beneath. There are no more beautiful leaves in any plant genus. The flowers are like those of African violets in shape, arrangement, and colors: small tubes whose ends flare into five contiguous lobes in colors of white, yellow, orange, pink, and red. Some petals are fringed and scalloped on their margins, and some are bi-colored.

These plants are completely intolerant of drought conditions and must have regular and ample supplies of moisture. In addition they relish and flourish in ambient air that is high in relative humidity. They do not tolerate full midday sun, especially in the hotter areas; but, at the same time, they need bright light to grow and bloom well. They thrive with regular applications of half-strength fish emulsion in spring, summer, and autumn. They are completely tropical in nature, and frost is anathema; indeed, temperatures below 40°F are not good. There are no more beautiful groundcovers for the gardener in tropical or frost-free climes than these little plants.

ERIOBOTRYA (er´-ee-o-BOAT-ree-a)
Rosaceae: The Rose Family
LOQUAT
Small trees; large deeply veined leaves; panicles of
    rose and white fragrant flowers; golden fruit
Zones vary according to species
Sun
Average but regular amounts of moisture
Average soil
Propagation by seed; cultivars are grafted

A genus of 10 evergreen shrubs and trees in the Himalayas, China, Japan, and Taiwan. They all have relatively large and leathery somewhat brittle leaves with strong veining, furry panicles of small usually fragrant five-petaled flowers with long stamens reminiscent of single roses, and relatively large fruit.

Eriobotrya deflexa (dee-FLEX-a) is native to Taiwan and adjacent mainland China, and is hardy in zones 8 through 11. It grows to 15 or sometimes 20 feet in height and should be trained when young if a tree form is wanted. New growth is covered in a beautiful rusty pubescence. The leaves are almost stalkless, 10 inches long, oblong to obovate in shape and pointed at the ends, with small indentations along the leaf margins. The new leaves are a beautiful copper to rosy copper in color, which they retain for some time before turning a dark and glossy green. The trees bloom in early spring with terminal panicles of small white slightly fragrant flowers. The fruit is about an inch wide, dark olive green changing to a dull orange; it is not, unlike the other commonly planted species, palatable. The species is sometimes called the bronze loquat because of the color of the new leaves. It makes an especially attractive large shrub or small tree, which should be sited to be seen close up; it also makes a wonderful espalier subject. There are several naturally occurring varieties of this tree that vary in size of leaf and fruit.

Eriobotrya japonica (ja-PAHN-i-ka) is indigenous to eastern China and southern Japan and is hardy in zones 7 through 11, although not as a fruiting tree in zones 7 and 8. This wonderfully tropical looking little tree is nevertheless quite hardy to cold. It grows to 20 feet or more with a short thick trunk, dense and spreading crown, and heavy ascending branches. The 12-inch-long deep green, rough, and deeply veined leaves are toothed on their margins and grayish pubescent on their undersides. Borne in early winter to early spring, the flowers are in pyramidal 6-inch-high panicles whose stems are covered in orange to rust-colored tomentum. Each little flower is like a white or rosy-white tiny single-flowered rose with a roselike fragrance. The time of flowering is unfortunate for the colder zones in which the tree grows because it usually means that the flowers are damaged by cold and do not set fruit; abortion of fruit and flowers often occurs even in zone 9a. The fruits are generally 1 to 2 inches wide and a deep yellow to a deep gold in color. They are edible and are sweetly acid and juicy. Several grafted cultivars on the market have varying degrees of acidity and sweetness of the fruit. Ornamentally the tree is hard to beat and is best planted where its beauty can be seen close up as a small shade or fruit tree; like *E. deflexa* it makes an excellent and dramatic espalier subject, and few such subjects are as beautiful when in fruit. It is sometimes called the Japanese medlar.

ERVATAMIA. See *Tabernaemontana.*

ERYTHEA. See *Brahea.*

ERYTHRINA (er-i-TRY-na)
Papilionaceae (Fabaceae, Leguminosae), subfamily
    Papilionoideae: The Bean, Pea Family
CORAL TREES
Shrubs to medium-sized trees; leaves of 3 broad
    leaflets; racemes of yellow, red, and orange flowers
Zones vary according to species
Sun
Average but regular amounts of moisture; some are
    drought tolerant when established
Average soil
Propagation by seed and cuttings

A large genus of about 100 species of shrubs and trees in tropical and subtropical regions around the world. All are thorny to some extent and have trifoliate leaves with the terminal leaflet usually larger than the other two. Many hail from semiarid areas with distinct dry seasons and, under such conditions, are deciduous and drought tolerant; others need an adequate and regular supply of moisture. All grow relatively fast with regular watering, and some grow very fast. Some species are indigenous to elevated regions and do not flourish in hot lowland areas with high relative humidity, although they grow and survive in such areas and often bloom well. All have relatively spectacular displays of terminal clusters of red or orange modified pealike flowers; usually one petal, the "banner," is much larger than the others and is boat-shaped. The flower spikes are erect except when they are so large as to bend over; many bloom in spring or summer, but many others bloom in winter and spring or even year-round. The flowers in each inflorescence open from the bottom upwards, and many have a candelabra shape. When in bloom, all the species attract hummingbirds. The fruits are beanlike pods, usually formed like a string of beads, with mostly large and scarlet seeds that are often poisonous. Most species have a corklike and fissured bark when they reach tree size; the wood, however, is often brittle and is easily damaged by high winds. The branches also are sometimes subject to inexplicable premature deaths, and the need for pruning can be frequent. Yet some of the world's most spectacular flowering trees are here included. Most visually effective are those species that bloom when leafless.

Erythrina abyssinica (ab-i-SIN-i-ka) (synonym *E. tomentosa*) is indigenous to savannah regions of tropical East Africa and is hardy in zones 10 and 11 and marginal in zone 10a. It grows to 30 or even 40 feet in height with an irregular and spreading crown. All parts of the tree except the older leaves and older trunk are covered with small black curved thorns and a gray to rusty-colored tomentum. The leaflets are broadly elliptic to almost round. The terminal leaflet is as much as 8 inches wide, and the other leaflets are 2 to 4 or 5 inches wide. The tree is deciduous unless the winter season is wet. The inflorescences form in spring when the tree is often leafless. They are erect and compact and look like round pompons from a distance; they slowly lengthen as the flowers successively open. The individual flowers are orange to scarlet in color, and are tubular and curved in shape because they do not fully open, which gives a distinctively shaggy appearance to the cluster. This tree is very spectacular when in bloom, and the common name of red hot poker tree is rather apropos.

Erythrina ×bidwillii (bid-WIL-lee-eye) is a cross between *E. crista-galli* and *E. herbacea*. From the former it inherits thorniness, a nearly year-round blooming period, and a nearly evergreen habit, and from the latter parent it inherits a shrublike growth form and its flower shape. The large shrub or small tree is hardy in zones 8b through 9a as a returning perennial shrub and in zones 9b through 11 as a permanent shrub or small tree. A finer large flowering shrub or small tree would be hard to come by.

Erythrina caffra (KAF-ra) (synonym *E. constantiana*) is native to eastern South Africa. Hardy in zones 10 and 11 and marginal in zone 10a, it is one of the most beautiful species in the genus because of its dependable form and showy flowers. The tree grows to 40 feet or so and has an ultimate and lovely umbrella-shaped spread of as much as 60 feet. What prickles and thorns exist are limited to the younger branches and petioles; the trunk is free of viciousness. This tree is de-

ciduous unless the winter season is wet, in which case it often still loses many of its leaves. The leaflets are broadly ovate, with the terminal leaflet larger than the other two. The tree blooms in mid to late winter, depending on the weather, with short compact inflorescences of mostly scarlet flowers, although they are sometimes creamy white to yellow. Gardeners should try to purchase the plants in bloom. Flower form is tubular and similar to that of *E. coralloides*. The tree is sometimes called kaffirbloom.

Erythrina constantiana. See *E. caffra.*

Erythrina coralloides (kor-a-LOY-deez) is indigenous to northeastern and central Mexico and is hardy as a tree form in zones 9b through 11 and as a perennially returning shrub in zones 8b and 9a. It grows to about 20 feet and makes a broad, spreading and open crown with usually contorted branches. The small curved prickles are not numerous, but are spread over all the newer growth. The leaflets are broad, more or less heart-shaped, and about 3 inches wide. The tree is usually deciduous in cold or dry winter areas in which it nevertheless survives as a tree. The pyramidal inflorescences come in the spring and summer and are similar to those of several other species, including *E. herbacea:* they are 6 to 12 inches long, shorter before the flowers are fully open. The scarlet blossoms open from the bottom of the spike upwards, but they do not fully open, and each flower is keel-shaped. The species is sometimes called the naked coral tree.

Erythrina crista-galli (krist´-a-GAHL-lee) is native to southern Brazil, Uruguay, Paraguay, and northern Argentina, and is hardy as a tree form in zones 9b through 11 and as a perennially returning shrub in zones 8b and 9a. It grows to 30 feet, sometimes more, if not cut back by cold and forms a very irregular crown that usually needs pruning to maintain a pleasing shape. It is drought tolerant when established, but this tree grows so fast with ample moisture that one is hard put to keep up with pruning it. All parts except the older trunks bear vicious curved thorns. The ovate to triangular leaflets are 3 or more inches wide and dark green, and even they have the prickles. Most of the literature indicates that the tree blooms only in the spring with the appearance of the deciduous leaves. This statement is not true in wet climates where the tree is evergreen and blooms all year in cycles of about 6 weeks. The inflorescences are perhaps the most spectacular of all the species, and their showiness is only slightly modified by the leaves, which are present when the tree is in bloom. The inflorescences, which are so long as to usually become pendent, consist of as many as 100 scarlet 2- to 3-inch long flowers (many of them open at the same time), whose shape is unusual and has led to the common names of fireman's cap (because the banner is so large and is puckered and creased like a cap), cockspur coral-tree, and cry-baby tree (the flowers often exude a sugary liquid). Some plants have flowers that are more pink than red; the gardener should try to purchase the plants when they are in bloom for color. Plate 190.

Erythrina falcata (fal-KAIT-a) is indigenous to parts of Bolivia, Peru, Argentina, and southern Brazil, and is hardy in zones 10 and 11 as a tree form and in zone 9b as a shrub. The tree is quite similar in form and flower to *E. crista-galli*, but is more tender to cold and the inflorescences are more erect and stand out from the leafy crown to a greater degree.

Erythrina flabelliformis (fla-bel′-li-FORM-is) is native to extreme southern Arizona and adjacent northern Mexico and is hardy as a tree form in zones 9b through 11 and as a perennially returning shrub in zones 8b and 9a. It grows to about 15 feet with a somewhat irregular crown and is often grown as a shrub even where it is completely hardy. Some individuals of this species are quite prickly, while others are barely so. The leaflets are triangular to almost round and 4 or more inches wide; they are usually deciduous no matter what the winter is like. The pyramidal inflorescences appear with or just before the leaves and consist of many bright red slender blossoms much like those of *E. coralloides*.

Erythrina fusca (FYOOS-ka) (synonyms *E. glauca, E. ovalifolia*) is native to the American, African, and Asian tropics and thus has the most widespread habitat in the genus; it is hardy in zones 10 and 11 and marginal in zone 10a. The tree grows to as much as 60 feet with a spread almost as wide. The leaflets are much like those of *E. crista-galli* in size and shape, leathery, dark green, and oval; they are deciduous only in dry or cold winters. The stems and trunk bear curved thorns when young, but mostly lose them when older. The 8- to 10-inch long inflorescences are densely flowered. Each blossom consists of a 2-inch-long orange-red banner with two velvety brown, red-tipped wings. They are some of the most magnificent flowers in the genus. The trees bloom in spring and summer.

Erythrina glauca. See *E. fusca*.

Erythrina herbacea (hur-BAY-see-a) is native to a wide area from coastal South Carolina down through Florida and the West Indies and westward to Texas and adjacent Mexico. It is hardy in zones 7 through 11. It is mostly a small prickly and deciduous shrub to 3 or 4 feet in height, but may reach a stature of 15 feet in the tropical parts of its range where it is also only partially deciduous. In spite of its specific epithet, it often forms soft wood. The triangular leaflets are 2 inches wide with prickles on the petiole. The flowers appear in early spring through May, depending on the weather, are in inflorescences as much as 2 feet long, and are always erect. Each flower is a deep red or deep orange, about 2 inches long, and narrowly keel-shaped very much like that of *E. flabelliformis* and *E. coralloides*. Most plants have only one bloom period, but some do a repeat show in mid or late summer. This plant is very spectacular in bloom.

Erythrina humeana (hyoo-mee-AHN-a) is indigenous to eastern South Africa and is hardy as a small tree form in zones 9b through 11 and as a perennially returning shrub in zones 8b and 9a. The natural inclination of this plant is a large shrub, but it can easily be trained to tree form when young in the nearly frost-free areas. The plant is prickly throughout except on the older branches, and the leaves are quite similar to those of *E. herbacea;* They are only deciduous in dry or cold winters. The inflorescence and individual flowers are also similar to those of *E. herbacea* except that they are both larger and the color is more orange than scarlet. The little tree blooms in summer and fall and is sometimes called the Natal coral-tree.

Erythrina ovalifolia. See *E. fusca*.

Erythrina poeppigiana (po-pij′-ee-AHN-a) is indigenous to slightly elevated areas of eastern Peru and adjacent Brazil and is hardy in zones 10 and 11 and marginal in zone 10a. It is one of the largest and most beautiful species in the genus, reaching a height of 60 or even 80 feet with a spread of at least 40 feet, a trunk diameter of 4 feet or more, and a dependable dome-shaped habit. The tree is deciduous in dry winters. The two lower leaflets are 4 or 5 inches wide, and the terminal leaflet is as much as 8 inches wide; all are ovate to almost orbicular in shape. The flowers come mainly in spring but sometimes also in mid to late summer and are the size and color of those of *E. crista-galli*, with much the same shape. Beautiful in and out of bloom, this is one of the world's most spectacular flowering trees.

Erythrina speciosa (spee-see-O-sa) is indigenous to southern Brazil along streams and rivers, often in swampy ground, and is hardy in zones 10 and 11. It grows to 20 or 25 feet in height with a short stout trunk and massive and often contorted branches that spread to form a wide crown of 9-inch-wide leaves with rhombic-shaped leaflets. The tree is deciduous in all but the wettest and mildest winters. The spring flowers come out before the leaves, are in terminal erect spikes 1 to sometimes 2 feet in height, and consist of many tubular and keeled brick red to scarlet blossoms. This species is one of the most spectacular in bloom because the trees are usually leafless.

Erythrina tomentosa. See *E. abyssinica*.

Erythrina variegata (vair′-ee-a-GAIT-a) (synonym *E. indica*) is native to a very large area of the Asian tropics, from tropical East Africa through the islands of the Indian Ocean, India, Southeast Asia, the islands of the South Pacific, and northwards to the Philippines and Taiwan. It is hardy in zones 10 and 11. One of the most beautiful species, it makes a large tree to 60 feet in height or even more with a broad and picturesque crown of dependable growth habit. The tree has strong black curved prickles on the branches and petioles. The leaflets are very broadly ovate to almost round and are large, to 6 or 8 inches wide. The tree is deciduous in dry or cold winters and sometimes even in wet winters. The crimson flowers come in late winter and early spring. The inflorescences are long and densely packed with 3-inch-long blossoms, each with a broad "banner" with a pointed tip and 10 long and protruding scarlet stamens. Most plants also bloom intermittently during the summer. The tree is sometimes called tiger's-claw.

Erythrina variegata **'Alba'**, a white-flowered cultivar, is not as attractive as the type. *Erythrina variegata* **var.** *orientalis* (synonyms *E. variegata* [or *indica*] var. *picta*, *E. variegata* [or *indica*] 'Rex'), a naturally occurring variety, has incredibly beautiful leaves with the shape and size of the type but with the leaf veins white or yellow. It does not, alas, grow as vigorously or as large as the type. Plate 191.

Erythrina vespertilio (ves´-pur-TIL-ee-o) is native in northern and western Australia and Queensland and is hardy in zones 10 and 11 and marginal in zone 10a. This stout-trunked tree grows to 30 feet or sometimes more with a spreading crown of somewhat irregular habit. The leaflets are quite variable, but are usually ovate to rhomboid in shape and are smaller than those of most other species; they are usually deciduous. The inflorescence is long and densely packed with perhaps the most beautiful individual flowers of any of the species. The blossoms have broad, elliptic banners and are pink to salmon or coral in color with long protruding black-tipped stamens. This very choice tree is almost thornless. It is most commonly termed the bat's-wing coral tree, supposedly because of the fluttering of the leaves in a breeze.

ESCONTRIA (es-KAHN-tree-a)
Cactaceae: The Cactus Family
No known English common name
Tall treelike green, ribbed cactus with spines along
    the rib crests; small yellow flowers
Zones 10 and 11
Sun
Drought tolerant
Average, sandy, well-drained soil
Propagation by seed

A monotypic cactus genus in southern Mexico and Guatemala. *Escontria chiotilla* (chee-o-TEE-ya) grows fairly quickly (for a cactus species) to as much as 20 feet with a stout trunk and several low, fat ascending branches. The trunk and branches are a deep olive green to dark green in color and bear six to eight regularly spaced ribs along whose crests the tufts of gray spines grow. The small 2-inch-long funnel-shaped flowers are yellow and appear in the summer near the tops of the fat green columns. This lovely species needs to be as dry as possible in the winter when it is not actively growing but should not be subjected to prolonged drought conditions in the summer. Because of these requirements, it is difficult to maintain in regions with wet winters.

ESPOSTOA
(es-POST-o-a / es-poas-TOE-a)
Cactaceae: The Cactus Family
Common names vary according to species
Columnar many-ribbed, spiny cactuses usually with
    hair; white and yellow nocturnal flowers
Zones 10 and 11
Sun
Drought tolerant
Average, sandy, well-drained soil
Propagation by seed

A genus of 10 columnar, sometimes branching, cactus species in Bolivia, Peru, and southern Ecuador. All have some woolly hairs on the stems, and most have enough to be covered in what appears to be spun wool or angel hair. The stems have many narrow ribs along the tops of which the spines are thick and long enough to almost form an enclosure. The plants are summer-bloomers, and the blossoms arise from the sides of the stems, not from the tops. The 2- to 3-inch-wide nocturnal flowers are open cup-shaped, few petaled, and white or yellowish in color with a distinct inner ring of yellow stamens and a protruding green or yellow stigma. These beautiful plants are difficult to grow in wet and humid climates where the winters are wet. They demand perfect drainage.

Espostoa lanata (la-NAHT-a) is native to northwestern Peru and can attain a height of 12 feet or more in its native habitat, although it is usually no more than 4 or 5 feet tall in cultivation. It is a spectacular treelike branching cactus whose columnar stems have as many as 30 narrow ribs that are covered in short white or yellowish hair. The areas of the stems where the white 3-inch-wide nocturnal flowers form are covered (at flowering time) with long thick and very dense hairs; the 2-inch-wide scarlet fruits projecting from this woolly mass can be a startling sight. The species is sometimes called the cotton-ball cactus, the snowball cactus, or the Peruvian old man cactus.

Espostoa melanostele (mel-a-NAHS-te-lee / mel´-a-no-STEEL-ee) is indigenous to western Peru and grows to 6 feet or more. It seldom branches and is more spiny-appearing than most other species because the wool covering is not as heavy. The spines are rusty red to golden brown in color and as much as 2 inches long. The white flowers are nocturnal and emerge from a dense patch of long hairs.

ETLINGERA (et-LING-e-ra)
Zingiberaceae: The Ginger Family
TORCH GINGER; PHILIPPINE WAXFLOWER
Tall clumping, reedlike stems; banana-like leaves;
    large globe of pink and red flowers
Zones 10 and 11; marginal in zone 10a
Partial shade
Water lover
Rich, moist, well-drained soil that is on the acidic side
Propagation by root division and by seed

A genus of more than 50 species of large rhizomatous and aromatic herbs in tropical Asia, from Sri Lanka through New Guinea. This genus was formerly known as *Nicolaia* and before that was called *Phaeomeria;* it is still likely to be found listed and for sale under one of these now invalid genus names. Only one species is common in cultivation; it is perhaps the most magnificent species in the whole ginger family. ***Etlingera elatior*** (ee-LAIT-ee-or) (synonym *Nicolaia elatior, Phaeomeria magnifica*) is native to the Indonesian islands of Java and Celebes. The stems can grow to 18 or 20 feet with leathery linear to oblong-lanceolate 3-foot-long leaves that are dark green above and reddish purple beneath. The leaves are arranged oppositely on the stem in one plane. In general appearance the plant looks like a giant version of most *Alpinia* species; with time the rhizomatous roots form a large clump of canes. The spectacular inflorescences appear in late summer or fall atop separate stems arising directly from the roots; they are sometimes as much as 6 feet tall but usually only about 3 or 4 feet. The waxy flower cluster is as much as 10 inches tall by 6 or 7 inches wide and consists of large basal bracts that are deep red with white margins, above which are the red smaller bracts (also margined in white) that form a cone and enclose the small yellow flowers at their bases. A naturally occurring deep pink flowered form is identical to the red-flowered form except for the flower color and for its bracts, which lack the white margins of the type. The plant in bloom is a universal symbol of the tropics and is among the world's most tropical looking, exotic, and spectacular garden subjects for frost-free regions. It is sometimes planted in the warmer parts of zone 9b, but does not often bloom there because the stems are intolerant of frost and the plants need two seasons of stem growth to flower. Plate 192.

EUGENIA (yoo-JEEN-ee-a)
Myrtaceae: The Myrtle, Eucalyptus Family
Common names vary according to species
Small to medium-sized trees; glossy foliage; flower
   clusters of mostly stamens; colorful fruit
Zones vary according to species
Sun to partial shade
Average but regular amounts of moisture
Humusy, non-alkaline soil
Propagation by seed and cuttings

A very large genus of more than 1000 species of large shrubs and small to medium-sized evergreen trees in tropical and subtropical regions around the world but mostly in tropical America. All have relatively large glossy undivided leaves arranged opposite each other and solitary flowers from the branches or, more often, flowers in lateral clusters. Each blossom consists of four small white petals and many long stamens. The fruits usually have the persistent sepals at their apical ends. Almost all species need a non-alkaline soil. This genus once was even more vast than it is now and, as may be observed from the synonyms cited below and under *Sygygium*, the names are still in a state of flux.

Eugenia aggregata (ag-re-GAIT-a) (synonym *Myrciaria edulis*) is native to Brazil, Colombia, and Ecuador and is surprisingly hardy, being adaptable to zones 9b through 11. It is an attractive large shrub or small tree, growing slowly to 15 feet with a rather narrow form. The lustrous dark green elliptic 3- to 4-inch-long leaves have strong midribs. The plant blooms in spring with solitary white flowers followed in early summer by the inch-long oblong berries, which are red but soon change to a deep wine color; their shape and the adherent calyx lobes give them a very strong resemblance to tiny cashew fruit. They are edible, taste like cherries, and are eaten fresh or used in making jams and jellies. The species is called cherry of the Rio Grande, from a river in Brazil, not the one in Texas and Mexico.

Eugenia australis. See *Syzygium paniculatum.*

Eugenia axillaris (ax-il-LAIR-is / axi-IL-la-ris) is native to southern Florida, the Bahamas, and the West Indies, and is hardy in zones 10 and 11. It grows slowly to about 20 feet and has bright green aromatic and leathery elliptic to ovate leaves with strong midveins. The leaves are odoriferous, especially when bruised or crushed, with a strange and exotic fragrance that some find offensive. The new growth is coppery red and most attractive. The small white flowers are in small clusters along the stems and branches and are sweetly fragrant. They are followed by bright red berries, which mature black and are said to be edible. The plant bears the vernacular name of white stopper because an infusion of the leaves supposedly cures diarrhea and because the color of the bark is gray to almost white.

Eugenia brasiliensis (bra-zil´-ee-EN-sis) is indigenous to the southern coastal areas of Brazil and is hardy in zones 10b and 11. It slowly grows to a height of 25, sometimes 35 feet, with a slender and erect shape. The elliptic to oblong leaves are leathery and shiny above, 3 to 4 inches long, and tinged with red when new. The tree blooms in spring with inch-wide white flowers in the leaf axils. The subsequent fruits are ripe in early summer. They are first green, then red, and finally dark purple or almost black when ripe and are round and usually less than an inch wide. They are edible and supposedly taste much like cherries. This species is called grumichama or Brazil cherry.

Eugenia confusa (kahn-FYOO-sa) is native to southern Florida, the Bahamas, and the West Indies and is hardy in zones 10 and 11 and marginal in zone 10a. The largest *Eugenia* species native to Florida, it can attain a height of 50 feet or more in the warmer parts of its native habitat but is seldom more than 25 feet tall in Florida. It makes a slender graceful tree form with somewhat pendulous branches. The 2-inch-long leathery leaves are elliptic to ovate and have a definite point at their ends; they somewhat resemble those of the camellia except the leaf margins are entire and not toothed. The flowers appear in spring and are white and very small. They are followed by tiny quarter-inch bright red berries in summer, which are not edible. This very attractive tree is sometimes called red-berry stopper and ironwood because of the heavy and durable heartwood.

Eugenia coronata (kor-o-NAIT-a) is native to tropical West Africa and is hardy in zones 10 and 11 and marginal in zone 10a. It grows slowly to as much as 20 feet and has an elongate crown of 3-inch-long leathery elliptic leaves. The flowers in spring are small white and fragrant, and the subsequent berries mature to an attractive bluish black color. Nothing distinguishes or elevates this species above the others in the landscape, but because of its relatively slow growth and because it holds its leaves well to the ground if it receives enough water, it makes a fine hedge subject.

Eugenia cumini. See *Syzygium cumini.*

Eugenia foetida (fee-TY-da / FET-i-da) (synonym *E. buxifolia, E. myrtoides*) is indigenous to southern Florida, the West Indies, and Central America, and is hardy in zones 10 and 11. It grows to a maximum of 20 feet or so and is mostly shrubby in all but the tropical parts of its range, but may be trained when young to tree form. The leathery dark green leaves are ovate to elliptic in shape, usually no more than an inch long, aromatic and almost stalkless; they have somewhat the appearance of *Pyracantha* leaves. The small white flowers are borne in summer, and the fruits are red, usually turning black when ripe. Like the above species the plant is used more for hedges than specimens. It is sometimes called Spanish stopper.

Eugenia jambolana. See *Syzygium cumini.*

Eugenia jambos. See *Syzygium jambos.*

Eugenia luschnathiana (lush-nay´-thee-AHN-a) is native to the state of Bahía in eastern central Brazil and is fully hardy in zones 10 and 11, although often surviving in zone 9b. The plant slowly grows into a small tree as much as 30 feet tall, but is usually little more than half that stature under cultivation. The oblong crown is dense with 3-inch-long narrowly elliptic leaves that have a long and often curled tip and a strong midrib. The flowers are borne in late spring. Each one is usually less than an inch wide, but quite attractive with four pure white satiny petals and many long yellowish stamens. The fruits are perhaps the most beautiful in the genus and make a delightful show because of their color. They are an inch or more wide, round to pear-shaped, and a deep golden yellow or orange. They are edible, slightly acidic, and "resinous" in flavor, and are mostly eaten fresh. The tree is called pitomba.

Eugenia malaccensis. See *Syzygium jambos, S. malaccense.*

Eugenia myrtifolia. See *Syzygium paniculatum.*

Eugenia paniculatum. See *Syzygium paniculatum.*

Eugenia rhombea (RAHM-bee-a / rahm-BAY-a) (synonyms *E. anthera, E. procera*) is native to the Florida Keys (but now quite rare there), the West Indies, and Central America, and is hardy in zones 10 and 11 and marginal in zone 10a. It grows to a maximum of 25 feet with a rather open crown of somewhat pendent branches and dark green ovate leaves about 3 inches long. The small white flowers are liable to appear at any time of the year, but usually most abundantly in the spring. The half-inch-wide round fruits are first yellow then red and finally black and, because the little tree can be in bloom almost constantly, there are often all three colors of fruit on a single tree. This very attractive small tree sometimes is called red stopper or spiceberry. It should be more widely planted than it now is.

Eugenia uniflora (yoo-ni-FLOR-a) is native to most of eastern Brazil and adjacent Surinam and French Guiana. It is hardy in zones 10 and 11 and often survives in zone 9b. This small tree to 20 feet or so wants to grow more as a shrub than a tree, although if trained early a tree form is possible. It has a rather slender crown of 3-inch-long stalkless, deep green, glossy, aromatic ovate to elliptic leaves. The white fragrant flowers in spring are small but attractive. The fruits mature in early summer and are quite attractive. Usually more than an inch wide and rounded, they have seven or eight distinct grooves and in their appearance remind one of tiny pumpkins. They are a deep red to almost black when mature and are edible and sweet to slightly acidic. They and the trees are called Surinam cherry or pitanga. This plant has been used very successfully as a hedge.

EUPHORBIA (yoo-FOR-bee-ah)
Euphorbiaceae: The Euphorbia, Spurge Family
Common names vary according to species
Incredibly diverse genus of herbs, trees, and
    succulents
Zones vary according to species
Light requirements vary according to species; most
    need sun
Water requirements vary according to species
Soil requirements vary according to species
Propagation by cuttings, unless otherwise stated

An immense and extremely diverse genus of about 2000 species from every region and almost every clime of the globe. Many species are annual or perennial herbs, some are tropical trees or shrubs, and very many others are succulent. The latter group of species is indigenous to dry regions in Africa and includes some large and treelike members that outwardly resemble the tree-form cactus species from the Americas. The only constant characteristic uniting these disparate plant forms is the structure of the flower, which consists of a fleshy usually cup-shaped organ that bears the tiny and much modified male and female flowers. The male flowers consist of a single stamen, and the female flowers consist of only the three-celled pistil usually on a stalk. These tiny flowers are often accompanied by much larger and much more colorful bracts. Most species have milky, sometimes quite poisonous sap, especially the cactuslike types. For landscape purposes the species are here divided into three plant body types: giant cactuslike succulent tree types, small succulent types, and tropical shrub and tree types. Some of the cactoid species (both treelike and the smaller species) look more like true cactus species than do many true cactus species and they are quite spectacular, exotic, and tropical looking.

GIANT CACTUSLIKE TREE TYPES: These are almost all indigenous to Africa, Madagascar, and the Canary Islands, with a few in the Arabian Peninsula over to the drier parts of India. Like true cactus species, they have ephemeral leaves that soon wither and fall off, swollen and succulent stems in which most photosynthesis occurs, and spines (highly modified leaves). Almost all have insignificant flower clusters, but some are quite attractive when in full bloom. In most of these species the little flower clusters appear on the crest of the rib (or angle) that grows out of the stem. None of these species are hardy outside zones 10b and 11, and all have cultural requirements identical to cactus species. They grow quite slowly, and the dimensions given are the maximum attained only with great age.

Euphorbia abyssinica (ab-i-SIN-i-ka) is native to Ethiopia. It is a gigantic and very impressive treelike succulent that can grow to 30 feet with several ascending dark green thick branches. Each branch has eight wavy deep ribs with lighter striations, and the crest of each rib bears downward-pointing paired and heavy spines. This plant is a very spectacular.

Euphorbia angularis (ang-yoo-LAIR-is) (synonym *E. lemaireana*) is native to South Africa. It grows ultimately to 15 or 20 feet with segmented three-angled ascending branches bearing spines along the wavy crests of the ribs.

Euphorbia canariensis (ka-nair´-ee-EN-sis) is indigenous only to the Canary Islands off the northwestern coast of Africa. It is one of the most beautiful and spectacular species in the genus. It grows to as much as 30 feet and makes a trunk in time from which grow many ascending and curved stems, with four to six ribs each. Each rib bears pairs of black spines along its crest. No one is likely to attempt eating this plant, but it is poisonous in all its parts.

Euphorbia candelabrum (kan-de-LAHB-rum) is indigenous to eastern South Africa, Tanzania, Kenya, Ethiopia, and the Sudan. It is one of the largest species in the genus, growing to as much as 60 feet in its native habitats and at least half that in cultivation. It makes a trunk atop which are the very many jointed four-angled dark green ascending stems with spines along the wavy crests of the ribs. Mature plants are almost overwhelmingly dramatic in the landscape and have a noble yet endearing effect in large scale plantings.

Euphorbia cooperi (KOOP-ur-eye) is native to South Africa. It grows to 15, sometimes 20 feet in height, with ascending light green jointed branches. Each segment is short, fat, and ovate, and marked with darker striations. The segments have four to six deep ribs whose crests are lined with pairs of dark spines. The plant is probably a variety of *E. ingens;* whatever its true inheritance, it is a very exotic and appealing species that is reputedly poisonous in all its parts. Plate 193.

Euphorbia dawei (DAW-ee-eye) is native to the Lake Region of Uganda. It grows to 30 feet with a tall and very straight trunk atop which is the umbrella-like canopy of three-ribbed dark green branches.

Euphorbia excelsa (ek-SEL-sa) is native to South Africa and is somewhat similar to *E. dawei*, although it does not grow quite as tall and the branches are more bluish green.

Euphorbia grandidens (GRAND-i-denz / gran-DY-denz) is indigenous to South Africa. It ultimately grows to 30 feet or more with a trunk and tiers of bright green four-angled somewhat twisted branches that are variegated in silver; the ribs are wavy-crested and bear short spines. This species is one of the prettiest of the tree types. It is sometimes called big-tooth euphorbia.

Euphorbia ingens (ING-enz) is native to tropical East Africa. It grows to 30 feet or more with a stout trunk and many light green ascending five-angled jointed branches. Each deep rib is striated with darker green and is wavy along its crest with triangular-shaped protuberances bearing short spines. This species is one of the most beautiful.

Euphorbia lemaireana. See *E. angularis.*

Euphorbia robecchii (ro-BEK-kee-eye) is native to Kenya. It can grow to 30 feet in time, with a straight tall trunk atop which are the long twisted three-angled dark green branches arranged in tiers with spines along the crests of the angles. This species is very picturesque when old, with a resemblance to some of the *Araucaria* (monkey-puzzle) tree species because of the way the branches grow in tiers.

Euphorbia tetragona (te-TRAG-o-na / tet-ra-GO-na) is native to South Africa. It ultimately grows to 30 feet or more with a trunk and long, somewhat twisted dark green five-angled branches in tiers. At the crest of each angle of the branches are spine-bearing tubercles. The species grows faster than most and is quite picturesque.

Euphorbia tirucalli (teer-oo-KAHL-lee) is native to Uganda, Zaire, and eastward into India and Indonesia. It is one of the strangest-looking species in the genus and grows to 30 feet with a green trunk (becoming brown and woody at the base). It has many smooth, rubbery, cylindrical and spineless green main branches and shorter, spineless cylindrical green branches near the ends of these. The terminal branches are about the thickness of a pencil, which has led to the most common vernacular names of pencil plant, milkbush, or pencil tree. The milky sap is poisonous and quite irritating to mucous membranes. The plant is quite tolerant of saline air and soil and is a very good choice for seaside plantings where an exotic and bizarre look is wanted.

SMALLER SUCCULENT TYPES: These are often similar structurally to the treelike forms but are significantly smaller. Like the larger types they have very ephemeral leaves, and most are indigenous to Africa. Some are more like the cylindrical or globose and clustering cactus species rather than like smaller versions of the tree types. All are indigenous to desert regions and have the same cultural requirements as the treelike species except that some of them are hardier to cold than the tree forms. Many species are resistant to salty air and spray as well as saline soils.

Euphorbia antiquorum (ant-i-KWOR-um) is native to southern India and is hardy in zones 10b and 11. It grows slowly to 10 feet with ascending jointed three-angled branches. The crest of each angle is scalloped and set with pairs of spines. The plant is tolerant of salty air and soil and makes an excellent seaside subject where it is often used as a hedge; it is also a prime candidate for drama in the cactus and succulent garden.

Euphorbia avasmontana (a-vas´-mahn-TAN-a) is indigenous to Namibia, Botswana, and adjacent South Africa, and is hardy in zones 10 and 11. It is one of the most beautiful cactuslike species and grows to about 6 feet. The many ascending bright green or bluish green fat stems have five to eight angles with a waxy coating, and come from the base of the plant. Each stem is only slightly constricted at the joints. The crests of the angles are tan-colored and consist of a horny chitinous substance bearing regularly spaced and very tough two-pronged half-inch-long thorns. This species is one of several that look more like a true cactus than do many true cactus species, and one of the most beautiful of the cactus species at that.

Euphorbia caput-medusae (kap´-ut-meh-DOO-see) (synonym *E. medusae*) is native to southwestern South Africa and is adapted to zones 10 and 11. It grows to about a foot in height and is usually 3 feet in width. It consists of many grayish green foot-long stems that first arch upwards, then downwards, and finally up again at their tips; the visual effect is like that of an octopus or some strange gorgonlike flower. The stems are covered in many small tubercles spirally arranged around their circumferences. The plant is completely spineless. It is a pretty, small species that makes a wonderful specimen for up-close sites, such as in the pockets of large rocks or alongside paths in the succulent and cactus garden. The plant is propagated by cuttings or seed.

Euphorbia cereiformis (seer´-ee-eye-FORM-is) is probably indigenous to South Africa, but may be a hybrid. It is unknown in the wild and is hardy in zones 10 and 11. It is a beautiful cactuslike species growing to about 3 feet in height with many dark olive green 3-foot-long stems branching from the base of the plant. Each stem has as many as 15 narrow and deep ribs. Each rib is crested with regularly spaced triangular tubercles, and each tubercle bears a stout straight spine.

Euphorbia coerulescens (see-roo-LES-senz) is native to southwestern South Africa and is hardy in zones 10 and 11 and marginal in zone 9b. It is a freely branching species with many stems rising from the ground. Each fat stem slowly grows to as much as 5 feet high, has four to six angles, and is divided into many joints. It is rather similar to *E. avasmontana,* but does not grow quite as large, the stem segments are shorter, the crests of the ribs have a dark (as opposed to a light-colored) horny chitinous ridge bearing two-pronged half-inch-long spines, and the color of the stems is never

bluish. It is nevertheless a beautiful plant and looks very much like a cactus species.

Euphorbia echinus (ee-KYN-us) is indigenous to southern Morocco and is hardy in zones 9b through 11. It is a wonderfully picturesque small clumping cactus-like species with many 2-foot-long six-ribbed curving stems rising from the ground. Each stem is dark green with a lighter colored chitinous ridge atop each rib, which is topped with short gray or red spines. The plant freely clumps and, in time, can make a large mat of stems.

Euphorbia enopla (ee-NOP-la) is native to southwestern South Africa and is hardy in zones 9b through 11. It is a lovely freely branching species that grows to about 3 feet. Each fat curved stem rises from the ground, is light green to bluish green in color, and bears six to eight plump ribs. Each rib is knobby-crested and bears 2-inch-long red spines. This species is beautiful, partly because of its color.

Euphorbia grandicornis (grand-i-KORN-is) is native to eastern South Africa, Mozambique, Tanzania, and Kenya, and is hardy in zones 10 and 11. It grows to about 6 feet with a few segmented three-ribbed branches. Each dark green segment is deeply constricted from its neighbor and is almost round in outline when new, elongating later into a more or less triangular shape. The ribs of the segments are thin wings whose crests are hard, bonylike, and lighter colored; they bear several groups of very stout 3-inch-long gray spines in pairs. The plant is often called cow-horn euphorbia and is almost startlingly exotic.

Euphorbia heptagona (hep-TAG-o-na) is native to southwestern South Africa and is hardy in zones 10 and 11. It is a beautiful species with a short trunk and a few ascending 5- to 10-ribbed light green to grayish green branches with long reddish brown spines emanating from the tubercled crests of the ribs.

Euphorbia hermentiana. See *E. trigona.*

Euphorbia hottentota (haht-en-TAHT-a) is indigenous to southwestern South Africa and Namibia and is hardy in zones 10 and 11. It grows to about 6 feet with only a few branches. Each branch is a waxy light green in color with a feathery pattern of dark green. The branches are five-angled, and each angle is somewhat twisted, with a scalloped crest bearing stout spine pairs on the outermost part of the scallop.

Euphorbia inermis (in-ER-mis) is native to southwestern Africa and is hardy in zones 10 and 11. It is quite similar in appearance to *E. caput-medusae,* but the stems are thinner. The plant is propagated by cuttings or seed.

Euphorbia lactea (LAK-tee-a / lak-TAY-a) is native to the drier areas of Sri Lanka and India and is hardy in zones 10b and 11. It is now naturalized in many tropical areas around the world. The plant grows to about 6 feet with many ascending candelabra-like three-angled or four-angled dark green branches. The areas between the angles are yellow-green in color, which sometimes extends in streaks into the angles. The crests of the ribs are scalloped and bear pairs of black spines. The plant is called false cactus, dragon-bone tree, candelabra cactus, and milkstripe euphorbia. Because it is quite tolerant of saline air and soil, it is a very good choice for seaside plantings where an exotic and tropical effect is desired. It is often planted as a defensive hedge at the vegetation line on tropical beaches.

Euphorbia ledienii (le-DEEN-ee-eye) is native to southwestern South Africa and is hardy in zones 10 and 11 and marginal in zone 9b. It is a very cactuslike plant in appearance and grows to 6 feet or so in height. The branches arise directly from the ground, are a waxy light green and five-angled, with the crests of the ribs deeply notched, and bear closely set brown or reddish pairs of spines.

Euphorbia medusae. See *E. caput-medusae.*

Euphorbia morinii. See *E. heptagona.*

Euphorbia obesa (oh-BEE-sa) is native to southwestern South Africa and is hardy in zones 10 and 11 and marginal in zone 9b. This fascinating spineless dwarf plant should be planted where its striking form and color can be appreciated up close. It forms a globular or sometimes slightly conical plant about 8 inches high with eight ribs and corresponding valleys circumnavigating the rounded body. The color is a waxy grayish to bluish green with many thin striations of purple, brown, dark green, or even red. The crests of the ribs bear many small brownish red tubercles. This little wonder is sometimes called the living baseball plant. It is propagated by seed.

Euphorbia pentagona (pen-TAG-o-na) is indigenous to southwestern South Africa and is hardy in zones 10 and 11 and marginal in zone 9b. It grows to as much as 9 feet with time and has many ascending and curved branches in whorls. Each branch is five-angled and bears a triangular protuberance at its crest and one long tough grayish-colored spine projecting from the tip of the protuberance. It is a very striking cactuslike plant.

Euphorbia polyacantha (pah-lee-a-KANTH-a) is native to Ethiopia and is hardy in zones 10b and 11. It makes a small cactuslike plant to 4 or 5 feet in height with ascending branches off a short trunk. Each branch has four or five angles and is dark green in color. The crests of each rib are covered in a grayish chitinous material and from this spring the 2-inch-long tough gray spine pairs. This species is another of the very cactus appearing types.

Euphorbia polygona (pah-LIG-o-na) is native to southwestern South Africa and is hardy in zones 10 and 11 and marginal in zone 9b. It is a beautiful cactuslike plant with many curved stems branching from the base of the plant and reaching 3 feet or sometimes more. Each stem has 12 to as many as 30 deep and thin winglike wavy-margined and slightly scalloped ribs. The crests of the ribs bear short single spines, although some stems are spineless or nearly so. Plate 194.

Euphorbia pseudocactus (soo-doe-KAK-tus) is indigenous to northeastern South Africa and is hardy in zones 10 and 11. This wonderful little shrub grows to a maximum of 4 or sometimes 5 feet. It has no trunk but many branches from the base. Each branch is four-angled, light yellow green in color with darker fan-shaped markings, and a few sharp white or gray spines along the crest of the wavy wings.

Euphorbia pulvinata (pul-vi-NAIT-a) is native to a wide area in South Africa and is hardy in zones 10 and 11. It is a tiny mat-forming species with 2- or 3-inch-high stems. Each stem has 7 to 10 ribs with red spines emanating from the wavy crests of the ribs. The species is sometimes called the pincushion euphorbia. It is an exquisite sight when planted in and among rocks where it can be appreciated up close.

Euphorbia symmetrica (sim-MET-ri-ka) is indigenous to southwestern South Africa and is hardy in zones 10 and 11 and marginal in zone 9b. This little beauty is very similar to *E. obesa* except that the plant body is usually wider. It has a long taproot, which soaks up water like a sponge, making it vulnerable to rot in all but the fastest draining soils. The plant is propagated by seed.

Euphorbia trigona (try-GO-na / TRY-go-na) is of unknown origin but probably is indigenous to tropical southwestern Africa and is hardy in zones 10b and 11. It grows to 8 or 10 feet in height and is very similar to and has the same cultural requirements as *E. lactea.*

Euphorbia tuberculata (too-burk´-yoo-LAIT-a) is native to southwestern South Africa and is hardy in zones 10 and 11. It is much like *E. caput-medusae* except that it bears fewer branches and looks like a starfish. It is very effective planted where it can be viewed up close. The plant is propagated by seed.

TROPICAL SHRUB & TREE TYPES: Included here are shrubs and trees like *Euphorbia pulcherrima* (poinsettia). These plants have varying cultural requirements. Many of them are somewhat succulent in nature and need conditions similar to those of the two preceding categories, others are intolerant of drought, and some need fertile and moist soil.

Euphorbia atropurpurea (at´-ro-poor-POOR-ee-a) is indigenous to the Canary Islands and is hardy in zones 10 and 11 and marginal in zone 9b. It is a quite attractive little shrub growing to 3 or 4 feet with succulent reddish brown branches and 4-inch-long waxy bluish green narrowly elliptic leaves crowded at the ends of the stems. It blooms off and on throughout most of the year with terminal, long-stalked few-flowered clusters of purplish red bracts. The plant is drought tolerant but needs more water than most of the more succulent types, especially when it is actively growing in the warmer months. It is propagated by cuttings or seed.

Euphorbia bubalina (boo-ba-LEEN-a) is native to South Africa and is hardy in zones 10 and 11 and marginal in zone 9b. It grows to 3 or 4 feet with a few knobby, tubercled branches ascending from a short trunk. The 6-inch-long narrowly elliptic light green leaves are crowded at the ends of the stems. The flowers are similar in form and size to those of *E. atropurpurea,* but the color of the bracts is green to greenish yellow with red margins. This species has cultural requirements similar to the succulent types.

Euphorbia cotinifolia (ko-tin´-i-FO-lee-a) is indigenous to the West Indies, Mexico, and Central America down to Venezuela and Peru, and is hardy in zones 10 and 11, although it will grow back from the root in zone 9b. It grows to 8 or 9 feet with an almost equal spread, but sometimes can attain the stature of a small tree to 15 feet or more in height. It needs guidance when young if it is to have a single trunk. The young branches are purplish red. The 4- to 6-inch-long blue-green to purplish leaves are ovate to diamond-shaped and are long-stalked; they occur in whorls of three along the stems. The young leaves are maroon-colored when new. ***Euphorbia cotinifolia*** **'Atropurpurea'** (at´-ro-poor-POOR-ee-a) is more widely available than the type and its leaves keep the maroon to pinkish orange color as they age. The type is prettier than the cultivar, in my opinion, because the latter has too much of a good thing. The flowers are white. All parts of the plant contain a milky sap, which is poisonous and a strong irritant. The plant is not drought tolerant and needs a humusy and fairly moist, well-draining soil and full sun to maintain the brilliant color of the leaves. It is propagated by cuttings or seed.

Euphorbia fulgens (FUL-gainz / FUL-jenz) is indigenous to southern Mexico and is hardy in zones 10 and 11 although it often comes back from the root in zone 9b. It grows to 6 feet or sometimes more and has thin wiry and gracefully arching stems that create a fountainlike effect. The leaves clothe the stems almost to their bases and are 4 to 6 inches long and narrowly elliptic to narrowly lanceolate. The plants bloom primarily in fall and winter but off and on all year. The stems are nearly hidden by the orange-bracted to scarlet-bracted flower clusters. The shrub is sometimes called scarlet plume. The plant has milky sap that is mildly poisonous and often a skin irritant to people who are sensitive to it. There are cultivars with white and yellow flowers as well as one with purplish leaves. The plant needs a humusy, moist, well-drained soil. It is propagated by cuttings or seed.

Euphorbia leucocephala (lyook-o-SEF-a-la) is native to southern Mexico and Central America and is hardy in zones 10 and 11 although it often comes back from the root in zone 9b. It grows to 9 or 10 feet and has 3-inch-long medium green leaves that grow in whorls around the stems with their margins usually upturned so that the entire leaf is V-shaped in cross section. The plant blooms in cycles in late fall, winter, and spring at which times it is covered in white-bracted flower clusters. It has cultural requirements similar to those of *E. fulgens* and is propagated by cuttings or seed. The milky sap is poisonous and an irritant to some people.

Euphorbia milii (MIL-ee-eye) is native to western Madagascar and is hardy only in zones 10 and 11 although sometimes coming back from the roots in zone 9b. It is a small and very spiny shrub that grows to 3 or 4 feet in height. The erect or sometimes sprawling woody gray stems are covered in more or less spirally arranged inch-long vicious black spines. The spatulate to obovate 2-inch-long leaves are found only on the new growth; the plant is often completely leafless, but this condition can be ameliorated with regular watering. One grows it for the resplendent red or pink flowers: this is the crown of thorns or Christ-thorn. The plants bloom in cycles throughout the year in truly tropical climes and most of the year (the warmer months) in subtropical areas; the bloom cycles mostly occur with rain after a period of drought. The flowers are tiny, fleshy, and yellow-green and, as with the other members of this genus, it is the bracts surrounding these flowers that make the show. The bract color ranges from red to orange and pink, and there are cultivars with white bracts and some with yellow bracts. There are also hybrids between this species and other *Euphorbia* species that make larger plants with much larger flower bracts. Besides being drought tolerant, the plants are quite immune to saline air and soil and are perfect choices for seaside plantings, especially in hedge form. The plant is propagated by cuttings or seed. Plate 313.

Euphorbia pulcherrima (pul-KER-ri-ma) is native to southern Mexico and Central America and is hardy in zones 10 and 11, but springs back from the roots in zone 9b and often in zone 9a. The poinsettia is normally seen as a large, multistemmed shrub to 10 feet or so in height, but in its native habitat and in completely frost-free climates it becomes a tree to as much as 30 feet tall. It needs guidance when young to train it to tree form. Unfortunately it is seldom allowed to grow into tree form even in the tropics, because its owners are eager to have the flowers at eye level and easily accessible for cutting. It is a truly magnificent sight when grown as a tree and in bloom. The 4- to 10-inch long leaves are long-stalked, ovate to lanceolate in shape, and generally a dark green in color; they are usually toothed or lobed on the margins and are generally found clustered at the ends of the stems. The flowers are terminal on the branches, and the scarlet elliptical bracts are spectacular, spreading to about a foot wide. There are hundreds of named cultivars whose distinctions are size and color of the bracts. The colors range from white through yellow to pink, salmon, and scarlet, and there are bi-colored types and "double-flowered" varieties. The plants usually bloom in late fall, winter, and early spring but are known to flower in the tropics year-round in cycles dependent upon rainfall. Almost all the cultivars are significantly smaller in ultimate stature than is the red-flowered type. The sap of the plants is milky, but its poisonous qualities are only myth, although the juice is not palatable. The plants do best with an adequate and regular supply of water and need a fairly rich and humusy, well-drained soil. They respond to fertilizers in late summer; fish emulsion is perfect for them. They bloom sparsely, if at all, without sun. If not grown as a tree where possible, the plants become leggy and leafless at the bottoms of the tall stems; sometimes the effect can be beautiful, especially if the bottoms of the plants are hidden by lower-growing plants. Plate 195.

Euphorbia punicea (pyoo-NIS-ee-a) is native to the West Indies and is hardy in zones 10b and 11. It is a large shrub that can grow to as much as 25 feet but is usually no more than 12 feet tall. The shrub or little tree is somewhat sparsely branched, and the younger branches are rubbery, turning woody with age and covered in the younger parts with rings of leaf scars. The 6-inch-long leathery leaves are obovate in shape and a dark green in color; they are clustered at the ends of the branches. The plant blooms whenever the weather is warm enough with terminal and few-flowered clusters of tiny greenish yellow flowers surrounded by two large ovate scarlet to pinkish orange bracts. The plants are somewhat drought tolerant, but grow and bloom much better with adequate and regular supplies of water, especially in the warmer months while they are actively growing. They are not very fussy about the type of soil in which they grow as long as it is freely draining. The plant is propagated by cuttings or seed. Plate 196.

Euphorbia splendens. See *E. milii.*

EUPHORIA (yoo-FOR-ee-a)
Sapindaceae: The Soapberry, Golden-Rain Tree
    Family
LONGAN; DRAGON'S-EYE
Medium-sized evergreen tree; glossy pinnate leaves;
    clusters of warty tan-colored fruit
Zones 10 and 11
Sun
Average but regular amounts of moisture
Humusy, well-drained soil
Propagation by seed and air-layering; named cultivars
    are grafted

A genus of about 15 species of trees in tropical Asia. All have pinnate leaves and globular warty-textured fruits, some of which are edible. Only one species is commonly planted in the United States. ***Euphoria longan*** (LAHN-gan) (synonym *Nephelium longan*) is native to southern tropical China and adjacent Myanmar (Burma) and India. This beautiful tree slowly grows to about 40 feet in height with a short rough-barked trunk and a dense and spreading crown usually wider than its height. The approximately foot-long leaves have 7 to 11 leaflets, which are 8 inches long, narrowly elliptic to lanceolate, glossy and dark green, with a strong reddish midvein and a pointed tip. The new leaves are usually orange to maroon-colored. The trees bloom in late winter and early spring with erect 8- to 10-inch-high terminal panicles of small white or yellowish six-petaled flowers. The fruits mature in mid to late summer and are in pendent clusters. Each round warty fruit is about an inch in diameter and a tan to reddish brown in color. The white flesh is edible and insipidly sweet. The single round seed is jet black with a white spot at one end, which has led to the vernacular

name of dragon's eye. ***Euphoria longan* 'Kohala'** is the most widely available of the named cultivars that are reputedly superior to the type in sweetness.

EUTERPE (yoo-TURP-ee)
Palmae (Arecaceae): The Palm Family
ASSAI PALM
Tall slender, ringed trunks with crownshafts; arching,
    pinnate leaves with long, drooping leaflets
Zone 10b and 11
Sun
Water lovers
Rich, moist, humusy, well-drained soil
Propagation by seed

A genus of about 25 pinnate-leaved palm species in the West Indies, Central America, and northern South America. Some species are clustering or suckering in habit; some have solitary trunks. Most species are indigenous to lowland rain forests, but some occur at elevations of 10,000 feet. Two of the species are commonly planted in the tropics and are similar to each other. The gross difference is that one is a suckering or clustering species and the other has a solitary trunk. Both species need warmth and moisture and, since they are denizens of the rain forest, appreciate protection from the midday sun when young. Both are unusually fast growing for palm species and are among the most beautiful and tropical looking of trees. The leaves of both species fall from the leaf crown almost immediately after dying, which fact adds to the elegant and nearly pristine look of these palm beauties.

Euterpe edulis (ED-yoo-lis) is indigenous to the Amazon region of Brazil. It has a solitary trunk to as much as 100 feet in its native habitat, but often attains no more than half that stature in cultivation. The elegantly slender trunk is no more than a foot in diameter in the tallest specimens and is usually only about 6 inches in diameter; it is a beautiful green in color in its upper part, gradually shading to a light or dark gray and is ringed with brown to white leaf scars. The slender dark green crownshaft is about 6 feet high in mature palms. The gracefully arching leaves are about 10 feet long with many regularly spaced 3-foot-long narrow tapering and pendent leaflets. The leaves are reminiscent of those of *Howea forsteriana* (kentia palm), but they are even more graceful because the leaflets are so limp and drooping. The palm is called palmito in Brazil because it is the source of palm hearts, the unfolded developing leaves in the very center of the palm's crown; since this is the tree's only growing point, the harvesting of this tissue unfortunately means the death of the palm.

Euterpe oleracea (o-le-RAYS-ee-a) is a clustering or suckering species native to the Amazon region of Brazil, southern Venezuela, and the Guyanas of northern South America. The trunk grows quickly to as much as 60 feet and often does not sucker until the original trunk is of that stature. The crown usually has fewer leaves than that of *E. edulis*, but their individual appearance and dimensions are quite similar. A beverage concocted from the purple fruits of this species is called locally "assai."

EXOTHEA (ex-OATH-ee-a / ex-o-THEE-a)
Sapindaceae: The Soapberry, Golden-Rain Tree
     Family
INKWOOD; IRONWOOD
Small to medium-sized evergreen tree; lustrous
     leaves; panicles of fragrant white flowers; red fruit
Zones 10 and 11; marginal in zone 10a
Sun
Average but regular amounts of moisture
Average, sandy, well-drained soil

A genus of only three tree species in southern Florida, the West Indies, Mexico, and Central America. Only one species is planted, and it is not planted enough. *Exothea paniculata* (pan-ik´-yoo-LAIT-a) grows to as much as 50 feet in the wetter parts of its range, but usually attains a maximum of 30 feet in cultivation. The tree has a slender dense crown and a cinnamon-colored trunk. The leaves are pinnate but not obviously so as they are short and bear only two or four leaflets when the tree is young and six when it is mature; there is no terminal leaflet. The 5-inch-long leaflets are elliptical in shape with a strong midrib and are a lustrous deep green in color. The tree blooms in spring and early summer with small panicles near the ends of the branches; the individual five-petaled flowers are small, white, and fragrant with centers of red stamens. The fruits mature in summer and fall and are in clusters of round half-inch-wide orange to red berries that age to a deep purple. This species is one of the finest native landscape subjects and warrants much greater use in warm climate gardens. It is somewhat drought tolerant when established, carefree, and of great beauty in the landscape.

FAGRAEA (fa-GREE-a)
Loganiaceae: The Buddleia, Carolina Jessamine
     Family
No known English common name
Large evergreen trees; spreading crowns of leathery
     leaves; white fragrant nocturnal flowers
Zones 10b and 11
Sun
Water lover
Humusy, moist, well-drained soil
Propagation by seed and air-layering

A genus of about 35 trees and shrubs in Southeast Asia, Malaysia, northern Australia, and the islands of the South Pacific. A few species are epiphytic. All have relatively large leathery leaves with prominent sheathing stipules and funnel-shaped flowers, usually in clusters.
Fagraea ceilanica (say-LAHN-i-ka) (synonym *F. zeylanica*) is native to Sri Lanka and southern India. It grows to as much as 50 feet in its native habitat, but is usually considerably smaller in cultivation and must often be trained and guided while young to a tree form. It has extraordinarily beautiful leaves that are as much as 14 inches long, a deep green in color, generally obovate in shape, and heavily veined with dark midrib and lateral veins. The very attractive flowers are in terminal clusters of three to more than a dozen. Each blossom is 4 or 5 inches long, pure white, and formed almost exactly like an Easter lily. The flowers are only slightly fragrant. This handsome species is unaccountably scarce in cultivation, at least in the United States. Plate 197.
Fagraea fragrans (FRAY-granz) is native to India and Malaysia. It grows slowly to 60 feet or more with a wide but oblong to pyramidal crown of stout spreading branches whose ends are somewhat upturned. The tree branches low, and in time (and unless pruned) the lower branches usually sweep the ground, much as some old limbs of *Quercus virginiana* (live oak) do. The dark green leaves, which are in whorls near the ends of the branches, are 6 inches long, elliptical in shape, dark green, and leathery, with a strong and lighter colored midrib. When the tree blooms in late spring or summer, it is almost covered with the panicles of fragrant 2-inch-wide yellowish white five-petaled tubular flowers, each with long protruding white stamens. The flowers open in the evening but last for several days and, because of the number of flowers in an inflorescence, the tree is in bloom for several weeks. The panicles of small red berries mature in the fall and create quite a spectacle. They are not palatable but are relished by the flying foxes (fruit bats) in their native habitat. This species is one of the world's most beautiful and should be much more widely planted in the American tropics than it currently is.
Fagraea zeylanica. See *F. ceilanica.*

×FATSHEDERA (fats-HED-e-ra)
Araliaceae: The Aralia, Schefflera Family
FATSHEDERA
Woody thick-stemmed sprawling shrub; large glossy
     English-ivy-like leaves
Zones 8b through 11
Partial shade
Average but regular amounts of moisture
Average soil
Propagation by cuttings

An intergeneric hybrid between the shrub *Fatsia japonica* and the vine *Hedera helix.* ×*Fatshedera lizei* (LIZ-ee-eye) combines some of the desirable attributes of both parent genera but, unlike either parent, it is neither a real shrub nor a true vine. The dark green thick and glossy leaves are wonderfully tropical looking, 6 to 8 inches wide and as long, and widely ovate in outline, with three to five deep and pointed lobes. The thick stems, which grow fairly quickly to 10 to 15 feet in length, are pliable when young but mature into stiff and woody ropelike branches. Because the stems tend to grow without branching, the tips should be pinched to cause such branching. The plants cling not neither do they twine and, if a vinelike subject is wanted, the stems must be tied to a strong support. A lattice is the perfect structure for training the miscreant as a vine. The bases of stems that are made to climb are usually bare of leaves, and it is usually visually advantageous to have low growing plants in front of the vine, although the bare-bottomed look is also sometimes what is wanted. This plant can be used as a groundcover, but doing so necessitates regular pruning of the errant and erect stems, and weighting those that do not stand to attention so that they behave in the manner desired. The plant is somewhat drought tolerant but almost stops growing and the leaves are smaller without a regular and adequate supply of moisture.

FATSIA (FAT-see-a)
Araliaceae: The Aralia, Schefflera Family
JAPANESE RICEPAPER PLANT; FATSIA
Evergreen shrub; very large glossy dark green deeply
    lobed leaves held horizontally
Zones 7 through 10
Shade to partial shade
Average but regular amounts of moisture
Average well-drained, slightly acidic soil
Propagation by seed and cuttings

A genus of only three species of evergreen small trees and shrubs in eastern China, southern Japan, and Taiwan. All have large lobed leaves and terminal panicles of many tiny white or yellowish flowers. Only one species is common in cultivation.

Fatsia japonica (ja-PAHN-i-ka) is native to the southern Japanese islands. It seldom grows to more than 10 feet and takes some time to attain that stature. It is usually about as wide as it is tall, not because it branches all that much, but because the leaves are so large and are carried on such long petioles. The tough and stiff, leathery but glossy and deep green leaves are a foot wide and are held on petioles a foot or more in length. The leaves are round but deeply lobed into 5 to 11 segments, and the lobes bear shallowly serrate margins. This bold and dramatic plant is very useful for creating a tropical look of some height in shaded non-tropical regions. The shrub is not at home in truly tropical regions without a period of cool temperatures. It is superb combined with finer-textured and lighter-colored foliage plants like ferns. There are several cultivars, some of which are dwarf in stature, and others which have variegated (white) leaves.

Fatsia papyrifera. See *Tetrapanax.*

FEIJOA (FAY-jo-a)
Myrtaceae: The Myrtle, Eucalyptus Family
PINEAPPLE GUAVA
Large evergreen shrub or small tree; reddish bark;
    white and red flowers; egg-shaped green fruit
Zones 8 through 11; marginal in zone 7b
Sun
Average but regular amounts of moisture
Sandy, humusy, well-drained soil
Propagation by seed; named cultivars are grafted

A genus of only two species of evergreen shrubs or small trees in southern Brazil, Uruguay, southern Paraguay, and northern Argentina. Only one species is planted outside botanical gardens. *Feijoa sellowiana* (sel-lo´-wee-AHN-a) (synonym *Acca sellowiana*) is native to northeastern Argentina and southern Brazil. It grows to 20 feet, sometimes more, in height and makes a compact large shrub or small tree with a picturesquely twisted reddish brown trunk. It needs to be trained when young to a single trunk if a tree form is desired. The 3-inch-long stiff and leathery leaves are bright green to grayish green above, with a white tomentum beneath. The exquisite and edible flowers come in late spring and are borne in the leaf axils. They consist of four petals. Each inch-long very fleshy and succulent velvety recurved white petal has a reddish purple back. Many long scarlet yellow-tipped stamens protrude from the center of the flower. The edible fruits ripen in early autumn and are 2- to 4-inch-long egg-shaped berries, olive green in color, usually with a reddish hue, and tasting somewhat like pineapple. This very beautiful little tree is sometimes used as a tall hedge but is most effective as a patio tree where its color, flowers, and fruit can be enjoyed up close. It is also espaliered like *Eriobotrya* (loquat) species against walls and lattices with great effect. The plant is unusually hardy to cold for a subtropical species and survives for many years in the warmer parts of zone 7.

FEROCACTUS (FER-o-kak-tus)
Cactaceae: The Cactus Family
BARREL CACTUS
Massive ribbed globular to columnar spiny cactuses;
    yellow, pink, and red flowers atop columns
Zones vary according to species
Sun
Drought tolerant
Average sandy, very well drained soil
Propagation by seed

A genus of about 24 large globular to cylindrical cactus species in the southwestern United States and Mexico. All have plant bodies with many ribs and large clusters of spines with a very large central spine that is usually hooked. The funnel-shaped yellow to red flowers are borne near the tops of the columns and have spreading petals. These plants exhibit the very essence of the tropical desert look, and few other subjects are more picturesque.

Ferocactus acanthodes (a-KANTH-o-deez / ak´-an-THO-deez) is indigenous to southern Nevada, adjacent California and Arizona, and northern Mexico, and is hardy in zones 8 through 11. The plant body starts out globose and about 2 feet in diameter, then becomes cylindrical, and finally becomes a very stout column to 8 or 10 feet high. It is a ribbed body with as many as 25 crests from which grow the many reddish spines in clusters. The largest spines reach almost 5 inches long from the center of the cluster. The flowers come in the summer and are red or yellow. This tawny-colored beauty is one of the finest and most picturesque in the genus.

Ferocactus chrysacanthus (kris-a-KANTH-us) is native to Baja California and is hardy in zones 10 and 11. It slowly grows to about 3 feet in height and 3 feet in diameter with about 20 ribs. Each rib bears many tubercles from which grow the brilliant yellow to reddish wide and hooked spines. The summer flowers are yellow and pink.

Ferocactus diguetii (dee-GET-ee-eye) is native to Baja California and is hardy in zones 10 and 11. It grows very large to 12 feet or more in height and 3 feet in diameter. The plant body has more than 30 dark green ribs with 3-inch-long reddish yellow hooked spines growing from the areoles atop the rib crests. The summer flowers are yellow. This grand plant is a superb desert symbol and gives dignity, scale, breadth, and nobility to any cactus and succulent collection.

Ferocactus emoryi. See *F. wislizenii.*

Ferocactus glaucescens (glaw-SES-senz) is indigenous to central Mexico and is hardy in zones 9b through 11. It does not grow much more than a foot in height but attains a diameter of almost 2 feet. The olive green plant body is divided into 11 to 15 wide and arching ribs from the crests of which grow the stout 3-inch-long golden spines. Unlike many other species in the genus, this one has more green showing than spine color, which simply highlights the beautiful color of the spines. The summer flowers are silky yellow. The species is stunningly attractive.

Ferocactus herrerae (er-ER-ee) is native to northwestern Mexico and is hardy in zones 9b through 11. It grows to 6 feet in height with a diameter of about 18 inches. The body has a dozen or so thin winglike and wavy ribs from which grow the clusters of inch-long gray spines with a central broad and hooked spine. The large summer flowers are red with yellow-tipped petals. This species is considered by some botanists to be but a variety of *F. wislizenii.*

Ferocactus histrix (HIS-trix) is native to northeastern and central Mexico and is hardy in zones 9 through 11. It grows to about 2 feet in height and 3 feet in diameter, and is always globular. It is also the essence of the vernacular name, barrel cactus. The body bears about two dozen narrow winglike ribs from which grow the 3-inch-long golden spines. The summer flowers are a brilliant yellow.

Ferocactus latispinus (lat-i-SPYN-us) is indigenous to central and southern Mexico and is hardy in zones 10 and 11. It is always globular in shape, growing only to a foot or so in height and slightly more in width. The deep olive green plant body has from 15 to 23 thin ribs from which grow the spectacular clusters of very wide and flat 2-inch-long tough spines. The shape of the spines has led to the plant's vernacular name of devil's tongue. The summer flowers are reddish purple. This species is choice and dramatic because of the great spines.

Ferocactus pilosus (py-LO-sus) (synonym *F. stainesii*) is native to central Mexico and is hardy in zones 10 and 11. It is arguably the most beautiful species in the genus because of its color and size. It grows to as much as 10 feet in height with a diameter of more than 2 feet. The deep green plant body has 15 to 20 deep ribs from which the clusters of 2-inch-long brilliant red to reddish brown thick spines arise. In addition, this is one of the few species in the genus that suckers or clusters, making immense and very impressive groups. The summer flowers are orange to red in color. ***Ferocactus pilosus*** var. ***pilosus*** is identical to the type, except that the plant body is covered (beneath the spines) with white hair; it is indeed beautiful.

Ferocactus rectispinus (rekt-i-SPYN-us) is indigenous to Baja California and is hardy in zones 10 and 11. A spectacular species because of the 3-inch-long red spines, it grows to 6 feet or more with a deep green plant body bearing two dozen thin ribs with tubercles. The summer flowers are large and a deep golden yellow with a prominent purple stigma in the center of the flower.

Ferocactus stainesii. See *F. pilosus.*

Ferocactus wislizenii (wis-li-ZEN-ee-eye) (synonym *F. emoryi*) occurs naturally from western Texas to Arizona and adjacent Mexico and is hardy in zones 8 through 11. It is a spectacular plant growing to more than 5 feet in height in the warmer parts of its range and to 3 feet in diameter. The plant body has about 30 ribs with clusters of spines atop each crest. Each cluster bears several gray to reddish spines about 2 inches long with one wide hooked central spine to 3 or 4 inches long. The spectacular summer flowers are 3 or more inches across, with scarlet, yellow, or orange petals and yellow tips. Plate 198.

FICUS (FYK-us / FEEK-us)
Moraceae: The Fig, Mulberry Family
FIG
Small to gigantic evergreen trees, shrubs, and vines
Zones 10b and 11 unless otherwise indicated
Sun to partial shade
Water requirements vary according to species
Deep, humusy soil
Propagation by seed, cuttings, and air-layering

A very large genus of at least 800 species and possibly as many as twice that number of mostly large trees but also shrubs and clinging vines, in tropical and subtropical areas throughout the world, predominantly the Asian tropics. Most species are evergreen; some are truly deciduous (usually briefly), but the time of leaf fall is quite variable and is dependent on a dry or cool season. Most species have large and often magnificently beautiful leaves, but some (mostly the vining forms) have small leaves. All species have leaves that unfold from large protective sheaths (technically called "stipules"), some of which are highly colored and most decorative.

The minute flowers are without petals, and the fruits (seeds) are formed inside a fleshy pear-shaped or globular hollow receptacle, the fig, that is enlarged at its apical end and bears a tiny opening through which pollinating insects enter the flower chamber. Many fig species are cauliflorous. Only one species produces fruit that is regularly eaten by humans, the common and usually deciduous fig, *Ficus carica,* although the fruits of many other species are relished by other animals, especially bats, monkeys, and birds.

Almost all species have sap that is thick and milky. This latex in some species has been utilized for making rubber, and the tree species are often referred to as rubber trees. The sap is not poisonous and very seldom is it even the slightest irritant to human skin. Indeed, the young shoots of many species are eaten by native peoples in tropical countries, and mature leaves and twigs are commonly used as feed for livestock.

Some of the world's largest trees are species of *Ficus,* not so much because of their height, although many attain a height of 100 feet and sometimes much more, but because of their girth. This massive girth results from the plant's remarkable ability to spread its mass over sometimes more than an acre of ground by aerial roots that descend from the pre-existing branches, reach the ground, turn into supporting trunks themselves, and then continue the process throughout the length of the tree's life, which can be a long time. The aerial roots, which are at first relatively thin, are usually very numerous and appear without close inspection to be the hanging parts of large vines. Few of the thin strandlike aerial roots metamorphose into supporting trunks, but in some very old specimens there may number more than 500. This "banyan" growth phenomenon (the proliferation and spread of secondary trunks by aerial roots) is invariable in some species, but is only seen in other species when they are grown in humid climates. In the drier tropics and subtropics, the descending aerial roots of the latter species often wither before they reach the ground. Some species, especially those indigenous to the drier climes, never form aerial roots no matter what the moisture content of the air.

Many large species have buttressed trunks and roots. These great winglike flanges of trunk near the base of the tree usually merge into sinuous and serpentine far-reaching surface roots of some height above the soil level. The buttresses may be as high as 6 feet or more where they originate from the main trunk, and the ends of the surface roots may reach out to a radial distance as great as that of the tree's canopy itself.

Many of the largest tree species start their spectacular long lives as epiphytes in soil pockets on other forest trees (including individuals of their own species) or palms and, guided by gravity, send down roots in search of the ground. When these roots find terra firma, they branch and expand around the host trunk and within a few years have formed a hollow cylinder of trunk. Unless something quickly kills or someone soon removes the fast growing fig, it is simply a matter of time before the host is completely engulfed and its tissues crushed by the enlarging epiphyte turned terrestrial, which now is of considerable size and no longer needs its host. It is therefore no wonder that this type of fig is often called "strangler." The host need not necessarily be another live plant. The stranglers are known to employ wooden fence posts, stone statues, and buildings as their host— any structure that provides a pocket of soil large enough to germinate a seed and a surface minutely porous enough for the absorptive geotropic (gravity-responsive) roots to cling to their habitat is fodder for these trees. Interestingly, when grown from the beginning in the open ground, most of these strangler species never achieve the great heights that their counterparts do when their life begins epiphytically high in the crotch or in a soil pocket of a large host tree. Occurrences of the epiphytic-strangler, buttressed, and banyan growth habits are not exclusive of one another. Many species exhibit all three phenomena, while some only two or one, and still others manifest none of these growth forms.

Many tree forms, even the tallest, sprout from the root after being frozen to the ground. Species such as *Ficus elastica* and *F. auriculata* are often grown as large returning-perennial shrubs in zone 9 because of their immense and wonderfully tropical looking foliage. The large tree species have roots on and near the surface that are truly invasive. These species should not be planted near buildings, although regular and ample supplies of water tend to decrease the range of their peregrinating roots. These species are, however, probably the most beautiful tree species for planting along avenues if there is sufficient room for the great roots. Nothing gives more of a sense of spaciousness than rows of these giants arching over a roadway.

The genus *Ficus* is rampant with species venerated and used by humankind. Some of the large tree species are simply the most glorious examples of the vegetable kingdom that the earth provides. There is nothing to compare with the sight of a single tree covering more than an acre of ground. The following species are hardy in zones 10 and 11 and marginal in zone 10a unless otherwise indicated. Also, they require average and regular amounts of moisture unless otherwise indicated in the individual descriptions.

Ficus afzelii (af-ZEL-ee-eye) (synonyms *F. eriobotryoides, F. saussureana*) is indigenous to tropical western, central, and southeastern Africa. In its native habitat it usually starts life as an epiphyte on larger trees or palms. It is, compared to many others, a modest grower, reaching a height of 30 feet or so. The dark green leathery leaves are about a foot long and are narrowly elliptic to narrowly oblanceolate in shape with a short abrupt tip and a prominent lighter colored midrib. The leaves are much larger on young trees, and the new growth on trees of all ages is a beautiful coppery maroon in color. The golden to orange figs are mostly hidden by the leaves but are borne in pairs and are covered in a fine pubescence. This species is one of the most beautiful of the smaller evergreen species. The most common vernacular name is loquat-leaved fig because of the shape and size of the leaves.

Ficus altissima (al-TIS-i-ma) is native to northeastern India, Myanmar (Burma), and Malaysia, and northeastward to the Philippines. While called the lofty fig in many parts of the world, the tree does not attain the height that many other species of *Ficus* do but rather is usually more spreading than towering although it nevertheless grows to 70 or 80 feet. It usually starts out as an epiphyte on larger trees and is a banyan but does not produce the multitude of aerial roots and subsidiary trunks as do many others. The young growth of twigs and small branches is pubescent and usually green, but the trunks and older branches have silvery gray bark. The dark green leaves, which are usually about a foot long but may be only half that size, are short-stalked, elliptic to ovate in shape with a short blunt tip, leathery, glossy, and heavily veined with white or red. The midrib is prominent with five to nine lateral pairs of veins. The bottommost pair of veins forms a distinctive large V. The round figs, borne in the leaf axils usually in pairs, are about a half inch in diameter and are orange to scarlet in color. This great tree grows fast with ample water and fertile soil. It is one of the most beautiful in the genus, but ultimately grows too large for the average home grounds. It is glorious in parks and on estates or anywhere a large tree can be accommodated. It seems to prefer the warmer and more humid tropical and subtropical areas over the drier and cooler ones. It is also sometimes called the council fig because of meetings held under its canopy in its native habitat. Plate 199.

Ficus aspera (a-SPER-a / AS-pe-ra) (synonym *F. parcellii*) is native to the islands of the South Pacific northeast of Australia. It is usually a large shrub to small tree, but sometimes attains a height of 50 feet in its native habitat. The leaves are quite variable in shape and color. At least two cultivars are much more common in cultivation than is the type. Typical leaves are 8 to 12 inches long, cordate to rhomboid in shape, and almost stalkless. They are rough but usually glossy above and pubescent beneath, sometimes coarsely toothed on the margins, and sometimes deeply lobed, although many individuals exhibit leaves neither lobed nor with serrated margins. The globose figs, which are borne on the trunk and branches, are yellow maturing to scarlet and are about an inch in diameter, sometimes larger. *Ficus aspera* 'Canonii' (ka-NOAN-ee-eye) has leaves colored a bronzy red above and purple beneath and bright red figs. *Ficus aspera* 'Parcellii' (par-SEL-lee-eye) is the most common form in cultivation. It has leaves that are marbled and speckled with white to a lesser or greater degree (some leaves are almost entirely white) and pink to purple figs. Because of the leaf variegation it is often called the clown fig or mosaic fig. The two cultivars are astonishingly attractive in the landscape. The tree is not a banyan. Plate 200.

Ficus aurea (AW-ree-a / OW-ree-a) is native to southern Florida and the West Indies and is one of only two *Ficus* species indigenous to the U.S. mainland. It is the famous (or infamous) strangler fig or Florida strangler fig. Not only does it usually start life as an epiphytic strangler, it is a banyan and usually makes buttressed trunks. The light brown trunk is short and squat when planted in the ground and attains a great diameter with time. The dark green leathery leaves are 6 to 8 inches long and elliptical in shape, with a short apical point and a strong and lighter colored midrib. The tiny stalkless round figs are yellow when mature, leading to another common name of golden fig. This tree is wonderful with its great horizontal limbs. It grows to 50 or 60 feet and is sometimes three times as wide, spreading itself by the descending aerial roots that metamorphose into pillar trunks after reaching the ground. The tree is drought tolerant when established. Plate 201.

Ficus auriculata (aw-rik′-yoo-LAIT-a) (synonym *F. roxburghii*) is indigenous to northeastern India through Myanmar (Burma), Thailand, southern China, and Southeast Asia. It is a low and spreading species whose trunks usually show no signs of buttressing and whose aerial roots are rare. It is often grown as an immense spreading shrub because of its very large and tropical looking leaves, which are often 15 inches wide and as long. The leaves are orbicular to broadly ovate to almost diamond-shaped with a cordate base, and they unfold with a gorgeous brownish red coloration, later turning bright green. The upper surfaces of the leaves are as rough as sandpaper, pubescent beneath, and blessed with a deep midrib and lateral veins. The leaves are extraordinarily attractive, and the leaf margins are sometimes remotely toothed. Most plants drop their leaves and become semi-dormant in cold or dry winters. Because of this habit, the species is often successfully grown in zone 9b with occasional damage. As if the marvelous giant leaves were not attraction enough, the figs, which are formed on the trunk and branches, are a wonderful deep red in color and sometimes as much as 3 inches in diameter. Although they are edible, they are not as palatable as the fruit of *F. carica*. This species is sometimes called the Roxburg fig. It is a water lover and one of the tropical world's finest landscape subjects.

Ficus australis. See *F. rubiginosa*.

Ficus benghalensis (ben-gal-ENS-is) (synonym *F. indica*) is native to a very wide area of Asia, from India through Myanmar (Burma), Thailand, Southeast Asia, southern China, and Malaysia. It is now naturalized in almost every wet tropical area of the earth. The trunks are tan colored to light gray or even white. This fig is the world's largest tree in terms of its spread. Some very old individuals cover more than an acre of ground and make a virtual forest from a single tree. The tree grows to as much as 100 feet with low, immense, leaning, and ponderously thick limbs from which descend curtains of reddish brown aerial roots. Some of these roots, after reaching the ground, thicken, grow stiff, and become secondary prop or pillar trunks. No one knows just how long this banyan process might be able to continue nor just how great a spread the tree might attain nor even how long the trees live, but some accounts from ancient Indian writings indicate at least 5000 years. The dark green and leathery leaves are as much as a foot long and ovate to elliptic to almost oblong in shape with a very small apical tip. The midrib and lateral veins are prominent and colored white to yellow. The beautiful red figs are stalkless and are borne in pairs along the branches. The tree is called the banyan (a word derived ultimately from Sanskrit through Portuguese and referring to the merchants who set up shop under the spreading trees), Indian banyan, and Indian fig tree. This awe-inspiring tree is drought tolerant and grows but does not thrive in frost-free Mediterranean climates like southern and coastal California where it grows much more slowly, produces few aerial roots (and the ones it does produce seldom reach the ground), and never even approaches the ultimate size of individuals grown in the wet tropics. Where the climate is favorable, there is nothing to compare to a mature banyan tree for large landscapes. Plates 202, 203, and 204.

Ficus benjamina (ben-ja-MYN-a) is indigenous to a vast area including India, southern China, Southeast Asia, Malaysia, the Philippines, northern Australia, and the islands of the South Pacific. It is a variable species, and several delightful cultivars are available. *Ficus benjamina* var. *benjamina,* the type, is a very large tree of banyan habit with relatively few auxiliary trunks. It reaches 80 feet or more with a spread of twice that in its native habitats where it begins its life as an epiphytic strangler. The great branches produce slender twigs at their ends, which are more or less pendent and which phenomenon has given rise to one of the vernacular names, weeping fig. The bark is a lovely gray to white, and in young trees the trunks are picturesque because they are erect but not straight columns. With age the tree form is a spreading banyan type that is broader than tall with a beautiful dense umbrella-like canopy of pendent branches, which often cascade to the ground. One of the world's finest shade trees, this fig is currently the most widely grown tree indoors, whether in a home or atrium. The tree produces surface roots that, in large and old specimens, are a problem in confined spaces. The thin, glossy medium green leaves are 3 to 5 inches long and ovate to elliptical in shape with long tapering apical "tails," and are borne on flexible petioles, which allow them to move and shimmer with the slightest breeze. The leaves are rather similar in shape to those of the poplar tree. The tiny stalkless figs are a beautiful dark red in color. Other common names for this species are Chinese banyan, Chinese weeping banyan, and laurel fig. This species and its cultivars are drought tolerant when established. *Ficus benjamina* 'Exotica' supposedly originated in Java. It has narrower, darker green leaves with longer tips that are somewhat twisted on quite pendulous slender branches. This cultivar

makes one of the most graceful trees in the genus. *Ficus benjamina* var. *nuda* (NOO-da) (synonym *F. philippinensis*) has large dark green oblong leathery and glossy leaves with a very long tip and a beautiful and graceful weeping habit. The new growth is a wonderful bronzy rose in color. *Ficus benjamina* 'Variegata' (vair-ee-a-GAIT-a) is a variegated (white) form. Plate 205.

Ficus brevifolia. See *F. citrifolia.*

Ficus callophylloides. See *F. subcordata.*

Ficus callosa (kal-LO-sa) is indigenous to a large area of tropical Asia from southern India and Sri Lanka, Southeast Asia, Indonesia, and the Philippines. It is a large and beautiful species that does not produce aerial roots but grows to 100 feet in its native habitats. The dark gray trunk is buttressed with age and is a stout and low-branching heavy column. The beautiful dark green leathery but glossy leaves are short-stalked, elliptical to ovate in shape, 8 to 10 inches long, with a short pointed tip, and are heavily veined with light green or yellow-green. The leaves drop in cold or dry winters. The small figs are green to yellow. This very beautiful tree is better "behaved" than the gigantic banyan types with their invasive roots and immense spread. It produces surface roots but not as abundantly as the banyan types, and the leaves are as beautiful as those of any *Ficus* species. Furthermore, it is unexcelled as a shade tree for large spaces. It is drought tolerant when established but does much better with ample and regular amounts of moisture.

Ficus carica (KAIR-i-ka / ka-REEK-a), the common fig or edible fig, is native to the Middle East eastward to Afghanistan. It is hardy in zones 8 through 11, with some cultivars adaptable to zone 7. Except in wet tropical climes, the tree is deciduous in the winter. It grows as high as 30 feet but is usually grown as a large multitrunked shrub. The trees are low branching with heavy gray and gnarled branches. The leaves are as much as a foot across and generally ovate to almost orbicular in outline but are shallowly to deeply lobed into three to five segments. Each segment has a lighter colored midrib and is often toothed. The leaves are light green to dark green in color and rough, almost sandpapery, to the touch. The young branches and leaves have a strong, almost indescribable warm and fecund "fig" odor, especially when bruised. The edible figs are large, pear-shaped, and yellowish to purple to brown in color. There are many cultivated varieties, varying in flavor of fig, size of tree, shape and size of leaf, and hardiness to cold. All forms of the species are drought tolerant when established. *Ficus carica* 'Mission' is one of the best for ornamental purposes as it is a large and strong grower. A very few varieties, called "caprifigs," need a pollinating wasp to form fruit. The most famous of these varieties in the United States is *Ficus carica* 'Calimyrna'. All other figs are self pollinating. All need sun and sandy, freely draining soil to thrive. They are drought tolerant when established although, like many other landscape subjects, grow faster and better with a regular and adequate supply of moisture. The species makes a broad umbrella-shaped crown of dense foliage, is excellent as a shade or patio tree, and is quite picturesque when bare of leaves in the winter. Like all other species in the genus, *F. carica* has a white milky latex to which a few people are allergic.

Ficus citrifolia (sit-ri-FO-lee-a) (synonyms *F. brevifolia*, *F. laevigata*) is native to a vast area including the Florida Keys, the Bahamas, the West Indies, Mexico, Central America, and South America. It is not a banyan type fig but produces aerial roots and grows to 80 feet or more in the more favorable and wetter parts of its range although it is drought tolerant when established. The trunk is stout, low-branched, and a beautiful light gray in color. In general appearance this species is reminiscent of *F. aurea*, but does not spread as wide and is usually smaller. What it most resembles when old is *Quercus virginiana* (live oak). The leaves are 4 to 5 inches long and ovate to elliptical in shape with a cordate base and a short pointed tip, and are borne on 1- to 2-inch-long petioles. A deep dark green in color with a prominent lighter colored midrib and lateral veins, the leaves are partly deciduous in cold or dry winters. The figs are long-stalked, a beautiful red to brownish red in color and reputedly edible. This species is another fine landscape subject with few transgressing surface roots, good drought tolerance, and an upright habit. It should be much more widely planted than it is at present. It endures the common names of shortleaf fig and, in Florida, wild fig and wild banyan, although it is not a tree with banyan growth habit.

Ficus columnaris. See *F. macrophylla* var. *columnaris.*

Ficus deltoidea (del-TOY-dee-a) (synonym *F. diversifolia*) is indigenous to the southern Philippines southward and westward to Southeast Asia, Malaysia, and Indonesia. This large shrub or small tree with aerial roots often begins its life as an epiphyte but is not a banyan. It grows only to 20 feet or so in height and is more often found as a shrub than a tree, even in nature. Indeed, it is usually seen as a large cascading epiphytic shrub on large trees, thus one of the common names of mistletoe fig. It is a spreading and somewhat sprawling shrub with slender zigzagging branches. The bark is gray and what trunk there is is slender and usually leaning. The leaf shape is probably the most variable in the whole genus and ranges from elliptical or lanceolate to obovate or spatulate, the two latter shapes being more common than the two former. Only the spatulate-shaped leaf form is regularly sold and cultivated. The 3-inch-long leaves are dark green thick and leathery, almost succulent, and the ends of the spatulate-shaped leaves are usually provided with a shallow notch. The plant loves warmth and humidity, and produces picturesque aerial roots under such conditions. It is a very good choice for a large cascading landscape subject, especially when the climatic conditions allow growing it on larger trees. It also makes a fine foreground subject for larger trees and shrubs and is superb as a container plant, especially when placed against a background where its form can be appreciated.

Ficus diversifolia. See *F. deltoidea.*
Ficus drupacea. See *F. mysorensis.*
Ficus elastica (ee-LAS-ti-ka) is native to Nepal, Bhutan, northeast India, Myanmar (Burma), Malaya, Sumatra, and Java. In its native habitat it usually begins life as an epiphyte, later strangling its host and becoming a gigantic banyan type fig. It grows to 100, sometimes 150, feet or even more, with great buttressed trunks covering large expanses of ground and serpentine surface roots snaking out far from the main trunk. It is one of the noblest and most awe-inspiring examples of tropical vegetation. Mature trees must be seen to be believed; with their great buttressed trunks, giant ascending limbs, and curtains of aerial roots, the trees make not only a forest within the forest, but are also veritable worlds unto themselves. They must be seen quickly in nature as the forests wherein they dwell are being decimated at an ever increasing and most alarming rate. As a landscape subject the tree obviously grows too large for the average homeowner in the wet tropics, but it is of such great beauty that it should be planted even more than it is on estates, in parks, and along great avenues. Part of the reason for its almost startling beauty is the size of the leaves. Commensurate with the size and beauty of the tree form, the leaves are a foot or more long, elliptic to oblong in shape, dark green, thick and leathery but glossy on the upper surface, with a very prominent and lighter colored midvein. They are short-stalked and, in mature trees, are found mostly at the ends of the branches. The leaf buds are covered by a pink-colored to red-colored stipule, which often persists for some time after the leaf emerges, and which adds to the great beauty of the tree. The oblong figs are light to dark green in color and about a half inch in diameter. The tree grows but does not thrive in frost-free Mediterranean climates like those of southern coastal California where it makes few aerial roots and does not spread. Specimens in these drier regions are nevertheless of great beauty and are more restrained and manageable than those grown in truly tropical climates. The most common vernacular name for the tree is simply the rubber tree, as its latex was once used as a substitute for the superior sap of *Hevea brasiliensis*. Other common names include Indian rubber tree, Assam tree, and snake tree (in allusion to the surface roots). There are several horticultural varieties or cultivars, none of which is capable of attaining the stature of the type. Some, such as *Ficus elastica* 'Decora' (de-KOR-a), have wider, thicker, much glossier leaves. Others have variegated leaves. *Ficus elastica* 'Doescheri' (DUR-shur-eye) has green, gray, white, and yellow leaves. *Ficus elastica* 'Schryvariana' (skree-vair-ee-AHN-a) has leaves with a background of ivory to yellow and a central pinnate variegation of dark and grayish green. *Ficus elastica* 'Tricolor' (TRY-kul-or), perhaps the most beautiful variegated form, has leaves mottled in green, yellow, and pink, with a bright red midrib. These cultivars are exceedingly beautiful of leaf but not always successful landscape subjects. For example, the leaves

of 'Decora' are stiff-looking and are not graceful in the landscape. The variegated forms are often more chlorotic appearing than beautiful. These varieties make wonderful houseplants, however, as does their ancestral type. Before *F. benjamina* became popular as an indoor tree subject, *F. elastica* was the most popular indoor member of the genus.

Ficus eriobotryoides. See *F. afzelii.*

Ficus fairchildii. See *F. subcordata.*

Ficus glomerata. See *F. racemosa.*

Ficus indica. See *F. benghalensis.*

Ficus laevigata. See *F. citrifolia.*

Ficus lutea. See *F. nekbudu, F. vogelii.*

Ficus lyrata (ly-RAIT-a) (synonym *F. pandurata*) is indigenous to tropical Central and West Africa. It is a small to medium-sized tree, never growing to more than 40 feet in height, with a mostly slender crown of gigantic leaves. The tree is not a banyan in habit and seldom produces aerial roots even in the most humid and wet climates. The bark is dark gray to almost black and is usually broken into vertical fissures. The overall visual and landscape effect is that of a very large leaved evergreen oak tree. The leaves are as much as 18 inches long and a foot wide, and the common name fiddle-leaf fig perfectly describes their shape: obovate with cordate or squared basal ends and slightly wavy and scalloped margins. The leaf texture is very tough and leathery, and the upper surface a dark deep glossy green with prominent and lighter colored midrib and lateral veins. The round inch-wide figs are green. The tree is stunning as a patio or shade tree or planted where the great decorative leaves and the formal silhouette can be appreciated up close. Because of the size and texture of the leaves, the tree seems too stiff and unnatural for most other landscape purposes. It is drought tolerant when established but languishes and does not grow unless it receives regular and adequate supplies of water.

Ficus macrophylla (mak-ro-FYL-la) (synonym *F. magnolioides*) is native to tropical Queensland and northern New South Wales in Australia where it is reported to grow to a height of 200 feet. Trees in cultivation in the United States are not nearly so great in stature, and their spread far exceeds their height. In Australia the tree is commonly called the Moreton Bay fig or the Australian banyan. It is indeed a banyan type fig and in its native habitat often starts its life as an epiphyte, eventually strangling and replacing its host. It does not, however, produce the prodigious amount of aerial roots that many other banyan figs do and, when grown in drier climates, tends to eschew the production of aerial roots and subsidiary trunks altogether. Yet the brown to light gray trunks of mature individuals are always massive and heavily buttressed no matter what the climate, and the surface roots are prominent and spectacular and often exceed the width of the canopy in their spread. The 6- to 12-inch-long leaves are long-stalked, ovate to elliptic in shape, leathery and glossy above, with a strong whitish or reddish midrib. Like those of *F. elastica,* the new leaves are clothed in bright

pink and persistent sheaths. Furthermore, the leaves are strongly reminiscent in shape and size to the leaves of *Magnolia grandiflora* (southern magnolia). The inch-wide figs are rounded, a reddish brown to sometimes purplish brown in color, and usually speckled with tiny white spots. It is hard to imagine a more beautiful landscape subject. It is as wonderfully picturesque as even the great spreading banyans of tropical Asia. There is something truly magical about the great meandering whitish surface roots winding their way out from the enchanting buttresses of the trunks, above which the dark green crown of large leaves looms with its massive light-colored limbs. The tree is hardier to cold than most other banyan species and is known to survive in zone 9b, although it is marginal there. Established trees are usually unharmed by temperatures of 28°F or above, although young trees are much more susceptible to cold. Because of the great interest and influx of landscape material from Australia, the trees have been growing in California for a longer period than in Florida. The tree is drought tolerant when established. **Ficus macrophylla** var. **columnaris** (ka-LUM-na-riss / kah-lum-NAIR-iss) (synonym *F. columnaris*), on Lord Howe Island off the northeastern coast of Australia, is as supreme an example of a great banyan tree as any tropical Asian species. It has leaves very similar in shape to those of the type, but they are larger and the tree produces copious amounts of aerial roots and is said to sometimes cover more than an acre of ground with its great auxiliary trunks. Photographs show it to be the equal of such glories as *F. benghalensis* and *F. elastica.* Plate 206.

Ficus magnolioides. See *F. macrophylla.*

Ficus microcarpa (myk-ro-KARP-a) (synonyms *F. nitida, F. retusa*) is indigenous to a wide area from the southern Japanese Islands, southeastern China, and southwards through the Philippines and Borneo to Southeast Asia and northern Australia. Common names for the tree include Indian laurel, Chinese banyan, and Cuban laurel. It grows to as much as 75 feet in its native haunts but is seldom over 50 feet in cultivation. It is a banyan but seldom produces aerial roots (and, therefore, subsidiary trunks) when grown in drier climates. Furthermore, the trunk does not buttress nearly to the extent that other banyan trees do. While surface roots are produced, they are not nearly so extensive as in the larger banyan species. These more "restrained" qualities of *F. microcarpa* make it a very desirable subject for street planting as well as for large yards. Indeed, it (especially the dense-crowned *F. microcarpa* var. *nitida*) is one of the most common street trees in warm climates around the world. The beautiful trunks are a light gray to almost white in color. The younger branches are slender and beautifully pendent, often touching the ground even in large specimens. The dark green leaves are short-stalked, leathery, 3 to 5 inches long, and broadly ovate to obovate in shape. The new growth is a light green, sometimes rosy-colored, which greatly adds to the beauty of the tree. The globose figs are a half inch in diameter and a dark purple when ripe. ***Ficus microcarpa* 'Green Gem'** has leaves larger than those of the type. ***Ficus microcarpa* var. *nitida*** (ni-TEE-da / ni-TY-da) has a much more erect form of growth with branches that are not pendent. It forms a low and wide crown similar to that of *Quercus virginiana* (live oak) and is one of the finest of street and shade trees for warm climate gardens. It is also much used for hedges (tolerating all but the severest amount of pruning) and in containers on streets and patios. The leaves are narrower (elliptic to obovate) than the type, and the tree's crown is more densely foliaged. ***Ficus microcarpa* 'Variegata'** is an attractive variegated cultivar. All forms of this species are drought tolerant when established. They are fairly hardy for a large *Ficus* species and have been successfully grown in the warmer parts of zone 9b for many years.

Ficus microphylla. See *F. rubiginosa.*

Ficus mysorensis (my-sor-ENS-is) (synonym *F. drupacea*) is indigenous to India, Myanmar (Burma), southern China, and Southeast Asia. It grows to as much as 75 feet in its native habitats but is seldom more than 40 to 50 feet in cultivation. The tree is not a banyan, although it produces a few aerial roots in the humidity of Southeast Asia. The light brown-colored trunk in older individuals is slightly buttressed and sends out far-ranging sinuous surface roots, which are similar in size and form to those of *F. macrophylla*. The leathery but glossy leaves, which are as much as a foot long, are a deep green in color and broadly elliptical in shape, with a prominent and lighter colored midrib and lateral veins. The figs are a bright orange to red or purple and are more than an inch in diameter. These beautiful trees withstand a few degrees of frost. Many are thriving in the warmer parts of zone 10a. The only common name seems to be Mysore fig. Plate 207.

Ficus nekbudu (nek-BOO-doo) (synonyms *F. lutea*, *F. utilis*) is native to tropical central and southeastern Africa from Congo, Zaire, and Tanzania to Mozambique and Natal (South Africa). This banyan produces copious aerial roots under wet tropical conditions and grows to 70 feet in height with a spread of 100 feet or more in its native haunts. The light brown-colored trunk is massive and buttressed, and the branches are ponderous. The dark green leaves are as beautiful as any in the genus. A foot, sometimes more, in length and broadly elliptical in shape, they are glossy and leathery above, with prominent lighter colored venation. The trees are at least partly deciduous in cold or dry winters but are not hardy to cold. The inch-wide figs are borne in clusters and are covered in a white pubescence. The tree is sometimes called Zulu fig or Nekbudu fig. Where there is space this is one of the finest of trees for landscape purposes in frost-free climates. It has the essence of the tropical look with its large, heavily veined leaves and massive trunk. The tree is drought tolerant when established.

Ficus nitida. See *F. microcarpa.*

Ficus nota (NOAT-a) is native to the Philippines and northern Borneo. It is a small spreading tree that grows only to about 30 feet with a dark-colored usually crooked trunk. The dark green leaves are leathery but thin in texture, heavily veined above, as much as a foot long, and narrowly ovate with a short apical tip and an unequally lobed cordate base. The leaf margins are finely to coarsely serrate. The reddish brown figs appear on the trunk and branches.

Ficus palmeri (PALM-ur-eye) is indigenous to Baja California. It often grows to no more than a few feet in the drier parts of its range (it is a favored bonsai subject) or where it seems to have sprouted on rocks, but it can attain a height of 50 or 60 feet when grown or found in regions with more rainfall. It forms a "caudex" type trunk that is nearly white in color and is often greatly swollen at the base. The leaves are 6 to 8 inches long, ovate in shape, and soft and leathery with prominent yellowish midrib and lateral veins. The figs are small, yellowish, and pubescent. The tree often begins its life as a strangler fig on cactus species or other shrubs in its native habitat, although it is not a banyan fig, and is often later found seemingly growing from atop rock piles or cliffs. It is a wonderfully picturesque thing with its stout white trunk that is usually bulbous at the base and its strangling roots grasping and enveloping rocks and soil. This fig is quite drought tolerant, and a soil with unimpeded drainage is essential for its well-being. The tree is called anaba in Mexico and desert fig in the United States. It is a wonderfully suitable large subject for the cactus and succulent garden and is also a beautiful shade tree. It should be much more widely planted in arid tropical regions as a street and park tree.

Ficus pandurata. See *F. lyrata.*

Ficus parcellii. See *F. aspera.*

Ficus petiolaris (peet-ee-o-LAIR-is) is native to western Mexico. It is similar in habit to *F. palmeri* and, like that species, its stature is dependent on how much water it can get: it is only a shrub in true desert areas but develops into a medium-sized or even large tree with an adequate and regular supply of moisture. The trunk, which is often swollen at the base, is a brownish yellow to dark gray in color and is seldom buttressed. The long-stalked leaves are very beautiful: about 6 inches wide, broadly ovate-cordate to round with a pointed tip, deep green or bluish green, leathery, and somewhat wavy on the margins with deep and very prominent midrib and lateral veins that are yellowish to scarlet in color. The small figs are a deep green speckled with white or pink. This species is unusually attractive for a fig in tropical arid regions and, if given enough water, is a superb landscape subject. Few trees have such remarkably beautiful leaves.

Ficus pseudopalma (soo-doe-PALM-a) is native to the Philippines. It is an unusual fig species in that it only grows to about 30 feet tall under optimum conditions, its few branches are bare of leaves except at their tips, and the leaves are relatively long and narrow. Thus, the overall appearance of the tree is similar to that of a palm or, more accurately, a large *Yucca* or *Dra-*

caena species. It reportedly grows unbranched in its native habitat, adding to the palm or dracaena-like effect. As seen in cultivation it is usually multitrunked and looks much better this way. The leaves at the ends of the branches or trunks are immense: 3 feet long and only about 6 inches wide. They are short-stalked and generally narrowly oblanceolate to narrowly obovate in shape, and leathery but glossy above, with small teeth along the margins towards the ends of the leaves. They are surprisingly tough for their size and are not easily tattered by wind, but strong, persistent winds mar their appearance, so the tree is best sited where it has some protection. The inch-wide figs are purplish green to purplish brown and are almost hidden by the leaves. They are reputedly edible. Common names are dracaena fig, Philippine fig, and palm fig. This species is striking and ornamental in the landscape, especially when planted where its form is silhouetted. Plate 208.

Ficus pumila (PYOO-mi-la) (synonym *F. repens*) is indigenous to a wide area of Asia from the southern Japanese Islands southwards through Taiwan, the Philippines, southeastern China and Southeast Asia, including Vietnam. One of the vining species in the genus, it is very widely planted in the tropics and subtropics. In spite of its almost completely tropical origin, it is hardy in zones 9 through 11 with only occasional damage in severe winters of zone 9a. It is one of the finest of the clinging vines as it is evergreen and, when established, grows fast and vigorously. It covers a great surface area if it receives enough water during the growing season. As a juvenile plant it is restrained and the leaves are small and restricted to a thin mat covering of the surface on which the stems cling. Once, however, the plant is established in a location (about a year—it helps to cut the plant back when it is first planted to incite new growth), its growth rate accelerates markedly and it forms mature fruiting branches, which arch out from the mat of small juvenile leaves and form larger mature dark green leaves that are oblong in shape and about 4 inches long. The beautiful 2-inch-long oblong figs are yellow to red and are borne only on the mature fruiting branches, which spread to 2 feet or so perpendicularly from the surface mat. The vine makes an incredibly beautiful and lush effect when mature and covers a very large space with time. Unless the vine can be pruned regularly, it should not be planted where it will transgress onto wooden surfaces as the clinging roots are invasive and will soon mar and even destroy such a substrate. This plant is called creeping fig and climbing fig. Because of its variability of form, it has several cultivars, of which two are noteworthy. *Ficus pumila* **'Minima'** (MIN-i-ma) remains small in leaf and fruit throughout its life and is a very attractive subject for tracery against light colored walls and up close. *Ficus pumila* **'Variegata'** (vair-ee-a-GAIT-a) has foliage with yellowish white variegation and does not grow as large or as vigorously as the type.

Ficus racemosa (ray-si-MO-sa) (synonym *F. glomerata*) is indigenous to India eastward through Southeast Asia, Indonesia, Malaysia, and northern Australia. It is not a banyan, but it sometimes produces aerial roots and grows to a height of 80 feet or even more with a spread at least as wide. When mature, the massive trunk is buttressed. The long-stalked leaves are 6 to 8 inches long, dark green, ovate to elliptical in shape, and are glossy above with a metallic sheen. The common name is cluster fig because the figs are borne on the trunk and lower branches in great bunches on a thick pendent stalk. Each fruit is more than an inch long and is pear-shaped and a beautiful scarlet speckled with white when mature. This highly ornamental tree is suitable for large spaces in the tropics and is somewhat drought tolerant when established.

Ficus religiosa (re-lij´-ee-O-sa) is native to northeastern India through Myanmar (Burma), Thailand, and Southeast Asia. It is a strangler species that starts its life as an epiphyte in its native haunts but seldom produces aerial roots and is not a banyan type fig species even in wet tropical climates. The great mature single trunks are only slightly buttressed. Surface roots are produced but not to the extent of the great strangler banyans like *F. benghalensis*, *F. elastica*, and *F. macrophylla*. The tree grows to a great size with age, sometimes reaching a height of 100 feet with an equal spread. The bark is a deep brown in color and contrasts wonderfully with the bluish green leaves. The thin, not leathery leaves are shaped rather like those of *Populus tremuloides* (quaking aspen) but are much larger and more distinctive because of their very long and tapering "tail" at the end of the leaf. The blade is about 6 inches wide and 8 inches long, ovate to cordate in outline (except for the "tail"), with a whitish yellow midrib and lateral veins. Because of their thin texture and the long and pliable petioles on which they are borne, the leaves rustle and flutter in the slightest breeze. The tree is usually deciduous and drops its leaves in the late winter or early spring, although wet and warm winters often see no or only a marginal leaf fall. The tiny dark brown figs are stalkless on the branches and are not conspicuous nor very ornamental. Because of the tree's natural semi-dormant period, it is hardier to cold than many other of the great tropical *Ficus* species but is only marginally hardy in zone 9b. The epithet *religiosa* reflects the belief in Asia that this is the tree under which the Buddha sat and attained enlightenment, and supposedly died. It is sometimes called, especially in Asia, the bo tree, the Bodhi tree, or peepul. The tree is drought tolerant but only thrives with an adequate and regular supply of moisture. It grows well in southern California but does not attain the proportions nor does it thrive there as it does in the wetter and warmer tropical and subtropical areas. It is one of the finest large trees for parks, estates, and great avenues.

Ficus repens. See *F. pumila*.

Ficus retusa. See *F. microcarpa*.

Ficus roxburghii. See *F. auriculata*.

Ficus rubiginosa (roo-bij´-i-NO-sa) (synonyms *F. australis*, *F. microphylla*) is native to New South Wales and southern Queensland in Australia. It is a banyan and, in its native habitat, usually starts its life as an epiphyte and strangles its host, ultimately producing auxiliary trunks by the aerial roots with some buttressing of the primary trunk. It is, however, a most variable species and, especially when planted in semiarid areas, usually evinces no banyan habit and very seldom produces aerial roots. Under optimum conditions the tree grows to as much as 60 feet with a spread of 80 feet or so but, planted in less favorable (drier) areas like southern California, it seldom grows to more than 40 feet with about an equal spread, does not produce aerial roots, has an unbuttressed trunk, and makes a compact and dense crown of leaves. The bark color is cinnamon on younger parts with a felt of short brownish red hairs, turning dark gray or almost black on the trunk and older branches. The dark green leathery leaves are borne on short petioles that are cinnamon-colored due to the rusty pubescence. The leaves are generally about 6 inches long and elliptic to oblong in shape, with a prominent midrib but without conspicuous lateral veins. Young leaves are rusty pubescent when new and retain the pubescence underneath. The figs are borne in pairs along the branches and are usually felt-covered and a yellowish green to cinnamon in color. The individual trees are quite variable as to size of leaf and the amount of pubescence on branches and leaves. Some taxonomists separate the species into varieties according to the amount of felt evident and the size of the leaf. Whatever the taxonomic status, the trees are extremely ornamental and are, especially in frost-free Mediterranean climates, some of the finest landscape subjects available as they are drought tolerant. This species seems to have all the virtues of the giant *Ficus* species and none of the disadvantages and, although it is not gloriously spectacular like the giant banyans, it is of such beauty that it cries out, like a puppy in a pet store, "Take me; plant me; enjoy me." Common names are rusty fig, botany bay fig, and rusty-leaf fig.

Ficus saussureana. See *F. afzelii*.

Ficus subcordata (sub-kor-DAIT-a) (synonyms *F. callophylloides*, *F. fairchildii*) is native to the Philippines, Southeast Asia, Indonesia, and New Guinea. It is one of the most beautiful of the giant banyan species with copious aerial roots and far-spreading surface roots and subsidiary trunks. The great trunks are light gray to light brown in color. The branches are beautifully pendulous and the 6- to 8-inch-long leaves are elliptical to oblong in shape and a deep and lustrous green in color. The leaf venation is not prominent, and only the lighter colored midrib is conspicuous. The oblong figs are greenish yellow changing to red or brown when mature. One of the synonyms honors David Fairchild, who in 1926 collected seed of the tree in Java and planted a seedling at his home in Coral Gables, Florida, where the wonderful and now mature tree lives still at the back of the beautiful house on that estate known as "The Kampong." The tree is somewhat drought tolerant when established.

Ficus sycomorus (sik-o-MOR-us) is probably originally native to tropical East Africa and the southern Arabian Peninsula but was carried into Egypt, Syria, and Israel in prehistoric times where it flourished. It is not a banyan type fig species and is rather small as *Ficus* species go. It grows to 60 feet or more in its native habitat with an equal spread. The trunk is short, stout, and a light yellowish brown in color with thick and heavy branches. Old trunks show some buttressing. In overall appearance the tree is not unlike a large evergreen *F. carica* (common fig). The 6-inch-long dark green leaves are ovate to almost diamond-shaped and rather thin and rough to the touch on their upper surfaces, and are carried on 2-inch-long stalks. The midrib and lateral veins are prominent. The edible figs are borne on the trunk and branches. Each inch-wide fruit is covered in a whitish tomentum. The tree is very drought tolerant when established and is a valuable addition to the landscape repertoire of arid and semiarid tropical areas. Some of the literature indicates that the species is frost tolerant, but this is not true as the tree is often severely damaged by temperatures below 30°F. It is called the sycamore fig, Egyptian sycamore, mulberry fig, and simply sycamore, spelled either "sycamore" or "sycomore."

Ficus utilis. See *F. nekbudu*.

Ficus vogelii (vo-GEL-ee-eye) (synonym *F. lutea*) is indigenous to tropical West Africa. Because it is rather similar to *F. nekbudu*, some taxonomists consider it but a variant of that species and usually put both species into the taxon *F. lutea*. It is a banyan in wet tropical climes but sometimes has no aerial roots when planted in drier regions. The tree grows to 60 feet or more and, in wet regions, has a spread of at least 100 feet when mature. The dark gray trunks are heavily buttressed when old, and there are many far-reaching surface roots. The leaves, which are similar to those of *F. nekbudu*, are some of the most beautiful of any tropical tree. They are as much as a foot long, a very deep almost bluish green in color, thick and leathery, very heavily veined with yellowish white, and oblong to elliptical in shape, and are carried on 6-inch-long brown stalks near the ends of the great branches.

FILICIUM (fi-LIS-ee-um)

Sapindaceae: The Soapberry, Golden-Rain Tree
    Family
FERN TREE
Medium-sized evergreen tree; spectacular large
    fernlike leaves; small purple fruit
Zones 10 and 11; marginal in zone 10a
Sun to partial shade
Average but regular amounts of moisture
Average well-drained soil
Propagation by seed and cuttings

A small genus of only three species of trees in tropical Africa and Asia. All have pinnate foliage, panicles of whitish flowers, and small blue or purple fruit. One is increasingly planted in nearly frost-free regions for its very attractive foliage. ***Filicium decipiens*** (de-SIP-ee-enz) is native to southern India and Sri Lanka. It grows rather slowly to as much as 70 feet in its native habitat but reaches half that height elsewhere. The trunk is dark gray to black in color and short in stature. The branches form low and create a rounded dense crown of large bright green foliage. The leathery leaves are 12 to 18 inches long and pinnate with 12 to 16 leathery bright green leaflets. Each leaflet is about 6 inches long and narrowly elliptic in shape with a strong midrib and wavy margins. The tiny flowers are insignificant in the landscape even though they are in 6-inch-long panicled clusters. The half-inch-long purplish oblong fruits are quite attractive, although they also do not show up well in the landscape. The tree is very beautiful because of the texture of the leaves and from a distance looks somewhat similar to a breadfruit tree. It is one of the finest subjects for patio planting or for lining streets and can be startlingly beautiful as an accent. It is an almost-too-good-to-be-true plant for tropical areas, not fussy about soil or watering although, like so many other plants, it looks better with regular and adequate supplies of moisture. Its only limitation is that it does not tolerate cold. Plate 209.

FIRMIANA (feer-mee-AHN-a)
Sterculiaceae: The Cacao, Cola-Nut Family
CHINESE PARASOL TREE
Deciduous tree to 40 feet; large lobed leaves; green trunk and bark; large papery fruit
Zones 8 through 11
Sun to partial shade
Average but regular amounts of moisture
Average well-drained soil

A genus of nine species of trees and large shrubs in eastern Asia and the western Pacific Islands. All have large usually lobed leaves, large clusters of orange or yellowish white flowers, and strange papery and flower-like fruit capsules that open to reveal seeds on the "petals." Only one species is planted outside botanical gardens in the United States. ***Firmiana simplex*** (SIM-plex) is native to the southernmost islands of Japan (Ryuku) southwards through Taiwan and the Philippines and westward into Southeast Asia. It looks very tropical when in leaf but is leafless for a long time. It grows to 50 feet or more in its native habitats but is usually no more than 30 feet tall in cultivation with a somewhat narrow and triangular crown. Except for the oldest wood, which is gray, the trunk is a striking green, smooth, and often shiny. The leaves are a foot or more across, very broadly ovate in outline, but deeply lobed into three to five segments. Each lobe ends in a point and has a prominent and lighter colored midrib. The leaves rather resemble large fig leaves or tropical maple leaves and turn a bright yellow before falling in November. The tree blooms in midsummer with terminal panicles of greenish white flowers. The strange fruits appear by early fall and consist of clusters of pendent bell-shaped greenish white papery capsules. Each capsule has four petal-like leaf parts that separate and show pealike seeds along their margins. The tree is drought tolerant when established but grows slowly and does not flourish. With an adequate and regular supply of water, however, it grows fairly quickly and is very lush and tropical looking in the summer.

FITTONIA (fit-TOE-nee-a)
Acanthaceae: The Acanthus Family
NERVE PLANT; MOSAIC PLANT; SILVER-NET PLANT
Small creeping plants with beautifully variegated leaves
Zones 10b and 11
Shade to partial shade
Water lovers
Humusy, moist, well-drained soil
Propagation by cuttings

A genus of only two species of creeping stem-rooting small herbs in low elevations of rain forests of the South American Andes. The small short-stalked leaves are elliptical in shape and heavily veined. Only one species is cultivated. ***Fittonia verschaffeltii*** (vur-sha-FELT-ee-eye) grows to only about 6 inches tall. It creeps along the ground with rooting stems and is a supreme ground-cover for frost-free regions. Each 4-inch-long elliptical leaf is dark green with a network of white or scarlet veins. It is difficult to imagine a more beautiful low groundcover. The unremarkable flowers are greenish white in short leafy bracts. The plant needs regular and ample water in a humus-rich well-drained soil and cannot take sun. There is nothing quite like the plant to brighten up shady areas, and it is a companion for almost any taller plant.

FORTUNELLA (for-too-NEL-la)
Rutaceae: The Citrus Family
KUMQUATS
Evergreen aromatic, mostly thorny trees and shrubs; fragrant white flowers; showy edible fruit
Zones vary according to species and variety
Sun
Average but regular amounts of moisture
Deep, sandy, humusy, well-drained soil
Propagation by seed and air-layering; most varieties are grafted

A small genus of four species, all of which are commonly called kumquats. The word *kumquat* is a transliteration of Chinese (Cantonese) words, which mean "golden orange" or "golden bean." The fruit is unique among the citrus tribe in having an edible skin, which is often more delicious and sweeter than the flesh within. All the species are originally native to southeastern China and parts of Southeast Asia. All are quite hardy to cold for citrus species and are dependably hardy in zones 9a through 11 and very often successful in zone

8b and even sometimes in zone 8a. This fortunate reality is partly due to their ability, unlike most other "citrus," to go into a dormant state with the approach of cold weather and shortened days. These plants also do wonderfully well in more tropical climates in which they seldom enter a period of dormancy. They are small trees that seldom grow taller than 12 or 15 feet, and there are dwarf forms of all the species. The standard forms make some of the prettiest trees the warm-climate gardener can grow as there is an ineluctable allure to these perfect little trees in and out bloom, somewhat like a loquat but more daintily graceful and refined. In fruit they are ornamental treasures. The dwarf forms are container subjects without equal and near-perfect foundation plants and hedge material.

Fortunella crassifolia (kras-si-FO-lee-a) is known as the meiwa kumquat and is a nearly thornless little tree reaching about 6 or 8 feet in height. The dark green 2- to 4-inch-long elliptic to lanceolate leaves are thick, leathery, stiff, and usually folded lengthwise to some extent to form a trough. The little fruits are a golden yellow to bright orange and are round to oblong in shape.

Fortunella hindsii (HYND-zee-eye) is known as the Hong Kong kumquat and is a very thorny small tree or, more usually, a bush only 6 or so feet high. The leaves are ovate-elliptic in shape and only 2 or 3 inches long. The fruits are almost perfectly round and usually less than an inch in diameter; they are reddish orange when ripe.

Fortunella japonica (ja-PAHN-i-ka) is known as the marumi kumquat. It grows to 9 or 10 feet in height and has small, 2-inch-long ovate-elliptic light green leaves and few thorns. The fruit is round and a golden yellow when ripe. The marumi kumquat is probably the hardiest kumquat.

Fortunella margarita (mar-ga-REET-a) is the largest kumquat, growing to 15 feet or more in height, with a dense crown. It is also the most widely grown species in the genus. The 4-inch-long dark green leaves are lanceolate to linear in shape and are usually somewhat folded lengthwise. The bright yellow fruit is about 2 inches long and oblong to obovate in shape. It is slightly less hardy to cold than the other kumquats but is a very strikingly attractive little tree.

FOUQUIERIA (foo-kee-ER-ee-a)
Fouquieriaceae: The Ocotillo Family
OCOTILLO; COACH WHIP
Trunkless shrub with tall, whiplike spiny branches; ephemeral leaves; spectacular red flowers
Zones 7 through 11; marginal in zone 6b
Sun
Drought tolerant
Sandy, very well drained soil
Propagation by cuttings, sometimes by seed

A genus of 11 species of columnar succulents and spiny shrubs and trees in Mexico and the southwestern United States. They all have ephemeral leaves and vicious spines that are the metamorphosed petioles of the quickly deciduous leaves. The leaves appear mainly in spring and summer, after rains. The plants also bloom with the advent of the rains. One species is eminently worthy of cultivation because of its attractive shape, size, and spectacular flowers. *Fouquieria splendens* (SPLEN-denz) is native to southwestern Texas, southern New Mexico, southern Arizona and adjacent Mexico, and desert areas of southern California and Baja California. The long spiny branches spring directly from the ground without benefit of any trunk and often reach a length of 20 feet, but the height of the plant is seldom that great as the whiplike stems usually arch and bend. It is nevertheless an imposing plant that needs some room. The mature stems are a deep gray to almost black, furrowed, angled, and covered with inch-long stout spines. The leaves, when they are evident, are inch-long bright green ovals bunched in groups along the stems. Appearing in spring, summer, and fall after rains, the leaves soon wither and fall. The spectacular scarlet to orange-red flowers are in short racemes along the top foot or so of the stems. Each flower is a narrow inch-long tube with many long protruding stamens. Like the leaves, the flower racemes appear principally after the spring, summer, or autumn rains. It seems hard to confuse this plant with a cactus species, but evidently some have as one of the common names is vine cactus; other and more common names are ocotillo (o-ko-TEE-yo) and coach whip. The plant is most dramatic and impressive in the cactus and succulent garden, especially when planted where its silhouette can be appreciated. It does not tolerate any soil with less than perfect drainage. It must have sun, and it is subject to rot in regions with heavy winter precipitation. Plate 210.

FREYCINETIA (fray-si-NET-ee-a)
Pandanaceae: The Pandanus, Screw-Pine Family
CLIMBING PANDANUS; CLIMBING SCREWPINE; FLOWERING PANDANUS
Large semi-climbing (twining) shrubs; tufts of linear leaves; showy purple, red, and yellow flowers
Zones 10b and 11
Partial shade to Sun
Water lover
Rich, humusy moist soil
Propagation by transplanting of suckers, cuttings, and seed

A large genus of about 175 species of small to very high climbing shrubs and trees in Madagascar, tropical Asia, northern Australia, northern New Zealand, the islands of the South Pacific, and Hawaii. They form fairly slender woody trunks from which arise aerial roots much like the species in the genus *Pandanus* to which they are related. In *Freycinetia*, however, the roots serve not only as props, but they also aid the plant's trunks in gaining a foothold on its support and provide minimal feeding organs while the plants twine around their supports. Without support, the plants mostly sprawl about, eventually forming an impenetrable groundcover thicket, but when they find a support, they grow up into it. In fact, they can climb to the tops of the tallest trees, at which point they tend to become trees themselves, although they are not strangling type plants and mostly coexist peacefully with their host. All species may be grown as nonclimbing shrubs or giant groundcovers.

The leaves are spaced regularly along the climbing trunks in one of two types of groups. One group consists of a very short single stem around which the leaves are spirally and densely arranged. The other type of group consists of several leaf stems along which leaves are arranged oppositely in pairs at right angles to one another (the pairs). The latter condition is termed "decussate." The leathery leaves are long and linear, elliptic to lanceolate in shape, and dark green in color with ridged longitudinal veins, and usually have regularly spaced small teeth along their margins.

The flowers are in terminal inflorescences, which consist of highly colored bracts surrounding a cone-shaped or cylindrical spadix of tiny unisexual blossoms that are rather similar to those of the arum family, Araceae, except that the flowers of *Freycinetia* are unisexual and the male and female flowers are on separate plants. The plants bloom mainly in winter in the Northern Hemisphere, sometimes in the fall or spring. The inflorescences are edible and supposedly quite sweet in taste.

These climbing trees are wonderfully tropical in appearance because of their leaves, growth habits, and brilliantly colored inflorescences. They are intolerant of frost but can withstand near-freezing conditions for short periods of time. Most of them need partial shade as they are understory plants but a few, which climb to the tops of tall trees, flourish in full sun. They are all indigenous to areas of high rainfall and cannot withstand drought conditions. They are not true epiphytes, deriving most of their nourishment from the soil and needing a fairly fertile medium that is rich in organic material. The plants are rare in cultivation in the United States but should certainly be more widely planted for their exotic form and brilliant inflorescences. Two or three species are sometimes available.

Freycinetia arborea (ahr-BOR-ee-a) is native to the low rain forests of the Hawaiian islands where it climbs to as much as 50 feet up moss covered trees and rock ledges with its orange-brown 2- to 3-inch-diameter trunks. The leaves are in spirals around the very short leaf stems and are as much as 3 feet long, linear-lanceolate in shape, and a deep green to deep olive green in color, and armed with short teeth on the margins. The terminal inflorescences are provided with deep pink to scarlet and orange-pink bracts surrounding a fat purple or violet-colored spadix. The plants relish sun or partial shade and are truly spectacular, spreading their beautiful spiral rosettes of leaves along and through tree trunks and canopies.

Freycinetia cumingiana (kum-in´-jee-AHN-a) (synonym *F. multiflora*) is indigenous to the Philippines. It grows rather slowly to as much as 20 or 30 feet but usually remains an understory plant in the rain forest biome. The trunks are slender and graceful, usually no more than an inch or so in diameter. The leafing stems arch out from the trunks and create hanging basketlike leafy aerial gardens. The leaves are arranged oppositely along the leaf stems and are no more than a foot long, linear in shape, very deep green in color with tapering tips and very tiny serrations along the margins. The terminal inflorescences consist of short fat deep orange to red bracts surrounding a pink spadix.

Freycinetia multiflora. See *F. cumingiana*.

GARCINIA (gar-SIN-ee-a)
Guttiferae (Clusiaceae): The Autograph Tree, Garcinia Family
IMBE
Small to medium-sized evergreen tree; large leaves; small clusters of flowers; orange fruit
Zones 10 and 11
Sun or partial shade
Average but regular amounts of moisture
Average well-drained soil
Propagation by seed

A large genus of about 200 species of evergreen trees and shrubs in tropical Asia, Polynesia, and Africa. All have relatively large and leathery leaves and flowers and large, colorful, and often edible fruit. Among the many fine fruit trees in this genus is the beautiful mangosteen, *Garcinia mangostana*, which is almost impossible to grow outside truly tropical areas and which is finicky as to soil. One species is now being planted in southern Florida where it seems to do quite well. *Garcinia livingstonei* (liv-ing-STOAN-ee-eye) is native to Zaire, Zambia, Tanzania, and northern Mozambique where it grows to as much as 40 feet. In Florida it seldom attains half this height. It forms a rather columnar crown but is variable in this respect, sometimes becoming a spreading small tree. The leathery 6-inch-long leaves are elliptical to oblong in shape with a pointed end and are almost stalkless, glossy above, and heavily veined with white. The small starlike flowers appear in axillary clusters in late spring, and the orange 2-inch-wide globular and edible fruits mature in midsummer. This small tree is quite attractive especially when in fruit and is one of the few species in the genus that is tolerant of any degree of frost and is also easy of culture. It makes a wonderful patio tree or specimen for any site where its form and color can be appreciated up close.

GARDENIA
(gar-DEEN-ee-a / gar-DEEN-ya)
Rubiaceae: The Coffee, Gardenia, Ixora Family
GARDENIA
Evergreen trees and large shrubs; large evergreen leaves; large fragrant white to orange flowers

Zones vary according to species
Sun to partial shade
Water lovers
Rich, humusy, moist, well-drained, slightly acidic soil
Propagation by cuttings, sometimes by seed

A large genus of about 250 species of trees and shrubs in the tropics and subtropics of Asia and Africa. All have large leaves and spectacular, fragrant flowers. The fruits are large berries, which often open while on the plant and release their seeds, but most species do not fruit in cultivation. Some of the most beautiful plants in the world are included here. Rare is it that a large group like this has so many representatives that are beautiful both in leaf and flower.

Gardenia augusta. See *G. jasminoides.*

Gardenia carinata (kair-i-NAIT-a) is indigenous to Malaysia and is hardy in zones 10 and 11. It grows slowly to about 30 feet in its native habitat and 20 feet or so in cultivation. The dark green glossy leaves are 6 to 8 inches long, elliptical to obovate in shape, heavily veined above and lighter colored and pubescent beneath. The wonderful flowers have five to six petals and appear singly near the ends of the branches in spring and summer and sporadically all year in tropical areas. They are 3 to 4 inches wide, and very fragrant, and open a creamy white but soon change to a deep yellow-orange. Few trees are more beautiful, and the fact that the flowers do not cover the tree seems to make them even more choice and beautiful.

Gardenia florida. See *G. jasminoides.*

Gardenia grandiflora. See *G. jasminoides.*

Gardenia imperialis (im-peer´-ee-AL-is) is native to tropical West Africa and is hardy in zones 10b and 11. This tree is large in its native haunts where it grows to 50 feet or even more with an oblong crown. In cultivation it can be expected to grow to at least half that stature. It has possibly the largest leaves in the genus; they are as much as 18 inches long, glossy dark green above, paler beneath, and elliptical to obovate in shape with deep veins on the upper surface. They are truly magnificent. The flowers appear all year in tropical climes, but there is a flush in early summer. They are white, fragrant 8-inch-long narrow tubes whose ends expand into 4-inch-wide disks of five to nine lobes. This tree is incredibly beautiful for tropical areas in and out of bloom. It is rare but well worth the search.

Gardenia jasminoides (jaz-mi-NOY-deez) (synonyms *G. augusta, G. florida, G. grandiflora, G. radicans*) is native to the southern Japanese islands, Taiwan, and eastern China. It is hardy in zones 9 through 11 and marginal in zone 8b. This species is the most widely planted species in the United States and most of the rest of the globe where it is hardy. It is known in the southern United States as cape jasmine or crepe jasmine. The former name has led many to think this species is native to South Africa, an error that is compounded and abetted by the use in Florida of *G. thunbergia,* a nematode-resistant South African species, as rootstock onto which *G. jasminoides* plants are (or should be) grafted. The unadulterated species is almost nonexistent in the nursery trade. ***Gardenia jasminoides* 'Fortuniana'** still is the most widely planted clonal form, although it is rapidly being surpassed in both availability and numbers of shrubs planted by several subsequent introductions. The plant grows to as much as 12 feet with an equal spread. The glossy dark green leaves are 4 to 8 inches long and elliptical to lanceolate in shape, with depressed main veins above and a short tip at the end. The intensely sweet-scented white and waxy flowers, which appear in cycles from spring to fall, are 3 to 5 inches wide and "double." Upon first opening, there are seven or eight large, more or less obovate-shaped outer petals and a center of similarly shaped petals forming a roselike cup. Within a day or so the center petals also have unfolded to create a flower shape like that of an open hybrid tea rose. The fragrance is legendary, haunting, and unforgettable, and has led to the flower being one of the florist's best-sellers for corsages. The several cultivars now available vary in the size of the plants; some forms attain a height of only 1 or 2 feet. These are very good for edging a bed and for stuffing a pretty plant into a small space. All varieties need a humusy soil that is of relatively low pH. Limestone soils must be amended with leaf mold or much compost and supplemented with a gardenia or azalea fertilizer or, better, regular applications of fish emulsion. The plants are intolerant of drought conditions but, at the same time, must be planted in a soil that is freely draining. The incredible flowers are worth the trouble.

Gardenia latifolia (lat-i-FO-lee-a) is native from India to Southeast Asia and is hardy in zones 10 and 11 and marginal in zone 10a. It grows to about 20 feet but is usually found as a shrub in nature and cultivation. It needs guidance when young to train to small tree form. The handsome large deep green leaves are as much as a foot long or wide, depending on the leaf shape, which varies, and is often almost round but usually obovate. The leaves are glossy with depressed veins above and lighter colored and felty beneath. The large fragrant flowers open white but soon change to an orange-yellow in color. They appear mostly in spring but sporadically all summer and consist of a 3- or 4-inch-long narrow tube whose ends flare into 5 to 11 lobes that create a disk about 6 inches wide.

Gardenia radicans. See *G. jasminoides.*

Gardenia spatulifolia (spat-yoo-li-FO-lee-a) is native to Mozambique and is hardy in zones 10 and 11. It slowly grows into a small tree to 20 feet but is more often a large shrub in form. The obovate to spatulate-shaped leaves are quite small, only about 2 inches long, and are stiff and a dark green in color. The fragrant white flowers make the plant worth growing. They appear in late winter and spring and occasionally in summer and fall and are narrow 4-inch-long tubes whose ends expand into 4-inch-wide disks of six to nine obovate white and waxy lobes.

Gardenia taitensis (ty-TEN-sis) is indigenous to the islands of the South Pacific including Tahiti and the Society Islands and is tender outside zones 10b and 11. It is a large shrub but can be trained to a small tree growing to about 20 feet. The very beautiful leathery but glossy dark green leaves are 4 to 8 inches long and elliptic to obovate in shape with prominent and lighter colored midrib and lateral veins above. The plants bloom intermittently all year. The intensely fragrant white flowers open at night but last for several days. They are slender 2-inch-long tubes whose ends flare into a 4-inch-wide disk of six to eight somewhat twisted waxy lobes. It is hard to imagine a more beautiful flowering shrub. Plate 211.

Gardenia thunbergia (toon-BERG-ee-a / thun-BUR-jee-a) is native to southeastern Africa and is hardy in zones 10 and 11. This large shrub grows to about 15 or 20 feet and can be trained to a small widespreading tree. The dark green elliptical leaves are about 6 inches long. The plant blooms in late winter and spring, sometimes in the fall, with very fragrant white flowers consisting of a 3-inch-long tube that expands into an eight-lobed disk with protruding and long-stalked yellowish ovary. The corolla lobes overlap to some extent and give somewhat the effect of a double flower. The plant is rather drought tolerant and quite easy of culture. It is much used as a rootstock for *G. jasminoides* (cape jasmine) in Florida but is more than worthy of being planted for its beauty, surpassing that of the cape jasmine in many respects.

Gardenia tubifera (too-BIF-e-ra) is indigenous to Malaysia and Indonesia and is hardy in zones 10b and 11. In its native habitat it is a large tree growing to 60 feet or even more. In cultivation in frost-free regions of the United States it can be expected to reach at least half that height. The 8-inch-long dark green, leathery, glossy leaves are obovate and heavily veined above. The small flowers, which make quite a show, are about an inch wide at the end of an inch-long tube and open white at night but turn a brilliant orange before they wither several days later. This most beautiful tree is spectacular in and out of bloom.

GAUSSIA (GOWS-see-a / GAWS-see-a)

Palmae (Arecaceae): The Palm Family
MAYA PALM
Tall palm with slender ringed trunk and feathery
    plumelike arching leaves
Zones 10b and 11
Sun to partial shade
Average but regular amounts of moisture
Humusy, well-drained soil
Propagation by seed

A genus of five species of pinnate-leaved palms in Mexico, Central America, and the West Indies. The genus now includes the one species that was formerly in the genus *Opsiandra*. *Gaussia maya* (MAH-ya) (synonym *Opsiandra maya*) is indigenous to Yucatán, Gua-

temala, and Belize. It grows to about 60 feet in its native lands but usually is no more than 40 feet tall in cultivation. The trunk is slender, swollen at the base, and beautifully ringed, and the 6- to 8-foot-long leaves have many bright green leaflets, which arise from the rachis from several angles, giving the leaf a lovely plumose effect. The palm's crown has but a few large leaves, which phenomenon gives it a rather sculptural aspect and makes it a beautiful silhouette in the landscape. The palm blooms for a long period with many flower spikes arching out from the upper trunk. The inflorescences wait several years to open while the trunk continues to grow above them, and then they start opening in succession from bottom to top, at which time the tree is festooned with greenish yellow flowers and yellow and red fruits. The palm thrives on limestone soils.

GENIPA. See *Casasia*.

GEOGENANTHUS

(jee-o-je-NANTH-us)
Commelinaceae: The Spiderwort Family
SEERSUCKER PLANT
Low-growing herbaceous plants with strikingly
    variegated leaves
Zones 10 and 11
Shade to partial shade
Water lover
Humusy, moist, well-drained soil
Propagation by seed, cuttings, and transplanting of
    suckers

A genus of only four species of short creeping and suckering plants with succulent stems and fleshy leaves at the ends of the unbranched stems. The small three-petaled flowers are blue or purple. One species is planted for its beautiful variegated leaves. *Geogenanthus poeppigii* (po-PIJ-ee-eye) (synonyms *Dichorisandra musaica*, *Geogenanthus undatus*) is native to the rain forests of Amazonas in Brazil and Peru. The plant never grows more than 8 or 10 inches tall and freely suckers. The 5- to 6-inch-long leaves are broadly elliptical to broadly ovate to almost round and are puckered and quilted on the very dark green surface and bear wavy longitudinal lines of silver or gray. The little plants are unexcelled as shady groundcovers and are almost startlingly beautiful in such situations, adding much needed brightness and variegation to the gloom.

GLIRICIDIA (gleer-i-SID-ee-a)

Papilionaceae (Fabaceae, Leguminosae), subfamily
    Papilionoideae: The Bean, Pea Family
MADRE-DE-CACAO
Small deciduous tree with large pinnate leaves;
    racemes of pink flowers appearing with new leaves
Zones 10 and 11; marginal in zone 9b
Sun
Average but regular amounts of moisture

Average well-drained soil
Propagation by seed and cuttings

A genus of six species of shrubs and trees in tropical America. All have pinnate leaves with an odd number of leaflets, small pink or white pealike flowers from the leaf axils, and flat twisted seed pods. Only one species is commonly planted in tropical regions. It is widely used as a shade tree for coffee and cacao plantations as these crops do not relish full sun in the true lowland tropics. This use of the tree has led to the vernacular "madre de cacao," which is Spanish for "mother of cacao." ***Gliricidia sepium*** (SEEP-ee-um) grows quickly to as much as 30 feet, branching low with long and somewhat pendent limbs that form a wide and usually umbrella-shaped crown of fine foliage. The tree usually requires pruning and guidance when young to form a single trunk. The large leaves are about 10 inches long with 3-inch-long bright green oblong to elliptical leaflets which, when bruised, emit a strong vegetable odor. There is often a bronzy cast to the upper surfaces of the leaves, especially the new leaves. The tree is deciduous in cold or dry winters. The flowers are produced with or just before the leaves appear in the spring and are much more floriferous after a dry winter. Indeed, the tree often blooms any time of year after a drought. The flowers are formed in short clusters all along the branches and are somewhat reminiscent of *Cercis canadensis* (redbud) of the eastern United States, although the flower color is more pleasing, being a lighter and brighter pink. All parts of these trees are poisonous except for the flowers, which are edible. Native peoples use the ground-up bark and seeds as a rat-killer, and the genus name means "rat-killer." There is a white-flowered form of this species, which is not as effective in the landscape as the type. This tree can be quite spectacular when in bloom and the leaves are beautiful, but it is usually necessary to prune it when young lest it become a rangy multitrunked mess. It is also one of the fastest growing landscape subjects available. It roots readily from cuttings in the growing season and is often used, with much pruning required, as a "living fence" in tropical areas.

GLOBBA (GLOAB-ba)
Zingiberaceae: The Ginger Family
GLOBBA
Small reedlike plants with cannalike leaves and
    terminal clusters of pink and yellow flowers
Zones 10 and 11 as permanent perennials; zone 9 as
    returning perennials
Shade to partial shade
Water lovers
Rich, humusy, moist, well-drained soil
Propagation by root division, rhizome division, and
    aerial bulbs

A genus of about 70 perennial rhizomatous herbs in tropical Asia. None of the species grows to more than about 5 feet, and all have succulent reedlike stems and relatively large lanceolate leaves arranged in opposite pairs at right angles to each other around the unbranching stems. The inflorescences are terminal and usually pendent, and consist of colored bracts and small yellow flowers. The stems of the inflorescences have rudimentary leaves near their bases, which sometimes produce bulbils in the leaf axils. These bulbils can be used to propagate the plants. Like those of many other genera in the Zingiberaceae (ginger family), the flowering stems should be cut back to the ground after the blooms wither as they only degenerate and eventually die. Several of the species with pendent inflorescences are called dancing ladies because of their graceful small flowers that flutter in the breeze.

Globba atrosanguinea (at´-ro-san-GWIN-ee-a) is native to Borneo. The stems reach a maximum height of about 3 feet, and the elliptical to lanceolate-shaped leaves are about 10 inches long, dark glossy green above, and purplish beneath. The erect inflorescence is about 3 inches high with scarlet bracts and small yellow flowers.

Globba bulbifera. See *G. marantina.*

Globba marantina (mar-an-TEEN-a) (synonyms *G. bulbifera, G. schomburgkii*) is indigenous to Southeast Asia and grows to about 2 feet. The elliptic leaves are about 10 inches long, dark green above, and paler green and hairy beneath. The inflorescences are 4 or 5 inches long, pendent, and gracefully arching, with bright yellow bracts and small yellow flowers. The species is one of the dancing ladies.

Globba schomburgkii. See *G. marantina.*

Globba wintii (WINT-ee-eye) is native to Thailand and Vietnam and grows to about 3 feet. The leaves are about a foot long, dark glossy green above, and cordate at the base. The inflorescences are 6 to 8 inches long and pendent, and composed of many light purple 3-"petaled" bracts from which peek the slender yellow to orange small flowers. Plate 212.

GMELINA (meh-LYN-a / meh-LEEN-a)
Verbenaceae: The Verbena, Lantana Family
PARROT'S BEAK
Climbing or sprawling thorny shrub; small leaves;
    exotic pendent brown and yellow flowers
Zones 10 and 11
Sun
Water lover
Average well-drained soil
Propagation by seed and cuttings

A genus of about three dozen spiny small trees and shrubs, many of them semiclimbing, in the Old World tropics. They have oppositely arranged leaves and terminal racemes of flowers. Each flower is accompanied by a large persistent bract. The corollas are bell-shaped to tubular with two usually somewhat scalloped lobes. One species is commonly grown in tropical and subtropical regions for its fascinatingly exotic flowers.

Gmelina philippensis (fil-i-PEN-sis) (synonym *G. hystrix*) is native to a vast area of tropical Asia, from the Philippines southward through Malaysia and eastward through Southeast Asia and into India. It is a sprawling shrub that, like bougainvillea, climbs to as much as 20 feet or may be grown as a shrub to 10 or 12 feet. It may even be grown as a small tree (a standard). The elliptic to obovate dark green leaves, which are 2 to 4 inches long and are deeply veined above, are accompanied by small spines in the leaf axils. The plant blooms in cycles all year in the tropics and in the warm months elsewhere. The foot-long raceme is pendulous and consists of large ovate brownish purple to greenish purple bracts from which emerge in pairs curious 2-inch-long yellow or orange-yellow tubular flowers. The flowers have greatly inflated corolla lobes that themselves terminate in two spreading lobes of very unequal size. Thus, the visual effect of each flower pair is that of a set of pincers. The flowers in the inflorescence open from the bottom upwards with never more than a pair of blossoms showing at one time. Each flower is accompanied by a reddish orange calyx. The plant is probably best grown as a mounding shrub but is quite effective as a vine or an espalier. It is not very frost tolerant but usually survives nicely in zone 10 and needs sun and regular and adequate amounts of moisture to bloom well.

GONIOPHLEBIUM
(go´-nee-o-FLEE-bee-um)
Polypodiaceae: The Largest Fern Family
No known English common name
Large evergreen epiphytic pinnate ferns
Zones 10b and 11
Shade to partial shade
Water lovers
Rich, humusy, well-drained soil or leaf mold
Propagation by root division, rhizome division, and
    spores

A genus of about 20 large epiphytic fern species in tropical Asia. They have large creeping rhizomes by which they make colonies on trees and other supports. The fronds are pinnate or simple and pinnately segmented. None of the species is hardy to cold, and they need fairly high relative humidity levels. They may be also grown terrestrially. This genus is a segregate from the formerly bloated *Polypodium*.

Goniophlebium persicifolium (pur-sis´-i-FO-lee-um) (synonym *Polypodium persicifolium*) is found naturally in a vast area of the Asian tropics from northern India and southern China into Southeast Asia through Malaysia and northwards to the Philippines. It is a magnificent epiphyte with great pendent pinnate fronds as long as 6 feet. The leaflets are a grassy glossy green and linear-lanceolate in shape, with toothed, wavy margins. This species is spectacular for growing on large trees or walls, or for planting in a hanging basket.

Goniophlebium subauriculatum (sub´-aw-rik-yoo-LAIT-um) (synonym *Polypodium subauriculatum*) occurs naturally from northern India through Myanmar (Burma), Southeast Asia, and Malaysia to northern Australia and the adjacent islands of the South Pacific. It grows as large as *G. persicifolium* but is a finer-textured species with longer and thinner leaflets that are somewhat sickle-shaped and have margins that are usually tiny-toothed. The fronds are even more pendent than those of *G. persicifolium* and are a stunning sight hanging from trees or walls because of their size and grace. *Goniophlebium subauriculatum* 'Knight-iae' is an outstanding cultivar whose leaves are narrower but as long and whose leaflets are broader but usually overlapping. It has the appearance of a giant form of one of the Boston fern varieties.

GORDONIA (gor-DOE-nee-a)
Theaceae: The Camellia, Tea Family
Common names vary according to species
Small to medium-sized evergreen trees; lustrous
    leaves; large white and yellow fragrant flowers
Zones vary according to species
Sun
Water lovers
Humusy, well-drained, slightly acidic soil
Propagation by seed

A genus of about 70 species of evergreen trees and shrubs in tropical and subtropical parts of Asia and the southeastern United States. All have leathery and relatively large leaves and showy bisexual flowers, which much resemble the single flowers of *Camellia sasanqua* to which the genus *Gordonia* is related. The trees are not, in general, spectacular like those of *Delonix regia* (royal poinciana) or *Jacaranda* species when in bloom, but it is hard to find a more pleasing and subtly beautiful group of trees and shrubs, both for their leaves as well as their lovely flowers. The plants are not drought tolerant and must not be allowed to suffer such conditions. In addition they need a slightly acidic soil. Calcareous and limy soils should be amended with peat moss or compost.

Gordonia anomala. See *G. axillaris*.

Gordonia axillaris (ax-IL-la-ris / axi-il-LAIR-is) (synonym *G. anomala*) is found naturally from Taiwan through the Philippines and southeastern China to Southeast Asia. It is hardy in zones 10 and 11 and marginal in zone 9b. It is seldom a tree except in the true tropics and is usually grown as a large spreading shrub, attaining a maximum height of 10 to 15 feet. The 6-inch-long elliptical leaves are a very dark green in color and leathery in texture, and have shallow serrations along their margins. The flowers are about 5 inches wide with five pure white crinkled petals surrounding a central mass of bright orange stamens; they are beloved of bees.

Gordonia lasianthus (lay-zee-ANTH-us) is native to the southeastern United States from the coastal areas of North Carolina to Florida and westward to Mississippi. It is hardy in zones 7b through 11. The tree grows to as much as 80 feet with great age but is slow, and most plants in cultivation attain no more than 40 feet with a rather columnar crown. The leaves, which are somewhat similar to those of *G. axillaris* but narrower, are about 6 inches long and have a strong and lighter colored midrib. They turn a bronzy to cherry red with the advent of cold weather. The flowers are somewhat smaller than those of *G. axillaris* but very similar and just as beautiful. The tree sometimes goes by the common names of loblolly bay and black laurel. This beauty should be much more widely planted than it is at present. It is of outstanding beauty and has a definitely tropical look. Plate 213.

GOSSYPIUM (go-SIP-ee-um)
Malvaceae: The Mallow, Hibiscus, Cotton Family
WILD COTTON
Large shrubs and small trees; large evergreen lobed
    leaves; white and pink hibiscus-like flowers
Zones 10 and 11 as permanent shrubs and trees;
    zone 9 as returning perennial shrubs
Sun
Average but regular amounts of moisture
Average well-drained soil
Propagation by seed

A genus of about 40 species of trees, shrubs, and perennial herbs in warm regions around the globe. All have leaves that are lobed to some degree and flowers similar to those of *Hibiscus*, to which the genus is related. *Gossypium* is the cotton genus. One species is occasionally planted for ornament in tropical and nearly tropical areas. ***Gossypium hirsutum*** (heer-SOOT-um) (synonym *G. punctatum*) is native to most of tropical America including the Florida Keys. It grows to 8 or 10 feet tall with an equal spread and must be trained to a single trunk when young if a small tree form is wanted. It is a fast-growing, soft-wooded plant that is easily pruned to any size and form. The 6-inch-long leaves are broadly cordate in shape and usually have two or three lobes. Borne on 5-inch-long pliable petioles, the leaves are usually felty on both upper and lower surfaces. The 2- to 3-inch-wide flowers have five somewhat twisted petals, which form a cup shape and open white or yellowish white with large scarlet spots at the base of each petal. The petals change color within a day to a rose or deep pink hue. The flowering period extends throughout the warm months. The fruits are small triangular capsules that split open to reveal white to brown cottonlike fibers. The plants are tolerant of drought and saline spray and soil and are very useful for quickly filling in sun-drenched spaces.

GRAPTOPHYLLUM
(grap-to-FYL-lum)
Acanthaceae: The Acanthus Family
CARICATURE PLANT; CAFE CON LECHE
Large shrub; large variegated leaves; small red
    tubular flowers in terminal clusters

Zones 10 and 11 as permanent perennials; zone 9b as
    returning perennial shrubs
Sun to partial shade
Average but regular amounts of moisture
Average well-drained soil
Propagation by cuttings, sometimes by seed

A genus of 10 evergreen shrubs in Australia and the islands of the South Pacific north and east of that continent. They have fairly large variegated leaves and short terminal clusters of red or purple-red tubular-shaped flowers with two corolla lobes. Only one species is in general cultivation. ***Graptophyllum pictum*** (PIK-tum) (synonym *G. hortense*) is probably indigenous to New Guinea. It grows to 6 or 8 feet with an equal spread. The plant is grown for its large and colorfully variegated leaves, although the flowers are quite attractive. The leaves are about 6 inches long, elliptical in shape, and purplish brown when new, changing to a bright deep green when mature. They have a feathery or splotchy line of white to yellow or red variegation along the midrib, and the combination of colors is astonishingly beautiful, showing up at a great distance in the landscape. The terminal flower clusters are 3 to 4 inches long and consist of 2-inch-long scarlet to purplish red tubes, which expand into two lobes at their ends. The leaves of one variety are green and yellow or white without the purple and brown. One of the choicest landscape subjects, this species is sometimes planted as an annual in cold zones because of its beauty, which is magnetic up close and from afar. In tropical regions it is often pruned into a hedge. The plants are not drought tolerant but can withstand somewhat dry periods when established. They appreciate a soil that is not too infertile. Plate 214.

GUAIACUM (GWAH-ya-kum)
Zygophyllaceae: The Lignum-Vitae Family
LIGNUM-VITAE; HOLY WOOD; TREE OF LIFE
Large shrubs and small evergreen trees; leathery
    pinnate leaves; blue and purple flowers
Zones 10 and 11
Sun
Average but regular amounts of moisture; drought
    tolerant
Average well-drained soil
Propagation by seed

A genus of six species of evergreen trees and shrubs in tropical America. All have leathery pinnate leaves and white, blue, or purple long-stalked flowers with four or five petals. The wood of *Guaiacum officinale* and *G. sanctum*, which is some of the densest and hardest known, is valued for making many *objets d'art* and articles that require absolute durability. The resinous wood is full of oil, so that ball-bearings made from it need no lubrication. The common names result from the great healing power once attributed to the resin. The trees inhabit the drier areas of the American tropics and therefore need a soil with excellent drainage. They also often grow near the seacoast and are quite tolerant of saline air and soil. Two species are planted in the United States, one of which is native to the Florida Keys. All species grow very slowly and take many years to make a tree form. The two species listed below are possibly the world's most beautiful blue-flowered trees. Both bloom almost year-round and both, because of their extremely slow growth, are more often seen as large shrubs than as small trees.

Guaiacum officinale (o-fis´-i-NAHL-ee) is native to the West Indies, Panama, and northern South America. It grows very slowly to about 30 feet with a short trunk, dark gray bark, and a dense and spreading crown. The leaves are 4 to 5 inches long and consist of four to six obovate dark green leathery leaflets that are 2 inches long. The inch-wide flowers, which have four or five petals, open sky blue or dark blue, sometimes almost violet, and fade to almost white. The petals are stalked and surround a circle of white stamens with beautiful golden anthers. Plate 215.

Guaiacum sanctum (SANK-tum) is indigenous to the same area as *G. officinale* except that it extends up to the Florida Keys. It usually grows smaller than *G. officinale*, but there are reports of trees 30 feet tall. The leaves are definitely smaller, and the tree's crown is usually more dense with a lighter colored trunk. Plate 216.

GUIHAIA (gwee-HAH-ya)

Palmae (Arecaceae): The Palm Family
No known English common name
Small clustering fan-leaved palm with silver-backed
    leaves
Zones 8b through 11
Sun to partial shade
Average but regular amounts of moisture; probably
    drought tolerant
Humusy, well-drained soil
Propagation by seed

A genus of only two palmate-leaved palm species in southern China and adjacent Vietnam where they usually occur on limestone cliff faces. One species is becoming available but no one seems to have completely determined its hardiness to cold as it is so far grown only in southern Florida and southern California. In Houston, Texas, it has survived unscathed a temperature of about 22°F in containers and 17°F in Waller, Texas, at Yucca Do Nursery. ***Guihaia argyrata*** (ahr-ji-RAIT-a) (synonym *Trachycarpus argyratus*) is indigenous to southern China. It is a slow-growing clustering short-trunked palm with very beautiful palmate leaves that are completely circular in outline but very deeply divided almost to the petiole into about two dozen linear tapering segments. Each segment is bright green above and shallowly pleated, the fold being roof-shaped rather than trough-shaped. The reverse of the leaves, like the newly unfolding leaves, is a beautiful tan color overlain with a bright and tangible white to silvery

chalky pubescence. The beauty of this small palm will doubtless result in its becoming more readily available soon. Plate 217.

GUILIELMA. See *Bactris*.

GUZMANIA

(goos-MAHN-ee-a / guz-MAIN-ee-a)
Bromeliaceae: The Pineapple, Bromeliad Family
GUZMANIA
Large rosettes of smooth, often highly colored
    straplike leaves; spikes of yellow and red flowers
Zones 10b and 11
Shade to partial shade
Water lovers
Humusy, porous, well-drained soil or leaf mold
Propagation by transplanting of suckers and by seed

A large genus of about 180 mostly epiphytic bromeliad species in South America, Central America, the West Indies, and southern Florida although most species are to be found in the mountainous rain forests of Colombia and Ecuador. All have full widespreading rosettes of smooth unarmed leaves, branched spikes of brilliant yellow, orange, or red bracts, and white or yellow flowers. The flower spikes are often branched, with the branches arising from all angles of the flower stem. The leaves are smooth, without teeth on the margins, and often highly colored, especially near the inflorescence at the time of flowering. Most species bloom in fall, winter, and early spring. They are spectacular plants, especially when in flower. All need warmth, moisture, and shade or partial shade with good air circulation as they are almost exclusively epiphytic on tall forest trees. These brilliant and remarkable species have only recently gained the popularity they deserve.

Guzmania berteroniana (ber´-te-ro-nee-AHN-a) is indigenous to Puerto Rico, Hispaniola, and Panama. It grows to about 18 inches tall with broadly oblong, bluntly tipped foot-long smooth and arching leaves, which are lime green above and reddish brown to brownish purple beneath. The inflorescence, which is about 9 inches long on a 6-inch spike, is lance-shaped and consists of large deep orange to red overlapping bracts from which emerge the bright yellow tubular flowers.

Guzmania bismarckii (biz-MARK-ee-eye) is native to the rain forests of northeastern Peru. It is of unparalleled beauty and size, growing to as much as 7 feet in height with narrowly lanceolate arching leaves that are as much as 4 feet long. Leaf color varies from pale almost whitish green to a bright apple green heavily speckled and lined with dark green above and below. The flower spike and inflorescence on any other member of the genus would be considered splendid, but compared to the vegetative glory of the present species it is merely beautiful, with the typical height and red bracts and yellow flowers.

Guzmania conifera (ko-NIF-e-ra) is indigenous to mountainous rain forests of eastern Ecuador and northern Peru. This unusual species is startlingly beautiful when in bloom. The leaves are broad and dark green and look rather more like those of *Eucharis* than a bromeliad. The rosette is wide and open in character. The incredible inflorescence is like fire and resembles a pincushion of molten lava: a globular to cone-shaped cluster of many pointed ovate-shaped vividly red bracts tipped with bright yellow. The yellow flowers are almost hidden deep in the overlapping bracts. Plate 218.

Guzmania daniellii (dan-ee-EL-ee-eye) is found naturally at elevations of up to a mile in the rain forests of the Colombian Andes. It is a large species often growing to a height of 5 feet with 3-foot-long straplike leaves that are green with a distinctly reddish hue. The flower spike is often 2 feet tall, and the cylindrical inflorescence about 9 inches high with red bracts and yellow flowers. It is one of the most spectacular species.

Guzmania lindenii (lin-DEN-ee-eye) is native to the Andean regions of northern and central Peru at elevations of well over a mile. It grows to 5 feet or more in height and is comparable in beauty to *G. bismarckii* but, alas, does not like hot climates. The narrow straplike leaves are as much as 3 feet long by only about 3 inches wide. They are a deep green with lovely horizontal swaths of white or light green. The flower spike is about 3 feet tall with light green bracts and white flowers.

Guzmania lingulata (ling-yoo-LATE-a) is indigenous to a large area from the West Indies and Central America down to Brazil. The type grows to about 2 feet with many solid green smooth 18-inch-long leaves. It is one of the most widely grown species. It is also one of the most variable, the forms differing in length and in color and variegation of leaves and inflorescences. All forms are beautiful of leaf and flower and extremely easy of culture. Some have much red coloration on the leaves, and some have unusually large flower spikes, but all have large red bracts and brilliant yellow flowers. Plate 219.

Guzmania monostachia (mo-no-STAIK-ee-a) has the largest natural range in the genus and is found from extreme southern Florida through the West Indies, Central America down to Brazil and from sea level to elevations of more than a mile. It is therefore quite adaptable to various growing conditions and one of the easiest plants to grow well. Fortunately for the plant lover, it is also quite beautiful. The smooth shiny leaves are a pure deep green in color and about 18 inches long and an inch wide. The flower spike is about 18 inches high, and the elliptical inflorescence about 6 inches long and of singular beauty. The lower bracts, which are large and ovate in shape with pointed tips, are light green in color with longitudinal dark brown stripes. The small white flowers peep out from between the bracts. Above them are the brilliant red or orange overlapping bracts from which emerge more small white flowers. *Guzmania monostachia* var. *variegata* has its leaves margined in creamy white.

Guzmania musaica (myoo-ZAY-i-ka) is native to Panama and Colombia. It is a medium-sized species growing to about 2 feet with beautiful deep olive green purplish hued 2-foot-long leaves that are marked with thin horizontal darker bands above. The under surfaces of the leaves are purplish red in color. The flower spike is 2 feet tall and bears a globular-shaped inflorescence with orange and red bracts and small white flowers.

Guzmania zahnii (ZAHN-ee-eye) is native to the cloud forest regions of Panama and Costa Rica where it grows to 2 feet with long, thin-textured arching 2-foot-long leaves that make an extended and open rosette resembling a small *Dracaena* species. The narrow leaves are marked with reddish brown longitudinal lines. The 3-foot-tall flower spike is composed of large glowing cherry red leaflike bracts below with a sulfur-yellow-branched inflorescence above. There is an incredibly beautiful cultivar, *Guzmania zahnii* 'Variegata' (vair-ee-a-GAIT-a), whose leaves are striped with pink, white, green, and yellow and are reminiscent of the vibrantly colored cultivars of *Ananas comosus* (pineapple). There is no more colorful plant.

HAMELIA (ha-MEL-ee-a)
Rubiaceae: The Coffee, Gardenia, Ixora Family
HUMMINGBIRD BUSH; SCARLET BUSH;
   FIREBUSH
Large spreading evergreen shrub; lance-shaped
   leaves; everblooming scarlet tubular flowers
Zones 10 and 11 as permanent shrubs; zone 9 as
   returning perennial shrubs
Sun
Average but regular amounts of moisture
Average well-drained soil
Propagation by seed and cuttings

A genus of about 40 species of small trees and shrubs from southern Florida through the West Indies, Mexico, Central America, and down into South America as far south as Paraguay. One species is now widely planted in the southern United States for its spectacular everblooming habit. *Hamelia patens* (PAY-tenz) is native from southern Florida to Paraguay. Under optimal conditions it grows into a small tree to 20 feet or more, but it is often found and grown as a large shrub. If not frozen back, it naturally forms several dark reddish brown trunks with a crown of foliage, in which form it is very beautiful. The stems and young parts of the trunk are of a definitely reddish hue. The leaves are 4 to 8 inches long and are mostly elliptical in shape with a short pointed tip, but they are somewhat variable, and ovate-shaped leaves are not uncommon. Leaf color is a medium green in late spring, summer, and early autumn, but changes to red or purplish-reddish bronze in cold weather. The plants bloom all year in constantly warm climates and they tend not to bloom in cycles or flushes, but rather parade a constant and great abundance of flowers as long as the weather is warm. The individual flowers are between 2 and 3 inches long and are rather narrow tubes with only tiny lobes at the ends of the blossoms. The throats are pinkish, with tiny yellow anthers at the mouth of the flower. Flower color ranges from scarlet to orange and the blossoms are in loose-flowered terminal clusters. The fruits are quarter-inch-wide scarlet berries, which turn black when mature. These blossoms are favorites of hummingbirds and butterflies, and the fruits are loved by many bird species. There is probably no more dependable flowering shrub for warm climates. The plants are almost foolproof and exceedingly easy of culture as all they demand are sun and a well-drained soil, with occasional irrigation in drought situations. Large shrubs are nothing short of amazing when in full bloom. Plate 220.

HARPEPHYLLUM (harp-e-FYL-lum)
Anacardiaceae: The Mango, Cashew, Pistachio, Sumac Family
KAFFIR PLUM
Medium-sized evergreen tree; dense rounded crown of pinnate leaves; red and purple fruit
Zones 10 and 11
Sun
Average but regular amounts of moisture
Average well-drained soil
Propagation by seed and cuttings

A monotypic genus in northern South Africa. *Harpephyllum caffra* (KAF-ra) grows to a maximum height of about 40 feet with a short, thick dark gray trunk and a very dense crown of dark green pinnate leaves. The plant is often pruned when young into just about any tree form the gardener desires, many of them attractive and picturesque. The individual leaves are 8 to 12 inches long and are composed of 5 to 17 somewhat sickle-shaped leaflets with pointed apices. The leaves are shiny dark green above with a prominent and lighter colored midrib, and are paler beneath. They look rather like those of *Fraxinus* (ash) species, but are so dense on the tree that the overall effect is completely different and definitely lush and tropical looking. The new leaves are a beautiful bronzy-rose in color, which adds to the beauty of the tree. The tiny greenish white flowers are insignificant in the landscape even though they are in fairly large clusters. The inch-long fruits, however, are beautiful, but a female tree is needed as the plants are single-sexed. The egg-shaped fruits are in clusters in the axils of the leaves (as also are the flowers) and mature from olive green through red to a deep purple. They are supposed to be edible and are much used for making jellies and jams. It is a very attractive tree that is easy of culture and mostly free of pests and diseases.

HARPULLIA (har-POOL-ee-a)
Sapindaceae: The Soapberry, Golden-Rain Tree Family
TULIPWOOD
Medium-sized evergreen trees with spreading crown; large pinnate leaves; large orange fruit
Zones 10 and 11; marginal in zone 10a
Sun
Average but regular amounts of moisture
Average well-drained soil
Propagation by seed

A genus of about 24 species of evergreen trees and shrubs in Madagascar, through India, Southeast Asia, Australia, and up to the Philippines. They all have large pinnate leaves, clusters of tiny yellowish flowers, and yellow or orange two-lobed leathery fruit capsules. Two similar species are planted in the United States. Both are outstandingly beautiful and tropical looking and are perfect street trees as well as small shade trees.

Harpullia arborea (ahr-BOR-ee-a) (synonym *H. cupanioides*) is native to India, Malaysia, and the Philippines. It slowly grows to 60 feet or more in its native habitat with a short dark brown trunk and a dense rounded crown of large pinnate leaves carried on spreading and ascending branches whose ends are somewhat pendent. The tree usually attains no more than 40 feet in cultivation. The leaves are as much as 2 feet long and are composed of 8 to 10 elliptical to obovate 6-inch-long dark green shiny leaflets with depressed veins above. The tiny yellowish flowers are in clusters among the leaves and are formed almost year-round in tropical climates. The bright red to orange fruits are two-lobed into inch-wide hollow rounded leathery segments. Each segment splits open when mature to reveal a single jet black seed. The overall form of each fruit is that of a dumbbell.

Harpullia cupanioides. See *H. arborea*.

Harpullia pendula is indigenous to Indonesia, Malaysia, and northeastern Australia north to the Philippines. It is quite similar to *H. arborea* except that it does not grow as tall. Plate 221.

HECHTIA (HEK-tee-a)
Bromeliaceae: The Pineapple, Bromeliad Family
HECHTIA
Medium-sized rosettes of tough succulent narrowly linear spiny leaves; tall spikes of tiny flowers
Zones vary according to species
Sun
Drought tolerant
Sandy, well-drained soil
Propagation by transplanting of suckers and by seed

A genus of about 50 succulent terrestrial aloelike xerophytic desert-dwelling bromeliad species in Central America, Mexico, and Texas. Some species are tiny and no more than 6 inches in height; others grow to 4 or 5 feet. All have dense rosettes of very many narrow succulent leaves (often more than 100) with spines on their margins. They are perfect in the cactus and succulent garden or a raised bed where rain does not collect and drainage is completely unimpeded. Leaf color is gray to dark green unless the plant is in full sun, where it ought to be, and in which case there is a beautiful rosy hue to the leaf. The plants are very easy of culture given their penchant for sun and perfectly draining soil and are as picturesque as most *Aloe* or *Agave* species.

Hechtia argentea (ahr-JEN-tee-a) is native to Central Mexico and is hardy in zones 9b through 11. The leaves grow to about 2 feet long and are only about an inch wide. They taper to a strong point and are beautifully arching and recurved. The plants are dark green in color, but this hue is almost totally obscured by the shiny silvery scales on the upper leaf surfaces. The undersides of the leaves are green with silvery lines, and regularly spaced vicious quarter-inch-long spines line the leaf margins. The flower spike is about 3 feet tall with small orange bracts in the inflorescence and tiny white flowers. The plant is very attractive when grown atop small rocky mounds or planted in stone walls where its drooping spidery form can be appreciated.

Hechtia desmetiana (dez-met´-ee-AHN-a) is indigenous to central and western Mexico and is hardy in zones 10 and 11. This species is especially beautiful because of its very thick 18-inch-long stiff leaves that are narrowly lanceolate in shape and reddish green in color with many strong spines along the margins. The flower spike is 3 feet or more in height and much branched, and bears orange to red bracts and flowers. This aloe-like bromeliad is very choice.

Hechtia ghiesbreghtii. See *H. glomerata*.

Hechtia glomerata (glahm-e-RAIT-a) (synonym *H. ghiesbreghtii*) occurs naturally from southwestern Texas to Guatemala and is hardy in zones 8 through 11. It is also one of the most attractive species in the genus because of the color of its leaves. The leaves are about 18 inches long, less than an inch wide, and a deep green in color suffused with red and brown on the upper surface near the margins where the regularly spaced stout spines originate. The leaves are armed with stiff points at their ends. The plants produce several flower spikes at once, which are 2 to 3 feet tall, with inflorescences that are green with white flowers.

Hechtia marnier-lapostollei (mahrn´-yay-lap-o-STOL-lee-eye) is indigenous to central Mexico and is hardy in zones 9b through 11. It is a small but beautiful clumping species. The leaves, which are no more than 6 inches long and recurved near their ends, are a wonderful silvery gray to almost bluish gray in color and are armed with relatively large teeth along their margins. The inflorescence is about 2 feet tall and consists of white flowers. Plate 222.

Hechtia podantha (po-DANTH-a) is native to southern and central Mexico and is hardy in zones 10 and 11. The plant is large, with 2- to 3-foot-long narrowly lanceolate thick and succulent dark green leaves, which are recurved at their ends and armed with stout spines along their margins. This species occurs in areas with more rainfall than the areas of most other species and is a wise choice for wet tropical areas, although it still needs a site with perfect drainage. The plant is spec-

tacular in and out of bloom. The red flower spike reaches as much as 7 feet in height and is much branched with hundreds of tiny white flowers along the branches.

Hechtia rosea (RO-zee-a / ro-ZAY-a) is native to southern Mexico and is hardy in zones 10 and 11. This outstandingly beautiful species has many 2-foot-long narrowly lanceolate leaves with a long tapering point and many curved whitish spines along the leaf margin. Leaf color is a beautiful bluish gray to brownish gray, which becomes heavily hued with a deep rose color in full sun in the summer. The flower spikes are as much as 3 feet tall with large branched inflorescences of brilliant scarlet bracts and flowers. This plant is extremely colorful and attractive for nearly frost-free gardens.

Hechtia schottii (SHAHT-tee-eye) is indigenous to southern Mexico and is hardy in zones 10 and 11. A large and beautiful plant, it has leaves to 3 feet or more in length, but less than 2 inches in width. The leaves are a deep green in color with a reddish brown hue near their bases and are armed with widely spaced stout spines along their margins. The flower spike is about 3 feet tall with green bracts and white flowers.

Hechtia texensis (tex-ENS-is) is indigenous to southwestern Texas and adjacent Mexico and is hardy in zones 8 through 11. It is a large and very choice plant with very many 18-inch-long leaves that are a bright and shiny deep green above and completely white with silvery scales beneath. The leaf margins are armed with strong curved brown spines, and most of the leaf surface turns a deep chocolate-maroon to scarlet and yellow in the heat and intensity of the sun. The flower spike is about 3 feet tall with many whitish green bracts and small white flowers.

HEDERA (HED-e-ra)
Araliaceae: The Aralia, Schefflera Family
Common names vary according to species
Large woody clinging vines with evergreen lobed
    leaves
Zones vary according to species
Shade to sun
Water lovers
Rich, humusy, well-drained soil
Propagation by cuttings

A genus of 11 species of large and woody evergreen vines in Europe, western Asia, and northern Africa. All have tiny whitish flowers in globular-shaped clusters and relatively large leaves that are lobed to at least some degree. The plants do not bloom until mature, and the leaves of flowering branches are dramatically different from those of the juvenile stems. Furthermore, the flowering and fruiting stems do not climb. One species, *Hedera helix* (English ivy), is probably the most widely planted groundcover and wallcover in the United States. The following species are very beautiful on walls and trees and as groundcovers. They should not be planted on wooden walls or walls that need painting, as the clinging aerial roots are invasive and seriously degrade wooden surfaces and are difficult to remove from brick surfaces that need regular painting. The problem is not so acute on trees where, if the vines threaten to take over the tree, the stems may be cut and, in a few months, the dead stems removed. These plants are very beautiful and tropical looking when they cascade down in their vigor from the tops of old oak trees. Many home gardeners have trouble getting the plants started on trees. The problem usually comes when the vines are planted too closely to the trunks where there is insufficient depth to the soil. If planted away from the surface roots in fairly deep soil and irrigated until established, success is almost guaranteed.

Hedera algeriensis. See *H. canariensis.*

Hedera canariensis (synonym *H. algeriensis*) is native to northern Africa and the Canary Islands and is hardy in zones 9 through 11 but often grown in zone 8b. It is a stout-stemmed vine that quickly grows to 30 or even 40 feet in height. The large cordate to diamond-shaped leaves are as much as 8 inches wide and a deep and glossy green above with prominent and lighter colored veins. The leaves are carried on thick reddish brown stalks and are rather widely spaced along the stems, which gives the vine an appealing tracery effect on walls. The plants also excel as groundcovers, making a very lush effect. They must not be allowed to suffer drought, and they do not relish the full sun of midsummer in hot climates. Because of its nativity the vine is called Algerian ivy. Variegated forms are available.

Hedera helix (HEE-lix) is native to most of Europe and parts of western Russia. It is very hardy to cold, the type being adaptable to zones 6 through 10, and is not comfortable in truly tropical areas. It is universally known as English ivy in the United States and is probably the most widely planted wallcover and groundcover. It will, in time, grow to at least 50 feet, sometimes more, with closely set dark green ovate leaves that have three to five lobes and are as much as 4 inches wide with lighter colored veins above. The vine makes an almost impenetrable groundcover and a very dense mat of foliage on walls, fences, and so forth. It grows quickly and dependably and needs regular and adequate moisture to do well. There are many cultivars, varying mainly in size and coloration of the leaf as well as degree of indentation of the lobes. The variegated cultivars are, in general, less hardy to cold than is the type, and some of them are of doubtful attractiveness in the landscape although very attractive as houseplants, in hanging baskets, and as tracery on walls and other structures up close. The non-variegated cultivars **Hedera helix 'Baltic', Hedera helix 'Bulgaria',** and **Hedera helix 'Rumania'** are hardier to cold than the type and are reputedly thriving in zones 5 and 4.

HEDYCHIUM (he-DIK-ee-um)
Zingiberaceae: The Ginger Family
GINGER LILY; BUTTERFLY GINGER

Tall reedlike stems; cannalike leaves in single plane; clusters of fragrant white to orange flowers
Zones 8 through 11
Sun to partial shade
Water lovers
Rich, humusy, moist soil
Propagation by root division and sometimes by seed

A genus of about 40 herbaceous and rhizomatous perennials in Madagascar, the Himalayas, and tropical Asia. All have reedlike stems with relatively large linear cannalike leaves growing in one plane along opposite sides of the stems. Some species grow to no more than 2 feet in height, while others attain 12 feet or sometimes more. The flowers are in large terminal clusters at the ends of the canes. The individual flowers are usually fragrant and always tubular, with expanded ends of three frilled or scalloped petals somewhat resembling birds or butterflies. The flowers are usually densely packed within the terminal cluster, and most have long colorful stamens that extend well beyond the flower's corolla. Unlike *Alpinia* species and some other ginger relatives, *Hedychium* species bloom on a season's cane growth, which accounts for their being listed as hardy in zone 8. In reality, they are hardy wherever the roots do not freeze in the ground. Where the growing season is long enough to allow maturity of the stems, whether frozen back the previous winter or not, the plants will bloom. Of course, a winter mulch helps in such situations. All species spread by the rootstock, although most do not spread rapidly. True water lovers, they must not be allowed to suffer from drought. Most thrive in boggy conditions. They also need a fairly rich soil. The leaves of the Himalayan species are subject to burning in the sun of hot climates and sometimes burn even when in partial shade. The sunburn seems to have no effect on the flowering of the plants.

Hedychium coccineum (kahk-SIN-ee-um) is native to northeastern India and Myanmar (Burma). It grows to 6 feet or more and has narrow 18-inch-long dark green leaves that have a bluish cast beneath. The flower clusters are oblong-shaped and as much as a foot long. The individual flowers are scarlet in color with very long protruding pink stamens. They all usually open at the same time, creating a spectacular floral display. **Hedychium coccineum var. aurantiaca** (aw´-ran-TY-a-ka) has deep orange flowers. Both the type and the variety have only a slight fragrance.

Hedychium coronarium (kor-o-NAHR-ee-um) is indigenous to India and southeastern China. It is probably the most widely grown species in the genus. It grows to 6 feet, sometimes more, with 2-foot-long lance-shaped medium green leaves. The flowers are pure white with a light yellow splotch near the base of the petals and are borne in foot-high globular to pyramidal spikes. The gardenia-like fragrance of this species is almost legendary and has resulted in its being used for making leis in Hawaii.

Hedychium flavescens (fla-VES-senz) is native to

eastern India. It is a large plant growing to 9 feet or more with narrow 2-foot-long dark green leaves. The flower clusters are a foot long and densely packed with large yellow very fragrant flowers.

Hedychium flavum (FLAY-vum) is native to northern India. It grows to about 6 feet in height with 2-foot-long narrow and pointed dark green leaves. The flower clusters are large but not densely packed, and the pure yellow flowers are arguably the most wonderfully fragrant of any species, a combination of gardenia and honeysuckle.

Hedychium gardnerianum (gard-ner´-ee-AHN-um) is indigenous to the Himalayan region of northern India. It grows to 6 feet with thick lanceolate to elliptic 18-inch-long leaves. The flower cluster is as much as 2 feet tall and is possibly the most beautiful in the whole genus, with large light yellow to light orange flowers and long protruding scarlet stamens. The flowers all open simultaneously, creating a real spectacle, and each one is deliciously fragrant. This very popular species is called the kahili ginger. Plate 223.

Hedychium greenei is indigenous to India. It grows to about 6 feet in height with thick reddish stems and narrow foot-long leaves that are deep green above and purplish red beneath. The leaves very much resemble banana leaves as both sides of the leaf are often pendent as are the leaves of most *Musa* species. The inflorescence is about 6 inches tall, and the individual blossoms are a vivid orange in color, usually with some red markings.

HELICONIA (heel-i-KO-nee-a)
Heliconiaceae: The Heliconia Family
LOBSTER CLAW; PARROT-BEAK
Tall reedlike stems; bananalike leaves; great clusters
    of colored boat-shaped flowers and bracts
Zones 10b and 11
Sun to partial shade
Water lovers
Rich, humusy, well-drained, acidic soil
Propagation by rhizome division and sometimes by
    seed

A genus of about 200 species of medium-sized to very large herbaceous and rhizomatous perennials mostly in the American tropics with 6 of the species in the South Pacific. The genus is allied to *Strelitzia* (bird-of-paradise) and *Musa* (banana) and was once included in one of these two families—Strelitziaceae or Musaceae. Some species grow to only 3 or 4 feet in height, while others reach 20 feet or more. All the species are clump-forming by the rhizomatous roots, but some clump slowly while others are much more aggressive. The leaves are relatively large and linear and are arranged along only two sides of the stems in a single plane. The leaves are usually ridged with horizontal slightly raised veins and have a stout midrib. The horizontal veins are sometimes differently colored from the rest of the leaf blade, and strong winds often tatter the

leaves along these veins. Some leaves are borne on fairly long stalks and are more or less ascending, looking much like banana leaves. Other species have leaves that are almost stalkless. Overall the individual plants look like a cross between a banana plant and a *Canna* species.

The inflorescences are terminal at the ends of the stems and are either erect or pendent. They consist of large bracts that are mostly boat-shaped and often very colorful—indeed, every hue of the rainbow is represented here—and from which the tiny clusters of coiled bisexual flowers peek out. Usually one basal bract is much larger than the rest, and it may or may not be colored like the others. The arrangement of the bracts around the flower stem is either spiral or on two opposite sides in one plane. Most species bloom in spring, summer, and autumn, but some can bloom at any time of the year and some are virtually ever-blooming.

All the species need warmth, regular, and abundant supplies of water and a rich humusy soil. Most are colonizers of opened sites or riverbanks in tropical rain forests and thrive in sun. Some are found as understory plants in the forest and need partial shade to do well. None tolerates frost, and most completely die off, roots and all, if frozen. A few species spring back from the rhizomatous roots if the freezing temperatures do not go too low and do not last too long, though these species, because they bloom only on year-old stems, will not bloom if frozen back in successive winters. Like the stems of many members of the Zingiberaceae (ginger family), the stems of *Heliconia*, having flowered once, die off as the flowers fade and the tiny knoblike fruits mature. It is, therefore, best to cut these stems to the ground after they bloom.

There is a myriad of naturally occurring varieties and cultivars as well as natural hybrids now available. Some are extraordinarily beautiful but difficult to identify as the cultivar forms often differ radically in appearance from the type. Several elegant dwarf cultivars have appeared, mostly with parentages of *Heliconia angusta, H. psittacorum, H. spathocircinata,* and *H. stricta.* These wonderful forms have the same cultural requirements as their parents. The visual aspect of every species is emblematic of the tropics and the tropical look. Some species are almost startlingly spectacular and exotic, adding a luminosity of color and gracefulness of form as few other landscape subjects can.

Heliconia acuminata (a-kyoo´-mi-NAIT-a) is indigenous to Brazil, Venezuela, and Peru. This small species never grows to more than 5 or 6 feet and has long-stalked banana-like deep green leaves with a prominent and darker-colored midrib. The inflorescences are borne on long red or yellow stalks and are distinctive in appearance with only a few long and tapering narrow boat-shaped bracts whose colors range from scarlet to deep orange-red to yellow. The bracts are arranged in a widely spaced zigzagging manner along the stem of the flower spike and have very large and showy flowers emerging from their interiors. The flowers range in color from green to yellow or white, often with a dark green band near their tips. This species and its forms are truly captivating and alluring, with flowers looking somewhat like birds in flight. The plants need sun to bloom.

Heliconia angusta (an-GUST-a) is indigenous to southeastern Brazil. It is a small plant usually growing to no more than about 5 feet with long-stalked dark green banana-like leaves. The inflorescence is erect and the bracts, which are in one plane along opposite sides of the flower spike, are boat-shaped, long, stiff, and narrow, and range in color from crimson through orange to pure yellow. The flowers are almost as large and showy as the bracts: they are white or yellow and protrude well out of the embrace of the stiff bracts. *Heliconia angusta* '**Holiday**', the most beautiful cultivar, has crimson bracts and large white flowers. It usually blooms at Christmas-time (actually from autumn to spring). The plants thrive in partial shade.

Heliconia bella (BEL-la) is indigenous to Panama. A small species that grows only to about 6 feet, it is a very choice and beautiful plant. The leaves are long-stalked and very dark green above, with a maroon midvein and fine variegation beneath. The erect pyramidal inflorescence is composed of many luminously scarlet closely set boat-shaped bracts. The lower bracts are long and tapered, the upper ones fatter and shorter. The visual effect is that of a lit torch. Unlike most other species, this one grows and blooms well with only a moderate amount of sunlight.

Heliconia bihai (bee-HA-ee) is native to the West Indies, Central America, and northern South America. It grows from 8 to 15 feet tall with long usually red-stalked 6-foot-long light green banana-like leaves. The erect inflorescence is short-stalked and consists of many triangular boat-shaped long-tapering scarlet yellow-tipped bracts arranged in a zigzagging manner in one plane along the stem of the flower spike. A larger basal bract is narrow and green. There are many cultivars; some have solid scarlet, pure golden-colored, or pure bluish green bracts. Some have as many as two dozen bracts, while others have as few as six. This species and its cultivars are among the most beautiful plants in the genus and need sun to bloom well. Plates 224 and 225.

Heliconia caribaea (kair-i-BEE-a) is native to the West Indies. The plant grows very large to as much as 20 feet with 6-foot-long dark green waxy banana-like leaves on 5-foot-long petioles. The bracts of the erect and almost stalkless inflorescence are closely set in one plane along the stem of the flower spike and are fat, boat-shaped, flat, and keel-like on the bottom, long-tapering from an almost rounded base, and bright reddish orange in color. A larger basal bract is green. There are cultivars with dark red to almost purple bracts, brilliant yellow and green bracts, and golden to scarlet-colored bracts. All have the same beautiful shape. The species needs at least a half day's full sun to bloom well.

Heliconia collinsiana (kahl-linz´-ee-AHN-a) is native to southern Mexico and adjacent Central America. It grows from 6 to 12 feet with long-stalked medium green banana-like leaves. The inflorescence is pendent with spirally arranged and widely separated red to orange long-tapered boat-shaped bracts with bright yellow flowers peeking out. The inflorescence as well as the younger leaves are covered in a shiny and waxy bloom. The species needs at least a half day's sun to bloom.

Heliconia indica (IN-di-ka) is one of six species not indigenous to the American tropics; it is naturally found in New Guinea and is one of the largest species in the genus, growing to 20 feet or more. The 7-foot-long oblong leaves are long-stalked, banana-like, thick, leathery, and very deep dark green. *Heliconia indica* '**Spectabilis**' (spek-TAB-i-liss) has leaves that are dark green to rose in color with a pink or maroon midrib and very many horizontal thin white, red, or pink lines on the surface. The undersides of the leaves are usually a brilliant orange-red or coppery orange in color. These leaves, which are among the world's most beautiful, are reason to grow this cultivar as the erect inflorescences, while pretty enough, are not colorful but rather are solid green. There are several other cultivars, but none with as incredibly beautiful leaves as this form. The plants need a half day's sun to look good.

Heliconia latispatha (lat-i-SPAYTH-a) occurs naturally from southern Mexico to northern South America. It grows from 6 to 15 feet in height with long-stalked yellow-green banana-like leaves that have a thin red margin. The inflorescence is erect with widely spaced long-triangular tapering boat-shaped bracts that are usually yellow to orange at their bases, changing to scarlet at the ends of the bracts. At least one cultivar has solid yellow bracts. The bracts are arranged spirally around the stem of the flower spikes and are held horizontally or somewhat ascending. This species needs a half day's sun to bloom.

Heliconia mariae (MAHR-ee-eye) is found naturally from Guatemala to Colombia. It is perhaps the largest species in the genus, often growing to well over 20 feet in height. The long-stalked deep green banana-like leaves are truly immense, often 10 or more feet long, and have prominent horizontal ridges on their upper surfaces. The gigantic pendent inflorescence is as long as 3 feet and is composed of closely set S-shaped brilliant red bracts in one plane along two sides of the flower stem. The plant is a truly astounding sight, especially when in bloom. It needs sun to bloom.

Heliconia orthotricha (or-toe-TRYK-a) is native to Colombia, Ecuador, and Peru. It grows from 3 to 15 feet with long-stalked light green banana-like leaves that have reddish stalks and dark midribs. The inflorescence consists of 6 to 12 triangular boat-shaped bracts, the lower ones very long-tapering. The bracts, which are regularly spaced along the stem of the flower spike, are not overlapping. Colored with glowing crimson or rose outlined in dark grayish green, they are usually covered in a fine pubescence. There is no more elegant-looking species. The plant needs some sun to bloom well.

Heliconia psittacorum (sit-ta-KOR-um) is native

to eastern Brazil northwards through the Virgin Islands. Quite variable, it is probably the most widely planted species in the genus. The plants grow from 2 to 6 feet with stalked deep green banana-like leaves that are only about 2 feet long. The inflorescence is fairly distinctive, although very variable as to color. The bracts are always sharply ascending, the lower ones much larger than the upper ones, and tapered. Ranging in color from scarlet to pink, yellow, or blue-green, the bracts are rather widely spaced along the zigzagging stem of the flower spike and are arranged in one plane along its two sides. This species is one of the few whose flowers are almost as showy as the bracts in which they reside. Some flowers are as long as or longer than the upper bracts. The flowers range in color from green to orange to yellow and almost white, and they usually have their tips marked in zones of dark green and white or yellow. Some of the color combinations of bracts and flowers are more than enchanting, and the form of the inflorescences often reminds one of birds in flight. Common names of the varieties of this species include parrot's plantain, parrot's flower, and parakeet flower. There are many cultivars and hybrids and several elegant dwarf forms. *Heliconia* **'Golden Torch'**, a cross between *H. psittacorum* and *H. spathocircinata*, grows from 4 to 6 feet in height with widely separated stiff and tapering golden-yellow bracts and flowers. It blooms year-round. The plants, both type and hybrids, need almost full sun to bloom. Plate 226.

Heliconia rostrata (ro-STRAYT-a / rah-STRAYT-a / ro-STRAHT-a) is indigenous to western Peru and Ecuador. It grows as small as 5 feet or as large as 20 feet with long-stalked medium green to bluish green, 5-foot-long banana-like leaves. The pendent inflorescence is the most beautiful in the genus. It is long-stalked with the bracts aligned in one plane on opposite sides of the flower spike and arranged in a zigzagging manner. Each bract is fat and boat-shaped. The basal bracts are more linear and long-pointed, while the other bracts are short-tipped. Their color is a brilliant scarlet with the lower surface outlined in luminous yellow. The inflorescence stands out splendidly in the landscape, and the plant is one of the most exotic and tropical looking subjects one can grow. The species needs at least a half day's sun. Plate 227.

Heliconia schiedeana (sheed-ee-AHN-a) is indigenous to southern Mexico. It grows to about 6 feet with long-stalked dark green 4-foot-long banana-like leaves. The erect inflorescence is long-stalked with 7 to 10 widely spaced long narrow tapering vivid red bracts arranged spirally around the stem of the flower spike. The bracts are held horizontally or they are pendent, never ascending. The flowers are large and yellowish green. This species is known to come back from the roots in zone 9 after being frozen to the ground. The plants need sun to bloom well. Plate 228.

Heliconia spathocircinata (spayth´-o-seer-si-NAIT-a) is native to northern South America. It is a rather small species, never growing to more than 6 feet with long-stalked deep olive green banana-like leaves. The inflorescences are erect, and the widely separated green, yellow, or red fat boat-shaped bracts are spirally arranged on the flower stem. The long-tapering basal bract usually ends in a small leaf. The species is not overly spectacular, but is widely grown, easy of culture, and a parent of several good hybrid forms and their cultivars.

Heliconia stricta (STRIK-ta) is native to northern South America. This variable species grows from 3 to 8 feet in height with long-stalked banana-like leaves that usually have a reddish midrib and are often colored red or purple beneath. The short inflorescences are composed of as few as four and as many as a dozen boat-shaped, long-tapering bracts, which usually are not overlapping and are arranged in a rather zigzagging manner in one plane along the stem of the flower spike. Their color ranges from pure red or scarlet to pure golden and to green with red and yellow variegation. The plants need nearly full sun to bloom well. There are several lovely dwarf cultivars of this species.

Heliconia wagneriana (wag-ner´-ee-AHN-a) is indigenous to Central America southwards to Colombia. This very beautiful species grows to as much as 15 feet in height with long-stalked banana-like leaves with dark red midribs. The erect inflorescence is closely set with very fat short-tapering boat-shaped bracts that are light green with a large blotch of red or pink in the fat center. The red zone is surrounded by a thin area of yellow. There is a very large and long-tapering green basal bract. The plants need sun.

Heliconia zebrina (ze-BREEN-a) is indigenous to the rain forests of Peru. It grows only to 3 or 4 feet in height with long-stalked 2- to 3-foot-long banana-like leaves that are a grayish green above with horizontal bands of very dark green. Each band surrounds a thin white line, and the backs of the leaves are purple. The erect inflorescence consists of five to seven widely spaced, long, narrow, and tapering red to orange boat-shaped bracts arranged in a zigzagging manner in one plane around the stem of the flower spike and from which the long greenish flowers protrude. This wonderful species is eminently worth growing for its exotic leaves. The lovely inflorescences are a remarkable lagniappe. The species thrives in partial shade.

HELIOCEREUS (hee´-lee-o-SEER-ee-us)
Cactaceae: The Cactus Family
SUN CACTUS
Sprawling angular, flat-stemmed spiny cactuses; large spectacular red and white flowers
Zones 10 and 11
Sun to partial shade
Average but regular amounts of moisture
Sandy, well-drained soil or sandy leaf mold
Propagation by cuttings

A small genus of about six cactus species in Mexico and Central America. They are not desert dwellers, even though most species have typically cactus-looking angled or ribbed stems with spines, and they should be treated more like *Epiphyllum* species to which they are related. They are often grown as epiphytic vines, but need some soil around their roots. They are equally happy sprawling over rocks or the ground, in which their stems root, and few things are lovelier than these stems hanging from atop a retaining wall or similar structure with their immense flowers. The blossoms are very similar to those of the genus *Epiphyllum* (orchid cactus), but all these species are diurnal. There are no more spectacular flowers, some of which are more than 6 inches wide. The plants do not like full sun, especially in hot climates, and need regular amounts of water.

HEMIGRAPHIS (heem-i-GRAF-is)
Acanthaceae: The Acanthus Family
RED IVY; RED-FLAME IVY
Groundcover plants; Coleus-like green, purplish, and
    reddish leaves; small spikes of white and red
    flowers
Zones 10 and 11
Partial shade to partial sun
Water lovers
Rich, humusy, moist, well-drained soil
Propagation by cuttings

A large genus of almost 100 species of herbs and shrubs in tropical Asia. The cultivated species are low-growing, creeping plants that root at the stem nodes. The ovate-cordate or linear leaves grow like many members of the Labiatae (mint family): they are borne on the stem in pairs, each pair at right angles to the ones above and below it. The flowers, which are in short terminal clusters, are tiny tubes with five small lobes at their ends. As with most members of the acanthus family, the individual flowers are accompanied by small leaflike bracts at their bases. Only one species is commonly planted in the United States. *Hemigraphis alternata* (all-tur-NAIT-a) (synonym *H. colorata*) is native to Malaysia. It never grows more than 16 inches high with 3-inch-long ovate leaves that are toothed on their margins. Leaf color is green overlain with a metallic luster of bronzy purple. The flowers are white. This beautiful groundcover grows in shade or nearly full sun and becomes more colorful with more light.

HEPTAPLEURUM.
See *Schefflera arboricola*.

HESPERALOE
(hess-pur-AY-lo-ee / hess-pur-AL-o)
Agavaceae: The Agave Family
RED YUCCA
Rosettes of thin wiry grasslike leaves; tall spikes of red
    flowers
Zones 7 through 11; marginal in zone 6b
Sun
Drought tolerant
Sandy, well-drained soil
Propagation by transplanting of suckers and by seed

A genus of only three species in southwestern Texas and adjacent Mexico. The plants do not even much resemble those of the genus *Yucca*. In fact, except for the flowers they look more like succulent grasses. Only one species is regularly planted, especially in Texas. ***Hesperaloe parviflora*** (par-vi-FLOR-a) makes a tuftlike rosette of wiry, succulent stiff, and narrow, usually arching leaves that are grayish green to brownish red, depending on the amount of sun and moisture. About 4 feet long and only an inch wide, they are somewhat channeled or grooved above with margins that usually fray into white threads. The plants slowly clump and, when in bloom, are spectacular. The flower spikes, which appear in early summer and often into the fall, are 4 to 6 feet or more in height, usually branched, with inch-long salmon to scarlet tubelike flowers along the upper half. The plants are very effective in the cactus and succulent garden, especially when in bloom, and are stunning when planted where their shape and color can be appreciated up close or against a contrasting background. All they need are sun and a very well draining sandy soil.

HIBISCUS (hi-BIS-kus / hy-BIS-kus)
Malvaceae: The Mallow, Hibiscus, Cotton Family
HIBISCUS
Evergreen shrubs and trees; large leaves; distinctive
    mallowlike flowers of every hue
Zones vary according to species
Sun
Average but regular amounts of moisture
Average well-drained soil
Propagation by seed and cuttings for species, and by
    cuttings and air-layering for hybrids

A large genus of about 250 species of perennial herbs, shrubs, and trees found in all the warmer parts of the globe. Most have relatively large and undivided leaves, although a few have deeply dissected leaves. Most have solitary flowers that are five-petaled disks with a relatively long and protruding central column of stamens and pistil. The stamens and anthers arise directly from the lower portion of the column atop which resides the stigma. The species are grown primarily for the usually large and very showy flowers, but some tropical tree species have remarkably beautiful leaves and noble statures.

Hibiscus abutiloides. See *H. tiliaceus*.
Hibiscus acetosella (a-seet′-o-SEL-la) (synonym *H. eetveldeanus*) is indigenous to tropical East and Central Africa. It is hardy as a permanent perennial in zones 10 and 11, and is grown as a returning perennial in zone 9 and often as an annual in colder zones. As a perennial, it is short-lived. It grows to 6 or 8 feet with many non-branching stems, which become woody at their bases.

The 6- to 8-inch-long leaves are variable in shape and color and may be unlobed, but more usually have three to five deep narrow lobes, which give an almost palmate appearance to the leaf. The leaves are a deep green suffused with a bronzy red or brownish red hue. The most commonly planted form has reddish purple to brownish purple leaves. Unlike most other species in the genus, this species is grown for its very ornamental leaves rather than for the small reddish purple or yellow flowers, which are nonetheless attractive. The leaves are supposedly edible and are used as is lettuce in salads and are cooked as spinach. The plants are fairly drought tolerant and need sun to bring out the leaf colors and to keep the stems from becoming leggy. Plate 229.

Hibiscus arnottianus (ahr-not-tee-AHN-us) is native to Hawaii and is hardy in zones 10 and 11, although it is grown as a returning perennial in zone 9b. It is similar in leaf and flower to the ubiquitous *H. rosa-sinensis* (Chinese hibiscus), but grows larger, usually forming a small tree to 25 or 30 feet in tropical areas. The smooth deep green leaves are about 6 inches wide and long and are ovate with a short tip at the end and depressed veins above. The flowers are 6 inches wide or more and are almost identical to several white-flowered cultivars of the Chinese hibiscus, with five white petals and a deep red staminal column. The little tree is not as freely blooming as most Chinese hibiscus cultivars, but blooms all year in cycles and is very choice and tropical looking.

Hibiscus chinensis. See *H. rosa-sinensis*.

Hibiscus eetveldeanus. See *H. acetosella*.

Hibiscus elatus (ee-LAIT-us) is native to Cuba and Jamaica and is hardy in zones 10b and 11. It is one of the largest species in the genus, growing to 70 or 80 feet in its native habitat with a large broad to irregularly shaped open crown of foliage. The very handsome dark green 10-inch-long by 8-inch-wide heart-shaped leaves have prominent and lighter colored or reddish veins above and are reason enough to grow the tree. The brilliant flowers are even more of a reason. The 4-inch-wide blossoms are borne singly near the ends of the branches and never completely cover the tree but, because of their size and color, create a wonderful spectacle. They exhibit the typical hibiscus form, with five petals and staminal column, and are open cup-shaped and orange, changing to a spreading form and to red and finally maroon by the end of the day. The petals, which are narrower than those of the Chinese hibiscus and do not overlap, are also strongly recurved at their ends by the time they turn dark red. Common names are Cuban bast, tree hibiscus, and mahoe. The latter two names are unfortunate because they are used for a related species, *H. tiliaceus*. The tree is of outstanding beauty and one of the glories of the world's tropical flowering trees. Plate 230.

Hibiscus macrophyllus (mak-ro-FYL-lus) is indigenous to a wide area from India eastward to Java and is hardy in zones 10b and 11. It is another of the giant species of *Hibiscus,* growing to 70 or 80 feet in its native habitats with a wide and open crown. The leaves are what make this species special. They are as much as 2 feet wide, broadly heart-shaped to almost round, and leathery but glossy, with deep and depressed veins above. The flowers are only about an inch across but quite attractive with lemon-yellow petals and dark red at their bases. The tree, because of the giant leaves, is incredibly spectacular, with the essence of the tropical look.

Hibiscus rosa-sinensis (ro´-za-sin-ENS-is) (synonym *H. chinensis*) is indigenous to a far-flung area of tropical Asia including southeastern China. It is hardy in zones 10 and 11 and is grown as a returning perennial shrub in zone 9b. It grows into a small tree from 20 to 30 feet tall in completely frost-free regions, but is often cultivated as a multitrunked large shrub even in the tropics. The leaves, which are somewhat variable in size and shape, are generally cordate in outline, about 6 inches long and dark green and shiny above with depressed veins. The margins are mostly smooth, but may be lobed to some extent and are often serrate. The large 5-inch-wide flowers have spreading red petals. This species is the most widely grown, and there are now so many cultivars and hybrids (principally between *H. rosa-sinensis* and *H. schizopetalus*) that it would almost require a separate book just to list them. Most cultivars and hybrids are nearly ever-blooming as long as the weather is warm. Some forms have gigantic flowers almost a foot wide, and the flower color includes every shade except true blue. The flower is the state flower of Hawaii and is synonymous with the tropics and the tropical look. Common names for this species are Chinese hibiscus and tropical hibiscus. These plants relish sun and rich soil with adequate and regular amounts of water in a well-draining soil that is not too alkaline. Plate 231.

Hibiscus schizopetalus (skits-o-PET-a-lus) is native to tropical East Africa, Mozambique, Tanzania, and Kenya, and is quite tender to cold and not adaptable outside zones 10b and 11, although marginal in zone 10a. It is a large shrub, growing to about 12 feet with gracefully drooping branches and rather small dark green narrowly heart-shaped leaves with shallowly serrate margins. The flower is the most unusual in the genus, if it is, indeed, a separate species. Some taxonomists think it is but a form of *H. rosa-sinensis*. The blossom is long-stalked and pendent and hangs completely vertically, not just at a nod. The scarlet to pink petals are deeply lobed into fine oblanceolate segments, which are themselves lobed and the petals are curled back from the protruding and downward pointing staminal column. The visual effect is simply stunning. Common names include fringed hibiscus, Japanese hibiscus, and Japanese lantern, even though the plants are not indigenous to those islands. The plants bloom year-round, but not with the abundance of flowers associated with the hybrids and cultivars of *H. rosa-sinensis*. There is nothing more attractive when planted where the form of the branches and flowers can be appreciated up close.

This plant is the perfect patio tree for tropical regions.

Hibiscus tiliaceus (til-ee-AYS-ee-us) (synonym *H. abutiloides*) is probably indigenous to tropical seashores of Africa and Polynesia, although its distribution now includes the entire tropical world and its precise points of origin are obscured. It is hardy in zones 10b and 11 as a permanent tree form and in zones 9b and 10 as a returning large shrub. This tree grows quickly to as much as 50 feet away from the coast with a dense and spreading crown of thick drooping branches. The leaves are a deep green, 5 to 8 inches wide and broadly cordate to almost round, and have prominent and lighter colored (often reddish) midribs and lateral veins above but are grayish green to almost white beneath. The tree blooms year-round in tropical areas with 5- or 6-inch-wide typical hibiscus-shaped flowers that never quite open to a flat face. The flowers are a pale to deep golden yellow when they first open but gradually change to a red or maroon color by day's end. The tree is similar in many ways to *H. elatus*, but the latter generally grows larger, is not found near the seacoast, and its flowers are orange upon opening and have narrower petals, whereas *H. tiliaceus* is a seashore inhabitant and its flowers open yellow changing to red before they fall and have broader petals that overlap and never open as wide. The fruit is an inch-long ovoid velvety capsule. Common names are sea hibiscus, mahoe, and tree hibiscus. This species is one of the finest trees for planting near tropical seashores where it is generally much shorter because it is windswept and where it sports a picturesquely contorted trunk. It also thrives inland with a sufficient amount of moisture—altogether a treasure of a landscape subject. It grows almost in the water, where it thrives on and binds sand dunes when its pendulous branches touch the wet sand and then set roots, and where it forms great thickets of beautiful leaves and flowers. Plate 232.

HOFFMANNIA (hahf-MAN-nee-a)
Rubiaceae: The Coffee, Gardenia, Ixora Family
TAFFETA PLANTS
Herbaceous shrubs; large spectacular quilted and
    variegated leaves; small clusters of tubular flowers
Zones 10b and 11
Partial shade
Water lovers
Rich, humusy, moist, well-drained soil
Propagation by cuttings

A genus of about 48 species of herbaceous shrubs in southern Mexico and Central America with large soft and felty obovate or oblanceolate corrugated or quilted leaves with short tips and lighter colored veins. The small tubular flowers are in clusters in the leaf axils and are white, yellow, or red. These denizens of tropical rain forests need warmth and humidity and must not dry out. The leaves are as exotic, dramatic, and beautiful as any on earth, and they are a wonderful treasure to come upon along a shady path or anywhere else.

Hoffmannia bullata (bul-LAIT-a) (synonym *H. refulgens*) is indigenous to southern Mexico and Central America. It grows to only about 2 feet with rounded reddish succulent, sparsely branching stems. The fleshy 6- to 8-inch-long leaves are obovate to oblanceolate in shape with very deeply depressed surface veins and with the velvety tissues between them ridged and puckered. The upper surface leaf color is a deep olive green with a bronzy purple suffusion and lighter colored veins, while the lower surface is a vivid maroon in color. The flowers are red. ***Hoffmannia bullata* 'Vittata'** (vi-TAIT-a), an outstanding cultivar, has its upper leaf surface veins hued with shining silver.

Hoffmannia ghiesbreghtii (geez-BREKH-tee-eye) is indigenous to southern Mexico and Guatemala. It grows to a maximum of 3 feet with four-angled purplish few-branching stems. The foot-long leaves are elliptic to oblanceolate in shape with the surface veins deeply depressed and the tissues between them puckered. The upper surface leaf color is a metallic and satiny green with a bronze or purplish hue, while the underside is reddish purple. The midvein is pink, and the lateral veins are usually silvery, always of a lighter color than the background of the leaf blade. The flowers are yellow. The plants usually look better if pinched back when they start to become leggy. There are several cultivars. ***Hoffmannia ghiesbreghtii* 'Variegata'** has its upper leaf surface splotched with pink and white, and its underside a deep rose color. Plate 233.

Hoffmannia refulgens. See *H. bullata*.

HOLMSKIOLDIA
(hoam-skee-OAL-dee-a)
Verbenaceae: The Verbena, Lantana Family
CHINESE HAT PLANT; MANDARIN HAT
Large sprawling evergreen shrub; clusters of large red
    and orange flowers
Zones 10 and 11
Sun
Average but regular amounts of moisture
Average well-drained soil
Propagation by cuttings

A genus of 10 species of scandent sometimes spiny shrubs in Africa and Asia with oppositely arranged leaves and clustered flowers with large and fused membranous sepals enclosing small solitary tubular flowers. Only one species is planted. ***Holmskioldia sanguinea*** (san-GWIN-ee-a) is native to lower elevations in the Himalayas. It is a sprawling shrub that can be made to behave as a vine if tied to a support of some kind. It also is suitable as a fountainlike shrub. Either form needs pruning lest the plant become a scraggly mess. As a vine it sometimes reaches a height of 15 feet, and as a shrub it is usually no more than 6 feet tall. The 4-inch-long leaves are ovate in shape with a pointed tip and are usually somewhat felty and a medium green in color. The plants bloom off and on all year but most heavily in winter and spring. The flower clusters are formed in the leaf axils and usually consist of six or so inch-wide, deep orange disks, which surround a solitary deep red tubular-shaped flower. This brilliantly flowered plant is best used as an espalier, a cascade atop walls, or tied to a trellis where it can be appreciated up close. When in full bloom it looks rather like an orange bougainvillea. Plate 234.

HOMALOCEPHALA.

See *Echinocactus texensis.*

HOWEA (HOW-ee-a)
Palmae (Arecaceae): The Palm Family
KENTIA PALMS; SENTRY PALMS
Ringed, solitary-trunked palms with spectacular dark
    green feather leaves
Zones vary according to species
Partial shade to sun
Average but regular amounts of moisture
Humusy, well-drained soil
Propagation by seed

A genus of only two pinnate-leaved slow-growing palm species on Lord Howe Island off the northeastern coast of Australia. Both are single-trunked, and the older trunks have rings of leaf scars. This palm genus was formerly named *Kentia,* and this cognomen has become the most frequently used common name of the genus. Both species need protection, especially when young, from the midday summer sun in hot climates, but may be planted in full sun at any age in cool but frost-free climates like those of the southern California coast. The palms are slow growing and, from the time they bloom, it takes about 4 years for the seeds to ripen. This explains why *Howea forsteriana* (kentia palm), while still one of the most popular palms for indoor plantings, is yet quite expensive.

Howea belmoreana (bel-mor´-ee-ANN-a) (synonym *Kentia belmoreana*) grows slowly to a maximum height of 20 to 25 feet with slender and very graceful trunks that are a beautiful light gray to almost white in color with closely set rings. The long-stalked leaves are 7 to 10 feet long and the rachis is stiffly arched and bears many stiff erect and upturned dark green evenly spaced leaflets, so that the leaf is V-shaped in cross section. The palm has unusual grace and a striking and quite exotic architectural aspect, which is not quite unique among palm species but is nevertheless of distinct and unequaled appeal, and which makes it unsurpassed for a silhouette display against the sky, large expanses of walls, or different background landscape colors. The palm is accommodating in this respect because of its slow growth and retains whatever proportions it has for a relatively long time. The species is not hardy to cold and is damaged by temperatures below 30°F and is usually killed by any temperature below 28°F. Thus it is safe only in zones 10b and 11.

Howea forsteriana (for-ster´-ee-AHN-a) grows larger and somewhat faster than *H. belmoreana* to a maximum height of 40 or 50 feet with a slender grayish brown trunk closely set with rings. The long-stalked leaves are 7 to 12 feet long with many regularly spaced dark green 2- to 3-foot-long limp leaflets. The large, heavy, beautifully arching leaves create an astoundingly graceful and attractive fountainlike effect to younger plants. There is likely nothing more elegant in nature than these wonderful curves accented by the great drooping leaflets. This plant should be sited where there are no other prima donna plants to compete with this visual perfection. They have been used for more than 100 years as indoor or "interiorscape" subjects, gracing every imaginable sort of chamber from saloons and cheap hotel lobbies to spacious presidential ballrooms. The plant can withstand much abuse including dry periods, but its full potential as one of the world's most beautiful palms will never be in evidence if it is not provided with regular and ample amounts of moisture and a soil that is fairly rich in nutrients. Older palms sometimes withstand a temperature of 28°F unharmed, but anything colder is trouble and temperatures in the low 20s (sometimes the mid 20s) are fatal. These palms are adaptable only to zones 10 and 11. Plate 235.

HURA (HYOOR-a)
Euphorbiaceae: The Euphorbia, Spurge Family
SANDBOX TREE
Gigantic tree; tall straight buttressed trunk, gloriously
    beautiful large leaves; large exotic fruit
Zones 10b and 11
Sun
Water lover
Average well-drained soil
Propagation by seed and cuttings

A genus of only two species of gigantic trees in tropical America, hardly distinguishable one from the other. ***Hura crepitans*** (KRAYP-i-tanz) is an immense tree in the West Indies, Central America, and northern South America that is said to grow to 200 feet. The straight and buttressed trunk is free of branches for the first 50 to 100 feet. There are short, fat, viciously pointed spines on the upper trunk and branches and on young trunks. The extraordinarily beautiful 8- to 24-inch-long leathery leaves, which are cordate to oblong to almost round with a pointed end, are finely pubescent and have prominent, depressed, and lighter colored veins on the upper surface. They are carried on petioles at least as long as the blades. The tree is at least partly deciduous in dry or cold winters. The flowers are of one sex but both sexes are found on the tree. The male flowers look rather like tiny dark red ears of corn, and the female flowers like small orange-red toadstools. The outrageous fruits are 3-inch-wide brown woody globes whose sides are deeply grooved into many segments; the whole looks something like a miniature stylized pumpkin. When mature, the fruits explode and scatter the many flat coinlike seeds far around the surrounding area.

There are as many seeds as fruit segments. The common name comes from an ancient use of the immature fruits, when filled with fine sand, as quill holders and blotting mechanisms. Supposedly the fruits are still used as paper weights by pouring molten lead into the unexploded capsules. All parts of the tree are poisonous, and the milky sap is a strong skin irritant. The tree is of breathtaking nobility and majesty and is extraordinarily beautiful of leaf and fruit, but, because of its ultimate size, is not for the average yard.

HYLOCEREUS (hy-lo-SEER-ee-us)
Cactaceae: The Cactus Family
NIGHT-BLOOMING CEREUS; QUEEN OF THE
  NIGHT
Sprawling jointed and triangular-stemmed cactuses;
  tiny spines, immense nocturnal white flowers
Zones 10 and 11
Sun to partial shade
Average but regular amounts of moisture
Humusy, sandy, well-drained soil
Propagation by seed and cuttings

A genus of 15 or so semi-epiphytic cactus species in tropical America. All have stems with three to five angles and with a few widely spaced tiny spines, and the branches usually form aerial roots. The nocturnal flowers are white and funnel-shaped with many widespreading petals and sepals surrounding a great circular mass of yellowish stamens and a central protruding yellowish pistil. These are some of the world's most alluring blossoms, and they are made even more romantic by their often intense fragrance and nocturnal habit. The plants bloom year-round in tropical climates but most heavily in the summer. These species are not true desert dwellers and need more water than do, say, *Ferocactus* (barrel cactus) species. They also need some humus in their soil (leaf mold is perfect). They are often found in forests climbing on trees by aerial rootlets; indeed, the genus name means "forest taper (candle)." They can be grown as climbers or shrubs and even hedges. Because of their tolerance to salty air, ocean spray, and slightly saline soil, they are perfect planted near the seacoast as long as they are out of range of the highest tides.

Hylocereus calcaratus (kal-ka-RAIT-us) is native to Costa Rica where it climbs to 20 feet or more on trees. The dark green soft stems are three-angled and the ridges scalloped. There may or may not be short bristly spines on the crests of the lobes. The white nocturnal flowers are about 7 inches long and spread about a foot wide including the greenish sepals. The plant needs very bright light and regular water, but does not like full sun in hot climates.

Hylocereus guatemalensis (gwaht´-e-ma-LEN-sis) is native to Guatemala and El Salvador. It grows to 20 feet or more, clambering up trees. The bluish or grayish green stems are three-angled and shallowly lobed with small spines on the ridges. The very fragrant flowers are more than a foot long and at least as wide

with pure white rather narrow petals and widespreading brownish sepals.

Hylocereus undatus (un-DAIT-us) is probably native to the West Indies, but has become so widespread in the American tropics and worldwide that its exact origins are unknown. It is the most popular species and has, along with night-blooming cereus, the common name of lady of the night. Unfortunately other cactus species are also burdened with the latter moniker as is at least one other non-cactus flowering shrub. The plant grows to 20 feet or more, scrambling on and over any substrate its rootlets can penetrate, usually the bark of shrubs and trees but also porous rocks. The stems are three-angled, and each joint is scalloped and carries a small group of short dark spines. The fragrant flowers are a foot long and as much as 18 inches wide including the yellowish green sepals. The 4-inch-wide round fruits are edible and sweet with many tiny black seeds. The cactus is extremely floriferous in the summer if given enough water and a fairly rich soil. A hedge of these plants in full bloom is one of the tropical world's unforgettable sights. Plate 236.

HYOPHORBE (hy-o-FOR-bee)
Palmae (Arecaceae): The Palm Family
BOTTLE PALM; SPINDLE PALM
Feather-leaved palms; short bulging trunks;
  crownshafts; dark green stiffly arching leaves
Zones vary according to species
Sun
Average but regular amounts of moisture
Average well-drained soil
Propagation by seed

A genus of five species of pinnate-leaved palms from the Mascarene Islands east of Madagascar in the Indian Ocean. All the species have thick trunks and most of them have trunks that are conspicuously swollen at the base or bulging in the middle. Atop the trunk is a thick and often swollen bright green to grayish green or bluish green crownshaft. The relatively few leaves arch stiffly and have a stout midrib. The crown of leaves is always beautiful and dramatically architectural. The trunks, however, are an acquired taste; some think them dumpy, insolent, and grotesque, while others think them shapely and dramatically architectural. In any case they could never be called "graceful." Where they are planted would seem to make all the difference whether they are pleasing in the landscape. Rather than trying to hide their unusual form, the latter should be accented. The plants thrive in saline conditions and are wise choices for seashore plantings. They are startlingly dramatic, as are most palm species, when trees of varying heights are planted in a group. In spite of their ability to thrive in salt spray and saline soil, the palms need regular and adequate amounts of water (not salt water).

Hyophorbe lagenicaulis (lahg´-en-i-KAW-lis / la-jen´-i-KAW-lis) slowly grows only to about 15 feet. Its trunk is greatly swollen at the base and at maturity truly deserves the common name of bottle palm. The crown of leaves is sparse with usually only about 6 leaves, each 10 feet long, deep green in color, and with many regularly spaced stiff tapering leaflets. The leaflets are carried on a thick stout rachis and are held upright at about a 45° angle, giving the leaf as a whole a distinct V shape in cross section. The species is quite tender to cold and is not adaptable outside of zones 10b and 11. Plate 237.

Hyophorbe verschaffeltii (ver-sha-FELT-ee-eye) grows larger than the above species, often reaching a maximum height of 30 feet. The trunk is thick and usually swollen in the middle or just beneath the crownshaft, which phenomenon occasions the common name of spindle palm. The leaves are, like those of other species, few, but each is large (to 10 feet long) and full. The dark green tapering leaflets spring from the stout rachis at several angles, giving a somewhat plumose look to the whole leaf. The leaflets are fairly limp and not as stiff as those of *H. lagenicaulis*, which further adds to the fuller and more graceful aspect of the blade. These palms look especially nice when trees of varying heights are planted in groups. The species is slightly hardier than the bottle palm, but is not adaptable outside zones 10 and 11.

HYPHAENE (hy-FEE-nee)
Palmae (Arecaceae): The Palm Family
GINGERBREAD PALMS; DOUM PALMS
Fan-leaved palms with erratically branching slender trunks; large colorful edible fruit
Zones 10b and 11
Sun
Average but regular amounts of moisture; drought tolerant
Sandy, well-drained soil
Propagation by seed

A genus of about 10 species of palmate-leaved palms, some with branching trunks, in Egypt, central sub-Saharan and East Africa, Madagascar, Arabia, and India. The genus has the world's only palms whose trunks branch naturally. The leaves are costapalmate, meaning that the petiole extends well into the leaf blade, often resulting in an arch to the blade (i.e., it is V-shaped in cross section). The palms naturally grow in arid or semiarid areas, often in poor soils with no natural drainage, allowing various salts to collect therein. It is important to note that the palms always grow (like *Washingtonia* species in the American Mojave and Sonoran deserts) near springs or other sources of underground water. Because the names of the various species are taxonomically in flux and it is difficult to determine the species from the present literature, the palms are rare in cultivation, although there are several in botanical gardens and many collectors are growing them. Other reasons for their scarcity are their very slow rate of growth and the tendency of the germinating seeds to throw down a sinker root to as much as 3 feet before the juvenile leaves sprout from the seed. *Hyphaene*

thebaica (thee-BAY-i-ka) is doubtless the most commonly planted species. From Egypt and northern Africa, it grows to 20 or 30 feet in height. Old specimens have black trunks that are branched, starting at 10 to 12 feet, into several successive forks. Each branch ends in a rather small rounded head of 3-foot-wide grayish green deeply segmented leaves.

HYPOESTES (hy-po-ES-teez)
Acanthaceae: The Acanthus Family
POLKA-DOT PLANTS
Small herbaceous perennials with variegated leaves and terminal spikes of blue and white flowers
Zones 10 and 11 as permanent perennials; zone 9 as returning perennials
Sun to partial shade
Average but regular amounts of moisture
Average well-drained soil
Propagation by seed or cuttings

A genus of about 40 species of herbaceous perennials and shrubs in South Africa, Madagascar, and Southeast Asia, only one of which is cultivated to any extent in the United States. *Hypoestes phyllostachya* (fyl-lo-STAIK-ee-a) (synonym *H. sanguinolenta*) is an herbaceous shrub from Madagascar that grows to as much as 3 feet in height. It has soft oppositely arranged small 2- or 3-inch-long linear-cordate leaves that are a deep green flecked with pink or purplish spots. A cultivar with green leaves heavily spotted with white stands out better in the landscape, but both type and cultivar are quite charming and just about carefree, thriving in sun or partial shade. They are beautiful in beds with small ferns and other tropical contrasting foliage plants like *Begonia* or *Impatiens* and they make a wonderful border plant. They usually need to be pinched or cut back as they become leggy when allowed to grow to their full height; and the flower spikes, while attractive enough, rob the plants of vigor and should be removed as they form. The only other care the plants need is occasional watering as they are not really drought resistant. Plate 240.

ICHTHYOMETHIA. See *Piscidia*.

ILLICIUM (il-LIS-ee-um)
Illiciaceae: The Star-Anise Family
ANISE TREES
Small and medium-sized evergreen trees; leathery leaves; small flowers; asterisk-shaped fruit
Zones vary according to species
Sun to partial shade
Water lovers
Humusy, moist, well-drained, acidic soil
Propagation by seed and cuttings

A genus of about 40 species of evergreen shrubs and small trees in southeastern Asia, the southeastern United States, and the West Indies. All have thick leathery leaves that are usually aromatic, small often fragrant flowers, and unusual rounded several-sectioned small fruit, usually shaped like a star or an asterisk, with each section containing a single seed. *Illicium* is the sole genus in the family Illiciaceae and it is related to the magnolia family, in which it was formerly included. Only three species are regularly planted, but they are all of exceptional ornamental quality.

Illicium anisatum (an-i-SAHT-um) (synonym *I. religiosum*) is native to Japan and Taiwan and is hardy in zones 7b through 11 and marginal in zone 7a. It grows to about 20 feet and is normally a large multistemmed shrub, but is easily trained when young to a small tree form with a dense crown of foliage about 10 feet wide. The thick, almost succulent-looking leathery but glossy light green to dark bluish green leaves are elliptical in shape, tapering to a point, and about 4 inches long with a strong midrib. When crushed or bruised, the leaves emit a heady odor of anise. The inch-wide flowers, which are found in the leaf axils and which are whitish to yellow-green with 20 or so linear petals, are not showy in the landscape nor are they fragrant. The inch-wide rounded and sectioned fruits are reddish brown when mature and quite attractive up close, but do not show up well in the landscape. The little tree is usually called the Japanese anise tree. Somber but elegant, this carefree plant is a nearly perfect subject for a patio tree. Grown as a large shrub, it is suitable for foundation plantings.

Illicium floridanum (flor-i-DAIN-um) is found naturally from southern Louisiana eastward along the Gulf Coast to north-central Florida. Hardy in zones 7 through 11, it grows to 20 feet or sometimes slightly taller and, like *I. anisatum,* is often a multistemmed shrub that is easily trained to small tree form. The leaves are also similar in shape to those of *I. anisatum* but are slightly longer and are not quite as thick. They have the same aroma when crushed or bruised. The flowers, which are similar in shape to but much more ornamental than the Japanese anise tree, are 2 or sometimes almost 3 inches wide and crimson to reddish purple in color with 20 or more petals. The fruits are the shape and color of those of *I. anisatum* but are, of course, larger. Common names are the Florida anise and the purple anise tree. This very choice small native tree or large shrub should be planted even more than it now is.

IMPATIENS (im-PAY-shenz)

Balsaminaceae: The Balsam, Impatiens Family
IMPATIENS
Evergreen herbaceous everblooming subshrubs;
    flowers in every hue except true blue
Zones 10 and 11; usually treated as annuals
    elsewhere
Partial shade to partial sun
Water lovers
Humusy, sandy, moist, well-drained soil
Propagation by seed and cuttings

A large genus of as many as 900 species of annual and perennial succulent-stemmed herbs and subshrubs in all parts of the globe but principally tropical Africa and tropical Asia. The leaves are generally ovate to elliptical in shape and usually toothed to some extent on the margins. The flowers are unusual in having one of the sepals much larger than the others and inflated into a small pouch with a curved or hooked spur. There are five petals, and the upper one is separated from the other four, which are fused. Because all the petals are about the same size, the petal arrangement is not always blatantly obvious in some tropical perennial species unless one pulls the flower apart. Each petal bears two lobes at its end.

The genus includes such longtime annual garden subjects as *Impatiens balsamina* (balsam) and *Impatiens capensis* (jewelweed), but we are here concerned only with the tropical perennial everblooming species known simply as New Guinea impatiens, which are indigenous to New Guinea and adjacent areas, and the sultana impatiens, which are of African origin. They are some of the loveliest of plants for adding color and form to shady and partially shady areas as they bloom almost continually with brilliantly colored flowers and, in the New Guinea forms, often strikingly attractive variegated leaves. Both forms are extremely popular now and widely grown as annual bedding plants in colder climates.

The **New Guinea impatiens** (Plate 238) are derived principally from *Impatiens hawkeri, I. linearifolia,* and *I. platypetala*. All these species (and their hybrids and cultivars) have wonderfully large and brilliant flowers, but produce fewer of them than the South African species (and their hybrids and cultivars). This trait is no drawback, but rather makes the plants more conspicuous and arresting, especially since the leaves are usually outstandingly beautiful. *Impatiens hawkeri* (HAWK-ur-eye) hails from mountainous regions of New Guinea and parts of Indonesia. It grows to 2 feet with reddish succulent stems and 6-inch-long ovate to elliptic quilted leaves, which are prominently serrate on their margins and which have a red midrib surrounded by a narrow feathery area of orange and yellow. The flowers are red to brownish red and about 2 inches wide. *Impatiens linearifolia* (lin´-ee-air-e-FO-lee-a) is also naturally found in elevated areas of New Guinea and grows to about 2 feet with 3-inch-long leaves in whorls near the ends of the wine-red succulent stems. The leaves are linearly elliptic in shape, remotely serrate on the margins, and a dark green above with a maroon midrib and a central area of yellow variegation. The flowers are 1 to 2 inches wide and a beautiful carmine-red. *Impatiens platypetala* (plat-ee-PET-a-la) is found naturally on the Indonesian island of Celebes where it grows to a foot or so with purplish succulent stems and 3-inch-long dark green elliptic to ovate leaves with a beautiful red midrib. The flowers are usually about 2 inches wide and range in color from white to pink and purple. The hybrids and cultivars of these species range in flower color from white to pink, red, violet, purple, and magenta, and the leaves are always variegated to some extent with yellow, orange, or red. All the plants have reddish succulent stems and leaves that are more linear and shorter-stalked than the African varieties. With parents originating in mountainous areas, they are less adaptable to hot climates but are possible with some shade and water every rainless day.

The **African impatiens**, also known as busy Lizzie or sultana impatiens, are derived from *Impatiens walleriana* and *I. marianae*. ***Impatiens marianae*** (mair-ee-AHN-ee) is found naturally in northern India where it grows as a creeping perennial to 1 or 2 feet in height. It has dark green ovate leaves with striking silvery variegation between the lateral veins. The flowers are small and mauve to purple. ***Impatiens walleriana*** (wahl´-'r-ee-AHN-a) is indigenous to tropical coastal East Africa, Tanzania, and Mozambique. It grows to 1 or 2 feet with long-stalked ovate leaves that are a deep medium green with finely serrate margins and are often found with some whitish variegation. The flowers are quite variable in color and may be white, pink, purple, or variegated. The hybrids and cultivars of these species are legion and range in flower color and form from white through orange, pink, and purple with many double forms and multicolored forms.

INGA (EEN-ga)
Mimosaceae (Fabaceae, Leguminosae), subfamily Mimosoideae: The Mimosa Family
ICE-CREAM BEAN TREE
Medium-sized evergreen tree; large pinnate leaves; large white mimosalike flowers
Zones 10b and 11
Sun to partial shade
Average but regular amounts of moisture
Humusy, well-drained soil
Propagation by seed

A genus of about 250 species of trees and shrubs in tropical America. All have big, lush pinnate leaves with few, large, even-numbered leaflets and large powder-puff-like clusters of white or yellow flowers. The flowers are rich in nectar and very attractive to bees and hummingbirds. The big flat, square or cylindrical leguminous pods of most species are edible. The genus is replete with choice shrubs and trees, most of which are unaccountably absent in tropical U.S. gardens. Only one species is planted, and it is not very common.

Inga edulis (ED-yoo-liss) is native to the West Indies, Central America, and northern South America. It is a fast-growing low-branching tree to 40 feet or more with dark gray smooth bark and a spreading crown. The 2-foot-long pinnate leaves have six to eight leaflets, which are 4 or 5 inches long, glossy dark green, and elliptical, with prominent and lighter colored midrib and lateral veins. The leaflets are borne on a winged rachis. The flower clusters appear year-round but mostly in spring and summer at the ends of the branches. Each

flower in the cluster is a mass of long white stamens projecting from small hairy brown petals. The fruit pods are 12 to 24 inches or more in length, oblong in outline with a hooked tip, fat, and four-angled with a sweet edible pulp, which leads to the vernacular name ice-cream bean tree. The tree is delicious-looking in every sense of the word and should be much more widely planted than it now is. It is perplexing why these wonderfully beautiful and carefree trees have been so neglected in American ornamental horticulture. Possibly it is because they are used mainly in their native habitats as shade for coffee plantations and, therefore, considered more utilitarian than beautiful.

Inga pulcherrima. See *Calliandra tweedii*.

IOCHROMA (eye-o-KROAM-a)
Solanaceae: The Petunia, Potato, Tomato Family
No known English common name
Sprawling evergreen shrub; clusters of large tubular purple or blue flowers
Zones 10 and 11 as permanent perennials; zone 9b as returning perennials
Sun to partial sun
Water lovers
Humusy, moist, well-drained soil
Propagation by seed and cuttings

A genus of about 20 species of evergreen shrubs and small trees in tropical America with relatively large leaves and terminal clusters of tubular or bell-shaped flowers. Only one is much planted. ***Iochroma cyaneum*** (sy-AYN-ee-um) is native to Panama and adjacent South America. It is a fast-growing sprawling shrub that attains a maximum height of about 12 feet but is often grown as a vine by guiding and tying it onto a trellis or other support. The 4- to 8-inch-long soft and felty leaves are ovate to lanceolate in shape and short-tipped. They are not exceptionally beautiful, but the summer flowers are most elegant. Borne in terminal and pendent clusters of a dozen or more blossoms, each flower is a 2- or 3-inch-long narrow tube with flaring but short corolla lobes. Flower color varies from violet or purple to almost pure blue. The plants in bloom are extraordinarily beautiful cascading from atop a retaining wall or planted in tall urns. This highly ornamental genus needs to be much more fully exploited for garden subjects. There are scarlet-flowered and orange-flowered species as beautiful as the one here discussed.

IPOMOEA (ip-o-MEE-a / ip-o-MOY-a)
Convolvulaceae: The Morning Glory Family
MORNING GLORY
Large twining vines; heart-shaped, lobed or dissected leaves; funnel-shaped and trumpet-shaped flowers
Zones vary according to species
Sun to partial shade
Average but regular amounts of moisture
Average well-drained soil
Propagation by seed and cuttings

A large genus of as many as 500 species of twining herbaceous to woody vines and a few erect growing shrubs or small trees. The species are mostly perennial, but there a few annual ones. They are found in all the tropical regions of the world. The leaves are usually large and cordate in shape, but may be deeply divided into lobes or even into threadlike segments. The flowers are all tubular, trumpet-shaped or bell-shaped, and often brilliantly colored. Every hue of the rainbow is represented in the flower colors of this genus. The typical morning glory flower shape is a funnel tube, which expands at the end into a rounded and usually flat disk with five shallow points and a line of slightly different color or texture radiating from the throat to each point. Some species and their cultivars and hybrids are very popular and widely planted as garden subjects all over the world. The perennial species are grown as annuals where winters are severe. All the species grow fast, some rampantly so, and many need a good amount of heat to flower well, although this is not true of all of them. Few bloom well without at least a half day's sun, but most are not particular as to soil fertility. They are mostly grown for their large flowers, but some have outstandingly beautiful leaves or fruit, and one is an important root crop, the sweet potato. Most are near perfect subjects for a lush and tropical look and are so easy of culture that they should not be overlooked even though they are common in gardens. Most annual cultivars and hybrids, of which there are hundreds, are derived from four species: *Ipomoea coccinea*, *I. nil*, *I. purpurea*, and *I. tricolor*. These are exceedingly easy of culture (except for the 'Imperial Japanese' forms) and need only be stuck in a sunny spot where the climate has a long enough growing season for the plant to thrive and flower. Many *Ipomoea* species have poisonous seeds.

Ipomoea acuminata. See *I. indica*.

Ipomoea alba (AL-ba) (synonyms *Calonyction aculeatum*, *Ipomoea bona-nox*) is probably originally native to tropical America but has been so widespread for so long in tropical regions that its precise origins are unknown. Known as the moonflower, it is a permanent perennial vine only in zones 10 and 11, but usually returns from the root in zone 9b and is very widely grown as an annual in colder climes. The vine twines very rapidly with heat to as much as 30 feet or more and is densely clothed with big beautiful heart-shaped leaves that are 8 or more inches long with a fairly long tapering point. The stunningly beautiful white fragrant nocturnal flowers are the typical morning glory shape but are very wide. They are as much as 8 inches across at the ends of their 6-inch-long funnels and have light yellow throats. The vine grows so fast that it is grown as an annual in cold climates, but it needs heat to grow and bloom.

Ipomoea arborescens (ahr-bo-RES-senz) is native to Mexico and is hardy in zones 10 and 11 although it usually springs back from the root in zone 9b. It is a large shrub or small tree with smooth gray bark that grows to as much as 30 feet in height and just about as wide with many pendent branches. The plant usually needs to be trained when young if a tree form is desired. The leaves are olive green to grayish green and felty, especially beneath. Cordate in shape with tapering ends, they are about 6 inches long. The tree is naturally deciduous in cold or dry winters. The flowers appear mostly in late winter and early spring when the tree is leafless, but some blossoms may be expected in the summer and fall. Each flower is pure white with a red throat that stands out like an eye and is about 5 inches long and as wide with the typical morning glory shape. This plant needs a relatively poor and very fast draining soil and full sun. The tree is called tree morning glory in the United States and palo blanco in Mexico.

Ipomoea batatas (ba-TAHT-us) is originally native to tropical America and, unless the roots are harvested, is a permanent perennial in zones 10 and 11 and a returning perennial in zones 8 and 9. In other zones it is grown as an annual. This plant is the sweet potato. Often and unfortunately, it is called a "yam" in the southern United States, although elsewhere around the world the yam is a species of *Dioscorea*. The 2-inch flowers are pink to violet and shaped like miniature morning glories. The plant is never grown for its flowers and rather seldom is it grown for its foliage, although the leaves are quite lush and handsome—6 inches long, felty, heart-shaped, and usually deeply lobed. Instead, the plant is grown worldwide in deep soil for its edible underground tubers. The tuber may be placed upright in a jar with water touching the lower part of the root, causing it to sprout and quickly grow as the more or less prostrate and stem-rooting vine it is. The tuber needs very good light to look good when grown this way, and it must have some water around the roots always. There is an increasingly popular cultivar named **Ipomoea batatas 'Blackie'** with leaves that are deeply lobed into three or five pointed segments. The new leaves open green with darker-colored veins, but soon the entire leaf turns a deep purple (sometimes almost black) with reddish purple undersides. The cultivar is effective in the landscape if planted where its color and form stand out, perhaps trailing over lighter colored rocks or anywhere it can be seen up close against a lighter colored background.

Ipomoea bona-nox. See *I. alba*.

Ipomoea cairica (KY-rik-a) is indigenous to tropical Africa and tropical Asia and is a permanent perennial in zones 10 and 11 and a returning perennial in zone 8 and 9; elsewhere it is grown as an annual. The tuberous-rooted vine climbs high and fast with slender stems. It has exquisite 4-inch-wide by 4-inch-long leaves that are a deep green and very deeply segmented into five pointed lobes, of which the lower lobe is largest. The appearance of the leaves is not entirely unlike that of the Hawaiian schefflera plant, *Schefflera arboricola*. The flowers are equally beautiful: light pink 2- or 3-inch-wide flaring funnels with red throats.

Ipomoea carnea subsp. *fistulosa*. See *I. fistulosa*.
Ipomoea crassicaulis. See *I. fistulosa*.

Ipomoea emarginata. See *I. pes-caprae.*

Ipomoea fistulosa (fist-yoo-LO-sa) (synonyms *I. carnea* subsp. *fistulosa, I. crassicaulis*) is indigenous to the West Indies, Mexico, Central America, and southwards to Brazil and is hardy in zones 10 and 11, although it usually springs back from the root in zone 9 and sometimes in zone 8. This species is a shrub, growing fast to 8 or 10 feet with slender stems that become woody at the base. The 6- to 8-inch-long narrowly ovate leaves, which are long-stemmed and a dull dark green in color, have a long tapering tip. The 5-inch-long by 5-inch-wide pink morning-glory-like flowers have a darker pink throat and are borne all year but especially during the summer. The plant now has an almost pantropical distribution and, in the United States, has escaped from cultivation in southern Texas and along the Gulf Coast to Florida. The plant is usually called the bush morning glory.

Ipomoea horsfalliae (hors-FAL-lee-eye) is native to the West Indies and, because of the large tuberous root, is a permanent perennial in zones 10 and 11 and a returning perennial in zone 9. Since, however, the vine blooms in the winter, it is seldom grown outside frost-free areas even though the leaves are exceptionally handsome. It quickly grows very large to 30 feet or more with beautiful 5-inch-long glossy dark green leaves that are rounded in outline but deeply cut into five or seven wavy-margined segments. The lowest lobe is the largest. The upper surface of each lobe has a prominent and lighter colored midrib. The flowers are sometimes pink to purple but mostly a deep cherry-red and are only about 3 inches long, tubular and narrow, with five distinct pointed lobes to the flaring end of the trumpet. The vine is covered with blossoms in December and January. *Ipomoea horsfalliae* **'Briggsii'** (BRIG-zee-eye) is a larger-flowered cultivar with wonderful scarlet to reddish purple flowers.

Ipomoea imperati (im-per-AHT-ee) is native to beaches in the tropics and subtropics worldwide. It is similar to and has the same climatic and cultural requirements as *I. pes-caprae* except that the leaves are sometimes palmately lobed into three to five segments (besides having the typical shape of those of *I. pes-caprae*), and the flowers are a wonderful pure white with yellow throats. The vine is as choice as *I. pes-caprae* and should receive the same consideration from the plant lover. Plate 239.

Ipomoea indica (IN-di-ka) (synonym *I. acuminata*) is native to a wide area of tropical America and is a permanent perennial in zones 10 and 11 and a returning perennial in zone 9; elsewhere it is grown as an annual. This very rapid grower climbs to 30 feet or more in a single season (with water and heat) or can be used as a groundcover. The large handsome dark green leaves are as much as 8 inches wide, and cordate to almost round, with the upper lobes almost touching each other. The flowers are the typical morning glory shape and are about 5 inches wide and pure blue to purplish blue when they open, but change to pink later in the day. The vine is sometimes called the blue dawn flower. There are several cultivars differing only in the color of the flowers: purple and white.

Ipomoea macrantha (ma-KRANTH-a) (synonyms *Calonyction tuba, Ipomoea tuba*) is found on all tropical and subtropical seashores and is a permanent perennial in zones 10 and 11 and a returning perennial in zone 9b. The vine is a strong-growing twiner to 20 feet or so that also creeps along the sand or soil, rooting at the stem nodes. The beautiful 6-inch-long leaves are cordate in shape and a deep glossy green above with a prominent and lighter colored midrib and lateral veins. The vine blooms in cycles all year with 4-inch-wide pure white nocturnal flowers. The plant is, appropriately enough, called the beach moonvine.

Ipomoea mauritiana (maw-rit´-ee-AHN-a) is indigenous to the West Indies and is hardy only in zones 10 and 11 but sometimes resprouts from the tuberous root in zone 9b. It grows to 30 feet in frost-free areas and has beautiful leaves, which are 6 inches wide and deeply dissected into five to nine segments. The leaves look like those of most varieties of *Abelmoschus esculentus* (okra). The flowers appear most of the year but most heavily in spring and summer with typical morning-glory-shaped blossoms that are a deep pink with dark crimson throats.

Ipomoea pes-caprae (pais-KAP-ree) (synonym *I. emarginata*) is found naturally on all tropical and subtropical beaches and is a permanent perennial in zones 10 and 11 and a returning perennial in zone 9b. It is also one of the finest plants for seashore planting, as it thrives in and binds soil above tide levels. In addition, the plant is of exceptional beauty. This very large-growing creeping, stem-rooting perennial has thick ropelike stems, which can reach a length of 70 feet or more. The wonderfully thick leathery bright green 5- to 6-inch-wide leaves are oblong to round in outline but deeply notched at the apex, giving a cloven-hoof likeness to the leaf blade. The leaves are usually found somewhat folded along the prominent midrib, especially at midday. The plants bloom year-round in frost-free areas but most heavily in summer. The pink to almost purple flowers with deep rose throats have the typical morning glory form and are about 2 inches wide and long. The vine, which does not require a saline environment to do well, is lovely creeping over rocks, or used as a groundcover in the sun, or guided up a lattice or trellis in any site with full sun. The plant is suitable for any very well draining soil that is on the poor side and thrives in almost pure sand. It is most commonly called the railroad vine (the allusion seems to be to the long straight-running stems), but also beach morning glory and goat's-foot morning glory. All parts of the plant are mildly poisonous. Plate 240.

Ipomoea tuba. See *I. macrantha.*
Ipomoea tuberosa. See *Merremia.*

IRESINE (i-REZ-i-nee / ir-e-ZYN-ee)
Amaranthaceae: The Amaranthus Family
Common names vary according to species
Red-stemmed herbaceous subshrubs; brilliantly
    colored long-stalked leaves; greenish flowers
Zones 10 and 11 as permanent perennials; zone 9b as
    returning perennials
Sun to partial shade
Average but regular amounts of moisture
Average well-drained soil
Propagation by cuttings and sometimes by seed

A genus of about 80 species of perennial herbs (a few
are annuals) and subshrubs in tropical America. All
have long-stalked leaves that are colored to some degree and small terminal spikes of insignificant greenish
white flowers. Two species are commonly planted. The
plants are spectacular as bedding subjects, for adding
color to sunny and relatively dry sites, and as colorful
accents with larger and green-leaved tropicals.

Iresine herbstii (HERB-stee-eye) is indigenous to
Brazil. It grows to as much as 6 feet with succulent red
stems. The ovate to round 3-inch-long leaves, which
are long-stalked and sometimes with fluted bases, are
often notched on their ends, depending on the variety.
They are purplish red to pink or green with darker red
striations or, in the green-leaved form, yellow. The
plants are sometimes called chicken gizzards or bloodleaf.

Iresine lindenii (lin-DEN-ee-eye) is native to
Ecuador where it grows to a maximum of 3 feet. The
long-stalked ovate leaves have pointed tips and are
green with a great amount of yellow or reddish variegation. The petioles as well as the plant's main stems are
succulent and red in color. The plants are often called
bloodleaf.

ISOLATOCEREUS.
See *Stenocereus dumortieri*.

IXORA (IX-or-a / ix-OR-a)
Rubiaceae: The Coffee, Gardenia, Ixora Family
IXORA
Small to medium-sized evergreen shrubs; glossy
    leaves; large rounded clusters of yellow and red
    flowers
Zones 10b and 11
Sun
Water lovers
Humusy, moist, well-drained, acidic soil
Propagation by cuttings

A very large genus of about 400 species of evergreen
trees and shrubs in tropical Africa, Asia, Australia, and
the islands of the South Pacific. All have leaves oppositely arranged or in whorls and large terminal clusters
of small tubular white, yellow, orange, pink, or red flowers. Most species bloom year-round, peaking in summer and fall in the subtropical parts of the United

States. The plants need a fairly rich moist acidic soil.
In areas like southern Florida, the soil usually needs
amendments of compost or peat moss. The shrubby
species are the most widely planted, but there are wonderful tree types. Some of the shrubby forms are possibly the most popular hedge subjects in subtropical climates, like that of southern Florida, where they are
overused for this purpose and often uncared for. Nonetheless, these are still some of the most beautiful flowering shrubs and trees.

Ixora acuminata (a-kyoo´-mi-NAIT-a) is native
to northern India. It is a shrub, only growing to about
12 feet, with large elliptic to oblong dark green glossy
leaves that are about 9 inches long. The plant blooms all
year with pure white flowers in clusters about 5 inches
wide. Unlike the flowers of most other species, the flowers of this one are extravagantly fragrant. Also unlike
many other *Ixora* species, the plant thrives in partial
shade.

Ixora casei (KAY-zee-eye) (synonym *I. macro-
thyrsa*) is native to Sumatra. It grows to 10 or 12 feet
with foot-long linearly elliptic medium green glossy
leaves with a prominent and lighter colored midrib. It is
possibly the most spectacular-flowered species with 6-
to 8-inch-wide globular clusters of glowing crimson
flowers with protruding stamens.

Ixora chinensis (chi-NEN-sis) is native to southern China, Southeast Asia, and Malaysia. It is similar to
I. coccinea but somewhat smaller. There are cultivars
with yellow, white, and pink flowers.

Ixora coccinea (kahk-SIN-ee-a) is indigenous to
India and Sri Lanka. It is a large shrub or small tree
growing to 12 or 15 feet in time. The leaves are cordate
to oblong in shape, about 6 inches long, dark glossy
green, and almost stalkless but clasping the stems. The
flowers are in terminal 5- to 6-inch-wide clusters and
are red or deep orange in color, although there are cultivars with yellow, pink, scarlet, and various shades of
orange flowers. There are also several dwarf cultivars.
Ixora coccinea 'Nora Grant' is the most popular
dwarf. *Ixora* 'Super King' is a popular hybrid between *I. coccinea* and *I. duffii*. It has slightly larger flower
clusters than the type. These lovely things are used
everywhere in southern Florida as hedge material with
much pruning, but the type and its color forms are
equally suited for small patio trees or specimens in a
large shrub border. The plant is sometimes called flame
of the forest, jungle flame ixora, or jungle geranium.
Plate 241.

Ixora congesta (kahn-JES-ta) is native to Myanmar (Burma), Thailand, and the Malay Peninsula. It
grows to 25 feet or sometimes more with wonderful
dark green and glossy lanceolate leaves that are as much
as a foot long. The flower clusters are 4 to 6 inches wide
and tightly packed with red or orange flowers. This exceptionally beautiful species is hard to find but well
worth the effort. It is intolerant of drought conditions.

Ixora duffii (DUF-fee-eye) is indigenous to the Mi-
cronesian Islands east of the Philippines. It is a shrub

growing to 10 feet with 6-inch-long linearly elliptic glossy leaves and terminal clusters of dark red flowers. Plate 242.

Ixora finlaysoniana (fin´-lay-so-nee-AHN-a) is indigenous to Thailand. It grows to as much as 20 feet with glossy dark green 6-inch-long elliptic to obovate leaves. The pure white flowers are in 6-inch-wide clusters and are wonderfully fragrant.

Ixora javanica (ja-VAHN-i-ka) is native to Java and adjacent Malaysia. It is a small tree growing to about 20 feet, but is usually grown as a large shrub with leathery narrowly elliptical leaves as much as a foot long. The flowers are orange-red to orange or even yellow in color and are borne in 6- to 8-inch-wide terminal clusters.

Ixora odorata (o-do-RAIT-a) is indigenous to Madagascar. It grows to 8 or 10 feet with elliptic dark green stiff leaves that are as much as a foot long. The loose flower clusters are immense, as much as a foot wide or more, with many 5-inch-long purple flower tubes expanding into light pinkish white disks. The flowers are wonderfully fragrant, but unfortunately they age to a dirty brownish pink.

JACARANDA

(zhahk-a-RAN-da / zhahk-a-RAHN-da)
Bignoniaceae: The Catalpa, Jacaranda, Trumpet-
    Vine Family
JACARANDA; FERN TREE
Medium-sized briefly deciduous trees; large pinnate
    leaves; large clusters of blue and purple flowers
Zones 10 and 11; marginal in zone 9b
Sun to partial shade
Average but regular amounts of moisture
Average sandy, well-drained soil
Propagation by seed

A genus of 45 or 50 species of shrubs and trees in the West Indies and South America. All have large bipinnate leaves and white, pink, blue, or purple bell-shaped or trumpet-shaped flowers in mostly terminal panicles. The blue-flowered species are possibly the most beautiful blue-flowering trees, of which there is a scarcity in the world; one other genus, *Guaiacum* (lignum-vitae), would be the other candidate. One species is much planted in almost all tropical and subtropical areas. *Jacaranda mimosifolia* (mi-mo´-si-FO-lee-a) (synonyms *J. acutifolia, J. ovalifolia*) is native to southern Brazil and northern Argentina. It grows to a maximum of 50 or sometimes 60 feet with a light brown or dark gray trunk and an open, often irregular, crown about as wide as the tree is high and of airy and very lacy foliage that is beautiful and reason enough to grow the tree. The leaves are as much as 18 inches long and bipinnate with innumerable small bright green oblong leaflets; they somewhat resemble those of *Delonix regia* (royal poinciana). The trees are deciduous in their native habitat, which has a winter-to-spring dry season, but in wetter climes leaf drop is often scant or nonexis-

tent. Flowering times are variable and depend on the amount of rainfall and the temperatures, but are generally in April and May in the southeastern United States. The blossoms are in pyramidal terminal clusters that are erect unless the number of flowers causes the tips of the clusters to droop. Individual flowers are trumpet-shaped and somewhat curved with an expanded end of five lobes. The color varies from almost pure blue to almost lavender, lavender-blue being the most common hue. The seed pods are a minor work of art, being mahogany-colored 2-inch-wide, flattish, slightly bent castanet-like affairs, the two halves separating when mature. A white-flowered form is, by almost universal accord, not as beautiful as the type. These lovely trees seem to bloom more profusely where there is a dry season in winter or spring and, while they grow very fast in wet and tropical areas, they also do not bloom as young or as profusely as they do in Mediterranean climates like that of southern California. Young wood is tender and is damaged by any temperature below 30°F, but older wood seems able to withstand 26°F or sometimes lower. These trees should not suffer prolonged drought, which may stunt their growth. The jacaranda is the perfect patio tree and, when in bloom, is more than magnificent against a background of dark green foliage or other dark background to set off the light blue flower display. There is no finer street tree in tropical and subtopical areas. Plate 243.

JACOBINIA. See *Justicia.*

JACQUEMONTIA

(jak-kwe-MAHNT-ee-a)
Convolvulaceae: The Morning Glory Family
No known English common name
Small twining vine; heart-shaped leaves; small
    morning-glory-like blue flowers
Zones 9b through 11 as perennials; almost anywhere
    as annuals
Sun to partial shade
Average but regular amounts of moisture
Average well-drained soil
Propagation by seed and cuttings

A large genus of about 120 twining herbaceous vines mostly in tropical America. The genus is closely related to *Ipomoea* and has similar leaves and flowers, except that the flowers of *Jacquemontia* are smaller and formed in larger clusters. Only one species is commonly planted. *Jacquemontia pentantha* (pen-TANTH-a) is indigenous to southern Florida, the West Indies, and northern South America. It grows only to about 10 feet and has beautiful, small, heart-shaped, leathery, glossy deep green leaves. The plant blossoms all year, unless there is a frost, with inch-wide light blue round morning-glory-like flowers with a white throat; they are formed in clusters of 6 to 12 or so. This lovely little thing needs to be planted where it can be seen up close.

JACQUINIA (jak-KWIN-ee-a)
Theophrastaceae: The Jacquinia Family
Common names vary according to species
Small evergreen trees; leathery leaves in whorls;
    fragrant white flowers; red and orange berries
Zones 10 and 11; marginal in zone 10a
Sun
Average but regular amounts of moisture; drought
    tolerant when established
Average sandy, well-drained, alkaline soil
Propagation by seed

A genus of about 30 species of evergreen shrubs and trees found in the drier regions of tropical America. All have stiff and leathery undivided leaves that are usually arranged in whorls and sometimes have spiny tips. The fragrant funnel-shaped white or yellow flowers have rounded five-lobed calyces and fringed five-lobed corollas, but the flower has the appearance of having 10 petals as the calyx and corolla are the same color and almost the same size. The fruits are showy yellow, orange, or red berries. These are wonderful little trees that are beautiful of leaf, flower, and fruit. All they require are sun, a warm climate, and a sandy, well-drained soil. All species are drought tolerant and thrive in the alkaline limestone soils of southern Florida and with saline conditions, making them near perfect subjects for seaside gardens.

Jacquinia arborea (ahr-BOR-ee-a) (synonym *J. barbasco*) is native to the West Indies where it slowly grows to 15 to 20 feet with dark gray usually multiple trunks. The light green stiff leathery leaves are about 4 inches long and obovate to almost spatulate in shape and are clustered mainly near the ends of the branches. The quarter-inch wide yellowish white flowers are borne year-round in terminal spikes, and the subsequent fruits are half-inch-wide round red-orange to scarlet berries whose weight causes the clusters to be pendent. One of the finest salt-tolerant small trees, it has an unusual refinement and elegance and is always in flower and usually in fruit. All parts of the plants are poisonous. The tree is sometimes called torchwood in the United States and barbasco in Jamaica, where its crushed fruit was once used to stun fish for harvesting. Plate 244.

Jacquinia keyensis (kee-YENS-is) (synonym *J. armillaris*) is native to the Florida Keys and the West Indies. It is rather similar to *J. arborea* except that its leaves, flowers, and fruits are not quite as large or as brilliantly colored, the leaf margins are rolled inward to a greater extent, the leaf tips are frequently notched, and the tree's bark is a darker gray, almost bluish gray. The tree is usually called joewood or cudjoe wood in the United States and barbasco in the West Indies.

JATROPHA (ja-TRO-fa)
Euphorbiaceae: The Euphorbia, Spurge Family
Common names vary according to species
Succulent cactuslike perennials or flowering shrubs
    or small flowering trees
Zones vary according to species
Sun to partial shade
Average but regular amounts of moisture; some
    species are drought tolerant
Average sandy, well-drained soil
Propagation by seed and cuttings

A genus of about 150 very variable plant forms found in all warm or tropical regions of the world; many are desert species. All these dissimilar plants are united only by the similarity of their flower structures. Some are succulent large-growing perennials rather similar to cactus or, more precisely, the succulent species of the genus *Euphorbia*; others are leafy shrubs or small trees. All these plants are exotic and tropical looking in one way or another, and some have spectacular leaves and flowers. Most species have poisonous fruits and sap.

Jatropha curcas (KOOR-kas) (synonym *Curcas curcas*) is native to a wide area of tropical America and is hardy in zones 10b and 11. This small tree to 12 or 15 feet in height is often grown as a large multitrunked shrub. As a tree it is broad crowned with a short light brown or dark gray trunk. The 4- to 8-inch-wide long-stalked leaves are broadly ovate in outline but always have three to five shallow lobes and are rough in texture, dark green above, and lighter beneath with prominent lighter colored raised venation. The tree is often winter deciduous with cold or drought conditions. The tiny greenish yellow flowers are borne in axillary clusters, and the fruits are 2-inch-long egg-shaped three-parted berries that mature from yellow to black. The seeds of this plant, while poisonous, especially raw, have been eaten as a tasty nut and used as a laxative, and the oil expressed from them is still used in the plant's native habitat as a torch fuel. The little tree is called physic nut (for its use as a purgative) and Barbados nut. The leaves are the reason to grow this plant; they are beautiful and quite tropical looking.

Jatropha gossypifolia (go-sip´-i-FO-lee-a) is found naturally in the West Indies and Mexico. It is hardy in zones 10b and 11 and successfully self sows in zone 9. It is an exquisitely beautiful little tree that grows to 12 to 15 feet with a smooth grayish rubbery trunk, a broad neat crown of foliage, and 6-inch-wide leaves that are broadly ovate in outline but deeply three-lobed and quite reminiscent in shape to those of *Gossypium* (cotton plant) species. The young leaves are entirely purple or mahogany-red in color with each lobe showing a deep red midrib; they mature to a glossy deep apple green or coppery green color with dark pink to red midribs. The plants bloom year-round with terminal few-flowered clusters of tiny red and yellow flowers. The combination of green leaves, purple to mahogany-colored leaves, and red and yellow flowers is exceptionally attractive. The fruits are about a half-inch wide, rounded, three-parted, and green in color maturing to yellow. The plant's only fault other than the typical poisonous sap and fruit is that it is intolerant to frost, but the seeds will survive a freeze and sprout with warm weather. The plants seem to thrive on poor soils, but are ever so much more attractive and grow very much faster with fertile soil and adequate water. Like the seeds of the physic nut, the seeds of this species (and, in this case, the leaves and sap) have been ingested by native peoples as a laxative and remedy for stomach distress. Because of these "medicinal" properties the tree is sometimes called the bellyache tree. Plate 245.

Jatropha integerrima (in-te-JER-i-ma) (synonyms *J. hastata, J. pandurifolia*) is native to the West Indies. It is hardy in zones 10 and 11 and is somewhat marginal in zone 10a. The plant grows naturally as a large multitrunked shrub, but may be trained when young to a small single-trunked tree specimen growing to about 12 feet in height with dark brown rather fissured bark. The leaves are quite variable in shape but usually about 6 inches long; they can be entire, elliptical or obovate and even ovate, but they can also be frequently found with several irregularly shaped and spaced lobes, often resembling a fiddle. In the past the leaf forms seem to have warranted separation into different species: *J. hastata* (*hastata* means "spear-shaped leaf") and *J. pandurifolia* (*pandurifolia* means "fiddle-shaped leaf"). In any case, it is not the leaves for which the plant is grown but rather the spectacular year-round flower display. The flowers are an inch wide and a brilliant scarlet to rosy red in color, and appear in large terminal clusters of many blossoms, each with five broad elliptical petals. Few shrubs or trees are as impressive as this species in bloom. The shrub is often called peregrina in Latin America. Plate 247.

Jatropha multifida (mul-TIF-i-da) is native to Mexico through Central America and down to Brazil and is hardy in zones 10b and 11. It is a small tree growing to 20 feet or sometimes more with a brown or gray trunk. The very beautiful leaves are a foot or more wide and round in outline but very deeply divided into 7 to 11 narrow segments. Each segment has widely spaced sharp lobes along its margins. The leaves would be more than enough reason to have this plant; the flowers make it almost irresistible. The plants flower intermittently all year but most heavily when the weather is hot. The large flat-topped inflorescences are terminal on the branches with many scarlet or coral-red flowers. This species is perfect in a cactus and succulent garden as well as a shrub border to give color and texture, and there is hardly a finer sunny patio tree. The little tree is usually called coral plant.

Jatropha podagrica (po-da-GREEK-a) is native to the drier areas of Central America and is hardy in zones 10 and 11 and marginal in zone 10a. It is a small shrub to about 4 or 5 feet. The plant has few stems or trunks, and the main one is greatly swollen at the base and knobby above. The leaves are found only at the ends of the stems and are enormous relative to the height of the plant; they are a bright green in color, 10 or more inches wide, and broadly ovate or round in out-

line but deeply lobed into three to five wide segments. Each segment is somewhat scalloped along its margin and sports a thick and lighter colored midrib. The plant is deciduous in cold or drought conditions. The flower spikes are terminal or sometimes arise directly from the side of the stems and are long-stalked with a flat cluster of many small red or orange-red blossoms. The plants bloom most of the year in cycles but never when the weather is cold. Because of the swollen stems the shrub is often called the gout plant. Plate 246.

JUSTICIA (jus-TIS-ee-a)

Acanthaceae: The Acanthus Family
Common names vary according to species
Medium-sized evergreen herbs or shrubs; large lance-
    shaped leaves; spikes of yellow and red flowers
Zones vary according to species
Light requirements vary according to species
Water requirements vary according to species
Soil requirements vary according to species
Propagation by seed and cuttings

A large genus of more than 400 species of herbaceous perennials or woody shrubs in all warm regions of the earth. All have oppositely arranged ovate to lance-shaped leaves, sometimes large. The flowers are mostly in terminal spikes or clusters and are tightly packed within these inflorescences; each flower is accompanied by a bract or bracts that are often larger and showier than the tubular flower.

Justicia adhatoda (ad-ha-TO-da) (synonym *Adhatoda vasica*) is native to India and Sri Lanka and is hardy in zones 10 and 11, although it usually comes back from the root in zone 9. It grows as a many-branched shrub to 6 or 8 feet in height with beautiful 8-inch-long elliptic medium green leaves that have deeply depressed veins above and are finely pubescent. The plants bloom in summer with terminal spikes that have white two-lipped flowers. The lower lip usually is streaked with red. The plant needs sun and moist rich soil.

Justicia aurea (OW-ree-a / AW-ree-a) (synonyms *Jacobinia aurea, Justicia umbrosa*) is indigenous to Mexico and central America and is hardy in zones 10 and 11, although it usually comes back from the root in zone 9b. This extraordinarily beautiful shrub grows to as much as 12 feet with foot-long lanceolate to broadly ovate deep green leaves with yellow midribs and deeply depressed lateral veins that are held on four-angled stems. The foot-tall fat flower spikes hold many 2-inch-long curved tubular golden flowers, an inflorescence of exceptional beauty. This choice plant needs at least a half day's sun and a rich soil with plenty of moisture, especially in the summer when blooming. Plate 248.

Justicia brandegeana (bran-dej´-ee-AHN-a) (synonym *Beloperone guttata*) is indigenous to Mexico and is hardy in zones 9 through 11 and usually sprouts from the root in zone 8b. Known as the shrimp plant, it is beloved of gardeners in the southern United States for many years. It is a broad shrub with wiry stems that grows to as much as 5 or 6 feet but is easily kept lower. The ovate leaves are about 3 inches long and of no great beauty, but the pendent inflorescences are very attractive. They are 6 inches long and consist of many overlapping greenish bronze to pink and coppery-colored ovate inch-long bracts. Each bract encloses a tubular white two-lipped flower with purplish red spots on the lower lip that peeks out from the shrimpy colors; the little flowers sometimes barely extend beyond the bracts. The plants seem to thrive with neglect in average soil, and they are somewhat drought tolerant but, if possible, should not be subjected to prolonged periods of aridity. They bloom in full sun or partial shade. Plate 249.

Justicia brasiliana (bra-zil´-ee-AHN-a) (synonyms *Beloperone amherstiae, B. brasiliana*) is native to Brazil and is hardy in zones 10 and 11. This rather small spreading shrub has gracefully arching branches growing to only about 3 or 4 feet. The 6-inch-long widely spaced leaves are in pairs along the stems, are ovate in shape and toothed on the margins, and end in a short point. The short inflorescences arise from the leaf axils and consist of 2-inch-long scarlet to pink tubular two-lipped flowers. The upper lips are straight and the lower lips are bent back and lobed. The plant is not fussy about soil but does not like drought and blooms well in partial shade.

Justicia carnea (KAR-nee-a) (synonyms *Jacobinia carnea, J. magnifica*) is indigenous to northern South America and northern Brazil and is hardy in zones 10 and 11 although it usually sprouts from the root in zone 9. This shrub grows to 6 or 8 feet and has four-angled reddish stems. The 10-inch-long leaves are linearly ovate in shape with a fine pubescence and prominent and lighter colored veins above. The flowers are pink to red in fat terminal spikes, and the plant blooms in summer and fall with flowers similar in shape to those of *Justicia aurea*. It needs partial shade and a rich moist soil to do well.

Justicia carthaginensis (kar-thaj´-i-NENS-is) (synonym *Beloperone violacea*) is native to the West Indies, Central America, and northern South America, and is hardy in zones 10 and 11, although it sometimes returns from the root in zone 9b. This herbaceous species only grows to about 3 feet with beautiful deep green narrowly elliptical leaves with a prominent and lighter colored midrib. The purple to lavender-colored flowers are in short fat terminal or axillary spikes, and each blossom is a narrow tube expanding into four inch-wide lobes. The plant thrives in partial shade and average soil that is not too dry.

Justicia coccinea. See *Odontonema strictum.*
Justicia ghiesbreghtiana. See *J. spicigera.*
Justicia spicigera (spi-SIJ-e-ra) (synonym *J. ghiesbreghtiana*) is indigenous to Mexico, central America, and Colombia and is hardy in zones 10 and 11, although it will sprout from the root in zone 9. It is an herbaceous shrub growing to as much as 6 feet with soft velvety four-angled stems and pubescent medium green 6- to 8-inch-long elliptical leaves with depressed veins. The inflorescence is axillary or terminal and is few-flowered with 2-inch-long orange-red tubular flowers. The plant needs sun, is not fussy about soil, and is fairly drought tolerant.

Justicia umbrosa. See *J. aurea.*

KALANCHOE
(KAL-an-ko-ee / ka-LAN-cho)
Crassulaceae: The Sedum, Sempervivum Family
Common names vary according to species
Succulent herbs and shrubs; flat scalloped or fat
    leaves; large panicles of tubular four-lobed flowers
Zones 10 and 11; mostly marginal in zone 10a
Sun to partial shade
Most are drought tolerant
Sandy, well-drained soil
Propagation by seed and cuttings; some produce
    plantlets on the leaves

A genus of about 125 species of succulent and semi-succulent herbs and subshrubs mainly in Africa and Madagascar. Some species have very thick, fat, and definitely succulent leaves; others have more typical flat leaves that can be called "fleshy." Some of the more succulent-leaved species produce plantlets on the leaf margins and flower spikes that may be used for propagation. All have relatively large terminal panicles of tubular or bell-shaped, often pendent flowers with corollas that expand into four linear lobes; most species bloom in late fall, winter, and spring. Some of these species are grown mainly for the curious and very attractive succulent leaves that are often large and scalloped; others are grown primarily for their large and spectacular flower panicles; and still others are grown both for the outstanding leaf forms and textures and for the flowers. All are superb subjects for rock gardens or cactus and succulent collections; most are equally suited to sunny, well-drained borders, the smaller species best sited where they can be seen up close. Most are best where their unusual forms are displayed against a differently colored background or near differently colored plants or stones.

Kalanchoe beharensis (bay-ha-RENS-is) is native to Madagascar. This large succulent-leaved shrubby type, which sometimes grows to 9 or 10 feet in height, has stems that turn woody at the base. It is grown for the magnificent fleshy triangular-cordate scalloped leaves that are as much as 16 inches long and are covered above with a rusty-colored felt and below with a silvery-colored felt. The attractive but not spectacular flowers are yellowish green. The plants are called velvet-leaf or feltbush. There are hybrids of this species with leaves of varying sizes and degrees of marginal indentations. One outstanding form is called oakleaf kalanchoe.

Kalanchoe blossfeldiana (blahs-feld´-ee-AHN-a) (synonym *K. globulifera*) is indigenous to Madagascar. This small fleshy-leaved herb seldom attains 2 feet in height and is grown for its flowers. The succulent and glossy leaves are 2 or 3 inches long, elliptic to oblong in shape with shallow indentations along the margins. The branched flower spikes reach well above the rather compact plants and consist of hemispherical clusters of small deep red flowers; the plants bloom in fall, winter, and spring. There are several cultivars and hybrids of this species—the other parents being *K. flammea* or *K. pumila*—that are more floriferous and usually more compact with yellow, red, or white blossoms and often with red-tinged leaves. These cultivars and hybrids are much sought after potted plants and are widely sold and bought in the Christmas holiday season, though they may be sold year-round. They flower according to the length of daylight, so commercial growers adjust the photoperiod (amount of light) to induce flowering. This species and its cultivars and hybrid forms are not as drought tolerant as many of the more succulent species. Plate 250.

Kalanchoe daigremontiana (dy´-gre-mont-ee-AHN-a) is native to Madagascar. It is a succulent fleshy-leaved subshrub growing to as much as 3 feet with very fleshy linear-lanceolate leaves that are as much as 10 inches long, notched on the margins, and somewhat concave in cross section; they are smooth and brownish green above and lighter beneath with purple splotches. The leaves are arched and curled backwards at their tips and grow only at the ends of the few stems much like a palm or *Yucca* species. This viviparous species bears tiny plantlets on the leaf margins. The plant has purple flowers. It is sometimes called the devil's backbone and because of the lavish production of plantlets, maternity plant. An outstanding hybrid between *K. daigremontiana* and *K. tubiflora* has shorter more erect leaves that are colored like those of *K. tubiflora* but shaped more like those of *K. daigremontiana* and are borne mostly atop the 3-foot tall stems, giving a palmlike aspect to the hybrid plant, much like that of *K. tubiflora*. This hybrid is sometimes called the good luck plant.

Kalanchoe delagonensis. See *K. tubiflora*.

Kalanchoe eriophylla (er´-ee-o-FYL-la) is indigenous to Madagascar. It is a small compact plant growing only to about 10 inches with fat, stalkless, closely set ovate and keel-shaped very succulent leaves that are covered with a mat of fine white cottonlike hairs and have purple-brown spots near the margins. The flowers are blue to purple.

Kalanchoe farinacea (fair-i-NAY-see-a) is native to the island of Socotra in the Arabian Sea south of the Arabian Peninsula. It is a small and very compact plant with stalkless fleshy smooth, lime green obovate inch-long leaves that are remotely notched at their tips, are covered with a silvery bloom, and have pinkish margins. The flower clusters are very compact with many beautiful inch-long scarlet tubular flowers with yellow bases.

Kalanchoe fedtschenkoi (fet-SHANK-oy) (synonym *Bryophyllum fedtschenkoi*) is indigenous to Madagascar. It grows to about 2 feet with wiry sprawling stems that may even be prostrate. The fleshy 2-inch-long leaves are obovate in shape with scalloped margins

and an intriguing color of metallic bluish green overlain with a violet bloom and margined with purple. The flowers are pinkish brown bells that are not too spectacular but are quite lovely with the bluish leaves. There are several cultivars of this species. ***Kalanchoe fedtschenkoi* 'Marginata'** is the most attractive of these.

Kalanchoe flammea (FLAM-mee-a) is native to Somalia and southern Ethiopia in northeastern Africa. It is similar to *K. blossfeldiana* but the flowers are usually larger and come in shades of yellow, orange, and red.

Kalanchoe gastonis-bonnieri (gas-TON-is-bahn-nee-ER-ee) is indigenous to Madagascar. It grows to a maximum height of 3 feet with a short stem and an immense rosette of 18-inch-long leaves. The leaves are thick and fleshy, oblanceolate to spatulate in shape, and bronzy green in color with a white bloom and scalloped margins. The plants are viviparous with plantlets produced along the margins of the older leaves. The flowers are bell-shaped and pink to orange in color. Plate 251.

Kalanchoe grandiflora (gran-di-FLOR-a) is native to tropical East Africa and southern India. It grows to 2 or 3 feet in height with 3-inch-long very fleshy ovate to spatulate grayish green leaves with a bluish bloom and scalloped margins. The yellow flowers are large and showy. There are hybrids with *K. flammea* and *K. blossfeldiana* that have even larger flowers and leaves.

Kalanchoe longiflora (lahn-ji-FLOR-a) is native to Mozambique and Tanzania. It grows only to about 2 feet with four-angled stems and short-stalked fleshy obovate 3-inch-long leaves that are a grayish to coppery green in color with an orange hue on the scalloped leaf margins. The bell-shaped flowers are orange.

Kalanchoe marmorata (mar-mo-RAIT-a) (synonym *K. somaliensis*) is indigenous to southern Ethiopia and Somalia. It grows to about 3 feet with closely set fleshy short-stalked obovate 5- to 10-inch-long leaves that are a bluish green in color often with a pinkish hue, scalloped margins, and many deep purple to almost black irregularly shaped spots. The flowers are white. Because of the purplish black markings on the leaves this old favorite is called the penwipe plant.

Kalanchoe pinnata (pin-NAIT-a) (synonyms *Bryophyllum calycinum*, *B. pinnatum*) is probably originally indigenous to India but is now so widespread in tropical regions that its exact origin is uncertain. This succulent shrub grows to as much as 6 feet and has few-branched hollow stems bearing extraordinarily attractive 4- to 6-inch-long fleshy oblong leaves that are regularly scalloped along the edges; they are a light grayish green in color with red margins. With age the new leaves tend to be truly pinnate with three to five scalloped leaflets. The plant freely produces rooting plantlets along the leaf margins. The flowers are not particularly showy, being a purplish green in color. This species is one of the most popular in the genus and has several common names including air plant, curtain plant (because a leaf or a portion of a leaf may be pinned to a curtain where the plantlets will root), miracle-leaf, and Mexican love plant.

Kalanchoe prolifera (pro-LIF-e-ra) is native to Madagascar. It is a magnificent succulent growing to 10 or even 12 feet with four-angled few-branched stems and 18-inch-long fleshy pinnate leaves with 7 to 11 oblong bright green leaflets with scalloped margins. The flowers are also beautiful, being clear yellow inch-long bells. The plant is viviparous, producing plantlets along the margins of the leaflets and in the leafy flower spike.

Kalanchoe pumila (PYOO-mi-la) is native to Madagascar. It is a small compact plant hardly growing to more than a foot in height with closely set fleshy obovate inch-long leaves that are scalloped on the margins and are a beautiful dark green in color overlain with a brownish purple hue. The flowers are a reddish purple.

Kalanchoe rhombopilosa (rahm´-bo-py-LO-sa) is native to Madagascar. It is a compact plant growing to about 18 inches with closely set short-stalked wedge or fan-shaped very succulent leaves that are green with a silvery bloom, the outer margin wavy and the whole leaf irregularly streaked with dark brown to dark reddish purple striations. The flowers are greenish yellow outlined in purplish red. This species is one of the most attractive in the genus.

Kalanchoe scapigera (ska-PIJ-e-ra) is native to Kenya, Tanzania, and the island of Socotra. It is a small and compact species growing to about 18 inches with many closely set obovate to almost round 2- to 3-inch-wide and long fleshy leaves that are a beautiful grayish green in color overlain with a silvery bloom. The compact flower spike is closely set with many beautiful half-inch-long tubular red and yellow flowers.

Kalanchoe somaliensis. See *K. marmorata.*

Kalanchoe synsepala (sin-SEP-a-la) is indigenous to Madagascar. It is a small plant never growing more than a foot or so in height with a short stem and a rosette of closely set very succulent obovate to spatulate-shaped 8-inch-long leaves that are somewhat keeled and cup-shaped, a pale green in color with very shallowly scalloped and purplish red margins. The flowers are white. This species is unique in the genus because of its habit of producing plantlets on the spreading roots and sending out rooting stems from the leaf axils; this habit makes it very good as a groundcover in semishady sites and perfect as a hanging basket subject.

Kalanchoe tomentosa (toe-men-TOE-sa) is native to Madagascar. It is a small branching succulent plant growing to about a foot in height and is entirely covered in a white velvety pubescence. The 3-inch-long leaves are fat and juicy, keeled, and generally obovate to spatulate in shape. The margins near the leaf tips are shallowly toothed and the scalloped areas are spotted with a dark brown color. The pendent bell-shaped flowers are beige with light brown stripes. The species is one of the most popular and beautiful. It has common names of panda plant, plush plant, pussy ears, and teddybear plant.

Kalanchoe tubiflora (tyoob-i-FLOR-a) (synonyms *Bryophyllum tubiflorum, Kalanchoe delagonensis, K. verticillata*) is native to South Africa and Madagascar. The plant has a distinctive shape, growing like a miniature coconut palm, the succulent almost cylindrical leaves remaining only at the tips of the stems and growing in a pseudo-rosette atop the 3-foot stems. The plant is seldom branched and the leaf "crown" consists of the upper leaves erect to horizontal and the lowest leaves pendent and drooping, an effect leading to a further palmlike aspect. The base of the stem slowly suckers and this gives a very beautiful aspect, rather like a grove of palms. The leaves are about 6 inches long, almost cylindrical with a groove on the upper surface, and grayish green in color with a pink suffusion and scattered purplish spots. The ends of the leaves bear a profusion of plantlets. The pendent bell-shaped flowers are red. This species is sometimes called the chandelier plant, but a better common name would be the coconut palm kalanchoe. Plate 252.

Kalanchoe uniflora (yoon-i-FLOR-a) is native to Madagascar. It is a prostrate-stemmed, spreading plant that roots at the leaf nodes with inch-long obovate fleshy leaves that are scalloped near the tips. The inch-long urn-shaped flowers appear in clusters at the ends of the trailing stems and are rosy red to purplish red.

Kalanchoe verticillata. See *K. tubiflora.*

KENTIA. See *Carpentaria* and *Howea.*

KIGELIA (ky-JEEL-ee-a / kee-GAIL-ee-a)
Bignoniaceae: The Catalpa, Jacaranda, Trumpet-Vine Family
SAUSAGE TREE
Evergreen tree; dense pinnate foliage; large clusters of red flowers; immense long fruit
Zones 10b and 11
Sun
Average but regular amounts of moisture; drought tolerant when established
Average well-drained soil
Propagation by seed

A monotypic genus that occurs naturally in a large area of tropical eastern Central Africa and East Africa. *Kigelia africana* (af-ri-KAHN-a) (synonym *K. pinnata*) grows to a maximum of 50 feet with a thick smooth gray trunk and a spreading dense crown of dark green 2-foot-long leaves composed of 7 to 11 six-inch-long oblong tough leathery leaflets. The leaves are sometimes deciduous in especially dry or cold winters. The tree blooms most of the year with immense 3- to 6-foot-long pendent clusters of 4-inch-wide broadly spreading irregularly bell-shaped velvety flowers with five-lobed corollas that are a very dark red in color; the blossoms are nocturnal and have a strange fragrance which some find pleasing but others rather dislike. The tree is usually grown for its spectacular fruit, although it is eminently gardenworthy for its overall ornamental quality, especially as a shade tree. The inedible fruits are as much as 3 feet long by 6 inches wide, light brown or dark gray, and sausage-shaped. They hang from cordlike stems that are often much longer than the fruit, sometimes as much as 20 feet, creating a sight unsurpassed for its exotic and tropical looking appeal. The tree has been in cultivation mostly as a curiosity in southern Florida and other tropical areas for a good while; it should, because of its unprecedented beauty, be much more widely planted than it is. About the only drawback to this wonderful tree is that the flowers usually need to be hand pollinated unless there are night-flying insects or bats to do the job. Plate 253.

KOELREUTERIA

(kel-roo-TER-ee-a / kurl-roy-TER-ee-a / kurl-ROY-tree-a)
Sapindaceae: The Soapberry, Golden-Rain Tree Family
GOLDEN RAIN TREE
Medium-sized deciduous trees; large pinnate leaves; large clusters of yellow flowers; pink fruit
Zones vary according to species
Sun to partial shade
Average but regular amounts of moisture
Average well-drained soil
Propagation by seed

A genus of only three species of medium-sized deciduous trees in China, Korea, Japan, and Taiwan. All have large bipinnate leaves, large terminal clusters of small yellow flowers and panicles of papery lantern-shaped showy three-sided seed pods that are pink to orange or red in color. All three species hold their leaves late into the fall and, if the weather remains warm and there is adequate moisture, they are almost evergreen. The trees are fast growing and beautiful of leaf, flower, and fruit.

Koelreuteria bipinnata (by-pin-NAIT-a) (synonym *K. integrifolia*) is native to southwestern China and is hardy in zones 8 through 11. It grows to a maximum height of 40 feet and makes an attractive spreading umbrella-shaped shade tree with a picturesque dark trunk. The 2-foot-long dark green leaves are quite beautiful, being bipinnate and fernlike in appearance. The large branched flower clusters appear in September or October atop the tree; they are triangular or pyramidal in shape, as much as 2 feet tall, and are composed of hundreds of tiny golden four-petaled starlike flowers. The seed pods mature in November (sometimes late October), each one a 2-inch-long three-sided bronzy pink capsule; they remain on the tree through the winter and provide a show equal to that of the fall flowers. Plate 254.

Koelreuteria elegans (EL-e-ganz) (synonym *K. formosana*) is, as the alternative specific epithet implies, indigenous to Taiwan (Formosa) and is hardy only in zones 9 through 11 although somewhat marginal in zone 9a. This species is the most beautiful in the genus. It grows to 60 feet or sometimes more with a dark and picturesquely nonstraight trunk and a broad and spreading crown of bipinnate triangular-shaped leaves

that are 2 or more feet long and have the appearance of large fern fronds. The flowers and flowering time are similar to that of *K. bipinnata*, but the subsequent seed pods are more colorful, a deep pink to scarlet in color. The tree is nearly evergreen in mild wet winters and is often grown as a very large multitrunked specimen tree, a specimen tree of which there are few equals in beauty. It is often planted and lasts for many years in zone 9a but about once every 30 or 40 years a severe freeze is liable to severely damage it; temperatures below 15°F are deadly. Plate 255.

Koelreuteria formosana. See *K. elegans.*
Koelreuteria integrifolia. See *K. bipinnata.*

LAGERSTROEMIA

(lahg-er-STREEM-ee-a / lahg-er-STRURM-ee-a)
Lythraceae: The Crepe-Myrtle Family
CREPE MYRTLE; CRAPE MYRTLE
Shrubs or small trees; evergreen or deciduous leaves; large terminal clusters of showy flowers
Zones vary according to species
Sun
Average but regular amounts of moisture
Average well-drained soil
Propagation by cuttings for hybrids and by seed for species

A genus of about 50 species of shrubs and trees in Asia and Australia. All have relatively large pyramidal-shaped terminal panicles of densely packed flowers that have six or more petals, all of which are clawed in shape and crinkled and ruffled like crepe paper; a few have large and attractive leaves. The fruits are small round woody five-sectioned capsules. All species are tropical or near tropical except one, *Lagerstroemia indica*, from China. They are easy of culture and require no special treatment except for the problem of mildew in the wetter and more humid areas; they reward the gardener with outstanding floral displays for much of the year. Only two species are commonly planted, but there are many more species worthy of the gardener's attention, like *L. subcostata* with its wonderful white gnarled trunk. While the species described below are somewhat drought tolerant when established, they grow better and flower better if not allowed to suffer from lack of moisture, especially *L. speciosa*.

Lagerstroemia faurei is a species from the humid southern Japanese islands with slightly larger leaves than those of *L. indica* and white to pinkish white flowers; it is a quite lush and attractive little tree that is becoming more popular and therefore more widely planted. It has the same cultural and climatic requirements as *L. indica*.

Lagerstroemia indica (IN-di-ka) is native to Japan and China and is hardy in zones 7b through 11. It is the crepe myrtle (also spelled "crape myrtle") so widely planted all over the southern and southwestern United States and California. This species is naturally a small deciduous tree that grows to 20 or 30 feet. It has gnarled trunks of reddish brown or gray outer bark that exfoliates, revealing an inner bark of a beautiful cream to pinkish tan coloration. The medium green slightly glossy leaves are elliptical in shape and about 3 inches long. The tree leafs out rather late in the spring, but in the autumn is one of the few trees that gives a modicum of "fall color" to subtropical regions, the leaves turning reddish brown, red, and yellow. The little trees are grown for the spectacular display of flowers that appear from early summer through fall. The flower clusters are terminal on the branches and, in the type of the species, the flowers are white, pink, or purple. There is probably no more dependable small flowering tree for the Deep South, southwestern United States, and most of California. While these trees are not as spectacular as *Delonix regia* (royal poinciana) or the flamboyant *Spathodea campanulata* (African tulip tree), they certainly rival both in their color and floriferousness. It is an all too common practice in the southern United States to keep cutting the trees back every year, the idea being that this pruning induces more flower production; this is not even true and results in hideously sheared monstrosities with weak branches that, in the summer, cannot even support the flower clusters and in the winter have the appearance of an unbearably ugly fagot of dead sticks. Left to assume its natural form as either a single-trunked specimen or a large multitrunked tree *Lagerstroemia indica* is one of the most beautiful of trees for the southern United States and similar climates, with its lovely form and colorful bark, not to mention the sight of a tree ablaze with color for much of the summer. There are many cultivars of this species, ranging in size from near dwarf shrubs and almost vinelike dwarf types to 30-foot (or more) trees, and every color is represented except true blue and yellow. The hybrids between *L. indica* and *L. faurei* show some resistance to mildew. All the trade names of these hybrids and their cultivars contain the name of an American Indian tribe, like "Cherokee" or "Seminole." Plate 256.

Lagerstroemia speciosa (spee-see-O-sa) is native to a wide area of the Asian tropics from India, southern China, Southeast Asia, New Guinea, and northern Australia, and is hardy only in zones 10 and 11, sometimes suffering damage in zone 10a. The specific epithet "speciosa" means "showy" or "spectacular" and spectacular these trees are, as much for the large lustrous leaves as for the wonderful pink to violet flower clusters. The tree grows to 60 feet or more in its native habitat with a broad, rounded, and dense crown of foliage carried by the smooth gray trunk that is mottled with white; in cultivation it is usually smaller and seldom reaches more than 30 to 40 feet. The foot-long leaves are lanceolate to oblong in shape, dark green above, and rough but glossy; they turn a bright red and drop when the temperature falls below 40°F, leading the uninitiated to think the tree is suddenly dying. This species is truly remarkable when in flower in the summer as the top of the tree is covered (as is that of *L. indica*) in the erect pyramidal 2-foot-tall pointed panicles of pink or

purplish flowers that fade somewhat as they age. The tree is usually called the queen's crepe myrtle and sometimes the pride of India.

LAGUNCULARIA
(la-gunk´-yoo-LAHR-ee-a)
Combretaceae: The Combretum Family
WHITE MANGROVE
Shrub or small evergreen seashore tree; thick
   succulent leaves; clusters of tiny white flowers
Zones 10 and 11
Sun
Water lover
Rich moist soil
Propagation by seed

A monotypic genus naturally occurring in southern Florida, the Florida Keys, the West Indies, Mexico, Central America, South America, and coastal areas of tropical West Africa. *Laguncularia racemosa* (ray-see-MO-sa) is a sprawling shrub or small tree in most of Florida but, in true tropical regions, grows to as much as 60 or even 80 feet in height; even as a tree the species is usually multitrunked in Florida with a fairly narrow and oblong dense crown. It is one of the mangroves, meaning that it thrives in salt water as long as there is no strong wave action, although the white mangrove is not as seaworthy as the black mangrove (*Avicennia* species) or the red mangrove (*Rhizophora* species); it is found on the landward side of these more nautical species. The tree's trunk is not white as the vernacular name suggests; rather it is a dark gray to deep reddish brown with prominent ridges in older trees. It is called white mangrove because of the heartwood, which is light-colored and dense and is used for making tools. Like the more maritime mangrove species, this one makes stilt-like roots that at high tide are usually covered by sea water. It produces pneumatophores, but not in the abundance that *Rhizophora* and *Avicennia* species do, and often these structures are entirely lacking with *Laguncularia*. The leaves are quite beautiful: 3 inches long, thick, smooth, and leathery, deep emerald green, and broadly elliptical to oblong in shape with a prominent midrib; they are borne on reddish brown petioles almost as long as the blade itself and, like the other mangrove species, are usually covered with encrustations of salt when grown in the sea water. The fragrant flowers are not showy but are attractive close up and borne in axillary racemes. Each tiny velvet-covered blossom is a greenish white in color. The leathery fruits are a half inch long greenish yellow to reddish yellow and, like the other mangrove species, start germinating while still hanging on the tree. The white mangrove is a beautiful tree for planting in tidal marshes and along lagoons and estuaries. Although it thrives near ocean beaches, its root system is shallow and strong winds will topple it. Like the other mangrove species it grows well inland as long as it has sufficient moisture, and it is often used as a large hedge.

LANTANA (lan-TAN-a)
Verbenaceae: The Verbena, Lantana Family
LANTANA

Evergreen shrubs; rough aromatic oval leaves; dome-shaped clusters of many-colored flowers

Zones 10 and 11 as permanent perennials; zone 9 as returning perennials; anywhere as annuals

Sun

Average but regular amounts of moisture; drought tolerant

Average well-drained soil

Propagation by seed and cuttings

A large genus of about 150 shrubs in tropical Africa and tropical America. All have rough and scented leaves and some have thorns or prickles. The many small tubular flowers have corollas with four or five lobes and are borne in usually rounded heads. The flower color is variable, and some species have several different colors in one inflorescence. The plants are ever-blooming in frost-free regions. There are no easier flowering plants to grow; all they desire is sun and a well-draining soil. Some people do not like the pungent aroma of these plants while others find it as delightful as that of anything in the herb garden. All parts of the following are mildly poisonous.

Lantana camara (ka-MAHR-a) (synonyms *L. hispida*, *L. horrida*) is native to the drier regions of a very wide area of tropical America. It is a shrub growing to 8 to 10 feet with thick tough, rough and hairy 3- to 5-inch-long ovate leaves that are toothed along the margins. The common name of these plants should be the rainbow shrub because each flower cluster contains yellow, orange, pink, and red blossoms. The flower clusters cover the plants when in bloom and they bloom all the time unless cut back by frost. The plant is more than common: it has become naturalized along the entire Gulf Coast and all Florida, the southwestern United States, and the warmer parts of California. It is very tolerant of salty spray and saline soil, and thrives in seaside gardens, but does not stand soggy soil. Although *L. camara* is one of the finest flowering shrubs ever introduced, it is very seldom seen for sale now, its hybrids and cultivars having taken over the trade. Some of the forms are nothing short of spectacular in flower; every color except true blue is found. In addition, there are dwarf and semi-dwarf forms that bloom in near drought conditions. ***Lantana camara* 'Radiation'**, a blazingly brilliant red and yellow-flowered 6-foot shrub, is prettier than any modern form of rose and much easier to grow. Plate 257.

Lantana hispida. See *L. camara.*

Lantana horrida. See *L. camara.*

Lantana montevidensis (mahnt´-e-vi-DENS-is) (synonym *L. sellowiana*) is native to a wide area of the South American continent. It is a scandent, sprawling shrub with trailing branches that root along the ground; seldom does it grow much over a foot in height. The leaves are similar to those of *L. camara* but smaller.

Flower color is a rosy pink to light purple with some white flowers in the cluster, a delicious combination. This species is often called weeping lantana. It is wonderful cascading down from retaining walls and perfect planted in tall pots or urns or used as a groundcover. This species is naturalized in the areas cited for *L. camara* and it is the parent of many of the more vinelike forms for sale now. It is completely drought tolerant, although it stops growing and blooming under such conditions.

Lantana sellowiana. See *L. montevidensis.*

LATANIA (la-TAIN-ee-a)
Palmae (Arecaceae): The Palm Family
LATAN PALM

Large solitary trunked fan palms with large stiff blue-green leaves

Zones 10 and 11; somewhat marginal in zone 10a

Sun to partial shade

Average but regular amounts of moisture

Average well-drained soil

Propagation by seed

A genus of only three species of robust solitary trunked palmate-leaved palms in the Mascarene Islands east of Madagascar. The leaves are large, stiff, and grayish or bluish green in color and the large fruits are brown or black and create a striking color combination with the leaves. The three species are quite similar to each other, especially when older, and are difficult to distinguish without detailed study of the flowers and close-up examination of the leaves and fruit. For landscaping purposes the three species are nearly identical. They grow to a maximum of 50 to 60 feet in height with light gray ringed trunks. The rings usually are raised and the trunks usually are somewhat swollen at the base. The leaves are about 8 feet wide and are partially folded into a trough shape from the center of the leaf due to the leaf stalk protruding well into the leaf blade; there is a cone-shaped projection of hard tissue near the base of the leaf that is referred to as a "hastula." This folding of the leaves along with the stiffness of the segments gives the visual impression of movement, even when there is none. The leaf blades are deeply divided into many very stiff tapering segments. When young, the three palm species are more easily distinguished from each other because of the coloration of leaves and leaf stalks. All three are somewhat similar in general appearance to *Bismarckia* (bismarck palm) species, but are distinguished by having relatively thicker trunks, somewhat smaller leaves, and leaves that are more folded than those of the bismarck palm. They are as outstandingly impressive in the landscape as the bismarck and, because of their color and form, stand out as do few other trees. Latan palms are as difficult to transplant when very young as are bismarck palms; like the latter they need to have formed some trunk before transplantation is attempted.

Latania loddigesii (lo-di-GEEZ-ee-eye), the blue

latan palm, has leaves that in seedlings are a purplish red, later changing to a bluish green with much whitish waxy scurf on the undersurface. Plate 258.

Latania lontaroides (loan-ta-ROY-deez), the red latan palm, has red leaf stalks when young. These retain the red color longer than do the stalks of *L. loddigesii*, which also are red when young.

Latania verschaffeltii (vur-sha-FELT-ee-eye), the yellow latan palm, has bright yellow to orange leaf stalks, especially when young.

LEMAIREOCEREUS

Although the genus name is no longer valid, it appears in all but the latest literature and is still used in the nursery trade. It therefore seems appropriate to provide a complete listing of the cultivated species with their current names.

Lemaireocereus cartwrightianus. See *Armatocereus cartwrightianus.*

Lemaireocereus dumortieri. See *Stenocereus dumortieri.*

Lemaireocereus eruca. See *Stenocereus eruca.*

Lemaireocereus hollianus. See *Pachycereus hollianus.*

Lemaireocereus laetus. See *Armatocereus laetus.*

Lemaireocereus marginatus. See *Pachycereus marginatus.*

Lemaireocereus thurberi. See *Stenocereus thurberi.*

Lemaireocereus weberi. See *Pachycereus weberi.*

LEPIDOZAMIA (lep-i-doe-ZAY-mee-a)

Zamiaceae: The Zamia (a Cycad) Family
No known English common name
Very large, dark green palmlike cycads with thick
    trunks and large flat leaves
Zones 10 and 11
Partial shade
Water lovers
Rich, humusy, well-drained, acidic soil
Propagation by seed

A small genus of only two species of large palmlike cycads in eastern Australia. Both species are solitary trunked, spineless and, except for ultimate size, quite similar to each other. They are spectacularly beautiful with the essence of the tropical look. The plants need warmth, moisture and a rich soil that is slightly on the acidic side; compost or peat moss is needed as an amendment in calcareous soils.

Lepidozamia hopei (HOAP-ee-eye) reportedly makes a trunk to 50 or 60 feet in height. The leaves are 6 to 10 feet long, flat, and 12 to 18 inches wide, with many linear deep green and glossy leaflets. Plate 259.

Lepidozamia peroffskyana (per-ahf´-skee-AHN-a) does not grow as tall as *L. hopei* and has slightly smaller leaves.

LEUCOPHYLLUM (lyook-o-FYL-lum)

Scrophulariaceae: The Snapdragon, Foxglove Family
PURPLE SAGE; CENIZA (se-NEE-sa); TEXAS
    RANGER; TEXAS SAGE; SILVERLEAF
Medium-sized gray to grayish green-leaved shrub;
    rose to purple flowers after rains in summer
Zones 8 through 11
Sun
Drought tolerant
Sandy, well-drained soil
Propagation by seed and cuttings

A genus of about 12 evergreen shrubs in southern New Mexico, southwestern and southern Texas, and adjacent Mexico. One species has become popular because of its foliage color and flowers. *Leucophyllum frutescens* (froo-TES-senz) grows to as much as 10 feet but is usually smaller. It makes a fairly compact shrub with inch-long elliptic to oblong almost stalkless leaves that are silvery to almost bluish gray in color because of the multitude of tiny hairs on both surfaces of the leaves. The plant blooms irregularly all year in the warmer parts of its range but chiefly in summer and fall, especially after rainy periods, with many inch-long rose to violet or purple bell-shaped flowers in the leaf axils. The bush is near perfect in rock gardens or anywhere that is dry and sunny. It is successfully grown in wet climates if planted in mounded or raised beds, but it suffers and eventually dies out if planted in sites with poor drainage. *Leucophyllum frutescens* 'Green Cloud', a green-leaved cultivar, has deep purple flowers and is not as showy in the landscape as the type.

LICUALA (li-KWAHL-a)

Palmae (Arecaceae): The Palm Family
LICUALA
Small clustering or solitary-trunked fan-leaved palms
    of exquisite beauty
Zones vary according to species
Partial shade to sun
Water lovers
Rich, humusy, well-drained soil
Propagation by seed

A genus of about 100 species of palmate-leaved palms in northeastern India, southern China, the Philippines, Southeast Asia, Indonesia, Malaysia, New Guinea, the islands of the South Pacific, and northern Australia. Once seen these palms are immediately recognizable and never forgotten. All have leaves that are mostly circular in outline, although the blade is sometimes deeply divided, and the leaves are borne on relatively long and slender petioles. When the leaves are divided, the segments are usually cleft all the way to the petiole and the divisions are more or less wedge-shaped and multiribbed or channeled. The fruits are mostly bright red, but they are often almost hidden among the leaves. These palms grow in tropical rain forests or along riverbanks, and one of their prime requirements is a regular and abundant supply of moisture; the other requirements are warmth (they are almost without exception intolerant of frost) and, for most of them, protection from the midday sun.

Licuala gracilis (GRAS-i-lis) is native to Java and is hardy in zones 10 and 11. It is a dwarf clustering species with trunks growing only to 3 or 5 feet. The leaves are orbicular in outline but are divided into 7 to 20 deep green wedge-shaped ribbed segments with jagged ends; the thin leaf stalks are about 30 inches long and are almost flat.

Licuala grandis (GRAN-dis) is native to the New Hebrides Islands (Vanuatu) southeast of the island of New Guinea and is adaptable only to zones 10b and 11. It is one of the most widely planted species. It is a solitary trunked palm whose stem grows only to about 10 feet. Because the leaves are closely set in the crown, they often appear to be round but in truth are more broadly diamond-shaped than round. The leaves are entire but have jagged ends and the blades are strongly ribbed or pleated and often wavy or undulating; wind sometimes breaks the unsegmented leaves into three or more large segments. There is a good reason this palm is popular: it is one of the world's most beautiful.

Licuala lauterbachii (law-tur-BAHK-hee-eye) is indigenous to New Guinea and is hardy in zones 10b and 11. It is a single-trunked species growing to a maximum height of about 15 feet with leaves that are nearly circular in outline but deeply divided into many closely set long wedge-shaped ribbed segments with jagged ends. There is nothing in nature more elegant than these wonderful leaves held on their very long thin and pliable leaf stalks.

Licuala orbicularis (or-bik´-yoo-LAIR-is) is native to the island of Borneo and is adaptable only to zones 10b and 11. It is a trunkless species, the fantastically beautiful leaves arising directly from the underground stem. The 4-foot-wide undivided leaves are held on long thin round petioles and are very broadly deltoid in shape: a semicircle with a flat base. They are deeply ribbed, and the margins are only remotely toothed.

Licuala paludosa (pal-oo-DOE-sa) is native to Thailand, Southeast Asia, and Malaysia, and is hardy in zones 10b and 11. It is one of the larger-growing species whose solitary trunks reach to as much as 15 feet. The leaves are borne on long spiny petioles and are about 4 feet wide, deeply divided into many wedge-shaped ribbed segments with jagged ends; they are very densely arranged in the crown and would be lovelier if they were not so dense. Yet the palm is beautiful.

Licuala ramsayi (RAM-say-eye) is native to northeastern Australia and New Guinea and is not adaptable outside zones 10b and 11. This wonderful palm is the tallest in the genus with solitary trunks growing to as much as 40 feet in height. The medium green leaves are perfectly circular in outline, 3 or 4 feet wide, and divided to the leaf stalk into several wedge-shaped ribbed segments, and borne on 5-foot-long petioles. They are incredibly attractive and graceful.

Licuala spinosa (spi-NO-sa) is native from the Philippines westward to Thailand but is, amazingly, adaptable to zones 9b through 11 although marginal in zone 9b. The trunks of this large clustering species grow to a maximum of 15 feet. The leaves are nearly circular in outline, about 3 feet wide, and deeply divided into many wedge-shaped segments, and are carried on 5-foot-long spiny stalks. This very handsome palm looks better if some of the trunks in a clump are thinned out to leave stems of varying heights and to allow the remarkable leaf shapes to be better seen. Plate 260.

LITCHI (LICH-ee)
Sapindaceae: The Soapberry, Golden-Rain Tree
  Family
LITCHI; LYCHEE; LEECHEE; LICHI
Medium-sized evergreen tree; dense crown of
  compound leaves; brilliant red fruit
Zones 10 and 11; marginal in zone 10a
Sun
Average but regular amounts of moisture
Sandy, humusy, well-drained, acidic soil
Propagation by seed and air-layering; named cultivars
  are grafted

A monotypic genus in southern China. *Litchi chinensis* (chi-NENS-is) slowly grows to 35 or 40 feet with a dense, rounded, and usually rather compact crown. The leaves are about a foot long and are pinnate. Each leaf consists of two to four pairs of 5- to 8-inch-long glossy, dark green pointed elliptical leaflets. The new leaves are bronzy red in color and are extraordinarily attractive. The trees usually bloom in spring with foot-long drooping clusters of tiny greenish white flowers. By July or August the flowers have ripened into beautiful red or orange 1- to 2-inch-wide round to oval leathery and pebbly skinned fruits with as many as 20 in each pendent grapelike cluster. The tree is unsurpassed for planting in close-up situations, as a patio tree or a small shade tree. It is not drought tolerant and needs a non-alkaline soil; limestone-based soils can be amended with much compost, and a 3-inch-deep mulch of pine needles or leaf mold around the tree's roots helps immensely, but the mulch should not touch the trunk. The tree is hardy to temperatures slightly below 30°F, but is subject to producing new growth in the winter months that may be burned by a temperature of freezing or below. Plate 261.

LIVISTONA (liv-i-STOAN-a)
Palmae (Arecaceae): The Palm Family
Common names vary according to species
Tall large-leaved fan palms with spiny leaf stalks, the
  leaves often with drooping segments
Zones vary according to species
Sun to partial shade
Average but regular amounts of moisture
Sandy, humusy, well-drained soil
Propagation by seed

A genus of 28 palmate-leaved solitary-trunked species. Most of these are in Australia but members of the genus are scattered over most of southern Asia and parts of Africa, Arabia, India, and as far north as the southern Japanese islands. Some species have beautifully ringed trunks, and all have straight and usually tall trunks. Most species have leaves that are obviously costapalmate and leaf segments that are more or less drooping at their ends; all have relatively large leaves that are carried on long and spiny petioles. The red, blue, or black fruits are relatively large and quite attractive, although none of the species produces flowers until the individual palms are of some age. All grow rather slowly unless they receive ample amounts of moisture and, while most of them can survive dry conditions, none of them likes such situations. They are quite impressive in the landscape as they are robust palms, with straight trunks and large leaves.

Livistona australis (aw-STRAL-is) is found naturally in Australia along the southern half of the eastern coastal area and is adaptable to zones 9b through 11, although often successfully grown in 9a. It grows rather slowly to 70 or even 80 feet in its native habitat but usually only to about 50 feet in cultivation. It forms with age a beautiful straight gray or brown ringed trunk that is usually no more than a foot in diameter. The dark green leaves are about 8 feet wide, almost circular in outline, and are deeply divided into many linear segments that are split and gracefully drooping at their ends. The leaf crown is dense with leaves. This species makes a wonderful lawn specimen tree but is even more attractive when planted in groups if the individuals are of varying heights so that their large heads are not in visual conflict. The fruits are black when mature. The plant is commonly called the Australian fan palm.

Livistona chinensis (chi-NENS-is), the Chinese fan palm, is native to the southern Japanese islands and Taiwan and is probably the hardiest species, being dependable in zones 9 through 11 and marginal in zone 8b. The palm is rather similar in appearance to *L. australis* but does not grow quite as tall, has slightly smaller but heavier leaves whose color is more yellow-green than deep green and whose leaf segments are somewhat wider but just as pendent as those of the Australian fan palm. The trunk of Chinese fan palm is not as conspicuously ringed as is that of Australian fan palm. The fruits are a rosy gray to grayish blue in color. This species is the most widely planted in the genus, especially in the United States. It, like the Australian fan palm, is wonderful when planted in groups with individuals of varying heights. Plate 262.

Livistona decipiens (de-SIP-ee-enz) is native to the central coastal area of Queensland in Australia and is hardy in zones 9b through 11. Its lovely brown to dark gray ringed trunk attains a height of 50 or 60 feet in its native habitat but is usually no more than 30 feet tall in cultivation. This species has very beautiful deep green leaves that are 8 or more feet wide with the leaf stalk protruding very deeply into the leaf blade. From a distance the leaves look almost pinnate in form because of the way the very long thin leaf segments are attached to the intrusive petiole and because their split ends hang vertically downwards for 3 feet or more. The fruits are black in color.

Livistona mariae (MAHR-ee-eye) is indigenous to central Australia in the Alice Springs area where it is found near permanent springs; it is hardy in zones 10 and 11, although it is planted and often survives in zone 9b. It is a very large and robust species growing to 70 or 80 feet in its native habitat and to about 50 feet in cultivation. The 6-foot-wide leaves are usually a silvery green in color and are held on very long red leaf stalks. They are only semicircular in outline with many segments cut halfway to the center of the blade; the ends of the segments are pendent but not as long as those of *L. australis*, *L. chinensis*, or *L. decipiens*. The leaves and leaf stalks are usually a deep purplish red on young plants, and the fruits are a deep black in color. The tree is fast growing compared to other species in the genus.

Livistona rotundifolia (ro-tund´-i-FO-lee-a) is native to the Philippines and parts of Indonesia, and is hardy in zones 10b and 11. It grows to 70 or 80 feet in the wild but usually only to about 50 feet in cultivation, with a slender trunk that is reddish brown in youth maturing to a smooth light gray with age. The remarkable 6- to 7-foot-wide deep green leaves are carried on 8-foot-long leaf stalks; they are completely circular in outline and are divided only to about a third or less of the width of the leaf blade into many nondrooping segments. Few palm leaves can match the elegance and grace of these, and they are stunningly beautiful when the palms are young and the leaves can be viewed up close. Mature palms are lovely in silhouette because of the gracefully long slender leaf stalks. The fruits are a deep scarlet in color maturing to black. The species is perhaps the fastest growing in the genus *Livistona*. Plate 263.

Livistona saribus (SAIR-i-bus) is indigenous to southern China, Southeast Asia, Borneo, and the Philippines, and is hardy in zones 10 and 11. It grows to about 60 feet in its native habitat but usually only to 40 feet or so in cultivation. The ringed trunks are a pale gray in color when mature, but are usually covered in adherent leaf bases when younger. The 6-foot-long leaf stalks are armed with large inch-long teeth that are more prominent in young plants than in older specimens. The tree's large crown is very dense with 5- to 6-foot-wide leaves that are divided to about half the depth of the blade into many segments with drooping ends. The fruits are bluish gray in color and are speckled with white spots.

LONCHOCARPUS
(lahnk-o-KARP-us / lahnch-o-KARP-us)
Papilionaceae (Fabaceae, Leguminosae), subfamily
Papilionoideae: The Bean, Pea Family
LANCEPOD

Medium-sized evergreen trees; pinnate leaves; large
    terminal clusters of rose or purple flowers
Zones 10 and 11; marginal in zone 10a
Sun to partial shade
Average but regular amounts of moisture
Humusy, well-drained, acidic soil
Propagation by seed

A large genus of about 150 species of shrubs and
small trees in tropical Africa, Madagascar, tropical
America, and Australia. All have large pinnate leaves
with an odd number of leaflets, terminal clusters of
white, pink, or purple pealike flowers, and leathery seed
pods. These beautiful trees are still and unaccountably
rather rare in the United States. They are very handsome when in bloom. Possibly their spread to most
home gardens has been limited because many species
are poisonous to humans.

Lonchocarpus latifolius (lat-i-FO-lee-us) is native
to the West Indies. It grows to as much as 50 feet with
a picturesquely nonstraight brown trunk and a dome-
shaped crown of foliage. The leaves are beautiful
enough to warrant planting the tree for their sake alone:
they are as much as 18 inches long with five to nine 6-
to 8-inch-long elliptic to oblong dark green leaflets with
prominent and lighter colored veins above and a lighter
colored pubescence beneath. The tree blooms during
most of the summer with erect terminal foot-high clusters of pink to light red pealike flowers.

Lonchocarpus violaceus (vee-o-LAYS-ee-us) is
native to the West Indies. It grows to 30 or 40 feet with
a dense crown of pendulous branches. The leaves are
about a foot long with 11 to 15 three- or four-inch-long
lance-shaped dark green glossy leaflets. The tree, like
L. latifolius, blooms in summer with erect terminal clusters of pink to purplish rose pealike flowers. Plate 264.

LOPHOCEREUS. See *Pachycereus*.

LUCUMA. See *Pouteria*.

LYCIANTHES. See *Solanum rantonnetii*.

LYGODIUM (ly-GO-dee-um)
Schizaeaceae: The Japanese Climbing Fern Family
JAPANESE CLIMBING FERN
High-climbing fern with finely cut dark green leaves
Zones 9b through 11 as permanent perennials; zones
    8b and 9a as returning perennials
Partial shade
Average but regular amounts of moisture
Sandy, humusy, moist, well-drained soil
Propagation by transplanting of suckers and by
    spores

A genus of about 40 species of twining fern species
distributed worldwide in warm and tropical regions.
Even though one species is native to the eastern United
States, it is reportedly difficult to grow. ***Lygodium***

japonicum (ja-PAHN-i-kum) is the only species commonly planted. Native to a very large area of Asia from
Japan southward to Australia and westward to India,
Japanese climbing fern climbs to 20 feet or more if given
something on which to twine. The sterile leaves are bipinnate, broadly triangular in shape, medium green in
color and about 12 inches square with finely cut leaflets.
The fertile leaves are about the same size but are more
leathery and usually a deeper green in color with the
leaflets three-lobed, the terminal lobe very long in relation to the other two. The plant makes a wonderful vertical contrast on stems of other plants or planted on
anything around which it can twine. The fern is quite
fast growing and it is often a good idea to cut the old
stems back every spring, if they have not been killed
back, to ensure a more vigorous and a more tidy growth
habit.

LYSILOMA (lys-i-LO-ma)
Mimosaceae (Fabaceae, Leguminosae), subfamily
    Mimosoideae: The Mimosa Family
Common names vary according to species
Small to medium-sized evergreen trees; even-pinnate
    leaves; round heads of white flowers
Zones 10 and 11; marginal in zone 10a
Sun
Average water; drought tolerant when established
Average well-drained soil
Propagation by seed

A genus of about 30 species of shrubs and trees in
tropical and subtropical America. All have bipinnate
leaves with an even number of leaflets, axillary ball-
shaped clusters of white flowers, and thin brown flat
seed pods. The leaves are semideciduous, dropping
with the onset of cold or drought in the winter and usually falling simultaneously with new growth in the
spring. *Hortus III* has the names confused: *Lysiloma
latisiliqua* actually is *L. sabicu* and *L. bahamensis* is *L.
latisiliqua*.

Lysiloma bahamensis. See *L. latisiliqua*.

Lysiloma latisiliqua (lat´-i-si-LIK-wa) (synonym
L. bahamensis) is native to southern Florida, the Bahamas, the West Indies, and Yucatán (Mexico), usually found near the ocean or near lagoons. It grows fast
to 40 or sometimes as much as 60 feet with a wonderfully whitish trunk and bark, somewhat zigzagging
branches that are pendulous at their ends, and a beautiful airy, rounded but open crown. The feathery fernlike leaves are bipinnate with many half-inch-long medium green leaflets that are oblong in shape and a much
paler green beneath. The tree blooms all spring and
summer with white flowers in perfectly round inch-wide
heads that are in few-headed branched clusters and are
quite attractive without being spectacular. The species
is tolerant of salt spray and saline soil and is wind resistant, making it a valuable subject for planting as a shade
tree near the beach. The tree is called wild tamarind in
its native habitat. Plate 265.

Lysiloma sabicu (SAB-i-koo) is native to most of the West Indies and is also found in Yucatán (Mexico). It grows to 30 or 40 feet with a slender and vaselike crown of ascending branches that are somewhat pendent near their ends. The leaves, flowers, and seed pods are similar to those of *L. latisiliqua*, but the leaflets are slightly larger. The young leaves unfold with beautiful bronzy red margins. The tree is called Cuban tamarind and sabicu.

MACADAMIA (mak-a-DAIM-ee-a)
Proteaceae: The Protea Family
MACADAMIA NUT
Small, dense-crowned evergreen tree; large leaves;
    clusters of round green fruit; edible nut
Zones 10 and 11
Sun
Average but regular amounts of moisture
Sandy, humusy, well-drained soil
Propagation by seed; named cultivars are grafted

A small genus of 10 species of shrubs and small trees from Madagascar eastward to Australia. Only two species are regularly planted, both from eastern Australia, for the delicious nuts. Unfortunately neither of the species bears fruit well in hot and humid climates like that of southern Florida, although the large-leaved trees are certainly attractive enough to warrant planting for their beauty alone. Both *Macadamia integrifolia* (in-teg´-ri-FO-lee-a) and *Macadamia tetraphylla* (tet-ra-FYL-la) are similar enough to each other that a single description suffices. They grow slowly to 50 or 60 feet in their native Australia (Queensland and northern New South Wales) but usually do not reach more than 20 or 30 feet in cultivation in the continental United States. They assume a rather dense and wide crown of very deep green leathery foot-long leaves that are wavy-margined and have widely scattered tiny teeth on the margins and a strong and lighter colored midrib. The trees bloom in late winter and spring with foot-long pendent clusters of tiny white or pinkish white flowers that look rather like gigantic oak tree catkins. These give way in summer to elongated and drooping clusters of inch-wide round green fruits, each with a pointed end. It is the nut inside the green husk and tough outer shell that is the delicious macadamia nut of commerce. The leaves, outer shell, and husk of the nuts are poisonous.

MACFADYENA (mak-fay-DEEN-a)
Bignoniaceae: The Catalpa, Jacaranda, Trumpet-
    Vine Family
CAT'S CLAW VINE; CAT-CLAW; YELLOW
    TRUMPET VINE
Clinging rampant evergreen vine; two-parted leaves;
    large yellow trumpet-shaped spring flowers
Zones 9 through 11; marginal in zone 8a
Sun to partial shade
Average but regular amounts of moisture

Average well-drained soil
Can be invasive
Propagation by cuttings, sometimes seed

A small genus of only four species of clinging vines, all with pinnate leaves reduced to only two leaflets with a terminal and three-pronged clawlike clinging tendril. Each tendril ends in a sharp curved point and resembles a cat's extended claw in appearance and in its ability to attach to anything. The flowers are all flaring trumpet-shaped and yellow. The genus was once known as *Doxantha*. Only one species is planted in the southern United States and in California. *Macfadyena unguis-cati* (oon´-gwiss-KAHT-ee) (synonym *Doxantha unguis-cati*) is native to a very large area of the American tropics from the West Indies and Mexico to Argentina and Uruguay. This very fast growing vine adheres to almost any surface including concrete and grows high and wide, sometimes to as much as 50 feet. The two leaflets are elliptical and pointed, dark green, and slightly wavy. The flowers appear with the advent of warm weather in the spring, anytime from March to May. Each blossom is 3 or 4 inches wide, deep yellow to almost gold, and one of several in clusters at the ends of the stems and in the leaf axils. The vine is seldom covered with flowers but nevertheless makes a grand show because of the size of the blossoms. It sometimes blooms off and on in the summer and even fall. The seed pods are about 18 inches long, thin, and green until they mature to a dark brown and release the many floating seeds. They are rather attractive because they hang vertically like a curtain. The leaves usually drop if the temperature falls below 25°F, and the vine is killed back if the temperature falls much below 20°F. The thickened roots resprout with the return of warm weather but, since the plants bloom in spring, there are seldom flowers from such comebacks. Because of its penetrating clinging tendrils, this vine should not be planted on or near painted wood structures. The vine also spreads along the ground, rooting from the leaf axils, and can become a nuisance under some circumstances unless the errant growth is checked.

MACHAEROCEREUS.
See *Stenocereus*.

MACROZAMIA (mak-ro-ZAIM-ee-a)
Zamiaceae: The Zamia (a Cycad) Family
No known English common name
Solitary palmlike cycads, with or without trunks;
    pinnate leaves
Zones vary according to species
Sun to partial shade
Average but regular amounts of moisture
Sandy, humusy, well-drained soil
Propagation by seed

A genus of about 25 species of cycads found naturally in the southern half of Australia. They are all solitary-trunked but the trunk is often underground and therefore, for landscape purposes, non-existent. All have typical pinnate leaves, and the leaflets, which are fairly widely spaced along the rachis, are sometimes divided into two lobes. A few species have a scant amount of leaves with twisted leaflets on twisted rachises and are weedy looking and not ornamental. Those that are palmlike can be very beautiful. The species have green male and female cones, with diamond-shaped scales with a long tapering point. The seeds are red or orange.

Macrozamia communis (KAHM-yoo-nis / kah-MYOO-nis) is found in southeastern New South Wales and is hardy in zones 9b through 11 and marginal in zone 9a. This species seldom has an emergent trunk. When it does it is no more than a foot or two in height. The leaves are numerous. Each is 4 to 6 feet long with many regularly spaced linear pointed leaflets arising from the rachis in an almost flat plane. This large and quite graceful species looks good in a container or in the ground, especially in groups of three or more plants of differing heights.

Macrozamia diplomera (dip-lo-MER-a) is indigenous to inland areas of New South Wales and is hardy in zones 9 through 11. It is a trunkless species with 10 to 50 leaves. Each leaf is 3 to 4 feet long and stiff but arching, with many narrow leaflets that are usually split into two linear segments near their bases. The species is somewhat drought tolerant.

Macrozamia macdonnellii (mak-DAHN-'l-lee-eye) is indigenous to the dry regions of central Australia and is hardy in zones 9b through 11 and marginal in zone 9a. It is a large species that slowly grows to 12 to 15 feet with a 3-foot-thick trunk. The leaf crown is dense with beautiful bluish green leaves that are flat, somewhat arching, and 5 to 7 feet long with regularly spaced thin bluish leaflets. This spectacular plant is drought tolerant.

Macrozamia moorei (MOR-ee-eye) is native to interior areas of Queensland and is hardy in zones 9b through 11. It is the largest species in the genus and arguably the most beautiful. It grows slowly to a maximum height of 30 feet with a 20-foot-tall trunk, although this stature should not be expected in cultivated plants. The narrow and flat leaves are as much as 9 feet long with many closely set linear bright green to bluish green leaflets. With age the plant looks similar to *Phoenix canariensis* (Canary Island date palm) but has many more and narrower leaves than that palm. It is one of the most impressive cycad species and makes a splendid specimen plant.

MAGNOLIA (mag-NOL-ya)
Magnoliaceae: The Magnolia Family
MAGNOLIA
Medium to large evergreen trees; large tough leathery leaves; large white, yellow, or pink flowers
Zones vary according to species
Sun to partial shade
Average but regular amounts of moisture
Rich, humusy, well-drained soil of relatively low pH
Propagation by seed for the species, cuttings or air-layering for the cultivars

A genus of about 125 species of trees and shrubs found principally in China, Japan, North America, and tropical America, although there are a few species in India, Myanmar (Burma), Malaysia, Indonesia, Borneo, and the Philippines. There are about as many deciduous species as there are evergreen species. Among the latter, none is more choice and beautiful than *Magnolia grandiflora* (southern magnolia), native to the southern United States. The new growth of all species is enveloped in the bud by large and usually pubescent stipules, and the leaves are large, leathery, usually stiff, and glossy. The flowers are relatively large and usually fragrant with many separate petals and a central usually cone-shaped structure bearing the male and female parts. The sepals and petals often merge imperceptibly into one another and are, as a whole, termed "tepals." The fruit is a conelike structure with large scalelike carpels in the center of the blossom. Each carpel bears a single seed, which is usually large and red in color and which is visible when the individual carpels mature and split open. The genus, as well as the entire family, is thought to be one of the oldest and most primitive of all the flowering plants because of the just-described flower characteristics. Other primitive flowering plants have somewhat similar blossoms, such as species of *Anemone*, *Nymphaea*, *Paeonia*, and *Ranunculus*, and *Liriodendron tulipifera* (tulip tree). These magnificent trees and their magnificent flowers are among the most beautiful in the world.

Magnolia coco (KO-ko) (synonym *M. pumila*) is native to Guangzhou in southeastern China and is hardy in zones 9b through 11. It is a large shrub, slowly growing to 8 or 12 feet and about as wide. The dark green leaves are elliptic to oblong in shape, leathery and smooth, and lack pubescence and strong venation. The plant blooms in the summer with inch-wide pure white tiny flowers that open at night and are exquisitely fragrant. Unfortunately, the petals usually fall the day after the flowers open.

Magnolia delavayi (del-a-VAY-eye) is native to the lower Himalayas of southern China and is hardy in zones 8b through 11 and marginal in zone 8a. It is an immense multitrunked shrub or a small tree slowly growing to 35 or 40 feet with rough dark brown bark and a dense and rounded crown. If a tree form is wanted the plant must be trained from youth to a single strong stem and the lower suckers constantly removed. The leaves are among the largest in the family; they are from 10 to 16 inches long, generally broadly ovate in shape, and a grayish lime-green in color with a strong lighter colored midrib. These leaves are extraordinarily attractive and tropical looking, even more so than those of *M. grandiflora*, from which they differ by being less rigid and much larger. The tree blooms all summer long. The flowers are almost as large as those of *M. grandiflora* and are similar in form, but there are not so many blossoms at a time, and the fragrance is less lemony. Furthermore, the flowers are short-lived, the petals usually dropping the same day they open.

Magnolia grandiflora (grand-i-FLOR-a) is found from North Carolina southward into central Florida and westward to southern Arkansas and eastern Texas. Except for the trees in Arkansas, most trees grow on the coastal plain. The tree is hardy in zones 7 through 11. It grows rather slowly to as much as 120 feet, but specimens of this stature are rare. Most cultivated trees reach no more than 70 or 80 feet and are usually half as broad. The tree naturally branches low and, when grown from youth in an open situation, makes a pyramidal form with branches and leaves usually to the ground. Trees whose life has been spent in the forest have trunks that branch only near the top of the bole, with widespreading crowns. With age the open-grown trees invariably have a rounded to oblong crown atop a thick dark gray to almost black trunk that is straight but gnarled and may be as much as 3 feet in diameter. Unless the soil is deep and irrigation is regular and adequate, the trees produce strong sinuous surface roots. In England and California the tree is sometimes espaliered against walls and fences to often stunning effect. Some trees have been "bonsaied" into 4-foot-tall very wide (20 feet) hedgelike specimens; the visual result is different but not beautiful. The natural form of this species makes one of the world's most beautiful trees. The leaves are very variable in size and shape. They may be ovate to obovate in shape but usually are elliptical to oblong and 5 to 10 inches long, more or less pointed at both ends, extremely stiff, tough, and leathery. They seem to take forever to decompose once they have fallen. Leaf color is a deep medium green to almost blackish or bronzy-green in some forms. Leaf texture is always lustrous above and somewhat to extremely rusty pubescent beneath, where the color ranges from yellow-green to tawny to cinnamon or dark reddish brown. The leaves may be curled at their margins or nearly flat, and the margins may be straight or wavy. The tree's flowering season may start as early as February or as late as mid May and may last in cycles throughout the summer and continue well into the autumn. It also may be confined only to late or early spring. The flowers are as much as 10 inches wide with many spatulate thick succulent petals that are cupped at their ends and are widespreading and quite separated from each other. The flowers are pure white when newly opened but turn buff to orange and sometimes brown just before they fall. The fragrance is legendary and nearly impossible to describe, but there is usually a strong lemony component to the bouquet. The most common vernacular names for the tree are southern magnolia and the bull bay. There are supposedly more than 100 cultivars varying in size and shape of tree, leaf, and flower. There are even forms with variegated leaves. *Magnolia grandiflora* **'Charles Dickens'** is a spreading tree with beautiful broadly ovate or elliptical, pointy-tipped very lustrous leaves, large white flowers, and very large, completely scarlet fruit. *Magnolia grandiflora* **'Little Gem'** grows only to about 20 feet with a compact and rather narrow crown. The 4- to 5-inch-long completely elliptical leaves have a beautiful bronzy tomentum beneath. The flowers are smaller than the type but otherwise similar. The plants bloom when small and make perfect "dooryard" trees. *Magnolia grandiflora* **'Majestic Beauty'** has slightly larger leaves and flowers than the type with the undersides of the leaves lacking the rusty color evident in the type. Plate 266.

Magnolia pumila. See *M. coco.*

MALLOTONIA (mal-lo-TOAN-ee-a)
Boraginaceae: The Heliotrope Family
SEA LAVENDER; BEACH HELIOTROPE; BAY
    LAVENDER
Dense shrub with fleshy silvery-green leaves; small
    clusters of white flowers
Zones 10 and 11
Sun
Drought tolerant
Sandy well-drained soil
Propagation by seed and cuttings

A monotypic genus that occurs naturally along beaches in southern Florida, the West Indies, Mexico, and Central America. *Mallotonia gnaphalodes* (naf-a-LO-deez) (synonym *Tournefortia gnaphalodes*) is a small shrub growing rather slowly to about 6 feet with thick dark branches, which root on touching the soil or sand, making a clumping, spreading, and dense growth. The grayish green leaves are thick, linear to spatulate in shape, and 3 to 5 inches long. Covered in a silvery silky down, the leaves are clustered in whorls near the ends of the branches. The tiny white bell-shaped flowers appear in cycles throughout the year but are not particularly showy. They are in densely packed terminal one-sided somewhat coiled spikes at the ends of the branch tips. The plant is quite picturesque with its silvery green leaves and contorted branches and is perfect for planting along sandy beaches outside the area of wave action. The genus was at one time named *Argusia* and at another time *Tournefortia*.

MALVAVISCUS (mal-va-VIS-kus)
Malvaceae: The Mallow, Hibiscus, Cotton Family
TURK'S CAP; MEXICAN TURK'S CAP;
    SLEEPY HIBISCUS
Sprawling evergreen shrub; tubular pendent scarlet
    flowers
Zones 10 and 11 as permanent perennials; zone 9 as
    returning perennials
Sun to partial shade
Average water; drought tolerant once established
Average well-drained soil
Propagation by cuttings, sometimes seed

A very small genus of only three species of sprawling or vinelike evergreen shrubs found from Mexico to Peru and Brazil. Only one species is planted in the United States. ***Malvaviscus arboreus*** (ahr-BOAR-ee-us) (synonym *M. drummondii*) is a wide and rather sprawling shrub, growing to as much as 10 feet and at least as wide with many unbranched stems densely clothed to the ground. The dark green 5- to 6-inch-long broadly ovate long-tipped leaves are shallowly toothed and softly pubescent. Unless frost occurs the plants bloom year-round with axillary clusters of 2- to 3-inch long hibiscus-like deep red flowers that do not fully open and thus assume a pendent bell-shape. The fruits are inch-wide scarlet berries but are seldom formed. The shrub is foolproof in any site that is well drained and gets at least a half day's sun. It is colorful enough that, although overused, it is a welcome sight through most of the year. It has become naturalized in southern Texas and most of peninsular Florida. The shrub is sometimes called sleeping hibiscus because of its flowers that do not fully open. Plate 267.

MAMMEA (MAM-mee-a)
Guttiferae (Clusiaceae): The Autograph Tree, Garcinia Family
MAMMEE; MAMEY; MAMMEE APPLE; SOUTH AMERICAN APRICOT
Large evergreen tree; large magnolia-like leaves; large fragrant white flowers; large edible fruit
Zones 10b and 11
Sun
Average but regular amounts of moisture
Average well-drained soil
Propagation by seed

A genus of about 50 species of evergreen trees in tropical Madagascar, Indonesia, Malaysia, the islands of the South Pacific and tropical America, most of them in Asia. Only one species is commonly planted in the United States for its beautiful leaves and large edible fruit. ***Mammea americana*** (a-mer-i-KAHN-a) is native to the West Indies and northern South America. It grows slowly to about 60 feet with a short massively thick trunk and relatively few large ascending branches that create a dense oblong or oval crown of dark green foliage. The leaves, which resemble those of *Magnolia grandiflora,* are about 8 inches long, broadly elliptical in shape, leathery, glossy and dark green above with a prominent and lighter colored midrib, and pale green beneath. The tree blooms in spring and early summer with beautiful 1- to 2-inch-wide fragrant white flowers in few-flowered clusters in the leaf axils. Each blossom has four to six ovate petals surrounding a central mass of orange stamens and pistils. The gorgeous round fruits appear in summer and, when mature, are 4 to 8 inches in diameter, light brown, grayish brown or reddish brown in color and leathery with tiny bumps on the skin. The flesh is a deep yellow or orange and is said to taste like apricots or raspberries. If not picked in sum-

mer or late summer when they are ripe, the fruits remain on the tree until the next flowering season, adding to the great beauty of this species. Because of the remarkably attractive leaves, flowers, and fruit the mamey is one of the world's most handsome trees. It is also easy to grow, thriving in most well-drained soils and, while more vigorous and healthy when given adequate and regular amounts of water, it is nevertheless somewhat drought tolerant and is also free of pests and diseases.

MANDEVILLA (man-de-VIL-la)
Apocynaceae: The Oleander, Frangipani, Vinca Family
MANDEVILLA
Evergreen vines and sprawling shrubs; leathery leaves; large pink or white trumpet-shaped flowers
Zones 10b and 11; sometimes root hardy in zones 9b and 10a; anywhere as annuals
Sun to partial shade
Water lovers
Rich, humusy, well-drained soil
Propagation by cuttings

A large genus of more than 100 species of tuberous-rooted herbs, shrubs, and twining vines in Central America and South America. All have somewhat milky sap, undivided and nearly stalkless leaves, and flowers with five broad petals, each with the twist characteristic of the oleander family. The cultivated species are vines of hybrid and garden origins whose parentages are sometimes uncertain. The genus was once named *Dipladenia.*

***Mandevilla* 'Alice du Pont'** is a sport from a hybrid of *M. ×amabilis* (which is a hybrid of *M. splendens* and an unknown *Mandevilla* species) and *M. splendens.* The vine grows to 12 or 15 feet with beautiful 4- to 8-inch-long ovate to elliptical thick, leathery dark green leaves with deeply depressed veins above. The plant blooms whenever the temperature is above 50°F at night. The flowers are in axillary clusters of as many as 12 blossoms. Each flower is about 4 inches wide at the end of a 2-inch tube and is a deep rose in color with an even deeper pink color at the opening of the light yellow throat. This spectacular flowering vine needs a rich moist soil with compost. It blooms constantly with adequate moisture and bi-monthly applications of fish emulsion or a 20–20–20 fertilizer. It can be pruned to almost any height and form but needs something around which to twine. Plate 268.

Mandevilla boliviensis (bo-liv-ee-ENS-is) is native to Bolivia and possibly Ecuador. This semi-climber is just as happy as a sprawling, mounding shrub as when trained to a trellis. The stems are more slender than those of *M.* 'Alice du Pont' and its relatives, and the dark green glossy ovate leaves are only 3 to 4 inches long. The flowers are in few-flowered axillary clusters. Each blossom is about 2 inches wide at the flaring end of its inch-long tube, and is pure white with a yellow throat. The plant is not as free-flowering as the *M. splen-*

dens hybrids and cultivars nor is its flowering period year-round. It has a very appealing quiet beauty and makes a near perfect foundation plant and or container plant for the patio. Plate 269.

Mandevilla **'Red Riding Hood'** is a sport from a hybrid of *M.* ×*amabilis* and *M. sanderi*. It is a sprawling shrub that can be trained on a trellis, but it also looks and does fine as a shrub. The dark green glossy leaves are only about 2 inches long and are ovate to elliptic in shape. The plant blooms almost as floriferously as *M.* 'Alice du Pont' with few-flowered clusters of 2-inch-wide very deep pink to red blossoms with a deep yellow throat. The flowers are shaped like those of *M.* 'Alice du Pont' except for the petals that are usually somewhat reflexed at their tips.

Mandevilla sanderi (SAN-dur-eye) is native to Brazil. It is similar to its hybrid *M.* 'Red Riding Hood', but the flowers are not as large nor as deeply colored and the species is more of a climber. *Mandevilla sanderi* **'My Fair Lady'** is a striking white-flowered cultivar.

Mandevilla splendens (SPLEN-denz) is indigenous to Brazil and is similar to its offspring *M.* 'Alice du Pont' except that the species is not nearly so floriferous and the color of its flowers is a much paler pink.

MANETTIA (ma-NET-tee-a)
Rubiaceae: The Coffee, Gardenia, Ixora Family
FIRECRACKER VINE
Slender vine with ovate leaves; tubular red and yellow flowers
Zones 10 and 11 as permanent perennials; zone 9 as returning perennials
Sun
Average but regular amounts of moisture
Sandy, humusy, well-drained soil
Propagation by cuttings, sometimes seed

A genus of about 80 species of evergreen twining vines in tropical America, mostly South America. They have oppositely arranged leaves and tubular flowers with four or five lobes. Only two species are commonly planted, although many others are worthy of cultivation.

Manettia cordifolia (kord-i-FO-lee-a) (synonym *M. glabra*) is indigenous to Peru, Bolivia, and northern Argentina. The vine grows to as much as 15 feet with ovate to lanceolate dark green leaves that are smooth above and pubescent beneath. The plant blooms spring, summer, and fall with 2-inch-long cigar-shaped crimson tubular flowers whose ends are five-lobed. If frosted back, the vine will not bloom in the spring.

Manettia luteorubra (loot-ee-o-ROOB-ra) (synonyms *M. bicolor*, *M. discolor*, *M. inflata*) is native to Paraguay and Uruguay. It grows only to about 8 or 10 feet and makes a dense mass of foliage. The leaves are 4 to 6 inches long, ovate-lanceolate in shape, almost stalkless, a very deep green, almost bluish, in color, and slightly pubescent. The plant blooms all summer and sometimes (if not frosted back) in spring and autumn. The flowers are about an inch long and cigar-shaped,

with five tiny pointed lobes at the end of the corolla tube. Crimson for most of the length of the tube, the flowers are bright yellow near the tip.

MANGIFERA
(man-JIF-e-ra / main-GIF-e-ra)
Anacardiaceae: The Mango, Cashew, Pistachio, Sumac Family
MANGO
Large evergreen tree; large linear leaves; great sprays of reddish flowers; large golden and red fruit
Zones 10b and 11
Sun
Average but regular amounts of moisture
Average well-drained soil
Propagation by seed; named cultivars are grafted

A genus of about 40 species of large trees in tropical Asia. Only one, the mango, is planted outside botanical gardens. *Mangifera indica* (IN-di-ka) is native to northern India, Myanmar (Burma), Thailand, and Malaya. In its native habitat it grows to 80 or 90 feet in height and as much as 100 feet in width with a very broad dome-shaped and dense canopy above a stout dark gray trunk that, with age, is somewhat buttressed. In cultivation the tree can be expected to attain 60 or 70 feet with a width of at least that much.

The leaves vary in shape and size, and each cultivar is more or less different from the typical characteristics. Generally the leaves are linear-elliptic in shape, pointed at the apex, and curved and somewhat drooping. Found mostly at the ends of the branches, they are as much as 14 inches long, are carried on 4- or 5-inch stalks, and are generally glossy above and a deep green in color with a prominent and lighter colored midrib. The new leaves of all forms are a different color from the mature leaves, usually a bronzy to wine red, sometimes orange or even yellow.

The terminal flower clusters appear on the tree any time from December to March. As much as 2 feet tall and pyramidal in shape, they may contain several thousand tiny pinkish white to yellowish to reddish yellow or even reddish brown five-petaled flowers. From each of these great clusters of flowers only a very few fruits mature in late summer to early fall but, because a large tree may have been covered in flowers earlier, there are usually many fruits on a single tree. The fruits are quite variable in shape, size, and coloration. They are hardly ever a single color, but are usually mottled and may have red, purple, gold, light or dark green, or yellow hues all on one fruit, although some are nearly a single color. The shape and size of the fruits vary from round to oblong or kidney-shaped and, unless round, the shape is always asymmetrical and often there is a distinct curved tip or beak. Weight and size of the fruit vary from as small as 3 inches to more than 10 inches and from a few ounces to 4 or 5 pounds. Fruiting trees make an outstanding spectacle in the landscape in part because of the very long stalks on which the fruits are held.

If the focus of this text were on the quality of these edible fruits we would indeed have a very long section on the subject as there are many varieties worldwide. Although many people consider the mango the world's finest edible fruit, some people simply do not like any of the varieties they have ever tasted. Moreover some people are allergic to the sap and fruit of the tree. In any case it is doubtful that anyone does not consider the tree to be of great beauty, especially when in fruit. When growing the tree for its fruit, gardeners should avoid seedlings as they seldom produce first-rate tasting fruit. Plate 270.

MANIHOT (MAN-ee-haht)
Euphorbiaceae: The Euphorbia, Spurge Family
CASSAVA; TAPIOCA; MANIOC; YUCA
Small deciduous or almost evergreen soft-wooded
    trees; large deeply cut leaves
Zones vary according to species
Sun to partial shade
Average but regular amounts of moisture
Average well-drained soil
Propagation by seed and cuttings

A genus of around 100 species of herbs, shrubs, and small, mostly soft-wooded trees in tropical America. All have mildly poisonous milky sap, and several species have large tuberlike roots that are quite poisonous unless cooked. Ironically, the most famous of these species is the source of cassava or tapioca, a dietary staple for many people. The leaves in this genus are quite variable, some being almost round and entire or shallowly lobed, others heart-shaped, and still others so deeply divided that they resemble those of a fan palm. The flowers, which are in terminal or axillary clusters, are white or greenish white, bell-shaped or lantern-shaped, and are relatively large for members of the euphorbia family. The fruits are small three-lobed capsules. Most species have outstandingly tropical looking leaves and are quite beautiful.

Manihot carthaginensis (kar-thaj´-i-NENS-is) is thought to be native from southern Texas to Argentina, but is most likely an escape from cultivation in Texas and is probably originally indigenous only to Central and South America. This small deciduous tree is completely hardy in zones 9 through 11, marginal as a tree in zone 9a, and a returning perennial shrub in zone 8. It grows quickly to 15 or sometimes 20 feet, often adding as much as 2 feet to its height in one month. The tree is sparsely branched, and the smooth trunk and older branches a beautiful reddish brown in color. The new growth, however, is a vivid emerald green and rather succulent. The tree's branching pattern is irregularly zigzagging and often produces very picturesque specimens, but also can be ungainly and grotesque. Corrective pruning when the tree is young or in the winter dormancy period can usually rectify the situation. The leaves are circular in outline, carried on stalks as long as the leaves are wide, dark green but not glossy above,

and pale green beneath. They are from 8 to 16 inches wide but very deeply and palmately segmented into 5 to 13 obovate to elliptical 3- to 10-inch-long lobes, each with a long tapering point. The lobes have a prominent and lighter colored midrib (as well as lateral veins) and extend almost to the leaf stalk. Because of the circular outline of the blade, the leaf looks almost as though the petiole is attached to the center of the blade, a condition referred to as "peltate." The main leaf segments are sometimes shallowly lobed, and the margins of the segments are often wavy. These leafy spheres are captivatingly tropical in appearance and rival the great *Cecropia* species in beauty of form. They are irresistible in silhouette against the sky or a contrasting background and serve to make the tree unexcelled for close-up situations like a patio tree, if the tree's deciduous nature is not a problem. The leaves start turning a clear yellow in late October to mid November and soon thereafter fall. Because of the winter dormancy the tree is unharmed by temperatures above 25°F, but there is often some dieback of the branch tips even in completely tropical regions. The tree is known to resprout from the root after being cut to the ground by temperatures in the low teens. The plant is reportedly grown in Brazil for the root clusters, which contain a great amount of starch. The roots are doubtless poisonous if uncooked and caution should be exercised or experimentation avoided by the gardener. *Manihot carthaginensis* 'Variegata' has leaves quite beautifully variegated with yellow or white but is not as hardy as the type and is only safe in zones 10 and 11. Plates 271 and 272.

Manihot esculenta (es-kyoo-LENT-a) is indigenous to southern Brazil and is dependably hardy only in zones 10 and 11, although it is often successfully grown in zone 9b. It is similar to *M. carthaginensis* except the tree does not usually grow as large. Indeed, it is as often a shrub as it is a small tree. The bark is gray to dark gray in color with the new growth green and succulent. The leaves are about the size of those of *M. carthaginensis* but are even more deeply lobed. The lobes usually are elliptic rather than obovate and are themselves not usually lobed. The large tuberlike roots of this tree are the source of cassava and tapioca. Cassava is the processed root or the meal prepared by grinding the cooked root; tapioca is the dried starch granules resulting from cooking the root which, after being recooked and rehydrated (and usually sweetened), makes a delicious type of pudding. *Manihot esculenta* 'Variegata' has variegated leaves that are very beautiful up close, but the cultivar's landscape value is less than spectacular. The plant makes, however, an exquisite subject for intimate locations. Plate 273.

Manihot grahamii (GRAM-ee-eye) is very similar to *M. carthaginensis* and may be but a variety of the latter, or vice-versa. It has the same cultural and climatic requirements as *M. carthaginensis*.

MANILKARA

(ma-NILK-a-ra / man-il-KAR-a)
Sapotaceae: The Sapodilla Family
Common names vary according to species
Medium-sized to large evergreen trees with large
    leathery leaves and colorful fruit
Zones 10b and 11
Sun
Average but regular amounts of moisture
Average well-drained soil
Propagation by seed; named cultivars are grafted

A genus of about 75 species of medium-sized to very large evergreen trees in the tropics of both hemispheres. All the species have a milky nontoxic sap, large alternately arranged leathery leaves, small white or yellowish flowers, and relatively large round and sometimes edible fruit. They are among the most dependable and beautiful trees for creating a lush tropical effect. The genus was formerly known as *Achras*.

Manilkara bahamensis (bah-ha-MENS-is) (synonyms *Achras emarginata, Manilkara jaimiqui, Mimusops emarginata*) is native to the Florida Keys and the West Indies. It grows to as much as 45 feet with a dense and rounded crown of foliage and a dark brown trunk, but is also found as a large multitrunked shrub. The 4-inch-long elliptic to oblong leathery leaves, which are mostly bunched at the ends of the branches, have a prominent midrib and are notched at the apex. They are not glossy and are a deep green to grayish green in color above and a lighter yellowish green with brownish closely set short hairs beneath. The pendent and hairy flower clusters spring from the leaf axils and are composed of 2-inch-long narrow tubes with six-lobed nonspreading corollas. The clusters are quite attractive up close but are not spectacular in the landscape. The 2-inch-wide round light brown fruits are rather spectacular in the landscape—a beautiful combination of gray-green leaves and brown fruit. They are reportedly edible, if not delicious, and contain a spongy and juicy pulp with a few flat black seeds. This native species is an outstandingly valuable and beautiful landscape subject and is tolerant of all but extreme saline conditions. The tree is called wild sapodilla as well as wild dilly.

Manilkara bidentata (by-den-TAIT-a) (synonym *Mimusops balata*) is indigenous to the West Indies, Panama, and northern South America. It is a noble tree attaining a height of almost 100 feet in its native haunts and more than half that height in cultivation. It forms a great oblong to rounded crown of foliage held on ponderous branches atop a fairly short massive light brown trunk. The 10-inch-long leaves are a deep green in color, elliptic to obovate in shape, thick and leathery with a very prominent and yellowish midrib. The flowers are small and white with six to eight corolla lobes and are formed in axillary clusters. The beautiful round golden inch-wide fruits are carried on 2-inch-long stalks and are reputedly edible. The wood of this tree is very hard, dense, and durable, and the latexlike sap is used as a substitute for gutta-percha and in the manufacture of golf balls and machine belts. Ornamentally, few trees are more impressive or beautiful.

Manilkara jaimiqui. See *M. bahamensis*.

Manilkara roxburghiana (rahx-burg´-ee-AHN-a) (synonym *Mimusops roxburghiana*) is indigenous to India. It grows to 30 or 40 feet in cultivation with a rounded dense crown of foliage when mature but is columnar in form when young. The oblong leaves are exceptionally beautiful and are somewhat reminiscent of those of *Pittosporum tobira* but are much larger. About 8 inches long, they are glossy dark green above with a prominent and lighter colored midrib and usually notched ends and are grayish green beneath. The small white flowers are borne in the leaf axils at the ends of the branches and are rather insignificant in the landscape but are wonderfully fragrant, especially at night. The 2-inch-wide yellow-green to bright yellow fruits are round and hang on rather long stalks from the ends of the branches, making a beautiful display. They are supposedly edible and sweet in taste but dry and mealy in texture. The tree is drought tolerant when established. Because it is quite tolerant of saline air, spray, and soil, it is a perfect candidate for seaside planting as well as along streets and avenues inland. Plate 274.

Manilkara zapota (sa-POAT-a) (synonyms *Achras zapota, Sapota achras*) is one of the world's most handsome trees because of the spectacularly beautiful leaves and large long-lasting light brown or reddish brown fruit. It is found naturally in southern and southeastern Mexico, Guatemala, and Belize. The tree attains a height of almost 100 feet in its native haunts but is usually not much over 50 feet tall in cultivation. It forms a relatively short gray to brownish trunk whose bark is composed of rectangular small plates. The tree's crown is rounded and dense when mature with the branches arranged in closely set tiers, but the form is usually pyramidal in shape when young. The gorgeous 5- to 6-inch-long elliptic leaves are pointed at the apex, leathery and thick in texture, and a deep olive to grayish and lustrous green, and have prominent midribs. They are found in a spiral or rosette arrangement near the ends of the picturesquely thick gray branches. The small greenish white flowers, which are extended narrow tubes with flaring rosebud-shaped corollas, are found in the leaf axils near the ends of the twigs. The lovely 4-inch-wide fruits are round to egg-shaped and a light brown to grayish brown in color. Their surfaces are pebbly in texture until old, at which time the fruit usually splits. One of the most beautiful sights in the vegetable kingdom is the combination of these fruits against the background of the dense crown of glossy grayish green leaves. The fruits are edible and often delicious. The superior varieties have a yellowish white to brownish or reddish brown juicy pulp that is slightly gritty but wonderfully sweet when ripe and suggestive of a combination of kiwi fruit (*Actinidia chinensis*) and the pear. Commonly sold cultivars are ***Manilkara zapota* 'Brown Sugar', *Manilkara zapota* 'Modello', *Manilkara zapota***

'Prolific', and *Manilkara zapota* 'Russell'. The black seeds have a small barb at one end but are easily removed from the sliced fruit. The thick sap (called "chicle") is used still in the manufacture of chewing gum for which it has been grown in large plantations in tropical America and the Far East. This species is tolerant of salty air and fairly saline soil but is not a true beachfront tree. It is most commonly called sapodilla (sap-o-DILL-a/ sap-o-DEE-ya) in the United States, but also bears the vernacular names of dilly, nispero, chicozapote (cheek´-o-sa-PO-tay) and, in Asia, naseberry. Plate 275.

MANSOA. See *Pseudocalymma.*

MARANTA (ma-RANT-a)
Marantaceae: The Maranta Family
Common names vary according to species
Small to medium-sized herbs with gorgeously
    variegated leaves
Zones 10 and 11; often sprouting from the roots in
    zone 9b
Partial to almost full shade
Water lovers
Rich, moist, well-drained soil
Propagation by root divisions, rhizome division, and
    (for some species) cuttings

A small genus of about 36 tropical American species of clumping herbs with thick roots and elliptic to oblong (rarely lanceolate) leaves growing from sparsely branching stems. The petioles are provided with sheaths and a cushionlike gland at the base of the leaf stalk, which often causes the leaf blade to draw inward with the advent of darkness. The leaves of these species are among the most exotic and colorful in the plant world because of their often amazing variegation. The small flowers are attractive and orchidlike but are not effective in the landscape. The genus is closely allied to *Calathea*, and the distinction between some of the species in the two genera is often nearly impossible for the untrained.

Maranta arundinacea (a-run-di-NAIS-ee-a) occurs naturally over a wide range of the American tropics, from the West Indies through Mexico, Central America, and into tropical South America. It is one of the largest species in the genus, reaching a height of 3 to 5 feet, with zigzagging branching stems and long-stalked elliptic-lanceolate foot-long dark green leaves with darker longitudinal markings and long tips. *Maranta arundinacea* 'Aurea' (OW-ree-a) has leaves mostly yellow with green markings. *Maranta arundinacea* 'Variegata' (vair-ee-a-GAIT-a), another beautiful cultivar, has leaves mostly green with yellow markings. The plant is sometimes called arrow-root as well as the obedience plant.

Maranta bicolor (BY-kul-or) is indigenous to northeastern South America. It is a low-growing species with beautiful mostly oblong 8-inch-long leaves that are a lovely olive green with feathery gray markings around the midrib and darker green blotches around this feathered variegation. The specific epithet *bicolor* refers to the undersides of the leaves, which are a beautiful shade of purplish red or a deep wine in color. The plant has tuberous roots that allow it to spring back from a freeze after the weather warms up in the spring in zone 9b. This clumping and slowly spreading species is unexcelled as a groundcover in nearly frost-free shady areas without traffic.

Maranta insignis. See *Calathea lancifolia.*
Maranta kegeljanii. See *Calathea bella.*
Maranta kerchoviana. See *M. leuconeura* var. *kerchoviana.*

Maranta leuconeura (loo-ko-NYOOR-a) is native to the wetter areas of tropical Brazil and is doubtless the most beautiful species in the genus. It is also a variable species with several naturally occurring resplendent forms. The plant grows to only 6 inches or, at most, a foot in height, with spreading succulent stems that are almost vinelike. This species is possibly the most beautiful groundcover for bright but shady and nearly frost-free areas where traffic is not a factor. The leaves are about 6 inches long and are oblong in shape. Their variegation is almost incredible, looking nearly artificial because it is so artistic and does not vary from one individual to another of the same variety or cultivar. The type has olive to deep green leaves with a white central midrib and regularly spaced brownish purple to purplish green blotches down through the center of each side of the blade; the undersides of the blades are purplish red. *Maranta leuconeura* var. *erythroneura* (e-rit´-ro-NYOO-ra) is so extraordinarily beautiful as to almost defy description. It is similar to the type except that the midrib and lateral veins are a bright cardinal red and the central feathery area is lime green. The blade is purplish red beneath. *Maranta leuconeura* var. *kerchoviana* (ker-chahf´-ee-AHN-a) (synonym *M. kerchoviana*) is similar to the type, but the colors are more pronounced and there are beautiful silvery curved lateral veins that extend to the margin of the blade. *Maranta leuconeura* var. *leuconeura* (synonym *M. massangeana*) is another variety so extraordinarily beautiful as to almost defy description. It has dark bluish green leaves with a shimmering and satiny patina. The dark gray midrib is surrounded by a silver feathery pattern with long curved lateral veins that extend to the leaf margins. The undersides of the leaves are the beautiful wine color of the type. The species and its various forms are called the prayer plant. Plate 276.

Maranta massangeana. See *M. leuconeura* var. *leuconeura.*

MARGINATOCEREUS.
See *Pachycereus.*

MARKHAMIA (mark-HAM-ee-a)

Bignoniaceae: The Catalpa, Jacaranda, Trumpet-
Vine Family
No known English common name
Small to medium-sized evergreen trees; pinnate
leaves; large clusters of yellow trumpet flowers
Zones 10 and 11; marginal in zone 10a
Sun
Average but regular amounts of moisture
Humusy, well-drained soil
Propagation by seed

A genus of about 12 species of small to medium-sized evergreen trees in tropical Africa and Asia. They have large odd-pinnate leaves, terminal racemes or panicles of bell-shaped or funnel-shaped five-lobed flowers accompanied by large spathelike calyces. Flower color is yellow, often with red or purple hues in the throat. The trees bloom at any time of the year in tropical regions but principally in spring or summer. The pods are exceptionally large and attractive, often covered in a velvety pubescence. The genus is closely allied to *Spathodea* and is sometimes confused with it because of the similar tree form and habit. All the species are spectacular in bloom as the blossoms nearly cover the plants, and the trees are pleasing of form and foliage when not in flower. These species are also easy to grow and are fast growing in tropical or nearly tropical regions.

Markhamia hildebrandtii. See *M. lutea.*

Markhamia lutea (LOOT-ee-a) (synonym *M. hildebrandtii*) is native to tropical Central and West Africa. It grows to 30 feet or sometimes more with wonderfully large leaves. Each leaf is about 18 inches long with 8-inch-long glossy dark green oblong leaflets. The flowers, borne in terminal rounded clusters, are a brilliant yellow with red lines in the throat.

Markhamia obtusifolia (ahb-tyoos´-i-FO-lee-a) is indigenous to tropical Africa. It is similar in size and leaf form to *M. lutea* but grows slightly larger and the individual blossoms have chocolate, purplish red, or reddish brown stripes in their throats rather than red stripes. Plate 277.

MASTICHODENDRON

(mast-i-ko-DEN-drun)
Sapotaceae: The Sapodilla Family
MASTIC; FALSE MASTIC; JUNGLE PLUM;
WILD OLIVE
Large evergreen tree; light green leaves; small round
yellow and orange fruit
Zones 10b and 11
Sun
Average water; drought tolerant when established
Average well-drained soil
Propagation by seed

A small genus of evergreen trees in tropical America with nontoxic milky sap, one of which extends into southern Florida. *Mastichodendron foetidissimum* (fet-i-DIS-i-mum) (synonym *Sideroxylon foetidissimum*) occurs naturally in extreme southern Florida, the West Indies, Gulf Coastal Mexico, and Central America. It grows to as much as 80 feet with a broad but usually open crown and a thick gray to almost white trunk. The bark is fissured into shaggy rectangular plates. The leathery elliptic leaves are 4 to 8 inches long, long stalked, a yellow green in color, with a prominent and lighter colored midrib, and are distinctly wavy margined. The leaves are usually found clustered near the ends of the massive branches. The ill-smelling tiny yellowish white flowers appear on the inner twigs behind the leaves and are not effective in the landscape, but the inch-wide yellow to orange round fruits are quite attractive although mostly hidden among the leaves. The fruits are reputedly edible but insipid in taste and an irritant in quantity. This native tree is magnificent when mature and should be more widely planted wherever the climate is suitable. It is drought tolerant and remarkably immune to salty air and saline soil.

MEDINILLA

(med-i-NEE-ya / med-i-NIL-la)
Melastomataceae: The Tibouchina Family
MEDINILLA
Herbaceous shrub; large fleshy lance-shaped leaves;
spectacular pendent pink flower clusters
Zone 11; marginal in zone 10b
Partial shade
Water lover
Rich, humusy, well-drained soil
Propagation by seed and cuttings

A large genus of about 150 species of herbaceous shrubs in tropical Africa, southeastern Asia, and the islands of the South Pacific. Many species are epiphytic or vinelike, and all have beautiful large leaves that are typical of the family and large and showy panicles of white or pink flowers. Only one is common in cultivation. *Medinilla magnifica* (mag-NIF-i-ka) is native to the Philippines where it grows as a gigantic epiphyte in soil pockets on the great tropical rain forest trees and terrestrially in cleared spots that are not in full sun. The plant grows to as much as 8 feet with succulent four-angled stems, another characteristic of many members of the family. The immense foot-long stalkless lanceolate to ovate deep green leaves have the distinct midrib and longitudinal lighter colored veins that are typical of the melastoma family and are arranged oppositely along the stem. The plant blooms year-round with pendent long-stalked inflorescences that consist of several large light pink leaflike bracts above (or below if the inflorescences were erect) branched clusters of coral red or deep pink small flowers with white stamens. This incredibly beautiful giant herb is usually grown terrestrially in cultivation or in containers. It needs near-constant high relative humidity, a soil or potting medium rich in compost and freely draining, good air circulation, and very bright shade but not direct sunlight. It cannot withstand frost and is sometimes injured by temperatures below 40°F. Plate 278.

MEGASKEPASMA
(meh-gas´-ke-PAZ-ma)
Acanthaceae: The Acanthus Family
BRAZILIAN RED-CLOAK
Large herbaceous shrub; immense ovate leaves;
    gigantic terminal red flower spikes
Zones 10b and 11 as a permanent perennial; zone 9b
    as a returning perennial
Sun to partial shade
Average but regular amounts of moisture
Average well-drained soil
Propagation by cuttings

A monotypic genus that occurs naturally in southern Venezuela. *Megaskepasma erythrochlamys* (e-rit´-ro-KLAY-mis) (synonym *Adhatoda cydoniifolia*) is a magnificent shrub with a grotesque botanical name. It grows to at least 6 feet in height and, without frost, often to 10 or even 12 feet. The leaves are a foot, sometimes more, long, and are elliptical to ovate in shape with a prominent and lighter colored (rarely pink) large midrib and slightly depressed lateral veins, which give somewhat of a quilted effect to the blade. The plants bloom mainly in the fall through the spring, but summer blooms are not uncommon. The erect terminal inflorescence is a foot or more tall and consists of closely packed large scarlet to purplish red bracts enclosing elongated arching two-lipped white flowers, which peek out in the same manner as those of *Justicia brandegeana* (shrimp plant). This shrub is breathtaking in the landscape as a tall background subject underplanted with almost anything that is not as tall; one of the most intriguing partners is the shrimp plant whose more subtle flower colors are extremely complementary with those of the red-cloak. The plant in bloom is shockingly spectacular when one first encounters it because of its unexpected size in leaf and flower cluster. This shrub has soared in popularity in the 1990s. Plate 279.

MERREMIA (mer-REEM-ee-a)
Convolvulaceae: The Morning Glory Family
WOOD ROSE; YELLOW MORNING GLORY
Twining vine with hand-shaped leaves; yellow
    trumpet flowers; woody fruit shaped like a rose
Zones 10 and 11
Sun
Average but regular amounts of moisture
Average well-drained soil
Propagation by seed, cuttings, and (sometimes) root
    division

A genus of about 75 species of twining vines in tropical or subtropical areas worldwide. All are closely related to those in the genus *Ipomoea* (morning glory) but, unlike most *Ipomoea* species, have yellow or white flowers rather than shades of red, pink, or blue. Like morning glories, many species form tuberous roots. Only one is commonly cultivated and attractive enough for the scope of this book, although several weedy species are naturalized in the southernmost parts of the United States. *Merremia tuberosa* (toob-e-RO-sa) (synonym *Ipomoea tuberosa*) is a rampantly growing large twiner that grows to 50 feet or more in two years. The attractive circular hand-shaped leaves are almost reason enough to grow this large vine. They are about 6 inches wide and are deeply divided into seven lance-shaped deep green spreading segments, which radiate 360° from the end of the leaf stalk and which create a blade that is circular in outline. The vine blooms in summer and fall with solitary perfectly formed morning-glory-like 2- to 3-inch wide trumpets that are a deep and clear yellow in color. These wonderful flowers and leaves would certainly be reason enough to grow the plant, but there is more. The sepals do not fall after the flowers fade; rather they enlarge, become leathery and almost woody, and then close over the ovary, forming a top-shaped yellowish "fruit." When they open after a few weeks or a couple of months, there is revealed a petal-like structure around the developing rounded chestnutlike fruit. The visual effect is that of an enchanting flower carved out of a golden to reddish brown wood with a satiny finish. Taken together these leaves, flowers, and fruit make the wood rose one of the world's most beautiful vines. Although the plant is rampant and large, it should have a place in any and every tropical or subtropical garden that has the space. With the return of warm weather the climber will sprout from the large roots after a freeze in zone 9b and often in zone 9a, but this is a moot point because it will often not have enough of a growing season to bloom and, even if it does, another freeze the following winter will most likely destroy the beautiful developing pods.

MERYTA (MER-i-ta / me-RYT-a)
Araliaceae: The Aralia, Schefflera Family
PUKA
Small tree with dense rounded crown of immense
    green leaves
Zones 10 and 11
Sun to partial shade
Water lover
Rich, moist, well-drained soil
Propagation by seed and cuttings

A small genus of about 15 species of small trees in Australia, New Zealand, and the islands of the South Pacific. All have large undivided leathery leaves that are bunched near the ends of the branches. The tiny flowers are in large panicles but are not particularly ornamental. Only one species is grown, and it is not often found, although it is eminently worth having. *Meryta sinclairii* (sin-KLAIR-ee-eye) is found in the tropical regions of the north island of New Zealand and the adjacent South Pacific islands north of it. The little tree grows to 20 or even 30 feet with time and forms a broad and rounded but sparsely branched crown. The immense leaves are elliptical to lanceolate in shape, tough and leathery but glossy above, and 12 to 18 inches long. Found in great clusters at the ends of the thick branches, the leaves have beautiful lighter colored midribs and lateral veins, and are wavy-margined. The effect is that of a giant-leaved *Ficus* species, although these trees do not make the forest giants that most fig species do. Nonetheless, they make spectacularly beautiful patio trees and are stunning when planted anywhere they can be seen and enjoyed up close.

MICHELIA

(mee-CHEL-ee-a / mee-SHEL-ee-a / meek-HEL-ee-a)
Magnoliaceae: The Magnolia Family
Common names vary according to species
Small to medium-sized evergreen trees or shrubs;
    fragrant flowers
Zones vary according to species
Sun to partial shade
Average but regular amounts of moisture
Average well-drained soil on the acidic side
Propagation by seed and cuttings

A genus of about 45 species of mostly evergreen shrubs and small to medium-sized trees in tropical and subtropical parts of Asia. They are related to the genus *Magnolia* and, while the flowers of most species are not as showy nor as large as most magnolias, the fragrance of almost all of them is extraordinary. In addition the blossoms mostly appear in the leaf axils and tend to be somewhat hidden by the foliage, whereas those of *Magnolia* tend to be terminal on the branches and more obvious.

Michelia champaca (shahm-PAHK-a / chahm-PAHK-a) is native to the Himalayan regions of northern India and southern China and is hardy in zones 10 and 11, although it is sometimes successfully grown in zone 9b. It is one of the tallest and fastest growing species, to 70 or 80 feet in its native habitat, but usually to no more than 30 or 40 feet in cultivation. The trunks are gray, sometimes quite light gray, in color and the tree makes an oblong crown of beautiful 8- to 10-inch-long narrowly ovate to lanceolate leaves that are glossy and light to medium green in color. In truly tropical areas the tree blooms most of the year but most heavily in summer. The flowers are 4 to 5 inches wide with 12 fairly narrow, spreading, and somewhat twisted deep yellow to orange petals. They have one of the sweetest fragrances known. The tree needs rich soil and slightly more than an average amount of water in a well-drained site. It is usually called the fragrant champaca.

Michelia doltsopa (dolt-SOAP-a) is indigenous to the Himalayan regions of northern India and western China and is hardy in zones 9b through 11, although marginal in zone 9a. It is a variable tree but usually grows fairly quickly to about 40 feet with a light brown or gray trunk and an oblong and fairly narrow crown. The 6- to 8-inch-long leathery elliptic to oblong leaves are dark and glossy green above and minutely brown fuzzy beneath. The wonderfully fragrant flowers are as much as 8 inches but usually 5 to 6 inches wide. The numerous white petals are ovate and surround a magnolia-like center of male and female flower parts. The trees bloom mostly in the late winter and early spring.

Michelia figo (FEE-go) (synonym *M. fuscata*), the banana shrub, is native to western China and is hardy in zones 7 through 9. It does not enjoy or flourish in tropical areas. A large slow-growing shrub, it reaches to as much as 15 feet or even more in height and half as wide. It is densely covered in 3-inch-long elliptic light green almost stalkless leaves. The plant is not extraordinarily attractive, but the fragrance of the flowers is reason enough to grow it even though the flowers usually appear only once a year (spring) and last for a month at the longest. The blossoms, which are usually less than 2 inches long and which are partially hidden by the foliage, are cup-shaped with yellow petals shaded in brownish purple. The fragrance is definitely "fruity" with a strong scent of banana, but more exhilarating and one of the world's finest. The shrub needs protection from the midday summer sun and a rich, moist but free-draining soil that is on the acidic side.

Michelia fuscata. See *M. figo.*

MICONIA (mi-KOAN-ee-a)

Melastomataceae: The Tibouchina Family
VELVET TREE
Large mostly herbaceous shrub; gigantic and
    gorgeously variegated leaves
Zone 11; marginal in zone 10b
Partial shade
Water lovers
Rich, humusy, moist, well-drained soil
Propagation by cuttings

A very large genus of about 1000 species of trees and shrubs in tropical America. All have large and showy leaves but usually insignificant flower clusters, which is unusual in this family noted both for the extraordinary beauty of the leaves as well as the flowers. Alas, only one species out of this very large genus is common in cultivation. *Miconia calvescens* (kal-VES-senz) (synonym *M. magnifica*) is native to much of tropical America from southern Mexico to northern South America. It is a large mostly herbaceous shrub growing to about 15 feet as an understory plant in the tropical rain forest. It is grown for its almost unimaginably beautiful ovate leaves, which are as much as 2 feet long with depressed veins above. The veins and midrib of the leaf are colored yellowish white, the undersides reddish purple. This magnificent shrub needs constant humidity and warmth. No other tropical genus warrants more attention than this one. It is almost unbelievable that more of these beauties have not been exploited for gardeners in frost-free regions. Plate 280.

MICROGRAMMA (myk-ro-GRAM-ma)
Polypodiaceae: The Largest Fern Family
No known English common name
Small epiphytic clumping and spreading ferns with
　dark green undivided fronds
Zones 10 and 11
Partial shade
Water lovers
Leaf mold
Propagation by root division

A small genus of about 20 species of epiphytic ferns with undivided leaf blades in tropical America and tropical West Africa. They all have creeping rhizomes, which serve as holdfasts, as moisture-gathering and nutrient-gathering organs, and to increase the plants' purview. All species are relatively small. The oblong, lanceolate or linear, and leathery fronds seldom are more than 10 inches long. The ferns may be planted in soil pockets on large trees and allowed to spread along the branches, which creates a lush tropical look of great beauty. This genus was formerly a part of the giant *Polypodium* genus, and many species are still listed there. The following is a list of the easily obtainable species with a brief description of each.

Microgramma heterophyllum (het-ur-o-FYL-lum) is found in southern Florida and the West Indies. It has fronds to about 6 inches long.

Microgramma lycopodioides (lyk´-o-poad-ee-OY-deez) occurs naturally in a wide area of tropical South and Central America. It has fronds to 10 inches long.

Microgramma nitida (ni-TY-da) is native to Central America. It has fronds to 8 inches long.

MICROLEPIA (myk-ro-LEEP-ee-a)
Dennstaedtiaceae: The Bracken Fern Family
LACE FERN
Medium-sized triangular-leaved light green fern
Zones 9 through 11
Partial shade to nearly full sun
Average but regular amounts of moisture
Humusy, well-drained soil
Propagation by root division, rhizome division, and
　spores

A genus of about 50 terrestrial fern species in tropical and subtropical regions of the Old World. They have finely dissected (four-pinnate or five-pinnate) lacy medium-sized leaves, usually quite triangular in shape. One species is becoming increasingly popular because of its ease of culture and exceptional grace. *Microlepia strigosa* (stry-GO-sa) occurs over a very large area of Asia, including the southern Japanese islands, the islands of the South Pacific, southern China, Malaysia, and India. This lacy and delicate-appearing plant is actually tough, dependable, and easy of culture, and is one of the few large and attractive ferns that can grow in full sun if it has enough water. It grows to 3 or even 4 feet in height and makes a fairly dense clump of tripinnate 3- to 4-foot-long triangular bright green fronds that have a metallic and sometimes bluish sheen when new.

MICROSORIUM (myk´-ro-SOR-ee-um)
Polypodiaceae: The Largest Fern Family
Common names vary according to species
Evergreen ferns with simple leaves
Zones 10 and 11
Shade to partial shade
Water lovers
Rich, humusy, well-drained soil or leaf mold
Propagation by rhizome division

A genus of about 40 species of mostly epiphytic ferns in tropical Africa, Asia, and Australia. All have creeping or climbing fleshy rhizomes and simple leaves, mostly unsegmented although some have fronds that are deeply three-lobed or even pinnately segmented. The species with unsegmented and simple leaves are somewhat similar to *Asplenium* (bird's-nest fern) species and are sometimes burdened with the vernacular name of climbing bird's-nest ferns. These ferns are easy of culture, provided the grower supplies warmth and humidity. They are often grown terrestrially as well as epiphytically.

Microsorium musifolium (myoos-i-FO-lee-um) (synonym *Polypodium musifolium*) is indigenous to Indonesia, Malaysia, New Guinea, and the Philippines. This beautiful epiphytic species has simple fronds that are as much as 3 feet long, stalkless, long linear-lanceolate in shape, and a light yellow-green in color. They are provided with prominent, very dark midribs and dark lateral veins, which create an unusual and most picturesque form. This species is exquisitely beautiful on trees or walls surrounded by dark green forms, and it may be grown terrestrially. The plant is sometimes called the banana-leaf fern.

Microsorium punctatum (punk-TAIT-um) (synonyms *Polypodium polycarpon, P. punctatum*) is indigenous to an immense area from tropical East Africa through India, Southeast Asia, Malaysia, Australia, and into Polynesia. It has stalkless fronds that are simple and undivided, narrowly linear-lanceolate in shape, a glossy pale yellow-green in color, and as much as 4 feet long. The spreading rhizomes in time will create large colonies on trees, walls, and even rocks that have depressions with soil or leaf mold in them. The plant is quite variable in nature and has sported into several cultivars. *Microsorium punctatum* 'Grandiceps' (GRAN-di-seps) is probably the most distinctive of the cultivars. Its fronds are terminated in several branched divisions. This cultivar is sometimes called elkhorn fern, another most unfortunate vernacular as this name also is used for species of *Platycerium*.

MILLETTIA (mil-LET-tee-a)
Papilionaceae (Fabaceae, Leguminosae), subfamily
　Papilionoideae: The Bean, Pea Family

Common names vary according to species
Evergreen vine and small evergreen tree; red and
     purple pealike flowers in pyramidal clusters
Zones vary according to species
Sun
Average but regular amounts of moisture
Average well-drained soil
Propagation by seed

A genus of almost 100 species of vines, shrubs, and small trees in tropical and subtropical regions of the Old World. All have odd-pinnate leaves and terminal clusters of pink, red, or purple pealike flowers.

Millettia grandis (GRAN-dis) is indigenous to South Africa and is hardy in zones 10 and 11. It is a small tree growing to 20 or 30 feet in height with a short trunk and a broad and dense crown of lovely foot-long leaves consisting of 11 to 15 bright green lance-shaped leaflets. The trees bloom in spring and early summer with erect narrow spikes of pure pink pealike flowers. This species likes a rich, humusy soil and is not drought tolerant.

Millettia ovalifolia (o-val´-i-FO-lee-a) is native to Myanmar (Burma) and is hardy in zones 10b and 11. It is a small tree in cultivation but grows fast to 50 or 60 feet in its native habitat. It forms a short gray trunk (or often multiple trunks) that is picturesquely not straight, and a round-headed and open crown. The beautiful large light green leaves consist of seven ovate 3-inch-long leaflets, making the entire blade about 12 inches long. The leaves are often briefly deciduous in dry or cold winters, and the new growth is an almost translucent rosy-bronze. The flowers appear in spring in terminal drooping panicles of pealike pink and purple blossoms.

Millettia pinnata. See *Pongamia pinnata.*

Millettia reticulata (re-tik´-yoo-LAIT-a) occurs naturally in Taiwan and southeastern China and is hardy in zones 9 through 11. It is a fast and strong-growing twining vine that eventually forms thick rope-like woody stems and can cover a large area. The leaves are exceptionally beautiful with five to nine glossy very dark green 3-inch-long elliptic to lanceolate leaflets. The vine blooms late spring and early summer and often sporadically throughout the summer and fall with 6- to 8-inch-long semi-erect pyramidal panicles of reddish to deep purple to almost black pealike flowers. The flowers have a light fragrance, which some think resembles cedar or camphor, but which others find more akin to burning rubber. The vine is called evergreen wisteria in the United States because, except for the flower color, it resembles that spring-flowering plant.

MIMUSOPS (MIM-yoo-sahps)
Sapotaceae: The Sapodilla Family
SPANISH CHERRY
Small dense evergreen tree; fragrant white flowers;
     showy red fruit
Zones 10b and 11
Sun
Average but regular amounts of moisture
Average well-drained soil
Propagation by seed and cuttings

A genus of about 60 trees and large shrubs in the Old World tropics. All have nontoxic milky sap, relatively large leathery leaves, small white flowers, and clusters of large berrylike fruit. One species is widely grown in the tropics for its beauty as well as its edible fruits.

Mimusops balata. See *Manilkara bidentata.*

Mimusops elengi (e-LANG-ee) is native to India, Myanmar (Burma), Malaysia, and the islands of the South Pacific. In its native habitats the tree attains a height of 80 feet or more, but in cultivation it is seldom more than 40 feet tall. It slowly forms a very dense oblong crown with a short trunk until it is mature, at which point the crown is usually broader. The 3- to 6-inch-long leaves are ovate to elliptic in shape, dark green above and a paler green beneath, leathery in texture with wavy margins, and a prominent and lighter colored midrib. The new leaves are a reddish bronze in color. The small white half-inch-wide starlike fragrant flowers are formed in small clusters from the leaf axils and, while quite attractive up close, are mostly hidden by the leaves. The fruits, however, are showy inch-long deep yellow to deep orange berries, which hang from 2-inch-long stalks in small clusters. They are reportedly edible but very astringent. This tree is a perfect candidate for a large patio as it is relatively small and neat in appearance, and has the year-round ornamental qualities of beautiful leaves, fragrant flowers, and attractive fruit.

Mimusops emarginata. See *Manilkara bahamensis.*

Mimusops roxburghiana. See *Manilkara roxburghiana.*

MONOCOSTUS (mahn-o-KAHST-us)
Costaceae: The Costus Family
MONOCOSTUS
Medium-sized shrub; fleshy thin stems; large
     succulent lanceolate leaves; large yellow flowers
Zones 10 and 11
Sun to partial shade
Average but regular amounts of moisture
Average well-drained soil

A monotypic genus from western Peru. ***Monocostus uniflorus*** (yoo-ni-FLOR-us) can attain a height of 6 or even 8 feet but is usually smaller. It is very similar vegetatively to members of the related genus *Costus*, but the curving *Monocostus* inflorescence arises from the leaf axils and is not terminally disposed. The pure yellow flowers are quite large, about 3 inches wide, and the three petals overlap to form a cup shape or a flat disk. The plant is much more tender to cold than are the *Costus* species and will not usually sprout from the root after being frozen to the ground. This most striking plant, especially in bloom, should be more widely cultivated. It is reportedly extinct in the wild in its native habitat.

MONODORA
(mo-no-DOR-a / mo-NOAD-o-ra)
Annonaceae: The Cherimoya Family
AFRICAN NUTMEG; CALABASH NUTMEG; JAMAICAN NUTMEG; ORCHID-FLOWER TREE
Large evergreen tree; immense leaves; yellow and red flowers; large fragrant fruit
Zones 10b and 11
Sun to partial shade
Water lover
Rich, moist, humusy, well-drained soil
Propagation by seed

A small genus of about 20 evergreen trees and shrubs in tropical Africa and Madagascar. All have rather large entire leaves and large pendent six-petaled flowers often with three of the petals highly modified into long trailing, twisted, and highly colored tail-like appendages. Despite the vernacular names, no species is related to the true nutmeg (*Myristica fragrans*), the calabash tree (*Crescentia cujete*), the orchids or the orchid tree genus *Bauhinia*. Rather they are kindred to *Annona cherimola* (cherimoya). One species is much planted as an ornamental in the tropics and was at one time imported into the West Indies for commercial production of the fruit, which is used as a substitute for the true nutmeg. ***Monodora myristica*** (my-RIST-i-ka) is indigenous to tropical Africa from Senegal through Nigeria into Kenya. The tree grows to 80 feet or more in its native habitats but is seldom more than 50 feet in cultivation. It forms a straight trunk with large horizontal branches. The pendent leaves are exceptionally beautiful and are as much as 2 feet long, elliptic to obovate in shape, a deep dark green in color, with prominent and lighter colored midribs and a short apical "tail"; the tree is often deciduous to some extent in drier areas. The fragrant flowers appear in spring before the leaves if the tree is deciduous. Hanging on 8-inch-long stalks, each flower is 8 or more inches wide with three exceptionally large frilled petals of basic yellow or white fringed with deep red and often with green flecks. The dark brown to black pendent fruits that follow are round to gourd-shaped, from 3 to 8 inches in diameter, and very hard shelled, and hang from cords that are sometimes 2 feet long. The flesh and seeds are redolent of the scent of nutmeg and have been used for centuries as a substitute for that more expensive spice. There is hardly a more tropical looking and exotic tree, in and out of flower or fruit.

MONSTERA (mahn-STER-a)
Araceae: The Calla Lily, Jack-in-the-Pulpit Family
Common names vary according to species
Great clinging vines; immense, usually dissected leaves; large spathelike inflorescences
Zones 10b and 11 as permanent vines; zone 9b as returning vines
Partial shade to sun
Water lovers
Rich, humusy, well-drained soil
Propagation by cuttings

A genus of 22 species of climbing plants in tropical America. They cling by aerial roots emanating from stout cylindrical stems. The leaves are almost invariably large and often pinnately dissected or exhibiting naturally formed holes in the leaf blade. The leaf stalk is winged on its lower portion and is somewhat flexible. All species have two leaf forms. In the juvenile stage the leaves are relatively small, almost completely unsegmented or perforated, nearly stalkless, and overlapping like shingles on the surface of the substrate. In the mature stage the leaves are very large, stalked, and typical of the species. It is fortunate that cuttings taken from mature-leaved vines tend to retain the mature leaf form. One side of the blade is usually larger than the other, a condition termed "inequilateral." The inflorescences are large with large white to yellowish spathes that nearly completely enclose the large whitish spadices. The spadix matures into a narrow brown cone-shaped fruit (actually an "aggregate" fruit composed of many small fruits), which in some species is edible. All species are completely tropical in nature, but most are capable of sprouting from their roots after a freeze and some form such thick and tough stems that it takes a severe freeze to kill them (the stems). *Monstera deliciosa* stems have survived brief encounters with temperatures in the low 20s when protected from the wind, and *M. friedrichstahlii* has sprouted from its roots with the same temperatures.

Monstera acuminata (a-kyoo-mi-NAIT-a) is indigenous to northern Central America where it grows to 30 or more feet up large forest trees. The mature leaves are a medium green, relatively thin in texture, a foot long, and long stalked. In shape they are inequilaterally ovate to lanceolate with a short tip and several elliptical perforations paralleling the lateral veins. The vine is often called the shingle plant because of the very different form and overlapping nature of the juvenile leaves.

Monstera adansonii (ad-an-SO-nee-eye) (synonym *M. pertusa*) occurs naturally in Panama, Colombia, Venezuela, and Guyana. It grows to 50 or more feet up the trunks of the giant rain forest trees. The leaves are as much as 3 feet long, a deep green in color, slightly wavy-margined, and leathery. In shape, they are somewhat inequilaterally ovate with a long curved tip and many irregularly shaped perforations in the blade. This species is one of the most spectacular and exotic climbing plants.

Monstera deliciosa (synonym *Philodendron pertusum*) was found naturally in southern Mexico and Central America where it grew to great heights up the rain forest trees although it is probably extinct in its natural habitat. The mature leaves, which are as much as 3 feet wide and of even greater length, are generally ovate to almost orbicular in outline. The blade is deeply divided into 12 to 24 mostly oblong and square-ended inequilateral segments. The lower and upper segments have a "tail" near their bottoms, as if the segments were trying to knit with their neighbors. In the largest leaves there are elliptic perforations between the upper segments near the lighter green to yellow midrib. The edible fruit smells and tastes vaguely of pineapple, but is not edible until mature, as indicated by its smell and by the ease of picking it apart. Before that the fruit contains the typical oxalic acid crystals and bites the mouth and digestive tract. There are variegated cultivars that are at least as attractive as the type. The leaf is one of the most familiar, beautiful, and exotic of leaves, and has the very essence of the tropical look. The giant vines are not only exquisite climbing trees, but also make one of the most spectacular gigantic groundcovers. The number of common names for this climber attests to its familiarity and popularity: ceriman, Swiss cheese plant, breadfruit vine, Mexican breadfruit, hurricane plant, window plant, and fruit-salad plant. The vine used to be (and sometimes still is) erroneously termed split leaf philodendron and cut-leaf philodendron. Plate 281.

Monstera dubia (DOO-bee-a) is native to southern Mexico, Nicaragua, and Costa Rica. It is an immense vine growing to the tops of the tallest rain forest trees. The leaves are proportionally immense: they are 4 or more feet long, generally oblong in outline but very deeply divided into many narrow linear segments, which create the appearance more of a palm frond than a *Monstera* species. It is an incredible experience to look up a soaring tree trunk and see these giant pinnate leaves issuing forth from the trunk through shade and sun.

Monstera epipremnoides (ep´-ee-prem-NOY-deez) (synonym *M. leichtlenii*) is indigenous to Costa Rica where it grows up the tallest rain forest trees. The immense leaves are 3 or more feet long, oblong in outline but very deeply divided into two dozen or more segments, each with the basic shape of that of the *M. deliciosa* blade. There are many small rounded perforations along both sides of the stout midrib. This climber is another truly spectacular species.

Monstera friedrichstahlii (freed-rik-SHTAHL-ee-eye) is native to Central America. It grows to 30 or 40 feet and has 2-foot-long relatively thin, medium green leaves. In shape they are somewhat inequilaterally ovate, with many regularly spaced elliptic-shaped perforations along both sides of the midrib. The visual effect of the leaf is stunning.

Monstera leichtlenii. See *M. epipremnoides.*
Monstera pertusa. See *M. adansonii.*

MONTEZUMA (mahnt-e-ZOO-ma)
Bombacaceae: The Bombax, Baobab Family
TREE HIBISCUS; MAGA

Large evergreen tree; large heart-shaped leaves; great red mallowlike flowers
Zones 10b and 11; marginal in zone 10a; may be grown as a shrub in zone 9b
Sun
Average but regular amounts of moisture
Average well-drained soil
Propagation by seed and cuttings

A monotypic genus found naturally only on the island of Puerto Rico, although it was formerly thought to have been indigenous to Mexico, thus the genus name. *Montezuma speciosissima* (spee´-see-o-SIS-i-ma) is a tree that grows to 50 feet or more and makes a short dark gray trunk carrying a broad and very dense crown. The wonderfully large leathery dark green heart-shaped long-stalked leaves may be as much as 12 inches wide. The primary veins and midrib of the leaf are a marvelous yellow to golden brown to red in color. The tree blooms most of the year but most heavily in late winter and spring. Each glossy scarlet blossom is hibiscus-shaped, about 6 inches wide, and has the staminal column characteristic of the hibiscus family, Malvaceae. Indeed, some botanists still place the tree in that family, so close are the similarities of the flowers. Some forms have flowers that are more pink than red and often have white streaks on the petals; these varieties, which have been cloned to some extent and which are infrequently available, are as beautiful in the landscape as the type. There is also a white-flowered form. The tree is a perfect lawn specimen but is even better where its striking beauty of form, leaf, and flower can be appreciated up close. The tree flourishes on the alkaline limestone soils of southern Florida.

MORINDA (mo-RIN-da)
Rubiaceae: The Coffee, Gardenia, Ixora Family
INDIAN MULBERRY; LIMBURGER TREE; AWL TREE; NONI

Small evergreen tree; large glossy leaves; clusters of white flowers; green and yellow fruit
Zones 10b and 11
Sun to partial shade
Average but regular amounts of moisture
Average well-drained soil
Propagation by seed and cuttings

A genus of about 80 species of trees, shrubs, and a few vines in all tropical parts of the globe, but principally Asia. All have dense clusters of white or red star-like flowers and compound fruits. One species is regularly planted in tropical regions for the beauty of its leaves, flowers, and edible fruit. *Morinda citrifolia* (sit-ri-FO-lee-a) is native to Malaysia, northern Australia, and the islands of the South Pacific. It grows to as much as 70 feet in its native habitats but is usually under 30 feet in cultivation. The extraordinarily beautiful leaves are large but very graceful, soft, pliable, and somewhat puckered on the surface. They are glossy and shining, 10 or more inches long, ovate to elliptic in shape, with a very prominent yellowish green midrib and lateral veins. The tiny white star-shaped flowers occur in tight dense clusters in the leaf axils. These flower clusters develop into single 2- to 4-inch-long aggregate yellowish white to greenish white fruits when the separate calyces in the cluster fuse together. The individual fruits are lumpy but generally oblong in shape, bumpy, and warty with small pits on their surfaces much like strawberries. They have somewhat the appearance of a small mutated pineapple and are reputedly edible but have a strange unappetizing odor. This species makes one of the most enchantingly beautiful small trees on earth. It cannot be praised enough.

MORINGA (mor-ING-a)
Moringaceae: The Horseradish-Tree Family
HORSERADISH TREE
Small evergreen tree; large ferny leaves; fragrant
    white pealike flowers; showy edible fruit
Zones 10 and 11; marginal in zone 10a
Sun
Average but regular amounts of moisture
Average well-drained soil
Propagation by seed and cuttings

A genus of 14 small soft-wooded trees in Africa, Madagascar, India, and Arabia. They have thick and somewhat succulent trunks and branches that are resinous and aromatic, large but delicate-appearing pinnate foliage, pendent clusters of small caperlike flowers, and long narrow seed pods. One species is commonly planted in the tropics for its flowers, edible seed pods, and large aromatic root, which is used as a substitute for horseradish (*Armoracia rusticana*). **Moringa oleifera** (o-lee-IF-e-ra) (synonym *M. pterygosperma*) grows to 20 or 30 feet in height with a thick light gray to light brown trunk and limbs. The bark is rather corklike. The tree forms a broad and open graceful crown of light green 2-foot-long bipinnate leaves with soft inch-long ovate to obovate leaflets. The foliage may be deciduous in drought or cold. The trees are virtually everblooming and the 6-inch-long pendent flower clusters are composed of inch-wide fragrant flowers with white or yellow protruding stamens and golden anthers. Each blossom has ten petals, nine descending and one erect. The tree, especially when in flower, somewhat resembles a locust, but the leaves are even lacier and larger. The seed pods, which are 18 inches long, narrow, and three-sided, contain many small seeds, which, when mature, are winged but when young are tender and cooked like beans, boiled in curries, or pickled like okra. In addition the leaves and flowers are edible and are sometimes used in salads, and the seeds are fried and eaten or used as one source of oil in making salad oil. This graceful and airy small tree is perfect for a sunny patio.

MUCUNA (moo-KOON-a)
Papilionaceae (Fabaceae, Leguminosae), subfamily
    Papilionoideae: The Bean, Pea Family
NEW GUINEA CREEPER; D'ALBERTIS
    CREEPER
Large twining vine; pinnate foliage; immense and
    magnificent pendent clusters of red flowers
Zones 10b and 11
Sun to partial shade
Water lover
Humusy, moist, well-drained soil
Propagation by seed

A genus of around 100 species of large climbers in tropical regions around the world. All have large leaves, which consist of only three leaflets, and large long-stalked flower clusters of modified pealike blossoms, which resemble the inflorescences of *Erythrina* trees more than those of sweet peas (although the *Mucuna* flower clusters are usually pendent and those of *Erythrina* are not). The large drooping seed pods of some of the species (including *M. bennettii*) are covered in short tawny hairs, which are quite attractive but also quite irritating to the skin of most persons. One uncommonly found species is generally considered to be the world's most spectacular flowering vine. A few species are grown for cattle fodder in the United States and other countries where the growing season is long enough. **Mucuna bennettii** (ben-NET-tee-eye) is a gigantic liana native to Malaysia and New Guinea. No one seems to know just how large it can get, but it can supposedly completely cover the largest rain forest trees in its native habitats. It, therefore, is not a fit subject for the average-sized garden nor the average gardener. It must be added, however, that in cultivation in all but truly tropical areas the vine does not grow so immense nor so fast as it does in the equatorial rain forests. The glossy deep green leaflets are about 6 inches long and are lanceolate to elliptic in shape with a curved apical point. The pendent inflorescence is as long as 2 feet and is carried on a peduncle that may be just as long. The cluster is made up of many densely packed upturned broad clawlike flowers that are a vivid scarlet to fiery orange red. Each blossom is about 5 inches long with the whitish yellow stamens shyly peeking out from the ends of the intensely red clawlike calyces. There really is nothing more spectacular in flower, although there are vines and trees as beautiful and as spectacular. It truly must be seen to be believed, so overwhelming is the size and color. It sometimes suffers under the vernacular names of New Guinea creeper, Bennett's mucuna, D'Albertis creeper, and flame of the forest. Plate 282.

MURRAYA (mur-RAY-ya / mur-RY-ya)
Rutaceae: The Citrus Family
ORANGE JESSAMINE; ORANGE JASMINE
Evergreen small trees or large shrubs; glossy pinnate
    leaves; clusters of small white fragrant flowers
Zones 9b through 11; marginal in zone 9a

Sun
Average but regular amounts of moisture
Rich, humusy, well-drained soil
Propagation by seed and cuttings

A small genus of four or five aromatic small trees and shrubs in tropical Asia. They have odd-pinnate leaves and four-petaled to five-petaled white flowers resembling those of the orange tree and other *Citrus* species to which they are related. One species is very common in tropical and subtropical regions and is grown for its beautiful leaves and fragrant flowers. Another species, *Murraya koenigii*, the true curry plant, is cultivated for culinary purposes.

Murraya panicluata (synonyms *Chalcas exotica*, *Murraya. exotica*) grows to 12 or 15 or even 20 feet without frost and is naturally a large multitrunked shrub, but it may be trained to a dense-crowned tree form. The leaves are about 10 inches long and are composed of six to nine glossy deep green oval to diamond-shaped 2-inch-long leaflets. The flower clusters usually form in late summer and into the fall, but the plant may also bloom in the spring. Each blossom is somewhat less than an inch wide with four or five white thick and succulent petals and a heavenly aroma of orange blossoms. Older plants sometimes form attractive small red fruits. The plant is widely used as hedge material because it stands up well to shearing and is naturally dense, although naturally shaped (unpruned) shrubs make a prettier picture. The little trees are drought tolerant once established but, like so many other plants, look and are ever so much healthier and grow faster with good soil and adequate and regular irrigation. There is a dwarf cultivar that is not nearly as attractive as the type.

MUSA (MYOOS-a / MOOS-a)
Musaceae: The Banana Family
BANANA; PLANTAIN
Giant clumping herbs; palm tree form; immense long
    leaves; huge flower stems; large yellow fruit
Zones vary according to species
Sun to partial shade
Water lovers
Rich, humusy, moist, well-drained soil
Propagation by root division

A genus of about 40 species of large to immense herbs in tropical Africa, India, Sri Lanka, Southeast Asia, and northern Australia. They are suckering, fast-growing plants with thick, succulent, and often tall stems atop which grow the large to very large oblong to elliptic-shaped soft leaves with strong and thick midribs. The stems are called "pseudostems" because they are not true stems but rather a columnar collection of the old leaf bases of the plant, which fact is easily seen when a trunk is cut in two. The pseudostem blooms once and then slowly dies after the formation of fruit. The trunk should be cut down after the fruit matures. The inflo-rescence is often gigantic and pendent, and is a terminal spike, which flowering position thereby ends further growth of the pseudostem and leaf development. There are always other suckering pseudostems from the same root system to continue growth of the original plant. The flower spike contains many large, colored bracts from which emerge the relatively small flowers. The first flowers formed and the first to blossom are the female or bisexual flowers, and then the male flowers emerge and open. The position of these blossoms in relation to the ground depends, of course, on whether the spike is long and heavy enough to become pendent or whether it remains erect in the center of the leaves. Most edible and all commercially valuable fruiting bananas have very large and pendulous inflorescences. The fruit, of course, develops only from the female flowers which, when they emerge, exhibit the "proto-bananas" beneath their corollas.

There are no more tropical looking subjects than the bananas. They are second only to palms and ferns for creating the look and feel of the tropics, especially when they are in flower or fruit. In addition, because of their suckering habit, the clumps usually have leaves from the ground up, making them unexcelled for creating a lush effect, especially when planted in the angle of the corner of a building or other structure.

Given a climate with a warm enough winter, there are few plants that are easier to grow and maintain at their best. Several of the species are root hardy in zone 9 and quite often in zone 8. This means that the pseudostems may not reach enough age to flower and fruit, but that the beauty of the leaves will be there for late spring, summer, and well into the autumn. It also means that sometimes, especially in zone 9b and even zone 9a, there will be flowers and fruit. The flowering of the stems does not depend on the season, but rather how old the pseudostem is. It usually takes two seasons or two years for a pseudostem to flower and fruit.

For the impatient gardener in love with the tropical look, these giant herbs cannot be beat as they are among the fastest growing plants. Many are faster than all but the most tropical and largest bamboo species. And the bananas do not need time to become established as do the bamboo species. Many bananas can grow more than a foot a week in warm weather with sufficient moisture and a reasonably rich soil. Their roots are shallow and the rich soil need not be that deep. The best thing the gardener can do is to mulch the plants with leaf mold, and this can be obtained from the growing plants themselves.

There are three flies in this ointment: banana leaves are easily tattered by wind; with time, the banana clump migrates and the center of the clump tends to become bare as the rhizomatous roots spread outward; and the sap of all species almost indelibly stains all fabrics. The solution for the first problem is to plant bananas where they are protected at least to some extent from high winds. For the second problem, if it is a problem, the only solution is to rearrange the position of the young suckers before they become too massive to dig and move. The third problem is best avoided by wearing old clothes when cutting leaves, stems, or fruit clusters.

The taxonomy of the genus *Musa* is somewhat uncertain and still in a state of flux. The names of some species are subject to change if further studies are ever undertaken (and funded).

Musa acuminata (a-kyoo´-mi-NAIT-a) and its varieties and forms are originally native to most of tropical Asia and possibly tropical East Africa. It is hardy in zones 10 and 11. A very variable species in nature, it is one of the species involved in many important commercial fruiting hybrids and cultivars. The type is a large plant forming pseudostems to 20 feet or even more with 10-foot-long leaves that, unlike the leaves of most other species and forms with this size of leaf, are fairly erect and relatively narrow. The stems and the upper surfaces of the leaves are sometimes spotted with a reddish brown or purplish black maculation, and the leaves are often a reddish purple beneath. The inflorescence and the fruit cluster are large and pendulous with the 6-inch-long fruits maturing to a deep yellow color. ***Musa acuminata* var. *sumatrana*** (soo-ma-TRAHN-a) (synonyms *M. sumatrana, M. zebrina*) and its cultivar ***Musa acuminata* var. *sumatrana* 'Rubra'** (ROOB-ra) grow smaller than the type (usually only to about 8 feet) and have beautiful leaves with red undersides and with red streaks and blotches above. They are both called blood banana. ***Musa acuminata* 'Dwarf Cavendish'** (synonym *M. nana*, 'Dwarf Chinese'), which grows only to about 6 feet with dark green leaves and delicious 6-inch-long fruit, is variously called dwarf banana, dwarf Chinese banana, ladyfinger banana, and Canary Island banana. ***Musa acuminata* 'Giant Cavendish'** is a large form of 'Dwarf Cavendish' with green leaves. ***Musa acuminata* 'Grand Nain',** another cultivar of 'Dwarf Cavendish', grows to 6 feet with golden yellow fruit. ***Musa acuminata* 'Green Red'** grows to 10 feet or more with dark green leaves and beautiful red and orange fruit. ***Musa acuminata* 'Gros Michel'** grows to 12 feet or more with very large leaves and fruit clusters. ***Musa acuminata* 'Lacatan'** grows to 12 feet or more with large fruit clusters. ***Musa acuminata* 'Valery'** grows to about 6 feet with very large fruit.

Musa arnoldiana. See *Ensete ventricosum.*

Musa basjoo (BAHS-joo) is indigenous to the southern Japanese islands. It is called Japanese banana and is possibly the hardiest species, being root hardy in zones 7 through 11. It is a relatively small banana, growing only to 8 or 10 feet at the most with small leaves to 5 feet long. The inflorescence is usually erect with clusters of 3-inch-long unpalatable greenish yellow fruit. ***Musa basjoo* 'Variegata',** a beautiful cultivar, has white lines and blotches on the upper surfaces of the leaves.

Musa coccinea (kahk-SIN-ee-a) (synonym *M. uranoscopus*) occurs naturally in Myanmar (Burma), Laos, Thailand, Vietnam, Cambodia, and mainland Malaya, and is hardy in zones 10 and 11. It is called the flowering banana because of the large and erect brilliant red, long-lasting torch-shaped inflorescence. The plant grows only to about 7 feet with 4-foot-long bright green leaves. The erect flower stalk is a foot or more in height and the densely packed glossy scarlet narrow bracts are 6 to 12 inches long and are often tipped with yellow. The little flowers are yellow. The small orange-pink rounded fruits are only about 3 inches long. Plate 283.

Musa ensete. See *Ensete ventricosum.*

Musa fehi (FAY-hee) (synonym *M. troglodytarum*) is originally native to New Guinea and the adjacent islands of the South Pacific. Hardy in zones 10 and 11, it grows 12 to 15 feet and produces 10- to 12-foot-long relatively narrow leaves atop green trunks with purplish bases. The sap is also purplish. The inflorescence is erect and consists of green bracts and pinkish white flowers. The 6-inch-long fruits are orange and unpalatable unless cooked. The plant is called fehi or fe'i.

Musa nana. See *M. acuminata* 'Dwarf Cavendish'.

Musa ornata (or-NAIT-a) (synonym *M. rosacea*) is native to India and Myanmar (Burma). It is hardy in zones 10 and 11, although the root is usually hardy in zone 9b. The trunks grow to 8 feet and are green with blackish purple blotches. The deep olive green leaves are about 6 feet long. The plant is grown mostly for the beautiful erect inflorescence, which consists of large narrowly ovate pink to deep rose bracts with orange-yellow flowers. The small fruits stand erect also and are orange in color.

Musa ×paradisiaca (pair´-a-deez-ee-AHK-a / pair-a-DIS-ya-ka) (synonym *M. sapientum*) is a hybrid between *M. acuminata* and *M. balbisiana,* a species from most of tropical Asia and esteemed for its resistance to diseases but not grown commercially or as an ornamental. *Musa ×paradisiaca* is root hardy in zones 8b through 11 but very seldom fruits in the colder parts of its range. It and its several hundred cultivars are probably the world's most widely grown banana and are the most common varieties in the market. The pseudostems grow to 20 feet or more with 10- to 12-foot-long deep green leaves. The inflorescence has large succulent purple and deep red bracts that unfurl to reveal the white or yellow-orange flowers. The fruit clusters are immense, and the individual fruits are large and yellow when mature. ***Musa ×paradisiaca* 'Ae Ae'** (synonym 'Koae') has its trunk, leaves, and fruit beautifully striped with white. According to W. O. Lessard, the plants need a soil relatively low in pH lest the leaves turn pure white and be unable to photosynthesize. ***Musa ×paradisiaca* 'Horse Banana'** (synonym 'Orinoco') is the most common variety planted for landscape purposes all over the Deep South, the Gulf Coast, Arizona, and California. It grows large and fast and is a beautiful and valuable addition to the tropical look with edible fruit that is best when cooked. ***Musa ×paradisiaca* 'Mysore'** has large densely packed clusters of small yellow fruit. ***Musa ×paradisiaca* 'Vittata'** (vi-TAHT-a) has supremely beautiful leaves that are irregularly variegated with white and lighter green and have red margins.

Musa sapientum. See *M. ×paradisiaca.*

Musa sumatrana. See *M. acuminata* var. *sumatrana.*

Musa troglodytarum. See *M. fehi.*

Musa uranoscopus. See *M. coccinea.*

Musa velutina (ve-LOOT-i-na) is native to northern India and is root hardy in zones 9 through 11. It is a dwarf species growing only to about 6 feet. The dark green leaves have midribs that are a vivid red on their undersides. The erect inflorescence consists of large pink bracts, yellow flowers, and rose-colored small fruits, and is very beautiful and long-lasting. Plate 284.

Musa zebrina. See *M. acuminata* var. *sumatrana.*

MUSSAENDA

(mus-SEEN-da / myoo-say-END-a)
Rubiaceae: The Coffee, Gardenia, Ixora Family
Common names vary according to species
Large-leaved shrubs; showy pink, red, yellow, or
    white flowers
Zones 10b and 11; marginal in zone 10a
Sun
Average but regular amounts of moisture; NOT
    drought tolerant
Humusy, well-drained soil
Propagation by cuttings

A large genus of about 200 species of shrubs and a few climbers in tropical Africa, Asia, and some islands of the South Pacific. All have unusual inflorescences that are broad clusters of small tubular flowers, each with one highly modified and colorful large sepal. The modified and leaflike sepals are in colors of white, yellow, pink, or red, and are what make the show. These spectacular shrubs are easy of culture, needing only some sun, moderately rich and well-drained soil, and a regular supply of moisture to provide a nearly year-round supply of color. The inflorescences should be removed after all their color fades to stimulate new flowering and because the wilted blossoms are not especially attractive.

Mussaenda erythrophylla (e-rit´-ro-FYL-la) is native to tropical West Africa where it grows as a sprawling shrub to as much as 30 feet, but it is usually no more than 15 feet tall in cultivation. The 6-inch-long elliptic velvety leaves are a deep green and very hairy beneath. The bracts are usually scarlet but may be pink to deep rose also. The enlarged sepals are about 3 inches long, and the calyx tubes are usually yellow but sometimes red. The plant is sometimes called Ashanti blood and red flag plant, but it is easier and seems more satisfying to just use the genus name with the addition of the word *red.* Plate 285.

Mussaenda glabra (GLAB-ra) (synonym *M. luteola*) is also native to tropical Africa and makes a small sprawling shrub with 3-inch-long elliptic leaves. The inflorescences of airy long-stalked yellowish white se-pals subtending bright yellow half-inch-wide corolla tubes give an extremely graceful aspect to the shrub in bloom.

Mussaenda luteola. See *M. glabra.*

Mussaenda philippica (fi-LIP-pi-ka) is indigenous to the Philippines. It grows to 10 or 12 feet and is quite similar to *M. erythrophylla* except that the large sepals are white. The shrub suffers under the vernacular names of Buddha's lamp and virgin tree. Plate 286.

MYRCIARIA (meer-see-AHR-ee-a)

Myrtaceae: The Myrtle, Eucalyptus Family
JABOTICABA (ja-boat-i-KAH-ba)
Small evergreen trees; glossy leaves; white flowers on
    trunk and branches; purple and black fruit
Zones 10 and 11; marginal in zone 9b
Sun to partial shade
Average but regular amounts of moisture
Rich, humusy, well-drained soil
Propagation by seed; named cultivars are grafted

A small genus of about 40 evergreen trees and shrubs in South America. The species are cauliflorous; that is, they produce flowers and fruit on the trunk and main branches of the plant. All these plants were formerly a part of the genus *Eugenia.* One species is widely grown in tropical regions for the delicious fruit. **Myrciaria cauliflora** (kawl-i-FLOR-a) (synonym *Eugenia cauliflora*) is native to southern Brazil. It grows naturally but rather slowly in cultivation into a large multitrunked shrub to 20 or 30 feet with ascending branches, a rounded and dense crown, and a light brown flaking bark. It is easily trained when young to tree form. The leaves are a deep glossy green, lance-shaped, and 2 to 3 inches long. The little trees flower in summer, and the trunk and primary branches are sometimes covered with the small green and white flowers with their many protruding white stamens. The fruits mature in late summer and are round, purplish black, and about an inch in diameter with the taste of a somewhat acidic grape. There are named cultivars. The tree is lovely as a patio subject or planted in small groups. It is intolerant of drought conditions and must never be allowed to suffer from that condition, which is another reason to use it as a patio subject. It is quite tender to frost when young and is likely to be killed at 28°F, but when mature can withstand about 25°F without severe damage.

Myrciaria edulis. See *Eugenia aggregata.*

MYRTILLOCACTUS

(mur-TIL-lo-kak-tus)
Cactaceae: The Cactus Family
Common names vary according to species
Large treelike ribbed columnar cactuses; small white
    flowers; red and red-purple edible fruit
Zones 10 and 11
Sun
Drought tolerant

Average well-drained soil
Propagation by seed and cuttings

A small genus of only four beautiful large, columnar, and ribbed, freely branching cactus species in western and southern Mexico and Guatemala. They have small white flowers and small round edible fruit. The stems (trunks) are relatively fat and gracefully ascending from near the bases of the plants. Each column has only a few ribs from which the small clusters of black spines grow.

Myrtillocactus cochal (ko-CHAHL) is found naturally in the Sonoran desert of Mexico and in Baja California. It grows to 10 feet with many curved trunks arising from near the base of the plant. Each greenish yellow stem has six to eight shallow ribs dotted with the regularly spaced small clusters of black spines, giving a very exotic and geometric effect. The white flowers appear in summer and are about an inch wide. The sweet-tasting dark red and round fruits are also about an inch wide.

Myrtillocactus geometrizans (jee-o-MET-ri-zanz) has very many nearly straight fat bluish green stems growing to 12 or sometimes 15 feet. Each stem has five or six fat ribs with many small reddish brown to black short spines radiating from regularly spaced tiny areoles. The new growth is almost a pure blue and has a glistening glaucous coating. The mature cactus plant looks remarkably like some of the large succulent *Euphorbia* species from Africa. The white summer flowers are an inch or slightly more wide and appear near the tops of the columns. The inch-wide round fruits are purple. This exceptionally beautiful species is sometimes called blue candle or blue flame.

Myrtillocactus schenckii (SHENK-ee-eye) is native to southwestern Mexico and grows to 15 feet or more with relatively slender trunks and many black and red spines. The white summer flowers are about 2 inches wide, and the inch-wide fruits are scarlet in color.

NANNORRHOPS (NAN-no-rahps)
Palmae (Arecaceae): The Palm Family
MAZARI PALM
Small clustering fan-leaved palm with bluish leaves
Zones 7b through 11
Sun
Drought tolerant
Average well-drained soil
Propagation by seed

A monotypic palm genus native to desert areas of Pakistan and the Arabian Peninsula. *Nannorrhops ritchiana* (rich-ee-AHN-a) is a palmate-leaved, short-trunked clumping species. Its individual trunks die off after flowering and fruiting, but this does not alter the landscape effect for it renews its short trunks at regular intervals. The bluish leaves are costapalmate and narrow, having an outline of generally less than a semicir-

cle, and the leaf segments are stiff. The great landscape value of this palm is as a small accent because of the leaf color. It grows very slowly and, with time, attains a height of 8 to 10 feet and a spread of that much or more. Being a desert species it demands perfect drainage but is otherwise not very particular as to soil type. It should not be planted in shade.

NEANTHE. See *Chamaedorea elegans.*

NELUMBO (nel-UM-bo)
Nymphaeaceae: The Water Lily Family
LOTUS; WATER LOTUS
Aquatic plants; giant round leaves above water surface; large fragrant flowers; decorative pods
Zones not indicative; water temperature more important
Sun
Aquatic
Very rich wet soil
Propagation by root division and seed

A small genus of only two aquatic species in North America and tropical Asia. The plants are usually placed into the family Nymphaeaceae, which includes the true water lilies. Some taxonomists think they should have their own family, Nelumbonaceae, and, according to Perry D. Slocum, there is genetic evidence to support this position. In any case lotus grow in mostly shallow water and have thick cylindrical roots from which the leaves and flowers grow. They can be grown anywhere their large roots do not freeze in winter. The warmer the climate, the deeper the water in which these plants will grow, as deep water in colder climates takes too long to warm up in the spring. If the roots are planted in shallow water in tropical and subtropical climates, the leaves will be very much above the water level and will create the impression of a large shrub growing atop the water.

The immense peltate round leaves are as much as 3 feet across and arise directly from the thick roots. They are held well above the surface of the water and have puckered centers corresponding to the attachment of the petiole beneath. The large flowers, which appear in late spring and summer and which are also held above the water's surface, are multipetaled. The many outer sepals grade almost imperceptibly into the true petals, which are generally wider than those of most true water lilies. The most distinctive aspect of these flowers is the large flat-topped yellow or green pistil in the center, which is surrounded by a mass of filamentous yellow stamens. This pistil becomes woody when the corolla has fallen and the seeds have matured at the top. The woody pods are long lasting and quite ornamental with their seed cavities and are used in flower arranging and other crafts.

Because of the leaf and flower sizes there are no more exotic and tropical looking aquatic plants than these.

Given a rich soil, sun, and a climate in which the roots will not freeze in winter, they are exceedingly easy of culture. One plants them and forgets them. They need a certain amount of summer heat to bloom but, according to Perry D. Slocum, severely hot summers like those found in the hot desert climates of the southwestern United States tend to retard the formation of blossoms as do high summer temperatures that do not reach 75°F (like those experienced in the U.S. Pacific Northwest). Lotus roots, leaves, and seeds are edible and are much relished in Asia.

Nelumbo lutea (LOOT-ee-a / loo-TEE-a) occurs naturally over the eastern United States from Minnesota to Florida and westward to eastern Texas. It has bluish green leaves 2 feet wide and pure deep yellow flowers that approach a foot in diameter. There are several cultivars available, all in shades of yellow. The plant is sometimes called water chinquapin or American lotus.

Nelumbo nucifera (noo-SIF-e-ra) is native to tropical Asia and Australia and has vernacular names of Egyptian lotus, sacred lotus, and Hindu lotus. It is a somewhat larger than *N. lutea*, with larger leaves and flowers. The leaves, which are as much as 3 feet wide and a deep yellowish green to viridian in color, are, like those of *N. lutea*, waxy and water repellent. The deliciously fragrant flowers are similar to those of the American lotus, but are slightly larger and are in shades of white, pink, rose, or red and combinations thereof. The typical color combination is deep pink invaded by yellowish white striations from the bases of the petals. There are several outstandingly beautiful, naturally occurring varieties and horticultural cultivars with pure white to almost pure red flowers. Some of these have double blossoms, the most beautiful of which is *Nelumbo nucifera* 'Mrs. Perry D. Slocum'. Plate 287.

NEODYPSIS (nee-o-DIP-sis)
Palmae (Arecaceae): The Palm Family
Common names vary according to species
Medium-sized feather-leaved palms with beautiful
    and unusual crownshafts
Zones vary according to species
Sun to partial sun
Average but regular amounts of moisture
Average well-drained soil
Propagation by seed

A small genus of 14 palm species in Madagascar. Most are solitary-trunked, but a few species are clustering. All have large pinnate leaves. Madagascar is a large island with several climates, and these palms occupy most of them, from semiarid savannahs to mountainous rain forests. All are magnificent palms, but only two are common in cultivation.

Neodypsis decaryi (de-KAHR-ee-eye) is native to the drier parts of Madagascar and is hardy in zones 10 and 11 and marginal in zone 9b. It makes a trunk of 20 feet in height or sometimes more that is dark in color

with gray rings. The crownshaft is unique among palms: it is three-sided (or three-angled) and is triangular in cross section, the leaves growing out from three points. This phenomenon creates a truly spectacular landscape subject because the leaf bases are light gray and the great arching leaves are a bluish to grayish green. The shape of the crownshaft has led to the common name of triangle palm. The leaves are fairly stiff and erect and are recurved only at their tips. The leaflets emerge from the rachis at an angle of somewhat less than 90°, making the leaves V-shaped in cross section. Another unusual feature of these leaves is the long persistent threads that hang from them. This sensational landscape subject has a great fountain sweep of grayish leaves that is seen to best advantage against a dark green background. This palm must have perfect drainage. It is intolerant of poor limestone-based soils and prefers a sandy and humusy soil. It grows fairly rapidly in warm climates but slower in cool Mediterranean regions. It is hardy to about 28°F, but any temperature below that causes significant damage. The plant is slow to recover from such damage, and usually languishes for a time before finally succumbing to the damage, especially in moister climes where fungus attacks the growing point.

Neodypsis lastelliana (la-stel´-lee-AHN-a) occurs naturally in approximately the same regions of Madagascar as *N. decaryi*, but is completely intolerant of frost. Thus it is not a good choice outside zones 10b and 11, although it is marginally hardy in zone 10a. It has but one outward characteristic in common with the triangle palm: the erect aspect of the leaves. It grows slightly taller than the triangle palm, to as much as 30 feet or more, and has trunks that are much lighter in color. The unbelievably beautiful light-colored (sometimes almost white) trunks have greenish rings of leaf scars. The crownshaft is supremely beautiful as it is fairly large and is covered in a tight reddish brown felt, a feature that has led to the common name of teddy bear palm. It is, alas, also sometimes called the redneck palm. The leaf rachises are erect and fairly stiff, but the bright green leaflets are pliable and emerge at right angles from the rachis, creating a single plane to the pinnate leaf. This lush and tropical looking palm species is tougher than it looks. It is adaptable to a wide variety of soil types, except for very poor and limy soils, and has some drought tolerance when established. Plate 288.

NEOREGELIA
(nee´-o-re-JEEL-ee-a / nee´-o-re-GAIL-ee-a)
Bromeliaceae: The Pineapple, Bromeliad Family
Common names vary according to species
Spreading rosettes of colorful straplike spiny-
    margined leaves; low flower heads in rosette center
Zones 10 and 11
Partial shade to full sun
Water lovers
Leaf mold or epiphytic mix
Propagation by transplanting of suckers and by seed

A genus of about 100 clumping epiphytic bromeliad species mostly in southeastern Brazil. Most have spreading rosettes of spiny-margined highly colored leaves, although a few are vase-shaped. Many species have long-ranging stolons that climb tree limbs or create breathtaking cascades (if there is nothing on which to cling) of plants that seem to dance in the air. The inflorescence is a densely packed cluster of purple, blue, or white (or combinations thereof) three-petaled flowers, which are individually gorgeous but generally tiny. These are some of the most dependably beautiful bromeliad species because of their usually highly colored leaves, although the dense flower spikes are mostly hidden by the leaves since the former do not normally rise above the plane of the leaf rosette. Leaf color ranges from all shades of green through yellow, orange, pink, and red, and there is usually variegation, sometimes exceedingly beautiful, especially during the flowering period when the center of the rosette changes color. The spinier species strongly resemble small colorful *Agave* species. Many of the most brilliantly colored species, hybrids, and cultivars need full or nearly full sun to bring out their beauty. They are easy of culture in partial shade to almost full sun with adequate moisture. All the plants listed here may be grown terrestrially with a loose and fast-draining medium, and the larger species are much used in tropical climes as bedding plants to add color and form.

Neoregelia ampullacea (am-pyool-LAIS-ee-a) is a beautiful small species that has long-running stolons and makes a wonderful cascade of plants. The light green 6-inch-long leaves are straplike to almost spatulate in shape and are spotted with reddish brown above and below. This species does not form a colored center when in flower, but the lovely violet blossoms are a remarkable complement to the green and brown leaves. There are wonderfully colored hybrids of this species with mostly deep red to deep wine red coloration; the other parent(s) are mostly unknown.

Neoregelia carcharodon (kar-KAIR-o-dahn) is one of the larger species, and its rosette can reach a diameter of 2 feet or more. The leaves are as much as 2 feet long and 6 inches wide and are armed with large forward pointing teeth along their margins. The plant is variable in color, ranging from pure green to a splendid bronzy orange. The non-green form should be sought, bought, and grown, as it is one of the most beautiful bromeliad species. The plants need partial sun to look their best.

Neoregelia carolinae (kair-o-LYN-ee) is perhaps the most common species, but the type, a large green rosette with brilliant red markings when in flower and probably of garden origin, is seldom available because of the many superior cultivars and hybrids. *Neoregelia carolinae* 'Medallion' has bright apple green leaves with the center of the rosette the most intense scarlet and bronzy red to brownish red. *Neoregelia carolinae* 'Meyendorffii' (my-en-DORF-fee-eye) is an extraordinarily brilliant cultivar whose large deep green leaves are wonderfully striped with longitudinal bands of red, orange, and deep yellow. The central and newest leaves are almost pure scarlet when the plant is in flower. *Neoregelia carolinae* 'Perfecta' (per-FEK-ta) is somewhat similar to 'Meyendorffii', but the leaf striations are more regular, making the plant even more elegant. *Neoregelia carolinae* 'Tricolor' (TRY-kul-or) has stunningly beautiful white and pink longitudinal striations on its leaves. The type and its cultivars are often called blushing bromeliad. Plates 289 and 290.

Neoregelia compacta (kahm-PAK-ta) is a small species with deep green narrowly strap-shaped leaves less than a foot long and forming a somewhat vaselike rosette. Fast growing, it propagates itself by long ranging stolons and is one of the species that makes such a beautiful cascade of plant material. *Neoregelia compacta* 'Bossa Nova' is one of the most handsome bromeliads with foot-long straplike leaves bordered with wide white bands on each margin. It is a thrilling experience to see this cultivar spilling from tree limbs, in a hanging basket, or cascading over a wall. It needs partial sun to keep its wonderful coloring.

Neoregelia concentrica (kahn-SENT-ri-ka) is one of the largest species in the genus. It can form a rosette 3 feet wide with wide light green prickly margined leaves that are spotted with purplish brown and have red tips. The unadorned species is now hard to find. *Neoregelia concentrica* 'Plutonis' (ploo-TON-is) is quite common and has a central core of deep violet-spotted leaves.

Neoregelia cruenta (kroo-ENT-a) is another large species, forming rosettes 3-feet wide or even more. The leaves are yellow-green with red tips and as much as 3 feet long but only 2 or 3 inches wide. This variable species has gradations in leaf color to pure red with red bands on the undersides of the leaves. A planting of differently colored forms is a stunning sight. The plants need much light to remain colorful.

Neoregelia kautskyi (KOWT-skee-eye) is an entrancing species with wide foot-long rather thin leaves, which are a beautiful yellow-green, shading to a deep lime-green at their bases. The leaves are heavily streaked and blotched with a wonderful brownish red color. The color combination is irresistible and makes a vibrant yet subtle statement in the landscape.

Neoregelia marmorata (mar-mo-RAIT-a) is a fairly large species with foot-long widespreading leaves of mint green spotted with irregular reddish brown maculations and tipped with vivid red. This beauty is quite common and easy of culture and is often termed marble plant.

Neoregelia pauciflora (paws-i-FLOR-a) is an enchanting little species with long-running stolons, which create a curtain of airy diminutive vase-shaped mint green plants. The leaves are usually notched at their apices and are always flecked with dark purple.

Neoregelia pendula (PEN-dyoo-la) is native to the rain forests of eastern Ecuador and northern Peru, and is a very tender species, adaptable only to zones 10b and

11. It has small rosettes, but produces long-ranging roots that form more rosettes, resulting in a veritable cascade of the small colorful plants. Each rosette consists of bright green shiny long and much recurved spiny-margined leaves, the center ones a vivid red and purplish red in color. This species is one of the choicest small bromeliads.

Neoregelia spectabilis (spek-TAB-i-lis) is one of the commonest species in the genus, and with good reason. The plant is fairly large with 2-foot-wide rosettes of broad thick tough olive green leaves that are tipped in red and banded with horizontal gray stripes beneath. ***Neoregelia spectabilis*** **'Variegata'** (vair´-ee-a-GAIT-a) is a superb form with orange to yellow longitudinal striations on the upper surfaces of the leaves. It needs good light to remain vividly colored. Because of the red tips on the leaves, this beauty is called fingernail plant and painted fingernail.

NEPHELIUM. See *Euphoria*.

NEPHROLEPIS
(nef-ro-LEEP-iss / nef-RO-le-pis)
Oleandraceae: The Sword Fern Family
SWORD FERNS
Fairly large terrestrial ferns with relatively narrow and
    long fronds
Zones vary according to species
Partial shade to sun
Water lovers
Humusy, well-drained soil
Propagation by root division and spores

A genus of about 30 species of terrestrial ferns found all over the tropical and subtropical world. The leaves of most species are pinnate, but some are as much as five-pinnate. The plants propagate themselves by creeping stolons and make beautiful clumps in a fairly short time. Most species are commonly referred to as sword ferns as the typical shape of the frond is relatively long and narrow. Ladder fern is also used, especially in Europe, as the leaflets of most species are fairly wide, regularly spaced, and mostly of equal size, giving, indeed, somewhat the look of a ladder to the individual frond. Not only is the genus widespread, but one of the species and its forms is possibly the most widely cultivated fern species in the world. All the species are bold and tropical looking ferns and, for the most part, among the easiest to grow.

Nephrolepis acuminata (a-kyoo-mi-NAIT-a) is native to Indonesia and Malaysia and is hardy in zones 10 and 11 although it often succeeds in zone 9b. It has long arching pinnate fronds with widely spaced leaflets. The fronds reach 3 feet in length and are a bright medium green in color.

Nephrolepis acutifolia (a-kyoot-i-FO-lee-a) is native to a very wide area of Malaysia and northern Australia, and is hardy in zones 10 and 11. It grows large and forms colonies rather quickly. The fronds are relatively erect and are as much as 5 feet long with closely and regularly spaced oblong light green leaflets. This bold and quite tropical looking beauty can grow in full sun and is somewhat resistant to dry conditions once it is established.

Nehprolepis biserrata (by-ser-RAIT-a) is indigenous to an immense area covering most parts of the tropical Southern Hemisphere and has become naturalized in almost every tropical region of the globe. It is usually hardy only in zones 10 and 11, but is often successful in zone 9b. The beautifully arching pinnate leaves are as much as 5 feet long with wide, evenly spaced lance-shaped dark green leaflets with remote teeth on their margins. The plants grow large and fast, and quickly make large colonies. They are mildly invasive, although easily removed from where they are not wanted. This species is one of the most beautiful and tropical looking in the genus. There are several cultivars, some with forked leaflets.

Nephrolepis cordifolia (kord-i-FO-lee-a) is so widespread in tropical regions that its original habitat is unknown. It is hardy in zones 9b through 11. The bright green erect fronds grow to 3 feet long with regularly spaced medium green lanceolate to oblong leaflets usually with wavy margins. The spacing of the leaflets has led to the vernacular name of ladder fern. This species is also called erect sword fern. It grows fast, readily colonizes ground, and can grow in partial shade or almost full sun. This variable species has produced several cultivars, which vary in plant size, leaf size, and leaf shape. Some of the forms are unrecognizable as belonging to the species. ***Nephrolepis cordifolia*** **'Duffii'**, in particular, looks as much like a *Selaginella* species as a fern. According to David L. Jones, this cultivar is more tender to cold than is the type.

Nephrolepis exaltata (ex-ahl-TAIT-a) is so widespread in tropical and subtropical regions that its original habitat is uncertain but is probably tropical America. It is hardy in zones 9b through 11 and is usually successful in zone 9a. The typical species is hard to find, but has produced a bewildering number and variety of cultivars, which probably make it the world's most widely grown fern species. Most cultivars are not as hardy as the type. The type has fronds that are as much as 5 or more feet long with regularly spaced lance-shaped light green leaflets. The leaflets are alternately arranged (in contradistinction to most other species) and united in a more or less parallel plane along the rachis. ***Nephrolepis exaltata*** **'Bostoniensis'** (bahsto´-nee-ENS-is), the Boston fern, was the first and original mutation to be named. It is somewhat more tender to cold than the species. This beautiful form has wider and more arching leaves than the type. There are now several cultivars of this cultivar with plant sizes from typical to dwarf and leaf color in varying shades of green. The other cultivars are so varied in appearance, ranging from pinnate to several-pinnate, and so many in number that only a few can be described here. Very few of these cultivars are as cold hardy as the type. Furthermore, some of the forms have such fine leaves that overhead watering tends to damage them. Other forms tend to revert to the type or the previous cultivar from whence they were derived, and some of the forms are true monstrosities although some others are exquisitely beautiful. *Nephrolepis exaltata* **'Dreyeri'** (DRY-ureye) is gracefully arching in form. *Nephrolepis exaltata* **'Elegantissima'** (el-e-gan-TIS-si-ma) has bipinnate leaves. *Nephrolepis exaltata* **'Randolphii'** (ran-DAHL-fee-eye) is gracefully arching in form. *Nephrolepis exaltata* **'Scholzelii'** (skoal-ZEL-eeeye) has bipinnate leaves. *Nephrolepis exaltata* **'Teddy Junior'** is compact with beautifully ruffled pinnate leaves. Plate 291.

　　Nephrolepis falcata (fal-KAIT-a) is indigenous to a wide area from India and Sri Lanka through Myanmar (Burma) and Southeast Asia to New Guinea and is hardy in zones 10 and 11. It is a lovely species with long and gracefully pendent dark green leathery pinnate fronds composed of very many dark green alternately arranged lanceolate leaflets. The plants are fairly tough, but not cold hardy and thrive in partial shade. *Nephrolepis falcata* forma *furcans* (FOOR-kanz) is a striking form whose leaflets are forked at their apices, giving an elegant and airy appearance to the long leaves. This form looks superb on a wall with soil pockets or in a hanging basket.

　　Nephrolepis pendula (PEN-dyoo-la) is native to tropical America and is hardy in zones 10 and 11. It is similar in form to *N. falcata* but is a somewhat smaller plant.

NEPHTHYTIS. See *Syngonium*.

NERIUM (NEER-ee-um)

Apocynaceae: The Oleander, Frangipani, Vinca
　　Family
OLEANDER
Evergreen shrubs and small trees; linear leaves;
　　masses of white, yellow, pink, and red flowers
Zones vary according to cultivar
Sun
Drought tolerant
Average well-drained soil
Propagation by cuttings

　　A monotypic genus native to a very large area of the subtropical Old World, from the Mediterranean region eastward through China and into Japan. *Nerium oleander* (o-lee-AN-dur) (synonym *N. indicum*) is a large shrub that may be trained to a small tree form when young. The bark and trunk are smooth and a deep gray in color, and the branches are semirubbery and pliable. The dark green leaves, which are linear-elliptic to lanceolate in shape with a prominent and lighter colored midrib, are as much as 12 inches long but usually no more than 8 inches. The leaves are borne on short petioles and grow in tiers or whorls of three around the stems. The type blooms prolifically in spring and early summer with flat-topped clusters of white to pink or red flowers. Each flower is funnel-shaped with flaring and twisted corolla lobes (the twist indicative and characteristic of the family). One to 3 inches wide, the flowers have fringed throats in the center of the blossom. There is a definite fragrance to the blossoms of most plants, somewhat similar to daffodils, but some people seem incapable of sensing it. The flowers usually but not always form linear ridged 6-inch-long seed pods, which contain many thin flaky seeds and which should be removed when they are forming. All parts of these plants are quite poisonous and there have been reports of several fatalities over the years. Even the smoke from the burning wood of oleander is poisonous.

　　The plants are famous for their tolerance of drought and other adverse conditions including poor soil and saline conditions. The two things they must have to bloom well are sun and summer heat. All the forms are supremely well adapted as hedges, both large and small, withstanding well almost any amount of shearing as the plants bloom on new growth. It is, however, as patio trees that the larger growing cultivars are so exquisite looking with their large evergreen leaves and masses of bright-colored flowers. In some areas oleanders are planted unwisely as specimen shrubs in the lawn or as foundation plantings, where they always look out of place in isolation, even when in full bloom.

　　There are now many cultivars ranging in size from no more than 3 feet in height to well over 20 feet and in flower color from pure white through yellow, pink, salmon, and fiery red. Some have double blossoms, which add nothing to the landscape value, and the spent flowers remain too long on the plant and create a quite messy appearance as they wilt. At least one form has leaves variegated with yellow striations. Some forms are almost ever-blooming, and there is a wide range of cold hardiness among the cultivars.

DWARF FORMS: *Nerium oleander* **'Hawaii'** grows to about 6 feet, has deep salmon-pink flowers, and is hardy to temperatures in the low 20s. *Nerium oleander* **'Little Red'** grows to about 6 feet, has pure red flowers, and is hardy to temperatures slightly below 20°F. *Nerium oleander* **'Marrakesh'** grows only to about 5 feet, has pure red flowers, and is hardy to about 22°F. *Nerium oleander* **'Morocco'** grows to about 6 feet maximum, has white flowers, and is hardy to about 20°F. *Nerium oleander* **'Petite Pink'** grows to 4 or 5 feet, has bright pure pink flowers, and is hardy to temperatures in the mid 20s. *Nerium oleander* **'Petite Salmon'** grows to about 4 feet high, has exquisite light salmon-pink flowers, and is hardy to temperatures in the mid 20s.

INTERMEDIATE-SIZED FORMS: *Nerium oleander* **'Algiers'** grows to about 8 feet, has dark red flowers, and is hardy to about 20°F. *Nerium oleander*

'Casablanca' grows from 6 to 8 feet in height, has pure white flowers, and is hardy to about 20°F. *Nerium oleander* 'Ruby Lace' grows to about 8 feet in height, has light red flowers, and is hardy to about 24°F. *Nerium oleander* 'Tangier' grows to 6 or 8 feet in height, has pure pink flowers, and is hardy to about 22°F.

LARGE FORMS: *Nerium oleander* 'Calypso' grows to 10 or 12 feet, has cherry flowers, and is hardy to temperatures somewhat below 20°F. *Nerium oleander* 'Cherry Ripe' grows to 12 feet or more, has bright red flowers, and is hardy to temperatures somewhat below 20°F. *Nerium oleander* 'Hardy Pink' grows to at least 12 feet, has deep pink to salmon-pink flowers, and is hardy to temperatures slightly below 20°F. *Nerium oleander* 'Hardy Red' grows to at least 12 feet, has large bright red flowers, and is hardy to temperatures slightly below 20°F. *Nerium oleander* 'Isle of Capri' grows to 10 feet or more, has pale yellow flowers, and is hardy to about 20°F. *Nerium oleander* 'Sister Agnes', one of the largest cultivars, grows to as much as 20 feet in height, has pure white crinkly flowers, and is hardy to temperatures slightly below 20°F.

NICOLAIA. See *Etlingera*.

NOLINA (no-LEEN-a / no-LYN-a)
Agavaceae: The Agave Family
BEAR GRASS; BASKET GRASS
Yuccalike thick-trunked rosettes; many narrow
   arching grasslike leaves; large panicles of flowers
Zones vary according to species
Sun
Average but regular amounts of moisture; drought
   tolerant when established
Average well-drained soil
Propagation by seed and transplanting of suckers

A small genus of about two dozen species of desert perennials, which grow palmlike with large and dense rosettes of long linear and very narrow recurving tough leaves usually atop thick trunks. Along their margins, the leaves have tiny teeth and curling brown or gray linear fibers. The innumerable tiny whitish flowers appear in tall panicles from the leaf crown and are held well above the leaves. These plants are spectacular forms for the cactus and succulent garden, especially when in bloom. They need a soil with unimpeded drainage and a site in full sun. The genus is closely allied to *Beaucarnea* and *Dasylirion* (sotols) and has been and is included therein by some taxonomists. *Nolina* species differ from *Dasylirion* species by having leaves that are generally much more pliable with very minute teeth along their margins as opposed to the large teeth on the sotol leaves. In addition, the inflorescences of *Nolina* species are much broader and showier.

Nolina bigelovii (big-e-LO-vee-eye) (synonym *Dasylirion bigelovii*) is indigenous to southern Arizona and adjacent Baja California, and is hardy in zones 9 through 11 and marginal in zone 8b. It seldom makes a trunk but has a large rosette, as much as 6 feet in height and somewhat more in width, of very many narrow and tough recurved deep green leaves, usually with a bluish cast. The summer inflorescence is plumelike and of majestic proportions standing as much as 10 feet tall.

Nolina erumpens (ee-RUMP-enz) is native to western Texas, southern New Mexico, and adjacent northern Mexico, and is hardy in zones 7 through 11. With great age the plants form trunks as much as 5 or even 6 feet tall, but for many years they are simply 5-foot-wide dense fountainlike rosettes of tough grassy dark green leaves. The inflorescence is about 6 feet tall.

Nolina longifolia (lahn-ji-FO-lee-a) (synonym *Dasylirion longifolium*) is native to Mexico and is hardy in zones 9b through 11 and marginal in zone 9a. With age the plant makes a thick trunk to as much as 9 feet tall, atop which grows the large rosette of typical narrow and tough linear leaves. The upper trunk may or may not form a few branches. The flower stalk of this species is not as tall as those of most others but is, nevertheless, impressive. This species is sometimes called the Mexican grass-tree.

Nolina microcarpa (myk-ro-KARP-a) naturally occurs in southern Arizona, New Mexico, Texas, and adjacent northern Mexico, and is hardy in zones 7b through 11. The plant is similar to *N. bigelovii* in form, but the flower spike is not quite as tall.

Nolina parryi (PAIR-ree-eye) is indigenous to southwestern California and is hardy in zones 8 through 11. It makes a short branched trunk with 4- to 5-foot-wide rosettes of bright green leaves that have tiny teeth rather than the splitting fibers. The inflorescence is tall, plumose, and massive.

NORONHIA
(no-ROAN-ee-a / no-ROAN-ya)
Oleaceae: Jasmine, Ligustrum, Olive Family
MADAGASCAR OLIVE
Small tree with large, leathery dark green leaves;
   clusters of inch-long purple fruit
Zones 10 and 11
Sun
Drought tolerant
Average well-drained soil
Propagation by seed

A genus of about 40 species of large shrubs and small trees in Madagascar and adjacent Indian Ocean islands. They all have relatively large leathery leaves, often of great beauty. The small whitish flowers, with four succulent petals, are in clusters. The fruit is a one-seeded berry with edible flesh. Only one species is planted to any extent in tropical regions. *Noronhia emarginata* (ee-mar-ji-NAIT-a) is indigenous to Madagascar and is a small tree with a smooth gray trunk and an open but fairly narrow crown of large leathery leaves. The beautiful, broadly elliptic to obovate leaves are 7 to 8 inches long, thick and leathery, and dark green above but lighter beneath. They are notched at their ends and borne on short leaf stalks, have a prominent and lighter colored midrib, and look much like the leaves of *Clusia rosea* (autograph tree). The yellowish white flowers appear in late spring in clusters in the leaf axils and, while not spectacular, are wonderfully fragrant and lovely to contemplate up close. The fruit is olive-shaped, about an inch long, and is a deep purple or purplish green in color, with reportedly edible and sweet flesh. These little trees are wonderfully attractive and, because of their drought tolerance and salt tolerance, are perfect choices for landscaping subjects near the beach or as patio trees.

NOTHOPANAX. See *Polyscias.*

NYMPHAEA (nim-FEE-a)
Nymphaeaceae: The Water Lily Family
WATER LILY
Aquatic plants with rounded floating leaves; large, many-petaled flowers of every color
Zones not indicative; water temperature more important
Sun
Aquatic
Rich soil
Propagation by root division and seed

A genus of about 50 species of aquatic plants distributed in all regions of the earth where the bottoms of ponds and lakes do not freeze. All the species have relatively large rounded floating peltate leaves with lobes on one end and showy many-petaled flowers that may be approximately level with the water's surface or may rise significantly above the water level. The leaf lobes may or may not be overlapping. The plants mostly bloom in spring, summer, and fall, but many tropical species flower almost year-round.

For horticultural purposes, water lilies are grouped into tropical and nontropical species. In general the tropical species and their hybrids have larger flowers that are held conspicuously above the water level, whereas the hardy types have generally smaller blossoms that are borne near the water's surface. In addition, the flowers of tropical *Nymphaea* species include a broader color palette than do the hardy species, adding true blue to the white, yellows, pinks, and reds. Some tropical species have nocturnal flowers that may remain open during the heat and brightness of the day, and some propagate viviparously by forming plantlets on their leaves. The diurnal bloomers sport flowers that open in the morning and usually close up with nightfall. All these species give a unique tropical look and color to ponds and lakes. No body of water of any size should be without at least one *Nymphaea* species. Most species and hybrids require about 36 square feet of water surface for each plant.

The tropical species and their hybrids and cultivars

can only be successfully grown where the sustained water temperatures remain above 60°F, which phenomenon roughly corresponds with zones 9b through 11, although many species and cultivars are successfully grown as annuals in almost all zones. However, it must be pointed out that the U.S.D.A. zones are only indicators of low temperatures to be expected in a normal winter and some regions that are climatically zone 9b do not have enough heat to raise water temperatures to the level at which tropical species of *Nymphaea* are happy. In truth, the tropicals survive anywhere that the bottom of the pond or lake does not freeze but, in areas with colder winters than zone 9, the plants tend to be sparse bloomers and die out rather quickly. The burdensome alternative for cold-winter water gardeners is to always plant the roots in submerged half-barrels and lift and store these containers in a warm place over the winter. This, of course, is quite labor intensive and requires an area which can accommodate the large containers and provide enough warmth and light to keep the plants healthy. Plates 293 and 294.

Nymphaea ampla (AMP-la) is native to tropical and subtropical America from southern Texas through Mexico, the Caribbean, Central America, and into Brazil. This beautiful species has nearly orbicular lobed leaves that approach 2 feet in width. The leaves have toothed margins and are a lovely bronzy red in color when new. The fragrant diurnal flowers are about 6 inches wide with many white petals and greenish sepals.

Nymphaea caerulea (see-ROOL-ee-a) is native to Egypt, Chad, Sudan, and Zaire. It has bright green 18-inch-wide leaves that are ovate in outline. The many-petaled diurnal flowers are 6 inches wide. Each petal is light blue at the tip, shading to purple at the base. The center of the blossom is composed of deep yellow stamens. This flower, which is not a lotus (*Nelumbo* species), is unfortunately called Egyptian lotus, blue lotus, and blue lotus of the Nile.

Nymphaea capensis (ka-PENS-is) is native to South Africa. The orbicular leaves are as much as 18 inches wide and are toothed along their margins. The diurnal exquisitely fragrant flowers are 8 inches wide with many light blue petals. The plant is called Cape water lily.

Nymphaea colorata (ko-lo-RAIT-a) occurs naturally in tropical East Africa. The round leaves are relatively small for the genus and are usually less than a foot wide with parted and rounded lobes. The flowers are also fairly small, only about 5 inches wide, but are a very beautiful deep blue to purple. The plant blooms for a long period. This species has produced several colorful modern hybrid water lilies.

Nymphaea flavovirens (flay-vo-VY-renz) is indigenous to Mexico. It has round leaves that are as much as 18 inches wide with rounded parted lobes. The 6-inch-wide diurnal flowers are pure white with a lovely center of dark yellow stamens.

Nymphaea gigantea (jy-GANT-ee-a) is native to tropical Australia and the great island of New Guinea.

It has leaves that are nearly round to egg-shaped and as much as 18 inches wide. The upper side is a bright green, the underside reddish purple. The leaf blade is cleft at one end with pointed lobes, making a V-shaped opening. The large diurnal flowers, which are held a foot or so above the water's surface, are about a foot wide, with very many petals. The inner petals are light blue and the outer ones a deep blue or violet in color; they contrast beautifully with the bright yellow stamens in the center of the blossom. There are several naturally occurring varieties. ***Nymphaea gigantea* var. *alba*** has pure white flowers. There are exquisitely beautiful cultivars with flowers mostly pink and white, although most cultivars have blossoms that are smaller than the type.

Nymphaea lotus (LO-tus) is native to a large part of tropical Africa. The leaves are as much as 2 feet wide (but usually smaller) and are round with small scallops along the margins. The widespreading nocturnal many-petaled flowers are white with pinkish sepals and are the better part of a foot wide with beautiful yellow stamens in the center of the blossom. This water lily is called Egyptian water lily, lotus, Egyptian water lotus, and white lotus. The word *lotus* in these names is unfortunate because the plant is not a lotus (*Nelumbo* species).

Nymphaea micrantha (my-KRANTH-a) is indigenous to tropical West Africa. The 10-inch-long light green leaves are red on their undersides, broadly cordate in outline, and deeply cleft into two equilateral widely separated and pointed lobes. The diurnal 4- or 5-inch-wide flowers are white or pale blue with white stamens in the center of the blossom. This viviparous species produces tiny but complete plants on the tops of the leaves near the petiole which, according to Perry D. Slocum, sometimes bloom while still attached to the "parent" leaf. Slocum also reports that, according to Kenneth Landon of San Angelo, Texas, it is doubtful that the species is actually in cultivation in the Americas and that what is thought to be *N. micrantha*, is in reality ***Nymphaea* 'Daubeniana'** (daw-ben´-ee-AHN-a), a cross between *N. micrantha* and *N. caerulea*.

Nymphaea pubescens (pyoo-BES-senz) is indigenous to a wide area of tropical Asia including the Philippines, Malaysia, India, Indonesia, and northern Australia. This quite beautiful species has 10-inch-long elliptically outlined scalloped-margined leaves that are dark green and heavily veined with purplish red undersides. The leaves are cleft into two equilateral pointed lobes and the undersides as well as the leaf stalks are softly pubescent. The fragrant pure white nocturnal flowers are as much as 10 inches wide and are adorned with many lanceolate petals.

Nymphaea rubra (ROOB-ra) is indigenous to southern India. The round leaves are as much as 18 inches wide and are a beautiful brownish green tending towards olive green. The 10-inch-wide nocturnal flowers are a deep reddish violet in color.

Nymphaea stuhlmannii (shtool-MAHN-nee-eye) is indigenous to tropical East Africa. It is a beautiful species with round to egg-shaped dark green leaves that are 10 inches long with rounded open lobes. The fragrant 6-inch-wide many-petaled flowers are a deep clear yellow with centers of orange stamens. This species is sometimes called the Indian red water lily.

NYMPHOIDES (nim-FOY-deez)
Menyanthaceae: The Floating-Hearts Family
FLOATING HEARTS; WATER SNOWFLAKE
Aquatic plants with small waterlily-like leaves; small
   white and yellow flowers held above water
Zones 8 through 11
Sun
Aquatic
Rich, humusy wet soil
Propagation by cuttings

A genus of about 20 species of aquatic plants resembling small waterlilies in their growth habit. They have floating leaves that are nearly round with two basal lobes at the juncture of the petiole. The plants have long wandering rhizomatous roots that are fairly invasive, leading some gardeners to grow the plants in submerged containers. One species is widely cultivated in warm climate regions. ***Nymphoides indica*** (IN-di-ka) is native to tropical and subtropical ponds and lakes around the world. It has floating 4- to 6-inch-wide leaves that are round with two basal lobes and dark to olive green in color with reddish purple undersides. The small inch-wide white five-petaled flowers are on side shoots from the leaf petiole and rise above the water level. The flowers have yellow centers and slightly fringed petals and are produced in abundance throughout the warm parts of the year. This plant, which is invaluable for providing a finer texture in large pools, ponds, and lakes, is of great beauty. Plate 292.

OCHNA (OK-na)
Ochnaceae: The Mickey Mouse Plant Family
MICKEY MOUSE PLANT; BIRD'S-EYE BUSH
Evergreen shrub; bright yellow flowers; spectacular
   red and black fruit
Zones 10 and 11
Sun
Average but regular amounts of moisture
Average well-drained soil
Propagation by seed and cutting

A fairly large genus of 80 or more species of shrubs and trees in Africa and Asia. All have rather small leaves but large yellow flowers and berrylike fruits that develop in the expanded calyx. The fruiting parts often are showier than the flowers. One species is commonly planted in tropical regions. ***Ochna serrulata*** (ser-roo-LAIT-a) is native to South Africa. It grows usually to no more than 8 feet with stiff and leathery oblong to elliptic 5-inch-long dark green leaves, which are minutely serrate on their margins and show a prominent and lighter colored midrib. The quite beautiful flowers are rather reminiscent of small yellow *Magnolia grandiflora* blossoms. They have five or six ovate greenish white sepals, five bright yellow spreading spatulate-shaped petals, and a central column of orange stamens and pistil. The 3- to 4-inch-wide flowers are borne in few-flowered clusters at the branch tips in midsummer. After the petals fall, the sepals thicken, enlarge, and eventually turn a brilliant scarlet, cupping the plum-shaped ovary (which gradually turns from green to black) within their center. The visual effect of the sepals is at least as spectacular as that of the flowers. The common name comes about because most people see a resemblance in these fruit clusters to the ears of the Disney character.

OCHROSIA (o-KROAZ-ee-a / o-KRO-zhya)

Apocynaceae: The Oleander, Frangipani, Vinca Family
KOPSIA
Small evergreen tree; beautiful large leathery leaves; clusters of yellow-white flowers; red fruit
Zones 10b and 11
Sun
Average but regular amounts of moisture; drought tolerant when established
Average well-drained soil
Propagation by seed and cuttings

A genus of 23 species of tropical trees and shrubs in Australasia. They have milky and sometimes poisonous sap, leathery entire leaves arranged in whorls along the branches, clusters of pinwheel-like flowers, and attractive but usually poisonous fruit. One species is commonly planted in the American tropics for its beautiful leaves and extraordinary bright red fruit. *Ochrosia elliptica* (el-LIP-ti-ka) (synonym *O. parviflora*) is native to northern Australia and the island of New Caledonia. It grows as a small tree to 20 feet or more with a rounded but fairly open canopy and a smooth gray trunk. The exquisitely beautiful dark green 6-inch-long leaves are leathery, heavily veined with a prominent and lighter colored midrib, and oblong to elliptic in shape. The fragrant flowers appear in flattish dense clusters usually in midsummer. Each tiny blossom is a small yellowish white little pinwheel. The late summer fruits are remarkable affairs in two parts. Each part is a bright red 2-inch-long plum-shaped drupe with a short curved tip, joined to its twin at the end opposite the tip. The tree, which is resistant to saline conditions and which is drought tolerant when established, is a perfect candidate for seaside plantings. One is hard put to find a more beautiful strand plant. The common name is most unfortunate as there is a validly named genus *Kopsia* with remotely similar plants. Plate 295.

ODONTONEMA (o-dahnt´-o-NEEM-a)

Acanthaceae: The Acanthus Family
Common names vary according to species
Evergreen herbaceous shrubs; long terminal spikes of brilliant red flowers
Zones 10b and 11 as permanent perennials; zone 9b as returning perennials; anywhere as annuals
Sun or part shade
Average but regular amounts of moisture
Average well-drained soil
Propagation by seed and cuttings

A genus of about two dozen herbs and shrubs in the American tropics with terminal spikes of white, yellow, or red flowers. These evergreen shrubs are bold and beautiful when in flower, and they are easy of culture, demanding only sun, regular irrigation, and a reasonably fertile soil. None is hardy to cold, but they will come back from the root if the temperatures do not long remain below the mid 20s. The genus *Odontonema*, like several other genera of the acanthus family, is still in taxonomic confusion. Its species have been placed in both *Jacobinia* and *Justicia*. Because of their extraordinary attractiveness, all the species should be much more widely planted than they are. They are prime attractors of bees, hummingbirds, and butterflies.

Odontonema callistachyum (kal-lis-STAIK-ee-um) is native to Mexico and Central America. It is a large and spectacular shrub growing to 15 feet or more with square stems, foot-long elliptic-ovate tomentose leaves, and tall brilliant pink to scarlet terminal spikes of urn-shaped flowers. This species should be more regularly planted in warm regions than it is. It grows large and fast and is possibly overwhelming to those with small gardens. It blooms from midsummer through autumn and is a truly glorious sight.

Odontonema schomburgkianum (shahm-burg´-kee-AHN-um) (synonym *Thyrsacanthus rutilans*) is native to northern South America. It grows to about 6 feet or so with oblong-lanceolate to elliptic heavily veined 10-inch-long leaves. The inflorescence is unusual in that it is very long (as much as 3 feet long), airy and drooping, with tubular or urn-shaped inch-long scarlet flowers. It makes a dramatic and splendid spectacle.

Odontonema strictum (STRIK-tum) is indigenous to Central America. It is one of the smaller species, growing only to about 6 feet, but is by far the most popular and widely planted species and is still growing in popularity and availability. The 6-inch-long bright green leaves are glossy and oblong to elliptic in shape. The inflorescences appear in late summer and are produced into late autumn and even winter. The erect spike is as much as 18 inches tall with many waxy orange-red to deep scarlet tubular flowers. There is a variegated-leaved form that adds nothing to the landscape value of the plant, although it is about as attractive as the type. The plant is common enough to have at least three vernacular names, cardinal flower, cardinal's guard, and firespike or firestick. It is sometimes incorrectly labeled as *Justicia coccinea*.

ONCOBA (AHNK-o-ba / ahn-KO-ba)

Flacourtiaceae: The Flacourtia, Governor's-Plum
    Family
Common names vary according to species
Small evergreen trees; lustrous leaves; white single-
    roselike fragrant flowers; green and yellow fruit
Zones 10 and 11
Sun
Average but regular amounts of moisture; drought
    tolerant when established
Average well-drained soil
Propagation by seed

A genus of about 40 species of usually spiny trees
and shrubs in Brazil, tropical Africa, and western Asia.
They have white, yellow, or red exceptionally attractive
flowers with many stamens and large hard berrylike
many-seeded fruit. This greatly underutilized group of
showy flowering plants should be much more widely
cultivated.

Oncoba kraussiana (krowss-ee-AHN-a) (synonym *Xylotheca kraussiana*) is native to northern South
Africa. It grows to 15 or sometimes 20 feet and should
be trained while young if a small tree form is wanted.
Otherwise it is naturally a very attractive large shrub.
The soft shiny dark green leaves are 2 to 3 inches long
with entire and smooth margins. The plant is nearly
everblooming in frost-free climates. Each 3-inch-wide
blossom has 9 to 13 pure white obovate notched petals
and a center of bright yellow stamens with orange anthers. The flowers resemble white Shasta daisies from a
distance, but the plant is, of course, unrelated to the
daisy family. The fruit is a 2-inch-wide round green oil-
rich and many-seeded berry that matures to a beautiful
orange color.

Oncoba spinosa (spi-NO-sa) is indigenous to tropical East and Central Africa into the Arabian peninsula.
It grows to 20 feet, sometimes more, and is naturally a
small tree. It has smooth gray bark and an open crown
of shiny foliage with sharp 2-inch-long thorns in most
leaf axils. The leaves are about 4 inches long, finely serrate on the margins, and reminiscent of those of a cherry
tree. They have a quite attractive deep reddish hue
when young. The tree is deciduous with cold or winter
drought conditions. The exceptional flowers appear in
late spring and early summer and resemble large single
roses or single-flowered camellias. Each blossom is 3
inches wide with six or seven white or yellowish white
notched petals surrounding a central mass of wonderful
deep yellow stamens. The fruits are beautiful hard-
shelled round to pear-shaped 3-inch-long berries hanging from stout 3-inch-long stalks. At first green, then
vivid yellow, the fruits finally turn reddish brown when
mature. This wonderful plant is known as fried egg tree
(for its flowers) or snuffbox tree (for its dried fruits,
which are used as containers for snuff and as rattle toys
for infants). The fruits are reportedly edible but not
delicious.

OPSIANDRA. See *Gaussia*.

OPUNTIA (o-PUNT-ee-a / o-POONT-ee-a)

Cactaceae: The Cactus Family
Common names vary according to species
Cactus plants with pads or knobby stems; large
    showy yellow, pink, purple, and red flowers
Zones vary according to species
Sun
Drought tolerant
Average well-drained soil
Propagation by seed and cuttings

Opuntia is the second largest cactus genus with nearly
500 species. All cactus species are American in origin,
most of them in the American tropics, but no cactus
genus is as widespread as *Opuntia*. Its members range
from Canada to Tierra del Fuego, the southernmost tip
of South America, and they have become naturalized all
over the world in arid and semiarid regions. The genus
is a varied one as to plant form. Its members have
jointed stems. Many species have the joints formed as
pads and are known as the prickly pear and tuna forms.
Other species have cylindrical joints that are usually
knobby; these are mostly referred to as cholla (CHO-
ya) cactus. Some of the tropical species form thick,
woody treelike trunks with or without branches. Many
Opuntia species are small and some are prostrate in
growth, but many others are treelike and, especially the
ones forming pads, quite spectacular, wonderfully exotic, and picturesquely tropical looking. A few of the
padded species have infrequent or tiny spines, but most
species have distinct and numerous spines, which are
exceptionally beautiful. All species have "glochids," that
is, clusters of tiny spines with nearly microscopic barbs
on their ends. These glochids make the plants difficult
to handle and onerous to deal with when these spines
puncture skin. The glochids also make these plants first-
rate candidates for barrier landscape subjects.

Opuntia species have more or less cup-shaped flowers
with numerous petals and many stamens. Like the flowers of almost every other species of cactus, these are of
exceptional beauty, in colors ranging from mostly yellow but also orange, red, purple, and even white in a few
species. Many *Opuntia* species produce large mostly
globular and colorful fruit called "tuna." Some of these
fruits are edible, delicious, and a near staple of native
peoples all over the continent. In addition, the joints of
many padded forms are eaten as vegetables or used for
cattle fodder after the spines are removed (usually by
burning the outer surface of the pads). Several almost
completely spineless cultivars are grown for this purpose.

Opuntia basilaris (bay-si-LAIR-iss) is native to
Nevada, Arizona, and adjacent Mexico and is hardy in
zones 7 through 11. It grows to a maximum height of
about 3 feet with 5- to 12-inch-long obovate pads that
are a beautiful bluish green to purplish rose in color.
Usually one inch-long spine arises from the purple-

colored glochids. The 3-inch-wide summer flowers are a deep rose to purple in color. This species, which is a very effective plant for adding color to the cactus and succulent garden, is called beaver tail or rose tuna.

Opuntia bigelovii (big-e-LO-vee-eye) is indigenous to southern Nevada, Arizona, southwestern California, and adjacent northern Mexico. It is hardy in zones 8 through 11. This much-branching cholla type species grows to as much as 6 feet with some of the world's loveliest spines. These spines, which are an inch-long and light yellow to golden, cover the stems and gleam in the sun. The summer flowers are about 2 inches wide and are a light purple in color. Because the plant looks as though it is covered in golden felt from a distance, it is usually called the teddy-bear cactus or the teddy-bear cholla. Plate 296.

Opuntia chlorotica (klo-RAHT-i-ka) is found naturally from southwestern California eastward to New Mexico and the northern regions of Mexico adjacent to that area. It is hardy in zones 8 through 11. This padded species has nearly orbicular 8-inch-wide pads that are a mint green to bluish green in color with purplish gray areoles from which protrude yellowish glochids and a few inch-long spines. The 3-inch-wide silken summer flowers are a translucent yellow, and the tips of the petals are flushed with red. Because of the round pads, this species is called the pancake cactus or flapjack cactus.

Opuntia cholla (CHO-ya) is native to Baja California and is hardy in zones 9 through 11. It grows to about 10 feet with freely branching stems whose surfaces are barely visible because of the very many handsome white inch-long spines. The summer flowers are a light rose color. The common name is, of course, cholla.

Opuntia echinocarpa (ee-kyn´-o-KARP-a) occurs naturally in southern Utah, southwestern Nevada, southern California, western Arizona, and down into Baja California, and is hardy in zones 6 through 11. This very spiny cholla type species grows to about 5 feet with many branches. The spines are as much as 10 inches long and sparkle and glow in the sun. The 2-inch-wide summer flowers are a greenish yellow. This is a very beautiful and hardy cactus. Plate 297.

Opuntia falcata (fal-KAIT-a) is native to Hispaniola and is hardy in zones 10 and 11. This very interesting and exotic-looking species has pads but also a definite and woody trunk, which can attain a height of 10 or 12 feet. The individual dark green pads are about a foot long, thin glossy-skinned, and lanceolate to obovate or sickle-shaped. Each areole bears two inch-long white or yellow spines. The 2-inch-wide red flowers appear in summer.

Opuntia ficus-indica (fy´-kus-IN-di-ka) has been cultivated for so long in the tropical areas of the Americas that its precise point of origin is obscure. It is definitely tropical and is adaptable only to zones 10 and 11, although marginally hardy in zone 9b. This treelike species has a woody trunk that reaches as much as 12 feet in height. It has large light green to grayish green 18-inch-long spatulate-shaped pads. The plant produces few or no spines apart from the glochids. The summer flowers are 3-inch-wide cups of luminous yellow, followed by the golden tuna, which are relished by people and animals. The specific epithet *ficus-indica* means "Indian fig," but few people seem to use this name, preferring either tuna or spineless cactus. This species is probably the world's most widely grown cactus species. Plate 298.

Opuntia fulgida (FUL-ji-da) is native to southern Arizona and adjacent Mexico and is hardy in zones 9 through 11. It is a cholla type species that grows to as much as 10 feet, usually producing a woody base. The joints are a foot long and deeply knobby with yellow areoles and glochids from which arise 10 brown or yellowish spines. The small inch-wide pink flowers are produced in late summer. This species is one of several referred to as jumping cholla or jumping cactus because the joints detach readily and cling by the barbed spines to whatever has caused their detachment. From there they are carried afar, where they can root when finally dislodged from their carrier.

Opuntia imbricata (im-bri-KAIT-a) is found naturally from eastern Colorado into Mexico and is hardy in zones 5 through 11. It is a much-branched cholla type species growing to as much as 10 feet and forming a woody base. The light green to deep bluish stems are deeply tubercled in a pattern that has led to the common name of chain-link cactus. The summer flowers are as much as 4 inches wide, and their color ranges from orange to vermilion. The plant has a wide natural range. Over this range there is a gradation of forms of differing heights, stem color, and flower color. The smaller forms are restricted to the colder parts of the range.

Opuntia leucotricha (lyook-o-TRYK-a) is indigenous to central Mexico and is adaptable to zones 9b through 11. It grows to as much as 15 feet with a basally woody trunk. This small tree type species has large and somewhat pubescent dusty green relatively thin pads that are usually paddle-shaped and longer than broad but may also be broadly obovate or almost round. There is only one radial spine on the mature joints or pads, but juvenile pads have more. The spines point downwards and create a deceptively soft and hairy aspect. The plants bloom in midsummer with very many 4-inch-wide yellow cup-shaped blossoms, each with a red style and bright green stigma.

Opuntia microdasys (myk-ro-DAY-sis) is native to southwestern Texas and adjacent Mexico and is hardy in zones 8 through 11. This species is one of the most attractive cactus species and with its several forms is widely grown in and out of doors. It is a pad type species that usually grows to around 3 feet in height. The pads are fairly thick and succulent, 6 to 8 inches long, round to spatulate in shape, and a beautiful clear yellow-green to bluish green in color. There are usually no radial spines, but many regularly spaced and closely set white or yellow soft-appearing fuzzy glochids that give a felty pubescent appearance to the pads. The summer flowers are 2-inch-wide yellow cups. There are several forms of this species differing mainly in the size, number, and color of the areoles and pads. The plant is called rabbit ears, bunny ears, yellow bunny ears, and goldblush. Its forms and cultivars are called polka-dot cactus, honey bunny, cinnamon cactus, blind pear (because of the lack of large spines), and red bunny ears.

Opuntia pilifera (py-LIF-e-ra) is native to Mexico and is hardy in zones 10 and 11. This pad-type species grows to as much as 15 feet and, with time, forms a cylindrical woody trunk. The foot-long pads are beautiful, fat, succulent, mint green, and ovate in shape. Regularly spaced along the pads are white areoles, which produce many short white hairs, and inch-long white spines, which radiate in a starlike fashion from the centers of the areoles. The 3-inch-wide flowers are scarlet in color. This species is noble and attractive.

Opuntia violacea is indigenous to southeastern Arizona, southwestern New Mexico, and southwestern Texas, and is hardy in zones 8 through 11. It grows to 3 or 4 feet in height with thick round to obovate pads and sometimes forms a short trunk when old. The pads are a beautiful bluish green to violet and sometimes are almost completely powdery blue in color. The areoles, the glochids, and the few spines are reddish brown to reddish purple. The summer flowers are as much as 4 inches wide and are a translucent clear yellow with red throats. This species is most highly recommended.

OREOCEREUS. See *Borzicactus*.

OREODOXA. See *Roystonea*.

PACHIRA (pa-KY-ra)
Bombacaceae: The Bombax, Baobab Family
GUIANA CHESTNUT; WATER CHESTNUT;
  PROVISION TREE; WILD COCOA
Large evergreen trees; great palmate leaves; fantastic
  foot-wide spidery flowers; attractive pods
Zones 10b and 11; usually survives as a non-
  flowering shrub in zones 10a and 9b
Sun
Water lovers
Rich, humusy, well-drained soil
Propagation by seed

A genus of about 24 species of trees in Mexico, Central America, and northern South America. These plants are among the world's most beautiful; no other plant surpasses the allure of these magnificent large-leaved trees with their gigantic and exotic flowers and fruit. They grow to more than 80 feet in their native habitats, often with great buttressed trunks; in cultivation they are seldom more than 50 feet in stature with relatively short stout trunks.

The large leaves are palmately compound and mostly round in outline, composed of five to seven elliptic to obovate leaflets, each as much as a foot long with prominent lighter colored midribs and lateral veins. The fragrant flowers open at night and are sometimes as much as 18 inches wide with five very long and relatively narrow great arching petals of white, yellow, pink, red, or purple. From the center of these blossoms protrudes a bundle of hundreds of very long (but not as long as the petals) silky white, pink, or purple stamens with red anthers. The unfortunate thing about the flowers is that the petals do not last very long, usually less than a day, but they are produced in abundance and for a long period; in some plants they are produced in cycles year-round, but mostly in winter.

The fruits are from 4 to 18 inches long and velvety brown to reddish brown football-shaped to nearly orbicular pods. Unlike the seeds of most other members of the bombax family, the relatively large seeds of *Pachira* are not surrounded by any sort of floss and are highly esteemed as a raw and a cooked food in many tropical areas.

None of these species is drought tolerant, and some—those found naturally along estuaries or lake shores in the tropical rain forests of the Americas—are almost aquatic. They are the most beautiful trees on the small islands in Lake Catemaco in the state of Veracruz, Mexico. Most thrive with regular and adequate supplies of moisture. I have grown one *Pachira* species in Houston, Texas (zone 9a), for several years now and find that the plants freeze to the ground when temperatures are below 30°F but that, amazingly, they resprout from their roots (unless they are in an exposed area) from temperatures above 22°F. They therefore can be used as beautiful non-flowering shrubs in zone 9b, as their growth rate is moderately fast.

The taxonomy of this genus has been much confused for quite a while, and almost all accounts seem to contradict one another. The trees considered here have been formerly placed into the genera *Bombax* and *Bombacopsis* and incorrectly distributed as members of the genus *Pseudobombax*. Even fairly up-to-date publications seem to contradict each other as to the differences between the two species. Even Edwin A. Menninger contributed to the bewilderment by writing that the petals of *P. insignis* are crimson, but then publishing a color plate that clearly shows the species with white or yellowish white petals. Menninger's photo of *P. aquatica* is not of sufficiently good quality to know (at least for me) if one is looking at a wilted flower that has lost most of its petals or a fresh flower with some petals removed.

Of the two trees listed in the literature as being grown in the United States—***Pachira aquatica*** and ***Pachira insignis***—it seems fairly certain that one species has purple or red petals, while the other has white, yellowish, or pinkish petals. And one is generally larger than the other in its leaves and stature. The problem is which is which. *Pachira aquatica* is the much more commonly labeled species. Indeed plant retailers in the southern states and California are now selling plants labeled as *P. aquatica* for indoor decoration, but these plants are never in flower or fruit. Plates 299, 300, 301, and 302.

PACHYCEREUS (pak-ee-SEER-ee-us)
Cactaceae: The Cactus Family
Common names vary according to species
Immense treelike columnar, ribbed cactus species; large white nocturnal flowers
Zones 10 and 11
Sun
Drought tolerant
Average well-drained soil
Propagation by seed and cuttings

A genus of maybe 10 giant columnar ribbed treelike cactus species in Mexico. They are somewhat similar to *Carnegiea gigantea* (sahuaro), but the "arms" of these great branching specimens are always held more closely together as they ascend from the main trunk and there are usually more of them. Like the sahuaro these are nocturnal-flowering cacti, and like *Carnegiea*, they form flowers at the tops of the columns. The fruits are large and very spiny. The spines are usually a bright yellow or golden in color. The larger species are fully as spectacular, as exotic, and as beautiful as the sahuaro. The smaller species are quite large for cactus plants and have a distinctive appeal, unsurpassed by any other genus. None of these plants is hardy to freezing temperatures, and they appreciate more moisture and a somewhat better soil than do many smaller cactus species.

Pachycereus hollianus (hahl-lee-AHN-us) (synonym *Lemaireocereus hollianus*) is found naturally in south central Mexico. It is an unusual species because of the basal branching, the columns very seldom or never branching. The resulting visual effect of a mature plant is that of a tall fence or stockade. Each grayish green column may attain a height of 15 feet and bear 8 to 10 ribs having red or black spines. The white flowers are 4 inches wide.

Pachycereus marginatus (mahr-ji-NAIT-us) (synonyms *Cereus marginatus*, *Lemaireocereus marginatus*, *Marginatocereus marginatus*, *Stenocereus marginatus*) is native to central and southern Mexico. It is an incredible cactus species with tall very straight columns branching out from the base of the plants. Each column is 25 feet tall, a bright green to grayish or bluish green, plump, and succulent with usually four but sometimes as many as seven ribs whose crests bear thick but deciduous spines. The bases of the columns are smooth and angled. These stems are unbranched unless injured, and the resulting visual aspect has led to the vernacular name of organ-pipe cactus. Although there is at least one other cactus with the same common name, the appellation is quite apt. The stems or columns grow in large segments each year, but the divisions between these joints are smoothed out with time, resulting in an appealing soft and succulent aspect to the older por-

tions, which look almost as if they were carved from soapstone. The plants bloom in the summer. The diurnal flowers are borne at the tops of the tall stems, are about 2 inches long and as wide with rose or brownish sepals and white petals, and are shaped much like the blossoms of *Carnegiea gigantea* (sahuaro). The round fruits are a brownish red in color.

Pachycereus pecten-aboriginum (pek´-ten-ab-o-RIJ-i-num) is native to Baja California and the northern and central Mexican states. This beauty grows to as much as 30 feet with a thick basal trunk and several closely set ascending subsidiary deep green columns, each with a dozen or so deep ribs bearing brown spines. The summer flowers are white with reddish brown exteriors. This very spectacular species rivals the size and majesty of *Carnegiea gigantea* (sahuaro).

Pachycereus pringlei (PRING-lee-eye) occurs naturally in Baja California and the state of Sonora in northwestern Mexico. It is the largest and most impressive species, a tree form with a stout trunk, growing to 40 feet or more in height. The many gray-green columns are heavily ribbed, the ribs carrying short reddish spines. The flowers are 3-inch-wide white cups with greenish red sepals. There is no more impressive cactus species.

Pachycereus schottii (SHAHT-tee-eye) (synonym *Lophocereus schottii*) is native to the states of Baja California and Sonora in northwestern Mexico and to extreme southwestern Arizona in the United States. It grows to 15 feet with many tall olive green to deep green stems or branches directly from the base of the plant whose trunk is hardly apparent. The branches are seven-ribbed and the spines along the crests of each rib are stout and few, except at the tops of the stems where they are bunched and quite bristly looking. This has led to one of the common names, whisker cactus. The cactus is also called locally senita. The nocturnal flowers are pink, and the plumlike fruits are red. This species is one of the finest landscape subjects for tropical and subtropical arid regions or a tropical cactus and succulent garden; the great clumps of branches lending an inimitable and most exotic aspect to the xerophytic panorama. ***Pachycereus schottii* 'Monstrosus'** (mahn-stro-sus) has ribs broken up into smooth knobby projections and mostly spineless stems. It is called the totem-pole cactus. Plates 303 and 304.

Pachycereus weberi (WEB-er-eye) (synonym *Lemaireocereus weberi*) is native to southwestern Mexico. It is one of the most picturesque cactus species. It is also a giant plant, growing to 30 feet in height or sometimes more, with very many closely set light bluish green deeply ribbed straight ascending columns borne atop a relatively tall and stout trunk. The 4-inch-wide flowers are greenish white. This great cactus is almost startling in appearance when mature. It wants rather greater amounts and more frequent rations of moisture than its sisters and brothers.

Plate 285. *Mussaenda erythrophylla*. Author's garden, Houston, Texas

Plate 283. *Musa coccinea* inflorescence. The Kampong, Coconut Grove, Florida. Photo by Larry Schokman

Plate 286. *Mussaenda philippica*. The Kampong, Coconut Grove, Florida. Photo by Larry Schokman

Plate 284. *Musa velutina* inflorescence. Mercer Arboretum, Houston, Texas

Plate 287. *Nelumbo nucifera* 'Mrs. Perry D. Slocum'. Photo by Perry D. Slocum

Plate 288. *Neodypsis lastelliana*. Fairchild Tropical Garden, Miami, Florida

Plate 289. *Neoregelia carolinae* 'Medallion'. Photo by Jim Racca

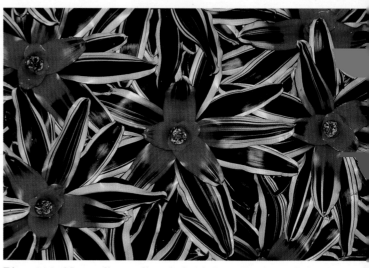

Plate 290. *Neoregelia carolinae* hybrid. Leu Gardens, Orlando, Florida

Plate 318. *Phoenix canariensis.* Berkley Botanic Garden, California. Photo by Diane Laird

Plate 319. *Phoenix reclinata.* Fairchild Tropical Garden, Miami, Florida

Plate 321. *Phyllostachys bambusoides* 'Allgold'. Mercer Arboretum, Houston, Texas

Plate 320. *Phoenix rupicola.* Edison estate, Fort Myers, Florida

Plate 322. *Phytolacca dioica.* San Antonio Botanic Gardens, San Antonio, Texas

Plate 324. *Pittosporum tobira.* San Antonio Botanic Gardens, San Antonio, Texas

Plate 326. *Plumeria* hybrid inflorescence. Alton Marshall garden, Houston, Texas

Plate 323. *Piper auritum.* Author's garden, Houston, Texas

Plate 325. *Platycerium bifurcatum.* Edison estate, Fort Myers, Florida

Plate 327. *Plumeria* hybrid inflorescence. Alton Marshall garden, Houston, Texas

Plate 328. *Plumeria alba.* Key West, Florida

Plate 330. *Podranea ricasoliana.* Brownsville, Texas

Plate 329. *Plumeria obtusa.* Mercer Arboretum, Houston, Texas

Plate 331. *Porana paniculata.* The Kampong, Coconut Grove, Florida

Plate 332. *Pseuderanthemum alatum.* Author's garden, Houston, Texas

Plate 333. *Pseudobombax ellipticum* (white form). Alton Marshall garden, Houston, Texas

Plate 334. *Pseudobombax ellipticum* (pink form). Photo by Larry Schokman

Plate 335. *Pseudocalymma alliacea*. Alton Marshall garden, Houston, Texas

Plate 337. *Psidium guajava*. Homestead, Florida. Photo by Roger Hammer

Plate 336. *Pseudophoenix lediniana*. Fairchild Tropical Garden, Miami, Florida

Plate 338. *Quisqualis indica.* Houston, Texas

Plate 340. *Rhapis excelsa* and *Dracaena fragrans* 'Lindenii'. Moody Gardens, Galveston, Texas

Plate 339. *Ravenala madagascariensis.* Edison estate, Fort Myers, Florida

Plate 341. *Rhizophora mangle.* Costa Rica. Photo by Larry Schokman

Plate 342. *Rhoeo spathacea.* Heathcote Botanic Garden, Fort Pierce, Florida

Plate 343. *Rhoeo spathacea* 'Variegata'. Mercer Arboretum, Houston, Texas

Plate 344. *Ricinus communis.* Author's garden, Houston, Texas

Plate 345. *Roystonea elata.* Fairchild Tropical Garden, Miami, Florida

Plate 346. *Sanchezia speciosa.* Fairchild Tropical Garden, Miami, Florida

Plate 347. *Saraca thaipingensis.* Photo by Larry Schokman

Plate 348. *Scaevola aemula* 'Blue Wonder'. Houston Plant and Garden Nursery, Houston, Texas

Plate 349. *Schefflera actinophylla.* Miami, Florida

Plate 350. *Schizolobium parahyba.* The Kampong, Coconut Grove, Florida

Plate 351. *Senecio confusus.* Leu Gardens, Orlando, Florida

Plate 352. *Serenoa repens* (blue form). Moody Gardens, Galveston, Texas

Plate 353. *Sesbania tripetii.* The Kampong, Coconut Grove, Florida. Photo by Larry Schokman

Plate 354. *Solandra grandiflora.* Fairchild Tropical Garden, Miami, Florida

Plate 355. *Solandra maxima.* Alton Marshall garden, Houston, Texas

Plate 356. *Sophora secundiflora.* San Antonio, Texas

Plate 357. *Spathodea campanulata.* The Kampong, Coconut Grove, Florida. Photo by Larry Schokman

Plate 358. *Spathodea campanulata* (yellow form). The Kampong, Coconut Grove, Florida. Photo by Larry Schokman

Plate 359. *Stapelia gigantea.* Gladys Porter Zoo, Brownsville, Texas

Plate 360. *Stenocereus thurberi.* Organ Pipe Cactus National Monument, Arizona

Plate 361. *Stenochlaena tenuifolia*. Leu Gardens, Orlando, Florida

Plate 364. *Stigmaphyllon ciliatum*. Houston, Texas

Plate 362. *Stephanotis floribunda*. Author's garden, Houston, Texas

Plate 363. *Sterculia foetida*. The Kampong, Coconut Grove, Florida. Photo by Larry Schokman

Plate 365. *Strelitzia nicolai*, *Piper auritum*, and *Caesalpinia pulcherrima*. Author's garden, Houston, Texas

Plate 366. *Strelitzia reginae.* Selby Botanic Garden, Sarasota, Florida

Plate 367. *Strelitzia reginae* var. *juncea.* South Africa. Photo by Sean Hogan

Plate 368. *Streptosolen jamesonii.* The Kampong, Coconut Grove, Florida. Photo by Larry Schokman

Plate 369. *Strobilanthes dyeranus* with *Alocasia* 'Hilo Beauty'. Author's garden, Houston, Texas

Plate 370. *Strongylodon macrobotrys* inflorescence. Photo by Larry Schokman

Plate 371. *Syzygium malaccense*. The Kampong, Coconut Grove, Florida. Photo by Larry Schokman

Plate 372. *Tabebuia caraiba*. Photo by Larry Schokman

Plate 373. *Tabebuia chrysantha*. Kauai, Hawaii. Photo by Larry Schokman

Plate 374. *Tabebuia chrysotricha* flowers and fruit. The Kampong, Coconut Grove, Florida. Photo by Larry Schokman

Plate 392. *Urechites lutea.* Author's garden, Houston, Texas

Plate 394. *Victoria amazonica* showing underside of leaf. Photo by Perry D. Slocum

Plate 393. *Veitchia mcdanielsii.* Fairchild Tropical Garden, Miami, Florida

Plate 395. *Victoria* 'Longwood Hybrid'. Kew Gardens, London, England. Photo by Perry D. Slocum

Plate 397. *Vriesea imperialis.* Fairchild Tropical Garden, Miami, Florida

Plate 396. *Vriesea fosteriana* in bloom with *Philodendron selloum.* Ganna Walska Lotus Land, Santa Barbara, California. Photo by Steven Timbrook

Plate 399. *Warszewiczia coccinea.* Photo by Larry Schokman

Plate 398. *Wagatea spicata.* Photo by Larry Schokman

Plate 400. *Washingtonia filifera* in its native habitat. Palm Springs, California

Plate 401. *Washingtonia robusta.* Fairchild Tropical Garden, Miami, Florida

Plate 402. *Wodyetia bifurcata.* Fairchild Tropical Garden, Miami, Florida

Plate 403. *Xanthosoma sagittifolium.* Author's garden, Houston, Texas

Plate 405. *Yucca aloifolia* 'Marginata'. Fairchild Tropical Garden, Miami, Florida

Plate 404. *Yucca aloifolia*. The Kampong, Coconut Grove, Florida. Photo by Larry Schokman

Plate 406. *Yucca brevifolia*. Joshua Tree National Monument, Arizona

Plate 407. *Yucca brevifolia* growth habit. Joshua Tree National Monument, Arizona

Plate 409. *Zombia antillarum* trunk. Selby Botanic Garden, Sarasota, Florida

Plate 408. *Zamia furfuracea.* Author's garden, Houston, Texas

PACHYPODIUM (pak-ee-PO-dee-um)

Apocynaceae: The Oleander, Frangipani, Vinca
    Family
MADAGASCAR PALM
Very spiny-trunked palmlike succulent; strap-shaped
    leaves atop trunks; white flowers
Zones 10 and 11
Sun
Drought tolerant
Average well-drained soil
Propagation by seed

A small genus of spiny succulent shrubs in south-eastern Africa and the island of Madagascar. They form swollen spine-covered trunks atop which grow the crowns of straplike leathery dark green leaves, giving to the plants the general aspect of a palm tree. The spines are borne atop cone-shaped tubercles that are spirally arranged and fairly densely set around the lengths of the trunks. The five-petaled flowers grow from the leaf crown and are red, yellow, or white in color.

Pachypodium lamerei (la-MER-ee-eye) is native to southern Madagascar. It grows to 10 or even 12 feet with time. The gray or tan-colored trunk is swollen at the base and tapers with height like an inverted carrot; it is usually completely unbranched but sometimes naturally forms a few branches near the top of the main trunk and usually branches if the main trunk is damaged or cut in two. The inch-long gray to black spines are in threes from atop the spirally arranged tubercles. There are as many as two dozen linear-elliptic arching leaves at the top of the trunk, each of which is from 10 to 18 inches long; they are a deep and lustrous green with a prominent and lighter colored midrib. The leaves are often deciduous in cold or drought conditions. The white five-petaled flowers grow from the midst of the leaf crown, each blossom as much as 4 inches across with obdeltoid-shaped petals and with the twisted-petal form that is characteristic of the family. These are quite remarkable plants, combining aspects of palms with those of a cactus, and are about as exotic-looking a plant as one can find. The other species are similar except in size of stem and leaf, *P. lamerei* being among the largest. Plate 305.

PACHYSTACHYS (pak-ee-STAIK-iss)

Acanthaceae: The Acanthus Family
Common names vary according to species
Small to medium-sized herbaceous shrubs; spikes of
    bright yellow or red flowers
Zones 10 and 11 as perennial landscape subjects;
    anywhere as annuals
Partial shade to sun
Average but regular amounts of moisture
Rich, humusy, well-drained soil
Propagation by cuttings

A small genus of about a dozen herbaceous shrubs in tropical America. They are closely allied to the genera *Jacobinia* and *Justicia* with minor technical details of the stamens differentiating these from the others; they are often confused with the two other genera by botanists and non-botanists alike and, in truth, one of the following species of *Pachystachys* has an overall appearance so similar to most *Justicia* species that its segregation seems almost perverse. The classification is further complicated by a vernacular name that is shared by a *Pachystachys* species and a species in the related genus *Odontonema*. These trivia matter not very much to the plant lover except for trying to find and acquire the desired plant. These most worthy garden subjects are valuable because they freely bloom in less than full sun; alas they are not as hardy to cold as most *Justicia* species, and they will seldom resprout from the root when frozen down. They need to be deadheaded and pinched or pruned back after each flush of flowers to encourage non-leggy growth and the development of more inflorescences.

Pachystachys coccinea (kahk-SIN-ee-a) naturally occurs from northern South America through the West Indies. It grows to 6 feet or so and has 6- to 8-inch-long dark green elliptic and acuminate heavily veined leaves. The inflorescences are terminal 6-inch-tall spikes of many closely set curved scarlet tubular two-lipped flowers. The lower lip is divided into three segments. There are ovate green bracts at the base of the inflorescence, and the entire cluster has an appearance decidedly similar to those of most *Justicia* species.

Pachystachys lutea (LOOT-ee-a) is native to Peru. It grows to as much as 3 feet and is naturally a rather compact everbloomer with linear-ovate 6-inch-long dark green heavily veined leaves. The 6-inch-tall flower spike is four-sided because of the arrangement of the intensely yellow large ovate bracts all along its length; a curved white tubular two-lipped flower protrudes from the center of each bract, much like *Justicia brandegeana* (shrimp plant) inflorescence. Indeed, the most common vernacular name of this species is the yellow shrimp plant, the other vernacular name being golden candle. This glorious flowering plant blooms most heavily in summer, but is actually ever-blooming as long as the weather is warm. Nothing surpasses it for brightening up partially shady sites, and it is nothing short of spectacular when planted in masses. Plate 306.

PANAX. See *Polyscias*.

PANDANUS (pan-DAN-us)

Pandanaceae: The Pandanus, Screw-Pine Family
PANDANUS; SCREW-PINE; WALKING PALM
Dense rosettes of linear leaves atop branching trunks;
    stilt roots; large fruit shaped like a pine cone
Zones 10b and 11
Sun to partial shade
Average but regular amounts of moisture; drought
    tolerant when established
Average well-drained soil

Propagation by cuttings, transplanting of suckers, and (sometimes) uncovered seed

A large genus of at least 600 small to large trees in the tropics of the Old World. They are not trees in the sense of a pine or an oak and are not related to those; rather they are monocots distantly affiliated with palms, bananas, true pineapples, and lilies. They make cylindrical trunklike stems, which are usually branching. At the end of the stem are compressed spirals of long linear leaves, which are usually razor sharp or armed with teeth. Aerial, stilt, and brace roots are produced from the lower portions of the trunks, and mature plants are usually broader than they are wide. with the branches spreading horizontally much like those of a strangler fig. Some species grow to 70 feet in height in their native haunts, but almost none reaches such dimensions in cultivation. The trees are single-sexed, with only male flowers on some trees and only female flowers on the others. The fragrant male flowers are in long spikes and are often accompanied by colorful bracts, while the female inflorescences are dense globose heads of petalless flowers. The large, round or elliptical, and compound fruits resemble orbicular pine cones or pineapples, and are green when young but usually mature to yellow, orange, or brownish orange. One of the common names, screw pine, arises from the spiral leaf scars on the trunks and the fruits (on the female plants) that are vaguely similar to those of a pine tree. The leaves have been and still are much used for fabric, cordage, and the construction of thatched roofs. The fruits of many species are eaten, and the large seeds have been used as paintbrushes by aboriginal peoples because of the tufted apical fibers. The plants are commonly found growing near the seashore just out of reach of the surf or around tidal lagoons and are therefore tolerant of saline soil and spray. They flourish, however, farther inland under all kinds of soil conditions. The trees are drought tolerant but, like so many others, thrive much better and grow faster and more lush with adequate and regular amounts of moisture, although none grow quickly. There are no more dramatically exotic plants for the tropical landscape; they are one of the symbols of the tropics and are the very essence of the tropical look.

Pandanus baptistii (bap-TIST-ee-eye) is native to the New Guinea region. It is atypical of most other species in that it is of dwarf stature, producing a trunk that is seldom more than 3 feet tall. Atypical also are its bluish green erect but arched 3- or 4-foot-long leaves, which lack teeth on their margins. The plants are used in tropical beds and hedges. *Pandanus baptistii* '**Aureus**', a beautiful cultivar with lovely yellow longitudinal stripes on the leaves, is much more widely planted than the type.

Pandanus dubius (DOOB-ee-us) (synonym *P. pacificus*) is indigenous to New Guinea, Indonesia, and Malaysia. Mature plants reportedly grow to 60 feet in their native habitat, but seldom attain more than 30 feet in cultivation. The trunks are straight with many aerial roots, and the very spiny leaves are as much as 12 feet long and almost a foot wide. These magnificent plants make dramatic specimens or wondrous large patio trees. The juvenile form of *P. dubius* has leaves that are significantly shorter than those of the mature specimens and resembles a giant bromeliad until it forms enough trunk to take on the adult characteristics. It was mistakenly named *P. pacificus* originally, and the error persists in much of the literature.

Pandanus pygmaeus (pig-MEE-us) is native to Madagascar. It is, as the specific epithet implies, of dwarf stature, forming no trunk or very short trunks. The leaves are also diminutive and usually no more than 18 inches long; they are narrow but marked with beautiful longitudinal yellow stripes. The small size and colorfulness of the species make it perfect in borders to create an exotic and tropical effect.

Pandanus sanderi (SAN-dur-eye) is native to eastern Malaysia and grows to about 15 feet in cultivation. It is probably the best tree-sized pandanus for the average garden as it is colorful and yet is not gigantic. The narrow leaves are about 3 feet long and exhibit charming thin yellow striations down their midribs.

Pandanus utilis (YOOT-i-lis) is probably originally indigenous to Madagascar, but its origins are obscured as it is the most widespread and most widely planted species in the tropics. It is a large tree, but grows only to about 30 feet in cultivation. It has many aerial roots and spreading branches whose tips bear the dense crowns of stiff dark green waxy-textured leaves. The 6-foot-long leaves bear small red teeth on their margins. Plates 307 and 308.

Pandanus veitchii (VEECH-ee-eye) is indigenous to the islands of the South Pacific. It is similar to *P. sanderi* except that the leaves have white instead of yellow coloration and the plant is somewhat larger.

PANDOREA (pan-DOR-ee-a)
Bignoniaceae: The Catalpa, Jacaranda, Trumpet-Vine Family
Common names vary according to species
Evergreen pinnate-leaved vines; white and pink trumpet-shaped flowers
Zones 9b through 11
Sun to partial shade
Water lovers
Rich, humusy, moist, well-drained soil
Propagation by seed and cuttings

A genus of six species of glossy pinnate-leaved twining vines in Australasia. They have terminal few-flowered inflorescences of fragrant funnel-shaped to bell-shaped flowers in colors of white, yellow, pink, or purple. This genus is yet another that has had a taxonomically checkered past. Some of its members were placed formerly into the genera *Bignonia* and *Tecoma*, and after it was determined that they deserved separate status, some were placed into the genus *Podranea* (an anagram of the word "pandorea").

Pandorea brycei. See *Podranea brycei.*

Pandorea jasminoides (jaz-mi-NOY-deez) (synonyms *Bignonia jasminoides, Tecoma jasminoides*) is native to northeastern Australia. It grows to as much as 30 feet with many slender stems clothed with leaves to the ground if it gets enough moisture, light, and nutrients. The leaves are composed of five to nine glossy and waxy deep green 2-inch-long ovate to lanceolate leaflets. The plants bloom in summer and fall and, in truly tropical areas, produce flowers at almost any time of the year. Each blossom is funnel-shaped and about 2 inches long with a flared five-lobed corolla; the color ranges from white to light pink but the throat of the flower is always a darker pink to almost red in color. This vine is neither very heavy nor dense, but it is perfect for arbors and trellises where flowers and an evergreen twiner are wanted. It also serves as a very good groundcover if it receives enough moisture, although it is not a control for erosion. *Pandorea jasminoides* 'Alba' is a pure white form whose blossom has no pink. The plant is usually called the jasmine pandorea, but also bower plant.

Pandorea pandorana (pan-dor-AN-a) (synonyms *Bignonia australis, B. pandorana, Tecoma australis*) is indigenous to Malaysia, Indonesia, and northern Australia. This vine is denser, heavier, lusher, and taller growing than *P. jasminoides,* with beautiful glossy leaves consisting of five to nine lanceolate 3-inch-long leaflets that are a wonderful bronzy to reddish green when new. It produces its flowers more abundantly than does *P. jasminoides,* but the individual flowers are not as large or showy as those of the former and they are somewhat obscured by the foliage mass. This species is sometimes called the wonga-wonga vine.

Pandorea ricasoliana. See *Podranea ricasoliana.*

PARKINSONIA (park-in-SO-nee-a)
Caesalpiniaceae (Leguminosae), subfamily
    Caesalpinioideae: The Cassia, Royal Poinciana
    Family
JERUSALEM THORN; MEXICAN PALO VERDE
Open, weeping, medium-sized semi-evergreen tree;
    tiny leaves; many yellow flowers in summer
Zones 9 through 11 as a tree; zone 8 as a shrub
Sun
Drought tolerant
Average well-drained soil; tolerant of alkalinity
Propagation by seed

A genus of six species of small to medium-sized spiny trees in warm and dry regions of the Americas and Africa. They have unusual pinnate or bipinnate leaves that consist mainly of the rachis, with the subsidiary leaf stalks of the leaflets reduced to almost non-existence and the leaflets quite tiny. The rachis is accompanied by a pair of thorns at its base where it joins the twig. Only one species is commonly planted. *Parkinsonia aculeata* (a-kyoo´-lee-AIT-a) occurs naturally in drier regions of southern Mexico and Central America. Some

of the literature indicates that it is indigenous to the southern parts of Texas and New Mexico; this is probably not the case but it has become naturalized in the warmer parts of these regions. It is a short-trunked spreading round-crowned tree with light bright green trunks and branches, except for the older wood, which is gray or brown. It grows to as much as 40 feet, but usually attains a maximum of only 30 feet; it grows fast when young and soon makes a fine landscape subject. The leaves are as much as 18 inches long with tiny quarter-inch-long leaflets. The landscape effect is that of having no leaves but only drooping green twigs, which create a fine, airy, and diaphanous green aspect. Often this aspect is not just an appearance, as the tiny leaflets are readily shed with the onset of drought or cold. From mid spring through early summer these trees are covered in short racemes of half-inch-wide five-petaled fragrant yellow flowers. The petals are claw-shaped, and one is larger than the other four and has red or orange streaks or dots at its base. The tree is not, of course, a shade tree, but its graceful form and long flowering period make it unexcelled for varying texture and color in the landscape. It would be the perfect patio tree were it not for the litter of fallen leaves; if that is not a problem then it is a perfect close-up or patio tree. In spite of its origins the tree thrives in areas of normal or even above-normal rainfall as long as the soil is freely draining. It seems to need alternating periods of water and the lack of it to flower at its best. The tree is perfectly at home near the beach as it is quite tolerant of saline as well as alkaline soil conditions. Plate 309.

PARMENTIERA (par-men-TEER-a)
Bignoniaceae: The Catalpa, Jacaranda, Trumpet-
    Vine Family
CANDLE TREE; PANAMA CANDLE TREE;
    CANDLEFRUIT
Small evergreen tree; three-parted leaves; long thin
    waxy yellowish fruit on trunk and branches
Zones 10 and 11; marginal in zone 10a
Sun
Average but regular amounts of moisture
Average well-drained soil
Propagation by seed

A small genus of nine often spiny evergreen shrubs and small trees in southern Mexico, Central America, and northern South America. They have compound leaves of three leaflets and produce their flowers and fruits on the trunks and larger branches of the trees, not at the ends of the branches or twigs. The funnel-shaped or bell-shaped flowers are white or greenish white and appear singly or in few-flowered clusters on the trunks. The fruits are long and narrow in shape and edible if not always tasty. One species is fairly commonly planted in tropical areas as a curiosity or for cattle fodder and sometimes for human consumption. *Parmentiera cereifiera* (ser-ee-IF-e-ra) is a spineless species native to Panama. It grows to 20 or 30 feet and naturally forms a multitrunked specimen, but usually must be trained to standard tree form. The leaves are held on winged stalks and have three ovate to elliptic short-tipped 2-inch-long thin dark green leaflets. The exceptionally beautiful flowers are not showy in the landscape as they are half hidden on the trunk(s) and larger branches; they are nearly stalkless on the trunk and major branches, 2 to 3 inches long, and curved open bell shapes with five scalloped waxy white corolla lobes enclosing the four long stamens. The calyx is a dull brown in color. The fruits are the reason most people grow this tree. They are short-stalked narrow yellow or white waxy cylinders, each of which may grow to 3 or even 4 feet long. The fruits have a strong vegetable odor that many people compare to that of ripe apples, and they are relished as a vegetable by some and grown in many places for cattle fodder. When first seen, these curtains of white or yellow are almost startlingly exotic. When one grows accustomed to them, they are merely fascinatingly or beautifully exotic. The fruit spectacle is best seen on open trees, which have either been thinned of some of the many trunks they tend to form or have been trained to a single trunk.

PASSIFLORA (PAS-i-flor-a)
Passifloraceae: The Passionflower Family
PASSIONFLOWER
Large evergreen vines; bold leaves; spectacular exotic
   flowers in every color; large fruit
Zones vary according to species
Sun to partial shade
Average but regular amounts of moisture
Average well-drained soil
Propagation by seed and cuttings

A very large genus of about 500 species of vines and scandent shrubs, mainly in tropical America but found in all tropical and subtropical regions around the world. They climb by stout tendrils—a very few having tendrils reduced to curved spines—and usually have large lobed leaves, always with a pair of stipules, although a few species have entire leaves. The bold and remarkable flowers are unlike those of any other genus of plants.

The flowers are organized into two main parts: the bracts, calyx tube, sepals, petals, and corona on one level, and a central column, called an "androgynophore" (an-dro-JYN-o-for), forming the upper or second level. All passionflower blossoms have three variously shaped bracts beneath the actual flower, which may wither and fall off at an early stage of the flower's development or which may be persistent. The corolla has five sepals and five petals and is borne atop a "calyx tube," which is simply a cylindrical or cup-shaped fusion of the lower parts of the sepals and petals. There are one or more circular rings of filaments growing from the center of the petals, a structure called a "corona" (Latin for "crown"), which constitutes the innermost part of the flower's "disk." The androgynophore is sim-

ply a straight tall fleshy column arising from the center of the whorl of sepals and petals (the blossom's disk) atop which are borne the male parts (stamens) and, above them, the female parts (ovary, styles, and stigmas). The fruits are relatively large (some very large) and are technically many-seeded juicy berries. Some of the fruits have edible and delicious flesh. Many of these species are prime butterfly attractors, but their beauty must be partially sacrificed for the butterflies, which seek the vines to lay their eggs on; when the eggs hatch, the ensuing caterpillars start eating the leaves and stems.

The derivation of the vernacular name for this genus comes from the very fanciful and anthropomorphic interpretations of the flowers by botanically oriented Christian missionaries in the newly discovered Americas of the early seventeenth century. The androgynophore is supposed to represent the crown of thorns, and the stamens and stigmas, the nails, used to pin Jesus Christ to the cross. It is not known upon which species all this imagination was expended, but every part of the flowers, including the three bracts (the Trinity), was explained at one time or another as representing a part of Christ's Passion.

The summarized description in the header of this encyclopedia entry may cause the reader to believe that the species in this genus constitute the perfect vines, with beautiful leaves and lush growth, fantastic and exquisite, often fragrant flowers, and beautiful and often edible fruit; and so they are. All *Passiflora* species are worthy of having; only space and climate can limit the choice. These plants are not only wondrously attractive, they are also exceptionally easy to grow given a warm enough climate and adequate and regular amounts of moisture. Almost without exception the species are not particular as to soil. Indeed, many require a nutrient-deficient sandy soil in which to thrive and to produce the maximum number and size of flowers. A nutrient-rich soil tends to promote foliage growth at the expense of the blossoms. The one almost universal requirement is warmth. According to passionflower expert John Vanderplank, there are only three species and a few cultivars that show any hardiness to cold. The following entries, which are but a sampling of the wonderful leaves, flowers, and fruits available in this genus, only mention the appropriate zones if they are other than zones 10 and 11, and the growth of the vines should be assumed to be lush, large, and vigorous unless indicated otherwise. Several of the species have vernacular names that include the word *pop*; this seems to be derived neither from the verb nor the regional use of the word for a bottled or carbonated beverage, but rather is a derivation from an Amerindian word for the species native to the United States.

Passiflora actinia (ak-TIN-ee-a) is native to southern Brazil but is hardy in zones 9b through 11 as a permanent perennial and sprouts from the root in zone 9 and possibly zone 8a. It is not one of the big species; it grows only to 10 or 15 feet with thin stems. The leaves are entire, ovate to almost round, and about 4 inches wide. The flower's petals are pure white and reflexed. The corona is composed of many thick long filaments that are banded with purple and white. The central column is flesh-colored with bright orange anthers.

Passiflora alata (a-LAIT-a) is native to eastern Brazil and is hardy in zones 10 and 11 but will sprout from the root in zone 9b. The leaves are entire, about 6 inches long, and ovate. The fragrant flowers are among the most beautiful in the genus. They have petals that are a deep red inside and white outside, and a light pink corona with thick long filaments that are each banded with white, red, and purple. The large anthers are yellow, and the pure white stigmas are borne on yellow-green styles. The 6-inch-long orange oval fruits are not only edible but reportedly delicious.

Passiflora ×alato-caerulea (a-lait´-o-see-ROOL-ee-a) (synonym *P. pfordtii*) is a hybrid between *P. alata* and *P. caerulea*. It is hardy in zones 9 through 11 and sometimes in zone 8b. One of the oldest and most popular hybrids, it is quite free flowering and easy of culture. The three-lobed leaves are about 5 inches wide. The very fragrant flowers have white sepals and light pink petals, the former alternating in arrangement with the latter so that the effect is that of 10 bicolored petals. The corona filaments are long, thin, and a deep purple, and the central column is pea-green with yellow stamens. Some people find the fragrance of this flower alluring and pleasant; others find it offensive. Plate 310.

Passiflora amethystina (am-e-THIST-i-na / am-e-this-TYN-a) is indigenous to eastern Brazil and is hardy in zones 10 and 11 but sprouts from the root in zone 9b. It is a slender-stemmed species growing only to about 15 feet. The leaves are deeply three-lobed and about 3 inches long. The flowers are symphonies of pink, rose, purple, white, and green, and are produced all year in tropical climes. The reflexed petals and sepals are a deep rose or purple in color. The corona is composed of relatively short thin dark purple filaments with one or two white bands. The central column is white at its base and light green on the column itself, and bears deep green and yellow anthers with ruddy-colored styles and stigmas above.

Passiflora antioquiensis (an´-tee-ahk-wee-EN-sis) is native to Colombia. Its juvenile leaves are not lobed, but the mature leaves are very deeply three-lobed and about 6 inches long by 3 inches wide; each lobe has serrate margins. The flowers, which are quite unusual for a *Passiflora* species and which were responsible for the species formerly being placed into a separate genus, *Tacsonia*, lack a distinct corona, but the petals and sepals are very long and a deep carmine red. The corona is much reduced to a short purple ring. The central column is very long and fleshy pink at its base, the thin anthers yellow, and the stigmas green atop white styles. The yellow edible fruits are shaped like small bananas, which fact results in the common names of banana passion fruit and banana passionflower.

Passiflora caerulea (see-ROOL-ee-a) is native to southern Brazil and northern Argentina. It is hardy in zones 9b through 11 and will resprout from the root in zone 9a and sometimes in zone 8b. One of the most widely grown species, it and most of its cultivars and hybrids are some of the most rampant and fastest growing species, covering a fairly large area in a relatively short time. In Houston, where it grows to the tops of the trees and "jumps" from there to anything else it wants to, there are camphor and oak trees with giant purplish blossoms! The beautiful leaves are deep green, glossy, and very deeply lobed into five to nine linear usually scalloped segments. The 4-inch-wide flowers have white or greenish white sepals and petals. The corona filaments are numerous and relatively thin, and deep purple to almost black at their bases with a band of white or pink above the purple; the upper halves are a deep lilac to purple. The central column carries large green and yellow anthers topped by reddish brown styles and stigmas. The fruits are edible but not delicious; they are about 3 inches long, oval in shape and orange in color when ripe. The type is called blue passionflower, although the overall color is more purple and white than blue. There are several hybrids and cultivars of this species. *Passiflora caerulea* 'Constance Elliott' has white to greenish white sepals and petals and many long yellow-white corona filaments. *Passiflora caerulea* 'Grandiflora' (gran-di-FLOR-a) has flowers that are almost twice as large as those of the type.

Passiflora coccinea (kahk-SIN-ee-a) is native to most of northern South America. The 5-inch-long leaves are unsegmented, oblong, acuminate, and shallowly serrate on the margins. The flowers, except for the yellow anthers, are almost entirely scarlet. The red corona filaments are clasped around the central column and may be partly pinkish or purplish. The round orange 2-inch-wide fruits are edible and reportedly delicious. The vine and its fruit are called the red granadilla (grahn-a-DEE-ya).

Passiflora edulis (ED-yoo-lis) is indigenous to southern Brazil, Paraguay, and northern Argentina. It is doubtless the most widely grown species because of the large edible fruit. The deep green glossy and very attractive leaves are about 10 inches long and three-lobed; the lobes have marginal serrations. The 3- to 4-inch-wide flowers are quite attractive but not the showiest in the genus. The petals and sepals are green and white. The corolla filaments are very numerous and lengthy, their apical halves curled and white, the lower halves lilac and purple. The central column and its parts are a dull yellow. The sweetly acidic round fruit is about 3 inches wide and a deep purple when ripe. There several cultivated varieties of the purple passionfruit or purple granadilla (grahn-a-DEE-ya). *Passiflora edulis* 'Flavicarpa' (flayv-i-KARP-a) has larger yellow fruit and larger flowers. All forms of this species have been known to recover from freezing temperatures in zone 9b.

Passiflora foetida (FET-i-da / fee-TYD-a) was

originally native to Central and South America and much of the West Indies, but is now naturalized in every tropical and subtropical region of the globe. It is hardy in zones 10 and 11, but resprouts from its roots in zone 9 and readily reseeds itself. It is a rank grower with rank-smelling hairy foliage and stems; but it is also a fascinating and beautiful species. The 6-inch-long leaves are three-lobed; each lobe is margined with teeth. The flower bracts are extremely large and divided into many fine segments like green feathers that extend beneath and beyond the width of the blossom itself. The sepals and petals may be white, pink, or lilac, and are semireflexed. The corona filaments are long and down-turned, purple at their bases, white in their middle zone, and pink on their outer zone. The central column is rose-colored on the stalk with bright green and yellow sexual parts. The fruits are inch-long usually globular berries that are reported to be edible; they are enclosed in the feathery and persistent bracts, and range in color from almost white through yellow, pink, and red. This species is very variable, with leaf shape and size, flower color, and fruit color and size varying from one form to another. The vernacular names for this species are many, the most common being love-in-a-mist (because of the great feathery bracts), wild water lemon, and running pop.

Passiflora incarnata (in-kar-NAIT-a) is native to the eastern and southern United States and is the hardiest species in the genus, being adaptable to zones 7 through 11 and probably root hardy in colder zones although it is naturally deciduous and dies back in all zones. The 6-inch-long leaves are three-lobed with fine serrations along the margins of each segment. The sepals and petals may be white, greenish white, pink, or purplish. The corona filaments are long, often longer than the corolla, twisted at their apical ends, usually white at their bases, and pink above that zone with purple maculation. The central column bears large whitish yellow anthers held by greenish, black spotted stamen filaments with large white and yellow styles and stigmas. The 2- to 3-inch-long oval fruits are yellowish when mature and insipidly sweet. *Passiflora incarnata* goes by the names maypop, wild passionflower, and May vine. *Passiflora* **'Incense'** is a hybrid between *P. incarnata* and *P. cincinnata* that is not as hardy as the maypop, being root hardy in zone 8b; it is a popular hybrid form with 8-inch-long five-lobed leaves and almost totally lilac or violet-colored flowers with a strong scent.

Passiflora mollissima is native to the Andean (low elevations) region of South America. It is quite similar to *P. antioquiensis* in all characters, but the flowers are light pink in color. It even has the same vernacular name as *P. antioquiensis*: banana passion fruit.

Passiflora pfordtii. See *P.* ×*alato-caerulea*.

Passiflora quadrangularis (kwa-drang'-yoo-LAIR-is) is indigenous to Central America and parts of the West Indies, but is so popular and has been so widely grown for so long that its range now is the entire tropical world. This gigantic and fast-growing vine has 10-inch-long broadly ovate soft, deep green heavily veined entire leaves. The 5-inch-wide fragrant flowers are sweet dreams of red, purple, and white. The slightly reflexed sepals and petals may be white or red. The incredible corona forms a broad cup in the center of the flower, and the individual filaments are banded with reddish brown and alternating zones of white and purple. The central column is relatively short and is provided with colors of ivory and chocolate. The fruits of this species, which are the largest in the genus and as much as a foot long, are oblong in shape and orange in color when ripe. Because of the sweet fruit, the species is known as the granadilla (grahn-a-DEE-ya) or giant granadilla.

Passiflora racemosa (rays-i-MO-sa) is indigenous to eastern Brazil. This free-flowering species has long pendent racemes of red flowers. The 5-inch-long mature leaves are three-lobed, but the immature plants bear entire leaves. The leaves are not dense on the vine, and almost every one stands out against its background. The flower is about 4 inches wide with deep red narrow sepals and petals. The corona is composed of short filaments that are violet basally and white on their upper halves. The central column is tall and light green in color except for the yellow anthers. The 3-inch-long four-sided fruits are light green when ripe. Because of the great long inflorescences (as much as 3 feet) this species is one of the most spectacular when in bloom. It is usually called the red passionflower.

Passiflora vitifolia (vit-i-FO-lee-a) is native to Central America and northern South America. It is a large, strong growing, and vigorous vine with 6-inch-long deep green three-lobed leaves; the lobes are irregularly and shallowly scalloped. The giant fragrant 8-inch-wide flowers are nothing short of breathtaking. The sepals and petals are a vivid deep red and, as the flower ages, become distinctly reflexed. The corona filaments are short and deep purplish red and pink. The central column is also red with yellow anthers and white stigmas. The small velvety fruits are supposedly edible. Plate 311.

PAUROTIS. See *Acoelorraphe*.

PEDILANTHUS (ped-i-LANTH-us)
Euphorbiaceae: The Euphorbia, Spurge Family
DEVIL'S BACKBONE; SLIPPER SPURGE;
    REDBIRD CACTUS; CHRISTMAS CANDLE
Succulent evergreen shrub; zigzagging fleshy stems;
    thick waxy leaves; starlike clusters of red flowers
Zones 10 and 11; marginal in zone 9b
Sun to partial shade
Drought tolerant
Average well-drained soil
Propagation by cuttings and (sometimes) seed

A genus of a dozen or so species of succulent shrubs found in semiarid regions of Mexico, Central America, northern South America, and parts of the West Indies. They contain a milky sap, which is mildly poisonous and to which many people are allergic. The leaves are alternate in arrangement and never segmented. The flowers are in unusual rounded and usually star-shaped clusters. The bracts, which enclose the tiny flowers, make whatever show there is. One species is very commonly planted in tropical regions for its cultivar with variegated leaves and red flowers (bracts). *Pedilanthus tithymaloides* (tith´-ee-ma-LOY-deez) is native to some of the Florida Keys and the West Indies, Mexico and southwards into northern South America. It grows to as much as 10 feet, but is usually 4 to 6 feet tall in cultivation and as wide or wider, with green rubbery zigzagging stems. The dark green 4-inch-long leaves are short-stalked and ovate, with a short apical "tail." They grow from opposite sides of the stems in a distinct and flat plane at 180° from one another and are deciduous with cold or prolonged drought conditions. The type is rather rare in cultivation. *Pedilanthus tithymaloides* **'Variegatus'** (vair´-ee-a-GAIT-a), an attractive cultivar, usually replaces the species in gardens. Its leaves are mottled with white and pink, and its stems are finely striated with white. There is a dwarf form of the type and the variegated cultivar. The star-shaped inflorescences are borne all over the ends of the stems and appear mostly in summer but, in truly topical regions, in cycles year-round; they consist of a dozen or so tiny red flowers peeking out from the ends of their slipper-shaped scarlet enclosures of overlapping bracts. Birds seem quite fond of the half-inch-wide ovoid striped seed pods. The plants are extremely easy of culture, needing only at least a half day's sun and a very well draining soil to thrive. They are mostly used for hedges, but are quite attractive in a raised bed with other tropicals and are superb for adding color in the cactus and succulent garden. Like most other drought tolerant plants, they do better with irrigation in periods of prolonged drought. The plants are grown in zone 9b where they usually quickly recover from sharp frosts.

PELLIONIA (pel-lee-O-nee-a)
Urticaceae: The Nettle, Pilea Family
Common names vary according to species
Low creeping succulent evergreen herbs; pink stems; beautiful variegated leaves
Zones 10b and 11
Shade to partial shade
Average but regular amounts of moisture
Rich, humusy, well-drained soil
Propagation by cuttings

A genus of about 50 mostly succulent low-growing herbs in tropical and subtropical Asia. They have nearly stalkless, alternately arranged, and undivided leaves. The tiny flowers are in small clusters and are insignificant in the landscape, but the size and variegation of the leaves in some species make them ideal and quite choice for groundcovers, borders, overhanging low shady walls, and hanging basket subjects in tropical areas. They are quite tender and are marginal in zone 10a but usually recover from the occasional frost in that zone.

Pellionia daveauana (da-vay´-a-WAHN-a) is indigenous to Southeast Asia. It grows only to about a foot in height, but the creeping 2-foot-long pink stems trail along the ground and tend to root at the nodes, making it an exquisite choice for a groundcover in shady or partially shaded areas. The 2- to 3-inch-long elliptic to lanceolate reddish purple to almost black leaves are shallowly scalloped on their margins and beautifully variegated with a wide central area of silver and light green streaks. This little beauty is unfortunately called trailing watermelon begonia; it is not a begonia.

Pellionia pulchra is indigenous to Vietnam. It is similar in size, shape, and landscape use to *P. daveauana*, but the stems are deep rose to purple in color and the upper sides of the leaves are grayish green with deep dark brown or black main veins and purple or rose undersides.

PELTOPHORUM
(pelt-o-FOR-um / pel-TAHF-o-rum)
Caesalpiniaceae (Leguminosae), subfamily Caesalpinioideae: The Cassia, Royal Poinciana Family
YELLOW POINCIANA; YELLOW-FLAME TREE; YELLOW FLAMBOYANT; COPPER POD
Medium-sized evergreen trees; large ferny foliage; spectacular giant sprays of yellow flowers
Zones 10 and 11; marginal in zone 9b
Sun
Average but regular amounts of moisture
Average well-drained soil
Propagation by seed

A genus of about 15 tree species in tropical areas worldwide. They are medium-sized to fairly large trees with large bipinnate foliage and majestic terminal panicles of yellow five-petaled slightly to very fragrant yellow flowers. The seed pods are flat and mostly oblong in shape. The two species that are commonly planted in tropical and subtropical areas are quite similar in general appearance including the flower panicles; one is arguably superior because of its slightly larger leaves whose youthful color is apparent and of exceptional beauty. It is hard to over praise these wonderful trees; they are fast growing, extremely easy of culture, spectacular of form, leaf, and flower, and the very essence of the tropical look. While somewhat drought tolerant when established, they look and thrive ever so much better with adequate and regular amounts of moisture.

Peltophorum dubium (DOO-bee-um) (synonym *P. vogelianum*) is native to Brazil. It is similar to *P. pterocarpum*, but has somewhat smaller leaflets and therefore somewhat smaller leaves, its new leaves have only a slight amount of or no rusty tomentum, and the tree is slightly hardier to cold. It blooms in late spring and summer and often into the autumn, as does *P. ptero-carpum*, and flowered magnificently in Houston, Texas, for two successive years following three mild winters. The tree is very fast growing.

Peltophorum ferrugineum. See *P. pterocarpum*.
Peltophorum inerme. See *P. pterocarpum*.

Peltophorum pterocarpum (ter-o-KARP-um) (synonyms *P. ferrugineum, P. inerme, P. roxburghii*) is indigenous to a wide area of tropical Asia from India through Malaysia to Australia and northwards to the Philippines. The tree naturally makes a broad dense crown of large ferny foliage atop a rather short massive gray trunk and grows to as much as 50 feet although 30 feet is more usual. It is unsurpassed as a shade or street tree as there is not much litter. The leaves are as much as 2 feet long with many half-inch-long dark green leaflets, reminiscent of but even more beautiful than those of *Jacaranda* species, partly because the new foliage is covered in a rusty tomentum that adds an entrancing color effect. The leaves drop in severe cold or drought conditions. The great 2- to 3-foot-tall flower panicles of this tree appear in late spring through autumn and put it in the same spectacular class as *Delonix regia* (royal poinciana), although it usually blooms over a longer period. As for the inch-wide individual clear yellow flowers, Kathryn Gough in *A Garden Book for Malaysia* (1928) is quoted by Edwin A. Menninger in *Flowering Trees of the World* (1962):

> Best of all for cutting are the luminous flowers; those that glow and hold light. I do not know what it is that gives some flowers a 'lit-up' look; not only does the light shine through their petals, but they seem to catch, reflect, and hold it. . . . Yellow and flame-colored dahlias hold light, and so do the fleeting single hibiscus, blue morning-glory, and above all, the golden spikes of *Peltophorum inerme*. Sprays of these flowers indoors seem liquid gold; they are wonderfully beautiful with their decorative, unopened, tight bronze buds and bronze stems, just touched with gilt. The fully opened flowers have crinkled golden petals and orange-tipped stamens. The light shines and glows in a mass of these beautiful flowers more intensely in the shade indoors than when they are growing outside.

This luminosity of the flower clusters is also apparent outdoors (see Plate 312). The fruits are flat 3-inch-long four-seeded oblong pods that turn a wine-brown color when ripe and are attractive in themselves. The only fault these enchanting trees have is that their trunks and branches are prone to damage in storms.

Peltophorum roxburghii. See *P. pterocarpum*.

PEPEROMIA (pep-e-ROAM-ee-a)
Piperaceae: The Black Pepper, Peperomia Family
Common names vary according to species

Small, mostly succulent herbs; fleshy, beautifully variegated and often tomentose leaves
Zones 10b and 11; some survive in zone 10a
Shade to partial shade
Average but regular amounts of moisture
Rich, humusy, very well drained soil
Propagation by cuttings

A very large genus of 1000 or more species of smallish mostly succulent and fleshy-leaved perennials in tropical areas worldwide but mostly the Americas. They are of such diverse leaf character and growth form as to cause the uninitiated to wonder what the botanical taxonomists were thinking of to lump them together into one genus; the answer is much more apparent when the plants flower. The inflorescences are quite typical of the pepper family: minute flowers without sepals or petals, very densely packed into thin tail-like—and, in genus *Peperomia*, prominently erect—spikes that are usually white, green, or yellowish in color. The leaves are usually long stalked, thick, and fleshy, always undivided, and usually with prominent venation and wondrous variegation. Many species are epiphytic with creeping, rooting stems and, while all are denizens of wet forests, some of them, especially the epiphytic species, absolutely demand perfect drainage in whatever medium they are planted.

This great genus of plants includes some of the most deliciously beautiful leaves in the world, making them unexcelled as shady groundcovers or for low bedding plants in shady tropical and subtropical regions. They are equally beautiful and appropriate planted among rocks in shady water garden areas. None of them can withstand much frost and, while they usually recover, are somewhat marginal even in zone 10a.

With at least a thousand species and innumerable cultivars and hybrids of these, only a cursory examination of their extraordinary diversity is possible and I have included only the more popular, more commonly grown species and varieties, especially those with striking variegation or color. But there is still a great world of beauty waiting for the adventurous tropical plant hunter or gardener.

Peperomia argyreia (ahr-ji-REE-a) (synonyms *P. peltifolia, P. sandersii*) is native to northern South America including the northern half of Brazil. It grows to no more than a foot and has thick peltate, ovate 6-inch-long bluish green leaves that are wonderfully marked with broad feathery bands of silver radiating downwards from the point of attachment to the red leaf stalk. This species does not quickly spread or creep as many others and is best used as a color accent for shady areas although, planted en masse, it makes one of the most attractive groundcovers. One of its unfortunate vernacular names is watermelon begonia, which should be eschewed in favor of watermelon peperomia.

Peperomia bicolor (BY-kul-or) is native to Ecuador. It grows to about a foot in height with many creeping and trailing succulent but pubescent reddish brown stems. The 2-inch-long broadly elliptical to broadly ovate leaves are a metallic grayish green above with a broad silver midrib and longitudinal veins. The upper surface of the leaf is finely pubescent and velvety to the touch, while the lower surface is a deep rose in color. This superb and almost unbelievably beautiful groundcover is also very lovely in a hanging basket or growing on a low wall. It is sometimes called the Inca princess or silver velvet peperomia.

Peperomia blanda (BLAN-da) (synonym *P. langsdorfii*) is native to northern South America and the West Indies. It is one of the larger species, growing to almost 2 feet, with beautiful felty red stems. The 4-inch-long elliptic to obovate felty leaves are deep green with longitudinal white veins above and a wine-red color beneath.

Peperomia caperata (kap-e-RAIT-a) is probably indigenous to Brazil. It (including its varieties) is possibly the most widely cultivated *Peperomia* species, especially as a house or greenhouse plant. It is a clumping species, superb as an accent but, like the other clumping species, is extraordinarily attractive planted en masse as a groundcover. The plant seldom grows to more than a foot in height. The leaves are deep green above, light red beneath, broadly ovate to almost orbicular in shape, and more or less peltate in attachment to the pink leaf stalk. They are thick and glossy with prominent veins between which the waxy leaf surface is distinctly puckered. There are several cultivars of this very popular species including forms with differently variegated leaves. Vernacular names for this species and some of its cultivars are emerald ripple, green ripple, red ripple, and little fantasy.

Peperomia clusiifolia (kloo´-see-eye-FO-lee-a) occurs naturally in the West Indies and northern South America. It grows usually to only a foot in height with thick elliptic to obovate 3- to 6-inch-long dark green leaves that are margined with a wine-red strip. It is usually called the red-edged peperomia.

Peperomia elongata (ee-lahn-GAIT-a) is native to northern South America. It grows to only 6 inches or so, spreads by its roots, and is a near perfect groundcover. The thick glossy 3-inch-long leaves are elliptic in shape and a deep green in color with wide silvery midrib and pale longitudinal veins.

Peperomia griseoargentea (griz´-ee-o-ahr-JEN-tee-a) (synonym *P. hederifolia*) is native to Brazil. It grows to usually less than a foot in height. The deep pink 4-inch-long petioles carry the 3-inch-wide ovate to orbicular thick and succulent leaves whose glossy light green surface is puckered between the raised and much darker veins. This beauty is sometimes called the ivy-leaf peperomia or ivy peperomia, but also the platinum peperomia and the silver-leaf peperomia. It is very tender to cold.

Peperomia hederifolia. See *P. griseoargentea*.

Peperomia hirta (HEER-ta) is indigenous to Cuba. It grows to only 6 inches or so and trails along the ground. The exquisite 2-inch-long obovate and somewhat cupped leaves are a deep mint green above and

are covered with a satiny plush of velvety short gray hairs.

Peperomia langsdorfii. See *P. blanda*.

Peperomia maculosa (mak-yoo-LO-sa) (synonym *P. variegata*) is native to parts of the West Indies, Panama, and northern South America. It is one of the most beautiful and one of the largest-leaved species in the genus. It grows to a foot or more in height, and its fleshy stems and petioles are maculated with reddish purple dots. The leaves are as much as 7 inches long and are variable in shape from elliptical to almost orbicular. Leaf color is a deep bluish green above with a wide silver-colored midrib and longitudinal veins and a pale greenish white to pink below. This gorgeous plant is sometimes called, for no apparent reason, the radiator plant.

Peperomia metallica (met-AL-lik-a) is indigenous to eastern Peru. It grows to about 6 inches, sometimes more, with pink stems, inch-long linear-lanceolate waxy coppery-green leaves bearing a fairly wide silvery and usually feathery-shaped midrib. This exceptionally attractive species creeps and trails along the ground, making it the perfect tropical groundcover for shady or partially shady sites.

Peperomia obtusifolia (ahb-tyoos´-i-FO-lee-a) is indigenous to southeastern Mexico down through northern South America and much of the West Indies. It is a variable species (to be expected with such a large natural range), but typically grows to less than a foot in height with 5- to 8-inch-long spatulate or obovate somewhat cup-shaped dark green waxy leaves that are usually wedge-shaped at the attachment to the leaf stalk. The mostly prostrate stems and short leaf stalks are streaked and splotched with or sometimes entirely maroon. There are many cultivated forms of this little plant varying mostly in leaf color. Some of them are so heavily variegated as to have no apparent green in the leaf. *Peperomia obtusifolia* **'Variegata'**, the most beautiful of these cultivars, has markings of ivory, some green, and rose or red. These plants are probably the second most, if not the most, widely grown and popular in the genus, and they carry several common names including baby rubber plant, American rubber plant, and pepper-face.

Peperomia ornata (or-NAIT-a) is found naturally in southern Venezuela and northern Brazil. It is a clumping non-creeping type that grows usually to only a foot. It has pseudorosettes of 5-inch-long wine-red petioles holding 6-inch-long elliptical leaves that are gray-green with deep green feathery veins above and even are an even paler green beneath with red veins.

Peperomia peltifolia. See *P. argyreia*.

Peperomia pseudovariegata (soo´-do-vair-ee-a-GAIT-a) is native to Ecuador and southwestern Colombia. It grows to a foot or so, but is mostly scandent and trailing. It has long-stalked red petioles carrying glossy 6-inch-long dark green elliptic leaves. *Peperomia pseudovariegata* **var. sarcophylla** (sahr-ko-FYL-la) (synonym *P. sarcophylla*) has leaves with a prominent gray midrib and gray-green longitudinal veins and is exceedingly attractive.

Peperomia puteolata (pyoo´-tee-o-LAIT-a) is native to Peru. It is an extraordinarily handsome plant, growing to a foot or so in height but having long trailing purplish red stems. The narrowly elliptic to narrowly ovate 5-inch-long leaves are long-tipped and a deep waxy green above with deeply depressed veins of yellowish white. This species is one of the most attractive groundcovers or hanging basket subjects, and it is superb planted in or cascading over low stone walls. It is sometimes called parallel peperomia.

Peperomia sandersii. See *P. argyreia*.

Peperomia sarcophylla. See *P. pseudovariegata* var. *sarcophylla*.

Peperomia variegata. See *P. maculosa*.

Peperomia velutina (ve-LOOT-in-a / vel-oo-TYN-a) is indigenous to Ecuador. It grows to a foot or so in height with many reddish purple zigzagging stems. The 3-inch-long velvety coppery-green ovate leaves have a prominent silver-colored midrib and longitudinal veins above; the undersides of the leaves are a salmon to red in color. Aptly called the velvet peperomia, it is a very lovely plant similar to *P. bicolor*.

PERESKIA (pe-RES-kee-a)
Cactaceae: The Cactus Family
LEAF CACTUS; BLADE APPLE
Very spiny-stemmed, leafy, shrubs or small trees;
    broad leaves; white, yellow, pink, or red flowers
Zones 10 and 11; zone 9b as root hardy shrubs
Sun
Average but regular amounts of moisture
Humusy, very well drained soil; somewhat drought
    tolerant
Propagation by cuttings and (sometimes) seed

An unusual cactus genus of fewer than 20 species of large leafy shrubs, many of them scandent or climbing, and a few erect small trees. They differ from almost all other cactus species in having unsegmented, mostly woody, cylindrical, only remotely succulent but very spiny stems and broad (not reduced, not early deciduous, and not tiny or scalelike) mostly evergreen leaves. These relatively large leaves naturally drop with cold or prolonged drought. Although these plants do not outwardly appear to be members of the cactus family, they indeed are true cactus plants. They are as beautiful as most other more traditional appearing cactus species, especially when in flower. The flowers are usually cup-shaped and rather similar in form and color to "single" roses, but they usually bloom more freely than those rose types. These plants tend to bloom in cycles of aridity followed by moisture. In their native habitats this can occur at intervals throughout the year, but in wetter climes they do not lose their leaves and will bloom in cycles unrelated to rainfall, mostly in the summer. The members of this cactus genus differ from the much more succulent cactus species in needing more regular amounts of moisture and, in general, a more nutritious soil. They do not grow in areas as arid as the true desert regions where species like *Ferocactus* (barrel cactus) thrive. Rather they are found in what are called "tropical thorn forests," semiarid areas in which many species of mostly deciduous tropical trees with thorns and some of the giant tree cactus species grow. For landscaping purposes, most of them are supreme large hedge material.

Pereskia aculeata (a-kyoo´-lee-AIT-a) is found naturally in the Florida Keys, most of the West Indies, through Brazil and Venezuela and into Paraguay. It is a giant scandent shrub type whose growth is too quick and loose to train to a standard tree form; it forms many very long and long-ranging spiny stems. The fleshy leaves are thick and dark green, ovate to lanceolate in shape and about 3 inches long. Black spines from 1 to 3 inches long grow from the leaf axils. The plants bloom in summer and fall with large clusters of cup-shaped 2-inch-wide fragrant flowers consisting of at least 10, sometimes as many as 20, white to yellowish white ovate sharp-tipped petals. The centers of the flowers are filled with many stamens with yellow or orange anthers surrounding the style and stigmas. Although the round inch-wide orange-yellow fruits are covered in spines, they are edible and are relished by many people. Common names are Barbados gooseberry, lemon vine, and leaf cactus. ***Pereskia aculeata* 'Godseffiana'** (gahd-sef´-fee-AHN-a) is a beautiful cultivar whose new foliage is a lovely coppery rose in color that slowly ages to a coppery olive green. The undersides of the leaves are a beautiful purplish in color.

Pereskia bleo (BLAY-o) is native to Panama and Colombia. It is a large shrub or small tree without much tendency to climb. It can be trained to an attractive standard, growing to as much as 25 feet, but this requires maintenance as the plants grow fast and tend to produce branches from almost any part of the trunk. The young stems are decidedly red in color, but turn green and then gray with age. The leaves are exceptionally beautiful and look more like those of a tropical rain forest tree than a denizen of semiarid areas and, indeed, this is almost the case. The species is found in relatively arid regions of its natural range, but Panama and Colombia cannot be said to be truly "arid" in anyone's book. The leaves are as much as 8 inches long, heavily veined, thin and soft, a deep green in color, and ovate to lanceolate in shape. There are several 2-inch-long black spines arising from the leaf axils. The flowers are among the loveliest in the family: 2-inch-wide deep pink to orange-red to scarlet blossoms borne in few-flowered clusters along the branches, with broadly ovate waxy petals and centers of clear yellow stamens and pistil. The spineless juicy fruits are globular in shape and about 2 inches in diameter. The plant is sometimes called the wax rose.

Pereskia grandifolia (grand-i-FO-lee-a) is native to Brazil. It grows from 8 to 15 feet in height with long-ranging scandent limbs and does not naturally make a tree form. The dark green leaves are as much as 8 inches long and are elliptic to oblong in shape with one or two black straight 2-inch-long spines in the axils. The 2-inch-wide flowers have obovate and usually notched pink petals with a white suffusion at their bases, and they surround a central mass of golden stamens and a pure white pistil. This species is probably the most commonly planted in the genus and is sometimes called the rose cactus. Plates 28 and 313.

Pereskia lychnidiflora (lik-nid´-i-FLOR-a) is a tree type from southern Mexico and Central America growing to 30 feet or more. The plant has very variable leaves that may be lanceolate to almost orbicular and are anywhere from half an inch to 4 inches in length and width. A single 2-inch-long black spine grows from each leaf axil. The flowers are exceptionally beautiful 3-inch-wide orange to deep yellow cups, whose petals are usually lighter colored at their bases. A perfect little tree for dry areas or a specimen in the cactus and succulent garden, this beautiful plant is somewhat less hardy to cold than the other species and should not be attempted outside zones 10b and 11.

Pereskia nemorosa (nee-mo-RO-sa) is indigenous to southern Brazil, Uruguay, Paraguay, and northern Argentina, and is slightly hardier to cold than most other species, being usually dependable in the warmer parts of zone 9b. It grows to as much as 25 feet, but is usually a shrub form and must be trained to a standard if a tree form is desired. The thick dark green 5-inch-long leaves are elliptic to obovate in shape and are accompanied by several 2-inch-long black spines in their axils. The 3- to 4-inch-wide flowers are pink, and the petals are usually white at their bases.

PERSEA (PURS-ee-a / PER-see-a)
Lauraceae: The Laurel, Avocado, Sassafras Family
AVOCADO; ALLIGATOR PEAR; AGUACATE; AHUACATE
Evergreen trees; large shiny leaves; clusters of tiny flowers; large green and purplish edible fruit
Zones vary according to species and variety
Sun
Average but regular amounts of moisture
Rich, humusy, sandy, very well drained soil
Propagation by seed and cuttings; named cultivars are usually grafted

A large genus of about 150 species of evergreen trees in warm and tropical parts of the Americas and Asia. They have alternately arranged entire usually large and glossy leaves, tiny flowers arising from the leaf axils, and usually large berrylike fruits. One tropical American species is grown in all tropical and subtropical regions for its large edible fruits; this is the avocado, an extremely attractive and tropical looking tree in and out of fruit.

Persea americana (a-mer´-i-KAHN-a) (synonym *P. gratissima*) is indigenous to tropical America, but has been cultivated for so very long that its original and exact habitats are unknown. It naturally grows into a broad and spreading tree to as much as 60 feet in height with a relatively short and fissured trunk that is dark in color. The overall appearance of a large avocado tree is like that of a live oak (*Quercus virginiana*). The ovate to elliptic leaves are from 6 to 12 or sometimes even 18 inches long, and usually glossy and heavily veined, with the midrib and lateral veins lighter in color. The leaves are almost invariably of a lighter color and somewhat pubescent on their undersides. The hardier races (the Mexican and some of the Guatemalan) usually have points at the leaf ends. Plate 314.

There are now very many forms of the avocado, and it has been determined that one large group, the Mexican race, is probably derived from a different species, namely, *Persea drymifolia* (drim-i-FO-lee-a / dry-mi-FO-lee-a) (synonym *P. americana* var. *drymifolia*). It occurs naturally in the Mexican highlands and into northern Mexico, whereas *P. americana* is indigenous to lower and wetter parts of tropical America. Mexican avocado trees usually are not as large as the forms and hybrids of *P. americana*, but their fruits are smaller, thicker-skinned, and darker in color than those of *P. americana*, and their leaves and young stems tend to be aromatic whereas those of *P. americana* are usually not. In addition, there is an intermediate form known as the Guatemalan race, which is a form of *P. americana* indigenous to somewhat elevated regions in Guatemala and other parts of Central America.

Avocado trees may bloom any time from late fall through spring; the Mexican forms usually bloom November to March, while the West Indian forms usually do not do so until early spring, and the Guatemalan types seem to bloom mostly in late spring and early summer. The avocado's tiny flowers are in many-flowered clusters from the leaf axils near the ends of the branches; individually they are greenish white and not effective in the landscape. The flowers are bisexual, but the male and female parts are functional at different times on different individual trees. Growing more than one avocado tree therefore increases fruit production.

The fruits of all races are quite variable in shape and size ranging from 2 inches in length to more than a foot. The shape may be from round to oblong, but most are oval or pear-shaped, often with distinct and elongated "necks." Fruit color ranges equally as wide, from light green through dark green to almost red and a deep brownish purple. The texture and thickness of the fruit's skin may be anything from quite thin, smooth and difficult to remove to very thick, leathery rough, and rather easy to remove. The fruits are oily, high in calories and protein, and very nutritious, those of the Mexican and Guatemalan forms usually containing the greatest oil content. All forms have a single central seed that may be small to large and round to ovate or sometimes even oblong. The flavor and texture of the flesh ranges from somewhat watery, fibrous, and insipid to creamy, thick, fiberless, and extremely delicious. The fruits are traditionally picked before they are completely ripe as they usually go rather quickly from ripeness to overripeness if allowed to remain on the tree too long.

For the ornamental gardener the important differences in the three races of avocado are hardiness and the appearance of the trees. While they are all quite ornamental in appearance, the West Indian race is the least hardy to cold, the Guatemalan slightly hardier, and the Mexican the hardiest. The West Indian race generally has larger and lusher leaves than either of the other two races, but this can vary, especially with the intermediate Guatemalan forms. The West Indian types are hardy in zones 10 and 11, although some of them are marginal in zone 9b; they are quite well adapted where the climate is hot and humid. The Guatemalan forms are generally hardy in zones 9b through 11 and are fairly well adapted to steamy tropical and subtropical regions as well as drier and cooler regions. The Mexican forms are generally hardy in zones 9 through 11, although some are marginal in zone 9a, and they are, in general, best adapted to the cooler areas without excessive summer heat and humidity. It should be remembered that almost all trees are more susceptible to cold damage when they are young than when they are mature, and the avocado is no exception. Most popular varieties now grown are hybrids between these races. Some of the following cultivars and hybrids (especially of the West Indian race) are now hard to find as they have been put out of favor because of their inferior shipping and keeping qualities. They are worth looking for because, for the home gardener, especially the lover of the tropical look, they are as fine and sometimes finer than the more readily available varieties.

'Anaheim' is a West Indian cultivar that is quite tender to cold and is only adaptable to zones 10b and 11. It is a relatively small growing tree with large leaves and very large green thick-skinned fruit that matures in summer.

'Booth 7', a hybrid between West Indian and Guatemalan forms, is hardy in zones 10 and 11 and marginal in zone 9b. It is a good-sized tree of open habit with large green fairly thick-skinned fruit that matures in the fall.

'Booth 8' is similar in all respects to 'Booth 7' except that it usually bears more fruit per tree in a season.

'Brogdon', a hybrid between West Indian and Guatemalan forms, is fairly hardy for having such heritage and is well adapted to zones 9b through 11. It grows to about 30 feet and produces fairly small purplish fruit that matures in midsummer. This tree is large and very beautiful.

'Choquette', a hybrid between West Indian and Guatemalan forms, is hardy in zones 10 and 11 and marginal in zone 9b. It grows to 20 or 30 feet with large leaves and very large green fruit that matures in winter. The fruit is borne heavily in alternate years with relatively small numbers in the intervening years.

'Fuerte', a hybrid between Guatemalan and Mexican forms, is hardy in zones 10 and 11. It is a fairly large broad-crowned tree. Its fruits are green and rather small but plentiful in alternate years; they mature in winter and spring. This hybrid is probably the most widely grown and popular avocado variety with delicious oily, buttery, nut-flavored flesh.

'Gainesville' is a Mexican cultivar that is one of the hardiest to cold, being adaptable in zones 9 through 11. It grows sometimes to 30 feet and produces small fruits, which are deep purple to almost black when mature in summer. This cultivar is quite attractive when in fruit.

'Hall', a hybrid between West Indian and Guatemalan forms, is hardy in zones 10 and 11. It is a medium-sized tree with large beautiful leaves and large green fruit that matures in the fall.

'Hass', a hybrid between Guatemalan and Mexican forms, is hardy in zones 10 and 11. It is a large and beautiful spreading tree, which forms medium-sized deep purple to almost black, thick-skinned, warty pear-shaped, and very delicious fruit that matures in spring through summer.

'Hayes' is a hybrid between Guatemalan and Mexican forms, one of which is the world-famous 'Hass'. It is hardy in zones 10 and 11. It forms a rather tall, very beautiful tree with pendent branches and large dark purple-brown warty fruits that mature in winter and spring.

'Lula', a hybrid between West Indian and Guatemalan forms, is surprisingly hardy to cold considering its parentage; it is hardy in zones 9b through 11. The tree grows tall, but makes a fairly narrow crown of beautiful leaves and produces large green fruit that matures in fall and winter.

'Mexicola' (synonym 'Young') is a Mexican cultivar that is, for an avocado variety, very hardy to cold, being adaptable to zones 9 through 11. It grows to as much as 30 feet in height and produces small very deep purplish brown or black fruit, which ripens in late summer and autumn.

'Monroe', a hybrid between West Indian and Guatemalan forms, is hardy in zones 9b through 11. It grows to about 25 feet and produces extremely large green fruit. This very beautiful tree is one of the finest landscape subjects available for hot and humid areas.

'Nabal' is a Guatemalan cultivar that is hardy in zones 10 and 11 and marginal in zone 9b. It grows large and tall and produces large green fruit maturing in early summer to fall.

'Pinkerton' is a Guatemalan cultivar that is hardy in zones 10 and 11. It is a spreading tree with attractive leaves and large green fruit that ripens in late winter and early spring.

'Pollock' is a West Indian cultivar that is hardy in zones 10 and 11. It makes one of the most beautiful trees of all the varieties, with large leaves and an open spreading habit, growing to 30 feet or so in height. The summer-ripening fruits are immense, green, and pear-shaped with a "neck" at the stem end. This cultivar is an exceptional ornamental.

'Sharwil', a hybrid between Guatemalan and Mexican forms, is hardy in zones 10 and 11. It grows to 20 or 25 feet in height with a spreading and open crown of beautiful leaves and fairly large green rough-skinned fruit that matures in winter and spring.

'**Simmonds**' is a West Indian cultivar that is hardy in zones 10b and 11. It is a beautiful large-leaved tree that grows to 30 or 40 feet. The very large green pear-shaped fruit ripens in late summer and fall.

'**Taylor**' is a Guatemalan cultivar that is hardy in zones 9b through 11, although it is often successful in the warmer parts of zone 9a. It grows to 30 or 40 feet and makes a dense crown of beautiful dark green leaves and medium-sized green fruit maturing in winter and spring.

'**Tonnage**' is a Guatemalan cultivar that is hardy in zones 9b through 11. It is a large and beautiful variety with medium-sized green fruit, which ripens in late summer.

'**Waldin**' is an outstandingly beautiful West Indian cultivar that is hardy in zones 10b and 11. It grows to 40 or sometimes even 50 feet in height and has large beautiful leaves. The fruits are large and green and mature in late summer.

'**Winter Mexican**', a hybrid between West Indian and Mexican forms, is hardy in zones 9b through 11 and marginal in zone 9a. It is a beautiful large spreading tree with large leathery leaves and large green fruit that matures in fall and winter.

'**Zutano**' is a Mexican cultivar that is hardy in zones 10 and 11 and marginal in zone 9b. It grows to 30 or 40 feet and makes a beautiful tree with shiny deep green leaves and 6-inch-long pear-shaped fruits that mature in winter.

PETREA (PET-ree-a)
Verbenaceae: The Verbena, Lantana Family
QUEEN'S WREATH; PURPLE WREATH; SANDPAPER VINE; BLUEBIRD VINE
Large evergreen vine; large very rough leaves; long spectacular clusters of blue and purple flowers
Zones 10 and 11; marginal in zone 9b
Sun
Average but regular amounts of moisture
Rich, humusy, well-drained, acidic soil
Propagation by seed, cuttings, and (in old plants) transplanting of suckers

A genus of perhaps 30 species of shrubs, small trees, and vines in tropical America. They have oppositely arranged entire leaves often in whorls and clusters of white, pink, or purple flowers in racemes, the persistent flower calyces providing most of the color. One species is very popular and is widely planted in tropical and subtropical regions because of its spectacular flowers. *Petrea volubilis* (vah-LOOB-i-lis) is native to Mexico, Central America, and parts of the West Indies. It is a strong and fast growing twiner, reaching heights of 40 feet or more with thick ropelike stems. The 4- to 9-inch-long elliptic leaves are a deep green to gray-green in color with a prominent and lighter colored midrib and

with very rough surfaces. The vine blooms in cycles in spring, summer, and fall with 6- to 12-inch-long pendent racemes of many inch-wide five-petaled lilac to light purple to almost pure blue starlike calyces with a short-lived small deep blue or purple cup-shaped corolla in the center of the star. The petals soon fall, but the calyx lobes remain for quite a while creating a real show but eventually fading to a pale blue. There is probably no more spectacular blue-flowered vine available, and it is simply gorgeous up close and from afar. *Petrea volubilis* '**Albiflora**' (al-bi-FLOR-a) is a white-flowered cultivar. Plate 315.

PHAEDRANTHUS. See *Distictis*.

PHAEOMERIA. See *Etlingera*.

PHILODENDRON (fil-o-DEN-drun)
Araceae: The Calla Lily, Jack-in-the-Pulpit Family
PHILODENDRON
Evergreen mostly large vines or shrubs; large exotic often immense leaves; often colorful flowers
Zones vary according to species
Shade to partial sun; arborescent species adaptable to nearly full sun
Water lovers
Rich, humusy, well-drained soil
Propagation by cuttings; root division for a few stoloniferous species; sometimes seed

A large genus with possibly as many as 400 species of herbs, lianas, and more or less herbaceous trunked shrubs in tropical America. Some of these species are immense climbers with thick and stout ropelike stems, ascending their supports by aerial roots. Others are semi-scandent or completely erect mostly herbaceous giant shrubs, usually forming ringed trunks and heavy stilt and aerial roots. A few are mostly stemless bushy, non-climbing herbs (these are called "self-heading" and are mostly found as hybrids now). Finally, some are completely epiphytic. All the species are mostly intolerant of cold, but a few have a modicum of hardiness, and some will come back from trunks or large roots in zone 9. All species have usually large, sometimes immense, gloriously beautiful leaves, mostly cordate in outline but many deeply divided. All produce inflorescences typical of the arum family; some of these are quite large and quite beautiful, painted with colors of red, yellow, and purple along with the basic green and white of most other aroid genera. Philodendrons, whether the great vining types or the large-leaved shrubs, are indispensable for the tropical or subtropical gardener in love with the tropical look; they simply can not be matched for effect and are in the same class as the species of *Monstera* and *Epipremnum* for this purpose. Like the monsteras, many *Philodendron* species produce leaves that are markedly different in form from their mature leaves, and the mature leaves are seldom formed in the true vining types until the plants find a support and start to climb. All species need warmth and moisture and high humidity levels. There are now nearly as many cultivars and hybrids of *Philodendron* species as there are true species. Plate 316.

Philodendron andreanum. See *P. melanochrysum.*

Philodendron bipennifolium (by-pen´-i-FO-lee-um) (synonyms *P. panduraeforme, P. panduriforme*) is native to southeastern Brazil where it climbs trees in the tropical rain forest, growing to their tops and reaching a length of more than 70 feet, often hanging down like a curtain once they reach the top of a tree. The dense olive green leaves are as much as 18 inches long and very ornately shaped with a squared four-angle top (near the petiole) and a long obovate lower lobe, causing the whole to rather resemble the shape of a fiddle. Leaf color is a light to deep green, and the texture is leathery. The vine is fast growing and lush, but is not hardy to cold, being happy only in zones 10b and 11 and marginal in zone 10a.

Philodendron bipinnatifidum. See *P. selloum.*

Philodendron 'Choco' is a cultivar or hybrid of undetermined parentage that is tender to cold and adaptable only in zones 10b and 11. It is a quite lovely climber with thick waxy heart-shaped foot-long leaves that are deep green with prominent midribs, the lateral veins a beautiful white or silver in color.

Philodendron cordatum (kor-DAIT-um) naturally occurs in eastern Brazil and is hardy in zones 10 and 11. It grows strong and high with great deep green leathery 18-inch-long leaves that are narrowly cordate with the basal lobes long and backward pointing; they are held on relatively long petioles. This species is very picturesque, the essence of the tropical look. Its nomenclature has been confused in the nursery trade; most plants offered as *P. cordatum* are varieties of *P. scandens.* It is sometimes called the heart-leaf philodendron.

Philodendron distantilobium (dis-tant´-i-LOAB-ee-um) is indigenous to the Amazon Basin of Brazil and is not adaptable outside zones 10b and 11. This unusual-looking species has 18-inch-long leaves that are very deeply and pinnately segmented with elliptic divisions, the lobes or segments reaching almost to the midrib. The leaves look as much like those of a pinnate-leaved palm as they do anything else. This vine grows to great heights.

Philodendron domesticum (do-MEST-i-kum) (synonym *P. hastatum*) is probably native to central Brazil, but its origins are obscured. The vine is hardy in zones 10 and 11. It grows to medium heights and sports very beautiful thick and leathery leaves of a deep dark green color growing densely on the vine. Each leaf is 2 feet long or longer and is shaped like a narrow *Colocasia* (elephant's-ear) species, a long triangular shape with backward facing lobes. It is extremely tropical looking and should be sought after for creating the look. It is sometimes called the elephant's-ear philodendron and spade-leaf philodendron.

Philodendron erubescens (er-oo-BES-senz) is native to Colombia and is hardy in zones 10b and 11, although it is often successful in zone 10a. It is a vigorous climber and creeper that scrambles up trees and covers the ground since it tends to root at the stem nodes. It is often found as a thriving epiphyte high up in trees after its connections to the ground below have somehow been severed. The foot-long waxy-textured leaves are beautifully arrow-shaped and are carried on red petioles as long as or longer than the leaf blades. Young leaf color is a vivid wine-red, which matures to a deep olive green with bronze overtones and a narrow red margin. This species is one of the loveliest in the genus and is invaluable for adding form and color to shady and partially shady sites either as a climber or as a groundcover. There are several outstanding cultivars and hybrids of this species. ***Philodendron erubescens* 'Burgundy'** has leaves that are a deep wine red at maturity. ***Philodendron erubescens* 'Golden Erubescens',** one of the most attractive cultivars, has mature leaves that are a wonderful pinkish orange to pinkish yellow.

Philodendron* ×*evansii (EV-'nz-ee-eye) is a hybrid between *P. selloum* and *P. speciosum* which, because of the *P. selloum* parent, is hardier to cold than it looks, being adaptable to zones 9b through 11, with occasional damage in the colder zone and occasional root survival even in zone 9a. This wonderful plant is bold and noble in its looks. The giant 3-foot-long leathery, deep green leaves are linearly sagittate in outline with wavy and somewhat scalloped margins and prominent and lighter colored midrib and lateral veins. The plant grows as a scandent, almost-climbing, almost-treelike large shrub that is superb in big tropical borders, tied to trees, or as a massive cascade from atop a large shady wall.

Philodendron fragrantissimum (fray´-gran-TIS-si-mum) is native to northern South America and is completely intolerant of cold, being adaptable only to zones 10b and 11. It is a nonclimbing species in its maturity and is often epiphytic on large rocks or tree trunks in the tropical rain forest. The lovely leaves are as much as 2 feet wide and a deep green in color with a broad ovate shape; the great rounded basal lobes and deeply depressed veins give the blade a corrugated look. This species is perfect for growing near pools or for creating accent in shady borders. It needs warmth, half shade, and a very loose and freely draining soil or leaf mold that should, at the same time, never completely dry out.

Philodendron giganteum (jy-GANT-ee-um) is native to the West Indies and is hardy in zones 10b and 11. It is an immense and spectacular climber in truly tropical areas, growing to the tops of large trees and forming very thick ropelike stems with long aerial roots. The deep green leathery leaves are at least 3 feet long and are held on long petioles; the blade is linear-cordate with the basal lobes almost overlapping. There is no more striking vine in existence, and a well-grown specimen is one of the glories of the entire tropical plant world. It is sometimes called the giant philodendron. Plate 317.

Philodendron gloriosum (glor-ee-O-sum) is native to Colombia and is hardy in zones 10b and 11. The plant is not a true climber, but rather a stout creeper, which adds profound beauty to a tropical bed or groundcover. The leaves are held on fairly long petioles and are about 18 inches wide, perfectly heart-shaped, satiny in texture, and deep green above with a wide pinkish white midrib and lateral veins—a truly stunning sight in shady areas. The vine is sometimes called the satin-leaf philodendron.

Philodendron goeldii (GOLD-ee-eye / GURL-dee-eye) (synonym *Thaumatophyllum spruceanum*) is native to the Amazon region of Brazil and is hardy in zones 10b and 11. This most unusual plant is unlike any other *Philodendron* species. It is neither a vine nor a shrub, although it may be treated in the landscape as either, and the long leaves will do a low scramble around a tree trunk. The leaves are compound, consisting of a long petiole and a great spiraling rachis (as much as 6 feet or more in length) along one side of which are the numerous foot-long almost stalkless elliptic shiny green leaflets with prominent and lighter colored midribs. The visual effect is more akin to that of a large *Costus* species (which see) than a *Philodendron*. The plant is not new to cultivation, but has never been as popular or as widely available as the more traditional looking *Philodendron* species. It is worth seeking out as it lends a graceful and attractive airy feeling to a shady planting.

Philodendron grandifolium (grand-i-FO-lee-um) is native to northern South America and is hardy in zones 10b and 11. It is a high climber with long-petioled thick leathery deep green linear-cordate, 2-foot-long leaves with slightly round-scalloped and definitely wavy margins. This fast and strong grower adds great tropical beauty to large landscapes.

Philodendron hastatum. See *P. domesticum.*

Philodendron imbe (IM-bee / IM-bay) (synonym *P. sellowianum*) is indigenous to southeastern Brazil and is hardy in zones 10b and 11. It is a tall climber with thick ropelike purplish red stems and leaves that are synonymous with the tropical look: 16 inches long, linear-ovate, long arrow-shaped, thin but leathery, and unfurling pink and bronzy but soon turning a deep olive green. No tropical foliage vine is more satisfying. It is a variable species and has several noteworthy variegated-leaved cultivars.

Philodendron imperiale. See *P. ornatum.*

Philodendton laciniatum. See *P. pedatum.*

Philodendron laciniosum. See *P. pedatum.*

Philodendron melanochrysum (mel'-a-no-KRY-sum) (synonym *P. andreanum*) is indigenous to Costa Rica, Panama, and Colombia, and is hardy in zones 10b and 11. This great climber has almost unbelievably beautiful leaves that are as much as 3 feet long, perfectly heart-shaped with short apical tips, and a deep and iridescent greenish black in color overlain with a difficult to describe coppery sheen. The midrib and lateral veins are a lovely ivory color, and the whole blade has a velvety feel and look. Common names of this beauty are velour philodendron and black gold philodendron. If your garden is tropical enough and you can provide the required amounts of moisture, a more spectacular-leaved plant cannot be found or grown. It is an unforgettable sight on large trees or walls.

Philodendron mello-barretoanum (mel'-lo-bair'-e-toe-AHN-um) is native to eastern tropical Brazil and is hardy in zones 10 and 11. Although the trunk will survive temperatures slightly below freezing and the plant will usually sprout from its roots after temperatures in the mid 20s, the magnificence of the tree is not apparent after such freezes and the hardier *P. selloum* should be substituted for these situations. This magnificent arborescent species forms trunks to as much as 20 feet in height and a foot in diameter. The areas between the rings of leaf scars are armed with stout spines. The 4- to 6-foot-long leaves are quite similar to those of *P. selloum,* but are larger and even more exotic looking. This small tree is incomparably dramatic and tropical looking.

Philodendron melinonii (mel-i-NO-nee-eye) is indigenous to northern South America where it grows on large rain forest trees as a giant epiphyte. It is not adaptable outside zones 10b and 11. The plant forms immense rosettes of thick leathery arrow-shaped 3-foot-long leaves with wavy margins and prominent and lighter colored midrib and lateral veins. The blades are held on long bright red petioles. This species is shockingly beautiful clumped on walls or tall trees with its masses of dangling aerial roots and vividly red leaf stalks.

Philodendron micans. See *P. scandens.*

Philodendron ornatum (or-NAIT-um) (synonyms *P. imperiale, P. sodiroi*) is native to eastern Brazil (possibly also in western Peru and parts of Venezuela) and is hardy in zones 10b and 11. It is a large climber with long-stalked 2-foot-long broad-cordate leathery deep green leaves with deeply depressed lateral veins above and a distinct reddish hue beneath. It is, like most great climbers in this genus, of outstanding beauty.

Philodendron oxycardium. See *P. scandens.*

Philodendron panduraeforme. See *P. bipennifolium.*

Philodendron panduriforme. See *P. bipennifolium.*

Philodendron pedatum (pe-DAIT-um) (synonyms *P. laciniatum, P. laciniosum*) occurs naturally in eastern Venezuela, Guyana, Surinam, French Guiana, and northeastern Brazil, and is hardy in zones 10b and 11. It is a large epiphytic species growing on rocks and tree trunks with long-stemmed 18-inch-long leathery leaves that are triangular or cordate in outline, but pinnately segmented, usually with five rounded segments, the lowermost being the largest. It is spectacular and dramatic perched on trees or walls along which it slowly creeps and forms large colonies. One of its attractions is the long exotic curtains of aerial roots it produces.

Philodendron pertusum. See *Monstera deliciosa.*

Philodendron pittieri. See *P. scandens.*

Philodendron **'Santa-Leopoldana'** is a cultivar,

possibly a hybrid, of undetermined parentage that is not hardy to cold, being adaptable to zones 10b and 11. It is an exceptionally beautiful climber that may reach great heights but is relatively slow growing. The leaves are linear and arrow-shaped, as much as 3 feet long, a very deep emerald green in color, with prominent and lighter colored midribs and lateral veins and a thin reddish leaf margin that is slightly wavy but not indented.

Philodendron scandens (SKAN-denz) (synonyms *P. micans, P. oxycardium, P. pittieri*) is native to parts of the West Indies, southeastern Mexico, and Central America, and is hardy in zones 10b and 11. This species is the most widely grown in the genus; it was formerly found in almost every home and greenhouse, its juvenile forms cascading from planters and hanging baskets around the world. It is a fast and strong growing climber which, in its native haunts, grows to the tops of the tallest trees and forms dense mats of sumptuously tropical looking foliage. The juvenile leaves are no more than 6 inches long, perfectly heart-shaped, and usually with an apical "tail"; in this form it is often sold as *P. oxycardium*. The mature leaves are usually more than a foot long with definite "tails" and depressed veins above. There are naturally occurring forms with more velvety leaf surfaces, some with a definite metallic sheen, as well as some with beautifully colored veins. There are also several cultivars with varying degrees of variegation. The plant has accrued several vernacular names over the years for the type and its several forms, including heart-leaf philodendron, velvet-leaf philodendron, common philodendron, and parlor ivy.

Philodendron selloum (sel-LO-um) (synonyms *P. bipinnatifidum, P. sellowianum*) is indigenous to southern Brazil and adjacent Paraguay, and is one of the hardiest species in the genus, being adaptable to zones 9b through 11 and usually successful in zone 9a. This shrubby or arborescent species forms, with age, a stout, ringed trunk that may reach 12 feet or even more in height and 6 or more inches in diameter. Old mature specimens of this species strongly resemble stylized palm trees. The great glossy deep green and leathery leaves are as much as 4 feet long, and linear-cordate in outline but very deeply and pinnately segmented. The many segments are sometimes divided almost to the midrib which is, as are the central veins of the segments, prominent and lighter colored than the blade. Each segment has more or less wavy margins and is often scalloped on its margin. The species is one of the most exotic-looking subjects for the tropical or subtropical garden, especially in zone 9. The leaves lend a texture and form to gardens that few other plants can match,' and they are unsurpassed for creating the tropical look. Degree of marginal indentation and amount of lobing of the leaves varies widely within the type, and some forms are marvelously attractive. There are several variegated forms, none of which are very satisfactory in the landscape. One of the forms has in the past been elevated to specific status, *P. bipinnatifidum*. This name is now the correct name for both forms, but almost all plants for sale are labeled with the old name, *P. selloum*. It is unfortunate also that forms of this species have also been sold as *P. sellowianum* (an erroneous spelling), which is also a synonym for *P. imbe*. The species has, in addition, contributed to myriad hybrids between itself and other species including *P. speciosum*. Plate 396.

Philodendron sellowianum. See *P. imbe, P. selloum*.

Philodendron sodiroi. See *P. ornatum*.

Philodendron speciosum (spee-see-O-sum) is indigenous to southern and western Brazil and is hardy in zones 10 and 11. It is a semi-arborescent species, forming a short trunk with age. Even when a trunk is formed it is usually mostly obscured by the gigantic leathery deep green leaves that may measure as long as 6 feet. The leaves are linear-cordate in outline with basal lobes that almost overlap and with large, prominent, and lighter colored midribs and lateral veins. The leaf margins are wavy. The visual effect of these colossal leaves is almost overwhelming and makes them somewhat difficult to blend in with the general landscape, even the general tropical landscape. Plants are spectacularly effective planted singly near water.

Philodendron tweedianum (tweed-ee-AHN-um) is native to southern Brazil, Uruguay, and northern Argentina, and is hardy in zones 9b through 11, usually surviving in zone 9a. It forms with age a short trunk bearing 18-inch-long arrow-shaped leaves with scalloped margins. The landscape value is that of a dwarf *P. speciosum*, a valuable addition to large borders and patio plantings.

Philodendron verrucosum (ver-roo-KO-sum) is indigenous to Costa Rica, Panama, Colombia, and Ecuador, and is hardy in zones 10b and 11. It is a tall climber with exquisite variegated leaves, which are 2 feet long and perfectly cordate in shape with scalloped margins. The leaf color is a deep and dark iridescent, metallic bronzy green with the midribs, lateral veins, and margin highlighted in feathery pale green to almost white variegation. The petioles are a deep red in color, and the undersides of the leaves are a pinkish violet color. This species is sometimes called the velvet-leaf philodendron. This vine has leaves as beautiful as any terrestrial *Alocasia* species; they are almost heartbreakingly elegant. The plant has the advantage of being much more prominent in the landscape than most *Alocasia* species. For the tropical garden I cannot recommend this vine highly enough.

Philodendron williamsii (WIL-yum-zee-eye) is native to eastern tropical Brazil and is hardy in zones 10b and 11. This large and magnificent epiphytic species can also be grown as a short-trunked arborescent form. The immense leaves are as much as 3 feet long, a brilliantly shining glossy deep green in color, linear and arrow-shaped, with scalloped and wavy margins and prominent and lighter colored midrib and lateral veins. The great length of the leaves in relation to their width causes them to curve backwards at both ends. This extraordinary plant is an almost unbelievable sight radiating out from large tree trunks or spilling out of large walls or wet hillsides and, as so many other giant-leaved *Philodendron* species, is a perfect complement to pools and water gardens.

Philodendron 'Xanadu' is a beautiful hybrid form, one of whose parents is *P. selloum*. It is self-heading and grows to 4 or 5 feet in frost-free climes but is hardy in zones 10 and 11 and will resprout from the thick roots in zone 9b, sometimes even in zone 9a. The leaves are about a foot long and resemble those of *P. selloum* but are smaller and usually more linear in shape with a prominent midrib that is either grayish or reddish in color.

PHLEBODIUM (flee-BO-dee-um)
Polypodiaceae: The Largest Fern Family
RABBIT'S-FOOT FERN; HARE'S-FOOT FERN
Large colony-forming fern; brownish hairy surface
    roots; large metallic green pinnate leaves
Zones 10 and 11; marginal in zone 9b
Partial shade to partial sun
Water lover
Rich, humusy, well-drained soil or leaf mold
Propagation by root division, rhizome division, and
    spores

A small genus of ferns in tropical America, previously included in the very large genus *Polypodium*. They have stout creeping rhizomes that are covered in rusty-colored hairlike scales, which have a slight resemblance to a cat's or rabbit's leg. One species is quite popular indoors as a hanging basket subject and outdoors to give a decidedly tropical look and texture to borders. It may also be treated as an epiphyte on trees or walls. **Phlebodium aureum** (OW-ree-um / AW-ree-um) (synonym *Polypodium aureum*) is native to a vast area of tropical America from southern Florida through the West Indies, Mexico, Central America, and down into northern South America. It grows both as an epiphyte and terrestrially. It is an almost unbelievably variable species. Some forms are so different from each other that they hardly seem to be of the same species. One form graces palm trunks in central and southern Florida, giving them an even greater appeal than they would otherwise have, especially the *Sabal palmetto* trunks. The typical form grows to 5 or even 6 feet in height and has shiny arching leaves that are 3 to 4 feet long. The leaves are not compound, but rather are deeply and pinnately segmented, with the segments usually somewhat lobed or toothed. Leaf color is a beautiful light bluish or silvery green with a metallic sheen, and the rachis bears a prominent silver streak along its upper surface. The wandering scaly rhizomes can cover a fairly large area of ground or trunk with time and form particularly beautiful masses of foliage. The fern is quite effective when grown as an epiphyte because the colonies are then usually more or less separated. The plant needs strong light to flourish and even adapts to full sun in all but hot regions.

PHOENIX (FEE-nix)
Palmae (Arecaceae): The Palm Family
DATE PALMS
Small to very large pinnate-leaved palms; single or
    clustering trunks; showy fruit clusters
Zones vary according to species
Sun to partial shade
Average but regular amounts of moisture; some are
    drought tolerant when established
Soil requirements vary according to species
Propagation by seed and (for some clumping species)
    transplanting of suckers

A small palm genus of 17 or more species in tropical and subtropical regions of the Old World in diverse habitats from desert oases to tropical rain forests. While small in number of species, some representatives of this genus truly dominate warm climate landscapes almost to the same extent as the coconut palm (*Cocos*) in the true tropics and the Mexican fan palm (*Washingtonia* species) in Mediterranean and subtropical climates. The form of these plants varies greatly from very tall and often massive palms to nearly dwarf types. A species may be solitary-trunked or clustering and suckering, and the individual trunks may be straight or gracefully curved. All have pinnate leaves, most of which are armed with vicious thorns on at least a part of the blade. The leaflets of most species grow at several different angles from the leaf's rachis, giving a somewhat stiff yet plumelike look to the individual leaves, while the leaflets of some species emerge from the rachis in a single plane. The male and female flowers are on separate plants, so that both sexes are needed for the females to set fruit. The most famous example in the genus is *Phoenix dactylifera* (date palm) of northern Africa and the Middle East, which has for millennia provided a staple food for the people indigenous to its original habitat and in more recent history an important confection for the rest of the world. The *Phoenix* species are notorious for readily hybridizing with one another if grown in proximity. Many specimens already planted and for sale are of mixed parentages.

Phoenix canariensis (ka-nair´-ee-ENS-is) occurs naturally only on some of the Canary Islands off the western coast of northern Africa and is hardy in zones 9 through 11, sometimes surviving in zone 8. It is one of the most imposing and majestic palm species and, in view of its tiny natural habitat, is remarkable for having been spread into every warm region of the globe. It grows usually to a height of about 40 feet, including the immense leaf crown, but very old specimens can have trunks of more than 50 feet and a total height of 60 to 70 feet. Until old age the tree has a quite thick and massive trunk; the trunks of old palms do not, of course, shrink, but in relation to their height they are not nearly so massive. The trunk of the tree is one of its most decorative features: very straight and, even when mature, with rings of flattened diamond-shaped leaf scars, its color a light to dark brown or orange brown. There is somewhat of an aesthetic problem with the trunk in hot and humid climates where the humidity tends to rot the outer fibers, causing them to fall off in patches. This results in a less than elegant appearance, but in drier areas, such as southern California, the trunks are as beautiful as the leaf crown. The crown is composed of 60 to more than 100 great 10- to 20-foot-long stiff but beautifully arching pinnate leaves which, in the type, are a deep yellowish green to olive green but, in those trees of hybrid origin (with *P. dactylifera*), a deeper and often bluish or grayish green. The individual leaflets are folded so that the leaflet in cross section is trough-shaped and forms a V. The lowermost leaflets are meta-morphosed into 2- to 3-inch-long green to black formidable spines. The large fruit clusters are long lasting and quite attractive, spilling from the crown with their many inch-wide round orange fruits; they are considered edible, but, as Desmond Muirhead writes in his wonderful little palm landscaping handbook, *Palms,* "so are cats in some societies." These palms are drought tolerant when established but, like almost every other drought-tolerant species, they grow faster and look ever so much better with regular and adequate amounts of moisture. They are not demanding as to soil fertility, but a good deep and somewhat sandy soil is their preference; it should be well draining. Next to *Phoenix dactylifera*, the true date palm, this tree has the most salt tolerance of any species in the genus. It will not adapt to truly saline conditions, but is a perfect candidate for areas that receive only occasional salty spray. The palm is almost universally known as Canary Island date palm in the English-speaking world. There is hardly a more beautiful sight than an avenue lined with these trees or several of varying heights in a large group on a lawn, and this palm is one of the few trees noble and yet elegant enough to look very good as a matched pair for a spacious entrance. The trees look grotesque unless they are allowed to keep their complete large and wonderful crowns of leaves. Removing the older leaves results in an unnatural, stiff, and very ungraceful appearance. While this palm is slow growing, it lives a long time and is a very valuable addition to any landscape other than a tiny one. Plate 318.

Phoenix dactylifera (dak-ti-LIF-e-ra) is the date palm. It has been cultivated for so long in the general region of what was probably its native habitat that its precise and original domain is obscured but was most likely northern Africa and the Middle East. The palm is hardy in zones 9 through 11, sometimes surviving in zone 8b. The tree typically grows to a fairly great height when old, forming as much as 60 feet of tall straight and relatively thin trunk. Younger trees form suckers at the base of the trunks, a happy circumstance for commercial date growers since all they need do is to remove the suckers to propagate an especially desirable form. Seedlings seldom exhibit the full characteristics of either parent. The leaves of the date palm are as large as those of *Phoenix canariensis* (Canary Island date palm) but fewer. The date palm's crown usually sports only about half as many (30 or 40) leaves, and they are also stiffer and

generally more erect than those of the Canary Island date palm, giving the true date palm a more formal and a stiffer appearance. Leaf color is a decidedly grayish green, sometimes almost silvery or bluish and, like most other species in the genus, the bases of the leaves are armed with stout spines. The great pendent fruit clusters are no showier than those of Canary Island date palm and contain no more fruits per cluster, but the individual fruits are slightly larger, a deep yellow to orange in color, more brownish when mature, and are not only edible but delicious. There are many named varieties. Trees that grow in wet and humid regions do not produce the quality nor the number of fruit as do those that grow in arid and semiarid areas with low relative humidity. The date palm, being indigenous to deserts, is drought tolerant once its roots are established, but it should not be treated as a cactus. Like almost every other drought-tolerant plant, it does best with regular and adequate amounts of water. In the deserts it is always found at oases (springs) and never in the truly arid parts of the desert. Because it is indigenous to arid areas, it also does not flourish in humid areas as well as it does in more Mediterranean regions, although there are at least two cultivars now that seem to do much better in areas like the Gulf Coast and Florida of the United States: ***Phoenix dactylifera* 'Medjool'** and ***Phoenix dactylifera* 'Zahedii'.** This palm is rather nonchalant about soil and grows well in almost any reasonably fertile medium as long as it is well drained. Because of little rainfall in most of its range, the tree is quite adaptable to saline conditions and is and should be much used near the seashore. Since the 1970s, this species and its cultivars have become one of the most frequently planted landscape palms in the tropical and subtropical areas of the United States, particularly in the southwestern desert areas. This phenomenon is partly due to the rapid development of the former date plantations in the desert areas of California and Arizona into ever-expanding tracts of suburbia, those great old palm groves now giving way to acres of new houses with many former occupants of the groves being transported to adorn further developments around the country and the world. I am told, however, by Dr. Henry Donselman that there are now as many commercial date palms as ever, the groves younger and in different locations. Most of these naturally stiff-looking trees are now being planted in the Sun Belt in straight rows, where each tree is the same height and the rows are trimmed to the look of colossal and stiff shaving brushes. Regrettably, this does not allow the trees to keep their naturally full and much more graceful crowns of leaves. Instead of lushness and quietude, coolness and gracefulness, these new plantings have an austere and irascible, a regimented and hostile, a quite tiring and an overbearing demeanor. These noble trees are capable of providing wonderfully graceful landscape accents with their full crowns giving form and texture to the skyline and, in groups of full-crowned trees of varying heights, can add much beauty to warm climate gardening, whether arid or not.

Phoenix reclinata (rek-li-NAHT-a) is native to tropical West, East, and Central Africa and is hardy only in zones 10 and 11 but will sometimes grow to maturity in zone 9b. This clumping or clustering palm species is one of the world's loveliest. The plants form many suckers or subsidiary trunks throughout their lives, and a single specimen may have as many as two dozen trunks. The trunks are not straight, but lean gracefully outward from their points of origin, attaining a maximum height of about 30 feet. Each beautifully ringed trunk usually carries between 20 and 30 leaves, each of which is about 15 feet long with many bright green leaflets growing at several angles from the rachis; the lower leaflets are reduced to very vicious spines 3 to 6 inches long. Few things are as beautiful as a large tuft of this palm, but the clumps are made even more graceful and dramatic if a few trunks are thinned out as the mass develops so that they are of differing heights and so that their individual beauty can be seen and appreciated to its fullest. I have seen this palm planted as a hedge, with the many young trunks of evenly spaced plants completely obscured by a tangled mass of foliage; the visual effect is anything but attractive. If a hedge is wanted using this palm, it is infinitely more aesthetically pleasing to let a few trunks of varying heights form first and then allow the many subsequent suckers to form the desired barrier at the base of the larger ones. There is probably no more perfect candidate for planting near ponds, lakes, or swimming pools, the gracefully reclining thin trunks lending a tropical and exotic essence that is only matched by something like the coconut palm (*Cocos*). *Phoenix reclinata* very readily hybridizes with other *Phoenix* species, and no other date palm has a wider spectrum of forms. None of the hybrids are as elegant as the type species (their trunks are usually thicker and their fronds seldom quite as languorously graceful), but gardeners outside tropical areas can rejoice at the opportunity they have to enjoy specimens almost as picturesque as those that might have just arrived on the boat from Senegal. This magnificent and yet ethereal tree appreciates a richer soil than either *P. dactylifera* (date palm) or *P. canariensis* (Canary Island date palm) and its owner will be highly rewarded with relatively fast and vigorous growth in addition to good form and color if its planting includes a deep soil. In its native habitat the tree grows along riverbanks at the edges of tropical forests, suggesting that in cultivation it loves water in a well-drained soil. The palm is universally called the Senegal date palm in the English-speaking world. Plate 319.

Phoenix roebelinii (ro-be-LIN-ee-eye) is native to Vietnam, Laos, Cambodia, and Thailand, and is hardy in zones 10 and 11, although it often survives unprotected for many years in zone 9b. It is an exquisitely beautiful solitary-trunked palm, semi-dwarf in stature, forming only 8 to 10 feet of trunk. It is perhaps the most graceful *Phoenix* species with its relatively thin knobby trunk and full rounded crown of 50 or more delicate and gossamer flat-planed leaves. Each leaf is about 6 feet long and has many regularly spaced deep green glossy leaflets, which turn into 2-inch-long sharp spines at the petiole end of the leaf. The leaves are unlike those of any other date palm in that they are lightweight and quite soft in texture. The young leaves are covered with a fine chalky grayish white bloom, which gives them a beautiful grayish green cast, while the mature leaves are glossy and a deep grassy green in color. This species is unexcelled for use as a silhouette, a small patio tree, or along a walkway where its elegance of form and detail can be appreciated up close. *Phoenix roebelinii* is more often than not sold in containers as a "double palm," meaning that there are two individuals to a pot. This practice is heartily encouraged as few things are lovelier than a planting of two or three palms of varying heights. The tree is native to tropical rain forests where it grows in clearings or along riverbanks. It is a water lover and needs a rich and humusy soil in which it grows moderately quickly. Without the abundant water and in a nonfertile soil the palm grows quite slowly and never develops the great beauty of which it is capable. It is usually and inelegantly called the pygmy date palm, miniature date palm, or dwarf date palm.

Phoenix rupicola (roop-i-KO-la) occurs naturally in northeastern India and is hardy in zones 10 and 11 but survives for many years and to maturity in warm areas of zone 9b. It is a solitary-trunked palm species that only forms about 20 or 25 feet of trunk which, unlike almost every other *Phoenix* species, is nearly free of distinctly apparent leaf bases or rings. The leaves are, next to those of the pygmy date, the most graceful and soft-textured of all the date palms. They are, like those of *P. robelenii* (miniature date palm) flat, the leaflets arising from the rachis in only one plane. The lower leaflets are spines, but they are few compared to other *Phoenix* species and in young palms are so soft and pliable as to constitute no threat of bodily harm. The leaf crown is full and round with as many as 50 or 60 wonderfully arching 10-foot-long bright green leaves. The tree is not terribly particular as to soil, but really appreciates a moderately fertile deep soil and, while it is somewhat drought tolerant when established, grows faster and is more lush with adequate and regular supplies of water. This species is arguably the most beautiful date palm. It combines the grace and elegance of miniature date palm with the nobility of *P. canariensis* (Canary Island date palm). A group of these palms with trunks of varying heights is one of the most beautiful sights the plant world has to offer. The vernacular English names for this wonderful tree are wild date palm, cliff date palm, and Indian date palm. Plate 320.

Phoenix sylvestris (sil-VES-tris) is native to a large part of India, but is nevertheless hardy in zones 9 through 11 with occasional damage in zone 9a. It is a solitary-trunked species, forming a ringed trunk to 30 feet in height, occasionally more. The leaves and tree are similar to those of *P. canariensis* (Canary Island date palm) and *P. dactylifera* (date palm) with the differences being that *P. sylvestris* is less stiff-looking than the date palm but less majestic than the Canary Island date palm. The leaf crown is, next to that of the Canary Island date palm, the fullest in the genus. The individual leaves are 10 to 12 feet long, grayish green, bluish green, or silvery green in color, and very thorny near the petioles. Mature trees create a superbly tropical effect in the landscape and, like so many other palm species, are exceptionally attractive planted in groups of individuals of varying heights. Common names for the tree are toddy palm and wild date palm. The people of India have for millennia used the sap from the palm's young inflorescences to make sugar which, when fermented leads to yet another instance of humankind's need for alcoholic beverages; hence the name toddy palm.

PHORMIUM (FORM-ee-um)
Agavaceae: The Agave Family
NEW ZEALAND FLAX; NEW ZEALAND HEMP; FLAX LILY
Giant fan-shaped clump of stiff swordlike gray-green red-margined leaves; tall spikes red flowers
Zones 9 through 11 as permanent perennials; zone 8 as returning perennials
Sun or partial shade
Average but regular amounts of moisture; drought tolerant
Average well-drained soil
Propagation by seed and transplanting of suckers

A genus of only two species of very large perennial evergreen herbs in New Zealand. One is commonly planted in warm climates around the globe for its dramatic landscape effect. *Phormium tenax* (TEN-ax) forms a two-sided fan-shaped clump of immense stiff swordlike leaves that are from 6 to 10 feet long and about 6 inches wide. The leaves are a deep green, grayish green, or brownish green in color with red or deep orange thin-lined margins that tend to split into thick separated fibers. The great branched flower spikes, which appear in summer from the center of the leaf group and which are showy in the landscape without being beautiful close up, may reach a height of 15 feet and carry several 2-inch-long bell-shaped rusty red or orange flowers with six spreading corolla lobes. The plant is singularly dramatic in appearance and is most effective as an accent in large plantings. It can also be used very effectively in the cactus and succulent garden or even near pools and streams, but must have good soil drainage and needs sun to look good. There are several highly ornamental cultivars and hybrids (with the other species, *P. colensoi*) in a variety of sizes and leaf colors including purple, orange, and bronze. One form is beautifully variegated with creamy white, which makes the plant look like a variegated species of *Dracaena*. The type is quite tolerant of salty spray and, to a large extent, saline soil. It is a choice and sensational landscape subject for plantings near the seashore.

PHYLLANTHUS (fyl-LANTH-us)
Euphorbiaceae: The Euphorbia, Spurge Family
OTAHEITE (o-ta-HEE-tee or o-ta-HAY-tee) GOOSEBERRY; GOOSEBERRY TREE
Shrub or tree with large false-pinnate leaves; masses of small flowers and multitudes of small fruit
Zones 10 and 11
Sun to partial shade
Average but regular amounts of moisture
Average well-drained soil
Propagation by seed and cuttings

A large genus of about 650 species of herbs, shrubs, and trees in tropical and subtropical regions around the world. Many of them have stems (besides the normal stems or trunks) that look like pinnate leaves and are called "cladophylls" or "cladodes." These are leaflike stems that often also bear the many small flowers and fruits. The genus name is from the Greek for "leaf" and "flower." The flowers are typical of the euphorbia family: tiny and without petals. Although there are many gardenworthy species, only one is commonly planted for its tart edible fruit and ornamental leaves. *Phyllanthus acidus* (AS-i-dus) (synonym *P. distichus*) is indigenous to a wide area of the Asian tropics from Madagascar eastward through India, into Southeast Asia, Indonesia, and up to the Philippines. It readily naturalizes in near-tropical regions and has been in cultivation for so long that its original habitat may be only a small part of this vast area. It grows to as much as 20 or 25 feet, but is usually smaller or kept smaller, and is a somewhat sprawling large shrub that is easily trained to a spreading small tree form. The 3-inch-long ovate to lanceolate nearly stalkless leaves are found on small terminal 12-inch-long branchlets and are arranged in a single plane along both sides of the little branches, giving the effect of foot-long pinnate leaves. The new leaves are a beautiful rosy-bronze in color. The tiny pinkish or greenish white flowers appear in small pendent clusters along the main branches and trunk in great profusion in late winter and spring. The fruit matures in early summer and is spectacular, nearly covering the branches and often parts of the tree's trunk with inch-wide pumpkin-shaped yellow or yellowish ribbed fruits. The fruit is edible but acidic in taste and is usually made into jams and, with the addition of sugar, tartly sweet sauces for meat. The tree is exceptionally attractive, especially when in fruit, and is quite tropical in appearance. It is often used in a shrubby border to give form and color to the border and is very endearing as a patio tree. The common name is Tahitian in origin.

PHYLLOSTACHYS
(fy-lo-STAIK-iss / fil-LAHS-ta-kis)
Gramineae (Poaceae): The Grass, Bamboo Family
BAMBOO
Mostly tall running bamboos
Zones vary according to species

Sun to partial sun
Average but regular amounts of moisture
Average well-drained soil
Can be invasive
Propagation by transplanting of suckers

A genus of 80 or more bamboo species mostly in China, but also in northern India and Myanmar (Burma). All the species are "running type" bamboo, meaning that their creeping rhizomes spread some distance each year before sending up new culms and with time form large colonies or groves of bamboo stems. This growth habit can be a problem for some gardens as the roots travel under sidewalks and other such barriers, and the strong new shoots often emerge in areas where they are not wanted. This invasiveness can also make bamboos excellent subjects for covering large outlying areas and for erosion control. As a whole these species are characterized by relatively short internodes, relatively small leaves, but often quite tall culms sometimes with a diameter of several inches. The groves of mature individuals can be remarkably attractive with their tall pillars of green or purplish to almost black ringed culms, leafless for several feet and supporting a canopy of great ferny foliage. Most species are hardy to cold and some are exceptionally so. Indeed, some species are not well adapted to tropical or nearly tropical areas and need a certain amount of winter chill to thrive. Some of them are more weedy and grasslike than noble. Only the larger species are discussed here, and they are all more at home in temperate regions than in the near-constantly warm regions of zones 10 and 11, although they do very well along the Upper Gulf Coast region of the United States and similar regions that are hot, wet and humid.

Phyllostachys bambusoides (bam-boo-SOY-deez) is native to a large area of eastern and central China. It is fully hardy in zones 7 through 11 and usually root hardy in zone 6, but it does not thrive in the tropical climates of zones 10b and 11. The culms grow usually to a maximum height of 30 or 35 feet, but in their native haunts can reach as much as 60 or 65 feet. The culms are a vivid dark green in the type and as much as 5 or 6 inches in diameter with the internodes a foot apart in mature canes. The leaves are on branches and emanate from the nodes for about the top half of the culm; they are as much as 6 inches long, and dark green, and have a tufted look in the landscape. The large mature groves are superbly ornamental. This species is called the giant timber bamboo, giant Japanese timber bamboo, Japanese timber bamboo, and madake (ma-DAH-kee). It is one of the most widely planted bamboo species, and the culms have many uses. ***Phyllostachys bambusoides* 'Allgold'** (synonym *P. sulphurea*) does not grow quite as large as the type nor is it quite as hardy to cold, but has gorgeous deep yellow to almost orange culms, sometimes with a few thin green stripes. ***Phyllostachys bambusoides* 'Castillon'**, like 'Allgold', does not grow as large as the type nor is it as cold hardy,

but is spectacular with golden-green-striped canes, a few of the leaves with gold stripes. Plate 321.

Phyllostachys edulis (ED-yoo-liss) (synonyms *P. heterocycla* var. *pubescens*, *P. pubescens*) is native to eastern and south central China and is hardy in zones 8 through 11. Known as the moso bamboo, it is one of the finest and most beautiful species in the genus. It grows to as much as 70 feet or even more with gorgeous 6- to 7-inch-wide dark green culms that are covered in a luscious velvety coat of tiny hairs. The culms mature to a deep olive green to grayish green with distinct and exquisite white rings at the nodes. The leaves are borne on branches on the top half or two-thirds of the culms, are unusually small, and create an unusually feathery and lacy effect. This bamboo is somewhat difficult to propagate and to establish and is, therefore, sometimes difficult to find and, when found, somewhat pricey. It is worth the effort for the warm-climate gardener with enough room to have a grove of these beautiful plants. A heavy or light clay soil and regular irrigation of new plantings go a long way to ensure success. The young shoots of established clumps are edible when cooked and are important in Asian cooking.

***Phyllostachys heterocycla* var. *pubescens*.** See *P. edulis*.

Phyllostachys nigra (NY-gra) is native to central and eastern China and is hardy in zones 9 through 11 and usually root hardy in zone 7. The culms attain a height of 20 or sometimes 30 feet. The most distinctive characteristic of the plant is the black or purplish black mature canes, which are 2 to 3 inches in diameter. The canes are first green but, within a season, turn dark, especially with sun. This bamboo makes an exceptionally graceful and ornamental grove if the culms are judiciously thinned after a year or two of growth. It is commonly called the black bamboo. ***Phyllostachys nigra* 'Bory'** grows taller than the type, sometimes to as much as 50 feet, and has canes as much as 4 inches in diameter. The culms are never entirely black, however, but are a deep green splotched with a darker color. ***Phyllostachys nigra* 'Henon'** grows much larger than the type, sometimes to 60 feet, and has 5-inch-wide culms that are rough (with tiny pits) to the touch and a whitish or silvery green in color when young, maturing to a glaucous bluish green. This cultivar is a far superior landscape subject than the type, growing strong and bold. A well-cared for and judiciously thinned grove is distinctly tropical and quite exotic in appearance.

Phyllostachys pubescens. See *P. edulis*.

Phyllostachys sulphurea. See *P. bambusoides* 'Allgold'.

PHYTOLACCA (fyt-o-LAK-ka)
Phytolaccaceae: The Pokeweed Family
OMBÚ; BELLA SOMBRE (BE-ya SOAM-bray)
Large evergreen tree; large tropical looking leaves;
  white trunk; immense aboveground roots

Zones 9b through 11 as a large tree; zone 9a as a
  small tree
Sun
Average but regular amounts of moisture; drought
  tolerant when established
Humusy, sandy, well-drained soil
Propagation by seed and cuttings

A genus of about 35 species of herbs, shrubs, and
trees in warm temperate, subtropical, and tropical regions of the world. They have large undivided leaves,
spikes of tiny flowers without petals, and clusters of
small berrylike fruits. One species is native to the
United States and is famous as the pokeweed: *Phytolacca americana* is cultivated occasionally for its edible
(when cooked) attractive leaves and purple-red berries.
Another species is a stunningly ornamental evergreen
tree that is unaccountably rare in cultivation in warm
and tropical regions of the United States. ***Phytolacca
dioica*** (dy-OYK-a) is native to the pampas of southern Brazil, Uruguay, Paraguay, and northern Argentina. It is a soft-wooded tree growing quickly to as much
as 60 feet. It is usually multitrunked, the trunk(s) massive, thick, and a light tan to almost white in color. The
spread of the tree is usually at least equal to its height
and may be considerably more, sometimes to more than
100 feet in zones 10 and 11. The crown is rounded and
massive but also open and airy. The trees are said to
live to a very great age, to be resistant to fire and wind,
and to repel insects and mosquitoes. The juvenile leaves
are as much as 18 inches long, and those of mature
plants no more than half that length. The leaves are
ovate-elliptic in shape, a deep dark green in color with a
strong red midrib when young, and are soft and thick.
The tree is deciduous with drought or cold, and male
and female flowers are on separate trees. The small
white flowers with extended stamens are in pendent terminal racemes. Only female trees, of course, bear the
clusters of small red berries. The glories of this tree are
its extraordinary lower trunk and surface roots, which
are truly massive and look like piled up and cooled lava
flows. These roots can be as much as 60 feet in diameter and 6 or even 8 feet high. In addition, the canopy is
exquisitely massive, open, and graceful. This wonderful
tree is not only an outstanding curiosity, but is also extremely beautiful and exotic looking. It is a near perfect
shade tree as it provides its own "benches" for resting in
its ethereal umbrage. This magnificent tree should be
more widely grown in the warmer parts of the United
States. I know of no trees in Florida. While it grows
magnificently in southern California, it is rare there. A
tree in the San Antonio (Texas) Botanic Garden is often
frozen back but grows very rapidly and has attained as
much as 30 feet of height in the past. The plant is almost worshipped in its native Argentina. Plate 322.

PILEA (PIL-ee-a / PY-lee-a)
Urticaceae: The Nettle Family
Common names vary according to species

Small somewhat succulent-looking herbs; variegated
  leaves
Zones 10 and 11
Partial shade to partial sun
Average but regular amounts of moisture
Humusy, moist, well-drained soil
Propagation by cuttings and (sometimes) seed

A large genus of more than 600 annual and perennial
herbs in every warm and tropical region of the world
except Australia. Leaf color and form are variable in this
genus. The one unvarying diagnostic is the tri-nerved
leaves, which always have a strong and usually depressed midrib and two other strong and depressed
curving longitudinal veins on the leaf surface. Many
species have variegations on the leaf surface and some
have a wonderful quilted effect caused by the leaf's surface bearing many small raised "puckered" areas. The
flowers are in axillary clusters of tiny white or pink blossoms and are not effective in the landscape. All these
plants make wonderful groundcovers, adding texture
and color to partially shady areas. Some of them are
creeping and rooting at the stem nodes, and these are
excellent as groundcovers, for edging, for hanging baskets, and for planting on low moist walls. They are easy
to grow in partially shaded and moist sites, but need a
certain amount of light to maintain their variegation
and to prevent legginess of form. Some species often
sprout from their roots if frozen to the ground and if the
soil remains unfrozen, but this phenomenon is not completely dependable.
  Pilea cardierei (kar-dee-ER-ee-eye) is native to
Vietnam. It grows to about a foot in height with thin
round stems and 2-inch-long elliptic to obovate deep
green to bluish green glossy leaves. The leaves have
shallowly toothed margins, a short pointed tip, and
beautiful silvery gray markings between the midrib and
the two outer veins. It is called, appropriately, the alu-
minum plant and the watermelon pilea. It is exceedingly easy of culture given regular amounts of moisture
in a well-drained soil and shade or partial shade where
it greatly brightens the gloom. *Pilea cardierei* **'Minima'** is a smaller and more compact cultivar. It has
slightly smaller leaves and stems with a pinkish hue.
This species is unusually hardy to cold and is usually
unharmed by temperatures of 30°F; it will also usually
come back from its roots if temperatures do not fall
below 25°F for very long.
  Pilea involucrata (in-vahl´-yoo-KRAIT-a) (synonym *P. spruceana*) is native to the West Indies, Panama,
and northern South America. It is a trailing and creeping
plant, which roots at the stem nodes and which never
grows to more than a foot in height. It is dense with beautiful quilted 2-inch-long velvety, ovate to elliptic, almost
stalkless leaves that are a wonderful coppery green to almost brown above and purple beneath. The plant is
sometimes called the friendship plant and panamiga,
panamica, or panamico. It needs bright shade to retain
its remarkable color and compact form.

Pilea microphylla (myk-ro-FYL-la) occurs naturally in a wide area of the American tropics from southern and eastern Mexico through Central America and southwards into Brazil. This creeping plant never grows more than a foot high, has succulent watery stems, and tiny, almost stalkless thick and fleshy, rounded deep green leaves less than a half inch wide. It is one of the finest plants available for stuffing into the spaces between stepping stones, for planting in and on walls, and for a fine-textured edging around foliage beds. It readily seeds itself in warm moist climates and is one of the ever-present adventive plants in moist greenhouses and conservatories, appearing in the soil of pots and on the greenhouse floor and in joints in the walls. It is called the artillery plant (because its tiny flowers tend to shoot pollen out in a cloud) and artillery fern (because of its beautiful fine and fernlike texture).

Pilea mollis (MAHL-lis) is native to Central America and northern South America and is one of the most beautiful species in the genus. It is a semi-trailing plant, growing to a foot or slightly more with thick ridged green stems and 2- to 3-inch-long ovate to elliptic thick leaves. The leaves are deeply quilted and puckered above with the three prominent veins a beautiful reddish brown or brownish purple. The puckering extends to the leaf margins and results in their being scalloped. This plant is outstanding in a spot where its gorgeous color and wonderful texture can be appreciated up close. It works extremely well as a large groundcover or planted in soil pockets in walls or spilling over their tops and is unexcelled as a textured edging subject.

Pilea nigrescens (ny-GRES-senz) is native to parts of the West Indies. It grows to a foot or so in height and makes a fine dense cover of 3-inch-long elliptic quilted leaves that are a deep coppery to bluish green in color with much gray to silvery variegation between the veins. This plant is strikingly beautiful for creating color in semi-shady areas.

Pilea nummulariifolia (num'-yoo-lair'-ee-eye-FO-lee-a) is indigenous to parts of the West Indies, Panama, and southwards to northern South America and Peru. It is a creeping and trailing plant, rooting at the stem nodes. It is perfect as a groundcover, a hanging basket subject, or planted in or on walls. It grows only to a foot in height, but makes a spreading mat of rounded, scallop-margined velvety apple-green leaves. It, along with several other plants of similar growth habits, is unfortunately called creeping Charlie.

Pilea serpyllacea (sur'-pil-LAY-see-a) (synonym *P. serpyllifolia*) is quite similar to *P. microphylla:* it is indigenous to the same general area and needs the same treatment culturally and aesthetically as the artillery plant. The main difference is that this species has slightly larger leaves, which are finely pubescent and which have a deeper green color to the leaf blade. It is perhaps even more attractive than the artillery plant, but is much less common in cultivation.

Pilea serpyllifolia. See *P. serpyllacea.*

Pilea spruceana. See *P. involucrata.*

PIMENTA (pi-MENT-a)
Myrtaceae: The Myrtle, Eucalyptus Family
ALLSPICE; PIMENTO; PIMIENTO; JAMAICAN
    PEPPER
Small evergreen tree; aromatic leaves and bark;
    clusters of white flowers; clusters of red-brown fruit
Zones 10 and 11; marginal in zone 9b
Sun
Average but regular amounts of moisture; drought
    tolerant when established
Average well-drained soil
Propagation by seed

A genus of perhaps five species of small trees in tropical America. All have aromatic leaves and stems, oppositely arranged leathery leaves, and clusters of tiny white flowers from the leaf axils. The berries are quite fragrant, and those of a couple of the species are much used as spices for flavoring liqueurs and curries. One species is widely planted in warm-climate regions for its beauty and its berries, especially in the American tropics. *Pimenta dioica* (dy-OYK-a) (synonym *P. officinalis*) is native to the West Indies, southern Mexico, and Central America. It grows to 30 or sometimes 40 feet in height with a fairly dense oblong crown of 7- or 8-inch-long leathery and shiny light green leaves atop a relatively short trunk of gray and whitish exfoliating bark. The trees bloom in spring and early summer with tiny white flowers in small pyramidal clusters from the leaf axils near the ends of the branches. The fruits, which mature in summer, are quarter-inch-wide green berries that turn brown or reddish brown and finally black and are picked when still green for the commercial trade in allspice. When crushed or bruised the fruit as well as the leaves smell strongly of cinnamon, nutmeg, and cloves. This beautiful but slow-growing tree is best used for a close-up effect as a patio tree, although it is equally effective in a large shrub border. The mature tree is undamaged by temperatures as low as 28°F, but temperatures of 24°F will do much damage and anything below that will usually result in the death of the tree.

PIPER (PY-pur)
Piperaceae: The Black Pepper, Peperomia Family
PEPPER
Large herbs or vines; large leaves; minute flowers in
    tail-like spikes; fruits in pendent clusters
Zones vary according to species
Sun to partial shade
Water lovers
Rich, humusy, well-drained soil
Propagation by root division, cuttings, and
    (sometimes) seed

A gigantic genus of more than 1000 species of large herbs, shrubs, vines, and small trees in tropical regions around the world. The most distinguishing feature of this group is the inflorescence, which is invariably a narrowly cylindrical stalked spike with many minute scalelike flowers without sepals or petals. Each flower rests on an equally tiny bract. The flowers are packed so densely onto the spike that a hand lens is usually needed to differentiate the separate blossoms. The color of the tiny flowers and, therefore, the spike is usually white, gray, or tan. Almost all the species have relatively large alternately arranged leaves with distinct sheaths at the bases of the petioles and a strong, usually pleasant and invigorating odor when bruised or crushed. The fruits are usually tiny but may also be much larger than the flowers and may be colored. The most famous species is probably *Piper nigrum,* the black pepper vine of tropical Asia. All the vining species grow very nicely as ground-covers (and are almost unparalleled for such use), unless they find something on which to climb by their clinging aerial roots.

Piper auritum (OW-ri-tum / AW-ri-tum) is native to southeastern Mexico and Central America. It is a large herbaceous shrub, growing to 15 feet or sometimes more with mostly unbranched thick stems having woody bases supplied with large stilt roots to keep the upper portions of the plants with their giant leaves from toppling the little trees in the wind. The enormous and exceptionally beautiful leaves are as much as 18 inches wide (or long depending on the shape of the leaf). They are generally cordate, but may also be nearly orbicular, and are a light to deep green in color, velvety with a prominent and lighter colored midrib above and a paler and more densely pubescent undersurface. The leaf margins are often somewhat scalloped and wavy. The freely produced flower spikes are an intense pure white and are startlingly beautiful. All parts of the plants are strongly aromatic when bruised or crushed, the odor reminding most people of root beer and leading to the most common vernacular name in the United States, the root beer plant. Mexicans and Central Americans use the plant in several culinary ways, including wrapping the leaves around meat and other vegetables, the whole to be cooked much as the Greeks do in making dolma. Their names for it include yerba santa and Santa Maria. It is one of the fastest growing foliage plants, reaching 15 feet within a 9-month growing season with plentiful moisture and a fairly decent soil. As far as I know it never sets seed in the United States (at least in zone 9), but propagates by wandering underground rhizomes, which earn it the distinction of being invasive. If the errant new plants are pulled up before they are more than a foot or so tall, the peregrination is easily controlled. This giant herb is one of the best for creating quick and spectacular tropical effects in the landscape and is a permanent perennial in zones 10 and 11 and a returning perennial anywhere else that its roots do not freeze, usually zones 8 and 9. It is often cut back even in frost-free regions to encourage more compact and even lusher growth, which usually exhibits even more enormous leaves than those on the old stems. Plates 323 and 365.

Piper betle (BET-lee / BEET-lee) is indigenous to eastern India, through Southeast Asia and down into Indonesia. It is hardy in zones 10 and 11, although it will sometimes return from the root in zone 9b. It is a large and dense vine, climbing by aerial rootlets, with beautiful thick 6-inch-long perfectly cordate glossy deep green leaves with depressed curved longitudinal veins above. The fruits enlarge only slightly from the flower size, but turn a bright red in color, creating an attractive red "tail." This plant is the betel or betle pepper vine, the leaves of which are infamous for being one of the ingredients of the reportedly narcotic and addictive "betel juice," made by chewing or sucking on slivers of *Areca catechu* (betel nut) wrapped in these leaves and mixed with a lime paste and tobacco.

Piper crocatum. See *P. ornatum.*

Piper futokadsura. See *P. kadsura.*

Piper kadsura (kad-SOO-ra) (synonym *P. futokadsura*) is native to the southern Japanese islands and southern Korea and is hardy in zones 9b through 11 and root hardy in zone 9a. It is a climbing shrub, growing to as much as 20 feet, with aerial rootlets. The lovely 4- to 5-inch-long deep bluish green waxy-shiny cordate leaves have deeply depressed curved longitudinal veins above and a short curved tip. The little berrylike fruits are green, maturing to red. This species is sometimes called the Japanese pepper.

Piper longum (LAHNG-um) is native to northeastern India, southwestern China, and adjacent Myanmar (Burma), and is hardy in zones 10b and 11. It is a slow-growing scandent shrub or vine reaching to about 20 feet when climbing. The extraordinarily beautiful foot-long elliptic to lanceolate-shaped deep green glossy leaves have depressed veins and a lighter colored midrib above and are pale green in color beneath. Plants need warmth and humid conditions and should not be allowed to dry out.

Piper macrophyllum (mak-ro-FYL-lum) is indigenous to parts of the West Indies, southern Mexico, Central America and southwards to Venezuela. It is similar to *P. auritum* in habit and cultural requirements with somewhat more beautiful but slightly smaller leaves that are decidedly glossy as opposed to the velvety pubescent leaves of the root beer plant. It is also not as fast growing nor as invasive as *P. auritum* and is altogether a very choice plant.

Piper magnificum (mag-NIF-i-kum) is native to eastern Peru and is hardy in zones 10 and 11. This shrub grows only to 4 or 6 feet in height, is sparsely branched, and has ridged, corky-textured stems. The 9- to 10-inch-long leaves are borne on short winged petioles that clasp the stem, and the leaf blade is heavy, leathery and fleshy, broadly oblong to obovate in shape, a very deep green above, and an intense purplish red and velvety pubescent beneath. The leaf surface is quilted and puckered between the deeply depressed and lighter colored lateral veins, and the midribs are stout and almost white as are the leaf's margins. This spectacular-leaved shrub is sometimes called the lacquered pepper tree because of the almost patent leather finish on the upper surface of the leaves.

Piper nigrum (NY-grum) is the black pepper, white pepper, or simply the pepper plant. It is originally native to southern India and Sri Lanka, but has been spread all over the world's tropical regions. It is hardy in zones 10 and 11, but is grown and often survives in zone 9b. This tall-growing vine has rather slender stems that bear clinging aerial rootlets at the nodes. The ovate to elliptic to almost round leaves are a smooth dark green above and are 6 to 8 inches wide or long with depressed veins, which give a ridged look to the leaf's surface. The leaves have a usually lighter colored midrib. The fruits are quarter-inch wide round berries (actually drupes) on long pendent spikes. Initially green, they turn red and finally black when fully mature. They are the peppercorns of commerce. The ground whole peppercorn yields black pepper, and removing the blackened fleshy pulp around the seed or stone before grinding it yields white pepper. The vine is one of the world's most important commercial plants—its importance to fifteenth-century Europeans changed the course of history—and is also of great beauty, lending an exotic and tropical appearance to anything on which it is allowed to climb.

Piper ornatum (or-NAIT-um) (synonym *P. crocatum*) is indigenous to the central islands of Indonesia and is hardy in zones 10 and 11. This slender-stemmed, high-climbing vine is exceptionally beautiful with its red stems and leaf stalks. The leaves are variable in shape and color, ranging from linear cordate and long-tipped to broadly cordate and almost orbicular. They are held peltate on the leaf stalks, and the leaf surfaces are smooth and waxy to the touch and much spotted with dark green, pinkish white and silver, while the undersurfaces are a gorgeous wine-red in color. The vine grows rather slowly, reaching heights of 30 feet. It demands nearly constant warmth and humidity, but can recover from a light and short frost. It grows in deep shade but needs bright light (not full sun) to bring out the lovely mottling.

Piper porphyrophyllum (por´-fi-ro-FYL-lum) (synonym *Cissus porphyrophyllum*) is native to Malaysia and is hardy in zones 10b and 11, although sometimes root hardy in zones 10a and 9b. It is a high-climbing vine with slender reddish stems bearing 4- to 6-inch-wide mint green broadly cordate to almost round leaves that are wine-colored beneath. The upper leaf surface is velvety pubescent and has deeply depressed curved longitudinal veins lined in yellowish white with pinkish white blotches. The leaf surface is raised between the veins, giving an overall quilted look to the blade. This exceptionally beautiful vine needs warmth and moisture and does not tolerate full sun.

Piper sylvaticum (sil-VAT-i-kum) is indigenous to northeastern India and adjacent Myanmar (Burma). It is hardy in zones 10 and 11, although often root hardy in zone 9b. This small vine grows to about 15 feet in height. It has slender wiry stems bearing 4-inch-long cordate grayish green leaves with a silvery and metallic sheen. The depressed curved longitudinal veins are a deep bluish green, and this color feathers out in a retic-ulated manner between these main veins. This strikingly beautiful vine needs to be planted where it can be enjoyed up close.

PISCIDIA (pis-SID-ee-a)
Papilionaceae (Fabaceae, Leguminosae), subfamily
    Papilionoideae: The Bean, Pea Family
JAMAICAN DOGWOOD; FISH-POISON TREE
Medium-sized semi-evergreen tree; pinnate leaves;
    pendent clusters of white or pink flowers
Zones 10b and 11
Sun
Average but regular amounts of moisture; drought
    tolerant when established
Average well-drained soil
Propagation by seed

A genus of eight small trees in southern Florida and the West Indies with pinnate leaves and panicles of pealike flowers. One species is fairly widely planted for its display of wisteria-like flowers in spring. *Piscidia piscipula* (pis-SIP-yoo-la) (synonym *Ichthyomethia piscidia*) naturally occurs in southern Florida and the West Indies. It grows to 40 or sometimes 50 feet and makes a somewhat irregularly shaped crown that is usually broad and open but may be oblong; the trunk is fairly stout and the bark is green on newer wood, becoming dark gray and scaly on the older wood. The foot-long leaves are pinnate with seven to nine oblong or elliptic grayish green 2- to 4-inch-long leaflets. The young leaves are a beautiful silky bronzy orange in color. Unless the winter season is unusually wet, the tree normally loses its leaves for a brief period in late winter. The tree blooms in February and March with dense and pendent clusters of inch-wide pealike flowers that are white with a couple of pink, purple, or red stripes. The bark and leaves are quite poisonous if ingested, and one of the vernacular names reveals a former use of this species. The tree is never what one would call "spectacular," but is attractive enough to warrant cultivation for its fast growth, beautiful foliage, lovely flowers, and picturesque habit. The trees are also tolerant of saline soil and salty spray and are perfect for seashore plantings.

PISTIA (PIST-ee-a)
Araceae: The Calla Lily, Jack-in-the-Pulpit Family
WATER LETTUCE; SHELLFLOWER
Floating aquatic or bog plants with rosettes of velvety
    scalloped leaves
Zones 8 through 11
Sun to partial shade
Water lover
Still or slowly moving ponds or wet humusy soil
Can be invasive
Propagation by transplanting of suckers

A monotypic genus found in subtropical and tropical ponds, lakes, and bogs around the world. *Pistia stratiotes* (stray-tee-O-teez) grows in a stemless rosette of

6- to 12-inch-long ridged yellow-green to deep olive green leaves that are obovate to spatulate in shape, usually with a squared-off apex, which is usually shallowly scalloped. The leaf surfaces are wonderfully velvety-pubescent. The tiny whitish flowers are rather typical of the family, but are mostly hidden between the overlapping leaves and are not important in the landscape. These lovely "floating roses" are found adrift in sluggish or still waters and along the edges of ponds or lakes, where they grow in the surrounding boggy conditions. They propagate by running stolons, which produce plantlets, and can virtually cover a pond. While the individual plants are beautiful enough, they not only look better with clear water between their groups of rosettes but they can also crowd out other floating plants. For small ponds it is no great problem to lift and cut masses of the plants but, in a large pond or lake, it can be a real chore.

PITHECELLOBIUM

(pith´-e-sel-LO-bee-um)
Mimosaceae (Fabaceae, Leguminosae), subfamily
    Mimosoideae: The Mimosa Family
TEXAS EBONY; EBONY APE'S-EARRING
Medium-sized spiny evergreen tree; small pinnate
    leaves; clusters of yellow or white flowers
Zones 9 through 11
Sun
Average but regular amounts of moisture; drought
    tolerant when established
Average well-drained soil
Propagation by seed

A small genus of about 20 mostly thorny shrubs and trees in tropical and subtropical America. They have bipinnate foliage and spikes or balls of tiny flowers with very long stamens, as is typical of the mimosa family, and podlike usually twisted or coiled fruits. Most species, while fast growing and attractive in bloom, are somewhat weedy, weak of trunk and limb, and generally not that desirable in the landscape. One species is slower-growing and makes a distinctive, almost noble tree that is attractive year-round.

Pithecellobium flexicaule (flex-i-KAW-lee) (synonym *P. ebano*) is native to southern Texas and adjacent Mexico. It usually grows to about 30 feet but can attain a height of 50 feet with a dense rounded crown of dark green foliage. The tree naturally grows with either a single trunk or several trunks and is attractive in both forms. The trunks are rough-textured and dark gray or brown in color and, when single, fairly massive. The dark green bipinnate leaves are mostly at the ends of the zigzagging twigs and are quite attractive, with two or three paired pinnae of from 8 to 12 elliptic to obovate half-inch-long leaflets. Each twig usually has a pair of half-inch-long straight spines. The tree blooms mostly in early summer, but flowers in spring, late summer, and fall, especially after periods of dryness followed by rain. The tiny yellowish white fragrant flowers are in 1-to 2-inch-long dense spikes at the ends of the branches. The curved pods are thick and fat, black when mature, and about 6 inches long; they are tough and last for a year or more on the tree. The tree is well adapted to arid or semiarid areas, but also thrives in wetter climes in a fast-draining soil. It is near perfect as a patio tree or, with its picturesque habit, lining streets or wide walkways. It is quite adaptable to seaside plantings as it is tolerant of fairly saline soil and salty spray and wind.

Pithecellobium saman. See *Samanea saman*.

PITTOSPORUM

(pit-TAHS-po-rum / pit´-to-SPOR-um)
Pittosporaceae: The Pittosporum Family
Common names vary according to species
Evergreen shrubs or small trees; leathery leaves; large
    fragrant white or yellow flower clusters
Zones vary according to species
Sun
Average but regular amounts of moisture
Humusy, sandy, well-drained soil
Propagation by cuttings and (sometimes) seed

A large genus of about 200 species of evergreen shrubs and trees in the tropics and subtropics of the Old World, mostly in the Southern Hemisphere. They have alternately arranged or whorled leathery undivided leaves and broad axillary clusters of five-petaled usually fragrant flowers that form two-parted or three-parted rounded often brilliantly colored fruits whose seeds are surrounded by a very sticky viscous substance. Most species are somewhat drought tolerant when established but do and look ever so much better with regular and adequate amounts of water.

Pittosporum rhombifolium (rahmb-i-FO-lee-um) is native to northeastern Australia and is hardy in zones 10 and 11 and marginal in zone 9b. It slowly grows in its native habitat to as much as 70 or 80 feet, but is usually no more than half that stature under cultivation. It makes a beautiful oblong fairly dense crown of deep green 4-inch-long ovate to diamond-shaped leathery leaves with widely spaced shallow teeth along their margins. The beautiful dark gray trunk is low-branched and, unless trained when young, is likely to form a multitrunked specimen as often as not. The tree blooms in late spring with 6-inch-wide clusters of small white flowers. The round half-inch-wide fruits are nothing short of spectacular. They are a vivid deep yellow to orange or red in color and persist on the tree through the autumn and winter. This lovely tree is attractive always and beautiful almost anywhere in the landscape, being unexcelled for street planting. It is called the diamond-leaf pittosposrum and the Queensland pittosporum.

Pittosporum tobira (to-BY-ra) is native to the southern Japanese islands and eastern and southern China. It is hardy in zones 8b through 11 and marginal in zone 8a. It is most often called Japanese pittosporum, but also sometimes just tobira. This large shrub or small tree usually grows to a maximum of 12 or 15 feet but occasionally to as much as 25 feet. The trunks are extremely picturesque, dark gray in color, smooth in texture, but gnarled and never straight. As a tree, either trained to multiple trunks or a single-trunked specimen, it has a character almost unequaled and looks like a giant bonsai subject. The leaves are clustered near the ends of the branches and grow almost in whorls there. Each leaf is 4 to 6 inches long, thick and leathery, but also glossy and obovate to spatulate, with a prominent and lighter colored midrib. The spectacular and intensely fragrant flowers appear in late spring and early summer, and are in 6-inch-wide clusters of small white waxy-petaled blossoms, which age to a deep yellow. Their fragrance is most akin to that of orange blossoms and attracts every bee within a quarter-mile radius. The plant does not often form fruit in wet humid regions but, when it does, it is a round half-inch-wide dark green berry that turns brown when mature and opens to exhibit an orange seed. This shrub is one of the most widely planted in the Deep South, along the Gulf Coast, in Florida, and in the warmer parts of California and Arizona. It is remarkably beautiful and, being tolerant of salinity, is exceptionally fine near the seashore where it is often the prettiest shrub or tree in the landscape, especially when windswept. *Pittosporum tobira* **'Variegata'** is of great beauty because of the grayish green foliage edged in creamy white, but it is slightly less hardy to cold. It is stunning in borders as it does not grow nearly so tall as the type (only to about 6 feet), and it is tolerant of partial shade where it gives some much needed color to shrubby borders. It is widely used as hedge material, but is not well suited to formal attire. *Pittosporum tobira* **'Wheeler's Dwarf'** is a tiny and very compact version of the type that grows only to about 2 feet. It is much used as edging material and along gravel paths and is interplanted among large stepping stones. Plate 324.

Pittosporum undulatum (un-dyoo-LAIT-um) is indigenous to the east coast of Australia and is hardy in zones 10 and 11 and marginal in zone 9b. The tree grows to as much as 40 feet with time and is, of course, a much larger tree in its native habitat. It forms a low-branched trunk carrying a wide and rounded dense crown of deep green foliage. The olive green leaves are fairly thin, narrowly elliptic to lanceolate, glossy, and about 6 inches long. Each leaf has a prominent and lighter colored midrib and a wavy margin. The leaves, like those of *P. tobira*, tend to be crowded at the ends of the branches. The tree blooms in early to mid-spring with few-flowered 6-inch-wide clusters of white to almost yellow very fragrant flowers whose scent, like that of most other species, is highly reminiscent of orange blossoms. The fruits mature in September and are round and a deep yellow in color, eventually splitting to reveal deep brown seeds. This wonderful tree is exquisite in any part of the landscape and is often used, with heavy shearing, as a hedge, which seems unfortunate as the tree form is of such great beauty. It unfortu-

nately is not very fond of hot and humid regions and looks best in the milder Mediterranean climates.

PLATYCERIUM (plat-ee-SER-ee-um)
Polypodiaceae: The Largest Fern Family
STAGHORN FERNS; ELKHORN FERNS; ANTELOPE EARS
Large epiphytic ferns; immense lobed mostly flat leaves
Zones vary according to species
Partial shade to śun
Water lovers
Rich, humusy, well-drained soil or leaf mold
Propagation (for most species) by transplanting of suckers and by spores

A genus of 18 large epiphytic fern species in tropical regions around the globe but mainly in the Old World and mainly in the Southern Hemisphere. Their growth habit and form are unique among the ferns. The individual fern leaves produce two radically differing leaf forms, one fertile and one infertile. The infertile fronds, usually called the "shield fronds," are relatively very large, have margins that are usually (and sometimes deeply) lobed, and are relatively flat in form. They stand erect from their support and have roots that hold the plant fast to its substrate, which may be a tree trunk (dead or alive) or a rock. The fertile fronds are smaller, hang downwards from the base of the shield fronds, and are never as broad as the infertile fronds but are usually forked into segments resembling a deer's antlers. These fronds produce the propagative spores. The shield fronds are smooth and waxy on their surfaces, while the fertile fronds have a velvety pubescence and the masses of spores on their undersurfaces in some species are large, brown, and velvety.

Almost all the species are indigenous to tropical rain forests and need constant moisture and a relatively large amount of soil or epiphytic mix around their roots to ensure proper nutrition and to hold moisture. In nature the plants begin life on and in the crotches of smooth-trunked large forest trees as tiny plantlets from newly sprouted spores. With time they build up their root systems and collect a large amount of leaf mold and debris to see them through drier periods in monsoonal areas. Growing the plants in this way is not usually an option for the home gardener, who purchases relatively large plants and must secure them to trees, rocks, or some other substrate. The only solution is to pin the plants to their new home, often with a mass of wire (if not already provided from the grower) around the roots to collect and hold leaf mold or soil. The procedure is straightforward enough with rocks, woodwork, and similar supports but, in the case of trees, care must be taken not to encircle the tree's trunk with wire. Instead, the wire should be hung on nails driven into the trunk. The nails may be driven directly through the shield fronds for attachment. If the tree is a palm, nails should not be used as the wounds in palm trunks never truly heal. In time the ferns often encircle the tree trunk with roots and the detritus constituting their food and drink. In climates without regular and adequate rainfall, the plants must be routinely sprayed with water, preferably collected rainwater. All but one species (*Platycerium superbum*) grow plantlets from their short rhizomes, and these little plants may be removed at the beginning of the growing season (spring to early summer) and used to form new clumps.

These ferns are among the most spectacular and fantastic looking plants the tropical gardener can grow. The smallest species are only about a foot wide, but the larger ones exceed 6 feet in breadth. They create an exotic and tropical look that can hardly be surpassed.

Platycerium andinum (an-DYN-um / an-DEEN-um) is native to eastern Peru and northern and northeastern Bolivia and is called the South American staghorn fern. It is a medium-sized species. The deeply divided grayish green shield fronds are 2 feet or more long, with deep green lobes on the upper half and with heavy veins. The plant needs constant warmth and humidity and is safe only in zones 10b and 11.

Platycerium bifurcatum (by-fur-KAIT-um) is native to Indonesia, New Guinea, eastern Australia, and the islands adjacent to that part of the continent. It is probably the most commonly grown species, mainly because it is very easy of culture and is relatively hardy to cold. It is adaptable to zones 10 and 11, but evidently only some southerly populations of the species are so hardy. Australian fern authority David L. Jones writes in *Encyclopedia of Ferns*: "In Australia the species extends into temperate regions and plants from such southerly collections are very cold-hardy and will tolerate severe frosts." The Northern Hemisphere reader must remember, however, that "severe frosts" in Australia are not as severe or as long as in the non-Mediterranean parts of North America. The common staghorn fern is a somewhat variable species but, in general, the type has foot-wide shield fronds that are more or less reniform (kidney-shaped) and a light green in color with relatively shallow lobes on the upper margin. The fertile fronds are a deep grayish green, segmented into two or three large forks, and often hang down 3 feet or more from the base of the shield fronds. The several cultivars of this species vary in size, color, and the form of the fronds. Plate 325.

Platycerium coronarium (kor-o-NAHR-ee-um) is native to Southeast Asia, Indonesia, Malaysia, and northward to the Philippines. Adaptable only to zones 10b and 11, it is a spectacular species whose shield fronds are more than 3 feet wide and deeply lobed on their upper margins. The fertile fronds may reach as much as 12 feet and are great curtains of many segmented dark green leaves. Few sights are as awesome as a mature clump of this mighty fern perched high on giant forest trees.

Platycerium superbum (soo-PURB-um) is indigenous to northeastern Australia and is hardy in zones 10b and 11. The grayish green shield fronds may attain a width of 5 feet or more, are deeply lobed, and exhibit prominent darker veins. The fertile fronds are a bright green and relatively short.

Platycerium veitchii (VEECH-ee-eye) is native to semiarid areas of northern Queensland outside the rain forests and is adaptable to zones 10 and 11. It is not a giant species. The deeply segmented and bright green shield fronds are usually about 18 inches wide, and the fertile fronds are as much as 2 feet long, much divided, and covered in a silky pubescence of matted hairs, which imparts an overall silvery or gray-green color. The plant grows on cliff faces and needs sun to do well. This trait along with the fern's slight frost tolerance and striking color makes it an exceptionally desirable plant.

PLECTRANTHUS (plek-TRANTH-us)
Labiatae (Lamiaceae): The Mint Family
Common names vary according to species
Creeping herbs; attractive fleshy leaves used as
    groundcovers; small flowers in whorls on a spike
Zones 10 and 11 as permanent perennials; zone 9b as
    returning perennials; anywhere as annuals
Partial shade to partial sun
Average but regular amounts of moisture
Average well-drained soil
Propagation by seed and cuttings

A large genus of about 350 species of herbs and herbaceous subshrubs with mostly square stems (diagnostic of the mint family), oppositely arranged fleshy leaves that are usually scalloped, and flowers in whorls around a terminal spike. These plants are used in the shady garden as bedding plants and especially as groundcovers and the more scandent types are beautiful cascading from atop low walls. Indoors they are used as hanging baskets or container plants. Many species and their forms have wonderfully attractive leaves. The flower spikes should be removed when they form as they are not showy or effective in the landscape and their continued growth tends to make the plants leggy.

Plectranthus australis. See *P. nummularius*.

Plectranthus coleoides (kol-ee-OY-deez) (synonym *P. forsteri*) is native to southern India through Indonesia and Malaysia to northern Australia. It is not a trailing groundcover type but rather a small subshrub growing to as much as 3 feet in height. The leaves are 2 inches long, held on purplish red stems, and are ovate in outline but scalloped along their margins. They are grayish green with darker green splotches along the veins and a creamy white margin. The plant is beautiful as a small bedding subject and as pleasing to the eye as many *Begonia* and all *Coleus* species.

Plectranthus forsteri. See *P. coleoides*.

Plectranthus nummularius (num-yoo-LAIR-ee-us) (synonyms *P. australis*, *P. parviflorus*, *P. verticillatus*) is native to tropical East Africa and is called Swedish ivy and (unfortunately) creeping Charlie. The plants are trailing and root at the leaf nodes, never growing to more than a foot tall, making them perfect for groundcovers as well as cascade plants either in baskets or spilling over walls. The succulent waxy rounded leaves are 2 to 3 inches wide and, scalloped on their margins. The upper surface is a beautiful metallic deep green, and the lower surface a grayish green with purple veins.

Plectranthus oertendahlii (urt-en-DAHL-ee-eye) is probably indigenous to tropical Africa but is not found there now except in cultivation. It is a trailing plant that grows only to a foot in height and roots at the nodes, making a perfect groundcover. The 3-inch-wide succulent bronzy-green leaves are almost stalkless and almost round with round-scalloped margins. Both surfaces of the leaves are velvety, and the main veins on the upper surface are outlined in a beautiful creamy white. The leaf undersurface is purple. The plants are sometimes called Brazilian coleus, prostrate coleus, and candle plant (for the tall flower spikes).

Plectranthus parviflorus. See *P. nummularius.*
Plectranthus verticillatus. See *P. nummularius.*

PLEOMELE. See *Dracaena.*

PLUMERIA (ploo-MER-ee-a)
Apocynaceae: The Oleander, Frangipani, Vinca
    Family
FRANGIPANI; PLUMERIA; TEMPLE TREE;
    PAGODA TREE; NOSEGAY; WEST INDIAN
    JASMINE
Semi-evergreen rubbery-trunked small trees; large
    bold leaves; splendid clusters fragrant flowers
Zones 10b and 11; marginal in zone 10a
Sun to partial sun
Average but regular amounts of moisture
Rich, humusy, sandy, well-drained soil
Propagation by cuttings

A genus of only eight species of shrubs and small trees in tropical America. They have milky latexlike sap, typical of most members of the Apocynaceae, to which some people are allergic. The leaves are large, thick, rather succulent, and heavily veined. The rubbery trunks and stems are marked with persistent leaf scars. The trees bear great terminal clusters of fragrant large, long-tubed salverform blossoms, each with five somewhat twisted corolla lobes. The contorted corolla lobes or petals, which are apparent in bud and often after the flowers are fully open, reflect another diagnostic feature of the family. The fruits are 6-inch-long narrowly cylindrical pods growing in pairs adjoined to each other at right angles and full of thin flaky seeds. The genus name is sometimes but erroneously spelled "Plumieria."

The members of this genus are found in the West Indies, southern Mexico through Central America, and into northern South America. They mostly occur on hillsides in very well draining, often poor soils and are exposed to the full brunt of the tropical sun. These hillsides are often near the seashore. Without exception, the species now in cultivation are tolerant of salty spray and slightly saline soil and are much planted near the coast. In much of their range there are distinct dry and wet seasons and, under these conditions, the trees become deciduous for at least part of the dry season. This phenomenon has led to much confusion for many gardeners, for in climates with more evenly distributed rainfall, these trees are often mostly evergreen. At least one species seems to resist losing its leaves no matter what the amount and regularity of rainfall; it would rather die than go deciduous. Furthermore in the areas with dry and wet seasons, the plants bloom mainly in the wet season, while in more moist regions they tend to bloom in cycles all year-round, depending partly on the species, cultivar, or hybrid.

Almost all the species are small trees that grow from 20 to 40 feet in their native habitats with an equal or even greater width, but a couple of species are more shrublike, attaining only 10 or 12 feet in height. There are now nearly dwarf cultivated forms, which are quite useful for the gardener who wants their beauty but must grow them in containers to be moved into a greenhouse or indoors. All have thick stems and trunks that are rubbery and limber but easily broken when young and immature. Mature trunks are woody and inflexible at their bases. The growth form is low-branching, usually open, with relatively few branches, and the shape of the trees in general is often candelabra-like.

The leaves are almost exclusively found at the ends of the branches in apparent whorls, although technically the leaves are alternately arranged along the stem. Leaf size ranges from 6 or 8 inches long to more than 24 inches, and the shape is generally elliptic but can vary from that to linear-oblong, obovate-emarginate to spatulate. The leaf's midrib is prominent and often lighter colored than the blade, which is light to deep green in color, smooth in texture above but often pubescent beneath, with distinct and darker lateral veins.

Some people find the relatively few branches and the thick and rubbery gray or almost white limbs to be lacking in aesthetic appeal, especially in climates where the trees have a deciduous period. Indeed, Edwin A. Menninger found their most usual form to be "an awkward set of wooden antlers topped with nosegays." But I find that the mature trees, even without their exceptional flowers, are more than beautiful when in leaf. The leaves are invariably large (sometimes immense), thick, leathery, and very tropical looking, and make a wonderful texture in the landscape. Most species, cultivars, and hybrids have much denser foliage crowns when they are near their maximum size than they do when they are juvenile.

The inflorescence is a loose broad panicle of long-tubed flowers. Each flower is salverform in overall shape with five widely expanding and usually overlapping elliptic to obovate waxy corolla lobes, which approximately exhibit the twist that is one of the characteristics of the family Apocynaceae. A few of the species that are extremely rare in the United States and a few cultivars and hybrids now in cultivation have narrow lobes that are widely separated one from the other. Flower color now includes every known color except true blue, with a truly wonderful spectrum of combinations and shadings in the individual flowers which may be from 2 to more than 6 inches wide when fully opened (Plates 326 and 327). Almost all are exquisitely fragrant but some cultivars and hybrids are exceptionally so while others are only faintly scented. The time of day seems to affect fragrance, with mornings, afternoons, and evenings providing the greatest excitement. Many varieties have an almost poignant fruity perfume, mostly of apricot or peach, while others are strongly reminiscent of gardenias or honeysuckle and some are simply indescribable.

Frangipani are exceedingly easy of culture and have only three requisites: a frost-free or nearly frost-free climate, a fast draining and non-compacted soil, and at least a half day's sun. They do well in average well-drained soil but appreciate one that is high in organic matter with leaf mold, compost, or rotted cow or horse manure. They are fairly drought tolerant but, like so many other plants of this type, do their best with adequate and regular supplies of moisture. The most important thing to remember regarding their water requirements is that they die in a compacted and poorly draining soil in which water stands. Frangipani should not be planted outdoors in climates that are basically frost-free but have a relatively cold and wet winter season. The reason is that, with the advent of cold weather, all species tend to go into dormancy and if they receive large amounts of moisture while in a dormant state, even in perfectly draining soil, are subject to root rot if the plants are not actively photosynthesizing.

The plants are as easy to propagate as they are to grow. Cuttings taken in late spring through summer are easily rooted in sand that is kept slightly moist but not wet. The cuttings should be from 15 inches to 2 feet long and should be from the ends of branches that are not in bloom. Most important is that the cuttings be allowed to form a callus on the cut end, which is easily done by placing the cutting in a dry spot out of the sun for a few days to a week. Frangipani plants do not produce many roots in relation to the size of the plants, and large specimens are easily transplanted in warm weather.

The average gardener is unlikely to ever come across more than three of the eight *Plumeria* species and, of these, most individual plants are cultivars or hybrids of only two of the species. In addition, all three commonly cultivated species are variable in growth and leaf form and in flower size and color. With modern hybridization, there is often more variation among the hybrids and cultivars than there is between the individuals of the several "pure" species that may be found in cultivation. Whatever the parentage, these plants are of incomparable beauty, especially when in bloom, and are one of the indispensable jewels in the crown of the tropical garden.

Plumeria acutifolia. See *P. rubra* forma *acutifolia*.

Plumeria alba (AL-ba) is native to the West Indies. It grows to as much as 40 feet with an equal or greater spread and is the largest species. The leaves are oblong to elliptic in shape and generally a foot long, but may approach 2 feet in length in some forms. Furthermore, the leaves are slightly to mostly pubescent underneath and often have their margins rolled down and under to some extent. The flowers are white with yellow centers. This species is one of the glories of the tropics, but is difficult to find now as the "pure" species and is not much used in hybridization. Plate 328.

Plumeria emarginata. See *P. obtusa*.

Plumeria lutea. See *P. rubra* forma *lutea*.

Plumeria obtusa (ahb-TYOOS-a) (synonyms *P. emarginata*, *P. obtusifolia*) is indigenous to Cuba, Jamaica, Puerto Rico, the Yucatán Peninsula of Mexico and Belize. This quite variable species may encompass more than one distinct species. In any case, the plants within this group are the most beautiful in the genus. They grow to 20 feet or sometimes more with age and form relatively compact widespreading little trees. The leaves are variable in shape, but the most typical form is oblanceolate to obovate or even spatulate. From 6 inches to 14 inches in length, the leaves are often emarginate and are very deep dark green in color, glossy in texture above, with a prominent and lighter colored midrib. In shape, texture, and color the leaves rather resemble those of *Pittosporum tobira*. The trees are naturally evergreen no matter what the amount of rainfall. The intensely fragrant flowers are pure white, sometimes with faint yellow in the center of the corolla lobes whose shapes vary from obovate to linear and may be overlapping or quite separated. One of the most beautiful sights in the plant kingdom is a mature tree of this species in bloom. The species is sometimes called the Singapore frangipani or Singapore plumeria. Plate 329.

Plumeria obtusifolia. See *P. obtusa*.

Plumeria rubra (ROOB-ra) occurs naturally from southern Mexico through Central America and into Panama. It grows to 20 feet or sometimes more with an open crown of elliptic to obovate leaves that vary in length from 10 to 20 inches and have prominent and often lighter colored midribs and distinct lateral veins. There is also usually apparent a vein that outlines the leaf shape just within the leaf margin and "contains" the other veins. There are evidently at least four distinct forms to this species. In the past these forms were often named as distinct and separate species. ***Plumeria rubra*** **forma** ***acutifolia*** (a-kyoot'-i-FO-lee-a) (synonym *P. acutifolia*) has white flowers with yellow centers and sometimes red or pink suffusions on the corolla lobes. ***Plumeria rubra*** **forma** ***lutea*** (LOOT-ee-a) (synonym *P. lutea*) has yellow flowers sometimes flushed pink. ***Plumeria rubra*** **forma** ***rubra*** is the most common natural form. It has deep pink flowers often with yellow centers. ***Plumeria rubra*** **forma** ***tricolor*** (TRY-kul-or) (synonym *P. tricolor*) has white flowers with yellow centers and a red or pink suffusion near the ends of the corolla lobes. The species is involved in almost all the many cultivars and hybrids between the various cultivars now sold and grown.

Plumeria tricolor. See *P. rubra* forma *tricolor.*

PODRANEA (po-DRAY-nee-a)
Bignoniaceae: The Catalpa, Jacaranda, Trumpet-
    Vine Family
PINK TRUMPET VINE
Twining vines; pinnate leaves; large terminal and
    pendent clusters of pink and red trumpet flowers
Zone vary according to species
Sun
Average but regular amounts of moisture
Average well-drained soil
Propagation by seed and cuttings

A genus of only two species of twining vines in Africa. They have odd-pinnate leaves and bell-shaped pink and red flowers in terminal pendent panicles. The genus is closely allied to and all too similar to *Pandorea* and is a segregate from that genus because of a few technical characters. It is most unfortunate that "*Podranea*" is an anagram of "*Pandorea.*" The similarity in names and the similarity in plants have led to great confusion and consternation for almost all warm-climate gardeners. *Podranea* species are distinguished from *Pandorea* species by their leaves and flowers. The pinnate leaves of *Pandorea* are glossy and leathery and the margins of the leaflets are completely smooth and entire, whereas those of *Podranea* are not glossy and the margins of the leaflets are shallowly toothed. In addition, the flowers of *Pandorea* are only remotely, if at all, striped, while those of *Podranea* are heavily veined. Unfortunately the flowers of *Podranea* are also similar to those of *Clytostoma,* another related genus in the bignonia family. The species described here are not as ornamental as those of the genus *Pandorea* except when in flower, at which time they are possibly more spectacular than those of the former genus.

Podranea brycei (BRYS-ee-eye) (synonyms *Pandorea brycei, Tecoma reginae-sabae*) is native to tropical southeastern Africa and is adaptable to zones 10 and 11. The vine grows to moderate heights of only 15 to 20 feet. It has pinnate leaves composed of 9 or 11 lanceolate to ovate-shaped 2-inch-long leaflets whose margins are somewhat toothed. The plants bloom in late winter, spring, and early summer. The flowers are borne in large terminal hanging panicles. Each flower is 2 to 3 inches long and a shallow and wide-flaring trumpet with five deep and scalloped lobes that are colored light pink with deep red veins and a yellow throat. The vine is sometimes called the Queen of Sheba vine.

Podranea ricasoliana (rik´-a-sol-ee-AHN-a) (synonyms *Pandorea ricasoliana, Tecoma ricasoliana*) is indigenous to South Africa and is hardy in zone 9 as a returning perennial vine and in zones 10 and 11 as a permanent perennial vine. The plant is fast growing and twines its way to 20 or 30 feet if frost does not cut it back. The pinnate leaves are composed of seven to eleven ovate and shallowly toothed 2-inch-long leaflets with long tapering tips. The plants are deciduous with cold or drought and tend to become bare of leaves at the base of the vines. The vine blooms in summer with great terminal and pendent panicles of 20 or more flowers. Each flower is a wide shallow five-lobed trumpet. The lobes are fairly deep and scalloped, and the flower color is pink with deep red veins and deep rose throats. In keeping with the general confusion attendant upon the *Pandorea-Podranea* question, it is sometimes called the ricasol pandorea. Plate 330.

POLYPODIUM. See *Drynaria, Goniophlebium, Microsorium, Phlebodium.*

POLYSCIAS (po-LIS-see-as)
Araliaceae: The Aralia, Schefflera Family
Common names vary according to species
Evergreen shrubs and small trees with large entire,
    segmented, or pinnate leaves
Zones 10b and 11; marginal in zone 10a
Partial shade to sun
Average but regular amounts of moisture
Humusy, well-drained soil
Propagation by cuttings

A genus of about 100 species of evergreen shrubs and trees in the Old World tropics. The plants in this genus are extremely diverse in form, especially regarding their leaves. The only characteristic uniting them into one genus is the structure of their individual flowers, which are tiny and usually borne in umbels that are not significant in the landscape. These plants were formerly included in the large genus *Aralia* and the smaller genus *Nothopanax;* the latter is no longer a valid generic name.

Polyscias balfouriana. See *P. scutellaria* 'Balfourii'.

Polyscias elegans. See *P. fruticosa* 'Elegans'.

Polyscias filicifolia (fi-lis´-i-FO-lee-a) (synonym *Aralia filicifolia*) is native to the islands of the South Pacific. It grows to 8 or 10 feet and is densely clothed with olive green pinnate leaves, each of which may be as much as 2 feet long with nine to seventeen 6-inch-long leaflets that are usually pinnately segmented. Because these shrubs keep their branches and leaves to the ground unless pruned, the plants are quite spectacular and are much used as impressive hedge material in tropical regions. They are, however, more beautiful as part of a tropical shrubbery border or planted as specimens for close-up viewing. The shrubs are not tolerant of frost and are sometimes damaged even in zone 10a. They are commonly called fern-leaf aralia or angelica.

Polyscias fruticosa (froot-i-KO-sa) (synonym *Aralia fruticosa*) is native to a vast area of tropical Asia from eastern India through Southeast Asia, Malaysia, Indonesia, and into Polynesia. It is a large shrub or small tree growing to 15 or even 20 feet and forming a vertical and columnar shape usually with the foliage in rounded whorls or tiers. It usually needs to be trained when young if a tree form is wanted and can be pruned into several shapes other than the columnar form it naturally assumes. The deep green leaves are 2 feet or more long and are tripinnate with many 4-inch-long ovate to lanceolate-shaped leaflets that are usually deeply toothed. All forms of the species are usually called ming aralia. This "designer plant" is suitable for silhouetting against a large wall or for use as a sculptured and picturesque patio tree. *Polyscias fruticosa* **'Elegans'** (synonyms *Panax elegans*, *Polyscias elegans*) is the most popular of several cultivars. Sometimes called the parsley aralia, it is a much smaller and more compact plant. It has bipinnate leaves with much-scalloped leaflets that resemble the leaves of parsley (*Petroselinum crispum*).

Polyscias guilfoylei (gil-FOIL-ee-eye) (synonym *Aralia guilfoylei*) is indigenous to the islands of the South Pacific. It is a large shrub or small tree growing to 20 or even 25 feet. It must usually be trained to one leader when young if a tree form is wanted. The leaves are as much as 2 feet long and are pinnate with seven to nine 5-inch-wide deep green linear-elliptic to ovate to almost orbicular toothed leaflets usually irregularly margined with white. The plant is not particularly tropical looking nor especially attractive, but is fairly popular as a houseplant and for growing outdoors in the tropics. The plant is sometimes called geranium-leaf aralia and roseleaf aralia. There are several cultivars with varying degrees of variegation and segmentation of the leaflets.

Polyscias pinnata. See *Polyscias scutellaria.*

Polyscias scutellaria (skut-el-LAHR-ee-a) (synonyms *Nothopanax scutellarium*, *Polyscias pinnata*) is indigenous to the islands of the South Pacific. It is a large shrub growing to 15 or even 20 feet in height with few branches and a vertical or columnar form with whitish or gray stems ringed with leaf scars. It has trifoliate leaves with broadly ovate to round leaflets each of which is as much as a foot wide. The leaves are leathery but very glossy and deep green with a prominent sunken midrib and lateral veins that are a lighter color. This species is by far the most beautiful in the genus. Its great shining leaves are very tropical appearing. Unlike most other *Polyscias* species, this one is tolerant of full sun and is widely used as a boundary or hedge subject. *Polyscias scutellaria* **'Balfourii'** (bal-FOOR-ee-eye) (synonym *P. balfouriana*) has rounded leaflets only 3 or 4 inches wide that are scalloped on their margins and show white variegation along the midrib and the leaf margins. This very attractive cultivar is used as a large and informal hedge, in large shrub borders, or as a patio tree. *Polyscias scutellaria* **'Cochleata'** (kahk-lee-AIT-a) has leaves that are simple or consist of only two leaflets. The 10-inch-wide leaves or leaflets are ovate to very broadly oblong (almost square in outline), with the edges somewhat rolled up, very glossy and leathery, with very shallow indentations along the margins and deeply sunken and lighter colored midrib and lateral veins.

POLYSTICHUM. See *Rumohra.*

PONGAMIA (pahn-GAM-ee-a)
Papilionaceae (Fabaceae, Leguminosae), subfamily
    Papilionoideae: The Bean, Pea Family
PONGAM; POONGA OIL TREE
Large round-topped evergreen pinnate-leaved tree;
    clusters of fragrant pink flowers
Zones 10 and 11; marginal in zone 10a
Sun
Water lover
Humusy, sandy, well-drained soil
Propagation by seed

A monotypic genus native to Southeast Asia, Indonesia, Malaysia, and northern Australia. *Pongamia pinnata* (pin-NAIT-a) (synonym *Millettia pinnata*) grows to as much as 80 feet in its native habitats, but is seldom more than 40 or 50 feet with an almost equal spread in cultivation. It forms a fairly massive short trunk with a broad dense umbrella-shaped crown. The branches are somewhat pendulous near their ends. The pinnate leaves are a foot long or slightly longer with five or seven elliptic to ovate and acuminate glossy deep green and deeply veined leaflets. The foliage is usually briefly deciduous in February in the Northern Hemisphere. The trees bloom in late spring with axillary racemes of fragrant blossoms near the ends of the branches. The racemes are usually heavy enough to be pendent. The individual flowers are shaped like those of the pea plant or wisteria and are light pink to light purple in color. The pods are short, only 1 or 2 inches long, and a deep brown in color with a hooked tip. Each pod contains only one seed, which is poisonous if eaten. The tree is superbly beautiful, especially when in bloom, and is one of the finest shade trees for tropical and subtropical regions. It has the drawback, however, of being somewhat messy with its pods and leaves.

PONTEDERIA (pahnt-e-DER-ee-a)
Pontederiaceae: The Water-Hyacinth, Pickerel-Weed
    Family
PICKEREL WEED
Aquatic bog plants with long-stalked cannalike
    leaves; tall spikes of deep blue flowers
Zones vary according to variety
Sun to partial shade
Aquatic or bog
Rich, humusy very moist soil
Propagation by root division and rhizome division

A genus of about five perennial herbs in and around the edges of ponds, pools, and lakes throughout North and South America. One species is native to the eastern half of the United States and is one of the world's finest bog and marginal plants. *Pontederia cordata* (kor-DAIT-a) is a very hardy bog plant that is adaptable in shallow water to zones 4 through 9. It has creeping rhizomatous roots and grows to about 2 feet in height with long-stalked rounded cordate-shaped light green leaves. The leaves die down in winter, but return with the warmth of spring. The inflorescences appear in summer and are spikes of light blue flowers arising from the tops of the leaf stalks. Each blossom has tiny yellow dots on the upper petals. ***Pontederia cordata* var. *lanceolata*** (lants-ee-o-LAIT-a) (synonym *P. lanceolata*) is a larger and more beautiful but less hardy form from the southeastern United States. It is hardy in zones 7 through 11 and grows to about 5 feet tall with narrowly lanceolate bright green leaves and larger, longer flower spikes with deeper blue flowers. These plants add great form and texture to the margins of ponds, pools, and lakes, and grow in as much as 6 inches of water or in the adjacent muck and mud if it is perennially moist. They look best if not completely encircling the perimeter of the pond or pool, but rather growing in large clumps or groups.

PORANA (po-RAHN-a)
Convolvulaceae: The Morning Glory Family
CHRISTMAS VINE; SNOW VINE; BRIDAL VEIL
Thin-stemmed but large evergreen vine; heart-shaped
    leaves; masses of white winter flowers
Zones 10b and 11
Sun
Average but regular amounts of moisture
Average well-drained soil
Propagation by seed and cuttings

A genus of 20 twining vines and shrubs in tropical Asia. They have large axillary panicles of small bell-shaped morning-glory-like flowers that are usually white. One species is widely planted in tropical and subtropical regions for its great masses of white winter flowers. ***Porana paniculata*** (pan´-ik-yoo-LAIT-a) is native to northeastern India and Myanmar (Burma). It grows quickly to 40 or even 50 feet with 6- to 8-inch-long, alternately arranged, short-tipped heart-shaped grayish green leaves with prominent midribs and lateral veins. The spaces between the veins are often somewhat puckered, and the undersides of the leaves are whitish pubescent. The vines bloom in late fall and early winter, usually from late November through December in the Northern Hemisphere, with great axillary panicles of tiny white strangely fragrant blossoms. The panicles are as much as 2 feet long and usually cover the entire vine. The seed pods are not always produced but, when they are, they are tiny and hairy propeller-shaped affairs. The vine returns from its roots even in zone 9b, but often does not make enough growth before autumn to bloom well. Plate 331.

PORTLANDIA (port-LAN-dee-a)
Rubiaceae: The Coffee, Gardenia, Ixora Family
PORTLANDIA
Evergreen shrubs; large glossy leaves; large white
    trumpet-shaped flowers
Zones 10 and 11
Sun
Average but regular amounts of moisture
Humusy, sandy, well-drained soil
Propagation by seed and cuttings

A genus of perhaps two dozen evergreen shrubs and trees in tropical America. They have large leathery oppositely arranged leaves and large funnel-shaped white or purple flowers. One species is planted in tropical regions (but not widely enough) for its large, pure white trumpet-shaped flowers. ***Portlandia grandiflora*** (grand-i-FLOR-a) is native to the West Indies. It grows rather slowly to 6 or 8 feet in height, usually with an equal spread. The very deep green glossy leaves are narrowly ovate to elliptic in shape and 8 to 10 or even 12 inches long. They are thick and leathery in texture and usually slightly wavy on their margins with a prominent midrib that is yellow or reddish in color. The young leaves are a beautiful deep wine-red in color. The plants bloom in cycles throughout the spring and summer, with the great flowers emerging from the leaf axils near the ends of the branches. Each flower is 6 to 8 inches long, funnel-shaped, pure satiny white when open, with five to eight corolla lobes. The flower buds are a deep rose shading to pink, and the opened flowers usually have the outside of their corolla tubes flushed with pale pink. The combination of rose, shell pink, and white flowers and buds with the deep green and red foliage creates an exquisite symphony of hues that must be seen to be appreciated. The flowers have a delicate and tantalizing fragrance during the day, which becomes alluring and mesmerizing at night. The world provides few flower spectacles to match this. One reason why the plant is not more widely grown where it is adapted is possibly because it seems quite difficult to propagate the plants from cuttings and the shrubs do not always set fruit. This beauty has survived freezes in zone 9b but usually grows too slowly to bloom in such areas.

PORTULACARIA
(port´-yoo-la-KAHR-ee-a)
Portulacaceae The Portulaca, Purslane Family
ELEPHANT BUSH; ELEPHANT FOOD
Large evergreen succulent shrub; rubbery reddish
    trunks, stems; small round fleshy leaves
Zones 10 and 11; marginal in zone 9b
Sun
Drought tolerant
Average well-drained soil
Propagation by cuttings and (sometimes) seed

A monotypic genus native to South Africa. ***Portulacaria afra*** (AF-ra) grows to as much as 12 or 15 feet in height with few branches and a spreading open habit. The short grayish brown trunks are stout and may turn woody at their bases; the stems are limber and rubbery and usually a reddish brown in color. The leaves are oppositely arranged along the outer stems and are half-inch-wide, dark green, fleshy, and round. The leaves are never dense on the tree, which fact lends a charming silhouette to the plant. The flowers are in rounded terminal clusters and are tiny, dainty, and pink in color, but the plant does not often bloom in cultivation. The little tree is quite picturesque planted where its silhouette can be appreciated. Because it has the overall appearance of a large bonsai subject, it is perfect for miniature "landscapes." It is equally at home in the cactus succulent garden, where it adds texture and form. It has some similarities to *Crassula argentea* (jade plant), but the stems are not as thick, the leaves are smaller, and the plant has a more open and delicate appearance. It must have a very freely draining soil, but is not very particular as to the fertility of the soil. It relishes full sun and heat and withstands temperatures to about 30°F, but anything colder damages it and temperatures at or below 26°F kill it outright. The plant is tolerant of a certain amount of soil salinity and looks and does very well planted near the seashore out of the dune area. There are cultivars with leaves variegated in white or yellow. These are much smaller and slower growing than the type and are quite attractive as potted plants and even better as large groundcovers for sunny sites.

POSOQUERIA (po-so-KWER-ee-a)
Rubiaceae: The Coffee, Gardenia, Ixora Family
NEEDLE-FLOWER; JASMINE TREE
Small evergreen tree; large leaves; large clusters of
    white tubular fragrant flowers
Zones 10b and 11
Sun
Average but regular amounts of moisture
Rich, humusy, well-drained soil
Propagation by cuttings

A genus of a dozen or so evergreen shrubs and small trees in tropical America. They have leathery oppositely arranged relatively large leaves and flowers in large terminal rounded clusters. The individual blossoms are long narrow and tubular with flaring five-parted corolla lobes. One species is planted in the tropics, especially the American tropics, for its beautiful leaves and pure white fragrant flowers. *Posoqueria latifolia* (lat-i-FO-lee-a) is indigenous to the West Indies, southern Mexico, Central America, and southwards into Brazil. It is a small fast growing tree attaining a height of 20 feet or sometimes more with a spread of equal width and a dense crown of foliage. The light green elliptic leaves are 8 to 10 inches long, very short-stalked, leathery, and glossy, and are provided with a heavy and lighter colored midrib and lateral veining. The leaf margins are usually somewhat rolled in (upwards) and very often outlined with a very thin line of yellow. The tree blooms in mid spring and later in the fall with terminal rounded many and densely flowered clusters of pure white very fragrant flowers. Each blossom is a very narrow 8-inch-long tube whose end flares into an inch-wide flat disk of five oblong corolla lobes. The flower buds are erect until open, at which time their unevenly distributed weight causes the blossoms to droop. The fragrance is akin to that of *Plumeria* flowers and is reason enough to grow these plants. When in bloom the little trees are covered with flowers and are a quite dazzling sight as well as scent. The fruits, when they form, are beautiful 3-inch-long yellow ovoid fleshy berries that are reportedly edible but insipid. This lovely thing is unaccountably rare in cultivation in the United States and greatly deserves to be much more widely planted. It is tender to frost, which may be one reason for its relative scarcity, but then so are many other more popular plants in the tropical garden.

POTHOS. See *Epipremnum*.

POUTERIA (poo-TER-ee-a)
Sapotaceae: The Sapodilla Family
Common names vary according to species
Large evergreen trees; large beautiful leaves; large
    colorful fruit
Zones 10b and 11
Sun
Moisture requirements vary according to species
Soil fertility requirements vary according to species
Propagation by cuttings; named cultivars are usually
    grafted

A genus of about 50 evergreen trees in tropical regions around the world but principally the Americas. They have thick milky sap that coagulates on exposure to the air, large heavily veined, alternately arranged elliptic leaves with short stalks, small flowers in axillary clusters, and large fleshy fruit. These are noble and impressive trees, and several of them produce important edible fruit.

Pouteria campechiana (kahm-pech´-ee-AHN-a) (synonyms *Lucuma nervosa*, *L. salicifolia*) is indigenous to southern Mexico and Central America. In its native haunts it quickly grows to as much as 90 feet, but in cultivation it seldom attains more than 30 feet with a broad and rounded crown above a short brown, somewhat fissured trunk. The narrowly elliptic leaves are mostly clustered near the ends of the branches and are as much as 10 inches long and heavily and deeply veined with a lighter colored midrib. The whitish flowers are tiny but fragrant and appear in small axillary clusters in summer and fall. They are followed in early winter by beautiful round to oval yellow or orange 3- to 5-inch-long smooth-skinned glossy fruits that usually have a rounded and somewhat curved tip. The fruits are edible and relished by some people, while others find the dry texture and cloyingly sweet yamlike flavor unappealing. The tree, however, is of great quiet beauty, and the large orange-colored fruits are spectacular in the landscape. This beautiful tree, which is not fussy as to soil type as long as it is fast draining, succeeds with average but regular supplies of moisture. It endures but slight frost. Temperatures below 30°F wreak havoc, and the tree is usually killed by anything lower than 28°F, making it adaptable only to zones 10b and 11. Common names are canistel and egg-fruit. There are named varieties with supposedly superior tasting fruits that are often larger than that of the type.

Pouteria mammosa. See *P. sapota.*

Pouteria sapota (sa-PO-ta) (synonyms *Calocarpum sapota, Lucuma mammosa, Pouteria mammosa*) is native to southern Mexico and Central America. It grows fast and attains heights of 100 feet or more in its native habitat, but is usually no more than 50 or 60 feet in cultivation. The trunk on large trees is massive and sometimes beautifully buttressed. The magnificent bright green leaves are clustered near the ends of the branches and are deciduous with cold or drought. The leaves are 6 to 12 inches long, elliptic to obovate in shape with short-pointed tips, and heavily veined with lighter colored midribs and lateral veins; the lower surface is grayish green. The small yellowish white flowers are in axillary clusters. The fruits are round to elliptic in shape and as much as 8 inches long, with a warty tan to dark brown skin; the flesh is edible and considered delicious by many people. This exceptionally handsome tree needs warmth and a rich, humusy, and well-drained soil. It is completely intolerant of drought conditions. The tree and its fruit are called sapote, marmalade fruit, mamee (mamey) sapote, and marmalade plum.

PRITCHARDIA (prit-CHARD-ee-a)

Palmae (Arecaceae): The Palm Family
Common names vary according to species
Medium-sized, solitary smooth-trunked fan palms; large deep green waxy palmate leaves
Zones 10b and 11
Sun
Water lovers
Humusy, sandy, well-drained soil
Propagation by seed

A genus of 37 species of fan palms in the South Pacific from the island of Tonga northwards to Hawaii. By far the greatest number of species are indigenous to the Hawaiian islands. They are some of the world's most beautiful fan palms, and they are quite distinctive because of the formal yet elegant stiff fan-shaped leaves. Once seen these plants are unforgettable. All have unarmed, deeply pleated, usually stiff, palmately segmented leaves that are generally divided to only about half the depth of the leaf blade. The leaf blade may be nearly circular in outline to less than 180 degrees of the arc. The leaves are costapalmate. The petiole extends for some distance into the blade, and the leaf segments are split into two parts at their tips. Many Hawaiian species are extremely rare because of their originally very small natural ranges and now the encroachment of modern civilization and its attendant development of their habitats. Two species from islands other than those of Hawaii are widely planted in all moist tropical regions for their almost indescribable beauty. Both (see descriptions below) are endemic to seashore areas and are tolerant of salty ocean spray and somewhat saline soil conditions. Besides the coconut, they are the most beautiful palms that can be grown near the shore. At the same time they are intolerant of drought and dry winds, not to mention cold, and neither thrive nor even look good in tropical arid regions even if they are near the seacoast. Alas, like many varieties of the coconut, the palm is highly susceptible to the dreaded lethal yellowing disease and should not be planted in areas in which it is rampant until a cure is found.

Pritchardia pacifica (pa-SIF-i-ka) is originally native only to the island of Tonga in the South Pacific, about 1700 miles east of mainland Australia. It grows slowly to a total height of about 30 feet with as much as 25 feet of brownish ringed trunk completely free of fibers and leaf bases and a very full crown of as many as 40 large leaves. The mature leaves are about 8 feet wide and deeply costapalmate with the many segmentations reaching only to about a foot into the blade. The blade is rather cup-shaped when young, but spreads out and even has pendent outer parts when mature. The leaf stalks and unfurled leaves are covered in a fantastically beautiful waxy white powdery bloom. This extraordinarily beautiful palm is usually called the Fiji fan palm and sometimes the Pacific fan palm. It was long thought to be indigenous to both Tonga and Fiji, but modern research has shown that it was introduced to the latter island by its aboriginal population centuries before the Western world discovered either location.

Pritchardia thurstonii (thur-STON-ee-eye) is indigenous to the island of Fiji in the South Pacific. It has about the same dimensions as the Fiji fan palm, but the leaf crown has fewer leaves. The leaves, which are perhaps even more lovely than those of *P. pacifica*, are borne atop a slender and wonderfully attractive gray to brownish trunk with faint rings. The leaf blade is the same size as that of the Fiji fan palm but is stiffer with more and finer segments that are divided to about one-third of the depth of the blade. The leaves are only slightly pendent at their tips, which lends to the palm's crown a stiff but thrillingly elegant aspect.

PSEUDERANTHEMUM
(soo-de-RANTH-e-mum)

Acanthaceae: The Acanthus Family
Common names vary according to species
Herbs and small shrubs with variegated leaves; spikes of white or purple flowers
Zones vary according to species
Light requirements vary according to species
Average but regular amounts of moisture
Sandy, humusy, well-drained soil
Propagation by seed, cuttings, and (for clumping species) transplanting of suckers

A genus of about 60 herbs and shrubs in tropical and subtropical regions around the globe. They have relatively large leaves, most of which are provided with some sort of variegation, often very colorful variegation. The small flowers are in terminal spikes of five-petaled (or five-lobed) blossoms in colors of white, pink, blue, and purple, some of which are quite showy. Two of the petals overlap to give the impression from any distance of only four petals.

Pseuderanthemum alatum (a-LAIT-um) (synonym *Chamaeranthemum alatum*) is native to the southeastern half of Mexico and into Central America. It is a permanent perennial in zones 10 and 11 and a returning perennial in zone 9 and sometimes in zone 8b. This colorful herb is called chocolate plant because that is the primary color of the leaves of most of its forms. It is a clumping plant, growing to as much as 18 inches but usually only to a foot or less. The leaves are held on long, winged petioles, and the blade is perfectly cordate in shape with a short and usually curved tip. Leaf size varies from about 6 inches in length to well over a foot. The veins are deeply depressed, and the blade is puckered and quilted between them and finely pubescent above. Leaf color varies from pure milk-chocolate brown to greenish brown to a bright pinkish or reddish brown, always with the midrib and parts of the lateral veins splotched with silver or gray. The color varies with the plant form and the amount of light the plant receives. Generally, with more sun the leaves are redder. The flower spikes rise well above the foliage, sometimes reaching a total height of 3 feet. The individual flowers are a brilliant blue to purple to violet in color and are about a half inch wide. The lowermost petal usually has a line of white dots down its center. The plant is adapted to light conditions ranging from shade to full sun, although most nursery salespeople tell the customer that it cannot take full sun. It makes one of the finest groundcovers for zones 9 through 11. When in bloom, the symphony of differently hued browns and the purple or blue of the flowers is breathtaking, especially up close. Chocolate plant needs regular and adequate amounts of moisture and, while somewhat drought tolerant when established, languishes with aridity. It readily reseeds itself and, within a year or so, becomes naturalized. Plate 332.

Pseuderanthemum atropurpureum (at´-ro-poor-POOR-ee-um) (synonyms *Eranthemum atropurpureum*, *Pseuderanthemum carruthersii* var. *atropurpureum*) is native to Polynesia although many erroneously think it originated in tropical America because it has been naturalized in the latter area for so long. The shrub is not hardy outside zones 10 and 11, although it recovers by sprouting from the root in zone 9b and sometimes in zone 9a. It grows to 5 or 6 feet, sometimes to as much as 10 feet, with 6-inch-long elliptic to ovate waxy-textured strong-veined leaves that are pure and deep carmine-colored when new but soon change to irregular combinations of wine-red, claret, brownish purple, pink, yellow, and orange. The plant is obviously grown for its highly colored foliage, but the flowers are also quite attractive. The short terminal spikes of inch-wide starry light purple or lilac-colored blossoms with deep purple spots are borne all year in tropical regions, but in the warm months in less tropical areas. The shrubs are adapted to sun or partial shade, although the leaf colors tend to fade in the intense sunlight of hot climate regions. The shrub is beautiful anywhere and is often used as a formal or informal hedge. It is sensational in groups and mass plantings for color. Unless grown in the sun, the plants tend to become bare at the base.

Pseuderanthemum carruthersii **var. *atropurpureum*.** See *P. atropurpureum*.

Pseuderanthemum reticulatum (re-tik´-yoo-LAIT-um) is also indigenous to Polynesia and is similar in size, form, and cultural requirements to *P. atropurpureum* but has leaves that are significantly larger (to 10 inches long) and more ovate than elliptic in shape. In addition the new leaves are completely yellow to orange-yellow in color, but change at full maturity to light green with yellow midrib and lateral veins. The flowers are of the same form and size as those of *P. atropurpureum*, but are white with red or purple spots, creating from any distance the overall effect of being pink in color. The shrub is used in the landscape the same as *P. atropurpureum* but, unlike the latter, is stunningly beautiful planted against a dark background. A planting of the two species is extraordinarily beautiful

PSEUDOBOMBAX

(soo-doe-BAHM-bax)
Bombacaceae: The Bombax, Baobab Family
SHAVINGBRUSH TREE
Medium-sized deciduous tree; large palmate leaves;
    large pompon white or pink flowers
Zones 10 and 11; marginal in zone 9b
Sun
Average but regular amounts of moisture
Average well-drained soil
Propagation by seed and cuttings

A genus of 20 species of small to large mostly deciduous trees in tropical America. Almost all have compound palmately divided large leaves (a few have simple leaves) and flowers with multitudinous and very long stamens. They are indigenous to areas with distinct wet (summer) and dry (winter) seasons. They are mostly deciduous in the dry season and usually maintain the habit of dropping their leaves in winter even when rainfall is copious. The botanical nomenclature of these trees has had an extremely checkered past. At one time they were considered to be species of *Pachira*, and they are still usually called "*Bombax*" by some. Two species are planted for their beautiful leaves, unusual and picturesque tree form, and startling flowers of winter to early spring, which usually appear on the leafless stems.

Pseudobombax ellipticum (el-LIP-ti-kum) (synonym *Bombax ellipticum*) is native to southern Mexico and Guatemala. It grows quickly to 30 feet in height, sometimes much more with a short very stout unarmed smooth dark green trunk, the limbs usually with lighter vertical striations. The plants form multiple trunks as often as they do solitary ones, and the shape of the tree with multiple stems is often octopus-like. The great leaves are long-stalked with five to seven palmately arranged deep green leaflets. The leaflets form a circular outline to the whole leaf. Each mature leaflet is very finely pubescent above and below, from 6 inches to a foot long, and elliptic to obovate in shape with a prominent and lighter colored midrib and lateral veins. The newly unfurled leaves usually but not always have a beautiful reddish bronzy hue. On older leaves the leaflets become so large that they are frequently somewhat pendent, although the younger ones mostly lie in a flat plane. They are extremely beautiful and are reason enough to have the tree. The leaves usually drop in late December or early January, leaving the green stems bare until some time in March. This condition varies and, in some years, the trees retain at least some leaves throughout this period. The terminal flower buds start forming in late autumn or early winter, at which time they resemble brown and succulent toy tops. In late February these buds expand into 6-inch-long velvety cigar-shaped affairs and open at dusk to reveal five half-inch-long, recurved, velvet brownish and white petals and hundreds of 6- to 8-inch-long white or pink stamens very reminiscent of the vernacular name. There are never two simultaneous colors on one tree, as the blossoms of an individual tree are either white or deep pink. The pink-flowered forms are more spectacular during daylight hours, but the white-flowered form is astonishingly attractive in the moonlight and is said to have larger blossoms. Plates 333 and 334.

Pseudobombax grandiflorum (grand-i-FLOR-um) is indigenous to Brazil and is much less common in cultivation, at least in the United States. It is a larger tree with leaves quite similar in size and form to those of *P. ellipticum*. The flowers are also quite similar but are only white in color, never pink.

PSEUDOCALYMMA
(soo-doe-ka-LYM-ma)
Bignoniaceae: The Catalpa, Jacaranda, Trumpet-
   Vine Family
GARLIC VINE
Large evergreen vine; glossy leaves of only 2 leaflets;
   large sprays of purple, pink, and white flowers
Zones 10 and 11 as permanent perennials; zone 9b as
   returning perennials
Sun
Average but regular amounts of moisture
Average well-drained soil
Propagation by seed and cuttings

A genus of a dozen or so evergreen vines in tropical America. They have compound leaves of three leaflets, the terminal leaflet usually reduced to a tendril. The flowers are in large terminal or axillary racemes, are funnel-shaped or bell-shaped, and have five lobes at the end. This group of plants has suffered several name changes. The genus was for years known as *Cydista* and

then changed to *Pseudocalymma.* The latest taxonomic research has placed it into yet a different genus, namely, *Mansoa,* but this name is still scarce in the literature and some nurseries still refer to the genus as "*Cydista.*" Only one species is commonly planted in warm-climate regions and its popularity seems to increase each year in the southern United States. *Pseudocalymma alliacea* (al-lee-AY-see-a) (synonyms *Cydista aequinoctialis, Mansoa alliacea*) occurs naturally in the West Indies, Central America, and down into Brazil. It is a large vine, growing to heights of 20 or 30 feet. The glossy bright green 4- or 5-inch-long leaves are composed of only two elliptic to ovate leaflets with a wavy margin and a strong and lighter colored midrib. The third leaflet is reduced to a tendril. The leaves and the stems exude a strong odor of garlic when crushed or bruised. Flowers may appear as early as April in tropical regions, but are found only in the hot months in less tropical areas. The plants bloom in cycles of about 6 weeks and the flowers are formed in large terminal racemes of 3- to 4-inch-long funnel-shaped blossoms with five corolla lobes. Flower color is pink or light purple, which changes to light pink or even white as the blossoms age. The corolla is usually marked with deeper-colored veins. The result of the flowers' changing colors with age, of course, is that there are several shades of color on the vine simultaneously. These plants are slow to start growth after being transplanted but, once they do, grow quickly. They do not bloom in any exposure that receives less than a half day's sun and, while drought tolerant to some extent when established, they appreciate adequate and regular supplies of moisture. A large well-grown vine in full bloom is as spectacular as any *Bougainvillea* variety and is of an overall color that is somewhat rare. Plate 335.

PSEUDOGYNOXIS. See *Senecio.*

PSEUDOPHOENIX (soo-doe-FEE-nix)
Palmae (Arecaceae): The Palm Family
Common names vary according to species
Small to medium-sized pinnate-leaved palms; stout
   bulging gray or green ringed trunks; large leaves
Zones 10b and 11
Sun
Average but regular amounts of moisture; drought
   tolerant
Average well-drained soil; thrives in sandy or
   limestone soils
Propagation by seed

A genus of only four species of solitary-trunked pinnate-leaved palms with crownshafts in extreme southern Florida, the Bahamas, Hispaniola, Jamaica, and along the coasts of Yucatán (Mexico), and Belize. All have quite thick and stout light-colored trunks with varyingly placed bulges and very beautiful rings of leaf scars. The large pinnate-leaved crowns do not carry many leaves, which adds to their stylistic charm. The leaves are stiff and long, and the leaflets arise from the rachis at different planes and are usually arranged in small groups. The plants produce many flowers and fruits, which are readily visible as the inflorescences are relatively long and pendent and are not hidden by the leaves. The fruits are invariably attractive, bright red, and about the size and shape of plums. The palms are extremely slow growers, which is the main reason that they are not more widely planted as they are expensive and take a long time to attain their characteristic beauty. Those with mature specimens on their property are indeed fortunate. These palms are adaptable only to near tropical conditions and should not be attempted in any zone colder than 10a where they are sometimes damaged. Because of their slow growth, they cannot usually recover from serious cold damage. All the species have at least part of their natural ranges within sight of the seashore and are, therefore, perfectly adapted to being grown in locations with salty ocean spray and somewhat saline soil conditions.

Pseudophoenix lediniana (le-din´-ee-AHN-a) is indigenous to Hispaniola. It is the largest species in the genus, growing to an overall height of 40 feet with a trunk of 30 feet or more. It is also arguably the finest looking species and grows somewhat faster than the others. The trunks are relatively thin for the genus. The youngest (upper) parts of the trunks and the crownshafts are a light grayish or bluish green in color, while the older parts of the trunks are almost pure white with beautiful bluish green rings. The trunk is distinctly but not greatly swollen or bulged below the leaf crown. The handsomely arching leaves in the canopy number about a dozen. Each leaf is as long as 12 feet with grassy green very thin leaflets. Plate 336.

Pseudophoenix sargentii (sahr-JENT-ee-eye) is indigenous to southern Florida, Mexico, and Belize. It is, alas, almost extinct in the wild in southern Florida. It grows slowly to as much as 30 feet in height. The trunk usually bears a distinct bulge along its upper part, but the bulge may be low on the trunk and is quite variable in its exact location. No two trunks seem to look the same. The trunks are beautifully ringed, and their color varies from greenish gray to tan and sometimes cinnamon brown, the older parts always a dark gray in color. The crownshafts are sometimes not obvious, but, when they are, they are short, stout, and a bluish green in color. The leaves are usually under 10 feet long and are held on silvery-colored petioles. The blades usually have somewhat twisted rachises, and the leaf is arching but stiff-looking with the blue-green leaflets arching upwards from the rachis and giving a more or less V shape to the leaf in cross section. The tree is sometimes called the buccaneer palm. It is variable in its growth habit depending on its origin. Several naturally occurring named forms were formerly elevated to species status. *Pseudophoenix sargentii* **subsp.** *saonae* **var.** *navassana* is one of them and supposedly grows taller and faster than the type.

Pseudophoenix vinifera is indigenous to Hispaniola and Cuba. It grows very slowly to as much as 30 feet with a trunk height of about 20 feet. The deep gray to tan-colored trunk usually bulges widely just beneath the leaf crown and at its base, and is very distinctly and beautifully ringed in shades of green to brown. The crownshaft is distinct and an attractive smooth grayish or bluish green in color. The leaves are only about 6 or 8 feet long, but the leaflets are large and relatively wide for the genus. Their dark green color and relative suppleness allow them to be somewhat drooping and give a rather plumose appearance to the leaf as a whole. The species is now almost extinct in Haiti, one of its native haunts, as it is felled by the indigenous people who use its sweet sap for making an alcoholic beverage. The specific epithet *vinifera* means "wine-bearing."

PSIDIUM (SID-ee-um)
Myrtaceae: The Myrtle, Eucalyptus Family
GUAVA
Small evergreen trees; beautiful large leaves; fragrant
    white flowers; yellow, pink, or red edible fruit
Zones vary according to species
Sun
Average but regular amounts of moisture
Average well-drained soil
Propagation by seed; named cultivars are grafted

A large genus of 100 or more evergreen shrubs and trees in tropical America. The species have oppositely arranged simple, relatively large and leathery leaves. The five-petaled white flowers are relatively large for the myrtle family and have the multitude of long stamens that are characteristic of the family. The fruits are large berries with persistent calyces at the apical ends. They are often edible, some being delectable.

Psidium cattleianum. See *P. littorale.*

Psidium guajava (gwa-YAH-va) is probably indigenous to southern Mexico and Central America, but has been in cultivation so long and so widely spread around tropical America that its precise points of origin are obscured. It is a small tree growing rather rapidly to 30 or 35 feet with an equal spread and a short trunk and tan or reddish brown bark that flakes and is easily pulled off to reveal the grayish green interior bark. The young stems are remotely four-angled. The oblong to elliptic to obovate light green leaves are short-stalked and 6 or 7 inches long with prominent and lighter colored midrib and lateral veins above and a fine pubescence beneath. The leaves are leathery but not glossy. The flowers may appear at almost any time of the year in tropical areas, but usually are most abundant in spring, summer, and early fall, and are solitary or in groups of two or three from the leaf axils. Each flower is slightly fragrant, more than an inch wide, with five recurved white or yellowish white sepals and short-lived petals, and several hundred long white stamens. The beautiful 4- to 6-inch-wide fruit is round to pear-shaped or egg-shaped. It is deep green until ripe, at which time it turns a yellowish green to golden or pale pink color and is fragrant with an earthy but sweet scent. It is not only edible, but is highly regarded by most people as a true delicacy and is much used for making preserves, jellies, and other confections and beverages. This truly beautiful tree, especially when in fruit, has a strongly tropical appearance. It is tender to all but the lightest frosts and is not suited to areas colder than zones 10 and 11, although the tree has sprouted from the root even in zone 9a. There are many named cultivars (and hybrids with some of the lesser known *Psidium* species) whose fruit qualities and colors are outside the scope of the present book. The tree is usually called simply the guava, but sometimes also the yellow guava or apple guava. Plate 337.

Psidium littorale (lit-toe-RAHL-ee) (synonym *P. cattleianum*) is native to eastern Brazil. It is hardy in zones 9b through 11 and springs back from its roots in zone 9a. It is a very large shrub or, if trained and pruned, a beautiful small tree, slowly growing to 20 feet or sometimes more. Because of its relatively slow growth, it is more often grown as a large shrub. The trunk(s) and bark are a deep brown to reddish brown in color, and the crown is dense. The elliptic to obovate leaves are 2 to 4 inches long, thick and leathery, a lustrous deep green above, and a grayish green beneath, with prominent and lighter colored midribs. The leaves are often notched at the apical end, but may also be acuminate. The shrubs bloom mainly in late spring, but sometimes also sporadically in the summer. The blossoms arise from the leaf axils and are either solitary or in groups of two or three. The flowers are white or yellowish white, about an inch wide, and quite similar to those of *P. guajava* (common guava) except that they are much more fragrant. The little round fruits are an inch to 2 inches wide and are green changing to red or yellow when mature. Because of the small but persistent calyx lobes, the fruits very much resemble miniature pomegranates. They are edible and taste like a combination of pear and acidic strawberry. The plants are most commonly called the strawberry guava, but also the cattley guava. Many people consider this little tree or shrub to be more beautiful than *P. guajava*, but, although I concur that the strawberry guava is indeed beautiful, the common guava seems to me more attractive because of its larger leaves and fruit and more interesting and larger form and texture.

PSYCHOTRIA (sy-KOAT-ree-a)
Rubiaceae: The Coffee, Gardenia, Ixora Family
WILD COFFEE
Medium-sized evergreen shrub; small white flowers; bright red berries
Zones 10 and 11; marginal in zone 9b
Partial shade to nearly full shade
Average but regular amounts of moisture
Humusy, sandy, well-drained soil
Propagation by seed

An immense genus of nearly 1000 species of herbs and evergreen shrubs and trees in tropical and subtropical regions around the world. What they have in common are flower details and oppositely arranged entire evergreen leaves. One shrub species is indigenous to southern Florida and the West Indies and is becoming popular as an ornamental in that area. ***Psychotria nervosa*** (ner-VO-sa) (synonym *P. undata*) grows to 6 or sometimes 10 feet in height and is densely clothed in 6-inch-long narrowly elliptic leathery and glossy deep green leaves. The leaves are so very deeply veined that the tissue between them is puckered and quilted in appearance. The shrub blooms spring and summer with small axillary panicled clusters of tiny white flowers, which give way to small brilliantly red berries in early autumn. The berries are edible but not palatable. Birds and other wildlife, however, relish and seek them out. Although a relative of the true coffee plants, wild coffee is not good as a substitute for making the world's most widely consumed non-alcoholic beverage. The shrub is very attractive and is almost invaluable for providing form, color, and texture in shady areas.

PTYCHOSPERMA (ty-ko-SPERM-a)
Palmae (Arecaceae): The Palm Family
Common names vary according to species
Medium-sized elegant solitary-stemmed or clumping slender-trunked pinnate-leaved palms
Zones 10b and 11
Sun to partial shade
Water lovers
Rich, humusy, well-drained soil
Propagation by seed

A genus of 28 solitary-trunked or clumping pinnate-leaved palm species of unusual elegance in Malaysia, New Guinea, northeastern Australia, and Polynesia. They all have exquisitely slender smooth ringed trunks, whether solitary or clustering, with prominent but slender crownshafts. The inflorescences are large and showy, the flowers often fragrant, and the shiny red, orange, or black fruits spectacular, hanging as they do beneath the crownshafts and leaf canopy. They have relatively sparse leaf crowns commensurate with their rarefied stems. All the species have the ends of the leaflets toothed to some extent, many of them to the point that the word "jagged" is appropriate to their description. These palms, because of their slender graceful forms of modest proportions and their relatively small crowns of leaves, make some of the most attractive landscape subjects for close-up planting in patios and dooryards of tropical regions. They need protection from strong and damaging winds and frost to look their best, but they are well adapted to fairly low light levels. In their native habitats they grow mostly as understory trees in the rain forest or along heavily vegetated riverbanks. This phenomenon makes them superb subjects for atriums and other large well-lit indoor areas, but they never look so wonderful in these spaces as they do planted outdoors. Some of the species were formerly placed into the genera *Actinophloeus*, *Kentia*, and *Seaforthia*, none of which are now valid names. The genus *Archontophoenix* was originally included in the genus *Ptychosperma*.

Ptychosperma elegans (EL-e-ganz) (synonym *Seaforthia elegans*) is indigenous to northeastern Queensland in Australia. It is a solitary-trunked palm, forming as much as 40 feet of trunk in its native habitat, but usually having a stem no more than 20 or 25 feet tall in cultivation. The trunk is wonderfully and evenly slender for its total height, being no more than 6 inches in diameter. The 2-foot-high velvety crownshaft is a beautiful grayish green or brown in color. The leaf crown seldom has more than a dozen 8-foot-long stiffly arching leaves. Each leaf has wide 2- or 3-foot-long yellowish green pleated leaflets with obliquely cut and jagged ends. The egg-shaped fruits are a bright orange-red in color. The palm is most often called the solitaire palm, but occasionally the Alexander palm. The tree is of unsurpassed grace, symmetry, and beauty of form, and is even more exquisite when planted two or three to a group of varying heights of trunk. One of the most splendid sights I have seen was a large Spanish-style courtyard with a small group of solitaire palms of varying heights in its center, surrounded at their bases with small *Alocasia* species, ginger relatives, *Phoenix roebelinii*, self-heading *Philodendron selloum*, and small ferns planted around the perimeter of the courtyard.

Ptychosperma macarthurii (mak´-ahr-THOOR-ee-eye) is native to northeastern Australia and the great island of New Guinea. This clumping or clustering species has gray or white and wonderfully black-ringed trunks that grow to as much as 20 or 25 feet in height. The trunks are usually completely straight except where they bend from the clump and are only 4 or 5 inches in diameter, which width does not vary from near the base to the bottom of the elegantly smooth waxy and light green crownshafts. The crown almost never has more than 10 stiffly arching leaves, each of which is only 5 or 6 feet long with bright green evenly spaced 2-foot-long leaflets with jagged ends. The fruits are a brilliant waxy red in color. A mature clump of this extraordinary palm combines the beauties of the stems of a timber bamboo with the fountainlike grace of a tropical palm, and one is hard put to find a more exquisite landscape subject for intimate areas like a patio. It should go without saying that the clumps are more beautiful when the separate trunks are of varying heights, which is accomplished by judicious removal of a few trunks as the clump grows and fills out. The result is breathtaking when the stems are not all the same height and when there are much smaller ones to fill in the base with their beautiful leaves.

PYROSTEGIA (py-ro-STEE-jee-a)
Bignoniaceae: The Catalpa, Jacaranda, Trumpet-
    Vine Family
FLAME VINE
Large evergreen tendril-climbing vine; spectacular
    orange-red flowers in winter through early spring

Zones 10 and 11; zone 10a as a marginal bloomer
Sun
Average but regular amounts of moisture
Average well-drained soil

Propagation by cuttings and (sometimes) seed

A genus of only four species of tendril-climbing vines in South America. They have compound leaves consisting of three leaflets, with the terminal leaflet usually reduced to a three-forked tendril. The flowers are in dense terminal or axillary clusters. Each flower has a narrow tubular five-lobed corolla and long stamens. One species is widely planted in frost-free regions for its spectacular display of orange-red flowers in late fall and winter. ***Pyrostegia venusta*** (ve-NOOS-ta) (synonyms *Bignonia ignea, B. venusta, Pyrostegia ignea*) is native to southern Brazil and Paraguay. It is a fast growing—some would say aggressively growing—vine, attaining 30 feet or more. The leaves are composed of two or three leaflets, usually two, with the third leaflet a coiling and three-parted tendril. Each glossy leaflet is 3 or 4 inches long and narrowly ovate in shape with an extended apical point. The vine is subject to bloom any time from mid December through May, but most often starts in January and continues to April, often giving a repeat but less showy performance in the summer. When it does bloom, there is probably no other flowering vine that is more spectacular, especially if one likes the color of deep orange. The blossoms are in dense and short terminal panicles, which become pendent with their weight. The individual flowers are narrow 3-inch-long orange-red tubes whose ends flare into five reflexed corolla lobes (the two uppermost lobes are joined so that the effect is that of four petals). The long yellow-orange stamens and style peek out from the end of the tube. As in the flowers of many other members of the bignonia family, the corollas as a whole often become detached from the calyx and slip down to hang suspended from the large and sticky stigma, which phenomenon gives from any distance a fringed and filigreed appearance to the flower clusters. Flame vine needs as much sun as possible to bloom well but is not fussy about soil and is somewhat drought tolerant when established. It is a perfect choice, with irrigation, for tropical desert areas as it truly loves heat and sun. The vine will resprout from its roots if frozen back, but this is usually a moot point considering its flowering season. It is usually a nonflowering plant in areas subject to freezes.

PYRRHEIMA. See *Siderasis*.

QUERCUS (KWER-kus)
Fagaceae: The Oak, Beech Family
LIVE OAKS
Large massive evergreen trees; low-branching
    massive trunks of picturesque character
Zones vary according to species

Sun
Average but regular amounts of moisture
Average well-drained soil
Propagation by seed and (sometimes) cuttings

A large genus of around 600 small to very large trees found in all areas of the globe except the Arctic and Antarctica, but mostly in the Northern Hemisphere. Related and similar genera in the same family, Fagaceae, are found in the Southern Hemisphere. *Quercus* species occupy just about every ecological niche except the frigid and the truly arid and are even found in desert areas near watercourses and in the mountains. Almost all oak trees are relatively large. Some of the largest and oldest trees on earth are oaks. All have alternately arranged leaves that are simple but may be very deeply segmented or lobed. Most species are deciduous, but several are evergreen. All species produce male and female flowers on the same tree. The male flower clusters, called "catkins," are much more evident than those with female flowers; the catkins are the long, narrow and pendent clusters of very tiny flowers seen on oaks in the spring in the United States and whose pollen grains often cause much distress to sufferers of hay-fever. The fruit of an oak is the acorn, which is a nut whose base (sometimes the whole nut) is enclosed in the cup-shaped remains of the bracts that are found at the base of the female flower; these bracts technically are termed an "involucre." The evergreen oaks are mostly found in the warmer areas of the earth. They are not, as a rule, especially tender to frost; most of them are found in the United States, Mexico, and China, with a few in Europe and, when indigenous to tropical regions, they are usually montane in origin.

Quercus agrifolia (ag-ri-FO-lee-a) is indigenous to the low coastal mountain ranges of California and is hardy in zones 7b through 11. Other than the unparalleled grandeur of the evergreen giants, *Sequoia sempervirens* (redwood) and *Sequoiadendron giganteum* (giant sequoia), *Q. agrifolia* is perhaps the most beautiful tree native to that state. The California live oak or the coast live oak grows to as much as 70 feet with an equal or greater spread. Like its more famous cousin *Q. virginiana* (southern live oak), the California live oak has a massive and low-branched dark gray or reddish brown trunk with massive branches growing nearly horizontally and picturesquely contorted. Unlike that of southern live oak, California live oak has a trunk that is usually not much fissured, at least until old. The tree's canopy is very broad but generally irregular in shape and is densely clothed with dark green foliage. The leathery elliptic leaves are about 3 inches long, toothed on their margins, and glossy above with a slight whitish pubescence beneath; they are usually somewhat rolled on their margins, and the edges turned under to form a slight convexity. This tree is one of the world's stateliest and most picturesque and rivals not only the southern live oak in impressiveness, but also some of the giant banyan trees of the tropics.

Quercus chrysolepis (kry-SAHL-e-pis / kry-so-LEEP-is) is indigenous to the west coast of the North American continent from Oregon down into Baja California where it is called the canyon live oak. It is hardy in zones 7 through 11. It grows to 70 or 80 feet, usually with an equal spread. It is not quite as massive as either *Q. virginiana* (southern live oak) or *Q. agrifolia* (California live oak) and its branches are not as massive or as horizontal as either of those two oaks but the tree is nevertheless quite impressive. The crown is more vertical than the crowns of the southern live oak and the California live oak, and it is also irregular in shape when old and quite picturesque. The trunk may be as relatively massive as the other so-called live oaks and the bark is lighter in color than that of those oaks and generally smoother with shallower fissures. The elliptic to oblong leaves are no more than 2 inches long and are usually untoothed on their margins; they are dark green and shiny above and pale green or grayish beneath. The tree is not well adapted to hot arid areas.

Quercus engelmannii (eng-el-MAHN-nee-eye) is native to southwestern California and Baja California and is hardy in zones 9 through 11. It is almost as impressive as the two preceding species but is of slightly smaller stature. The oblong leathery leaves are 2 inches long with remotely toothed margins and are dark green and shiny above but a pale grayish green beneath. In California, this oak is sometimes called the mesa oak. This beautiful tree does not tolerate hot arid climates and is not well adapted to hot and humid ones either.

Quercus suber (SOO-bur) is native to the Mediterranean regions of southern Europe and northern Africa and is hardy in zones 8b through 11. This amazing tree is one of the most impressive oak species. It grows to 80 feet in height, usually with an equal width, but the tree's dense canopy is not as spreading nor as open as those of many other live oaks; the massive trunk is usually higher-branched and the limbs not so horizontal although they are almost as massive. A considerable portion of the girth of the trunk and the larger limbs is composed of the spongy dark brown bark, as much as 6 inches or more thick, which is greatly and deeply but irregularly fissured and which is the commercial source of true cork. Not surprisingly, the tree is called the cork oak. The ovate to elliptic 3-inch-long leaves are a deep lustrous green above and grayish pubescent beneath, and the leaf margins are toothed. This majestic and imposing tree is adapted to almost all types of climate other than cold ones but seems least happy in hot and humid regions where its remarkable and beautiful bark is subject to attack by fungus.

Quercus virginiana (veer-jin´-ee-AHN-a) is indigenous to a large area of North America from the coastal regions of southern Virginia and North Carolina southwards into the West Indies, eastward into the southern half of Arkansas and the eastern half of Texas and southwards from there into Mexico. It is hardy in zones 7 through 11. The live oak or southern live oak is the world's most beautiful and impressive *Quercus* species, as well as one of the most adaptable trees, and thrives in cool and moist climates as well as in hot and arid ones if it is watered. It is most at home in hot and humid regions and these areas, especially the Gulf Coast region of the southern United States, are where it attains its greatest proportions. Some of the largest and most venerable old trees are found within 100 feet of the seashore along the Gulf of Mexico and show that the tree is tolerant of salty spray as well as a low degree of salinity in the soil; these trees have several times been flooded with salt water during hurricanes and tropical storms. Almost all oaks live to great ages and the evergreen species, as a whole, live longer than the deciduous forms, but none are known to reach the age and size of the southern live oak. There are trees still alive that are estimated to be more than 2000 years old. The tree grows to as much as 70 feet and its spread is sometimes the better part of 200 feet in very old specimens. The trunk is exceedingly massive for a tree not indigenous to hot tropical rain forests, and some old trees have trunk diameters of more than 8 feet. The trunk is very low branched and, in old trees, the great horizontal lower limbs often sweep the ground; on southern estates and the few remaining old plantations of Louisiana, Mississippi, Alabama, and Georgia this phenomenon is often accompanied by cabling or other structures to hold the limbs off the ground and to allow the grass to be mowed beneath them. The limbs of the tree grow almost entirely in a horizontal fashion and they are more or less contorted, especially on old trees. The bark of the live oak is deep gray to almost black in color and is distinctly fissured and longitudinally ridged. The deep green leathery leaves are 3 to 6 inches long, elliptic to mostly oblong in shape and more or less glossy above but grayish or white and pubescent beneath; leaf margins are mostly smooth but can also be remotely toothed, and the edge of the leaf is sometimes rolled under to some extent. The live oak naturally sheds its leaves in late winter to mid spring as the new ones start to grow and the beauty of an immense old tree covered in the luminous light green of its new growth is one of the great botanical wonders the world has to offer. The tree is also reported to be naturally deciduous for a considerable period during the winter in the coldest parts of its range and zones of adaptability. The tree is fast growing, especially when young, if provided with adequate and regular amounts of moisture and a soil that is not too limy. The species is variable as to size and form and there are several different naturally occurring varieties at the extremities of the tree's range, none of which in any way matches the glory of the type as they are generally much smaller in stature and slower growing. There is no more beautiful thing on earth than an old southern live oak; it matches the grandeur and beauty of even the largest tropical banyans, especially when festooned with *Tillandsia usneoides* (Spanish moss).

QUISQUALIS (kwis-KWAH-lis)
Combretaceae: The Combretum Family
RANGOON CREEPER

Large evergreen vine; large leaves; clusters of very
   long tubed white, pink, and red flowers
Zones 10 and 11 as permanent perennials; zone 9b as
   returning and flowering perennials
Sun to part shade
Average but regular amounts of moisture
Average well-drained soil
Propagation by cuttings, transplanting of suckers
   from older plants, and (sometimes) seed

A genus of about 17 climbing shrubs in tropical Africa, India, Malaysia, and the Philippines. They have large simple leaves and large terminal clusters of long-tubular flowers with five expanded corolla lobes. One species is commonly planted in tropical and subtropical regions for its truly lovely large sprays of flowers. ***Quisqualis indica*** (IN-di-ka) is native to southern Myanmar (Burma), the Malay Peninsula, Malaysia, New Guinea, and up to the Philippines. It is a very large and fast growing semiclimbing vine that scrambles its way up and into a proper support like a trellis, pergola, or other structure into which it can grow its stems. The beautiful leaves are large, soft, and usually somewhat pendent and grow densely on the horizontally spreading secondary stems that grow out from the main clambering stem; they are 5 to 6 inches long, deeply veined, short-stalked, light green in color, and ovate to elliptic in shape, and cause the horizontal secondary stems to look like immense compound pinnate leaves. The bases of the leaf stalks are provided with distinct stipules and these often (but not always) turn into short thorns that help the vine to get a foothold on its support. The leaves are deciduous with the advent of cold or drought and sometimes fall without assistance from either phenomenon, although they are persistent in many winter seasons if there is no frost. The plants bloom from late spring (unless cut back by winter frost) through the fall. The terminal flower clusters are composed of as many as a dozen 3-inch-long narrowly tubular strangely fragrant flowers whose ends expand into five corolla lobes; the narrow tubes are usually green but the expanded corolla lobes are white quickly changing to pink and finally to red, resulting in multicolored inflorescences. In moist and truly tropical areas the vine becomes colossal in size and must usually be pruned at least once a year to keep it from taking over all but the largest gardens; it is reported that in such climates the plants bloom in cycles year-round. The literature consistently indicates that rangoon creeper can not be grown to flowering size in any but almost completely tropical climates; this has not been my experience in Houston, Texas, where almost every winter sees a frost, sometimes severe. The vine comes back from temperatures in the low 20s and by midsummer is so fast growing that it usually blooms the same season; it rather sulks for a few months in spring and early summer but by August is growing rampantly enough to climb 15 feet. Contrary to the advice of some authors, it does not like drought and, while it withstands and survives that condition, it never attains its full potential without adequate and regular supplies of moisture. The plant is, after all, native to wet tropical areas of Asia. Plate 338.

RADERMACHERA

(ray-dur-MAHK-e-ra)
Bignoniaceae: The Catalpa, Jacaranda, Trumpet-
    Vine Family
CHINA DOLL
Evergreen shrubs and small trees; large fine bipinnate
    leaves; yellow trumpet-shaped flowers
Zones 10b and 11
Sun to partial shade
Water lover
Rich, humusy, well-drained soil
Propagation by cuttings and (sometimes) seed

A genus of about 15 species of small evergreen trees in tropical Asia. They have oppositely arranged pinnate leaves and clusters of trumpet-shaped flowers. One species is widely sold as an indoor foliage plant and is planted out in tropical or near tropical regions for its fernlike foliage and occasional yellow flowers. *Radermachera sinica* (SIN-i-ka) occurs naturally in southeastern China and Southeast Asia. In its native habitat it is a rather large tree, but in cultivation it is a small tree that usually grows as a large shrub to as much as 20 feet with stems densely clothed in very attractive leaves, which are about 2 feet long, triangular in outline, and bipinnate with very deep green glossy 2-inch-long ovate leaflets that are slightly toothed on their margins. The plant seems to bloom rather seldom in cultivation; when it does, it produces terminal clusters of 3-inch-long deep yellow funnel-shaped fragrant blossoms with five crinkly corolla lobes in spring, summer, or fall. It is beautiful as a small patio tree or planted in large borders for the textured and tropical looking effect of its foliage. The plant is intolerant of frost, does not like full sun in hot climates, and must not suffer drought. It also needs a humusy, well-drained soil that is not alkaline; the incorporation of humus, leaf mold, compost, or peat moss into the limestone soils found throughout southern Florida is necessary to ensure the shrub's health. It is a temperamental but beautiful addition to close-up gardening in tropical areas.

RANDIA (RAN-dee-a)

Rubiaceae: The Coffee, Gardenia, Ixora Family
RANDIA
Evergreen shrub; glossy leaves; long-tubed white
    fragrant flowers; attractive green and white fruit
Zones 10 and 11; marginal in zone 10a
Sun to partial shade
Average but regular amounts of moisture
Average well-drained soil
Propagation by seed and cuttings

A large genus of 200 or more species of shrubs and trees in all tropical regions of the globe. They have oppositely arranged leaves often accompanied by spines in the axils. The flowers are tubular or funnel-shaped and are usually solitary in the leaf axils but may also be in clusters and may be terminal in placement. Almost all species have white flowers and most of them are very fragrant. One species is sometimes planted in tropical gardens for its exquisite flowers. *Randia formosa* (for-MO-sa) is native to parts of Central America southwards into northern South America. It is an angular-branched spineless shrub growing fairly slowly to 6 or 8 feet in height. The 2-inch-long leaves are ovate to elliptic in shape, a dark green in color, and deeply veined and glossy on their upper surfaces. In tropical regions the plant blooms year-round with wonderful solitary pure white flowers in the leaf axils. Each blossom is about 3 inches long and consists of a very narrow tube whose end expands into four or five lanceolate-shaped corolla lobes. Each lobe is half white and half mint green on its outer surface, the two colors separated longitudinally. The flowers are outstandingly fragrant, especially at night. The fruits are entirely captivating: 2-inch-long little ovoid berries with a persistent apical calyx and a mottling of dark green, gray-green, and sometimes white; they eventually turn a deep yellow and are said to be edible and sweet. The shrub is beautiful because of its leaves, flowers, and fruit but is somewhat stiff looking because of its growth habit and is probably best interplanted with other shrubs and perennials in a border, although it makes a very nice informal hedge and infrequent pruning does not harm it.

RAPHIA (RAF-ee-a)

Palmae (Arecaceae): The Palm Family
RAFFIA PALM
Immense suckering pinnate-leaved palms; leaves of
    gargantuan proportions
Zones 10b and 11
Sun to partial shade
Water lover
Rich, humusy moist soil
Propagation by seed

A genus of 28 species of very large pinnate-leaved palms in tropical Africa, the northern part of the island of Madagascar, and one species in the Amazon region of Brazil. The plants are mostly suckering or clumping in nature, but several species form only solitary trunks; the emergent trunks are almost invariably covered with the old leaf bases whose remains become black, tough, and sometimes spiny. These plants exhibit some of the largest leaves in the vegetable kingdom, and one species has the largest leaves among the palms and, therefore, among all plants; true, the leaf is compound, but it is by far the largest. Some of these palms form no trunk above ground and all have trunks that are relatively short for the incredible size of their leaves. They are not appropriate for the average-sized garden; besides their colossal size, the individual trunks die after flowering and fruiting, presenting an aesthetic quandary and the mechanical problem of their removal. In botanical gardens and on large estates the larger species are breathtaking in their visual effect and draw spectators like no other plants. The inflorescence is exceedingly bizarre in appearance, consisting of several thick and snaky, segmented, ropelike affairs from which the feathery sprays of both male and female flowers peek. The fruits are fairly large and are very attractive toy-top-shaped masses covered in shiny brown or black scales. Aboriginal peoples in Africa, Madagascar, and South America have many uses for raffia palms, and the fibers from the leaves were once used in the West as twine and cordage but the natural product is now largely replaced by synthetic and other naturally occurring materials. None of the species can withstand frost, and all need warmth and an ample and continuous supply of moisture.

Raphia farinifera (fair-i-NIF-e-ra) (synonym *R. ruffia*) is indigenous to Madagascar. It is the second largest growing species, the trunks reaching a height of 20 or sometimes 30 feet and a diameter of more than 3 feet before flowering and fruiting. The leaves may reach a length of 70 feet and are 10 feet or more in width and, on mature plants, are always at least 40 feet long. The leaf as a whole is erect, stiff, and ascending, never pendent and never falling beneath an angle of 45° from the plane and its emergence from the top of the trunk. The petioles, which are longer than the leaves of most other pinnate palms, are as much as 15 feet long; they are armed with teeth on their lower parts where they are 10 feet or more in diameter. The leaflets are as much as 8 feet long but only 3 or 4 inches wide; they are deep green above and whitish and mealy or floury beneath (*farinifera* means "bearing flour"). The strange and exotic inflorescences may be as much as 12 feet long, and it takes several years for the various clusters to emerge and for the fruit to mature. There is nothing on earth more spectacular than a mature raffia palm.

Raphia hookeri (HOOK-er-eye) has 8-foot suckering trunks and 20- to 30-foot-long leaves. It is smaller than *R. farinifera* but requires the same climatic conditions and culture.

Raphia vinifera (vi-NIF-e-ra) also is smaller than *R. farinifera* with a solitary trunk to 20 feet in height and leaves to 30 or even 40 feet long. Like *R. hookeri,* it may be occasionally found for sale and is planted in tropical regions to some extent.

RAVENALA (rav-e-NAL-a)
Strelitziaceae: The Bird-of-Paradise, Traveler's Tree Family
TRAVELER'S TREE; TRAVELER'S PALM
Large, trunked, fan-shaped plant; immense banana-like leaves; bird-of-paradise-like flowers
Zones 10 and 11
Sun
Average but regular amounts of moisture
Average well-drained soil
Propagation by transplanting of suckers and by seed

A monotypic genus native to northern Madagascar. *Ravenala madagascariensis* (mad´-e-gas-kair´-ee-ENS-is) is an immense, suckering mostly herbaceous banana-like herb which, with age, makes woody trunks as much as 40 feet tall. Atop the trunk spring giant long-stalked 10- to 12-foot long stiff erect banana-like leaves in one plane on opposite sides of the stem, forming a great semicircle or symmetrical fan shape. The very stout leaf stalks are usually longer than the great leaves, and the colossal and spectacular fan created by both is the reason the plant is grown. The new leaves have entire margins, but on larger plants the wind soon tears the leaves along their lateral and parallel veins, creating the look of a large pinnate leaf from a distance. The trunk is tightly wrapped in old leaf bases in its younger (upper) parts but becomes smooth near the base and is woody, unlike the trunk of *Strelitzia nicola* (white bird-of-paradise) that has a hollow trunk. The plants bloom more or less all year, but especially in the winter in the Northern Hemisphere. The inflorescences arise from the top of the trunk, among and half hidden by the leaf stalks, and consist of spikes of about a dozen great foot-long greenish boat-shaped pointed bracts that cradle small white flowers. The overall aspect of each bract is that of the bird-of-paradise flower, but these are much larger and not as colorful. The fruits are large black seeds covered with pointed deep blue-beaked arils; they reside in the now woody bracts from which their stalks eventually become detached and they fall to the ground. There are few things in the vegetable kingdom that can be compared to this plant: it has some palmlike qualities, such as the enormous fan of leaves at the top of the trunk; it has leaves similar to the banana and the giant white bird-of-paradise, and its flowers are quite similar to but larger than that plant. What is unique is the tremendous flat fan of leaves. The "traveler's" part of the common names comes about because the concavities at the bases of the overlapping leaf stalks each hold a liter or so of water, which supposedly has been used to quench the thirst of wayfarers in the wilderness. While quite spectacular and definitely exotic, these plants are difficult to integrate into the general landscape precisely because of their unique and very bold countenance. In my opinion they look best treated as palms. If allowed to keep their suckers and form clumps of individuals of varying heights, they can create a tableau like that (but not as graceful) of a group of coconuts, whether the group be isolated or mixed in with other vegetation. A single large specimen of traveler's palm in a broad expanse of lawn is simply a curiosity and is never an integral part of the landscape. Plate 339.

RAVENEA (ra-VEN-ee-a)
Palmae (Arecaceae): The Palm Family
MAJESTY PALM

Short thick-trunked pinnate-leaved palm with dark
    green leaves
Zones 10 and 11; marginal in zone 9b
Partial shade to sun
Water lover
Rich, humusy moist soil on the acidic side
Propagation by seed

A genus of only 10 solitary trunked palm species in
Madagascar and the Comores Islands. These are pinnate-leaved palms inhabiting wet as well as dry regions
and growing from sea level to well over a mile in elevation. Only one species is much cultivated outside botanical gardens and it has soared in popularity since its
introduction in the 1980s. *Ravenea rivularis* (riv-
yoo-LAIR-is) is native to southern Madagascar where it
grows along the edges of rivers. It quickly reaches a total
height of 15 or 20 feet with 10 or 12 feet of trunk. The
trunk is swollen at the base, a deep gray or tan in color,
and strongly ringed. The pinnate leaves are 6 to 8 feet
long, a deep green in color and fairly erect but gracefully
arching, usually with a twist to the rachis near the end of
the blade. This lovely palm is quite fast growing and
surprisingly hardy for such a tropical looking species;
although usually damaged by a temperature of 28°F, it
has survived a temperature of 24°F in Houston, Texas,
and, because of its fast growth, makes a quick recovery
from frost damage. It needs a rich humus-laden soil and
is not tolerant of drought. It is stunted and subject to
disease and insect attack in poor limy soils, which need
to be amended with much organic material. The palm
tolerates fairly shady conditions very well and is especially beautiful when grown as an understory subject to
give texture and a tropical feel to woodland type settings. It is equally at home in the sun.

RHAPHIDOPHORA. See *Epipremnum.*

RHAPIDOPHYLLUM
    (rap´-i-doe-FYL-lum)
Palmae (Arecaceae): The Palm Family
NEEDLE PALM
Small suckering slow growing fan palm with long
    black sharp spines on its leaf stalks
Zones 7b through 10a
Partial shade to Sun
Average but regular amounts of moisture
Average well-drained soil
Propagation by transplanting of suckers and by seed

A monotypic genus native to the southeastern
United States from South Carolina to central Florida
and westward through southern Georgia and the southern halves of Alabama and Mississippi. *Rhapidophyllum hystrix* (HIS-trix) is a low, bushy suckering fan-
leaved palm. It has leaves as much as 5 feet wide that are
deeply and palmately divided into 20 or more linear,
deep green segments that form usually slightly less than

180° of a circle; the undersides of the leaves are usually
gray to silver in color. The bases of the petioles (actually
the sheaths around the petioles) are armed with long
black needles. The palm seldom forms a true aboveground trunk, but the mass of leaf bases and fibers
builds a stout trunklike structure that may attain 6 feet
in height and is covered in the needlelike spines. The
palm grows very slowly, but in time forms relatively
large colonies. In nature it grows as an understory subject in tall forests and is usually found in low wet areas;
it grows in full sun and in drier sites but is not as picturesque under such conditions where the leaf crown is
not as open and graceful. In part shade and with regular and adequate supplies of water it makes a very lovely
open-crowned specimen with long graceful leaf stalks
and, if suckers are judiciously removed occasionally, a
very attractive silhouette. The plant is one of the world's
hardiest palm species, being successfully grown by
some adventurous gardeners in zone 6b with minor protection; it somewhat languishes in perennially hot and
truly tropical climes where there is no winter chill.

RHAPIS (RAP-is)
Palmae (Arecaceae): The Palm Family
LADY PALM
Elegant clumping slender-stemmed fan palms
Zones vary according to species
Partial shade to sun
Average but regular amounts of moisture
Average well-drained, slightly acidic soil
Propagation by transplanting of suckers

A genus of 12 fan-leaved palm species in southeastern China and Southeast Asia. These are clumping
palms; an individual plant often makes a large clump
wider than its height. The trunks are wonderfully slender and quite exquisite, especially when the clusters are
thinned to some extent. Almost all species have their
delicate trunks clothed in beautiful "woven" dark fibers.
The leaf stalks are also especially narrow and graceful,
and the relatively large many-fingered leaves dance and
shimmer in the breeze. Two species are very widely
planted in tropical and warm climate regions, but several others are being introduced now and more are waiting to make their debuts. The plants are most easily
propagated by dividing large clumps; male and female
plants are needed to produce seed and for one species
this is impossible as there are no female plants. Seedling
plants grow very slowly.
    Rhapis excelsa (ek-SEL-sa) (synonyms *Chamae-
rops excelsa, Rhapis flabelliformis*) is native to Taiwan and
southeastern China. The plant is completely hardy in
zones 9b through 11 and marginal in zone 9a, surviving
temperatures in the mid to low 20s unscathed. The
trunks grow to as much as 10 feet and are almost completely covered with dark tan-colored fibers that age to
a dark gray or even black color; this gives the stems a
total diameter of about an inch. The plants produce

hundreds of stems that grow quite close together, and a single clump can reach 10 or even 12 feet in diameter. The leaves grow all along the stems except on the oldest and most crowded trunks; they are carried on very thin petioles that are about 18 inches long. The leaf blade is 12 to 18 inches wide with 12 to 20 or more very deep linear segments that form an almost complete circle. That the leaves grow from the trunks for most of the trunk length and that the new canes or trunks grow mostly from the perimeter of a clump make this little palm species near perfection for informal tall hedge material in partially shaded sites. It is also almost unexcelled as a close-up specimen where its grace can be fully appreciated; like many other clumping palm species, it is more graceful and artistic if some of the crowded trunks are removed to better show off its wonderful silhouette. This beauty is sometimes called the bamboo palm because of its clumping habit and fanned leaves. The name is unfortunate because at least three other palm genera also bear this name; a better common name occasionally in use is large lady palm. The large lady palm grows in full sun, even in hot climates, but its leaves will not be the beautiful deep green hue they are with partial shade and protection from the midday sun. The palm is not drought tolerant, and it grows faster and more luxuriantly with adequate and regular supplies of moisture. The species has many variegated-leaved cultivars that the Japanese favor almost to the point of mania, creating very high prices for some of them. Some of these are quite beautiful especially up close, but not necessarily in a landscaping sense. There are also dwarf cultivars that are astoundingly beautiful in partially shady rock gardens and bordering semi-shady paths and walkways as an accent. The species is perhaps the perfect palm for indoor cultivation, thriving without sun, though it still needs bright light, and with resistance to insect infestations that make having other palms a chore. Plate 340.

Rhapis flabelliformis. See *R. excelsa.*

Rhapis humilis (HYOO-mi-lis) suffers the same uncertainty of origin that *R. excelsa* (large lady palm) does and for the same reasons; it is most likely indigenous to the same general area but is still unknown in the wild. The palms are hardy in zones 9 through 11 and marginal in zone 8b. This species is arguably the most beautiful in the genus. "Humilis" translates as "small" or "humble" while "excelsa" means "tall"; this is an anomaly since *R. humilis* grows considerably taller than the large lady palm The trunks grow to as much as 20 feet and are even more slender than those of the large lady palm; the leaf segments are also pointed on their ends, unlike those of the large lady palm. In addition the adherent fibers are more tightly woven onto the stems and are lighter colored resulting in light brown (as opposed to dark gray or even black) trunks. The clumps are not quite as wide as those of the large lady palm but the trunks are even more crowded in a clump. The leaves of this palm do not envelop the trunks to the degree that those of *R. excelsa* do and this adds to the graceful and more palmlike aspect of the plant. The leaves are not significantly larger than those of the large lady palm but they are more deeply divided, have more segments, and the ends of the divisions are usually pendulous to some extent, adding even more charm. The genus produces male and female flowers on separate plants, which presents a real problem as there are no known female plants of *R. humilis,* all plants in cultivation being divisions from original plants in China centuries ago. This unfortunate fact makes the slender lady palm rare and expensive to obtain. The species does not, alas, flourish in hot and steamy climates like those of Florida, the U.S. Gulf Coast, and wet lowland tropical regions. It wants cooler summers and grows to perfection (and actually grows faster than the large lady palm) along the coast of California and in other Mediterranean regions. It is perfectly adapted to areas that are tropical or subtropical but elevated and moist like those of the north island of New Zealand and the low areas of the eastern Andes.

RHIZOPHORA

(ry-ZAHF-o-ra / ry-zo-FOR-a)
Rhizophoraceae: The Red Mangrove Family
RED MANGROVE; AMERICAN MANGROVE
Large stilt-rooted tree in lagoons and bays; large
    glossy leaves; strange exotic root-forming fruits
Zones 10b and 11
Sun
Water lover
Semi-aquatic of seashores, brackish lakes, lagoons,
    and estuaries
Propagation by seed

A genus of only three mangrove species on tropical seacoasts around the world. *Rhizophora mangle* (MANG-lay / MANG-lee), the one American species in the genus, is also found on the shores of tropical West Africa. The plants are among the wonders of the world's tropical coastal areas for their beauty and for their importance to the coastal ecology. The trees grow on all the tropical coasts of the Western Hemisphere except those where the bottom of the sea drops off sharply or the surf is great enough to dislodge and carry away their seeds (although once established, they can withstand the winds of most hurricanes). They luxuriate in the quieter waters of lagoons, estuaries, and brackish lakes and, on the coast itself, they grow as far into the sea as the mark of low tide if the surf is not too rough.

The trees produce large aerial prop roots in abundance from their trunks and, when mature, from the branches themselves. These roots are arching, they divide dichotomously near the usual water level, and they can form impenetrable thickets in a fairly short time. They are covered with whitish lenticels that allow the exchange of gases between bark and the air and, in the case of the genus *Rhizophora,* the extrusion of salts accumulated from the sea water. These roots en masse trap the silt and other debris that pass their way and, with time, build the land seaward. In addition, the underwater root environment provides protection for young shellfish, fry, and all stages of mollusk growth, making these trees one of the most important in the world ecologically. Their beauty is exceptional.

Mature trees have been known to reach heights of 100 feet or more in truly tropical and protected areas and, at one time, there were specimens at least 80 feet tall on the southwesternmost part of the Florida peninsula in the Everglades region of the Ten Thousand Islands. Today, with severe hurricanes striking the East Coast, bad freezes over all the peninsula, and the acceleration of real estate development everywhere, one is hard put to find specimens over 40 feet in stature. In some places these trees are even being torn "out of the way" so that the new owners of property along the coast may more easily see the water!

The trunks and prop roots are a cinnamon-red in color when young but mature to a gray or dark gray color. The tree's canopy is always above any but hurricane water levels and is broad and irregular or dome-shaped. The branches grow more or less horizontally and are never straight but rather always contorted in some manner, making the tree one of the most picturesque forms in the whole world.

The deep green elliptic leaves are arranged oppositely on the stems and are 3 to as much as 8 inches long and are usually found mostly at the ends of the branches; they are thick, leathery but glossy on their upper surface, which also exhibits a prominent and lighter colored midrib, and a much paler shade of green on their lower surface.

The succulent flowers have four petals and four sepals and are produced year-round; in extra-tropical areas they are produced less abundantly in the cooler months. They are yellow or whitish yellow in color and usually less than an inch wide, occurring in pairs or in groups of three from the axils of the leaves. The amazing inch-long green and fleshy fruits form quickly. They are triangular or conical in shape and contain but one seed. Within a few weeks the surface of the fruit hardens and changes to a definite brown color and the seed within sprouts while the fruits are still on the tree. The emerging green cigar-shaped reddish-brown-tipped sprout grows to as much as a foot before its weight detaches the fruit and seedling, at which time the whole affair plunges into the water where it may penetrate the soil beneath the water. If it does not enter the soil, the fruit and seedling float away to another site where they can find soil and generate another land-building colony. The seedlings can remain viable for as long as a year in or out of the water. Plate 341.

RHOEO (RO-ee-o)
Commelinaceae: The Spiderwort Family
MOSES-IN-A-BOAT; OYSTER PLANT; MOSES-IN-A-CRADLE; PURPLE-LEAVED SPIDERWORT

Small clumping perennial; lance-shaped green and purple leaves; white and purple flowers
Zones 10 and 11; marginal in zone 9b
Sun to partial shade
Average but regular amounts of moisture; drought tolerant when established
Average well-drained soil
Propagation by transplanting of suckers

A monotypic genus that technically is a part of the large genus *Tradescantia*, but is here retained under *Rhoeo* because the latter name is so widespread in the literature and the nursery trade. ***Rhoeo spathacea*** (spath-AY-see-a) (synonyms *R. discolor*, *Tradescantia bicolor*) is native to the West Indies, southern Mexico, and Guatemala. It grows to about 18 inches in height, never more than 2 feet, and forms clumping rosettes on very short stems of 18-inch-long lanceolate to elliptic stiff but succulent and fleshy leaves, shiny deep green above and a deep purple or purplish red beneath. The small white flowers have three papery petals and are borne inside and almost hidden by a purple boat-shaped envelope consisting of two bracts. This useful and colorful small groundcover and border or bedding plant has a succulent and tender appearance that belies its true durability. Once planted it requires almost no care and will form large clumps with time. Indeed, its seeds are very easily dispersed, and it is often found growing epiphytically on trees, the joints in sidewalks, buildings, and rocks. It is drought tolerant, indifferent to soil conditions as long as the medium is well drained, and grows almost anywhere except deep shade; soggy soil usually leads to root and stem rot. It looks especially good planted among and in rocks as it takes only a small pocket of soil on large rocks or boulders to sustain it. It is equally attractive among stones near water, although it should never be planted in boggy conditions. There is a very attractive cultivar, ***Rhoeo spathacea* 'Variegata'**, with red and yellowish white longitudinal lines on the leaf surface as well as a dwarf and more compact form. Some people are allergic to the sap of this plant. Plates 342 and 343.

RHYTICOCOS. See *Syagrus amara*.

RICINUS (RIS-i-nus)
Euphorbiaceae: The Euphorbia, Spurge Family
CASTOR-BEAN; CASTOR-OIL PLANT; PALMA CHRISTI

Small tree or large shrub; large to immense hand-shaped leaves; colorful flower spikes and spiny fruit
Zones 10 and 11 as a permanent perennial; zones 9 and 8b as a returning perennial; anywhere as an annual
Sun
Average but regular amounts of moisture
Average well-drained soil
Propagation by seed

A monotypic genus native to a large area of tropical Africa. **_Ricinus communis_** (KAHM-yoo-nis) is now naturalized and often considered a weed in all tropical and subtropical regions including the southeastern and southwestern United States. It is poisonous in all its parts, but especially its seeds, which are deadly if eaten. Therefore, the species should not be planted where small children have access to it. Castor-bean very quickly grows into a small to medium-sized tree in wet tropical regions, reaching as much as 40 feet, with a much-branched flat or dome-shaped dense crown of leaves and a trunk to a foot in diameter and woody at its base. In less favorable areas it seldom grows to more than 20 feet, with or without occasional light frost. It is naturally a very variable plant when it comes to leaf size, leaf color, and ultimate height, exhibiting leaves that range from less than a foot in diameter to 3 feet or more in width. The leaves are alternately arranged on the stems and are borne on long petioles; they are normally a deep green in color and almost round in outline but deeply cleft into eight or nine triangular and toothed segments, giving the blade a distinctly palmate appearance. Leaf color is usually deep green, and each lobe has a prominent and lighter colored or reddish midrib as well as lateral veins that are so marked and usually depressed. There are several smaller-leaved forms with brilliant red, reddish purple, reddish bronze and bronzy-colored leaves. The plants bloom year-round in frost-free regions. The large flower spikes are terminal on the branches and consist of elongated panicles of small red and yellow flowers, with the male blossoms on the bottom and the females near the top of the spike. The fruits form into three-sectioned, three-seeded inch-long oblong or cylindrical burlike capsules usually covered with soft but pointed spines; the capsules range from brown to deep red in color and the inch-long oblong seeds within are beautifully mottled with brown, green, red, and white. The seeds are the source of castor oil, a universal but harsh and vile-tasting purgative. The oil extracted from the deadly poisonous seeds is also much used in the making of paints, varnishes, and lacquers, and was formerly used in the manufacture of soaps. There is hardly a more tropical appearing tree and the plants grow incredibly fast with heat, sun, water, and a fairly fertile soil, making them unsurpassed for creating quick screen, small shade trees, and large tropical accents. They survive on poor soil and are even somewhat drought tolerant when established but, with adequate and regular amounts of moisture and a rich soil, grow phenomenally fast and lush. Plate 344.

ROYSTONEA (roy-STOAN-ee-a)
Palmae (Arecaceae): The Palm Family
ROYAL PALM
Tall solitary, columnar usually bulging-trunked
    palms with great pinnate leaves
Zones 10b and 11
Sun
Water lovers
Rich, humusy, moist, well-drained soil
Propagation by seed

A genus of perhaps a dozen tall pinnate-leaved palms with massive columnar and usually bulging trunks found in tropical America. Some of the world's tallest palm species are in this genus, and several of them are considered by many people to be the most beautiful palms in the world. They are all distinguished by their smooth and faintly but beautifully ringed light-colored trunks that mostly grow to great heights, their great smooth dark green crownshafts, and their large, lissome, and usually plumose pinnate leaves on relatively short stalks. None of them can withstand much cold and, as young trees, they need protection from frost; they also need good soil and regular and adequate supplies of moisture to fulfill their great potential. Many of these palm species have been planted throughout the tropical world and are among the most widely recognized emblems of the tropics and the tropical look. Unlike many other palms, royal palms have adapted to the hurricane-prone regions to which they are indigenous by readily shedding their leaves in strong winds, thus allowing their trunks to remain standing long after those of other species have toppled. The genus was formerly known as _Oreodoxa_.

Roystonea borinqueana (bo-rin´-kee-AHN-a) is indigenous only to the island of Puerto Rico. It is similar in all respects to _R. regia_ (Cuban royal palm), except that it usually does not grow as tall, seldom reaching more than 50 feet, and its leaflets are glossier. Even though it is much less common than the Cuban royal palm, it is as beautiful.

Roystonea elata (ee-LAIT-a) is indigenous to the Everglades region of southern Florida. In addition to _Quercus virginiana_ (live oak), _Taxodium distichum_ (bald cypress), _Rhizophora mangle_ (red mangrove), and _Magnolia grandiflora_ (southern magnolia), it is one of the most beautiful and impressive trees indigenous to Florida and certainly the most beautiful species that is endemic to the state. It grows to as much as 100 feet with a magnificent gray-ringed to almost white-ringed trunk with a bulging base and sometimes a slight bulging at or just above the middle of the stem. The glorious crownshaft is as much as 8 feet tall and is very smooth and a deep glossy green in color. The crown is full and usually round with 10 to 15 great arching leaves. The leaves are 10 to 12 feet long and consist of hundreds of 3-foot-long deep green drooping leaflets that emerge from the rachis at almost every angle and create a wonderful plumed aspect to each giant blade. The native habitat is mostly wet with fairly rich soil and is very nearly tropical—clues to making this palm happy in cultivation. Development and human intervention as transplanting from the wild have nearly decimated these trees in nature. Wonderful specimens are still to be seen in the Everglades National Park and the Big Cypress National Preserve northwest of the national park. Most palms for sale and labeled as *Roystonea elata* or Florida royal palm are probably *R. regia* (Cuban royal palm). Some botanists consider the Florida roayl palm only a form of the more widespread Cuban royal. Plate 345.

Roystonea oleracea (o-le-RAY-see-a) is native to Trinidad, Barbados, Venezuela, and Colombia in South America. It is the tallest growing species, often reaching heights of more than 100 feet with an almost straight but slightly tapering smooth white or gray closely ringed trunk bulging only at its base. Atop the trunk, the long tall, smooth, and dark green crownshaft resides, and atop it spring the 15 or more 20-foot-long arching leaves. Unlike the leaves of most other species, the 4- to 5-foot-long drooping leaflets of these leaves emerge from the rachis in a single plane on the two opposite sides of the rachis, creating a flat leaf surface somewhat like that of the coconut palm. The leaf crown is not as rounded as are those of the Cuban and Florida royals. There is no more noble and impressive tree in a landscape than this one.

Roystonea regia (REEJ-ya / REE-jee-a) is indigenous only to Cuba, but is now so widely planted throughout the lowland tropics of the world that its origin may seem pantropical. It is similar in all its characteristics to *R. elata* (Florida royal palm), except that it is shorter (usually to no more than 60 feet) and it always has a distinct bulge somewhere above the middle of the great white or gray and closely ringed trunk. It is the most widely planted *Roystonea* species and, once seen, it is not difficult to fathom the reason.

RUELLIA

Acanthaceae: The Acanthus Family
Common names vary according to species
Small herbaceous shrubs; flowers of white, yellow,
    pink, red, blue, and purple
Zones 10 and 11
Partial shade to partial sun
Average but regular amounts of moisture
Average well-drained soil
Propagation by seed and cuttings

A genus of about 150 species of evergreen perennial herbs, shrubs, and subshrubs found in all tropical and subtropical areas but most abundantly in tropical America. They have oppositely arranged leaves with five-lobed trumpet-shaped flowers quite similar in form to those of the petunia, although some species have more exotically shaped flowers with curved asymmetrical corollas and long protruding stamens. The flowers are borne in the axils of the leaves and are usually single, but also occur in small clusters. Many species are rather weedy in appearance, especially the ones indigenous to the southern and southwestern United States where they are usually called Mexican petunia, but many others have attractive flowers in colors of every hue in the rainbow and some are exceedingly attractive with both flowers and leaves that are definitely tropical and exotic looking. All species survive in poor and rather dry soil

but only look good and flourish with adequate and regular amounts of moisture and a soil that is rich in organic matter. Although quite tender to frost, most species reseed themselves in zone 9 if they grow long enough to bloom and set seed.

Ruellia affinis (AF-fi-nis) is native to eastern Brazil. It is a small shrub growing to as much as 6 feet with pendent, long wiry branches; it is easily espaliered or tied and trained to a support to simulate a vine. The 5-inch long short-stalked elliptic leaves are a medium green in color with deeply depressed veins above. The plant blooms most of the year in tropical areas. The 4-inch-long glowing scarlet salverform flowers have wide-spreading lobes borne singly in the leaf axils. The flower color is one of the nicest reds in existence.

Ruellia amoena. See *R. graecizans*.

Ruellia colorata (kul-o-RAIT-a) is native to the Amazon region of Brazil. It grows 3 to 4 feet and has 6-inch-long elliptic deep green leaves with deeply depressed veins that are of a lighter shade than the rest of the blade. It blooms year-round with axillary spikes of fiery red flowers whose corolla tubes are curved on top, giving the flower a hooded look; the throat of the blossom is a deep yellow and exhibits long protruding red stamens tipped with yellow anthers. This beautiful plant luxuriates in partial shade.

Ruellia devosiana (de-vo´-zee-AHN-a) is native to eastern Brazil. It grows to only 2 feet and is rather prostrate in habit. The 3-inch-long elliptic nearly stalkless leaves are exceptionally beautiful: deep green with silvery green midrib and lateral veins above and reddish purple beneath. The plant blooms year-round and has 2-inch-long salverform white or pale pink flowers with lavender lines in the throat. This species is a wonderfully exotic groundcover for moist semishady areas. It is equally effective as a cascade on stone walls and in hanging baskets.

Ruellia graecizans (GREEK-i-zanz) (synonym *R. amoena*) is indigenous to a vast area of South America, generally in clearings of rain forests. It grows to 2 or 3 feet in height and is a sprawling weak-stemmed subshrub with nearly stalkless 3- to 4-inch-long medium green elliptic quilted and usually pubescent leaves. The plant blooms year-round but most heavily in late winter and spring. It has long-stalked axillary inflorescences of several salverform inch-long scarlet blooms with throats spotted yellow. The plant is somewhat weedy in appearance and tends to die out early. It is best cut back or renewed from seed or cuttings each year.

Ruellia macrantha (mak-RANTH-a) is native to eastern Brazil. It grows to 6 feet or sometimes more with a dense and rounded habit in sun or partial shade. The 6-inch-long leaves are nearly stalkless, linear-ovate to linear-elliptic in shape and lime-green with prominent and lighter colored midribs. The plant blooms year-round but most heavily in fall, winter, and spring with large solitary flowers in the leaf axils. Each blossom is funnel-shaped and about 3 inches long with a 4-inch-wide five-lobed flaring end. The flower color is rose with orange flushes and red veins inside the flower's throat. This species is perhaps the showiest-flowered in the genus.

Ruellia makoyana (mak-o-YAHN-a) is native to a large area of tropical Brazil. It grows only to 12 or 18 inches in height and has trailing and mostly prostrate stems. The 3-inch-long, nearly stalkless lanceolate-shaped leaves are deep emerald green, often with a purplish cast and creamy white midribs and lateral veins. The solitary flowers appear year-round in the leaf axils and are 2 inches long, pink or red, and salverform in shape. This makes an exquisite groundcover in half-shaded moist sites and is equally beautiful as a cascade from rocky walls or in a hanging basket. For reasons unknown, the plant is sometimes called monkey plant.

RUMOHRA (roo-MOR-a)
Dryopteridaceae: The Wood Fern Family
LEATHERLEAF FERN; LEATHER FERN
Medium-sized clumping terrestrial or epiphytic fern;
    leathery bipinnate to tripinnate leaves
Zones 9b through 11; marginal in zone 9a
Partial shade to nearly full sun
Water lover
Rich, humusy moist soil
Propagation by transplanting of suckers and by
    spores

A genus of six terrestrial or epiphytic fern species in tropical regions around the world but mainly in the Southern Hemisphere. Only one species is much planted outside botanical gardens. *Rumohra adiantiformis* (ad´-ee-ant-i-FORM-is) (synonyms *Aspidium capense*, *Polystichum adiantiforme*, *P. capense*) is indigenous to a vast area of the Southern Hemisphere, from Africa to Australia, New Zealand, Polynesia, and South America. It is an epiphytic or terrestrial species and grows to about 3 feet in height with 3-foot-long spreading triangular-shaped bipinnate or tripinnate leathery but glossy medium green leaves. The fern is quite easy to grow given a humusy, moist, well-drained soil or epiphytic mix and adequate moisture. As a terrestrial subject it makes a wonderful groundcover as its rhizomatous roots slowly spread to create small colonies. As a terrestrial it flourishes in almost full sun if it receives enough moisture. It is slightly hardier to cold with its roots in the ground. It is undamaged by temperatures of 26°F or above and will usually return from temperatures of 20°F or above. The leaves are favorites of florists and floral designers because of their artful and graceful form and long-lasting qualities after being cut.

SABAL (SAY-bal / SAH-bal)
Palmae (Arecaceae): The Palm Family
PALMETTO
Small to very tall fan-leaved palms
Zones vary according to species
Sun to partial sun
Average but regular amounts of moisture
Average well-drained soil
Propagation by seed

A genus of 16 species of solitary-trunked palmate-leaved palms in tropical and subtropical America. They have costapalmate leaves. None of the species grows fast, and many are truly slow. All take several years to form an aboveground trunk, having to first grow an elaborate root system that sometimes includes underground development of the trunk. All the species are capable of withstanding drought and indifferent soil, but only flourish in appearance with adequate and regular amounts of moisture and a decent soil that is high in organic matter.

Sabal causiarum (kow-see-AHR-um) is native to the Caribbean island of Puerto Rico and is hardy in zones 9 through 11 although somewhat marginal in zone 9a. One of the largest species, it grows to as much as 40 feet with a truly massive columnar gray to almost white trunk that is, except in young specimens, free of leaf bases. The leaves are 6 feet wide and are borne on petioles as long. The leaf blade is strongly costapalmate and often twisted to some extent, and the leaf crown is large, rounded, and as much as 20 feet wide with as many as 50 leaves. This imposing and very beautiful species looks quite nice as a single large specimen but, like most palms, looks even better when individuals of varying heights are planted in a group. It is sometimes called the Puerto Rican hat palm or simply the hat palm as the indigenous inhabitants are wont to make straw hats from its leaves.

Sabal glaucescens. See *S. mauritiiformis*.

Sabal mauritiiformis (maw-rit´-ee-eye-FORM-is) (synonym *S. glaucescens*) occurs naturally in southern Mexico, Central American, and northern South America and is hardy in zones 10 and 11. It is perhaps the most graceful and elegant species in the genus, growing to as much as 50 or 60 feet in height but with a trunk that is only a foot or slightly more in diameter. The glossy medium green leaves are as much as 6 feet wide but, because they are so deeply segmented and because the segments are so limp and pendulous, the leaves look almost pinnate from a distance. The leaves are borne on petioles as long as or longer than the leaves are wide. This palm is of exceptional beauty and should be much more widely planted than it is at present.

Sabal mexicana (mex-i-KAHN-a) (synonym *S. texana*) is native to extreme southern Texas along the Rio Grande and adjacent northern Mexico, down into Central America, but, when mature, is hardy in zones 7b through 11 and marginal in zone 7a. This species is similar in appearance to *S. palmetto* (palmetto palm), except that it is not quite as tall, has a more massive trunk, and has larger leaves (to more than 6 feet wide) with broader and darker-colored segments that usually have a bluish cast. Perhaps the most desirable aspect of the Texas palmetto is that the trunk tends to keep its criss-crossed leaf bases and stalks for a longer period than do most other *Sabal* species. The 2- to 3-foot-diameter trunks have a tan-colored wickerwork look, which is quite picturesque.

Sabal minor (MY-nor) is indigenous to a large portion of the southeastern United States, from central and southeast Texas northwards to southern Oklahoma, the southern half of Arkansas, and eastward to the North Carolina coast, always in moist and sometimes swampy areas. It is the hardiest species in the genus and is adaptable to zones 7 through 11 and marginal in zone 6b. Seldom does this palm form an aboveground stem, and when it does, the stem is usually only a few feet tall. It grows naturally as an understory species in partial to almost deep shade and is called the dwarf palmetto. The medium green to deep green to bluish green leaves, which are 3 feet to almost 6 feet wide, are held on 3-foot-long stalks and are nearly round in outline but deeply divided into many tapering segments. Unlike the petiole of most other *Sabal* species, the petiole of the dwarf palmetto does not extend very far into the leaf blade. The plant is used as a large shrub. It is also used as a very tall groundcover, since the spread of its leaf crown is usually 8 to 10 feet. The dwarf palmetto is valuable for creating a very tropical look to large shady areas, either as a bold groundcover or as an accent, where most other palms do not flourish, and it is adaptable to almost boggy conditions where, again, most palms do not like to be. Although it survives in sun and dry soil, it never grows as large nor looks as happy under such conditions.

Sabal palmetto (pahl-MET-toe) is native to the southern half of the South Carolina coast southwards into southern Florida, the Bahamas, and Cuba, and is hardy in zones 8 through 11. It is sometimes called the cabbage palm because its terminal buds were once cooked like cabbage and used for food. This species is one of the tallest in the genus, sometimes attaining a height of 90 feet. The trunk is usually no more than a foot in diameter and may be completely covered in the criss-crossing wickerwork pattern of old leaf bases in younger palms or relatively smooth and closely ringed, especially in older palms. The leaf crown is dense and round and composed of 20 to 40 deeply costapalmate dark green leaves held on 6-foot-long petioles. The blade is divided to about half its depth into many stiff segments whose ends are usually pendent. This palm is quite graceful, especially when it is mature and when it is grown in a moist site. Towering above the great live oaks in its native haunts, its silhouette is nearly awe-inspiring. The tree survives near the seacoast and is tolerant of ocean spray. It is doubtless the most widely planted *Sabal* species, at least in the United States. It is often enough neglected in cultivation, resulting in stunted and starved, tired-looking specimens. Furthermore, it is often planted in straight rows of stems of equal height, like giant toothpicks with little top tufts of green and yellow leaves, or in twos with the trunks leaning and crossed over each other into a giant X. Both plantings are aesthetic and landscaping nightmares.

This beauty needs to be integrated into a landscape with small groups of palms of differing heights and, if possible, lower contrasting vegetation around to thwart the lean and mean effect created by having its slender trunks exposed to the ground.

Sabal texana. See *S. mexicana.*

SAMANEA (sa-MAN-ee-a)

Mimosaceae (Fabaceae, Leguminosae), subfamily Mimosoideae: The Mimosa Family
RAIN TREE; MONKEYPOD; SAMAN TREE
Large, majestic spreading tree; dense bipinnate foliage; pink and red powder-puff flowers
Zones 10 and 11; marginal in zone 10a
Sun
Water lover but somewhat drought tolerant when mature
Average well-drained soil
Propagation by seed

This species is now technically subsumed into the genus *Albizia*, but this change of name is barely yet reflected in the literature and is not in the trade and is therefore included here under the old name. *Samanea saman* (sa-MAHN) (synonyms *Albizia saman*, *Enterolobium saman*, *Pithecellobium saman*) is indigenous to Central America, Trinidad, and Tobago, and adjacent northern South America, and is one of the tropical world's most magnificently beautiful trees. In its native rain forest habitats it grows quickly to as much as 100 or even 150 feet in height with an ultimate spread of more than 200 feet. In cultivation, however, it is usually about half these dimensions in the open, although the tree is always much wider than tall, and when grown as an understory subject becomes much taller than when it is planted in the open. The trunk is very thick and low-branched when grown in the open. The great horizontally ascending branches fork in a rather zigzagged manner, giving to mature trees the look of colossal bonsai subjects. The crown is almost invariably umbrella-shaped or dome-shaped. The even-bipinnate leaves are as much as a foot long and consist of six or eight pairs of 1- to 2-inch-long elliptic to diamond-shaped to obovate medium green leaflets that are smooth and shiny above but grayish green and pubescent beneath. The leaflets farthest from the stem are the largest. The tree is sometimes deciduous in the winter with drought or cold. It is named rain tree for two reasons. First, the leaves, like those of very many other members in the super-family Leguminosae, close up with the advent of darkness or when raindrops touch them. Second, at one time it was thought that the honeydew dropping from the ends of the branches was discharged by the tree when, in fact, it is the exudations of aphids and other sap-sucking insects feeding on the foliage. The tree blooms in cycles for most of the year, but most heavily from late spring through the summer, with mimosa-like heads of blossoms whose calyces and corollas are insignificant compared with the long stamens, which constitute the bulk of the individual inflorescence. The stamens are in bundles of 8 to 10. Each stamen is red or pink for half its length and white at its base. The fruit is a 6- to 10-inch-long flat pod that, when immature and still green, is edible, supposedly sweet, and much used as cattle fodder. This splendid tree is not for the small garden. It is adapted to very large specimen plantings in parks and on large estates as well as great avenues. In addition, the roots are deep and widespread and, especially in regions subject to drought conditions, surface and can interfere with patios, roadways, and the like. Everyone who has seen a mature specimen of *Samanea*, either in photos or "in the flesh," has exclaimed in awe at its superb form and extraordinary size and color. It is one of the most strikingly beautiful trees in the world.

SANCHEZIA

(sahn-CHAYS-ee-a / san-CHEEZ-ee-a)
Acanthaceae: The Acanthus Family
SANCHEZIA
Medium-sized herbaceous shrub; beautiful variegated large leaves; spikes of red flowers
Zones 10b and 11 as permanent perennials; zone 9b as returning perennials
Partial shade to partial sun
Water lover
Average well-drained soil
Propagation by cuttings and (sometimes) seed

A genus of about 20 species of herbs and subshrubs in tropical America. They have oppositely arranged heavily veined large leaves and terminal spikes of white, yellow, or red tubular flowers. One species is very widely planted in tropical regions for its outstandingly beautiful large leaves and lovely red and yellow flowers. *Sanchezia speciosa* (spee-see-O-sa) (synonym *S. nobilis*) is native to Ecuador and northeastern Peru. It grows to 6 or sometimes as much as 8 feet in height with square reddish stems carrying beautifully variegated leaves. The 18-inch-long short-stalked (red) broadly elliptic leaves are pointed at both ends. The midrib and lateral veins are colored yellow or sometimes red. The plants bloom at any time of the year if the weather is warm and they are large enough, which means 2 or 3 feet in height with full-sized leaves. The inflorescences are terminal one-sided spikes of 2-inch-wide ovate red bracts enclosing several narrowly tubular 2-inch-long deep yellow flowers, only two of which are open at any given time. This exceedingly attractive shrub for semi-shady areas is possibly the most spectacular shrub that can be grown under such conditions. The plants suffer damage at freezing or below temperatures but, with the return of warm weather, grow back from their root system if the temperature does not fall below nor stay in the low 20s for very long. They do not, however, grow fast enough to usually form flowers in zone 9. Plate 346.

SANSEVIERIA (san-se-VEER-ee-a)

Agavaceae: The Agave Family
SNAKE PLANT; MOTHER-IN-LAW'S TONGUE; BOWSTRING HEMP
Rosettes of stiff, tough, succulent, variegated leaves; spikes of spidery white fragrant flowers
Zones 10 and 11
Partial shade to sun
Average but regular amounts of moisture; drought tolerant when established
Average well-drained soil
Propagation by root division, transplanting of suckers, and cuttings

A genus of about 70 clumping herbaceous plants with rhizomatous roots and usually stemless rosettes of tough, fibrous, stalkless, stiff, erect, and succulent leaves that are usually variegated to some extent. The inflorescence is a scape of very fragrant small narrowly tubular greenish white flowers. These species occur in the drier regions of tropical Asia and Africa and are used in the garden to add texture and color to drier but not necessarily fully sunny sites. They are striking and often bold-appearing plants that are easily overused because of their harsh features. Mass plantings tend to be tiresome rather than beautiful. All species are tolerant of seacoast conditions where they are much planted and where they usually flourish in full sun. *Sansevieria arborescens* (ahr-bo-RES-senz) is indigenous to tropical East Africa. It is one of the few species that makes a stem. It grows to 4 or 5 feet in height with clumping stems and 18-inch-long flat or cylindrical grayish green linear-lanceolate leaves that are spirally arranged around the stems. It flourishes in full sun, but is more a curiosity than beautiful, although it fits well into rock or succulent and cactus gardens. *Sansevieria trifasciata* (try-fay´-see-AIT-a) occurs naturally in tropical northeastern South Africa, Mozambique, Zaire, and Zimbabwe. It is a clumping stemless rosette of erect stiff and thick 3- to 4-foot-long linear-lanceolate long-tipped leaves that are somewhat twisted and a light silvery green with jagged horizontal bands of deep green. This species, with its many cultivars, is by far the most widely grown snake plant. Among the multitude of forms are some far removed from the looks of the type and hardly recognizable as its ancestors. *Sansevieria trifasciata* '**Hahnii**' (HAHN-ee-eye) is a dwarf with short wide leaves of various variegations. *Sansevieria trifasciata* '**Laurentii**' (law-RENT-ee-eye), with thick beautiful margins of deep yellow, is probably the most widespread cultivar. Other cultivars have completely linear leaves about a half inch wide. The smaller cultivars look good in the cactus and succulent garden.

SAPOTA. See *Manilkara*.

SARACA

(SAH-ra-ka / sa-RAK-a / sa-RAHK-a)
Caesalpiniaceae (Leguminosae), subfamily
    Caesalpinioideae: The Cassia, Royal Poinciana
    Family
Common names vary according to species
Small evergreen trees; large glossy pinnate leaves;
    large clusters of fragrant red and yellow flowers
Zones 10b and 11
Partial shade to partial sun
Water lovers
Rich, humusy, well-drained soil
Propagation by seed and air-layering

A genus of eight slow-growing evergreen shrubs and trees in tropical Asia from India to southern China and through Malaysia. The leaves are large, alternately arranged, even-pinnate, and leathery. The new leaves are limp and colored pink, bronzy-orange, or bronzy-violet. The inflorescences appear on the branches, twigs, and sometimes the trunks, and are large globose heads of yellow, pink, or red fragrant four-"petaled" blossoms with long protruding stamens. The fruit is a linear-oblong tough red or purple-red pod which is, itself, quite attractive. The flowers lack petals or corollas, and it is the sepals that make the show. These trees usually bloom several times a year according to the monsoonal periods in their native haunts, but in the mainland United States seem to bloom only in spring. They are almost unbelievably beautiful of both leaf and flower and deserve much greater attention from tropical gardeners in the United States than what they presently get.

Saraca declinata (dek-li-NAIT-a / dek-li-NAHT-a) is indigenous to Malaysia and Indonesia. It grows to about 30 or sometimes 40 feet in height with 18-inch-long leaves composed of four to eight pairs of foot-long lanceolate heavily veined leaflets on 4-inch-long petioles. The tree blooms in spring with 6-inch-wide clusters of deep yellow flowers, which turn a deep red before they fall.

Saraca indica (IN-di-ka) is native to Southeast Asia through Malaysia and Indonesia, where it grows along riverbanks to about 30 feet in height with a dense oblong crown. The leaves are as much as a foot long and are composed of four to six pairs of 6- to 8-inch-long oblong to narrowly lanceolate nearly stalkless leathery but glossy leaflets. The new leaves are limp, drooping, and a beautiful rose to bronzy purple in color. In the United States the trees usually bloom in spring with 4-inch-wide densely packed almost stalkless heads of orange-yellow red-stamened flowers that change to a scarlet color as they age. The tree is called asoka and sorrowless tree in India, where Hindus believe that it wards off adversity. Hindus also believe that the Buddha was born under an asoka tree.

Saraca thaipingensis (ty-ping-ENS-is) occurs naturally along the Malay Peninsula. It grows to about 20 feet with leaves as much as 2 or even 3 feet long and consisting of five to eight pairs of lanceolate heavily veined drooping almost stalkless leaflets. The species blooms in March and April in the United States with foot-wide flower heads consisting of deep yellow blossoms with a red "eye" which, with time, turn a fiery orange-red. Plate 347.

SARITAEA (sair-i-TEE-a)

Bignoniaceae: The Catalpa, Jacaranda, Trumpet-
    Vine Family
No known English common name
Large tendril-climbing vine; glossy leaves; pink and
    purple trumpet-shaped flowers
Zones 10b and 11
Sun to partial sun
Average but regular amounts of moisture
Average well-drained soil
Propagation by seed and cuttings

A monotypic genus indigenous to Colombia and Ecuador. *Saritaea magnifica* (mag-NIF-i-ka) (synonyms *Arrabidaea magnifica*, *Bignonia magnifica*) is a vigorous twiner and tendril-climbing vine that can grow to the tops of large trees. It has leaves consisting of only two leathery but glossy elliptic, ovate or obovate 4-inch-long dark green leaflets with a terminal tendril replacing the middle or third leaflet. The vine blooms several times a year, but primarily and most abundantly in the winter. The flowers are in few-flowered terminal clusters of 3-inch-long by 4-inch-wide, rose to light purple tubular to funnel-shaped blossoms. Each flower has a white or yellow throat marked with darker lines and five corolla lobes. This beautiful vine will not usually recover from being frozen to the ground. It is not drought tolerant and needs a fairly humusy soil to grow and flower at its best.

SCAEVOLA (SEE-vo-la)

Goodeniaceae: The Scaevola Family
Common names vary according to species
Small to large evergreen shrubs; distinctive white,
    blue, or purple fan-shaped "half" flowers
Zones vary according to species
Sun
Moisture requirements vary according to species
Average well-drained soil
Propagation by seed and cuttings

A genus of almost 100 species of herbs and shrubs in tropical and subtropical regions around the globe. They have alternately arranged or whorled simple and entire leaves, and flowers that are solitary or in few-flowered clusters in the leaf axils. Each blossom has a deeply five-lobed corolla that circumscribes only a semicircle of about 180°, giving the blossom the appearance of a half-opened fan.

Scaevola aemula (EEM-yoo-la) is indigenous to a very large area of tropical Asia and is hardy in zones 10 and 11 as a permanent perennial and in zone 9 as a returning perennial. It grows to as much as 3 feet but is mostly smaller and can be pruned to be so. It has a sprawling and trailing habit, which makes it a very good subject for rock gardens and for planting on or atop walls. The 2-inch-long bright green leaves are somewhat nondescript: elliptic to lanceolate to obovate in shape, usually toothed on the margins, and slightly pubescent. The 1- to 2-inch-wide bluish lavender flowers cover the plant when in bloom. Each corolla segment has a band of white or yellow at its base, giving the flower an "eye." The plants bloom year-round in frost-free climates but mainly in the spring, summer, and fall. There are now superior cultivars available, such as *Scaevola aemula* **'Blue Wonder'** and *Scaevola aemula* **'Purple Fanfare',** which are more floriferous and which have slightly darker and larger flowers. Plate 348.

Scaevola frutescens. See *S. taccada.*

Scaevola koenigii. See *S. taccada.*

Scaevola plumieri (ploom-ee-ER-ee) occurs naturally on the tropical coasts of the Gulf of Mexico and the Caribbean as far north as the southern portion of Florida and southernmost Texas. In Florida it grows on the Atlantic coast as well as that of the Gulf of Mexico, where it is called the inkberry. It is adaptable to zones 10 and 11 but is grown and often survives in zone 9b. This beautiful woody-clumping shrub grows to as much as 6 feet in height. It has succulent mostly trailing stems that are woody at their bases but root at the nodes where they touch the sand. In time, these stems make large and dense colonies. The leaves are stiff but succulent and leathery, a deep olive green to light yellow green in color, 1 to 3 inches long, and obovate to spatulate in shape with a strong midrib. They are bunched at the ends of the branches. The few-flowered inflorescences occur in the leaf axils year-round but mostly in the warmer months. Each "half" flower is about an inch wide, and the corolla lobes are white to a pale pinkish white in color. The fruits are usually less than a half inch long and are like green olives in shape and color until they mature, at which time they are jet black. There are few lovelier shrubs for planting near the seacoast, but the plants demand full sun. This species is often used as a low and informal hedge as it is not injured by pruning once or twice a year, and it is unequaled as a large groundcover for the seashore. The plants do not require a seacoast to thrive, but are equally at home inland if the soil is fast-draining and the plants are not over watered.

Scaevola taccada (ta-KAHD-a) (synonyms *S. frutescens, S. koenigii*) is very widespread, occurring naturally on most coasts and islands of both the Pacific and the Indian Oceans. It is hardy in zones 10 and 11, although it has been known to sprout from the root in zone 9b. It is sometimes called the beach plum or naupaka. It grows to 15 feet or sometimes more in sites protected from the wind and is quite possibly the perfect beach plant, growing on dunes and very near the salt water. In fact, it may grow too well near the seacoast, where it is crowding out the native *S. plumieri* in Florida. It is a magnificent shrub, similar to *S. plumieri* but growing much larger and definitely more treelike with

somewhat larger flowers whose corolla lobes are white but have pink blotches and lines. The plants bloom year-round. The beautiful leaves are 6 to 10 inches long, similar to those of *S. plumieri*, but are usually notched on their ends. This large shrub is easily trained to tree form if that is desired and older plants along the windswept coasts have the look of 100-year-old bonsai subjects. The fruits, unlike those of *S. plumieri*, are white when mature and slightly larger than those of the native inkberry. Naupaka does not tolerate shade, must have sun, and should not be watered unless real drought ensues.

SCHAUERIA

(SHOW-'r-ee-a / show-ER-ee-a
Acanthaceae: The Acanthus Family
No known English common name
Small herbaceous shrub; large glossy leaves; large
    spikes of golden spidery flowers
Zones 10 and 11 as permanent perennials; zone 9b as
    returning perennials
Sun to partial sun
Water lover
Rich, humusy, moist, well-drained soil
Propagation by cuttings and (sometimes) seed

A genus of only eight evergreen species of subshrubs in tropical eastern Brazil. They have large oppositely arranged heavily veined leaves and terminal spikes of narrowly tubular red or yellow flowers that are interspersed with long narrow bracts, which give a shaggy or spidery appearance to the inflorescences. One species is fairly common in cultivation in tropical and subtropical regions. *Schaueria flavicoma* (flay-vi-KO-ma) grows to as much as 6 feet tall and is densely covered with 6- to 8-inch-long lanceolate deep green leaves with deeply depressed midrib and lateral veins that are usually a lighter color than the blade. The plant blooms most of the year with 5-inch-tall spikes of 2-inch-long very narrow tubular bright yellow flowers and many inch-long threadlike yellow bracts. The flowers are most attractive against the dark green foliage. Given regular and adequate supplies of moisture and a fairly decent soil, these plants are quite easy to grow and maintain, and they look especially good close-up.

SCHEFFLERA

(SHEF-fle-ra / shef-FLER-a)
Araliaceae: The Aralia, Schefflera Family
SCHEFFLERA
Shrubs and small trees; large palmate compound
    leaves; large terminal spikes of red and yellow
    flowers
Zones vary according to species
Light requirements vary according to species
Average but regular amounts of moisture
Average well-drained soil
Propagation by cuttings, air-layering, and
    (sometimes) seed

An immense genus of more than 700 species of shrubs, trees, and even a few vines in tropical America, tropical Asia, tropical Australia, and the Pacific Islands. All have palmately compound leaves that are generally circular in outline with long-stalked leaflets. The tiny flowers are in small umbels along a spikelike raceme or panicle. The relatively few species in cultivation are used mainly as foliage plants and are exceedingly bold and tropical in appearance. The genus was originally as large as it is now, but underwent much division and segregation of its various groups in the early twentieth century. These various genera have mostly been reunited into this very large super-genus, including the ubiquitous umbrella tree, which was formerly put into the genus *Brassaia*.

Schefflera actinophylla (ak-tin´-o-FYL-la) (synonym *Brassaia actinophylla*) is indigenous to northeastern Australia and southern New Guinea and is hardy only in zones 10b and 11 and marginal in zone 10a. This species is one of the world's most popular plants both as a houseplant and as a small tree outdoors in tropical regions. Indeed, it has become naturalized in most truly tropical areas. The umbrella tree, Queensland umbrella tree, or octopus tree grows to as much as 60 or even 80 feet in its native habitat, but is usually about half that height in cultivation. It grows fast into a single-trunked or multitrunked tree with a mostly oblong crown. When it is of age, the tree forms a spreading canopy of relatively few thick branches. The stout trunks and larger branches sometimes form aerial roots when older, especially in wet climates. The bark is tan-colored to medium brown. In wet tropical regions the tree sometimes begins life as an epiphytic strangler, much like so many members of the genus *Ficus*. Then, when mature, it usually forms thick surface roots, again much like many *Ficus* species. Although quite impressive as a single-trunked specimen, it seems even more picturesque when trained to three to five trunks. The 2-foot-wide leaves are some of the world's most spectacular and beautiful. They consist of 9 to 15 oblong glossy deep green foot-long drooping leaflets on stalks 3 inches long and radiating in a circular fashion from the end of the 1- to 2-foot-long main petiole. The midrib of each leaflet is prominent and usually of a lighter color than the rest of the blade. The general size and shape of the leaves have led to the comparison to an umbrella in one of the common names. The trees generally bloom in the summer in the Northern Hemisphere with terminal and spectacular, erect but spreading 2- to 3-foot-long spikelike inflorescences from the highest branches. The tiny red flowers are bunched into rounded umbels along the six to more than a dozen spikes radiating from the end of the each branch. Each group of inflorescences has an appearance rather like the arms of an octopus. The fruits are a half inch wide, round, and scarlet in color. Trees in flower or fruit are an unforgettable sight and one of the glories of the tropical plant world. There are several cultivars in the trade.

Schefflera actinophylla **'Amate'**, with thicker and wider leaflets, is the most worthy. These trees look and perform their best only in sunny and moist sites with a fairly fertile soil. They are intolerant of frost and are damaged by temperatures at or below freezing, although they often survive to maturity in zone 10a and in zone 9b can be maintained for years as a returning multibranched shrub until a devastating freeze occurs. If frozen to the ground, they are slow to recover and often succumb to fungus and insect damage before they can attain any size. The tree is usually pruned to a multistemmed shrub form for use as a houseplant. Plate 349.

Schefflera arboricola (ahr-bor´-i-KO-la / ahr-bo-RIK-o-la) (synonym *Heptapleurum arboricolum*) is native to Taiwan and is hardy in zones 10 and 11 and marginal in zone 9b as a medium-sized shrub. In frost-free regions it can attain a height of 15 or even 20 feet with an equal or greater spread. Like its larger relative *S. actinophylla* (umbrella tree), the plant often forms aerial roots from the trunks and larger branches when mature, and it more often than not starts its life as an epiphyte on large trees. It is possible to train the shrub when young to a single-trunked or few-trunked small tree, although its natural penchant is to grow as a large multistemmed shrub. Its stems are pliable and tend to be almost vinelike. The leaves, which are similar to those of the umbrella tree but smaller, are carried on 4- to 6-inch-long petioles. The 7 to 11 elliptic to obovate leathery dark green leaflets, radiating from and forming a circle at the ends of the leaf stalks, are each from 2 to 6 inches long and are held on short petioles usually less than an inch long, thus giving this species a completely different landscape look from that of the umbrella tree The plants do not often bloom in cultivation but, when they do, the terminal inflorescences are about a foot wide, flat or dome-shaped, and dense with umbels of tiny yellow or orange flowers. The flowers are nothing as spectacular as those of the umbrella tree, and the fruits are small orange to black berries. The plant is invaluable for creating a tropical look in large shrub borders or as an accent because of its ability to flourish in partial shade. It also makes a beautiful espalier against semishady walls where its beautiful leaf form can be silhouetted, and there are few more beautiful large groundcovers, especially in the marginal parts of its climatic range. These little trees are usually called Hawaiian schefflera or dwarf schefflera, though they are neither Hawaiian in origin nor especially dwarf in habit.

Schefflera arboricola **'Variegata'** (vair-ee-a-GAIT-a) has variegated leaves with a wonderful yellow, but it is somewhat more tender to cold and tends to revert to the type. There is nothing finer for adding tropical color to shady situations. This species is not drought tolerant and needs a good and friable soil to do its best. It is somewhat hardier to cold than its great relative the umbrella tree, is usually undamaged by temperatures above 30°F, and recovers well from temperatures above 25°F, although it does not grow nearly as fast as the umbrella tree. It has been grown in zone 9b as a large groundcover in sun and shade where it has recovered, albeit slowly, from occasional temperatures in the low 20s.

Schefflera elegantissima. See *Dizygotheca elegantissima.*

Schefflera pueckleri (PYOOK-lur-eye) (synonym *Tupidanthus calyptratus*) is native to northeast India, Myanmar (Burma), southeastern China, and Southeast Asia, where it grows to 30 or 40 feet usually as a multi-trunked tree. It is hardy only in zones 10b and 11 and marginal in zone 10a. The plant was introduced into horticulture in the 1960s as *Tupidanthus calyptratus,* and this is still its name in almost all nurseries. It is similar to *S. actinophylla* (umbrella tree) but is, if possible, even more attractive except for its less spectacular inflorescences. The tree's canopy is naturally rather oblong in form, but it can also be wide and spreading, and the trunk is low-branched and massive in older specimens. The tree also sometimes becomes scandent and acts almost as if it were a giant liana. Its habit mostly is determined by pruning (or acts of nature) when young. Its leaves, while strongly resembling those of the umbrella tree, are slightly larger with more pendulous and more evenly sized oblong deep green and glossy leaflets. The usually 10 leaflets form a complete circle from the ends of the main petiole. The leaves are borne on red petioles, the leaflets have red stalks, and the prominent midrib of each leaflet is of a lighter color than the blade or is sometimes red in color. The inflorescence seems rare in cultivation. It is terminal on the branch ends and consists of a spreading panicle of strange yellowish green cup-shaped fleshy flower receptacles whose outer perimeter bears a semicircle of white stamens. This odd flower form has resulted in the vernacular name of mallet flower in some regions. Whether trained as a narrow-crowned small tree, a multitrunked silhouette, or a widespreading dense shade tree, there is nothing more spectacular and tropical looking than a large "tupidanthus." Its beauty is simply stunning.

SCHISMATOGLOTTIS

(shis-mat´-o-GLAHT-tis)
Araceae: The Calla Lily, Jack-in-the-Pulpit Family
DROP-TONGUE
Low herbaceous perennials; lance-shaped variegated
    leaves
Zones 10b and 11; marginal in zone 10a
Shade to partial shade
Water lovers
Humusy, moist, well-drained, acidic soil
Propagation by transplanting of suckers

A genus of about 100 species of dieffenbachia-like herbaceous perennials mostly in tropical Asia with a few in tropical America. This genus is closely allied to and quite similar to *Dieffenbachia.* Most species have above-ground stems bearing relatively large ovate to lanceolate-shaped, usually variegated leaves, but some have underground stems. All have long leaf stalks that wrap around the stem. They have inflorescences characteristic of the family: a spathe and spadix, the former usually long and trailing and soon deciduous. The genus name is Greek for "falling tongue." Several species such as ***Schismatoglottis concinna*** (kahn-SIN-na), ***Schismatoglottis emarginatus*** (ee-mar´-ji-NAIT-us), and ***Schismatoglottis picta*** (PIK-ta), are widely used in tropical shady sites for their beautiful green and white leaves, often bluish green and silver. There are several gorgeous hybrids and cultivars, including ***Schismatoglottis* 'King of Hearts'**, ***Schismatoglottis* 'Queen of Spades'**, and ***Schismatoglottis* 'Sliver Light'**, that have larger and more colorful leaves than the unadulterated species. These lovely plants grow from 1 to 2 feet in height with ovate to lance-shaped leaves and are intolerant of full sun. They need warmth, moisture, and a rich soil to look their best. All species make stupendously beautiful groundcovers as well as accents in shady borders.

Schismatoglottis roebelinii. See *Aglaonema crispum.*

SCHIZOLOBIUM (skits-o-LO-bee-um

Caesalpiniaceae (Leguminosae), subfamily
    Caesalpinioideae: The Cassia, Royal Poinciana
    Family
BRAZILIAN FERN TREE
Tall evergreen or deciduous tree; immense fernlike
    foliage; spectacular yellow flowers
Zones 10b and 11; marginal in zone 10a
Sun to partial sun
Water lover
Average well-drained soil
Propagation by seed

A genus of only two species of immense evergreen trees in rain forests of tropical America. The two species are quite similar, with one growing slightly larger than the other. Indeed, there may be only one distinct species. ***Schizolobium parahyba*** (par-a-HY-ba) is found naturally in southern Mexico, Central America, and southwards through Colombia, eastern Peru, and Brazil north of São Paulo. Although its total range is vast, like many tropical lowland rain forest trees it is nowhere abundant. In climax growth the tree may reach heights of 150 feet or more in its stretch for the tree canopy, and under these conditions its trunk is truly massive and buttressed like many other rain forest giants. Planted or growing in the open, however, the tree seldom attains much more than half that height, and its smooth light brown to gray trunk is not so massive. It is one of the world's fastest growing large trees, usually making as much as 6 feet of trunk growth a year, especially when young. The tree's crown is wide and spreading, but has few branches. In youth it often grows to a height of 20 feet or more before it first branches, giving it the aspect of a giant tree fern because of its extraordinary foliage. The light green bipinnate leaves, which are clustered near the ends of the branches, are each as much as 5 feet long. They are the second largest pinnate leaves among flowering plants, right behind the pinnate-leaved palms. Some ferns have larger pinnate leaves, but they are not included in the flowering plants. The trees are often deciduous briefly in midwinter, especially with drought or cold, but they are as likely to retain their leaves through the winter if the season is wet and warm. They usually bloom in early spring, sometimes as early as February but usually in March, with large spreading but erect terminal panicles of golden yellow five-petaled flowers. This glorious tree is obviously not for tiny gardens, but if there is room for it there is no more breathtaking sight in or out of bloom for the tropical gardener. It should be more widely planted in southern Florida. It is sometimes grown in zones 10a and 9b as a giant tree fern or palmlike shrub because of its fantastic and gargantuan foliage. It never, of course, blooms under such environmental conditions. Plate 350.

SCINDAPSUS. See *Epipremnum*.

SEAFORTHIA. See *Ptychosperma*.

SELENICEREUS (se-len´-i-SEER-ee-us)
Cactaceae: The Cactus Family
NIGHT-BLOOMING CEREUS; QUEEN-OF-
   THE-NIGHT; SNAKE CACTUS
Rounded or angled sprawling thick stemmed
   cactuses; immense white nocturnal flowers
Zones 10 and 11
Partial shade to sun
Average but regular amounts of moisture
Sandy, humusy, well-drained soil
Propagation by seed and cuttings

A genus of about 20 scandent and sprawling, semi-epiphytic cactus species with long slender ribbed stems bearing clusters of short spines and aerial roots that help support the long stems in their climbing and clambering habit. Members of the genus are found mostly in Mexico, but also in the West Indies, Central America, and northern South America. The various species are mostly quite similar, differing mainly in the number of ribs or angles on the stem and the exact shape of the flowers. The most widely grown and available species is *Selenicereus grandiflorus* (gran-di-FLOR-us). Other species that will be found are *Selenicereus hamatus* (ha-MAHT-us), *Selenicereus macdonaldiae* (mak-DAHN-'l-dee-eye), and *Selenicereus pteranthus* (ter-ANTH-us). These cactuses are grown only for their flowers, which are more than a foot wide by about as long and shaped like a slender scaly slightly spiny tube that expands at its end into a great starburst of petals. The numerous 8-inch-long obovate pure white petals are surrounded by many linear and longer brownish white or greenish white sepals, and in the center is a great mass of yellow stamens and anthers surrounding a many-parted yellow stigma. All species are summer-blooming. They are best grown where these flowers can be viewed at close range. A trellis is perfect for this as is a low wall over which they can cascade. Needless to add, they are exceptionally stunning in bloom when snaking their way through and over other succulents, rocks, and cactus plants if they can be grown out of full sun. They tolerate the sun in cool coastal Mediterranean climates like that of the southern California coast, but they need protection from the blazing midday orb in hot climates. They withstand slight frost and are nearly impossible as year-round garden subjects outside zones 10 and 11, although they often survive for years in the warmer parts of zone 9b. Unlike true desert dwellers, these species need regular amounts of moisture, and they enjoy high relative humidity as well. They do well near the seacoast, but are not as tolerant of saline conditions as some other genera like *Hylocereus* and need to be out of reach of the ocean spray.

SENECIO (se-NEE-see-o)
Compositae (Asteraceae): The Daisy Family
MEXICAN FLAME VINE; ORANGE-GLOW
   VINE
Tall evergreen twining vine; glossy fleshy leaves;
   spectacular red, orange, and yellow flowers
Zones 10b and 11 as permanent perennials; zones
   10a and 9b as returning perennials
Sun
Average but regular amounts of moisture
Average well-drained soil
Propagation by seed and cuttings

An immense and very varied genus of small trees, shrubs, herbaceous subshrubs, vines, and xerophytic succulent species found in almost all parts of the world. The name of the genus has been changed to "*Pseudogynoxis*" but this change is quite recent and not in most of the literature and it seems best here to keep it in *Senecio*. The only things these species have in common are the alternately arranged leaves and the particular form of their daisylike flowers. Most species are not particularly tropical in appearance, but some are, including *Senecio johnstonii* (giant groundsel) of Africa's equatorial mountains and *S. petasitis* (California geranium). Most of these species are adaptable only to Mediterranean or even cooler and frost-free climates because they occur naturally in such climes. *Senecio confusus* (kahn-FYOO-sus) is native to tropical Mexico. It grows to 30 feet or more in frost-free climates and also trails and covers the ground if a support is not available. It makes a dense cover of 3- to 5-inch-long lanceolate fleshy dark green leaves with toothed margins. The vine blooms year-round in tropical regions with terminal clusters of inch-wide or wider daisylike flowers whose rays are a vivid orange to orange-red in color that ages to a deep red. The central disk flowers are a wonderful gold color. The plant is carefree but not drought tolerant and will often grow quickly back from the roots after being frozen to the ground, even in zone 9a. Plate 351.

SENNA. See *Cassia*.

SERENOA (ser-e-NO-a / se-RAYN-o-a)
Palmae (Arecaceae): The Palm Family
SAW PALMETTO
Small clumping fan-leaved palm; stiff leaves of green
    or silvery blue green
Zones 7 through 11; marginal in zone 6b
Sun to partial sun
Average but regular amounts of moisture; drought
    tolerant when established
Average well-drained soil
Propagation by seed

A monotypic palm genus native to the coastal plain areas of South Carolina and Georgia, westward through southern Alabama to southern Mississippi and in all parts of Florida. *Serenoa repens* (REE-penz) is a low-growing clumping species never more than 10 feet tall whose trunks are usually underground and branching subterraneously to form large colonies of leaves. The result is a dense mass of stiff palmately segmented 3-foot-wide light green or blue-green leaves carried on leaf stalks longer than the blade is wide. The margins of the petioles are serrate, leading to the vernacular name saw palmetto. Each leaf, whether blue or green, is quite beautiful as its outline is usually a complete circle. This suggests that the leaf masses might look better if occasionally thinned out. The clumps can be as much as 15 feet wide by 10 feet tall. Occasionally the shaggy trunks on some individuals emerge and grow mostly prostrate along the ground for as much as 8 or 10 feet. The flowers and fruits are mostly hidden by the densely packed leaf clusters, but the fruits are noticeable by their unpleasant odor when they are ripening. The form with silvery blue or blue-green leaves is quite a bit more attractive than the plain green-colored form, but both make a dramatic and tropical looking accent in the landscape. Great masses of the plants are somewhat tiresome to contemplate, however. Neither form is very attractive when isolated. The great clumps look ever so much better when integrated into a shrub border or mixed with tall trees. In its native haunts the palm grows mostly under tall pine trees whose shade is ephemeral. It is very tolerant of seashore conditions as long as it is above the highest tide lines. The transplanting of large specimens from the wild is seldom successful. Plate 352.

SESBANIA (ses-BAIN-ee-a)
Papilionaceae (Fabaceae, Leguminosae), subfamily
    Papilionoideae: The Bean, Pea Family
Common names vary according to species
Large shrubs and small trees; pinnate leaves; large
    wisteria-like clusters of white, yellow, or red
    flowers
Zones 10 and 11 as permanent perennials or trees;
    anywhere as annuals
Sun
Average but regular amounts of moisture
Sandy, well-drained soil
Propagation by seed

A genus of about 50 species of mostly herbaceous large shrubs and a few small woody trees in tropical and subtropical regions. The mostly evergreen leaves are even-pinnate and often large. Some species enter a period of dormancy and lose their leaves with the advent of cold weather. The inflorescences are axillary racemes consisting of many pealike flowers mostly in colors of red and yellow, a few with white or purplish blossoms. The pods are usually large, but not especially attractive and their removal, if possible, from the plants as they form allows these shrubs and little trees to flower for a longer period. The plants are often called rattlebox because the seeds in the mature pods are usually loose and make noises when the fruits are shaken. Many shrubby species are somewhat weedy in habit and are short-lived. These often are treated as very large annuals as they grow quickly and bloom within one season. The tree species are also relatively short-lived for trees, but they are fast growing and invariably beautiful of leaf and blossom. All species revel in sun and warmth and usually are prolific self sowers. The genus was for many years known as "*Daubentonia*." Although the seeds of a few species are sometimes used by poor southerners in the United States as a coffee substitute, most species have poisonous seeds and the grower is advised against experimentation.

Sesbania grandiflora (gran-di-FLOR-a) is indigenous to tropical areas of Asia but has become naturalized in most tropical and subtropical regions including southern Florida and the West Indies. It is the largest-growing species in the genus, attaining a height of 40 feet in its native habitats and in tropical areas to which it is well adapted. It usually is no more than 20 feet tall in the continental United States. This fast-growing tree has a rather picturesque flat-topped aspect and shaggy furrowed contorted trunk and branches. The leaves, which are usually a foot long with as many as 60 inch-long deep green oblong leaflets, are reason enough to grow the plant. The tree blooms year-round in tropical regions but most heavily in spring and summer. The inflorescences are few-flowered, but the individual blossoms are large (as much as 4 inches long). Their color varies from light pink to deep red or maroon, and they are typically pea-shaped. The amazing pods are as much as 2 feet long. The tree goes under the colloquial names of parrot flower, vegetable hummingbird, sesban, and corkwood tree.

Sesbania punicea (poo-NEES-ee-a) (synonym *Daubentonia punicea*) is native to southeastern Brazil, Uruguay, and northeastern Argentina. It grows to as much as 12 feet and is usually a large shrub but may be easily trained into a small tree form. The leaves are as much as 8 inches long and consist of as many as 20 pairs of oblong medium to dark green inch-long leaflets. The leaves are deciduous in cold or dry winters. The plants bloom in spring and summer with beautiful wisteria-like pendent clusters of scarlet to brick red or purplish red pea-shaped blossoms. These are some of the most beautiful flowers in the genus. The pods are rather small for the genus, usually no more than 4 inches long and four-angled (or four-squared). The little tree seeds itself profusely, especially in warm regions where it has become somewhat of a pest. It is very fast growing. Common names include dwarf poinciana, false poinciana, and purple rattlebox.

Sesbania tripetii (try-PET-ee-eye) (synonym *Daubentonia tripetii*) is indigenous to northern Argentina and southern Brazil. It is a small usually flat-topped tree growing to a maximum of 15 feet or so in height with fernlike pinnate foot-long leaves with as many as 24 pairs of inch-long oblong medium to dark green leaflets. The leaves usually are deciduous in cold or dry winters. The plants bloom whenever the weather is hot. The pendent racemes of pealike orange to reddish orange blossoms are followed by elongated squared (or four-winged) pods that turn almost black before dropping. Although the blossoms are never scarlet in color, the most common vernacular name for the plant is scarlet wisteria tree; red wisteria is also applied. Plate 353.

SETCREASEA. See *Callisia*.

SIDERASIS (sy-de-RAY-sis)
Commelinaceae: The Spiderwort Family
No known English common name
Low clumping rosettes of large colorful fleshy hairy
    leaves; pink and violet flowers half hidden by
    leaves
Zones 10b and 11
Partial shade to partial sun
Average but regular amounts of moisture
Humusy, well-drained soil
Propagation by transplanting of suckers and
    (sometimes) by seed

A genus of only two species of low-growing fleshy-leaved herbs in tropical eastern Brazil. *Siderasis fuscata* (fyoos-KAIT-a) (synonyms *Pyrrheima fuscata*, *Tradescantia fuscata*) is a clustering rosette of foot-long ovate fleshy leaves that are a dark olive green to chocolate green above with central gray or silvery longitudinal markings. The underside of the leaf is a vivid dark purplish red in color and the entire leaf, above and below, is covered in soft reddish orange hairs that give an iridescent sheen to both surfaces. The plants bloom in cycles year-round with small clusters of inch-wide deep rose to blue-violet three-petaled flowers in the leaf axils. The blossoms are often half hidden by the leaves, but they are quite beautiful. The plant makes a very beautiful groundcover in tropical regions and looks especially good interplanted with rocks and small ferns or planted in soil pockets on stone walls. It may also be grown on large trees as an epiphyte if soil can be provided. Small plants with yellow-variegated leaves or yellow flowers seem to bring out the leaf colors of *Siderasis*. This species does not tolerate frost, but usually returns from its rhizomatous roots if the temperature does not go much below 30°F.

SIDEROXYLON. See *Mastichodendron*.

SIMAROUBA (sim-a-ROO-ba)
Simaroubaceae: The Quassia, Paradise Tree, Tree-
    of-Heaven Family
PARADISE TREE; BITTERWOOD
Tall evergreen tree; smooth reddish bark; large
    leathery pinnate leaves; red and black fruit
Zones 10 and 11; marginal in zone 10a
Sun to partial sun
Average but regular amounts of moisture
Average well-drained soil
Propagation by seed

A genus of six evergreen shrubs and trees in tropical America. They have alternately arranged even-pinnate leaves, erect panicles of small five-petaled white or yellow flowers, and clusters of berrylike fruit. One species is planted in southern Florida for its beauty. *Simarouba glauca* (GLAWK-a) is indigenous to southern Florida, the West Indies, Mexico, and northern Central America. It grows slowly to 50 feet or sometimes more with a dense and rounded or oblong crown atop a generally smooth but minutely scaly barked straight gray or more often reddish brown trunk. The leaves are large and exceptionally beautiful, to as much as 18 inches long, and are composed of 10 to 16 oblong to slightly obovate leathery leaflets. Each leaflet is short-stalked, 2 to 5 inches long, dark green and glossy above, and grayish green beneath with a prominent and lighter colored midrib. The leaflets are progressively larger from the bottom to the apex of the rachis and often have their margins turned under. The new foliage is a very lovely reddish bronze in color. The trees bloom in spring and early summer with large axillary or terminal panicles of many small pale yellow starlike flowers. The inch-long ovoid rosy-orange berrylike fruits ripen to a blackish purple color. They are reputedly edible but insipid. This tree occurs naturally near the coast as well as inland and is nicely adapted to seaside plantings. Indeed it is very beautiful in any sort of planting and is one of the finest native trees for landscape purposes.

SINOCALAMUS. See *Dendrocalamus*.

SOLANDRA (so-LAN-dra)
Solanaceae: The Petunia, Potato, Tomato Family
CUP-OF-GOLD VINE; CHALICE VINE;
    GOLDCUP VINE
Large, heavy evergreen vines; large lustrous leaves;
    large trumpet-shaped gold and yellow flowers

Zones 10 and 11 as permanent perennials; zone 9b as
    returning perennials
Sun to partial sun
Average but regular amounts of moisture
Average well-drained soil
Propagation by cuttings and (sometimes) seed

A genus of eight large heavy-stemmed lianas in tropical America. They have large mostly lanceolate leathery but glossy alternately arranged leaves and large
yellow or golden long bell-shaped wide-flaring flowers
with five-lobed corollas. There are often purple-brown
stripes in the flower's throat. The plants bloom mostly
in the late autumn, winter, and early spring, almost
never in the summer. The flowers of all species are similar to each other and are, as a group, quite distinctive
and easily recognized once seen. While the blossoms
are fragrant, especially at night, the scent is neither that
sweet nor powerful; it is reminiscent of vanilla or coconut. In the West Indies and on the coasts of Mexico
these vines can be seen clambering and rooting along
rocky ledges and cliffs above the churning surf, which is
to say that they are tolerant of ocean spray and, to some
extent, saline soil and that they make magnificent subjects for seashore plantings. The beautiful thick ropelike
stems grow very fast and range very far (200 feet according to Edwin A. Menninger). They root at the
nodes and simply scramble over almost anything including other vegetation. They look best when trained
against walls or onto some sort of trellis, pergola, or
fence, and nothing is more spectacular for training up
the walls of houses to spill out over roofs and windows.
These species may be severely pruned for any purpose
as they grow very fast and bloom on new growth. All do
best with regular and adequate supplies of moisture,
but are not particular as to soil. While they luxuriate in
full sun in all but hot arid regions, they seem to prefer
having their roots shaded from the sun and heat. The
specific names are very much confused in the nursery
trade, partly because the flowers of all species are so
much alike. The flowers are said to be poisonous.

Solandra grandiflora (gran-di-FLOR-a) (synonym *S. nitida*) is indigenous to the West Indies. It has
leaves that are about 8 inches long and elliptic to obovate in shape, with prominent and lighter colored
midribs. The flower is 8 to 10 inches long, a great elongated bell shape with a quite narrow bottom end in the
calyx. The corolla lobes are scalloped and distinctly
rolled back towards the stem, creating a tall goblet
shape. The blossoms open pale yellow to almost white,
but change to a deep golden yellow. The inside of the
flower sports five rather narrow brownish purple lines
down the middle of each corolla lobe. Plate 354.

Solandra guttata (gut-TAHT-a) is native to Mexico. It has elliptic to oblong leaves similar to those of *S.
grandiflora* but not exceeding 6 inches in length. The
undersides of the leaves as well as the stems are covered
in a fine pubescence. The flowers are slightly larger than
those of *S. grandiflora* and usually a deeper color, oth-

erwise they are quite similar. Many plants offered for
sale as "*S. guttata*" are, in reality, *S. maxima*.

Solandra hartwegii. See *S. maxima*.

Solandra laevis. See *S. longiflora*.

Solandra longiflora (lahn-ji-FLO-ra) (synonyms
S. laevis, *S. macrantha*) is native to the West Indies. Its
leaves and flowers are quite similar to those of *S. grandiflora* except that its corolla is narrower, longer, and
more narrowly funnel-shaped rather than bell-shaped,
sometimes to a foot long, and the flowers seldom
deepen in color from the near-white color with which
they open nor are they ever golden in color.

Solandra macrantha. See *S. longiflora*.

Solandra maxima (MAX-i-ma) (synonyms *S.
hartwegii*, *S. nitida*) is indigenous to Mexico. It is the
most widely grown and widely available of the species.
In fact, much of the material offered for sale as other
species turns out to be this one. The glossy 6- or 7-inch-
long leaves are elliptic in shape, glabrous, and about 6
inches long, with a prominent and lighter colored
midrib and depressed lateral veins. The 6- to 7-inch-
long flowers resemble those of the other species except
that they are more open and flaring, and the corolla
wider and flatter, thus allowing the inside of the flower
with its narrow chocolate-purple lines to be more easily
seen. The blossoms age to a deeper golden color than
that of the other species. This species most resembles
the so-called chalice shape. Plate 355.

Solandra nitida. See *S. maxima*.

SOLANUM (so-LAHN-um / so-LAIN-um)
Solanaceae: The Petunia, Potato, Tomato Family
Common names vary according to species
Herbs, shrubs, vines and small trees; usually hairy or
    felty; distinctive flattish flowers with corona
Zones vary according to species
Sun to partial sun
Average but regular amounts of moisture
Average well-drained soil
Propagation by seed and cuttings

An immense genus of 1500 or more species of herbs,
herbaceous shrubs, trees, and vines in all regions of the
globe except for the Arctic and Antarctic, but especially
well represented in the warmer parts of the earth. The
only constant and defining characteristics are the alternate arrangement of the leaves and the structure of the
white, yellow, blue, or purple flower: a disk, flat or not,
of five corolla lobes with a central column of anthers
adherent to the pistil. Most species, whatever their
form, are weedy in nature, although many have bold
and often segmented if coarse foliage. Almost all can be
grown as annuals in colder climates and most reseed
themselves in all but cold regions.

Solanum giganteum (jy-GANT-ee-um) is native
to tropical East Africa, India, and Sri Lanka, and is
hardy only in zones 10 and 11 although it often survives
and returns from the root in zone 9b. This large shrub
quickly grows to 8 or 10 feet and has large roselike

prickles on the stems. It can be pruned to simulate a small tree. It has thick soft grayish green leaves that are 10 inches long, lance-shaped, heavily veined above, and white pubescent beneath. The plant blooms irregularly most of the year but heaviest in the warm months. The small clusters of pale bluish violet flowers give way to half-inch-wide round scarlet succulent cherrylike fruits. The plant provides nice texture and form to shrub borders and is quite attractive, especially in fruit. It usually self seeds.

Solanum hispidum (HIS-pi-dum) (synonym *S. warscewiczii*) is indigenous to southeastern and southern Mexico and is hardy in zones 10 and 11, although it usually recovers in zone 9b. It grows to about 6 feet and has very bold and dramatic foliage along with spiny stems covered in reddish brown hairs. The deep olive green leaves are felty with the reddish brown hairs and are about a foot long and broadly ovate in shape, but are deeply divided into about 10 lance-shaped lobed segments. The plants bloom most of the year with small clusters of white flowers followed by tiny round yellow fruits. The plant can be used in the landscape as *S. giganteum* is used and provides a dramatic accent of texture and color. It is sometimes called the devil's fig.

Solanum jasminoides (jaz-min-OY-deez) is indigenous to a large area of eastern Brazil and is hardy in zones 9 through 11, although it is often killed back in zone 9. The potato vine is a sprawling, slender-stemmed wispy-looking but fast-growing vine that twines its way to 20 or even 30 feet if not frozen back. The leaves, which are about 3 inches long, lance-shaped, and glossy bright green in color, drop if exposed to near-freezing temperatures. The older leaves are sometimes lobed. The plant is nearly everblooming in frost-free regions. It has large but loose-flowered clusters of inch-wide satiny white starlike blossoms. It makes a nice pergola cover and is attractive but not spectacular. Its delicacy is not appropriate to every situation and it looks best as a filler or light screen, especially with a background of darker foliage that highlights the delicate white flowers.

Solanum macranthum. See *S. wrightii.*

Solanum marginatum (mar-ji-NAIT-um) is native to Ethiopia and is adaptable to zones 10 and 11. It grows to 6 or 8 feet and is a coarse but fascinating large-leaved shrub with yellow or white sharp spines and velvety white hairs on every part of the plant including the leaves. The leaves are 8 to 10 inches long, lobed like many deciduous oak tree leaves, deep green with white veins, and covered in a white velvety pubescence. Later, this pubescence, except for the very margins of the leaf surface, falls off the top surface of the leaf, leaving the green and white veins prominently displayed. The plant blooms mainly in the summer with small white flowers that form small yellow fruits. The shrub is drought tolerant and is a stunning subject for sunny and somewhat arid areas of the rock garden or as a loud accent in the flower border.

Solanum melongena (mel-ahn-JEN-a) is native to southern India and Sri Lanka and is hardy in zones 10 and 11. Known as the eggplant of vegetable gardeners, it is usually grown as an annual. It is, or at least some forms of it are, of great beauty with large lobed leaves, purplish new growth, and large colorful fruits of white, green, yellow, and especially purple. The type grows to 4 or 5 feet, and the cultivars with extra large dark purple fruits need to be staked as the very heavy fruits ripen. The pendent 2-inch-wide flowers are violet to almost blue in color. More ornamental and more manageable are the smaller-fruited cultivars whose fruit comes in just about every color including red, except for true blue. These smaller-fruited varieties have more rounded, truly egg-shaped fruit. The plants need a soil fairly rich in organic matter, are not drought tolerant, and require almost full sun to bloom and fruit well.

Solanum pseudocapsicum (soo-doe-KAPS-i-kum) occurs naturally in northern Africa and extreme southern Europe, but has now become naturalized in almost every tropical and subtropical region of the world. It is hardy only in zones 10 and 11, but is widely grown as an annual and is known to many gardeners as the Jerusalem cherry. It grows only to 3 or 4 feet in height with deep green glossy elliptic to obovate 4- or 5-inch-long leaves with prominent and lighter colored midrib and lateral veins. It blooms year-round with tiny white flowers that form beautiful scarlet or golden fruits about the size of cherry tomatoes. There are several named very dwarf and compact cultivars with usually larger and deeper-colored fruit. These little plants add great color to any sunny or half-sunny site and are virtually carefree. They should not be planted where children are liable to pick and eat of the mildly poisonous little "cherries."

Solanum quitoense (kee-toe-ENS-is) is indigenous to the lower slopes of the eastern Andes Mountains in South America, primarily in Peru, and is hardy in zones 10 and 11. This scrambling shrub with spectacular leaves and fruit usually needs to have its growing tips pinched back, especially in hot climates, to maintain a decent shape. The plant grows to 6 or even 8 feet in height, and the beautiful leaves are from 10 to almost 24 inches long and are broadly ovate to broadly lanceolate in shape, with large rounded scallops along the leaf margin. New growth is densely covered in a lovely purple pubescence, which often lasts on the leaf to maturity. Otherwise the leaves age to a deep olive green color with reddish purple to yellowish white midribs and lateral veins. The tiny white flowers, formed on the stems and branches, are mostly hidden by the leaves and are not important in the landscape, but they form beautiful 2-inch-wide rounded fruits that look like small tomatoes and are equally edible and rather sweet in taste. People in this plant's native haunts call it naranjillo (nah´-rahn-HEE-yo) or lulu and make several beverages from the little fruits and eat them fresh. This very interesting plant is not completely at home in hot regions as it hails from low mountainous areas. It needs partial shade in hotter areas, and the soil, which should be rich in organic matter, should never be allowed to completely dry out.

Solanum rantonnetii (ran-toe-NET-ee-eye) is native to northern Argentina and Paraguay and is hardy in zones 9b through 11 and marginal in zone 9a. The correct name for this plant is now *Lycianthes rantonnetii* (liss-ee-ANTH-eez) in the solanum family. It is a fast-growing scrambling almost vinelike shrub that is used as a vine, a shrub, a large groundcover, and even a "standard" small tree form. It grows to as much as 20 feet in height as an espalier or trained to a trellis, but is usually only 6 to 8 feet tall as a shrub or standard. The leaves are about 4 inches long, ovate to lanceolate in shape, and a dull green above and below; they drop in freezing weather. The plant blooms year-round in frost-free regions, with large loose-flowered clusters of bright violet blossoms. It needs sun, regular moisture, and good drainage. It looks its best grown as an espalier or a vine.

Solanum robustum (ro-BUS-tum) is indigenous to eastern Brazil and is hardy in zones 10 and 11. Except for the lack of white venation and tomentum and for having slightly larger and more elongated leaves, it is similar to, is used for the same landscaping purposes as, and needs the same culture as *S. marginatum*.

Solanum seaforthianum (see-forth´-ee-AHN-um) is indigenous to a large area of Brazil and is also found in Paraguay. It has been naturalized in many tropical and subtropical regions of the world. This vine is hardy in zones 10 and 11. It is a small slender-stemmed thing, which rarely grows to more than 12 feet. The leaves are as much as 8 inches long and are a dull smooth green. Quite variable in shape, the leaves are usually pinnately segmented, but the lobes or segments may be so deep as to create a false compound pinnate leaf. The vine loses its leaves with the approach of freezing temperatures and, if the mercury falls much below freezing, is killed to the roots and does not usually resprout. The plant blooms in cycles all year with loose clusters of inch-wide violet to almost blue flowers. Each flower has narrowly lanceolate corolla lobes that do not usually overlap. The small fruits are round and red but not edible. The plant is sometimes called the Brazilian nightshade.

Solanum warscewiczii. See *S. hispidum*.

Solanum wendlandii (wend-LAN-dee-eye) is native to Costa Rica and is hardy in zones 10b and 11 and marginal in zone 10a. This beautiful vine is a rampant and fast grower to as much as 50 feet. It tends to become bare at the base of the stems when older and should be underplanted with smaller growing vegetation to mask the stems. The leaves are as much as a foot long. Older leaves are usually pinnately segmented to the point that the leaf looks compound and even-pinnate, while the younger leaves are mostly only shallowly segmented, usually into three parts. The petioles are fairly long and, like the midribs of the leaves, are often armed with small hooked spines. This great vine usually suffers leaf drop when temperatures fall below 40°F and is killed by temperatures much below freezing. The plant blooms in summer and fall with large panicles of light blue to violet 2- to 3-inch-wide blossoms. It is called variously Costa Rican nightshade, marriage vine, divorce vine, and paradise flower. This species is one of the most beautiful flowered in the genus. It needs a fairly rich soil and is not drought tolerant.

Solanum wrightii (RYT-ee-eye) (synonym *S. macranthum*) is native to tropical Brazil and Bolivia and is hardy in zones 10 and 11. It is naturally a small tree, growing very quickly to 20 feet or sometimes more, but may also be grown as a large shrub. The leaves are from 10 to 18 inches long and are ovate in outline, but the margins are fairly deeply and pinnately segmented, giving the blade the general form of an acanthus leaf. There are usually short sharp spines along the prominent and lighter colored midrib. The plant blooms year-round, but most heavily in the summer with clusters of 3-inch-wide pale violet to almost white flowers. This potato tree has beautiful leaves and flowers and makes a truly spectacular small tree in tropical regions.

SOLESTEMON. See Coleus.

SOPHORA (so-FOR-a)
Papilionaceae (Fabaceae, Leguminosae), subfamily
   Papilionoideae: The Bean, Pea Family
Common names vary according to species
Large evergreen shrub and small evergreen tree; large
   pinnate leaves; wisteria-like flowers
Zones vary according to species
Sun to partial sun
Average but regular amounts of moisture; drought
   tolerant when established
Average well-drained soil
Propagation by seed and cuttings

A genus of about 50 deciduous and evergreen shrubs in all but cold regions of the world. They have odd-pinnate leaves, pealike flowers in terminal clusters, and cylindrical usually four-angled pods that are constricted between the relatively large seeds.

Sophora secundiflora (se-kun´-di-FLOR-a) is indigenous to southern New Mexico, central, western, and southern Texas, and adjacent northern Mexico. It is hardy in zones 7 though 11 and marginal in zone 6. This evergreen large shrub or small tree grows slowly to as much as 30 feet in height. It naturally makes a tree form in all but the coldest parts of its range and is very picturesque. The trunk is low-branched, the branches are sharply ascending, the bark is black and fissured, and the tree's dense crown is usually oblong but may be somewhat spreading. The tree grows very slowly and is easily kept as a wide dense shrub. The odd-pinnate leaves are usually no more than 6 inches long with 5 to 13 pairs of elliptic to oblong leathery but glossy very deep green and almost stalkless leaflets. The tree blooms in late winter and spring anytime from early February to April with 5-inch-long densely packed terminal mostly one-sided racemes of bluish violet pealike flowers. The extremely fragrant flowers smell of grape Kool-Aid, almost to the point of being overpowering. The 6- to 8-inch-long pods, which are formed by early summer, are light brown and pubescent when young but soon turn bluish gray, resulting for most of the hot months in an appearance that suggests the tree is again in flower. The pods do not open for many months, but when they do they reveal beautiful shiny scarlet rock hard seeds. The tree demands perfect drainage and is drought tolerant when established but appreciates irrigation under such conditions. It grows naturally on mostly limestone-based soils, but seems indifferent to the pH level as long as it is nonacidic. The tree does not look good nor does it grow well or bloom in shade. It would seem to be a perfect small tree for southern Florida as it flourishes in limy soils but, as it turns out, it seems to need a winter chill to some extent to flower well. It should, however, be more widely planted in central and northern Florida. It is generally called Texas mountain-laurel or mescal-bean in its natural habitats as the seeds are very poisonous and supposedly narcotic and hallucinogenic. It is not, of course, in any way related to the true mountain laurel, *Kalmia latifolia*, of the Appalachian Mountains. Plate 356.

Sophora tomentosa (toe-men-TOE-sa) is almost worldwide in its tropical distribution and no one seems certain just what its original habitat might have been. In the Americas it is found in virtually every tropical or subtropical locality, from southern Florida and extreme southern Texas down through much of South America. It is hardy in zones 10 and 11 and marginal in zone 9b but often survives even in zone 9a. This shrubby species grows to as much as 15 feet or more and usually as wide. In the warmer parts of its range it is often a small tree and can be trained to that form when young in tropical areas. The beautiful odd-pinnate leaves are about a foot long and consist of 9 to 23 elliptic leathery but deep glossy green and slightly pubescent leaflets. Each leaflet is nearly stalkless and exhibits a prominent and somewhat depressed midrib. The new growth is silvery pubescent. The plant blooms year-round in frost-free regions with terminal mostly one-sided racemes of golden yellow pealike flowers. These flower spikes are erect when first formed but soon become non-erect to almost pendent because of the many blossoms and the length of the raceme, which is as much as 18 inches long. The pods are as much as 8 inches long and are similar in appearance and habit to those of the mescal-bean, originating as brownish and furry but later turning gray. The pods are constricted between the seeds, leading to the most common vernacular name, necklace-pod. The shrub readily self sows in tropical and subtropical regions. This spectacular plant is carefree in its requirements, needing only sun and warmth to flourish. It is drought tolerant but also luxuriates in moist soil as long as it is well drained, and it tolerates

salinity in the soil as well as the air—a hard-to-beat combination.

SPATHIPHYLLUM

(spayth-i-FYL-lum)
Araceae: The Calla Lily, Jack-in-the-Pulpit Family
PEACE LILY
Small to large herbaceous perennials; large leaves; tall
  calla-lily-like white flowers
Zones 10b and 11; marginal in zone 10a
Bright shade
Water lovers
Humusy, well-drained soil
Propagation by transplanting of suckers and by seeds

A genus of 36 evergreen slow-clumping large-leaved rhizomatous herbs in tropical America, the Philippines, and Indonesia. None of the plants has aboveground stems as the leaves arise directly from the ground in dense clusters. Each leaf is on a stalk that is usually as long as the blade, which may be as much as 3 feet long. The fleshy and leathery dark green leaves, which are oblong, lanceolate, or ovate in shape and always have a tapering point, have prominent and depressed veins so deep as to give a corrugated look to the blade. The plants bloom year-round as long as the weather is warm. The single-stalked flowers rise well above the pseudo-rosette of foliage. Each flower is typical of the family: a large white spathe half surrounding the cream-colored to green spadix of tiny bisexual flowers. The plants vary from the above description only in size, leaves, and flowers among the many cultivars and hybrids. Some of the plant bodies are scarcely more than a foot tall, while others exceed 5 feet in height. Some leaves are narrow, others are broad, ranging in length from less than a foot to well over 3 feet. Some of the flowers are relatively narrow and as small as 3 inches long, while others may be the better part of a foot long.

These plants have three requirements that must be met if they are to be grown successfully: fertile but friable soil rich in organic matter such as compost or leaf mold and one that drains very freely; very bright or high shade but no direct sun unless it be very late afternoon or very early morning sun; and a constant supply of moisture and humidity. They benefit greatly from regular applications of organic fertilizers such as diluted fish emulsion. Anything stronger is liable to push green growth at the expense of flower production and may also burn the leaves. Some species often sprout from their roots if frozen to the ground and the soil remains unfrozen, but this phenomenon is not completely dependable and the plants usually do not grow fast enough to bloom the season after being cut back. These are not plants for arid regions, including frost-free deserts. Although they flourish in warmth, they tolerate occasional cold snaps and still look good. There are few more exciting and lovely sights than a mass of the smaller varieties used as a large groundcover in bright shade, or a large cultivar used as an accent in bright shady borders, especially when in flower. In such plantings the larger cultivars, which are superb, imposing, and spectacular, are as regal as small palms.

SPATHODEA (spa-THO-dee-a)
Bignoniaceae: The Catalpa, Jacaranda, Trumpet-
Vine Family
AFRICAN TULIP TREE
Large evergreen tree; large pinnate leaves; spectacular
clusters of red, orange, and yellow flowers
Zones 10b and 11; marginal in zone 10a
Sun
Average but regular amounts of moisture
Sandy, humusy, well-drained soil
Propagation by seed and cuttings

A monotypic genus native to tropical Central Africa, principally Uganda and western Kenya. After *Delonix regia* (royal poinciana), **Spathodea campanulata** (kam-pan´-yoo-LAIT-a) is the world's most beautiful flowering tree. It is a large tree growing very quickly to as much as 75 feet in its native habitat and to at least 50 feet in cultivation. It usually forms a more or less vase-shaped but broad-topped crown of a few large branches atop a smooth light-colored high-branching trunk. The crown may also assume a more oblong or narrow shape. Although there are relatively few branches, the tree's canopy is fairly dense because of the very large leaves. These great closely set leaves occur mostly along the terminal one-third of the thick smooth branches, leaving much beautiful trunk and branch material visible. Each odd-pinnate leaf is as much as 2 feet long and consists of 9 to 21 leathery but glossy deep green ovate-lanceolate 5-inch-long leaflets, each with a prominent red or cream-colored midrib and depressed lateral veins. The tree generally blooms in winter and spring, usually from early December through March, but sometimes sporadically during the rest of the year. The great round and flattish flower clusters are terminal on the branches and are composed of a multitude of claw-like or keel-shaped cinnamon-colored flower buds, which open from the rim of the cluster inward. Each bud splits apart to allow the 5-inch-long by 3-inch-wide bell-shaped corolla to emerge. The tulip-shaped corolla is five-lobed but divided into two main parts (i.e., it is two-lipped). Each lobe is somewhat fringed and a deep orange-red to pure scarlet in color with usually yellow margins. The erect slender brown pods are 6 to 8 inches long and two-sectioned and, at maturity, split in two to release hundreds of wafer-thin flat seeds that float in the wind. There is a pure yellow-flowered form of the tree that is almost as spectacular as the more common red-flowered form and it comes true from seed. As they form, the flower buds are often turgid with rainwater. Then, when the brown leathery calyx starts to split in efflorescence, it can discharge the collected water all at once. This phenomenon has led to the common name of fountain tree. Occasionally the name flame of the forest is used, which is unfortunate as there are at least two other tropical trees burdened with this appellation. This landscape subject is nearly carefree once established. It flourishes in wet or dry soils but prefers regular and adequate amounts of moisture. It requires nearly full sun to bloom well. The tree is intolerant of frost, and young trees are especially prone to such damage. Yet the tree survives as a giant shrub in the warmer parts of zone 9 and is so fast growing that it often makes enough growth in one season to bloom before the next freeze occurs; it is never a real tree in regions subject to frost, however. As is often the case, such beauty as that of the African tulip tree does not come without a price tag of some sort and in this case it is in the form of fairly weak and brittle wood that is vulnerable to hurricane and other storm damage. Plates 357 and 358.

SPHAEROPTERIS. See *Cyathea*.

SPIRONEMA. See *Callisia*.

SPONDIAS (SPAHN-dee-as)
Anacardiaceae: The Mango, Cashew, Pistachio,
Sumac Family
Common names vary according to species
Small and medium evergreen trees; large pinnate
foliage; orange, red, and purple edible fruit
Zones 10b and 11; marginal in zone 10a
Sun to partial sun
Average but regular amounts of moisture
Average well-drained soil
Propagation by seed and cuttings

A genus of 10 evergreen or deciduous small to large trees in tropical Asia and tropical America. They have large odd-pinnate leaves, terminal panicles of small flowers, and large berrylike edible fruit.

Spondias axillaris. See *S. mombin*.
Spondias cytherea. See *S. dulcis*.
Spondias dulcis (DOOL-sis) (synonym *S. cytherea*) is indigenous to Indonesia eastward through Polynesia. It grows to a height of 60 feet or even more in its native habitat, but is usually no more than 40 feet tall in cultivation. It forms a spreading but open crown of foliage carried on few branches above a beautiful smooth gray or tan-colored trunk. The pinnate leaves are very large and very beautiful. They are rather bunched at the ends of the large branches and are as much as 30 inches long, with 9 to 27 ovate to elliptic to lanceolate 4-inch-long glossy deep green leaflets whose margins are remotely toothed. The tree is briefly deciduous in midwinter if the weather is cold or dry. The tree blooms in the spring with large terminal panicles of tiny greenish white flowers. The fruits, which mature in autumn or even early winter, are formed in pendent clusters of two to three. Each fruit is plum-shaped to round, light green to pale yellow, and about 3 inches long but maturing to a golden color suffused with red and speckled with dark

red and purplish brown. The edible fruits are reportedly sweet but also acidic with a hint of pineapple, and they usually fall from the tree while still green. The tree is superbly beautiful in the fall and quite attractive the rest of the year, even if bare of leaves. It is sometimes called the ambarella or the otaheite apple.

Spondias lutea. See *S. mombin.*

Spondias mombin (MAHM-bin) (synonyms *S. axillaris, S. lutea*) occurs naturally in rain forests of the West Indies, southern Mexico, Central America, and southwards into northern Brazil and Peru. It grows to 60 feet or more and forms a spreading canopy above a large stout trunk that may be 3 feet in diameter with very thick light cinnamon-brown-colored fissured and somewhat patchy bark. The leaves are 12 to 18 inches long with 9 to 19 lanceolate to obovate 6-inch-long light green leaflets. Each leaflet has a prominent and lighter colored midrib, lateral veins, and a tapering point. Like most other *Spondias* species, this one is deciduous in cold or drought conditions. The tree usually blooms in late spring and early summer with large terminal panicles of tiny greenish white fragrant flowers. The fruits, which are in pendulous clusters, are 1 to 2 inches long, ovoid, and orange-yellow in color. They look like the fruits of *Eriobotrya japonica* (loquat) and are edible but supposedly quite acidic, often with a tinge of turpentine to the taste. This species is the grandest and most beautiful in the genus and should be much more widely used as a landscape subject.

Spondias purpurea (poor-POOR-ee-a) is indigenous to a wide expanse of tropical America from southern Mexico through Central America into northern Brazil and Peru, where it may grow to 50 feet in height. In cultivation it is usually no more than 20 feet tall with an open broad canopy and is sometimes only a sprawling giant shrub. The leaves are 4 to 10 inches long and consist of 7 to 19 small 2-inch-long elliptic to oblong or even obovate light green nearly stalkless leaflets. The terminal leaflet usually is ovate to almost deltoid in shape, and the new growth is a beautiful bronzy red to bronzy purple color. Like *S. dulcis,* this species may be deciduous in midwinter with cold or drought. The trees bloom in spring with terminal hairy panicles of tiny pinkish or purplish flowers. The fruits usually mature in late summer and are small irregularly shaped, yellow-orange to red to purple in color, and supposedly taste like acidic plums. The tree is called the purple mombin, red mombin, Spanish plum, or hog plum.

STAPELIA (sta-PEL-ee-a)

Asclepiadaceae: The Milkweed, Madagascar Jasmine
   Family
STARFISH FLOWER; STARFISH PLANT;
   CARRION FLOWER
Small low clumps of fleshy four-angled stems; large
   five-petaled red, yellow, brown, or purple flowers
Zones 10 and 11; marginal in zone 10a
Partial to full sun

Drought tolerant
Sandy, well-drained soil
Propagation by seed and cuttings

A genus of about 100 species of small succulent herbs in tropical eastern and southeastern Africa eastward through Madagascar, the Arabian Peninsula, and into India. They form sometimes large basally branching clusters of linear, very fleshy four-angled usually curving, ascending, and usually waxy but also often pubescent stems. The ridges of the stem angles are scalloped into upward-pointing soft "teeth." Stem color varies from bright green to olive green to a definite brownish green, and stem length is from 4 or 5 inches to as much as 18 inches. The plants bloom in summer with solitary or small-clustered flowers mostly at the base of but also along the length of the stems. The flowers are as much as 18 inches wide on short pedicels and cup-shaped or more often star-shaped, with five ovate spreading corolla lobes. The yellow, orange, red, brown, or purple lobes are usually mottled or striped with varying hues of the above colors and are often covered in long hairs. The flowers often have a small star within the star. This small five-pointed growth in the center of the flower is actually the stamens grown together and is called a "corona." These blossoms have, for the most part, a fetid odor reminiscent of decaying meat, which attracts flies, their only pollinators. In spite of the usual odor, which does not, fortunately, carry in the air very far from its source, the flowers are extremely attractive and exotic. The large-flowered plants are almost startlingly spectacular, especially in relation of the flower size to that of the plant stems. These fantastic succulent plants are too often neglected in tropical and subtropical gardening and should be much more widely planted for their picturesque form and dazzlingly exotic blossoms. They are wonderfully outlandish in rock gardens or the cactus and succulent garden, where they create a miniature landscape of their own if planted with even smaller succulents, since they look like Lilliputian models of tree cactus species. Because of their arching stems and habit of forming fairly wide clusters of stems, they are also superb as semi-cascading subjects atop stone walls, especially when in bloom as the flowers are often bigger and more pendulous than the plant's stems. Besides warmth, these plants need at least a half day's sun to bloom and a very freely draining sandy soil. They need to be watered when dry in the summer growing season, but wet and cold winters often lead to stem rot, which is usually fatal. They should never be planted where water is liable to stand, even in the summer.

Stapelia ambigua (am-BIG-yoo-a) is indigenous to southern South Africa and will withstand a touch of frost. The stems are to 10 inches tall, olive green in color, and pubescent. The flowers form at the base of the stems and are 5 inches wide, pinkish brown to light pink in color, with horizontal red stripes. The margins and center of the flowers have dark red hairs.

Stapelia asterias (a-STER-ee-as) occurs naturally

in southwestern South Africa. The pubescent stems are as much as a foot tall and are pale green in color. The flowers are borne at the base of the stem. Each blossom is about 4 inches wide and brownish red to purplish red in color with horizontal yellow lines, and is covered in purplish red hairs.

Stapelia gigantea (jy-GANT-ee-a) is native to northwestern South Africa. Its stems are about 10 inches tall, pale green in color, and pubescent. The flowers form at the base of or along the stems. Each blossom is 18 inches wide, yellow in color with horizontal red stripes, and covered in purplish red hairs. Plate 359.

Stapelia glandulifera. See *S. glanduliflora.*

Stapelia glanduliflora (glan´-dyoo-li-FLOR-a) (synonym *S. glandulifera*) is native to eastern South Africa. Its stems are about 8 inches tall, dark green in color, and waxy in texture. The flowers form at the base of the stems. Each blossom is about 2 inches wide and pale yellow in color with small purple-red dots and red horizontal lines. The blossoms are densely covered in long milky white nearly translucent hairs.

Stapelia hirsuta (heer-SOOT-a) is indigenous to South Africa. The stems are 12 inches tall and grayish green in color, with flowers forming at their bases. Each blossom is 5 inches wide and light purple-brown with horizontal lines of yellow and purple. The margins are covered with purplish red hairs.

Stapelia nobilis (NO-bil-is) occurs naturally in central East Africa. Its stems are 8 inches tall, pale green in color, and pubescent. The flowers are borne at the base of or along the stems. Each blossom is 12 inches wide and brownish yellow in color with horizontal red stripes, and is densely covered in purplish red hairs.

Stapelia variegata (vair´-ee-a-GAIT-a) is native to southwestern South Africa. The stems grow to 8 inches in height and are dark green in color with a waxy texture. The plant flowers at the base of its stems with 3-inch-wide blossoms that are more or less cup-shaped and greenish yellow in color, with dark purple-brown spots, a dark purplish ring in the center of the flower, and a yellow starlike corona in the very center.

STEMMADENIA (stem-ma-DEN-ee-a)

Apocynaceae: The Oleander, Frangipani, Vinca
 Family
No known English common name
Small evergreen trees; beautiful large glossy leaves;
 white or yellow fragrant pinwheel-like flowers
Zones 10b and 11; marginal in zone 10a
Sun to partial sun
Water lovers
Average well-drained soil
Propagation by seed and cuttings

A genus of seven evergreen or deciduous trees and shrubs in tropical America. They are characterized by large oppositely arranged elliptic or lance-shaped leathery but glossy leaves, small terminal clusters of large fra-grant salverform five-lobed white or yellow flowers, and strange two-parted colorful fruits.

Stemmadenia galleottiana. See *S. littoralis.*

Stemmadenia glabra. See *S. obovata.*

Stemmadenia littoralis (lit-toe-RAL-lis) (synonym *S. galleottiana*) occurs naturally in rain forests from southern Mexico through Central America and into northern South America. This small tree grows rather slowly to about 25 feet, with a spreading and irregular crown of glorious foliage atop a short pinkish-tan-colored smooth trunk. The glossy and thin but leathery leaves are elliptic in shape, to 6 inches long, more or less pendulous, a bright to olive green in color with deeply depressed and lighter colored midrib and lateral veins. The leaves are found mostly at the ends of the tiered branches. The plants bloom usually in late summer and early autumn, but a few flowers are sporadically produced all year. The terminal inflorescences are few-flowered and consist of three or four flowers, which are 5 inches long by 3 inches wide, and salverform in shape. The five overlapping slightly fringed corolla lobes are pure white in color with yellow throats. Their powerful fragrance suggests *Plumeria* (frangipani) species. The strange fruits, which form shortly after the corolla falls away, consist of two golden yellow half-inch-long parts held horizontally and directly opposite each other, each one shaped like an orange fruit segment. For a small tree this one has to rank high on the list of the world's most beautiful trees. Its form is reminiscent of the frangipani, but even more appealing, and the little orange fruits add an almost poignant touch of elegance.

Stemmadenia obovata (ahb-o-VAIT-a) (synonym *S. glabra*) is native to rain forests from southeastern Mexico southwards to Ecuador. It grows fairly slowly to about 30 feet or sometimes more, with a spreading canopy of tiered foliage atop a short smooth tan-colored trunk. The gorgeous leaves are about 8 inches long, elliptic to obovate in shape, leathery but glossy, and deeply veined above. The tree blooms year-round but mainly in the summer with terminal few-flowered clusters of 5-inch-long by 4-inch-wide pale yellow salverform flowers with a sweet and penetrating fragrance. The fruits are similar to those of *S. littoralis* but darker in color. This tree is, if possible, even more beautiful than *S. littoralis*.

STENOCEREUS (sten-o-SEER-ee-us)

Cactaceae: The Cactus Family
Common names vary according to species
Shrubby or treelike columnar ribbed spiny cactus
Zones vary according to species
Sun to partial sun
Drought tolerant
Sandy, well-drained soil
Propagation by seed and cuttings

A genus of about 24 cactus species. All have columnar and ribbed stems that are mostly ascending, and many are tree forms. They are usually very spiny. The diurnal or nocturnal flowers are bell-shaped or funnel-shaped, and the fruits are always spiny. Here included are some of the most striking large tree-form cactus species. They were once all in the genus *Lemaireocereus*, which is no longer a valid name.

Stenocereus dumortieri (doo-mor´-tee-ER-ee) (synonyms *Isolatocereus dumortieri, Lemaireocereus dumortieri*) is native to central and western Mexico and is hardy in zones 10 and 11. One of the largest cactus species, this tree grows to as much as 40 feet with many ascending bluish green branches. The stems or branches have usually six ribs (occasionally five and sometimes as many as nine) with whitish spines that age to black along their crests. The flowers are nocturnal and are about 2 inches long with white petals and brown sepals. This very picturesque and spectacular cactus species is alluringly dramatic against the skyline, as forceful as *Carnegiea gigantea* (sahuaro) and faster growing.

Stenocereus eruca (e-ROOK-a) (synonyms *Lemaireocereus eruca, Machaerocereus eruca*) is indigenous to Baja California and is hardy in zones 9b through 11. This species has more or less prostrate stems that may reach 20 feet in length. The stems root along the ground and, because of their spininess, have led to the plant's common name, creeping devil. The growing tips of the branches are erect and, because of their length, look like giant worms or snakes winding their way through the desert with their heads raised queryingly. The branches are about 4 inches thick with usually 12 ribs. The crests of these ribs are covered with very many large gray spines that age to yellow. The longest spines are about 2 inches. The stems tend to die at their points of origin after some years and this can leave a gap in the garden that can be filled with some contrasting type of plant or another stem of the creeping devil cactus. The large white or yellowish flowers are nocturnal and as much as 6 inches long. The egg-shaped fruits are about 2 inches long and scarlet in color. While drought tolerant, the plant is not completely happy in the hottest desert regions where it tends to be stunted unless given some shade during the hottest part of the day. The cactus is superb when planted en masse and lends a unique aspect to the cactus and succulent garden because of the creeping and very spiny stems that appear to be writhing.

Stenocereus marginatus. See *Pachycereus marginatus.*

Stenocereus thurberi (THURB-er-eye) (synonyms *Cereus thurberi, Lemaireocereus thurberi, Marshallocereus thurberi*) is native to extreme southwestern Arizona and the adjacent state of Sonora in Mexico. It is hardy in zones 9b through 11. One of the most beautiful cactus species, it forms a wide clump of 15-foot-tall sharply ascending grayish green stems. Each stem is unbranched, arises from the base of the plant, and has 12 to 17 deep ribs. Because of its form, this cactus is universally referred to as the organ-pipe cactus. Apart from *Carnegiea gigantea* (sahuaro), it is the most dominant and beautiful plant in the Organ-Pipe Cactus National Monument in southwestern Arizona. The numerous spines are black changing with age to gray. The flowers are diurnal and about 3 inches long with cream-colored to deep pink petals and dark red sepals. The round, scarlet, about 3-inch-wide fruits are said to be edible. Plates 296 and 360.

STENOCHLAENA (sten-o-KLEEN-a)
Blechnaceae: The Dwarf Tree Fern Family
No known English common name
Large magnificent climbing ferns with immense pinnate leaves
Zones 10 and 11; marginal in zone 9b
Partial shade to partial sun
Water lovers
Humusy, well-drained soil, leaf mold, or epiphytic mix
Propagation by root division and spores

A genus of only five fern species in tropical Africa through Malaysia and into Australia. They are ultimately epiphytic, but usually start life as terrestrial. Some of the largest fern fronds are found in this genus, which has been segregated from the giant fern family Polypodiaceae and is now scientifically grouped with the *Blechnum* ferns.

Stenochlaena palustris (pa-LUS-tris) is indigenous to eastern India eastwards through Australasia. It is similar to and is much more common in cultivation than *S. tenuifolia* but is smaller and not as impressive in the landscape.

Stenochlaena tenuifolia (ten´-yoo-eye-FO-lee-a) is native to Malaysia. There is no better tropical landscape subject than this magnificent and massive fern species. It grows as a terrestrial or spectacular groundcover and, climbing to the tops of the tallest trees, it flaunts its great 3- to 6-foot-long glossy light green pinnate fronds into the misty heights, creating the look of primal creation in a tropical or subtropical garden. Nothing is more tropical looking or adds more sense of depth and expanse to a garden than a plant like this when used as a groundcover that ascends into the trees. It grows fast with moisture, warmth, and humidity. Its slender stems are virtually hidden by the dense cover of noble fronds. This climbing fern does not like the full midday sun of hot climates, but luxuriates in bright shade with direct afternoon or morning sun. It is tender to frost but recovers quickly from ambient air temperatures slightly below freezing, temperatures which damage the fronds but not the stems. It even recovers at the base from a sharp frost below 30°F if planted in the ground and mulched. Plate 361.

STENOLOBIUM. See *Tecoma.*

STEPHANOTIS (stef-a-NOAT-is)
Asclepiadaceae: The Milkweed, Madagascar Jasmine Family

MADAGASCAR JASMINE; BRIDAL WREATH;
WAX-FLOWER
Large heavy evergreen vine; beautiful leathery glossy
    leaves; waxy white fragrant flowers
Zones 10 and 11
Sun to partial sun
Average but regular amounts of moisture
Average well-drained soil
Propagation by seed and cuttings

A genus of five evergreen twining vines in Madagascar eastward to Malaysia. They have oppositely arranged undivided leathery leaves, axillary clusters of funnel-shaped or salverform usually fragrant flowers, and large fleshy fruits. One species is very popular as an indoor or greenhouse plant and as a florist's flower. It is widely planted out in tropical regions for its beautiful leaves and fragrant flowers. *Stephanotis floribunda* (flor-i-BUN-da) is indigenous to the great island of Madagascar. It is a heavy vine with woody but ropelike stems that slowly twine to 12 or sometimes 15 feet in frost-free regions. The leathery, glossy, thick leaves are about 4 inches long, a very deep green in color, and oblong in shape with a short tip and a prominent and lighter colored midrib. The plant blooms off and on all year in tropical regions, but primarily in summer and autumn in about 2-month cycles or flushes. The flower cluster is formed on a long stalk from the end of which radiate in a circular fashion the long-stalked waxy pure white salverform and very fragrant blossoms. Each flower is about 2 inches long with a 2-inch-wide flare of the five ovate and pointed corolla lobes at the end. The flowers are quite long-lasting on the vine and when cut. In warm wet climates the plant occasionally produces fruits that are 6 inches long, very heavy and fat, and shaped like a ribbed cucumber. These fruits take at least 2 years to mature. The vine is relatively slow growing and needs a strong support as the thick stems and leaves are heavy. It usually needs to be tied at first to a lattice or other support around which it will twine, and it will not twine around any object more than about 2 inches in diameter. It tends to cascade as much as it twines and makes a beautiful display flowing over low walls and similar objects. It seems to flourish best when planted in a site where its roots are shaded and where its top is in sun or partial sun. Although it is capable of surviving mild drought conditions, it does not like such situations. It loves a fairly rich soil that is high in organic matter and appreciates monthly applications of diluted fish emulsion in the spring and summer. It is very tender to frost. Although it is fine at temperatures near freezing for short periods, anything below freezing severely knocks it back. A temperature of 25°F kills it to the ground, and it does not usually recover even with the return of warm weather in the spring. Plate 362.

STERCULIA (ster-KYOO-lee-a)
Sterculiaceae: The Cacao, Cola-Nut Family
INDIAN ALMOND; BANGAR NUT

Large deciduous tree; large compound leaves;
    malodorous flowers; colorful red and black fruit
Zones 10b and 11; marginal in zone 10a
Sun
Average but regular amounts of moisture
Humusy, well-drained soil
Propagation by seed

A large genus of about 200 species of evergreen and deciduous trees in tropical regions around the world but primarily in tropical Asia. They have various types of leaves, from simple and entire to compound. The small flowers do not have petals but rather enlarged sepals and are in large axillary panicles. The often colorful woody fruits, which are usually divided into several parts, are wont to split open before falling to reveal large black seeds. One species is widely planted as a shade tree and for the beauty of its leaves. *Sterculia foetida* (fee-TY-da / FET-i-da) is indigenous to an immense area of the Old World tropics, from tropical Central Africa eastward through Madagascar, India, Malaysia and into northern Australia. It grows quickly to almost 100 feet in its native haunts, but is usually not more than 60 feet tall in cultivation. The tree's crown is generally about as wide as the tree is tall, but may also be more elongated in shape. The smooth trunk is gray to cinnamon-brown, and the branches are mostly horizontal. The compound leaves are generally found near the ends of the large branches and look like a cross between the leaves of a *Schefflera* species and a *Castanea* (chestnut) species. They are long-stalked and the five to nine almost stalkless leaflets radiate from the end of the stalk in a circular fashion. Each leaflet is as much as 6 inches long, elliptic in shape, and a deep green in color with a very prominent yellowish midrib. The tree is usually deciduous from mid-December or early January until March, when the flowers appear in large drooping axillary panicles. Each blossom is 1 or 2 inches wide and lacks petals but has five petal-like orange or red fleshy sepals. The inflorescences are beautiful, but the flowers emit a truly unpleasant odor, one that is not easily overlooked and that reaches out from the tree along the breeze. The word *sterculia* is a form of the Latin word for "excrement" and *foetida* means "stinking." The fruit, which develops fairly quickly after the smelly blossoms fall, is a 3- to 5-inch-long rounded to greenish yellow pear-shaped two-sectioned woody pod that ages to a bright carmine red color and then splits open to reveal several bluish black to jet black half-inch-long hard seeds. The tree is intolerant of all but very light frosts. If one can endure the repellent odor of the flowers in the spring, this tree is most noble and beautiful in and out of leaf. Need one add that it is best planted away from living areas? Plate 363.

STETSONIA (stet-SO-nee-a)
Cactaceae: The Cactus Family
TOOTHPICK CACTUS
Immense tree-form cactus with many long spines;
    large nocturnal white flowers

Zones 10 and 11
Sun
Drought tolerant
Sandy, well-drained soil
Propagation by seed

A monotypic cactus genus native to northern Argentina and southern Bolivia. **Stetsonia coryne** (ko-RY-nee) is a tree-form cactus that grows to as much as 30 feet tall and as wide with a short stout gray trunk and many ascending branches. The trunk in mature specimens is as much as 2 feet thick. Each 4- to 6-inch-wide bluish green to gray-green branch sports eight or nine deep and narrow ribs whose crests bear numerous black and gray 4-inch-long spines. The visual aspect of mature plants is that of a cross between *Carnegiea gigantea* (sahuaro) and a giant cholla cactus. The long-necked nocturnal flowers are white and as much as 6 inches long with brownish or pinkish sepals. This outstanding landscape subject for the large cactus and succulent garden is almost overwhelming in its beauty and size. It is drought tolerant, but appreciates relief from severe conditions, especially in the summer. It is tolerant of saline spray and slightly saline soil and is superb for seashore gardens if protected from high winds.

STIGMAPHYLLON

(stig-ma-FYL-lahn)
Malpighiaceae: The Malpighia Family
BUTTERFLY VINE; BRAZILIAN GOLDEN
    VINE; ORCHID VINE
Large slender-stemmed evergreen twining vines; large
    clusters of bright yellow flowers
Zones 10 and 11 as permanent perennials; zone 9 as
    returning perennials
Sun to partial sun
Average but regular amounts of moisture
rich, humusy, well-drained soil
Propagation by seed and cuttings

A large genus of as many as 100 species of large twining vines in tropical America. They have oppositely arranged leaves, rounded showy clusters of yellow flowers, and samara-like fruits (i.e., dry, papery propeller-shaped winged fruits like those of elm and maple trees).

Stigmaphyllon ciliatum (sil-ee-AIT-um) occurs naturally from eastern Central America southwards to eastern Uruguay. It grows quickly to 20 or 30 feet in frost-free regions with slender stems covered in deep green paired, ovate 3-inch-long leaves whose margins have tiny hairlike teeth and whose midribs are a pale green. The vine blooms year-round in tropical areas, but always most heavily in summer with rounded 4- or 5-inch-wide axillary flower clusters. The individual flowers, which are a pure bright yellow and an inch or slightly more wide, consist of five fluted and fringed clawlike petals. Each petal is a narrow tube at its base that suddenly expands into a squared lobe. The flowers

are supposed to resemble those of the orchid genus *Oncidium*, but if they did *Oncidium* would not be so popular. I find the flowers shaped like blossoms of *Bauhinia* and even more like *Delonix regia* (royal poinicana). The color, however, is more like that of *Oncidium*. In any case the vine is almost covered by these lovely airy flowers when it is in bloom. Because of its nearly carefree cultural requirements, this species is a major landscape subject for tropical and subtropical regions. Plate 364.

Stigmaphyllon littorale (lit-toe-RAHL-ee) is native to southeastern Brazil, Uruguay, Paraguay, and northeastern Argentina. It is reasonably similar to *S. ciliatum*, but it is a larger and more vigorous vine. Growing to as much as 30 feet, it has larger but similarly shaped leaves and smaller flowers in larger clusters. Although it seems to be a better choice for the gardener, its flowering season is shorter, confined to the summer only. It is, nevertheless, a spectacular plant and if a larger vine is needed, it is a very good choice. It is possibly also slightly hardier to cold than is *S. ciliatum*.

STRELITZIA (stre-LITZ-ee-a)

Strelitziaceae: The Bird-of-Paradise, Traveler's Tree
    Family
BIRD OF PARADISE; BIRD-OF-PARADISE
    FLOWER
Clumping banana-like long-stalked leaves in one
    plane, with or without trunk; fantastic birdlike
    flowers
Zones vary according to species
Sun
Average but regular amounts of moisture
Rich, humusy, well-drained soil
Propagation by transplanting of suckers, root
    division, and (sometimes) seed

A genus of only four species of large clumping herbs in South Africa, two of them very large and forming trunks. The leaves are arranged opposite each other in one plane and are long-stalked, more or less banana-like but stiff and leathery, and held more or less erect. The few-flowered inflorescences arise from the leaf axils on short or long stalks, and the flowers are cradled in large stiff boatlike horizontally held bracts (or spathes). Each blossom, and there are usually six or more in a given bract, consists of three sepals and three petals. The three sepals are relatively very large; two of them stand erect and the third is lance-shaped or tail-like and held horizontally or pendent. The three petals are more or less united and constitute the flower's "tongue"; one of them is short, the other two are long and united into a stiff arrow or lance-shaped affair, which encloses the stamens and through which the very long style and three-parted stigma protrude. The fruits are tough three-parted capsules containing several small fringed seeds. For many years this genus was placed in the Musaceae (banana family). Flowers of *Strelitzia*, however, are quite different from those of bananas and so are the fruits. Two species are very widely grown. They are planted out in tropical or subtropical regions, and in houses, greenhouses, and public places as "decorator plants" and for the spectacular flowers.

Strelitzia nicolai (nik-o-LAH-ee) is a spectacular clumping and trunk-forming species that may grow to a height of 30 feet, with each trunk capable of attaining about 20 feet. The trunks are, like in banana plants, pseudostems. Mostly hollow, they are generally cinnamon-brown in color because of the adherent leaf bases. After these fall away, the lower trunks are smooth and grayish green to bluish green. The leaves arise from the tops of these stems and grow on two opposite sides of the stem in a single plane. The visual and landscaping effect is that of a clumping pinnate-leaved palm. These trees have a slight resemblance to *Ravenala madagascariensis* (travelers palm) and are sometimes mistaken for younger plants of the latter, although they do not make nearly as great a fan of leaves as does the travelers palm The heavy leaf stalks are as long as the leaves, are erect but beautifully arching, and are grooved or channeled on their upper sides. Their bases wrap around the trunk or stem. The leaf blade is usually about 4 feet long but may be as much as 6 feet long. It is linear-oblong in shape, very leathery and tough, a deep grass green or grayish green in color, smooth and waxy looking, and often cupped or concave in cross section, especially when young. The wind sometimes tears these great leaves along their transverse veins, leaving them segmented into rectangular strips on either side of the midrib and looking almost pinnate in structure. The plants bloom primarily in winter but may produce flower spikes at any time of the year. The inflorescences are identical in structure to those of the smaller and somewhat more colorful *S. reginae*, but are larger. They also are half hidden by the leaf stalks as the peduncle of the inflorescence is much shorter than the leaf petiole. The boatlike bract or spathe is as much as 18 inches long and a deep bluish purple in color. The three giant sepals are snow white and give to the plant one of its common names, white bird-of-paradise. The "tongue" (the petals) is purplish and grayish brown. The plants are hardy in zones 10 and 11 and marginal in zone 9b. They are generally unharmed by temperatures as low as 28°F, but are damaged at 26°F. They are severely damaged by temperatures in the low 20s, but usually recover, although they never grow to size if these conditions persist year after year. Whether it has formed trunks or not, this is one of the most dramatic landscape subjects for the tropical or subtropical gardener. It should be treated in a landscaping sense as a palm, and it does not look its best isolated in the middle of a large lawn. While grown mostly for its bold foliage and form, its flowers are also very beautiful, although not as colorful nor nearly so dominant in the landscape as those of the more diminutive *S. reginae*. This species makes a wonderful close-up subject and is perfection itself planted where its silhouette can be viewed against walls or other backgrounds and where it is afforded some protection from fraying winds. It can survive short droughts, but it really needs and appreciates regular and adequate amounts of water, especially when young. This giant herb grows fairly fast with regular watering and in a good soil, especially when young. Plate 365.

Strelitzia reginae (re-JY-nee) is a trunkless species whose dense clumps seldom attain more than 5 feet of height. Its leaves are similar in shape and color to those of *S. nicolai* (white bird-of-paradise), but are not nearly as large. The petiole usually is 3 feet long at the most and the blade a foot or 18 inches long with depressed lateral veins and often a reddish midrib. Although the leaves grow in a single plane as do those of all *Strelitzia* species, the phenomenon is not nearly so recognizable as with the white bird-of-paradise because the density of the clumps tends to hide the leaf orientation. The plants bloom mostly in fall, winter, and early spring, but form flowers intermittently all year. The inflorescence is typical of the genus, and its form is the most colorful in the genus and instantly recognized by almost everyone as a symbol of the tropics. The flower stalks also reach well above the leaves and thus display well the radiance of the blooms. The 8-inch-long boatlike bract or spathe is usually mint green in color (sometimes a darker green) and is suffused with purple or red. The gigantic sepals are a deep yellow or vibrant silky orange, and the arrow-shaped "tongue" (the petals) is a deep royal blue with the protruding stigma and style pure white. The plant, which is more tender to cold than is the giant white bird-of-paradise, is hardy only in zones 10 and 11 and is somewhat marginal in zone 10a. It is fairly slow to recover when frosted back and does not make a good landscape subject again for at least a season. In fact, if the following winter sees the same low temperatures, the plants will usually be lost. This species looks good planted almost anywhere, especially when in bloom, but is at its best when not isolated in a large space. It can add a resplendent accent of color to large borders and, with a green backdrop of large ferns or other tropical looking leaves, its sumptuous flowers are unsurpassed in beauty. It needs at least a half day's sun to bloom well and, like the giant bird-of-paradise, is somewhat drought tolerant but looks and blooms better with adequate supplies of moisture. Several cultivars are occasionally encountered, the most valuable for the landscape probably being the dwarf *Strelitzia reginae* 'Humilis' (HYOO-mi-lis) or *Strelitzia reginae* 'Pygmaea' (pig-MEE-a), which grows only to 18 or 20 inches tall but bears flowers about as large as the type. *Strelitzia reginae* var. *juncea* (JUN-see-a) has no leaf blades, only leaf stalks, and the petioles, which are very erect and stiff, give the plant the look of a rush or some stiff strange succulent. The flowers of this variety are almost identical to those of the type, but their peduncles are not as long and the spathes with their loads of blossoms are not generally held above the dramatic blue-green or gray-green strange foliage. Nonetheless, the stems (leaves) create a perfect foil for the display of the flowers, and this variety is highly recommended. Because of the reduced chlorophyll-making areas, it needs more sun than the type if it is to bloom well. Plates 366 and 367.

STREPTOSOLEN (strep-toe-SO-len)
Solanaceae: The Petunia, Potato, Tomato Family
MARMALADE BUSH; FIREBUSH; YELLOW
    HELIOTROPE
Sprawling evergreen shrub that can be used as a
    small vine; petunia-like yellow and orange flowers
Zones 10 and 11 as a permanent perennial; zone 9b
    as a returning perennial
Sun to partial sun
Average but regular amounts of moisture
Average well-drained soil
Propagation by cuttings

A monotypic genus native to low elevations of the Andes Mountains in Colombia and Peru. *Streptosolen jamesonii* (jaim-e-SO-nee-eye) is a sprawling and semiclimbing shrub that makes a wonderfully colorful groundcover, espalier, or cascade atop a wall. The leaves are about an inch long, ovate in shape, and a glossy green with depressed veins. The plant blooms year-round in tropical regions, but most heavily from spring to fall. The flowers are in rounded terminal panicles. Each blossom is about an inch wide and an inch long, salverform to funnel-shaped, with five corolla lobes. The flowers open a bright tangerine orange and fade to a clear yellow, resulting in a bi-colored effect (or almost tri-colored as the darker blossoms retain their yellow throats). As a sprawling shrub the plant grows to 6 or 7 feet. As an espalier or trained over a wall or trellis, it "climbs" to 15 feet or sometimes more. The plant also looks wonderful in a rock garden, where the shape and color of the flowers blend perfectly with rocks of almost any color and with gray or subdued foliage colors. Plate 368.

STROBILANTHES
    (stro-bi-LANTH-eez)
Acanthaceae: The Acanthus Family
PERSIAN SHIELD
Small herbaceous shrub; beautiful green, silver, pink,
    and purple leaves; small purple flowers
Zones 10 and 11 as permanent perennials; zone 9 as
    returning perennials; anywhere as annuals
Partial shade to partial sun
Average but regular amounts of moisture
Rich, humusy, well-drained soil
Propagation by cuttings and (sometimes) seed

A large genus of more than 250 herbs and subshrubs in tropical Asia. They have alternately arranged usually entire leaves and terminal spikes or panicles of small tubular flowers. One species has become very popular as a greenhouse plant. It is planted out as a color accent in tropical and subtropical areas and treated as an annual in colder climates. *Strobilanthes dyeranus* (dy-er-AN-us) (sometimes misspelled as "dyerianus") is native to Myanmar (Burma). This herb grows to as much as 4 feet and is planted for its beautiful 8-inch-long elliptic to ovate-lanceolate leaves, which are colored mostly in varying degrees of purple beneath but exhibit iridescent shades of purple, silver, pink, and green above. The midrib and lateral veins are always outlined in green, and the leaf margins are usually, but not invariably, shallowly scalloped. The plants bloom year-round, but the small tubular purple flower spikes are rather insignificant looking and not important in the landscape. In fact, the flowers are best removed as they form to keep the plants from becoming leggy and to direct vigor from flower maturation to that of stem and leaf growth. The plants are usually recommended for partial shade to almost total shade, but they grow equally well in partial sun and flourish even in full sun in cooler climates. They have better color with some sun no matter what the climate. They usually need to be pinched back as they grow upwards to avoid legginess and to maintain a compact shape if that is what is wanted. They are not drought tolerant and look good only with regular amounts of moisture. Some fertility to the soil helps promotes leaf color. Plate 369.

STRONGYLODON
    (strahn-GIL-o-dahn)
Papilionaceae (Fabaceae, Leguminosae), subfamily
    Papilionoideae: The Bean, Pea Family
JADE VINE
Large evergreen vine; immense hanging clusters of
    large claw-shaped blue-green flowers
Zones 10b and 11
Sun
Water lover
Humusy, moist, well-drained soil
Propagation by seed and cuttings

A genus of about 20 species of shrubs but mainly large vines in southeastern Asia and the islands of the South Pacific. One species is sparingly planted in tropical Florida, but is much more common in truly tropical regions. *Strongylodon macrobotrys* (mak-ro-BOAT-ris / ma-KRAHB-o-tris) is indigenous to the rain forests of the Philippines. It is a large and vigorous grower once established and can grow to 30 or 40 feet in height with thick woody serpentine stems. The leaves are dense on the stems except for the bottoms and consist of three elliptical to ovate 5-inch-long leaflets, which open a bronzy rose in color but quickly change to a deep green. The vine blooms in spring and early summer in the Northern Hemisphere with incredible pendent racemes that are 2 to 5 feet long and consist of many 4-inch-long stylized pea-shaped blue-green flowers. Each flower is 4 or 5 inches long with a much recurved swept-back banner and a claw-shaped keel. The vine needs a large support and, of course, looks best planted on a pergola where its gigantic flower clusters may be viewed from below. It is one of the most subtly spectacular plants when in bloom. Jade vine will stand no frost or drought and needs a rich, moist soil where its roots are shaded and its top is in the sun. Plate 370.

SWIETENIA (swee-TEN-ee-a)
Meliaceae: The Mahogany, Chinaberry Family
MAHOGANY
Large evergreen trees; large pinnate leaves; small
    clusters fragrant flowers; large brown and red fruit
Zones vary according to species
Sun
Moisture requirements vary according to species
Average well-drained soil
Propagation by seed

A small genus of only three species of small to large trees in tropical America. They have alternately arranged even-pinnate glossy leaves, axillary or terminal panicles of small five-petaled flowers, and large woody fruits that split open to release many winged seeds. One species is the most valuable timber tree in tropical America. Both species described below grow near the shore as well as inland, and both are tolerant of ocean spray and slightly saline soil conditions and are fairly resistant to hurricane force winds. They are among the most magnificent of tropical American forest trees and are superb shade as well as avenue trees.

Swietenia candollea. See *S. macrophylla.*

Swietenia macrophylla (mak-ro-FYL-la) (synonym *S. candollea*) is originally native to a large area of tropical America from Veracruz and Yucatán in Mexico through northern Guatemala, coastal Central America, and into Venezuela, Colombia, northern Ecuador, eastern Peru, northern Bolivia, and west central Brazil. Hardy in zones 10b and 11, this giant rain forest species grows to a height of 150 feet or more. It usually has an extraordinarily tall, straight, dark, and fissured trunk that, in age, is swollen and buttressed at its base. The canopy is open and spreading. The 12- to 18-inch-long leaves consist of 8 to 12 lance-shaped glossy green 6-inch-long leaflets with a tapering point. The leaves may be deciduous with the advent of drought or cold. The trees bloom in late spring and early summer with axillary panicles of small greenish yellow or orange flowers. The fruits are 6- to 8-inch-long fig-shaped light brown capsules dangling from foot-long cords; they split into five segments when mature. This species is, or was, the most important timber tree in the Americas. Vast areas of its original range have almost been depleted for the valuable reddish brown wood. This great beauty needs near constant warmth and humidity, hailing as it does from tropical wet lowland forests. It grows fast with proper moisture levels, especially when young. The tree is called Honduran mahogany or big-leaf mahogany.

Swietenia mahagoni (ma-HAHG-o-nee / ma-ha-GO-nee) is indigenous to extreme southern Florida, the Bahamas, and the northern West Indies. It is hardy in zones 10 and 11 and somewhat marginal in zone 10a. The tree grows to 60 or 70 feet with time and has a generally straight trunk, which is swollen and often buttressed at the base, with a dark gray to black fissured bark. The crown is open and spreading with age but usually fairly dense, rounded, and compact when the tree is young. The leaves are 8 to 10 inches long with 12 or 14 ovate-lanceolate dark green leaflets. Each leaflet has a prominent and lighter colored midrib and a yellowish green underside. Like those of the Honduran mahogany, the leaves fall with cold or drought and usually do so anyway in late winter. The trees bloom in late spring and early summer with axillary panicles of white or greenish yellow fragrant flowers. The fruits are similar to those of the Honduran mahogany, but are only about 5 inches long. This species was the first to be exploited for its valuable wood, probably because it was the first to be found by European explorers. It is a threatened species in all its original habitat. It is usually called the West Indian mahogany or Spanish mahogany to distinguish it from the larger Honduran mahogany tree. The tree is fast growing but not as fast as *S. macrophylla*, and it can tolerate drier conditions than can the Honduran mahogany. Of course, it grows faster and looks its best with ample and regular amounts of moisture.

SYAGRUS (sy-AG-rus)
Palmae (Arecaceae): The Palm Family
Common names vary according to species
Small to tall feather-leaved palms
Zones vary according to species
Sun to partial sun
Average but regular amounts of moisture
Average well-drained soil
Propagation by seed

A genus of 32 species of pinnate-leaved palm species in South America, mostly Brazil. Almost all the species are solitary-trunked, but a few have clustering trunks. The palms lack crownshafts, and the leaflets of most species arise from the rachis at different angles, thus effecting the look of an ostrich plume in their fullness.

Syagrus amara (a-MAHR-a) (synonym *Rhyticocos amara*) is native to the Lesser Antilles islands of Dominica and Martinique in the West Indies and is hardy only in zones 10 and 11 and marginal in zone 10a. It grows to 60 feet in height, sometimes more, with an aspect that is probably nearer that of *Cocos nucifera* (coconut) than any other palm. Like the coconut, it grows near the shore as well as inland and is extremely tolerant of ocean spray and saline soil. Thus, it is a premier landscaping subject for tropical seashores. Unlike that of the coconut, the trunk of the overtop palm does not lean and bend to such a great extent and it shows much less distinct rings of leaf scars on the trunk. The leaves, which seldom exceed 12 feet in length, are not as large as those of the coconut. In addition, *S. amara* does not produce coconuts. Instead, its seeds are in fairly large clusters of 2-inch-long, egg-shaped bright orange-colored fruits. The palm does not have the grandeur nor the unrivaled grace of the coconut, but it is a good substitute and should be more widely planted. This beautiful tree is drought tolerant but, as with so very many other palms and landscape subjects, grows faster—indeed, it is a fast growing palm, especially when young—and looks better with regular and adequate supplies of water. It flourishes in limestone soils.

Syagrus romanzoffiana (ro´-man-zahf-fee-AHN-a) (synonyms *Arecastrum romanzoffianum, Cocos plumosa*) is native to southern Brazil, Paraguay, Uruguay, and northeastern Argentina and is hardy in zones 9 through 11 although marginal in zone 9a. One of the world's most widely planted palms, this species is almost universally known in English-speaking regions as the queen palm. For many years the scientific name of the palm was *Arecastrum* and before that it was part of the large genus *Cocos*, which now includes only the coconut palm. It is often still listed in nurseries under the older name *Cocos plumosa*, occasionally under *Arecastrum*, and almost never under *Syagrus*. This beauty grows to as much as 50 or even 60 feet and is one of the world's fastest growing palms. Two feet of trunk growth per year is not unheard of under good cultural conditions. It is also one of the world's most beautiful species when well grown. The light gray trunk is smooth except for the uppermost parts and is beautifully ringed from its bulging base to its top. The trunk is not quite as beautiful as that of *Roystonea* (royal palm) species, but it is quite lovely and its rings are generally as widely spaced as are those of the royal palms. Two varieties once recognized may still be in the nursery trade but are no longer valid botanically: *Arecastrum romanzoffianum* var. *australis* and *A. romanzoffianum* var. *bortyophorum*, the former variety having relatively thin trunks and the latter variety with unusually thick and robust trunks. The great arching and very plumose deep green leaves of the queen palm are as long as 20 feet with 3-foot-long pendulous leaflets. The palm generally blooms in the spring, but flowering may occur at almost any time in tropical regions. The inflorescence is a large panicle of small white flowers emerging from a large boat-shaped bract or spathe. The inch-wide rounded fruits are orange in color when mature. The tree is somewhat drought tolerant, although it hails from regions that are not prone to drought, and it really does not live up to its potential in the landscape when starved of water. It needs a rich, humusy soil that is on the acidic side, as limy and dry soils cause the leaves to be more yellow than green and much smaller than those of healthy specimens. It is better not to plant this palm if it cannot be supplied with the environmental conditions it needs. The mature palm is relatively hardy to cold and is unscathed by temperatures above 25°F. It is usually damaged by temperatures in the low 20s and anything below 20°F is likely to be devastating, although mature palms have many times recovered from temperatures of 18°F if the freezing is not prolonged. Although much planted in the hot desert areas of the southwestern United States, the tree is subject to leaf burn in the summer in these regions.

Syagrus schizophylla (skits-o-FYL-la) (synonyms *Arikuryroba schizophylla, Cocos schizophylla*) is native to eastern Brazil and is hardy in zones 10 and 11, although it sometimes survives in zone 9b. It is another segregate from the old genus *Cocos* and later carried for many years the unwieldy generic name of *Arikuryroba,* which is a Latinized form of its aboriginal name. This beautiful palm grows slowly to about 15 feet in height with 10 or sometimes 12 feet of trunk. The trunk is an interior or exterior designer's dream come true: it is covered in the thin straight sticklike brown or brownish gray leaf bases that create the look of fine wicker. The 6-foot-long deep green leaves are fairly stiff, and the leaflets, which are neither pendulous nor plumose, are arranged in one plane. The leaf crown is dense and full, and there are usually several dozen long-stalked leaves that grow from the trunk extended for as much as 3 feet, not just from the very top of the trunk. The little palm makes one of the most beautiful intimate or close-up subjects available. It is perfect in partial shade, which it seems to prefer as it grows mostly in forests in its native habitat. The tree is somewhat drought tolerant but does not like such conditions and its leaves respond very favorably to a humusy, moist, well-drained soil by taking on a deep almost bluish hue. The palm is sometimes referred to as the arikury palm, although this is rare. It is, alas, not enough widely planted to have a more descriptive vernacular. It deserves to be much more widely planted.

SYNADENIUM (sin-a-DEN-ee-um)
Euphorbiaceae: The Euphorbia, Spurge Family
AFRICAN MILKBUSH
Medium-sized succulent evergreen shrub; rubbery
   red stems; fleshy leaves; red flowers
Zones 10 and 11
Sun to partial sun
Drought tolerant
Average well-drained soil
Propagation by cuttings and (sometimes) seed

A genus of about 20 species of succulent shrubs and small trees with a milky latexlike sap in tropical America and tropical Africa eastward through Madagascar and the Mascarene Islands. One species is grown both as a greenhouse and indoor plant in northern regions and planted as a shrub in tropical and subtropical regions for its attractive succulence and red flowers. *Synadenium grantii* (GRANT-ee-eye) is native to tropical East Africa. It is a succulent shrub with rubbery wine-colored stems growing to as much as 12 feet in height but usually no more than half that in cultivation. The milky sap is mildly poisonous and is a skin irritant to many people. The dark grayish green fleshy leaves are 5 to 8 inches long, diamond-shaped to obovate with a prominent midrib and lateral veins, and almost stalkless. The small carmine-red flowers appear year-round in terminal panicles. *Synadenium grantii* '**Rubra**', the form usually sold and planted, has bright red stems and leaves that open wine-red before turning brownish red. The plant grows in almost any well-drained site, and it seems completely indifferent as to soil, flourishing even in mortar or saline soil. It is widely planted and is a very good subject for beachfront properties where it gives color and texture to difficult areas. The two things it is intolerant of are soggy soil and frost, although it survives and quickly returns from light freezes.

SYNGONIUM (sin-GO-nee-um)
Araceae: The Calla Lily, Jack-in-the-Pulpit Family
ARROWHEAD VINE
Large, strong-growing evergreen vine or
    groundcover; large three-parted arrow-shaped
    leaves
Zones 10 and 11 as permanent perennials; zone 9 as
    returning perennials
Shade to partial sun
Average but regular amounts of moisture
Average well-drained soil
Propagation by cuttings

A genus of 33 vines in tropical America. The members of this genus are very similar to the seven species of *Nephthytis* and are mostly indistinguishable for the nonbotanist. Within each genus the species are confusingly similar, with the differences between a given form of one species often greater than the differences between the separate species. Plants for sale may be labeled as either "*Nephthytis*" or "*Syngonium*" and may be correctly labeled or not. All these plants require the same cultural conditions and are used for identical landscaping purposes. The most widely available species is *Syngonium podophyllum*. The juvenile foliage is usually relatively small, arrow-shaped, and undivided even when the mature leaves are segmented. Most forms have leaves with some variegation, which may or may not be retained as the plants mature. The juvenile forms especially have the appearance of small green and white caladiums and are much used as house plants. **Syngonium podophyllum** (po-do-FYL-lum) is indigenous from southeastern Mexico through Central America and southwards through most of Brazil and into western Bolivia. The mature leaves are ovate in outline, but are deeply three-parted, with two of the segments relatively small and mostly horizontal and with a third and much larger segment in the middle, giving the whole leaf somewhat the look of a giant arrowhead. Often the leaves have more than three segments, sometimes as many as nine in older plants. The complete leaf may attain a length of well over a foot with an almost equal width. This vine grows to great heights outdoors in frost-free regions—50 feet is not uncommon and 100 feet has been recorded. The stems may attain a diameter of 2 or even 3 inches and become woody at their bases. The vine, which climbs and holds to its substrate with strong aerial roots, grows similarly to and fills the same ecological role as a climbing *Philodendron* or *Monstera* species in the tropical rain forest. It is spectacular and soul-satisfying climbing large palms and other trees and makes one of the best tropical groundcovers the

gardener can find. With adequate and regular supplies of moisture and a fairly fertile and humusy soil, the plant is extremely fast growing. The vine does not bloom when juvenile and must grow fairly tall before doing so. When it does bloom, the small inflorescence is typical of the family: a yellowish green spathe mostly surrounding a shorter spadix of unisexual flowers. The fruits, if they are produced, are spikes of small black berrylike seeds. There are several variegated clones, some of them startlingly beautiful. Most of these lose all or most of their color when mature and far-climbing; they will, however, tend to maintain the color even as large groundcovers if they do not climb. Few plants are more tropical looking or as useful and easy to grow.

SYZYGIUM (si-ZIJ-ee-um)
Myrtaceae: The Myrtle, Eucalyptus Family
Common names vary according to species
Small to large evergreen trees; glossy leaves; shaving-
    brush-like flowers; colorful edible fruit
Zones vary according to species
Sun to partial sun
Average but regular amounts of moisture
Average well-drained soil
Propagation by seed

A large genus of about 500 species of aromatic evergreen trees in the tropics of Asia, Africa, Australia, and the Pacific Islands. They have oppositely arranged entire leaves, axillary or terminal clusters of white, yellow, or red five-lobed almost stalkless flowers with many long stamens, and large colorful and edible berries.
Syzygium australe. See *S. paniculatum.*
Syzygium cumini (KYOO-mi-ny) (synonyms *Eugenia cumini, E. jambolana, Syzygium jambolana*) is native to India, Sri Lanka, Myanmar (Burma), and Indonesia, and is hardy only in zones 10 and 11 and marginal in zone 10a. This magnificent tree grows quickly to more than 100 feet in its native habitat and usually to about 70 feet in cultivation. It forms a broad to oblong dense canopy above a short thick dark gray trunk. Young trees often need to be trained to one trunk unless a multitrunked specimen is desired. The leaves are elliptic, leathery but silky and glossy, dark green, and 6 to 10 inches long with a very prominent and yellowish midrib and a short and abrupt "tail." The new growth is a beautiful bronze-pink in color. The tree blooms from early spring into summer in the Northern Hemisphere. The small clusters of fragrant flowers have a fleshy funnel-shaped inch-long calyx, which is white changing to pink, with many pink stamens. The fruits mature from midsummer to fall and are also formed in pendent clusters. Each berry is oblong in shape, 1 to 2 inches long, and green changing to pink, red, purple, and almost black when ripe. There are usually several degrees of ripeness and colors in a single fruit cluster. The berries are edible and reportedly sweet but acidic and are used for making jams and jellies. The tree is usually called the jambolan or jambolan plum. This

almost incredibly beautiful tree has but one fault: its abundant fruits are messy when they fall. Although they are beautiful and beloved of birds, the fruits limit for most people the tree's use to sites away from pavements or parking areas.

Syzygium jambolana. See *S. cumini.*

Syzygium jambos (JAHM-bos) (synonyms *Eugenia jambos, E. malaccensis*) is native to southern China, Southeast Asia, Malaysia, and Indonesia into northern Australia, and is hardy in zones 10 and 11, although it occasionally survives in zone 9b. This small tree with a dense and spreading crown grows slowly to about 30 or 40 feet in cultivation. If a standard form is desired, it usually must be trained to a single trunk when young. The deep green short-stalked leaves, which are elliptic to lanceolate in shape with tapering and usually curved tips, are 4 to 9 inches long and are leathery but glossy with a prominent and lighter colored midrib. The new leaves are a shiny pink or red in color. The tree blooms in late spring with terminal clusters of 3-inch-wide fluffy white or greenish white flowers that are mostly very many long stamens. The round 2-inch-wide fruits mature in the summer and are a pale yellow to almost white in color with the persistent darker-colored calyx lobes at the ends. They are edible and smell and taste like rose water, leading to the common name of rose apple.

Syzygium malaccense (ma-la-KEN-see) (synonym *Eugenia malaccensis*) is indigenous to Malaysia and is hardy in zones 10b and 11. Called the Malay apple, it is a wonderful tree species that grows to 40 feet or more with a dense but not compact crown. The incredibly beautiful leaves are 6 to 18 inches long, elliptic to lanceolate, bright green, leathery, and glossy, with prominent midribs and depressed lateral veins. The leaves are so large that they are usually pendulous. The trees bloom year-round, producing flowers and fruits anywhere on the trunk and branches. The blossoms are as much as 3 inches wide and consist mainly of very many red or purplish red stamens. The shiny red fruits are pear-shaped, about 4 inches long, and edible, reportedly being sweet without acidity. This tree is one of the world's most beautiful, but it is, alas, quite tender to cold. Plate 371.

Syzygium paniculatum (pan-ik´-yoo-LAIT-um) (synonyms *Eugenia australis, E. myrtifolia, E. paniculatum, Syzygium australe*) is indigenous to eastern Australia and is hardy in zones 10 and 11. This small tree to 30 or sometimes 50 feet is often grown as a shrub or large clipped hedge. As a tree it must usually be trained to form, either single or multitrunked, when young. It makes a dense oblong crown atop a short dark trunk. The nearly stalkless leaves are about 4 inches long, elliptic to lanceolate in shape, dark glossy green in color, usually with a pinkish bronzy hue when young, and bearing a prominent and lighter colored midrib. The plant blooms most of the year in tropical climes and mostly in the warm months elsewhere. The inch-wide white fluffy flowers are in small terminal and axillary clusters. The fruits are inch-long pink to reddish purple, upside-down apple-shaped edible berries that are said to be sweet but insipid. This species is usually called the brush cherry or Australian brush cherry. The tree is beautiful but somewhat formal in appearance. There is a variegated cultivar that is less attractive.

TABEBUIA (tab-e-BOO-ya)
Bignoniaceae: The Catalpa, Jacaranda, Trumpet-Vine Family
TRUMPET TREES
Evergreen and deciduous small to large trees; spectacular trumpet-shaped flowers
Zones vary according to species
Sun
Average but regular amounts of moisture
Average well-drained soil
Propagation by seed and cuttings

A genus of about 100 species of shrubs and small trees in tropical America. The leaves are usually palmately compound but a few have simple leaves; most are evergreen but some are at least briefly deciduous. The flowers, which are in terminal clusters of funnel-shaped or bell-shaped five-lobed blossoms, range from white through yellow, orange, red, and purple. The lobes are divided into two groups, three lobes on the bottom and two on the top. All these species bloom most heavily in the dry season of their native habitats, which varies from one region to the next but is usually from December through March if, indeed, there is a dry season for some of these areas. Most species bloom in late fall, winter, and spring in the Northern Hemisphere. The fruits are linear capsules that resemble those of *Catalpa bignonioides* (catalpa tree), although the pods are usually more ornamental and often fur-covered. These trees are favorites in tropical and near-tropical regions because of their spectacular floral displays. Most smaller species bloom when quite young. The members of this genus were formerly dispersed among the genera *Cybistax, Stenolobium,* and *Tecoma. Stenolobium* is no longer a valid genus name, but the other two are and one of the following species is technically in the genus *Cybistax.* In addition almost all species show a remarkable variation in their leaf form and size as well as in size and exact color of the flowers, all depending on the climate, the soil, the exposure, and so forth. The larger species are (or were) important timber trees because of their very heavy and durable wood. None of the species is truly fast growing, although the larger trees approach what might be called fast growth.

Tabebuia argentea. See *T. caraiba.*

Tabebuia avellanedae. See *T. impetiginosa.*

Tabebuia caraiba (ka-RY-ba) (synonyms *T. argentea, Tecoma argentea*) is native to southern Brazil, Paraguay, and Uruguay, and is hardy in zones 10 and 11 and marginal in zone 9b. It is called the silver trumpet tree and sometimes the tree of gold or golden bell. The little tree grows fairly slowly to 25 or 30 feet with a slender and irregular crown above a grayish brown short somewhat crooked, ridged, and corky-barked trunk. The leaves are digitately or palmately compound and consist of five to seven oblong to lanceolate 6-inch-long leaflets with prominent and lighter colored midribs and lateral veins. The leaves are exceptionally beautiful because of their color, a silvery gray-green. The tree is wonderful even when not in bloom because of its "designer's" form, color of leaves, and bark. The leaves are usually deciduous in early spring, but this is not a surety, especially in wet winters. The trees produce scattered flowers year-round, but are at the height of bloom in early winter through mid spring. The golden yellow flowers are formed in large terminal clusters. Few small trees are as beautiful as this one. It is simply delicious year-round and is one of the finest sunny patio subjects. It even looks good planted alone in an expanse of lawn surrounded by space. Plate 372.

Tabebuia chrysantha (kris-ANTH-a) is indigenous in all of tropical Mexico southwards into Venezuela and is hardy in zones 10 and 11 and marginal in zone 9b. It grows to as much as 100 feet in its native haunts but is seldom more than 35 or 40 feet tall in cultivation. The trunk is seldom truly straight, at least in cultivation in the open, and the canopy is open and spreading. The leaves are as much as 10 inches wide with five ovate leaflets. Each leaflet is as long as 7 inches and bears a short curved tip. The tree, which is deciduous in late winter and spring unless the winter is unusually warm and wet, usually starts blooming in midwinter and may continue until summer. The somewhat fragrant flowers are golden yellow in color with rose-colored streaks in the throat. Plate 373.

Tabebuia chrysotricha (kris-o-TRYK-a / kry-so-TRIK-a) (synonyms *T. pulcherrima*, *Tecoma chrysotricha*) is indigenous to Colombia and adjacent Brazil and is hardy in zones 10 and 11 and marginal in zone 9b. It grows to about 30 feet with a spreading crown atop a short grayish brown somewhat crooked but picturesquely ridged trunk. The leaves are palmately compound, divided into five or seven deep green 4-inch-long leaflets that form a circular or semicircular outline. The leaves are usually deciduous in the spring but may be persistent, especially if the weather is wet. The tree blooms sporadically year-round but most heavily in winter and late spring. The flowers are as much as 4 inches long and are a bright yellow, sometimes with indistinct purplish lines on the corolla lobes. The tree is exquisite and graceful when in bloom, especially if the leaves have fallen. It is usually called the golden trumpet tree in English-speaking regions. Plate 374.

Tabebuia donnell-smithii (dahn´-nel-SMITH-ee-eye) (synonyms *Cybistax donnell-smithii*) is native to southern Mexico and adjacent Central America. Hardy in zones 10 and 11 and marginal in zone 10a, this magnificent tree grows to as much as 100 feet in its native haunts, but usually to no more than 60 or 70 feet in cultivation. It produces an open and irregular crown of large leaves atop a tall smooth immensely thick trunk with light to dark gray bark. The leaves are as much as 18 inches wide and circular in outline, but palmately compound with five or seven ovate-oblong 10-inch-long dark green leaflets. The leaves are deciduous unless the winter is warm and wet. The trees bloom sporadically year-round but most heavily in mid to late winter or spring. The pure yellow flowers light up the sky and the landscape on large trees especially if the trees are leafless at the time. There are few things on earth more magnificent than this tree, which is usually called primavera in the Americas. This species is now correctly known as *Cybistax donnell-smithii*; it was also once placed in the genus *Roseodendron*. Since it so much resembles the trees in *Tabebuia*, it would seem best for the purposes of this book to include it here.

Tabebuia dugandii. See *T. impetiginosa*.
Tabebuia eximia. See *T. impetiginosa*.
Tabebuia heptaphylla. See *T. impetiginosa*.
Tabebuia heterophylla (het´-e-ro-FYL-la) (synonym *T. triphylla*) is native to the West Indies and is hardy in zones 10 and 11 and marginal in zone 9b. The tree grows to as much as 20 feet or more but is often kept as a large shrub. The leaves are palmately compound with five obovate 3-inch-long leaflets although, when young, the plant often has single simple foliage. The little tree is not normally deciduous. It blooms year-round but most heavily in late spring through the summer with clusters of white to rosy-colored flowers. There are forms and cultivars with pure white flowers as well as pure deep pink blossoms. Plate 375.

Tabebuia impetiginosa (im´-pe-ty-ji-NO-sa) (synonyms *T. avellanedae*, *T. dugandii*, *T. eximia*, *T. heptaphylla*, *T. ipe*, *T. nicaraguensis*, *T. palmeri*, *T. shunkerigoi*) is the most widespread species in the genus, occurring naturally from northern Mexico to northern Argentina. It is hardy only in zones 10 and 11 although often grown and surviving as a large shrub in zone 9b. It is a variable species as can be seen from the number of synonyms, and in its native haunts attains heights from 30 to 120 feet, depending on the climate, exposure, and soil conditions. In cultivation the tree is usually from 30 to 60 feet tall. The massive trunk may be 6 feet in diameter in very old trees and is often buttressed at its base. It is tall and straight, dark gray to dark brown in color, and generally smooth with a spreading and open canopy. The leaves are as much as a foot wide and palmately compound, and consist of five to seven ovate to obovate dark green leaflets. Like many other *Tabebuia* species, this one is deciduous in late winter and early spring unless the weather is unusually warm and wet. The trees bloom sporadically for most of the year, but there is almost nothing to compare to them when, at the height of their efflorescence in late winter or early spring, the tops of the trees are covered with the scintillating pink, deep rose, or purple trumpet flowers. Each flower is about 4 inches long with an orange or yellow throat. Plate 376.

Tabebuia ipe. See *T. impetiginosa*.
Tabebuia mexicana. See *T. rosea*.

Tabebuia nicaraguensis. See *T. impetiginosa.*

Tabebuia pallida (PAL-li-da), which has the same natural range as and is very similar to *T. heterophylla,* is probably identical to it.

Tabebuia palmeri. See *T. impetiginosa.*

Tabebuia pentaphylla. See *T. rosea.*

Tabebuia pulcherrima. See *T. chrysotricha.*

Tabebuia punctatissima. See *T. rosea.*

Tabebuia rosea (ROZ-ee-a / ro-ZAY-a) (synonyms *T. mexicana, T. pentaphylla, T. punctatissima*) is native to tropical Mexico southwards into northern Venezuela and Colombia and is hardy in zones 10b and 11. In its natural range it grows to as much as 80 feet in height, but seldom attains more than 50 feet in cultivation. Its trunk is tall and straight and, in the wetter parts of its range, is often buttressed at the base. The leaves are about a foot wide with five ovate to obovate leaflets forming a circle. The tree blooms most heavily in March and April but sporadically all year, especially in dry periods. The 4-inch-long flowers are white outside but pink or deep rose inside the corolla lobes, and they usually have a yellow throat. Plate 377.

Tabebuia serratifolia (ser-rait´-i-FO-lee-a) is indigenous to northern South America and the islands of Trinidad and Tobago southwards through eastern and central Brazil and into Bolivia. It is hardy only in zones 10 and 11 and marginal in zone 10a. One of the most impressive trees in the tropics, it grows slowly to heights of well over 100 feet in its native habitats with a thick and buttressed trunk, and to as much as 60 or so feet in cultivation. The leaves are about 10 inches wide with five ovate 7-inch-long leaflets with toothed margins. The tree is only briefly deciduous, if at all. The flowers appear anywhere from January until May (often through this whole period) and cover the tree with their great terminal yellow clusters.

Tabebuia shunkerigoi. See *T. impetiginosa.*

Tabebuia triphylla. See *T. heterophylla.*

TABERNAEMONTANA

(tab´-ur-nee-mahn-TAN-a)

Apocynaceae: The Oleander, Frangipani, Vinca
 Family

CARNATION OF INDIA; CRAPE-JASMINE;
 CRAPE-GARDENIA; PINWHEEL-FLOWER

Large evergreen shrub; large glossy leaves; white
 fragrant pinwheel-like or gardenia-like flowers

Zones 10 and 11 as permanent shrubs; zone 9b as
 returning shrubs

Sun to partial shade

Water lover

Average well-drained soil

Propagation by cuttings and (sometimes) seed

A large genus of about 100 trees and shrubs in the tropics of Africa, Asia, and Australia. They have milky sap, oppositely arranged leaves (a given pair often unequal in size), and terminal or axillary clusters of yellow or white salverform flowers with twisted corolla lobes. The fruit when it forms is a double ovoid or half-moon-shaped yellow or orange pod with many thin seeds. One species is very widely planted in tropical and subtropical regions for its large shiny foliage and showy white fragrant flowers. The rest of the members of this genus are remarkable for their absence in American horticulture; there are many lovely species crying out for exploitation. *Tabernaemontana divaricata* (di-vair´-i-KAIT-a) (synonyms *Ervatamia coronaria, Tabernaemontana coronaria*) is indigenous to northern India, Myanmar (Burma), and Thailand. It is a large much-branched shrub growing to as much as 15 feet in frost-free areas. It may be trained to a superbly attractive small tree with one or more crooked gray trunks. The leaves are elliptic to lanceolate in shape, 6 to 8 inches long, leathery in texture, and a deep glossy green in color with a prominent and lighter colored midrib and depressed lateral veins. The plants bloom year-round in tropical regions with small axillary and terminal clusters of tubular pure white waxy blossoms. Each blossom has five large expanded and twisted corolla lobes as much as 3 inches wide. The flowers are fragrant, especially at night, with a carnation-like aroma. There are double-flowered cultivars with several overlapping crinkled petals that look remarkably like the flowers of most cultivars of *Gardenia jasminoides;* these are preferred by most people, although some find the single pinwheel-shaped blossoms of the type to be startlingly effective and romantic against the dark green foliage. The plants survive in poor soil and even withstand mild drought conditions, but they never look good under such circumstances. The shrub is basically unaffected by temperatures above 30°F and is damaged by anything lower but sprouts from its roots if the temperature does not fall nor stay very long below 22°F. Since this plant grows fairly fast and blooms on new wood, it makes an attractive landscape specimen and blooms profusely in one season. For these reasons, it makes a fine hedge for sun or partial shade but is always most beautiful as a small tree or in a mixed shrub border. It is also quite attractive as a large container plant for entranceways or patios. Plate 378.

TAMARINDUS (tam-a-RIN-dus)

Caesalpiniaceae (Leguminosae), subfamily
 Caesalpinioideae: The Cassia, Royal Poinciana
 Family

TAMARIND

Large evergreen tree; large pinnate ferny leaves; small
 yellow flowers; large edible brown pods

Zones 10b and 11

Sun

Average but regular amounts of moisture

Average well-drained soil

Propagation by seed and cuttings

A monotypic genus probably originally native to tropical Africa. *Tamarindus indica* (IN-di-ka) has been so widely cultivated for so long all over the tropical world that its origins are now obscure. It is a large tree attaining a height of as much as 80 or 90 feet but usually no more than 60 feet with an equally wide umbrella-shaped dense crown above a relatively short massive light gray to dark gray rough trunk. The even-pinnate leaves are about 10 inches long with two to three dozen inch-long regularly spaced light green to grayish green oblong leaflets. The tree is sometimes deciduous for brief periods if the weather turns dry. The beauty blooms mainly in the summer with terminal clusters of inch-wide pale yellow three-petaled flowers usually striped with red. The fat pods that follow are about 8 inches long, usually curved, and a beautiful cinnamon in color. They contain 5 to 10 seeds, and the surrounding pulp is sweet but also quite acidic and tart in taste and is used to make beverages, sauces, and chutney. The tree is not drought tolerant and needs a deep soil with regular irrigation when dry. It is majestic and yet graceful and, although fairly slow growing, it is one of the finest shade trees for tropical regions. It is also highly wind resistant.

TAPEINOCHILUS (ta-payn´-o-KYL-us)
Costaceae: The Costus Family
PINEAPPLE GINGER; GIANT SPIRAL
    GINGER; INDONESIAN WAX GINGER
Large herbs with fleshy-caned stems; large leaves;
    large red cone-shaped flower heads
Zones 10 and 11
Sun to partial shade
Water lover
Rich, humusy, well-drained soil
Propagation by root division, rhizome division, and
    stem cuttings

A genus of about 15 species of large rhizomatous herbs with reedlike segmented stems from which spiraling one-sided compound leaves grow. The inflorescence arises directly from the ground on a stalk at the end of which is a large cylindrical head of nearly overlapping tough waxy bracts enclosing the small flowers. One species is sometimes planted. *Tapeinochilus ananassae* (ahn-a-NAHS-see) is indigenous to eastern Indonesia and northern Australia. It grows to 6 or 8 feet in height with clumping jointed reedlike fleshy stems that are usually reddish in color. The leaves are one-sided pinnate spirals of fleshy dark green 6-inch-long obovate leaflets (i.e., the rachis of the compound leaf is spiral, not straight, and the leaflets grow on only one side of this rachis). The inflorescence usually appears in late summer or fall and consists of a foot-long cylinder of ovate tough waxy red bracts whose upper ends are tubular and densely packed onto the spike and which almost hide the small and ephemeral yellow flowers. The apical ends of the bracts are pointed and somewhat drooping. The peduncle is segmented and jointed like the leafy stems and may be from less than a foot in height to 5 or 6 feet tall. The flower head does look somewhat like a red pineapple, but it looks even more

like a pine cone. The plants grow best with protection from the midday sun in hot climates. The stems slowly increase from the roots to make small clumps with time. They survive freezes as long as the rhizomatous roots are not damaged, but these are near the surface of the soil and are usually not hardy outside zone 9b. Mulching improves the survival rate, but the plants may not bloom the following summer if frozen back. This beautiful and exotic-looking plant should be more widely grown than it is at present in tropical and near-tropical regions of the United States.

TAXODIUM (tax-O-dee-um)
Taxodiaceae: The Bald Cypress Family
BALD CYPRESS; SWAMP CYPRESS
Large deciduous and evergreen coniferous trees;
    picturesque form; ferny leaves; aerial roots; cones
Zones vary according to species
Sun
Water lovers
Rich, humusy wet soil on the acidic side
Propagation by seed

A genus of only two species of large coniferous trees in the eastern and southern areas of the United States and most of Mexico. Old specimens make some of the most magnificent trees native to the continent with truly immense trunks reaching heights of well over 100 feet. Both species occur naturally in wet and often quite swampy areas. In these environments their form is quite picturesque and their roots form large and very attractive pneumatophores usually called "knees." They also grow in soil that is not flooded; here they do not form the knees but become more traditional-looking although still very large trees.

Taxodium ascendens. See *T. distichum* var. *nutans.*

Taxodium distichum (DIS-ti-kum) occurs naturally along rivers and in swamps from southern New England southwards through Florida, westward to Texas and northwards from there to southern Illinois. There are more trees in the state of Florida than anywhere else. This species is hardy in zones 5 through 11. In the northern parts of its range it does not grow to the proportions it attains in the subtropical areas, where it can grow to a height of 150 feet with a trunk diameter of 10 feet or even more. The trunks are much enlarged at their bases with great buttresslike flanges and indentations, above which they are very tall and straight. The scaly bark is a light gray to a reddish tan in color. The leaves are needlelike, usually slightly less than an inch long, very narrow, and are arranged on two opposite sides of the twigs in a single plane. They are light green when new and the leafy twigs look especially fernlike then. They turn a brownish red in late fall and by the first of January are usually gone from the trees along the Gulf Coast, but younger trees, especially in swampy subtropical areas, often have green leaves year-round. The cones are round, usually only about an inch in diameter, and are usually mature by the first of the year.

The tree forms a distinct pyramidal shape when young and retains it for a long period if grown out of swampy areas. Older trees have dense oblong to pyramidal crowns when grown in dry soil, but old patriarchs in the swamps have a great tiered branching that is very picturesque. The trees live for a very long time; some are more than 1000 years old. ***Taxodium distichum* var. nutans** (NYOO-tanz) (synonym *T. ascendens*) is smaller and slower growing than the type and has smaller almost scalelike leaves. It is called the pond cypress and is inferior to the type in every way. Plate 379.

Taxodium mucronatum (myook-ro-NAIT-um) is indigenous from southern Texas through Mexico into Guatemala and is hardy in zones 8 through 11. It is called Montezuma cypress to distinguish it from *T. distichum*. It is similar to *T. distichum* in overall appearance with four exceptions: the tree is more massive but not as tall; its branch tips and twigs are pendulous, giving the tree the aspect of a slightly weeping form; the leaves are evergreen in frost-free or nearly frost-free regions; and the trunk is incredibly more massive with age. There are 1000-year-old trees in Mexico that have heights of 120 feet, trunk diameters of 40 feet, and trunk circumferences of 110 feet. These measurements make them the widest-spreading trees on earth, after the giant banyan *Ficus* species. Some people, when first seeing such trees near Oaxaca and Mexico City, refuse to believe they are looking at a single tree, the same phenomenon is noted when the uninitiated first see a giant spreading banyan.

TECOMA (te-KO-ma)
Bignoniaceae: The Catalpa, Jacaranda, Trumpet-
  Vine Family
YELLOW ELDER; YELLOW BELLS; YELLOW
  TRUMPET-FLOWER
Large evergreen shrubs and small trees; pinnate
  leaves; large golden yellow trumpet-shaped flowers
Zones 10 and 11 as permanent shrubs and trees;
  zone 9b as returning shrubs
Sun
Average but regular amounts of moisture
Average well-drained soil
Propagation by seed and cuttings

A genus of about 12 evergreen trees and shrubs in tropical and subtropical America. The genus is closely allied to several others in the bignonia family and is a segregate from several much larger genera including *Tabebuia*, which it most closely resembles. The biggest and most important difference to the gardener is that the leaves of *Tabebuia* species are digitately (or palmately) compound whereas those of *Tecoma* are pinnately compound. Only one species is commonly planted outside botanical gardens.

Tecoma capensis. See *Tecomaria capensis*.
Tecoma reginae-sabae. See *Podranea brycei*.
Tecoma ricasoliana. See *Podranea ricasoliana*.
Tecoma stans (stahns) (synonyms *Bignonia stans*, *Stenolobium stans*) is indigenous to southern Florida, the West Indies, southern Texas, Mexico, Central America, and southwards through Brazil and into northern Argentina. The type grows to 15 or even 20 feet and is mostly a large shrub form but is easily trained to a small tree form when young. The odd-pinnate leaves are 8 to 10 inches long and are composed of from 5 to 13 ovate to linear-lanceolate, glabrous to pubescent, toothed bright green leaflets. The plants bloom year-round in tropical regions but mostly in the spring and fall. The flowers are in dense many-flowered terminal rounded racemes. Each blossom is about 2 inches long, trumpet-shaped with five corolla lobes of unequal sizes, and a clear light to deep golden yellow often with five light red lines inside the corolla. The pods are about 6 to 8 inches long, very narrow, and thin, and look very much like those of *Catalpa bignonioides* (catalpa tree). There are two naturally occurring varieties of this species, one of which is significantly hardier to cold than the other. ***Tecoma stans* var. angustata** (synonym *T. incisa*) is the hardier shrub, possibly safe in zone 8b. It is found naturally in Texas and northern Mexico and has leaflets that are narrower than the other variety. ***Tecoma stans* var. velutina** is less hardy to cold, has wider ovate leaflets that are pubescent beneath, and has slightly larger and deeper-colored flowers. This species is one of the most spectacular and dependable flowering shrubs or trees. It is easy of culture and breathtakingly beautiful in bloom. The blossoms seem to glow with molten gold when they are at their peak. The plants are quite fast growing and bloom when young and only 2 or 3 feet in height. The little trees are drought tolerant when established but do better, of course, with adequate and regular supplies of moisture. They are not particular as to soil as long as its drainage is unimpeded, and they grow and flourish in poor and stony sites. Plate 380.

TECOMANTHE (tek-o-MANTH-ee)
Bignoniaceae: The Catalpa, Jacaranda, Trumpet-
  Vine Family
PINK TRUMPET VINE
Large woody evergreen vines; large pinnate leaves;
  large clusters of pink and red flowers
Zones 10b and 11
Sun
Average but regular amounts of moisture
Humusy, moist, well-drained soil
Propagation by seed and cuttings

A genus of five large vine species in eastern Indonesia, New Guinea, the Solomon Islands, northern Australia, and the north island of New Zealand. They have large odd-pinnate leaves and pendulous, rounded clusters of bell-shaped rose or red flowers. They are still fairly rare in cultivation, but one species (*Tecomanthe dendrophila*) seems to be, fortunately, growing in popularity.

Tecomanthe argentea. See *Tabebuia caribaea*.
Tecomanthe chrysotricha. See *Tabebuia chrysotricha*.

Tecomanthe dendrophila (den-dro-FYL-la / den-DRAHF-i-la) (synonym *T. venusta*) is indigenous to eastern Indonesia, New Guinea, and the Solomon Islands. It is a twining vine that grows to 30 feet or more, making beautiful gray woody ropelike pliable stems. The odd-pinnate leaves consist of three or five elliptic to lanceolate-shaped shiny light green leaflets with beautifully depressed veins. The terminal leaflet is larger than the other leaflets. The plants bloom sporadically all year in tropical climes but most heavily in spring and summer in the Northern Hemisphere. The pendent flower clusters are axillary in position and occur only on the older mature and often leafless wood. The rounded flower clusters may be as much as a foot across and each contains about two dozen bell-shaped five-lobed blossoms. Each blossom is 3 or 4 inches long, a deep rose to purplish red or maroon in color on the outside of the corolla, and a creamy white to pale orange on the inside of the tube. This species likes its head in the sun and its feet in the shade. It is not especially fast growing. It is very tender to frost, intolerant of drought conditions, and needs a moist, friable soil with compost or leaf mold added. When young, it usually needs to be helped along to climb by tying it to a support until it gets going. It is not spectacular in bloom, but is quite beautiful, especially up close, and is a perfect choice for a protected but sunny position in tropical areas.

TECOMARIA (tek-o-MAHR-ee-a)
Bignoniaceae: The Catalpa, Jacaranda, Trumpet-
    Vine Family
CAPE HONEYSUCKLE
Evergreen scandent shrub and vine; large glossy
    pinnate leaves; spectacular orange or red flowers
Zones 9b through 11 as a permanent perennial; zone
    9a as a returning perennial
Sun to part sun
Average but regular amounts of moisture
Average well-drained soil
Propagation by cuttings and (sometimes) seed

A monotypic genus native to northeastern South Africa and southern Mozambique. *Tecomaria capensis* (ka-PENS-is) (synonyms *Bignonia capensis*, *Tecoma capensis*) is a sprawling scandent shrub with pliable stems that may be trained as a vine, espalier, hedge, or fountainlike shrub. It also can be used as a large groundcover since it freely suckers. The leaves are almost beautiful enough to have the plant around for their sake alone: they are odd-pinnate with seven or nine ovate dark glossy green leaflets that are strongly toothed on their margins and exhibit depressed midribs and lateral veins. The plant blooms in cycles year-round but most abundantly in fall, winter, and early spring. The bloom cycles seem to be triggered by dry periods followed by wet periods. The inflorescence is an erect terminal raceme consisting of many 2- to 3-inch-long deep orange to brick red curved tubular blossoms with five spreading corolla lobes in two groups. The upper group

has two lobes and the lower has three. The long protruding stamens are yellow-orange, and the blossoms are favorites of hummingbirds. The pods are thin, narrow, and about 6 inches long, and contain many flaky seeds, which are best removed unless they are desired for propagation. There are several very attractive cultivars with flowers ranging from orange-apricot to pure yellow. None of these are as vigorous or as free-blooming as the type, but they make excellent groundcovers or bedding plants. The plant does not twine or cling and, to simulate a vine, its pliable woody stems must first be tied to or guided through a support. In this manner the plant grows to as much as 20 feet. Left as a sprawling shrub, it grows only to about 6 feet high. It is especially beautiful cascading atop and over stone walls or similar forms, and nicely simulates a red or orange bougainvillea. It has been trained to a small tree or standard, which is exquisitely beautiful when in bloom, but such a form needs nearly constant pruning. The plant is not particular as to soil, needing only one that is well drained, but it must have at least a half day's sun to bloom well. It takes quite well to heavy pruning, which keeps it in bounds and (since it blooms on new wood) induces flowering. Plate 381.

TECTONA (tek-TOAN-a)
Verbenaceae: The Verbena, Lantana Family
TEAK
Tall semi-evergreen tree; beautiful gigantic elliptic
    leaves; large panicles of white and purple flowers
Zones 10b and 11
Sun
Average but regular amounts of moisture
Average well-drained soil
Propagation by seed and transplanting of suckers

A genus of four species of immense trees in India, Southeast Asia, Malaysia, and the Philippines. They have oppositely arranged leaves or leaves in whorls that are borne on four-angled stems. The flowers are formed in large terminal panicles of small white or blue five-petaled blossoms and produce four-sectioned dry berries. One species is very widely planted in tropical regions mainly for its very durable wood, which has many uses. *Tectona grandis* (GRAN-dis) is native to northeastern India, Myanmar (Burma), and Malaya, and grows to as much as 150 feet in its native habitats but usually only attains somewhat less than 100 feet in cultivation. It forms an oblong crown of tiered branches above a tall straight gray or light brown trunk. The trees are deciduous in monsoonal climates like those to which it is native but are often evergreen in constantly moist regions. The very widely elliptical, very short-stalked leaves are immense, as much as 3 feet long by at least 18 inches in width. The leaves are pubescent and bright green, with very prominent and yellowish midribs and lateral veins above, and a velvety and tawny color beneath. They lose most of their pubescence, especially on their upper surfaces, when they are mature.

These are among the most beautiful leaves in the plant kingdom. The trees bloom in summer in the Northern Hemisphere with great broad terminal panicles of small purple and white flowers. Many authors claim that the inflorescences are not showy, but I find them as pretty as those of many flowering trees. The round brown fruits are neither showy nor unattractive. This great magnificence seems not particular as to soil and grows quite well in those that are somewhat limy and relatively high in pH. It does not tolerate frost, especially when young, but recovers fast from temperatures above 30°F when older and if the subfreezing is not prolonged. It grows quickly when young but slows down in middle age to a mere medium-fast growth rate. It is not truly drought tolerant and, although it hails from monsoonal regions, this does not mean that the dry season is usually drought-ridden.

TERMINALIA (turm-i-NAL-ee-a)
Combretaceae: The Combretum Family
TROPICAL ALMOND; INDIAN ALMOND
Large evergreen and deciduous tree; tiered branches; large glossy green and red leaves; red fruit
Zones 10b and 11 as a tree; zones 10a and 9b as a shrub
Sun
Average but regular amounts of moisture; drought tolerant
Average well-drained soil
Propagation by seed

A large genus of about 200 species of evergreen mostly large trees in tropical regions around the world. They have large entire leaves that are crowded at the ends of the mostly horizontal branches, axillary spikes of small petal-less flowers, and berrylike large-seeded fruits. One species is very widely planted for its shade, beauty, and ability to flourish on the seacoast. *Terminalia catappa* (ka-TAP-pa) is native to Malaysia, Indonesia, northern Australia, and Polynesia. It grows to more than 100 feet in its native habitats but is usually no more than half that height on the tropical U.S. mainland. It forms one of the most distinctive tree silhouettes: a massive and short dark trunk bearing tiers of completely horizontal branches at the ends of which are clustered the large glossy leaves. Its canopy is pyramidal overall but, except in very old trees, is usually wider than tall. The foot-long nearly stalkless stiff leaves are leathery but glossy above, obovate to spatulate in shape, sometimes with truncated or emarginate ends, and dark green in color with prominent and lighter colored midribs and lateral veins. In its native lands the tree is completely deciduous about twice a year, usually corresponding with the onset of a dry season, but new leaves are added so quickly thereafter that for all practical purposes it is evergreen. The old leaves turn completely orange, orange-red, or purplish carmine before dropping, and this phenomenon may be witnessed to some degree at almost any time of the year in all re-

gions. The tree blooms mostly in spring and summer in the Northern Hemisphere with tail-like terminal spikes of tiny greenish white flowers. The 2-inch-long almond-shaped fruits are green turning rosy or red when they ripen. The seeds are edible and are mostly eaten roasted for the oily kernel, although they are also eaten raw. There is hardly a better tree for seaside planting as the beautiful tropical almond thrives in ocean spray and soil salinity. It grows equally well inland and seems to flourish in almost any soil, including limy ones, and is drought tolerant when established.

TETRAPANAX (tet-ra-PAN-ax)
Araliaceae: The Aralia, Schefflera Family
RICE-PAPER PLANT; CHINESE RICE-PAPER PLANT
Large evergreen multitrunked shrub; immense felty scalloped leaves; giant white flower clusters
Zones 10 and 11 as a large permanent shrub; zones 8 through 9 as a returning smaller shrub
Sun to partial shade
Average but regular amounts of moisture
Average well-drained soil
Invasive
Propagation by seed and transplanting of suckers

A monotypic genus native to Taiwan and adjacent southern China. The stems of *Tetrapanax papyriferus* (pap-i-RIF-e-rus) (synonyms *Aralia papyrifera*, *Fatsia papyrifera*) grow fairly quickly to as much as 15 feet or more in frost-free regions, the total height of the plants being more than 20 feet. The trunks are 2 to 3 inches wide, light brown or gray in color, ridged with many narrow fissures, never straight but always leaning, picturesquely curved to some extent, and very light in weight. The soft pith within is used in Asia for making the finest quality rice paper. Unless the trunks branch (and they do not usually do so without some sort of injury), the great leaves grow only from the ends of these tall thin trunks, creating a definite palmlike aspect. The plants sucker and usually create a wide clump of stems of varying heights, although there may be only one or two tall palmlike growths. The suckering is not limited to the immediate area of the original clump; it may occur at great distances from the clump, as much as 20 feet, especially if the original roots of the clump are disturbed.

The yellowish green to gray-green leaf stalks are as much as 3 feet long and they carry leaves that are as much as 30 inches wide. The leaves are circular or very broadly ovate in outline but are deeply lobed into seven to nine wide pleated segments, which are nearly overlapping and scalloped with smaller lobes that have shallowly toothed margins. Leaf color is medium to deep green above and a light grayish green beneath. The color is always greener in shade and more grayish green in full sun. Each segment shows a depressed and yellowish green midrib and lateral veins above, and is greenish yellow beneath. All the veins are stout and much raised on their undersurfaces. The leaves are pubescent above and below but especially beneath, and the new growth is covered in a fine white loose powdery substance that is irritating to the eyes and noses of some persons. *Tetrapanax papyriferus* 'Variegata', a spectacular cultivar, is very desirable in intimate settings, especially with a background of dark green or other color to set off its wonderful cream, green, and white coloring. It is not so successful however in other sites.

The plants bloom in winter or late fall, usually starting in early December, with immense terminal panicles of very many globose clusters of strangely but sweetly fragrant small white flowers. The panicles may be as much as 3 feet long, and there is usually more than one panicle at the end of a stem. The weight of these flower clusters sometimes causes the taller stems to bend. The fruits are small greenish round berries that ripen to black.

There are few more tropical looking landscape subjects, and the plants are basically carefree and grow quickly, especially with regular supplies of moisture. They are exceptionally handsome treated as small palms in the landscape, and the silhouettes of the giant leaves are stunning against walls or other similar backgrounds. Suckering can be a problem if the unwanted and errant growths are not removed when they first appear, and yet the groves they create are wonderfully beautiful. The plants do not like the full sun of very hot climates and are seldom successfully transplanted in the height of summer in such regions. They are damaged by temperatures below 30°F and are cut to the ground by temperatures in the low 20s, but they return vigorously with the advent of warm weather if the temperature does not fall below 10°F. They never attain the stature in climates subject to such temperatures that they do in truly subtropical areas; they will, however, sucker just as readily. Plates 382 and 383.

TETRASTIGMA (tet-ra-STIG-ma)
Vitaceae: The Grape Family
CHESTNUT VINE
Large evergreen succulent tendril-climbing vine;
    large palmately compound fleshy leaves
Zones 10 and 11
Shade to partial sun
Average but regular amounts of moisture
Average well-drained soil
Propagation by cuttings and (sometimes) seed

A genus of 90 species of large mostly evergreen vines in Southeast Asia, Malaysia, Indonesia, northern Australia, and the Philippines. They have large alternately arranged palmately (or digitately) compound fleshy leaves, rounded axillary clusters of small unisexual four-petaled flowers, and small berrylike fruits. One species is very widely planted in tropical and subtropical regions for its beautiful fleshy compound leaves. *Tetrastigma voinieranum* (voyn-yer-AHN-um) (synonyms *Cissus voinieranum*, *Vitis voinieranum*) is native to

Laos. It is a very vigorous high climbing liana that is used as much for a groundcover as it is for a vine. The fleshy reddish stems become ropelike as a mature climber, and the leaves are a foot or even more wide and consist of five (sometimes three) elliptic to obovate 8-inch-long fleshy leaflets with toothed margins. The new growth is covered in a wonderful cinnamon-colored pubescence. The plants do not often bloom in cultivation. The small yellowish flowers are in rounded axillary clusters and give way to small black berries. The vine climbs by thick stout coiling tendrils, but it also sprawls along the ground, rooting at the stem nodes, and is breathtakingly beautiful as a large groundcover. It climbs fairly quickly to great heights, clinging to any surface into or around which the tendrils can get a holdfast. It is especially beautiful cascading from atop walls, eaves, and similar forms. The plant looks as though it needs constant moisture and does not resent such conditions, but it is almost (but not quite) drought tolerant and requires only an average amount of water. It is not particular as to soil but appreciates one amended with humus. It is tender to frost but quickly grows back from temperatures above 28°F if the subfreezing does not last too long.

TETRAZYGIA (tet-ra-ZIJ-ee-a)
Melastomataceae: The Tibouchina Family
No known English common name
Evergreen shrub; beautifully veined leaves; terminal
    clusters of white and yellow flowers
Zones 10 and 11; marginal in zone 9b
Sun to partial sun
Average but regular amounts of moisture
Average well-drained soil
Propagation by seed

A genus of 12 or more species of small trees and shrubs in Florida and the West Indies. They have the beautifully veined leaf that is typical of this family, terminal panicles of flowers with large colorful stamens that are also typical of the family, and small berries. One species is planted as an ornamental for its beautiful leaves and flower clusters. *Tetrazygia bicolor* (BY-kul-or) is indigenous to southern Florida, the Bahamas, Cuba, Jamaica, and Hispaniola. It usually grows to about 15 feet as a large shrub but may occasionally reach twice that height and is easily trained to a standard tree form when young. The long-stalked leaves are narrowly lanceolate in shape, a glossy deep green above and a pale grayish green beneath, about 8 inches long, and usually somewhat curved with tapering ends. They are graced with three distinct longitudinal curved veins, and the leaf blade is somewhat puckered between the less distinct lateral veins. The tree blooms in spring and summer with erect pyramidal terminal panicles of half-inch-wide pure white four-petaled or five-petaled flowers, each with 10 protruding jointed golden stamens. Among native U.S. mainland plants, this is one of the most beautiful and should be much more widely grown.

It is not particular as to soil and is drought tolerant when established. It is an excellent hedge subject but is much more beautiful as a free-form shrub or small tree.

THALIA (THAL-ee-a / THAIL-ee-a)
Marantaceae: The Maranta Family
THALIA
Perennial bog plants; reedlike stems; *Canna*-like
   leaves; tall spikes of orchidlike purple flowers
Zones vary according to species
Sun to partial shade
Aquatic or bog plant
Rich, humusy, wet soil
Can be invasive
Propagation by root division, rhizome division,
   transplanting of suckers, and (sometimes) seed

A genus of 12 species of perennial rhizomatous and clumping bog plants with reedy stems and *Canna*-like but long-stemmed leaves arranged spirally around the stem. The terminal inflorescence is a loose-flowered panicle of small three-lobed violet or purple flowers. Although similar in form to *Canna* varieties, these plants are more delicate and graceful, more architectural, a sort of "designer's canna." They are quite handsome growing in the shallow edges of ponds or pools, where they add a valuable tall texture. They also grow out of shallow water as long as the soil is constantly moist. These plants are mostly ignored in horticulture, probably because their flowers are not spectacular. This situation should be changed, since the plants are lovely and tropical looking and deserve a much wider acceptance, especially for bog and water gardeners. The clumps spread quickly and can sometimes be invasive, but the stems are easily pulled up and pose no real threat to the landscape.

Thalia dealbata (day-al-BAHT-a) is native to the southeastern United States from South Carolina southwards through most of Florida and westward through Georgia, Alabama, Mississippi, Louisiana, southern Arkansas, and eastern Texas. It is hardy in zones 7 through 11 and marginal in zone 6. The plant grows to 6 or 8 feet in height with long-stalked 18- to 24-inch-long broadly lanceolate deep green to bluish green leaves that are covered in a powdery bloom when new and usually show a violet margin. The margins of the leaf blades are also generally somewhat upturned, giving a concavity to the blade. The plants bloom mostly in the fall with 2-foot-tall terminal spikes atop which are the closely set blossoms with pale blue bracts and violet-colored flowers. The stems die down to the ground with frost but return when constant warm weather ensues in the spring.

Thalia divaricata. See *T. geniculata.*

Thalia geniculata (jen-ik´-yoo-LAIT-a) (synonym *T. divaricata*) is native to central and southern Florida, the West Indies, northern South America, Central America, and most of Mexico. It is hardy in zones 10 and 11 as a permanent perennial and in zone 9 as a returning perennial. The plant is similar to *T. dealbata*, but the leaves are larger, up to 3 or more feet long, somewhat narrower and flatter, lack the white powdery covering, and are generally a lighter green in color. The flower spikes are taller and looser, and the individual flower clusters pendent. The attractive blossoms are basically the same color as those of *T. dealbata* but are slightly larger. This plant is very attractive and graceful for wet areas, especially if its form and flower color can be silhouetted against the water or a similar background. Plate 379.

THAUMATOPHYLLUM. See *Philodendron goeldii.*

THELYPTERIS (theh-LIP-te-ris)
Thelypteridaceae: The Maiden Fern or Wood Fern
   Family
WOOD FERN; MAIDEN FERN; SOUTHERN
   WOOD FERN
Medium-sized evergreen lacy clump-forming ferns
Zones 10 and 11 as permanent perennials; zones 8
   and 9 as returning perennials
Shade to sun
Average but regular amounts of moisture
Average well-drained soil
Propagation by root division, rhizome division,
   transplanting of suckers, and spores

A large genus of terrestrial ferns worldwide in its distribution but primarily in the tropics and subtropics. The scientific names of these ferns are in terrible disarray, and the common names do not help the situation as there are very many duplicates and similarities from other genera. Most plants now labeled in the trade as *Dryopteris* or *Thelypteris* are likely to change in the not-too-distant future as more botanical research is done. All the species are very easy of culture and quite ferny and tropical looking. One species is very widely available and planted. *Thelypteris kunthii* (KOONT-ee-eye) (synonyms *Cyclosorus kunthii, Dryopteris kunthii, D. normalis, Thelypteris normalis*) is native to the Gulf Coast region of the United States, the West Indies, and Central America. The pubescent bipinnate fronds are as much as 4 feet long, lanceolate in outline, and a bright light green in color. This fern grows fast in shade or sun and quickly makes large clumps or colonies. It is not particular as to soil and thrives in boggy conditions as well as almost dry sites. It is cut to the ground by temperatures at or below 28°F but quickly returns from the roots with the advent of warm weather. It is normally called wood fern or southern wood fern, but in regions to which it is not native it may be termed southern maiden fern. As a landscape subject it is fine, carefree, and dependable.

THESPESIA (thes-PEEZ-ee-a)
Malvaceae: The Mallow, Hibiscus, Cotton Family
PORTIA TREE; SEASIDE MAHOE; CORK
   TREE; FALSE ROSEWOOD

Small to medium-sized evergreen tree; beautiful large leaves; spectacular hibiscus-like flowers

Zones 10b and 11 as permanent trees; zones 10a and 9b as returning shrubs

Sun

Average but regular amounts of moisture

Average well-drained soil

Propagation by seed and cuttings

A genus of about 17 species of trees and shrubs in tropical regions around the world. They have relatively large cordate and often lobed leaves and axillary cup-shaped hibiscus-like flowers. One species is so widely grown in tropical coastal regions that its origins are obscured, although it is probably originally indigenous to the Old World tropics. ***Thespesia populnea*** (po-PUL-nee-a) grows quickly to 40 or 50 feet and, inland, forms a dense spreading round-topped canopy atop a low thick dark-colored trunk. When grown on the seashore, it is low and spreading with a windswept and contorted trunk. The beautiful long-stalked 4- or 5-inch-long leaves are perfectly cordate with tapering ends, deep green leathery and glossy above, with striking and lighter colored midrib and lateral veins in a radiating pattern. The tree blooms year-round in tropical areas with solitary 2-inch-long cup-shaped hibiscus-like yellow flowers that mature to pink or red. The petals do not unfold to a flat face as do those of *Hibiscus rosa-sinensis* blossoms but rather remain half-rolled; the petals overlap to form a bell-shaped tube. The fruit is a 1- or 2-inch-wide brown leathery cup-shaped affair that is flat on the top. This tree is about as salt-tolerant as any but mangrove species and grows not in the surf but near it, even on the sand dunes. It thrives in almost any well-drained soil and is drought tolerant. There are few more beautiful seaside subjects. It is similar to and often confused with *Hibiscus tiliaceus;* both trees grow in the same coastal areas but the seaside mahoe has smaller and less rounded leaves and smaller flowers that do not open as wide as those of *H. tiliaceus.*

THEVETIA

(theh-VEE-tee-a / theh-VET-ee-a)

Apocynaceae: The Oleander, Frangipani, Vinca Family

YELLOW OLEANDER; LUCKY NUT; BE-STILL TREE

Large evergreen shrubs and small trees; oleander-like leaves; yellow funnel-shaped fragrant flowers

Zones 10 and 11 as small tree; zone 9b as returning shrub

Sun

Average but regular amounts of moisture

Sandy, humusy, well-drained soil

Propagation by seed and cuttings

A genus of eight evergreen shrub and tree species in tropical America. They have milky poisonous sap, alternately arranged leaves, terminal clusters of funnel-shaped flowers with twisted petals, and flattish hard seed pods. All parts of these plants are very poisonous. One species is widely planted for its attractive foliage and beautiful flowers. ***Thevetia peruviana*** (pe-roo´-vee-AHN-a) (synonym *T. neriifolia*) is indigenous to the West Indies, southeastern Mexico, and Belize. It is a large shrub or small tree growing quickly to as much as 20 or sometimes 30 feet in the warmest regions and is easily trained to tree form when young. The bright green and glossy linear leaves are 6 or 7 inches long and look much like those of *Nerium oleander* (oleander). The plants bloom year-round in tropical regions but mostly in the summer and fall. The terminal inflorescence is few-flowered, but the flowers are relatively large, up to 3 inches long and bell-shaped or funnel-shaped with the five overlapping corolla lobes somewhat twisted (a characteristic of the family). The flowers are usually a clear, bright yellow in color, but may also be somewhat more orange or peach-colored. Some blossoms are fragrant with the scent of roses, but others are unaccountably lacking in aroma. The fruit is a rounded to almost flat four-sided hard black pod containing flat seeds, which are deadly poisonous. The little tree is severely damaged by temperatures of 30°F or lower but quickly recovers if the temperature does not fall below 25°F for very long. It cannot be maintained as a tree form in climates subject to freezing temperatures. It grows well in almost any soil and has a slight tolerance to salt spray, but it seems to appreciate a sandy humusy soil. The plant is a beauty either as a standard with one or several trunks or as a large shrub clothed to the ground in branches. Shrub forms that are bare at the base are not very handsome. The narrow leaves add great texture to shrub borders, and the large yellow flowers make this plant irresistibly attractive. As a patio tree in sunny sites it is almost unexcelled. It should never be planted where inquisitive children might have access to its allure.

THRINAX (TRY-nax)

Palmae (Arecaceae): The Palm Family

THATCH PALMS

Small to medium-sized solitary thin-trunked fan-leaved palms of exquisite gracefulness

Zones 10 and 11; marginal in zone 10a

Sun to partial sun

Average but regular amounts of moisture; drought tolerant

Average well-drained soil

Propagation by seed

A small genus of only seven species of slender-trunked palmate-leaved palms in tropical America. They have smooth and slender very straight gray to light brown trunks atop which are poised rounded crowns of nearly circular segmented leaves that are carried on slender petioles. The inflorescences are long, erect panicles of whitish flowers, which give way to drooping clusters of white berries. These palms are without exception exceedingly graceful and beautiful and, because of the thin straight trunks, have a diminutive stateliness matched by few other plants. They have only one fault: they are quite slow-growing and because of this usually do not recover from temperatures below 30°F. The trees, which are quite tolerant of salt spray, grow near the seacoast as well as inland. They are tolerant of slightly saline soil and revel in calcareous and alkaline soils as well as those of neutral pH. The following species are drought tolerant when established.

Thrinax altissima. See *Coccothrinax alta.*

Thrinax ekmanii. See *T. morrisii.*

Thrinax excelsa (ek-SEL-sa) (synonym *T. rex*) is native only to the island of Jamaica. One of the largest species, it forms as much as 30 feet of slender trunk and attains a total height approaching 40 feet. The 6- to 7-foot-wide bright green to bluish green leaves are perhaps the largest in the genus. They are completely circular in outline, and the segments are definitely and beautifully pendent at their ends. The petioles are longer than the width of the leaves, resulting in one of the most beautiful leaf crowns of any palm species: completely round and open. There are very few more beautiful palms or trees of any kind in this world. Plate 384.

Thrinax floridana. See *T. radiata.*

Thrinax keyensis. See *T. morrisii.*

Thrinax microcarpa. See *T. morrisii.*

Thrinax morrisii (mor-RIS-ee-eye) (synonyms *T. ekmanii, T. keyensis, T. microcarpa*) is indigenous to the Florida Keys and the West Indies. It grows to as much as 20 feet with almost that height of slender trunk. The leaves are as much as 5 feet wide and nearly circular in outline with deep and stiff segments that are bright green above with varying degrees of silver beneath. The petioles are about 6 feet long, giving the leaf crown a rounded and full aspect. The palm is sometimes called the Key thatch palm or the peaberry palm.

Thrinax parviflora (par-vi-FLOR-a) is indigenous to the small island of Jamaica. This incredibly beautiful small palm grows to 20 or sometimes 25 feet in height with a full and rounded or oblong leaf crown. The 3- or 4-foot-wide deep green leaves are circular in outline with deep but broad segments that are somewhat pliable and often twisted to some extent. The leaves are carried on 5-foot-long petioles and are constantly shimmering in the slightest breeze.

Thrinax radiata (ray-dee-AIT-a / ray-dee-AHT-a) (synonyms *T. floridana, T. wendlandiana*) is native to southern Florida, the West Indies, southeastern Mexico, and Belize. It grows to 20 or 25 feet with time. The leaf canopy is rounded and consists of as many as 18 or 20 leaves whose stalks are not as long as those of most other *Thrinax* species, giving a compact but beautiful aspect to the palm's crown. Each leaf is nearly circular in outline with long broad and pendulous bright green to yellow green segments. This species seems slightly more hardy to cold than the others.

Thrinax rex. See *T. excelsa.*

Thrinax wendlandiana. See *T. radiata.*

THUNBERGIA

(thun-BURJ-ee-a / toon-BERG-ee-a)
Acanthaceae: The Acanthus Family
Common names vary according to species
Evergreen vines and scandent shrubs; large trumpet-shaped flowers in every color
Zones vary according to species
Sun to partial shade
Average but regular amounts of moisture
Rich, humusy, moist, well-drained soil
Propagation by seed and cuttings

A genus of about 100 species of herbs, shrubs, and mostly twining vines in tropical Africa, Madagascar, and tropical Asia. They have oppositely arranged usually large simple leaves, flowers that are funnel-shaped to salverform with five spreading corolla lobes in every color of the rainbow, and small round seed capsules.

Thunbergia alata (a-LAIT-a) is native to tropical East Africa and is hardy as a permanent vine in zones 10b and 11, as a returning perennial vine in zones 9b and 10a, and as an annual anywhere the growing season is 5 months or more. This small, slender-stemmed twining or trailing plant seldom grows to more than 10 feet and is universally called the black-eyed-Susan vine in English-speaking countries. The long-stalked leaves are triangular-ovate in shape, about 3 inches long, rough, and hairy, with deeply depressed veins above. The leaves are a bright light green in color and usually have a few sharp lobes on the leaf margins. The solitary funnel-shaped flowers are formed year-round in tropical regions but mostly in summer and fall elsewhere. They cover the vine when it is in bloom. Each blossom is about 2 inches long and slightly more than an inch wide with a five-lobed corolla. Each lobe is notched at its apex. Flower color is white or ivory with a deep purple throat, but several cultivars, which have yellow or orange flowers with black throats, are more popular then the type. The vine grows rapidly and blooms the first season from seed. It is not drought tolerant and needs at least a half day's sun to bloom well. It is often pruned back almost to the ground in winter, even in tropical areas, to renew its vigor and bloom capacity. It is as easily grown as an annual even in frost-free regions. It is quite attractive and free-flowering on small trellises or even more so as a cascade atop walls or in hanging baskets and makes a superb groundcover for sunny frost-free areas if regular amounts of water can be supplied.

Thunbergia erecta (e-REK-ta) is indigenous to most of tropical Africa and is hardy in zones 10 and 11 as a permanent perennial and in zone 9 as a returning perennial. This herbaceous shrub grows to 6 or 8 feet in height. It is seldom sprawling enough to use as a vine. The little shrub is burdened with the oxymoronic vernacular of bush clock-vine and sometimes king's mantle. The deep green 3-inch-long leaves are ovate to elliptic in shape with long-tapering ends and are remotely and shallowly lobed or completely unlobed. The plant blooms year-round in frost-free regions with 3-inch-long blue to violet flowers with yellow or orange throats. The outside of the long corolla tube is usually white. The color of the blue-flowered form is extremely pleasing, but the plants are not spectacular in the landscape. They are best used as close-up subjects. The shrub is not very particular as to soil but needs some sun to bloom well and usually requires some pruning to maintain a desired shape. Plate 385.

Thunbergia fragrans (FRAY-granz) is native to Sri Lanka and tropical India and is hardy only in zones 10 and 11 as a permanent vine and zone 9b as a returning perennial. It is a twining vine that grows quickly but only to about 12 or 15 feet in height with many slender stems. The leaves are similar to those of *T. alata*, about 3 inches long, deep green, ovate-triangular in shape with remote and shallowly lobed margins. The plants bloom mostly in warm weather with 2-inch-wide white five-lobed flowers that are only very slightly fragrant, if at all. The corolla lobes are scalloped and sometimes deeply notched, and the flower's throat is usually a pale yellow. This plant is as often used for a groundcover in full sun as it is as a vine.

Thunbergia gibsonii. See *T. gregorii.*

Thunbergia grandiflora (gran-di-FLOR-a) is indigenous to tropical India and is hardy in zones 10 and 11 as a permanent vine and in zone 9b (and sometimes zone 9a) as a returning vine. One of the world's most beautiful twining vines, it is strong growing and very large, often attaining heights of 50 feet or more in tropical regions. The beautiful 6- to 8-inch-long leaves are thick and succulent yet rough to the touch, broadly ovate to lanceolate in shape, with long-tapering ends and scalloped margins. The plant blooms year-round in cycles in frost-free areas but always most heavily in summer and fall. The pure blue to mauve-blue funnel-shaped flowers are in pendent loose and few-flowered clusters. Each blossom is about 3 inches long with a flat disk of five expanded corolla lobes often marked with white or darker stripes, especially the lowermost lobe. The throat of each flower is white to yellow. There is a pure white cultivar that is at least as beautiful and is even more outstanding in the landscape. While the stems of the sky flower or blue trumpet vine are fairly slender, the vine makes a dense mass of heavy thick leaves and needs a strong support to which it must usually be tied at first. It needs adequate and regular supplies of moisture and a rich humusy soil, and does not bloom well without at least a half day's sun. This species is also sometimes called Bengal clock-vine. Plate 386.

Thunbergia gregorii (gray-GOR-ee-eye) (synonym *T. gibsonii*) is native to tropical East Africa and is hardy only in zones 10 and 11 as a permanent vine and in zone 9b as a returning vine. This twining climber or trailer grows to 15 feet or more and is similar in every respect to *T. alata* (black-eyed Susan vine) except for the color of the flowers which, in this case, are a vivid deep orange with no "eye." This vine is usually called the orange clock vine.

Thunbergia laurifolia (law-ri-FO-lee-a) is native to tropical India and is hardy in zones 10 and 11, somewhat marginal in zone 10a, and usually returns from the roots in zone 9b. Compared with *T. grandiflora*, it is perhaps even more beautiful, grows to even greater heights, has leaves without scalloped margins, and has larger, lighter blue flowers. Both species have the same cultural requirements. In addition, the deep green 6-inch-long leaves of *T. laurifolia* are ovate-lanceolate in shape, thick, and leathery.

Thunbergia mysorensis (my´-sor-EN-sis) is also indigenous to tropical India and is hardy in zones 10 and 11, although it often returns from the root in zone 9b. It is a rampantly growing large vine that may reach heights of 50 feet or more and has a dense cover of heavy foliage. The deep green 6-inch-long leaves are ovate-lanceolate in shape, leathery in texture, and shallowly scalloped on their margins. The vine blooms all year in tropical regions with long and pendent inflorescences of rather strange 2- or 3-inch-long red and yellow blossoms. The corolla tube is curved and elongated into a hooded fashion and is somewhat flattened overall, glistening red or brownish red on the outside and a bright canary yellow within with immense yellowish white stamens and anthers peeking from inside the tube. This vine is quite spectacular in bloom and is possibly the most spectacular *Thunbergia* species in the landscape.

THYRSACANTHUS. See *Odontonema schomburgkianum.*

TIBOUCHINA (tib-oo-CHEEN-a)
Melastomataceae: The Tibouchina Family
Common names vary according to species
Large evergreen shrubs and small trees; beautifully
    veined leaves; large purple and pink flowers
Zones vary according to species
Sun to partial sun
Average but regular amounts of moisture
Rich, humusy, well-drained, acidic soil
Propagation by cuttings

A large genus of about 350 species of evergreen shrubs and trees in tropical America, mostly Brazil. They have mostly four-angled stems and beautiful short-stalked leaves (as is characteristic of the family) with deep longitudinal veins. The blade is somewhat quilted between the veins, and the leaves usually turn a bright orange or orange-red before falling. The five-petaled flowers have jointed stamens typical of the family and are terminal on the stems, usually in loose panicles colored white, yellow, orange, pink, red, blue, or purple. This is yet another wonderful genus of plants whose members are lamentably mostly absent in horticulture. The genus is rife with wondrous species of greatly varying character and should be much more widely exploited for gardens in the tropics and subtropics.

Tibouchina grandiflora. See *T. urvilleana.*

Tibouchina granulosa (gran-yoo-LO-sa) is indigenous to western Brazil and eastern Bolivia and is hardy as a tree in zones 10b and 11 and as a returning shrub in zone 10a and 9b. It grows quickly to as much as 40 feet in its native habitat but is usually about half that height in cultivation. The stems are four-angled, and the new growth is clothed in a reddish bronze felt. The wonderful 8-inch-long leaves are narrowly elliptic to lanceolate in shape and a dark green in color, pubescent beneath but usually smooth and almost glossy above. The little tree blooms year-round but most heavily in summer and fall. The flowers are in erect terminal panicles and each five-petaled 2-inch-wide blossom is a deep rose to violet in color. The plant is sometimes called the purple glory tree.

Tibouchina semidecandra. See *T. urvilleana.*

Tibouchina urvilleana (ur-vil´-lee-AHN-a) (synonyms *T. grandiflora, T. semidecandra*) is native to southern and eastern Brazil. It is hardy in zones 10 and 11 as a permanent perennial, marginal in zone 9b, and as a returning perennial in zone 9a. It grows quickly to as much as 18 or even 20 feet in height but is usually somewhat smaller and is easily trained to a small tree form in frost-free areas. The stems are four-angled and pubescent, and the new growth is densely covered in glistening orange to reddish hairs. The leaves are narrowly ovate to mostly elliptic in shape, about 6 inches long, a medium green in color, slightly and silvery pubescent above but densely so beneath. The leaves are margined with red or orange in the summer in hot regions and with the advent of cold weather. The plant blooms year-round but most heavily in early summer into late fall. The flowers are in few-flowered erect and terminal panicles. Each five-petaled velvety-textured blossom is 3 to 5 inches wide and a wonderful royal purple in color. The contrast with the golden stamens is truly magnificent. The shrub does not like hot summer regions but nevertheless blooms more or less dependably in those areas, especially in the cooler months. It is at its best in cooler Mediterranean climates like that of coastal southern California and is almost universally termed the princess flower in English-speaking countries but sometimes also glory-bush.

TILLANDSIA (til-LAND-zee-a)
Bromeliaceae: The Pineapple, Bromeliad Family
Common names vary according to species
Epiphytic strap or linear and wiry-leaved plants of
    greatly varying sizes; showy spikes of flowers
Zones vary according to species
Partial shade to sun
Moisture requirements vary greatly according to
    species
Leaf mold or epiphytic mix or no soil
Propagation by root division, transplanting of
    suckers, and stem division

An immense genus of more than 500 species, the largest and most widespread genus (from coastal Virginia to Tierra del Fuego) in the bromeliad family. The individual plants range in size and form from tiny and threadlike to very large rosettes of strap-shaped leaves. The flowers may be tiny and solitary or in 10-foot-tall spikes, and flower color spans the entire spectrum. *Tillandsia* species inhabit areas from sea level to well over 2 miles in elevation, and their hardiness ranges from complete intolerance of frost to that of most pine trees. Many species are xerophytic and grow on cactus trees or rocks in the hot Latin American or South American deserts. Indeed, one species grows on desert sands in what is possibly the driest if not the hottest desert in the world, the Atacama of Peru. Others luxuriate in the moist half-shade of tropical rain forests. The xeric species have silvery scalelike hairs covering their wiry leaves. These scales not only absorb whatever moisture comes their way, but also protect the chlorophyll areas of the leaf from the ultraviolet of the tropical sun. Most species, being true "air plants," do not need any soil to flourish. Almost all are clumping plants that form offsets at the base of the plants, by stolons, or sometimes from the inflorescence or the stem of the plant. All have tubular flowers encased in colorful bracts, and on most inflorescences the flowers are arranged on opposite sides in one plane. Almost all species bloom in late autumn through winter, and some of the inflorescences are quite long lasting. Some species are monocarpic, but most are not. A few produce only very few if any offshoots but the plants do not die after flowering. The seeds (fruits) have propeller-like wings by which they are dispersed far and wide. The following are selections of the larger and easier grown species and those which, because of their spectacular inflorescences, make some statement in the landscape.

Tillandsia cacticola (kak-ti-KO-la) is native to northwestern Peru where it grows on cactus plants, thorny *Acacia* species, and other bush and tree-form vegetation. It is not adaptable outside zones 10 and 11. The lance-shaped leaves are as much as 18 inches long, usually somewhat twisted and grayish green to silvery green in color, and form a rather flat rosette. The inflorescence is of exceptional beauty: a branched spike as much as 2 feet tall with lovely waxy and iridescent pink to lavender, fat lance-shaped bracts enclosing delicate white flowers, which reach out some distance from their housing. This species is one of the most beautiful in the genus when in bloom. Plate 387.

Tillandsia capitata (kap-i-TAIT-a) is indigenous to the West Indies, eastern Mexico, and eastern Central America, and is hardy in zones 10 and 11. It forms a rosette that is 18 to 24 inches wide and consists of many grayish green recurved and arching leaves, each of which is concave in cross section and 12 to 16 inches long. The plants turn orange or red, especially near the center of the rosette, when they bloom. The inflorescence is formed atop the lengthening stem with its colored leaves and is relatively small and compact but, because of the change in leaf color, is spectacular. The flowers are a vivid purple with protruding yellow stamens. The plant grows on rocks and trees in full sunlight and is drought tolerant but needs relatively high humidity in the air. It thrives near the seashore.

Tillandsia caput-medusae (kap´-ut-MED-yoo-sy / kap´-ut-me-DOO-see) is native to southern Mexico and Central America in tropical deciduous forests of low mountains and is hardy in zones 10 and 11. It forms a rosette as much as 2 feet wide with a bulbous base and soft pliable grooved foot-long and much twisted bright green leaves with silvery scales. The inflorescence is sparsely branched with several linear spikes of intensely red bracts and small blue flowers. The plant, which needs some sun to bloom, is spectacular when in flower and is always interesting because of the tentacle-like leaves.

Tillandsia cyanea (sy-AIN-ee-a) is indigenous to coastal areas of Ecuador and is hardy in zones 10b and 11. It forms a 2-foot-wide rosette of narrow, arching, and recurved deep green grasslike leaves. The inflorescence is among the most beautiful in the genus: it is a foot tall with a flat obovate fan that turns a brilliant cerise to deep rose in color. The large deep rose to deep purple three-petaled flowers emerge from the fan of bracts. This plant needs constant humidity and partial shade, and must never dry out. There are several cultivars of this popular species, including one with leaves beautifully variegated with longitudinal yellow stripes.

Tillandsia dasylirifolia (day´-zee-leer-i-FO-lee-a) occurs naturally from central and southern Mexico through Central America to Colombia, and is hardy in zones 10 and 11. This urn-shaped plant has a distinctly bulbous base to the rosette. The narrowly lanceolate leaves are fairly stiff and are about a foot long and an inch wide at their bases; they are grayish green to bluish green in color. The great flower spike is branched and resembles more that of the genus *Aechmea* than most *Tillandsia* species; it is as much as 4 feet tall and is pink in color with narrowly cylindrical purple and white flowers. The plant needs sun and is quite drought tolerant.

Tillandsia deppeana (dep-pee-AHN-a) is native to a vast area of tropical America from the West Indies and southern Mexico through Central America and into Colombia and Ecuador and is hardy in zones 10 and 11. It grows from near sea level to altitudes exceeding 2 miles. Because of its range, it is a variable species forming rosettes from 3 to 6 feet wide that consist of bright green strap-shaped leaves from 2 to 4 feet long. The inflorescence may attain a height of 6 feet or be as short as 2 feet and consists of a panicle of fan-shaped spikes that are orange to rose in color with bright purple flowers. The plant is adaptable in sun or semishade and to wet or dry conditions.

Tillandsia fasciculata (fas-sik´-yoo-LAIT-a) occurs naturally from southern Florida through the West Indies and into northern South America, Central America, and eastern Mexico. It is adaptable to zones 9b through 11. The plant is epiphytic on all manner of trees and is a quite variable species. The leaves vary in length from 1 to 3 feet or more and the inflorescence

from 1 to 4 feet in height. The leaves are stiff but pliable and form a full and widespreading rosette. They are usually a dusty or grayish green but may also have a beautiful reddish hue, especially in bright sun. The inflorescence consists of branching racemes of green, yellow, or red bracts and small purple flowers. The species is very easy to grow and requires nearly constantly high relative humidity and protection from hard freezes. It is one of the most spectacular species indigenous to the mainland United States. Plate 388.

Tillandsia flexuosa (flex-yoo-O-sa) is native to southern Florida, the West Indies, Panama, and northern South America. It is hardy in zones 9b through 11. The plant forms an urn-shaped 2-foot-wide rosette of grayish green narrowly lanceolate recurved and twisted leaves that have transverse bands of silver. The erect inflorescence is as much as 3 feet tall and consists of a few branched spikes of flat lance-shaped clusters of pale green bracts with white, pink, or purple flowers. This one likes sun or shade and tolerates wet or dry conditions as long as the relative humidity level is fairly high.

Tillandsia grandis (GRAN-dis) occurs naturally from the states of Veracruz and Yucatán in Mexico, northern Guatemala, Belize, eastern Honduras, and northern Nicaragua, and is hardy in zones 10b and 11. It is the largest species in the genus, growing to as much as 15 feet when in bloom. It forms a broad rosette, and the leaves are about 5 feet long by 2 to 6 inches wide, and straplike with tapering ends. Leaf color is a deep bluish green usually with purplish undersides. The inflorescence may reach a height of 12 or 15 feet and is a giant candelabra form with widely spaced and long-stalked flat fan-shaped spikes of green and yellow bracts with white nocturnal flowers. This great bromeliad is adapted to sun and high humidity levels.

Tillandsia lampropoda (lamp-ro-PO-da) is native to mountains of central Mexico and is hardy in zones 9b through 11. It forms a rosette of foot-long narrow grayish green erect and long tapering leaves. The inflorescence is about 2 feet tall and is a wide flat lanceolate-shaped fan of scarlet, yellow, and green bracts with small yellow flowers. The plant is drought tolerant and is adapted to sun or semi-shade.

Tillandsia lindenii (lin-DEN-ee-eye) is native to the mountains of Ecuador and Peru and is hardy in zones 10 and 11. It forms a full rosette of 1- to 2-foot-long narrow recurved deep green grasslike leaves. The inflorescence rises a foot or more above the foliage and is a narrowly lanceolate-shaped flat fan of greenish bronzy orange bracts. Emerging from the bracts are the extraordinarily large three-petaled blue to lilac-colored flowers usually with a patch of white at the base of each petal. The plant flourishes in partial shade and high humidity.

Tillandsia streptophylla (strep-toe-FYL-la) is indigenous to montane forests in the West Indies, southern Mexico, and Central Mexico, and is hardy in zones 10 and 11. It is a relatively broad-leaved species, and the velvety grayish green to brownish green leaves bizarrely curl and twist. The species makes a stem to some extent and can reach a height of 2 feet. The inflorescence is exceptional: a much-branched and quite tall red-stemmed spike with white and rose bracts and small purple flowers.

Tillandsia tricolor (TRY-kul-or) is indigenous to southeastern Mexico southwards through Belize and into Nicaragua and is hardy in zones 10 and 11. It forms a foot-wide full and rounded rosette of stiff narrow tapering scaly olive green leaves. The inflorescence is a single tall erect coral-red spike with a narrowly linear group of bracts at its end. The bracts, which change from a vivid green to yellow and then red as they age, exhibit all three colors on the stem. The flowers are violet in color. The plant needs some sun or very bright light and humidity.

Tillandsia usneoides (oos-nee-OY-deez) has a greater natural range than any bromeliad species—from coastal Virginia to southern Argentina. Few plants of any type have such a wide range. The species is hardy in zones 7 through 11. It is the Spanish moss of the American South, famous for festooning the great live oaks of the Gulf Coast region. The individual plants are rootless, very thin and threadlike, much-branching light green stems covered in silver-colored scales. The 1- to 2-inch-long thin, curved and scaly silvery green leaves occur on the stems at intervals of an inch or so. The stems normally reach a length of 4 to 10 feet but may, in rare instances, be as long as 100 feet. They hang mostly from trees but, in sufficiently humid and favorable regions, may adorn rock faces, cave entrances, telephone lines, houses, or almost any other structure. The flowers are tiny, green, blue, or violet-colored, and nocturnally fragrant. The plants grow in sun or shade. Their only requirements are high humidity and winters in which the temperature does not fall below 0°F or remain below freezing for long periods. These plants add an inimitable atmosphere to the landscape, one which no other plant can reproduce and one whose great beauty is easily forgotten or overlooked by people living in the plant's range. Plate 379.

Tillandsia utriculata (oo-trik´-yoo-LAIT-a) is indigenous to southern Florida, the West Indies, and northern Venezuela, and is hardy in zones 10 and 11. It forms a 1- to 2-foot-wide rosette of long and pliable 2- to 3-foot-long lanceolate-shaped light green leaves that are pendent and usually long drooping. The inflorescence is as much as 4 feet tall and regularly and widely branches into lanceolate spikes of yellow-green bracts with white flowers. The plant flourishes in sunny to shady conditions but needs high humidity.

Tillandsia wagneriana (wag-ner´-ee-AHN-a) is native to eastern Peru and is adaptable only to zones 10b and 11. It forms open 2-foot-wide rosettes of thick very broad strap-shaped 18-inch-long deep green leaves. The inflorescence is about 2 feet tall and consists of a light pink stem and a whorl of flat lance-shaped spikes of pink bracts from which emerge the small purple or violet-colored flowers. The plant flourishes in shade to semishade and must have high humidity, regular water, and warmth.

Tillandsia xerographica (zer-o-GRAF-i-ka) is native to coastal areas of southern Mexico and Central America and is hardy in zones 10b and 11. This spectacular plant forms light gray to almost white or pinkish white rosettes that are 2 feet or more in width. The 2-foot-long linear leaves are recurved and often coiled to some extent at their ends, and are covered with white powdery scales. At blooming time the stem of the rosette elongates to as much as 3 feet to form an inflorescence well above the rosette. The bracts are red and green, and the flowers are purple. The plant needs sun to bloom and is drought tolerant.

TIPUANA (tip-oo-AHN-a)

Papilionaceae (Fabaceae, Leguminosae), subfamily
    Papilionoideae: The Bean, Pea Family
TIPU TREE; ROSEWOOD; PRIDE OF BOLIVIA
Large evergreen tree; pinnate dark green leaves; large
    clusters of yellow flowers
Zones 10 and 11; marginal in zone 9b
Sun
Average but regular amounts of moisture
Average well-drained soil
Propagation by seed

A monotypic genus native to southern Bolivia and northwestern Argentina. In the forests of its native habitat, *Tipuana tipu* (TIP-oo) often grows to 100 feet with a massive, buttressed, tall, and straight trunk, but in cultivation and planted in open sites it always forms a broad rather open, flat-topped or dome-shaped canopy above a massive short dark brown trunk. Some old trees are intensely, almost heartbreakingly beautiful and picturesque with the form of old *Delonix* (royal poinciana) or *Samanea* (rain tree) species: low-branched with massive and horizontally growing but contorted zigzagging limbs. The odd-pinnate leaves are about a foot long and consist of 13 to 21 olive green to yellowish green oblong 1- to 2-inch-long leaflets. The tree is often deciduous in its native habitat where there is usually a distinct dry season, but is mostly evergreen in regions with regular rainfall. It flowers from late spring through most of the summer with axillary racemes of butterfly-like light yellow to orange-yellow flowers. The fruits are 2-inch-long winged pods. The tree is frost sensitive, especially when young, but can usually withstand a temperature of 28°F without severe damage. Old wood is immune to temperatures as low as 24°F or even 22°F if the subfreezing does not last too long, but the tree is cut back by such temperatures. It is fast growing and not terribly particular as to soil, but is not drought tolerant.

TOURNEFORTIA. See *Mallotonia*.

TRACHYCARPUS (traik-ee-KAR-pus)
Palmae (Arecaceae): The Palm Family
WINDMILL PALM; CHINESE WINDMILL
   PALM; MONKEY PALM; CHUSAN PALM
Medium-sized slender solitary-trunked fan-leaved
   palm with furry trunk
Zones 7b through 11; marginal in zone 7a
Sun to partial shade
Average but regular amounts of moisture
Average well-drained soil
Propagation by seed

A small genus of only four to six species of palmate-leaved palms in northern India, northern Myanmar (Burma), northern Thailand, and southern China. They are slow-growing solitary-trunked palms with their trunks often covered, except at the base, in a thick mat of furry leaf base fibers. The leaf crowns are rounded and compact. One species is widely planted in subtropical and warm-temperate regions. *Trachycarpus fortunei* (for-TYOON-ee-eye) (synonyms *Chamaerops excelsa*, *Trachycarpus excelsus*) is native to southern China. Very old palms grow to as much as 40 feet in their native haunts but this is rare in cultivation, 20 to 25 feet usually being the maximum. The trunk is very straight and quite slender, although when covered with the brown to gray leaf base fibers it may appear to have two or three times its actual diameter. The 2- to 3-foot-wide deep green leaves are almost circular in outline and are divided to more than halfway to the center of the blade into many linear stiff segments whose ends do not usually droop; however, some individual palms have pendent leaf segments. The leaf crown is dense and rounded with two dozen or more leaves. Each leaf is carried on a 1- to 2-foot-long toothed petiole. These trees do not flourish in hot climates where they are shorter-lived and the furry trunks are usually messier looking. They are much more at home in Mediterranean and cool-summer regions like the Riviera and coastal California, Oregon, and Washington, although they are widely planted in hot and humid climes like the Upper Gulf Coast region. This palm is one of the world's hardiest and the hardiest of the tree-form palms. There are mature specimens in Vancouver, British Columbia, Canada; Scotland; Ireland; and even in the lower elevations of Switzerland. Because of its slow growth and neat, almost formal appearance, the palm is exceptionally beautiful in close-up sites and is almost as beautiful planted singly as in small groups of palms of varying heights. Its silhouette is stunningly attractive.

TRADESCANTIA. See *Callisia*.

TREVESIA (tre-VEE-zee-a)
Araliaceae: The Aralia, Schefflera Family
Common names vary according to species
Evergreen shrubs and small trees; immense rounded and lobed leaves; large clusters of yellow flowers
Zones 10 and 11
Sun to partial shade
Average but regular amounts of moisture
Rich, humusy, well-drained, acidic soil
Propagation by cuttings

A small genus of about a dozen evergreen trees and shrubs in southern Asia, Malaysia, Indonesia, and the islands of the South Pacific. They are often armed with thorns, and the leaves are round in outline and quite large for plants of this stature: usually 2 feet or even more wide and always lobed or pseudocompound. The small flowers are in terminal panicles of rounded clusters, and the fruits are small berries. These are some of the boldest and most tropical looking plants in the world. So massive and intricate are their leaves that they are sometimes difficult to "place" in the landscape. The plants are frost sensitive and die back from temperatures below 30°F but usually sprout from the roots if the temperature does not fall below the mid 20s. Doing so, of course, results in a multitrunked shrub form and precludes a tree form.

Trevesia palmata (pahl-MAHT-a) is indigenous to northern India, southern China, Vietnam, and Thailand. It grows to as much as 30 feet in its native habitats but is usually no more than 20 feet tall in cultivation and is often grown as a large shrub. As a tree form it is sparsely branched (sometimes completely unbranched) and forms a loose broad open canopy. The branches are white pubescent, prickly, and somewhat pendent and weeping. The 2-foot-wide leaves are carried on prickly petioles that are longer than the width of the blade. The leathery dark green leaf is pseudocompound with the false leaflets radiating from the end of the petiole in a circle. At the juncture of the petiole is a more or less circular web of leaf blade, through which the false leaflet stems extend. At their ends are 7 to 11 lanceolate five-lobed false leaflets whose lobes are so deep as to cause them to look like pinnately segmented oak leaves. The midribs of the false leaflets are distinctly lighter colored than the rest of the leaf, and the leaf tissue is puckered and quilted between the midribs and lateral veins. The new growth is white tomentose. *Trevesia palmata* 'Micholitzii', an outstanding cultivar, has leaves that keep much of the white pubescence and are heavily speckled with white dots. The general shape and the frosty color of the leaves of this cultivar have led to the vernacular name of snowflake tree or snowflake plant. The type can be grown in full sun as a silhouette or close-up specimen, whether planted in a tub or planted out, but the cultivar needs at least partial shade and protection from the hot afternoon sun in all but cool regions. Both forms are spectacular plants and are about as exotic and tropical looking a subject as one can find.

Trevesia sundaica (soon-DAY-i-ka) is native to Java and Sumatra. It grows to 15 or 20 feet tall and is similar to *T. palmata* in many respects, including growth habit, pubescence (which is reddish in this species), and size of leaves. It is different, however, in that the leaves are less compound looking and only deeply and palmately lobed. The rounded web of tissue at the juncture of the petiole continues out to the "false leaflets" (the lobes), which are lanceolate to oblanceolate in shape with tapering ends. The overall effect is not so massively lacy as that of *T. palmata*. This species looks more like a glossy-leaved and branching *Tetrapanax* species.

TRICHOCEREUS. See *Echinopsis.*

TRIPLARIS (TRIP-la-ris / trip-LAIR-is)
Polygonaceae: The Buckwheat, Sea-Grape Family
LONG JOHN; PALO SANTO TREE; ANT TREE
Medium-sized to large evergreen tree; large long
   leaves; spectacular clusters of red flowers and fruit
Zones 10 and 11; marginal in zone 10a
Sun
Average but regular amounts of moisture
Average well-drained soil
Propagation by seed

A genus of 17 species of trees in Central America and tropical South America. They have hollow stems, alternately arranged large heavily veined leaves, large terminal racemes of red flowers, and showy red three-winged fruits. The male and female flowers are on separate trees. Several species are now in cultivation, but only one is common in the United States. *Triplaris americana* (a-mer´-i-KAHN-a) occurs naturally from Panama through northern South America to southeastern Brazil. The tree grows to as much as 70 or 80 feet in its native haunts but is usually only about 50 or 60 feet in height in cultivation. The tree's canopy is irregularly oblong and never widespreading. Furthermore, the smooth dark gray bark tends to peel off in irregular patches, leaving whitish areas along the tall straight trunk. Thus, the tree's general aspect from a distance is that of a very large-leaved *Eucalyptus* species. The short-stalked leaves are as much as 24 inches long, dark (sometimes almost bluish) green, and oblong to elliptic in shape, with a prominent and lighter colored midrib and beautiful depressed lateral veins. The leaves are as magnificent as those of any large-leaved *Ficus* species, and the new growth is a resplendent bronzy purple in color. In mid to late winter and early spring the trees form their foot-long racemes of vivid red or purplish red urn-shaped flowers, and the show often continues through April. The blossoms of the male trees are, alas, not as deeply colored as those of the female trees, and there is no way of knowing the sex of the trees until they bloom. The female trees produce fruits as colorful as the flowers themselves: three-angled rounded and nutlike with three brilliant red 2-inch-long propeller-like wings that allow the winged seeds to spin in space as they fall. The tree is doubtless one of the world's most beautiful. It is more than pleasing year-round and has not a single fault. It needs sun to bloom and is not drought tolerant. Even though the center of its natural distribution is equatorial, mature trees are usually unharmed by temperatures of 28°F. Young trees are more tender to cold and are usually damaged by any temperatures below freezing. The other species in this genus should be much more greatly exploited for they are all of outstanding and distinctive beauty. Plates 389 and 390.

TRITHRINAX (try-TRY-nax)
Palmae (Arecaceae): The Palm Family
Common names vary according to species
Small palmate-leaved palms with trunks covered in
   spiny fibers
Zones 9 through 11
Sun
Average but regular amounts of moisture; drought
   tolerant
Average well-drained soil
Propagation by seed

A genus of five palmate-leaved palms in South America. All but one species are solitary-trunked. They are slow-growing and have compact rounded crowns of stiffly segmented leaves atop trunks covered in spiraling woven fibers with spinelike projections. All species flourish in fairly poor soils of relatively high pH, and all are intolerant of soggy soils. They are all fairly tolerant of frost but, if damaged by cold, are slow to recover and are subject to fungal attack, especially in warm humid climates.

Trithrinax acanthocoma (a-kanth´-o-KO-ma) is indigenous to southern Brazil, Paraguay, Uruguay, and northern Argentina, and is the most common species in cultivation. It grows slowly to 15 or 20 feet with fairly stout trunks completely covered in a beautiful wicker-like pattern of brown woven fibers with spiraling grayish spiny projections. The 3-foot-wide leaves are very stiffly segmented, each describing a half circle in outline and are dark green above and pale green to gray beneath. They are held on petioles that are as long as the leaf is wide. This palm is architectural looking and is quite attractive up close or against backgrounds of beige or white that show off its intricate trunks. It is a good candidate for large-scale rock gardens, with or without cactus or succulents. It is sometimes called the spiny fiber palm.

Trithrinax brasiliensis (bra-zil´-ee-EN-sis) occurs naturally in southern Brazil and northern Argentina. It grows to 15 or 18 feet and is rather similar to *T. acanthocoma* in overall appearance but usually is smaller growing. The inflorescences are large and showy with many small white flowers, and the plant blooms at an early age. Some botanists think this is but a form or variety of *T. acanthocoma*.

Trithrinax campestris (kam-PES-tris) is a beautiful clumping species that occurs naturally in northern

Argentina. The palm grows to as much as 20 feet tall and has wonderful leaves that are stiff (like the other species) but covered on top in a beautiful bluish white short tomentum and a deep glossy green beneath. This species is most choice and should be sought out and planted as it is about as hardy as the others and is very beautiful. Plate 391.

TUPIDANTHUS. See *Schefflera pueckleri*.

URECHITES
(oo-REK-i-teez / oor-e-KYT-eez / yoo-REK-i-teez / yoor-e-KYT-eez)
Apocynaceae: The Oleander, Frangipani, Vinca Family
WILD ALLAMANDA; HAMMOCK VIPERTAIL
Tall evergreen vine; lustrous leaves; beautiful yellow trumpet-shaped flowers
Zones 10 and 11; marginal in zone 10a
Sun
Water lover that grows with average but regular amounts of moisture
Average well-drained soil
Propagation by seed and cuttings

A genus of only two vine species in southern Florida, the West Indies, and Central America. They have stems with milky, sticky, and poisonous sap, simple oppositely arranged entire leaves, few-flowered axillary and terminal clusters of bell-shaped or funnel-shaped yellow or white flowers, and small linear pods. Only one species is in cultivation and it is still, alas, too rare. *Urechites lutea* (LOOT-ee-a) (synonym *Echites andrewsii*) is native to extreme southern Florida and the Florida Keys. It is a very fast growing and tall twining vine, to as much as 50 feet. Its lustrous elliptic leaves have prominent and lighter colored midribs and depressed lateral veins. The plant blooms year-round in tropical regions, but only in warm weather elsewhere. The flowers are in terminal and axillary few-flowered clusters. Each blossom is bell-shaped to salverform with five spreading, slightly twisted, pure bright yellow corolla lobes. The vine has the distinct advantage of twining "widely," which is to say that its stems encircle objects of relatively great diameters, including palm trunks. This most worthwhile and beautiful native plant deserves much wider acceptance. It is unfortunately quite tender to frost and is the type of plant, like species of *Allamanda* and *Mandevilla*, that does not usually sprout from its roots if frozen to the ground. Plate 392.

VEITCHIA (VEECH-ee-a)
Palmae (Arecaceae): The Palm Family
Common names vary according to species
Medium to tall solitary and slender-trunked feather-leaved palms
Zones 10b and 11
Sun
Average but regular amounts of moisture
Average well-drained soil
Propagation by seed

A genus of 18 species of pinnate-leaved palms from Fiji northwestward through New Caledonia and Vanuatu (New Hebrides) and thence into the Philippines. They have straight, slender light-colored trunks with lovely rings on all but the oldest parts of the stems; large, slender, and prominent, not to mention beautiful, crownshafts; and usually colorful and quite attractive fruits. The taller-growing species are fast growing and are as graceful as coconut palms, lending an almost unexcelled tropical and exotic look to the landscape. All species have half crowns of short-stalked leaves, the old leaves falling away before they recline much below the horizontal plane. All have long and relatively thick leaflets that are almost universally pliant and drooping. Very few have stiff and upturned leaflets. None is tolerant of frost and all are usually severely damaged by temperatures below 30°F. They are not very particular about soil conditions as long as the medium is well drained.

Veitchia arecina (air-e-SEEN-a) is native to New Caledonia and the Philippines. It grows to 25 or 30 feet in height, has a slender light gray to almost white closely but somewhat indistinctly ringed trunk and a nonbulging smooth greenish white crownshaft atop which is the sparsely leaved and open canopy of flattish fronds. The leaves are from 7 to 9 feet long with 3-inch-wide by 2-foot-long deep green lance-shaped and tapering leaflets that are not as pliable nor as pendent as those of many other species. The deep orange to bright red 2-inch-long fruits are egg-shaped. This very graceful, airy, mid-sized, fast-growing species looks best when individuals of varying heights are planted in a group.

Veitchia joannis (jo-AN-nis) is indigenous to the Fiji Islands. It is one of the tallest species, quickly growing to as much as 90 feet in its native habitat but usually to no more than 60 feet in cultivation. Its slender trunk is dark gray to medium brown in color with beautiful dark rings, especially on the newer growth. The crownshaft is very slender, barely bulging at its base, and a light gray to light tan in color. The 10-foot-long bright green leaves are beautifully arching, and the wide leaflets are wonderfully pendulous. This species is one of the few in the genus in which the leaves, at least in older palms, hang below the horizontal plane. The fruits are ovoid and a deep red in color. This tree is a noble palm with exceptional grace, closely rivaling the coconut in beauty and allure.

Veitchia mcdanielsii (mak-dan-YEL-zee-eye) is indigenous to Vanuatu (New Hebrides) in the South Pacific. It grows fast to 70 or 80 feet in its native habitat and to as much as 60 feet in cultivation in the United States. The palm is similar to *V. joannis* except for the trunk, which is even thinner and lighter colored, and the beautiful leaves, which do not lie beneath the horizontal plane. The leaflets are at least as pendulous as those of *V. joannis* and create one of the world's most beautiful silhouettes. The tree's only common name seems to be the sunshine palm. Plate 393.

Veitchia merrillii (mer-RIL-lee-eye) (synonym *Adonidia merrillii*) is native to the Philippines. It is one of the smaller species in the genus, growing only to 20 or 25 feet, and slower growing than the taller species. The dark gray ringed trunks are slender but not as ethereally graceful as those of the tall species. The crownshaft, which is relatively shorter and definitely thicker than those of most other *Veitchia* species, is a light olive green in color and is somewhat swollen at its base. The leaf crown is much fuller than those of most other *Veitchia* species and consists of more leaves. The leaf rachis is stiffly and very much arching, creating great curves to the palm's crown. The leaflets are stiff and upright, arching from the rachis at an angle that creates a V shape for most of the leaf's length. The red fruit clusters are at the height of their color around Christmas, which has led to the vernacular name of Christmas palm. This species is by far the most popular in the genus, possibly because of its diminutive stature, but not nearly as elegant as the others. It seems stiff, too formal, and lacking in gracefulness. The tree is also sometimes referred to as the Manilla palm because of its origin.

Veitchia montgomeryana (mahnt-gum´-ree-AHN-a) is indigenous to Vanuatu and is so similar to *V. joannis* that most tropical gardeners wonder why it was ever segregated from that species. The main landscaping difference between the two is that *V. montgomeryana* does not grow as tall as *V. joannis*, usually only to about 30 feet, and its leaves do not lie below the horizontal. In any case it is a very beautiful palm.

Veitchia winin (WIN-in) is native to Vanuatu and is also very similar to *V. joannis*. It has a more open and spreading leaf crown, and its trunks are usually slightly darker in color. Its leaves do not descend from the horizontal plane as much as do those of *V. joannis*, the leaf color is usually a darker green, and the bright red fruits are smaller. It is at least as beautiful and as graceful as *V. joannis*.

VICTORIA (vik-TOR-ee-a)
Nymphaeaceae: The Water Lily Family
GIANT WATER LILY
Immense floating pads with upturned edges; giant water lilylike white and pink fragrant flowers
Zones not indicative; water temperature more important
Sun to partial sun
Aquatic
Rich, humusy wet soil
Propagation by seed

A genus of only two species of giant aquatics in tropical South America related to the genus *Nymphaea* (water lily). Both species have large rhizomes of immense flat floating round pads with upturned edges and large supportive air-filled veins on the undersides. There are spines on the leaf stalks, the undersides of the leaves, and the flower stems. The fragrant white and pink flowers are similar to those of the water lily and lotus species, but usually larger, and they are nocturnal. The blossoms are borne on long stems from the erect rhizome in the mud and float on the water. The plants need water that is 3 feet or more in depth. The petioles of the leaves are longer than the depth of the water and adjust to varying water depths. Both species are tropical. *Victoria cruziana* does not grow in regions where the water temperature never goes above 75°F, and *V. amazonica* needs water temperatures of around 80°F or even above. These species are impossible in areas where the night temperatures fall drastically from those of midday, chilling the water. The U.S.D.A. zones are not reliable indicators for these plants. San Francisco, for example, is in zone 10 and yet the climate is cool to the point that water temperatures do not get warm enough for these beauties. In general, if the climate is such that night temperatures fall below 65°F for more than a month, then these plants are impossible.

Victoria amazonica (am-a-ZAHN-i-ka) (synonym *V. regia*) occurs naturally in the vast Amazon River Basin of Brazil and northern Bolivia. The floating pads are as much as 6 feet wide and have upturned edges, which may be as tall as 8 inches. There are two notches directly opposite each other along the rim of the leaf, both reaching down to within an inch of the water level. The leaf stalk is attached to the bottom center of the leaf. The upper surface of the leaves is not completely smooth but is covered in small puckered concavities, which match the correlative convexities of the leaf's lower surface. Leaf color is yellowish green to a deep olive green above and a reddish purple color beneath. The massive hollow veins are a deep red, and the outside of the upturned edges is usually a pale purple or pink color. The plants bloom constantly as long as the water temperature is 85°F or more. The flowers, which are borne on spiny stalks from the rhizome, are as much as 18 inches wide with very many oblong, somewhat twisted and curling petals that are pure white upon first opening but change to pink the next day. The flowers open at night and close up by noon of the next day, but last for at least 48 hours. There are small spines even on the exterior surface of the yellowish white sepals. This "equatorial" species will not survive in areas where the water temperature falls below 70°F for any appreciable time. Plate 394.

Victoria cruziana (krooz-ee-AHN-a) is indigenous to south central Brazil, Paraguay, north central Argentina, and southern Bolivia. It is quite similar to *V. amazonica*, except that its leaves and flowers are almost but not quite as large, the flower's sepals are spineless, and the plant tolerates lower water temperatures than does *V. amazonica*. This species grows well where water temperature does not fall below 60°F for long periods.

Victoria **'Longwood Hybrid'**, a hybrid between *V. amazonica* and *V. cruziana*, was produced at Longwood Gardens, Kennett Square, Pennsylvania, in 1961.

It has leaves that are as much as 8 feet wide. Its flowers are as large as those of *V. amazonica,* and it tolerates the same water temperature range as does *V. cruziana.* According to Perry D. Slocum, it "in many respects is superior to its parents." Plate 395.

Victoria regia. See *V. amazonica.*

VITIS. See *Tetrastigma.*

VRIESEA (VREEZ-ee-a)

Bromeliaceae: The Pineapple, Bromeliad Family
Common names vary according to species
Fairly large rosettes of smooth often variegated
 leaves; tall flat spikes of many-colored flowers
Zones vary according to species
Partial shade to sun
Water lovers
Leaf mold or epiphytic mix
Propagation by transplanting of suckers, root
 division, and seed

A genus of about 250 mostly epiphytic bromeliad species from Mexico to Argentina with most species in Brazil. They have smooth leathery straplike and entire leaves. The inflorescence is usually erect but sometimes pendent and consists of yellow, orange, or red bracts that are usually arranged on two opposite sides of the spike into a fan shape. The flowers are small three-petaled white, yellow, pink, red, or purplish. These plants are, in general, of easy cultivation and almost all can be grown as terrestrials as well as epiphytes. Some of the variegated-leaved species and hybrids are among the world's most beautiful plants of any type.

Vriesea conferta. See *V. ensiformis.*

Vriesea ensiformis (ens-i-FORM-is) (synonym *V. conferta*) is native to eastern and southeastern Brazil and is hardy in zones 10 and 11. It forms a widespreading rosette of bright green strap-shaped leaves, each 18 to 24 inches in length. The flat inflorescence is linear-pyramidal in shape with many beautiful scarlet bracts, often margined with orange or yellow, that are arranged on two opposite sides of the spike into a fan shape. The flowers are three-petaled, long stamened, and yellow. The plant needs high humidity and partial to almost total shade with bright light.

Vriesea fenestralis (fen-e-STRAL-is) is indigenous to southern Brazil and is hardy in zones 10 and 11. It forms a large rosette of fairly stiff but nevertheless gracefully arching thick and leathery but shiny, very dark green 2-foot-long leaves that, when new, are almost pure chartreuse with many fine dark green longitudinal striations. As the leaves lengthen and mature, the yellowish variegation is reduced to large speckles and then almost disappears from the oldest and lowermost leaves in the rosette. The combination of form and color is nearly incomparable. The inflorescence only adds to the symphony of green and yellow: a 3-foot-tall spike with large green bracts and large pure yellow flowers. The plant can be grown terrestrially as well as epi-

phytically and is one of the most beautiful bromeliad species. It does not like the full sun of hot climates and flourishes in high humidity.

Vriesea fosteriana (fahs-ter´-ee-AHN-a) is native to southern Brazil and is hardy in zones 10b and 11. It is an immense and very beautiful plant with stiff leathery but glossy and arching leaves as much as 3 feet long. The leaves are light green banded with irregular wavy horizontal darker lines above and chocolate colored matching bands beneath. The leaf margins are usually maroon. Leaf color is very variable. Some plants have a purplish red suffusion when immature, and some have leaves banded with white or silver. The inflorescence is as much as 7 feet tall with loosely spaced bright green bracts and yellow flowers. There are several cultivars of this variable plant and some are extraordinarily beautiful. *Vriesea fosteriana* **'Red Chestnut'** is the most famous and most beautiful. Its new leaves are almost completely reddish brown with a few irregular transverse wavy yellow bands, and its older leaves are progressively more green with reddish brown and yellow horizontal wavy lines. These exceptionally attractive giants relish sun and humidity. Plate 396.

Vriesea glutinosa (gloot-i-NO-sa) occurs naturally only on the island of Trinidad and is hardy in zones 10b and 11. It forms a widespreading rosette of 2-foot-long deep green shiny leaves that have deep brownish purple horizontal bands on their undersides. The stalk of the inflorescence is also speckled with this color and is branched but flat, each branch being a very narrow and linear spike of shiny scarlet bracts with small orange flowers. The plant wants partial shade and humidity.

Vriesea hieroglyphica (hy-ro-GLIF-i-ka) is native to the forests of southern Brazil and is not adaptable outside zones 10b and 11. It is a gigantic species with rosettes 5 feet wide and as tall. The leaves are 3 or more feet long, stiff and leathery but arching, and yellow-green in color with regularly spaced horizontal wavy markings of dark purple or black both above and below. The undersides of the leaves are also somewhat bronzy-orange. The 3-foot-tall inflorescence has green bracts and golden yellow flowers. This noble and quite beautiful species needs partial shade and high humidity. There is no more beautiful bromeliad!

Vriesea imperialis (im-peer´-ee-AL-is) is a terrestrial species from east central Brazil and is adaptable only to zones 10b and 11. It is another very large plant with 6- or even 8-foot-wide rosettes of quite broad thick and leathery leaves that have an abrupt point at their ends. The leaves are a smooth dark olive green to almost bluish green above and maroon beneath. When plants are grown in sun, the upper leaf surfaces usually show bronze and reddish hues on the new growth as well. The inflorescence is about 6 feet tall with scarlet to wine-red bracts and whitish yellow flowers. This gigantic and superb bromeliad needs sun and is somewhat drought tolerant. Plate 397.

Vriesea inflata (in-FLAIT-a) is indigenous to the forests of southeastern Brazil and is hardy in zones 10b and 11. It forms an urn-shaped rosette of foot-long purplish or bluish metallic green shiny leaves. The long-lasting inflorescence is a thing of wonder: a 3-foot-tall great elliptic fan-shaped flat spike of lime green bracts margined with yellow and with a beautiful orange-red base to each bract. The flowers are a bright yellow. The plant wants partial shade and high humidity.

Vriesea platynema (plait-ee-NEEM-a) occurs naturally from the West Indies to Venezuela and northern Brazil and is not adaptable outside zones 10 and 11. It forms a broad and spreading 5-foot-wide rosette of thick leathery and smooth deep green to bluish green 2-foot-long leaves with purplish undersides and thin wavy transverse lime green striations above. The inflorescence is about 2 feet tall and consists of reddish purple bracts and greenish white flowers. *Vriesea platynema* var. *rosea* is a beautiful naturally occurring variety that has light, almost chartreuse, green-ridged leaves with purplish fingernail-like tips.

Vriesea simplex (SIM-plex) is native to the island of Trinidad, northern South America, and northern Brazil, and is hardy in zones 10b and 11. It forms a small rosette with foot-long soft deep green straplike leaves that are wine-red beneath. Some forms have deep red or purplish red on both sides of the leaf. The inflorescence is pendent with widely spaced yellow bracts, each of which has a deep rose or scarlet base from which emerge the yellow-petaled flowers with dark green stamens. The plant needs partial shade, moisture, and high humidity.

Vriesea speciosa. See *V. splendens.*

Vriesea splendens (SPLEN-denz) (synonym *V. speciosa*) is native to the island of Trinidad and adjacent northern South America and is hardy in zones 10b and 11. The specific epithet says it all: "splendid!" The rosette is fairly spreading, and the leaves are as much as 2 feet long. The type is hardly available any longer, several cultivars having replaced it in popularity. These have silvery or chocolate-purple and wavy transverse bands on the leaves, which create some of the world's most beautiful. The inflorescence is as much as 3 feet tall and is a single great sword-shaped spike of intense crimson or pure yellow bracts (according to the cultivar) with tiny yellow flowers. The darker-banded forms are spectacular, especially when in bloom. The plants demand partial to almost full shade (with bright indirect light) and ample moisture and humidity.

WAGATEA (wa-GAHT-ee-a)
Caesalpiniaceae (Leguminosae), subfamily
    Caesalpinioideae: The Cassia, Royal Poinciana
    Family
CANDY CONE VINE
Immense tall, fast growing spiny vine; pinnate leaves;
    tall spikes of yellow and red flowers
Zones 10b and 11
Sun to partial shade
Average but regular amounts of moisture

Humusy, well-drained soil
Propagation by seed and cuttings

A monotypic genus native to the northwestern region of the subcontinent of India. *Wagatea spicata* (spy-KAIT-a) grows to as much as 100 feet or even more and it grows quickly, often producing stems a foot or more in diameter. All but the oldest parts of this vine are covered in hooked spines, which allow it to quickly gain a foothold on other vegetation. The bipinnate leaves are as much as a foot long with 2-inch-long oblong to elliptic leaflets that are bright green to dark green above and paler and pubescent beneath. The plant blooms mostly in spring with 2-foot-long tail-like racemes of urn-shaped flowers whose fiery orange-red calyces open to reveal five brilliant yellow petals and stamens. The vine is overwhelmingly spectacular when in bloom, but is immense and rampant and definitely not for small gardens. Plate 398.

WARSZEWICZIA (war-say-WIK-zee-a)
Rubiaceae: The Coffee, Gardenia, Ixora Family
WILD POINSETTIA
Large evergreen shrub or small tree; immense
    corrugated leaves; spectacular red flowers
Zones 10b and 11
Sun to partial shade
Water lover
Average well-drained, acidic soil
Propagation by seed and cuttings

A genus of only four species of shrubs and trees in tropical America. They have very large oppositely arranged leaves and large terminal clusters of small flowers, some of which develop a much-enlarged and very showy calyx lobe similar to those of the flowers in the genus *Mussaenda*. One species is planted in truly tropical areas. *Warszewiczia coccinea* (kahk-SIN-ee-a) (synonym *Calycophyllum coccinea*) is native to the island of Trinidad, adjacent northern South America, and southwards to interior Brazil. It is a large shrub or small tree growing rather quickly to 20 feet or sometimes more. It is sparsely limbed, and the branches are long and arching, with an almost weeping form. The immense leaves are spectacular: elliptic to obovate in shape, glossy dark green above, paler and pubescent beneath, and 2 or more feet long. The prominent midrib is a lighter color than the leaf, the lateral veins are depressed above, and the leaf tissue between the veins is quilted. The plant blooms year-round in cycles of about 2 months. The blossoms are in 2-foot-long terminal racemes of nearly overlapping clusters of small tubular orange flowers. Some flowers develop extraordinarily large, long-stalked leaflike brilliantly red sepals, which are very showy. There are a couple of double-flowered cultivars, which are the plants usually seen in cultivation, although they seem no more spectacular than the type. The immense and gorgeous leaves of this small tree are reason enough to grow and possess it. The spectacular inflorescences are more than a convincing lagniappe. The species is completely intolerant of frost and is anything but drought tolerant. Furthermore, it needs a soil on the acidic side; limestone soils should be amended with organic matter. Plate 399.

WASHINGTONIA

(wash-ing-TOAN-ee-a)
Palmae (Arecaceae): The Palm Family
Common names vary according to species
Very tall fan-leaved palms
Zones vary according to species
Sun
Average but regular amounts of moisture; drought
    tolerant when established
Average well-drained soil

A genus of only two species of solitary-trunked palms in southern California, western Arizona, and northwestern Mexico. These are relatively fast-growing trees with fairly stout trunks and large full crowns of thorny-stalked palmately segmented costapalmate leaves. They are denizens of desert areas but are always found near or at permanently flowing springs, which are usually located in arroyos and canyons or at the bases of hills. Both species tend to have much of their trunks clothed in dead and pendent leaves, which create a haystack or skirt around the trunk. This characteristic has led to the vernacular name of petticoat palm. Wind or fire often remove the shaggy coats, and some people regularly have the dead leaves pruned away to reveal the trunk. The two species hybridize quite freely when grown together. Of the many such hybrids in cultivation, those with strong characteristics of *Washingtonia robusta* are especially valuable horticulturally in the colder parts of that species' range. Both species are eminently adapted to arid regions if the trees are supplied with enough irrigation. They luxuriate with their tops in hot dry air, but grow wonderfully well with only minimum degradation of trunk beauty in more humid climes. They are rather difficult to distinguish from each other when very young, the trunks and leaves looking almost identical.

Washingtonia filamentosa. See *W. filifera*.

Washingtonia filifera (fil-IF-e-ra) (synonym *W. filamentosa*) occurs naturally in desert regions of central southern California and adjacent southwestern Arizona and is hardy in zones 8b through 11 and marginal in zone 8a. It is often called the California fan palm. Some of the literature (from the United Kingdom) cites the moniker cotton palm, a name never used in the Americas. The tree grows moderately fast to as much as 50 feet or more with a full and rounded crown of 25 to 40 long and spiny-stalked 6-foot-wide grayish green leaves. The fairly massive trunk, which is usually about 2 feet in diameter but often more, is a deep gray in color with closely set rings on the newer wood. The older wood usually is fissured with thin cracks. The trunks of older palms are not especially attractive up close, and the trees look better planted as avenue trees or relatively

distant landscape subjects where their wonderful crowns accent the horizon. A group of the palms planted as trees of varying heights is stunningly attractive and tropical looking. The tree is noble and massive looking and is one of the most widely planted palm species in the United States as it flourishes throughout Florida, along the Gulf Coast, in the warmer desert regions, and in almost all the non-mountainous areas of California. The trees are, like almost every other plant, much more tender to cold when young and, although they are usually unscathed by temperatures below 20°F when mature, may be severely damaged or even killed by the same temperatures when in the seedling stage. Plate 400.

Washingtonia robusta (ro-BUS-ta) (synonym *W. sonorae*) is indigenous to Baja California and the state of Sonora in Mexico. It is hardy in zones 9 through 11, although somewhat marginal in zone 9a. It is usually called the Mexican fan palm to distinguish it from *W. filifera* (California fan palm). The palm grows quickly and to great heights of more than 100 feet in its native habitat and to at least 70 feet where it is at home in cultivation. Its trunk is not as massive or robust as that of the California fan palm, a nomenclatural irony, and is usually scarcely more than a foot in diameter although always somewhat swollen at its base. The older parts of the trunk are gray in color, and the newer trunk growth is clothed in deep chestnut red or brown leaf bases, which are often laboriously cut away to reveal the almost smooth and usually reddish-colored younger trunk. The leaves are never grayish green in color, but always a bright or deep green. Compared to California fan palm, the leaf stalks are shorter; the leaf crown is not so massive but more compact and usually does not have as many leaves although it is equally beautiful and rounded; and the ends of the leaf segments are more pendulous and almost astonishingly beautiful, especially in silhouette. Mature palms are some of the most elegant and graceful subtropical landscape subjects, their thin and extremely tall forms completely and ineluctably arresting in the landscape. This species is, by far, the most common palm in southern California and far southern Texas as well as the cities of Phoenix and Tucson. The palm is much more tender to cold than is *W. filifera*, especially young trees, and mature palms do not survive temperatures below 15°F and are often killed by any temperature below 20°F, and seedlings may be killed by 25°F. Plate 401.

Washingtonia sonorae. See *W. robusta*.

WINTERANA. See *Canella*.

WODYETIA (woad-YET-ee-a)
Palmae (Arecaceae): The Palm Family
FOXTAIL PALM
Tall, smooth, ringed and solitary-trunked fast-
    growing plumose feather-leaved palm
Zones 10 and 11

Sun
Average but regular amounts of moisture; not
    drought tolerant
Average well-drained soil
Propagation by seed

A monotypic palm genus native to northeastern Queensland in Australia. ***Wodyetia bifurcata*** (by-foor-KAIT-a) was unknown to horticulture and almost unknown to botanists, even Australian botanists, in the early 1980s. It is now in great demand because of its extraordinary beauty, fast growth, and adaptability. There may not be an equivalent example of such immediate acceptance and dissemination of horticultural material from its discovery in the wild. The palm is quite similar in most respects to a closely allied palm genus from the same region, *Normanbya,* which has been known to botanists and horticulturists for a while. *Normanbya* never caught the imagination of horticulturists and landscapers, probably because it is more demanding in its cultural requirements than is the foxtail palm. This fast-growing tree reaches as much as 50 feet in its native habitat, but usually only about 30 feet in cultivation. The smooth, gray to tan trunk has beautiful darker colored and widely spaced rings. It is somewhat bulging at the base and very gradually tapers to the non-bulbous smooth olive green and tapering crownshaft, which has a white bloom on its surface. The leaf crown usually consists of only 10 to 12 leaves, but it is full because the former are full-bodied, plumelike, and beautifully arching. Each leaf is about 10 feet long and rather short-stalked. The many dark green jagged-ended leaflets grow from the rachis at all angles, creating the cylindrical and foxtail-like visual effect. The inflorescence is not spectacular, but the clusters of orange or red fruits are very attractive. This palm has striking similarities to *Roystonea* species (royal palms), but the trunk is not as massive, as columnar, or as stately looking. It grows faster than almost all royal palms and is a good landscape substitute for a royal except for use as an avenue tree for which absolutely nothing matches the grandeur of the royals. It looks its best as a "canopy-scape" subject, its beautiful leaf crown floating above lower masses of vegetation. The palm is amazingly tolerant of cold to be so tropical looking. Mature trees are seldom damaged by temperatures above 29°F and often recover quickly from temperatures above 26°F, although that is about the limit. The foxtail palm occurs naturally in Australia's rain forest and does well only in cultivation in areas with adequate and regular rainfall or in sites where the gardener can supply such moisture requirements. The good news is that the palm seems to thrive in a wide range of soil types. Plate 402.

XANTHOSOMA (zanth-o-SO-ma)
Araceae: The Calla Lily, Jack-in-the-Pulpit Family
Common names vary according to species
Large evergreen elephant-ear-like plants with very
    large usually variegated leaves

Zones 10b and 11 as permanent perennials; zones 9
    through 10a as returning perennials
Partial shade to sun
Water lovers
Rich, humusy, well-drained soil
Propagation by root division, rhizome division

A genus of about 50 species of large and rhizomatous herbs in tropical America. They have broad peltate arrowhead-shaped leaves that are sometimes pinnately segmented. Most form no trunk or stem, but a few form short trunks. Many have incredibly beautiful and variegated leaves, some of which are gigantic. The inflorescences are typical of the family and are quite similar to those of the genus *Caladium.* Most are superior in beauty of leaf to *Colocasia* species, but no more difficult to grow and maintain.

Xanthosoma atrovirens. See *X. sagittifolium.*

Xanthosoma jacquinii. See *X. undipes.*

Xanthosoma lindenii (lin-DEN-ee-eye) (synonym *Caladium lindenii*) is native to rain forests of Colombia. The long-stalked thin but leathery leaves are 18 to 20 inches long and are linear-ovate in outline but deeply lobed at their bases into a linear arrowhead shape. The midrib and lateral veins are heavily marked with silvery white to create one of the world's most beautiful leaves that is almost startlingly elegant and exotic looking in shady sites among other vegetation. There are several cultivars varying only in the amount of silvery white variegation in the leaf. This species is arguably the most beautiful subject for brightening shady and semishady sites. Nothing is more beautiful and exotic for such purposes. The plants are heavy feeders and demand regular supplies of moisture. This gorgeous thing is sometimes prosaically called Indian kale or spoon flower.

Xanthosoma mafaffa. See *X. sagittifolium.*

Xanthosoma sagittifolium (sa-jit´-i-FO-lee-um) (synonyms *X. atrovirens, X. mafaffa*) is probably indigenous to the West Indies but has been naturalized all over tropical America for so long that its exact origins are uncertain. In frost-free regions this gigantic-leaved species slowly forms a stout dark-colored stem to as much as 3 feet tall, covered with the remains of the old leaf base sheaths. The thick and leathery long-stalked leaves frequently attain a length of 4 or even 5 feet in truly tropical regions with much water and a rich soil. Leaf shape is broadly sagittate, and leaf color is a very deep bluish green above and a pale light green beneath, with deep chocolate purple or almost black petioles that are as long as the leaf. A grown person can stand under the leaf canopy of mature plants. The type has leaves with slightly depressed midribs and lateral veins above but with no difference in coloration between the blade and the veins. There are several cultivars, however, with the veins a lighter color and one with the leaf margins white. The large tuberous rhizome of this plant is reportedly edible and is often grown as a vegetable in tropical regions. It thrives in shady or sunny sites, but needs copious amounts of water and a rich soil. It is quite successful as a bog subject or lining the margins of pools and ponds, its roots in a couple of inches of water, where it is possibly the most spectacular and dramatic bog subject. The most common of the vernacular names seems to be yautia. Plate 403.

Xanthosoma undipes (UN-di-peez) (synonym *X. jacquinii*) occurs naturally from Mexico through Central America southwards to Peru. This gigantic species is similar in most respects to *X. sagittifolium* but with broader and thicker leaves with white streaks between the lateral veins. In tropical areas with lots of water and a rich soil the leaves are sometimes even larger than those of *X. sagittifolium*. This plant is a superb bog and shallow aquatic subject.

Xanthosoma violaceum (vee-o-LAY-see-um) is probably native to the West Indies, but has been naturalized all over tropical America for so long that its exact origins are uncertain. It is similar to *X. sagittifolium* but its leaves are not quite as large, the leaf margins have a purplish hue, and the midrib and lateral veins are lighter colored than the leaf blade. This very beautiful species needs the same environmental conditions as *X. sagittifolium* and makes one of the most dramatic and beautiful bog or shallow aquatic landscape subjects. It is sometimes called the blue taro or blue ape (AH-pay).

XYLOTHECA. See *Oncoba*.

YUCCA (YUK-ka)
Agavaceae: The Agave Family
YUCCA
Large rosettes of swordlike leaves often atop palmlike
    trunks; tall spikes of white flowers
Zones vary according to species
Sun
Average but regular amounts of moisture; many are
    drought tolerant
Average well-drained soil
Propagation by seed, cuttings, and transplanting of
    suckers

A genus of about 40 perennial and evergreen plants in the Americas with large rosettes of tough, often rigid, and usually sharp-pointed sword-shaped leaves. Most make a stem or trunk of varying heights, often branching, but a few are trunkless. They grow mostly in arid or semiarid regions. Many are true desert plants, but some are indigenous to fairly moist climates, although always found on high and well-drained sites. They have showy, terminal, erect, and unusually tall racemes or panicles of mostly pendulous and fairly large white six-petaled flowers, the separate petals often forming a cup shape. Some of the flowers are delightfully fragrant, and all are edible and were often eaten by the aboriginal peoples. All the species bloom in spring, summer, or early autumn, and some of the more tropical species are subject to flowering at any time of the year. The fruits are usually dry multisectioned capsules, but they may also be smooth, leathery, and undivided on the outside. Almost all species live on after flowering, but a few are monocarpic. Only one species grows at a rate that could be called "fast." Most grow slowly to moderately and some are exceedingly slow. Almost without exception these plants are quite tropical looking and very dramatic in the landscape. When in bloom, they add a wonderful vertical and colorful accent. The plants are especially beautiful in silhouette, and the best part is that many of them are quite hardy to cold. Many trunkless species are easily confused with the sotol genus, *Dasylirion*. but up close the differences are obvious as *Yucca* species very rarely have teeth on the leaf margins. Most species form long taproots and therefore should be transplanted only when young and only when container grown. Digging plants out of the wild not only is unconscionable in an environmental sense, but the plants also usually die within a few months because of the root damage.

Yucca aloifolia (a-lo´-i-FO-lee-a) is native from the southern coastal region of Virginia southwards through Florida and the West Indies and eastward into the southern half of Texas and most of eastern Mexico. It is hardy in zones 8 through 11 and marginal in zone 7. It forms a trunk to as much as 8 or 10 feet that is usually but not always branched and, when unbranched, is often reclining on the ground because of the top-heaviness of the leaves. The leaves, which are closely and spirally set along most of the stem length, are 2 to 3 feet long but only about 2 inches wide at the base, tapering to a very sharp point like a dagger. They are stiff and tough and a very deep dark green color in the type. The plant is called Spanish bayonet or Spanish dagger and, by botanists, aloe yucca. There are several worthy cultivars. ***Yucca aloifolia*** '**Marginata**' has leaves margined in yellow. ***Yucca aloifolia*** '**Tricolor**' has a central longitudinal stripe of yellow on the leaves. The plants are very effective as accents in raised beds or the cactus and succulent garden and are widely used as hedge material and barriers. They are beautiful anywhere their silhouettes can be seen, but are less effective against a green background, even the variegated cultivars. The plants may be kept relatively low and very bushy by cutting back the taller trunks. In addition the species is very tolerant of salty ocean spray and saline soil and makes a perfect beach plant, thriving even on the dunes. Old tall-trunked and branched trees have a very picturesque and tropical look reminiscent of the more tender dragon tree, *Dracaena draco*. Spanish dagger does not do well where there is not much summer heat and, while it is drought tolerant to some degree, tends to die out in extreme and prolonged dry periods. Plates 404 and 405.

Yucca angustissima (an-gus-TIS-si-ma) is native to New Mexico, northern Arizona, and southern Utah, and is adaptable to zones 7 through 9 and marginal in zone 6. This trunkless species grows to about 2 feet. The stiff but somewhat outwardly curved 2-foot-long yellowish green to dark green leaves have some coiling white fibers adherent to the margins and a short but stout and dangerous spiny tip. The inflorescence is as much as 8 feet tall.

Yucca arborescens. See *Y. brevifolia.*

Yucca arizonica (air-i-ZOAN-i-ka) is native to southern Arizona and the adjacent state of Sonora in Mexico, and is hardy in zones 9 through 11. This short-trunked species grows to about 10 feet, and the sometimes branched stem is usually clothed in old leaves. The leaves are deep green in color and about 2 feet long, linear-lanceolate in shape and stiff but somewhat pliable except for the short spiny tip. This species is quite drought tolerant and needs full sun and a very freely draining site.

Yucca arkansana (ark-an-SAHN-a) is indigenous to southwestern Texas northwards to central and eastern Oklahoma and western Arkansas and down into northwestern Louisiana. It is hardy in zones 7 through 11 and marginal in zone 6. It is a somewhat insignificant plant in the landscape mixed with other vegetation, but if featured in the rock garden surrounded by sand, rocks, or differently colored vegetation it can be quite effective in a small-scale way. The leaves are very narrow and thin, pliant and grasslike, and are about 2 feet long with sharp spiny points and a few coiling white fibers on their margins.

Yucca australis. See *Y. filifera.*

Yucca baccata (ba-KAHT-ta) occurs naturally in southern Colorado, southern Utah and Nevada, western California, Arizona, southern New Mexico, western Texas, and adjacent northern Mexico. It is a very hardy species adaptable in zones 6 through 9. It does not usually form a trunk, but the rosette is large and striking with 3-foot-long very stiff, somewhat curved, thick, concave, dark green to bluish green spiny-tipped leaves whose margins have many curling white fibers. The inflorescence is large and full but does not ascend much above the leaf rosette. The plant is a formidable accent in the cactus and succulent garden. It is extremely drought tolerant and thrives in almost any sunny site with well-drained soil. The fruits are edible and were prized by the native Americans. The most common name is the datil yucca, but it is occasionally referred to as the banana yucca because of the long yellowish and leathery edible fruits.

Yucca brevifolia (brev-i-FO-lee-a) (synonym *Y. arborescens*) is indigenous only to the Mojave Desert of the western United States, a roughly circular area whose center is at the juncture of the boundaries of California, Utah, Nevada, and Arizona. Hardy in zones 9 through 11 and marginal in zone 8, this species is the famous and picturesque Joshua tree with branched trunk and contorted limbs ending in stiff rosettes of daggerlike leaves. The trunk, which grows slowly to as much 30 or even 35 feet but is usually less, is clothed except on its oldest parts in the shag of old dead leaves. The leaves of the terminal rosettes are relatively short, growing only to 12 or 18 inches in length. They are very stiff, rigid, and a dark gray green in color. The terminal inflorescences are unusual for the genus in that they are pendent at maturity. The tree is inordinately picturesque in a way that few others are. It also has, to some people, an almost menacing and ghostlike or phantomlike aspect because of the contorted arms (branches) that seem to be beseeching or writhing, Nowhere is its gloominess more pronounced than in its native haunt where its form seems to match and even exacerbate the brooding lonely high desert solitude. The tree is quite drought tolerant and must have sun and a site in which the drainage is completely unimpeded. It does not thrive in humid regions. It makes an incredibly picturesque lawn specimen, patio tree, or focal point in the cactus and succulent garden. There are at least two naturally occurring varieties of this species, one of which is radically different in growth form from the type. ***Yucca brevifolia*** var. ***herbertii*** is a clumping species with mostly unbranching trunks growing only to about 15 feet. Its trunk is clothed for most of its length with the stiff, swordlike leaves. Plates 406 and 407.

Yucca campestris (kam-PES-tris) is indigenous to central western Texas and is hardy in zones 7 through 11 and marginal in zone 6. It is a suckering species with short shaggy trunks to 3 feet or so in height. The leaves are as much as 3 feet long and quite slender, almost grasslike but unarching. Leaf color is a dark olive green to bluish green. The leaf rosette is rather full and attractive and makes a fine-textured statement in the landscape if silhouetted against contrasting colors. It looks good in the cactus and succulent garden or in a low shrub or perennial border for accent. The plants are drought tolerant but tend to look puny under severe conditions.

Yucca carnerosana (kar´-ne-ro-SAHN-a) is native to southwestern Texas and adjacent Mexico and is hardy in zones 8 through 11 and marginal in zone 7. This massive tree-form yucca grows to an ultimate height of 20 or 30 feet with a thick and sparsely branched trunk and immense rosettes of very stout 2- to 4-foot-long deep green very stiff leaves that are 3 inches wide at the base and taper to a sharp point. The trunk is usually completely clothed in the old dead leaves, which increases the massive aspect of the plant. Even without the leaf shag, the trunks of mature plants are very thick, as much 30 inches in diameter. The inflorescence is tall and robust. This imposing species is so massive in form and so dominating in the landscape that it is somewhat difficult to place. It is perfectly at home as a focal point in a large cactus and succulent garden and, in arid regions, may be used as a small specimen tree. Even though its natural range experiences occasional temperatures near 0°F, this species will not survive prolonged stretches of these subfreezing conditions. It must have sun and a freely draining site. Its only vernacular names seem to be giant dagger and Spanish dagger.

Yucca constricta (kahn-STRIK-ta) (synonym *Y. tenuistyla*) is native to southern and southwestern Texas and adjacent Mexico, and is hardy in zones 8 through 11 and marginal in zone 7. This trunkless but suckering species has small rosettes of stiff daggerlike dark green leaves about 18 inches long with many curling whitish fibers on the margins. The attractive agavelike plant is drought tolerant although, like many other *Yucca* species, loses vigor and color under extreme drought conditions.

Yucca elata (ee-LAIT-a) is native to the southern halves of New Mexico and Arizona and southwards through western Texas and adjacent Mexico. It is hardy in zones 7 through 11. This arborescent species takes many years to form its usually unbranched trunk, which may attain a height of 25 feet. The beauty of the tree is its softly shaggy, relatively thin and tall trunk and its very narrow, grasslike, and gracefully arching leaves in the full, dense, and rounded rosettes. The leaves are yellowish green in color, usually with a silvery suffusion. The landscape effect is especially fine and delicate. This tree is superb anywhere the color and form can be appreciated against a darker background. It is one of the finest native *Yucca* species. It has the vernacular name of soaptree yucca or soapweed because its mucilaginous sap was used by Native Americans as a substitute for soap.

Yucca elephantipes (el-e-FANT-i-peez) (synonyms *Y. gigantea*, *Y. guatemalensis*) is native to southern Mexico and Guatemala and is hardy in zones 10 and 11, although it sometimes survives to maturity in zone 9b. It is one of the largest species in the genus, growing to as much as 30 or sometimes even 40 feet in height. Its lovely light brown to gray corky-textured cylindrical trunk is usually free of the thatch of old dead leaves. The deep green leaves are 3 to 4 feet long, as much as 4 inches wide at their bases, relatively soft and pliable, and usually recurved or bent. They are spiny-pointed but soft-tipped and not vicious, although running into them at full force can hurt. The plants tend to sucker at the base to create a complete giant mound of foliage. The pups may be removed without harm to the parent plant if the more picturesque form of a branching and large-headed tree is desired. This species is probably the fastest growing in the genus, outpacing many more traditional looking trees in its growth. Because the plant is very lush looking, it does not seem a denizen of desert areas like most other *Yucca* species and, indeed, it is not. It is not drought tolerant and dies in prolonged periods without water and can be damaged by the midday sun of tropical desert regions where it needs some shade during the hottest part of the day. It does, however, demand a fast-draining soil that is never waterlogged. This species is also tolerant of salty ocean spray and slightly saline soil and is a very beautiful candidate for seaside gardens landward from the dunes. The tree looks good in the cactus and succulent garden but, because of its size and lush appearance, it looks even better as a patio tree, specimen tree, or a very large component of a shrub border. It also is a "canopy-scape" subject; that is, mature trees are unexcelled at creating a "floating" form above lower masses of foliage, much as many palm species do. Few other plants surpass this

one as a silhouette subject. The tree is usually called the spineless yucca or giant yucca.

Yucca faxoniana (fax-o´-nee-AHN-a) is indigenous to southwestern Texas and adjacent Mexico and is hardy in zones 7 through 11. It is another giant species, the mostly unbranched trunk attaining as much as 40 feet of height with time. The trunks are stout and usually covered with the orange-brown shag of dead leaves. The living leaves are from 2 to 4 feet long, as much as 4 inches wide, very stiff and rigid, a deep dark green in color, and bear very sharp apical points. This specimen tree is very beautiful when mature and is somewhat similar to *Y. carnerosana* but more graceful. The plants are drought tolerant, but not extremely so and they must have full sun.

Yucca filamentosa (fil´-a-men-TOE-sa) is native to the coastal area of North Carolina southwards to central Florida. It is hardy in zones 7 through 11 and marginal in zone 6a. The rosettes of this trunkless species consist of 2-foot-long bluish green stiff and slightly outwardly curved spiny-tipped leaves. The plant makes a very good accent, especially for the colder regions, and the inflorescence is large and dramatic. The plants are drought tolerant, although they tend to look emaciated in severe conditions. They thrive in full sun to partial shade. The plant is called the Adam's needle or the needle palm. The latter is a quite unfortunate moniker as there is a true palm species (*Rhapidophyllum hystrix*) with the same name.

Yucca filifera (fi-LIF-e-ra) (synonyms *Y. australis*, *Y. flaccida*) is native to central and central eastern Mexico and is hardy in zones 9 through 11 and marginal in zone 8b. This giant arborescent species grows to as much as 35 feet with much branching and rather resembles *Y. brevifolia* (Joshua tree) except that its limbs are not so numerous nor as contorted. The trunk is covered with the skirt of dead leaves on all but its oldest parts and is one of the finest aspects of the plant. The leaves are stiff, dark green in color, and fairly short, only reaching about 2 feet long, but are provided with sharp short points. The inflorescences from the ends of the rosettes are, unlike those of almost all other *Yucca* species, pendent when fully formed. This species is perhaps the finest and most beautiful large species in the genus and is unfailingly attractive and picturesque when grown in full sun and freely draining sites. It is quite drought tolerant, but always looks better when supplied with irrigation in severe drought conditions.

Yucca flaccida. See *Y. filifera*.

Yucca gigantea. See *Y. elephantipes*.

Yucca glauca (GLAWK-a) (synonym *Y. intermedia*) is native to a vast area of the western and midwestern United States and is probably the hardiest *Yucca* species, being adaptable in zones 3 through 9. Alas, it is also one of the smallest species. It is trunkless and forms a full radiating rosette about 3 feet tall with very thin dark green or bluish green stiff but somewhat arching 2- to 3-foot-long leaves that terminate in short but sharp points and have beautiful white margins. The inflorescence rises as much as 3 feet above the leaf rosette. The plant is useful in cold areas to create an accent in beds or in rock gardens and looks superb with rocks and on or atop stone walls. It is one of the most drought tolerant *Yucca* species and is sometimes called the dwarf soapweed or dwarf soapweed yucca.

Yucca gloriosa (glor-ee-O-sa) (synonym *Y. gigantea*) is native to the coastal area of northeastern Mexico, coastal Texas, extreme southern Louisiana, Alabama, and northeastern Florida but is an escape from cultivation all along the Gulf Coast. It is hardy in zones 9 through 11 as a permanent large shrub or small tree and in zone 8 as a returning perennial. This low arborescent species is found naturally along the coast and is extremely tolerant of beach conditions. It usually grows to no more than 10 feet in height but occasionally forms 15 feet of trunk. The trunk is branched and usually clothed in recumbent dead leaves. The plant freely suckers, creating full-leaved clumps with time. If the old dead leaves are removed, the trunk is found to be a beautiful dark tan or dark gray in color and smooth except for the leaf scars. The rosettes appear very tropical, especially in silhouette, when the trunk has been freed of the dead leaf masses. The leaves are many and grow along the stem much like those of *Y. aloifolia*. In fact, the leaves of the two species are similar enough to cause gardeners some confusion in identification. The leaves of *Y. gloriosa* are wider at their bases than those of *Y. aloifolia,* they are more pliable, and they carry sharp tips that, although fairly soft and supple, can do much damage. This species is called Spanish bayonet, Spanish dagger, palm lily, Roman candle, and sea-island yucca. There are several variegated-leaved cultivars as well as more dwarf and more compact forms.

Yucca guatemalensis. See *Y. elephantipes*.

Yucca intermedia. See *Y. glauca*.

Yucca louisianensis (loo-ee´-zee-a-NEN-sis) occurs naturally in eastern Texas, eastern Oklahoma, northeastern Louisiana, and southern Arkansas, and is hardy in zones 7 through 10 and marginal in zone 6b. It is a trunkless rosette of 4-foot-long narrow and nicely arching grasslike olive green to grass green leaves with somewhat twisted apices ending in a sharp point. The inflorescence reaches a height of 8 or 9 feet.

Yucca macrocarpa. See *Y. schottii*.

Yucca mohavensis. See *Y. schidigera*.

Yucca pendula. See *Y. recurvifolia*.

Yucca recurvifolia (ree-kurv´-i-FO-lee-a) (synonym *Y. pendula*) is indigenous to the Gulf Coast region from northeastern Mexico, Texas, southern Louisiana along the coast to northern Florida and northward into coastal Georgia. It is hardy in zones 7 through 11 and marginal in zone 6b. This species is a superb landscape subject because of the color and form of the leaves, which are blue green to grayish green, thick and leathery but pliable and gracefully arching. The leaves are about 3 feet long and narrowly lanceolate with a pliable but very sharp point and make beautiful full rosettes. The relatively fast-growing plants sucker by running

stolons and make fairly extensive clumps in time. They produce stems as much as 5 feet tall, but the stems are usually hidden by the suckering habit. These are tough and carefree plants that thrive in full sun or partial shade and are not particular as to soil as long as it is fast-draining. They are reasonably drought tolerant and very well adapted to seaside conditions.

Yucca rigida (RIJ-i-da) is native to northern and northwestern Mexico and is hardy in zones 7 through 11 and marginal in zone 6b. This sparsely branching arborescent species grows to as much as 20 feet but usually only to 12 or 15 feet. The trunks are covered in a light brown thatch of old dead leaves. The 2- to 3-foot-long leaves are many and narrow, a deep bluish green, and very stiff. They create a very full and beautifully rounded shape to the leaf rosettes. This species is one of the few in the genus with tiny teeth along the leaf margin; the teeth are noticeable only up close. The inflorescence is short but full and often does not exceed the height of the leaves. The plant is very effective in the landscape because of its fine-textured rosettes with their striking bluish color. It is sometimes called the blue yucca.

Yucca rostrata (ro-STRAHT-a) is indigenous to southwestern Texas and adjacent northern Mexico and is hardy in zones 8 through 11 and marginal in zone 7. It is one of the most beautiful species in the genus and the loveliest of the ones native to Texas. It grows to as much as 15 feet or even 20 feet, usually with few branches. The trunks are clothed in the orange-brown shag of old dead leaves. The living leaves are thin and slightly grasslike as they are fairly supple. They are beautifully arching and reach about 2 feet in length with spiny tips and are a yellowish green to almost gray in color. The leaf rosettes are full and fine-textured. The inflorescence is large and very tall and one of the glories of whatever site in which the tree grows. The plant, which is quite drought tolerant and thrives in almost any well-drained soil, is perfectly at home near the shore and a valuable addition to the repertory of plants that are somewhat tolerant of salty air and saline soil.

Yucca rupicola (roop-i-KO-la) is indigenous to central Texas and is hardy in zones 7 through 11. This small trunkless species has few leaves to a rosette. The plant slowly suckers, however, and makes a pleasing show after a few years. The leaves are very dark green with a very thin yellow to brown margin. They are twisted along the upper half of their length, which leads to the vernacular name of twisted-leaf yucca. The inflorescence, while not especially full, reaches heights of 8 feet or more and makes quite a show in late spring and early summer.

Yucca schidigera (shy-DIJ-e-ra) (synonym *Y. mohavensis*) is native to southern Arizona and northern Baja California and is hardy in zones 8 through 11. It is an arborescent species that can attain a height of 15 or even 20 feet. The trunk is sparsely branched and may or may not be clothed in the shag of the dead leaves. The leaves, which are as much as 4 feet long, very stiff, and armed with sharp apical points, are a deep olive green in color, and concave in cross section, and bear very many long and coiling white fibers on their margins. The tree is very drought tolerant.

Yucca schottii (SHAHT-tee-eye) (synonym *Y. macrocarpa*) occurs naturally in the mountains of southern New Mexico, southern Arizona, and the state of Sonora in Mexico, and is adaptable to zones 7 through 9 and marginal in zone 6b. This short arborescent species slowly clumps from the base. The trunks are usually leaning to some extent and may attain a height of 20 feet, but are more often smaller, mostly unbranched, and covered in the shag of the old dead leaves although older trees often have a few branches. The 2- to 3-foot-long leaves are grayish green to yellowish green linear-lanceolate in shape and slightly flexible, with the long tapering apices somewhat rolled inward and provided with a very sharp point. This very picturesque little tree gives an exotic look to the cactus and succulent garden. The plant is drought tolerant but not extremely so. It does not do very well in humid climates, where it should be planted high and dry.

Yucca smalliana (smahl-lee-AHN-a) occurs naturally in coastal South Carolina southwards to northeastern Florida and westward to Mississippi. It is hardy in zones 7 through 11 and marginal in zone 6b. The plant is very similar to *Y. filamentosa*. It serves the same landscape purposes and has the same cultural requirements. The two species are often confused in the trade, are seldom correctly identified, and may be the same species botanically.

Yucca tenuistyla. See *Y. constricta*.

Yucca thompsoniana (tahmp-so´-nee-AHN-a) is native to southwestern Texas and adjacent Mexico and is hardy in zones 8 through 11 and marginal in zone 7b. It is a small tree-type yucca with sparse branching and a thatch-covered trunk. The leaves are usually no more than 18 inches long, a yellowish to almost bluish green, very stiff, fairly narrow, and sharp pointed. The leaf rosette is full and attractive. The plant blooms when quite young, and the inflorescence is large and beautiful. Branched specimens are very attractive and picturesque. Branching may be stimulated by injury or pruning of single-stemmed trunks. This very drought tolerant species looks and does better if watered during extreme conditions.

Yucca torreyi occurs naturally in western Texas, southern New Mexico, and adjacent northern Mexico and is adaptable to zones 7 through 10. This very tall columnar but usually unbranched arborescent species attains a height of as much as 25 feet. The leaves are somewhat similar to those of *Y. aloifolia* and usually cover a large portion of the stem. The rest of the trunk is clothed in the shag of old dead leaves. The inflorescence is quite large, but it often scarcely rises above the leaf rosettes.

Yucca treculeana (tree-kyool´-ee-AHN-a) is indigenous to central, southern, and southwestern Texas and adjacent northern Mexico. Hardy in zones 8 through 11 and marginal in zone 7, it is a tall columnar arborescent species that is usually unbranched but one that suckers to form giant clumps. The trunks are usually enveloped in the shag of old dead leaves but, with age, are usually clean and a dark gray in color. The inflorescences are large and full, but they usually do not rise much above the leaf rosettes. This is an impressive plant when old and has some similarities to both *Y. aloifolia* and *Y. gloriosa*. It grows inland and along the coast, and makes one of the finest seaside landscape subjects.

Yucca whipplei (WHIP-lee-eye) is native to southern California and adjacent Baja California and is hardy in zones 7 through 11 and marginal in zone 6b. It is a trunkless but very beautiful species with very full rosettes of very stiff thick bluish or grayish green 4-foot-long spiny-tipped leaves radiating out in all directions. The plant suckers to form attractive clumps, and the magnificent inflorescence is immense and almost overwhelming, as much as 15 feet tall, the largest in the genus *Yucca*. Although the plant is monocarpic, the offsets make it a permanent landscape subject. It is one of the hardiest and most carefree *Yucca* species and is very drought tolerant and even thrives in slightly saline soil. This species is usually called our Lord's candle.

ZAMIA (ZAYM-ee-a / ZAHM-ee-a)
Zamiaceae: The Zamia (a Cycad) Family
Common names vary according to species
Low evergreen fernlike cycads
Zones vary according to species
Sun to partial shade
Average but regular amounts of moisture
Average well-drained soil
Propagation by seed and (for clumping species) transplanting of suckers

A genus of about 60 cycad species in tropical and subtropical America. They have stout and short or completely subterranean trunks and pinnate leaves usually with broad thick leaflets. The cones are relatively fat and brown, reddish, or gray with vertical rows of large diamond-shaped segments and red seeds. Some species sucker and at least one species is epiphytic. These are exceptionally beautiful cycads because of the large leaflets, which are often a lovely yellowish green or bronzy color when new.

Zamia fischeri (FISH-ur-eye) is indigenous to central Mexico and is hardy in zones 10 and 11 and marginal in zone 9b. This small species grows to only about 3 feet in height. When mature it usually has a short stout trunk about 6 inches tall. The arching light green leaves are about 18 inches long with widely spaced lance-shaped thin leaflets whose margins are finely serrate. This lovely little fernlike cycad thrives in partial shade.

Zamia floridana. See *Z. pumila*.

Zamia furfuracea (fur-fyoo-RAY-see-a) is native to southeastern Mexico and is hardy in zones 9b through 11 and marginal in zone 9a. This species is perhaps the most common in the genus in cultivation. It is a clumping species that grows to as much as 4 or 5 feet but produces no aboveground trunk. The erect leaves are 3 to 4 feet long and the rosette is fairly dense with them. The closely set leaflets are oblong to obovate or obdeltoid in shape with finely serrate margins. When mature, the leaves are a medium green above and a brownish green beneath, but new leaves are a beautiful light greenish yellow. The leaves are almost flat when the plant is grown in partial shade, but the leaflets turn upwards from the plane of the leaf stalk to as much as 45° when grown in the sun. Because the texture of the mature leaves is slightly rough and because the leaflets are thick, the plant is usually called the cardboard palm. It looks superb almost anywhere in sun to partial shade and gives a wonderful textural accent because of the broad light-colored leaflets. The plant is tolerant of salty ocean spray and slightly saline soil and is a fine coastal garden subject. Plate 408.

Zamia integrifolia. See *Z. pumila.*

Zamia lindenii (lin-DEN-ee-eye) is indigenous to Ecuador and northern Peru and is hardy in zones 10b and 11. This species is one of the largest in the genus, growing to as much as 10 or 12 feet in height with a thick trunk to as much as 6 feet. The gorgeous leaves are as much as 7 or even 8 feet long and are erect but gracefully arching. The numerous opposite stalkless bright green elliptic foot-long leaflets have tapering and pointed tips and finely serrate margins. The leaf petiole has widely scattered prickly hairs, and the rachis is usually a reddish brown in color. The plant revels in partial shade and needs a rich and humusy soil. It should not be allowed to dry out but, at the same time, it needs a freely draining soil.

Zamia pumila (PYOO-mi-la) (synonyms *Z. floridana, Z. integrifolia*) occurs naturally from the southern Georgia coast through Florida, the Bahamas, and into the West Indies, and is hardy in zones 8 through 11. This trunkless but clumping species is one of the smallest *Zamia* species, growing only to about 2 feet with leaves that are about the same length. The leaves, except for their size, are rather similar to those of *Z. furfuracea,* but the leaflets are narrower and usually a darker green. The plant grows near the sea as well as inland and is quite tolerant of saline spray and soil. It likes sun and is drought tolerant. Its only drawback is its diminutive size, but it is quite attractive in the rock garden and along sunny paths. This cycad is most often called coontie.

Zamia skinneri (SKIN-nur-eye) is indigenous to Central American rain forests and is hardy in zones 10 and 11 and somewhat marginal in zone 10a. This trunk-forming species is one of the most beautiful cycads. The trunk is fairly slender for the genus and is as much as 6 feet tall. The leaves, which are about 6 feet long, have very large 18-inch-long leaflets that are a deep green when mature and quite glossy on their upper surfaces. Their shape is linear-ovate to broadly lanceo-

late with long tapering tips. The species is one of the finest and most tropical looking plants for shady to partially shady sites when planted where its lovely silhouette can be appreciated. It should not be allowed to dry out, and it needs a rich and humusy soil.

ZANTEDESCHIA
(zant-e-DEESH-ya / zant-e-DEESH-ee-a)
Araceae: The Calla Lily, Jack-in-the-Pulpit Family
CALLA LILY
Evergreen stemless plants with large arrow-shaped
    leaves; large white, yellow, and pink flowers
Zones 8 through 11; marginal in zone 7
Partial shade to partial sun
Water lovers
Rich, humusy, well-drained, acidic soil
Propagation by transplanting of suckers and by seed

A genus of only six species of clumping evergreen perennial rhizomatous and stemless herbs in southern Africa. They have large ovate-sagittate leaves that are often variegated and terminal flowers that are borne on long tall stalks well above the foliage. The flowers are typical of the family but are much more showy than those of most members, having open, flared, and highly colored or pure white cuplike spathes. The plants are evergreen only in warm winter regions. In climates in which the plants go dormant, the site should have perfect drainage if the winter season is cold and wet, as the rhizomes tend to rot when dormant or semi-dormant in wet ground. There are many hybrids between the several species and they are usually more robust with larger and deeper-colored flowers than those of the type.

Zantedeschia aethiopica (eeth-ee-OAP-i-ka) is native to northeastern South Africa. Known as the white-flowered calla lily, it is the most widely grown species. It grows to 3 feet or sometimes more. The 18-inch-long dark green leaves are long-stalked, ovate in outline, with deep sagittate basal lobes that give the leaf the overall shape of an arrowhead. The inflorescences are borne in spring and early summer on 3-foot-long stalks and are 8 to 10 inches long, pure white with a golden-yellow spadix, and somewhat fragrant. There are several cultivars varying in size of plant and flower. *Zantedeschia aethiopica* 'Green Goddess' has flowers with green hues near the top of the oversized inflorescence. The plants are easy to grow in partial shade to partial sun except in hot desert areas where the foliage always looks less than perfect. They should not be allowed to dry out while growing in the spring and summer, and they luxuriate in a soil enriched with compost or manure. This species is adaptable as a bog or shallow aquatic landscape subject in regions with winters warm enough to keep the plants from going dormant.

Zantedeschia albomaculata (al´-bo-mak´-yoo-LAIT-a) is indigenous to central South Africa. It is similar to *Z. aethiopica* but smaller in stature and has narrower leaves. Its long-stalked leaves have white spots, which make them exceptionally suitable for brightening up shady areas. The plants bloom in early summer with 6-inch-long white or yellow inflorescences that usually have a deep red suffusion at the base of the "cup."

Zantedeschia elliottiana (el´-lee-aht-tee-AN-a) is native to South Africa and is a smaller plant than the preceding two species. Its leaves are spotted as are those of *Z. albomaculata,* and the 6-inch-long summer inflorescence is a deep golden yellow. The plant tolerates more sun than the other species in the genus.

Zantedeschia rehmannii (ray-MAHN-nee-eye) occurs naturally in northeastern South Africa and grows only to about 2 feet in height with narrow sagittate-lanceolate leaves and beautiful rose-colored inflorescences. A cultivar with deeper-colored flowers is more common in cultivation than the type.

ZANTHOXYLUM (zan-THAHX-i-lum)
Rutaceae: The Citrus Family
WILD LIME; LIME PRICKLY-ASH
Large thorny evergreen shrub or small tree; pinnate
    leaves; tiny white flowers; small brown berries
Zones 10 and 11; marginal in zone 9b
Sun
Average but regular amounts of moisture
Average well-drained soil
Propagation by seed

A large genus of about 250 spiny evergreen or deciduous trees and shrubs on all continents except Antarctica. They are characterized by aromatic bark and usually aromatic pinnate leaves. The flowers are small but are borne in clusters. One species is widely grown in the American tropics for its beautiful foliage. ***Zanthoxylum fagara*** (fa-GAHR-a) occurs naturally in extreme southern Texas, Mexico, Central America, northern South America, the West Indies, and southern Florida. It grows to 25 or even 30 feet, but is more often a large shrub. For a tree form, it is usually necessary to train to a central leader when the plant is young. As a tree it makes a slender dense crown above a thin, mostly smooth dark gray trunk that is seldom completely straight and erect. The twigs are a light brownish yellow in color (*zanthoxylum* is derived from two Greek words and means "yellow wood"). The leaves are odd-pinnate with 7 to 14 stalkless elliptic to obovate to almost orbicular dark green shiny leaflets whose margins bear tiny and shallow indentations and whose tips are usually notched. Two distinctive characteristics of the leaves are the winged rachis and petiole with broadened green tissue between each leaflet and the pair of short recurved thorns at the bottom of each complete leaf. The leaves are wonderfully aromatic when crushed or bruised and smell of citrus. The little trees bloom in spring and early summer with small spikes of tiny greenish white flowers in the leaf axils, which quickly give way to small clusters of orange-brown small berries on the female trees. The tree makes a wonderful patio subject and, as a large shrub, gives texture to any border planting. The species grows near the coast as well as inland in its native haunts and is perfectly adapted to seaside plantings.

ZOMBIA (ZAHM-bee-a)
Palmae (Arecaceae): The Palm Family
ZOMBIE PALM
Small clumping spiny-trunked fan-leaved palm
Zones 10 and 11; marginal in zone 10a
Sun
Average but regular amounts of moisture
Average well-drained soil
Propagation by seed

A monotypic genus native to Hispaniola. A clumping spiny-trunked palm species, ***Zombia antillarum*** (an-TIL-la-rum / an-til-LAIR-um) grows slowly to 10 to 15 feet with several relatively thin trunks, each trunk wrapped in an intricate and most beautiful matting of gray to silvery fibers whose ends project outward in sharp spines. The leaves are usually about 3 feet wide, about 210° of a circle in outline, grass green in color, and divided about halfway to the petiole into many slightly drooping segments. The inflorescences are usually mostly hidden by the leaves, but the inch-wide fruits are a beautiful and striking white color. This palm is incredibly beautiful, especially if some of the stems are judiciously removed from a specimen to show off the form and beauty of the individual trunks. It is unaccountably rare outside botanical gardens, possibly because of the spines on the trunks, but is so choice that its wider planting is most heartily encouraged. It is carefree, drought tolerant, not particular as to soil and, because it grows near the shore as well as inland in Haiti, is one of the finest seaside landscape subjects. It usually sprouts from the base after being frozen to the ground by temperatures of 26°F but is sufficiently slow-growing that it is not of much use outside zones 10 and 11. Plate 409.

Landscape Lists

Aquatic, Bog, and Marsh Plants

Water is intimately associated with tropical gardens whether as the seas and their coasts or the lagoons, estuaries, rivers, and inland lakes. It is at and in these regions that some of the most spectacular and appealing tropical looking subjects are to be found. Furthermore, many purely terrestrial plants look ever so wonderful near water with their images reflected in ponds or streams. Among these are bananas, lobster claws, palms, and bamboos. In addition, water and the plants associated with it are havens for all manner of wildlife from fish and amphibians to the beasts of the fields and, even more importantly in a human aesthetic sense, birds. The world of water and plants is a complete one, both of beauty and of ecological harmony.

The purely aquatic subjects like waterlilies and other floating plants and the bog and marsh plants at the edges of ponds and lakes create a world of quiet grace, nobility, and startling color. Some of the world's most beautiful flowers are those of aquatics like species of *Eichornia*, *Nymphaea*, and *Victoria*, and they are made all the more spectacular because the plants that bear them are never of great treelike stature but always nearer the earth or water. It is a wonderful irony that the blossoms of almost all cactus species are equally dramatic and beautiful. The water world is complete with such wonders as majestic bald cypresses, the spectacular Guiana chestnut, and the great and dramatic papyrus.

Another wonderful irony is that many tropical seacoast plants are not only partially aquatic but are also drought tolerant. This strange phenomenon is due to the plants' metabolic mechanisms by which they separate the salt from the water and excrete the former. This process takes great amounts of plant energy and water, resulting in the plants' ability to carry on without a great deal of pure water.

Here included are marine as well as brackish and fresh water subjects. Many of them grow just as well on dry land.

Aquatics

Avicennia	*Nymphaea*
Cyperus	*Nymphoides*
Eichornia	*Pistia*
Laguncularia	*Pontederia*
Nelumbo	*Rhizophora*

Taxodium   *Victoria*
Thalia

Bog and Marsh

Acrostichum   *Hedychium*
Alocasia cucullata   *Laguncularia*
Alocasia 'Hilo Beauty'   *Pistia*
Alocasia macrorrhiza   *Pontederia*
Annona glabra   *Taxodium distichum*
Colocasia affinis   *Taxodium mucronatum*
Colocasia antiquorum   *Thalia dealbata*
Colocasia esculenta   *Thalia geniculata*
Cyperus alternifolius   *Thelypteris kunthii*
Cyperus papyrus   *Xanthosoma*
Cyrtosperma   *Zantedeschia aethiopica*
Eichornia

Bamboo and Large Grasses

Bamboo species are all grasses; which is to say that they are members of the family Gramineae (or Poaceae). All grasses have thick roots from which the stems and linear, sheathing leaves grow. These roots allow all perennial species to recover and grow again if the upper portions of the plants are killed back. In nature this has allowed the grasses to attain dominance and in some cases supremacy in regions where other plants are constantly cut back by fire or grazing animals and thus cannot sustain themselves

Bamboo species for the most part produce unusually large and tall stems for grasses. Some stems or canes (technically called "culms") attain heights of more than 100 feet. The stems are hollow except at the nodes or joints from which the branches and leaves grow. The culm nodes usually produce branches only on their upper parts, and leaves are produced only from the branches.

The tropical bamboo species generally do not produce new culms in spring or early summer; rather they wait until fall or even early winter to send up the new shoots that do not usually branch and leaf out until the following spring or summer. The temperate climate species on the other hand generally produce their new stems, branches, and leaves mostly simultaneously and principally in the spring and summer. The canes of all types of bamboo last for many years but eventually die and should then be removed. Removing these is a not-too-easy accomplishment for the very large tropical varieties and for some of the timber types from temperate regions.

The new stems or culms are almost unique in that they emerge from the ground with their maximum diameter already established and, in some tropical species, then grow upwards at a phenomenal rate. All species, however, require a period of adjustment after planting in which the plants will not grow much and in which, if new culms are produced, the stems will not be of maximum size. The period of adjustment is usually about a year, sometimes shorter for the temperate species and often longer for the giant tropical types. In hot and frostless or nearly frostless climates, bamboo should be planted in the late autumn or early winter. In cool and nearly frostless regions planting is successful at any time of year.

In regions with a temperate climate and varying seasons planting should be done only at times of the year in which the newly planted clumps will soon thereafter suffer neither frost nor high heat, usually early fall and early spring.

The roots of the bamboo species are exceptional in size and endurance. Like the roots of many other grass family members, they spread the individual bamboo plants by traveling on or under the ground and outward from the original point of the sprouting seed or original plant. The plants and their root systems are of two basic types: those whose roots each year spread far from the original point and are called "running types," and those whose roots each season spread only a short distance from the original point and are called "clumping types." The clumping types are, almost without exception, tropical or subtropical in origin while the running types are, almost without exception, from temperate climates.

The running types of bamboo can present a problem for the gardener as the habits of their roots make most of them invasive. This spreading habit also makes them exceptionally beautiful landscape subjects as they can form wonderfully attractive groves. They can be controlled only by a barrier through which and over which their roots cannot spread or by the laborious digging out of roots and stems from where they are not wanted. All bamboo species are especially beautiful near water. In addition, their roots will not spread into the aqueous environment, which means that as landscape subjects for the perimeters of ponds or pools their spread is at least partially controlled.

The temperate climate and running type bamboo species in this book are *Arundinaria*, *Arundo* and *Phyllostachys*. The tropical and clumping types are *Bambusa* and *Dendrocalamus*. *Arundo* is not a true bamboo but behaves as does an invasive running type.

Bromeliads and Other Epiphytes

Few groups of plants can compare to the bromeliads in beauty of form and flower. Their mostly succulent rosettes and spectacular spikes of flowers are unmatched for creating texture and color on the ground as well as in the trees of tropical landscapes. Even the smallest epiphytes lend allure to tree trunks while the larger epiphytes occasion the sense of nature primordial and supreme, the world in a former age of pristine and unpolluted glory.

All bromeliads are members of one family, Bromeliaceae. Their provenance, like that of the cactus family, is limited to the Western Hemisphere, indicating among other things that their evolution was, in geological time, relatively recent.

Most bromeliads are epiphytic, but quite a few are terrestrial, and many are adaptable to either life style. In form the plants range from wide and open rosettes (mostly the terrestrials), whose leaves are separated sufficiently from one another that they do not form reservoirs at their bases, to closely set rosettes (some of which are narrow and urn-shaped) whose leaf bases form reservoirs that collect water and organic matter, to elongated stems bearing leaves at regular intervals. Some species have very tight leaf rosettes, and a few are so tight that they almost form orchidlike pseudobulbs. These pseudobulbs have no function, however, other than to protect the leaves from heat and desiccation. The species whose leaves form water-collecting reservoirs are often referred to as "tank bromeliads." Their reservoirs, which provide water for the plants in times of drought, also collect organic matter and often serve as the breeding ground for tree frogs and as the sole habitat of many microscopic organisms.

Most species are inhabitants of mesic environments or even rain forest regions and need a regular supply of moisture whether they are epiphytic, terrestrial, or both. Others, especially species in the genus *Tillandsia*, are xerophytes. Some of these xerophytes are capable of withstanding more drought than most cactus species. They accomplish this feat by having their stems and leaves covered in moisture-conserving hairs and scales and the capability to draw any moisture from the air.

All bromeliads are capable of producing roots, but only the terrestrial and rosette forms have feeding type roots. The wiry-stemmed "air plants" (mainly of the genus *Tillandsia*) form only holdfast type roots. All but the solely terrestrial species are capable of forming holdfast roots, and some of these roots are rhizomatous and spreading, and form colonies of the individual plants.

The terrestrial species need a loose and freely draining soil with much organic material; leaf mold is especially desirable. The tank type bromeliads also relish leaf mold when grown terrestrially, but in addition need a more open and very freely draining medium amended with coarse sand, perlite, bark, or tree fern fiber, a mixture usually termed an "epiphytic mix." The true air plants, of course, require only a perch into which they will usually project holdfast roots if the substrate is porous enough. Favorite perches are dead tree limbs.

All species of rosette-forming tank type bromeliads are monocarpic. The rosettes are, however, maintained in the landscape by offsets, usually called "pups" by bromeliad fanciers. The pups are separate rosette-forming shoots that grow from the roots of the "mother" rosette. These pups are, of course, a primary method of propagation by collectors. Some tank type species form their pups in the middle of the pre-existing rosette at the time of flowering, and some form pups on the flower stems. All species form flowers, fruits, and seeds. The seeds can spread the plants over relatively large areas.

Bromeliads

Aechmea
Ananas
Androlepis
Billbergia
Bromelia
Canistrum
Cryptanthus

Deuterocohnia
Dyckia
Guzmania
Hechtia
Neoregelia
Tillandsia
Vriesea

Epiphytic Species Other than Bromeliads

Asplenium bulbiferum
Cochliostema
Cryptocereus
Davallia divaricata
Davallia fejeensis
Davallia mariesii
Davallia trichomanoides
Drynaria
Epiphyllum
Goniophlebium

Microgramma
Microsorium
Philodendron erubescens
Philodendron fragrantissimum
Philodendron melinonii
Philodendron pedatum
Philodendron williamsii
Phlebodium
Platycerium
Rumohra

Drought-Tolerant Plants

These plants are not just for arid climates. In all but true rain forest regions there are times of the year when nature does not provide the needed water for people, animals, and plants. Some of the following subjects, such as *Adansonia* (baobab tree) species, have immensely large trunks that store copious amounts of water. When mature, these plants survive for a year or more without a drop of rain. This would be an instance of extreme drought tolerance. Mature specimens of plants like *Carnegiea* (sahuaro) species are also capable of storing great quantities of water in their stems and can withstand periods of many months of drought; this is an example of great drought tolerance. Examples of medium drought tolerance are numerous and include vegetation that is capable of enduring monsoon climates (those in which there are distinct wet and dry seasons, the latter of which may last several months with little or no rain). Some tolerance to drought is most common, of course, and indicates a propensity for surviving without regular and adequate amounts of moisture. The last condition (termed "mesic") is one in which adequate moisture is found year-round in at least part of the root zone of the plant.

Acacia (most) Medium to great
Acrocomia Medium
Adansonia Extreme
Adenium Medium
Aeonium Medium
Agave Medium
Albizia lebbeck Medium
Aleurites fordii Medium
Aloe Medium to great
Aporocactus Medium
Armatocereus Great
Beaucarnea Some
Bismarckia Some
Borzicactus Medium
Brachychiton Medium
Brahea Medium
Bromelia Medium
Bucida Medium
Bulnesia Medium
Bursera Medium
Butea Medium
Butia Medium
Caesalpinia bonduc Great
Caesalpinia gilliesii Medium
Calotropis Medium
Canavalia Great
Canella Medium
Carissa Medium
Carnegiea Great
Casasia Great
Cassia didymobotrya Medium
Ceiba Medium
Cephalocereus Great
Cereus Medium

Chamaerops Medium
Chorisia Medium
Cissus incisa Medium
Cleistocactus Medium
Clusia Medium
Coccoloba Medium
Coccothrinax Medium
Cochlospermum Great
Cocos Medium
Codiaeum Some
Conocarpus Great
Copernicia Medium
Cordia Medium
Cordyline australis Medium
Cotyledon Some
Crassula Some
Dalbergia sissoo Some
Dasylirion Great to extreme
Deuterocohnia Medium
Dioon edule Medium
Dracaena draco Great
Dyckia Great
Echeveria Medium
Echinocactus Great to extreme
Echinopsis Great to extreme
Ehretia anacua Medium
Encephalartos lehmannii Medium
Encephalartos longifolius Medium
Erythrina (some) Medium to great
Escontria Great
Espostoa Great
Euphorbia (succulents) Great to extreme
Ferocactus Great to extreme
Ficus benghalensis Some

Ficus carica Medium
Ficus citrifolia Medium
Ficus palmeri Great
Ficus petiolaris Great
Ficus religiosa Medium
Ficus rubiginosa Some
Ficus sycomorus Medium
Fouquieria Great
Gossypium Medium
Guaiacum Medium
Hechtia Great
Hesperaloe Great
Hibiscus acetosella Medium
Hyphaene Medium
Jacquinia Medium
Jatropha podagrica Medium
Justicia brandegeana Some
Justicia spicigera Medium
Kalanchoe (most) Medium to great
Kigelia Medium
Lantana camara Medium
Lantana montevidensis Great
Leucophyllum Great
Lysiloma Medium
Macrozamia macdonnellii Great
Mallotonia Great
Malvaviscus Medium
Manilkara roxburghiana Great
Mastichodendron Great
Murraya Medium
Myrtillocactus Great
Nannorrhops Medium
Nerium Great
Nolina Great to extreme
Noronhia Great
Ochrosia Medium
Oncoba Medium
Opuntia Medium to great

Pachycereus Great
Pachypodium Great
Pandanus Medium
Parkinsonia Medium
Pedilanthus Medium
Phoenix canariensis Medium
Phoenix dactylifera Medium
Phormium Medium
Phytolacca Medium
Pimenta Medium
Piscidia Medium
Pithecellobium Great
Portulacaria Great
Pseudophoenix Medium
Rhoeo Medium
Sabal Some
Serenoa Medium
Solanum marginatum Medium
Sophora Great
Stapelia Medium to great
Stenocereus Great
Stetsonia Great
Syagrus amara Medium
Synadenium Medium
Tecoma Medium
Terminalia Great
Tetrazygia Medium
Thespesia Great
Thrinax Medium
Tillandsia capitata Extreme
Tillandsia dasylirifolia Extreme
Tillandsia lampropoda Extreme
Tillandsia xerographica Extreme
Trithrinax Medium
Washingtonia Medium
Yucca (most) Medium to great
Zamia pumila Medium
Zombia Medium

Erosion-Controlling Plants

These are plants that bind the soil along windswept, waterswept, or sloping ground. Of course, almost any plant can perform this function, but the plants listed here start the process and they are of sizes and forms that are not easily discouraged by wind, water, or degree of slope.

Acrostichum
Arundinaria argenteostriata
Arundinaria disticha
Arundinaria gigantea
Arundinaria pygmaea

Arundo
Aspidistra
Avicennia
Caesalpinia bonduc
Canavalia

Carissa macrocarpa
Freycinetia
Hedera canariensis
Hedera helix
Ipomoea indica
Ipomoea pes-caprae
Laguncularia
Lantana montevidensis
Phyllostachys bambusoides
Phyllostachys bambusoides 'Allgold'

Phyllostachys bambusoides 'Castillon'
Phyllostachys edulis
Phyllostachys nigra
Phyllostachys nigra 'Bory'
Phyllostachys nigra 'Henon'
Rhizophora
Scaevola plumieri
Tecomaria
Tetrastigma

Fast-Growing Plants

The word *fast* is, alas, a relative term, especially considering the various large groups of plants. For example, all palms are relatively slow growers compared to other groups of plants, so no palm can match the speed of growth of the fastest dicotyledonous trees. Some palms, however, are definitely fast growing. Just how fast any plant's growth is depends, of course, on the environmental conditions in which it finds itself. It is assumed that the plants below will be grown in conditions to their liking, else they might be as slow as or slower than many of the plants considered as slow.

Acacia auriculiformis
Acacia baileyana
Acacia nilotica
Acalypha
Albizia julibrissin
Albizia lebbeck
Aleurites fordii
Aleurites moluccana
Allamanda cathartica
Alocasia macrorrhiza
Alocasia odora
Alocasia plumbea
Alpinia purpurata
Alpinia zerumbet
Alstonia
Andira
Antigonon
Argyreia
Aristolochia durior
Aristolochia grandiflora
Barleria
Bauhinia ×*blakeana*
Bauhinia corymbosa
Bauhinia forficata
Bauhinia monandra
Bauhinia purpurea
Bauhinia variegata
Beaumontia
Bignonia
Bischofia

Blighia
Bombacopsis
Bougainvillea
Brachychiton
Brugmansia
Caesalpinia bonduc
Caesalpinia pulcherrima
Calophyllum
Campsis
Cananga
Carica
Carpentaria
Cassia
Cecropia
Ceiba
Chorisia
Cissus
Clematis
Clerodendrum bungei
Clerodendrum philippinum
Clerodendrum quadriloculare
Clerodendrum speciosissimum
Clerodendrum trichotomum
Clytostoma
Cobaea
Cochlospermum
Colocasia
Combretum
Cornutia
Costus

Crescentia alata
Datura
Delonix
Diospyros digyna
Distictis
Dombeya
Echites
Ensete
Enterolobium
Epipremnum
Erythrina
Etlingera
Euphorbia cotinifolia
Euphorbia leucocephala
Euphorbia pulcherrima
Euterpe
Ficus altissima
Ficus aurea
Ficus benghalensis
Ficus benjamina
Ficus callosa
Ficus citrifolia
Ficus macrophylla
Ficus microcarpa
Ficus pumila
Ficus religiosa
Firmiana
Gliricidia
Gossypium
Graptophyllum
Hamelia
Hedera
Heliconia
Hibiscus
Hura
Inga
Iochroma
Ipomoea
Iresine
Jacaranda
Jatropha gossypifolia
Koelreuteria
Lantana
Lonchocarpus
Lygodium
Macfadyena
Malvaviscus
Mandevilla
Markhamia
Michelia champaca
Millettia ovalifolia
Millettia reticulata
Moringa
Mucuna

Muntingia
Musa
Nephrolepis biserrata
Nephrolepis cordifolia
Ochna
Odontonema callistachyum
Pachystachys
Parkinsonia
Passiflora
Peltophorum
Pereskia
Persea
Petrea
Philodendron (most)
Phormium
Piper auritum
Piscidia
Podranea ricasoliana
Pongamia
Posoqueria
Pouteria campechiana
Pouteria sapota
Pseudobombax
Pseudocalymma
Psychotria
Pyrostegia
Quisqualis
Radermachera
Ravenea
Rhoeo
Ricinus
Samanea
Schizolobium
Sesbania
Solandra
Solanum jasminoides
Solanum rantonnetii
Solanum wendlandii
Spathodea
Stenochlaena
Sterculia
Swietenia macrophylla
Syagrus romanzoffiana
Syngonium
Syzygium cumini
Taxodium
Tecoma
Tecomaria
Tectona
Thespesia
Thevetia
Thunbergia alata
Thunbergia fragrans
Thunbergia grandiflora

Tipuana
Urechites
Veitchia (all but *V. merrillii*)
Wagatea
Washingtonia robusta

Wodyetia
Xanthosoma
Yucca elephantipes
Yucca recurvifolia

Ferns

The ferns are a large and varied group of plants. Their lovely and graceful genera and species span several plant families, and their growth forms are terrestrial or epiphytic. Many are climbing plants, and a few are completely aquatic. They are not flowering plants but rather propagate themselves sexually by spores, which form on the undersides or margins of the leaves in special organs called "sporangia" (the singular form of the word is "sporangium"). Most fern species have only one basic form of frond, but many others have two forms: the sterile, non-spore-producing fronds and the fertile, spore-producing leaves.

The spores are only somewhat analogous to seeds. Their germination produces not a mature fern plant but rather a special type of plant called the "prothallus." This prothallus, when mature, is usually heart-shaped and produces both male and female sexual parts that mature at different stages in the life of the prothallus; thus self fertilization is avoided. After fertilization of the female part of the prothallus, a complete fern plant is created within the saclike female organ and starts growing on its own, soon overtaking the prothallus that then withers away. The new plant, which is called the "sporophyte" (meaning a plant that bears spores), is the plant with fronds and sporangia that we normally call a fern, although most young sporophytes do not have fronds typical of their species until they have grown for a while.

For the egg in the female sexual organ (called an "archegonium") of the prothallus to be fertilized by sperm to create the new sporophyte, there must be water present as the sperms cannot otherwise move from one prothallus to another. This need for water indicates that the ferns are an ancient group of plants, one which evolved when the earth was more watery than it now is, and that ferns grow and thrive mostly in moist places. Their greatest size and diversity are reached in rain forests, both tropical and temperate.

Because of the unique life cycle and forms of ferns, botanists have had to create several special terms to describe them. Most of these terms are not needed by the average gardener to grow ferns properly. But anyone who reads the literature and is interested in the special beauty of these plants might well want to know that the stem of the fern frond is called the "stipe" and that, as for other pinnate leaves, the terms "rachis" and "leaflet" apply to ferns as well as to flowering plants with pinnate leaves. Not all ferns, of course, have compound pinnate leaves; several species have undivided leaves, many of which are among the grandest and most beautiful in the plant kingdom.

Acrostichum
Adiantum
Angiopteris
Asplenium
Blechnum
Cyathea
Davallia

Dicksonia
Drynaria
Goniophlebium
Lygodium
Microgramma
Microlepia
Microsorium

Nephrolepis   *Rumohra*
Phlebodium   *Stenochlaena*
Platycerium   *Thelypteris*

Fragrant Plants

Here included are not only plants whose flowers emit fragrance but also those whose other parts are deemed by a majority of persons to be pleasing to the nose.

Acacia (most)   *Clerodendrum bungei*
Agave sisalana   *Clerodendrum philippinum*
Aiphanes erosa   *Clerodendrum trichotomum*
Albizia julibrissin   *Cleyera*
Albizia lebbeck   *Coccothrinax fragrans*
Allamanda cathartica   *Cochliostema*
Alpinia   *Coffea*
Alstonia   *Combretum fruticosum*
Amyris   *Cordyline australis*
Andira   *Cornutia*
Annona   *Couroupita*
Areca catechu   *Dalbergia sissoo*
Arenga engleri   *Datura*
Artabotrys   *Dillenia*
Averrhoa carambola   *Diospyros digyna*
Avicennia   *Distictis laxiflora*
Azadirachta   *Dombeya*
Barringtonia   *Dracaena fragrans*
Beaumontia   *Dracaena surculosa*
Begonia deliciosa   *Echites*
Begonia grandis   *Ehretia anacua*
Begonia heracleifolia   *Epiphyllum*
Bischofia   *Eriobotrya*
Blighia   *Etlingera*
Brugmansia   *Eugenia axillaris*
Brunfelsia   *Exothea*
Caesalpinia coriaria   *Fagraea*
Caesalpinia mexicana   *Gardenia*
Calliandra surinamensis   *Gordonia*
Callisia fragrans   *Hedychium*
Calodendrum   *Hylocereus guatemalensis*
Calophyllum   *Hylocereus undatus*
Calyptranthes   *Illicium*
Cananga   *Ipomoea alba*
Canella   *Ixora acuminata*
Carissa   *Ixora finlaysoniana*
Casasia   *Ixora odorata*
Cassia excelsa   *Jacquinia*
Cereus peruvianus   *Laguncularia*
Cinnamomum   *Lantana*
Citharexylum   *Ligustrum*
Citrus   *Magnolia coco*
Clematis   *Magnolia delavayi*

Magnolia grandiflora
Mammea
Manilkara roxburghiana
Michelia
Mimusops
Monodora
Moringa
Murraya
Nelumbo
Noronhia
Nymphaea
Ochrosia
Oncoba
Pachira
Pandanus
Pandorea
Parkinsonia
Passiflora alata
Passiflora ×alato-caerulea
Passiflora quadrangularis
Passiflora vitifolia
Peltophorum
Pereskia aculeata
Pimenta
Piper auritum
Pithecellobium
Pittosporum

Plumeria
Pongamia
Porana
Posoqueria
Pouteria campechiana
Pouteria sapota
Psidium littorale
Quisqualis
Radermachera
Randia
Saraca
Solandra
Sophora secundiflora
Spondias mombin
Stemmadenia
Stephanotis
Swietenia
Syzygium cumini
Tabebuia chrysantha
Tabernaemontana
Tetrapanax
Thevetia
Victoria
Yucca
Zantedeschia aethiopica
Zanthoxylum

Groundcover Plants

Groundcover is a vague term in horticulture and, technically, just about any plant species or variety can be a groundcover. The pilot of a low-flying plane over the Amazon rain forest might well call the 200- to 300-foot canopy trees "groundcovers" when he or she looks down on the top of the forest. This, of course, is not what we usually mean by the term. As normally used, the term applies to plants of relatively low stature and often those that are creeping or spreading of form by means of their aboveground or underground stems. This last characteristic is certainly not the delimiting characteristic of the following species and varieties; some of the most beautiful covers consist of plants that do not normally spread their respective masses by these means. Yet, they are eminently amenable because of their size and form for mass plantings that do cover ground.

Adiantum
Aglaonema
Arundinaria argenteostriata
Arundinaria disticha
Arundinaria pygmaea
Aspidistra
Asystasia
Barleria
Begonia

Bertolonia
Bougainvillea
Burbidgea
Calathea
Callisia
Carissa macrocarpa (dwarf)
Chamaeranthemum
Chlorophytum
Cissus hypoglauca

Cissus incisa
Clerodendrum splendens
Cryptanthus
Ctenanthe
Davallia trichomanoides
Dieffenbachia
Dracaena surculosa
Epipremnum
Episcia
×*Fatshedera*
Fittonia
Freycinetia
Geogenanthus
Hedera
Hemigraphis
Ipomoea imperati
Ipomoea indica
Ipomoea macrantha
Ipomoea pes-caprae
Kalanchoe synsepala
Lantana montevidensis
Maranta
Monstera
Pandorea

Pellionia
Peperomia
Philodendron
Pilea
Piper (vining types)
Plectranthus
Portulacaria (low form)
Pseuderanthemum alatum
Rhoeo
Ruellia
Rumohra
Sabal minor
Scaevola plumieri
Schefflera arboricola
Schismatoglottis
Siderasis
Solanum rantonnetii
Spathiphyllum
Stenochlaena
Streptosolen
Syngonium
Tecomaria
Tetrastigma

Hedge and Screening Plants

Hedges can be practical or aesthetic in basic function and many are often both. Screens are by definition more practical than aesthetic, but they need not partake of the former characteristic to the exclusion of the latter. In general the slower growing plants are best for hedges, while the faster growing species are best for screening. It also helps for both functions if the particular plant tends to hold its leaves from top to bottom.

Acalypha
Allamanda cathartica
Amphitecna
Antigonon
Arundinaria
Bambusa
Barleria
Beaumontia
Bignonia
Bixa
Calotropis
Calyptranthes pallens
Carissa
Cereus
Citrus
Cleyera
Cobaea
Coccoloba uvifera

Cochlospermum
Conocarpus
Cryptostegia
Eugenia coronata
Eugenia foetida
Eugenia uniflora
Euphorbia antiquorum
Euphorbia lactea
Euphorbia milii
Feijoa
Ficus microcarpa var. *nitida*
Hylocereus
Ixora
Laguncularia
Ligustrum
Murraya
Nerium
Pandanus baptistii

Pedilanthus
Pereskia
Phoenix reclinata
Pittosporum tobira
Pittosporum undulatum
Polyscias filicifolia
Polyscias scutellaria
Pseuderanthemum atropurpureum
Randia

Rhapis
Ricinus
Scaevola plumieri
Syzygium paniculatum
Tabernaemontana
Tecomaria
Tetrazygia
Yucca

Invasive Plants

Invasive landscape plants are not usually appropriate for small or "tidy" gardens. They are bold not only of form but also of habit; this is a nice way of saying that some of them might take over a small plot. It is somewhat a matter of taste, but some gardeners find the size of a plant or its invasive roots to be much less onerous to deal with than the seeds of the great seed-dispersing species. Some species have more than one method of being ruffianly, but great amounts of seeds can be distributed almost literally overnight whereas roots take at least *some* time to grow. The following list indicates manner and degree of invasiveness for each plant or plant group.

Arundinaria Creeping rootstocks; high
Arundo Creeping rootstocks; medium
Bambusa vulgaris Creeping rootstocks; low
Campsis Size of vine, seeds; medium
Clerodendrum bungei Creeping rootstocks; high
Clerodendrum philippinum Creeping rootstocks; medium
Eichornia Creeping rootstocks; high
Hedera helix Creeping rootstocks, size of vines; medium

Macfadyena Creeping rootstocks, size of vines; medium
Nymphoides Creeping rootstocks; medium
Phyllostachys Creeping rootstocks; high
Piper auritum Creeping rootstocks; medium
Pistia Creeping rootstocks; medium
Sesbania Seeds; medium
Tetrapanax Creeping rootstocks; medium
Thalia Creeping rootstocks; low

Large Trees

Large trees are, of course, the ultimate superstructure of any landscape or garden. There are no very large trees that can flourish in shade when past the seedling stage, a fact that a moment's thought will show to be *a priori*: what plant would shade any of them in their maturity? A tree is "large" if it is more than 40 feet in height. A quick glance down the following list will reveal that there are several species whose maximum height is given as 40 feet. These are unusually massive or broad trees that in no true sense of the word can be called other than "large." The reader should note that the category of "tall trees" has been avoided. This is partly because some trees will grow unusually tall under certain stressful conditions and partly because of the breadth of some of these 30- or 40-footers. The heights given in the descriptions indicate a tree's normal height under normal conditions.

Acacia albida
Acacia galpinii

Acacia giraffe
Acacia koa

Adansonia
Albizia lebbeck
Aleurites moluccana
Alstonia
Andira
Antidesma
Artocarpus
Astrocaryum aculeatum
Avicennia
Bactris
Barringtonia
Bischofia
Bismarckia
Bombacopsis
Bombax
Borassus
Brachychiton
Bursera
Cananga
Carnegiea
Caryota rumphiana
Cassia grandis
Castanospermum
Ceiba
Chrysophyllum
Cinnamomum camphorum
Coccoloba diversifolia
Coccoloba pubescens
Cocos
Copernicia alba
Corypha
Couroupita
Dalbergia
Dillenia
Diospyros ebenum
Enterolobium
Erythrina fusca
Erythrina poeppigiana
Erythrina variegata
Euphorbia candelabrum
Euterpe
Fagraea fragrans
Ficus altissima
Ficus aurea
Ficus benghalensis
Ficus benjamina
Ficus callosa
Ficus citrifolia
Ficus elastica
Ficus macrophylla
Ficus microcarpa
Ficus mysorensis
Ficus nekbudu
Ficus racemosa

Ficus religiosa
Ficus rubiginosa
Ficus subcordata
Ficus sycomorus
Ficus vogelii
Gordonia lasianthus
Harpullia
Hibiscus elatus
Hibiscus macrophyllus
Hibiscus tiliaceus
Hura
Hyphaene
Jacaranda
Kigelia
Koelreuteria elegans
Latania
Lagerstroemia speciosa
Laguncularia
Lepidozamia
Livistona
Magnolia grandiflora
Mammea
Mangifera
Manilkara bidentata
Manilkara zapota
Mastichodendron
Millettia ovalifolia
Mimusops elengi
Monodora
Montezuma
Pachira
Persea (some)
Phoenix canariensis
Phoenix dactylifera
Phoenix sylvestris
Phytolacca
Pongamia
Pouteria campechiana
Pouteria sapota
Quercus agrifolia
Quercus chrysolepis
Quercus suber
Quercus virginiana
Raphia
Ravenala
Rhizophora
Roystonea
Sabal causiarum
Sabal mauritiiformis
Sabal mexicana
Sabal palmetto
Samanea
Schizolobium
Simarouba

Spathodea

Spondias dulcis

Spondias mombin

Sterculia

Swietenia

Syagrus amara

Syagrus romanzoffiana

Syzygium cumini

Tabebuia donnell-smithii

Tabebuia impetiginosa

Tabebuia rosea

Tabebuia serratifolia

Tamarindus

Taxodium

Tectona

Terminalia

Tipuana

Triplaris

Veitchia joannis

Veitchia mcdanielsii

Veitchia winin

Washingtonia

Palms and Cycads

All palm species are found in but one plant family, the Palmae (or Arecaceae). There are somewhat more than 200 genera and almost 3000 known palm species. It should come as no surprise that almost all species are tropical or subtropical in origin.

Palm species range in size and form from small trunkless shrubs to towering 200-foot-tall trees. Some are vines, and many have clumping or clustering trunks. Those species that produce aboveground stems (trunks) may have trunks that are as thin as half an inch or as stout as 4 feet or more in diameter. Only one genus of palm has naturally branching stems, although several species will branch as a result of injury to the trunk. Many palms have spines, teeth, or prickles on their stems, leafstalks, and sometimes on the leaves themselves.

The leaves of palms are among the glories of the entire plant kingdom. They range from 6 inches to more than 70 feet long and are of two basic forms: palmate and pinnate. Palmate leaves are round or semicircular in outline and may or may not be deeply segmented, while pinnate leaves are linear or oblong in outline with segments arranged in the fashion of a feather and sometimes fused into an apparent undivided blade. All palm leaves have stalks, although some are short. Almost all palm species have leaves only at the end of the trunks, but a few of the climbing types have their large leaves spaced at regular intervals for considerable distances along the stems.

Palm flowers are always in clusters, sometimes truly gigantic many-branched clusters, although the individual blossoms are usually quite small. The inflorescences of all species are accompanied and often subtended by large and often woody bracts. The flower clusters may arise from the trunk below the leaf crown, among the leaves in the crown, or rarely from the very top of the stem, the latter condition resulting in the death of the trunk after the fruits mature. Most palm fruits have a fleshy covering with only one seed but a few are multi-seeded. Fruit size ranges from a quarter-inch-wide berry to the 2-foot-wide double coconut.

Palm habitats include all types of environment except the subaqueous or submersed aquatic, the very cold montane regions, and the polar. The family has representatives in the mangrove coastal environment, estuaries and fresh water swamps, the oases of deserts, tropical and subtropical coastal plains and grasslands, deciduous tropical forests, rain forests (both lowland and montane and both tropical or subtropical and warm temperate), and even in the drier regions of mountains. The greatest diversity of the family is attained in tropical forest regions, especially humid and moist forests where many of the smaller palm species are understory subjects, the larger species finding homes in clearings and along riverbanks. The only growth form not represented in the family is that of the true epiphyte. The natural range of the palm family is as far north as southern Europe and as far south as the North Island of New Zealand.

Palms are monocots and, as such, do not produce successive layers of growth in their trunks or stems. The trunks may enlarge with time, but not because new wood is being created. Rather, they increase with the expansion of the tissues first formed. This fact has one important implication for the gardener: injuries to palm trunks are permanent and are not repaired by the plants. Therefore caution should be exercised in dealing with the trunks, especially in the transplanting of large specimens. Also, since very few trunked palms naturally branch, killing or removing the growing point means the death of that stem or trunk and, for the solitary-trunked species, death of the plant.

The roots of palms grow in a manner similar to that of the trunks; they branch but very little and do not increase in size with the growth of the aboveground parts. But most importantly the roots of palms originate after the seedling stage only from the trunk itself. There is no greatly dichotomizing underground root network as there is with an oak or other dicot tree, although the root systems of large palms may range far from the trunk near the surface of the ground. The implication is that palms are mainly surface feeders and usually need regular supplies of moisture and soil nutrients. Desert palms are never found away from streams or underground sources of water.

Very few palm species are not amenable to indoor cultivation, especially when young, and most are easily grown from seed although a few types are slow to germinate. They are slower growing in containers than they are planted out, but if their modest needs are attended to they are quite adaptable to such conditions and even the large species will make for some time beautiful potted subjects. Even the coconut may be grown for a while as a container plant, although it will soon die if permanently confined to the indoors. The coconut is difficult even in an atrium.

There is now in Florida, western Africa, southern Texas, and many parts of the Caribbean an always fatal disease to which several palm species are susceptible; it is called "lethal yellowing." The disease is caused by a *Mycoplasma* species, a microscopic organism with traits of both viruses and bacteria. It is thought to be transferred from one palm to another by a plant-juice-sucking leaf hopper, much like mosquitoes transfer malaria from human to human. The symptoms usually but not always include a sudden yellowing of the leaves of the palm, and death of the entire plant usually occurs within a few months after the first symptoms are evident, although there is an incubation period of as long as a year after transferal of the organism. There is presently no cure for this fatal palm disease, and the only prevention involves inoculation of uninfected palms with tetracycline antibiotics, an expensive and labor-intensive undertaking. Until a cure or better means of prevention is found, it is better to not plant susceptible palm species in regions which are known to have the disease. Palms susceptible to lethal yellowing are *Allagoptera, Arenga engleri, Borassus, Caryota, Chrysalidocarpus cabadae, Cocos, Corypha, Dictyosperma, Hyophorbe, Latania, Livistona chinensis, L. rotundifolia, Nannorrhops, Neodypsis decaryi, Phoenix, Pritchardia, Syagrus schizophylla, Trachycarpus,* and *Veitchia.*

Cycads are a unique group of plants, one that is much older than the flowering plants like morning glories, palms, and the royal poinciana. For many years botanists considered them distantly related to ferns, but it is now known that their nearest relatives—although far from close relatives—are the conifers, like the pine trees, spruces, redwoods and the monkey puzzle trees. What the conifers and cycads have in common are seed-bearing cones; they do not form flowers.

In many garden books and in the minds of many uninitiated gardeners, the palms and the cycads are included together—and there is a good reason for this: except for their sexual parts the two groups of plants have much in common in a landscaping sense. They are mostly palmlike in their gross appearances, although many more cycad species have hidden trunks or no trunks than do true palms. All have evergreen leaves that are pinnate and palmlike or fernlike. Thus are they included in this palm section of landscaping lists.

Palms

Acoelorraphe	*Guihaia*
Acrocomia	*Howea*
Aiphanes	*Hyophorbe*
Allagoptera	*Hyphaene*
Archontophoenix	*Latania*
Areca	*Licuala*
Arenga	*Livistona*
Astrocaryum	*Nannorrhops*
Bactris	*Neodypsis*
Bismarckia	*Phoenix*
Borassus	*Pritchardia*
Brahea	*Pseudophoenix*
Butia	*Ptychosperma*
×*Butiagrus*	*Raphia*
Carpentaria	*Ravenea*
Caryota	*Rhapidophyllum*
Chamaedorea	*Rhapis*
Chamaerops	*Roystonea*
Chrysalidocarpus	*Sabal*
Coccothrinax	*Serenoa*
Cocos	*Syagrus*
Copernicia	*Thrinax*
Corypha	*Trachycarpus*
Cryosophila	*Trithrinax*
Cyrtostachys	*Veitchia*
Dictyosperma	*Washingtonia*
Elaeis	*Wodyetia*
Euterpe	*Zombia*
Gaussia	

Cycads

Bowenia	*Encephalartos*
Ceratozamia	*Lepidozamia*
Cycas	*Macrozamia*
Dioon	*Zamia*

Poisonous Plants

Some poisonous plants are of supreme beauty and are staples of the tropical looking landscape. They are listed here, with their degree of toxicity, for those gardeners with small and inquisitive children or pets, who may wish to avoid such plants.

Adenium Low
Aleurites fordii Low
Allamanda Low
Annona Low
Arenga Medium
Barringtonia Medium
Blighia Great
Bowenia Medium
Brugmansia Medium
Canella Medium
Cassia bicapsularis Medium
Cassia fistula Medium
Cassia siamea Medium
Castanospermum Medium
Cerbera Medium
Clusia Medium
Cocculus Medium
Colocasia Medium
Crescentia cujete Medium
Cryptostegia Low
Datura DEADLY
Dieffenbachia Medium
Echites Great
Erythrina (many) Medium

Euphorbia (most) Great
Gliricidia Great
Hura Great
Ipomoea (many) Great
Jacquinia arborea Medium
Jatropha (most) Medium
Lantana Medium
Lonchocarpus Great
Macadamia Medium
Manihot Great
Nerium DEADLY
Ochrosia Medium
Pedilanthus Medium
Piscidia Great
Pongamia Great
Ricinus DEADLY
Sesbania (some) Medium
Solandra Medium
Solanum pseudocapsicum Low
Sophora secundiflora Great
Synadenium Medium
Thevetia DEADLY
Urechites Great

Salt-Tolerant Plants

Salinity is a feature not only of seacoasts, but also of areas in many desert regions. As has been noted in the introduction to the list of aquatic plants, many salt-tolerant species are drought tolerant as well. Following each plant name is the degree of salt tolerance. "Some" salt tolerance indicates that the plant is able to thrive in soil that contains only a minimum of briny substances. "Medium" salt tolerance is appropriate for plants that occasionally receive mild doses of saline ocean spray or inhabit a soil that contains some salinity but is far from saturated with it. "Great" salt tolerance is here applied to those species that live at the edge of the ocean or in or on the edges of salt pans in desert regions. "Complete" salt tolerance is reserved for such things as mangrove species that grow in the salty sea.

Acacia auriculiformis Some
Acacia choriophylla Great
Acacia farnesiana Some
Acacia pinetorum Great
Acoelorraphe Some
Acrocomia Some
Acrostichum Great
Aechmea fosteriana Some
Aechmea sphaerocephala Some
Aeonium Some
Agave americana Medium
Agave angustifolia Great
Agave attenuata Some
Agave neglecta Great

Agave sisalana Some
Albizia lebbeck Some
Allagoptera Great
Aloe Medium
Amphitecna latifolia Great
Amyris elemifera Great
Amyris madrensis Medium
Annona glabra Some
Annona muricata Some
Avicennia Complete
Barringtonia asiatica Great
Bougainvillea Medium
Bromelia Great
Bucida buceras Great

Bursera simaruba Great
Butea monosperma Some
Caesalpinia bonduc Complete
Calophyllum Great
Canavalia Great
Carissa macrocarpa Great
Casasia clusiifolia Great
Cerbera Great
Chrysobalanus icaco Great
Cissus incisa Medium
Clusia rosea Great
Coccoloba Great
Coccothrinax Great
Cocos Great
Conocarpus erectus Great
Cordia sebestena Medium
Cryptostegia grandiflora Medium
Cupaniopsis anacardioides Some
Dracaena draco Great
Echeveria Some
Encephalartos ferox Medium
Erythrina herbacea Medium
Eugenia axillaris Great
Eugenia confusa Great
Eugenia foetida Great
Eugenia rhombea Great
Euphorbia fulgens Medium
Euphorbia grandicornis Medium
Euphorbia lactea Great
Euphorbia milii Great
Euphorbia polyacantha Medium
Euphorbia punicea Medium
Euphorbia tirucalli Medium
Euphorbia trigona Medium
Gossypium hirsutum Great
Guaiacum Great
Hibiscus tiliaceus Great
Hylocereus Great
Hyophorbe Medium
Hyphaene Great
Ipomoea imperati Complete
Ipomoea macrantha Complete
Ipomoea pes-caprae Complete
Jacquinia Great
Laguncularia Complete
Lantana Great
Lysiloma latisiliqua Great
Mallotonia Great
Manilkara bahamensis Some
Manilkara roxburghiana Great

Manilkara zapota Great
Mastichodendron Great
Nerium Great
Noronhia Great
Ochrosia elliptica Great
Opuntia (most) Medium
Pandanus Great
Parkinsonia Medium
Phoenix dactylifera Medium
Phoenix canariensis Some
Phormium tenax Great
Piscidia Great
Pithecellobium flexicaule Medium
Pittosporum tobira Great
Plumeria Medium
Portulacaria afra Medium
Pritchardia Great
Pseudophoenix Great
Quercus virginiana Medium
Rhizophora Complete
Scaevola plumieri Great
Scaevola taccada Great
Serenoa Great
Simarouba glauca Great
Solandra Some
Sophora tomentosa Great
Stetsonia Medium
Swietenia mahogani Medium
Syagrus amara Great
Synadenium Great
Terminalia catappa Great
Thespesia populnea Great
Thevetia peruviana Great
Thrinax Great
Tillandsia capitata Medium
Tillandsia usneoides Medium
Yucca aloifolia Great
Yucca elephantipes Some
Yucca filamentosa Great
Yucca gloriosa Great
Yucca recurvifolia Medium
Yucca rostrata Medium
Yucca smalliana Great
Yucca treculeana Great
Yucca whipplei Some
Zamia furfuracea Great
Zamia pumila Great
Zanthoxylum fagara Great
Zombia Great

Shade-Tolerant Plants

Just as there are no large trees that flourish in shade, most smaller plants—outside of desert regions—are capable of this feat since that is the ecological niche they have filled to survive in a world of sun-hogging giants. No flowering plant, fern, or cycad can live without at least a modicum of light, of course, and none discussed in this book can tolerate complete gloom. "Full" shade means that the plant can tolerate and often prefers or is limited to areas that do not receive the sun's direct rays; it does not mean total lack of light. "Partial" shade (which is equivalent to "partial sun") means that the plant will tolerate or require sites that receive only the "milder" rays, those of the morning or late afternoon sun, or situations in which there are seldom if ever direct rays of the sun. These sites are nevertheless bright from high overhead shade or nearby reflected surfaces.

Achimenes Partial
Adiantum Partial
Aglaonema Full
Alocasia Partial
Angiopteris Partial
Anthurium Full
Aspidistra Full
Asplenium Full
Aucuba Full
Begonia (some) Partial
Bertolonia Partial
Blechnum Full
Bowenia Full
Brunfelsia pauciflora Partial
Burbidgea Partial
Caladium (most) Full
Calathea Full
Callisia Full
Carludovica Full
Chamaedorea Full
Chamaeranthemum Full
Chlorophytum Partial
Cissus adenopoda Partial
Cissus amazonica Partial
Cissus antarctica Partial
Cissus discolor Partial
Cissus gongylodes Partial
Cissus incisa Partial
Cissus rhombifolia Full
Cissus sicyoides Full
Cleyera Partial
Clivia Partial
Cocculus Full
Cochliostema Partial
Coffea Partial
Colocasia Partial
Cordyline stricta Full
Costus Partial
Crossandra Partial

Ctenanthe Partial
Curculigo Partial
Cyathea Partial
Cyperus alternifolius Full
Cyrtosperma Partial
Davallia Partial
Dicksonia Full
Dieffenbachia Partial
Dizygotheca Partial
Dracaena arborea Partial
Dracaena deremensis Partial
Dracaena fragrans Partial
Dracaena goldieana Partial
Dracaena marginata Partial
Dracaena surculosa Partial
Epipremnum Partial
Episcia Partial
×*Fatshedera* Partial
Fatsia Full
Ficus deltoidea Partial
Ficus pumila Full
Fittonia Full
Geogenanthus Full
Globba Full
Goniophlebium Full
Hedera Full
Hoffmannia Partial
Howea forsteriana Partial
Impatiens Partial
Lepidozamia Partial
Lygodium Partial
Maranta Full
Medinilla Partial
Miconia Partial
Microgramma Partial
Microlepia Partial
Microsorium Full
Monstera Partial
Nephrolepis Partial

Pellionia Full
Peperomia Full
Philodendron (most) Full
Phlebodium Partial
Pilea Partial
Piper Partial
Pittosporum tobira 'Variegata' Partial
Platycerium Partial
Plectranthus Partial
Polyscias Partial
Pseuderanthemum alatum Full
Psychotria Full
Ravenea Partial
Rhapidophyllum Partial
Rhapis Partial

Rumohra Partial
Sabal minor Full
Sanchezia Partial
Schefflera arboricola Partial
Schismatoglottis Full
Siderasis Partial
Spathiphyllum Partial
Stenochlaena Partial
Strobilanthes Partial
Syngonium Full
Tetrapanax Partial
Tetrastigma Full
Thelypteris Full
Xanthosoma Partial

Shrubs

The dictionary defines a shrub as a woody plant of relatively low height, having several stems arising from the base and lacking a single trunk. This is the most widely accepted definition of a shrub, but it is a narrower definition than the one used in this book since neither woodiness nor multiple stems is necessary, only the size and use of the plant. That is, in this volume a shrub is any landscape subject that is more than 3 feet in height but no more than 15 feet in height.

Acacia berlandieri
Acacia tortuosa
Acalypha
Acrostichum
Adenium
Agave (many)
Allagoptera
Allamanda
Alocasia macrorrhiza
Alocasia odora
Alocasia plumbea
Aloe
Alpinia
Amphiblemma
Amyris elemifera
Ananas
Androlepis
Aphelandra
Arenga engleri
Arenga tremula
Aspidistra
Asplenium
Asystasia
Aucuba
Barleria (most)
Bauhinia punctata

Bixa
Blechnum
Bocconia
Borzicactus
Bougainvillea
Bowenia
Breynia
Bromelia
Brugmansia
Brunfelsia
Bucida spinosa
Caesalpinia
Calliandra
Calotropis
Calyptranthes
Carissa
Carludovica
Casasia
Cassia alata
Cassia bicapsularis
Cassia corymbosa
Cassia didymobotrya
Cassia excelsa
Cassia multijuga
Cassia surattensis
Ceratozamia

Cereus
Chamaedorea
Chamaerops
Citrus (many)
Cleistocactus
Clerodendrum (most)
Cleyera
Coccoloba uvifera
Cocculus
Codiaeum
Coffea
Combretum fruticosum
Combretum microphyllum
Cordia lutea
Cordyline stricta
Cordyline terminalis
Curculigo
Cyperus
Dasylirion glaucophyllum
Dasylirion leiophyllum
Dasylirion texanum
Dasylirion wheeleri
Datura
Davallia
Dioon edule
Dizygotheca
Dombeya
Doryanthes
Dracaena arborea
Dracaena deremensis
Dracaena fragrans
Dracaena marginata
Dracaena reflexa
Dracaena sanderiana
Dracaena surculosa
Dracaena thalioides
Echinocactus
Echinopsis huascha
Echinopsis spachianus
Echinopsis thelegonus
Encephalartos (most)
Erythrina ×bidwillii
Erythrina crista-galli
Erythrina falcata
Erythrina flabelliformis
Erythrina herbacea
Erythrina humeana
Espostoa
Etlingera
Eugenia (most)
Euphorbia antiquorum
Euphorbia atropurpurea
Euphorbia avasmontana
Euphorbia bubalina

Euphorbia cereiformis
Euphorbia coerulescens
Euphorbia cotinifolia
Euphorbia echinus
Euphorbia enopla
Euphorbia fulgens
Euphorbia grandicornis
Euphorbia heptagona
Euphorbia hottentota
Euphorbia lactea
Euphorbia ledienii
Euphorbia leucocephala
Euphorbia milii
Euphorbia pentagona
Euphorbia polyacantha
Euphorbia polygona
Euphorbia pulcherrima
Euphorbia punicea
Euphorbia trigona
×Fatshedera
Fatsia
Feijoa
Ferocactus
Ficus auriculata
Ficus deltoidea
Fouquieria
Gardenia jasminoides
Gardenia latifolia
Gardenia spatulifolia
Gardenia taitensis
Gardenia thunbergia
Gordonia axillaris
Gossypium
Graptophyllum
Guaiacum
Guihaia
Hamelia
Hedychium
Heliconia
Hesperaloe
Hibiscus acetosella
Hibiscus arnottianus
Hibiscus rosa-sinensis
Hibiscus schizopetalus
Hoffmannia
Holmskioldia
Illicium
Iochroma
Ixora
Jacquinia
Jatropha curcas
Jatropha gossypifolia
Jatropha integerrima
Jatropha multifida

Jatropha podagrica
Justicia
Kalanchoe beharensis
Kalanchoe prolifera
Lagerstroemia indica (some)
Lantana
Leucophyllum
Licuala gracilis
Licuala orbicularis
Licuala spinosa
Ligustrum japonicum
Magnolia coco
Mallotonia
Malvaviscus
Mandevilla boliviensis
Mandevilla 'Red Riding Hood'
Megaskepasma
Michelia figo
Miconia
Murraya
Mussaenda
Myrtillocactus
Nannorrhops
Nephrolepis
Nerium
Ochna
Ochrosia
Odontonema
Oncoba kraussiana
Opuntia (most)
Pachystachys
Pandanus baptistii
Pandanus pygmaeus
Pedilanthus
Pereskia (most)
Philodendron (self-heading types)
Phlebodium
Phormium
Phyllanthus
Piper auritum
Piper longum
Piper macrophyllum
Piper magnificum
Pittosporum tobira
Polyscias
Portlandia
Portulacaria
Pseuderanthemum atropurpureum
Pseuderanthemum reticulatum

Psychotria
Radermachera
Randia
Rhapidophyllum
Rhapis
Ricinus
Ruellia
Sabal minor
Sanchezia
Scaevola aemula
Scaevola plumieri
Scaevola taccada
Schaueria
Schefflera arboricola
Selenicereus
Serenoa
Sesbania punicea
Sesbania tripetii
Solanum giganteum
Solanum hispidum
Solanum marginatum
Solanum melongena
Solanum pseudocapsicum
Solanum quitoense
Solanum rantonnetii
Solanum robustum
Solanum wrightii
Sophora tomentosa
Stenocereus eruca
Stenocereus thurberi
Strelitzia reginae
Streptosolen
Synadenium
Tabebuia heterophylla
Tabernaemontana
Tapeinochilus
Tecoma
Tecomaria
Tetrapanax
Tetrazygia
Thevetia
Thunbergia erecta
Tibouchina
Trevesia
Warszewiczia
Xanthosoma (most)
Yucca (many)
Zamia (most)
Zanthoxylum

Small Plants

These plants are often called "fillers" or "herbaceous perennials." Criteria for this volume are size and lack of true wood. Included below are plants that are from a few inches tall (true "ground huggers") to those 6 feet or less.

Achimenes
Adiantum
Aechmea (most)
Aeonium (most)
Agave echinoides
Agave filifera
Agave lechuguilla
Agave macroacantha
Agave parryi
Agave victoriae-reginae
Aglaonema
Allamanda 'Golden Sprite'
Alocasia (most)
Aloe (some)
Alpinia (many)
Ananas comosus
Androlepis
Anthurium (most)
Aphelandra
Aporocactus
Arundinaria argenteostriata
Arundinaria disticha
Arundinaria pygmaea
Arundinaria viridistriata
Aspidistra
Asystasia
Begonia (most)
Bertolonia
Billbergia
Blechnum
Bowenia
Burbidgea
Caladium
Calathea
Callisia
Canavalia
Canistrum
Chamaeranthemum
Chamaedorea metallica
Chlorophytum
Clivia
Cochliostema
Coleus
Colocasia affinis
Colocasia antiquorum
Colocasia fallax
Costus (most)

Cotyledon (most)
Crossandra
Cryptanthus
Cryptocereus
Ctenanthe
Cuphea hyssopifolia
Cyrtosperma
Datura
Davallia mariesii
Davallia trichomanoides
Deuterocohnia
Dichorisandra reginae
Dieffenbachia (many)
Dracaena goldieana
Dracaena sanderiana
Dracaena surculosa
Dracaena thalioides
Dyckia
Echeveria
Eichornia
Epiphyllum
Episcia
Euphorbia atropurpurea
Euphorbia bubalina
Euphorbia caput-medusae
Euphorbia cereiformis
Euphorbia echinus
Euphorbia enopla
Euphorbia heptagona
Euphorbia inermis
Euphorbia milii
Euphorbia obesa
Euphorbia polygona
Euphorbia pulvinata
Euphorbia symmetrica
Euphorbia tuberculata
Fittonia
Geogenanthus
Globba
Guzmania
Hechtia
Heliocereus
Hemigraphis
Hesperaloe
Hoffmannia
Hypoestes
Impatiens

Iresine
Justicia brandegeana
Justicia brasiliana
Justicia carthaginensis
Justicia spicigera
Kalanchoe (most)
Lantana montevidensis
Maranta
Medinilla
Microgramma
Microlepia
Microsorium
Monocostus
Neoregelia
Nephrolepis (most)
Odontonema strictum
Opuntia (many)
Pachystachys
Pandanus pygmaeus
Pedilanthus
Pellionia
Peperomia
Pilea
Pittosporum tobira 'Wheeler's Dwarf'
Plectranthus
Pontederia
Pseuderanthemum alatum
Rhapis excelsa (dwarf cultivars)

Rhoeo
Ruellia
Rumohra
Sanchezia
Scaevola aemula
Schismatoglottis
Siderasis
Solanum melongena
Solanum pseudocapsicum
Spathiphyllum (most)
Stapelia
Strelitzia reginae
Streptosolen
Strobilanthes
Thelypteris
Tillandsia (most)
Vriesea (many)
Xanthosoma lindenii
Yucca angustissima
Yucca arkansana
Yucca constricta
Yucca filamentosa
Yucca glauca
Yucca louisianensis
Yucca rupicola
Yucca smalliana
Zamia (most)
Zantedeschia

Small Trees

Small trees are those 40 feet in height or less. Some trees with these heights, such as *Delonix regia* (royal poinciana), are much too massive or spreading to ever be called "small" and are therefore listed under "Large Trees."

Acacia abyssinica
Acacia auriculiformis
Acacia baileyana
Acacia choriophylla
Acacia farnesiana
Acacia karroo
Acacia macracantha
Acacia nilotica
Acacia pinetorum
Acacia smallii
Acacia tortuosa
Acacia wrightii
Acoelorraphe
Acrocomia
Adenanthera
Aiphanes

Albizia julibrissin
Aleurites cordata
Aleurites fordii
Aleurites montana
Aloe dichotoma
Aloe excelsa
Aloe marlothii
Aloe speciosa
Amherstia
Amphitecna
Amyris madrensis
Annona
Areca
Arenga pinnata
Armatocereus
Astrocaryum alatum

Astrocaryum mexicanum
Averrhoa carambola
Bauhinia ×blakeana
Bauhinia forficata
Bauhinia monandra
Bauhinia purpurea
Bauhinia tomentosa
Bauhinia variegata
Beaucarnea
Blighia
Bocconia arborea
Brahea dulcis
Brownea
Brugmansia
Bucida buceras
Butea
Butia
×Butiagrus
Caesalpinia coriaria
Caesalpinia granadillo
Caesalpinia mexicana
Caesalpinia pulcherrima
Calliandra haematocephala
Calodendrum
Calotropis gigantea
Calyptranthes
Canella
Carica
Carissa edulis
Carissa macrocarpa
Carpentaria
Caryota urens
Casimiroa
Cassia excelsa
Cassia fistula
Cassia javanica
Cassia multijuga
Cassia siamea
Cassia spectabilis
Cephalocereus
Cerbera
Cereus argentinensis
Cereus forbesii
Cereus jamacaru
Chamaerops
Chorisia
Chrysalidocarpus cabadae
Chrysalidocarpus lucubensis
Chrysalidocarpus lutescens
Chrysobalanus
Cinnamomum aromaticum
Cinnamomum zeylanicum
Citharexylum spinosum
Citrus (most)

Clerodendrum quadriloculare
Clerodendrum trichotomum
Cleyera
Clusia
Coccoloba uvifera
Coccothrinax
Cocculus
Cochlospermum
Coffea
Copernicia baileyana
Copernicia hospita
Copernicia macroglossa
Copernicia pruinifera
Cordia boissieri
Cordia sebestena
Cordyline australis
Cornutia
Crescentia
Cryosophila
Cupaniopsis
Cyathea
Cyrtostachys
Dicksonia
Dictyosperma
Dioon spinulosum
Diospyros
Dombeya
Dracaena arborea
Dracaena draco
Dracaena marginata
Dracaena reflexa
Echinopsis pasacana
Echinopsis santiaguensis
Echinopsis terscheckii
Ehretia
Ensete
Eriobotrya
Erythrina abyssinica
Erythrina caffra
Erythrina coralloides
Erythrina crista-galli
Erythrina falcata
Erythrina humeana
Erythrina speciosa
Erythrina vespertilio
Eugenia
Euphorbia abyssinica
Euphorbia angularis
Euphorbia canariensis
Euphorbia cooperi
Euphorbia dawei
Euphorbia excelsa
Euphorbia grandidens
Euphorbia ingens

Euphorbia pulcherrima
Euphorbia punicea
Euphorbia robecchii
Euphorbia tetragona
Euphorbia tirucalli
Euphoria
Exothea
Fagraea ceilanica
Feijoa
Ficus afzelii
Ficus aspera
Ficus auriculata
Ficus carica
Ficus deltoidea
Ficus lyrata
Ficus nota
Ficus palmeri
Ficus petiolaris
Ficus pseudopalma
Filicium
Firmiana
Garcinia
Gardenia carinata
Gardenia imperialis
Gardenia latifolia
Gardenia spatulifolia
Gardenia taitensis
Gardenia thunbergia
Gardenia tubifera
Gaussia
Guaiacum
Hamelia
Harpephyllum
Hibiscus arnottianus
Howea
Hyophorbe
Illicium
Inga
Ixora congesta
Jacquinia
Jatropha curcas
Jatropha gossypifolia
Jatropha multifida
Koelreuteria
Lagerstroemia (some)
Licuala grandis
Licuala lauterbachii
Licuala paludosa
Licuala ramsayi
Ligustrum
Litchi
Lonchocarpus
Lysiloma
Macadamia

Macrozamia macdonnellii
Macrozamia moorei
Magnolia delavayi
Manihot carthaginensis
Manihot esculenta
Manilkara roxburghiana
Markhamia
Meryta
Michelia doltsopa
Millettia grandis
Morinda
Moringa
Muntingia
Murraya
Musa (most)
Myrciaria
Neodypsis
Nerium (some)
Newbouldia
Noronhia
Ochrosia
Oncoba
Opuntia pilifera
Pachycereus
Pandanus dubius
Pandanus utilis
Parkinsonia
Parmentiera
Peltophorum
Pereskia bleo
Pereskia lychnidiflora
Pereskia nemorosa
Persea (some varieties)
Phoenix reclinata
Phoenix rupicola
Phyllanthus
Pimenta
Piscidium
Pithecellobium
Pittosporum rhombifolium
Pittosporum tobira
Pittosporum undulatum
Plumeria
Polyscias
Portulacaria
Posoqueria
Pritchardia
Pseudobombax
Pseudophoenix
Psidium
Ptychosperma elegans
Ptychosperma macarthurii
Radermachera
Ravenea

Ricinus
Saraca
Schefflera actinophylla
Sesbania grandiflora
Solanum wrightii
Sophora secundiflora
Spondias purpurea
Stemmadenia
Stenocereus dumortieri
Stetsonia
Strelitzia nicolai
Syagrus schizophylla
Syzygium jambos
Syzygium malaccense
Syzygium paniculatum
Tabebuia caraiba
Tabebuia chrysantha
Tabebuia chrysotricha
Tabebuia heterophylla

Tecoma
Thespesia
Thevetia
Thrinax
Tibouchina
Trachycarpus
Trevesia
Trithrinax acanthocoma
Trithrinax brasiliensis
Trithrinax campestris
Veitchia arecina
Veitchia merrillii
Veitchia montgomeryana
Warszewiczia
Wodyetia
Yucca (some)
Zanthoxylum
Zombia

Succulent and Cactusy Looking Plants

All cactus species are members of one family, Cactaceae. Their provenance, like that of the bromeliad family, is limited to the Western Hemisphere, indicating among other things that their evolution was, in geological time, relatively recent. The range of these species is from British Columbia in southwestern Canada to Patagonia in South America and on the East Coast of the United States as far north as Cape Cod, Massachusetts. The center of their distribution is approximately halfway between British Columbia and Patagonia, namely, Mexico.

In form the members of this family range from tree and shrub types with stems and leaves to minute fleshy leafless globes to epiphytic and more or less climbing fleshy, usually spineless and leafless stems, to shrubby types with greatly flattened and spiny stems with very ephemeral leaves, and to giant treelike fleshy, spiny, often branching ribbed columns lacking permanent leaves. Two constant characteristics of all the species are the flower form and the areoles, which are the counterparts of stem nodes in other types of plants.

In those species with permanent spines there are two types of spines, the radial spines and the central spines. The former are relatively short and originate from the perimeter of an areole, while the central spines are relatively long and originate from the center of an areole. Many central spines are hooked at their ends, and in the genus *Opuntia* the areoles produce (often along with large spines) many fine and very small spines that are barbed on the end. Most cactus species have permanent spines. The spineless types mainly are confined to the epiphytic species, although some of the terrestrial dwellers are also spineless, notably *Lophophora* (peyote), which, along with some other spineless species, produce poisonous juices to protect the plants in the absence of spines.

No cactus species is a true "air plant" comparable to many of the bromeliads, and all need at least a modicum of soil in which to grow. All need some organic material in their soil; it is an onerous myth that they grow well in pure sand. A generally sandy compost with small rocks added is one of the best and, if the compost is lacking, any good garden soil will do well as a substitute. In fact, a combination of soil, compost, and sand is nearly ideal for most species. Cactus seldom need feeding with commercial fertilizers, except for the epiphytic forms, which need somewhat more nitrogen than do the completely terrestrial types. A good fertilizer for the epiphytics is half-strength fish emulsion supplemented alternately with half-strength seaweed solutions. The ideal soil pH is nearly neutral to slightly acidic for most species. These guidelines for soil and feeding apply only to cactus that are "planted out." Potted specimens are a different matter and one with which this author is not that familiar.

As for moisture requirements it is impossible to give an all-encompassing single rule; some species require abundant and regular supplies of water, while other species thrive receiving moisture only a few times a year. In general the more globular (succulent) types need less frequent watering, while the columnar, epiphytic, and bushy types appreciate more regular supplies of moisture. Almost all cactus species will "notify" their owners when they are stressed for water by the cessation of growth and the shrinking of stems. Most important for the succulent types is whether they have a dormant period. Only the truly tropical species do not have such a period. Succulents with a dormant period should not be watered in the winter unless there are prolonged drought conditions. Again, these guidelines for moisture requirements apply only to cactus that are "planted out." Potted specimens are a different matter as the containers dry out much more quickly and the soil much more readily becomes depleted of minerals and nutrients.

Because the great and desirable sahuaro (*Carnegiea gigantea*) cactus is so threatened and is so slow growing, gardeners may wish to consider four cactus species that serve as good substitutes for it: *Armatocereus rauhii*, *Echinopsis pasacana*, *E. terscheckii*, and *Stenocereus dumortieri*.

Included here are true cactus species, cactusy looking *Euphorbia* species, and all shrubs and trees that tend to create the look of a tropical desert. Almost all these plants need full sun, and they are xerophytic and drought tolerant for the most part.

Adenium	*Echinopsis*
Agave	*Escontria*
Aloe	*Espostoa*
Aporocactus	*Euphorbia abyssinica*
Armatocereus	*Euphorbia angularis*
Beaucarnea	*Euphorbia antiquorum*
Borzicactus	*Euphorbia avasmontana*
Calotropis	*Euphorbia canariensis*
Carnegiea	*Euphorbia candelabrum*
Cephalocereus	*Euphorbia caput-medusae*
Cereus	*Euphorbia cereiformis*
Cleistocactus	*Euphorbia coerulescens*
Cordyline australis	*Euphorbia cooperi*
Cotyledon	*Euphorbia dawei*
Crassula	*Euphorbia echinus*
Dasylirion	*Euphorbia enopla*
Deuterocohnia	*Euphorbia excelsa*
Doryanthes	*Euphorbia grandicornis*
Dracaena draco	*Euphorbia grandidens*
Dyckia brevifolia	*Euphorbia heptagona*
Echeveria	*Euphorbia hottentota*
Echinocactus	*Euphorbia inermis*

Euphorbia ingens
Euphorbia lactea
Euphorbia ledienii
Euphorbia milii
Euphorbia obesa
Euphorbia pentagona
Euphorbia polyacantha
Euphorbia polygona
Euphorbia pseudocactus
Euphorbia pulvinata
Euphorbia robecchii
Euphorbia symmetrica
Euphorbia tetragona
Euphorbia tirucalli
Euphorbia trigona
Euphorbia tuberculata
Ferocactus acanthodes
Fouquieria
Hechtia

Heliocereus
Hesperaloe
Hylocereus
Jatropha podagrica
Kalanchoe
Myrtillocactus
Nolina
Opuntia
Pachycereus
Pachypodium
Pereskia
Phormium
Portulacaria
Selenicereus
Stapelia
Stenocereus
Stetsonia
Synadenium
Yucca

Variegated or Colored Leaves

Color in the garden can be overdone but a garden or a landscape without any is monotonous at best. Many of the plants listed below have leaves of only one color, but that color is decidedly other than a shade of pure green.

Acalypha wilkesiana
Aechmea (many)
Aeonium (some)
Agave (most)
Aglaonema
Alocasia (many)
Aloe (many)
Alpinia luteocarpa
Alpinia sanderae
Alpinia zerumbet 'Variegata'
Ananas (most)
Androlepis
Anthurium (many)
Aphelandra
Arundinaria argenteostriata
Arundinaria viridistriata
Arundo donax 'Variegata'
Aspidistra elatior 'Variegata'
Aucuba japonica (cultivars)
Bambusa multiplex 'Silverstripe'
Bambusa vulgaris var. *striata*
Begonia (many)
Bertolonia
Billbergia (some)
Bismarckia
Bougainvillea (cultivars)

Brahea armata
Breynia
Bromelia
Burbidgea
Butia
Caladium
Calathea (most)
Callisia (some)
Calotropis
Canistrum
Canna (a few cultivars)
Chamaeranthemum
Chlorophytum (cultivars)
Chrysophyllum
Cissus adenopoda
Cissus amazonica
Cissus discolor
Coccothrinax
Cochliostema
Codiaeum
Colocasia affinis
Colocasia antiquorum
Colocasia fallax
Conocarpus
Cordyline (cultivars)
Costus arabicus

Costus cuspidatus
Costus malortieanus
Cotyledon (most)
Crassula
Cryosophila argentea
Cryptanthus
Ctenanthe (most)
Cyrtosperma
Deuterocohnia
Dieffenbachia
Dioscorea discolor
Dioscorea dodecaneura
Dracaena (cultivars)
Dyckia (most)
Echeveria (most)
Encephalartos eugene-maraisii
Encephalartos horridus
Encephalartos lehmannii
Encephalartos longifolius
Ensete ventricosum 'Maurellii'
Epipremnum aureum
Episcia (many)
Erythrina variegata var. *orientalis*
Euphorbia cotinifolia 'Atropurpurea'
Fatsia japonica (cultivars)
Ficus aspera (cultivars)
Ficus benjamina 'Variegata'
Ficus elastica (cultivars)
Ficus microcarpa 'Variegata'
Ficus pumila 'Variegata'
Ficus rubiginosa
Fittonia
Geogenanthus
Graptophyllum
Guihaia
Guzmania (most)
Hamelia (much of the year)
Hechtia (most)
Hedera helix (cultivars)
Heliconia indica 'Spectabilis'
Heliconia zebrina
Hemigraphis
Hoffmannia
Impatiens ("New Guinea")
Ipomoea batatas 'Blackie'
Iresine
Jatropha gossypifolia
Kalanchoe (most)
Latania
Leucophyllum
Mallotonia
Manihot (variegated cultivars)
Maranta (most)
Miconia

Musa acuminata var. *sumatrana*
Musa acuminata var. *sumatrana* 'Rubra'
Musa basjoo 'Variegata'
Musa ×*paradisiaca* 'Vittata'
Nannorrhops
Neoregelia (most)
Pandanus baptistii 'Aureus'
Pandanus pygmaeus
Pandanus veitchii
Pedilanthus tithymaloides 'Variegatus'
Pellionia
Peperomia (most)
Philodendron 'Choco'
Philodendron erubescens
Philodendron imbe (cultivars)
Philodendron melanochrysum
Philodendron ornatum
Philodendron verrucosum
Phormium
Pilea (most)
Piper magnificum
Piper ornatum
Piper porphyrophyllum
Piper sylvaticum
Pittosporum tobira 'Variegata'
Plectranthus
Polyscias (some)
Portulacaria afra (cultivars)
Pseuderanthemum alatum
Pseuderanthemum atropurpureum
Pseuderanthemum reticulatum
Rhapis excelsa (cultivars)
Rhoeo
Ricinus (cultivars)
Ruellia devosiana
Sanchezia
Schefflera arboricola 'Variegata'
Schismatoglottis (most)
Serenoa (some forms)
Siderasis
Solanum marginatum
Solanum quitoense
Strobilanthes
Synadenium grantii 'Rubra'
Terminalia
Thrinax (most)
Tillandsia (most)
Trevesia palmata 'Micholitzii'
Vriesea (most)
Xanthosoma lindenii
Yucca aloifolia (cultivars)
Zantedeschia albomaculata
Zantedeschia elliottiana

Vines

No type of plant gives more of a tropical look and feel than does a vine, especially the large evergreen vines, the homes of most of which are tropical. Vines ascend structures in several ways that are important for the gardener to understand. These climbing devises are not exclusive one from the other; many vines partake of more than one method, and some partake of all methods.

Some vines have no special adaptations for climbing on other plants or structures, but rather simply produce much-elongated stems that lean against whatever supports they can find. These "sprawling" plants are often not true vines, but rather scrambling shrubs that sometimes even turn into trees. An example is the genus *Freycinetia*. Several scrambling type plants have spines, often hooked spines, that help the plant obtain a foothold in its sprawling manner. *Bougainvillea* is a good example of this type.

One of the most common methods by which vines climb and one that is by far much more "supportive" is by means of twining their stems around another plant or other structure. Plants that use twining to climb are definitely vines and are much more tenacious than any scrambling type climber. *Ipomoea* (morning glory) is a prime example of a twiner.

Even more sure-footed are those plants that produce tendrils, usually from the leaf axils. Tendrils are specialized organs, smaller coiling stems, which reach out and wrap themselves around whatever structure they can to lift and support the vining plant. Some tendrils also produce devices almost like suction cups that drastically increase the strength of the hold the plant has. In addition, some tendrils are equipped with spines (usually hooked), which are a further aid in clinging to their support.

Finally, there are very many vines, especially tropical vines, that produce aerial roots (or rootlets) that grow out from the stem's nodes and penetrate whatever structure on which they find themselves. Obviously these roots do not penetrate substances like steel but, if there is any porosity to the substrate, these roots can gain a strong foothold. They also in many cases act as absorptive organs, furnishing further moisture to the plant from the air or from the interstices of the substrate.

Many vines serve very well not only as climbers, but also as groundcovers since their lengthy wandering stems usually form roots along the ground from the stem nodes if they do not find something on which to climb. It should be noted that some of these climbing methods can be inimical to whatever structure the plant chooses to climb upon; tendrils, suction cup devices, and aerial roots can often quickly deteriorate or at least disfigure wooden surfaces. And if that is not a problem for the gardener, the removal of these plants can be a problem as their clinging supports are quite tenacious. It is usually best to kill them from the bottom up (that is, sever their connection to the soil) and wait until the tops and the clinging devices have died and degenerated to the point that their removal is made easier.

Allamanda cathartica Small to large evergreen; sprawling

Anemopaegma Large evergreen; tendriled

Antigonon Large evergreen; tendriled

Argyreia Large evergreen; twining

Aristolochia Small to large; evergreen; twining

Bauhinia corymbosa Large evergreen; tendriled

Bauhinia punctata 10-foot evergreen; twining

Beaumontia Large massive evergreen; twining

Bignonia Large massive deciduous; tendriled with adhesive suckers

Bougainvillea Large evergreen; sprawling

Campsis Large deciduous with invasive aerial rootlets

Canavalia Large spreading evergreen; creeping and rooting

Cissus Medium to large evergreen and deciduous; tendriled

Clematis Medium evergreen; twining

Clerodendrum ×speciosum 20-foot semi-evergreen; twining

Clerodendrum splendens Small evergreen; twining

Clerodendrum thomsoniae Medium evergreen; twining

Clitoria 12-foot evergreen; twining

Clytostoma 20-foot evergreen; tendriled

Cobaea Large evergreen; clinging tendrils

Combretum coccineum Large evergreen; sprawling

Combretum grandiflorum Large evergreen; sprawling

Combretum microphyllum Large evergreen; sprawling

Congea Large evergreen; sprawling

Cryptostegia 20-foot heavy evergreens; twining

Dioscorea Large evergreen and semi-evergreen; twining

Distictis Large evergreen; tendriled

Echites Large evergreen; twining

Epipremnum Very large evergreen; clinging aerial rootlets

×Fatshedera Small heavy evergreen; sprawling

Ficus pumila Very large evergreen; clinging aerial rootlets

Freycinetia Large evergreen; sprawling

Gmelina 20-foot evergreen; sprawling

Hedera Large evergreen; clinging aerial rootlets

Heliocereus Large cactus; sprawling

Holmskioldia Large evergreen; sprawling

Hylocereus Large cactus; sprawling

Ipomoea Medium to large evergreen; twining

Jacquemontia Small evergreen; twining

Lygodium Tall evergreen; twining

Macfadyena Very large rampant evergreen; clinging rootlets

Mandevilla (most) Small to medium evergreen; twining

Manettia 15-foot evergreen; twining

Merremia Very large evergreen; twining

Millettia reticulata Large evergreen; twining

Monstera Very large massive evergreen; clinging rootlets

Mucuna Large evergreen; twining

Pandorea Large evergreen; twining

Passiflora Medium to large evergreen; tendriled

Petrea Large evergreen; twining

Philodendron (most) Medium to very large evergreens; clinging rootlets

Piper betle Large evergreen; clinging rootlets

Piper kadsura 20-foot evergreen; clinging rootlets

Piper longum 20-foot evergreen; clinging rootlets

Piper nigrum Large evergreen; clinging rootlets

Piper ornatum Tall evergreen; clinging rootlets

Piper porphyrophyllum Large evergreen; clinging rootlets

Piper sylvaticum 15-foot evergreen; clinging rootlets

Podranea 20- to 30-foot evergreens; twining

Porana Very large evergreen; twining

Pseudocalymma Large evergreen; tendriled

Pyrostegia Large evergreen; tendriled

Quisqualis Large scrambling evergreen

Saritaea Large evergreen; tendriled

Selenicereus Large cactus; sprawling

Senecio Tall evergreen; twining

Solandra Immense evergreen; sprawling

Solanum jasminoides 30-foot scrambling semi-evergreen

Solanum wendlandii Very large evergreen; twining

Stenochlaena Very large evergreen; aerial rootlets

Stephanotis Large heavy evergreen; twining

Stigmaphyllon Large evergreen; twining

Streptosolen Small evergreen; sprawling

Strongylodon Immense evergreen; twining

Syngonium Large evergreen; aerial rootlets

Tecomanthe Large evergreen; twining

Tecomaria Medium evergreen; sprawling

Tetrastigma Large evergreen; tendriled

Thunbergia (most) Small to large evergreens; twining

Urechites Large evergreen; twining

Wagatea Immense evergreen; hooked spines

Conversion Charts

Fahrenheit / Celsius		Inches / Centimeters		Feet / Meters	
0°F	−18°C	1 in	2.5 cm	1 ft	0.3 m
5°F	−15°C	2 in	5 cm	2 ft	0.6 m
10°F	−12°C	3 in	8 cm	3 ft	1.0 m
15°F	−9°C	4 in	10 cm	4 ft	1.2 m
20°F	−7°C	5 in	13 cm	5 ft	1.5 m
22°F	−6°C	6 in	15 cm	6 ft	1.8 m
24°F	−5°C	7 in	18 cm	7 ft	2.0 m
25°F	−4°C	8 in	20 cm	8 ft	2.4 m
26°F	−3°C	9 in	23 cm	9 ft	2.7 m
28°F	−2°C	10 in	25 cm	10 ft	3.0 m
30°F	−1°C	11 in	28 cm	15 ft	4.5 m
32°F	0°C	12 in	31 cm	20 ft	6.0 m
40°F	5°C	13 in	33 cm	25 ft	7.5 m
45°F	7°C	14 in	35 cm	30 ft	9.0 m
50°F	10°C	15 in	38 cm	35 ft	10.5 m
55°F	13°C	16 in	40 cm	40 ft	12.0 m
60°F	16°C	17 in	43 cm	45 ft	13.5 m
65°F	18°C	18 in	45 cm	50 ft	15.0 m
70°F	21°C	19 in	48 cm	55 ft	16.5 m
75°F	24°C	20 in	50 cm	60 ft	18.0 m
80°F	27°C	25 in	63 cm	70 ft	21.0 m
85°F	30°C	30 in	75 cm	80 ft	24.0 m
90°F	32°C	35 in	88 cm	90 ft	27.0 m

Formulas

$$°C = °F - 32 \times 5 \div 9$$
$$cm = inches \times 2.5$$
$$cm = feet \times 30$$
$$m = feet \times 0.3$$
$$m^2 = feet^2 \times 10.8$$
$$km = miles \times 0.62$$
$$ha = acres \times 2.5$$

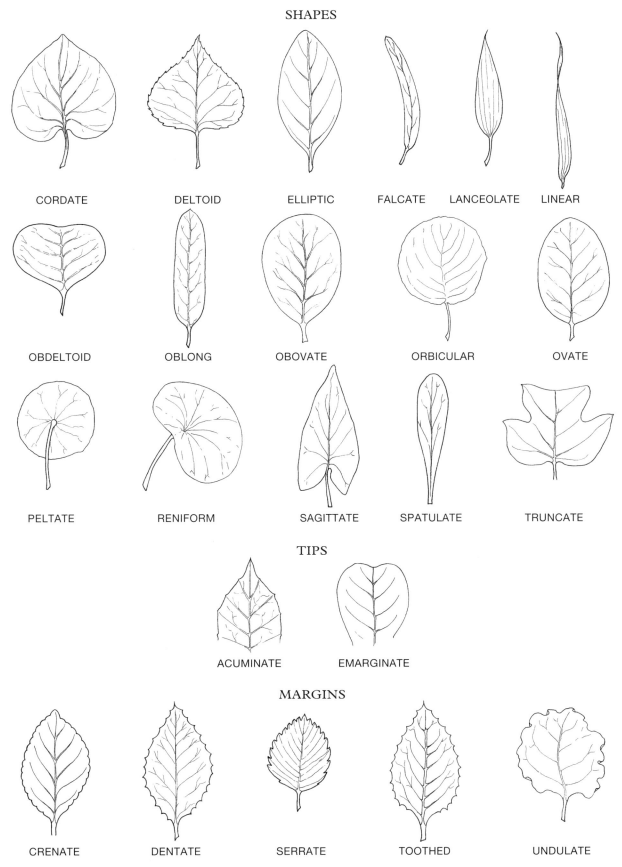

Figure 2. Leaf shapes, tips, and margins.

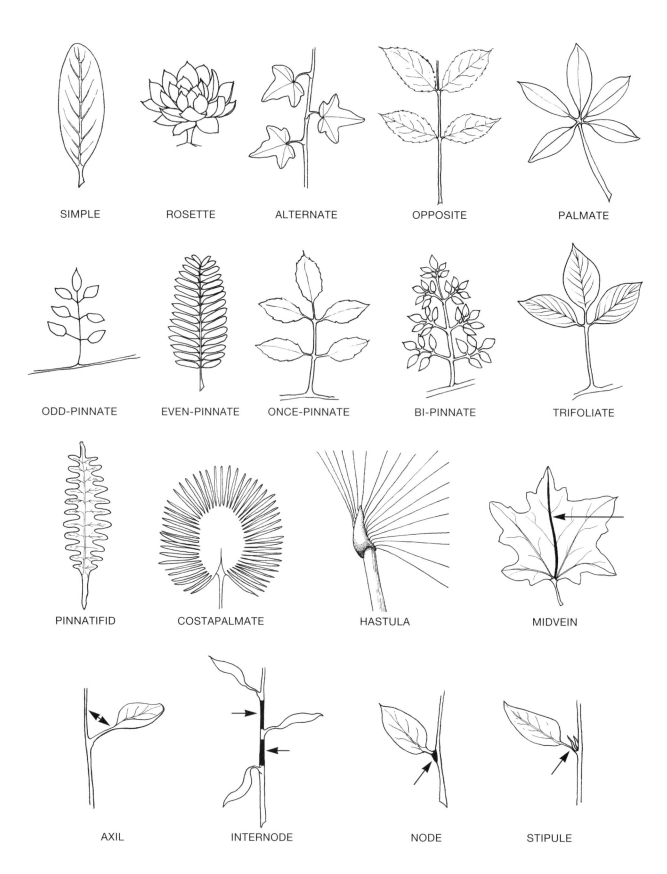

SIMPLE ROSETTE ALTERNATE OPPOSITE PALMATE

ODD-PINNATE EVEN-PINNATE ONCE-PINNATE BI-PINNATE TRIFOLIATE

PINNATIFID COSTAPALMATE HASTULA MIDVEIN

AXIL INTERNODE NODE STIPULE

Figure 3. Other leaf terms.

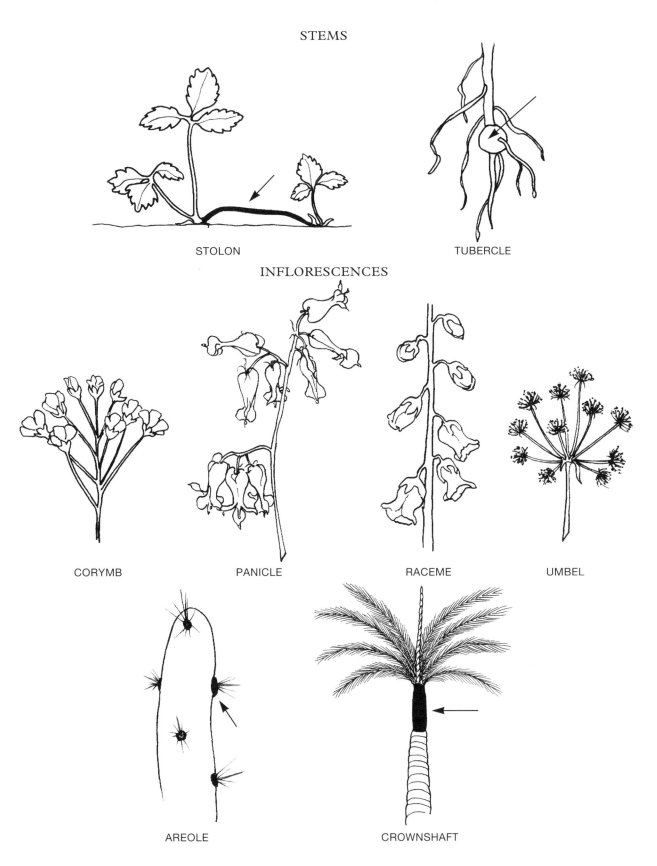

STEMS

STOLON   TUBERCLE

INFLORESCENCES

CORYMB   PANICLE   RACEME   UMBEL

AREOLE   CROWNSHAFT

Figure 4. Inflorescences and stems.

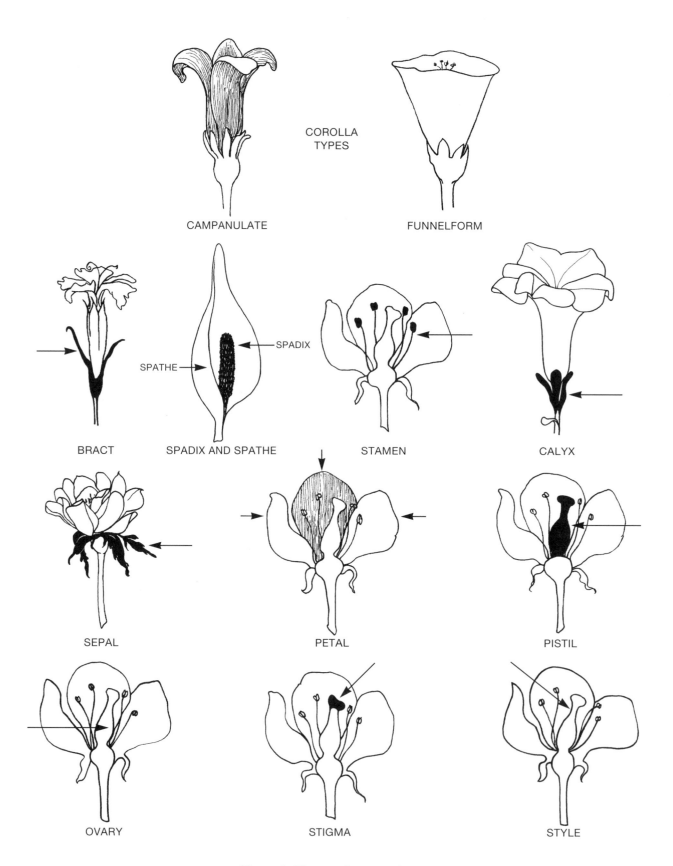

COROLLA
TYPES

CAMPANULATE

FUNNELFORM

BRACT

SPATHE — SPADIX

SPADIX AND SPATHE

STAMEN

CALYX

SEPAL

PETAL

PISTIL

OVARY

STIGMA

STYLE

Figure 5. Flowers shapes and parts.

Glossary

Acuminate. Tapering gradually to a sharp point; the sides of the tapering portion (usually a leaf is being discussed) are more or less concave.

Adventive. Locally naturalized.

Aerial root. A root formed on the stem or trunk of a plant, often but not always reaching to the ground.

Aggregate fruit. A compound fruit consisting of the several ripened ovaries of a single flower.

Air layering. A method of propagating plants with stems that involves the making of an incision along the stem or branch, covering the wound in damp sphagnum moss, wrapping the whole in plastic until the formation of roots from the stem into the damp moss after which event the stem is severed beneath the root mass and planted in either a container or in the ground.

Alternate (AHL-tur-nat). Leaf arrangement consisting of single leaves placed at differing heights along a stem; the converse of opposite arrangement. The term applies to all leaves whether they are simple or compound.

Annual. A plant that grows to maturity, flowers, and fruits in one year or one growing season and then dies.

Arboreal (ahr-BOR-ee-ul). Resembling a tree; treelike.

Arborescent (ahr-bo-RES-sent). Treelike; resembling a tree in size and form.

Areole (AIR-ee-ol). A cushionlike area on the stem of a cactus species consisting of tiny spines and/or hairs. These areas may be depressed or (more usually) raised. They are the origins of the shoots, stems, and flowers of cactus species.

Aril (AIR-il). A more or less fleshy and often highly colored appendage covering or partially covering a seed.

Aroid (AIR-oid). Any plant in the family Araceae, the arum family.

Axil (AX-il). The upper angle at which a leaf or other organ joins its stem, as in "axillary flowers," meaning that the flowers originate from the leaf axils.

Banyan (BAN-yan). A gigantic *Ficus* (fig) species whose individual plants spread over vast areas by aerial roots growing and descending from the main branches. The aerial roots, after reaching the ground, metamorphose into columnar pseudo-trunks farther and farther from the original trunk. Some individual banyan trees cover an area of more than an acre.

Binomial (by-NOAM-ee-ul). A name consisting of two parts: genus and species; the genus name is known as the "generic" name, and the species name is often referred to as the "specific epithet."

Bipinnate (by-PIN-nait). A pinnate leaf whose primary leaflets have been replaced by separate and smaller stalks that then bear their leaflets with or without individual stalks.

Brace roots. Aerial roots near the base of a tree's trunk or along its larger branches that reach the ground and serve to balance and hold fast the plant in its substrate.

Bract (brakt). A modified leaf below a flower or an inflorescence.

Bulb. A subterranean and modified leafy stem serving as a storage organ and consisting of overlapping leaf and often flower buds.

Bulbil. A small bulb produced above ground on stems or in inflorescences and serving the same function as the larger and subterranean bulbs.

Bulbous (BUL-bus). Having a bulb or resembling the shape of a bulb.

Calyces (KAY-li-seez). The plural of "calyx."

Calyx (KAY-lix). A collective term for a flower's sepals.

Capsule. A non-fleshy fruit that opens naturally and is composed of two or more sections but, unlike an aggregate fruit, is derived from a single ovary.

Carpel (KAR-pul). A primary division of an ovary. Some flowers have ovaries with a single seed-bearing part or carpel; others have compound ovaries consisting of two or more carpels or seed-bearing parts.

Caudex (KAW-dex). Technically the underground stem of a perennial plant, especially a palm; but, as used in horticulture, the term refers to any plant that produces a much thickened portion of trunk near its base.

Cauliflorous (kaw-li-FLOR-us). A term used to describe any tree or shrub that produces flowers—and therefore fruit—on its trunk or main branches.

Cauliflory (KAW-li-flor-ee). The condition of being cauliflorous.

Chlorosis (klor-O-sis). The loss of green color in a leaf, which condition is usually due to disease, insect attack, or nutrient deficiency.

Cladode (KLAD-oad). A synonym for "cladophyll."

Cladophyll (KLAD-o-fil / KLAD-o-fyl). A flattened branch or stem having the appearance and function of a leaf.

Clawed. Said of a sepal or petal whose base is constricted into a narrow and more or less tubular form but whose upper part is expanded and often fringed.

Clone. A plant (or any other organism) that is derived asexually from another plant and has the identical genetic material.

Compound leaf. A leaf that is composed of two or more separate and differentiated leaflets.

Concave. Trough-shaped.

Cordate (KOR-dait). Heart-shaped; a descriptive term for the outline of a simple leaf or leaflet, the lobes of the "heart" being near the point of attachment to the leafstalk.

Coriaceous (kor-ee-AY-see-us / kor-ee-AYSH-us). Leathery in texture.

Corolla (ko-ROAL-la). A collective term for the petals of a flower. In many flowers the petals are not separate but rather are united into a tube, a cup shape, and so forth, in which case there are usually but not always corolla lobes.

Corona (ko-RO-na). A crown-shaped appendage inside a flower consisting of united stamens or other flower parts.

Corymb (KOR-imb). A short broad inflorescence that is usually more or less flat-topped, with the individual flowers opening from the perimeter inward.

Corymbose (KOR-im-bos). In the form of a corymb.

Costapalmate (koast-a-PAHL-mait). A term used only with palmate-leaved palm species to denote the intrusion of the petiole into the blade of the leaf, thus giving the leaf a midrib to some extent that it otherwise would not have.

Crenate (KREN-ait). A term used to describe leaf margins that are scalloped.

Crownshaft. A term used only with pinnate-leaved palm species to denote an area just above the woody part of the trunks of certain palms; the area is more or less columnar in shape and usually smooth, and consists of the expanded and very tightly packed leaf bases of the leaves presently on the palm.

Crozier. The unexpanded and coiled new frond in the center of a fern's crown.

Cultivar. A variety or form of a species that originates in cultivation and is not found naturally.

Cuneate (KYOO-nee-ait). Triangular-shaped with the narrow end at the point of attachment; wedge-shaped.

Cyme (sym). An inflorescence identical in shape to a corymb but with the flowers opening from the center outward.

Deadheading. The act of removing spent flowers from a plant.

Deciduous (dee-SID-yoo-us). A term used to describe trees or shrubs whose leaves fall after a certain period. The opposite of "evergreen."

Deltoid (DEL-toid). Triangular-shaped, with the broader part near the point of attachment.

Dichotomous. Arranged in a succession of two-forked divisions.

Dicot (DY-kaht). An abbreviated form of the word "dicotyledon." A dicot seed produces seedlings with two seed leaves (cotyledons) as opposed to those of monocots (an abbreviated form of the word "monocotyledon"), which produce seedlings with only one seed leaf or cotyledon. Dicots have woody tissues as opposed to monocots; almost all true tree species are dicots. In addition the flowers of dicot (dicotyledonous) plants have their parts in fours or fives as opposed to those of monocots whose flower parts are in threes or multiples of three.

Digitate (DIJ-i-tait). A term used to describe a leaf with deeply cut lobes arranged as a splayed hand, the lobes radiating from the tip of the leafstalk.

Digitately compound. A term used to describe a compound leaf whose leaflets are arranged as a splayed hand, the leaflets radiating from the tip of the leafstalk.

Diurnal. A term used to describe flowers that open in the daytime.

Double flower. A flower that has—or seems to have—more than its normal number of petals. These extra "petals" are sometimes modified petal-like stamens.

Elliptic (el-LIP-tik). With the shape of an ellipse: an elongated oval with the middle part the widest and both ends tapering.

Endemic. A term used to describe a species whose natural range is confined to a certain described area as in ". . . the endemic Hawaiian flora."

Epithet. A word in a botanical binomial that follows the genus ("generic") name and denotes a species, variety, or cultivar.

Drupe (droop). A single-seeded fruit whose seed is enclosed in a stony layer that is surrounded by a fleshy area. The fruit of a peach tree is a drupe and is also often called a "stone fruit."

Emarginate (ee-MAR-ji-nait). A term used to describe a leaf that has a notch or shallow depression at its apex.

Entire. A descriptive term for the margin of a leaf that is smooth and unlobed, and lacks any sort of indentation.

Epiphyte (EP-i-fyt). A plant that grows upon another plant without invading the tissues of the latter plant.

Even-pinnate. An even number of leaflets in a pinnate leaf; the phenomenon results in a leaf that ends in a pair of leaflets rather than in a terminal (final) leaflet.

Genera (JIN-e-ra). The plural of "genus."

Glabrous (GLAB-rus). Smooth and not hairy.

Glaucous (GLAWK-us). Covered with a whitish or bluish bloom or a waxy and powdery substance that is easily rubbed away.

Glochid (GLAHK-id). Very small and fine spines provided with barbs; found in the cactus genus *Opuntia*.

Hastula (HAS-tyoo-la). A term used only with palmate-leaved palm species to denote an organ found on some palmate leaves. This organ is more or less pyramidal in shape and protrudes from the point at which the petiole joins the leaf blade. The protruding organ may be tiny or quite large and may be found on either the upper or lower surface of the leaf, or on both surfaces.

Herbaceous (hur-BAISH-yus). A term used to describe plants lacking woody parts.

Hybrid (HY-brid). The offspring of two species or of two different forms of a species.

Inflorescence (in'-flor-ES-sens). A cluster of flowers originating from a single point on the stem, branch or trunk.

Intergeneric (in'-tur-je-NER-ik). Between two genera.

Internode (IN-tur-noad). The area on a stem between one leaf node and the next.

Involucre (IN-va-look-'r). A whorl (or whorls) of leaflike bracts beneath a flower or an inflorescence.

Keel. The two lowermost petals of a papilionaceous flower. These petals are usually joined into a seemingly single and usually somewhat tubelike organ.

Keeled. Thicker on the bottom than on the top.

Lanceolate (LANTS-ee-o-lait). A term used to describe a leaf shape that is longer than wide, with the widest part of the blade near the point of attachment.

Lenticels. Raised pores on bark.

Lip. A petal or modified stamen that is usually larger than the other petals.

Leaflet (LEEF-let). One of the distinct divisions (blades) of a compound leaf.

Linear (LIN-ee-ur). A term used to describe a leaf that is longer than wide and whose margins are more or less parallel.

Mesic. Of average rainfall, being neither wet nor arid.

Midrib. A synonym for "midvein."

Midvein. The central main vein of a leaf or leaflet; it is usually the largest and most visually prominent vein in the leaf.

Monocarpic (mo-no-KARP-ik). A term used to describe a plant or part of a plant that flowers only once, sets fruit, and then dies off.

Monocot (MAHN-o-kaht / MO-no-kaht). An abbreviated form of the word "monocotyledon." A monocot produces seedlings with only one seed leaf (cotyledon) as opposed to those of dicots (an abbreviated form of the word "dicotyledon"), which produce seedlings with two seed leaves or cotyledons. Monocots do not usually produce woody tissues as opposed to dicots and, except for palms and a few other large monocots like the dragon tree (*Dracaena draco*), do not result in tree forms. In addition, the flowers of monocotyledonous plants have their parts in threes or multiples of three as opposed to dicots whose flower parts are in twos, fours, fives, or multiples thereof.

Monotypic (mo-no-TIP-ik). Said of a genus or family of plants that consists of only one species.

Nocturnal. A term used to describe flowers that open at night.

Node. The point on a stem from which a leaf or single group of leaves emerges.

Obdeltoid (ahb-DEL-toyd). Triangular-shaped with the narrowest part at the point of attachment; a reversely placed triangle.

Oblong (AHB-lahng). Longer than wide with sides more or less parallel, but whose width if somewhat greater than that implied by "linear."

Obovate (AHB-o-vait). A reversed ovate shape, the narrower part being near the point of attachment.

Obtuse (ahb-TYOOS). Blunt; not pointed.

Odd-pinnate. An uneven number of leaflets in a pinnate leaf; the phenomenon results in a leaf with a final terminal leaflet which apically projects farther from the stem than the other leaflets.

Ovary. The lower and usually expanded part of the pistil of a flower, the part in which the seeds form and which becomes the main part of a fruit.

Ovate (O-vait). Egg-shaped with the broader part being near the point of attachment.

Palmate (PAHL-mait). Descriptive term for the overall shape of a splayed hand or a compound or segmented leaf denoting a hand or fan-shaped placement of the leaflets or segments.

Panicle (PAN-i-k'l). A branched and elongated inflorescence of stalked flowers.

Papilionaceous (pa-pil´-yo-NAYSH-yus). A descriptive adjective for flowers of plants in the family Papilionaceae.

Pedicel (PED-i-sel). A flower stalk.

Peduncle (PEE-dunk'l). The stalk of an inflorescence.

Peltate (PEL-tait). A term used to describe a leaf whose stalk is attached to the leaf's lower surface rather than to any part of its margin; the stalk is usually attached to the center of the leaf's underside and the leaf is usually rounded in outline.

Perianth (PER-ee-anth). A collective term for the calyx and corolla—assuming the blossom has both—of a flower.

Perennial. A plant that lives for at least 3 years. The term is usually used to denote an herbaceous plant or an herbaceous shrubby plant.

Petal (PET-ul). A modified leaf of the corolla. A flower consists of a series of highly modified leaves arranged in whorls. The outermost (lowest) whorl is collectively called "the sepals" or "the calyx" and its parts are usually the most leaflike in nature. The next whorl is referred to as "the petals" or "corolla" and its parts are less leaflike and usually colored other than green. The inner whorls are the flower's sexual parts and may or may not consist of separate organs. The calyx and corolla also may have fused parts or, in some flowers, one or both of these whorls may be completely lacking.

Petiole (PEET-ee-ol). The primary stalk of a simple or compound leaf.

pH. An acronym for "potential of hydrogen." The pH scale, which ranges from 0 to 14, is used to indicate the alkalinity or acidity of a substance such as soil. The bottom of the scale, 0, is the ultimate in acidity and is assigned to substances such as sulfuric acid. The top of the scale, 14, is the ultimate in alkalinity and is applied to such substances as pure lye. The middle of the scale, 7, represents neutral. Most soils have a pH value of from 5 to 9, anything outside these limits usually being inimical to the health of any plant. Acid-loving plants usually need a value no less than 6, and alkaline-loving plants usually need one no greater than 8. Under all circumstances "organic" and "natural" amendments to the soil are much better than temporary "chemical" amendments; the organic amendments last longer and do not raise or lower the pH value suddenly and unnaturally.

Phyllode (FYL-load). A modified and leafless petiole having the appearance and often the function of a leaf.

Pinnae. The main divisions of a bipinnate leaf.

Pinnate (PIN-nait) leaf. A compound leaf whose leaflets are arranged on opposite sides of the rachis and consist of more than three leaflets.

Pinnatifid (pin-NAT-i-fid). A lobed leaf whose indentations are parallel and deep but never reach the midrib of the leaf.

Pistil (PIS-til). The female reproductive organ of a flower consisting of the ovary, the style, and the stigma. The ovary is the portion in which the seeds and fruit develop usually with expansion of the ovary. The style is usually a relatively elongated extension of the ovary atop which the stigma resides. The stigma receives pollen (the flower's analogue to animal sperm) and stimulates the pollen grains to fertilize—by means of a pollen tube—the ovules in the ovary, which then develop into the seeds.

Plumose (PLOO-moas). Feather-like with the segments arising from the midrib in more than one plane, resulting in a boa-like appearance.

Pneumatophore (nyoo-MAT-o-for). A specialized root that grows from normal subterranean roots but which rises above the water or soil surface and serves to aerate the subterranean or subaquatic root system.

Pyriform. Pear-shaped.

Raceme (ra-SEEM). An unbranched inflorescence of stalked flowers opening from the bottom upwards.

Rachis (RAIK-is). The primary and central stem of a compound leaf from which leaflets or subsidiary leafstalks arise; the midrib.

Recurved (ree-KURVD). Curved backwards or downwards.

Reflexed (ree-FLEXD). A synonym for "recurved."

Reniform (REN-i-form). Kidney-shaped.

Rhizome (RY-zoam). An underground or on-ground stem growing horizontally and giving rise to roots, stems, and leaves at its nodes or growing tips.

Rhizomatous (ry-ZOAM-a-tus). Provided with rhizomes.

Rootstock. A synonym for "rhizome."

Rosette (ro-ZET). A term usually referring to a plant form in which the leaves arise directly from the ground in a circular or radiating fashion. The term may also be used for a cluster of leaves on a trunk or branch.

Sagittate (SAJ-i-tait). Shaped like an arrow's head, the lobes relatively narrow and positioned at the point of attachment.

Salverform (SAL-vur-form). A corolla form that is tubular but ends apically in a more or less flat disk.

Scape (skaip). A leafless flower stem that rises directly from the ground (the root).

Scapose (SKAP-oas). Provided with a scape.

Sepal (SEEP-'l). See "petal."

Serrate (SER-rait). A term used to describe a leaf whose margin is toothed, the points oriented towards the leaf's apex.

Serrulate (SER-roo-lait). Minutely serrate.

Sheathing. Said of a leaf whose base is constricted into an almost tubular shape clasping and surrounding a stem.

Simple. Not compound. Used to describe a leaf that has but a single blade and is not divided into separate leaflets; the single blade may, however, be deeply lobed or partially segmented.

Solitary. Said of flowers (or other plant parts) that are borne singly, alone and not in clusters.

Spadices (SPAY-di-seez). The plural of "spadix."

Spadix (SPAY-dix). A usually cylindrical and relatively thick and fleshy spike of tiny densely set flowers usually surrounded or subtended by a large bract called a "spathe."

Spathe (spayth). A relatively large and often colored bract surrounding or found at the base of an inflorescence.

Spatulate (SPAT-yoo-lait). Spatula-shaped; a modified oblong shape with the apical end much larger than the tapering base; an exaggerated obovate shape.

Specific epithet. A word in a botanical binomial that follows the genus name (the "generic") and denotes a species, variety, or cultivar.

Sport. A plant that is significantly different from its parents due to mutation and not the recombination of genetic material involved in sexual reproduction.

Stamen (STAY-men). The male reproductive organ of a flower consisting of the filament and the anther, the latter organ producing and sometimes dispersing the pollen grains.

Staminode (STAM-i-noad). A highly modified stamen that is often large, colorful and petal-like and is usually sterile (that is, not producing pollen).

Standard. A large and erect petal, especially that of a papilionaceous flower.

Standard. A shrub or sometimes a vine that has been trained and pruned into a form with a single trunk.

Stigma (STIG-ma). The apical (terminal) end of the pistil; the part of the pistil that receives pollen grains and initiates their germination.

Stilt roots. Aerial roots emerging from near the base of a trunk that serve to stabilize the trunk and often to lift it above flood stage water.

Stipe (styp). The main stalk (petiole) of a fern leaf.

Stipule (STIP-yool). A leaflike appendage at the base of a leafstalk where the petiole attaches to the plant's stem. Stipules usually occur in pairs and are usually much smaller than the leaf blade, although in some (citrus) species the stipules are quite large and often larger than the leaf blade.

Stolon (STO-lun). A rootlike but aboveground stem that creeps along the surface of the soil and roots at specific nodes, creating new plants that are, of course, genetically identical to the parent plant.

Stoloniferous (sto-lu-NIF-e-rus). A term used to describe a plant that bears stolons.

Style (styl). The usually elongated portion of a pistil; the portion above the ovary and beneath the stigma.

Subtend (sub-TEND). To grow directly beneath.

Syncarp (SIN-karp). A synonym for "aggregate fruit."

Taxa (TAX-a). Plural form of the word *taxon*.

Taxon (TAX-ahn). A taxonomic category of any rank, such as "genus" or "family."

Tepal (TEEP-ul). A sepal or petal that is intermediate in form and not readily distinguished from either.

Terete (te-REET). Circular in cross section. Cylindrical.

Terrestrial (ter-RES-tree-ul). Of or from the ground or earth; growing in the ground or soil.

Tomentose (TOE-men-toas). Covered in dense short hairs.

Tomentum (toe-MENT-um). A covering of short, densely matted hairs.

Trifoliate (try-FO-lee-ait). A term used to describe a leaf with three leaflets.

Tuber (TOO-bur). A relatively short swollen root that is usually but not always subterranean. It has "eyes" or growing points from which emerge the shoots of new plants and is considered a food storage organ.

Tubercle (TOO-bur-k'l). A small rounded protuberance usually on a stem or trunk of a plant.

Type. The standard and definitive form of a species.

Umbel (UM-b'l). An inflorescence with stalked flowers radiating from the end of the flower stalk, forming an umbrella-shaped cluster or a semicircular (but never globular) mass.

Unifoliate. Having compound leaves that are reduced to one leaflet.

Vegetative. A term used to refer to the stems and leaves of a plant as opposed to its flowers.

Vernacular. The common non-scientific name of a plant.

Viviparous (vi-VIP-a-rus). A term used to describe a plant that bears on its parts plantlets that are viable and able to grow to maturity themselves.

Whorl. A circular arrangement of leaves, flowers, bracts, and so forth around a single point or node.

Wing. One of the side or lateral petals of a papilionaceous flower.

Xeric (ZER-ik). Of, from, or adapted to quite dry habitats.

Xerophyte (ZER-o-fyt). A plant indigenous to and adaptable to an arid environment.

Bibliography

Adams, Nancy M. *The Fiat Book of New Zealand Trees*. Wellington, New Zealand: A.H. & W. Reed, 1972.

Arp, Gerald K. *Tropical Gardening Along the Gulf Coast*. Houston, Texas: Gulf Publishing Company, 1978.

Audas, James Wales. *Native Trees of Australia*. Melbourne, Victoria, Australia: Whitcombe and Tombs, n.d.

Austin, Daniel. *Coastal Dune Plants: A Pocket Guide to the Common Plants of Southeast Florida's Ocean-Side Communities*. Gumbo Limbo Nature Center of South Palm Beach County, 1991.

———. *Scrub Plant Guide: A Pocket Guide to the Common Plants of Southern Florida's Scrub Community*. Gumbo Limbo Nature Center of South Palm Beach County, 1993.

———. *Coastal Park Plant Guide: A Pocket Guide to the Native Trees, Shrubs and Vines of Boca Raton's Hammock and Mangrove Parklands*. City of Boca Raton Department of Parks & Recreation, n.d.

Baensch, Ulrich, and Ursula Baensch. *Blooming Bromeliads*. Nassau, Bahamas: Tropic Beauty Publishers, 1994.

Bailey, Liberty Hyde. *The Standard Cyclopedia of Horticulture*. London: Macmillan Company, 1925.

Bailey, Liberty Hyde, and Ethel Zoe Bailey. *Hortus Third*. New York: Macmillan Publishing Company, 1976.

Bar-Zvi, David. *Tropical Gardening*. New York: Pantheon Books, 1996.

Barton, Barbara J. *Gardening by Mail: A Source Book*. Houghton Mifflin, 1994.

Berry, Fred, and John W. Kress. *Heliconia: An Identification Guide*. Washington, D.C.: Smithsonian Institution Press, 1991.

Blombery, Alec, and Tony Rodd. *Palms of the World, Their Care, Cultivation and Landscape Use*. North Ryde, N.S.W. Australia: Angus and Robertson Publishers, 1982.

Boyer, Keith. *Palms and Cycads Beyond the Tropics*. Milton, Queensland: The Publication Fund, Palm and Cycad Societies of Australia, 1992.

Britton, N. L., and J. N. Rose. *The Cactaceae*. New York: Dover Publications, 1963.

Broschat, Timothy K., and Alan Meerow. *Betrock's Reference Guide to Florida Landscape Plants*. Cooper City, Florida: Betrock Information Systems, 1994.

Buchanan, Rita, and Roger Holmes, eds. *Taylor's Guide to Gardening in the South*. Houghton Mifflin Company, 1992a.

———, eds. *Taylor's Guide to Gardening in the Southwest*. Houghton Mifflin Company, 1992b.

Callaway, Dorothy J. *The World of Magnolias*. Portland, Oregon: Timber Press, 1994.

Capon, Brian. *Botany for Gardeners*. Portland, Oregon: Timber Press, 1990.

Chapman, Timothy Sean. *Ornamental Gingers: A Guide to Selection and Cultivation*. St. Gabriel, Louisiana: Timothy Sean Chapman, 1995.

Clay, Horace F., and James C. Hubbard. *The Hawai'i Garden: Tropical Exotics*. Honolulu: University of Hawaii Press, 1977a.

———. *The Hawai'i Garden: Tropical Shrubs*. Honolulu: University of Hawaii Press, 1977b.

Condit, Ira J. *Ficus: The Exotic Species*. University of California, Division of Agricultural Sciences, 1969.

Consolino, Francesca, and Enrico Banfi. *The Simon & Schuster Guide to Climbing Plants*. New York: Simon & Schuster, 1993.

Coombes, Allen J. *Dictionary of Plant Names*. Portland, Oregon: Timber Press, 1985.

Corner, E. J. H. *The Life of Plants*. Cleveland, Ohio: The World Publishing Company, 1964.

———. *The Natural History of Palms*. Berkeley, California: University of California Press, 1966.

Courtwright, Gordon. *Tropicals*. Portland, Oregon: Timber Press, 1988.

Cronquist, Arthur. *An Integrated System of Classification of Flowering Plants*. New York: Columbia University Press, 1981.

Cullman, Willy, Erich Götz, and Gerhard Gröner. *The Encyclopedia of Cacti*. Portland, Oregon: Timber Press, 1987.

Dajun, Wang, and Shen Shao-Jin. *Bamboos of China*. Portland, Oregon: Timber Press, 1987.

DeFreitas, Stan. *Complete Guide to Florida Gardening*. Dallas, Texas: Taylor Publishing Company, 1987.

de Wit, H. C. D. *Plants of the World: The Higher Plants*. 2 volumes. New York: E.P. Dutton & Company, 1966, 1967

Doutt, Richard L. *Cape Bulbs*. Portland, Oregon: Timber Press, 1994.

Duffield, Mary Rose, and Warren D. Jones. *Plants for Dry Climates*. Los Angeles, California: HPBooks, 1992.

Dunk, Gillean. *Ferns*. Sydney, Australia: Angus & Robertson, 1994.

Eggenberger, Richard, and Mary Helen Eggenberger. *The Handbook on Plumeria Culture*. Houston, Texas: The Plumeria People, 1988.

Emboden, William A. *Bizarre Plants*. New York: Macmillan Publishing Company, 1974.

Everett, Rhomas H. *Living Trees of the World*. New York: Chanticleer Press, n.d.

Farrelly, David. *The Book of Bamboo*. San Francisco: Sierra Club Books, 1984.

Folsom, Debra Brown, John N. Trager, James Folsom, Joe Clements, and Nancy Scott. *Dry Climate Gardening with Succulents*. New York: Pantheon Books, 1995.

Foster, F. Gordon. *Ferns to Know and Grow*. Portland, Oregon: Timber Press, 1984.

Frear, Mary Dillingham. *Our Familiar Island Trees*. Boston: The Gorham Press, 1929.

Gardiner, James M. *Magnolias*. Chester, Connecticut: The Globe Pequot Press, 1989.

Gibbons, Martin. *Palms*. Seacaucus, New Jersey: Chartwell Books, 1993.

Giddy, Cynthia. *Cycads of South Africa*. Cape Town, South Africa: Purnell and Sons, 1974.

Gledhill, D. *The Names of Plants*. Cambridge: University Press, 1989.

Graf, Alfred Byrd. *Tropica*. East Rutherford, New Jersey: Roehrs Company, 1981.

———. *Exotica*. East Rutherford, New Jersey: Roehrs Company, 1982.

Griffiths, Mark. *Index of Garden Plants*. Portland, Oregon: Timber Press, 1994.

Hanly, Gil, and Jacqueline Walker. *The Subtropical Garden*. Portland, Oregon: Timber Press, 1992.

Hargreaves, Dorothy, and Bob Hargreaves. *Tropical Blossoms of the Caribbean*. Lahaina, Hawaii: Ross-Hargreaves, 1960.

———. *Tropical Trees Found in the Caribbean, South America, Central America, Florida*. Lahaina, Hawaii: Ross-Hargreaves, 1965.

———. *African Trees*. Kailua, Hawaii: Hargreaves Company, 1972.

———. *Hawaii Blossoms*. Portland, Oregon: Hargreaves Industrial, n.d.

Harrar, Elwood S., and J. George Harrar. *Guide to Southern Trees*. New York: Dover Publications, 1962.

Harris, James G., and Melinda Woolf Harris. *Plant Identification Terminology: An Illustrated Glossary*. Spring Lake, Utah: Spring Lake Publishing, 1994.

Hay, Roy, and Patrick M. Synge. *The Color Dictionary of Flowers and Plants for Home and Garden*. London: George Rainbird, 1969.

Henderson, Andrew, Gloria Galeano, and Rodrigo Bernal. *Field Guide to the Palms of the Americas*. Princeton, New Jersey: Princeton University Press, 1995.

Hertrich, William. *Palms and Cycads: Their Culture in Southern California*. San Marino, California: The Henry E. Huntington Library and Art Gallery, 1951.

Hobbs, Jack, and Terry Hatch. *Best Bulbs for Temperate Climates*. Portland, Oregon: Timber Press, 1994.

Hodel, Donald R. *Exceptional Trees of Los Angeles*. California Arboretum Foundation, 1988.

Höhn, Reinhardt, and Johannes Petermann. *Curiosities of the Plant Kingdom*. New York: Universe Books, 1980.

Holttum, R. E., and Ivan Enoch. *Gardening in the Tropics*. Portland, Oregon: Timber Press, 1991.

Hotchkiss, Neil. *Common Marsh, Underwater and Floating-Leaved Plants of the United States and Canada*. New York: Dover Publications, 1967.

Howard, Frances. *Landscaping with Vines*. New York: Macmillan Company, 1959.

Hutchinson, James. *The Families of Flowering Plants: Dicotyledons*. London: Macmillan & Company, 1926.

———. *The Families of Flowering Plants: Monocotyledons*. London: Macmillan & Company, 1934.

Hyam, R., and R. Pankhurst. *Plants and Their Names: A Concise Dictionary*. Oxford: University Press, 1995.

Innes, Clive, and Charles Glass. *Cacti*. New York: Portland House, 1991.

Isley, Paul T. *Tillandsia*. Gardena, California: Botanical Press, 1987.

Iredell, Jan. *Growing Bougainvilleas*. East Roseville, N.S.W., Australia: Simon & Schuster Australia, 1994.

Jones, David L. *Encyclopedia of Ferns*. Portland, Oregon: Timber Press, 1987.

———. *Cycads of the World*. Washington, D.C.: Smithsonian Institution Press, 1993.

Kingsbury, John M. *200 Conspicuous, Unusual, or Economically Important Tropical Plants of the Caribbean*. Ithaca, New York: Bullbrier Press, 1988.

Krempin, Jack L. *Palms and Cycads Around the World*. Sydney: Horwitz Grahame Pty., 1990.

Kriegel, John, ed. *Houston Garden Book*. Fredericksburg, Texas: Shearer Publishing, 1991.

Kuck, Loraine E., and Richard C. Tongg. *Hawaiian Flowers and Flowering Trees*. Rutland, VT & Tokyo: Charles E. Tuttle Company, 1960.

Lawrence, George H. M. *Taxonomy of Vascular Plants*. New York: Macmillan Company, 1951.

Lessard, W. O. *The Complete Book of Bananas*. Homestead, Florida: W. O. Lessard, 1992.

Lyons, Jr., Calvin G. *Successful Gardening in the Magic Valley of Texas*. Texas Garden Clubs, 1976.

Macaboy, Stirling. *What Flower is That?* New York: Crown Publishers, 1969.

———. *What Tree is That?* New York: Crescent Books, 1991.

Macmillan, H. F. *Tropical Planting and Gardening*. Kuala Lumpur: Malayan Nature Society, 1991.

Mason, Jr., Charles T., and Patricia B. Mason. *A Handbook of Mexican Roadside Flora*. Tucson, Arizona: The University of Arizona Press, 1987.

Matthews, J. W. *New Zealand Trees*. Wellington, New Zealand: A.H. & W. Reed, 1951.

Maxwell, Lewis S., and Betty M. Maxwell. *Florida Fruit*. Tampa, Florida: Lewis S. Maxwell, 1984a.

———. *Florida Trees and Palms*. Tampa, Florida: Lewis S. Maxwell, 1984b.

———. *Florida Plant Selector*. Tampa, Florida: Lewis S. Maxwell, 1988.

McCurrach, James C. *Palms of the World*. New York: Harper & Bros., 1960.

McDonald, Elvin. *The New Houseplant*. New York: Macmillan Publishing Company, 1993.

McGeachy, Beth. *Handbook of Florida Palms*. St. Petersburg, Florida: Great Outdoors Publishing Company, 1955.

Meerow, Alan W. *Betrock's Guide to Landscape Palms*. Cooper City, Florida: Betrock Information Systems, 1992.

Menninger, Edwin A. *Flowerig Trees of the World*. New York: Hearthside Press, 1962.

———. *Flowering Vines of the World*. New York, 1970.

———. *Color in the Sky: Flowering Trees in Our Landscape*. Stuart, Florida: Horticultural Books, 1975.

———. *Edible Nuts of the World*. Stuart, Florida: Horticultural Books, 1977.

———. *Fantastic Trees*. Portland, Oregon: Timber Press, 1995.

Merrill, Elmer D. *Plant Life of the Pacific World*. New York: Macmillan Company, 1945.

Mickel, John T. *Ferns for American Gardens*. New York: Macmillan Publishing Company, 1994.

Milne, Lorus, and Margery Milne. *Living Plants of the World*. New York: Chanticleer Press, n.d.

Mohlenbrock, Robert. *You Can Grow Tropical Fruit*. St. Petersburg, Florida: Great Outdoors Publishing Company, 1980.

Morton, Julia F. *500 Plants of South Florida*. Miami, Florida: E. A. Seemann Publishing, 1974.

———. *Exotic Plants for House and Garden*. Racine, Wisconsin: Western Publishing Company, 1977.

———. *Fruits of Warm Climates*. Miami, Florida: Julia F. Morton, 1987.

Muirhead, Desmond. *Palms*. Globe, Arizona: Dale Stuart King, n.d.

Nagle, J. Stewart. *Citrus for the Gulf Coast*. Clear Lake Shores, Texas: DT Press, 1994.

Neal, Bill. *Gardener's Latin*. Chapel Hill, North Carolina: Algonquin Books, 1992.

Nellis, David W. *Seashore Plants of South Florida and the Caribbean*. Sarasota, Florida: Pineapple Press, 1994.

Nelson, Gil. *The Trees of Florida*. Sarasota, Florida: Pineapple Press, 1994.

Ogden, Scott. *Garden Bulbs for the South*. Dallas, Texas: Taylor Publishing Company, 1994.

Ortho Books. *The World of Cactus and Succulents and Other Water-Thrifty Plants*. California: Chevron Chemical Company, 1977.

———. *All About Citrus and Subtropical Fruits*. California: Chevron Chemical Company, 1985.

Padilla, Victoria. *Bromeliads*. New York: Crown Publishers, 1966.

Page, P. E. *Tropical Tree Fruits for Australia*. Brisbane, Queensland: Queensland Department of Primary Industries, 1983.

Pesman, M. Walter. *Meet Flora Mexicana*. Globe, Arizona: Dale Stuart King, 1962.

Popenoe, Wilson. *Manual of Tropical and Subtropical Fruits*. New York: Hafner Press, 1920.

Ray, Richard, and Lance Walheim. *Citrus*. Los Angeles, California: Horticultural Publishing Company, 1980.

Recht, Christine, and Max F. Wetterwald. *Bamboos*. Portland, Oregon: Timber Press, 1992.

Record, Samuel J., and Robert W. Hess. *Timbers of the New World*. New Haven, Connecticut: Yale University Press, 1943.

Richards, M. A. *The Tropical Rain Forest: an Ecological Study*. London: Cambridge University Press, 1966.

Richardson, Alfred. *Plants of the Rio Grande Delta*. Austin: University of Texas Press, 1995.

River Oaks Garden Club. *A Garden Book for Houston*. Houston, Texas: Gulf Publishing Company, 1989.

Rupp, Rebecca. *Red Oaks and Black Birches*. Pownell, Vermont: Storey Communications, 1990.

Sajeva, Maurizio, and Mariangela Costanzo. *Succulents: The Illustrated Dictionary*. Portland, Oregon: Timber Press, 1994.

Schloss, Sue, ed. *The Hibiscus Handbook*. Cocoa Beach, Florida: The American Hibiscus Society, 1990.

Schuetz, Maxine Fortune. *Flowering Trees for Central and South Florida Gardens*. St. Petersburg, Florida: Great Outdoors Publishing, 1990.

Schulz, Peggie, ed. *Gesneriads and How to Grow Them*. Grandview, Missouri: Diversity Books, 1967.

Scurlock, J. Paul. *Native Trees and Shrubs of the Florida Keys*. Bethel Park, Pennsylvania: Laurel Press, 1987.

Seddon, S. A., and G. W. Lennox. *Trees of the Caribbean*. London: Macmillan Education, 1980.

Simmons, Alan E. *Growing Unusual Fruit*. New York: Walker & Company, 1972.

Slocum, Perry D., and Peter Robinson. *Water Gardening, Water Lilies and Lotuses*. Portland, Oregon: Timber Press, 1996.

Smith, Lyman B. *The Bromeliads: Jewels of the Tropics*. Cranbury, New Jersey: A. S. Barnes & Company, 1969.

Sohmer, S. H., and R. Gustafson. *Plants and Flowers of Hawai'i*. Honolulu: University of Hawaii Press, 1987.

Sperry, Neil. *Neil Sperry's Complete Guide to Texas Gardening*. Dallas, Texas: Taylor Publishing Company, 1991.

Squire, Sally McQueen. *The Complete Guide to Growing Bulbs in Houston*. Houston, Texas: Bayland Publishing, 1978.

Standley, Paul C. *Trees and Shrubs of Mexico*. Washington, D.C.: Smithsonian Press, 1920, 1922, 1923, 1924, 1926.

Stearn, William T. *Stearn's Dictionary of Plant Names for Gardeners*. London: Cassell Publishers, 1992.

Stevenson, George B. *Palms of South Florida*. Miami, Florida: George B. Stevenson, 1974.

Stresau, Frederic B. *Florida, My Eden*. Port Salerno, Florida: Florida Classics Library, 1986.

Sunset Books. *Sunset Western Garden Book*. Menlo Park, California: Sunset Publishing Corporation, 1995.

Sunset Magazine. *Cactus and Other Succulents*. Menlo Park, California: Sunset Publishing Corporation, 1994.

Tasker, Georgia B. *Enchanted Ground: Gardening with Nature in the Subtropics*. Kansas City, Kansas: Andrews and McMeel, 1994.

Taylor, Jane. *Climbing Plants*. Portland, Oregon: Timber Press, 1987.

Texas Forest Service. *Famous Trees of Texas*. Texas A&M University System, 1970.

Tomlinson, P. B. *The Biology of Trees Native to Tropical Florida*. Alton, Massachusetts: Harvard University Printing Office, 1980.

Uhl, Natalie W., and John Dransfield. *Genera Palmarum*. Lawrence, Kansas: Allen Press, 1987.

Vanderplank, John. *Passion Flowers*. Cambridge, Massachusetts: MIT Press, 1991.

Vines, Robert A. *Trees, Shrubs and Woody Vines of the Southwest*. Austin: University of Texas Press, 1960.

Walheim, Lance. *Citrus*. Tucson, Arizona: Ironwood Press, 1996.

Walters, James E., and Balbir Backhaus. *Shade and Color with Water-Conserving Plants*. Portland, Oregon: Timber Press, 1992.

Wardman, Elfrida L., ed. *The Bermuda Jubilee Garden*. The Garden Club of Bermuda, 1971.

Warnock, Barton H. *Plants of Big Bend National Park*. Washington, D.C.: United States Department of the Interior, 1951.

———. *Wildflowers of the Big Bend Country, Texas*. Alpine, Texas: Sul Ross State University, 1970.

———. *Wildflowers of the Guadeloupe Mountains and the Sand Dune Country, Texas*. Alpine, Texas: Sul Ross State University, 1974.

Watkins, John V., and Thomas J. Sheehan. *Florida Landscape Plants*. Gainesville, Florida: University Presses of Florida, 1975.

Watkins, John V., and Herbert S. Wolfe. *Your Florida Garden*. Gainesville, Florida: University Presses of Florida, 1986.

Willis, J. C. *A Dictionary of the Flowering Plants and Ferns*. London: Cambridge University Press, 1973.

Wilson, Robert Gardner, and Catherine Wilson. *Bromeliads in Cultivation*. Coconut Grove, Florida: Hurricane House Publishers, 1963.

Woman's Club of Havana, The Garden Section. *Flowering Plants from Cuban Gardens*. New York: Criterion Books, 1958.

Wunderlin, Richard P. *Guide to the Vascular Plants of Central Florida*. Tampa, Florida: University Presses of Florida, 1982.

Index

Names listed in alphabetical order in the descriptions, whether main entries or synonyms, are not repeated in this index; however, all common names in the text, any synonyms not cross-referenced in the alphabetized descriptions, and all plants mentioned apart from their main entries are included here. Thus, to locate a plant when its scientific name is known, one should look first in the text, then in the index.